The Complete Book of

HIT ▶▶

SINGLES

Compiled from

THE TOP 20 CHARTS
From 1954 to the Present Day

Dave McAleer

THIS IS A CARLTON BOOK

This edition published 2010 by Carlton Books Limited,
20 Mortimer Street,
London W1T 3JW

ISBN 978-1-84732-526-6

UK charts and facts to April 1998 and from April 2001 compiled by Dave McAleer
US charts and facts to March 1996 and from April 2001 compiled by Dave McAleer
UK and US charts and facts April 2001 to December 2006 compiled by Dave McAleer
UK charts & facts April 1998 to March 2001 & US charts & facts April 1996 to March 2001
    compiled by Danny Scott & Terry Burrows.
UK and US Facts January 2007 to December 2009 compiled by Matthew White.

Produced under licence from the Official UK Charts Company

Printed and bound in Dubai

Contents

INTRODUCTION

Johnny Mathis

Most of the world's top recording artists between 1954 and 2009 hailed from either America or Britain, and it has always been these two countries setting the vast majority of musical trends that keep pop record buyers entertained around the globe.

The major musical happening during the period was undoubtedly the growth of rock. It evolved out of late 1940s R&B and C&W music and was spread world-wide in the mid-1950s by acts like Bill Haley and Elvis Presley. In the 1960s, The Beatles and other British bands, weaned on American rock'n'roll and R&B, gave it a new lease of life. Rock then diversified into scores of successful sub-genres, making many more American and British recording artists international household names.

These 55 years have seen countless musical changes, all of which are chronicled in this book. The way we buy music has also altered drastically in this period. Initially, the vast majority of sales (especially in the UK) were on breakable 10" 78 rpm singles. These were replaced by 45 rpm vinyl singles, and then cassette singles ruled until the 1990s when CDs took over. Nonetheless, you may be surprised to know that single tracks have never sold better than they do right now, and that's solely thanks to digital downloads which today account for almost every sale. Not only are current chart entries selling in good quantities, but many of the other hits in this book are still regularly earning money thanks to their easy availability on the internet. In fact, the new all time top UK chart single, the 1987 Pogues and Kirsty MacColl hit 'Fairytale Of New York', is only in that position because of its download sales (and subsequent high Christmas time chart positions) every year between 2005-2009. Perhaps the only things you could be sure of during this period was that there would be no shortage of pop idols, TV and movie exposure would greatly influence record sales, a good 'novelty' would always sell and that most people would consider the music of their early teens to be the best there ever was.

The aim of this book is to try and put the 21,000 plus records that have reached the UK and US Top 20 charts since 1954 into some kind of perspective. The monthly Top 20s are based on a record's performance on the best sellers charts not on actual sales, since sales are impossible to verify for the full period. The transatlantic chart careers of every American or British hit can be checked in these easy-to-follow, fact-packed lists, and at a glance you can see all the similarities and indeed differences between the tastes of the two most important and influential countries in the world of music.

CHART FILES The Top 20 UK and US charts are compiled by means of a complex and comprehensive points system which considers not only a record's weekly chart positions and peak position, but also the number of weeks it spent on the Top 20, Top 10 and its weeks at No. 1 (if applicable).

Apart from the normal chart features these Top 20s also show:

(a) The total number of weeks a record spent in the country's Top 20 during that chart run.

(b) The record's equivalent position in the UK/US.

(c) Whether it was the artist's first (F) Top 20 entry in that country. In the case of duos the (F) refers to the first named act, or in the case of duos with several hits i.e. Marvin Gaye & Tammi Terrell, it refers to the duo as such.

(d) Whether it sold over a million (G) or two million (P) in that country. Gold records were first officially certified in the US by the RIAA in 1958, and even then some companies (including Motown) did not believe in certifying sales figures, and so some educated guesses have had to be made. Platinum certification was not introduced in the US until 1976, and so any two million plus sellers before that date (and there were quite a few) only carry a (G) designation.

The chart positions used for compiling the monthly Top 20s were those accepted at the time as the most accurate in the UK and America. If a single's title was spelt differently in the USA and Britain, it is listed on the chart as it was spelt in that country. However, in the index it can be found under the American spelling. Equivalent US or UK chart positions are not included if there was a gap of three years or more, as this would give a false impression of the record's success at that time.

LISTING BY ARTIST'S NAME This easy-to-check index lists an artist's hits in alphabetical order and shows the act's nationality and the month the hit entered this book's UK and US Top 20. Therefore, it is a simple matter to check the charts concerned for more information about the record. If the record was a remix or a re-issue of a previous Top 20 entry, it states (remix) or has a * symbol. If it is a shared hit, the chart information can be found under the first named artist on the track.

LISTING BY SONG TITLE An alphabetical listing of every single hit in this book with the artist's name.

The lists below reflect a track's chart performance and not its sales figures, and each chart run is treated individually. Therefore, if a record has been a hit on more than one occasion, which is a lot more common in the UK (especially at Christmas time), it may amass more points than a higher peaking record that has only had one chart run. Also, as proof that records have had longer US chart lives in recent years, you will notice that many of the All Time US Top 100 were released this century.

US Top 100 Singles 1954-2009

Pos	Title	Artist
1	The Twist	Chubby Checker
2	Smooth	Santana Featuring Rob Thomas
3	Macarena	Los Del Rio
4	We Belong Together	Mariah Carey
5	One Sweet Day	Mariah Carey & Boyz II Men
6	I'll Make Love To You	Boyz II Men
7	Yeah!	Usher Featuring Ludacris & Lil Jon
8	Candle In The Wind 1997/Something About The Way You Look Tonight	Elton John
9	Low	Flo Rida Featuring T-Pain
10	End Of The Road	Boyz II Men
11	I Will Always Love You	Whitney Houston
12	Un-Break My Heart	Toni Braxton
13	The Boy Is Mine	Brandy & Monica
14	Boom Boom Pow	The Black Eyed Peas
15	Hound Dog/Don't Be Cruel	Elvis Presley
16	I Swear	All-4-One
17	Cherry Pink And Apple Blossom White	Perez Prado
18	I'll Be Missing You	Puff Daddy & Faith Evans (featuring 112)
19	Lose Yourself	Eminem
20	Gold Digger	Kanye West Featuring Jamie Foxx
21	Dilemma	Nelly Featuring Kelly Rowland
22	Independent Women Part 1	Destiny's Child
23	Let Me Love You	Mario
24	Little Things Mean A Lot	Kitty Kallen
25	Maria Maria	Santana Featuring The Product G&B
26	Foolish	Ashanti
27	No One	Alicia Keys

Whitney Houston   The Bee Gees

Pos	Title	Artist
28	Irreplaceable	Beyoncé
29	Too Close	Next
30	In Da Club	50 Cent
31	Hey Ya!	OutKast
32	Baby Boy	Beyoncé Featuring Sean Paul
33	Rock Around The Clock	Bill Haley & His Comets
34	I Gotta Feeling	The Black Eyed Peas
35	Physical	Olivia Newton-John
36	Singing The Blues	Guy Mitchell
37	Wanted	Perry Como
38	Burn	Usher
39	You Light Up My Life	Debby Boone
40	The Sign	Ace Of Base

Pos	Title	Artist
41	Mack The Knife	Bobby Darin
42	Whatever You Like	T.I.
43	Crank Dat (Soulja Boy)	Soulja Boy Tellem
44	How You Remind Me	Nickelback
45	Oh! My Pa-Pa (O Mein Papa)	Eddie Fisher
46	Crazy In Love	Beyoncé Featuring Jay-Z
47	Hot In Herre	Nelly
48	Hey There	Rosemary Clooney
49	Waterfalls	TLC
50	Fantasy	Mariah Carey
51	Sh-Boom	The Crew-Cuts
52	Goodies	Ciara Featuring Petey Pablo
53	Hey Jude	The Beatles
54	Candy Shop	50 Cent Featuring Olivia
55	Bette Davis Eyes	Kim Carnes
56	Monster Mash	Bobby 'Boris' Pickett & The Crypt Kickers
57	Endless Love	Diana Ross & Lionel Richie
58	Heartbreak Hotel/I Was The One	Elvis Presley
59	Fallin'	Alicia Keys
60	Truly Madly Deeply	Savage Garden
61	My Boo	Usher & Alicia Keys
62	Dreamlover	Mariah Carey
63	Family Affair	Mary J. Blige
64	Take A Bow	Madonna
65	Because You Loved Me	Celine Dion
66	U Got It Bad	Usher
67	Live Your Life	T.I. Featuring Rihanna
68	Theme From 'A Summer Place'	Percy Faith
69	That's The Way Love Goes	Janet Jackson
70	I'm Real	Jennifer Lopez
71	Can't Help Falling In Love	UB40
72	December 1963 (Oh, What A Night)	The Four Seasons
73	On Bended Knee	Boyz II Men
74	Mr. Sandman	The Chordettes
75	Sixteen Tons	Tennessee Ernie Ford
76	Can't Nobody Hold Me Down	Puff Daddy (featuring Mase)
77	Every Breath You Take	The Police
78	Jump	Kris Kross
79	Run It!	Chris Brown
80	Bleeding Love	Leona Lewis
81	Jailhouse Rock/Treat Me Nice	Elvis Presley
82	Sexyback	Justin Timberlake
83	Promiscuous	Nelly Furtado Featuring Timbaland
84	Night Fever	The Bee Gees
85	The Yellow Rose Of Texas	Mitch Miller
86	All For You	Janet
87	This Is How We Do It	Montell Jordan
88	Teddy Bear/Loving You	Elvis Presley
89	Creep	TLC
90	Umbrella	Rihanna Featuring Jay-Z
91	I Kissed A Girl	Katy Perry
92	How Do I Live	LeAnn Rimes
93	Autumn Leaves	Roger Williams
94	Love Letters In The Sand/Bernadine	Pat Boone
95	Tha Crossroads	Bone Thugs-N-Harmony
96	Lollipop	Lil Wayne Featuring Static Major
97	Eye Of The Tiger	Survivor
98	The Wayward Wind	Gogi Grant
99	Le Freak	Chic
100	Ain't It Funny	Jennifer Lopez Featuring Ja Rule

Pos	Title	Artist
1	**Fairytale Of New York**	The Pogues
		Featuring Kirsty MacColl
2	**Rock Around The Clock**	Bill Haley & His Comets
3	**Bohemian Rhapsody**	Queen
4	**Imagine**	John Lennon
5	**It's Now Or Never**	Elvis Presley
6	**You've Lost That Lovin' Feelin'**	The Righteous Brothers
7	**You're The One That I Want**	John Travolta
		& Olivia Newton-John
8	**Relax**	Frankie Goes To Hollywood
9	**Jailhouse Rock**	Elvis Presley
10	**Wooden Heart**	Elvis Presley
11	**A Fool Such As I**	Elvis Presley
	/I Need Your Love To-Night	
12	**One Night/I Got Stung**	Elvis Presley
13	**You Got The Love**	The Source
		Featuring Candi Staton
14	**All I Want For Christmas Is You**	Mariah Carey

Madonna   *John Travolta*

Pos	Title	Artist
15	**Holiday**	Madonna
16	**The Wonder Of You**	Elvis Presley
17	**Rock-A-Hula Baby**	Elvis Presley
18	**(Everything I Do) I Do It For You**	Bryan Adams
19	**Sailing**	Rod Stewart
20	**Way Down**	Elvis Presley
21	**Two Tribes**	Frankie Goes To Hollywood
22	**Do They Know It's Christmas?**	Band Aid
23	**Take My Breath Away**	Berlin
24	**Albatross**	Fleetwood Mac
25	**Mysterious Girl**	Peter Andre
26	**Love Is All Around**	Wet Wet Wet
27	**Are You Lonesome Tonight?**	Elvis Presley
28	**Surrender**	Elvis Presley
29	**Reet Petite**	Jackie Wilson
30	**You Sexy Thing**	Hot Chocolate
31	**(Marie's The Name) His Latest Flame**	Elvis Presley
32	**I Will Survive**	Gloria Gaynor
33	**Young Girl**	Gary Puckett & The Union Gap
34	**Blue Monday**	New Order
35	**In The Air Tonight**	Phil Collins
36	**He Ain't Heavy, He's My Brother**	The Hollies
37	**She's Not You**	Elvis Presley
38	**A Little Less Conversation**	Elvis Vs JXL
39	**Secret Love**	Doris Day
40	**You To Me Are Everything**	The Real Thing
41	**Crying In The Chapel**	Elvis Presley
42	**Last Christmas**	Wham!
43	**Return To Sender**	Elvis Presley
44	**Billie Jean**	Michael Jackson
45	**(You're The) Devil In Disguise**	Elvis Presley
46	**Cara Mia**	David Whitfield With
		Mantovani & His Orchestra
47	**Space Oddity**	David Bowie
48	**Tainted Love**	Soft Cell
49	**Mary's Boy Child**	Harry Belafonte

Pos	Title	Artist
50	**All Right Now**	Free
51	**Leader Of The Pack**	The Shangri-Las
52	**You Spin Me Round (Like A Record)**	Dead Or Alive
53	**When I Fall In Love**	Nat 'King' Cole
54	**Rose Marie**	Slim Whitman
55	**Young At Heart**	The Bluebells
56	**Let's Twist Again**	Chubby Checker
57	**I Heard It Through The Grapevine**	Marvin Gaye
58	**Crazy For You**	Madonna
59	**Oh, Mein Papa**	Eddie Calvert
60	**I Feel Love**	Donna Summer
61	**A Whiter Shade Of Pale**	Procol Harum
62	**Diana**	Paul Anka
63	**I Will Always Love You**	Whitney Houston
64	**Give Me Your Word**	Tennessee Ernie Ford
65	**Umbrella**	Rihanna Featuring Jay-Z
66	**She Loves You**	The Beatles
67	**Three Lions**	Baddiel & Skinner &
		The Lighning Seeds
68	**When A Man Loves A Woman**	Percy Sledge
69	**Dancing Queen**	Abba
70	**Temptation**	Heaven 17
71	**Merry Xmas Everybody**	Slade
72	**Unchained Melody**	The Righteous Brothers
73	**Think Twice**	Celine Dion
74	**Reach Out I'll Be There**	The Four Tops
75	**Y.M.C.A.**	The Village People
76	**Happy Xmas (War Is Over)**	John & Yoko
		& The Plastic Ono Band
77	**Sugar, Sugar**	The Archies
78	**Good Luck Charm**	Elvis Presley
79	**All I Have To Do Is Dream / Claudette**	The Everly Brothers
80	**Cars**	Gary Numan
81	**Mull Of Kintyre/Girls' School**	Paul McCartney
82	**I Remember You**	Frank Ifield
83	**All Shook Up**	Elvis Presley
84	**Heartbreak Hotel**	Elvis Presley
85	**Wonderful Land**	The Shadows
86	**Hey Jude**	The Beatles
87	**Don't You Want Me**	Human League

Cliff Richard   *The Jackson Five*

Pos	Title	Artist
88	**Magic Moments**	Perry Como
89	**Just Walkin' In The Rain**	Johnnie Ray
90	**Who's Sorry Now**	Connie Francis
91	**Rivers Of Babylon /Brown Girl In The Ring**	Boney M
92	**Living Doll**	Cliff Richard
93	**Stay**	Shakespear's Sister
94	**Can't Get By Without You**	The Real Thing
95	**Crazy**	Gnarls Barkley
96	**I'll Be There For You**	The Rembrandts
97	**Young Love**	Tab Hunter
98	**What Do You Want To**	Emile Ford &
	Make Those Eyes At Me For?	The Checkmates
99	**Whatever Will Be, Will Be (Que Sera, Sera)**	Doris Day
100	**The Israelites**	Desmond Dekker & The Aces

Top All Time Singles Artists In The US

Pos	Name	First Hit	Last Hit
1	Elvis Presley	1956	77
2	The Beatles	1964	96
3	Madonna	1984	08
4	Mariah Carey	1990	09
5	Elton John	1971	98
6	Janet Jackson	1986	08
7	Michael Jackson	1971	02

Rolling Stones

Pos	Name	First Hit	Last Hit
8	Stevie Wonder	1963	87
9	Whitney Houston	1985	01
10	The Rolling Stones	1964	89
11	Paul McCartney	1971	86
12	The Supremes	1964	72
13	Usher	1997	08
14	The Bee Gees	1967	89
15	Chicago	1970	90
16	Prince	1980	95
17	Puff Daddy	1996	07
18	Rod Stewart	1971	94
19	Daryl Hall & John Oates	1976	90
20	Marvin Gaye	1963	83
21	Olivia Newton-John	1973	85
22	Aretha Franklin	1967	89
23	Jay-Z	1997	09
24	R. Kelly	1993	07
25	Beyoncé	2003	09
26	The Four Seasons	1962	94
27	Ricky Nelson	1957	72
28	The Beach Boys	1962	88
29	The Temptations	1964	73
30	Ludacris	2001	07
31	50 Cent	2002	09
32	Neil Diamond	1966	82
33	Kanye West	2004	09
34	Boyz II Men	1991	98
35	Phil Collins	1981	90
36	Pat Boone	1955	62
37	George Michael	1985	96
38	Nelly	2000	06
39	Connie Francis	1958	63
40	T-Pain	2005	09
41	Rihanna	2005	09
42	Diana Ross	1970	85
43	Donna Summer	1975	89
44	Carpenters	1970	81
45	Billy Joel	1978	93
46	Akon	2004	09
47	The Everly Brothers	1957	62
48	Kenny Rogers	1968	84
49	Lionel Richie	1981	87
50	Paul Anka	1957	76
51	The Jackson Five/The Jacksons	1969	84
52	Bryan Adams	1983	97
53	Brenda Lee	1960	66
54	Justin Timberlake	2002	09
55	Barbra Streisand	1964	97
56	Three Dog Night	1969	74
57	Destiny's Child	1998	05
58	Eminem	2000	09
59	Alicia Keys	2001	08
60	Lil Wayne	2004	09
61	Cher	1965	99
62	Ashanti	2001	05
63	Celine Dion	1991	00
64	Dionne Warwick	1964	87
65	TLC	1992	99
66	Jennifer Lopez	1999	06
67	Duran Duran	1983	93
68	T.I.	2005	09
69	Huey Lewis & The News	1982	91
70	Bobby Vinton	1962	74
71	Eagles	1972	80
72	Christina Aguilera	1999	08
73	John Cougar Mellencamp	1981	96
74	Ray Charles	1959	90
75	Barry Manilow	1974	84
76	Gloria Estefan	1986	99
77	Herman's Hermits	1964	67
78	Chubby Checker	1960	64
79	Richard Marx	1987	94
80	Chris Brown	2005	08
81	Foreigner	1977	88
82	P!nk	2000	09
83	Bobby Darin	1958	66
84	Bon Jovi	1986	95
85	Kool & The Gang	1974	87
86	Missy Elliott	1997	07
87	The Four Tops	1964	81
88	Paula Abdul	1989	92
89	Linda Ronstadt	1975	90
90	Bruce Springsteen	1980	97
91	Monica	1995	04
92	Neil Sedaka	1959	80
93	The Commodores	1975	85
94	The Platters	1955	67
95	Fleetwood Mac	1976	88
96	Gladys Knight & The Pips	1961	88
97	Bob Seger & The Silver Bullet Band	1969	87
98	Brook Benton	1959	70
99	Simon & Garfunkel	1965	75
100	Smokey Robinson & The Miracles	1961	76

Top All Time Singles Artists In The UK

Pos	Name	First Hit	Last Hit
1	Elvis Presley	1956	07
2	Cliff Richard	1958	08
3	Madonna	1984	09
4	The Shadows	1958	80
5	Michael Jackson	1972	09
6	The Beatles	1963	96
7	Elton John	1971	09
8	Kylie Minogue	1988	08
9	U2	1983	09
10	Queen	1974	03
11	Rod Stewart	1971	98
12	David Bowie	1969	02
13	Westlife	1999	09
14	Paul McCartney	1971	05
15	Robbie Williams	1996	09
16	George Michael	1984	09
17	The Rolling Stones	1964	05
18	Mariah Carey	1990	09
19	Pet Shop Boys	1985	09
20	Status Quo	1968	05
21	Diana Ross	1967	05
22	Abba	1974	04
23	Tom Jones	1965	09
24	Oasis	1994	09
25	Take That	1992	09
26	The Bee Gees	1967	01
27	Britney Spears	1999	09
28	Stevie Wonder	1966	05
29	Whitney Houston	1985	09
30	Lonnie Donegan	1956	62
31	Slade	1971	07
32	Eminem	1999	09
33	The Hollies	1963	88
34	Janet Jackson	1986	06
35	The Everly Brothers	1957	65
36	Erasure	1986	05
37	Girls Aloud	2002	09
38	Shakin' Stevens	1980	05
39	Boyzone	1994	08
40	UB40	1980	05
41	Sugababes	2000	09
42	Frank Sinatra	1954	86
43	Depeche Mode	1981	06
44	Madness	1979	99
45	Bon Jovi	1986	06
46	Iron Maiden	1982	07
47	Prince	1984	99
48	Pat Boone	1955	62
49	R. Kelly	1994	07
50	Wet Wet Wet	1987	08
51	Phil Collins	1981	07
52	McFly	2004	08
53	Roy Orbison	1960	92
54	Duran Duran	1981	05
55	Perry Como	1954	73
56	T. Rex	1970	91
57	Celine Dion	1992	02
58	Manic Street Preachers	1992	07
59	Hot Chocolate	1970	98
60	Blondie	1978	03
61	The Supremes	1964	74
62	Rihanna	2005	09
63	Christina Aguilera	1999	08
64	The Kinks	1964	83
65	Beyoncé	2002	09
66	Jennifer Lopez	1999	07
67	Backstreet Boys	1996	05
68	Connie Francis	1958	62
69	Bryan Adams	1985	02
70	Steps	1997	01
71	Electric Light Orchestra	1972	83
72	P!nk	2000	09
73	Petula Clark	1954	88
74	Adam Faith	1959	64
75	Manfred Mann	1964	73
76	Olivia Newton-John	1971	98
77	Justin Timberlake	2002	09
78	Spice Girls	1996	07
79	Puff Daddy	1997	07
80	Ronan Keating	1999	06
81	The Beach Boys	1964	87
82	Simply Red	1985	03
83	The Police	1979	97
84	Stereophonics	1997	07
85	Frankie Laine	1954	60
86	Nelly	2000	08
87	Cher	1965	01
88	Frankie Vaughan	1954	67
89	East 17	1992	99
90	Kanye West	2004	09
91	Donna Summer	1976	96
92	Gary Glitter	1972	84
93	Blur	1991	03
94	Billy Fury	1959	65
95	The Prodigy	1991	09
96	Shirley Bassey	1957	07
97	The Four Tops	1966	89
98	Jay-Z	1997	09
99	Craig David	1999	07
100	Showaddywaddy	1974	79

David Bowie

UK 1954 JAN-MAR

◆ Swiss song 'Oh Mein Papa' (aka 'Oh! My Pa-Pa') was the top transatlantic hit. In the USA Eddie Fisher's vocal topped the chart with British-based trumpeter Eddie Calvert's version runner-up. In Britain the roles were reversed.

◆ American songwriter Joe Darion had a hot winter with his compositions 'Changing Partners' (Patti Page, Kay Starr, Bing Crosby) and 'Ricochet' (Teresa Brewer, Joan Regan) hitting on both sides of the Atlantic.

◆ Mixed quintet The Stargazers became the first British group to rack up two No. 1s; a feat that was not repeated until 1963 by The Beatles. The former group were produced by Dick Rowe, the Decca A&R man who turned down The Beatles.

January 1954

This Mnth	Prev Mnth	Title	Artist	Label	Wks 20	(US Pos)	
1	12	Oh Mein Papa	Eddie Calvert	Columbia	21	(9)	F
2	1	Answer Me	Frankie Laine	Philips	17		
3	4	Let's Have A Party	Winifred Atwell	Philips	9		
4	3	Swedish Rhapsody	Mantovani	Decca	18		
5	15	Cloud Lucky Seven	Guy Mitchell	Philips	15		
6	-	Blowing Wild	Frankie Laine	Philips	12		
7	-	Rags To Riches	David Whitfield	Decca	11		
8	6	Chika Boom	Guy Mitchell	Philips	15		
9	2	Answer Me	David Whitfield	Decca	14		
10	18	Ricochet	Joan Regan	Decca	5		F
11	10	Poppa Piccolino	Diana Decker	Columbia	10		F L
12	-	Happy Wanderer	Obernkirchen Children's Choir	Parlophone	26		F L
13	-	That's Amore	Dean Martin	Capitol	11	(2)	
14	11	Crying In The Chapel	Lee Lawrence	Decca	6		F
15	-	The Creep	Ken Mackintosh	HMV	2		F
16	7	Swedish Rhapsody	Ray Martin	Columbia	4		L
17	8	I Saw Mommy Kissing Santa Claus	Beverley Sisters	Philips	5		F
18	5	I Saw Mommy Kissing Santa Claus	Jimmy Boyd	Columbia	6	(1)	F L
19	-	Oh! My Pa-Pa	Eddie Fisher	HMV	3	(1)	
20	16	Dragnet	Ray Anthony	Capitol	2	(3)	F L

February 1954

This Mnth	Prev Mnth	Title	Artist	Label	Wks 20	(US Pos)	
1	1	Oh Mein Papa	Eddie Calvert	Columbia	21	(9)	F
2	6	Blowing Wild	Frankie Laine	Philips	12		
3	5	Cloud Lucky Seven	Guy Mitchell	Philips	15		
4	13	That's Amore	Dean Martin	Capitol	11	(2)	
5	7	Rags To Riches	David Whitfield	Decca	11		
6	-	Tennessee Wig Walk	Bonnie Lou	Parlophone	10		F L
7	12	Happy Wanderer	Obernkirchen Children's Choir	Parlophone	26		F L
8	-	Man	Rosemary Clooney	Philips	5		
9	2	Answer Me	Frankie Laine	Philips	17		
10	4	Swedish Rhapsody	Mantovani	Decca	18		
11	-	Skin Deep	Ted Heath	Decca	3		
12	8	Chika Boom	Guy Mitchell	Philips	15		
13	-	Don't Laugh At Me	Norman Wisdom	Columbia	15		F
14	-	The Book	David Whitfield	Decca	15		
15	-	I See The Moon	Stargazers	Decca	15		
16	-	Ebb Tide	Frank Chacksfield	Decca	2	(2)	
17	-	Woman (Uh-Huh)	Jose Ferrer	Philips	4	(18)	F L
18	19	Oh! My Pa-Pa	Eddie Fisher	HMV	3	(1)	
19	-	Cuff Of My Shirt	Guy Mitchell	Philips	3		
20	-	Sippin' Soda	Guy Mitchell	Philips	1		

March 1954

This Mnth	Prev Mnth	Title	Artist	Label	Wks 20	(US Pos)	
1	15	I See The Moon	Stargazers	Decca	15		
2	1	Oh Mein Papa	Eddie Calvert	Columbia	21	(9)	F
3	7	Happy Wanderer	Obernkirchen Children's Choir	Parlophone	26		F L
4	6	Tennessee Wig Walk	Bonnie Lou	Parlophone	10		F L
5	13	Don't Laugh At Me	Norman Wisdom	Columbia	15		F
6	4	That's Amore	Dean Martin	Capitol	11	(2)	
7	14	The Book	David Whitfield	Decca	15		
8	2	Blowing Wild	Frankie Laine	Philips	12		
9	3	Cloud Lucky Seven	Guy Mitchell	Philips	15		
10	-	Changing Partners	Kay Starr	Capitol	14	(13)	
11	17	Woman (Uh-Huh)	Jose Ferrer	Philips	4	(18)	F L
12	-	Bell Bottom Blues	Alma Cogan	HMV	9		F
13	-	Skin Deep	Duke Ellington	Philips	2		F L
14	5	Rags To Riches	David Whitfield	Decca	11		
15	-	Changing Partners	Bing Crosby	Brunswick	3	(17)	
16	-	Granada	Frankie Laine	Philips	2		
17	8	Man	Rosemary Clooney	Philips	5		
18	19	Cuff Of My Shirt	Guy Mitchell	Philips	3		
19	-	Moonlight Serenade	Glenn Miller	HMV	1		F
20	-	From Here To Eternity	Frank Sinatra	Capitol	9		

January 1954

This Mnth	Prev Mnth	Title	Artist	Label	Wks 20	(UK Pos)	
1	10	Oh! My Pa-Pa	Eddie Fisher	RCA	19	(9)	
2	1	Rags To Riches	Tony Bennett	Columbia	24		
3	2	That's Amore	Dean Martin	Capitol	22	(2)	
4	5	Changing Partners	Patti Page	Mercury	19		
5	12	Stranger In Paradise	Tony Bennett	Columbia	19	(1)	
6	4	Ricochet	Teresa Brewer	Coral	19	(18)	
7	14	Stranger In Paradise	Four Aces	Decca	16	(6)	
8	3	Ebb Tide	Frank Chacksfield	London	23	(9)	
9	-	The Gang That Sang 'Heart Of My Heart'	Four Aces	Decca	15		
10	11	Oh, Mein Papa	Eddie Calvert	Essex	9	(1)	F
11	-	Stranger In Paradise	Tony Martin	RCA	9	(6)	
12	-	Secret Love	Doris Day	Columbia	20	(1)	
13	8	Eh Cumpari	Julius La Rosa	Cadence	20		
14	17	Changing Partners	Kay Starr	Capitol	9	(4)	
15	-	What Is Was, Was Football	Andy Griffith	Capitol	6		F L
16	6	You You You	Ames Brothers	RCA	8		
17	7	Vaya Con Dios	Les Paul & Mary Ford	Capitol	7	(7)	
18	16	You Alone	Perry Como	RCA	12		
19	9	Santa Baby	Eartha Kitt	RCA	5		
20	-	Till We Two Are One	Georgie Shaw	Decca	12		F L

February 1954

This Mnth	Prev Mnth	Title	Artist	Label	Wks 20	(UK Pos)	
1	1	Oh! My Pa-Pa	Eddie Fisher	RCA	19	(9)	
2	12	Secret Love	Doris Day	Columbia	20	(1)	
3	3	That's Amore	Dean Martin	Capitol	22	(2)	
4	5	Stranger In Paradise	Tony Bennett	Columbia	19	(1)	
5	4	Changing Partners	Patti Page	Mercury	19		
6	7	Stranger In Paradise	Four Aces	Decca	16	(6)	
7	-	Make Love To Me!	Jo Stafford	Columbia	20	(8)	
8	9	The Gang That Sang 'Heart Of My Heart'	Four Aces	Decca	15		
9	-	From The Vine Came The Grape	Gaylords	Mercury	12		
10	20	Till We Two Are One	Georgie Shaw	Decca	12		F L
11	2	Rags To Riches	Tony Bennett	Columbia	24		
12	-	Till Then	Hilltoppers	Dot	11		
13	-	I Get So Lonely	Four Knights	Capitol	21	(5)	L
14	11	Stranger In Paradise	Tony Martin	RCA	9	(6)	
15	6	Ricochet	Teresa Brewer	Coral	19	(18)	
16	-	At The Darktown Strutters' Ball	Lou Monte	RCA	7		F
17	-	Young-At-Heart	Frank Sinatra	Capitol	21	(12)	
18	-	From The Vine Came The Grape	Hilltoppers	Dot	11		
19	15	What Is Was, Was Football	Andy Griffith	Capitol	6		F L
20	-	Woman (Uh-Huh)	Jose Ferrer	Columbia	4	(7)	F L

March 1954

This Mnth	Prev Mnth	Title	Artist	Label	Wks 20	(UK Pos)	
1	7	Make Love To Me!	Jo Stafford	Columbia	20	(8)	
2	2	Secret Love	Doris Day	Columbia	20	(1)	
3	13	I Get So Lonely	Four Knights	Capitol	21	(5)	L
4	1	Oh! My Pa-Pa	Eddie Fisher	RCA	19	(9)	
5	17	Young-At-Heart	Frank Sinatra	Capitol	21	(12)	
6	3	That's Amore	Dean Martin	Capitol	22	(2)	
7	-	Cross Over The Bridge	Patti Page	Mercury	18	(13)	
8	4	Stranger In Paradise	Tony Bennett	Columbia	19	(1)	
9	-	Wanted	Perry Como	RCA	21	(4)	
10	5	Changing Partners	Patti Page	Mercury	19		
11	9	From The Vine Came The Grape	Gaylords	Mercury	12		
12	10	Till We Two Are One	Georgie Shaw	Decca	12		F L
13	-	Answer Me, My Love	Nat 'King' Cole	Capitol	18		
14	16	At The Darktown Strutters' Ball	Lou Monte	RCA	7		F
15	18	From The Vine Came The Grape	Hilltoppers	Dot	11		
16	12	Till Then	Hilltoppers	Dot	11		
17	8	The Gang That Sang 'Heart Of My Heart'	Four Aces	Decca	15		
18	-	Somebody Bad Stole De Wedding Bell	Eartha Kitt	RCA	4		L
19	6	Stranger In Paradise	Four Aces	Decca	16	(6)	
20	-	Cuddle Me	Ronnie Gaylord	Mercury	12		F L

◆ After a relatively quiet sales period, Frank Sinatra started a run of hits with his first Top 10 entry of the decade 'Young At Heart'.

▲ Trucker Elvis Presley recorded 'I'll Never Stand In Your Way' and 'Casual Love Affair' at a "make your own record" service at Sun Records, Memphis.

◆ Atlantic Records veteran R&B performer Joe Turner recorded the rock'n'roll standard, 'Shake, Rattle & Roll' which Bill Haley & The Comets would turn into the first transatlantic rock'n'roll hit.

UK 1954

APR-JUNE

◆ Al Martino was one of several American singers who covered US hits just for the British market. His own version of 'Wanted' sold just as well as original hitmaker Perry Como's recording in the UK.

▲ British songstress Petula Clark made her UK chart debut with the French song, 'The Little Shoemaker'. This foot-tapping composition also gave The Gaylords their biggest American hit.

◆ American heart-throbs Frankie Laine, Guy Mitchell and Johnnie Ray had British hits with records that failed in their homeland. Among these was Ray's No. 1 'Such A Night', banned by the BBC for being too suggestive.

April 1954

This Mnth	Prev Mnth	Title	Artist	Label	Wks 20	(US Pos)	
1	1	I See The Moon	Stargazers	Decca	15		
2	3	Happy Wanderer	Obernkirchen Children's Choir	Parlophone	26		F L
3	-	Secret Love	Doris Day	Philips	29	(1)	
4	10	Changing Partners	Kay Starr	Capitol	14	(13)	
5	5	Don't Laugh At Me	Norman Wisdom	Columbia	15		F
6	12	Bell Bottom Blues	Alma Cogan	HMV	9		F
7	2	Oh Mein Papa	Eddie Calvert	Columbia	21	(9)	F
8	-	Such A Night	Johnnie Ray	Philips	18		
9	7	The Book	David Whitfield	Decca	15		
10	-	The Kid's Last Fight	Frankie Laine	Philips	10		
11	-	Bimbo	Ruby Wright	Parlophone	5		F
12	4	Tennessee Wig Walk	Bonnie Lou	Parlophone	10		F L
13	15	Changing Partners	Bing Crosby	Brunswick	3	(17)	
14	6	That's Amore	Dean Martin	Capitol	11	(2)	
15	-	Dime And A Dollar	Guy Mitchell	Philips	5		
16	16	Granada	Frankie Laine	Philips	2		
17	-	Tenderly	Nat 'King' Cole	Capitol	1		
18	18	Cuff Of My Shirt	Guy Mitchell	Philips	3		
19	-	Friends And Neighbours	Billy Cotton & His Band	Decca	12		L
20	-	Happy Wanderer	Stargazers	Decca	1		

May 1954

1	3	Secret Love	Doris Day	Philips	29	(1)	
2	8	Such A Night	Johnnie Ray	Philips	18		
3	2	Happy Wanderer	Obernkirchen Children's Choir	Parlophone	26		F L
4	10	The Kid's Last Fight	Frankie Laine	Philips	10		
5	4	Changing Partners	Kay Starr	Capitol	14	(13)	
6	1	I See The Moon	Stargazers	Decca	15		
7	19	Friends And Neighbours	Billy Cotton & His Band	Decca	12		L
8	5	Don't Laugh At Me	Norman Wisdom	Columbia	15		F
9	-	Someone Else's Roses	Joan Regan	Decca	8		
10	-	Heart Of My Heart	Max Bygraves	HMV	8		
11	15	Dime And A Dollar	Guy Mitchell	Philips	5		
12	11	Bimbo	Ruby Wright	Parlophone	5		F
13	6	Bell Bottom Blues	Alma Cogan	HMV	9		F
14	9	The Book	David Whitfield	Decca	15		
15	-	Make Love To Me!	Jo Stafford	Philips	1	(1)	
16	7	Oh Mein Papa	Eddie Calvert	Columbia	21	(9)	F
17	-	Cross Over The Bridge	Patti Page	Oriole	8	(3)	L
18	-	Deadwood Stage	Doris Day	Columbia	7		
19	-	Shadow Waltz	Mantovani	Decca	5		
20	-	Heartless	Frankie Vaughan	HMV	5		

June 1954

1	1	Secret Love	Doris Day	Philips	29	(1)	
2	2	Such A Night	Johnnie Ray	Philips	18		
3	7	Friends And Neighbours	Billy Cotton & His Band	Decca	12		L
4	3	Happy Wanderer	Obernkirchen Children's Choir	Parlophone	26		F L
5	9	Someone Else's Roses	Joan Regan	Decca	8		
6	-	I Get So Lonely	Four Knights	Capitol	11	(3)	F L
7	-	Wanted	Perry Como	HMV	15	(1)	
8	10	Heart Of My Heart	Max Bygraves	HMV	8		
9	4	The Kid's Last Fight	Frankie Laine	Philips	10		
10	5	Changing Partners	Kay Starr	Capitol	14	(13)	
11	-	Cara Mia	David Whitfield	Decca	25	(10)	
12	-	Wanted	Al Martino	Capitol	15		
13	14	The Book	David Whitfield	Decca	15		
14	-	The Little Shoemaker	Petula Clark	Polygon	10		F
15	-	Idle Gossip	Perry Como	HMV	15		
16	11	Dime And A Dollar	Guy Mitchell	Philips	5		
17	17	Cross Over The Bridge	Patti Page	Oriole	8	(3)	L
18	-	The Happy Wanderer	Frank Weir	Decca	3	(4)	F
19	18	Deadwood Stage	Doris Day	Columbia	7		
20	-	Friends And Neighbours	Max Bygraves & The Tanner Sisters	HMV	3		

April 1954

This Mnth	Prev Mnth	Title	Artist	Label	Wks 20	(UK Pos)	
1	9	Wanted	Perry Como	RCA	21	(4)	
2	1	Make Love To Me!	Jo Stafford	Columbia	20	(8)	
3	7	Cross Over The Bridge	Patti Page	Mercury	18	(13)	
4	3	I Get So Lonely	Four Knights	Capitol	21	(5)	L
5	2	Secret Love	Doris Day	Columbia	20	(1)	
6	5	Young-At-Heart	Frank Sinatra	Capitol	21	(12)	
7	13	Answer Me, My Love	Nat 'King' Cole	Capitol	18		
8	-	A Girl, A Girl	Eddie Fisher	RCA	11		
9	-	Here	Tony Martin	RCA	15		L
10	-	There'll Be No Teardrops Tonight	Tony Bennett	Columbia	6		
11	11	From The Vine Came The Grape	Gaylords	Mercury	12		
12	-	The Man With The Banjo	Ames Brothers	RCA	13		
13	4	Oh! My Pa-Pa	Eddie Fisher	RCA	19	(9)	
14	15	From The Vine Came The Grape	Hilltoppers	Dot	11		
15	20	Cuddle Me	Ronnie Gaylord	Mercury	12		F L
16	-	Little Things Mean A Lot	Kitty Kallen	Decca	25	(1)	F
17	6	That's Amore	Dean Martin	Capitol	22	(2)	
18	8	Stranger In Paradise	Tony Bennett	Columbia	19	(1)	
19	-	Anema E Core	Eddie Fisher	RCA	4		
20	-	Man Upstairs	Kay Starr	Capitol	16		

May 1954

This Mnth	Prev Mnth	Title	Artist	Label	Wks 20	(UK Pos)	
1	1	Wanted	Perry Como	RCA	21	(4)	
2	6	Young-At-Heart	Frank Sinatra	Capitol	21	(12)	
3	2	Make Love To Me!	Jo Stafford	Columbia	20	(8)	
4	4	I Get So Lonely	Four Knights	Capitol	21	(5)	L
5	3	Cross Over The Bridge	Patti Page	Mercury	18	(13)	
6	16	Little Things Mean A Lot	Kitty Kallen	Decca	25	(1)	F
7	7	Answer Me, My Love	Nat 'King' Cole	Capitol	18		
8	-	If You Love Me (Really Love Me)	Kay Starr	Capitol	17		
9	12	The Man With The Banjo	Ames Brothers	RCA	13		
10	20	Man Upstairs	Kay Starr	Capitol	16		
11	9	Here	Tony Martin	RCA	15		L
12	8	A Girl, A Girl	Eddie Fisher	RCA	11		
13	-	The Happy Wanderer	Frank Weir	London	17		F L
14	-	Jilted	Teresa Brewer	Coral	7		
15	5	Secret Love	Doris Day	Columbia	20	(1)	
16	-	Three Coins In The Fountain	Four Aces	Decca	16	(5)	
17	-	The Happy Wanderer	Henri Rene	RCA	12		F L
18	15	Cuddle Me	Ronnie Gaylord	Mercury	12		F L
19	-	Poor Butterfly	Hilltoppers	Dot	4		
20	10	There'll Be No Teardrops Tonight	Tony Bennett	Columbia	6		

June 1954

This Mnth	Prev Mnth	Title	Artist	Label	Wks 20	(UK Pos)	
1	6	Little Things Mean A Lot	Kitty Kallen	Decca	25	(1)	F
2	16	Three Coins In The Fountain	Four Aces	Decca	16	(5)	
3	1	Wanted	Perry Como	RCA	21	(4)	
4	13	The Happy Wanderer	Frank Weir	London	17		F L
5	-	Hernando's Hideaway	Archie Bleyer	Cadence	16		F L
6	8	If You Love Me (Really Love Me)	Kay Starr	Capitol	17		
7	2	Young-At-Heart	Frank Sinatra	Capitol	21	(12)	
8	7	Answer Me, My Love	Nat 'King' Cole	Capitol	18		
9	10	Man Upstairs	Kay Starr	Capitol	16		
10	4	I Get So Lonely	Four Knights	Capitol	21	(5)	L
11	11	Here	Tony Martin	RCA	15		L
12	5	Cross Over The Bridge	Patti Page	Mercury	18	(13)	
13	-	Three Coins In The Fountain	Frank Sinatra	Capitol	10	(1)	
14	9	The Man With The Banjo	Ames Brothers	RCA	13		
15	17	The Happy Wanderer	Henri Rene	RCA	12		F L
16	-	I Understand Just How You Feel	Four Tunes	Jubilee	13		L
17	-	Crazy 'Bout You, Baby	Crew-Cuts	Mercury	14		F
18	3	Make Love To Me!	Jo Stafford	Columbia	20	(8)	
19	-	Isle Of Capri	Gaylords	Mercury	6		
20	-	Steam Heat	Patti Page	Mercury	2		

US 1954
APR-JUNE

◆ Bill Haley & The Comets recorded 'Rock Around The Clock' (originally released in March by Sonny Dae & The Knights). It was initially only a minor US hit.

◆ Mercury Records became the first label to stop supplying 78 rpm records to radio stations.

◆ As *Billboard* announced "Teenagers Demand Music With A Beat", 'Gee' by The Crows (considered by many to be the first rock 'n' roll record) entered the pop and R&B charts.

◆ The Crew-Cuts debuted on the chart with their self composed 'Crazy 'Bout Ya Baby'. The Canadian quartet followed this with a long string of cover versions of R&B hits including the doo-wop songs 'Sh-Boom', 'Oop Shoop' and 'Earth Angel'.

UK 1954 JULY-SEPT

▲ Many US pop acts covered R&B hits: The McGuire Sisters (above) scored with The Spaniels' 'Goodnight, Sweetheart, Goodnight', June Valli's 'I Understand' joined the original by The Four Tunes on the American chart, and Canadian quartet The Crew-Cuts had a US No. 1 with The Chords' scat smash, 'Sh-Boom'. The latter becoming the first rock-related hit in Britain.

◆ American vocalist Kitty Kallen failed to chart again after hitting the top.

July 1954

This Mnth	Prev Mnth	Title	Artist	Label	Wks 20	(US Pos)	
1	11	Cara Mia	David Whitfield	Decca	25	(10)	
2	1	Secret Love	Doris Day	Philips	29	(1)	
3	-	Little Things Mean A Lot	Kitty Kallen	Brunswick	23	(1)	F L
4	15	Idle Gossip	Perry Como	HMV	15		
5	12	Wanted	Al Martino	Capitol	15		
6	7	Wanted	Perry Como	HMV	15	(1)	
7	2	Such A Night	Johnnie Ray	Philips	18		
8	14	The Little Shoemaker	Petula Clark	Polygon	10		F
9	6	I Get So Lonely	Four Knights	Capitol	11	(3)	F L
10	3	Friends And Neighbours	Billy Cotton & His Band	Decca	12		L
11	-	Three Coins In The Fountain	Frank Sinatra	Capitol	19	(7)	
12	4	Happy Wanderer	Obernkirchen Children's Choir	Parlophone	26		F L
13	-	The Story Of Three Loves	Winifred Atwell	Decca	9		
14	-	Three Coins In The Fountain	Four Aces	Brunswick	6	(2)	F
15	5	Someone Else's Roses	Joan Regan	Decca	8		
16	8	Heart Of My Heart	Max Bygraves	HMV	8		
17	-	Young-At-Heart	Frank Sinatra	Capitol	1	(2)	F
18	-	Never Never Land	Frank Weir	Decca	13		
19	-	Charleston	Winifred Atwell	Decca	8		
20	-	The Little Shoemaker	Frank Weir	Decca	4		

August 1954

This Mnth	Prev Mnth	Title	Artist	Label	Wks 20	(US Pos)	
1	1	Cara Mia	David Whitfield	Decca	25	(10)	
2	3	Little Things Mean A Lot	Kitty Kallen	Brunswick	23	(1)	F L
3	11	Three Coins In The Fountain	Frank Sinatra	Capitol	19	(7)	
4	4	Idle Gossip	Perry Como	HMV	15		
5	2	Secret Love	Doris Day	Philips	29	(1)	
6	5	Wanted	Al Martino	Capitol	15		
7	14	Three Coins In The Fountain	Four Aces	Brunswick	6	(2)	F
8	6	Wanted	Perry Como	HMV	15	(1)	
9	-	My Friend	Frankie Laine	Philips	15		
10	13	The Story Of Three Loves	Winifred Atwell	Decca	9		
11	8	The Little Shoemaker	Petula Clark	Polygon	10		F
12	9	I Get So Lonely	Four Knights	Capitol	11	(3)	F L
13	-	Black Hills Of Dakota	Doris Day	Philips	7		
14	-	Little Things Mean A Lot	Alma Cogan	HMV	5		
15	7	Such A Night	Johnnie Ray	Philips	18		
16	18	Never Never Land	Frank Weir	Decca	13		
17	-	Midnight	Eddie Calvert	Columbia	7		
18	-	Three Coins In The Fountain	Tony Brent	Columbia	6		
19	-	Destiny	Johnnie Ray	Columbia	4		
20	19	Charleston	Winifred Atwell	Decca	8		

September 1954

This Mnth	Prev Mnth	Title	Artist	Label	Wks 20	(US Pos)	
1	3	Three Coins In The Fountain	Frank Sinatra	Capitol	19	(7)	
2	1	Cara Mia	David Whitfield	Decca	25	(10)	
3	2	Little Things Mean A Lot	Kitty Kallen	Brunswick	23	(1)	F L
4	9	My Friend	Frankie Laine	Philips	15		
5	-	Hold My Hand	Don Cornell	Vogue	21	(5)	F
6	4	Idle Gossip	Perry Como	HMV	15		
7	5	Secret Love	Doris Day	Philips	29	(1)	
8	-	Smile	Nat 'King' Cole	Capitol	14	(14)	
9	13	Black Hills Of Dakota	Doris Day	Philips	7		
10	-	Gilly Gilly Ossenfeffer Katzenellen Bogen By The Sea	Max Bygraves	HMV	8		
11	-	West Of Zanzibar	Anthony Steel & The Radio Revellers	Polygon	6		F L
12	6	Wanted	Al Martino	Capitol	15		
13	10	The Story Of Three Loves	Winifred Atwell	Decca	9		
14	14	Little Things Mean A Lot	Alma Cogan	HMV	5		
15	8	Wanted	Perry Como	HMV	15	(1)	
16	-	Story Of Tina	Ronnie Harris	Columbia	2		F
17	-	Some Day	Frankie Laine	Columbia	3	(18)	
18	16	Never Never Land	Frank Weir	Decca	13		
19	-	Dixieland	Winifred Atwell	Decca	4		
20	-	Little Things Mean A Lot	Jimmy Young	Decca	2		

July 1954

This Mnth	Prev Mnth	Title	Artist	Label	Wks 20	(UK Pos)	
1	1	Little Things Mean A Lot	Kitty Kallen	Decca	25	(1)	F
2	5	Hernando's Hideaway	Archie Bleyer	Cadence	16		F L
3	2	Three Coins In The Fountain	Four Aces	Decca	16	(5)	
4	4	The Happy Wanderer	Frank Weir	London	17		F L
5	-	Sh-Boom	Crew-Cuts	Mercury	21	(12)	
6	6	If You Love Me (Really Love Me)	Kay Starr	Capitol	17		
7	-	The Little Shoemaker	Gaylords	Mercury	18		L
8	13	Three Coins In The Fountain	Frank Sinatra	Capitol	10	(1)	
9	16	I Understand Just How You Feel	Four Tunes	Jubilee	13		L
10	3	Wanted	Perry Como	RCA	21	(4)	
11	-	Sh-Boom	Chords	Cat	11		F L
12	17	Crazy 'Bout You, Baby	Crew-Cuts	Mercury	14		F
13	-	Goodnight, Sweetheart, Goodnight	McGuire Sisters	Coral	10		F
14	15	The Happy Wanderer	Henri Rene	RCA	12		F L
15	9	Man Upstairs	Kay Starr	Capitol	16		
16	-	Hey There	Rosemary Clooney	Columbia	23	(4)	
17	-	In The Chapel In The Moonlight	Kitty Kallen	Decca	12		
18	-	The Little Shoemaker	Hugo Winterhalter	RCA	7		
19	-	I Understand	June Valli	RCA	4		L
20	7	Young-At-Heart	Frank Sinatra	Capitol	21	(12)	

August 1954

This Mnth	Prev Mnth	Title	Artist	Label	Wks 20	(UK Pos)	
1	5	Sh-Boom	Crew-Cuts	Mercury	21	(12)	
2	7	The Little Shoemaker	Gaylords	Mercury	18		L
3	1	Little Things Mean A Lot	Kitty Kallen	Decca	25	(1)	F
4	16	Hey There	Rosemary Clooney	Columbia	23	(4)	
5	2	Hernando's Hideaway	Archie Bleyer	Cadence	16		F L
6	17	In The Chapel In The Moonlight	Kitty Kallen	Decca	12		
7	3	Three Coins In The Fountain	Four Aces	Decca	16	(5)	
8	13	Goodnight, Sweetheart, Goodnight	McGuire Sisters	Coral	10		F
9	-	The High And The Mighty	Les Baxter	Capitol	9		
10	-	I'm A Fool To Care	Les Paul & Mary Ford	Capitol	12		
11	-	The High And The Mighty	Leroy Holmes	MGM	11		F L
12	-	The High And The Mighty	Victor Young	Decca	11		
13	4	The Happy Wanderer	Frank Weir	London	17		F L
14	11	Sh-Boom	Chords	Cat	11		F L
15	-	This Ole House	Rosemary Clooney	Columbia	23	(1)	L
16	12	Crazy 'Bout You, Baby	Crew-Cuts	Mercury	14		F
17	18	The Little Shoemaker	Hugo Winterhalter	RCA	7		
18	9	I Understand Just How You Feel	Four Tunes	Jubilee	13		L
19	-	Sway	Dean Martin	Capitol	6	(6)	
20	-	They Were Doin' The Mambo	Vaughn Monroe	RCA	12		L

September 1954

This Mnth	Prev Mnth	Title	Artist	Label	Wks 20	(UK Pos)	
1	1	Sh-Boom	Crew-Cuts	Mercury	21	(12)	
2	4	Hey There	Rosemary Clooney	Columbia	23	(4)	
3	2	The Little Shoemaker	Gaylords	Mercury	18		L
4	-	Skokiaan	Ralph Marterie	Mercury	14		L
5	15	This Ole House	Rosemary Clooney	Columbia	23	(1)	L
6	6	In The Chapel In The Moonlight	Kitty Kallen	Decca	12		
7	12	The High And The Mighty	Victor Young	Decca	11		
8	3	Little Things Mean A Lot	Kitty Kallen	Decca	25	(1)	F
9	-	Skokiaan	Four Lads	Columbia	11		
10	9	The High And The Mighty	Les Baxter	Capitol	9		
11	11	The High And The Mighty	Leroy Holmes	MGM	11		F L
12	-	I Need You Now	Eddie Fisher	RCA	21	(13)	
13	-	Shake, Rattle And Roll	Bill Haley & His Comets	Decca	20	(4)	G
14	10	I'm A Fool To Care	Les Paul & Mary Ford	Capitol	12		
15	20	They Were Doin' The Mambo	Vaughn Monroe	RCA	12		L
16	-	Hold My Hand	Don Cornell	Coral	15	(1)	
17	8	Goodnight, Sweetheart, Goodnight	McGuire Sisters	Coral	10		F
18	-	Hey There	Sammy Davis Jr.	Decca	4	(19)	F
19	-	If I Give My Heart To You	Doris Day	Columbia	15	(4)	
20	5	Hernando's Hideaway	Archie Bleyer	Cadence	16		F L

◆ The suggestive lyrics of top R&B hits, 'Honey Love' by Clyde McPhatter & The Drifters, 'Work With Me Annie', 'Sexy Ways' and 'Annie Had A Baby' by The Midnighters, and 'Shake, Rattle & Roll' by Joe Turner attracted bad publicity. Incidentally, Bill Haley's cleaned-up version of the latter became a transatlantic pop hit.

◆ Elvis Presley signed to Sun Records and released his version of R&B singer Arthur 'Big Boy' Crudup's 'That's All Right Mama' coupled with C&W performer Bill Monroe's 'Blue Moon Of Kentucky'.

◆ The Chords' original version of 'Sh-Boom' was the first R&B hit on an independent label to reach the Top 10.

UK 1954
OCT-DEC

◆ Both of West Indian pianist Winifred Atwell's Christmas hits, 'Let's Have A Party' and 'Let's Have Another Party', sold over a million copies worldwide.

◆ Elvis Presley, who had yet to have a UK release, was voted eighth Most Promising New C&W Singer in *Billboard's* US DJ poll – Tommy Collins took the crown.

◆ The flagging dance hall business on both sides of the Atlantic was revitalized firstly by the growth in interest in Latin American dances like the tango and mambo, and secondly by rock'n'roll. The latter was just starting to make an impression in the UK thanks to records like 'Sh-Boom' by The Crew-Cuts and 'Shake, Rattle And Roll' by Bill Haley & The Comets.

October 1954

This Mnth	Prev Mnth	Title	Artist	Label	Wks 20	(US Pos)	
1	5	Hold My Hand	Don Cornell	Vogue	21	(5)	F
2	8	Smile	Nat 'King' Cole	Capitol	14	(14)	
3	1	Three Coins In The Fountain	Frank Sinatra	Capitol	19	(7)	
4	4	My Friend	Frankie Laine	Philips	15		
5	3	Little Things Mean A Lot	Kitty Kallen	Brunswick	23	(1)	F L
6	2	Cara Mia	David Whitfield	Decca	25	(10)	
7	-	If I Give My Heart To You	Doris Day	Philips	10	(4)	
8	-	Sway	Dean Martin	Capitol	7	(15)	
9	-	My Son My Son	Vera Lynn	Decca	14		
10	-	The Story Of Tina	Al Martino	Capitol	8		
11	-	This Ole House	Rosemary Clooney	Philips	18	(1)	
12	-	This Ole House	Billie Anthony	Columbia	15		F
13	-	There Must Be A Reason	Frankie Laine	Philips	9		
14	-	Sh-Boom	Crew-Cuts	Mercury	9	(1)	F
15	10	Gilly Gilly Ossenfeffer Katzenellen Bogen By The Sea	Max Bygraves	HMV	8		
16	9	Black Hills Of Dakota	Doris Day	Philips	7		
17	7	Secret Love	Doris Day	Philips	29	(1)	
18	-	Rain Rain Rain	Frankie Laine	Philips	16		
19	-	If I Give My Heart To You	Joan Regan	Decca	11		
20	-	Make Her Mine	Nat 'King' Cole	Capitol	2		

November 1954

This Mnth	Prev Mnth	Title	Artist	Label	Wks 20	(US Pos)	
1	9	My Son My Son	Vera Lynn	Decca	14		
2	11	This Ole House	Rosemary Clooney	Philips	18	(1)	
3	1	Hold My Hand	Don Cornell	Vogue	21	(5)	F
4	19	If I Give My Heart To You	Joan Regan	Decca	11		
5	2	Smile	Nat 'King' Cole	Capitol	14	(14)	
6	7	If I Give My Heart To You	Doris Day	Philips	10	(4)	
7	12	This Ole House	Billie Anthony	Columbia	15		F
8	18	Rain Rain Rain	Frankie Laine	Philips	16		
9	6	Cara Mia	David Whitfield	Decca	25	(10)	
10	5	Little Things Mean A Lot	Kitty Kallen	Brunswick	23	(1)	F L
11	4	My Friend	Frankie Laine	Philips	15		
12	-	Santo Natale	David Whitfield	Decca	10		
13	-	No One But You	Billy Eckstine	MGM	17		F
14	13	There Must Be A Reason	Frankie Laine	Philips	9		
15	3	Three Coins In The Fountain	Frank Sinatra	Capitol	19	(7)	
16	14	Sh-Boom	Crew-Cuts	Mercury	9	(1)	F
17	-	I Need You Now	Eddie Fisher	HMV	10	(1)	
18	-	Let's Have Another Party	Winifred Atwell	Decca	8		
19	8	Sway	Dean Martin	Capitol	7	(15)	
20	-	Sh-Boom	Stan Freberg	Capitol	2		F L

December 1954

This Mnth	Prev Mnth	Title	Artist	Label	Wks 20	(US Pos)	
1	18	Let's Have Another Party	Winifred Atwell	Decca	8		
2	12	Santo Natale	David Whitfield	Decca	10		
3	29	This Ole House	Rosemary Clooney	Philips	18	(1)	
4	13	No One But You	Billy Eckstine	MGM	17		F
5	-	I Still Believe	Ronnie Hilton	HMV	14		F
6	1	My Son My Son	Vera Lynn	Decca	14		
7	3	Hold My Hand	Don Cornell	Vogue	21	(5)	F
8	8	Rain Rain Rain	Frankie Laine	Philips	16		
9	7	This Ole House	Billie Anthony	Columbia	15		F
10	4	If I Give My Heart To You	Joan Regan	Decca	11		
11	-	Heartbeat	Ruby Murray	Columbia	16		F
12	-	Let's Get Together No. 1	Big Ben Banjo Band	Columbia	4		F
13	-	Finger Of Suspicion	Dickie Valentine	Decca	15		
14	17	I Need You Now	Eddie Fisher	HMV	10	(1)	
15	-	I Can't Tell A Waltz From A Tango	Alma Cogan	HMV	11		
16	5	Smile	Nat 'King' Cole	Capitol	14	(14)	
17	-	Shake, Rattle And Roll	Bill Haley & His Comets	Brunswick	14	(7)	
18	6	If I Give My Heart To You	Doris Day	Philips	10	(4)	
19	-	Veni Vidi Vici	Ronnie Hilton	HMV	8		
20	-	Let's Have A Party	Winifred Atwell	Philips	6		

October 1954

This Mnth	Prev Mnth	Title	Artist	Label	Wks 20	(UK Pos)	
1	2	Hey There	Rosemary Clooney	Columbia	23	(4)	
2	12	I Need You Now	Eddie Fisher	RCA	21	(13)	
3	5	This Ole House	Rosemary Clooney	Columbia	23	(1)	L
4	1	Sh-Boom	Crew-Cuts	Mercury	21	(12)	
5	19	If I Give My Heart To You	Doris Day	Columbia	15	(4)	
6	4	Skokiaan	Ralph Marterie	Mercury	14		L
7	16	Hold My Hand	Don Cornell	Coral	15	(1)	
8	13	Shake, Rattle And Roll	Bill Haley & His Comets	Decca	20	(4)	G
9	9	Skokiaan	Four Lads	Columbia	11		
10	-	Cara Mia	David Whitfield	London	12	(1)	F L
11	3	The Little Shoemaker	Gaylords	Mercury	18		L
12	-	Papa Loves Mambo	Perry Como	RCA	16	(16)	
13	7	The High And The Mighty	Victor Young	Decca	11		
14	-	If I Give My Heart To You	Denise Lor	Majar	9		F L
15	15	They Were Doin' The Mambo	Vaughn Monroe	RCA	12		L
16	-	Smile	Nat 'King' Cole	Capitol	6	(2)	
17	-	Teach Me Tonight	De Castro Sisters	Abbott	17		F L
18	-	Whither Thou Goest	Les Paul & Mary Ford	Capitol	8		
19	6	In The Chapel In The Moonlight	Kitty Kallen	Decca	12		
20	-	Oop-Shoop	Crew-Cuts	Mercury	4		

November 1954

This Mnth	Prev Mnth	Title	Artist	Label	Wks 20	(UK Pos)	
1	2	I Need You Now	Eddie Fisher	RCA	21	(13)	
2	3	This Ole House	Rosemary Clooney	Columbia	23	(1)	L
3	1	Hey There	Rosemary Clooney	Columbia	23	(4)	
4	12	Papa Loves Mambo	Perry Como	RCA	16	(16)	
5	7	Hold My Hand	Don Cornell	Coral	15	(1)	
6	5	If I Give My Heart To You	Doris Day	Columbia	15	(4)	
7	-	Mr. Sandman	Chordettes	Cadence	19	(11)	F
8	17	Teach Me Tonight	De Castro Sisters	Abbott	17		F L
9	8	Shake, Rattle And Roll	Bill Haley & His Comets	Decca	20	(4)	G
10	-	Muskrat Ramble	McGuire Sisters	Coral	7		
11	6	Skokiaan	Ralph Marterie	Mercury	14		L
12	10	Cara Mia	David Whitfield	London	12	(1)	F L
13	-	Mambo Italiano	Rosemary Clooney	Columbia	8	(1)	
14	-	Count Your Blessings	Eddie Fisher	RCA	13		
15	4	Sh-Boom	Crew-Cuts	Mercury	21	(12)	
16	18	Whither Thou Goest	Les Paul & Mary Ford	Capitol	8		
17	-	(Bazoom) I Need Your Lovin'	Cheers	Capitol	5		F
18	9	Skokiaan	Four Lads	Columbia	11		
19	-	Hajji Baba	Nat 'King' Cole	Capitol	4		
20	-	Mr. Sandman	Four Aces	Decca	12	(9)	

December 1954

This Mnth	Prev Mnth	Title	Artist	Label	Wks 20	(UK Pos)	
1	7	Mr. Sandman	Chordettes	Cadence	19	(11)	F
2	1	I Need You Now	Eddie Fisher	RCA	21	(13)	
3	2	This Ole House	Rosemary Clooney	Columbia	23	(1)	L
4	8	Teach Me Tonight	De Castro Sisters	Abbott	17		F L
5	4	Papa Loves Mambo	Perry Como	RCA	16	(16)	
6	14	Count Your Blessings	Eddie Fisher	RCA	13		
7	-	Let Me Go, Lover	Joan Weber	Columbia	14	(16)	F L
8	-	The Naughty Lady Of Shady Lane	Ames Brothers	RCA	14	(6)	
9	9	Shake, Rattle And Roll	Bill Haley & His Comets	Decca	20	(4)	G
10	-	Mr. Sandman	Four Aces	Decca	12	(9)	
11	3	Hey There	Rosemary Clooney	Columbia	23	(4)	
12	5	Hold My Hand	Don Cornell	Coral	15	(1)	
13	6	If I Give My Heart To You	Doris Day	Columbia	15	(4)	
14	13	Mambo Italiano	Rosemary Clooney	Columbia	8	(1)	
15	-	Make Yourself Comfortable	Sarah Vaughan	Mercury	14		F
16	-	Dim, Dim The Lights (I Want Some Atmosphere)	Bill Haley & His Comets	Decca	12		
17	-	Hearts Of Stone	Fontane Sisters	Dot	16		F G
18	-	Let Me Go, Lover!	Teresa Brewer	Coral	9	(9)	
19	-	That's All I Want From You	Jaye P. Morgan	RCA	18		F
20	-	Hearts Of Stone	Charms	Deluxe	7		F

US
1954
OCT-DEC

◆ R&B radio stations, juke box operators and trade papers agreed it was time to halt "off-color and offensive" records – The Midnighters were the main scapegoats.

◆ Despite the fact that at times this quarter she had two records in the Top 3, Rosemary Clooney's 'This Ole House' was destined to be her last Top 20 hit.

▲ The Chordettes had their first and biggest transatlantic hit with 'Mr. Sandman', one of the catchiest tunes of the era.

UK 1955 JAN-MAR

▲ Bill Haley's 'Rock Around The Clock' had a two-week chart run in Britain. In the US, it became the theme to the controversial film, *The Blackboard Jungle*.

◆ Not only were several versions of 'Let Me Go Lover' and 'Mr. Sandman' battling it out, but there were also a couple of hit recordings of 'Mambo Italiano', 'This Ole House', 'Naughty Lady Of Shady Lane', 'A Blossom Fell' and 'Happy Days And Lonely Nights'.

◆ 'Give Me Your Word', which was the B-side of Tennessee Ernie Ford's minor US success, 'River Of No Return', surprised many people by topping the British chart.

January 1955

This Mnth	Prev Mnth	Title	Artist	Label	Wks 20	(US Pos)	
1	13	Finger Of Suspicion	Dickie Valentine	Decca	15		
2	-	Mambo Italiano	Rosemary Clooney	Philips	16	(10)	
3	4	No One But You	Billy Eckstine	MGM	17		F
4	5	I Still Believe	Ronnie Hilton	HMV	14		F
5	11	Heartbeat	Ruby Murray	Columbia	16		F
6	17	Shake, Rattle And Roll	Bill Haley & His Comets	Brunswick	14	(7)	
7	-	Mr. Sandman	Dickie Valentine	Decca	12		
8	15	I Can't Tell A Waltz From A Tango	Alma Cogan	HMV	11		
9	-	Mr. Sandman	Chordettes	Columbia	9	(1)	F
10	8	Rain Rain Rain	Frankie Laine	Philips	16		
11	-	Mr. Sandman	Four Aces	Brunswick	5	(10)	
12	3	This Ole House	Rosemary Clooney	Philips	18	(1)	
13	1	Let's Have Another Party	Winifred Atwell	Decca	8		
14	2	Santo Natale	David Whitfield	Decca	10		
15	7	Hold My Hand	Don Cornell	Vogue	21	(5)	F
16	-	Give Me Your Word	Tennessee Ernie Ford	Capitol	24		F
17	-	Count Your Blessings	Bing Crosby	Brunswick	3		
18	19	Veni Vidi Vici	Ronnie Hilton	HMV	8		
19	-	Softly Softly	Ruby Murray	Columbia	23		
20	9	This Ole House	Billie Anthony	Columbia	15		F

February 1955

This Mnth	Prev Mnth	Title	Artist	Label	Wks 20	(US Pos)	
1	19	Softly Softly	Ruby Murray	Columbia	23		
2	2	Mambo Italiano	Rosemary Clooney	Philips	16	(10)	
3	1	Finger Of Suspicion	Dickie Valentine	Decca	15		
4	16	Give Me Your Word	Tennessee Ernie Ford	Capitol	24		F
5	5	Heartbeat	Ruby Murray	Columbia	16		F
6	6	Shake, Rattle And Roll	Bill Haley & His Comets	Brunswick	14	(7)	
7	-	Naughty Lady Of Shady Lane	Dean Martin	Capitol	10		
8	-	The Naughty Lady Of Shady Lane	Ames Brothers	HMV	6	(3)	F L
9	3	No One But You	Billy Eckstine	MGM	17		F
10	7	Mr. Sandman	Dickie Valentine	Decca	12		
11	-	Happy Days And Lonely Nights	Ruby Murray	Columbia	8		
12	-	Let Me Go, Lover	Teresa Brewer	Vogue/Coral	10	(8)	F
13	-	Beyond The Stars	David Whitfield	Decca	9		
14	4	I Still Believe	Ronnie Hilton	HMV	14		F
15	-	Mobile	Ray Burns	Columbia	13		F
16	-	A Blossom Fell	Dickie Valentine	Decca	10		
17	-	Happy Days And Lonely Nights	Frankie Vaughan	HMV	3		
18	-	Majorca	Petula Clark	Polygon	5		
19	-	Mambo Italiano	Dean Martin	Capitol	2		
20	-	Drinking Song	Mario Lanza	HMV	1		

March 1955

This Mnth	Prev Mnth	Title	Artist	Label	Wks 20	(US Pos)	
1	4	Give Me Your Word	Tennessee Ernie Ford	Capitol	24		F
2	1	Softly Softly	Ruby Murray	Columbia	23		
3	-	Let Me Go, Lover	Dean Martin	Capitol	9		
4	2	Mambo Italiano	Rosemary Clooney	Philips	16	(10)	
5	-	A Blossom Fell	Nat 'King' Cole	Capitol	10	(2)	
6	15	Mobile	Ray Burns	Columbia	13		F
7	7	Naughty Lady Of Shady Lane	Dean Martin	Capitol	10		
8	3	Finger Of Suspicion	Dickie Valentine	Decca	15		
9	5	Heartbeat	Ruby Murray	Columbia	16		F
10	-	Let Me Go, Lover	Ruby Murray	Columbia	7		
11	13	Beyond The Stars	David Whitfield	Decca	9		
12	12	Let Me Go, Lover	Teresa Brewer	Vogue/Coral	10	(8)	F
13	11	Happy Days And Lonely Nights	Ruby Murray	Columbia	8		
14	16	A Blossom Fell	Dickie Valentine	Decca	10		
15	-	Tomorrow	Johnny Brandon	Polygon	8		F
16	-	Wedding Bells	Eddie Fisher	HMV	11		
17	18	Majorca	Petula Clark	Polygon	5		
18	-	If Anyone Finds This I Love You	Ruby Murray	Columbia	11		
19	8	The Naughty Lady Of Shady Lane	Ames Brothers	HMV	6	(3)	F L
20	6	Shake, Rattle And Roll	Bill Haley & His Comets	Brunswick	14	(7)	

US 1955
JAN-MAR

January 1955

This Mnth	Prev Mnth	Title	Artist	Label	Wks 20	(UK Pos)	
1	1	Mr. Sandman	Chordettes	Cadence	19	(11)	F
2	7	Let Me Go, Lover	Joan Weber	Columbia	14	(16)	F L
3	8	The Naughty Lady Of Shady Lane	Ames Brothers	RCA	14	(6)	
4	17	Hearts Of Stone	Fontane Sisters	Dot	16		F G
5	4	Teach Me Tonight	De Castro Sisters	Abbott	17		F L
6	18	Let Me Go, Lover!	Teresa Brewer	Coral	9	(9)	
7	3	This Ole House	Rosemary Clooney	Columbia	23	(1)	L
8	2	I Need You Now	Eddie Fisher	RCA	21	(13)	
9	15	Make Yourself Comfortable	Sarah Vaughan	Mercury	14		F
10	6	Count Your Blessings	Eddie Fisher	RCA	13		
11	10	Mr. Sandman	Four Aces	Decca	12	(9)	
12	-	Melody Of Love	Billy Vaughn	Dot	21		F G
13	19	That's All I Want From You	Jaye P. Morgan	RCA	18		F
14	16	Dim, Dim The Lights (I Want Some Atmosphere)	Bill Haley & His Comets	Decca	12		
15	-	Sincerely	McGuire Sisters	Coral	17	(14)	G
16	9	Shake, Rattle And Roll	Bill Haley & His Comets	Decca	20	(4)	G
17	-	(My Baby Don't Love Me) No More	DeJohn Sisters	Epic	9		F L
18	5	Papa Loves Mambo	Perry Como	RCA	16	(16)	
19	-	Earth Angel (Will You Be Mine)	Penguins	Dootone	11		F L
20	20	Hearts Of Stone	Charms	Deluxe	7		F

February 1955

This Mnth	Prev Mnth	Title	Artist	Label	Wks 20	(UK Pos)	
1	15	Sincerely	McGuire Sisters	Coral	17	(14)	G
2	4	Hearts Of Stone	Fontane Sisters	Dot	16		F G
3	12	Melody Of Love	Billy Vaughn	Dot	21		F G
4	2	Let Me Go, Lover	Joan Weber	Columbia	14	(16)	F L
5	13	That's All I Want From You	Jaye P. Morgan	RCA	18		F
6	-	Ko Ko Mo (I Love You So)	Perry Como	RCA	12		
7	1	Mr. Sandman	Chordettes	Cadence	19	(11)	F
8	19	Earth Angel (Will You Be Mine)	Penguins	Dootone	11		F L
9	-	Tweedle Dee	Georgia Gibbs	Mercury	17	(20)	G
10	3	The Naughty Lady Of Shady Lane	Ames Brothers	RCA	14	(6)	
11	-	Melody Of Love	David Carroll	Mercury	11		F L
12	-	Ko Ko Mo (I Love You So)	Crew-Cuts	Mercury	9		
13	-	The Crazy Otto (Medley)	Johnny Maddox	Dot	16		F L
14	9	Make Yourself Comfortable	Sarah Vaughan	Mercury	14		F
15	-	Earth Angel	Crew-Cuts	Mercury	10	(4)	
16	-	Melody Of Love	Four Aces	Decca	13		
17	17	(My Baby Don't Love Me) No More	DeJohn Sisters	Epic	9		F L
18	-	Open Up Your Heart (And Let The Sunshine In)	Cowboy Church Sunday School	Decca	16		F L
19	6	Let Me Go, Lover!	Teresa Brewer	Coral	9	(9)	
20	11	Mr. Sandman	Four Aces	Decca	12	(9)	

March 1955

This Mnth	Prev Mnth	Title	Artist	Label	Wks 20	(UK Pos)	
1	1	Sincerely	McGuire Sisters	Coral	17	(14)	G
2	13	The Crazy Otto (Medley)	Johnny Maddox	Dot	16		F L
3	3	Melody Of Love	Billy Vaughn	Dot	21		F G
4	9	Tweedle Dee	Georgia Gibbs	Mercury	17	(20)	G
5	-	The Ballad Of Davy Crockett	Bill Hayes	Cadence	20	(2)	F L
6	6	Ko Ko Mo (I Love You So)	Perry Como	RCA	12		
7	2	Hearts Of Stone	Fontane Sisters	Dot	16		F G
8	15	Earth Angel	Crew-Cuts	Mercury	10	(4)	
9	-	How Important Can It Be?	Joni James	MGM	13		
10	5	That's All I Want From You	Jaye P. Morgan	RCA	18		F
11	11	Melody Of Love	David Carroll	Mercury	11		F L
12	12	Ko Ko Mo (I Love You So)	Crew-Cuts	Mercury	9		
13	18	Open Up Your Heart (And Let The Sunshine In)	Cowboy Church Sunday School	Decca	16		F L
14	8	Earth Angel (Will You Be Mine)	Penguins	Dootone	11		F L
15	-	Ballad Of Davy Crockett	Fess Parker	Columbia	17		F
16	16	Melody Of Love	Four Aces	Decca	13		
17	-	Pledging My Love	Johnny Ace	Duke	3		F L
18	-	Darling Je Vous Aime Beaucoup	Nat 'King' Cole	Capitol	13		
19	-	Cherry Pink And Apple Blossom White	Perez Prado	RCA	22	(1)	F G
20	-	Ballad Of Davy Crockett	Tennessee Ernie Ford	Capitol	15	(3)	

◆ Alan Freed's first *Rock'n'Roll Party* with an all-star bill including Fats Domino, Joe Turner and The Drifters, attracted a record 15,000 fans. It was an all-R&B show – as yet, rock'n'roll had no stars of its own.

◆ R&B songs were having unprecedented success on the charts, albeit with pop cover versions. Among them were 'Hearts Of Stone', 'Sincerely', 'Shake, Rattle & Roll', 'Earth Angel', 'Tweedle Dee' and 'Pledging My Love' which gave R&B idol Johnny Ace a posthumous debut hit.

◆ With the aim of slowing down the number of pop versions of R&B records, vocalist Lavern Baker appealed to Congress to legally put an end to note-for-note cover versions of original songs.

◆ A bi-weekly Top 15 album chart was introduced by *Billboard*.

UK 1955 APR-JUNE

◆ Less than four months after making her chart debut, distinctive Irish vocalist Ruby Murray had a record five singles simultaneously on the UK chart.

◆ Latin American dance craze the mambo had its finest moment thanks to Perez Prado's transatlantic smash 'Cherry Pink And Apple Blossom White'.

◆ Sixteen months after they had simultaneously climbed the American Top 20, versions of 'Stranger In Paradise' by Tony Bennett, Tony Martin and The Four Aces also battled it out on the British chart. The song which was adapted from classical composer Borodin's 'Polovtsian Dances' came from the musical *Kismet*. The only local version to hit was by trumpeter Eddie Calvert, whose 'Oh, Mein Papa' had previously sold a million in the USA.

April 1955

This Mnth	Prev Mnth	Title	Artist	Label	Wks 20	(US Pos)	
1	1	Give Me Your Word	Tennessee Ernie Ford	Capitol	24		F
2	-	Cherry Pink And Apple Blossom White	Perez Prado	HMV	17	(1)	F
3	2	Softly Softly	Ruby Murray	Columbia	23		
4	18	If Anyone Finds This I Love You	Ruby Murray	Columbia	11		
5	16	Wedding Bells	Eddie Fisher	HMV	11		
6	-	Under The Bridges Of Paris	Dean Martin	Capitol	8		
7	-	Cherry Pink And Apple Blossom White	Eddie Calvert	Columbia	21		
8	6	Mobile	Ray Burns	Columbia	13		F
9	-	Prize Of Gold	Joan Regan	Decca	8	(55)	
10	5	A Blossom Fell	Nat 'King' Cole	Capitol	10	(2)	
11	-	Under The Bridges Of Paris	Eartha Kitt	HMV	10		F L
12	-	Stranger In Paradise	Tony Bennett	Philips	16	(2)	F
13	-	Ready Willing And Able	Doris Day	Philips	9		
14	3	Let Me Go, Lover	Dean Martin	Capitol	9		
15	-	Earth Angel	Crew-Cuts	Mercury	20	(8)	L
16	-	Stranger In Paradise	Tony Martin	HMV	13	(10)	F
17	15	Tomorrow	Johnny Brandon	Polygon	8		F
18	14	A Blossom Fell	Dickie Valentine	Decca	10		
19	-	A Blossom Fell	Ronnie Hilton	HMV	5		
20	10	Let Me Go, Lover	Ruby Murray	Columbia	7		

May 1955

This Mnth	Prev Mnth	Title	Artist	Label	Wks 20	(US Pos)	
1	12	Stranger In Paradise	Tony Bennett	Philips	16	(2)	F
2	2	Cherry Pink And Apple Blossom White	Perez Prado	HMV	17	(1)	F
3	7	Cherry Pink And Apple Blossom White	Eddie Calvert	Columbia	21		
4	1	Give Me Your Word	Tennessee Ernie Ford	Capitol	24		F
5	15	Earth Angel	Crew-Cuts	Mercury	20	(8)	L
6	16	Stranger In Paradise	Tony Martin	HMV	13	(10)	F
7	3	Softly Softly	Ruby Murray	Columbia	23		
8	-	Unchained Melody	Al Hibbler	Brunswick	17	(5)	F L
9	5	Wedding Bells	Eddie Fisher	HMV	11		
10	-	Unchained Melody	Jimmy Young	Decca	19		
11	-	If You Believe	Johnnie Ray	Philips	11		
12	4	If Anyone Finds This I Love You	Ruby Murray	Columbia	11		
13	13	Ready Willing And Able	Doris Day	Philips	9		
14	11	Under The Bridges Of Paris	Eartha Kitt	HMV	10		F L
15	-	Unchained Melody	Les Baxter	Capitol	9	(2)	F L
16	-	Melody Of Love	Ink Spots	Parlophone	4		F L
17	-	Stranger In Paradise	Four Aces	Brunswick	6	(5)	
18	6	Under The Bridges Of Paris	Dean Martin	Capitol	8		
19	-	Stranger In Paradise	Eddie Calvert	Columbia	4		
20	-	Where Will The Baby's Dimple Be	Rosemary Clooney	Philips	13		

June 1955

This Mnth	Prev Mnth	Title	Artist	Label	Wks 20	(US Pos)	
1	3	Cherry Pink And Apple Blossom...	Eddie Calvert	Columbia	21		
2	8	Unchained Melody	Al Hibbler	Brunswick	17	(5)	F L
3	10	Unchained Melody	Jimmy Young	Decca	19		
4	1	Stranger In Paradise	Tony Bennett	Philips	16	(2)	F
5	5	Earth Angel	Crew-Cuts	Mercury	20	(8)	L
6	2	Cherry Pink And Apple Blossom...	Perez Prado	HMV	17	(1)	F
7	-	Dreamboat	Alma Cogan	HMV	16		
8	6	Stranger In Paradise	Tony Martin	HMV	13	(10)	F
9	20	Where Will The Baby's Dimple Be	Rosemary Clooney	Philips	13		
10	11	If You Believe	Johnnie Ray	Philips	11		
11	17	Stranger In Paradise	Four Aces	Brunswick	6	(5)	
12	4	Give Me Your Word	Tennessee Ernie Ford	Capitol	24		F
13	15	Unchained Melody	Les Baxter	Capitol	9	(2)	F L
14	-	I Wonder	Dickie Valentine	Decca	15		
15	-	Sing It With Joe	Joe 'Mr. Piano' Henderson	Polygon	4		F
16	-	You My Love	Frank Sinatra	Capitol	7		
17	7	Softly Softly	Ruby Murray	Columbia	23		
18	-	Cool Water	Frankie Laine	Philips	22		
19	-	Crazy Otto Rag	Stargazers	Decca	3		
20	-	Stowaway	Barbara Lyon	Columbia	8		F

US 1955 APR-JUNE

April 1955

This Mnth	Prev Mnth	Title	Artist	Label	Wks 20	(UK Pos)	
1	5	The Ballad Of Davy Crockett	Bill Hayes	Cadence	20	(2)	F L
2	2	The Crazy Otto (Medley)	Johnny Maddox	Dot	16		F L
3	19	Cherry Pink And Apple Blossom White	Perez Prado	RCA	22	(1)	F G
4	4	Tweedle Dee	Georgia Gibbs	Mercury	17	(20)	G
5	15	Ballad Of Davy Crockett	Fess Parker	Columbia	17		F
6	1	Sincerely	McGuire Sisters	Coral	17	(14)	G
7	-	Dance With Me Henry (Wallflower)	Georgia Gibbs	Mercury	16		L
8	3	Melody Of Love	Billy Vaughn	Dot	21		F G
9	20	Ballad Of Davy Crockett	Tennessee Ernie Ford	Capitol	15	(3)	
10	9	How Important Can It Be?	Joni James	MGM	13		
11	18	Darling Je Vous Aime Beaucoup	Nat 'King' Cole	Capitol	13		
12	-	Unchained Melody	Les Baxter	Capitol	20	(10)	F G
13	13	Open Up Your Heart (And Let The Sunshine In)	Cowboy Church Sunday School	Decca	16		F L
14	-	Unchained Melody	Al Hibbler	Decca	18	(2)	F G
15	6	Ko Ko Mo (I Love You So)	Perry Como	RCA	12		
16	16	Melody Of Love	Four Aces	Decca	13		
17	8	Earth Angel	Crew-Cuts	Mercury	10	(4)	
18	-	The Breeze And I	Caterina Valente	Decca	11	(5)	F L
19	-	Play Me Hearts And Flowers (I Wanna Cry)	Johnny Desmond	Coral	5		F
20	11	Melody Of Love	David Carroll	Mercury	11		F L

May 1955

This Mnth	Prev Mnth	Title	Artist	Label	Wks 20	(UK Pos)	
1	3	Cherry Pink And Apple Blossom...	Perez Prado	RCA	22	(1)	F G
2	12	Unchained Melody	Les Baxter	Capitol	20	(10)	F G
3	7	Dance With Me Henry (Wallflower)	Georgia Gibbs	Mercury	16		L
4	1	The Ballad Of Davy Crockett	Bill Hayes	Cadence	20	(2)	F L
5	14	Unchained Melody	Al Hibbler	Decca	18	(2)	F G
6	5	Ballad Of Davy Crockett	Fess Parker	Columbia	17		F
7	9	Ballad Of Davy Crockett	Tennessee Ernie Ford	Capitol	15	(3)	
8	2	The Crazy Otto (Medley)	Johnny Maddox	Dot	16		F L
9	-	Unchained Melody	Roy Hamilton	Epic	13		F
10	11	Darling Je Vous Aime Beaucoup	Nat 'King' Cole	Capitol	13		
11	-	Honey-Babe	Art Mooney	MGM	16		F L
12	4	Tweedle Dee	Georgia Gibbs	Mercury	17	(20)	G
13	-	Whatever Lola Wants	Sarah Vaughan	Mercury	11		
14	-	A Blossom Fell/If I May	Nat 'King' Cole	Capitol	18	(3)	G
15	18	The Breeze And I	Caterina Valente	Decca	11	(5)	F L
16	-	Don't Be Angry	Crew-Cuts	Mercury	7		
17	-	Rock Around The Clock	Bill Haley & His Comets	Decca	22	(1)	G
18	6	Sincerely	McGuire Sisters	Coral	17	(14)	G
19	8	Melody Of Love	Billy Vaughn	Dot	21		F G
20	-	Two Hearts	Pat Boone	Dot	6		F

June 1955

This Mnth	Prev Mnth	Title	Artist	Label	Wks 20	(UK Pos)	
1	1	Cherry Pink And Apple Blossom...	Perez Prado	RCA	22	(1)	F G
2	2	Unchained Melody	Les Baxter	Capitol	20	(10)	F G
3	14	A Blossom Fell/If I May	Nat 'King' Cole	Capitol	18	(3)	G
4	3	Dance With Me Henry (Wallflower)	Georgia Gibbs	Mercury	16		L
5	17	Rock Around The Clock	Bill Haley & His Comets	Decca	22	(1)	G
6	5	Unchained Melody	Al Hibbler	Decca	18	(2)	F G
7	-	Learnin' The Blues	Frank Sinatra	Capitol	18	(2)	G
8	11	Honey-Babe	Art Mooney	MGM	16		F L
9	4	The Ballad Of Davy Crockett	Bill Hayes	Cadence	20	(2)	F L
10	6	Ballad Of Davy Crockett	Fess Parker	Columbia	17		F
11	9	Unchained Melody	Roy Hamilton	Epic	13		F
12	13	Whatever Lola Wants	Sarah Vaughan	Mercury	11		
13	7	Ballad Of Davy Crockett	Tennessee Ernie Ford	Capitol	15	(3)	
14	-	It's A Sin To Tell A Lie	Somethin' Smith & The Redheads	Epic	16		F L
15	-	Something's Gotta Give	McGuire Sisters	Coral	10		
16	15	The Breeze And I	Caterina Valente	Decca	11	(5)	F L
17	-	Love Me Or Leave Me	Sammy Davis Jr.	Decca	3	(8)	
18	-	Something's Gotta Give	Sammy Davis Jr.	Decca	9	(11)	
19	16	Don't Be Angry	Crew-Cuts	Mercury	7		
20	-	Heart	Eddie Fisher	RCA	7		

◆ For the only time in history two songs filled six slots on the US Top 10, 'Unchained Melody' and 'The Ballad Of Davy Crockett'. In the UK, three acts also reached the Top 10 with the former song and two with the latter.

▲ Perry Como, who was charting with a cover version of Gene & Eunice's R&B hit, 'Ko Ko Mo (I Love You So)', signed a lucrative 12 year TV contract with NBC.

◆ American Juke Box operators announced that there were 60% more R&B records being selected than a year ago.

21

UK 1955
JULY-SEPT

◆ Despite its failure in the US, 'Rose Marie' (from the 1925 musical of the same name) by Florida C&W artist Slim Whitman, held the top spot in Britain for 11 successive weeks – a record he held until 1991 when it was broken by Bryan Adams.

◆ Among the earliest R&B songs to chart in Britain were 'Earth Angel' and 'Sincerely', albeit the sanitized American pop versions by the Crew-Cuts and the McGuire Sisters respectively.

◆ Slim Whitman was not the only American artist hitting with a recording that had either failed in their homeland or had not merited release there. Other acts with Anglo-aimed singles included Rosemary Clooney, Johnnie Ray, Frank Sinatra and Frankie Laine. The latter was enjoying two UK-only successes 'Strange Lady In Town' and 'Cool Water'.

July 1955

This Mnth	Prev Mnth	Title	Artist	Label	Wks 20	(US Pos)	
1	7	Dreamboat	Alma Cogan	HMV	16		
2	3	Unchained Melody	Jimmy Young	Decca	19		
3	2	Unchained Melody	Al Hibbler	Brunswick	17	(5)	F L
4	1	Cherry Pink And Apple Blossom White	Eddie Calvert	Columbia	21		
5	14	I Wonder	Dickie Valentine	Decca	15		
6	-	Evermore	Ruby Murray	Columbia	17		
7	18	Cool Water	Frankie Laine	Philips	22		
8	5	Earth Angel	Crew-Cuts	Mercury	20	(8)	L
9	9	Where Will The Baby's Dimple Be	Rosemary Clooney	Philips	13		
10	-	Rose Marie	Slim Whitman	London	19		F
11	4	Stranger In Paradise	Tony Bennett	Philips	16	(2)	F
12	-	Every Day Of My Life	Malcolm Vaughan	HMV	16		F
13	-	Ev'rywhere	David Whitfield	Decca	20		
14	20	Stowaway	Barbara Lyon	Columbia	8		F L
15	6	Cherry Pink And Apple Blossom White	Perez Prado	HMV	17	(1)	F
16	8	Stranger In Paradise	Tony Martin	HMV	13	(10)	F
17	-	Strange Lady In Town	Frankie Laine	Philips	13		
18	-	Sincerely	McGuire Sisters	Vogue Coral	4	(1)	
19	10	If You Believe	Johnnie Ray	Philips	11		
20	13	Unchained Melody	Les Baxter	Capitol	9	(2)	F L

August 1955

This Mnth	Prev Mnth	Title	Artist	Label	Wks 20	(US Pos)	
1	10	Rose Marie	Slim Whitman	London	19		F
2	7	Cool Water	Frankie Laine	Philips	22		
3	6	Evermore	Ruby Murray	Columbia	17		
4	1	Dreamboat	Alma Cogan	HMV	16		
5	13	Ev'rywhere	David Whitfield	Decca	20		
6	12	Every Day Of My Life	Malcolm Vaughan	HMV	16		F
7	-	Learnin' The Blues	Frank Sinatra	Capitol	13	(2)	
8	17	Strange Lady In Town	Frankie Laine	Philips	13		
9	2	Unchained Melody	Jimmy Young	Decca	19		
10	5	I Wonder	Dickie Valentine	Decca	15		
11	4	Cherry Pink And Apple Blossom White	Eddie Calvert	Columbia	21		
12	3	Unchained Melody	Al Hibbler	Brunswick	17	(5)	F L
13	-	Mama	David Whitfield	Decca	11		
14	-	Indian Love Call	Slim Whitman	London American	12	(10)	
15	-	John And Julie	Eddie Calvert	Columbia	11		
16	-	The Breeze And I	Caterina Valente	Polydor	14	(13)	F L
17	8	Earth Angel	Crew-Cuts	Mercury	20	(8)	L
18	9	Where Will The Baby's Dimple Be	Rosemary Clooney	Philips	13		
19	14	Stowaway	Barbara Lyon	Columbia	8		F L
20	-	You My Love	Frank Sinatra	Capitol	7		

September 1955

This Mnth	Prev Mnth	Title	Artist	Label	Wks 20	(US Pos)	
1	1	Rose Marie	Slim Whitman	London	19		F
2	7	Learnin' The Blues	Frank Sinatra	Capitol	13	(2)	
3	2	Cool Water	Frankie Laine	Philips	22		
4	5	Ev'rywhere	David Whitfield	Decca	20		
5	16	The Breeze And I	Caterina Valente	Polydor	14	(13)	F L
6	3	Evermore	Ruby Murray	Columbia	17		
7	8	Strange Lady In Town	Frankie Laine	Philips	13		
8	15	John And Julie	Eddie Calvert	Columbia	11		
9	6	Every Day Of My Life	Malcolm Vaughan	HMV	16		F
10	14	Indian Love Call	Slim Whitman	London American	12	(10)	
11	-	Close The Door	Stargazers	Decca	9		
12	-	The Man From Laramie	Jimmy Young	Decca	12		
13	-	Love Me Or Leave Me	Sammy Davis Jr.	Brunswick	6	(10)	
14	-	Stars Shine In Your Eyes	Ronnie Hilton	HMV	7		
15	-	Something's Gotta Give	Sammy Davis Jr.	Brunswick	7	(9)	F
16	-	That's How A Love Song Was Born	Ray Burns	Columbia	6		L
17	-	Blue Star	Cyril Stapleton	Decca	12		
18	13	Mama	David Whitfield	Decca	11		
19	4	Dreamboat	Alma Cogan	HMV	16		
20	-	China Doll	Slim Whitman	London American	2		

July 1955

This Mnth	Prev Mnth	Title	Artist	Label	Wks 20	(UK Pos)	
1	5	Rock Around The Clock	Bill Haley & His Comets	Decca	22	(1)	G
2	1	Cherry Pink And Apple Blossom White	Perez Prado	RCA	22	(1)	F G
3	3	A Blossom Fell/If I May	Nat 'King' Cole	Capitol	18	(3)	G
4	7	Learnin' The Blues	Frank Sinatra	Capitol	18	(2)	G
5	2	Unchained Melody	Les Baxter	Capitol	20	(10)	F G
6	15	Something's Gotta Give	McGuire Sisters	Coral	10		
7	8	Honey-Babe	Art Mooney	MGM	16		F L
8	-	Hard To Get	Giselle Mackenzie	X	15		F L
9	6	Unchained Melody	Al Hibbler	Decca	18	(2)	F G
10	14	It's A Sin To Tell A Lie	Somethin' Smith & The Redheads	Epic	16		F L
11	18	Something's Gotta Give	Sammy Davis Jr.	Decca	9	(11)	
12	-	Ain't That A Shame	Pat Boone	Dot	18	(7)	G
13	-	Sweet And Gentle	Alan Dale	Coral	7		F L
14	4	Dance With Me Henry (Wallflower)	Georgia Gibbs	Mercury	16		L
15	11	Unchained Melody	Roy Hamilton	Epic	13		F
16	20	Heart	Eddie Fisher	RCA	7		
17	-	The House Of Blue Lights	Chuck Miller	Mercury	10		F L
18	9	The Ballad Of Davy Crockett	Bill Hayes	Cadence	20	(2)	F L
19	-	A Story Untold	Crew-Cuts	Mercury	4		
20	-	Hummingbird	Les Paul & Mary Ford	Capitol	9		L

August 1955

This Mnth	Prev Mnth	Title	Artist	Label	Wks 20	(UK Pos)	
1	1	Rock Around The Clock	Bill Haley & His Comets	Decca	22	(1)	G
2	12	Ain't That A Shame	Pat Boone	Dot	18	(7)	G
3	4	Learnin' The Blues	Frank Sinatra	Capitol	18	(2)	G
4	3	A Blossom Fell/If I May	Nat 'King' Cole	Capitol	18	(3)	G
5	8	Hard To Get	Giselle Mackenzie	X	15		F L
6	-	The Yellow Rose Of Texas	Mitch Miller	Columbia	19	(2)	G
7	10	It's A Sin To Tell A Lie	Somethin' Smith & The Redheads	Epic	16		F L
8	-	Seventeen	Boyd Bennett & His Rockets	King	13	(16)	F L
9	20	Hummingbird	Les Paul & Mary Ford	Capitol	9		L
10	17	The House Of Blue Lights	Chuck Miller	Mercury	10		F L
11	2	Cherry Pink And Apple Blossom White	Perez Prado	RCA	22	(1)	F G
12	5	Unchained Melody	Les Baxter	Capitol	20	(10)	F G
13	-	The Yellow Rose Of Texas	Johnny Desmond	Coral	14		L
14	6	Something's Gotta Give	McGuire Sisters	Coral	10		
15	-	Domani (Tomorrow)	Julius La Rosa	Cadence	4		L
16	-	Maybellene	Chuck Berry	Chess	10		F
17	11	Something's Gotta Give	Sammy Davis Jr.	Decca	9	(11)	
18	13	Sweet And Gentle	Alan Dale	Coral	7		F L
19	-	Wake The Town And Tell The People	Les Baxter	Capitol	11		
20	-	I'll Never Stop Loving You	Doris Day	Columbia	4	(17)	

September 1955

This Mnth	Prev Mnth	Title	Artist	Label	Wks 20	(UK Pos)	
1	6	The Yellow Rose Of Texas	Mitch Miller	Columbia	19	(2)	G
2	2	Ain't That A Shame	Pat Boone	Dot	18	(7)	G
3	1	Rock Around The Clock	Bill Haley & His Comets	Decca	22	(1)	G
4	16	Maybellene	Chuck Berry	Chess	10		F
5	-	Autumn Leaves	Roger Williams	Kapp	23		F G
6	13	The Yellow Rose Of Texas	Johnny Desmond	Coral	14		L
7	8	Seventeen	Boyd Bennett & His Rockets	King	13	(16)	F L
8	-	Seventeen	Fontane Sisters	Dot	11		
9	-	Love Is A Many-Splendored Thing	Four Aces	Decca	20	(2)	G
10	-	Tina Marie	Perry Como	RCA	13	(24)	
11	19	Wake The Town And Tell The People	Les Baxter	Capitol	11		
12	3	Learnin' The Blues	Frank Sinatra	Capitol	18	(2)	G
13	5	Hard To Get	Giselle Mackenzie	X	15		F L
14	-	Gum Drop	Crew-Cuts	Mercury	7		
15	-	Moments To Remember	Four Lads	Columbia	23		G
16	-	The Longest Walk	Jaye P. Morgan	RCA	6		L
17	-	Song Of The Dreamer	Eddie Fisher	RCA	5		
18	9	Hummingbird	Les Paul & Mary Ford	Capitol	9		L
19	4	A Blossom Fell/If I May	Nat 'King' Cole	Capitol	18	(3)	G
20	-	The Bible Tells Me So	Don Cornell	Coral	12		L

US 1955
JULY-SEPT

◆ Rock'n'roll had its first No. 1 hit, 'Rock Around The Clock' by Bill Haley & The Comets. It was estimated that Haley would earn $500,000 in 1955 from shows alone.

◆ Pat Boone debuted in the US Top 20 with Fats Domino's R&B No. 1, 'Ain't That A Shame', as Elvis Presley's name first appeared on the C&W chart with 'Baby Let's Play House'.

▲ *Rock 'N' Roll Revue*, arguably the first rock'n'roll film, was premiered. It starred Nat 'King' Cole (above) and Joe Turner.

◆ The 1950s most successful record producer, Mitch Miller, had his biggest hit as an artist with 'The Yellow Rose Of Texas'.

UK 1955
OCT-DEC

American composer Jerry Ross died aged 29, as his compositions, 'Hernando's Hideaway' and 'Hey There', held three places in the UK Top 5.

Thanks to its exposure in the hit film *The Blackboard Jungle*, 'Rock Around The Clock' by Bill Haley & The Comets became the first rock'n'roll record to top the UK chart.

The price of singles in Britain went up to 5s 7d (53 cents/27p).

Balladeer Jimmy Young became the first British artist to clock up two successive UK No. 1s. The record that completed the double was his version of the American film theme 'The Man From Laramie', a song which failed to chart Stateside.

October 1955

This Mnth	Prev Mnth	Title	Artist	Label	Wks 20	(US Pos)	
1	12	The Man From Laramie	Jimmy Young	Decca	12		
2	17	Blue Star	Cyril Stapleton	Decca	12		
3	1	Rose Marie	Slim Whitman	London	19		F
4	3	Cool Water	Frankie Laine	Philips	22		
5	-	Yellow Rose Of Texas	Mitch Miller	Philips	13	(1)	F L
6	4	Ev'rywhere	David Whitfield	Decca	20		
7	5	The Breeze And I	Caterina Valente	Polydor	14	(13)	F L
8	-	Hernando's Hideaway	Johnston Brothers	Decca	13		
9	2	Learnin' The Blues	Frank Sinatra	Capitol	13	(2)	
10	11	Close The Door	Stargazers	Decca	9		
11	-	Hey There	Rosemary Clooney	Philips	11	(1)	
12	-	Rock Around The Clock	Bill Haley & His Comets	Brunswick	17	(1)	G
13	-	Hernando's Hideaway	Johnnie Ray	Philips	5	(24)	
14	-	Hey There	Johnnie Ray	Philips	9		
15	10	Indian Love Call	Slim Whitman	London American	12	(10)	
16	-	I'll Come When You Call	Ruby Murray	Columbia	7		
17	9	Every Day Of My Life	Malcolm Vaughan	HMV	16		F
18	6	Evermore	Ruby Murray	Columbia	17		
19	13	Love Me Or Leave Me	Sammy Davis Jr.	Brunswick	6	(10)	
20	-	Go On By	Alma Cogan	HMV	4		

November 1955

This Mnth	Prev Mnth	Title	Artist	Label	Wks 20	(US Pos)	
1	8	Hernando's Hideaway	Johnston Brothers	Decca	13		
2	12	Rock Around The Clock	Bill Haley & His Comets	Brunswick	17	(1)	G
3	1	The Man From Laramie	Jimmy Young	Decca	12		
4	14	Hey There	Johnnie Ray	Philips	9		
5	11	Hey There	Rosemary Clooney	Philips	11	(1)	
6	2	Blue Star	Cyril Stapleton	Decca	12		
7	5	Yellow Rose Of Texas	Mitch Miller	Philips	13	(1)	F L
8	16	I'll Come When You Call	Ruby Murray	Columbia	7		
9	-	Let's Have A Ding Dong	Winifred Atwell	Decca	10		
10	6	Ev'rywhere	David Whitfield	Decca	20		
11	-	Song Of The Dreamer	Johnnie Ray	Philips	5		
12	-	Love Is A Many Splendoured Thing	Four Aces	Brunswick	13	(1)	
13	4	Cool Water	Frankie Laine	Philips	22		
14	-	Twenty Tiny Fingers	Stargazers	Decca	11		L
15	3	Rose Marie	Slim Whitman	London	19		F
16	-	Yellow Rose Of Texas	Gary Miller	Nixa	5		F
17	7	The Breeze And I	Caterina Valente	Polydor	14	(13)	F L
18	-	Ain't That A Shame	Pat Boone	London American	9	(2)	F
19	-	Meet Me On The Corner	Max Bygraves	HMV	11		
20	-	Yellow Rose Of Texas	Ronnie Hilton	HMV	2		

December 1955

This Mnth	Prev Mnth	Title	Artist	Label	Wks 20	(US Pos)	
1	2	Rock Around The Clock	Bill Haley & His Comets	Brunswick	17	(1)	G
2	-	Christmas Alphabet	Dickie Valentine	Decca	7		
3	12	Love Is A Many Splendoured Thing	Four Aces	Brunswick	13	(1)	
4	9	Let's Have A Ding Dong	Winifred Atwell	Decca	10		
5	19	Meet Me On The Corner	Max Bygraves	HMV	11		
6	14	Twenty Tiny Fingers	Stargazers	Decca	11		L
7	7	Yellow Rose Of Texas	Mitch Miller	Philips	13	(1)	F L
8	1	Hernando's Hideaway	Johnston Brothers	Decca	13		
9	-	Suddenly There's A Valley	Petula Clark	Nixa	10		
10	18	Ain't That A Shame	Pat Boone	London American	9	(2)	F
11	-	Hawkeye	Frankie Laine	Philips	8		
12	-	When You Lose The One You Love	David Whitfield	Decca	11	(62)	
13	-	Suddenly There's A Valley	Jo Stafford	Philips	6	(21)	L
14	-	The Singing Dogs (Medley)	Singing Dogs	Nixa	4		F L
15	-	Never Do A Tango With An Eskimo	Alma Cogan	HMV	5		
16	4	Hey There	Johnnie Ray	Philips	9		
17	5	Hey There	Rosemary Clooney	Philips	11	(1)	
18	-	Suddenly There's A Valley	Lee Lawrence	Columbia	3		L
19	6	Blue Star	Cyril Stapleton	Decca	12		
20	-	On With The Motley	Harry Secombe	Philips	3		F

October 1955

This Mnth	Prev Mnth	Title	Artist	Label	Wks 20	(UK Pos)	
1	9	Love Is A Many-Splendored Thing	Four Aces	Decca	20	(2)	G
2	1	The Yellow Rose Of Texas	Mitch Miller	Columbia	19	(2)	G
3	5	Autumn Leaves	Roger Williams	Kapp	23		F G
4	15	Moments To Remember	Four Lads	Columbia	23		G
5	2	Ain't That A Shame	Pat Boone	Dot	18	(7)	G
6	-	The Shifting Whispering Sands (Pts 1 & 2)	Billy Vaughn	Dot	13	(20)	
7	10	Tina Marie	Perry Como	RCA	13	(24)	
8	20	The Bible Tells Me So	Don Cornell	Coral	12		L
9	6	The Yellow Rose Of Texas	Johnny Desmond	Coral	14		L
10	8	Seventeen	Fontane Sisters	Dot	11		
11	-	Black Denim Trousers	Cheers	Capitol	8		L
12	-	The Shifting, Whispering Sands	Rusty Draper	Mercury	13		
13	-	Only You	Platters	Mercury	18	(5)	F G
14	-	He	Al Hibbler	Decca	20		
15	4	Maybellene	Chuck Berry	Chess	10		F
16	3	Rock Around The Clock	Bill Haley & His Comets	Decca	22	(1)	G
17	11	Wake The Town And Tell The People	Les Baxter	Capitol	11		
18	7	Seventeen	Boyd Bennett & His Rockets	King	13	(16)	F L
19	-	My Bonnie Lassie	Ames Brothers	RCA	7		
20	-	Suddenly There's A Valley	Gogi Grant	Era	9		F

November 1955

This Mnth	Prev Mnth	Title	Artist	Label	Wks 20	(UK Pos)	
1	3	Autumn Leaves	Roger Williams	Kapp	23		F G
2	1	Love Is A Many-Splendored Thing	Four Aces	Decca	20	(2)	G
3	4	Moments To Remember	Four Lads	Columbia	23		G
4	2	The Yellow Rose Of Texas	Mitch Miller	Columbia	19	(2)	G
5	13	Only You	Platters	Mercury	18	(5)	F G
6	-	Sixteen Tons	Tennessee Ernie Ford	Capitol	17	(1)	G L
7	-	I Hear You Knocking	Gale Storm	Dot	16		F G
8	12	The Shifting, Whispering Sands	Rusty Draper	Mercury	13		
9	14	He	Al Hibbler	Decca	20		
10	-	At My Front Door (Crazy Little Mama)	Pat Boone	Dot	9		
11	6	The Shifting Whispering Sands (Pts 1 & 2)	Billy Vaughn	Dot	13	(20)	
12	19	My Bonnie Lassie	Ames Brothers	RCA	7		
13	11	Black Denim Trousers	Cheers	Capitol	8		L
14	-	Forgive My Heart	Nat 'King' Cole	Capitol	5		
15	-	Love And Marriage	Frank Sinatra	Capitol	13	(3)	
16	20	Suddenly There's A Valley	Gogi Grant	Era	9		F
17	8	The Bible Tells Me So	Don Cornell	Coral	12		L
18	-	He	McGuire Sisters	Coral	10		
19	7	Tina Marie	Perry Como	RCA	13	(24)	
20	-	It's Almost Tomorrow	Dream Weavers	Decca	18	(1)	F L

December 1955

This Mnth	Prev Mnth	Title	Artist	Label	Wks 20	(UK Pos)	
1	6	Sixteen Tons	Tennessee Ernie Ford	Capitol	17	(1)	G L
2	1	Autumn Leaves	Roger Williams	Kapp	23		F G
3	7	I Hear You Knocking	Gale Storm	Dot	16		F G
4	3	Moments To Remember	Four Lads	Columbia	23		G
5	2	Love Is A Many-Splendored Thing	Four Aces	Decca	20	(2)	G
6	-	Memories Are Made Of This	Dean Martin	Capitol	17	(1)	G
7	5	Only You	Platters	Mercury	18	(5)	F G
8	9	He	Al Hibbler	Decca	20		
9	15	Love And Marriage	Frank Sinatra	Capitol	13	(3)	
10	20	It's Almost Tomorrow	Dream Weavers	Decca	18	(1)	F L
11	8	The Shifting, Whispering Sands	Rusty Draper	Mercury	13		
12	18	He	McGuire Sisters	Coral	10		
13	10	At My Front Door (Crazy Little Mama)	Pat Boone	Dot	9		
14	-	Nuttin' For Christmas	Barry Gordon	MGM	3		F G L
15	-	Band Of Gold	Don Cherry	Columbia	16	(6)	L
16	11	The Shifting Whispering Sands (Pts 1 & 2)	Billy Vaughn	Dot	13	(20)	
17	-	Only You (And You Alone)	Hilltoppers	Dot	5	(3)	
18	-	The Great Pretender	Platters	Mercury	17	(5)	G
19	4	The Yellow Rose Of Texas	Mitch Miller	Columbia	19	(2)	G
20	-	Daddy-O	Fontane Sisters	Dot	3		

◆ RCA Records paid $40,000 to sign Elvis Presley – a small fortune for an artist who had yet to have a pop hit. His final Sun single, 'I Forgot To Remember To Forget You', topped the C&W chart.

▲ Buddy Holly was signed by Decca Records. He had been a support act for both Elvis Presley and Bill Haley & The Comets when they performed in his home town, Lubbock, Texas.

◆ Tennessee Ernie Ford's revival of Merle Travis's late 1940s coal mining opus '16 Tons', broke the record for the fastest selling single. It sold over 600,000 in less than two weeks and rocketed to the top in just three weeks.

UK 1956 JAN-MAR

◆ As Mercury Records had no UK outlet, the Platters' US smashes, 'Only You' and 'The Great Pretender', were not released in the UK until Autumn 1956. This left the way clear for The Hilltoppers and Jimmy Parkinson.

▲ Lonnie Donegan's 'Rock Island Line' introduced the transatlantic public to skiffle – a do-it-yourself folk/blues based music that launched a thousand British groups.

◆ George Martin had three productions simultaneously in the UK Top 20. The records being by TV personality Eamonn Andrews, Eve Boswell and (later Beatles' publisher) Dick James.

January 1956

This Mnth	Prev Mnth	Title	Artist	Label	Wks 20	(US Pos)	
1	1	Rock Around The Clock	Bill Haley & His Comets	Brunswick	17	(1)	G
2	3	Love Is A Many Splendoured Thing	Four Aces	Brunswick	13	(1)	
3	-	Rock-A-Beatin' Boogie	Bill Haley & His Comets	Brunswick	8	(23)	
4	-	Sixteen Tons	Tennessee Ernie Ford	Capitol	11	(1)	
5	-	The Ballad Of Davy Crockett	Bill Hayes	London American	9	(1)	F L
6	5	Meet Me On The Corner	Max Bygraves	HMV	11		
7	-	Love And Marriage	Frank Sinatra	Capitol	8	(6)	
8	-	The Ballad Of Davy Crockett	Tennessee Ernie Ford	Capitol	7	(6)	L
9	15	Never Do A Tango With An Eskimo	Alma Cogan	HMV	5		
10	12	When You Lose The One You Love	David Whitfield	Decca	11	(62)	
11	6	Twenty Tiny Fingers	Stargazers	Decca	11		L
12	9	Suddenly There's A Valley	Petula Clark	Nixa	10		
13	-	Rock Island Line	Lonnie Donegan	Decca	14	(8)	F
14	-	The Tender Trap	Frank Sinatra	Capitol	9	(24)	
15	-	Pickin' A Chicken	Eve Boswell	Parlophone	10		F L
16	-	Sixteen Tons	Frankie Laine	Philips	3		
17	11	Hawkeye	Frankie Laine	Philips	8		
18	-	Someone On Your Mind	Jimmy Young	Decca	5		
19	10	Ain't That A Shame	Pat Boone	London American	9	(2)	F
20	2	Christmas Alphabet	Dickie Valentine	Decca	7		

February 1956

This Mnth	Prev Mnth	Title	Artist	Label	Wks 20	(US Pos)	
1	4	Sixteen Tons	Tennessee Ernie Ford	Capitol	11	(1)	
2	14	The Tender Trap	Frank Sinatra	Capitol	9	(24)	
3	5	The Ballad Of Davy Crockett	Bill Hayes	London American	9	(1)	F L
4	-	Memories Are Made Of This	Dean Martin	Capitol	14	(1)	
5	-	Zambesi	Lou Busch	Capitol	15	(75)	F L
6	7	Love And Marriage	Frank Sinatra	Capitol	8	(6)	
7	-	Only You	Hilltoppers	London American	21	(15)	F
8	13	Rock Island Line	Lonnie Donegan	Decca	14	(8)	F
9	8	The Ballad Of Davy Crockett	Tennessee Ernie Ford	Capitol	7	(6)	L
10	-	Dreams Can Tell A Lie	Nat 'King' Cole	Capitol	9		
11	-	It's Almost Tomorrow	Dream Weavers	Brunswick	16	(8)	F L
12	3	Rock-A-Beatin' Boogie	Bill Haley & His Comets	Brunswick	8	(23)	
13	-	Rock And Roll Waltz	Kay Starr	HMV	18	(1)	L
14	-	Band Of Gold	Don Cherry	Philips	11	(5)	F L
15	-	Robin Hood	Gary Miller	Nixa	6		
16	2	Love Is A Many Splendoured Thing	Four Aces	Brunswick	13	(1)	
17	-	Robin Hood	Dick James	Parlophone	8		F
18	15	Pickin' A Chicken	Eve Boswell	Parlophone	10		F L
19	-	Memories Are Made Of This	Dave King	Decca	13		F
20	-	Young And Foolish	Edmund Hockridge	Nixa	7		F

March 1956

This Mnth	Prev Mnth	Title	Artist	Label	Wks 20	(US Pos)	
1	11	It's Almost Tomorrow	Dream Weavers	Brunswick	16	(8)	F L
2	4	Memories Are Made Of This	Dean Martin	Capitol	14	(1)	
3	13	Rock And Roll Waltz	Kay Starr	HMV	18	(1)	L
4	5	Zambesi	Lou Busch	Capitol	15	(75)	F L
5	7	Only You	Hilltoppers	London American	21	(15)	F
6	19	Memories Are Made Of This	Dave King	Decca	13		F
7	14	Band Of Gold	Don Cherry	Philips	11	(5)	F L
8	-	See You Later Alligator	Bill Haley & His Comets	Brunswick	11	(6)	
9	20	Young And Foolish	Edmund Hockridge	Nixa	7		F
10	8	Rock Island Line	Lonnie Donegan	Decca	14	(8)	F
11	-	The Great Pretender	Jimmy Parkinson	Columbia	10		F
12	-	Poor People Of Paris	Winifred Atwell	Decca	15		
13	2	The Tender Trap	Frank Sinatra	Capitol	9	(24)	
14	1	Sixteen Tons	Tennessee Ernie Ford	Capitol	11	(1)	
15	-	Chain Gang	Jimmy Young	Decca	5		
16	-	Theme From 'The Three Penny Opera'	Dick Hyman Trio	MGM	9	(10)	F L
17	10	Dreams Can Tell A Lie	Nat 'King' Cole	Capitol	9		
18	-	Zambesi	Eddie Calvert	Columbia	5		
19	-	In Old Lisbon	Frank Chacksfield	Decca	4		L
20	18	Pickin' A Chicken	Eve Boswell	Parlophone	10		F L

January 1956

This Mnth	Prev Mnth	Title	Artist	Label	Wks 20	(UK Pos)	
1	6	Memories Are Made Of This	Dean Martin	Capitol	17	(1)	G
2	1	Sixteen Tons	Tennessee Ernie Ford	Capitol	17	(1)	G L
3	18	The Great Pretender	Platters	Mercury	17	(5)	G
4	3	I Hear You Knocking	Gale Storm	Dot	16		F G
5	15	Band Of Gold	Don Cherry	Columbia	16	(6)	L
6	-	Lisbon Antigua	Nelson Riddle	Capitol	20		F G L
7	9	Love And Marriage	Frank Sinatra	Capitol	13	(3)	
8	4	Moments To Remember	Four Lads	Columbia	23		G
9	-	Rock And Roll Waltz	Kay Starr	RCA	16	(1)	G L
10	10	It's Almost Tomorrow	Dream Weavers	Decca	18	(1)	F L
11	8	He	Al Hibbler	Decca	20		
12	2	Autumn Leaves	Roger Williams	Kapp	23		F G
13	-	Dungaree Doll	Eddie Fisher	RCA	12		
14	-	Angels In The Sky	Crew-Cuts	Mercury	12		L
15	7	Only You	Platters	Mercury	18	(5)	F G
16	-	See You Later, Alligator	Bill Haley & His Comets	Decca	13	(7)	
17	-	Teenage Prayer	Gale Storm	Dot	8		
18	14	Nuttin' For Christmas	Barry Gordon	MGM	3		F G L
19	-	Are You Satisfied?	Rusty Draper	Mercury	5		
20	5	Love Is A Many-Splendored Thing	Four Aces	Decca	20	(2)	G

February 1956

This Mnth	Prev Mnth	Title	Artist	Label	Wks 20	(UK Pos)	
1	9	Rock And Roll Waltz	Kay Starr	RCA	16	(1)	G L
2	1	Memories Are Made Of This	Dean Martin	Capitol	17	(1)	G
3	3	The Great Pretender	Platters	Mercury	17	(5)	G
4	6	Lisbon Antigua	Nelson Riddle	Capitol	20		F G L
5	16	See You Later, Alligator	Bill Haley & His Comets	Decca	13	(7)	
6	2	Sixteen Tons	Tennessee Ernie Ford	Capitol	17	(1)	G L
7	-	No, Not Much!	Four Lads	Columbia	15		G
8	5	Band Of Gold	Don Cherry	Columbia	16	(6)	L
9	10	It's Almost Tomorrow	Dream Weavers	Decca	18	(1)	F L
10	13	Dungaree Doll	Eddie Fisher	RCA	12		
11	14	Angels In The Sky	Crew-Cuts	Mercury	12		L
12	-	I'll Be Home	Pat Boone	Dot	14	(1)	G
13	-	The Poor People Of Paris	Les Baxter	Capitol	17		G L
14	-	Moritat (A Theme From 'The Three Penny Opera')	Dick Hyman	MGM	11	(9)	F L
15	17	Teenage Prayer	Gale Storm	Dot	8		
16	19	Are You Satisfied?	Rusty Draper	Mercury	5		
17	-	Why Do Fools Fall In Love	Frankie Lymon & The Teenagers	Gee	15	(1)	F G
18	11	He	Al Hibbler	Decca	20		
19	4	I Hear You Knocking	Gale Storm	Dot	16		F G
20	-	Go On With The Wedding	Patti Page	Mercury	3		

March 1956

This Mnth	Prev Mnth	Title	Artist	Label	Wks 20	(UK Pos)	
1	4	Lisbon Antigua	Nelson Riddle	Capitol	20		F G L
2	13	The Poor People Of Paris	Les Baxter	Capitol	17		G L
3	1	Rock And Roll Waltz	Kay Starr	RCA	16	(1)	G L
4	7	No, Not Much!	Four Lads	Columbia	15		G
5	3	The Great Pretender	Platters	Mercury	17	(5)	G
6	12	I'll Be Home	Pat Boone	Dot	14	(1)	G
7	5	See You Later, Alligator	Bill Haley & His Comets	Decca	13	(7)	
8	17	Why Do Fools Fall In Love	Frankie Lymon & The Teenagers	Gee	15	(1)	F G
9	-	Hot Diggity (Dog Ziggity Boom)	Perry Como	RCA	17	(4)	G
10	2	Memories Are Made Of This	Dean Martin	Capitol	17	(1)	G
11	14	Moritat (... 'The Three Penny Opera')	Dick Hyman	MGM	11	(9)	F L
12	8	Band Of Gold	Don Cherry	Columbia	16	(6)	L
13	-	Blue Suede Shoes	Carl Perkins	Sun	14	(10)	F G L
14	-	Heartbreak Hotel	Elvis Presley	RCA	20	(2)	F G
15	-	A Tear Fell	Teresa Brewer	Coral	15	(2)	
16	-	A Theme From 'The Three Penny Opera' (Moritat)	Richard Hayman & Jan August	Mercury	6		L
17	9	It's Almost Tomorrow	Dream Weavers	Decca	18	(1)	F L
18	10	Dungaree Doll	Eddie Fisher	RCA	12		
19	-	Eddie My Love	Teen Queens	RPM	4		F L
20	-	Why Do Fools Fall In Love	Gale Storm	Dot	3		

◆ Despite being described as "immoral" and "part of a plot to undermine the morals of our youth", rock'n'roll was achieving a measure of respectability, and starting to receive the media coverage its sales merited.

◆ The second "rock" title to head the chart was 'Rock And Roll Waltz' by veteran vocalist Kay Starr. Among the other early 1950s stars who moved into Big Beat territory were Eddie Fisher, who covered The Rock Brothers' 'Dungaree Doll', and TV personality Gale Storm whose string of R&B covers started with 'I Hear You Knocking', first cut by Smiley Lewis.

◆ Elvis Presley and Carl Perkins achieved the supposed impossible when 'Heartbreak Hotel' and 'Blue Suede Shoes' respectively, shot up the pop, C&W and R&B charts.

UK 1956 APR-JUNE

◆ For the first time in Britain an album sold enough copies to enter the best selling records chart. The LP **Songs For Swinging Lovers** contained such standards as 'Pennies From Heaven', 'Makin' Whoopee' and 'I've Got You Under My Skin'.

◆ In the month that Elvis and Carl Perkins debuted on the British chart and Alan Freed was first heard in Europe, the first Eurovision Song Contest was held: it was won by Lys Assia from Switzerland with a song called 'Refrains'.

◆ The British singles chart was extended to a Top 30.

◆ As Elvis Presley was first seen on the front cover of *NME*, Britain's Lonnie Donegan appeared on the cover of the noted US music magazine *Cash Box*. On returning from his American tour, Donegan left Chris Barber's Jazz Band and formed his own skiffle group.

April 1956

This Mnth	Prev Mnth	Title	Artist	Label	Wks 20	(US Pos)	
1	12	Poor People Of Paris	Winifred Atwell	Decca	15		
2	1	It's Almost Tomorrow	Dream Weavers	Brunswick	16	(8)	F L
3	3	Rock And Roll Waltz	Kay Starr	HMV	18	(1)	L
4	5	Only You	Hilltoppers	London American	21	(15)	F
5	6	Memories Are Made Of This	Dave King	Decca	13		F
6	4	Zambesi	Lou Busch	Capitol	15	(75)	F L
7	2	Memories Are Made Of This	Dean Martin	Capitol	14	(1)	
8	8	See You Later Alligator	Bill Haley & His Comets	Brunswick	11	(6)	
9	16	Theme From 'The Three Penny Opera'	Dick Hyman Trio	MGM	9	(10)	F L
10	-	My September Love	David Whitfield	Decca	21		
11	11	The Great Pretender	Jimmy Parkinson	Columbia	10		F
12	-	A Tear Fell	Teresa Brewer	Vogue/Coral	15	(9)	
13	-	Willie Can	Alma Cogan	HMV	7		
14	-	No Other Love	Ronnie Hilton	HMV	13		
15	-	Theme From 'The Threepenny Opera'	Billy Vaughn	London American	5	(37)	L
16	15	Chain Gang	Jimmy Young	Decca	5		
17	18	Zambesi	Eddie Calvert	Columbia	5		
18	-	Theme From The Threepenny Opera	Louis Armstrong	Philips	7		
19	7	Band Of Gold	Don Cherry	Philips	11	(5)	F L
20	-	You Can't Be True To Two	Dave King	Decca	7		

May 1956

This Mnth	Prev Mnth	Title	Artist	Label	Wks 20	(US Pos)	
1	14	No Other Love	Ronnie Hilton	HMV	13		
2	1	Poor People Of Paris	Winifred Atwell	Decca	15		
3	12	A Tear Fell	Teresa Brewer	Vogue/Coral	15	(9)	
4	3	Rock And Roll Waltz	Kay Starr	HMV	18	(1)	L
5	10	My September Love	David Whitfield	Decca	21		
6	2	It's Almost Tomorrow	Dream Weavers	Brunswick	16	(8)	F L
7	4	Only You	Hilltoppers	London American	21	(15)	F
8	-	I'll Be Home	Pat Boone	London American	23	(6)	
9	-	Lost John/Stewball	Lonnie Donegan	Pye Nixa	14	(58)	
10	-	Main Title Theme From The Man With The Golden Arm	Billy May	Capitol	6	(49)	F L
11	18	Theme From The Threepenny Opera	Louis Armstrong	Philips	7		
12	20	You Can't Be True To Two	Dave King	Decca	7		
13	-	Heartbreak Hotel	Elvis Presley	HMV	19	(1)	F
14	-	The Happy Whistler	Don Robertson	Capitol	7	(9)	F L
15	8	See You Later Alligator	Bill Haley & His Comets	Brunswick	11	(6)	
16	5	Memories Are Made Of This	Dave King	Decca	13		F
17	7	Memories Are Made Of This	Dean Martin	Capitol	14	(1)	
18	-	Blue Suede Shoes	Carl Perkins	London American	7	(3)	F L
19	-	Mountain Greenery	Mel Torme	Vogue/Coral	17		F
20	9	Theme From 'The Three Penny Opera'	Dick Hyman Trio	MGM	9	(10)	F L

June 1956

This Mnth	Prev Mnth	Title	Artist	Label	Wks 20	(US Pos)	
1	8	I'll Be Home	Pat Boone	London American	23	(6)	
2	9	Lost John/Stewball	Lonnie Donegan	Pye Nixa	14	(58)	
3	1	No Other Love	Ronnie Hilton	HMV	13		
4	13	Heartbreak Hotel	Elvis Presley	HMV	19	(1)	F
5	3	A Tear Fell	Teresa Brewer	Vogue/Coral	15	(9)	
6	-	Hot Diggity	Perry Como	HMV	12	(2)	
7	-	The Saints Rock 'n Roll	Bill Haley & His Comets	Brunswick	22	(18)	
8	5	My September Love	David Whitfield	Decca	21		
9	-	Blue Suede Shoes	Elvis Presley	HMV	8	(20)	
10	-	Too Young To Go Steady	Nat 'King' Cole	Capitol	10		
11	14	The Happy Whistler	Don Robertson	Capitol	7	(9)	F L
12	-	Moonglow/Theme From 'Picnic'	Morris Stoloff	Brunswick	8	(2)	F L
13	2	Poor People Of Paris	Winifred Atwell	Decca	15		
14	4	Rock And Roll Waltz	Kay Starr	HMV	18	(1)	L
15	18	Blue Suede Shoes	Carl Perkins	London American	7	(3)	F L
16	7	Only You	Hilltoppers	London American	21	(15)	F
17	10	Main Title Theme From The Man With The Golden Arm	Billy May	Capitol	6	(49)	F L
18	-	Songs For Swinging Lovers (L.P.)	Frank Sinatra	Capitol	5		
19	-	Hot Diggity	Michael Holliday	Columbia	4		
20	-	Gal With The Yaller Shoes	Michael Holliday	Columbia	3		

April 1956

This Mnth	Prev Mnth	Title	Artist	Label	Wks 20	(UK Pos)	
1	2	The Poor People Of Paris	Les Baxter	Capitol	17		G L
2	14	Heartbreak Hotel	Elvis Presley	RCA	20	(2)	F G
3	9	Hot Diggity (Dog Ziggity Boom)	Perry Como	RCA	17	(4)	G
4	13	Blue Suede Shoes	Carl Perkins	Sun	14	(10)	F G L
5	1	Lisbon Antigua	Nelson Riddle	Capitol	20		F G L
6	8	Why Do Fools Fall In Love	Frankie Lymon & The Teenagers	Gee	15	(1)	F G
7	6	I'll Be Home	Pat Boone	Dot	14	(1)	G
8	4	No, Not Much!	Four Lads	Columbia	15		G
9	-	Rock Island Line	Lonnie Donegan	Imperial	8	(8)	F
10	15	A Tear Fell	Teresa Brewer	Coral	15	(2)	
11	3	Rock And Roll Waltz	Kay Starr	RCA	16	(1)	G L
12	-	(You've Got) The Magic Touch	Platters	Mercury	11		
13	-	Long Tall Sally	Little Richard	Specialty	9	(3)	G
14	-	Moonglow And Theme From 'Picnic'	Morris Stoloff	Decca	18	(7)	F G L
15	5	The Great Pretender	Platters	Mercury	17	(5)	G
16	11	Moritat (A Theme From 'The Three Penny Opera')	Dick Hyman	MGM	11	(9)	F L
17	-	Themes From 'The Man With The Golden Arm'	Richard Maltby	Vik	6		F L
18	-	Ivory Tower	Cathy Carr	Fraternity	14		F L
19	-	Eddie My Love	Fontane Sisters	Dot	3		L
20	-	Main Title From 'The Man With The Golden Arm'	Elmer Bernstein	Decca	6		F L

May 1956

This Mnth	Prev Mnth	Title	Artist	Label	Wks 20	(UK Pos)	
1	2	Heartbreak Hotel	Elvis Presley	RCA	20	(2)	F G
2	3	Hot Diggity (Dog Ziggity Boom)	Perry Como	RCA	17	(4)	G
3	14	Moonglow And Theme From 'Picnic'	Morris Stoloff	Decca	18	(7)	F G L
4	4	Blue Suede Shoes	Carl Perkins	Sun	14	(10)	F G L
5	1	The Poor People Of Paris	Les Baxter	Capitol	17		G L
6	12	(You've Got) The Magic Touch	Platters	Mercury	11		
7	-	Moonglow And Theme From 'Picnic'	George Cates	Coral	13		F L
8	18	Ivory Tower	Cathy Carr	Fraternity	14		F L
9	6	Why Do Fools Fall In Love	Frankie Lymon/The Teenagers	Gee	15	(1)	F G
10	13	Long Tall Sally	Little Richard	Specialty	9	(3)	G
11	-	Standing On The Corner	Four Lads	Columbia	14	(26)	
12	-	The Wayward Wind	Gogi Grant	Era	19	(9)	G L
13	-	I'm In Love Again	Fats Domino	Imperial	15	(12)	G
14	10	A Tear Fell	Teresa Brewer	Coral	15	(2)	
15	9	Rock Island Line	Lonnie Donegan	Imperial	8	(8)	F
16	5	Lisbon Antigua	Nelson Riddle	Capitol	20		F G L
17	-	The Happy Whistler	Don Robertson	Capitol	10	(8)	F L
18	-	Ivory Tower	Charms	Deluxe	7		L
19	-	I Want You To Be My Girl	Frankie Lymon/The Teenagers	Gee	6		
20	7	I'll Be Home	Pat Boone	Dot	14	(1)	G

June 1956

This Mnth	Prev Mnth	Title	Artist	Label	Wks 20	(UK Pos)	
1	12	The Wayward Wind	Gogi Grant	Era	19	(9)	G L
2	3	Moonglow And Theme From 'Picnic'	Morris Stoloff	Decca	18	(7)	F G L
3	1	Heartbreak Hotel	Elvis Presley	RCA	20	(2)	F G
4	11	Standing On The Corner	Four Lads	Columbia	14	(26)	
5	13	I'm In Love Again	Fats Domino	Imperial	15	(12)	G
6	7	Moonglow And Theme From 'Picnic'	George Cates	Coral	13		F L
7	8	Ivory Tower	Cathy Carr	Fraternity	14		F L
8	2	Hot Diggity (Dog Ziggity Boom)	Perry Como	RCA	17	(4)	G
9	-	I Want You, I Need You, I Love You	Elvis Presley	RCA	18	(14)	G
10	17	The Happy Whistler	Don Robertson	Capitol	10	(8)	F L
11	-	I Almost Lost My Mind	Pat Boone	Dot	15	(14)	G
12	-	Transfusion	Nervous Norvus	Dot	8		F L
13	6	(You've Got) The Magic Touch	Platters	Mercury	11		
14	-	On The Street Where You Live	Vic Damone	Columbia	12	(1)	L
15	-	More	Perry Como	RCA	12	(10)	
16	-	Picnic	McGuire Sisters	Coral	7		
17	4	Blue Suede Shoes	Carl Perkins	Sun	14	(10)	F G L
18	10	Long Tall Sally	Little Richard	Specialty	9	(3)	G
19	19	I Want You To Be My Girl	Frankie Lymon/The Teenagers	Gee	6		
20	-	The Church Bells May Ring	Diamonds	Mercury	4		

US 1956

APR-JUNE

▲ R&B veterans Fats Domino (above) and Little Richard made their Top 10 debuts as Gene Vincent and Roy Orbison had their first Top 100 entries.

◆ Despite being banned on several radio stations, the morbid novelty 'Transfusion' by Nervous Norvus cracked the US chart and started a spate of "sick" or "death" songs. In the song Norvus (Jimmy Drake) somehow made the subject of car crashes and resulting blood transfusions humorous.

◆ Columbia Records announced that they would gradually drop 78 rpm production.

UK 1956
JULY–SEPT

◆ Britain's first rock'n' roll riots were reported, as the film *Rock Around The Clock* went on general release. The film had teenagers jiving in the aisles and, sometimes, slashing cinema seats.

▲ At a time when American artists ruled the UK charts, Frankie Lymon & The Teenagers became the first black American act to top the British hit parade.

◆ Surprisingly, the first British hit with "rock" in the title came from the very popular radio comedy team The Goons (Peter Sellers, Harry Secombe and Spike Milligan). The B-side, 'Ying Tong Song', returned to the Top 10 in 1973.

July 1956

This Mnth	Prev Mnth	Title	Artist	Label	Wks 20	(US Pos)	
1	1	I'll Be Home	Pat Boone	London American	23	(6)	
2	4	Heartbreak Hotel	Elvis Presley	HMV	19	(1)	F
3	-	All Star Hit Parade	Various Artists	Decca	8		F L
4	-	Why Do Fools Fall In Love	Frankie Lymon & The Teenagers	Columbia	15	(6)	F
5	-	I'm Walking Backwards For Christmas/Bluebottle Blues	Goons	Decca	8		F
6	6	Hot Diggity	Perry Como	HMV	12	(2)	
7	2	Lost John/Stewball	Lonnie Donegan	Pye Nixa	14	(58)	
8	-	Experiments With Mice	Johnny Dankworth	Parlophone	8	(61)	F
9	-	The Wayward Wind	Gogi Grant	London American	9	(1)	F L
10	7	The Saints Rock 'n Roll	Bill Haley & His Comets	Brunswick	22	(18)	
11	-	Wayward Wind	Tex Ritter	Capitol	11	(28)	F L
12	8	My September Love	David Whitfield	Decca	21		
13	-	Who Are We	Ronnie Hilton	HMV	8		
14	-	Walk Hand In Hand	Tony Martin	HMV	13	(21)	L
15	-	Whatever Will Be Will Be	Doris Day	Philips	20	(3)	
16	12	Moonglow/Theme From 'Picnic'	Morris Stoloff	Brunswick	8	(2)	F L
17	3	No Other Love	Ronnie Hilton	HMV	13		
18	18	Songs For Swinging Lovers (L.P.)	Frank Sinatra	Capitol	5		
19	5	A Tear Fell	Teresa Brewer	Vogue/Coral	15	(9)	
20	10	Too Young To Go Steady	Nat 'King' Cole	Capitol	10		

August 1956

This Mnth	Prev Mnth	Title	Artist	Label	Wks 20	(US Pos)	
1	15	Whatever Will Be Will Be	Doris Day	Philips	20	(3)	
2	4	Why Do Fools Fall In Love	Frankie Lymon/The Teenagers	Columbia	15	(6)	F
3	14	Walk Hand In Hand	Tony Martin	HMV	13	(21)	L
4	-	Sweet Old-Fashioned Girl	Teresa Brewer	Vogue/Coral	13	(12)	L
5	-	Mountain Greenery	Mel Torme	Vogue/Coral	17		F
6	2	Heartbreak Hotel	Elvis Presley	HMV	19	(1)	F
7	1	I'll Be Home	Pat Boone	London American	23	(6)	
8	11	Wayward Wind	Tex Ritter	Capitol	11	(28)	F L
9	10	The Saints Rock 'n Roll	Bill Haley & His Comets	Brunswick	22	(18)	
10	13	Who Are We	Ronnie Hilton	HMV	8		
11	-	Rockin' Through The Rye	Bill Haley & His Comets	Brunswick	19	(78)	
12	3	All Star Hit Parade	Various Artists	Decca	8		F L
13	-	Serenade	Slim Whitman	London American	8		
14	5	I'm Walking Back.../Bluebottle...	Goons	Decca	8		F
15	-	Walk Hand In Hand	Ronnie Carroll	Philips	7		F
16	9	The Wayward Wind	Gogi Grant	London American	9	(1)	F L
17	8	Experiments With Mice	Johnny Dankworth	Parlophone	8	(61)	F
18	6	Hot Diggity	Perry Como	HMV	12	(2)	
19	-	I Almost Lost My Mind	Pat Boone	London American	6	(2)	
20	-	Left Bank	Winifred Atwell	Decca	5		

September 1956

This Mnth	Prev Mnth	Title	Artist	Label	Wks 20	(US Pos)	
1	1	Whatever Will Be Will Be	Doris Day	Philips	20	(3)	
2	-	Lay Down Your Arms	Anne Shelton	Philips	13	(59)	
3	11	Rockin' Through The Rye	Bill Haley & His Comets	Brunswick	19	(78)	
4	2	Why Do Fools Fall In Love	Frankie Lymon/The Teenagers	Columbia	15	(6)	F
5	4	Sweet Old-Fashioned Girl	Teresa Brewer	Vogue/Coral	13	(12)	L
6	3	Walk Hand In Hand	Tony Martin	HMV	13	(21)	L
7	-	The Great Pretender/Only You	Platters	Mercury	10	(2)	F
8	-	Bloodnok's Rock 'n' Roll Call/ Ying Tong Song	Goons	Decca	8		
9	5	Mountain Greenery	Mel Torme	Vogue/Coral	17		F
10	9	The Saints Rock 'n Roll	Bill Haley & His Comets	Brunswick	22	(18)	
11	-	Bring A Little Water Sylvie/ Dead Or Alive	Lonnie Donegan	Pye Nixa	8		
12	-	A Woman In Love	Frankie Laine	Philips	19	(19)	
13	-	Born To Be With You	Chordettes	London American	8	(8)	
14	13	Serenade	Slim Whitman	London American	8		
15	-	Hound Dog	Elvis Presley	HMV	22	(1)	
16	-	I Want You I Need You I Love You	Elvis Presley	HMV	6	(1)	
17	6	Heartbreak Hotel	Elvis Presley	HMV	19	(1)	F
18	19	I Almost Lost My Mind	Pat Boone	London American	6	(2)	
19	-	Rock Around The Clock	Bill Haley & His Comets	Brunswick	11		
20	-	I'm In Love Again	Fats Domino	London American	5	(4)	F

July 1956

This Mnth	Prev Mnth	Title	Artist	Label	Wks 20	(UK Pos)	
1	1	The Wayward Wind	Gogi Grant	Era	19	(9)	G L
2	11	I Almost Lost My Mind	Pat Boone	Dot	15	(14)	G
3	9	I Want You, I Need You, I Love You	Elvis Presley	RCA	18	(14)	G
4	15	More	Perry Como	RCA	12	(10)	
5	2	Moonglow And Theme From 'Picnic'	Morris Stoloff	Decca	18	(7)	F G L
6	5	I'm In Love Again	Fats Domino	Imperial	15	(12)	G
7	-	Be-Bop-A-Lula	Gene Vincent & His Blue Caps	Capitol	14	(16)	F
8	-	Born To Be With You	Chordettes	Cadence	12	(8)	
9	14	On The Street Where You Live	Vic Damone	Columbia	12	(1)	L
10	4	Standing On The Corner	Four Lads	Columbia	14	(26)	
11	-	My Prayer	Platters	Mercury	17	(4)	G
12	-	Allegheny Moon	Patti Page	Mercury	16		G
13	-	Whatever Will Be Will Be (Que Sera Sera)	Doris Day	Columbia	20	(1)	G
14	-	A Sweet Old Fashioned Girl	Teresa Brewer	Coral	11	(3)	L
15	12	Transfusion	Nervous Norvus	Dot	8		F L
16	6	Moonglow And Theme From 'Picnic'	George Cates	Coral	13		F L
17	3	Heartbreak Hotel	Elvis Presley	RCA	20	(2)	F G
18	7	Ivory Tower	Cathy Carr	Fraternity	14		F L
19	-	It Only Hurts For A Little While	Ames Brothers	RCA	11		
20	-	Stranded In The Jungle	Cadets	Modern	3		F L

August 1956

This Mnth	Prev Mnth	Title	Artist	Label	Wks 20	(UK Pos)	
1	11	My Prayer	Platters	Mercury	17	(4)	G
2	-	Hound Dog/Don't Be Cruel	Elvis Presley	RCA	23	(2)	G
3	13	Whatever Will Be Will Be (Que...)	Doris Day	Columbia	20	(1)	G
4	3	I Want You, I Need You, I Love You	Elvis Presley	RCA	18	(14)	G
5	2	I Almost Lost My Mind	Pat Boone	Dot	15	(14)	G
6	12	Allegheny Moon	Patti Page	Mercury	16		G
7	1	The Wayward Wind	Gogi Grant	Era	19	(9)	G L
8	7	Be-Bop-A-Lula	Gene Vincent & His Blue Caps	Capitol	14	(16)	F
9	-	The Flying Saucer (Parts 1 & 2)	Buchanan & Goodman	Luniverse	8		F G
10	4	More	Perry Como	RCA	12	(10)	
11	-	Canadian Sunset	Hugo Winterhalter & Eddie Heywood	RCA	19		G L
12	8	Born To Be With You	Chordettes	Cadence	12	(8)	
13	14	A Sweet Old Fashioned Girl	Teresa Brewer	Coral	11	(3)	L
14	9	On The Street Where You Live	Vic Damone	Columbia	12	(1)	L
15	5	Moonglow And Theme From 'Picnic'	Morris Stoloff	Decca	18	(7)	F G L
16	-	Theme Song From 'Song For A Summer Night'	Mitch Miller	Columbia	9		
17	6	I'm In Love Again	Fats Domino	Imperial	15	(12)	G
18	-	The Fool	Sanford Clark	Dot	12		F L
19	19	It Only Hurts For A Little While	Ames Brothers	RCA	11		
20	20	Stranded In The Jungle	Cadets	Modern	3		F L

September 1956

This Mnth	Prev Mnth	Title	Artist	Label	Wks 20	(UK Pos)	
1	2	Hound Dog/Don't Be Cruel	Elvis Presley	RCA	23	(2)	G
2	1	My Prayer	Platters	Mercury	17	(4)	G
3	3	Whatever Will Be Will Be (Que...)	Doris Day	Columbia	20	(1)	G
4	11	Canadian Sunset	Hugo Winterhalter & Eddie Heywood	RCA	19		G L
5	-	Tonight You Belong To Me	Patience & Prudence	Liberty	15	(28)	F G
6	9	The Flying Saucer (Parts 1 & 2)	Buchanan & Goodman	Luniverse	8		F G
7	6	Allegheny Moon	Patti Page	Mercury	16		G
8	-	Honky Tonk (Parts 1 & 2)	Bill Doggett	King	18		F G L
9	18	The Fool	Sanford Clark	Dot	12		F L
10	8	Be-Bop-A-Lula	Gene Vincent & His Blue Caps	Capitol	14	(16)	F
11	16	Theme From 'Song For A Summer...'	Mitch Miller	Columbia	9		
12	-	Canadian Sunset	Andy Williams	Cadence	9		F
13	4	I Want You, I Need You, I Love You	Elvis Presley	RCA	18	(14)	G
14	5	I Almost Lost My Mind	Pat Boone	Dot	15	(14)	G
15	-	Just Walking In The Rain	Johnnie Ray	Columbia	21	(1)	G
16	-	Soft Summer Breeze	Eddie Heywood	Mercury	9		F L
17	-	You Don't Know Me	Jerry Vale	Columbia	9		F L
18	7	The Wayward Wind	Gogi Grant	Era	19	(9)	G L
19	10	More	Perry Como	RCA	12	(10)	
20	13	A Sweet Old Fashioned Girl	Teresa Brewer	Coral	11	(3)	L

US 1956 JULY-SEPT

◆ Rock'n'roll and R&B were becoming separate entities. A multi-racial rock'n'roll show in Maryland starring Carl Perkins, The Teenagers and Chuck Berry attracted nearly 70,000 fans. Meanwhile, an R&B DJ association decided to disassociate R&B from rock'n'roll – since rock's bad publicity was affecting their business.

◆ As Pat Boone and Elvis raided the R&B archives for, 'I Almost Lost My Mind' and 'Hound Dog', R&B stars, The Platters and Fats Domino, revived pop faves, 'My Prayer' and 'Blueberry Hill'.

◆ After vowing that he would never have Elvis on his TV show, Ed Sullivan relented. The first of Presley's three appearances on the show was watched by 82% of the US TV audience.

UK 1956 OCT-DEC

▲ In the *NME* poll, Elvis was runner-up to Bill Haley as World's Most Outstanding Vocal Personality, and to Frank Sinatra (above) as World's Outstanding Singer. In the *Billboard* DJ poll he was voted Most Played Male Pop and C&W Artist.

◆ Although they failed to enter the Top 100 in their homeland, American rock'n'roll records by Freddie Bell and The Bellboys ('Giddy-Up-A-Ding-Dong') and Mitchell Torok ('When Mexico Gave Up The Rhumba') were big British hits.

◆ For several weeks Bill Haley & The Comets had five singles in the UK Top 20.

October 1956

This Mnth	Prev Mnth	Title	Artist	Label	Wks 20	(US Pos)	
1	12	A Woman In Love	Frankie Laine	Philips	19	(19)	
2	2	Lay Down Your Arms	Anne Shelton	Philips	13	(59)	
3	15	Hound Dog	Elvis Presley	HMV	22	(1)	
4	1	Whatever Will Be Will Be	Doris Day	Philips	20	(3)	
5	-	Giddy-Up-A-Ding-Dong	Freddie Bell & The Bellboys	Mercury	8		F L
6	3	Rockin' Through The Rye	Bill Haley & His Comets	Brunswick	19	(78)	
7	7	The Great Pretender/Only You	Platters	Mercury	10	(2)	F
8	8	Bloodnok's Rock 'n' Roll Call/ Ying Tong Song	Goons	Decca	8		
9	11	Bring A Little Water Sylvie/ Dead Or Alive	Lonnie Donegan	Pye Nixa	8		
10	19	Rock Around The Clock	Bill Haley & His Comets	Brunswick	11		
11	-	Just Walkin' In The Rain	Johnnie Ray	Philips	18	(3)	
12	-	When Mexico Gave Up The Rumba	Mitchell Torok	Brunswick	15		F L
13	10	The Saints Rock 'n Roll	Bill Haley & His Comets	Brunswick	22	(18)	
14	-	More	Perry Como	HMV	8	(4)	
15	13	Born To Be With You	Chordettes	London American	8	(8)	
16	-	Razzle Dazzle	Bill Haley & His Comets	Brunswick	4	(15)	
17	-	See You Later Alligator	Bill Haley & His Comets	Brunswick	6	(6)	
18	4	Why Do Fools Fall In Love	Frankie Lymon & The Teenagers	Columbia	15	(6)	F
19	-	More	Jimmy Young	Decca	14		
20	5	Sweet Old-Fashioned Girl	Teresa Brewer	Vogue/Coral	13	(12)	L

November 1956

This Mnth	Prev Mnth	Title	Artist	Label	Wks 20	(US Pos)	
1	11	Just Walkin' In The Rain	Johnnie Ray	Philips	18	(3)	
2	1	A Woman In Love	Frankie Laine	Philips	19	(19)	
3	3	Hound Dog	Elvis Presley	HMV	22	(1)	
4	-	My Prayer	Platters	Mercury	10	(1)	
5	19	More	Jimmy Young	Decca	14		
6	6	Rockin' Through The Rye	Bill Haley & His Comets	Brunswick	19	(78)	
7	10	Rock Around The Clock	Bill Haley & His Comets	Brunswick	11		
8	12	When Mexico Gave Up The Rumba	Mitchell Torok	Brunswick	15		F L
9	-	Green Door	Frankie Vaughan	Philips	15		
10	2	Lay Down Your Arms	Anne Shelton	Philips	13	(59)	
11	-	Rip It Up	Bill Haley & His Comets	Brunswick	14	(25)	
12	-	Make It A Party	Winifred Atwell	Decca	10		
13	4	Whatever Will Be Will Be	Doris Day	Philips	20	(3)	
14	5	Giddy-Up-A-Ding-Dong	Freddie Bell & The Bellboys	Mercury	8		F L
15	-	St. Therese Of The Roses	Malcolm Vaughan	HMV	18		
16	-	The Green Door	Jim Lowe	London American	5	(2)	F L
17	-	Love Me As If There Were No Tomorrow	Nat 'King' Cole	Capitol	7		
18	-	Blue Moon	Elvis Presley	HMV	8	(55)	
19	14	More	Perry Como	HMV	8	(4)	
20	-	Cindy, Oh Cindy	Eddie Fisher	HMV	13	(10)	L

December 1956

This Mnth	Prev Mnth	Title	Artist	Label	Wks 20	(US Pos)	
1	1	Just Walkin' In The Rain	Johnnie Ray	Philips	18	(3)	
2	9	Green Door	Frankie Vaughan	Philips	15		
3	15	St. Therese Of The Roses	Malcolm Vaughan	HMV	18		
4	11	Rip It Up	Bill Haley & His Comets	Brunswick	14	(25)	
5	20	Cindy, Oh Cindy	Eddie Fisher	HMV	13	(10)	L
6	4	My Prayer	Platters	Mercury	10	(1)	
7	-	True Love	Bing Crosby & Grace Kelly	Capitol	23	(5)	
8	2	A Woman In Love	Frankie Laine	Philips	19	(19)	
9	12	Make It A Party	Winifred Atwell	Decca	10		
10	3	Hound Dog	Elvis Presley	HMV	22	(1)	
11	5	More	Jimmy Young	Decca	14		
12	18	Blue Moon	Elvis Presley	HMV	8	(55)	
13	8	When Mexico Gave Up The Rumba	Mitchell Torok	Brunswick	15		F L
14	-	Christmas Island	Dickie Valentine	Decca	3		
15	-	Love Me Tender	Elvis Presley	HMV	9	(1)	
16	-	Two Different Worlds	Ronnie Hilton	HMV	7		
17	-	A House With Love In It	Vera Lynn	Decca	6		
18	-	Cindy Oh Cindy	Tony Brent	Columbia	3		
19	-	Moonlight Gambler	Frankie Laine	Philips	9	(5)	
20	-	Singing The Blues	Guy Mitchell	Philips	20	(1)	

32

October 1956

This Mnth	Prev Mnth	Title	Artist	Label	Wks 20	(UK Pos)	
1	1	Hound Dog/Don't Be Cruel	Elvis Presley	RCA	23	(2)	G
2	8	Honky Tonk (Parts 1 & 2)	Bill Doggett	King	18		F G L
3	4	Canadian Sunset	Hugo Winterhalter & Eddie Heywood	RCA	19		G L
4	15	Just Walking In The Rain	Johnnie Ray	Columbia	21	(1)	G
5	-	The Green Door	Jim Lowe	Dot	21	(8)	F G
6	5	Tonight You Belong To Me	Patience & Prudence	Liberty	15	(28)	F G
7	3	Whatever Will Be Will Be (Que Sera Sera)	Doris Day	Columbia	20	(1)	G
8	2	My Prayer	Platters	Mercury	17	(4)	G
9	-	Friendly Persuasion/Chains Of Love	Pat Boone	Dot	13	(3)	G
10	-	Love Me Tender	Elvis Presley	RCA	18	(11)	G
11	12	Canadian Sunset	Andy Williams	Cadence	9		F
12	9	The Fool	Sanford Clark	Dot	12		F L
13	-	True Love	Bing Crosby & Grace Kelly	Capitol	19	(4)	G
14	-	Blueberry Hill	Fats Domino	Imperial	20	(6)	G
15	16	Soft Summer Breeze	Eddie Heywood	Mercury	9		F L
16	-	You'll Never Ever Know/It Isn't Right	Platters	Mercury	8	(23)	
17	7	Allegheny Moon	Patti Page	Mercury	16		G
18	-	Cindy, Oh Cindy	Vince Martin With The Tarriers	Glory	12	(26)	F L
19	-	True Love	Jane Powell	Verve	7		F L
20	17	You Don't Know Me	Jerry Vale	Columbia	9		F L

November 1956

This Mnth	Prev Mnth	Title	Artist	Label	Wks 20	(UK Pos)	
1	10	Love Me Tender	Elvis Presley	RCA	18	(11)	G
2	5	The Green Door	Jim Lowe	Dot	21	(8)	F G
3	1	Hound Dog/Don't Be Cruel	Elvis Presley	RCA	23	(2)	G
4	4	Just Walking In The Rain	Johnnie Ray	Columbia	21	(1)	G
5	-	Singing The Blues	Guy Mitchell	Columbia	19	(1)	G
6	14	Blueberry Hill	Fats Domino	Imperial	20	(6)	G
7	2	Honky Tonk (Parts 1 & 2)	Bill Doggett	King	18		F G L
8	13	True Love	Bing Crosby & Grace Kelly	Capitol	19	(4)	G
9	9	Friendly Persuasion/Chains Of Love	Pat Boone	Dot	13	(3)	G
10	3	Canadian Sunset	Hugo Winterhalter & Eddie Heywood	RCA	19		G L
11	6	Tonight You Belong To Me	Patience & Prudence	Liberty	15	(28)	F G
12	18	Cindy, Oh Cindy	Vince Martin With The Tarriers	Glory	12	(26)	F L
13	-	Hey! Jealous Lover	Frank Sinatra	Capitol	11		
14	16	You'll Never Ever Know/It Isn't Right	Platters	Mercury	8	(23)	
15	-	Cindy, Oh Cindy	Eddie Fisher	RCA	11	(5)	L
16	7	Whatever Will Be Will Be (Que...)	Doris Day	Columbia	20	(1)	G
17	19	True Love	Jane Powell	Verve	7		F L
18	-	I Walk The Line	Johnny Cash	Sun	3		F
19	-	A Rose And A Baby Ruth	George Hamilton IV	ABC Paramount	13		F G
20	-	Garden Of Eden	Joe Valino	Vik	7	(23)	F L

December 1956

This Mnth	Prev Mnth	Title	Artist	Label	Wks 20	(UK Pos)	
1	5	Singing The Blues	Guy Mitchell	Columbia	19	(1)	G
2	1	Love Me Tender	Elvis Presley	RCA	18	(11)	G
3	2	The Green Door	Jim Lowe	Dot	21	(8)	F G
4	6	Blueberry Hill	Fats Domino	Imperial	20	(6)	G
5	4	Just Walking In The Rain	Johnnie Ray	Columbia	21	(1)	G
6	8	True Love	Bing Crosby & Grace Kelly	Capitol	19	(4)	G
7	19	A Rose And A Baby Ruth	George Hamilton IV	ABC Paramount	13		F G
8	13	Hey! Jealous Lover	Frank Sinatra	Capitol	11		
9	3	Hound Dog/Don't Be Cruel	Elvis Presley	RCA	23	(2)	G
10	-	Love Me	Elvis Presley	RCA	11		
11	7	Honky Tonk (Parts 1 & 2)	Bill Doggett	King	18		F G L
12	15	Cindy, Oh Cindy	Eddie Fisher	RCA	11	(5)	L
13	-	Rock-A-Bye Your Baby With A Dixie Melody	Jerry Lewis	Decca	12	(12)	F L
14	9	Friendly Persuasion/Chains Of Love	Pat Boone	Dot	13	(3)	G
15	12	Cindy, Oh Cindy	Vince Martin With The Tarriers	Glory	12	(26)	F L
16	-	Since I Met You Baby	Ivory Joe Hunter	Atlantic	9		F L
17	20	Garden Of Eden	Joe Valino	Vik	7	(23)	F L
18	-	Gonna Get Along Without Ya Now	Patience & Prudence	Liberty	4	(22)	L
19	-	The Banana Boat Song	Tarriers	Glory	12	(15)	L
20	-	Mama From The Train	Patti Page	Mercury	5		

◆ Elvis Presley's 'Hound Dog' sold over three million while his record breaking 'Love Me Tender' amassed a million advance orders entering the best sellers at No. 2 (behind 'Hound Dog'). In 1956, Elvis put 17 different sides into the chart and held the top spot for six months. Presley products earned $20 million and he closed the year with 10 separate records on the US Top 100.

◆ In October four British acts were simultaneously situated in the Top 100; They were Anne Shelton and the orchestras of Ted Heath, Bob Sharples and Cyril Stapleton.

◆ Elvis Presley was not the only country artist to create a stir in the pop market. Johnny Cash, George Hamilton IV and Sanford Clark were all climbing the Top 20 and the C&W song 'Singing The Blues' (originally by Marty Robbins) by Guy Mitchell headed the list.

UK 1957

JAN-MAR

◆ Less than three months after his chart debut, Tommy Steele (who was already filming his life story!) became the first British rock'n'roll artist to top the charts. His version of 'Singing The Blues' replaced Guy Mitchell's at No. 1.

◆ Britain launched its first pop TV shows: *Cool For Cats*, where professional dancers performed choreographed routines to current records, and the very influential *6-5 Special* which featured live artists.

◆ Bill Haley & The Comets received an amazing media welcome to Britain, where *Rock Around The Clock* had became the first million seller. However, UK interest in them quickly faded and they left with minimal press coverage, and no future recordings made the Top 20.

January 1957

This Mnth	Prev Mnth	Title	Artist	Label	Wks 20	(US Pos)	
1	20	Singing The Blues	Guy Mitchell	Philips	20	(1)	
2	-	Singing The Blues	Tommy Steele	Decca	10		
3	3	St. Therese Of The Roses	Malcolm Vaughan	HMV	18		
4	1	Just Walkin' In The Rain	Johnnie Ray	Philips	18	(3)	
5	2	Green Door	Frankie Vaughan	Philips	15		
6	7	True Love	Bing Crosby & Grace Kelly	Capitol	23	(5)	
7	5	Cindy, Oh Cindy	Eddie Fisher	HMV	13	(10)	L
8	-	Friendly Persuasion	Pat Boone	London American	17	(9)	
9	-	Garden Of Eden	Frankie Vaughan	Philips	12		
10	10	Hound Dog	Elvis Presley	HMV	22	(1)	
11	4	Rip It Up	Bill Haley & His Comets	Brunswick	14	(25)	
12	15	Love Me Tender	Elvis Presley	HMV	9	(1)	
13	-	Blueberry Hill	Fats Domino	London American	10	(3)	
14	19	Moonlight Gambler	Frankie Laine	Philips	9	(5)	
15	8	A Woman In Love	Frankie Laine	Philips	19	(19)	
16	-	Don't You Rock Me Daddy-O	Lonnie Donegan	Pye Nixa	16		
17	-	Garden Of Eden	Gary Miller	Pye Nixa	2		
18	13	When Mexico Gave Up The Rumba	Mitchell Torok	Brunswick	15		F L
19	11	More	Jimmy Young	Decca	14		
20	9	Make It A Party	Winifred Atwell	Decca	10		

February 1957

This Mnth	Prev Mnth	Title	Artist	Label	Wks 20	(US Pos)	
1	9	Garden Of Eden	Frankie Vaughan	Philips	12		
2	1	Singing The Blues	Guy Mitchell	Philips	20	(1)	
3	8	Friendly Persuasion	Pat Boone	London American	17	(9)	
4	6	True Love	Bing Crosby & Grace Kelly	Capitol	23	(5)	
5	16	Don't You Rock Me Daddy-O	Lonnie Donegan	Pye Nixa	16		
6	3	St. Therese Of The Roses	Malcolm Vaughan	HMV	18		
7	13	Blueberry Hill	Fats Domino	London American	10	(3)	
8	-	Young Love	Tab Hunter	London American	17	(1)	F
9	2	Singing The Blues	Tommy Steele	Decca	10		
10	-	Don't Forbid Me	Pat Boone	London American	14	(3)	
11	7	Cindy, Oh Cindy	Eddie Fisher	HMV	13	(10)	L
12	-	Don't Knock The Rock	Bill Haley & His Comets	Brunswick	7	(45)	
13	-	Don't You Rock Me Daddy-O	Vipers Skiffle Group	Parlophone	6		F
14	10	Hound Dog	Elvis Presley	HMV	22	(1)	
15	5	Green Door	Frankie Vaughan	Philips	15		
16	-	Rock-A-Bye Your Baby (With A Dixie Melody)	Jerry Lewis	Brunswick	5	(10)	F L
17	4	Just Walkin' In The Rain	Johnnie Ray	Philips	18	(3)	
18	11	Rip It Up	Bill Haley & His Comets	Brunswick	14	(25)	
19	-	Adoration Waltz	David Whitfield	Decca	8		
20	-	You Don't Owe Me A Thing	Johnnie Ray	Philips	10	(10)	

March 1957

This Mnth	Prev Mnth	Title	Artist	Label	Wks 20	(US Pos)	
1	8	Young Love	Tab Hunter	London American	17	(1)	F
2	10	Don't Forbid Me	Pat Boone	London American	14	(3)	
3	-	Knee Deep In The Blues	Guy Mitchell	Philips	11	(21)	
4	5	Don't You Rock Me Daddy-O	Lonnie Donegan	Pye Nixa	16		
5	2	Singing The Blues	Guy Mitchell	Philips	20	(1)	
6	-	Long Tall Sally	Little Richard	London American	14	(6)	F
7	1	Garden Of Eden	Frankie Vaughan	Philips	12		
8	4	True Love	Bing Crosby & Grace Kelly	Capitol	23	(5)	
9	-	Banana Boat Song	Harry Belafonte	HMV	14	(5)	F
10	3	Friendly Persuasion	Pat Boone	London American	17	(9)	
11	-	Banana Boat Song	Shirley Bassey	Philips	6		.F
12	19	Adoration Waltz	David Whitfield	Decca	8		
13	-	Young Love	Sonny James	Capitol	7	(2)	F L
14	12	Don't Knock The Rock	Bill Haley & His Comets	Brunswick	7	(45)	
15	7	Blueberry Hill	Fats Domino	London American	10	(3)	
16	-	The Girl Can't Help It	Little Richard	London American	10	(49)	
17	-	Wisdom Of A Fool	Norman Wisdom	Columbia	4		L
18	6	St. Therese Of The Roses	Malcolm Vaughan	HMV	18		
19	20	You Don't Owe Me A Thing	Johnnie Ray	Philips	10	(10)	
20	16	Rock-A-Bye Your Baby (With A Dixie Melody)	Jerry Lewis	Brunswick	5	(10)	F L

January 1957

This Mnth	Prev Mnth	Title	Artist	Label	Wks 20	(UK Pos)	
1	1	Singing The Blues	Guy Mitchell	Columbia	19	(1)	G
2	3	The Green Door	Jim Lowe	Dot	21	(8)	F G
3	4	Blueberry Hill	Fats Domino	Imperial	20	(6)	G
4	2	Love Me Tender	Elvis Presley	RCA	18	(11)	G
5	19	The Banana Boat Song	Tarriers	Glory	12	(15)	L
6	-	Don't Forbid Me	Pat Boone	Dot	16	(2)	G
7	5	Just Walking In The Rain	Johnnie Ray	Columbia	21	(1)	G
8	6	True Love	Bing Crosby & Grace Kelly	Capitol	19	(4)	G
9	-	Moonlight Gambler	Frankie Laine	Columbia	12	(13)	G L
10	10	Love Me	Elvis Presley	RCA	11		
11	-	Young Love	Sonny James	Capitol	13	(11)	F G L
12	7	A Rose And A Baby Ruth	George Hamilton IV	ABC Paramount	13		F G
13	-	Young Love	Tab Hunter	Dot	13	(1)	F G
14	13	Rock-A-Bye Your Baby With A Dixie Melody	Jerry Lewis	Decca	12	(12)	F L
15	-	Blue Monday	Fats Domino	Imperial	10	(23)	G
16	-	Banana Boat (Day-O)	Harry Belafonte	RCA	12	(2)	G
17	12	Cindy, Oh Cindy	Eddie Fisher	RCA	11	(5)	L
18	8	Hey! Jealous Lover	Frank Sinatra	Capitol	11		
19	16	Since I Met You Baby	Ivory Joe Hunter	Atlantic	9		F L
20	-	Jamaica Farewell	Harry Belafonte	RCA	8		

February 1957

This Mnth	Prev Mnth	Title	Artist	Label	Wks 20	(UK Pos)	
1	-	Too Much	Elvis Presley	RCA	10	(6)	G
2	13	Young Love	Tab Hunter	Dot	13	(1)	F G
3	11	Young Love	Sonny James	Capitol	13	(11)	F G L
4	6	Don't Forbid Me	Pat Boone	Dot	16	(2)	G
5	1	Singing The Blues	Guy Mitchell	Columbia	19	(1)	G
6	16	Banana Boat (Day-O)	Harry Belafonte	RCA	12	(2)	G
7	5	The Banana Boat Song	Tarriers	Glory	12	(15)	L
8	9	Moonlight Gambler	Frankie Laine	Columbia	12	(13)	G L
9	15	Blue Monday	Fats Domino	Imperial	10	(23)	G
10	3	Blueberry Hill	Fats Domino	Imperial	20	(6)	G
11	-	You Don't Owe Me A Thing	Johnnie Ray	Columbia	4	(12)	L
12	-	Love Is Strange	Mickey & Sylvia	Groove	11		F L
13	2	The Green Door	Jim Lowe	Dot	21	(8)	F G
14	-	Marianne	Terry Gilkyson & The Easy Riders	Columbia	11		F G L
15	4	Love Me Tender	Elvis Presley	RCA	18	(11)	G
16	14	Rock-A-Bye Your Baby With A Dixie Melody	Jerry Lewis	Decca	12	(12)	F L
17	10	Love Me	Elvis Presley	RCA	11		
18	-	Wringle Wrangle	Fess Parker	Disneyland	3		L
19	12	A Rose And A Baby Ruth	George Hamilton IV	ABC Paramount	13		F G
20	20	Jamaica Farewell	Harry Belafonte	RCA	8		

March 1957

This Mnth	Prev Mnth	Title	Artist	Label	Wks 20	(UK Pos)	
1	2	Young Love	Tab Hunter	Dot	13	(1)	F G
2	-	Teen-Age Crush	Tommy Sands	Capitol	11		F G
3	4	Don't Forbid Me	Pat Boone	Dot	16	(2)	G
4	-	Butterfly	Charlie Gracie	Cameo	14	(12)	F G
5	1	Too Much	Elvis Presley	RCA	10	(6)	G
6	14	Marianne	Terry Gilkyson & The Easy Riders	Columbia	11		F G L
7	6	Banana Boat (Day-O)	Harry Belafonte	RCA	12	(2)	G
8	3	Young Love	Sonny James	Capitol	13	(11)	F G L
9	-	Round And Round	Perry Como	RCA	15		G
10	-	Party Doll	Buddy Knox	Roulette	14	(29)	F G
11	-	Butterfly	Andy Williams	Cadence	12	(1)	G
12	-	I'm Walkin'	Fats Domino	Imperial	10	(19)	G
13	-	Marianne	Hilltoppers	Dot	8	(20)	L
14	12	Love Is Strange	Mickey & Sylvia	Groove	11		F L
15	7	The Banana Boat Song	Tarriers	Glory	12	(15)	L
16	8	Moonlight Gambler	Frankie Laine	Columbia	12	(13)	G L
17	9	Blue Monday	Fats Domino	Imperial	10	(23)	G
18	-	Little Darlin'	Diamonds	Mercury	16	(3)	G
19	-	Come Go With Me	Dell-Vikings	Dot	17		F G
20	-	Why Baby Why	Pat Boone	Dot	10	(17)	G

▲ Parentally approved rock'n'roll star Pat Boone performed at President Eisenhower's Inaugural Ball and signed a $1 million TV deal.

◆ Fats Domino scored his third successive R&B No 1 with 'I'm Walkin'' (which followed 'Blueberry Hill' and 'Blue Monday') – holding the top slot for 23 out of 24 weeks!

◆ Many pundits tipped calypso to replace rock'n'roll as the West Indian influence could be heard in hits by artists such as Harry Belafonte, The Tarriers, Terry Gilkyson & The Easy Riders, Eddie Fisher and The Hilltoppers.

UK
1957
APR-JUNE

▲ In April, Little Richard (above) had three singles in the UK Top 20 and 14-year-old Frankie Lymon & The Teenagers had two. The youthful group, who successfully toured Britain and topped the bill at the London Palladium, were not to chart again.

◆ Skiffle, now reaching its peak of popularity, had its first chart topper with Lonnie Donegan's adaptation of the traditional American folk song 'Cumberland Gap'.

◆ Amazingly, Nat 'King' Cole's version of the 1952 film theme 'When I Fall In Love' (which did not chart in America) returned to the UK Top 5 in 1987.

April 1957

This Mnth	Prev Mnth	Title	Artist	Label	Wks 20	(US Pos)	
1	1	Young Love	Tab Hunter	London American	17	(1)	F
2	-	Cumberland Gap	Lonnie Donegan	Pye Nixa	11		
3	9	Banana Boat Song	Harry Belafonte	HMV	14	(5)	F
4	2	Don't Forbid Me	Pat Boone	London American	14	(3)	
5	6	Long Tall Sally	Little Richard	London American	14	(6)	F
6	3	Knee Deep In The Blues	Guy Mitchell	Philips	11	(21)	
7	-	Look Homeward Angel	Johnnie Ray	Philips	10	(36)	
8	4	Don't You Rock Me Daddy-O	Lonnie Donegan	Pye Nixa	16		
9	8	True Love	Bing Crosby & Grace Kelly	Capitol	23	(5)	
10	16	The Girl Can't Help It	Little Richard	London American	10	(49)	
11	-	Baby Baby	Frankie Lymon & The Teenagers	Columbia	8		L
12	-	Ninety-Nine Ways	Tab Hunter	London American	10	(12)	L
13	-	Heart	Max Bygraves	Decca	7		
14	5	Singing The Blues	Guy Mitchell	Philips	20	(1)	
15	-	Cumberland Gap	Vipers Skiffle Group	Parlophone	4		
16	-	I'm Not A Juvenile Delinquent	Frankie Lymon & The Teenagers	Columbia	4		L
17	19	You Don't Owe Me A Thing	Johnnie Ray	Philips	10	(10)	
18	-	I'll Take You Home Again Kathleen	Slim Whitman	London American	11	(93)	
19	-	When I Fall In Love	Nat 'King' Cole	Capitol	19		
20	-	Freight Train	Chas McDevitt Skiffle Group	Oriole	14	(40)	F L

May 1957

This Mnth	Prev Mnth	Title	Artist	Label	Wks 20	(US Pos)	
1	-	Rock-A-Billy	Guy Mitchell	Philips	11	(10)	
2	-	Butterfly	Andy Williams	London American	12	(4)	F
3	2	Cumberland Gap	Lonnie Donegan	Pye Nixa	11		
4	19	When I Fall In Love	Nat 'King' Cole	Capitol	19		
5	12	Ninety-Nine Ways	Tab Hunter	London American	10	(12)	L
6	11	Baby Baby	Frankie Lymon & The Teenagers	Columbia	8		L
7	-	Yes Tonight Josephine	Johnnie Ray	Philips	15		
8	3	Banana Boat Song	Harry Belafonte	HMV	14	(5)	F
9	20	Freight Train	Chas McDevitt Skiffle Group	Oriole	14	(40)	F L
10	18	I'll Take You Home Again Kathleen	Slim Whitman	London American	11	(93)	
11	-	Too Much	Elvis Presley	HMV	8	(1)	
12	1	Young Love	Tab Hunter	London American	17	(1)	F
13	7	Look Homeward Angel	Johnnie Ray	Philips	10	(36)	
14	5	Long Tall Sally	Little Richard	London American	14	(6)	F
15	-	Chapel Of The Roses	Malcolm Vaughan	HMV	7		
16	10	The Girl Can't Help It	Little Richard	London American	10	(49)	
17	-	Mr. Wonderful	Peggy Lee	Brunswick	13	(25)	F
18	-	Butterfly	Charlie Gracie	Parlophone	3	(3)	F
19	-	Butterfingers	Tommy Steele	Decca	15		
20	4	Don't Forbid Me	Pat Boone	London American	14	(3)	

June 1957

This Mnth	Prev Mnth	Title	Artist	Label	Wks 20	(US Pos)	
1	7	Yes Tonight Josephine	Johnnie Ray	Philips	15		
2	4	When I Fall In Love	Nat 'King' Cole	Capitol	19		
3	2	Butterfly	Andy Williams	London American	12	(4)	F
4	-	Gamblin' Man/Putting On The Style	Lonnie Donegan	Pye Nixa	18		
5	-	Around The World	Ronnie Hilton	HMV	15		
6	-	Around The World	Bing Crosby	Brunswick	14	(25)	
7	1	Rock-A-Billy	Guy Mitchell	Philips	11	(10)	
8	-	Little Darlin'	Diamonds	Mercury	15	(2)	F L
9	9	Freight Train	Chas McDevitt Skiffle Group	Oriole	14	(40)	F L
10	17	Mr. Wonderful	Peggy Lee	Brunswick	13	(25)	F
11	-	Around The World	Gracie Fields	Columbia	7		F L
12	-	A White Sport Coat	King Brothers	Parlophone	11		F
13	-	We Will Make Love	Russ Hamilton	Oriole	16		F
14	11	Too Much	Elvis Presley	HMV	8	(1)	
15	10	I'll Take You Home Again Kathleen	Slim Whitman	London American	11	(93)	
16	15	Chapel Of The Roses	Malcolm Vaughan	HMV	7		
17	-	All Shook Up	Elvis Presley	HMV	18	(1)	
18	-	Fabulous	Charlie Gracie	Parlophone	13	(16)	
19	-	Island In The Sun	Harry Belafonte	RCA	22	(30)	
20	3	Cumberland Gap	Lonnie Donegan	Pye Nixa	11		

April 1957

This Mnth	Prev Mnth	Title	Artist	Label	Wks 20	(UK Pos)	
1	18	Little Darlin'	Diamonds	Mercury	16	(3)	G
2	9	Round And Round	Perry Como	RCA	15		G
3	-	All Shook Up	Elvis Presley	RCA	17	(1)	G
4	10	Party Doll	Buddy Knox	Roulette	14	(29)	F G
5	19	Come Go With Me	Dell-Vikings	Dot	17		F G
6	12	I'm Walkin'	Fats Domino	Imperial	10	(19)	G
7	-	Gone	Ferlin Husky	Capitol	14		F G
8	11	Butterfly	Andy Williams	Cadence	12	(1)	G
9	20	Why Baby Why	Pat Boone	Dot	10	(17)	G
10	4	Butterfly	Charlie Gracie	Cameo	14	(12)	F G
11	2	Teen-Age Crush	Tommy Sands	Capitol	11		F G
12	-	Mama Look At Bubu	Harry Belafonte	RCA	7		L
13	-	Party Doll	Steve Lawrence	Coral	8		F
14	6	Marianne	Terry Gilkyson & The Easy Riders	Columbia	11		F G L
15	-	School Day	Chuck Berry	Chess	11	(24)	G
16	1	Young Love	Tab Hunter	Dot	13	(1)	F G
17	-	I'm Stickin' With You	Jimmy Bowen	Roulette	9		F L
18	-	I'm Sorry/He's Mine	Platters	Mercury	6	(18)	
19	-	Ninety-Nine Ways	Tab Hunter	Dot	4	(5)	L
20	-	So Rare	Jimmy Dorsey	Fraternity	21		G L

May 1957

This Mnth	Prev Mnth	Title	Artist	Label	Wks 20	(UK Pos)	
1	3	All Shook Up	Elvis Presley	RCA	17	(1)	G
2	1	Little Darlin'	Diamonds	Mercury	16	(3)	G
3	15	School Day	Chuck Berry	Chess	11	(24)	G
4	2	Round And Round	Perry Como	RCA	15		G
5	7	Gone	Ferlin Husky	Capitol	14		F G
6	5	Come Go With Me	Dell-Vikings	Dot	17		F G
7	4	Party Doll	Buddy Knox	Roulette	14	(29)	F G
8	-	A White Sport Coat (And A Pink Carnation)	Marty Robbins	Columbia	13		F G
9	20	So Rare	Jimmy Dorsey	Fraternity	21		G L
10	-	Love Letters In The Sand	Pat Boone	Dot	20	(2)	G
11	-	A Teenagers Romance/I'm Walkin'	Ricky Nelson	Verve	13		F G
12	9	Why Baby Why	Pat Boone	Dot	10	(17)	G
13	-	Dark Moon	Bonnie Guitar	Dot	7		F L
14	-	Rock-A-Billy	Guy Mitchell	Columbia	8	(1)	
15	12	Mama Look At Bubu	Harry Belafonte	RCA	7		L
16	-	Dark Moon	Gale Storm	Dot	15		L
17	6	I'm Walkin'	Fats Domino	Imperial	10	(19)	G
18	10	Butterfly	Charlie Gracie	Cameo	14	(12)	F G
19	8	Butterfly	Andy Williams	Cadence	12	(1)	G
20	18	I'm Sorry/He's Mine	Platters	Mercury	6	(18)	

June 1957

This Mnth	Prev Mnth	Title	Artist	Label	Wks 20	(UK Pos)	
1	10	Love Letters In The Sand	Pat Boone	Dot	20	(2)	G
2	11	A Teenagers Romance/I'm Walkin'	Ricky Nelson	Verve	13		F G
3	8	A White Sport Coat (And A Pink Carnation)	Marty Robbins	Columbia	13		F G
4	1	All Shook Up	Elvis Presley	RCA	17	(1)	G
5	9	So Rare	Jimmy Dorsey	Fraternity	21		G L
6	-	Bye Bye Love	Everly Brothers	Cadence	19	(6)	F G
7	3	School Day	Chuck Berry	Chess	11	(24)	G
8	16	Dark Moon	Gale Storm	Dot	15		L
9	2	Little Darlin'	Diamonds	Mercury	16	(3)	G
10	-	Searchin'/Young Blood	Coasters	Atco	19	(30)	F G
11	-	Start Movin' (In My Direction)	Sal Mineo	Epic	7	(16)	F L
12	5	Gone	Ferlin Husky	Capitol	14		F G
13	6	Come Go With Me	Dell-Vikings	Dot	17		F G
14	13	Dark Moon	Bonnie Guitar	Dot	7		F L
15	-	Four Walls	Jim Reeves	RCA	8		F
16	-	I Like Your Kind Of Love	Andy Williams	Cadence	6	(16)	
17	4	Round And Round	Perry Como	RCA	15		G
18	-	It's Not For Me To Say	Johnny Mathis	Columbia	15		F G
19	-	Old Cape Cod	Patti Page	Mercury	9		
20	-	Valley Of Tears/It's You I Love	Fats Domino	Imperial	6		

◆ With the drop from popularity of Bill Haley & The Comets, the media on both sides of the Atlantic prophesied the speedy demise of rock'n'roll.

◆ *The Alan Freed Show* premiered on US TV. His first guests included The Dell-Vikings and Guy Mitchell, who, like label-mate Johnnie Ray, scored his last British No. 1 hit this quarter.

◆ Richard Berry & The Pharaohs unsuccessfully released Berry's composition 'Louie Louie' – which went on to become one of the most recorded songs in rock history.

◆ Not only did Buddy Knox & The Rhythm Orchids' debut hit, 'Party Doll', beat a handful of cover versions to reach the top, But the B-side 'I'm Sticking With You', which featured group member Jimmy Bowen, also made the Top 20.

UK 1957 JULY-SEPT

◆ The first successful British rock-related group were The King Brothers. This youthful trio scored the first of their hits with a cover of Marty Robbins' 'A White Sport Coat'.

◆ John Lennon and Paul McCartney met for the first time at a Church Garden Fete as fellow Merseyside singer/songwriter Russ Hamilton earned a pot of gold for his double sided transatlantic smash, 'We Will Make Love'/'Rainbow'.

▲ Fifteen-year-old Paul Anka topped the transatlantic chart with his composition 'Diana' (written about his childhood baby-sitter), which went on to sell over a million in Britain.

July 1957

This Mnth	Prev Mnth	Title	Artist	Label	Wks 20	(US Pos)	
1	17	All Shook Up	Elvis Presley	HMV	18	(1)	
2	4	Gamblin' Man/Putting On The Style	Lonnie Donegan	Pye Nixa	18		
3	8	Little Darlin'	Diamonds	Mercury	15	(2)	F L
4	13	We Will Make Love	Russ Hamilton	Oriole	16		F
5	5	Around The World	Ronnie Hilton	HMV	15		
6	1	Yes Tonight Josephine	Johnnie Ray	Philips	15		
7	12	A White Sport Coat	King Brothers	Parlophone	11		F
8	2	When I Fall In Love	Nat 'King' Cole	Capitol	19		
9	6	Around The World	Bing Crosby	Brunswick	14	(25)	
10	-	Butterfingers	Tommy Steele	Decca	15		
11	10	Mr. Wonderful	Peggy Lee	Brunswick	13	(25)	F
12	-	Teddy Bear	Elvis Presley	HMV	18	(1)	
13	-	Love Letters In The Sand	Pat Boone	London American	21	(1)	
14	18	Fabulous	Charlie Gracie	Parlophone	13	(16)	
15	9	Freight Train	Chas McDevitt Skiffle Group	Oriole	14	(40)	F L
16	-	Lucille	Little Richard	London American	7	(21)	
17	19	Island In The Sun	Harry Belafonte	RCA	22	(30)	
18	-	Bye Bye Love	Everly Brothers	London American	13	(2)	F
19	3	Butterfly	Andy Williams	London American	12	(4)	F
20	-	I Like Your Kind Of Love	Andy Williams	London American	2	(10)	

August 1957

This Mnth	Prev Mnth	Title	Artist	Label	Wks 20	(US Pos)	
1	13	Love Letters In The Sand	Pat Boone	London American	21	(1)	
2	1	All Shook Up	Elvis Presley	HMV	18	(1)	
3	12	Teddy Bear	Elvis Presley	HMV	18	(1)	
4	17	Island In The Sun	Harry Belafonte	RCA	22	(30)	
5	2	Gamblin' Man/Putting On The Style	Lonnie Donegan	Pye Nixa	18		
6	4	We Will Make Love	Russ Hamilton	Oriole	16		F
7	3	Little Darlin'	Diamonds	Mercury	15	(2)	F L
8	18	Bye Bye Love	Everly Brothers	London American	13	(2)	F
9	-	Last Train To San Fernando	Johnny Duncan & The Blue Grass Boys	Columbia	16		F L
10	-	Diana	Paul Anka	Columbia	23	(1)	F G
11	5	Around The World	Ronnie Hilton	HMV	15		
12	-	With All My Heart	Petula Clark	Pye Nixa	16		
13	10	Butterfingers	Tommy Steele	Decca	15		
14	9	Around The World	Bing Crosby	Brunswick	14	(25)	
15	16	Lucille	Little Richard	London American	7	(21)	
16	14	Fabulous	Charlie Gracie	Parlophone	13	(16)	
17	6	Yes Tonight Josephine	Johnnie Ray	Philips	15		
18	8	When I Fall In Love	Nat 'King' Cole	Capitol	19		
19	7	A White Sport Coat	King Brothers	Parlophone	11		F
20	-	Start Movin'	Sal Mineo	Philips	6	(9)	F L

September 1957

This Mnth	Prev Mnth	Title	Artist	Label	Wks 20	(US Pos)	
1	10	Diana	Paul Anka	Columbia	23	(1)	F G
2	1	Love Letters In The Sand	Pat Boone	London American	21	(1)	
3	9	Last Train To San Fernando	Johnny Duncan & The Blue Grass Boys	Columbia	16		F L
4	4	Island In The Sun	Harry Belafonte	RCA	22	(30)	
5	12	With All My Heart	Petula Clark	Pye Nixa	16		
6	-	Water Water/Handful Of Songs	Tommy Steele	Decca	13		
7	2	All Shook Up	Elvis Presley	HMV	18	(1)	
8	-	Wanderin' Eyes/I Love You So Much It Hurts	Charlie Gracie	London American	12	(71)	L
9	-	Paralysed	Elvis Presley	HMV	9	(59)	
10	8	Bye Bye Love	Everly Brothers	London American	13	(2)	F
11	-	Tammy	Debbie Reynolds	Vogue Coral	15	(1)	F L
12	3	Teddy Bear	Elvis Presley	HMV	18	(1)	
13	5	Gamblin' Man/Putting On The Style	Lonnie Donegan	Pye Nixa	18		
14	16	Fabulous	Charlie Gracie	Parlophone	13	(16)	
15	-	Jenny Jenny	Little Richard	London American	5	(10)	
16	6	We Will Make Love	Russ Hamilton	Oriole	16		F
17	-	Stardust	Billy Ward & His Dominoes	London American	6	(14)	F L
18	-	Shiralee	Tommy Steele	Decca	3		
19	7	Little Darlin'	Diamonds	Mercury	15	(2)	F L
20	-	Build Your Love	Johnnie Ray	Philips	3	(58)	L

July 1957

This Mnth	Prev Mnth	Title	Artist	Label	Wks 20	(UK Pos)	
1	-	Teddy Bear	Elvis Presley	RCA	16	(3)	G
2	1	Love Letters In The Sand	Pat Boone	Dot	20	(2)	G
3	6	Bye Bye Love	Everly Brothers	Cadence	19	(6)	F G
4	5	So Rare	Jimmy Dorsey	Fraternity	21		G L
5	10	Searchin'/Young Blood	Coasters	Atco	19	(30)	F G
6	20	Valley Of Tears/It's You I Love	Fats Domino	Imperial	6		
7	18	It's Not For Me To Say	Johnny Mathis	Columbia	15		F G
8	8	Dark Moon	Gale Storm	Dot	15		L
9	-	Over The Mountain; Across The Sea	Johnnie & Joe	Chess	8		F L
10	-	Send For Me/My Personal Possession	Nat 'King' Cole	Capitol	13		
11	19	Old Cape Cod	Patti Page	Mercury	9		
12	-	Jenny, Jenny/Miss Ann	Little Richard	Specialty	8	(11)	
13	4	All Shook Up	Elvis Presley	RCA	17	(1)	G
14	3	A White Sport Coat (And A Pink Carnation)	Marty Robbins	Columbia	13		F G
15	-	Short Fat Fannie	Larry Williams	Specialty	12	(21)	F G
16	2	A Teenagers Romance/I'm Walkin'	Ricky Nelson	Verve	13		F G
17	-	I'm Gonna Sit Right Down And Write Myself A Letter	Billy Williams	Coral	11	(22)	F G L
18	16	I Like Your Kind Of Love	Andy Williams	Cadence	6	(16)	
19	-	C.C. Rider	Chuck Willis	Atlantic	5		F
20	9	Little Darlin'	Diamonds	Mercury	16	(3)	G

August 1957

This Mnth	Prev Mnth	Title	Artist	Label	Wks 20	(UK Pos)	
1	1	Teddy Bear	Elvis Presley	RCA	16	(3)	G
2	2	Love Letters In The Sand	Pat Boone	Dot	20	(2)	G
3	-	Tammy	Debbie Reynolds	Dot	19	(2)	G L
4	3	Bye Bye Love	Everly Brothers	Cadence	19	(6)	F G
5	5	Searchin'/Young Blood	Coasters	Atco	19	(30)	F G
6	4	So Rare	Jimmy Dorsey	Fraternity	21		G L
7	10	Send For Me/My Personal...	Nat 'King' Cole	Capitol	13		
8	17	I'm Gonna Sit Right Down...	Billy Williams	Coral	11	(22)	F G L
9	-	Diana	Paul Anka	ABC Paramount	15	(1)	F G
10	-	White Silver Sands	Don Rondo	Jubilee	8		F L
11	15	Short Fat Fannie	Larry Williams	Specialty	12	(21)	F G
12	-	Whispering Bells	Dell-Vikings	Dot	9		L
13	-	Rainbow	Russ Hamilton	Kapp	11		F L
14	7	It's Not For Me To Say	Johnny Mathis	Columbia	15		F G
15	-	Stardust	Billy Ward & His Dominoes	Liberty	10	(13)	
16	-	Remember You're Mine/There's A Gold Mine In The Sky	Pat Boone	Dot	11	(5)	G
17	11	Old Cape Cod	Patti Page	Mercury	9		
18	-	Whole Lot Of Shakin' Going On	Jerry Lee Lewis	Sun	13	(8)	F G
19	-	That'll Be The Day	Crickets	Brunswick	10	(1)	F G
20	-	Love Me To Pieces	Jill Corey	Columbia	2		F L

September 1957

This Mnth	Prev Mnth	Title	Artist	Label	Wks 20	(UK Pos)	
1	3	Tammy	Debbie Reynolds	Dot	19	(2)	G L
2	9	Diana	Paul Anka	ABC Paramount	15	(1)	F G
3	19	That'll Be The Day	Crickets	Brunswick	10	(1)	F G
4	18	Whole Lot Of Shakin' Going On	Jerry Lee Lewis	Sun	13	(8)	F G
5	-	Honeycomb	Jimmie Rodgers	Roulette	14	(30)	F G
6	1	Teddy Bear	Elvis Presley	RCA	16	(3)	G
7	13	Rainbow	Russ Hamilton	Kapp	11		F L
8	-	Mr. Lee	Bobbettes	Atlantic	9		F L
9	-	In The Middle Of An Island/I Am	Tony Bennett	Columbia	6		
10	5	Searchin'/Young Blood	Coasters	Atco	19	(30)	F G
11	16	Remember You're Mine/There's A...	Pat Boone	Dot	11	(5)	G
12	7	Send For Me/My Personal...	Nat 'King' Cole	Capitol	13		
13	4	Bye Bye Love	Everly Brothers	Cadence	19	(6)	F G
14	2	Love Letters In The Sand	Pat Boone	Dot	20	(2)	G
15	-	Chances Are/The Twelfth Of Never	Johnny Mathis	Columbia	19		G
16	15	Stardust	Billy Ward & His Dominoes	Liberty	10	(13)	
17	14	It's Not For Me To Say	Johnny Mathis	Columbia	15		F G
18	12	Whispering Bells	Dell-Vikings	Dot	9		L
19	-	Happy, Happy Birthday Baby	Tune Weavers	Checker	9		F L
20	11	Short Fat Fannie	Larry Williams	Specialty	12	(21)	F G

◆ More R&B acts than ever were breaking onto the pop chart. Among them were seasoned performers Billy Ward & His Dominoes, Little Richard, Chuck Willis and Fats Domino as well as relative newcomers like The Coasters, Johnnie & Joe and Larry Williams.

◆ CBS TV premiered *The Big Record* hosted by Patti Page, and *American Bandstand* debuted nationally. However, Jerry Lee Lewis' wildly outrageous performance on the Steve Allen and short-lived Alan Freed TV shows caused the biggest sensation.

◆ For the first time the top four artists on the R&B chart were all white: Paul Anka, Jimmie Rodgers, Jerry Lee Lewis and The Crickets. However, the year's top R&B record was 'Searchin''/'Young Blood', which gave The Coasters their first major hit.

UK 1957 OCT-DEC

▲ *NME* readers voted Pat Boone World's Outstanding Male Singer, Elvis Presley World's Outstanding Musical Personality, Doris Day (above) World's Top Female Singer and The Platters World's Top Group.

◆ Elvis Presley had a record seven singles in the UK Top 30. In America **Elvis' Christmas Album,** which had unprecedented American advance orders, replaced his **Lovin' You** at the top.

◆ Johnny Otis, who had been America's top R&B act of 1950, had a surprise British hit with a revival of 'Ma He's Making Eyes At Me', a flop in the USA.

October 1957

This Mnth	Prev Mnth	Title	Artist	Label	Wks 20	(US Pos)	
1	1	Diana	Paul Anka	Columbia	23	(1)	F G
2	2	Love Letters In The Sand	Pat Boone	London American	21	(1)	
3	11	Tammy	Debbie Reynolds	Vogue Coral	15	(1)	F L
4	4	Island In The Sun	Harry Belafonte	RCA	22	(30)	
5	-	That'll Be The Day	Crickets	Vogue Coral	12	(1)	F
6	3	Last Train To San Fernando	Johnny Duncan & The Blue Grass Boys	Columbia	16		F L
7	8	Wanderin' Eyes/I Love You So...	Charlie Gracie	London American	12	(71)	L
8	5	With All My Heart	Petula Clark	Pye Nixa	16		
9	-	Party	Elvis Presley	RCA	14		
10	6	Water Water/Handful Of Songs	Tommy Steele	Decca	13		
11	12	Teddy Bear	Elvis Presley	HMV	18	(1)	
12	-	Remember You're Mine/There's A Goldmine In The Sky	Pat Boone	London American	13	(10)	
13	7	All Shook Up	Elvis Presley	HMV	18	(1)	
14	-	Man On Fire/Wanderin' Eyes	Frankie Vaughan	Philips	11		
15	-	Whole Lotta Shakin' Goin' On	Jerry Lee Lewis	London American	7	(3)	F
16	9	Paralysed	Elvis Presley	HMV	9	(59)	
17	-	My Dixie Darling	Lonnie Donegan	Pye Nixa	8		
18	17	Stardust	Billy Ward & His Dominoes	London American	6	(14)	F L
19	15	Jenny Jenny	Little Richard	London American	5	(10)	
20	-	Call Rosie On The Phone	Guy Mitchell	Philips	3		

November 1957

This Mnth	Prev Mnth	Title	Artist	Label	Wks 20	(US Pos)	
1	5	That'll Be The Day	Crickets	Vogue Coral	12	(1)	F
2	9	Party	Elvis Presley	RCA	14		
3	3	Tammy	Debbie Reynolds	Vogue Coral	15	(1)	F L
4	12	Remember You're Mine/There's A...	Pat Boone	London American	13	(10)	
5	-	Be My Girl	Jim Dale	Parlophone	12		F L
6	1	Diana	Paul Anka	Columbia	23	(1)	F G
7	14	Man On Fire/Wanderin' Eyes	Frankie Vaughan	Philips	11		
8	-	Mary's Boy Child	Harry Belafonte	RCA	9	(12)	G
9	-	I Love You Baby	Paul Anka	Columbia	13	(97)	
10	-	Gotta Have Something In The Bank Frank	Frankie Vaughan & The Kaye Sisters	Philips	7		
11	-	Wake Up Little Susie	Everly Brothers	London American	11	(1)	
12	17	My Dixie Darling	Lonnie Donegan	Pye Nixa	8		
13	15	Whole Lotta Shakin' Goin' On	Jerry Lee Lewis	London American	7	(3)	F
14	10	Water Water/Handful Of Songs	Tommy Steele	Decca	13		
15	2	Love Letters In The Sand	Pat Boone	London American	21	(1)	
16	7	Wanderin' Eyes/I Love You So...	Charlie Gracie	London American	12	(71)	L
17	-	Santa Bring My Baby Back To Me	Elvis Presley	RCA	7		
18	8	With All My Heart	Petula Clark	Pye Nixa	16		
19	-	Alone	Petula Clark	Pye Nixa	9		
20	-	Ma He's Making Eyes At Me	Johnny Otis Show	Capitol	15		F

December 1957

This Mnth	Prev Mnth	Title	Artist	Label	Wks 20	(US Pos)	
1	8	Mary's Boy Child	Harry Belafonte	RCA	9	(12)	G
2	20	Ma He's Making Eyes At Me	Johnny Otis Show	Capitol	15		F
3	11	Wake Up Little Susie	Everly Brothers	London American	11	(1)	
4	9	I Love You Baby	Paul Anka	Columbia	13	(97)	
5	-	My Special Angel	Malcolm Vaughan	HMV	14		
6	5	Be My Girl	Jim Dale	Parlophone	12		F L
7	-	Let's Have A Ball	Winifred Atwell	Decca	5		
8	19	Alone	Petula Clark	Pye Nixa	9		
9	-	Reet Petite	Jackie Wilson	Coral	11	(62)	F
10	2	Party	Elvis Presley	RCA	14		
11	-	All The Way	Frank Sinatra	Capitol	16	(15)	
12	4	Remember You're Mine/There's A...	Pat Boone	London American	13	(10)	
13	17	Santa Bring My Baby Back To Me	Elvis Presley	RCA	7		
14	6	Diana	Paul Anka	Columbia	23	(1)	F G
15	-	Great Balls Of Fire	Jerry Lee Lewis	London American	11	(2)	
16	-	He's Got The Whole World In His Hands	Laurie London	Parlophone	7	(2)	F L
17	1	That'll Be The Day	Crickets	Vogue Coral	12	(1)	F
18	10	Gotta Have Something In The Bank...	Frankie Vaughan/Kaye Sisters	Philips	7		
19	-	April Love	Pat Boone	London American	17	(1)	
20	7	Man On Fire/Wanderin' Eyes	Frankie Vaughan	Philips	11		

This Mnth	Prev Mnth	Title	Artist	Label	Wks 20	(UK Pos)	
1	-	Wake Up Little Susie	Everly Brothers	Cadence	13	(2)	G
2	5	Honeycomb	Jimmie Rodgers	Roulette	14	(30)	F G
3	1	Tammy	Debbie Reynolds	Dot	19	(2)	G L
4	15	Chances Are/The Twelfth Of Never	Johnny Mathis	Columbia	19		G
5	2	Diana	Paul Anka	ABC Paramount	15	(1)	F G
6	-	Jailhouse Rock	Elvis Presley	RCA	17	(1)	G
7	19	Happy, Happy Birthday Baby	Tune Weavers	Checker	9		F L
8	4	Whole Lot Of Shakin' Going On	Jerry Lee Lewis	Sun	13	(8)	F G
9	3	That'll Be The Day	Crickets	Brunswick	10	(1)	F G
10	-	Be-Bop Baby/Have I Told You Lately That I Love You	Ricky Nelson	Imperial	15		G
11	8	Mr. Lee	Bobbettes	Atlantic	9		F L
12	-	Keep A Knockin'	Little Richard	Specialty	7	(21)	
13	-	Hula Love	Buddy Knox	Roulette	7		L
14	-	Fascination	Jane Morgan	Kapp	10		F L
15	-	Lotta Lovin'/Wear My Ring	Gene Vincent & His Blue Caps	Capitol	7		L
16	11	Remember You're Mine/There's A Gold Mine In The Sky	Pat Boone	Dot	11	(5)	G
17	-	Silhouettes	Rays	Cameo	16		F G L
18	7	Rainbow	Russ Hamilton	Kapp	11		F L
19	-	You Send Me	Sam Cooke	Keen	14	(29)	F G
20	6	Teddy Bear	Elvis Presley	RCA	16	(3)	G

This Mnth	Prev Mnth	Title	Artist	Label	Wks 20	(UK Pos)	
1	6	Jailhouse Rock	Elvis Presley	RCA	17	(1)	G
2	1	Wake Up Little Susie	Everly Brothers	Cadence	13	(2)	G
3	19	You Send Me	Sam Cooke	Keen	14	(29)	F G
4	17	Silhouettes	Rays	Cameo	16		F G L
5	10	Be-Bop Baby/Have I Told You...	Ricky Nelson	Imperial	15		G
6	4	Chances Are/The Twelfth Of Never	Johnny Mathis	Columbia	19		G
7	-	Little Bitty Pretty One	Thurston Harris	Aladdin	8		F L
8	-	My Special Angel	Bobby Helms	Decca	14	(22)	F G
9	2	Honeycomb	Jimmie Rodgers	Roulette	14	(30)	F G
10	-	April Love/When The Swallows Come Back To Capistrano	Pat Boone	Dot	17	(7)	G
11	3	Tammy	Debbie Reynolds	Dot	19	(2)	G L
12	-	Melodie D'Amour	Ames Brothers	RCA	9		
13	14	Fascination	Jane Morgan	Kapp	10		F L
14	12	Keep A Knockin'	Little Richard	Specialty	7	(21)	
15	-	Just Born/Ivy Rose	Perry Como	RCA	8		
16	5	Diana	Paul Anka	ABC Paramount	15	(1)	F G
17	7	Happy, Happy Birthday Baby	Tune Weavers	Checker	9		F L
18	-	Raunchy	Bill Justis	Phillips	11	(11)	F L
19	-	Rock & Roll Music	Chuck Berry	Chess	9		
20	-	Raunchy	Ernie Freeman	Imperial	7		F L

This Mnth	Prev Mnth	Title	Artist	Label	Wks 20	(UK Pos)	
1	1	Jailhouse Rock	Elvis Presley	RCA	17	(1)	G
2	10	April Love/When The Swallows Come Back To Capistrano	Pat Boone	Dot	17	(7)	G
3	3	You Send Me	Sam Cooke	Keen	14	(29)	F G
4	18	Raunchy	Bill Justis	Phillips	11	(11)	F L
5	-	Peggy Sue	Buddy Holly	Coral	14	(6)	F G
6	6	Chances Are/The Twelfth Of Never	Johnny Mathis	Columbia	19		G
7	4	Silhouettes	Rays	Cameo	16		F G L
8	-	At The Hop	Danny & The Juniors	ABC Paramount	15	(3)	F G
9	-	Great Balls Of Fire	Jerry Lee Lewis	Sun	11	(1)	G
10	19	Rock & Roll Music	Chuck Berry	Chess	9		
11	2	Wake Up Little Susie	Everly Brothers	Cadence	13	(2)	G
12	-	Kisses Sweeter Than Wine	Jimmie Rodgers	Roulette	11	(7)	G
13	5	Be-Bop Baby/Have I Told You...	Ricky Nelson	Imperial	15		G
14	8	My Special Angel	Bobby Helms	Decca	14	(22)	F G
15	20	Raunchy	Ernie Freeman	Imperial	7		F L
16	7	Little Bitty Pretty One	Thurston Harris	Aladdin	8		F L
17	-	All The Way/Chicago	Frank Sinatra	Capitol	9	(3)	
18	-	Bony Moronie/You Bug Me, Baby	Larry Williams	Specialty	7	(11)	L
19	15	Just Born/Ivy Rose	Perry Como	RCA	8		
20	-	Liechtensteiner Polka	Will Glahe	London	2		F L

US 1957
OCT-DEC

◆ Rock'n'roll was riding high with major hits from such greats as Elvis, Chuck Berry, Little Richard, The Everly Brothers, Gene Vincent and Jerry Lee Lewis. There was, however, still room for left-field records like 'Liechtensteiner Polka' by veteran German accordionist Will Glahe.

◆ Thanks partly to the rise of Top 40 radio, 1957 saw the boundaries between pop, R&B and C&W become blurred. In fact, at one time, the Top 6 on the pop and R&B charts were identical.

◆ For the first time, two female-led R&B groups found themselves in the US Top 10. New York schoolgirls The Bobbettes (aged 11-15) sang about their fifth grade teacher, 'Mr. Lee', while Massachusetts family combo The Tune Weavers, had a one-off hit with their composition, 'Happy Happy Birthday Baby'.

UK 1958
JAN-MAR

◆ Petula Clark had a hat-trick of hits with covers of US pop songs, 'With All My Heart', 'Alone' and 'Baby Lover'. When she recorded original material in the mid-1960s she became one of the top acts in America.

◆ Elvis Presley's 'Jailhouse Rock', with record advance orders of 250,000, became the first record to enter the chart at No. 1. Meanwhile, in America, 'Don't', became Presley's tenth chart topper in less than two years.

◆ Successful song-writer Hal David's collaboration with new-comer Burt Bacharach produced two successive UK No. 1s: 'The Story Of My Life' and 'Magic Moments'.

◆ Buddy Holly & The Crickets had a very successful tour of Britain, at a time when they were charting with four hits: 'Oh, Boy!', 'Peggy Sue', 'Maybe Baby' and 'Listen To Me'.

January 1958

This Mnth	Prev Mnth	Title	Artist	Label	Wks 20	(US Pos)	
1	2	Ma He's Making Eyes At Me	Johnny Otis Show	Capitol	15		F
2	15	Great Balls Of Fire	Jerry Lee Lewis	London American	11	(2)	
3	11	All The Way	Frank Sinatra	Capitol	16	(15)	
4	5	My Special Angel	Malcolm Vaughan	HMV	14		
5	9	Reet Petite	Jackie Wilson	Coral	11	(62)	F
6	-	Peggy Sue	Buddy Holly	Coral	12	(3)	F
7	-	Oh, Boy!	Crickets	Coral	12	(11)	
8	3	Wake Up Little Susie	Everly Brothers	London American	11	(1)	
9	4	I Love You Baby	Paul Anka	Columbia	13	(97)	
10	-	Kisses Sweeter Than Wine	Jimmie Rodgers	Columbia	10	(8)	F
11	-	Kisses Sweeter Than Wine	Frankie Vaughan	Philips	8		
12	19	April Love	Pat Boone	London American	17	(1)	
13	-	Jailhouse Rock	Elvis Presley	RCA	13	(1)	
14	-	The Story Of My Life	Michael Holliday	Columbia	14		
15	1	Mary's Boy Child	Harry Belafonte	RCA	9	(12)	G
16	8	Alone	Petula Clark	Pye Nixa	9		
17	-	Jack O' Diamonds	Lonnie Donegan	Pye Nixa	6		
18	14	Diana	Paul Anka	Columbia	23	(1)	F G
19	-	At The Hop	Danny & The Juniors	HMV	13	(1)	F L
20	-	Story Of My Life	Gary Miller	Pye Nixa	5		L

February 1958

This Mnth	Prev Mnth	Title	Artist	Label	Wks 20	(US Pos)	
1	14	The Story Of My Life	Michael Holliday	Columbia	14		
2	13	Jailhouse Rock	Elvis Presley	RCA	13	(1)	
3	19	At The Hop	Danny & The Juniors	HMV	13	(1)	F L
4	7	Oh, Boy!	Crickets	Coral	12	(11)	
5	-	Magic Moments	Perry Como	RCA	15	(3)	
6	3	All The Way	Frank Sinatra	Capitol	16	(15)	
7	-	Love Me Forever	Marion Ryan	Pye Nixa	10		F L
8	6	Peggy Sue	Buddy Holly	Coral	12	(3)	F
9	12	April Love	Pat Boone	London American	17	(1)	
10	-	You Are My Destiny	Paul Anka	Columbia	10	(9)	
11	2	Great Balls Of Fire	Jerry Lee Lewis	London American	11	(2)	
12	-	Bony Moronie	Larry Williams	London American	7	(14)	F L
13	1	Ma He's Making Eyes At Me	Johnny Otis Show	Capitol	15		F
14	4	My Special Angel	Malcolm Vaughan	HMV	14		
15	-	Raunchy	Bill Justis	London American	4	(2)	F L
16	10	Kisses Sweeter Than Wine	Jimmie Rodgers	Columbia	10	(8)	F
17	-	Witchcraft	Frank Sinatra	Capitol	6	(20)	
18	11	Kisses Sweeter Than Wine	Frankie Vaughan	Philips	8		
19	-	Sugartime	McGuire Sisters	Coral	3	(7)	
20	-	Mandy	Eddie Calvert	Columbia	11		L

March 1958

This Mnth	Prev Mnth	Title	Artist	Label	Wks 20	(US Pos)	
1	5	Magic Moments	Perry Como	RCA	15	(3)	
2	1	The Story Of My Life	Michael Holliday	Columbia	14		
3	2	Jailhouse Rock	Elvis Presley	RCA	13	(1)	
4	-	Don't	Elvis Presley	RCA	10	(1)	
5	3	At The Hop	Danny & The Juniors	HMV	13	(1)	F L
6	10	You Are My Destiny	Paul Anka	Columbia	10	(9)	
7	-	Nairobi	Tommy Steele	Decca	10		
8	7	Love Me Forever	Marion Ryan	Pye Nixa	10		F L
9	-	Good Golly Miss Molly	Little Richard	London American	7	(13)	
10	9	April Love	Pat Boone	London American	17	(1)	
11	4	Oh, Boy!	Crickets	Coral	12	(11)	
12	6	All The Way	Frank Sinatra	Capitol	16	(15)	
13	-	Whole Lotta Woman	Marvin Rainwater	MGM	14	(60)	F
14	-	Catch A Falling Star	Perry Como	RCA	7	(3)	
15	-	Can't Get Along Without You/ We're Not Alone	Frankie Vaughan	Philips	3		
16	-	Baby Lover	Petula Clark	Pye Nixa	4		
17	20	Mandy	Eddie Calvert	Columbia	11		L
18	-	Maybe Baby	Crickets	Coral	8	(18)	
19	-	La Dee Dah	Jackie Dennis	Decca	7		F L
20	8	Peggy Sue	Buddy Holly	Coral	12	(3)	F

January 1958

This Mnth	Prev Mnth	Title	Artist	Label	Wks 20	(UK Pos)	
1	8	At The Hop	Danny & The Juniors	ABC Paramount	15	(3)	F G
2	-	Stood Up/Waitin' In School	Ricky Nelson	Imperial	9	(27)	G
3	9	Great Balls Of Fire	Jerry Lee Lewis	Sun	11	(1)	G
4	2	April Love/When The Swallows Come Back To Capistrano	Pat Boone	Dot	17	(7)	G
5	5	Peggy Sue	Buddy Holly	Coral	14	(6)	F G
6	1	Jailhouse Rock	Elvis Presley	RCA	17	(1)	G
7	4	Raunchy	Bill Justis	Phillips	11	(11)	F L
8	12	Kisses Sweeter Than Wine	Jimmie Rodgers	Roulette	11		G
9	3	You Send Me	Sam Cooke	Keen	14	(29)	F G
10	7	Silhouettes	Rays	Cameo	16		F G L
11	-	Oh, Boy!	Crickets	Brunswick	6	(3)	
12	-	Jingle Bell Rock	Bobby Helms	Decca	2		L
13	-	The Stroll	Diamonds	Mercury	9		G
14	-	Sail Along Silvery Moon/Raunchy	Billy Vaughn	Dot	14		G
15	-	La Dee Dah	Billy & Lillie	Swan	7		F
16	-	Sugartime	McGuire Sisters	Coral	15	(14)	G
17	6	Chances Are/The Twelfth Of Never	Johnny Mathis	Columbia	19		G
18	-	Buzz-Buzz-Buzz	Hollywood Flames	Ebb	3		F L
19	-	Get A Job	Silhouettes	Ember	9		F G L
20	14	My Special Angel	Bobby Helms	Decca	14	(22)	F G

February 1958

This Mnth	Prev Mnth	Title	Artist	Label	Wks 20	(UK Pos)	
1	-	Don't/I Beg Of You	Elvis Presley	RCA	11	(2)	G
2	1	At The Hop	Danny & The Juniors	ABC Paramount	15	(3)	F G
3	19	Get A Job	Silhouettes	Ember	9		F G L
4	2	Stood Up/Waitin' In School	Ricky Nelson	Imperial	9	(27)	G
5	14	Sail Along Silvery Moon/Raunchy	Billy Vaughn	Dot	14		G
6	-	Short Shorts	Royal Teens	ABC Paramount	8		F L
7	16	Sugartime	McGuire Sisters	Coral	15	(14)	G
8	-	Catch A Falling Star/Magic Moments	Perry Como	RCA	14	(9)	G
9	13	The Stroll	Diamonds	Mercury	9		G
10	5	Peggy Sue	Buddy Holly	Coral	14	(6)	F G
11	3	Great Balls Of Fire	Jerry Lee Lewis	Sun	11	(1)	G
12	-	You Are My Destiny	Paul Anka	ABC Paramount	6	(6)	
13	-	Dede Dinah	Frankie Avalon	Chancellor	5		F
14	4	April Love/When The Swallows Come Back To Capistrano	Pat Boone	Dot	17	(7)	G
15	15	La Dee Dah	Billy & Lillie	Swan	7		F
16	-	Oh Julie	Crescendos	Nasco	8		F L
17	-	Don't Let Go	Roy Hamilton	Epic	4		
18	8	Kisses Sweeter Than Wine	Jimmie Rodgers	Roulette	11	(7)	G
19	-	A Wonderful Time Up There/It's Too Soon To Know	Pat Boone	Dot	12	(2)	G
20	-	Maybe	Chantels	End	4		F

March 1958

This Mnth	Prev Mnth	Title	Artist	Label	Wks 20	(UK Pos)	
1	1	Don't/I Beg Of You	Elvis Presley	RCA	11	(2)	G
2	-	Sweet Little Sixteen	Chuck Berry	Chess	9	(16)	G
3	19	A Wonderful Time Up There/It's Too Soon To Know	Pat Boone	Dot	12	(2)	G
4	8	Catch A Falling Star/Magic Moments	Perry Como	RCA	14	(9)	G
5	-	Tequila	Champs	Challenge	12	(5)	F G L
6	-	26 Miles	Four Preps	Capitol	10		F G
7	16	Oh Julie	Crescendos	Nasco	8		F L
8	5	Sail Along Silvery Moon/Raunchy	Billy Vaughn	Dot	14		G
9	-	Who's Sorry Now	Connie Francis	MGM	10	(1)	F G
10	3	Get A Job	Silhouettes	Ember	9		F G L
11	6	Short Shorts	Royal Teens	ABC Paramount	8		F L
12	-	Lollipop	Chordettes	Cadence	9	(6)	G
13	7	Sugartime	McGuire Sisters	Coral	15	(14)	G
14	-	The Walk	Jimmy McCracklin	Checker	5		F L
15	-	Dinner With Drac (Part 1)	John Zacherle	Cameo	3		F L
16	-	Breathless	Jerry Lee Lewis	Sun	6	(8)	L
17	2	At The Hop	Danny & The Juniors	ABC Paramount	15	(3)	F G
18	9	The Stroll	Diamonds	Mercury	9		G
19	-	Good Golly, Miss Molly	Little Richard	Specialty	3	(8)	L
20	12	You Are My Destiny	Paul Anka	ABC Paramount	6	(6)	

▲ TV star and teen idol Ricky Nelson topped the album chart with his debut LP, **Ricky**. Incidentally his father, Ozzie, had topped the charts in 1933 and his sons, Gunnar and Matthew, did so in 1990.

◆ Dick Clark's whose *American Bandstand* had become America's most watched daytime TV show (average audience of 8.5 million), launched *The Dick Clark Saturday Night Show*.

◆ One of rock's oddest hits was 'Dinner With Drac', which consisted of ghoulish and gory limericks spoken over a wild rocking backing track. Performer John Zacherle was host of TV's *Shock Theater*.

UK 1958 APR-JUNE

▲ Jerry Lee Lewis's British tour was cut short when the media discovered that his bigamously married third wife was his 14-year-old second cousin.

◆ Jack Good, producer of *6-5 Special*, launched *Oh Boy!*, a TV show which first introduced the public to such acts as Cliff Richard and Billy Fury.

◆ A track recorded on the streets of South Africa by a tin-whistle band in 1956, 'Tom Hark' by Elias & His Zigzag Jive Flutes, was the year's most unexpected UK hit.

April 1958

This Mnth	Prev Mnth	Title	Artist	Label	Wks 20	(US Pos)	
1	1	Magic Moments	Perry Como	RCA	15	(3)	
2	13	Whole Lotta Woman	Marvin Rainwater	MGM	14	(60)	F
3	7	Nairobi	Tommy Steele	Decca	10		
4	-	Swingin' Shepherd Blues	Ted Heath	Decca	10		L
5	18	Maybe Baby	Crickets	Coral	8	(18)	
6	19	La Dee Dah	Jackie Dennis	Decca	7		F L
7	-	Tequila	Champs	London American	7	(1)	F L
8	4	Don't	Elvis Presley	RCA	10	(1)	
9	-	A Wonderful Time Up There	Pat Boone	London American	14	(4)	
10	-	Who's Sorry Now	Connie Francis	MGM	20	(5)	F
11	2	The Story Of My Life	Michael Holliday	Columbia	14		
12	-	It's Too Soon To Know	Pat Boone	London American	8	(4)	
13	17	Mandy	Eddie Calvert	Columbia	11		L
14	14	Catch A Falling Star	Perry Como	RCA	7	(3)	
15	-	Breathless	Jerry Lee Lewis	London American	6	(9)	
16	9	Good Golly Miss Molly	Little Richard	London American	7	(13)	
17	-	To Be Loved	Malcolm Vaughan	HMV	8		
18	5	At The Hop	Danny & The Juniors	HMV	13	(1)	F L
19	3	Jailhouse Rock	Elvis Presley	RCA	13	(1)	
20	-	Lollipop	Chordettes	London American	5	(2)	L

May 1958

This Mnth	Prev Mnth	Title	Artist	Label	Wks 20	(US Pos)	
1	10	Who's Sorry Now	Connie Francis	MGM	20	(5)	F
2	2	Whole Lotta Woman	Marvin Rainwater	MGM	14	(60)	F
3	9	A Wonderful Time Up There	Pat Boone	London American	14	(4)	
4	-	Tom Hark	Elias & His Zigzag Jive Flutes	Columbia	12		F L
5	-	Wear My Ring Around Your Neck	Elvis Presley	RCA	7	(2)	
6	-	Lollipop	Mudlarks	Columbia	9		F
7	-	Grand Coolie Dam	Lonnie Donegan	Pye Nixa	9		
8	4	Swingin' Shepherd Blues	Ted Heath	Decca	10		L
9	20	Lollipop	Chordettes	London American	5	(2)	L
10	15	Breathless	Jerry Lee Lewis	London American	6	(9)	
11	7	Tequila	Champs	London American	7	(1)	F L
12	1	Magic Moments	Perry Como	RCA	15	(3)	
13	12	It's Too Soon To Know	Pat Boone	London American	8	(4)	
14	-	You Need Hands/ Tulips From Amsterdam	Max Bygraves	Decca	21		
15	-	On The Street Where You Live	Vic Damone	Philips	15	(8)	F L
16	-	I May Never Pass This Way Again	Robert Earl	Philips	9		F
17	-	Kewpie Doll	Perry Como	RCA	5	(12)	
18	17	To Be Loved	Malcolm Vaughan	HMV	8		
19	-	Kewpie Doll	Frankie Vaughan	Philips	9		
20	5	Maybe Baby	Crickets	Coral	8	(18)	

June 1958

This Mnth	Prev Mnth	Title	Artist	Label	Wks 20	(US Pos)	
1	1	Who's Sorry Now	Connie Francis	MGM	20	(5)	F
2	15	On The Street Where You Live	Vic Damone	Philips	15	(8)	F L
3	4	Tom Hark	Elias & His Zigzag Jive Flutes	Columbia	12		F L
4	-	Stairway Of Love	Michael Holliday	Columbia	11		
5	14	You Need Hands/ Tulips From Amsterdam	Max Bygraves	Decca	21		
6	-	All I Have To Do Is Dream/Claudette	Everly Brothers	London American	19	(1)	
7	-	Witch Doctor	Don Lang	HMV	10		L
8	3	A Wonderful Time Up There	Pat Boone	London American	14	(4)	
9	-	Army Game	TV Cast	HMV	6		F L
10	6	Lollipop	Mudlarks	Columbia	9		F
11	19	Kewpie Doll	Frankie Vaughan	Philips	9		
12	7	Grand Coolie Dam	Lonnie Donegan	Pye Nixa	9		
13	-	Twilight Time	Platters	Mercury	12	(1)	
14	-	Book Of Love	Mudlarks	Columbia	7		L
15	5	Wear My Ring Around Your Neck	Elvis Presley	RCA	7	(2)	
16	-	I May Never Pass This Way Again	Perry Como	RCA	4		
17	-	Big Man	Four Preps	Capitol	12	(6)	F L
18	17	Kewpie Doll	Perry Como	RCA	5	(12)	
19	-	Witch Doctor	David Seville	London	5	(1)	F
20	16	I May Never Pass This Way Again	Robert Earl	Philips	9		F

April 1958

This Mnth	Prev Mnth	Title	Artist	Label	Wks 20	(UK Pos)	
1	5	Tequila	Champs	Challenge	12	(5)	F G L
2	-	He's Got The Whole World (In His Hands)	Laurie London	Capitol	13	(12)	F G L
3	3	A Wonderful Time.../It's Too Soon...	Pat Boone	Dot	12	(2)	G
4	12	Lollipop	Chordettes	Cadence	9	(6)	G
5	-	Twilight Time	Platters	Mercury	13	(3)	G
6	-	Believe What You Say/ My Bucket's Got A Hole In It	Ricky Nelson	Imperial	8		G
7	4	Catch A Falling Star/Magic Moments	Perry Como	RCA	14	(9)	G
8	2	Sweet Little Sixteen	Chuck Berry	Chess	9	(16)	G
9	9	Who's Sorry Now	Connie Francis	MGM	10	(1)	F G
10	-	Book Of Love	Monotones	Argo	9		F L
11	-	Witch Doctor	David Seville	Liberty	13	(11)	F G L
12	-	Wear My Ring Around Your Neck	Elvis Presley	RCA	10	(3)	G
13	-	Don't You Just Know It	Huey (Piano) Smith & The Clowns	Ace	6		F L
14	13	Sugartime	McGuire Sisters	Coral	15	(14)	G
15	8	Sail Along Silvery Moon/Raunchy	Billy Vaughn	Dot	14		G
16	16	Breathless	Jerry Lee Lewis	Sun	6	(8)	L
17	-	Oh Lonesome Me/ I Can't Stop Lovin' You	Don Gibson	RCA	11		F L
18	1	Don't/I Beg Of You	Elvis Presley	RCA	11	(2)	G
19	-	Are You Sincere	Andy Williams	Cadence	5		
20	6	26 Miles	Four Preps	Capitol	10		F G

May 1958

This Mnth	Prev Mnth	Title	Artist	Label	Wks 20	(UK Pos)	
1	-	All I Have To Do Is Dream	Everly Brothers	Cadence	13	(1)	G
2	11	Witch Doctor	David Seville	Liberty	13	(11)	F G L
3	12	Wear My Ring Around Your Neck	Elvis Presley	RCA	10	(3)	G
4	5	Twilight Time	Platters	Mercury	13	(3)	G
5	2	He's Got The Whole World (In His...)	Laurie London	Capitol	13	(12)	F G L
6	-	Return To Me	Dean Martin	Capitol	13	(2)	
7	10	Book Of Love	Monotones	Argo	9		F L
8	-	Looking Back/Do I Like It	Nat 'King' Cole	Capitol	11		
9	1	Tequila	Champs	Challenge	12	(5)	F G L
10	17	Oh Lonesome Me/I Can't Stop...	Don Gibson	RCA	11		F L
11	-	Johnny B. Goode	Chuck Berry	Chess	8		
12	-	Kewpie Doll	Perry Como	RCA	7	(9)	
13	6	Believe What You Say/My Bucket's...	Ricky Nelson	Imperial	8		G
14	-	Chanson D'Amour (Song Of Love)	Art & Dotty Todd	Era	8		F L
15	4	Lollipop	Chordettes	Cadence	9	(6)	G
16	3	A Wonderful Time.../It's Too Soon...	Pat Boone	Dot	12	(2)	G
17	-	Sugar Moon/Cherie I Love You	Pat Boone	Dot	8	(6)	
18	-	Big Man	Four Preps	Capitol	9	(2)	G
19	-	Secretly	Jimmie Rodgers	Roulette	11		G
20	-	For Your Love	Ed Townsend	Capitol	4		F L

June 1958

This Mnth	Prev Mnth	Title	Artist	Label	Wks 20	(UK Pos)	
1	1	All I Have To Do Is Dream	Everly Brothers	Cadence	13	(1)	G
2	-	The Purple People Eater	Sheb Wooley	MGM	9	(12)	F G L
3	2	Witch Doctor	David Seville	Liberty	13	(11)	F G L
4	19	Secretly	Jimmie Rodgers	Roulette	11		G
5	6	Return To Me	Dean Martin	Capitol	13	(2)	
6	-	Do You Want To Dance	Bobby Freeman	Josie	10		F
7	8	Looking Back/Do I Like It	Nat 'King' Cole	Capitol	11		
8	18	Big Man	Four Preps	Capitol	9	(2)	G
9	4	Twilight Time	Platters	Mercury	13	(3)	G
10	-	Yakety Yak	Coasters	Atco	10	(12)	G
11	3	Wear My Ring Around Your Neck	Elvis Presley	RCA	10	(3)	G
12	-	Jennie Lee	Jan & Arnie	Arwin	6		F
13	17	Sugar Moon/Cherie I Love You	Pat Boone	Dot	8	(6)	
14	11	Johnny B. Goode	Chuck Berry	Chess	8		
15	5	He's Got The Whole World (In His...)	Laurie London	Capitol	13	(12)	F G L
16	-	Endless Sleep	Jody Reynolds	Demon	9		F L
17	14	Chanson D'Amour (Song Of Love)	Art & Dotty Todd	Era	8		F L
18	-	What Am I Living For	Chuck Willis	Atlantic	9		G L
19	7	Book Of Love	Monotones	Argo	9		F L
20	-	Patricia	Perez Prado	RCA	15	(8)	G L

◆ Chart newcomers included 14-year-old Londoner Laurie London, with his revival of 'He's Got The Whole World In His Hands', and Connie Francis with her tenth release, 'Who's Sorry Now'.

◆ Notwithstanding the continued popularity of the big beat artists, early 1950s stars such as Nat 'King' Cole, Perry Como, Dean Martin and the McGuire Sisters were still able to add to their hit tallies.

◆ Riots (including stabbings, rapes, looting and drug taking) allegedly took place after an Alan Freed show, and he was charged with incitement to riot. Some states then banned Freed shows.

◆ Two records using sped-up vocal gimmicks topped the chart: David Seville's 'Witch Doctor' and cowboy actor/singer Sheb Wooley's 'The Purple People Eater'.

UK 1958
JULY-SEPT

◆ One of the most recorded songs of the year, 'On The Street Where You Live', took noted US balladeer Vic Damone to the top. His version had also outpaced all the competition in the USA two years earlier.

◆ Cliff Richard's debut single, 'Move It' (composed by Ian Samwell from his backing group, The Drifters), only narrowly missed topping the chart.

◆ Johnny Otis's biggest American hit, 'Willie & The Hand Jive', was inspired by a digital dance started in British coffee bars and popularized on *6-5 Special*.

◆ In August, the month that both Michael Jackson and Madonna were born, George Harrison joined John Lennon and Paul McCartney's group, The Quarry Men.

July 1958

This Mnth	Prev Mnth	Title	Artist	Label	Wks 20	(US Pos)	
1	6	All I Have To Do Is Dream/Claudette	Everly Brothers	London American	19	(1)	
2	2	On The Street Where You Live	Vic Damone	Philips	15	(8)	F L
3	5	You Need Hands/Tulips From Amsterdam	Max Bygraves	Decca	21		
4	17	Big Man	Four Preps	Capitol	12	(6)	F L
5	13	Twilight Time	Platters	Mercury	12	(1)	
6	1	Who's Sorry Now	Connie Francis	MGM	20	(5)	F
7	-	Sugar Moon	Pat Boone	London American	10	(10)	
8	14	Book Of Love	Mudlarks	Columbia	7		L
9	-	Rave On	Buddy Holly	Coral	12	(41)	
10	7	Witch Doctor	Don Lang	HMV	10		L
11	4	Stairway Of Love	Michael Holliday	Columbia	11		
12	-	Sally Don't You Grieve/Betty, Betty, Betty	Lonnie Donegan	Pye Nixa	6		
13	-	The Purple People Eater	Sheb Wooley	MGM	6	(1)	F L
14	3	Tom Hark	Elias & His Zigzag Jive Flutes	Columbia	12		F L
15	-	Endless Sleep	Marty Wilde	Philips	12		F
16	-	I'm Sorry I Made You Cry	Connie Francis	MGM	7	(36)	
17	9	Army Game	TV Cast	HMV	6		F L
18	-	On The Street Where You Live	David Whitfield	Decca	8		L
19	-	Hard Headed Woman	Elvis Presley	RCA	8	(1)	
20	11	Kewpie Doll	Frankie Vaughan	Philips	9		

August 1958

This Mnth	Prev Mnth	Title	Artist	Label	Wks 20	(US Pos)	
1	1	All I Have To Do Is Dream/Claudette	Everly Brothers	London American	19	(1)	
2	-	When	Kalin Twins	Brunswick	16	(5)	F L
3	19	Hard Headed Woman	Elvis Presley	RCA	8	(1)	
4	-	Return To Me	Dean Martin	Capitol	16	(4)	
5	3	You Need Hands/Tulips From Amsterdam	Max Bygraves	Decca	21		
6	15	Endless Sleep	Marty Wilde	Philips	12		F
7	4	Big Man	Four Preps	Capitol	12	(6)	F L
8	9	Rave On	Buddy Holly	Coral	12	(41)	
9	5	Twilight Time	Platters	Mercury	12	(1)	
10	-	Patricia	Perez Prado	RCA	11	(2)	L
11	7	Sugar Moon	Pat Boone	London American	10	(10)	
12	6	Who's Sorry Now	Connie Francis	MGM	20	(5)	F
13	-	Think It Over	Crickets	Coral	5	(27)	
14	2	On The Street Where You Live	Vic Damone	Philips	15	(8)	F L
15	16	I'm Sorry I Made You Cry	Connie Francis	MGM	7	(36)	
16	-	Splish Splash	Charlie Drake	Parlophone	9		F
17	12	Sally Don't You Grieve/Betty, Betty, Betty	Lonnie Donegan	Pye Nixa	6		
18	-	Fever	Peggy Lee	Capitol	8	(8)	L
19	-	Carolina Moon/Stupid Cupid	Connie Francis	MGM	17	(14)	
20	-	Poor Little Fool	Ricky Nelson	London American	13	(1)	F

September 1958

This Mnth	Prev Mnth	Title	Artist	Label	Wks 20	(US Pos)	
1	2	When	Kalin Twins	Brunswick	16	(5)	F L
2	19	Carolina Moon/Stupid Cupid	Connie Francis	MGM	17	(14)	
3	4	Return To Me	Dean Martin	Capitol	16	(4)	
4	-	Volare	Dean Martin	Capitol	12	(15)	
5	1	All I Have To Do Is Dream/Claudette	Everly Brothers	London American	19	(1)	
6	18	Fever	Peggy Lee	Capitol	8	(8)	L
7	20	Poor Little Fool	Ricky Nelson	London American	13	(1)	F
8	6	Endless Sleep	Marty Wilde	Philips	12		F
9	16	Splish Splash	Charlie Drake	Parlophone	9		F
10	10	Patricia	Perez Prado	RCA	11	(2)	L
11	-	Volare	Domenico Modugno	Oriole	8	(1)	F L
12	-	Mad Passionate Love	Bernard Bresslaw	HMV	9		F L
13	-	Yakety Yak	Coasters	London American	7	(2)	F
14	5	You Need Hands/Tulips From...	Max Bygraves	Decca	21		
15	-	Bird Dog	Everly Brothers	London American	16	(2)	
16	3	Hard Headed Woman	Elvis Presley	RCA	8	(1)	
17	8	Rave On	Buddy Holly	Coral	12	(41)	
18	-	Trudie	Joe 'Mr. Piano' Henderson	Pye Nixa	6		L
19	-	Girl Of My Dreams	Tony Brent	Columbia	5		L
20	-	Born Too Late	Poni-Tails	HMV	10	(7)	F L

July 1958

This Mnth	Prev Mnth	Title	Artist	Label	Wks 20	(UK Pos)	
1	-	Hard Headed Woman	Elvis Presley	RCA	8	(2)	G
2	10	Yakety Yak	Coasters	Atco	10	(12)	G
3	2	The Purple People Eater	Sheb Wooley	MGM	9	(12)	F G L
4	20	Patricia	Perez Prado	RCA	15	(8)	G L
5	-	Splish Splash	Bobby Darin	Atco	10	(18)	F G
6	-	Poor Little Fool	Ricky Nelson	Imperial	12	(4)	G
7	16	Endless Sleep	Jody Reynolds	Demon	9		F L
8	4	Secretly	Jimmie Rodgers	Roulette	11		
9	-	Rebel-'Rouser	Duane Eddy	Jamie	8	(19)	F G
10	1	All I Have To Do Is Dream	Everly Brothers	Cadence	13	(1)	G
11	-	When	Kalin Twins	Decca	10	(1)	F G
12	6	Do You Want To Dance	Bobby Freeman	Josie	10		F
13	-	For Your Precious Love	Jerry Butler & The Impressions	Abner	5		F
14	-	Guess Things Happen That Way/ Come In Stranger	Johnny Cash	Sun	4		
15	-	My True Love/Leroy	Jack Scott	Carlton	13	(9)	F G
16	5	Return To Me	Dean Martin	Capitol	13	(2)	
17	3	Witch Doctor	David Seville	Liberty	13	(11)	F G L
18	18	What Am I Living For	Chuck Willis	Atlantic	9		G L
19	-	Willie And The Hand Jive	Johnny Otis Show	Capitol	8		F L
20	7	Looking Back/Do I Like It	Nat 'King' Cole	Capitol	11		

August 1958

This Mnth	Prev Mnth	Title	Artist	Label	Wks 20	(UK Pos)	
1	6	Poor Little Fool	Ricky Nelson	Imperial	12	(4)	G
2	4	Patricia	Perez Prado	RCA	15	(8)	G L
3	15	My True Love/Leroy	Jack Scott	Carlton	13	(9)	F G
4	-	Nel Blu Dipinto Di Blu (Volare)	Domenico Modugno	Decca	13	(10)	F G L
5	11	When	Kalin Twins	Decca	10	(1)	F G
6	-	Just A Dream	Jimmy Clanton	Ace	12		F G
7	5	Splish Splash	Bobby Darin	Atco	10	(18)	F G
8	9	Rebel-'Rouser	Duane Eddy	Jamie	8	(19)	F G
9	-	Little Star	Elegants	Apt	14	(25)	F G L
10	-	Fever	Peggy Lee	Capitol	7	(5)	
11	19	Willie And The Hand Jive	Johnny Otis Show	Capitol	8		F L
12	1	Hard Headed Woman	Elvis Presley	RCA	8	(2)	G
13	-	Ginger Bread	Frankie Avalon	Chancellor	7	(30)	
14	2	Yakety Yak	Coasters	Atco	10	(12)	G
15	-	If Dreams Came True	Pat Boone	Dot	6	(16)	
16	-	Bird Dog	Everly Brothers	Cadence	13	(2)	G
17	-	Born Too Late	Poni-Tails	ABC Paramount	10	(5)	F L
18	-	Everybody Loves A Lover	Doris Day	Columbia	8	(25)	L
19	-	Western Movies	Olympics	Demon	6	(12)	F L
20	-	Left Right Out Of Your Heart	Patti Page	Mercury	2		

September 1958

This Mnth	Prev Mnth	Title	Artist	Label	Wks 20	(UK Pos)	
1	4	Nel Blu Dipinto Di Blu (Volare)	Domenico Modugno	Decca	13	(10)	F G L
2	16	Bird Dog	Everly Brothers	Cadence	13	(2)	G
3	9	Little Star	Elegants	Apt	14	(25)	F G L
4	6	Just A Dream	Jimmy Clanton	Ace	12		F G
5	-	Rock-In' Robin/Over And Over	Bobby Day	Class	13	(29)	F G L
6	-	It's All In The Game	Tommy Edwards	MGM	14	(1)	F G
7	17	Born Too Late	Poni-Tails	ABC Paramount	10	(5)	F L
8	-	Tears On My Pillow	Little Anthony & The Imperials	End	10		F G
9	2	Patricia	Perez Prado	RCA	15	(8)	G L
10	3	My True Love/Leroy	Jack Scott	Carlton	13	(9)	F G
11	1	Poor Little Fool	Ricky Nelson	Imperial	12	(4)	G
12	-	Susie Darlin'	Robin Luke	Dot	9	(23)	F G L
13	19	Western Movies	Olympics	Demon	6	(12)	F L
14	-	Devoted To You	Everly Brothers	Cadence	6		
15	-	Summertime Blues	Eddie Cochran	Liberty	7	(18)	F L
16	13	Ginger Bread	Frankie Avalon	Chancellor	7	(30)	
17	5	When	Kalin Twins	Decca	10	(1)	F G
18	-	Are You Really Mine	Jimmie Rodgers	Roulette	4		
19	-	Near You	Roger Williams	Kapp	7		
20	10	Fever	Peggy Lee	Capitol	7	(5)	

◆ An anti-rock backlash at radio level resulted in many labels and artists softening their sound in order to get airplay (and therefore sales).

◆ Stereo, previously considered a gimmick for sound enthusiasts, was being taken seriously by labels like RCA, Columbia and Atlantic who started recording stereo pop singles.

◆ The first Hot 100 chart was launched by *Billboard*. Ricky Nelson stood at No. 1 with 'Poor Little Fool' and Britain's Frankie Vaughan peaked at No. 100 with his only US chart entry, 'Judy'.

◆ Mambo King Perez Prado's 'Patricia' spearheaded the Cha Cha Cha dance craze. Astoundingly his chart topping composition also reached the UK, R&B and even C&W listings!

UK 1958 OCT-DEC

▲ *NME* poll winners included Elvis (World's Outstanding Male), Connie Francis (World's Outstanding Female), the Everly Brothers (World's Outstanding Group) and Cliff Richard (above), whose act had been labelled "crude" and "vulgar" was Favourite New Singer.

◆ Italian songs were enjoying an unprecedented amount of success in the UK. Three versions of Domenico Modugno's US chart topper, 'Volare', charted alongside two recordings of 'Come Prima' and Dean Martin's multi-lingual transatlantic best seller, 'Return To Me'.

October 1958

This Mnth	Prev Mnth	Title	Artist	Label	Wks 20	(US Pos)	
1	2	**Carolina Moon/Stupid Cupid**	Connie Francis	MGM	17	(14)	
2	15	**Bird Dog**	Everly Brothers	London American	16	(2)	
3	4	**Volare**	Dean Martin	Capitol	12	(15)	
4	-	**King Creole**	Elvis Presley	RCA	9		
5	-	**Move It**	Cliff Richard	Columbia	11		F
6	20	**Born Too Late**	Poni-Tails	HMV	10	(7)	F L
7	-	**A Certain Smile**	Johnny Mathis	Fontana	14	(21)	F
8	1	**When**	Kalin Twins	Brunswick	16	(5)	F L
9	7	**Poor Little Fool**	Ricky Nelson	London American	13	(1)	F
10	12	**Mad Passionate Love**	Bernard Bresslaw	HMV	9		F L
11	-	**Come Prima**	Marino Marini	Durium	13		L
12	-	**It's All In The Game**	Tommy Edwards	MGM	15	(1)	F L
13	3	**Return To Me**	Dean Martin	Capitol	16	(4)	
14	-	**More Than Ever (Come Prima)**	Malcolm Vaughan	HMV	13		
15	11	**Volare**	Domenico Modugno	Oriole	8	(1)	F L
16	-	**Volare**	Marino Marini	Durium	5		F
17	-	**Western Movies**	Olympics	HMV	7	(8)	F L
18	-	**Hoots Mon**	Lord Rockingham's XI	Decca	16		F
19	9	**Splish Splash**	Charlie Drake	Parlophone	9		F
20	6	**Fever**	Peggy Lee	Capitol	8	(8)	L

November 1958

This Mnth	Prev Mnth	Title	Artist	Label	Wks 20	(US Pos)	
1	12	**It's All In The Game**	Tommy Edwards	MGM	15	(1)	F L
2	18	**Hoots Mon**	Lord Rockingham's XI	Decca	16		F
3	2	**Bird Dog**	Everly Brothers	London American	16	(2)	
4	11	**Come Prima**	Marino Marini	Durium	13		L
5	7	**A Certain Smile**	Johnny Mathis	Fontana	14	(21)	F
6	14	**More Than Ever (Come Prima)**	Malcolm Vaughan	HMV	13		
7	1	**Carolina Moon/Stupid Cupid**	Connie Francis	MGM	17	(14)	
8	5	**Move It**	Cliff Richard	Columbia	11		F
9	-	**Tea For Two Cha Cha**	Tommy Dorsey Orchestra	Brunswick	16	(7)	F L
10	-	**It's Only Make Believe**	Conway Twitty	MGM	14	(1)	F
11	4	**King Creole**	Elvis Presley	RCA	9		
12	-	**My True Love**	Jack Scott	London American	8	(3)	F
13	-	**Love Makes The World Go Round**	Perry Como	RCA	13	(33)	
14	-	**Tom Dooley**	Lonnie Donegan	Pye Nixa	12		
15	6	**Born Too Late**	Poni-Tails	HMV	10	(7)	F L
16	-	**Someday**	Jodie Sands	HMV	8	(95)	F L
17	-	**Someday**	Ricky Nelson	London American	8		
18	3	**Volare**	Dean Martin	Capitol	12	(15)	
19	17	**Western Movies**	Olympics	HMV	7	(8)	F L
20	-	**Come On Let's Go**	Tommy Steele	Decca	11		

December 1958

This Mnth	Prev Mnth	Title	Artist	Label	Wks 20	(US Pos)	
1	10	**It's Only Make Believe**	Conway Twitty	MGM	14	(1)	F
2	2	**Hoots Mon**	Lord Rockingham's XI	Decca	16		F
3	14	**Tom Dooley**	Lonnie Donegan	Pye Nixa	12		
4	1	**It's All In The Game**	Tommy Edwards	MGM	15	(1)	F L
5	9	**Tea For Two Cha Cha**	Tommy Dorsey Orchestra	Brunswick	16	(7)	F L
6	-	**Tom Dooley**	Kingston Trio	Capitol	12	(1)	F L
7	13	**Love Makes The World Go Round**	Perry Como	RCA	13	(33)	
8	-	**High Class Baby**	Cliff Richard	Columbia	9		
9	6	**More Than Ever (Come Prima)**	Malcolm Vaughan	HMV	13		
10	5	**A Certain Smile**	Johnny Mathis	Fontana	14	(21)	F
11	17	**Someday**	Ricky Nelson	London American	8		
12	20	**Come On Let's Go**	Tommy Steele	Decca	11		
13	4	**Come Prima**	Marino Marini	Durium	13		L
14	-	**The Day The Rains Came**	Jane Morgan	London American	13	(21)	F L
15	-	**Mary's Boy Child**	Harry Belafonte	RCA	5		G
16	3	**Bird Dog**	Everly Brothers	London American	16	(2)	
17	-	**Mandolins In The Moonlight**	Perry Como	RCA	8	(47)	
18	-	**More Party Pops**	Russ Conway	Columbia	3		F
19	-	**Real Love**	Ruby Murray	Columbia	3		
20	8	**Move It**	Cliff Richard	Columbia	11		F

October 1958

This Mnth	Prev Mnth	Title	Artist	Label	Wks 20	(UK Pos)	
1	6	It's All In The Game	Tommy Edwards	MGM	14	(1)	F G
2	5	Rock-In' Robin/Over And Over	Bobby Day	Class	13	(29)	F G L
3	2	Bird Dog	Everly Brothers	Cadence	13	(2)	G
4	8	Tears On My Pillow	Little Anthony & The Imperials	End	10		F G
5	12	Susie Darlin'	Robin Luke	Dot	9	(23)	F G L
6	-	Tea For Two Cha Cha	Tommy Dorsey Orchestra	Decca	10	(3)	G L
7	1	Nel Blu Dipinto Di Blu (Volare)	Domenico Modugno	Decca	13	(10)	F G L
8	3	Little Star	Elegants	Apt	14	(25)	F G L
9	-	Topsy Ii	Cozy Cole	Love	11	(29)	F G L
10	-	The End	Earl Grant	Decca	11		F L
11	-	It's Only Make Believe	Conway Twitty	MGM	13	(1)	F G
12	-	Chantilly Lace	Big Bopper	Mercury	10	(12)	F L
13	-	Tom Dooley	Kingston Trio	Capitol	15	(5)	F G
14	19	Near You	Roger Williams	Kapp	7		
15	15	Summertime Blues	Eddie Cochran	Liberty	7	(18)	F L
16	-	You Cheated	Shields	Dot	4		F L
17	4	Just A Dream	Jimmy Clanton	Ace	12		F G
18	-	How Time Flies	Jerry Wallace	Challenge	4		F
19	-	To Know Him, Is To Love Him	Teddy Bears	Dore	15	(2)	F G L
20	7	Born Too Late	Poni-Tails	ABC Paramount	10	(5)	F L

November 1958

This Mnth	Prev Mnth	Title	Artist	Label	Wks 20	(UK Pos)	
1	11	It's Only Make Believe	Conway Twitty	MGM	13	(1)	F G
2	13	Tom Dooley	Kingston Trio	Capitol	15	(5)	F G
3	1	It's All In The Game	Tommy Edwards	MGM	14	(1)	F G
4	9	Topsy Ii	Cozy Cole	Love	11	(29)	F G L
5	19	To Know Him, Is To Love Him	Teddy Bears	Dore	15	(2)	F G L
6	10	The End	Earl Grant	Decca	11		F L
7	6	Tea For Two Cha Cha	Tommy Dorsey Orchestra	Decca	10	(3)	G L
8	12	Chantilly Lace	Big Bopper	Mercury	10	(12)	F L
9	-	Lonesome Town	Ricky Nelson	Imperial	14		
10	-	I Got A Feeling	Ricky Nelson	Imperial	8	(27)	
11	2	Rock-In' Robin/Over And Over	Bobby Day	Class	13	(29)	F G L
12	-	Queen Of The Hop	Bobby Darin	Atco	10	(24)	G
13	-	Beep Beep	Playmates	Roulette	11		G
14	-	I Got Stung	Elvis Presley	RCA	10	(1)	G
15	-	One Night	Elvis Presley	RCA	11	(1)	
16	5	Susie Darlin'	Robin Luke	Dot	9	(23)	F G L
17	4	Tears On My Pillow	Little Anthony & The Imperials	End	10		F G
18	3	Bird Dog	Everly Brothers	Cadence	13	(2)	G
19	-	Forget Me Not	Kalin Twins	Decca	6		L
20	-	Mexican Hat Rock	Applejacks	Cameo	5		F L

December 1958

This Mnth	Prev Mnth	Title	Artist	Label	Wks 20	(UK Pos)	
1	5	To Know Him, Is To Love Him	Teddy Bears	Dore	15	(2)	F G L
2	2	Tom Dooley	Kingston Trio	Capitol	15	(5)	F G
3	15	One Night	Elvis Presley	RCA	11	(1)	
4	-	Problems	Everly Brothers	Cadence	9	(6)	G
5	13	Beep Beep	Playmates	Roulette	11		G
6	9	Lonesome Town	Ricky Nelson	Imperial	14		
7	-	Smoke Gets In Your Eyes	Platters	Mercury	13	(1)	G
8	1	It's Only Make Believe	Conway Twitty	MGM	13	(1)	F G
9	14	I Got Stung	Elvis Presley	RCA	10	(1)	G
10	-	The Chipmunk Song	Chipmunks	Liberty	7		F G
11	-	A Lover's Question	Clyde McPhatter	Atlantic	14		G
12	-	Whole Lotta Loving	Fats Domino	Imperial	9		G
13	4	Topsy Ii	Cozy Cole	Love	11	(29)	F G L
14	12	Queen Of The Hop	Bobby Darin	Atco	10	(24)	G
15	-	Bimbombey	Jimmie Rodgers	Roulette	7		L
16	10	I Got A Feeling	Ricky Nelson	Imperial	8	(27)	
17	3	It's All In The Game	Tommy Edwards	MGM	14	(1)	F G
18	-	Gotta Travel On	Billy Grammer	Monument	12		F G L
19	-	Love Is All We Need	Tommy Edwards	MGM	5		
20	-	My Happiness	Connie Francis	MGM	11	(4)	G

◆ Tommy Edwards' new "beat ballad" recording of his 1951 Top 20 hit, 'It's All In The Game', topped the transatlantic charts and started a rush of re-recordings.

◆ At times eight of the Top 10 acts were new to the chart. Among them was Conway Twitty, who amassed more country No. 1 hits than any other artist during his career, and the Teddy Bears, whose leader Phil Spector, became one of pop music's most successful producers and songwriters.

◆ The Kingston Trio's revival of the nine-teenth century song 'Tom Dooley' started the late 1950s folk revival. They were to have five chart topping albums in the next three years.

◆ Sales of records slipped by 15% as pur-chases of transistor radios and tape recorders increased.

UK 1959 JAN-MAR

◆ Among the acts charting with revivals of standard songs were US acts Little Richard, Paul Anka, the late Tommy Dorsey's Orchestra, Tommy Edwards, The Platters, Connie Francis and chart debutante Rosemary June.

◆ Lonnie Donegan, whose UK hit 'Does Your Chewing Gum Lose Its Flavour' reached the American Top 3 in 1961, signed a record £10,000 recording deal.

◆ For the first time three British records simultaneously made the US Top 20: 'Petite Fleur' by Chris Barber, 'The Children's Marching Song' by Cyril Stapleton and 'Manhattan Spiritual' by Reg Owen - all instrumentals.

◆ Both the Beverly Sisters and The Harry Simone Chorale clicked with the Christmas song 'The Little Drummer Boy'.

January 1959

This Mnth	Prev Mnth	Title	Artist	Label	Wks 20	(US Pos)	
1	1	It's Only Make Believe	Conway Twitty	MGM	14	(1)	F
2	14	The Day The Rains Came	Jane Morgan	London American	13	(21)	
3	2	Hoots Mon	Lord Rockingham's XI	Decca	16		F
4	5	Tea For Two Cha Cha	Tommy Dorsey Orchestra	Brunswick	16	(7)	F L
5	3	Tom Dooley	Lonnie Donegan	Pye Nixa	12		
6	-	Baby Face	Little Richard	London American	10	(41)	
7	-	To Know Him, Is To Love Him	Teddy Bears	London American	11	(1)	F L
8	6	Tom Dooley	Kingston Trio	Capitol	12	(1)	F L
9	-	Kiss Me Honey Honey Kiss Me	Shirley Bassey	Philips	13		
10	7	Love Makes The World Go Round	Perry Como	RCA	13	(33)	
11	12	Come On Let's Go	Tommy Steele	Decca	11		
12	8	High Class Baby	Cliff Richard	Columbia	9		
13	-	One Night/I Got Stung	Elvis Presley	RCA	10	(4)	
14	-	As I Love You	Shirley Bassey	Philips	16		
15	17	Mandolins In The Moonlight	Perry Como	RCA	8	(47)	
16	4	It's All In The Game	Tommy Edwards	MGM	15	(1)	F L
17	-	You Always Hurt The One You Love	Connie Francis	MGM	5		
18	-	Smoke Gets In Your Eyes	Platters	Mercury	19	(1)	
19	-	Chantilly Lace	Big Bopper	Mercury	4	(6)	F L
20	-	Problems	Everly Brothers	London American	9	(2)	

February 1959

1	14	As I Love You	Shirley Bassey	Philips	16		
2	13	One Night/I Got Stung	Elvis Presley	RCA	10	(4)	
3	9	Kiss Me Honey Honey Kiss Me	Shirley Bassey	Philips	13		
4	18	Smoke Gets In Your Eyes	Platters	Mercury	19	(1)	
5	7	To Know Him, Is To Love Him	Teddy Bears	London American	11	(1)	F L
6	-	Does Your Chewing Gum Lose It's Flavour	Lonnie Donegan	Pye Nixa	11	(5)	
7	6	Baby Face	Little Richard	London American	10	(41)	
8	20	Problems	Everly Brothers	London American	9	(2)	
9	2	The Day The Rains Came	Jane Morgan	London American	13	(21)	F L
10	-	(All Of A Sudden) My Heart Sings	Paul Anka	Columbia	12	(15)	
11	-	A Pub With No Beer	Slim Dusty	Columbia	13		F L
12	-	Petite Fleur	Chris Barber's Jazz Band	Pye Nixa	18	(5)	F L
13	-	The Little Drummer Boy	Beverley Sisters	Decca	11		
14	-	High School Confidential	Jerry Lee Lewis	London American	4	(22)	
15	1	It's Only Make Believe	Conway Twitty	MGM	14	(1)	F
16	4	Tea For Two Cha Cha	Tommy Dorsey Orchestra	Brunswick	16	(7)	F L
17	-	My Happiness	Connie Francis	MGM	13	(2)	
18	-	Little Drummer Boy	Harry Simeone Chorale	Top Rank	4	(13)	F L
19	-	Apple Blossom Time	Rosemary June	Pye-Int	3		F L
20	-	Gigi	Billy Eckstine	Mercury	12		

March 1959

1	4	Smoke Gets In Your Eyes	Platters	Mercury	19	(1)	
2	1	As I Love You	Shirley Bassey	Philips	16		
3	-	Side Saddle	Russ Conway	Columbia	25		
4	11	A Pub With No Beer	Slim Dusty	Columbia	13		F L
5	12	Petite Fleur	Chris Barber's Jazz Band	Pye Nixa	18	(5)	F L
6	17	My Happiness	Connie Francis	MGM	13	(2)	
7	13	The Little Drummer Boy	Beverley Sisters	Decca	11		
8	6	Does Your Chewing Gum Lose It's Flavour	Lonnie Donegan	Pye Nixa	11	(5)	
9	-	Stagger Lee	Lloyd Price	HMV	11	(1)	F
10	10	(All Of A Sudden) My Heart Sings	Paul Anka	Columbia	12	(15)	
11	-	It Doesn't Matter Anymore	Buddy Holly	Coral	21	(13)	
12	2	One Night/I Got Stung	Elvis Presley	RCA	10	(4)	
13	20	Gigi	Billy Eckstine	Mercury	12		
14	3	Kiss Me Honey Honey Kiss Me	Shirley Bassey	Philips	13		
15	-	Tomboy	Perry Como	RCA	10	(29)	
16	8	Problems	Everly Brothers	London American	9	(2)	
17	-	C'mon Everybody	Eddie Cochran	London American	10	(35)	
18	5	To Know Him, Is To Love Him	Teddy Bears	London American	11	(1)	F L
19	-	Wonderful Secret Of Love	Robert Earl	Philips	4		L
20	18	Little Drummer Boy	Harry Simeone Chorale	Top Rank	4	(13)	F L

January 1959

This Mnth	Prev Mnth	Title	Artist	Label	Wks 20	(UK Pos)	
1	7	Smoke Gets In Your Eyes	Platters	Mercury	13	(1)	G
2	20	My Happiness	Connie Francis	MGM	11	(4)	G
3	10	The Chipmunk Song	Chipmunks	Liberty	7		F G
4	18	Gotta Travel On	Billy Grammer	Monument	12		F G L
5	11	A Lover's Question	Clyde McPhatter	Atlantic	14		G
6	1	To Know Him, Is To Love Him	Teddy Bears	Dore	15	(2)	F G L
7	12	Whole Lotta Loving	Fats Domino	Imperial	9		G
8	-	Donna	Ritchie Valens	Del-Fi	14	(29)	F G L
9	-	16 Candles	Crests	Coed	11		F G
10	3	One Night	Elvis Presley	RCA	11	(1)	
11	4	Problems	Everly Brothers	Cadence	9	(6)	G
12	-	Lonely Teardrops	Jackie Wilson	Brunswick	11		F G
13	6	Lonesome Town	Ricky Nelson	Imperial	14		
14	-	Stagger Lee	Lloyd Price	ABC Paramount	12	(7)	F G
15	2	Tom Dooley	Kingston Trio	Capitol	15	(5)	F G
16	-	Goodbye Baby	Jack Scott	Carlton	7		
17	15	Bimbombey	Jimmie Rodgers	Roulette	7		L
18	5	Beep Beep	Playmates	Roulette	11		G
19	-	Manhattan Spiritual	Reg Owen	Palette	7	(20)	F L
20	-	All American Boy	Bill Parsons	Fraternity	9	(22)	F L

February 1959

This Mnth	Prev Mnth	Title	Artist	Label	Wks 20	(UK Pos)	
1	14	Stagger Lee	Lloyd Price	ABC Paramount	12	(7)	F G
2	8	Donna	Ritchie Valens	Del-Fi	14	(29)	F G L
3	9	16 Candles	Crests	Coed	11		F G
4	20	All American Boy	Bill Parsons	Fraternity	9	(22)	F L
5	1	Smoke Gets In Your Eyes	Platters	Mercury	13	(1)	G
6	2	My Happiness	Connie Francis	MGM	11	(4)	G
7	12	Lonely Teardrops	Jackie Wilson	Brunswick	11		F G
8	4	Gotta Travel On	Billy Grammer	Monument	12		F G L
9	16	Goodbye Baby	Jack Scott	Carlton	7		
10	19	Manhattan Spiritual	Reg Owen	Palette	7	(20)	F L
11	-	Tall Paul	Annette	Disneyland	8		F
12	-	I Cried A Tear	Lavern Baker	Atlantic	9		G L
13	-	Hawaiian Wedding Song	Andy Williams	Cadence	10		
14	5	A Lover's Question	Clyde McPhatter	Atlantic	14		G
15	-	Peter Gunn	Ray Anthony	Capitol	9		L
16	-	Petite Fleur (Little Flower)	Chris Barber Jazz Band	Laurie	6	(3)	F G L
17	-	Charlie Brown	Coasters	Atco	10	(6)	G
18	-	The Children's Marching Song (Nick Nack Paddy Wack)	Cyril Stapleton	London	4		F L
19	-	(All Of A Sudden) My Heart Sings	Paul Anka	ABC Paramount	5	(10)	
20	-	The Children's Marching Song	Mitch Miller	Columbia	5		L

March 1959

This Mnth	Prev Mnth	Title	Artist	Label	Wks 20	(UK Pos)	
1	-	Venus	Frankie Avalon	Chancellor	11	(16)	G
2	17	Charlie Brown	Coasters	Atco	10	(6)	G
3	-	Alvin's Harmonica	Chipmunks	Liberty	7		G
4	1	Stagger Lee	Lloyd Price	ABC Paramount	12	(7)	F G
5	-	It's Just A Matter Of Time	Brook Benton	Mercury	9		F G
6	2	Donna	Ritchie Valens	Del-Fi	14	(29)	F G L
7	-	I've Had It	Bell Notes	Time	8		F L
8	-	Tragedy	Thomas Wayne	Fernwood	8		F L
9	16	Petite Fleur (Little Flower)	Chris Barber Jazz Band	Laurie	6	(3)	F G L
10	12	I Cried A Tear	Lavern Baker	Atlantic	9		G L
11	15	Peter Gunn	Ray Anthony	Capitol	9		L
12	-	Never Be Anyone Else But You	Ricky Nelson	Imperial	9	(14)	
13	-	Come Softly To Me	Fleetwoods	Dolphin	10	(6)	F G
14	13	Hawaiian Wedding Song	Andy Williams	Cadence	10		
15	3	16 Candles	Crests	Coed	11		F G
16	11	Tall Paul	Annette	Disneyland	8		F
17	-	Pink Shoe Laces	Dodie Stevens	Crystalette	12		F G L
18	4	All American Boy	Bill Parsons	Fraternity	9	(22)	F L
19	-	It's Late	Ricky Nelson	Imperial	6	(3)	G
20	-	Please Mr. Sun	Tommy Edwards	MGM	3		

▲ Berry Gordy, composer of several of Jackie Wilson's (above) hits including his current R&B No. 1, 'Lonely Teardrops', launched his own label Tamla with 'Come To Me' by Marv Johnson.

◆ The plane crash that killed Buddy Holly, Ritchie Valens and The Big Bopper merited front page stories in Britain, but received less coverage Stateside. Interestingly, of the three stars, only Holly did not have one of his songs in the British Top 20 on the day he (and the music?) died.

◆ Mercury Records, who helped pioneer the 45rpm single, claimed to have released the first stereo singles and EPs.

UK 1959 APR–JUNE

▲ American rockers faring better in Britain included Little Richard, Eddie Cochran (above, whose 'C'mon Everybody' revisited the UK Top 20 in 1988) and the late Buddy Holly, whose 'It Doesn't Matter Anymore' topped the chart.

◆ The year's most successful singles artist in the UK was not a rock performer but easy-on-the-ear honky tonk pianist Russ Conway, whose self composed singles 'Side Saddle' and 'Roulette' both headed the chart.

April 1959

This Mnth	Prev Mnth	Title	Artist	Label	Wks 20	(US Pos)	
1	3	Side Saddle	Russ Conway	Columbia	25		
2	11	It Doesn't Matter Anymore	Buddy Holly	Coral	21	(13)	
3	1	Smoke Gets In Your Eyes	Platters	Mercury	19	(1)	
4	5	Petite Fleur	Chris Barber's Jazz Band	Pye Nixa	18	(5)	F L
5	6	My Happiness	Connie Francis	MGM	13	(2)	
6	9	Stagger Lee	Lloyd Price	HMV	11	(1)	F
7	-	Donna	Marty Wilde	Philips	11		
8	2	As I Love You	Shirley Bassey	Philips	16		
9	13	Gigi	Billy Eckstine	Mercury	12		
10	-	Charlie Brown	Coasters	London American	11	(2)	
11	4	A Pub With No Beer	Slim Dusty	Columbia	13		F L
12	17	C'mon Everybody	Eddie Cochran	London American	10	(35)	
13	15	Tomboy	Perry Como	RCA	10	(29)	
14	7	The Little Drummer Boy	Beverley Sisters	Decca	11		
15	-	Wait For Me	Malcolm Vaughan	HMV	8		L
16	-	Sing Little Birdie	Pearl Carr & Teddy Johnson	Columbia	5		F
17	-	A Fool Such As I/ I Need Your Love Tonight	Elvis Presley	RCA	14	(2)	
18	8	Does Your Chewing Gum Lose It's Flavour	Lonnie Donegan	Pye Nixa	11	(5)	
19	-	By The Light Of The Silvery Moon	Little Richard	London American	3		
20	10	(All Of A Sudden) My Heart Sings	Paul Anka	Columbia	12	(15)	

May 1959

This Mnth	Prev Mnth	Title	Artist	Label	Wks 20	(US Pos)	
1	17	A Fool Such As I/ I Need Your Love Tonight	Elvis Presley	RCA	14	(2)	
2	2	It Doesn't Matter Anymore	Buddy Holly	Coral	21	(13)	
3	1	Side Saddle	Russ Conway	Columbia	25		
4	7	Donna	Marty Wilde	Philips	11		
5	-	It's Late	Ricky Nelson	London American	18	(9)	
6	4	Petite Fleur	Chris Barber's Jazz Band	Pye Nixa	18	(5)	F L
7	-	I've Waited So Long	Anthony Newley	Decca	13		
8	-	Come Softly To Me	Fleetwoods	London American	8	(1)	F L
9	10	Charlie Brown	Coasters	London American	11	(2)	
10	-	Come Softly To Me	Frankie Vaughan/Kaye Sisters	Philips	8		
11	-	I Go Ape	Neil Sedaka	RCA	10	(42)	F
12	-	Mean Streak	Cliff Richard	Columbia	8		
13	3	Smoke Gets In Your Eyes	Platters	Mercury	19	(1)	
14	12	C'mon Everybody	Eddie Cochran	London American	10	(35)	
15	-	Fort Worth Jail	Lonnie Donegan	Pye Nixa	4		
16	-	Roulette	Russ Conway	Columbia	18		
17	-	Guitar Boogie Shuffle	Bert Weedon	Top Rank	8		F L
18	-	May You Always	McGuire Sisters	Coral	5	(11)	L
19	-	Idle On Parade (EP)	Anthony Newley	Decca	2		F
20	6	Stagger Lee	Lloyd Price	HMV	11	(1)	F

June 1959

This Mnth	Prev Mnth	Title	Artist	Label	Wks 20	(US Pos)	
1	1	A Fool Such As I/ I Need Your Love Tonight	Elvis Presley	RCA	14	(2)	
2	16	Roulette	Russ Conway	Columbia	18		
3	2	It Doesn't Matter Anymore	Buddy Holly	Coral	21	(13)	
4	7	I've Waited So Long	Anthony Newley	Decca	13		
5	5	It's Late	Ricky Nelson	London American	18	(9)	
6	-	Dream Lover	Bobby Darin	London American	17	(2)	
7	3	Side Saddle	Russ Conway	Columbia	25		
8	-	A Teenager In Love	Marty Wilde	Philips	13		
9	17	Guitar Boogie Shuffle	Bert Weedon	Top Rank	8		F L
10	12	Mean Streak	Cliff Richard	Columbia	8		
11	11	I Go Ape	Neil Sedaka	RCA	10	(42)	F
12	-	May You Always	Joan Regan	HMV	10		L
13	6	Petite Fleur	Chris Barber's Jazz Band	Pye Nixa	18	(5)	F L
14	4	Donna	Marty Wilde	Philips	11		
15	10	Come Softly To Me	Frankie Vaughan/Kaye Sisters	Philips	8		
16	-	Peter Gunn Theme	Duane Eddy	London American	10	(27)	
17	8	Come Softly To Me	Fleetwoods	London American	8	(1)	F L
18	-	Battle Of New Orleans	Lonnie Donegan	Pye	14		
19	9	Charlie Brown	Coasters	London American	11	(2)	
20	-	A Teenager In Love	Craig Douglas	Top Rank	8		F

April 1959

This Mnth	Prev Mnth	Title	Artist	Label	Wks 20	(UK Pos)	
1	13	Come Softly To Me	Fleetwoods	Dolphin	10	(6)	F G
2	1	Venus	Frankie Avalon	Chancellor	11	(16)	G
3	17	Pink Shoe Laces	Dodie Stevens	Crystalette	12		F G L
4	-	A Fool Such As I	Elvis Presley	RCA	9	(1)	G
5	12	Never Be Anyone Else But You	Ricky Nelson	Imperial	9	(14)	
6	-	Guitar Boogie Shuffle	Virtues	Hunt	9		F L
7	-	I Need Your Love Tonight	Elvis Presley	RCA	8	(1)	
8	5	It's Just A Matter Of Time	Brook Benton	Mercury	9		F G
9	8	Tragedy	Thomas Wayne	Fernwood	8		F L
10	19	It's Late	Ricky Nelson	Imperial	6	(3)	G
11	2	Charlie Brown	Coasters	Atco	10	(6)	G
12	-	The Happy Organ	Dave 'Baby' Cortez	Clock	10		F G
13	-	Since I Don't Have You	Skyliners	Calico	6		F L
14	-	Tell Him No	Travis & Bob	Sandy	6		F L
15	-	Tijuana Jail	Kingston Trio	Capitol	5		
16	-	Sea Cruise	Frankie Ford	Ace	5		F L
17	-	Turn Me Loose	Fabian	Chancellor	8		F
18	3	Alvin's Harmonica	Chipmunks	Liberty	7		G
19	-	Sorry (I Ran All The Way Home)	Impalas	Cub	9	(28)	F G L
20	7	I've Had It	Bell Notes	Time	8		F L

May 1959

This Mnth	Prev Mnth	Title	Artist	Label	Wks 20	(UK Pos)	
1	19	Sorry (I Ran All The Way Home)	Impalas	Cub	9	(28)	F G L
2	12	The Happy Organ	Dave 'Baby' Cortez	Clock	10		F G
3	-	Kansas City	Wilbert Harrison	Fury	10		F G L
4	-	Kookie, Kookie (Lend Me Your Comb)	Edward Byrnes & Connie Stevens	Warner	8	(27)	F G L
5	4	A Fool Such As I	Elvis Presley	RCA	9	(1)	G
6	3	Pink Shoe Laces	Dodie Stevens	Crystalette	12		F G L
7	6	Guitar Boogie Shuffle	Virtues	Hunt	9		F L
8	1	Come Softly To Me	Fleetwoods	Dolphin	10	(6)	F G
9	17	Turn Me Loose	Fabian	Chancellor	8		F
10	-	A Teenager In Love	Dion & The Belmonts	Laurie	10	(28)	F G L
11	-	Dream Lover	Bobby Darin	Atco	11	(1)	G
12	-	The Battle Of New Orleans	Johnny Horton	Columbia	14	(16)	F G
13	7	I Need Your Love Tonight	Elvis Presley	RCA	8	(1)	
14	-	Quiet Village	Martin Denny	Liberty	9		F G L
15	-	Enchanted	Platters	Mercury	7		
16	14	Tell Him No	Travis & Bob	Sandy	6		F L
17	2	Venus	Frankie Avalon	Chancellor	11	(16)	G
18	-	Only You	Frank Pourcel's French Fiddles	Capitol	7		F L
19	-	Three Stars	Tommy Dee	Crest	4		F L
20	-	Take A Message To Mary	Everly Brothers	Cadence	5	(20)	

June 1959

This Mnth	Prev Mnth	Title	Artist	Label	Wks 20	(UK Pos)	
1	12	The Battle Of New Orleans	Johnny Horton	Columbia	14	(16)	F G
2	-	Personality	Lloyd Price	ABC Paramount	11	(9)	G
3	11	Dream Lover	Bobby Darin	Atco	11	(1)	G
4	3	Kansas City	Wilbert Harrison	Fury	10		F G L
5	14	Quiet Village	Martin Denny	Liberty	9		F G L
6	10	A Teenager In Love	Dion & The Belmonts	Laurie	10	(28)	F G L
7	-	Tallahassee Lassie	Freddy Cannon	Swan	8	(17)	F G
8	-	Lonely Boy	Paul Anka	ABC Paramount	12	(3)	G
9	4	Kookie, Kookie (Lend Me Your Comb)	Edward Byrnes & Connie Stevens	Warner	8	(27)	F G L
10	18	Only You	Frank Pourcel's French Fiddles	Capitol	7		F L
11	-	Along Came Jones	Coasters	Atco	6		
12	-	Lipstick On Your Collar	Connie Francis	MGM	10	(3)	G
13	-	So Fine	Fiestas	Old Town	5		F L
14	2	The Happy Organ	Dave 'Baby' Cortez	Clock	10		F G
15	-	Frankie	Connie Francis	MGM	7		
16	1	Sorry (I Ran All The Way Home)	Impalas	Cub	9	(28)	F G L
17	-	Endlessly	Brook Benton	Mercury	5	(28)	
18	-	Goodbye Jimmy, Goodbye	Kathy Linden	Felsted	4		L
19	-	Bobby Sox To Stockings	Frankie Avalon	Chancellor	7		
20	-	I'm Ready	Fats Domino	Liberty	4		

◆ Stars who appeared in Alan Freed's final film, *Go, Johnny, Go*, included Chuck Berry, the late Ritchie Valens, Jackie Wilson and Jimmy Clanton.

◆ Dodie Stevens, who started recording when she was eight, turned 'Pink Shoe Laces' into gold, while fellow 13-year-old Dolly Parton's debut disc, 'Puppy Love' went unnoticed.

◆ As Chubby Checker's first single, 'The Class' charted, Hank Ballard's original recording of 'The Twist' hit the R&B Top 20. A year later Checker closely cloned Ballard's record and made musical history.

◆ A diverse group of instrumentalists found themselves with pop hits: Frank Pourcel's French string orchestra, R&B organist Dave 'Baby' Cortez, guitar driven rock group The Virtues and Martin Denny's exotic Hawaiian combo.

UK 1959
JULY-SEPT

◆ As Cliff Richard scored his first No. 1 with 'Living Doll', Duane Eddy hit with his version of 'Peter Gunn Theme' – in 1986 both artists returned to the Top 10 with re-recordings of these compositions.

◆ Mantovani, who had five albums on the US Top 30 stereo album chart, became the first British-based act to top the American LP chart when **Film Encores** moved into the top slot.

◆ The 1950s was truly the decade of the cover version and some of the art's most successful exponents - Marty Wilde, Frankie Vaughan, Craig Douglas and Tommy Steele - continued to add to their UK hits with their versions of songs from the American charts.

◆ To avoid confusion with US hit makers The Drifters, Cliff Richard's group changed their name to The Shadows.

July 1959

This Mnth	Prev Mnth	Title	Artist	Label	Wks 20	(US Pos)	
1	6	Dream Lover	Bobby Darin	London American	17	(2)	
2	18	Battle Of New Orleans	Lonnie Donegan	Pye	14		
3	8	A Teenager In Love	Marty Wilde	Philips	13		
4	2	Roulette	Russ Conway	Columbia	18		
5	16	Peter Gunn Theme	Duane Eddy	London American	10	(27)	
6	-	Personality	Anthony Newley	Decca	9		
7	-	Living Doll	Cliff Richard	Columbia	19	(30)	
8	1	A Fool Such As I/ I Need Your Love Tonight	Elvis Presley	RCA	14	(2)	
9	-	Goodbye Jimmy, Goodbye	Ruby Murray	Columbia	11		L
10	5	It's Late	Ricky Nelson	London American	18	(9)	
11	-	Lipstick On Your Collar	Connie Francis	MGM	15	(5)	
12	4	I've Waited So Long	Anthony Newley	Decca	13		
13	7	Side Saddle	Russ Conway	Columbia	25		
14	-	Personality	Lloyd Price	HMV	7	(2)	L
15	12	May You Always	Joan Regan	HMV	10		L
16	-	Big Hunk O' Love	Elvis Presley	RCA	8	(1)	
17	3	It Doesn't Matter Anymore	Buddy Holly	Coral	21	(13)	
18	20	A Teenager In Love	Craig Douglas	Top Rank	8		F
19	-	Poor Jenny	Everly Brothers	London American	7	(22)	
20	-	I Know	Perry Como	RCA	12	(47)	

August 1959

This Mnth	Prev Mnth	Title	Artist	Label	Wks 20	(US Pos)	
1	7	Living Doll	Cliff Richard	Columbia	19	(30)	
2	1	Dream Lover	Bobby Darin	London American	17	(2)	
3	2	Battle Of New Orleans	Lonnie Donegan	Pye	14		
4	11	Lipstick On Your Collar	Connie Francis	MGM	15	(5)	
5	-	Lonely Boy	Paul Anka	Columbia	13	(1)	
6	16	Big Hunk O' Love	Elvis Presley	RCA	8	(1)	
7	3	A Teenager In Love	Marty Wilde	Philips	13		
8	4	Roulette	Russ Conway	Columbia	18		
9	-	The Heart Of A Man	Frankie Vaughan	Philips	12		
10	-	Only Sixteen	Craig Douglas	Top Rank	14		
11	-	Someone	Johnny Mathis	Fontana	13	(35)	
12	6	Personality	Anthony Newley	Decca	9		
13	-	Ragtime Cowboy Joe	Chipmunks	London American	5	(16)	L
14	20	I Know	Perry Como	RCA	12	(47)	
15	5	Peter Gunn Theme	Duane Eddy	London American	10	(27)	
16	10	It's Late	Ricky Nelson	London American	18	(9)	
17	9	Goodbye Jimmy, Goodbye	Ruby Murray	Columbia	11		L
18	-	China Tea	Russ Conway	Columbia	10		
19	-	Tallahassee Lassie	Tommy Steele	Decca	3		
20	-	Mona Lisa	Conway Twitty	MGM	12	(29)	L

September 1959

This Mnth	Prev Mnth	Title	Artist	Label	Wks 20	(US Pos)	
1	10	Only Sixteen	Craig Douglas	Top Rank	14		
2	1	Living Doll	Cliff Richard	Columbia	19	(30)	
3	5	Lonely Boy	Paul Anka	Columbia	13	(1)	
4	-	Here Comes Summer	Jerry Keller	London American	12	(14)	F L
5	18	China Tea	Russ Conway	Columbia	10		
6	4	Lipstick On Your Collar	Connie Francis	MGM	15	(5)	
7	11	Someone	Johnny Mathis	Fontana	13	(35)	
8	20	Mona Lisa	Conway Twitty	MGM	12	(29)	L
9	9	The Heart Of A Man	Frankie Vaughan	Philips	12		
10	3	Battle Of New Orleans	Lonnie Donegan	Pye	14		
11	2	Dream Lover	Bobby Darin	London American	17	(2)	
12	-	40 Miles Of Bad Road	Duane Eddy	London American	9	(9)	
13	-	('Til) I Kissed You	Everly Brothers	London American	14	(4)	
14	-	Just A Little Too Much	Ricky Nelson	London American	8	(9)	
15	-	Sal's Got A Sugar Lip	Lonnie Donegan	Pye	3		
16	14	I Know	Perry Como	RCA	12	(47)	
17	6	Big Hunk O' Love	Elvis Presley	RCA	8	(1)	
18	-	The Three Bells	Browns	RCA	11	(1)	F L
19	-	High Hopes	Frank Sinatra	Capitol	12	(30)	
20	8	Roulette	Russ Conway	Columbia	18		

July 1959

This Mnth	Prev Mnth	Title	Artist	Label	Wks 20	(UK Pos)	
1	8	Lonely Boy	Paul Anka	ABC Paramount	12	(3)	G
2	1	The Battle Of New Orleans	Johnny Horton	Columbia	14	(16)	F G
3	-	Waterloo	Stonewall Jackson	Columbia	9		F G L
4	2	Personality	Lloyd Price	ABC Paramount	11	(9)	G
5	-	Tiger	Fabian	Chancellor	8		G
6	12	Lipstick On Your Collar	Connie Francis	MGM	10	(3)	G
7	-	My Heart Is An Open Book	Carl Dobkins Jr.	Decca	11		F G L
8	3	Dream Lover	Bobby Darin	Atco	11	(1)	G
9	7	Tallahassee Lassie	Freddy Cannon	Swan	8	(17)	F G
10	19	Bobby Sox To Stockings	Frankie Avalon	Chancellor	7		
11	-	A Boy Without A Girl	Frankie Avalon	Chancellor	5		
12	-	I Only Have Eyes For You	Flamingos	End	7		F L
13	-	Forty Miles Of Bad Road	Duane Eddy	Jamie	7	(11)	
14	-	Big Hunk O' Love	Elvis Presley	RCA	9	(4)	G
15	15	Frankie	Connie Francis	MGM	7		
16	-	There Goes My Baby	Drifters	Atlantic	10		F G
17	11	Along Came Jones	Coasters	Atco	6		
18	-	M.T.A.	Kingston Trio	Capitol	4		
19	-	Just A Little Too Much	Ricky Nelson	Imperial	4	(11)	
20	-	Lavender-Blue	Sammy Turner	Big Top	8		F

August 1959

This Mnth	Prev Mnth	Title	Artist	Label	Wks 20	(UK Pos)	
1	14	Big Hunk O' Love	Elvis Presley	RCA	9	(4)	G
2	20	Lavender-Blue	Sammy Turner	Big Top	8		F
3	7	My Heart Is An Open Book	Carl Dobkins Jr.	Decca	11		F G L
4	16	There Goes My Baby	Drifters	Atlantic	10		F G
5	1	Lonely Boy	Paul Anka	ABC Paramount	12	(3)	G
6	-	What'd I Say (Pt. 1)	Ray Charles	Atlantic	7		F G
7	-	The Three Bells	Browns	RCA	12	(6)	F G
8	-	What A Difference A Day Makes	Dinah Washington	Mercury	8		F
9	-	Sea Of Love	Phil Phillips With The Twilights	Mercury	9		F G L
10	5	Tiger	Fabian	Chancellor	8		G
11	2	The Battle Of New Orleans	Johnny Horton	Columbia	14	(16)	F G
12	13	Forty Miles Of Bad Road	Duane Eddy	Jamie	7	(11)	
13	-	Sleep Walk	Santo & Johnny	Canadian American	11	(22)	F G L
14	3	Waterloo	Stonewall Jackson	Columbia	9		F G L
15	19	Just A Little Too Much	Ricky Nelson	Imperial	4	(11)	
16	-	It Was I	Skip & Flip	Brent	6		F
17	-	My Wish Came True	Elvis Presley	RCA	4		
18	-	I'm Gonna Get Married	Lloyd Price	ABC Paramount	10	(23)	G
19	-	Sweeter Than You	Ricky Nelson	Imperial	5	(19)	
20	-	I Want To Walk You Home	Fats Domino	Imperial	7	(14)	

September 1959

This Mnth	Prev Mnth	Title	Artist	Label	Wks 20	(UK Pos)	
1	13	Sleep Walk	Santo & Johnny	Canadian American	11	(22)	F G L
2	7	The Three Bells	Browns	RCA	12	(6)	F G
3	18	I'm Gonna Get Married	Lloyd Price	ABC Paramount	10	(23)	G
4	9	Sea Of Love	Phil Phillips With The Twilights	Mercury	9		F G L
5	-	('Til) I Kissed You	Everly Brothers	Cadence	11	(2)	
6	-	Red River Rock	Johnny & The Hurricanes	Warwick	10	(3)	F
7	-	Broken-Hearted Melody	Sarah Vaughan	Mercury	8	(7)	G L
8	-	Mack The Knife	Bobby Darin	Atco	19	(1)	G
9	20	I Want To Walk You Home	Fats Domino	Imperial	7	(14)	
10	-	Baby Talk	Jan & Dean	Dore	6		
11	-	Kissin' Time	Bobby Rydell	Cameo	5		F
12	-	Put Your Head On My Shoulder	Paul Anka	ABC Paramount	12	(7)	
13	-	Poison Ivy	Coasters	Atco	9	(15)	G L
14	2	Lavender-Blue	Sammy Turner	Big Top	8		F
15	6	What'd I Say (Pt. 1)	Ray Charles	Atlantic	7		F G
16	-	Teen Beat	Sandy Nelson	Original Sound	10	(9)	F G
17	4	There Goes My Baby	Drifters	Atlantic	10		F G
18	-	Just Ask Your Heart	Frankie Avalon	Chancellor	8		
19	-	Mr. Blue	Fleetwoods	Dolton	14		G
20	-	Morgen	Ivo Robic	Laurie	6	(23)	F L

US 1959
JULY-SEPT

◆ *Billboard* slated fears that rock'n'roll was ready for the rockin' chair', pointing out that 50% of hits were still rock-related.

▲ Soulful, gospel-influenced R&B was taking off. Examples included 'What'd I Say' by Ray Charles (above), 'There Goes My Baby' by The Drifters and 'Shout' by the Isley Brothers – all musical milestones.

◆ Country performers Stonewall Jackson, Johnny Horton and The Browns notched up million selling pop hits in the USA. The latter two also scored in Britain, where Horton's anti-British Revolutionary War saga, 'The Battle Of New Orleans' was covered by Lonnie Donegan.

UK 1959 OCT-DEC

◆ Emile Ford became the first British-based black male performer to top the charts. His Johnny Otis-styled revival of 'What Do You Want To Make Those Eyes At Me For' sold over a million in the UK alone.

◆ Among the many other new groups in Britain were Johnny & The Moondogs (members included three Beatles) who reached the final in a TV *Star Search*.

▲ Transatlantic star Guy Mitchell, who had made his chart debut in 1950, ended the decade with the No. 1 single in America, 'Heartaches By The Number'.

October 1959

This Mnth	Prev Mnth	Title	Artist	Label	Wks 20	(US Pos)	
1	-	Mack The Knife	Bobby Darin	London American	14	(1)	
2	4	Here Comes Summer	Jerry Keller	London American	12	(14)	F L
3	13	('Til) I Kissed You	Everly Brothers	London American	14	(4)	
4	1	Only Sixteen	Craig Douglas	Top Rank	14		
5	2	Living Doll	Cliff Richard	Columbia	19	(30)	
6	18	The Three Bells	Browns	RCA	11	(1)	F L
7	-	Sea Of Love	Marty Wilde	Philips	11		
8	-	Travellin' Light	Cliff Richard	Columbia	16		
9	19	High Hopes	Frank Sinatra	Capitol	12	(30)	
10	-	Broken Hearted Melody	Sarah Vaughan	Mercury	12	(7)	F
11	8	Mona Lisa	Conway Twitty	MGM	12	(29)	L
12	7	Someone	Johnny Mathis	Fontana	13	(35)	
13	3	Lonely Boy	Paul Anka	Columbia	13	(1)	
14	5	China Tea	Russ Conway	Columbia	10		
15	14	Just A Little Too Much	Ricky Nelson	London American	8	(9)	
16	-	Red River Rock	Johnny & The Hurricanes	London American	13	(5)	F
17	12	40 Miles Of Bad Road	Duane Eddy	London American	9	(9)	
18	-	Peggy Sue Got Married	Buddy Holly	Coral	5		
19	-	Makin' Love	Floyd Robinson	RCA	7	(20)	F L
20	9	The Heart Of A Man	Frankie Vaughan	Philips	12		

November 1959

This Mnth	Prev Mnth	Title	Artist	Label	Wks 20	(US Pos)	
1	8	Travellin' Light	Cliff Richard	Columbia	16		
2	1	Mack The Knife	Bobby Darin	London American	14	(1)	
3	16	Red River Rock	Johnny & The Hurricanes	London American	13	(5)	F
4	-	What Do You Want To Make Those Eyes At Me For	Emile Ford & The Checkmates	Pye	18		F
5	3	('Til) I Kissed You	Everly Brothers	London American	14	(4)	
6	7	Sea Of Love	Marty Wilde	Philips	11		
7	-	Put Your Head On My Shoulder	Paul Anka	Columbia	10	(2)	
8	10	Broken Hearted Melody	Sarah Vaughan	Mercury	12	(7)	F
9	9	High Hopes	Frank Sinatra	Capitol	12	(30)	
10	6	The Three Bells	Browns	RCA	11	(1)	F L
11	19	Makin' Love	Floyd Robinson	RCA	7	(20)	F L
12	-	Oh! Carol	Neil Sedaka	RCA	14	(9)	
13	-	One More Sunrise (Morgen)	Dickie Valentine	Pye	7		L
14	-	Teen Beat	Sandy Nelson	Top Rank	8	(4)	F
15	-	What Do You Want	Adam Faith	Parlophone	15		F
16	2	Here Comes Summer	Jerry Keller	London American	12	(14)	F L
17	-	Mr. Blue	Mike Preston	Decca	5		F
18	-	Snow Coach	Russ Conway	Columbia	8		
19	11	Mona Lisa	Conway Twitty	MGM	12	(29)	L
20	4	Only Sixteen	Craig Douglas	Top Rank	14		

December 1959

This Mnth	Prev Mnth	Title	Artist	Label	Wks 20	(US Pos)	
1	15	What Do You Want	Adam Faith	Parlophone	15		F
2	4	What Do You Want To Make Those Eyes At Me For	Emile Ford & The Checkmates	Pye	18		F
3	12	Oh! Carol	Neil Sedaka	RCA	14	(9)	
4	1	Travellin' Light	Cliff Richard	Columbia	16		
5	-	Seven Little Girls Sitting In The Back Seat	Avons	Columbia	10		F L
6	3	Red River Rock	Johnny & The Hurricanes	London American	13	(5)	F
7	7	Put Your Head On My Shoulder	Paul Anka	Columbia	10	(2)	
8	18	Snow Coach	Russ Conway	Columbia	8		
9	-	Rawhide	Frankie Laine	Philips	13		L
10	-	More And More Party Pops	Russ Conway	Columbia	5		
11	2	Mack The Knife	Bobby Darin	London American	14	(1)	
12	-	Little White Bull	Tommy Steele	Decca	12		
13	-	Piano Party	Winifred Atwell	Decca	5		L
14	14	Teen Beat	Sandy Nelson	Top Rank	8	(4)	F
15	-	Among My Souvenirs	Connie Francis	MGM	6	(7)	
16	-	Staccato's Theme	Elmer Bernstein	Capitol	10		F L
17	-	Jingle Bell Rock	Max Bygraves	Decca	3		
18	5	('Til) I Kissed You	Everly Brothers	London American	14	(4)	
19	-	Little Donkey	Beverley Sisters	Decca	4		L
20	6	Sea Of Love	Marty Wilde	Philips	11		

October 1959

This Mnth	Prev Mnth	Title	Artist	Label	Wks 20	(UK Pos)	
1	8	Mack The Knife	Bobby Darin	Atco	19	(1)	G
2	12	Put Your Head On My Shoulder	Paul Anka	ABC Paramount	12	(7)	
3	19	Mr. Blue	Fleetwoods	Dolton	14		G
4	16	Teen Beat	Sandy Nelson	Original Sound	10	(9)	F G
5	1	Sleep Walk	Santo & Johnny	Canadian American	11	(22)	F G L
6	5	('Til) I Kissed You	Everly Brothers	Cadence	11	(2)	
7	13	Poison Ivy	Coasters	Atco	9	(15)	G L
8	-	Lonely Street	Andy Williams	Cadence	10		
9	18	Just Ask Your Heart	Frankie Avalon	Chancellor	8		
10	2	The Three Bells	Browns	RCA	12	(6)	F G
11	-	Primrose Lane	Jerry Wallace	Challenge	11		G
12	6	Red River Rock	Johnny & The Hurricanes	Warwick	10	(3)	F
13	3	I'm Gonna Get Married	Lloyd Price	ABC Paramount	10	(23)	G
14	-	Don't You Know	Della Reese	RCA	10		F G
15	-	Deck Of Cards	Wink Martindale	Dot	9	(18)	F G L
16	-	Battle Hymn Of The Republic	Mormon Tabernacle Choir	Columbia	5		F L
17	4	Sea Of Love	Phil Phillips With The Twilights	Mercury	9		F G L
18	7	Broken-Hearted Melody	Sarah Vaughan	Mercury	8	(7)	G L
19	20	Morgen	Ivo Robic	Laurie	6	(23)	F L
20	-	The Battle Of Kookamonga	Homer & Jethro	RCA	5		F L

November 1959

This Mnth	Prev Mnth	Title	Artist	Label	Wks 20	(UK Pos)	
1	1	Mack The Knife	Bobby Darin	Atco	19	(1)	G
2	3	Mr. Blue	Fleetwoods	Dolton	14		G
3	14	Don't You Know	Della Reese	RCA	10		F G
4	2	Put Your Head On My Shoulder	Paul Anka	ABC Paramount	12	(7)	
5	-	Heartaches By The Number	Guy Mitchell	Columbia	12	(5)	G L
6	15	Deck Of Cards	Wink Martindale	Dot	9	(18)	F G L
7	8	Lonely Street	Andy Williams	Cadence	10		
8	-	So Many Ways	Brook Benton	Mercury	9		
9	-	In The Mood	Ernie Fields	Rendezvous	10	(13)	F L
10	4	Teen Beat	Sandy Nelson	Original Sound	10	(9)	F G
11	11	Primrose Lane	Jerry Wallace	Challenge	11		G
12	-	Seven Little Girls Sitting In The Back Seat	Paul Evans & The Curls	Guaranteed	7	(25)	F
13	-	We Got Love	Bobby Rydell	Cameo	9		
14	-	Danny Boy	Conway Twitty	MGM	7		
15	-	Be My Guest	Fats Domino	Imperial	5	(11)	
16	-	Oh! Carol	Neil Sedaka	RCA	8	(3)	
17	-	Misty	Johnny Mathis	Columbia	7	(12)	
18	9	Just Ask Your Heart	Frankie Avalon	Chancellor	8		
19	7	Poison Ivy	Coasters	Atco	9	(15)	G L
20	-	The Enchanted Sea	Islanders	Mayflower	3		F L

December 1959

This Mnth	Prev Mnth	Title	Artist	Label	Wks 20	(UK Pos)	
1	5	Heartaches By The Number	Guy Mitchell	Columbia	12	(5)	G L
2	1	Mack The Knife	Bobby Darin	Atco	19	(1)	G
3	-	Why	Frankie Avalon	Chancellor	10	(20)	G L
4	-	El Paso	Marty Robbins	Columbia	12	(19)	G
5	13	We Got Love	Bobby Rydell	Cameo	9		
6	-	The Big Hurt	Miss Toni Fisher	Signet	12	(30)	F L
7	-	It's Time To Cry	Paul Anka	ABC Paramount	9	(28)	
8	9	In The Mood	Ernie Fields	Rendezvous	10	(13)	F L
9	2	Mr. Blue	Fleetwoods	Dolton	14		G
10	-	Way Down Yonder In New Orleans	Freddy Cannon	Swan	9	(3)	G
11	3	Don't You Know	Della Reese	RCA	10		F G
12	8	So Many Ways	Brook Benton	Mercury	9		
13	-	Hound Dog Man	Fabian	Chancellor	7		L
14	-	Among My Souvenirs	Connie Francis	MGM	6	(11)	G
15	16	Oh! Carol	Neil Sedaka	RCA	8	(3)	
16	-	Scarlet Ribbons	Browns	RCA	5		
17	15	Be My Guest	Fats Domino	Imperial	5	(11)	
18	-	Uh! Oh! Part 2	Nutty Squirrels	Hanover	5		F L
19	-	Pretty Blue Eyes	Steve Lawrence	ABC Paramount	11		
20	14	Danny Boy	Conway Twitty	MGM	7		

◆ Bobby Darin's transatlantic No. 1 'Mack The Knife' won the Grammy for Best Record of 1959 despite being banned by some stations who felt it might encourage gang warfare.

◆ The biggest group to sing on a Top 20 record were the 375 voiced Mormon Tabernacle Choir with their stirring version of the 97-year-old American fave 'Battle Hymn Of The Republic'.

◆ The US government stepped up its probe into payola (DJs receiving payments for playing records). Rock'n' roll's No. 1 DJ, Alan Freed, was to become the main scapegoat.

◆ One of the year's most unusual hits was TV personality Wink Martindale's revival of 'Deck Of Cards'. This monologue about a soldier playing cards in church was a Top 40 hit in Britain in 1959, 1963 and 1973!

UK 1960
JAN-MAR

◆ Cliff Richard & The Shadows set a new record when 19.5 million people watched them on *Sunday Night At The London Palladium*. The following day they flew to the USA to tour with American chart stars Frankie Avalon, Freddy Cannon and Bobby Rydell.

◆ Elvis Presley set foot in Britain for the only time when changing planes in Scotland on his way back to the US from Germany to be demobbed.

▲ British teen idol Adam Faith scored his second successive No. 1 single.

◆ *Record Retailer* introduced Britain's first Top 50 single and Top 20 album charts.

January 1960

This Mnth	Prev Mnth	Title	Artist	Label	Wks 20	(US Pos)	
1	2	What Do You Want To Make Those Eyes At Me For	Emile Ford & The Checkmates	Pye	18		F
2	1	What Do You Want	Adam Faith	Parlophone	15		F
3	3	Oh! Carol	Neil Sedaka	RCA	14	(9)	
4	16	Staccato's Theme	Eimer Bernstein	Capitol	10		F L
5	5	Seven Little Girls Sitting In The Back Seat	Avons	Columbia	10		F L
6	12	Little White Bull	Tommy Steele	Decca	12		
7	-	Starry Eyed	Michael Holliday	Columbia	9		L
8	9	Rawhide	Frankie Laine	Philips	13		L
9	-	Why	Anthony Newley	Decca	12		
10	-	Way Down Yonder In New Orleans	Freddy Cannon	Top Rank	11	(3)	
11	-	Heartaches By The Number	Guy Mitchell	Philips	9	(1)	L
12	-	Bad Boy	Marty Wilde	Philips	7	(45)	
13	6	Travellin' Light	Cliff Richard	Columbia	16		
14	-	Be My Guest	Fats Domino	London American	7	(8)	
15	-	Voice In The Wilderness	Cliff Richard	Columbia	10		
16	-	In The Mood	Ernie Fields	London American	5	(4)	F L
17	-	Some Kind-A Earthquake	Duane Eddy	London American	5	(37)	
18	15	Among My Souvenirs	Connie Francis	MGM	6	(7)	
19	-	Reveille Rock	Johnny & The Hurricanes	London American	4	(25)	
20	10	More And More Party Pops	Russ Conway	Columbia	5		

February 1960

This Mnth	Prev Mnth	Title	Artist	Label	Wks 20	(US Pos)	
1	9	Why	Anthony Newley	Decca	12		
2	15	Voice In The Wilderness	Cliff Richard	Columbia	10		
3	10	Way Down Yonder In New Orleans	Freddy Cannon	Top Rank	11	(3)	
4	-	Poor Me	Adam Faith	Parlophone	11		
5	7	Starry Eyed	Michael Holliday	Columbia	9		L
6	-	Pretty Blue Eyes	Craig Douglas	Top Rank	8		
7	-	On A Slow Boat To China	Emile Ford	Pye	9		
8	1	What Do You Want To Make Those Eyes At Me For	Emile Ford & The Checkmates	Pye	18		F
9	-	Beyond The Sea (La Mer)	Bobby Darin	London American	6	(6)	
10	11	Heartaches By The Number	Guy Mitchell	Philips	9	(1)	L
11	-	Running Bear	Johnny Preston	Mercury	12	(1)	F
12	-	Summer Set	Acker Bilk	Columbia	10		F
13	-	Misty	Johnny Mathis	Fontana	6	(12)	
14	2	What Do You Want	Adam Faith	Parlophone	15		F
15	-	Harbour Lights	Platters	Mercury	7	(8)	L
16	4	Staccato's Theme	Elmer Bernstein	Capitol	10		F L
17	6	Little White Bull	Tommy Steele	Decca	12		
18	-	You Got What It Takes	Marv Johnson	London American	10	(10)	F
19	8	Rawhide	Frankie Laine	Philips	13		L
20	3	Oh! Carol	Neil Sedaka	RCA	14	(9)	

March 1960

This Mnth	Prev Mnth	Title	Artist	Label	Wks 20	(US Pos)	
1	4	Poor Me	Adam Faith	Parlophone	11		
2	11	Running Bear	Johnny Preston	Mercury	12	(1)	F
3	-	Delaware	Perry Como	RCA	8	(22)	
4	1	Why	Anthony Newley	Decca	12		
5	7	On A Slow Boat To China	Emile Ford & The Checkmates	Pye	9		
6	18	You Got What It Takes	Marv Johnson	London American	10	(10)	F
7	-	Theme From 'A Summer Place'	Percy Faith	Philips	12	(1)	F L
8	12	Summer Set	Acker Bilk	Columbia	10		F
9	2	Voice In The Wilderness	Cliff Richard	Columbia	10		
10	-	What In The World's Come Over You	Jack Scott	Top Rank	7	(5)	L
11	3	Way Down Yonder In New Orleans	Freddy Cannon	Top Rank	11	(3)	
12	6	Pretty Blue Eyes	Craig Douglas	Top Rank	8		
13	-	Be Mine	Lance Fortune	Pye	7		F L
14	-	Fings Ain't What They Used T'be	Max Bygraves	Decca	10		
15	-	My Old Man's A Dustman	Lonnie Donegan	Pye	9		
16	-	Who Could Be Bluer	Jerry Lordan	Parlophone	5		F L
17	9	Beyond The Sea (La Mer)	Bobby Darin	London American	6	(6)	
18	-	Beatnik Fly	Johnny & The Hurricanes	London American	9	(15)	
19	-	Bonnie Came Back	Duane Eddy	London American	4	(26)	
20	-	Royal Event	Russ Conway	Columbia	3		

January 1960

This Mnth	Prev Mnth	Title	Artist	Label	Wks 20	(UK Pos)	
1	4	El Paso	Marty Robbins	Columbia	12	(19)	G
2	3	Why	Frankie Avalon	Chancellor	10	(20)	G L
3	-	Running Bear	Johnny Preston	Mercury	12	(1)	F G
4	6	The Big Hurt	Miss Toni Fisher	Signet	12	(30)	F L
5	10	Way Down Yonder In New Orleans	Freddy Cannon	Swan	9	(3)	G
6	-	Go Jimmy Go	Jimmy Clanton	Ace	8		
7	7	It's Time To Cry	Paul Anka	ABC Paramount	9	(28)	
8	19	Pretty Blue Eyes	Steve Lawrence	ABC Paramount	11		
9	14	Among My Souvenirs	Connie Francis	MGM	6	(11)	G
10	-	The Village Of St. Bernadette	Andy Williams	Cadence	7		
11	-	Teen Angel	Mark Dinning	MGM	11	(28)	F G L
12	1	Heartaches By The Number	Guy Mitchell	Columbia	12	(5)	G L
13	13	Hound Dog Man	Fabian	Chancellor	7		L
14	-	You Got What It Takes	Marv Johnson	UA	8	(5)	F
15	-	Where Or When	Dion & The Belmonts	Laurie	9		L
16	2	Mack The Knife	Bobby Darin	Atco	19	(1)	G
17	-	Sandy	Larry Hall	Strand	5		F L
18	5	We Got Love	Bobby Rydell	Cameo	9		
19	-	Not One Minute More	Della Reese	RCA	4		L
20	-	Smokie-Part 2	Bill Black's Combo	Hi	3		F

February 1960

This Mnth	Prev Mnth	Title	Artist	Label	Wks 20	(UK Pos)	
1	11	Teen Angel	Mark Dinning	MGM	11	(28)	F G L
2	3	Running Bear	Johnny Preston	Mercury	12	(1)	F G
3	-	Handy Man	Jimmy Jones	Cub	12	(3)	F G
4	15	Where Or When	Dion & The Belmonts	Laurie	9		L
5	-	He'll Have To Go	Jim Reeves	RCA	16	(11)	G L
6	-	What In The World's Come Over You	Jack Scott	Top Rank	10	(6)	G
7	-	Theme From 'A Summer Place'	Percy Faith	Columbia	15	(4)	G L
8	-	Lonely Blue Boy	Conway Twitty	MGM	6		L
9	-	Let It Be Me	Everly Brothers	Cadence	8	(18)	
10	1	El Paso	Marty Robbins	Columbia	12	(19)	G
11	-	Beyond The Sea	Bobby Darin	Atco	8	(8)	G
12	14	You Got What It Takes	Marv Johnson	UA	8	(5)	F
13	-	Down By The Station	Four Preps	Capitol	8		
14	6	Go Jimmy Go	Jimmy Clanton	Ace	8		
15	2	Why	Frankie Avalon	Chancellor	10	(20)	G L
16	8	Pretty Blue Eyes	Steve Lawrence	ABC Paramount	11		
17	-	Baby (You Got What It Takes)	Brook Benton & Dinah Washington	Mercury	10		G
18	-	Wild One	Bobby Rydell	Cameo	10	(12)	G
19	4	The Big Hurt	Miss Toni Fisher	Signet	12	(30)	F L
20	10	The Village Of St. Bernadette	Andy Williams	Cadence	7		

March 1960

This Mnth	Prev Mnth	Title	Artist	Label	Wks 20	(UK Pos)	
1	7	Theme From 'A Summer Place'	Percy Faith	Columbia	15	(4)	G L
2	5	He'll Have To Go	Jim Reeves	RCA	16	(11)	G L
3	18	Wild One	Bobby Rydell	Cameo	10	(12)	G
4	3	Handy Man	Jimmy Jones	Cub	12	(3)	F G
5	17	Baby (You Got What It Takes)	Brook Benton & Dinah Washington	Mercury	10		G
6	6	What In The World's Come Over You	Jack Scott	Top Rank	10	(6)	G
7	-	Puppy Love	Paul Anka	ABC Paramount	9		G
8	-	Sweet Nothin's	Brenda Lee	Decca	11	(4)	F G
9	11	Beyond The Sea	Bobby Darin	Atco	8	(8)	G
10	-	Harbor Lights	Platters	Mercury	8	(11)	
11	1	Teen Angel	Mark Dinning	MGM	11	(28)	F G L
12	-	Forever	Little Dippers	University	6		F L
13	9	Let It Be Me	Everly Brothers	Cadence	8	(18)	
14	-	Lady Luck	Lloyd Price	ABC Paramount	7		
15	2	Running Bear	Johnny Preston	Mercury	12	(1)	F G
16	-	O Dio Mio	Annette	Vista	5		
17	-	Beatnik Fly	Johnny & The Hurricanes	Warwick	5	(8)	L
18	-	Mama	Connie Francis	MGM	5	(8)	G
19	4	Where Or When	Dion & The Belmonts	Laurie	9		F L
20	-	Midnite Special	Paul Evans	Guaranteed	4		

◆ The success of Mark Dinning's moving ballad, 'Teen Angel' (about a 16-year-old girl who was killed by a speeding locomotive) inspired many similar death-discs.

◆ The Grammy for Best Record Of 1960 went to Percy Faith's transatlantic success, 'Theme From A Summer Place', which topped the US chart for nine weeks.

◆ As album sales grew, for the first time, the public demanded that certain tracks were released as singles. 'El Paso', 'Mack The Knife', 'Beyond The Sea' and 'Mama' were examples of this new trend.

◆ Jimmy Jones had a transatlantic smash with his own composition 'Handy Man'. He had originally recorded the song without success in 1956 with the group The Sparks Of Rhythm. The song returned to the Top 5 seventeen years later, by James Taylor.

UK 1960 APR-JUNE

◆ The Everly Brothers' initial release on Warner Brothers, their own composition 'Cathy's Clown', topped the chart on both sides of the Atlantic.

◆ Gene Vincent was injured and Eddie Cochran killed in a car crash in England. Cochran's first posthumous release, 'Three Steps To Heaven' topped the UK chart.

◆ The Silver Beetles (Beatles) toured Scotland as backing band to little heralded rocker Johnny Gentle, and appeared alongside Gerry & The Pacemakers at a gig on Merseyside.

◆ 'My Old Man's A Dustman', which Lonnie Donegan recorded live on stage in Doncaster, became the first British record to enter the chart at No. 1. It was a feat only Elvis had achieved previously.

April 1960

This Mnth	Prev Mnth	Title	Artist	Label	Wks 20	(US Pos)	
1	15	My Old Man's A Dustman	Lonnie Donegan	Pye	9		
2	-	Fall In Love With You	Cliff Richard	Columbia	11		
3	-	Handy Man	Jimmy Jones	MGM	17	(2)	F
4	-	Do You Mind	Anthony Newley	Decca	12	(91)	
5	14	Fings Ain't What They Used T'Be	Max Bygraves	Decca	10		
6	-	Stuck On You	Elvis Presley	RCA	8	(1)	
7	7	Theme From 'A Summer Place'	Percy Faith	Philips	12	(1)	F L
8	2	Running Bear	Johnny Preston	Mercury	12	(1)	F
9	18	Beatnik Fly	Johnny & The Hurricanes	London American	9	(15)	
10	-	Someone Else's Baby	Adam Faith	Parlophone	10		
11	-	Cathy's Clown	Everly Brothers	Warner	14	(1)	
12	3	Delaware	Perry Como	RCA	8	(22)	
13	-	Wild One	Bobby Rydell	Columbia	8	(2)	F
14	6	You Got What It Takes	Marv Johnson	London American	10	(10)	F
15	-	Sweet Nothin's	Brenda Lee	Brunswick	13	(4)	F
16	10	What In The World's Come Over You	Jack Scott	Top Rank	7	(5)	L
17	-	Clementine	Bobby Darin	London American	6	(21)	
18	-	Standing On The Corner	King Brothers	Parlophone	6		
19	1	Poor Me	Adam Faith	Parlophone	11		
20	-	Footsteps	Steve Lawrence	HMV	10	(7)	F

May 1960

This Mnth	Prev Mnth	Title	Artist	Label	Wks 20	(US Pos)	
1	11	Cathy's Clown	Everly Brothers	Warner	14	(1)	
2	10	Someone Else's Baby	Adam Faith	Parlophone	10		
3	3	Handy Man	Jimmy Jones	MGM	17	(2)	F
4	4	Do You Mind	Anthony Newley	Decca	12	(91)	
5	15	Sweet Nothin's	Brenda Lee	Brunswick	13	(4)	F
6	-	Cradle Of Love	Johnny Preston	Mercury	11	(7)	
7	-	Shazam	Duane Eddy	London American	9	(45)	
8	2	Fall In Love With You	Cliff Richard	Columbia	11		
9	18	Standing On The Corner	King Brothers	Parlophone	6		
10	20	Footsteps	Steve Lawrence	HMV	10	(7)	F
11	6	Stuck On You	Elvis Presley	RCA	8	(1)	
12	-	Three Steps To Heaven	Eddie Cochran	London American	12		
13	-	Heart Of A Teenage Girl	Craig Douglas	Top Rank	5		
14	7	Theme From 'A Summer Place'	Percy Faith	Philips	12	(1)	F L
15	1	My Old Man's A Dustman	Lonnie Donegan	Pye	9		
16	-	Stairway To Heaven	Neil Sedaka	RCA	7	(9)	
17	5	Fings Ain't What They Used T'be	Max Bygraves	Decca	10		
18	-	Mama	Connie Francis	MGM	11	(8)	
19	9	Beatnik Fly	Johnny & The Hurricanes	London American	9	(15)	
20	-	Let The Little Girl Dance	Billy Bland	London American	3	(7)	F L

June 1960

This Mnth	Prev Mnth	Title	Artist	Label	Wks 20	(US Pos)	
1	1	Cathy's Clown	Everly Brothers	Warner	14	(1)	
2	6	Cradle Of Love	Johnny Preston	Mercury	11	(7)	
3	3	Handy Man	Jimmy Jones	MGM	17	(2)	F
4	12	Three Steps To Heaven	Eddie Cochran	London American	12		
5	5	Sweet Nothin's	Brenda Lee	Brunswick	13	(4)	F
6	-	Robot Man	Connie Francis	MGM	11		
7	-	I Wanna Go Home	Lonnie Donegan	Pye	9		
8	7	Shazam	Duane Eddy	London American	9	(45)	
9	18	Mama	Connie Francis	MGM	11	(8)	
10	2	Someone Else's Baby	Adam Faith	Parlophone	10		
11	-	Ain't Misbehavin'	Tommy Bruce & The Bruisers	Columbia	11		F L
12	-	Sixteen Reasons	Connie Stevens	Warner	7	(3)	F L
13	-	He'll Have To Go	Jim Reeves	RCA	6	(2)	F
14	16	Stairway To Heaven	Neil Sedaka	RCA	7	(9)	
15	10	Footsteps	Steve Lawrence	HMV	10	(7)	F
16	-	Good Timin'	Jimmy Jones	MGM	13	(3)	L
17	-	Down Yonder	Johnny & The Hurricanes	London American	5	(48)	
18	-	Lucky Five	Russ Conway	Columbia	4		
19	4	Do You Mind	Anthony Newley	Decca	12	(91)	
20	20	Let The Little Girl Dance	Billy Bland	London American	3	(7)	F L

April 1960

This Mnth	Prev Mnth	Title	Artist	Label	Wks 20	(UK Pos)	
1	1	Theme From 'A Summer Place'	Percy Faith	Columbia	15	(4)	G L
2	7	Puppy Love	Paul Anka	ABC Paramount	9		G
3	2	He'll Have To Go	Jim Reeves	RCA	16	(11)	G L
4	-	Greenfields	Brothers Four	Columbia	11	(26)	F G L
5	-	Sink The Bismarck	Johnny Horton	Columbia	10		
6	8	Sweet Nothin's	Brenda Lee	Decca	11	(4)	F G
7	3	Wild One	Bobby Rydell	Cameo	10	(12)	G
8	-	Sixteen Reasons	Connie Stevens	Warner	11	(11)	G L
9	-	Footsteps	Steve Lawrence	ABC Paramount	6	(7)	
10	18	Mama	Connie Francis	MGM	5	(8)	G
11	-	Stuck On You	Elvis Presley	RCA	11	(2)	G
12	-	I Love The Way You Love	Marv Johnson	UA	8	(28)	
13	-	White Silver Sands	Bill Black's Combo	Hi	9		G
14	-	The Old Lamplighter	Browns	RCA	8		L
15	5	Baby (You Got What It Takes)	Brook Benton & Dinah Washington	Mercury	10		G
16	10	Harbor Lights	Platters	Mercury	8	(11)	
17	-	Cradle Of Love	Johnny Preston	Mercury	9	(2)	
18	16	O Dio Mio	Annette	Vista	5		
19	-	Step By Step	Crests	Coed	6		
20	-	Night	Jackie Wilson	Brunswick	10		G

May 1960

This Mnth	Prev Mnth	Title	Artist	Label	Wks 20	(UK Pos)	
1	11	Stuck On You	Elvis Presley	RCA	11	(2)	G
2	4	Greenfields	Brothers Four	Columbia	11	(26)	F G L
3	-	Cathy's Clown	Everly Brothers	Warner	12	(1)	G
4	20	Night	Jackie Wilson	Brunswick	10		G
5	8	Sixteen Reasons	Connie Stevens	Warner	11	(11)	G L
6	17	Cradle Of Love	Johnny Preston	Mercury	9	(2)	
7	-	Good Timin'	Jimmy Jones	Cub	9	(1)	G L
8	-	Let The Little Girl Dance	Billy Bland	Old Town	8	(15)	F L
9	5	Sink The Bismarck	Johnny Horton	Columbia	10		
10	14	The Old Lamplighter	Browns	RCA	8		L
11	-	He'll Have To Stay	Jeanne Black	Capitol	7		F G L
12	-	Stairway To Heaven	Neil Sedaka	RCA	7	(12)	
13	-	Paper Roses	Anita Bryant	Carlton	9	(25)	F
14	-	Burning Bridges	Jack Scott	Top Rank	10		L
15	13	White Silver Sands	Bill Black's Combo	Hi	9		G
16	-	Cherry Pie	Skip & Flip	Brent	6		L
17	-	Love You So	Ron Holden	Donna	7		F L
18	12	I Love The Way You Love	Marv Johnson	UA	8	(28)	
19	6	Sweet Nothin's	Brenda Lee	Decca	11	(4)	F G
20	1	Theme From 'A Summer Place'	Percy Faith	Columbia	15	(4)	G L

June 1960

This Mnth	Prev Mnth	Title	Artist	Label	Wks 20	(UK Pos)	
1	3	Cathy's Clown	Everly Brothers	Warner	12	(1)	G
2	-	Everybody's Somebody's Fool	Connie Francis	MGM	12	(7)	G
3	14	Burning Bridges	Jack Scott	Top Rank	10		L
4	7	Good Timin'	Jimmy Jones	Cub	9	(1)	G L
5	13	Paper Roses	Anita Bryant	Carlton	9	(25)	F
6	-	Swingin' School	Bobby Rydell	Cameo	6		
7	17	Love You So	Ron Holden	Donna	7		F L
8	11	He'll Have To Stay	Jeanne Black	Capitol	7		F G L
9	1	Stuck On You	Elvis Presley	RCA	11	(2)	G
10	-	Alley-Oop	Hollywood Argyles	Lute	10		F G L
11	-	Because They're Young	Duane Eddy	Jamie	9	(2)	G
12	4	Night	Jackie Wilson	Brunswick	10		G
13	-	Happy-Go-Lucky-Me	Paul Evans	Guaranteed	6		L
14	-	My Home Town	Paul Anka	ABC Paramount	7		
15	-	A Rockin' Good Way	Dinah Washington & Brook Benton	Mercury	7		L
16	-	I'm Sorry	Brenda Lee	Decca	13	(10)	G
17	-	Young Emotions	Ricky Nelson	Imperial	6		
18	-	Wonderful World	Sam Cooke	Keen	7	(2)	
19	2	Greenfields	Brothers Four	Columbia	11	(26)	F G L
20	5	Sixteen Reasons	Connie Stevens	Warner	11	(11)	G L

US 1960 APR-JUNE

◆ Before filming 'G.I. Blues', Elvis Presley appeared on a television special with Frank Sinatra, Dean Martin and Sammy Davis Jr. Elvis's label, RCA, announced that all singles, starting with Presley's 'Stuck On You' would be issued in both mono and stereo.

▲ Tony Williams, who had sung lead on all of The Platters' five million sellers, left to start a solo career. Neither Williams nor The Platters achieved gold status again.

◆ Jackie Wilson, one of Elvis's best-loved acts, had his biggest hit with 'Night' – a contemporary interpretation of a classical aria. Later in the year, Elvis followed suit with 'It's Now Or Never' and 'Surrender'.

61

UK 1960 JULY-SEPT

◆ After several unsuccessful singles, Cliff Richard's backing group, The Shadows, had a No. 1 hit with 'Apache'. They also recorded one of the earliest video discs, which was seen on European video juke boxes.

◆ The Beatles, with Pete Best on drums, played outside of Liverpool for the first time when they started a three month stand at the Indra club in Hamburg, Germany.

▲ Sam Cooke's current US hit, 'Wonderful World' (which he had written with Herb Alpert), was a transatlantic Top 10 hit for Herman's Hermits in 1965, and became a major British hit by Cooke in 1986 (21 years after his death!)

July 1960

This Mnth	Prev Mnth	Title	Artist	Label	Wks 20	(US Pos)	
1	16	Good Timin'	Jimmy Jones	MGM	13	(3)	L
2	-	Please Don't Tease	Cliff Richard	Columbia	13		
3	11	Ain't Misbehavin'	Tommy Bruce & The Bruisers	Columbia	11		F L
4	-	Shakin' All Over	Johnny Kidd & The Pirates	HMV	12		F
5	-	What A Mouth	Tommy Steele	Decca	7		L
6	6	Robot Man	Connie Francis	MGM	11		
7	-	Made You	Adam Faith	Parlophone	7		
8	4	Three Steps To Heaven	Eddie Cochran	London American	12		
9	-	Angela Jones	Michael Cox	Triumph	7		F L
10	-	Look For A Star	Garry Mills	Top Rank	7	(26)	F L
11	1	Cathy's Clown	Everly Brothers	Warner	14	(1)	
12	-	When Will I Be Loved	Everly Brothers	London American	12	(8)	
13	9	Mama	Connie Francis	MGM	11	(8)	
14	-	When Johnny Comes Marching Home	Adam Faith	Parlophone	7		
15	7	I Wanna Go Home	Lonnie Donegan	Pye	9		
16	17	Down Yonder	Johnny & The Hurricanes	London American	5	(48)	
17	-	If She Should Come To You	Anthony Newley	Decca	9	(67)	
18	-	Itsy Bitsy Teenie Weenie Yellow Polka Dot Bikini	Brian Hyland	London American	9	(1)	F
19	2	Cradle Of Love	Johnny Preston	Mercury	11	(7)	
20	3	Handy Man	Jimmy Jones	MGM	17	(2)	F

August 1960

This Mnth	Prev Mnth	Title	Artist	Label	Wks 20	(US Pos)	
1	2	Please Don't Tease	Cliff Richard	Columbia	13		
2	-	Apache	Shadows	Columbia	15		F
3	-	A Mess Of Blues	Elvis Presley	RCA	14	(32)	
4	4	Shakin' All Over	Johnny Kidd & The Pirates	HMV	12		F
5	-	Because They're Young	Duane Eddy	London American	14	(4)	
6	12	When Will I Be Loved	Everly Brothers	London American	12	(8)	
7	1	Good Timin'	Jimmy Jones	MGM	13	(3)	L
8	17	If She Should Come To You	Anthony Newley	Decca	9	(67)	
9	-	Tie Me Kangaroo Down Sport	Rolf Harris	Columbia	8	(3)	F
10	18	Itsy Bitsy Teenie Weenie Yellow Polka Dot Bikini	Brian Hyland	London American	9	(1)	F
11	10	Look For A Star	Garry Mills	Top Rank	7	(26)	F L
12	-	I'm Sorry	Brenda Lee	Brunswick	8	(1)	
13	-	Paper Roses	Kaye Sisters	Philips	10		L
14	-	Girl Of My Best Friend	Elvis Presley	RCA	12		
15	3	Ain't Misbehavin'	Tommy Bruce & The Bruisers	Columbia	11		F L
16	-	As Long As He Needs Me	Shirley Bassey	Columbia	22		
17	-	Everybody's Somebody's Fool	Connie Francis	MGM	10	(1)	
18	6	Robot Man	Connie Francis	MGM	11		
19	-	Mais Oui	King Brothers	Parlophone	3		
20	14	When Johnny Comes Marching Home	Adam Faith	Parlophone	7		

September 1960

This Mnth	Prev Mnth	Title	Artist	Label	Wks 20	(US Pos)	
1	2	Apache	Shadows	Columbia	15		F
2	5	Because They're Young	Duane Eddy	London American	14	(4)	
3	-	Tell Laura I Love Her	Ricky Valance	Columbia	12		F L
4	3	A Mess Of Blues	Elvis Presley	RCA	14	(32)	
5	14	Girl Of My Best Friend	Elvis Presley	RCA	12		
6	-	Only The Lonely	Roy Orbison	London American	15	(2)	F
7	16	As Long As He Needs Me	Shirley Bassey	Columbia	22		
8	1	Please Don't Tease	Cliff Richard	Columbia	13		
9	17	Everybody's Somebody's Fool	Connie Francis	MGM	10	(1)	
10	6	When Will I Be Loved	Everly Brothers	London American	12	(8)	
11	-	How About That	Adam Faith	Parlophone	10		
12	13	Paper Roses	Kaye Sisters	Philips	10		L
13	-	Nine Times Out Of Ten	Cliff Richard	Columbia	8		
14	-	Love Is Like A Violin	Ken Dodd	Decca	7		F
15	8	If She Should Come To You	Anthony Newley	Decca	9	(67)	
16	-	Walk-Don't Run	Ventures	Top Rank	8	(2)	F
17	4	Shakin' All Over	Johnny Kidd & The Pirates	HMV	12		
18	-	Walk Don't Run	John Barry Seven	Columbia	9		
19	12	I'm Sorry	Brenda Lee	Brunswick	8	(1)	
20	9	Tie Me Kangaroo Down Sport	Rolf Harris	Columbia	8	(3)	F

July 1960

This Mnth	Prev Mnth	Title	Artist	Label	Wks 20	(UK Pos)	
1	16	I'm Sorry	Brenda Lee	Decca	13	(10)	G
2	10	Alley-Oop	Hollywood Argyles	Lute	10		F G L
3	2	Everybody's Somebody's Fool	Connie Francis	MGM	12	(7)	G
4	-	Only The Lonely	Roy Orbison	Monument	10	(1)	F G
5	11	Because They're Young	Duane Eddy	Jamie	9	(2)	G
6	-	Mule Skinner Blues	Fendermen	Soma	9	(27)	F L
7	-	That's All You Gotta Do	Brenda Lee	Decca	6		
8	14	My Home Town	Paul Anka	ABC Paramount	7		
9	15	A Rockin' Good Way	Dinah Washington & Brook Benton	Mercury	7		L
10	-	When Will I Be Loved	Everly Brothers	Cadence	5	(5)	
11	-	Tell Laura I Love Her	Ray Peterson	RCA	7		F
12	-	Please Help Me, I'm Falling	Hank Locklin	RCA	10	(13)	F L
13	1	Cathy's Clown	Everly Brothers	Warner	12	(1)	G
14	-	Itsy Bitsy Teenie Weenie Yellow Polka Dot Bikini	Brian Hyland	Leader	10	(10)	F G
15	3	Burning Bridges	Jack Scott	Top Rank	10		L
16	-	Image Of A Girl	Safaris	Eldo	8		F L
17	18	Wonderful World	Sam Cooke	Keen	7	(2)	
18	-	Walkin' To New Orleans	Fats Domino	Imperial	7	(22)	
19	5	Paper Roses	Anita Bryant	Carlton	9	(25)	F
20	-	Alley-Oop	Dante & The Evergreens	Madison	5		F L

August 1960

This Mnth	Prev Mnth	Title	Artist	Label	Wks 20	(UK Pos)	
1	-	It's Now Or Never	Elvis Presley	RCA	14	(1)	G
2	14	Itsy Bitsy Teenie Weenie Yellow Polka Dot Bikini	Brian Hyland	Leader	10	(10)	F G
3	1	I'm Sorry	Brenda Lee	Decca	13	(10)	G
4	4	Only The Lonely	Roy Orbison	Monument	10	(1)	F G
5	-	Walk-Don't Run	Ventures	Dolton	12	(9)	F G
6	-	The Twist	Chubby Checker	Parkway	13	(9)	F G
7	16	Image Of A Girl	Safaris	Eldo	8		F L
8	-	Finger Poppin' Time	Hank Ballard & The Midnighters	King	10		F
9	18	Walkin' To New Orleans	Fats Domino	Imperial	7	(22)	
10	12	Please Help Me, I'm Falling	Hank Locklin	RCA	10	(13)	F L
11	11	Tell Laura I Love Her	Ray Peterson	RCA	7		F
12	-	Volare	Bobby Rydell	Cameo	8	(18)	G
13	2	Alley-Oop	Hollywood Argyles	Lute	10		F G L
14	-	Mission Bell	Donnie Brooks	Era	9		F L
15	6	Mule Skinner Blues	Fendermen	Soma	9	(27)	F L
16	-	In My Little Corner Of The World	Anita Bryant	Carlton	6		
17	3	Everybody's Somebody's Fool	Connie Francis	MGM	12	(7)	G
18	-	Feel So Fine	Johnny Preston	Mercury	5	(18)	L
19	-	(You Were Made For) All My Love	Jackie Wilson	Brunswick	4		
20	-	Dreamin'	Johnny Burnette	Liberty	7	(3)	F

September 1960

This Mnth	Prev Mnth	Title	Artist	Label	Wks 20	(UK Pos)	
1	6	The Twist	Chubby Checker	Parkway	13	(9)	F G
2	1	It's Now Or Never	Elvis Presley	RCA	14	(1)	G
3	-	My Heart Has A Mind Of Its Own	Connie Francis	MGM	12	(5)	G
4	5	Walk-Don't Run	Ventures	Dolton	12	(9)	F G
5	-	Mr. Custer	Larry Verne	Era	8		F G L
6	12	Volare	Bobby Rydell	Cameo	8	(18)	G
7	-	Chain Gang	Sam Cooke	RCA	10	(7)	G
8	-	Kiddio	Brook Benton	Mercury	8	(29)	
9	-	Theme From The Appartment	Ferrante & Teicher	UA	11		F
10	-	Yogi	Ivy Three	Shell	6		F L
11	-	A Million To One	Jimmy Charles	Promo	9		F L
12	14	Mission Bell	Donnie Brooks	Era	9		F L
13	20	Dreamin'	Johnny Burnette	Liberty	7	(3)	F
14	-	So Sad (To Watch Good Love Go Bad)	Everly Brothers	Warner	8	(5)	
15	2	Itsy Bitsy Teenie Weenie Yellow...	Brian Hyland	Leader	10	(10)	F G
16	8	Finger Poppin' Time	Hank Ballard & The Midnighters	King	10		F
17	3	I'm Sorry	Brenda Lee	Decca	13	(10)	G
18	16	In My Little Corner Of The World	Anita Bryant	Carlton	6		
19	-	Save The Last Dance For Me	Drifters	Atlantic	12	(2)	G
20	-	Pineapple Princess	Annette	Vista	5		L

◆ The 33⅓ RPM single was unsuccessfully launched. It appeared that the public preferred their singles and albums to run at different speeds.

◆ The Ventures had a transatlantic hit with 'Walk, Don't Run' – a guitar instrumental which influenced the instrumental sound of many early surf music bands.

◆ Teenage chart toppers included Brenda Lee (15), Bryan Hyland (16) and Chubby Checker (19). For the record, Checker's 'The Twist' also returned to the top in 1962 and is the most successful US chart single of all time.

◆ 18-year-old gospel singer Aretha Franklin recorded her first secular songs. The tracks, which included 'Over The Rainbow', helped secure her a five year deal with Columbia.

UK 1960 OCT-DEC

◆ Elvis Presley's 'It's Now Or Never', which had record UK advance orders, sold over 750,000 copies in its first week and passed the million mark 40 days later. Meanwhile, in America, his revival of 'Are You Lonesome Tonight' became his 15th chart topping single, and **G.I. Blues** his fifth No. 1 album.

◆ Instrumentals were big business in Britain – at times accounting for 30% of the chart. The hottest instrumental acts were The Shadows, Johnny & The Hurricanes, Duane Eddy and American session-group The Piltdown Men.

◆ Frankie Vaughan, one of the top UK singers of the 1950s, became the first UK pop performer to be the subject of the US TV show *This Is Your Life* – an estimated 40 million viewers saw the show.

October 1960

This Mnth	Prev Mnth	Title	Artist	Label	Wks 20	(US Pos)	
1	6	Only The Lonely	Roy Orbison	London American	15	(2)	F
2	3	Tell Laura I Love Her	Ricky Valance	Columbia	12		F L
3	7	As Long As He Needs Me	Shirley Bassey	Columbia	22		
4	11	How About That	Adam Faith	Parlophone	10		
5	13	Nine Times Out Of Ten	Cliff Richard	Columbia	8		
6	-	So Sad (To Watch Good Love Go Bad)	Everly Brothers	Warner	8	(7)	
7	18	Walk Don't Run	John Barry Seven	Columbia	9		
8	1	Apache	Shadows	Columbia	15		F
9	-	Chain Gang	Sam Cooke	RCA	8	(2)	F
10	-	Let's Think About Living	Bob Luman	Warner	9	(7)	F L
11	16	Walk-Don't Run	Ventures	Top Rank	8	(2)	F
12	5	Girl Of My Best Friend	Elvis Presley	RCA	12		
13	-	Dreamin'	Johnny Burnette	London American	12	(11)	F
14	-	Please Help Me, I'm Falling	Hank Locklin	RCA	7	(8)	F L
15	-	Rocking Goose	Johnny & The Hurricanes	London American	15	(60)	
16	4	A Mess Of Blues	Elvis Presley	RCA	14	(32)	
17	2	Because They're Young	Duane Eddy	London American	14	(4)	
18	-	MacDonald's Cave	Piltdown Men	Capitol	6		F
19	9	Everybody's Somebody's Fool	Connie Francis	MGM	10	(1)	
20	-	My Love For You	Johnny Mathis	Fontana	11	(47)	

November 1960

This Mnth	Prev Mnth	Title	Artist	Label	Wks 20	(US Pos)	
1	-	It's Now Or Never	Elvis Presley	RCA	14	(1)	G
2	3	As Long As He Needs Me	Shirley Bassey	Columbia	22		
3	13	Dreamin'	Johnny Burnette	London American	12	(11)	F
4	1	Only The Lonely	Roy Orbison	London American	15	(2)	F
5	15	Rocking Goose	Johnny & The Hurricanes	London American	15	(60)	
6	-	My Heart Has A Mind Of Its Own	Connie Francis	MGM	8	(1)	
7	-	Save The Last Dance For Me	Drifters	London American	14	(1)	
8	10	Let's Think About Living	Bob Luman	Warner	9	(7)	F L
9	-	Goodness Gracious Me	Peter Sellers & Sophia Loren	Parlophone	12		
10	20	My Love For You	Johnny Mathis	Fontana	11	(47)	
11	18	MacDonald's Cave	Piltdown Men	Capitol	6		F
12	-	Man Of Mystery	Shadows	Columbia	10		
13	9	Chain Gang	Sam Cooke	RCA	8	(2)	F
14	4	How About That	Adam Faith	Parlophone	10		
15	-	Mr. Custer	Charlie Drake	Parlophone	4		
16	7	Walk Don't Run	John Barry Seven	Columbia	9		
17	-	The Stranger	Shadows	Columbia	4		
18	-	Kommotion	Duane Eddy	London American	3	(78)	
19	6	So Sad (To Watch Good Love Go Bad)	Everly Brothers	Warner	8	(7)	
20	5	Nine Times Out Of Ten	Cliff Richard	Columbia	8		

December 1960

This Mnth	Prev Mnth	Title	Artist	Label	Wks 20	(US Pos)	
1	1	It's Now Or Never	Elvis Presley	RCA	14	(1)	G
2	7	Save The Last Dance For Me	Drifters	London American	14	(1)	
3	-	I Love You	Cliff Richard	Columbia	12		
4	-	Strawberry Fair	Anthony Newley	Decca	8		
5	9	Goodness Gracious Me	Peter Sellers & Sophia Loren	Parlophone	12		
6	-	Little Donkey	Nina & Frederick	Columbia	7		F
7	5	Rocking Goose	Johnny & The Hurricanes	London American	15	(60)	
8	12	Man Of Mystery	Shadows	Columbia	10		
9	-	Poetry In Motion	Johnny Tillotson	London American	13	(2)	F L
10	-	Lonely Pup (In A Christmas Shop)	Adam Faith	Parlophone	7		
11	-	Gurney Slade	Max Harris	Fontana	6		F L
12	6	My Heart Has A Mind Of Its Own	Connie Francis	MGM	8	(1)	
13	2	As Long As He Needs Me	Shirley Bassey	Columbia	22		
14	-	Perfidia	Ventures	London American	9	(15)	L
15	3	Dreamin'	Johnny Burnette	London American	12	(11)	F
16	10	My Love For You	Johnny Mathis	Fontana	11	(47)	
17	-	Blue Angel	Roy Orbison	London American	8	(9)	
18	-	Lively	Lonnie Donegan	Pye	6		
19	-	Ol' Macdonald	Frank Sinatra	Capitol	4	(25)	
20	-	Counting Teardrops	Emile Ford & The Checkmates	Pye	9		L

October 1960

This Mnth	Prev Mnth	Title	Artist	Label	Wks 20	(UK Pos)	
1	3	My Heart Has A Mind Of Its Own	Connie Francis	MGM	12	(5)	G
2	19	Save The Last Dance For Me	Drifters	Atlantic	12	(2)	G
3	7	Chain Gang	Sam Cooke	RCA	10	(7)	G
4	1	The Twist	Chubby Checker	Parkway	13	(9)	F G
5	-	I Want To Be Wanted	Brenda Lee	Decca	9		
6	-	Devil Or Angel	Bobby Vee	Liberty	9		F
7	5	Mr. Custer	Larry Verne	Era	8		F G L
8	14	So Sad (To Watch Good Love Go Bad)	Everly Brothers	Warner	8	(5)	
9	11	A Million To One	Jimmy Charles	Promo	9		F L
10	-	Let's Think About Living	Bob Luman	Warner	7	(6)	F L
11	2	It's Now Or Never	Elvis Presley	RCA	14	(1)	G
12	9	Theme From The Appartment	Ferrante & Teicher	UA	11		F
13	8	Kiddio	Brook Benton	Mercury	8	(29)	
14	-	Georgia On My Mind	Ray Charles	ABC Paramount	8	(18)	G
15	4	Walk-Don't Run	Ventures	Dolton	12	(9)	F G
16	-	You Talk Too Much	Joe Jones	Roulette	6		F L
17	-	Don't Be Cruel	Bill Black's Combo	Hi	7	(30)	
18	20	Pineapple Princess	Annette	Vista	5		L
19	-	Three Nights A Week	Fats Domino	Imperial	3		
20	-	Poetry In Motion	Johnny Tillotson	Cadence	9	(1)	F G

November 1960

This Mnth	Prev Mnth	Title	Artist	Label	Wks 20	(UK Pos)	
1	20	Poetry In Motion	Johnny Tillotson	Cadence	9	(1)	F G
2	-	Stay	Maurice Williams & The Zodiacs	Herald	8	(10)	F G L
3	14	Georgia On My Mind	Ray Charles	ABC Paramount	8	(18)	G
4	2	Save The Last Dance For Me	Drifters	Atlantic	12	(2)	G
5	-	Last Date	Floyd Cramer	RCA	13		F G
6	-	Let's Go, Let's Go, Let's Go	Hank Ballard & The Midnighters	King	7		L
7	5	I Want To Be Wanted	Brenda Lee	Decca	9		
8	16	You Talk Too Much	Joe Jones	Roulette	6		F L
9	-	A Thousand Stars	Kathy Young With The Innocents	Indigo	12		F L
10	-	New Orleans	Gary U.S. Bonds	Legrand	8	(17)	F
11	-	Are You Lonesome Tonight?	Elvis Presley	RCA	12	(1)	G
12	-	North To Alaska	Johnny Horton	Columbia	14	(21)	L
13	-	Alone At Last	Jackie Wilson	Brunswick	6		
14	-	Blue Angel	Roy Orbison	Monument	4	(10)	
15	17	Don't Be Cruel	Bill Black's Combo	Hi	7	(30)	
16	-	Sleep	Little Willie John	King	4		F L
17	1	My Heart Has A Mind Of Its Own	Connie Francis	MGM	12	(5)	G
18	-	He Will Break Your Heart	Jerry Butler	Vee Jay	9		
19	-	The Hucklebuck	Chubby Checker	Parkway	4		
20	6	Devil Or Angel	Bobby Vee	Liberty	9		F

December 1960

This Mnth	Prev Mnth	Title	Artist	Label	Wks 20	(UK Pos)	
1	11	Are You Lonesome Tonight?	Elvis Presley	RCA	12	(1)	G
2	5	Last Date	Floyd Cramer	RCA	13		F G
3	9	A Thousand Stars	Kathy Young/The Innocents	Indigo	12		F L
4	12	North To Alaska	Johnny Horton	Columbia	14	(21)	L
5	-	Wonderland By Night	Bert Kaempfert	Decca	13		F G
6	-	Sailor (Your Home Is The Sea)	Lolita	Kapp	10		F L
7	-	Many Tears Ago	Connie Francis	MGM	9	(12)	
8	18	He Will Break Your Heart	Jerry Butler	Vee Jay	9		
9	-	Exodus	Ferrante & Teicher	UA	14	(6)	G
10	1	Poetry In Motion	Johnny Tillotson	Cadence	9	(1)	F G
11	-	You're Sixteen	Johnny Burnette	Liberty	7	(4)	
12	2	Stay	Maurice Williams/The Zodiacs	Herald	8	(10)	F G L
13	10	New Orleans	Gary U.S. Bonds	Legrand	8	(17)	F
14	-	Lonely Teenager	Dion	Laurie	6		F
15	-	Sway	Bobby Rydell	Cameo	6	(12)	
16	6	Let's Go, Let's Go, Let's Go	Hank Ballard/The Midnighters	King	7		L
17	13	Alone At Last	Jackie Wilson	Brunswick	6		
18	-	Perfidia	Ventures	Dolton	6	(5)	
19	-	My Girl Josephine	Fats Domino	Imperial	3		
20	-	Corinna, Corinna	Ray Peterson	Dunes	7		L

▲ 'Bye Bye Baby', by Mary Wells, was the first single on Motown to reach the US Hot 100.

◆ Three years before the British invasion there was a short-lived German chart attack. Bert Kaempfert & His Orchestra headed the list, and Lolita became the first female vocalist to take a German language recording into the Top 20.

◆ 'North To Alaska' hit maker Johnny Horton died in a car crash after playing Austin's Skyline club, which was the last venue C&W legend Hank Williams played. Spookily, Horton's widow had also been married to Williams.

UK 1961

JAN-MAR

◆ Trad (based on old-time New Orleans-styled traditional jazz) was the latest UK music craze, with Acker Bilk, Kenny Ball and Chris Barber at the forefront of it.

▲ New transatlantic stars included the Buddy Holly-influenced 17-year-old Bobby Vee (above) and singer/songwriter Johnny Tillotson whose 'Poetry In Motion' topped the chart on both sides of the Atlantic.

◆ The Allisons were the most talked about new act. The duo's self-composed 'Are You Sure' dethroned Elvis at the top and came runner-up in the most publicized Eurovision Song Contest to date.

January 1961

This Mnth	Prev Mnth	Title	Artist	Label	Wks 20	(US Pos)	
1	9	Poetry In Motion	Johnny Tillotson	London American	13	(2)	F L
2	3	I Love You	Cliff Richard	Columbia	12		
3	2	Save The Last Dance For Me	Drifters	London American	14	(1)	
4	-	Portrait Of My Love	Matt Monro	Parlophone	10		F
5	1	It's Now Or Never	Elvis Presley	RCA	14	(1)	G
6	14	Perfidia	Ventures	London American	9	(15)	L
7	20	Counting Teardrops	Emile Ford & The Checkmates	Pye	9		L
8	-	Are You Lonesome Tonight?	Elvis Presley	RCA	10	(1)	
9	5	Goodness Gracious Me	Peter Sellers & Sophia Loren	Parlophone	12		
10	-	Buona Sera	Acker Bilk	Columbia	8		
11	-	Pepe	Duane Eddy	London American	8	(18)	
12	10	Lonely Pup (In A Christmas Shop)	Adam Faith	Parlophone	7		
13	-	Stay	Maurice Williams & The Zodiacs	Top Rank	6	(1)	F L
14	7	Rocking Goose	Johnny & The Hurricanes	London American	15	(60)	
15	-	Sway	Bobby Rydell	Columbia	5	(14)	
16	17	Blue Angel	Roy Orbison	London American	8	(9)	
17	4	Strawberry Fair	Anthony Newley	Decca	8		
18	8	Man Of Mystery	Shadows	Columbia	10		
19	-	You're Sixteen	Johnny Burnette	London American	8	(8)	
20	-	Sailor	Petula Clark	Pye	9		

February 1961

This Mnth	Prev Mnth	Title	Artist	Label	Wks 20	(US Pos)	
1	8	Are You Lonesome Tonight?	Elvis Presley	RCA	10	(1)	
2	20	Sailor	Petula Clark	Pye	9		
3	-	Rubber Ball	Bobby Vee	London American	7	(6)	F
4	19	You're Sixteen	Johnny Burnette	London American	8	(8)	
5	11	Pepe	Duane Eddy	London American	8	(18)	
6	4	Portrait Of My Love	Matt Monro	Parlophone	10		F
7	-	F.B.I.	Shadows	Columbia	11		
8	1	Poetry In Motion	Johnny Tillotson	London American	13	(2)	F L
9	-	Walk Right Back	Everly Brothers	Warner	11	(7)	
10	-	Sailor	Anne Shelton	Philips	5		L
11	-	Rubber Ball	Marty Wilde	Philips	4		L
12	-	Who Am I/This Is It	Adam Faith	Parlophone	9		
13	10	Buona Sera	Acker Bilk	Columbia	8		
14	-	Will You Love Me Tomorrow	Shirelles	Top Rank	9	(1)	F L
15	-	Calendar Girl	Neil Sedaka	RCA	8	(4)	
16	2	I Love You	Cliff Richard	Columbia	12		
17	-	Many Tears Ago	Connie Francis	MGM	5	(7)	
18	7	Counting Teardrops	Emile Ford & The Checkmates	Pye	9		
19	13	Stay	Maurice Williams & The Zodiacs	Top Rank	6	(1)	F L
20	-	Riders In The Sky	Ramrods	London American	7	(30)	F L

March 1961

This Mnth	Prev Mnth	Title	Artist	Label	Wks 20	(US Pos)	
1	9	Walk Right Back	Everly Brothers	Warner	11	(7)	
2	-	Are You Sure	Allisons	Fontana	12		F L
3	-	Theme For A Dream	Cliff Richard	Columbia	9		
4	14	Will You Love Me Tomorrow	Shirelles	Top Rank	9	(1)	F L
5	-	Wooden Heart	Elvis Presley	RCA	14		
6	7	F.B.I.	Shadows	Columbia	11		
7	20	Riders In The Sky	Ramrods	London American	7	(30)	F L
8	-	My Kind Of Girl	Matt Monro	Parlophone	7	(18)	
9	2	Sailor	Petula Clark	Pye	9		
10	15	Calendar Girl	Neil Sedaka	RCA	8	(4)	
11	-	Exodus	Ferrante & Teicher	London American	10	(2)	F L
12	12	Who Am I/This Is It	Adam Faith	Parlophone	9		
13	1	Are You Lonesome Tonight?	Elvis Presley	RCA	10	(1)	
14	-	Wheels	String-A-Longs	London American	6	(3)	F L
15	-	Samantha	Kenny Ball	Pye Jazz	10		F
16	-	And The Heavens Cried	Anthony Newley	Decca	7		
17	-	Lazy River	Bobby Darin	London American	8	(14)	
18	-	Let's Jump The Broomstick	Brenda Lee	Brunswick	4		
19	-	Ja-Da	Johnny & The Hurricanes	London American	3	(86)	L
20	3	Rubber Ball	Bobby Vee	London American	7	(6)	F

January 1961

This Mnth	Prev Mnth	Title	Artist	Label	Wks 20	(UK Pos)	
1	5	Wonderland By Night	Bert Kaempfert	Decca	13		F G
2	9	Exodus	Ferrante & Teicher	UA	14	(6)	G
3	1	Are You Lonesome Tonight?	Elvis Presley	RCA	12	(1)	G
4	-	Will You Love Me Tomorrow	Shirelles	Scepter	12	(3)	F G
5	-	Angel Baby	Rosie & The Originals	Highland	9		F L
6	2	Last Date	Floyd Cramer	RCA	13		F G
7	-	Rubber Ball	Bobby Vee	Liberty	9	(3)	
8	-	Calcutta	Lawrence Welk	Dot	11		F G L
9	4	North To Alaska	Johnny Horton	Columbia	14	(21)	L
10	20	Corinna, Corinna	Ray Peterson	Dunes	7		L
11	3	A Thousand Stars	Kathy Young With The Innocents	Indigo	12		F L
12	-	Shop Around	Miracles	Tamla	9		F G
13	-	Calendar Girl	Neil Sedaka	RCA	8	(8)	
14	11	You're Sixteen	Johnny Burnette	Liberty	7	(4)	
15	7	Many Tears Ago	Connie Francis	MGM	9	(12)	
16	6	Sailor (Your Home Is The Sea)	Lolita	Kapp	10		F L
17	-	Emotions	Brenda Lee	Decca	6	(29)	
18	-	Wonderland By Night	Louis Prima	Dot	6		L
19	8	He Will Break Your Heart	Jerry Butler	Vee Jay	9		
20	-	Once In A While	Chimes	Tag	4		F L

February 1961

This Mnth	Prev Mnth	Title	Artist	Label	Wks 20	(UK Pos)	
1	8	Calcutta	Lawrence Welk	Dot	11		F G L
2	4	Will You Love Me Tomorrow	Shirelles	Scepter	12	(3)	F G
3	12	Shop Around	Miracles	Tamla	9		F G
4	-	Pony Time	Chubby Checker	Parkway	11		G
5	2	Exodus	Ferrante & Teicher	UA	14	(6)	G
6	13	Calendar Girl	Neil Sedaka	RCA	8	(8)	
7	-	There's A Moon Out Tonight	Capris	Old Town	7		F L
8	17	Emotions	Brenda Lee	Decca	6	(29)	
9	-	Dedicated To The One I Love	Shirelles	Scepter	11		G
10	5	Angel Baby	Rosie & The Originals	Highland	9		F L
11	-	Where The Boys Are	Connie Francis	MGM	9	(8)	G
12	1	Wonderland By Night	Bert Kaempfert	Decca	13		F G
13	-	Wings Of A Dove	Ferlin Husky	Capitol	8		L
14	-	Wheels	String-A-Longs	Warwick	8	(11)	F G L
15	-	Baby Sittin' Boogie	Buzz Clifford	Columbia	7	(14)	F L
16	-	Don't Worry	Marty Robbins	Columbia	9		
17	20	Once In A While	Chimes	Tag	4		F L
18	-	Surrender	Elvis Presley	RCA	9	(1)	G
19	-	Ebony Eyes	Everly Brothers	Warner	7	(17)	
20	-	My Empty Arms	Jackie Wilson	Brunswick	4		

March 1961

This Mnth	Prev Mnth	Title	Artist	Label	Wks 20	(UK Pos)	
1	4	Pony Time	Chubby Checker	Parkway	11		G
2	18	Surrender	Elvis Presley	RCA	9	(1)	G
3	16	Don't Worry	Marty Robbins	Columbia	9		
4	14	Wheels	String-A-Longs	Warwick	8	(11)	F G L
5	9	Dedicated To The One I Love	Shirelles	Scepter	11		G
6	11	Where The Boys Are	Connie Francis	MGM	9	(8)	G
7	-	Apache	Jorgen Ingmann	Atco	10		F L
8	19	Ebony Eyes	Everly Brothers	Warner	7	(17)	
9	15	Baby Sittin' Boogie	Buzz Clifford	Columbia	7	(14)	F L
10	-	Walk Right Back	Everly Brothers	Warner	7	(1)	
11	1	Calcutta	Lawrence Welk	Dot	11		F G L
12	-	Spanish Harlem	Ben E. King	Atco	5		F
13	-	Gee Whiz (Look At His Eyes)	Carla Thomas	Atlantic	5		F
14	-	Good Time Baby	Bobby Rydell	Cameo	5	(27)	
15	7	There's A Moon Out Tonight	Capris	Old Town	7		F L
16	-	Think Twice	Brook Benton	Mercury	5		
17	-	On The Rebound	Floyd Cramer	RCA	9	(3)	
18	-	Blue Moon	Marcels	Colpix	9	(1)	F G
19	-	You Can Have Her	Roy Hamilton	Epic	2		L
20	-	Little Boy Sad	Johnny Burnette	Liberty	3	(15)	

◆ A doo-wop revival resulted in hits for groups like The Capris, Rosie & The Originals, The Chimes and The Marcels, whose up-date of 'Blue Moon' was a transatlantic No. 1.

◆ 'Shop Around' by The Miracles became Motown's first million seller.

◆ The world's most popular performer, Elvis Presley, decided to call a halt to live shows so that he could concentrate on his movie career. He signed a five year film contract with Hal Wallis and played his last stage show for eight years at Pearl Harbor in Hawaii.

◆ Frank Sinatra announced that he would soon be launching his own label, Reprise. Among the acts who joined him on the label were fellow rat-pack members Sammy Davis Jr and Dean Martin. He vowed never to release any rock'n'roll on Reprise.

UK 1961
APR-JUNE

◆ Ex-Drifter Ben E. King released 'Stand By Me' a song he had originally written for the group. It was a US Top 10 hit in both 1961 and 1986, and even topped the UK chart in 1987!

◆ Elvis Presley's 'Surrender', which like its predecessor, 'It's Now Or Never', was based on an old Italian ballad, had a record 460,000 advance orders.

◆ The first American artist to appear on new pop TV show *Thank Your Lucky Stars* was Gene Vincent. This show, more than any other, would spread the Merseybeat sound.

◆ British teen idol Billy Fury clocked up his biggest hit to date with a cover of Tony Orlando's 'Halfway To Paradise'. Unluckily for Fury, a proposed appearance on Dick Clark's show in the USA was cancelled at the eleventh hour.

April 1961

This Mnth	Prev Mnth	Title	Artist	Label	Wks 20	(US Pos)	
1	5	Wooden Heart	Elvis Presley	RCA	14		
2	2	Are You Sure	Allisons	Fontana	12		F L
3	17	Lazy River	Bobby Darin	London American	8	(14)	
4	-	You're Driving Me Crazy	Temperance Seven	Parlophone	12		F
5	11	Exodus	Ferrante & Teicher	London American	10	(2)	F L
6	3	Theme For A Dream	Cliff Richard	Columbia	9		
7	-	Where The Boys Are	Connie Francis	MGM	6	(4)	
8	-	Blue Moon	Marcels	Pye International	9	(1)	F L
9	1	Walk Right Back	Everly Brothers	Warner	11	(7)	
10	16	And The Heavens Cried	Anthony Newley	Decca	7		
11	-	Gee Whiz It's You	Cliff Richard	Columbia	8		
12	8	My Kind Of Girl	Matt Monro	Parlophone	7	(18)	
13	6	F.B.I.	Shadows	Columbia	11		
14	15	Samantha	Kenny Ball	Pye Jazz	10		F
15	-	Warpaint	Brook Brothers	Pye	9		F
16	-	African Waltz	Johnny Dankworth	Columbia	8		L
17	4	Will You Love Me Tomorrow	Shirelles	Top Rank	9	(1)	F L
18	-	A Hundred Pounds Of Clay	Craig Douglas	Top Rank	6		
19	-	Don't Treat Me Like A Child	Helen Shapiro	Columbia	11		F
20	-	Baby Sittin' Boogie	Buzz Clifford	Fontana	3	(6)	F L

May 1961

This Mnth	Prev Mnth	Title	Artist	Label	Wks 20	(US Pos)	
1	8	Blue Moon	Marcels	Pye International	9	(1)	F L
2	4	You're Driving Me Crazy	Temperance Seven	Parlophone	12		F
3	-	On The Rebound	Floyd Cramer	RCA	9	(4)	F L
4	-	Runaway	Del Shannon	London American	16	(1)	F
5	-	More Than I Can Say	Bobby Vee	London American	9	(61)	
6	19	Don't Treat Me Like A Child	Helen Shapiro	Columbia	11		F
7	1	Wooden Heart	Elvis Presley	RCA	14		
8	-	Theme From Dixie	Duane Eddy	London American	6	(39)	
9	-	Frightened City	Shadows	Columbia	11		
10	-	Easy Going Me	Adam Faith	Parlophone	5		
11	18	A Hundred Pounds Of Clay	Craig Douglas	Top Rank	6		
12	-	What'd I Say	Jerry Lee Lewis	London American	6	(30)	L
13	16	African Waltz	Johnny Dankworth	Columbia	8		L
14	-	You'll Never Know	Shirley Bassey	Columbia	8		
15	11	Gee Whiz It's You	Cliff Richard	Columbia	8		
16	15	Warpaint	Brook Brothers	Pye	9		F
17	3	Lazy River	Bobby Darin	London American	8	(14)	
18	-	Surrender	Elvis Presley	RCA	10	(1)	
19	-	But I Do	Clarence 'Frogman' Henry	Pye International	13	(4)	F
20	5	Exodus	Ferrante & Teicher	London American	10	(2)	F L

June 1961

This Mnth	Prev Mnth	Title	Artist	Label	Wks 20	(US Pos)	
1	4	Runaway	Del Shannon	London American	16	(1)	F
2	18	Surrender	Elvis Presley	RCA	10	(1)	
3	19	But I Do	Clarence 'Frogman' Henry	Pye International	13	(4)	F
4	9	Frightened City	Shadows	Columbia	11		
5	14	You'll Never Know	Shirley Bassey	Columbia	8		
6	-	Hello Mary Lou/Travellin' Man	Ricky Nelson	London American	15	(9)	
7	-	Halfway To Paradise	Billy Fury	Decca	18		
8	-	Have A Drink On Me	Lonnie Donegan	Pye	8		
9	-	Pasadena	Temperance Seven	Parlophone	12		
10	5	More Than I Can Say	Bobby Vee	London American	9	(61)	
11	-	Temptation	Everly Brothers	Warner	12	(27)	
12	-	Little Devil	Neil Sedaka	RCA	6	(11)	
13	3	On The Rebound	Floyd Cramer	RCA	9	(4)	F L
14	-	I've Told Every Little Star	Linda Scott	Columbia	6	(3)	F L
15	-	Running Scared	Roy Orbison	London American	9	(1)	
16	12	What'd I Say	Jerry Lee Lewis	London American	6	(30)	L
17	-	A Girl Like You	Cliff Richard	Columbia	12		
18	-	Pop Goes The Weasel	Anthony Newley	Decca	6	(85)	
19	-	Well I Ask You	Eden Kane	Decca	16		F
20	1	Blue Moon	Marcels	Pye International	9	(1)	F L

US 1961 APR-JUNE

April 1961

This Mnth	Prev Mnth	Title	Artist	Label	Wks 20	(UK Pos)	
1	18	Blue Moon	Marcels	Colpix	9	(1)	F G
2	-	Runaway	Del Shannon	Big Top	10	(1)	F G
3	7	Apache	Jorgen Ingmann	Atco	10		F L
4	17	On The Rebound	Floyd Cramer	RCA	9	(3)	
5	-	But I Do	Clarence 'Frogman' Henry	Argo	7	(3)	
6	5	Dedicated To The One I Love	Shirelles	Scepter	11		G
7	-	Mother-In-Law	Ernie K-Doe	Minit	9	(22)	F L
8	2	Surrender	Elvis Presley	RCA	9	(1)	G
9	-	Asia Minor	Kokomo	Felsted	5		F L
10	1	Pony Time	Chubby Checker	Parkway	11		G
11	-	Take Good Care Of Her	Adam Wade	Coed	8		F
12	-	Please Love Me Forever	Cathy Jean & The Roommates	Valmor	5		F L
13	-	A Hundred Pounds Of Clay	Gene McDaniels	Liberty	10		F G
14	3	Don't Worry	Marty Robbins	Columbia	9		
15	10	Walk Right Back	Everly Brothers	Warner	6	(1)	
16	-	One Mint Julep	Ray Charles	Impulse	6		
17	-	You Can Depend On Me	Brenda Lee	Decca	7		
18	-	I've Told Every Little Star	Linda Scott	Canadian American	7	(8)	F G
19	16	Think Twice	Brook Benton	Mercury	5		
20	-	Baby Blue	Echoes	Seg-Way	6		F L

May 1961

This Mnth	Prev Mnth	Title	Artist	Label	Wks 20	(UK Pos)	
1	2	Runaway	Del Shannon	Big Top	10	(1)	F G
2	7	Mother-In-Law	Ernie K-Doe	Minit	9	(22)	F L
3	13	A Hundred Pounds Of Clay	Gene McDaniels	Liberty	10		F G
4	-	Daddy's Home	Shep & The Limelites	Hull	8		F L
5	18	I've Told Every Little Star	Linda Scott	Canadian American	7	(8)	F G
6	1	Blue Moon	Marcels	Colpix	9	(1)	F G
7	-	Mama Said	Shirelles	Scepter	7		
8	-	Travelin' Man	Ricky Nelson	Imperial	12	(20)	G
9	17	You Can Depend On Me	Brenda Lee	Decca	7		
10	-	Breakin' In A Brand New Broken Heart	Connie Francis	MGM	6	(16)	
11	11	Take Good Care Of Her	Adam Wade	Coed	8		F
12	-	Portrait Of My Love	Steve Lawrence	UA	6		
13	-	Running Scared	Roy Orbison	Monument	9	(9)	G
14	16	One Mint Julep	Ray Charles	Impulse	6		
15	4	On The Rebound	Floyd Cramer	RCA	9	(3)	
16	5	But I Do	Clarence 'Frogman' Henry	Argo	7	(3)	
17	-	Hello Mary Lou	Ricky Nelson	Imperial	8	(3)	
18	-	I Feel So Bad	Elvis Presley	RCA	6	(20)	
19	-	Tragedy	Fleetwoods	Dolton	3		L
20	-	Little Devil	Neil Sedaka	RCA	3	(9)	

June 1961

This Mnth	Prev Mnth	Title	Artist	Label	Wks 20	(UK Pos)	
1	8	Travelin' Man	Ricky Nelson	Imperial	12	(20)	G
2	-	Moody River	Pat Boone	Dot	9	(14)	G
3	-	Raindrops	Dee Clark	Vee Jay	10		G L
4	-	Stand By Me	Ben E. King	Atco	7	(27)	
5	13	Running Scared	Roy Orbison	Monument	9	(9)	G
6	-	Quarter To Three	Gary U.S. Bonds	Legrand	10	(7)	G
7	-	The Writing On The Wall	Adam Wade	Coed	7		
8	18	I Feel So Bad	Elvis Presley	RCA	6	(20)	
9	-	Every Beat Of My Heart	Gladys Knight & The Pips	Vee Jay	7		F
10	-	The Boll Weevil Song	Brook Benton	Mercury	10	(28)	G
11	-	Tossin' And Turnin'	Bobby Lewis	Beltone	15		F G
12	-	Those Oldies But Goodies (Remind Me Of You)	Little Caesar & The Romans	Del-Fi	6		F L
13	-	You Always Hurt The One You Love	Clarence 'Frogman' Henry	Argo	5	(6)	L
14	7	Mama Said	Shirelles	Scepter	7		
15	-	Barbara Ann	Regents	Gee	6		F L
16	4	Daddy's Home	Shep & The Limelites	Hull	8		F L
17	17	Hello Mary Lou	Ricky Nelson	Imperial	8	(3)	
18	-	Yellow Bird	Arthur Lyman	Hi Fi	7		F L
19	3	A Hundred Pounds Of Clay	Gene McDaniels	Liberty	10		F G
20	-	Hello Walls	Faron Young	Capitol	5		F L

◆ Bob Dylan made his New York debut as opening act for blues great John Lee Hooker. Dylan also played harmonica on a recording session for Harry Belafonte.

▲ Among acts debuting on the Hot 100 were later superstars Paul Revere & The Raiders, Tony Orlando (who later had a string of hits with Dawn) and Gladys Knight & The Pips. The most successful new chart entrant, however, was singer/songwriter Del Shannon (above) whose 'Runaway' was a transatlantic topper.

◆ The Regents, who split up in 1958 after failing to get a deal for their song 'Barbara Ann', re-united when it became a surprise hit.

UK 1961 JULY-SEPT

◆ 'Michael', a 19th century slave song, gave American folk quintet The Highwaymen an unexpected transatlantic No. 1, despite heavy British competition from Lonnie Donegan. Incidentally, Donegan's 1959 UK hit 'Chewing Gum' was now huge in the USA.

◆ The Shadows became the first British rock act to top the UK album chart. Their boss, Cliff Richard, would be the second with his **21 Today** LP.

◆ In Liverpool, alternative pop magazine *Mersey Beat* was launched and The Beatles started playing regularly at the Cavern Club.

◆ 15-year-old London schoolgirl Helen Shapiro had two successive chart toppers with the British songs 'You Don't Know' and 'Walkin' Back To Happiness'. Both records sold over a million copies worldwide.

July 1961

This Mnth	Prev Mnth	Title	Artist	Label	Wks 20	(US Pos)	
1	11	Temptation	Everly Brothers	Warner	12	(27)	
2	1	Runaway	Del Shannon	London American	16	(1)	F
3	19	Well I Ask You	Eden Kane	Decca	16		F
4	6	Hello Mary Lou/Travellin' Man	Ricky Nelson	London American	15	(9)	
5	17	A Girl Like You	Cliff Richard	Columbia	12		
6	9	Pasadena	Temperance Seven	Parlophone	12		
7	7	Halfway To Paradise	Billy Fury	Decca	18		
8	3	But I Do	Clarence 'Frogman' Henry	Pye International	13	(4)	F
9	15	Running Scared	Roy Orbison	London American	9	(1)	
10	-	You Don't Know	Helen Shapiro	Columbia	14		
11	-	You Always Hurt The One You Love	Clarence 'Frogman' Henry	Pye International	9	(12)	L
12	2	Surrender	Elvis Presley	RCA	10	(1)	
13	-	Time	Craig Douglas	Top Rank	10		
14	18	Pop Goes The Weasel	Anthony Newley	Decca	6	(85)	
15	-	Romeo	Petula Clark	Pye	11		
16	-	Moody River	Pat Boone	London American	6	(1)	
17	4	Frightened City	Shadows	Columbia	11		
18	-	Weekend	Eddie Cochran	London American	3		L
19	-	Don't You Know It	Adam Faith	Parlophone	6		
20	-	Breakin' In A Brand New Broken Heart	Connie Francis	MGM	2	(7)	

August 1961

This Mnth	Prev Mnth	Title	Artist	Label	Wks 20	(US Pos)	
1	10	You Don't Know	Helen Shapiro	Columbia	14		
2	3	Well I Ask You	Eden Kane	Decca	16		F
3	-	Johnny Remember Me	John Leyton	Top Rank	11		F
4	7	Halfway To Paradise	Billy Fury	Decca	18		
5	15	Romeo	Petula Clark	Pye	11		
6	11	You Always Hurt The One You Love	Clarence 'Frogman' Henry	Pye International	9	(12)	L
7	6	Pasadena	Temperance Seven	Parlophone	12		
8	1	Temptation	Everly Brothers	Warner	12	(27)	
9	19	Don't You Know It	Adam Faith	Parlophone	6		
10	13	Time	Craig Douglas	Top Rank	10		
11	5	A Girl Like You	Cliff Richard	Columbia	12		
12	4	Hello Mary Lou/Travellin' Man	Ricky Nelson	London American	15	(9)	
13	-	Quarter To Three	Gary U.S. Bonds	Top Rank	9	(1)	L
14	-	Reach For The Stars/Climb Ev'ry Mountain	Shirley Bassey	Columbia	11		
15	2	Runaway	Del Shannon	London American	16	(1)	F
16	-	Climb Ev'ry Mountain	Shirley Bassey	Columbia	6		
17	-	Baby I Don't Care	Buddy Holly	Coral	6		
18	-	Marcheta	Karl Denver	Decca	7		F
19	-	That's My Home	Acker Bilk	Columbia	9		
20	-	Cupid	Sam Cooke	RCA	7	(17)	

September 1961

This Mnth	Prev Mnth	Title	Artist	Label	Wks 20	(US Pos)	
1	3	Johnny Remember Me	John Leyton	Top Rank	11		F
2	1	You Don't Know	Helen Shapiro	Columbia	14		
3	14	Reach For The Stars/Climb Ev'ry Mountain	Shirley Bassey	Columbia	11		
4	-	Wild In The Country	Elvis Presley	RCA	8	(26)	
5	-	Kon-Tiki	Shadows	Columbia	8		
6	20	Cupid	Sam Cooke	RCA	7	(17)	
7	2	Well I Ask You	Eden Kane	Decca	16		F
8	-	Michael	Highwaymen	HMV	10	(1)	F L
9	19	That's My Home	Acker Bilk	Columbia	9		
10	5	Romeo	Petula Clark	Pye	11		
11	-	Michael Row The Boat	Lonnie Donegan	Pye	6		
12	-	Jealousy	Billy Fury	Decca	8		
13	4	Halfway To Paradise	Billy Fury	Decca	18		
14	-	Get Lost	Eden Kane	Decca	8		
15	13	Quarter To Three	Gary U.S. Bonds	Top Rank	9	(1)	L
16	-	How Many Tears	Bobby Vee	London American	5	(63)	
17	-	Together	Connie Francis	MGM	8	(6)	
18	-	Hats Off To Larry	Del Shannon	London American	8	(5)	
19	11	A Girl Like You	Cliff Richard	Columbia	12		
20	-	You'll Answer To Me	Cleo Laine	Fontana	9		F L

70

July 1961

This Mnth	Prev Mnth	Title	Artist	Label	Wks 20	(UK Pos)	
1	11	Tossin' And Turnin'	Bobby Lewis	Beltone	15		F G
2	10	The Boll Weevil Song	Brook Benton	Mercury	10	(28)	G
3	6	Quarter To Three	Gary U.S. Bonds	Legrand	10	(7)	G
4	3	Raindrops	Dee Clark	Vee Jay	10		G L
5	18	Yellow Bird	Arthur Lyman	Hi Fi	7		F L
6	-	Hats Off To Larry	Del Shannon	Big Top	8	(8)	
7	-	I Like It Like That (Pt.1)	Chris Kenner	Instant	8		F G L
8	-	Dum Dum	Brenda Lee	Decca	9	(20)	
9	9	Every Beat Of My Heart	Gladys Knight & The Pips	Vee Jay	7		F
10	-	San Antonio Rose	Floyd Cramer	RCA	7		L
11	2	Moody River	Pat Boone	Dot	9	(14)	G
12	7	The Writing On The Wall	Adam Wade	Coed	7		
13	-	Together	Connie Francis	MGM	8	(10)	
14	-	Dance On Little Girl	Paul Anka	ABC Paramount	5		
15	1	Travelin' Man	Ricky Nelson	Imperial	12	(20)	G
16	-	Let's Twist Again	Chubby Checker	Parkway	7	(1)	G
17	-	Last Night	Mar-Keys	Satellite	7		F G L
18	-	Please Stay	Drifters	Atlantic	4		
19	12	Those Oldies But Goodies (...)	Little Caesar & The Romans	Del-Fi	6		F L
20	4	Stand By Me	Ben E. King	Atco	7	(27)	

August 1961

This Mnth	Prev Mnth	Title	Artist	Label	Wks 20	(UK Pos)	
1	1	Tossin' And Turnin'	Bobby Lewis	Beltone	15		F G
2	17	Last Night	Mar-Keys	Satellite	7		F G L
3	7	I Like It Like That (Pt.1)	Chris Kenner	Instant	8		F G L
4	-	Wooden Heart	Joe Dowell	Smash	9		F G L
5	-	Michael	Highwaymen	UA	10	(1)	F G
6	-	Pretty Little Angel Eyes	Curtis Lee	Dunes	5		F L
7	8	Dum Dum	Brenda Lee	Decca	9	(20)	
8	-	You Don't Know What You Got (Until You Lose It)	Ral Donner	Gone	7	(21)	
9	16	Let's Twist Again	Chubby Checker	Parkway	7	(1)	G
10	-	School Is Out	Gary U.S. Bonds	Legrand	6		
11	13	Together	Connie Francis	MGM	8	(10)	
12	-	Don't Bet Money Honey	Linda Scott	Canadian Am.	5		
13	-	Hurt	Timi Yuro	Liberty	7		F
14	6	Hats Off To Larry	Del Shannon	Big Top	8	(8)	
15	-	I'll Be There	Damita Jo	Mercury	4		F L
16	-	Never On Sunday	Chordettes	Cadence	6		L
17	-	As If I Didn't Know	Adam Wade	Coed	4		L
18	-	Let The Four Winds Blow	Fats Domino	Imperial	3		L
19	-	I'm Gonna Knock On Your Door	Eddie Hodges	Cadence	3	(27)	F
20	-	I Fall To Pieces	Patsy Cline	Decca	3		F

September 1961

This Mnth	Prev Mnth	Title	Artist	Label	Wks 20	(UK Pos)	
1	5	Michael	Highwaymen	UA	10	(1)	F G
2	-	Take Good Care Of My Baby	Bobby Vee	Liberty	8	(1)	G
3	-	My True Story	Jive Five	Beltone	6		F L
4	-	Does Your Chewing Gum Lose It's Flavor (On The Bedpost Over Night)	Lonnie Donegan	Dot	6	(3)	L
5	-	Cryin'	Roy Orbison	Monument	10	(26)	G
6	4	Wooden Heart	Joe Dowell	Smash	9		F G L
7	8	You Don't Know What You Got (...)	Ral Donner	Gone	7	(21)	
8	-	Little Sister	Elvis Presley	RCA	7	(18)	
9	-	Who Put The Bomp (In The Bomp, Bomp, Bomp)	Barry Mann	ABC	5		F L
10	-	The Mountain's High	Dick & Deedee	Liberty	6	(25)	F G
11	-	Without You	Johnny Tillotson	Cadence	6		
12	13	Hurt	Timi Yuro	Liberty	7		F
13	1	Tossin' And Turnin'	Bobby Lewis	Beltone	15		F G
14	-	(Marie's The Name) His Latest Flame	Elvis Presley	RCA	2	(1)	
15	-	When We Get Married	Dreamlovers	Heritage	3		F L
16	-	One Track Mind	Bobby Lewis	Beltone	3		L
17	17	As If I Didn't Know	Adam Wade	Coed	4		L
18	10	School Is Out	Gary U.S. Bonds	Legrand	6		
19	12	Don't Bet Money Honey	Linda Scott	Canadian Am.	5		
20	-	A Little Bit Of Soap	Jarmels	Laurie	2		F L

▲ The Supremes (including Diana Ross), who had previously recorded as The Primettes on Lupine, released their earliest Motown single, 'Buttered Popcorn'.

◆ The Dick Clark Caravan Of Stars Summer Tour hit the road. Headlining the show were Chubby Checker, Bobby Rydell, Gary US Bonds, The Shirelles, Duane Eddy and Johnny & The Hurricanes.

◆ As Chubby Checker's Grammy winning 'Let's Twist Again' hit, the twist (1960s teen dance sensation) was reported to be catching on with American adults.

UK 1961 OCT-DEC

◆ Unusually. three hits by British acts also reached the US Top 10: 'Midnight In Moscow' by Kenny Ball, 'Stranger On The Shore' by Acker Bilk and 'Let's Get Together' by 14-year-old Hayley Mills.

◆ Mantovani received five American gold albums while fellow Briton Matt Monro was voted Most Promising Artist in the *Billboard* DJ Poll.

◆ American hits from C&W stars Leroy Van Dyke, Jimmy Dean and Patsy Cline also scored in Britain, although, in the case of Cline's 'Crazy' it was 30 years later!

◆ EMI Records proudly announced that **The Black And White Minstrel Show** by The George Mitchell Minstrels (which was based on the act's very popular TV series) was the company's first album to sell over 100,000 copies in the UK.

October 1961

This Mnth	Prev Mnth	Title	Artist	Label	Wks 20	(US Pos)	
1	-	Walkin' Back To Happiness	Helen Shapiro	Columbia	15	(100)	
2	8	Michael	Highwaymen	HMV	10	(1)	F L
3	-	Wild Wind	John Leyton	Top Rank	6		
4	20	You'll Answer To Me	Cleo Laine	Fontana	9		F L
5	12	Jealousy	Billy Fury	Decca	8		
6	-	Sucu-Sucu	Laurie Johnson	Pye	10		F L
7	5	Kon-Tiki	Shadows	Columbia	8		
8	18	Hats Off To Larry	Del Shannon	London American	8	(5)	
9	4	Wild In The Country	Elvis Presley	RCA	8	(26)	
10	-	When The Girl In Your Arms Is The Girl In Your Heart	Cliff Richard	Columbia	7		
11	-	Bless You	Tony Orlando	Fontana	7	(15)	F L
12	14	Get Lost	Eden Kane	Decca	8		
13	-	Mexicali Rose	Karl Denver	Decca	9		
14	1	Johnny Remember Me	John Leyton	Top Rank	11		F
15	-	You Must Have Been A Beautiful Baby	Bobby Darin	London American	8	(5)	
16	-	Granada	Frank Sinatra	Reprise	4	(64)	
17	-	Hit The Road Jack	Ray Charles	HMV	8	(1)	
18	17	Together	Connie Francis	MGM	6	(6)	
19	-	My Boomerang Won't Come Back	Charlie Drake	Parlophone	6	(21)	L
20	2	You Don't Know	Helen Shapiro	Columbia	14		

November 1961

This Mnth	Prev Mnth	Title	Artist	Label	Wks 20	(US Pos)	
1	-	His Latest Flame	Elvis Presley	RCA	8	(4)	
2	1	Walkin' Back To Happiness	Helen Shapiro	Columbia	15	(100)	
3	-	Take Good Care Of My Baby	Bobby Vee	London American	11	(1)	
4	-	Big Bad John	Jimmy Dean	Philips	11	(1)	F L
5	10	When The Girl In Your Arms Is The Girl In Your Heart	Cliff Richard	Columbia	7		
6	-	Take Five	Dave Brubeck Quartet	Fontana	10	(25)	F
7	17	Hit The Road Jack	Ray Charles	HMV	8	(1)	
8	-	The Time Has Come	Adam Faith	Parlophone	8		
9	6	Sucu-Sucu	Laurie Johnson	Pye	10		F L
10	13	Mexicali Rose	Karl Denver	Decca	9		
11	-	Tower Of Strength	Frankie Vaughan	Philips	10		
12	-	Moon River	Danny Williams	HMV	12		F
13	11	Bless You	Tony Orlando	Fontana	7	(15)	F L
14	15	You Must Have Been A Beautiful Baby	Bobby Darin	London American	8	(5)	
15	3	Wild Wind	John Leyton	Top Rank	6		
16	-	Runaround Sue	Dion	Top Rank	5	(1)	F
17	-	The Savage	Shadows	Columbia	5		
18	-	Let's Get Together	Hayley Mills	Decca	5	(8)	F L
19	-	Midnight In Moscow	Kenny Ball	Pye Jazz	11	(2)	
20	4	You'll Answer To Me	Cleo Laine	Fontana	9		F L

December 1961

This Mnth	Prev Mnth	Title	Artist	Label	Wks 20	(US Pos)	
1	11	Tower Of Strength	Frankie Vaughan	Philips	10		
2	12	Moon River	Danny Williams	HMV	12		F
3	3	Take Good Care Of My Baby	Bobby Vee	London American	11	(1)	
4	19	Midnight In Moscow	Kenny Ball	Pye Jazz	11	(2)	
5	-	Stranger On The Shore	Mr. Acker Bilk	Columbia	33	(1)	G
6	-	I'll Get By	Shirley Bassey	Columbia	6		
7	2	Walkin' Back To Happiness	Helen Shapiro	Columbia	15	(100)	
8	1	His Latest Flame	Elvis Presley	RCA	8	(4)	
9	-	Johnny Will	Pat Boone	London American	8	(35)	
10	6	Take Five	Dave Brubeck Quartet	Fontana	10	(25)	F
11	-	Let There Be Drums	Sandy Nelson	London American	9	(7)	L
12	4	Big Bad John	Jimmy Dean	Philips	11	(1)	F L
13	8	The Time Has Come	Adam Faith	Parlophone	8		
14	-	My Friend The Sea	Petula Clark	Pye	4		
15	-	So Long Baby	Del Shannon	London American	6	(28)	
16	-	Don't Bring Lulu	Dorothy Provine	Warner	6		F L
17	-	Happy Birthday, Sweet Sixteen	Neil Sedaka	RCA	11	(6)	
18	-	I Cried For You	Ricky Stevens	Columbia	4		F L
19	17	The Savage	Shadows	Columbia	5		
20	-	I'd Never Find Another You	Billy Fury	Decca	11		

October 1961

This Mnth	Prev Mnth	Title	Artist	Label	Wks 20	(UK Pos)	
1	-	Hit The Road Jack	Ray Charles	ABC Paramount	9	(4)	G
2	-	Bristol Stomp	Dovells	Parkway	11		F G
3	-	Runaround Sue	Dion	Laurie	11	(10)	G
4	5	Cryin'	Roy Orbison	Monument	10	(26)	G
5	2	Take Good Care Of My Baby	Bobby Vee	Liberty	8	(1)	G
6	-	Mexico	Bob Moore & His Orchestra	Monument	7		F L
7	-	Big Bad John	Jimmy Dean	Columbia	12	(3)	F G
8	-	Let's Get Together	Hayley Mills	Vista	7	(15)	F L
9	-	Ya Ya	Lee Dorsey	Fury	7		F
10	-	You Must Have Been A Beautiful Baby	Bobby Darin	Atco	5	(10)	
11	-	Sad Movies (Make Me Cry)	Sue Thompson	Hickory	7		F
12	-	I Love How You Love Me	Paris Sisters	Gregmark	6		F L
13	-	This Time	Troy Shondell	Liberty	10	(17)	F L
14	10	The Mountain's High	Dick & Deedee	Liberty	6	(25)	F G
15	8	Little Sister	Elvis Presley	RCA	7	(18)	
16	-	The Fly	Chubby Checker	Parkway	8		
17	-	The Way You Look Tonight	Lettermen	Capitol	6		F
18	1	Michael	Highwaymen	UA	10	(1)	F G
19	-	Tower Of Strength	Gene McDaniels	Liberty	8		
20	-	Look In My Eyes	Chantels	Carlton	4		L

November 1961

This Mnth	Prev Mnth	Title	Artist	Label	Wks 20	(UK Pos)	
1	7	Big Bad John	Jimmy Dean	Columbia	12	(3)	F G
2	3	Runaround Sue	Dion	Laurie	11	(10)	G
3	-	Fool #1	Brenda Lee	Decca	8		
4	2	Bristol Stomp	Dovells	Parkway	11		F G
5	19	Tower Of Strength	Gene McDaniels	Liberty	8		
6	13	This Time	Troy Shondell	Liberty	10	(17)	F L
7	16	The Fly	Chubby Checker	Parkway	8		
8	-	Please Mr. Postman	Marvelettes	Tamla	11		F G
9	1	Hit The Road Jack	Ray Charles	ABC Paramount	9	(4)	G
10	-	Goodbye Cruel World	James Darren	Colpix	10	(22)	F G
11	11	Sad Movies (Make Me Cry)	Sue Thompson	Hickory	7		F
12	-	You're The Reason	Bobby Edwards	Crest	5		F L
13	-	A Wonder Like You	Ricky Nelson	Imperial	4		
14	-	Heartaches	Marcels	Colpix	4		L
15	-	Crazy	Patsy Cline	Decca	5		
16	12	I Love How You Love Me	Paris Sisters	Gregmark	6		F L
17	8	Let's Get Together	Hayley Mills	Vista	7	(15)	F L
18	-	Tonight	Ferrante & Teicher	UA	6		
19	-	I Understand (Just How You Feel)	G-Clefs	Terrace	7	(16)	F L
20	9	Ya Ya	Lee Dorsey	Fury	7		F

December 1961

This Mnth	Prev Mnth	Title	Artist	Label	Wks 20	(UK Pos)	
1	8	Please Mr. Postman	Marvelettes	Tamla	11		F G
2	10	Goodbye Cruel World	James Darren	Colpix	10	(22)	F G
3	-	The Twist	Chubby Checker	Parkway	15	(14)	G
4	-	Walk On By	Leroy Van Dyke	Mercury	10	(5)	F L
5	-	Run To Him	Bobby Vee	Liberty	11	(8)	G
6	-	The Lion Sleeps Tonight	Tokens	RCA	10	(13)	G L
7	1	Big Bad John	Jimmy Dean	Columbia	12	(3)	F G
8	-	Let There Be Drums	Sandy Nelson	Imperial	7	(3)	L
9	-	Happy Birthday, Sweet Sixteen	Neil Sedaka	RCA	8	(3)	
10	18	Tonight	Ferrante & Teicher	UA	6		
11	-	Peppermint Twist (Pt. 1)	Joey Dee & The Starliters	Roulette	13	(11)	F G
12	-	Moon River	Jerry Butler	Vee Jay	5		
13	2	Runaround Sue	Dion	Laurie	11	(10)	G
14	3	Fool #1	Brenda Lee	Decca	8		
15	-	Moon River	Henry Mancini	RCA	4	(17)	F
16	15	Crazy	Patsy Cline	Decca	5		
17	19	I Understand (Just How You Feel)	G-Clefs	Terrace	7	(16)	F L
18	5	Tower Of Strength	Gene McDaniels	Liberty	8		
19	-	When I Fall In Love	Lettermen	Capitol	8		
20	-	Can't Help Falling In Love	Elvis Presley	RCA	10	(3)	G

◆ Motown, who scored their first No. 1 with 'Please Mr. Postman' by The Marvelettes, were excited about 11-year-old Steveland Judkins, whom they renamed Little Stevie Wonder.

◆ The Beach Boys performed their first show under that name and released their debut single, 'Surfin''. Fellow newcomer Bob Dylan only attracted four dozen fans to his first Carnegie Hall concert while across the Atlantic, The Beatles drew just 18 people to their first south of England gig in Aldershot.

◆ Phil Spector launched his own label Philles with the Top 20 hit 'There's No Other' by The Crystals. Less successful was the launching by some other labels of "Little LPs" – six track 7-inch 33 rpm records.

UK 1962 JAN-MAR

◆ The theme from Cliff Richard's film *The Young Ones* racked up 500,000 advance orders and entered the UK chart at No. 1. It went on to sell over a million in Britain. The sound-track album also topped the chart.

◆ Elvis Presley earned his 29th gold single with the double-sided 'Rock-A-Hula Baby' and 'Can't Help Falling In Love'. The single came from the sound-track album to the film *Blue Hawaii*, which topped the chart for four months on both sides of the Atlantic. 'Can't Help Falling In Love' charted again later for Andy Williams, The Stylistics and UB40.

◆ Alexis Korner's group, Blues Incorporated (which at times included Charlie Watts, Jack Bruce, Ginger Baker, Mick Jagger and Brian Jones), played their debut gig at a club in Ealing.

January 1962

This Mnth	Prev Mnth	Title	Artist	Label	Wks 20	(US Pos)	
1	5	Stranger On The Shore	Mr. Acker Bilk	Columbia	33	(1)	G
2	20	I'd Never Find Another You	Billy Fury	Decca	11		
3	11	Let There Be Drums	Sandy Nelson	London American	9	(7)	L
4	-	The Young Ones	Cliff Richard	Columbia	13		G
5	17	Happy Birthday, Sweet Sixteen	Neil Sedaka	RCA	11	(6)	
6	-	Multiplication	Bobby Darin	London American	8	(30)	
7	-	Let's Twist Again	Chubby Checker	Columbia	18	(8)	
8	2	Moon River	Danny Williams	HMV	12		F
9	4	Midnight In Moscow	Kenny Ball	Pye Jazz	11	(2)	
10	9	Johnny Will	Pat Boone	London American	8	(35)	
11	-	Run To Him	Bobby Vee	Liberty	9	(2)	
12	-	The Twist	Chubby Checker	Columbia	5	(1)	F
13	1	Tower Of Strength	Frankie Vaughan	Philips	10		
14	-	The Lion Sleeps Tonight	Tokens	RCA	4	(1)	F L
15	-	Walk On By	Leroy Van Dyke	Mercury	9	(5)	F L
16	15	So Long Baby	Del Shannon	London American	6	(28)	
17	-	Forget Me Not	Eden Kane	Decca	9		
18	-	Language Of Love	John D. Loudermilk	RCA	4	(32)	F L
19	-	Toy Balloons	Russ Conway	Columbia	5		L
20	-	Cryin' In The Rain	Everly Brothers	Warner	9	(6)	

February 1962

This Mnth	Prev Mnth	Title	Artist	Label	Wks 20	(US Pos)	
1	4	The Young Ones	Cliff Richard	Columbia	13		G
2	7	Let's Twist Again	Chubby Checker	Columbia	18	(8)	
3	-	Rock-A-Hula-Baby	Elvis Presley	RCA	9	(23)	
4	17	Forget Me Not	Eden Kane	Decca	9		
5	15	Walk On By	Leroy Van Dyke	Mercury	9	(5)	F L
6	5	Happy Birthday, Sweet Sixteen	Neil Sedaka	RCA	11	(6)	
7	20	Cryin' In The Rain	Everly Brothers	Warner	9	(6)	
8	2	I'd Never Find Another You	Billy Fury	Decca	11		
9	1	Stranger On The Shore	Mr. Acker Bilk	Columbia	33	(1)	G
10	11	Run To Him	Bobby Vee	Liberty	9	(2)	
11	6	Multiplication	Bobby Darin	London American	8	(30)	
12	-	A Little Bitty Tear	Burl Ives	Brunswick	6	(9)	F L
13	-	Peppermint Twist	Joey Dee & The Starliters	Columbia	5	(1)	F L
14	-	Wimoweh	Karl Denver	Decca	10		
15	-	Lonesome	Adam Faith	Parlophone	4		
16	-	Can't Help Falling In Love	Elvis Presley	RCA	13	(2)	
17	-	The Comancheros	Lonnie Donegan	Pye	4		
18	-	March Of The Siamese Children	Kenny Ball	Pye Jazz	8	(88)	
19	3	Let There Be Drums	Sandy Nelson	London American	9	(7)	L
20	12	The Twist	Chubby Checker	Columbia	5	(1)	F

March 1962

This Mnth	Prev Mnth	Title	Artist	Label	Wks 20	(US Pos)	
1	18	March Of The Siamese Children	Kenny Ball	Pye Jazz	8	(88)	
2	-	Tell Me What He Said	Helen Shapiro	Columbia	10		
3	2	Let's Twist Again	Chubby Checker	Columbia	18	(8)	
4	-	Wonderful Land	Shadows	Columbia	16		
5	16	Can't Help Falling In Love	Elvis Presley	RCA	13	(2)	
6	14	Wimoweh	Karl Denver	Decca	10		
7	1	The Young Ones	Cliff Richard	Columbia	13		G
8	3	Rock-A-Hula-Baby	Elvis Presley	RCA	9	(23)	
9	9	Stranger On The Shore	Mr. Acker Bilk	Columbia	33	(1)	G
10	-	Hole In The Ground	Bernard Cribbins	Parlophone	7		F
11	-	Twistin' The Night Away	Sam Cooke	RCA	12	(9)	
12	-	Dream Baby	Roy Orbison	London American	11	(4)	
13	-	Softly As I Leave You	Matt Monro	Parlophone	8		
14	-	Hey! Baby	Bruce Channel	Mercury	9	(1)	F
15	7	Cryin' In The Rain	Everly Brothers	Warner	9	(6)	
16	-	The Wanderer	Dion	HMV	6	(2)	
17	4	Forget Me Not	Eden Kane	Decca	9		
18	12	A Little Bitty Tear	Burl Ives	Brunswick	6	(9)	F L
19	5	Walk On By	Leroy Van Dyke	Mercury	9	(5)	F L
20	-	Hey Little Girl	Del Shannon	London American	12	(38)	

January 1962

This Mnth	Prev Mnth	Title	Artist	Label	Wks 20	(UK Pos)	
1	3	The Twist	Chubby Checker	Parkway	15	(14)	G
2	11	Peppermint Twist (Pt. 1)	Joey Dee & The Starliters	Roulette	13	(11)	F G
3	6	The Lion Sleeps Tonight	Tokens	RCA	10	(13)	G L
4	20	Can't Help Falling In Love	Elvis Presley	RCA	10	(3)	G
5	-	I Know (You Don't Love Me No More)	Barbara George	AFO	8		F L
6	9	Happy Birthday, Sweet Sixteen	Neil Sedaka	RCA	8	(3)	
7	5	Run To Him	Bobby Vee	Liberty	11	(8)	G
8	4	Walk On By	Leroy Van Dyke	Mercury	10	(5)	F L
9	19	When I Fall In Love	Lettermen	Capitol	8		
10		Unchain My Heart	Ray Charles	ABC Paramount	6		
11	-	When The Boy In Your Arms (Is The Boy In Your Heart)	Connie Francis	MGM	6		
12	-	Norman	Sue Thompson	Hickory	9		G
13	-	Baby It's You	Shirelles	Scepter	9		
14	8	Let There Be Drums	Sandy Nelson	Imperial	7	(3)	L
15	1	Please Mr. Postman	Marvelettes	Tamla	11		F G
16	-	The Wanderer	Dion	Laurie	11	(13)	G
17	-	Town Without Pity	Gene Pitney	Musicor	4		F
18	-	A Little Bitty Tear	Burl Ives	Decca	8	(7)	F
19	2	Goodbye Cruel World	James Darren	Colpix	10	(22)	F G
20	-	Cotton Fields	Highwaymen	UA	7		L

February 1962

This Mnth	Prev Mnth	Title	Artist	Label	Wks 20	(UK Pos)	
1	-	Duke Of Earl	Gene Chandler	Vee Jay	11	(29)	F G
2	2	Peppermint Twist (Pt. 1)	Joey Dee & The Starliters	Roulette	13	(11)	F G
3	1	The Twist	Chubby Checker	Parkway	15	(14)	G
4	12	Norman	Sue Thompson	Hickory	9		G
5	16	The Wanderer	Dion	Laurie	11	(13)	G
6	4	Can't Help Falling In Love	Elvis Presley	RCA	10	(3)	G
7	-	Break It To Me Gently	Brenda Lee	Decca	9		
8	5	I Know (You Don't Love Me No More)	Barbara George	AFO	8		F L
9	-	Dear Lady Twist	Gary U.S. Bonds	Legrand	8		
10	18	A Little Bitty Tear	Burl Ives	Decca	8	(7)	F
11	13	Baby It's You	Shirelles	Scepter	9		
12	-	Cryin' In The Rain	Everly Brothers	Warner	8	(6)	
13	20	Cotton Fields	Highwaymen	UA	7		L
14	3	The Lion Sleeps Tonight	Tokens	RCA	10	(13)	G L
15	-	Hey! Baby	Bruce Channel	Smash	10	(2)	F G L
16	-	Chip Chip	Gene McDaniels	Liberty	5		L
17	-	Irresistible You	Bobby Darin	Atco	3		
18	17	Town Without Pity	Gene Pitney	Musicor	4		F
19	9	When I Fall In Love	Lettermen	Capitol	8		
20	7	Run To Him	Bobby Vee	Liberty	11	(8)	G

March 1962

This Mnth	Prev Mnth	Title	Artist	Label	Wks 20	(UK Pos)	
1	15	Hey! Baby	Bruce Channel	Smash	10	(2)	F G L
2	-	Midnight In Moscow	Kenny Ball	Kapp	9	(5)	F L
3	-	Don't Break The Heart That Loves You	Connie Francis	MGM	8	(28)	G
4	1	Duke Of Earl	Gene Chandler	Vee Jay	11	(29)	F G
5	-	Let Me In	Sensations	Argo	8		F L
6	-	What's Your Name	Don & Juan	Big Top	7		F L
7	12	Cryin' In The Rain	Everly Brothers	Warner	8	(6)	
8	-	Her Royal Majesty	James Darren	Colpix	5		
9	7	Break It To Me Gently	Brenda Lee	Decca	9		
10	5	The Wanderer	Dion	Laurie	11	(13)	G
11	-	Slow Twistin'	Chubby Checker	Parkway	10	(19)	G
12	-	Dream Baby	Roy Orbison	Monument	6	(3)	
13	-	Twistin' The Night Away	Sam Cooke	RCA	7	(4)	
14	-	Johnny Angel	Shelley Fabares	Colpix	10	(27)	F G L
15	-	Percolator (Twist)	Billy Joe & The Checkmates	Dore	5		F L
16	9	Dear Lady Twist	Gary U.S. Bonds	Legrand	8		
17	3	The Twist	Chubby Checker	Parkway	15	(14)	G
18	4	Norman	Sue Thompson	Hickory	9		G
19	16	Chip Chip	Gene McDaniels	Liberty	5		L
20	-	Good Luck Charm	Elvis Presley	RCA	10	(1)	G

US 1962 JAN-MAR

▲ The twist took off internationally. Chubby Checker signed to appear in the low-budget movie *Twist Around The Clock* (as did Dion) and Joey Dee filmed *Hey Let's Twist*. Countless artists climbed on the twist bandwagon. In America Checker's 1960 chart topper 'The Twist' returned and outsold all the competition, while in Britain his 'Let's Twist Again' reached No. 1. Checker also monopolized the US album chart with a record five LPs in the Top 12!

◆ Songwriter/trumpeter Herb Alpert, who had composed Sam Cooke's recent hit 'Wonderful World', formed his own Carnival label (he soon re-named it A&M).

UK 1962 APR-JUNE

British trad star Acker Bilk topped the US chart with 'Stranger On The Shore'. In the 1962 *Billboard* DJ poll he won awards for Top Instrumentalist and Top Instrumental Single.

Three years after his first tour was scrapped (following the discovery that he had married his 14-year-old second cousin), Jerry Lee Lewis made a triumphant return to the UK. The piano-pounding performer helped re-awaken interest in wild rock'n'roll and breathed more life into the burgeoning British beat boom.

The Beatles, attracted a record 900 crowd to the Cavern Club after their successful EMI audition. Meanwhile, the Dave Clark Five released their debut single 'That's What I Said'.

Mick Jagger met Brian Jones for the first time at the Ealing Jazz Club and decided to form a group called The Rollin' Stones.

April 1962

This Mnth	Prev Mnth	Title	Artist	Label	Wks 20	(US Pos)	
1	4	Wonderful Land	Shadows	Columbia	16		
2	14	Hey! Baby	Bruce Channel	Mercury	9	(1)	F
3	12	Dream Baby	Roy Orbison	London American	11	(4)	
4	-	When My Little Girl Is Smiling	Jimmy Justice	Pye	9		F
5	11	Twistin' The Night Away	Sam Cooke	RCA	12	(9)	
6	2	Tell Me What He Said	Helen Shapiro	Columbia	10		
7	20	Hey Little Girl	Del Shannon	London American	12	(38)	
8	5	Can't Help Falling In Love	Elvis Presley	RCA	13	(2)	
9	-	Never Goodbye	Karl Denver	Decca	7		
10	-	Speak To Me Pretty	Brenda Lee	Brunswick	9		
11	3	Let's Twist Again	Chubby Checker	Columbia	18	(8)	
12	6	Wimoweh	Karl Denver	Decca	10		
13	-	When My Little Girl Is Smiling	Craig Douglas	Top Rank	6		
14	-	Dr. Kildare Theme	Johnny Spence	Parlophone	5		F L
15	9	Stranger On The Shore	Mr. Acker Bilk	Columbia	33	(1)	G
16	1	March Of The Siamese Children	Kenny Ball	Pye Jazz	8	(88)	
17	-	Love Letters	Ketty Lester	London American	9	(5)	F L
18	-	Nut Rocker	B. Bumble & The Stingers	Top Rank	11	(23)	F L
19	-	Wonderful World Of The Young	Danny Williams	HMV	7		L
20	-	Ev'rybody's Twistin'	Frank Sinatra	Reprise	5	(75)	

May 1962

This Mnth	Prev Mnth	Title	Artist	Label	Wks 20	(US Pos)	
1	18	Nut Rocker	B. Bumble & The Stingers	Top Rank	11	(23)	F L
2	1	Wonderful Land	Shadows	Columbia	16		
3	17	Love Letters	Ketty Lester	London American	9	(5)	F L
4	-	Good Luck Charm	Elvis Presley	RCA	14	(1)	
5	10	Speak To Me Pretty	Brenda Lee	Brunswick	9		
6	-	I'm Looking Out The Window	Cliff Richard	Columbia	11		
7	7	Hey Little Girl	Del Shannon	London American	12	(38)	
8	4	When My Little Girl Is Smiling	Jimmy Justice	Pye	9		F
9	-	As You Like It	Adam Faith	Parlophone	10		
10	2	Hey! Baby	Bruce Channel	Mercury	9	(1)	F
11	19	Wonderful World Of The Young	Danny Williams	HMV	7		L
12	3	Dream Baby	Roy Orbison	London American	11	(4)	
13	5	Twistin' The Night Away	Sam Cooke	RCA	12	(9)	
14	-	Come Outside	Mike Sarne & Wendy Richard	Parlophone	14		F
15	-	Last Night Was Made For Love	Billy Fury	Decca	11		
16	-	The Party's Over	Lonnie Donegan	Pye	5		
17	15	Stranger On The Shore	Mr. Acker Bilk	Columbia	33	(1)	G
18	20	Ev'rybody's Twistin'	Frank Sinatra	Reprise	5	(75)	
19	-	Let's Talk About Love	Helen Shapiro	Columbia	3		
20	-	I Don't Know Why	Eden Kane	Decca	7		

June 1962

This Mnth	Prev Mnth	Title	Artist	Label	Wks 20	(US Pos)	
1	4	Good Luck Charm	Elvis Presley	RCA	14	(1)	
2	14	Come Outside	Mike Sarne & Wendy Richard	Parlophone	14		F
3	6	I'm Looking Out The Window	Cliff Richard	Columbia	11		
4	-	A Picture Of You	Joe Brown & The Bruvvers	Piccadilly	14		F
5	-	Ginny Come Lately	Brian Hyland	HMV	10	(21)	
6	15	Last Night Was Made For Love	Billy Fury	Decca	11		
7	20	I Don't Know Why	Eden Kane	Decca	7		
8	9	As You Like It	Adam Faith	Parlophone	10		
9	1	Nut Rocker	B. Bumble & The Stingers	Top Rank	11	(23)	F L
10	-	The Green Leaves Of Summer	Kenny Ball	Pye Jazz	9	(87)	
11	-	Do You Wanna Dance	Cliff Richard	Columbia	6		
12	17	Stranger On The Shore	Mr. Acker Bilk	Columbia	33	(1)	G
13	-	I Can't Stop Loving You	Ray Charles	HMV	12	(1)	
14	3	Love Letters	Ketty Lester	London American	9	(5)	F L
15	-	Theme From Dr. Kildare (Three Stars Will Shine Tonight)	Richard Chamberlain	MGM	4	(10)	F
16	-	Ain't That Funny	Jimmy Justice	Pye	8		L
17	-	A Little Love, A Little Kiss	Karl Denver	Decca	3		
18	2	Wonderful Land	Shadows	Columbia	16		
19	-	Here Comes That Feeling	Brenda Lee	Brunswick	8	(89)	
20	-	Follow That Dream E.P.	Elvis Presley	RCA	6	(15)	

April 1962

This Mnth	Prev Mnth	Title	Artist	Label	Wks 20	(UK Pos)	
1	14	Johnny Angel	Shelley Fabares	Colpix	10	(27)	F G L
2	20	Good Luck Charm	Elvis Presley	RCA	10	(1)	G
3	11	Slow Twistin'	Chubby Checker	Parkway	10	(19)	G
4	-	Mashed Potato Time	Dee Dee Sharp	Cameo	12		F G
5	-	Young World	Rick Nelson	Imperial	7	(21)	
6	-	Love Letters	Ketty Lester	Era	7	(4)	F G L
7	-	Lover Please	Clyde McPhatter	Mercury	8		L
8	-	Soldier Boy	Shirelles	Scepter	10	(27)	G
9	3	Don't Break The Heart That Loves You	Connie Francis	MGM	8	(28)	G
10	2	Midnight In Moscow	Kenny Ball	Kapp	9	(5)	F L
11	-	Shout (Pt. 1)	Joey Dee & The Starliters	Roulette	7		
12	-	Love Me Warm And Tender	Paul Anka	RCA	5	(14)	
13	1	Hey! Baby	Bruce Channel	Smash	10	(2)	F G L
14	-	Stranger On The Shore	Acker Bilk	Atco	13	(1)	F G L
15	12	Dream Baby	Roy Orbison	Monument	6	(3)	
16	-	Dear One	Larry Finnegan	Old Town	4		F L
17	-	Twist, Twist Senora	Gary U.S. Bonds	Legrand	6		
18	13	Twistin' The Night Away	Sam Cooke	RCA	7	(4)	
19	5	Let Me In	Sensations	Argo	8		F L
20	6	What's Your Name	Don & Juan	Big Top	7		F L

May 1962

This Mnth	Prev Mnth	Title	Artist	Label	Wks 20	(UK Pos)	
1	8	Soldier Boy	Shirelles	Scepter	10	(27)	G
2	14	Stranger On The Shore	Acker Bilk	Atco	13	(1)	F G L
3	4	Mashed Potato Time	Dee Dee Sharp	Cameo	12		F G
4	1	Johnny Angel	Shelley Fabares	Colpix	10	(27)	F G L
5	-	She Cried	Jay & The Americans	UA	8		F
6	-	Old Rivers	Walter Brennan	Liberty	6		F L
7	-	P.T. 109	Jimmy Dean	Columbia	6		L
8	2	Good Luck Charm	Elvis Presley	RCA	10	(1)	G
9	-	Shout! Shout! (Knock Yourself Out)	Ernie Maresca	Seville	6		F L
10	-	Everybody Loves Me But You	Brenda Lee	Decca	6		
11	11	Shout (Pt. 1)	Joey Dee & The Starliters	Roulette	7		
12	-	Funny Way Of Laughin'	Burl Ives	Decca	5		
13	17	Twist, Twist Senora	Gary U.S. Bonds	Legrand	6		
14	3	Slow Twistin'	Chubby Checker	Parkway	10	(19)	G
15	7	Lover Please	Clyde McPhatter	Mercury	8		L
16	-	Lovers Who Wander	Dion	Laurie	7		
17	-	The One Who Really Loves You	Mary Wells	Motown	7		F
18	-	I Can't Stop Loving You	Ray Charles	ABC Paramount	12	(1)	G
19	-	Conscience	James Darren	Colpix	5	(27)	L
20	-	Uptown	Crystals	Philles	5		

June 1962

This Mnth	Prev Mnth	Title	Artist	Label	Wks 20	(UK Pos)	
1	18	I Can't Stop Loving You	Ray Charles	ABC Paramount	12	(1)	G
2	2	Stranger On The Shore	Acker Bilk	Atco	13	(1)	F G L
3	-	It Keeps Right On A-Hurtin'	Johnny Tillotson	Cadence	9		
4	-	(The Man Who Shot) Liberty Valence	Gene Pitney	Musicor	6		
5	-	Palisades Park	Freddy Cannon	Swan	9	(22)	G
6	-	The Stripper	David Rose & His Orchestra	MGM	11		F G L
7	16	Lovers Who Wander	Dion	Laurie	7		
8	-	Playboy	Marvelettes	Tamla	7		
9	-	Second Hand Love	Connie Francis	MGM	5		
10	17	The One Who Really Loves You	Mary Wells	Motown	7		F
11	1	Soldier Boy	Shirelles	Scepter	10	(27)	G
12	-	Cindy's Birthday	Johnny Crawford	Del-Fi	4		F
13	-	That's Old Fashioned (That's The Way Love Should Be)	Everly Brothers	Warner	3		L
14	3	Mashed Potato Time	Dee Dee Sharp	Cameo	12		F G
15	-	Al Di La	Emilio Pericoli	Warner	7	(23)	F L
16	-	Don't Play That Song (You Lied)	Ben E. King	Atco	4		
17	10	Everybody Loves Me But You	Brenda Lee	Decca	6		
18	-	Snap Your Fingers	Joe Henderson	Todd	6		F L
19	-	Roses Are Red (My Love)	Bobby Vinton	Epic	12	(13)	F G
20	19	Conscience	James Darren	Colpix	5	(27)	L

US 1962
APR-JUNE

◆ Arranger Ernie Freeman considered actor Walter Brennan's recording of 'Old Rivers' to be the worst song he ever worked on. Nonetheless the tear jerking narration about a farmer and his mule ploughed its way up the chart.

◆ Latest American artists to score No. 1s were newcomer Bruce Channel with his composition 'Hey! Baby' and Ray Charles, with a revival of 'I Can't Stop Loving You'.

▲ The Freewheelin' Bob Dylan album was released. *Billboard* said, "Dylan could have a big following when he finds his own style."

UK 1962

JULY-SEPT

◆ Ringo Starr replaced drummer Pete Best in The Beatles, who recorded their Parlophone debut, 'Love Me Do'. The record, which took 17 takes, was a US No. 1 in 1964 and finally made the UK Top 10 twenty years later! Another group who were to change 1960s music, The Rolling Stones, made their live debut at the Marquee club in London.

◆ Frank Ifield scored the first of three successive No. 1s with 'I Remember You', which spent seven weeks at No. 1 in Britain and sold over a million copies.

◆ Despite the fact that their current UK singles failed to enter the US Top 100, American performers Jimmie Rodgers, The Crickets (with a vocal from Glen Campbell), Eydie Gormé and Nat 'King' Cole had major British hits. Also faring far better in Britain were new releases from Brenda Lee, Duane Eddy and Carole King.

July 1962

This Mnth	Prev Mnth	Title	Artist	Label	Wks 20	(US Pos)	
1	12	I Can't Stop Loving You	Ray Charles	HMV	12	(1)	
2	4	A Picture Of You	Joe Brown & The Bruvvers	Piccadilly	14		F
3	2	Come Outside	Mike Sarne & Wendy Richard	Parlophone	14		F
4	-	I Remember You	Frank Ifield	Columbia	19	(5)	F G
5	1	Good Luck Charm	Elvis Presley	RCA	14	(1)	
6	18	Here Comes That Feeling	Brenda Lee	Brunswick	8	(89)	
7	-	English Country Garden	Jimmie Rodgers	Columbia	9		L
8	5	Ginny Come Lately	Brian Hyland	HMV	10	(21)	
9	-	Don't Ever Change	Crickets	Liberty	9		L
10	-	Speedy Gonzales	Pat Boone	London American	12	(6)	
11	-	Our Favourite Melodies	Craig Douglas	Columbia	6		
12	10	The Green Leaves Of Summer	Kenny Ball	Pye Jazz	9	(87)	
13	3	I'm Looking Out The Window	Cliff Richard	Columbia	11		
14	15	Ain't That Funny	Jimmy Justice	Pye	8		L
15	6	Last Night Was Made For Love	Billy Fury	Decca	11		
16	-	Yes My Darling Daughter	Eydie Gorme	CBS	5		F
17	12	Stranger On The Shore	Mr. Acker Bilk	Columbia	33	(1)	G
18	-	Right Said Fred	Bernard Cribbins	Parlophone	6		L
19	19	Follow That Dream E.P.	Elvis Presley	RCA	6	(15)	
20	-	Ya Ya Twist	Petula Clark	Pye	5		

August 1962

This Mnth	Prev Mnth	Title	Artist	Label	Wks 20	(US Pos)	
1	4	I Remember You	Frank Ifield	Columbia	19	(5)	F G
2	10	Speedy Gonzales	Pat Boone	London American	12	(6)	
3	-	Guitar Tango	Shadows	Columbia	10		
4	-	Things	Bobby Darin	London American	12	(3)	
5	1	I Can't Stop Loving You	Ray Charles	HMV	12	(1)	
6	-	Roses Are Red	Ronnie Carroll	Philips	11		
7	2	A Picture Of You	Joe Brown & The Bruvvers	Piccadilly	14		F
8	9	Don't Ever Change	Crickets	Liberty	9		L
9	-	Once Upon A Dream	Billy Fury	Decca	8		
10	-	Little Miss Lonely	Helen Shapiro	Columbia	7		L
11	-	Let There Be Love	Nat 'King' Cole	Capitol	7		
12	-	Breaking Up Is Hard To Do	Neil Sedaka	RCA	11	(1)	
13	-	Sealed With A Kiss	Brian Hyland	HMV	8	(3)	
14	6	Here Comes That Feeling	Brenda Lee	Brunswick	8	(89)	
15	3	Come Outside	Mike Sarne & Wendy Richard	Parlophone	14		F
16	17	Right Said Fred	Bernard Cribbins	Parlophone	6		L
17	-	Roses Are Red (My Love)	Bobby Vinton	Columbia	4	(1)	F
18	-	Vacation	Connie Francis	MGM	4	(9)	L
19	7	English Country Garden	Jimmie Rodgers	Columbia	9		L
20	-	So Do I	Kenny Ball	Pye Jazz	3		

September 1962

This Mnth	Prev Mnth	Title	Artist	Label	Wks 20	(US Pos)	
1	-	She's Not You	Elvis Presley	RCA	11	(5)	
2	1	I Remember You	Frank Ifield	Columbia	19	(5)	F G
3	6	Roses Are Red	Ronnie Carroll	Philips	11		
4	-	It'll Be Me	Cliff Richard	Columbia	8		
5	4	Things	Bobby Darin	London American	12	(3)	
6	13	Sealed With A Kiss	Brian Hyland	HMV	8	(3)	
7	12	Breaking Up Is Hard To Do	Neil Sedaka	RCA	11	(1)	
8	-	Telstar	Tornados	Decca	19	(1)	F
9	2	Speedy Gonzales	Pat Boone	London American	12	(6)	
10	3	Guitar Tango	Shadows	Columbia	10		
11	-	Don't That Beat All	Adam Faith	Parlophone	8		
12	-	Sheila	Tommy Roe	HMV	11	(1)	F
13	-	The Loco-Motion	Little Eva	London American	12	(1)	F
14	-	Ballad Of Paladin	Duane Eddy	RCA	7	(33)	
15	9	Once Upon A Dream	Billy Fury	Decca	8		
16	-	Pick A Bale Of Cotton	Lonnie Donegan	Pye	5		L
17	-	Main Title Theme From 'Man With The Golden Arm'	Jet Harris	Decca	6		F
18	-	You Don't Know Me	Ray Charles	HMV	8	(2)	
19	-	Will I What	Mike Sarne with Billie Davis	Parlophone	5		L
20	-	It Might As Well Rain Until September	Carole King	London American	9	(22)	F

78

July 1962

This Mnth	Prev Mnth	Title	Artist	Label	Wks 20	(UK Pos)	
1	19	Roses Are Red (My Love)	Bobby Vinton	Epic	12	(13)	F G
2	6	The Stripper	David Rose & His Orchestra	MGM	11		F G L
3	1	I Can't Stop Loving You	Ray Charles	ABC Paramount	12	(1)	G
4	-	The Wah-Watusi	Orlons	Cameo	9		F G
5	-	Sealed With A Kiss	Brian Hyland	ABC Paramount	8	(5)	G
6	-	Wolverton Mountain	Claude King	Columbia	10		F G L
7	5	Palisades Park	Freddy Cannon	Swan	9	(22)	G
8	-	Johnny Get Angry	Joanie Sommers	Warner	7	(28)	F L
9	-	Gravy (For My Mashed Potatoes)	Dee Dee Sharp	Cameo	5		
10	15	Al Di La	Emilio Pericoli	Warner	7	(23)	F L
11	3	It Keeps Right On A-Hurtin'	Johnny Tillotson	Cadence	9		
12	-	Speedy Gonzales	Pat Boone	Dot	7	(2)	L
13	-	Breaking Up Is Hard To Do	Neil Sedaka	RCA	9	(7)	G
14	18	Snap Your Fingers	Joe Henderson	Todd	6		F L
15	-	Ahab, The Arab	Ray Stevens	Mercury	8		F
16	-	Theme From Doctor Kildare (Three Stars Will Shine Tonight)	Richard Chamberlain	MGM	7	(11)	F
17	8	Playboy	Marvelettes	Tamla	7		
18	-	Dancin' Party	Chubby Checker	Parkway	4	(17)	
19	-	I'll Never Dance Again	Bobby Rydell	Cameo	4		
20	12	Cindy's Birthday	Johnny Crawford	Del-Fi	4		F

August 1962

This Mnth	Prev Mnth	Title	Artist	Label	Wks 20	(UK Pos)	
1	13	Breaking Up Is Hard To Do	Neil Sedaka	RCA	9	(7)	G
2	1	Roses Are Red (My Love)	Bobby Vinton	Epic	12	(13)	F G
3	-	The Loco-Motion	Little Eva	Dimension	10	(2)	F G
4	4	The Wah-Watusi	Orlons	Cameo	9		F G
5	15	Ahab, The Arab	Ray Stevens	Mercury	8		F
6	-	Things	Bobby Darin	Atco	6	(3)	
7	5	Sealed With A Kiss	Brian Hyland	ABC Paramount	8	(5)	G
8	-	You Don't Know Me	Ray Charles	ABC Paramount	6	(6)	
9	12	Speedy Gonzales	Pat Boone	Dot	7	(2)	L
10	-	You'll Lose A Good Thing	Barbara Lynn	Jamie	5		F L
11	-	Little Diane	Dion	Laurie	5		
12	2	The Stripper	David Rose & His Orchestra	MGM	11		F G L
13	6	Wolverton Mountain	Claude King	Columbia	10		F G L
14	-	Party Lights	Claudine Clark	Chancellor	6		F L
15	-	Sheila	Tommy Roe	ABC Paramount	9	(2)	F G
16	-	She's Not You	Elvis Presley	RCA	7	(1)	
17	3	I Can't Stop Loving You	Ray Charles	ABC Paramount	12	(1)	G
18	16	Theme From Doctor Kildare (Three Stars Will Shine Tonight)	Richard Chamberlain	MGM	7	(11)	F
19	-	Vacation	Connie Francis	MGM	4	(13)	
20	8	Johnny Get Angry	Joanie Sommers	Warner	7	(28)	F L

September 1962

This Mnth	Prev Mnth	Title	Artist	Label	Wks 20	(UK Pos)	
1	15	Sheila	Tommy Roe	ABC Paramount	9	(2)	F G
2	-	Ramblin' Rose	Nat 'King' Cole	Capitol	10	(4)	G
3	3	The Loco-Motion	Little Eva	Dimension	10	(2)	F G
4	-	Sherry	Four Seasons	Vee Jay	10	(7)	F G
5	16	She's Not You	Elvis Presley	RCA	7	(1)	
6	-	Teenage Idol	Ricky Nelson	Imperial	6		
7	-	Green Onions	Booker T. & The M.G.'s	Stax	8	(7)	F G
8	8	You Don't Know Me	Ray Charles	ABC Paramount	6	(6)	
9	-	You Belong To Me	Duprees	Coed	6		F
10	-	Patches	Dickey Lee	Smash	9		F
11	14	Party Lights	Claudine Clark	Chancellor	6		F L
12	-	Let's Dance	Chris Montez	Monogram	7	(2)	F G
13	-	Rinky Dink	Dave 'Baby' Cortez	Chess	4		L
14	-	You Beat Me To The Punch	Mary Wells	Motown	5		
15	-	Alley Cat	Bent Fabric	Atco	5		F G L
16	6	Things	Bobby Darin	Atco	6	(3)	
17	-	Monster Mash	Bobby 'Boris' Pickett & The Crypt Kickers	Garpax	9	(3)	F G L
18	1	Breaking Up Is Hard To Do	Neil Sedaka	RCA	9	(7)	G
19	19	Vacation	Connie Francis	MGM	4	(13)	
20	2	Roses Are Red (My Love)	Bobby Vinton	Epic	12	(13)	F G

◆ David Rose recorded 'The Stripper' in ten minutes for use as background music in the 1958 TV production *Burlesque*. In 1962 it was tucked away on the B-side of the London born orchestra leader's 'Ebb Tide'. It was unearthed by some astute radio DJs and became one of the year's top sellers.

▲ The twist still ruled but many new dance crazes surfaced Stateside, including the successful Mashed Potato, Watusi, Popeye and Locomotion, the latter popularized by Little Eva.

◆ Singles sold at 98c and albums were $3.98 (mono) and $4.98 (stereo).

UK 1962

OCT-DEC

◆ Rock'n'roll great Little Richard played his first shows on British shores. He was supported by The Beatles, whom he thought "sounded like a black American act".

▲ Big winners at the *NME* poll were Elvis, Brenda Lee and The Everly Brothers, with The Beatles being voted 8th most popular British group.

◆ The first British group to top the American charts were instrumental combo The Tornados with 'Telstar'. The record's producer/composer, Joe Meek, earlier turned down a chance to work with The Beatles.

October 1962

This Mnth	Prev Mnth	Title	Artist	Label	Wks 20	(US Pos)	
1	8	Telstar	Tornados	Decca	19	(1)	F
2	12	Sheila	Tommy Roe	HMV	11	(1)	F
3	13	The Loco-Motion	Little Eva	London American	12	(1)	F
4	20	It Might As Well Rain Until September	Carole King	London American	9	(22)	F
5	1	She's Not You	Elvis Presley	RCA	11	(5)	
6	-	Ramblin' Rose	Nat 'King' Cole	Capitol	10	(2)	
7	18	You Don't Know Me	Ray Charles	HMV	8	(2)	
8	4	It'll Be Me	Cliff Richard	Columbia	8		
9	-	What Now My Love	Shirley Bassey	Columbia	8		
10	-	Venus In Blue Jeans	Mark Wynter	Pye	9		F
11	2	I Remember You	Frank Ifield	Columbia	19	(5)	F G
12	11	Don't That Beat All	Adam Faith	Parlophone	8		
13	-	Let's Dance	Chris Montez	London American	13	(4)	F
14	-	Sherry	Four Seasons	Stateside	10	(1)	F
15	-	Lonely	Acker Bilk	Columbia	5		
16	3	Roses Are Red	Ronnie Carroll	Philips	11		
17	-	Swiss Maid	Del Shannon	London American	12	(64)	
18	-	Lovesick Blues	Frank Ifield	Columbia	14	(44)	
19	5	Things	Bobby Darin	London American	12	(3)	
20	-	It Started All Over Again	Brenda Lee	Brunswick	3	(29)	

November 1962

This Mnth	Prev Mnth	Title	Artist	Label	Wks 20	(US Pos)	
1	18	Lovesick Blues	Frank Ifield	Columbia	14	(44)	
2	13	Let's Dance	Chris Montez	London American	13	(4)	F
3	1	Telstar	Tornados	Decca	19	(1)	F
4	17	Swiss Maid	Del Shannon	London American	12	(64)	
5	10	Venus In Blue Jeans	Mark Wynter	Pye	9		F
6	3	The Loco-Motion	Little Eva	London American	12	(1)	F
7	-	Bobby's Girl	Susan Maughan	Philips	12		F L
8	14	Sherry	Four Seasons	Stateside	10	(1)	F
9	-	Devil Woman	Marty Robbins	CBS	10	(16)	L
10	6	Ramblin' Rose	Nat 'King' Cole	Capitol	10	(2)	
11	-	No One Can Make My Sunshine Smile	Everly Brothers	Warner	7		
12	4	It Might As Well Rain Until September	Carole King	London American	9	(22)	F
13	2	Sheila	Tommy Roe	HMV	11	(1)	F
14	-	Dance With The Guitar Man	Duane Eddy	RCA	11	(12)	
15	-	Sun Arise	Rolf Harris	Columbia	11	(61)	
16	-	Oh Lonesome Me	Craig Douglas	Decca	4		L
17	9	What Now My Love	Shirley Bassey	Columbia	8		
18	-	Return To Sender	Elvis Presley	RCA	11	(2)	
19	-	A Forever Kind Of Love	Bobby Vee	Liberty	5		
20	-	Kid Galahad E.P.	Elvis Presley	RCA	3		

December 1962

This Mnth	Prev Mnth	Title	Artist	Label	Wks 20	(US Pos)	
1	18	Return To Sender	Elvis Presley	RCA	11	(2)	
2	1	Lovesick Blues	Frank Ifield	Columbia	14	(44)	
3	15	Sun Arise	Rolf Harris	Columbia	11	(61)	
4	-	The Next Time	Cliff Richard	Columbia	12		
5	14	Dance With The Guitar Man	Duane Eddy	RCA	11	(12)	
6	2	Let's Dance	Chris Montez	London American	13	(4)	F
7	7	Bobby's Girl	Susan Maughan	Philips	12		F L
8	4	Swiss Maid	Del Shannon	London American	12	(64)	
9	-	Rockin' Around The Christmas Tree	Brenda Lee	Brunswick	4	(14)	
10	3	Telstar	Tornados	Decca	19	(1)	F
11	-	Dance On	Shadows	Columbia	10		
12	-	Bachelor Boy	Cliff Richard	Columbia	12	(99)	
13	-	It Only Took A Minute	Joe Brown & The Bruvvers	Piccadilly	8		
14	9	Devil Woman	Marty Robbins	CBS	10	(16)	L
15	-	The Main Attraction	Pat Boone	London American	5		L
16	8	Sherry	Four Seasons	Stateside	10	(1)	F
17	-	Your Cheatin' Heart	Ray Charles	HMV	4	(29)	
18	-	Up On The Roof	Kenny Lynch	HMV	7		F
19	5	Venus In Blue Jeans	Mark Wynter	Pye	9		F
20	19	A Forever Kind Of Love	Bobby Vee	Liberty	5		

October 1962

This Mnth	Prev Mnth	Title	Artist	Label	Wks 20	(UK Pos)	
1	17	Monster Mash	Bobby 'Boris' Pickett & The Crypt Kickers	Garpax	9	(3)	F G L
2	4	Sherry	Four Seasons	Vee Jay	10	(7)	F G
3	2	Ramblin' Rose	Nat 'King' Cole	Capitol	10	(4)	G
4	10	Patches	Dickey Lee	Smash	9		F
5	-	Do You Love Me	Contours	Gordy	8		F G
6	-	I Remember You	Frank Ifield	Vee Jay	5	(1)	F L
7	12	Let's Dance	Chris Montez	Monogram	7	(2)	F G
8	7	Green Onions	Booker T. & The M.G.'s	Stax	8	(7)	F G
9	-	He's A Rebel	Crystals	UA	10	(19)	G
10	-	Only Love Can Break A Heart	Gene Pitney	Musicor	8		G
11	-	Venus In Blue Jeans	Jimmy Clanton	Ace	7		L
12	-	If I Had A Hammer	Peter, Paul & Mary	Warner	5		F
13	-	All Alone Am I	Brenda Lee	Decca	9	(11)	G
14	14	You Beat Me To The Punch	Mary Wells	Motown	5		
15	-	Surfin' Safari	Beach Boys	Capitol	3		F
16	1	Sheila	Tommy Roe	ABC Paramount	9	(2)	F G
17	-	Popeye (The Hitchhiker)	Chubby Checker	Parkway	5		
18	-	Gina	Johnny Mathis	Columbia	7		
19	-	Rain Rain Go Away	Bobby Vinton	Epic	4		
20	15	Alley Cat	Bent Fabric	Atco	5		F G L

November 1962

This Mnth	Prev Mnth	Title	Artist	Label	Wks 20	(UK Pos)	
1	-	Big Girls Don't Cry	Four Seasons	Vee Jay	13	(14)	G
2	9	He's A Rebel	Crystals	UA	10	(19)	G
3	13	All Alone Am I	Brenda Lee	Decca	9	(11)	G
4	-	Return To Sender	Elvis Presley	RCA	12	(1)	G
5	-	Next Door To An Angel	Neil Sedaka	RCA	6	(24)	
6	18	Gina	Johnny Mathis	Columbia	7		
7	10	Only Love Can Break A Heart	Gene Pitney	Musicor	8		G
8	-	Limbo Rock	Chubby Checker	Parkway	14	(29)	G
9	1	Monster Mash	Bobby 'Boris' Pickett & The Crypt Kickers	Garpax	9	(3)	F G L
10	5	Do You Love Me	Contours	Gordy	8		F G
11	-	Bobby's Girl	Marcie Blane	Seville	11		F G L
12	-	The Cha Cha Cha	Bobby Rydell	Cameo	6		
13	-	Don't Hang Up	Orlons	Cameo	8		
14	-	Close To Cathy	Mike Clifford	UA	5		F L
15	-	Nothing Can Change This Love	Sam Cooke	RCA	3		
16	17	Popeye (The Hitchhiker)	Chubby Checker	Parkway	5		
17	-	Ride	Dee Dee Sharp	Cameo	6		
18	2	Sherry	Four Seasons	Vee Jay	10	(7)	F G
19	-	The Lonely Bull	Herb Alpert	A&M	9		F
20	-	James (Hold The Ladder Steady)	Sue Thompson	Hickory	3		L

December 1962

This Mnth	Prev Mnth	Title	Artist	Label	Wks 20	(UK Pos)	
1	1	Big Girls Don't Cry	Four Seasons	Vee Jay	13	(14)	G
2	4	Return To Sender	Elvis Presley	RCA	12	(1)	G
3	11	Bobby's Girl	Marcie Blane	Seville	11		F G L
4	8	Limbo Rock	Chubby Checker	Parkway	14	(29)	G
5	-	Telstar	Tornados	London	11	(1)	F G L
6	13	Don't Hang Up	Orlons	Cameo	8		
7	19	The Lonely Bull	Herb Alpert	A&M	9		F
8	-	Release Me	Little Esther Phillips	Lenox	7		F
9	17	Ride	Dee Dee Sharp	Cameo	6		
10	-	Go Away Little Girl	Steve Lawrence	Columbia	12		G L
11	-	You Are My Sunshine	Ray Charles	ABC Paramount	5		
12	-	Keep Your Hands Off My Baby	Little Eva	Dimension	6		
13	3	All Alone Am I	Brenda Lee	Decca	9	(11)	G
14	-	Love Came To Me	Dion	Laurie	4		
15	2	He's A Rebel	Crystals	UA	10	(19)	G
16	-	Hotel Happiness	Brook Benton	Mercury	7		
17	-	Rumors	Johnny Crawford	Del-Fi	4		L
18	-	Dear Lonely Hearts	Nat 'King' Cole	Capitol	4		
19	-	Zip-A-Dee Doo-Dah	Bob B. Soxx & The Blue Jeans	Philles	6		F L
20	-	(Dance With The) Guitar Man	Duane Eddy	RCA	3	(4)	L

◆ Bobby 'Boris' Pickett's debut hit 'Monster Mash' was to reappear in the Top 20 eleven years later, and similarly the million selling 'Do You Love Me' by newcomers The Contours returned to the US Top 20 in 1988!

◆ The fastest selling LP of the time was President Kennedy impersonator Vaughn Meader's **The First Family**. The album broke existing records by selling over three million copies in its first month – not surprisingly it went on to earn a handful of Grammy awards.

◆ Notable chart newcomers included Peter, Paul & Mary (whose eponymous debut album hit No. 1), the Beach Boys and Herb Alpert, whose 'The Lonely Bull' was recorded in his garage at a cost of $65.

◆ "Hot Country Singles" was the new name of the C&W chart in *Billboard*.

UK 1963 JAN-MAR

The Beatles' second single 'Please Please Me' topped the chart. It put Merseybeat on the musical map and launched the Beat Boom. In America it was rush released but failed to click.

◆ Rock instrumentals reached new heights in February when records by (ex-Shadows) Jet Harris & Tony Meehan, The Tornados and The Shadows took the top three spots.

◆ The Scopitone video juke box was launched – it cost 5p a play to see acts like Craig Douglas and The Mudlarks – it proved to be a five minute wonder.

◆ Word came from Australia that The Bee Gees, an Everly Brothers influenced act, who originally hailed from Manchester, had signed with Festival Records. After making a name for themselves down under they became international superstars later on in the decade.

January 1963

This Mnth	Prev Mnth	Title	Artist	Label	Wks 20	(US Pos)	
1	11	Dance On	Shadows	Columbia	10		
2	1	Return To Sender	Elvis Presley	RCA	11	(2)	
3	4	The Next Time	Cliff Richard	Columbia	12		
4	12	Bachelor Boy	Cliff Richard	Columbia	12	(99)	
5	5	Dance With The Guitar Man	Duane Eddy	RCA	11	(12)	
6	-	Like I Do	Maureen Evans	Oriole	9		F L
7	3	Sun Arise	Rolf Harris	Columbia	11	(61)	
8	2	Lovesick Blues	Frank Ifield	Columbia	14	(44)	
9	-	Globetrotter	Tornados	Decca	8		
10	-	Diamonds	Jet Harris & Tony Meehan	Decca	10		F
11	-	Go Away Little Girl	Mark Wynter	Pye	7		
12	18	Up On The Roof	Kenny Lynch	HMV	7		F
13	10	Telstar	Tornados	Decca	19	(1)	F
14	-	Coming Home Baby	Mel Tormé	London American	4	(36)	L
15	13	It Only Took A Minute	Joe Brown & The Bruvvers	Piccadilly	8		
16	7	Bobby's Girl	Susan Maughan	Philips	12		F L
17	-	Don't You Think It's Time	Mike Berry	HMV	7		F
18	6	Let's Dance	Chris Montez	London American	13	(4)	F
19	-	Little Town Flirt	Del Shannon	London American	8	(12)	
20	-	Desafinado	Stan Getz & Charlie Byrd	HMV	5	(15)	F L

February 1963

This Mnth	Prev Mnth	Title	Artist	Label	Wks 20	(US Pos)	
1	10	Diamonds	Jet Harris & Tony Meehan	Decca	10		F
2	-	Wayward Wind	Frank Ifield	Columbia	10		
3	19	Little Town Flirt	Del Shannon	London American	8	(12)	
4	-	Please Please Me	Beatles	Parlophone	10	(3)	F
5	9	Globetrotter	Tornados	Decca	8		
6	4	Bachelor Boy	Cliff Richard	Columbia	12	(99)	
7	-	Loop De Loop	Frankie Vaughan	Philips	8		
8	17	Don't You Think It's Time	Mike Berry	HMV	7		F
9	-	The Night Has A Thousand Eyes	Bobby Vee	Liberty	8	(3)	L
10	-	All Alone Am I	Brenda Lee	Brunswick	7	(3)	
11	-	Island Of Dreams	Springfields	Philips	12		F
12	6	Like I Do	Maureen Evans	Oriole	9		F L
13	1	Dance On	Shadows	Columbia	10		
14	3	The Next Time	Cliff Richard	Columbia	12		
15	-	Sukiyaki	Kenny Ball	Pye Jazz	5		
16	-	Walk Right In	Rooftop Singers	Fontana	5	(1)	F L
17	-	That's What Love Will Do	Joe Brown & The Bruvvers	Piccadilly	9		L
18	-	Big Girls Don't Cry	Four Seasons	Stateside	5	(1)	
19	2	Return To Sender	Elvis Presley	RCA	11	(2)	
20	-	Summer Holiday	Cliff Richard	Columbia	11		

March 1963

This Mnth	Prev Mnth	Title	Artist	Label	Wks 20	(US Pos)	
1	20	Summer Holiday	Cliff Richard	Columbia	11		
2	4	Please Please Me	Beatles	Parlophone	10	(3)	F
3	-	Like I've Never Been Gone	Billy Fury	Decca	10		
4	17	That's What Love Will Do	Joe Brown & The Bruvvers	Piccadilly	9		L
5	9	The Night Has A Thousand Eyes	Bobby Vee	Liberty	8	(3)	L
6	-	Foot Tapper	Shadows	Columbia	9		
7	11	Island Of Dreams	Springfields	Philips	12		F
8	2	Wayward Wind	Frank Ifield	Columbia	10		
9	-	Charmaine	Bachelors	Decca	9		F
10	-	One Broken Heart For Sale	Elvis Presley	RCA	5	(11)	
11	7	Loop De Loop	Frankie Vaughan	Philips	8		
12	-	Hey Paula	Paul & Paula	Philips	7	(1)	F
13	-	From A Jack To A King	Ned Miller	London American	12	(6)	F L
14	-	Tell Him	Billie Davis	Decca	5		F L
15	1	Diamonds	Jet Harris & Tony Meehan	Decca	10		F
16	-	Say Wonderful Things	Ronnie Carroll	Philips	8	(91)	L
17	-	Rhythm Of The Rain	Cascades	Warner	10	(3)	F L
18	-	How Do You Do It?	Gerry & The Pacemakers	Columbia	11	(9)	F
19	-	Brown Eyed Handsome Man	Buddy Holly	Coral	10		
20	16	Walk Right In	Rooftop Singers	Fontana	5	(1)	F L

January 1963

This Mnth	Prev Mnth	Title	Artist	Label	Wks 20	(UK Pos)	
1	10	Go Away Little Girl	Steve Lawrence	Columbia	12		G L
2	5	Telstar	Tornados	London	11	(1)	F G L
3	4	Limbo Rock	Chubby Checker	Parkway	14	(29)	G
4	-	Tell Him	Exciters	UA	7		F L
5	16	Hotel Happiness	Brook Benton	Mercury	7		
6	-	The Night Has A Thousand Eyes	Bobby Vee	Liberty	8	(3)	G
7	-	My Dad	Paul Peterson	Colpix	7		L
8	-	Pepino The Italian Mouse	Lou Monte	Reprise	5		L
9	-	Two Lovers	Mary Wells	Motown	7		
10	19	Zip-A-Dee Doo-Dah	Bob B. Soxx & The Blue Jeans	Philles	6		F L
11	-	Walk Right In	Rooftop Singers	Vanguard	9	(11)	F G
12	-	Hey Paula	Paul & Paula	Philips	10	(11)	F G
13	1	Big Girls Don't Cry	Four Seasons	Vee Jay	13	(14)	G
14	-	It's Up To You	Rick Nelson	Imperial	6	(25)	
15	3	Bobby's Girl	Marcie Blane	Seville	11		F G L
16	-	Up On The Roof	Drifters	Atlantic	7	(29)	
17	2	Return To Sender	Elvis Presley	RCA	12	(1)	G
18	-	I Saw Linda Yesterday	Dickey Lee	Smash	5		
19	11	You Are My Sunshine	Ray Charles	ABC Paramount	5		
20	-	Loop De Loop	Johnny Thunder	Diamond	7		F L

February 1963

This Mnth	Prev Mnth	Title	Artist	Label	Wks 20	(UK Pos)	
1	12	Hey Paula	Paul & Paula	Philips	10	(11)	F G
2	11	Walk Right In	Rooftop Singers	Vanguard	9	(11)	F G
3	-	Ruby Baby	Dion	Columbia	8		
4	-	Walk Like A Man	Four Seasons	Vee Jay	9	(12)	G
5	6	The Night Has A Thousand Eyes	Bobby Vee	Liberty	8	(3)	G
6	-	You've Really Got A Hold On Me	Miracles	Tamla	7		
7	20	Loop De Loop	Johnny Thunder	Diamond	7		F L
8	-	Rhythm Of The Rain	Cascades	Valiant	11	(4)	F G L
9	-	From A Jack To A King	Ned Miller	Fabor	6	(2)	F L
10	16	Up On The Roof	Drifters	Atlantic	7	(29)	
11	1	Go Away Little Girl	Steve Lawrence	Columbia	12		G L
12	-	He's Sure The Boy I Love	Crystals	Philles	4		
13	-	You're The Reason I'm Living	Bobby Darin	Capitol	10		
14	14	It's Up To You	Rick Nelson	Imperial	6	(25)	
15	4	Tell Him	Exciters	UA	7		F L
16	-	Half Heaven-Half Heartache	Gene Pitney	Musicor	6		
17	9	Two Lovers	Mary Wells	Motown	7		
18	-	Wild Weekend	Rebels	Swan	6		F L
19	-	Little Town Flirt	Del Shannon	Big Top	3	(4)	
20	-	Blame It On The Bossa Nova	Eydie Gormé	Columbia	8		F L

March 1963

This Mnth	Prev Mnth	Title	Artist	Label	Wks 20	(UK Pos)	
1	4	Walk Like A Man	Four Seasons	Vee Jay	9	(12)	G
2	-	Our Day Will Come	Ruby & The Romantics	Kapp	8	(26)	F G
3	13	You're The Reason I'm Living	Bobby Darin	Capitol	10		
4	8	Rhythm Of The Rain	Cascades	Valiant	11	(4)	F G L
5	-	The End Of The World	Skeeter Davis	RCA	9	(20)	F G
6	3	Ruby Baby	Dion	Columbia	8		
7	20	Blame It On The Bossa Nova	Eydie Gormé	Columbia	8		F L
8	1	Hey Paula	Paul & Paula	Philips	10	(11)	F G
9	-	What Will My Mary Say	Johnny Mathis	Columbia	7		
10	-	He's So Fine	Chiffons	Laurie	11	(11)	F G
11	-	In Dreams	Roy Orbison	Monument	8	(5)	
12	18	Wild Weekend	Rebels	Swan	6		F L
13	-	South Street	Orlons	Cameo	7		G
14	-	One Broken Heart For Sale	Elvis Presley	RCA	5	(8)	
15	-	Our Winter Love	Bill Pursell	Columbia	6		F L
16	2	Walk Right In	Rooftop Singers	Vanguard	9	(11)	F G
17	-	Mama Didn't Lie	Jan Bradley	Chess	6		F L
18	9	From A Jack To A King	Ned Miller	Fabor	6	(2)	F L
19	-	Send Me Some Lovin'	Sam Cooke	RCA	5		
20	-	Baby Workout	Jackie Wilson	Brunswick	7		

▲ Plane crash victim Patsy Cline's funeral was attended by 25,000 people. Over 30 years later her albums still sold in enormous quantities on both sides of the Atlantic.

◆ Elvis Presley re-signed with RCA Records; the ten year deal guaranteed him $1 million. Both his current hits, 'Return To Sender' and 'One Broken Heart For Sale', were penned by noted R&B writers Otis Blackwell and Winifred Scott.

◆ In March, the Top 4 US albums were all by humorists: Alan Sherman (two entries), Frank Fontaine and Vaughn Meader.

UK 1963 APR-JUNE

◆ The Beatles' manager Brian Epstein also looked after Billy J. Kramer & The Dakotas who had two successive No. 1s and Gerry & The Pacemakers who achieved three.

◆ Early examples of R&B covers in the "Beat Boom" included Freddie & The Dreamers' 'If You Gotta Make a Fool Of Somebody' and The Rolling Stones' version of Chuck Berry's 'Come On'. The late Buddy Holly hit the Top 5 with revivals of Chuck's 'Brown Eyed Handsome Man' and Bo Diddley's eponymous song, while in America The Beach Boys turned Berry's 'Sweet Little 16' into 'Surfin' USA' and Lonnie Mack charted with Chuck's 'Memphis'.

◆ Ned Miller's 'From A Jack To A King', which was now a big hit with dealers, had been lost in the shuffle when originally released in 1957.

April 1963

This Mnth	Prev Mnth	Title	Artist	Label	Wks 20	(US Pos)	
1	18	How Do You Do It?	Gerry & The Pacemakers	Columbia	11	(9)	F
2	13	From A Jack To A King	Ned Miller	London American	12	(6)	F L
3	6	Foot Tapper	Shadows	Columbia	9		
4	19	Brown Eyed Handsome Man	Buddy Holly	Coral	10		
5	17	Rhythm Of The Rain	Cascades	Warner	10	(3)	F L
6	-	Say I Won't Be There	Springfields	Philips	8		L
7	16	Say Wonderful Things	Ronnie Carroll	Philips	8	(91)	L
8	1	Summer Holiday	Cliff Richard	Columbia	11		
9	-	The Folk Singer	Tommy Roe	HMV	7	(84)	
10	-	Nobody's Darlin' But Mine	Frank Ifield	Columbia	8		
11	-	From Me To You	Beatles	Parlophone	15	(41)	
12	3	Like I've Never Been Gone	Billy Fury	Decca	10		
13	-	In Dreams	Roy Orbison	London American	13	(7)	
14	9	Charmaine	Bachelors	Decca	9		F
15	-	Walk Like A Man	Four Seasons	Stateside	6	(1)	
16	-	Can't Get Used To Losing You	Andy Williams	CBS	10	(2)	
17	7	Island Of Dreams	Springfields	Philips	12		F
18	-	Robot	Tornados	Decca	5		
19	4	That's What Love Will Do	Joe Brown & The Bruvvers	Piccadilly	9		L
20	-	Let's Turkey Trot	Little Eva	London American	6	(20)	

May 1963

This Mnth	Prev Mnth	Title	Artist	Label	Wks 20	(US Pos)	
1	11	From Me To You	Beatles	Parlophone	15	(41)	
2	-	Scarlett O'Hara	Jet Harris & Tony Meehan	Decca	11		
3	16	Can't Get Used To Losing You	Andy Williams	CBS	10	(2)	
4	1	How Do You Do It?	Gerry & The Pacemakers	Columbia	11	(9)	F
5	13	In Dreams	Roy Orbison	London American	13	(7)	
6	10	Nobody's Darlin' But Mine	Frank Ifield	Columbia	8		
7	-	Do You Want To Know A Secret	Billy J. Kramer & The Dakotas	Parlophone	10		F
8	-	Two Kinds Of Teardrops	Del Shannon	London American	8	(50)	
9	-	Lucky Lips	Cliff Richard	Columbia	9	(62)	
10	2	From A Jack To A King	Ned Miller	London American	12	(6)	F L
11	-	Losing You	Brenda Lee	Brunswick	9	(6)	
12	6	Say I Won't Be There	Springfields	Philips	8		L
13	-	He's So Fine	Chiffons	Stateside	5	(1)	F
14	-	Deck Of Cards	Wink Martindale	London American	15		L
15	-	When Will You Say I Love You	Billy Fury	Decca	7		
16	-	Young Lovers	Paul & Paula	Philips	6	(6)	L
17	5	Rhythm Of The Rain	Cascades	Warner	10	(3)	F L
18	-	Take These Chains From My Heart	Ray Charles	HMV	13	(8)	
19	4	Brown Eyed Handsome Man	Buddy Holly	Coral	10		
20	9	The Folk Singer	Tommy Roe	HMV	7	(84)	

June 1963

This Mnth	Prev Mnth	Title	Artist	Label	Wks 20	(US Pos)	
1	-	I Like It	Gerry & The Pacemakers	Columbia	12	(17)	
2	7	Do You Want To Know A Secret	Billy J. Kramer & The Dakotas	Parlophone	10		F
3	1	From Me To You	Beatles	Parlophone	15	(41)	
4	18	Take These Chains From My Heart	Ray Charles	HMV	13	(8)	
5	-	If You Gotta Make A Fool Of Somebody	Freddie & The Dreamers	Columbia	9		F
6	-	Atlantis	Shadows	Columbia	11		
7	15	When Will You Say I Love You	Billy Fury	Decca	7		
8	14	Deck Of Cards	Wink Martindale	London American	15		L
9	2	Scarlett O'Hara	Jet Harris & Tony Meehan	Decca	11		
10	9	Lucky Lips	Cliff Richard	Columbia	9	(62)	
11	-	Falling	Roy Orbison	London American	8	(22)	
12	5	In Dreams	Roy Orbison	London American	13	(7)	
13	-	Bo Diddley	Buddy Holly	Coral	8		
14	8	Two Kinds Of Teardrops	Del Shannon	London American	8	(50)	
15	16	Young Lovers	Paul & Paula	Philips	6	(6)	L
16	-	Da Doo Ron Ron	Crystals	London American	10	(3)	
17	-	The Ice Cream Man	Tornados	Decca	4		L
18	-	It's My Party	Lesley Gore	Mercury	8	(1)	F
19	-	Forget Him	Bobby Rydell	Cameo Parkway	9	(4)	L
20	-	Confessin'	Frank Ifield	Columbia	11	(58)	

April 1963

This Mnth	Prev Mnth	Title	Artist	Label	Wks 20	(UK Pos)	
1	10	He's So Fine	Chiffons	Laurie	11	(11)	F G
2	-	Can't Get Used To Losing You	Andy Williams	Columbia	9	(3)	G
3	20	Baby Workout	Jackie Wilson	Brunswick	7		
4	13	South Street	Orlons	Cameo	7		G
5	-	Puff The Magic Dragon	Peter, Paul & Mary	Warner	10		G
6	-	I Will Follow Him	Little Peggy March	RCA	9		F G L
7	5	The End Of The World	Skeeter Davis	RCA	9	(20)	F G
8	-	Young Lovers	Paul & Paula	Philips	5	(12)	L
9	2	Our Day Will Come	Ruby & The Romantics	Kapp	8	(26)	F G
10	-	Pipeline	Chantays	Dot	8	(16)	F L
11	-	Don't Say Nothin' (Bad About My Baby)	Cookies	Dimension	5		L
12	-	Do The Bird	Dee Dee Sharp	Cameo	5		L
13	11	In Dreams	Roy Orbison	Monument	8	(5)	
14	-	On Broadway	Drifters	Atlantic	4		
15	4	Rhythm Of The Rain	Cascades	Valiant	11	(4)	F G L
16	-	Watermelon Man	Mongo Santamaria	Battle	4		F L
17	3	You're The Reason I'm Living	Bobby Darin	Capitol	10		
18	15	Our Winter Love	Bill Pursell	Columbia	6		F L
19	-	Mecca	Gene Pitney	Musicor	5		
20	-	Surfin' U.S.A.	Beach Boys	Capitol	10	(28)	G

May 1963

This Mnth	Prev Mnth	Title	Artist	Label	Wks 20	(UK Pos)	
1	6	I Will Follow Him	Little Peggy March	RCA	9		F G L
2	-	If You Wanna Be Happy	Jimmy Soul	SPQR	9		F G L
3	5	Puff The Magic Dragon	Peter, Paul & Mary	Warner	10		G
4	20	Surfin' U.S.A.	Beach Boys	Capitol	10	(28)	G
5	-	Foolish Little Girl	Shirelles	Scepter	7		L
6	10	Pipeline	Chantays	Dot	8	(16)	F L
7	2	Can't Get Used To Losing You	Andy Williams	Columbia	9	(3)	G
8	-	Losing You	Brenda Lee	Decca	7	(12)	
9	-	Reverend Mr. Black	Kingston Trio	Capitol	6		L
10	1	He's So Fine	Chiffons	Laurie	11	(11)	F G
11	-	Take These Chains From My Heart	Ray Charles	ABC Paramount	6	(4)	
12	-	Two Faces Have I	Lou Christie	Roulette	7		F
13	-	I Love You Because	Al Martino	Capitol	7		F
14	19	Mecca	Gene Pitney	Musicor	5		
15	14	On Broadway	Drifters	Atlantic	4		
16	11	Don't Say Nothin' (Bad About My Baby)	Cookies	Dimension	5		L
17	-	Hot Pastrami	Dartells	Dot	6		F L
18	-	Another Saturday Night	Sam Cooke	RCA	5	(25)	
19	3	Baby Workout	Jackie Wilson	Brunswick	7		
20	-	Charms	Bobby Vee	Liberty	4		

June 1963

This Mnth	Prev Mnth	Title	Artist	Label	Wks 20	(UK Pos)	
1	-	It's My Party	Lesley Gore	Mercury	9	(9)	F G
2	-	Sukiyaki	Kyu Sakamoto	Capitol	11	(8)	F G L
3	-	You Can't Sit Down	Dovells	Parkway	9		L
4	-	Da Doo Ron Ron	Crystals	Philles	8	(4)	G
5	13	I Love You Because	Al Martino	Capitol	7		F
6	-	Those Lazy-Hazy-Crazy Days Of Summer	Nat 'King' Cole	Capitol	7		
7	-	Hello Stranger	Barbara Lewis	Atlantic	7		F
8	-	Blue On Blue	Bobby Vinton	Epic	8		
9	-	Still	Bill Anderson	Decca	7		F L
10	2	If You Wanna Be Happy	Jimmy Soul	SPQR	9		F G L
11	12	Two Faces Have I	Lou Christie	Roulette	7		F
12	4	Surfin' U.S.A.	Beach Boys	Capitol	10	(28)	G
13	-	18 Yellow Roses	Bobby Darin	Capitol	4		
14	-	One Fine Day	Chiffons	Laurie	6		
15	8	Losing You	Brenda Lee	Decca	7	(12)	
16	-	Birdland	Chubby Checker	Parkway	3		
17	-	Easier Said Than Done	Essex	Roulette	9		F G
18	18	Another Saturday Night	Sam Cooke	RCA	5	(25)	
19	1	I Will Follow Him	Little Peggy March	RCA	9		F G L
20	17	Hot Pastrami	Dartells	Dot	6		F L

▲ Del Shannon charted with a cover of The Beatles' UK No. 1, 'From Me To You', and Bobby Rydell's (above) last major hit, 'Forget Him', was produced in Britain by its composer Tony Hatch.

◆ Roy Orbison returned home raving about The Beatles and Gerry & The Pacemakers who had supported him on his UK tour.

◆ Fifteen-year-old Little Peggy March topped the US chart with 'I Will Follow Him' and 17-year-old Lesley Gore had a No. 1 with the Quincy Jones-produced 'It's My Party'.

UK 1963 JULY-SEPT

▲ The Beatles' debut LP **Please Please Me** topped the chart for 30 weeks and the single 'She Loves You', which had record advance orders and sold over a million in the UK, cemented their position as Britain's top group.

◆ *Ready Steady Go* was launched – it was the British pop TV show which best reflected the times. Early guests included the Rolling Stones.

◆ Eric Clapton and Tom McGuinness (later of Manfred Mann) joined Casey Jones & The Engineers, and John Mayall launched The Bluesbreakers which included John McVie (later a founder of Fleetwood Mac.)

July 1963

This Mnth	Prev Mnth	Title	Artist	Label	Wks 20	(US Pos)	
1	20	Confessin'	Frank Ifield	Columbia	11	(58)	
2	1	I Like It	Gerry & The Pacemakers	Columbia	12	(17)	
3	6	Atlantis	Shadows	Columbia	11		
4	-	Devil In Disguise	Elvis Presley	RCA	8	(3)	
5	16	Da Doo Ron Ron	Crystals	London American	10	(3)	
6	4	Take These Chains From My Heart	Ray Charles	HMV	13	(8)	
7	-	Sweets For My Sweet	Searchers	Pye	10		F
8	8	Deck Of Cards	Wink Martindale	London American	15		L
9	-	Welcome To My World	Jim Reeves	RCA	9		
10	18	It's My Party	Lesley Gore	Mercury	8	(1)	F
11	-	Twist And Shout	Brian Poole & The Tremeloes	Decca	9		F
12	13	Bo Diddley	Buddy Holly	Coral	8		
13	5	If You Gotta Make A Fool Of Somebody	Freddie & The Dreamers	Columbia	9		F
14	3	From Me To You	Beatles	Parlophone	15	(41)	
15	11	Falling	Roy Orbison	London American	8	(22)	
16	-	Twist And Shout E.P.	Beatles	Parlophone	15	(2)	
17	-	Sukiyaki	Kyu Sakamoto	HMV	9	(1)	F L
18	2	Do You Want To Know A Secret	Billy J. Kramer & The Dakotas	Parlophone	10		F
19	19	Forget Him	Bobby Rydell	Cameo Parkway	9	(4)	L
20	-	You Can Never Stop Me Loving You	Kenny Lynch	HMV	6		L

August 1963

This Mnth	Prev Mnth	Title	Artist	Label	Wks 20	(US Pos)	
1	7	Sweets For My Sweet	Searchers	Pye	10		F
2	1	Confessin'	Frank Ifield	Columbia	11	(58)	
3	16	Twist And Shout E.P.	Beatles	Parlophone	15	(2)	
4	-	Bad To Me	Billy J. Kramer & The Dakotas	Parlophone	10	(9)	
5	11	Twist And Shout	Brian Poole & The Tremeloes	Decca	9		F
6	-	In Summer	Billy Fury	Decca	8		
7	4	Devil In Disguise	Elvis Presley	RCA	8	(3)	
8	-	Wipe Out	Surfaris	London American	8	(2)	F L
9	-	I'm Telling You Now	Freddie & The Dreamers	Columbia	7	(1)	
10	-	Theme From 'The Legion's Last Patrol'	Ken Thorne & His Orchestra	HMV	10		F L
11	5	Da Doo Ron Ron	Crystals	London American	10	(3)	
12	17	Sukiyaki	Kyu Sakamoto	HMV	9	(1)	F L
13	-	I'll Never Get Over You	Johnny Kidd & The Pirates	HMV	10		L
14	-	It's All In The Game	Cliff Richard	Columbia	9	(25)	
15	3	Atlantis	Shadows	Columbia	11		
16	-	You Don't Have To Be A Baby To Cry	Caravelles	Decca	7	(3)	F L
17	2	I Like It	Gerry & The Pacemakers	Columbia	12	(17)	
18	-	She Loves You	Beatles	Parlophone	24	(1)	G
19	6	Take These Chains From My Heart	Ray Charles	HMV	13	(8)	
20	20	You Can Never Stop Me Loving You	Kenny Lynch	HMV	6		L

September 1963

This Mnth	Prev Mnth	Title	Artist	Label	Wks 20	(US Pos)	
1	18	She Loves You	Beatles	Parlophone	24	(1)	G
2	14	It's All In The Game	Cliff Richard	Columbia	9	(25)	
3	4	Bad To Me	Billy J. Kramer & The Dakotas	Parlophone	10	(9)	
4	-	I Want To Stay Here	Steve Lawrence & Eydie Gormé	CBS	8	(28)	L
5	13	I'll Never Get Over You	Johnny Kidd & The Pirates	HMV	10		L
6	9	I'm Telling You Now	Freddie & The Dreamers	Columbia	7	(1)	
7	-	Just Like Eddie	Heinz	Decca	10		F
8	16	You Don't Have To Be A Baby To Cry	Caravelles	Decca	7	(3)	F L
9	-	Applejack	Jet Harris & Tony Meehan	Decca	8		L
10	-	Do You Love Me	Brian Poole & The Tremeloes	Decca	11		
11	10	Theme From 'The Legion's Last Patrol'	Ken Thorne & His Orchestra	HMV	10		F L
12	8	Wipe Out	Surfaris	London American	8	(2)	F L
13	-	Then He Kissed Me	Crystals	London American	10	(6)	
14	-	If I Had A Hammer	Trini Lopez	Reprise	10	(3)	F L
15	1	Sweets For My Sweet	Searchers	Pye	10		F
16	-	Still	Karl Denver	Decca	6		L
17	3	Twist And Shout E.P.	Beatles	Parlophone	15	(2)	
18	-	Dance On	Kathy Kirby	Decca	5		F
19	-	Shindig	Shadows	Columbia	7		
20	-	Wishing	Buddy Holly	Coral	5		L

This Mnth	Prev Mnth	Title	Artist	Label	Wks 20	(UK Pos)	
1	17	Easier Said Than Done	Essex	Roulette	9		F G
2	-	Surf City	Jan & Dean	Liberty	10	(24)	G
3	-	So Much In Love	Tymes	Parkway	9	(17)	F G
4	-	Tie Me Kangaroo Down, Sport	Rolf Harris	Epic	7	(7)	F L
5	-	Memphis	Lonnie Mack	Fraternity	8		F L
6	2	Sukiyaki	Kyu Sakamoto	Capitol	11	(8)	F G L
7	-	Fingertips (Pt. 2)	Stevie Wonder	Tamla	10		F G
8	-	Wipe Out	Surfaris	Dot	9	(8)	F G
9	8	Blue On Blue	Bobby Vinton	Epic	8		
10	14	One Fine Day	Chiffons	Laurie	6		
11	7	Hello Stranger	Barbara Lewis	Atlantic	7		F
12	-	Pride And Joy	Marvin Gaye	Tamla	6		F
13	-	(You're The) Devil In Disguise	Elvis Presley	RCA	8	(2)	G
14	1	It's My Party	Lesley Gore	Mercury	9	(9)	F G
15	-	Not Me	Orlons	Cameo	5		
16	-	Blowin' In The Wind	Peter, Paul & Mary	Warner	8	(14)	G
17	-	Just One Look	Doris Troy	Atlantic	6		F L
18	-	On Top Of Spaghetti	Tom Glazer & The Do-Re-Mi Children's Chorus	Kapp	3		F L
19	3	You Can't Sit Down	Dovells	Parkway	9		L
20	6	Those Lazy-Hazy-Crazy Days Of Summer	Nat 'King' Cole	Capitol	7		

1	7	Fingertips (Pt. 2)	Stevie Wonder	Tamla	10		F G
2	16	Blowin' In The Wind	Peter, Paul & Mary	Warner	8	(14)	G
3	-	Judy's Turn To Cry	Lesley Gore	Mercury	7		
4	-	Candy Girl	Four Seasons	Vee Jay	8		
5	13	(You're The) Devil In Disguise	Elvis Presley	RCA	8	(2)	G
6	8	Wipe Out	Surfaris	Dot	9	(8)	F G
7	3	So Much In Love	Tymes	Parkway	9	(17)	F G
8	-	Hello Mudduh, Hello Fadduh	Allan Sherman	Warner	8	(17)	F L
9	-	More	Kai Winding	Verve	6		F L
10	-	My Boyfriend's Back	Angels	Smash	10	(28)	G L
11	2	Surf City	Jan & Dean	Liberty	10	(24)	G
12	1	Easier Said Than Done	Essex	Roulette	9		F G
13	-	Mockingbird	Inez Foxx	Symbol	6		F L
14	-	If I Had A Hammer	Trini Lopez	Reprise	8	(4)	F G
15	-	Denise	Randy & The Rainbows	Rust	5		F L
16	4	Tie Me Kangaroo Down, Sport	Rolf Harris	Epic	7	(7)	F L
17	17	Just One Look	Doris Troy	Atlantic	6		F L
18	5	Memphis	Lonnie Mack	Fraternity	8		F L
19	-	Danke Schoen	Wayne Newton	Capitol	4		F
20	-	Hopeless	Andy Williams	Columbia	4		

1	-	Blue Velvet	Bobby Vinton	Epic	10		G
2	10	My Boyfriend's Back	Angels	Smash	10	(28)	G L
3	14	If I Had A Hammer	Trini Lopez	Reprise	8	(4)	F G
4	-	Heat Wave	Martha & The Vandellas	Gordy	9		F G
5	8	Hello Mudduh, Hello Fadduh	Allan Sherman	Warner	8	(17)	F L
6	-	Then He Kissed Me	Crystals	Philles	8	(2)	L
7	-	Sally, Go 'Round The Roses	Jaynetts	Tuff	7		F L
8	-	Surfer Girl	Beach Boys	Capitol	9		
9	-	The Monkey Time	Major Lance	Okeh	6		F
10	-	Mickey's Monkey	Miracles	Tamla	5		
11	-	Cry Baby	Garnet Mimms & The Enchanters	UA	8		F L
12	13	Mockingbird	Inez Foxx	Symbol	6		F L
13	-	Wonderful! Wonderful!	Tymes	Parkway	5		
14	-	Be My Baby	Ronettes	Philles	9	(3)	F G L
15	-	Hey, Girl	Freddie Scott	Colpix	5		F L
16	4	Candy Girl	Four Seasons	Vee Jay	8		
17	-	A Walkin' Miracle	Essex	Roulette	3		L
18	-	Frankie And Johnny	Sam Cooke	RCA	4	(24)	
19	2	Blowin' In The Wind	Peter, Paul & Mary	Warner	8	(14)	G
20	15	Denise	Randy & The Rainbows	Rust	5		F L

US 1963
JULY-SEPT

◆ Little Stevie Wonder became the first artist to simultaneously top both the single and album chart with 'Fingertips (Pt. 2)' and **The 12 year old Genius** respectively.

◆ Bob Dylan, Joan Baez and Peter, Paul & Mary, who headlined the Newport Folk Festival, joined 200,000 civil rights demonstrators in Washington.

◆ Bobby Vinton's revival of Tony Bennett's 1951 hit 'Blue Velvet', which rocketed to the top in a matter of weeks, took until 1990 to crack the UK Top 10 (following its use in an advert for skin cream).

◆ The Monkey was the biggest of the current dance crazes, with hits coming from Major Lance ('The Monkey Time') and The Miracles ('Mickey's Monkey').

UK 1963 OCT–DEC

◆ As the year ended, The Beatles had five records in the Top 20 singles (including 2 EPs and an album) and the top two albums. The **LP With The Beatles** entered at No. 1 as did 'I Want To Hold Your Hand', which smashed all UK sales records, selling a million copies in three days. A big US launch was planned for early 1964.

◆ For the first time, British acts, The Beatles and Cliff Richard (who had been voted Most Promising Male Singer in the top US teen magazine, *16*), won awards in the World section of the *NME* readers poll.

◆ UK acts scoring with US songs included Brian Poole & The Tremeloes, Gerry & The Pacemakers, Cliff Richard, Shirley Bassey, Kathy Kirby, Mark Wynter, The Hollies, The Searchers ('Ain't Gonna Kiss Ya') and The Beatles ('Twist And Shout').

October 1963

This Mnth	Prev Mnth	Title	Artist	Label	Wks 20	(US Pos)	
1	10	Do You Love Me	Brian Poole & The Tremeloes	Decca	11		
2	13	Then He Kissed Me	Crystals	London American	10	(6)	
3	1	She Loves You	Beatles	Parlophone	24	(1)	G
4	14	If I Had A Hammer	Trini Lopez	Reprise	10	(3)	F L
5	-	Blue Bayou	Roy Orbison	London American	10	(29)	
6	-	The First Time	Adam Faith	Parlophone	8		
7	-	You'll Never Walk Alone	Gerry & The Pacemakers	Columbia	15	(48)	
8	19	Shindig	Shadows	Columbia	7		
9	-	I (Who Have Nothing)	Shirley Bassey	Columbia	9		
10	9	Applejack	Jet Harris & Tony Meehan	Decca	8		L
11	17	Twist And Shout E.P.	Beatles	Parlophone	15	(2)	
12	2	It's All In The Game	Cliff Richard	Columbia	9	(25)	
13	7	Just Like Eddie	Heinz	Decca	10		F
14	-	Hello Little Girl	Fourmost	Parlophone	6		F
15	4	I Want To Stay Here	Steve Lawrence & Eydie Gormé	CBS	8	(28)	L
16	-	Ain't Gonna Kiss Ya (E.P.)	Searchers	Pye	4		
17	-	Searchin'	Hollies	Parlophone	4		F
18	-	Everybody	Tommy Roe	HMV	4	(3)	
19	-	Memphis Tennessee	Chuck Berry	Pye International	7		
20	-	Be My Baby	Ronettes	London American	7	(2)	F

November 1963

This Mnth	Prev Mnth	Title	Artist	Label	Wks 20	(US Pos)	
1	3	She Loves You	Beatles	Parlophone	24	(1)	G
2	7	You'll Never Walk Alone	Gerry & The Pacemakers	Columbia	15	(48)	
3	-	Sugar And Spice	Searchers	Pye	7	(44)	
4	20	Be My Baby	Ronettes	London American	7	(2)	F
5	9	I (Who Have Nothing)	Shirley Bassey	Columbia	9		
6	5	Blue Bayou	Roy Orbison	London American	10	(29)	
7	-	Don't Talk To Him	Cliff Richard	Columbia	10		
8	-	Secret Love	Kathy Kirby	Decca	12		
9	19	Memphis Tennessee	Chuck Berry	Pye International	7		
10	1	Do You Love Me	Brian Poole & The Tremeloes	Decca	11		
11	-	I'll Keep You Satisfied	Billy J. Kramer & The Dakotas	Parlophone	6	(30)	
12	-	You Were Made For Me	Freddie & The Dreamers	Columbia	11	(21)	
13	2	Then He Kissed Me	Crystals	London American	10	(6)	
14	-	Maria Elena	Los Indios Tabajaras	RCA	12	(6)	F L
15	-	Fools Rush In	Rick Nelson	London American	5	(12)	
16	6	The First Time	Adam Faith	Parlophone	8		
17	4	If I Had A Hammer	Trini Lopez	Reprise	10	(3)	F L
18	-	Blowin' In The Wind	Peter, Paul & Mary	Warner	5	(2)	F
19	-	It's Almost Tomorrow	Mark Wynter	Pye	6		L
20	-	I Only Want To Be With You	Dusty Springfield	Philips	14	(12)	F

December 1963

This Mnth	Prev Mnth	Title	Artist	Label	Wks 20	(US Pos)	
1	-	I Want To Hold Your Hand	Beatles	Parlophone	13	(1)	G
2	1	She Loves You	Beatles	Parlophone	24	(1)	G
3	8	Secret Love	Kathy Kirby	Decca	12		
4	-	Glad All Over	Dave Clark Five	Columbia	14	(6)	F
5	12	You Were Made For Me	Freddie & The Dreamers	Columbia	11	(21)	
6	7	Don't Talk To Him	Cliff Richard	Columbia	10		
7	20	I Only Want To Be With You	Dusty Springfield	Philips	14	(12)	F
8	-	Dominique	Singing Nun	Philips	8	(1)	F L
9	14	Maria Elena	Los Indios Tabajaras	RCA	12	(6)	F L
10	-	Twenty Four Hours From Tulsa	Gene Pitney	UA	13	(17)	F
11	11	I'll Keep You Satisfied	Billy J. Kramer & The Dakotas	Parlophone	6	(30)	
12	2	You'll Never Walk Alone	Gerry & The Pacemakers	Columbia	15	(48)	
13	-	Geronimo	Shadows	Columbia	6		
14	-	With The Beatles L.P.	Beatles	Parlophone	5		
15	-	Swinging On A Star	Big Dee Irwin	Colpix	10	(38)	F L
16	-	I Wanna Be Your Man	Rolling Stones	Decca	8		
17	19	It's Almost Tomorrow	Mark Wynter	Pye	6		L
18	-	All I Want For Christmas Is A Beatle	Dora Bryan	Fontana	3		F L
19	4	Be My Baby	Ronettes	London American	7	(2)	F
20	-	Beatles Hits E.P.	Beatles	Parlophone	5		

October 1963

This Mnth	Prev Mnth	Title	Artist	Label	Wks 20	(UK Pos)	
1	-	Sugar Shack	Jimmy Gilmer & The Fireballs	Dot	12		F G
2	14	Be My Baby	Ronettes	Philles	9	(3)	F G L
3	1	Blue Velvet	Bobby Vinton	Epic	10		G
4	-	Busted	Ray Charles	ABC Paramount	7	(20)	
5	11	Cry Baby	Garnet Mimms & The Enchanters	UA	8		F L
6	7	Sally, Go 'Round The Roses	Jaynetts	Tuff	7		F L
7	-	Mean Woman Blues	Roy Orbison	Monument	8	(14)	
8	-	Donna The Prima Donna	Dion	Columbia	7		
9	2	My Boyfriend's Back	Angels	Smash	10	(28)	G L
10	-	Honolulu Lulu	Jan & Dean	Liberty	5		
11	-	Deep Purple	Nino Tempo & April Stevens	Atco	9	(20)	F G
12	-	Don't Think Twice It's All Right	Peter, Paul & Mary	Warner	4		
13	4	Heat Wave	Martha & The Vandelias	Gordy	9		F G
14	-	That Sunday, That Summer	Nat 'King' Cole	Capitol	5		L
15	13	Wonderful! Wonderful!	Tymes	Parkway	5		
16	-	I Can't Stay Mad At You	Skeeter Davis	RCA	6		L
17	6	Then He Kissed Me	Crystals	Philles	8	(2)	L
18	-	Washington Square	Village Stompers	Epic	9		F L
19	-	Talk To Me	Sunny & The Sunglows	Tear Drop	5		F L
20	10	Mickey's Monkey	Miracles	Tamla	5		

November 1963

This Mnth	Prev Mnth	Title	Artist	Label	Wks 20	(UK Pos)	
1	1	Sugar Shack	Jimmy Gilmer & The Fireballs	Dot	12		F G
2	18	Washington Square	Village Stompers	Epic	9		F L
3	11	Deep Purple	Nino Tempo & April Stevens	Atco	9	(20)	F G
4	-	I'm Leaving It Up To You	Dale & Grace	Montel	10		F G
5	-	It's All Right	Impressions	ABC Paramount	8		
6	-	She's A Fool	Lesley Gore	Mercury	9		
7	-	Maria Elena	Los Indios Tabajaras	RCA	6	(7)	F L
8	-	Bossa Nova Baby	Elvis Presley	RCA	4	(11)	
9	-	Everybody	Tommy Roe	ABC Paramount	8	(13)	
10	7	Mean Woman Blues	Roy Orbison	Monument	8	(14)	
11	16	I Can't Stay Mad At You	Skeeter Davis	RCA	6		L
12	-	Dominique	Singing Nun (Soeur Sourire)	Philips	11	(3)	F G L
13	-	Fools Rush In	Rick Nelson	Decca	6	(12)	
14	-	(Down At) Papa Joe's	Dixiebelles	SS7	5		F
15	8	Donna The Prima Donna	Dion	Columbia	7		
16	-	500 Miles Away From Home	Bobby Bare	RCA	4		L
17	-	Walking The Dog	Rufus Thomas	ABC	6		F L
18	4	Busted	Ray Charles	ABC Paramount	7	(20)	
19	-	Hey Little Girl	Major Lance	Okeh	4		
20	-	Little Red Rooster	Sam Cooke	RCA	5		

December 1963

This Mnth	Prev Mnth	Title	Artist	Label	Wks 20	(UK Pos)	
1	12	Dominique	Singing Nun (Soeur Sourire)	Philips	11	(3)	F G L
2	-	Louie Louie	Kingsmen	Wand	9	(26)	F G
3	-	You Don't Have To Be A Baby To Cry	Caravelles	Smash	7	(6)	F L
4	-	Since I Fell For You	Lenny Welch	Cadence	10		F L
5	4	I'm Leaving It Up To You	Dale & Grace	Montel	10		F G
6	-	Be True To Your School	Beach Boys	Capitol	7		
7	9	Everybody	Tommy Roe	ABC Paramount	8	(13)	
8	-	There I've Said It Again	Bobby Vinton	Epic	10		G
9	-	Drip Drop	Dion	Columbia	6		
10	6	She's A Fool	Lesley Gore	Mercury	9		
11	-	Popsicles And Icicles	Murmaids	Chattahoochee	9		F L
12	17	Walking The Dog	Rufus Thomas	ABC	6		F L
13	-	Talk Back Trembling Lips	Johnny Tillotson	MGM	6		L
14	1	Sugar Shack	Jimmy Gilmer & The Fireballs	Dot	12		F G
15	-	Loddy Lo	Chubby Checker	Parkway	4		
16	-	Forget Him	Bobby Rydell	Cameo	8	(15)	L
17	20	Little Red Rooster	Sam Cooke	RCA	5		
18	2	Washington Square	Village Stompers	Epic	9		F L
19	-	Wonderful Summer	Robin Ward	Dot	5		F L
20	-	Quicksand	Martha & The Vandellas	Gordy	4		

US 1963
OCT-DEC

◆ London-based female duo The Caravelles were already in the US Top 20 when The Beatles "officially" started the British invasion of America.

▲ The year when the coffee house folk circuit boomed came to an end with Grammy winners Peter, Paul & Mary (above) holding the top two places on the album chart, and Bob Dylan selling out Carnegie Hall.

◆ Belgian Nun, Soeur Sourire, topped the single and album chart as the country mourned President Kennedy. A budget priced JFK memorial album sold a reported four million copies in six days.

UK 1964 JAN-MAR

◆ *Top Of The Pops* was launched. The TV show based on the Top 20 chart is still running thirty years later. Soon afterwards the first pirate radio station Radio Caroline started broadcasting from a ship in the North Sea.

▲ The Dave Clark Five's (above) 'Bits And Pieces' had 250,000 advance orders and The Beatles 'Can't Buy Me Love' piled up record UK advance orders of over a million.

◆ Blue beat was in with 'Madness' (Prince Buster) and 'Oh Carolina' (Folkes Brothers) selling well. A top 1980s band named themselves after the first track and the latter was a No. 1 in 1993 for Shaggy.

January 1964

This Mnth	Prev Mnth	Title	Artist	Label	Wks 20	(US Pos)	
1	4	Glad All Over	Dave Clark Five	Columbia	14	(6)	F
2	1	I Want To Hold Your Hand	Beatles	Parlophone	13	(1)	G
3	7	I Only Want To Be With You	Dusty Springfield	Philips	14	(12)	F
4	-	Hippy Hippy Shake	Swinging Blue Jeans	HMV	10	(24)	F
5	2	She Loves You	Beatles	Parlophone	24	(1)	G
6	10	Twenty Four Hours From Tulsa	Gene Pitney	UA	13	(17)	F
7	15	Swinging On A Star	Big Dee Irwin	Colpix	10	(38)	F L
8	5	You Were Made For Me	Freddie & The Dreamers	Columbia	11	(21)	
9	8	Dominique	Singing Nun	Philips	8	(1)	F L
10	-	Stay	Hollies	Parlophone	7		
11	3	Secret Love	Kathy Kirby	Decca	12		
12	9	Maria Elena	Los Indios Tabajaras	RCA	12	(6)	F L
13	16	I Wanna Be Your Man	Rolling Stones	Decca	8		
14	-	Kiss Me Quick	Elvis Presley	RCA	6	(34)	
15	-	We Are In Love	Adam Faith	Parlophone	6		
16	6	Don't Talk To Him	Cliff Richard	Columbia	10		
17	-	As Usual	Brenda Lee	Brunswick	10	(12)	
18	-	Needles And Pins	Searchers	Pye	9	(13)	
19	13	Geronimo	Shadows	Columbia	6		
20	-	I'm The One	Gerry & The Pacemakers	Columbia	9	(82)	

February 1964

This Mnth	Prev Mnth	Title	Artist	Label	Wks 20	(US Pos)	
1	18	Needles And Pins	Searchers	Pye	9	(13)	
2	20	I'm The One	Gerry & The Pacemakers	Columbia	9	(82)	
3	4	Hippy Hippy Shake	Swinging Blue Jeans	HMV	10	(24)	F
4	-	Diane	Bachelors	Decca	11	(10)	
5	1	Glad All Over	Dave Clark Five	Columbia	14	(6)	F
6	17	As Usual	Brenda Lee	Brunswick	10	(12)	
7	-	5-4-3-2-1	Manfred Mann	HMV	7		F
8	-	Don't Blame Me	Frank Ifield	Columbia	7		L
9	-	Anyone Who Had A Heart	Cilla Black	Parlophone	11		F
10	-	I Think Of You	Merseybeats	Fontana	11		F
11	6	Twenty Four Hours From Tulsa	Gene Pitney	UA	13	(17)	F
12	2	I Want To Hold Your Hand	Beatles	Parlophone	13	(1)	G
13	-	Baby I Love You	Ronettes	London American	7	(24)	L
14	3	I Only Want To Be With You	Dusty Springfield	Philips	14	(12)	F
15	-	I'm The Lonely One	Cliff Richard	Columbia	4	(92)	
16	10	Stay	Hollies	Parlophone	7		
17	-	Bits And Pieces	Dave Clark Five	Columbia	9	(4)	
18	-	Candy Man	Brian Poole & The Tremeloes	Decca	6		
19	-	For You	Rick Nelson	Brunswick	4	(6)	L
20	7	Swinging On A Star	Big Dee Irwin	Colpix	10	(38)	F L

March 1964

This Mnth	Prev Mnth	Title	Artist	Label	Wks 20	(US Pos)	
1	9	Anyone Who Had A Heart	Cilla Black	Parlophone	11		F
2	17	Bits And Pieces	Dave Clark Five	Columbia	9	(4)	
3	-	Little Children	Billy J. Kramer & The Dakotas	Parlophone	9	(7)	
4	-	Not Fade Away	Rolling Stones	Decca	9	(48)	
5	4	Diane	Bachelors	Decca	11	(10)	
6	-	Just One Look	Hollies	Parlophone	9	(44)	
7	10	I Think Of You	Merseybeats	Fontana	11		F
8	-	Boys Cry	Eden Kane	Fontana	7		L
9	1	Needles And Pins	Searchers	Pye	9	(13)	
10	-	I Love You Because	Jim Reeves	RCA	26		
11	18	Candy Man	Brian Poole & The Tremeloes	Decca	6		
12	-	Let Me Go, Lover	Kathy Kirby	Decca	6		
13	-	That Girl Belongs To Yesterday	Gene Pitney	UA	7	(49)	
14	2	I'm The One	Gerry & The Pacemakers	Columbia	9	(82)	
15	-	Stay Awhile	Dusty Springfield	Philips	6	(38)	
16	-	Over You	Freddie & The Dreamers	Columbia	5		
17	6	As Usual	Brenda Lee	Brunswick	10	(12)	
18	-	Can't Buy Me Love	Beatles	Parlophone	9	(1)	G
19	7	5-4-3-2-1	Manfred Mann	HMV	7		F
20	-	Theme For Young Lovers	Shadows	Columbia	6		

January 1964

This Mnth	Prev Mnth	Title	Artist	Label	Wks 20	(UK Pos)	
1	8	There I've Said It Again	Bobby Vinton	Epic	10		G
2	2	Louie Louie	Kingsmen	Wand	9	(26)	F G
3	11	Popsicles And Icicles	Murmaids	Chattahoochee	9		F L
4	16	Forget Him	Bobby Rydell	Cameo	8	(15)	L
5	1	Dominique	Singing Nun (Soeur Sourire)	Philips	11	(3)	F G L
6	-	Surfin' Bird	Trashmen	Garrett	7		F L
7	4	Since I Fell For You	Lenny Welch	Cadence	10		F L
8	-	The Nitty Gritty	Shirley Ellis	Congress	5		F
9	-	Midnight Mary	Joey Powers	Amy	5		F L
10	-	Drag City	Jan & Dean	Liberty	5		
11	-	As Usual	Brenda Lee	Decca	6	(5)	
12	13	Talk Back Trembling Lips	Johnny Tillotson	MGM	6		L
13	-	Hey Little Cobra	Rip Chords	Columbia	7		F L
14	-	Out Of Limits	Marketts	Warner	7		F G
15	-	Whispering	Nino Tempo & April Stevens	Atco	6	(20)	L
16	20	Quicksand	Martha & The Vandellas	Gordy	4		
17	-	Um, Um, Um, Um, Um, Um	Major Lance	Okeh	8	(40)	
18	-	I Want To Hold Your Hand	Beatles	Capitol	13	(1)	F G
19	3	You Don't Have To Be A Baby To Cry	Caravelles	Smash	7	(6)	F L
20	-	Wives And Lovers	Jack Jones	Kapp	4		F

February 1964

This Mnth	Prev Mnth	Title	Artist	Label	Wks 20	(UK Pos)	
1	18	I Want To Hold Your Hand	Beatles	Capitol	13	(1)	F G
2	-	You Don't Own Me	Lesley Gore	Mercury	8		G
3	17	Um, Um, Um, Um, Um, Um	Major Lance	Okeh	8	(40)	
4	-	She Loves You	Beatles	Swan	12	(1)	G
5	14	Out Of Limits	Marketts	Warner	7		F G
6	13	Hey Little Cobra	Rip Chords	Columbia	7		F L
7	-	Java	Al Hirt	RCA	9		F
8	-	For You	Rick Nelson	Decca	6	(14)	
9	-	Dawn (Go Away)	Four Seasons	Philips	8		
10	-	Anyone Who Had A Heart	Dionne Warwick	Scepter	6	(42)	F
11	6	Surfin' Bird	Trashmen	Garrett	7		F L
12	-	What Kind Of Fool (Do You Think I Am)	Tams	ABC	5		F L
13	-	California Sun	Rivieras	Riviera	6		F L
14	-	Talking About My Baby	Impressions	ABC Paramount	5		
15	1	There I've Said It Again	Bobby Vinton	Epic	10		G
16	-	Stop And Think It Over	Dale & Grace	Montel	5		L
17	-	Navy Blue	Diane Renay	20th Century	6		F L
18	-	A Fool Never Learns	Andy Williams	Columbia	5	(40)	
19	-	Please Please Me	Beatles	Vee Jay	8	(1)	G
20	-	See The Funny Little Clown	Bobby Goldsboro	UA	5		F

March 1964

This Mnth	Prev Mnth	Title	Artist	Label	Wks 20	(UK Pos)	
1	1	I Want To Hold Your Hand	Beatles	Capitol	13	(1)	F G
2	4	She Loves You	Beatles	Swan	12	(1)	G
3	19	Please Please Me	Beatles	Vee Jay	8	(1)	G
4	9	Dawn (Go Away)	Four Seasons	Philips	8		
5	-	Fun, Fun, Fun	Beach Boys	Capitol	7		
6	7	Java	Al Hirt	RCA	9		F
7	17	Navy Blue	Diane Renay	20th Century	6		F L
8	-	I Love You More And More Every Day	Al Martino	Capitol	5		
9	13	California Sun	Rivieras	Riviera	6		F L
10	-	Twist And Shout	Beatles	Tollie	9	(4)	G
11	-	Hello, Dolly!	Louis Armstrong	Kapp	16	(4)	F G L
12	20	See The Funny Little Clown	Bobby Goldsboro	UA	5		F
13	-	Kissin' Cousins	Elvis Presley	RCA	4	(10)	
14	-	Hi-Heel Sneakers	Tommy Tucker	Checker	4	(23)	F L
15	-	Good News	Sam Cooke	RCA	4		
16	16	Stop And Think It Over	Dale & Grace	Montel	5		L
17	-	My Heart Belongs To Only You	Bobby Vinton	Epic	4		
18	-	Glad All Over	Dave Clark Five	Epic	9	(1)	F
19	-	Suspicion	Terry Stafford	Crusader	9	(31)	F G L
20	-	I Only Want To Be With You	Dusty Springfield	Philips	4	(4)	F

◆ No one has had so many American hits in so short a time as The Beatles. Although unknown on New Year's Day, they had the top four singles and top two albums as March closed, and accounted for 60% of all records sold in the USA. A record breaking 73 million people watched their TV debut on the *Ed Sullivan Show* and their US tour was a resounding success.

◆ Youthful group The Osmonds appeared on TV with Mickey Rooney in *The Seven Little Foys*. Another young performer, 14-year-old Hank Williams Jr., signed with MGM (the label his legendary father had recorded for). Also, British teenager Davy Jones (later of The Monkees) was seen on the *Ed Sullivan Show* in the cast of *Oliver*.

UK 1964 APR-JUNE

◆ Mods and Rockers clashed on British beaches, teenagers and drugs were linked for the first time in the press and the first drug-related British records, Mickey Finn's 'Pills' and 'Purple Pill Eater' by The Wild Ones, were released.

◆ The Rolling Stones' eponymous debut album knocked The Beatles off the top after 51 consecutive weeks at the top.

◆ Peter & Gordon's 'World Without Love' was the eighth Lennon & McCartney song to top the UK chart in 14 months, and their fifth in the USA in less than five months.

◆ Mary Wells's last recording for Motown, 'My Guy', gave the label their first major transatlantic hit.

◆ Irish trio The Bachelors had two singles in the UK Top 10 while The Beatles had nine in the equivalent Canadian chart!

April 1964

This Mnth	Prev Mnth	Title	Artist	Label	Wks 20	(US Pos)	
1	18	Can't Buy Me Love	Beatles	Parlophone	9	(1)	G
2	-	I Believe	Bachelors	Decca	11	(33)	
3	3	Little Children	Billy J. Kramer & The Dakotas	Parlophone	9	(7)	
4	-	A World Without Love	Peter & Gordon	Columbia	9	(1)	F
5	10	I Love You Because	Jim Reeves	RCA	26		
6	6	Just One Look	Hollies	Parlophone	9	(44)	
7	4	Not Fade Away	Rolling Stones	Decca	9	(48)	
8	-	Tell Me When	Applejacks	Decca	8		F
9	13	That Girl Belongs To Yesterday	Gene Pitney	UA	7	(49)	
10	-	My Boy Lollipop	Millie	Fontana	10	(2)	F L
11	2	Bits And Pieces	Dave Clark Five	Columbia	9	(4)	
12	1	Anyone Who Had A Heart	Cilla Black	Parlophone	11		F
13	5	Diane	Bachelors	Decca	11	(10)	
14	-	Good Golly Miss Molly	Swinging Blue Jeans	HMV	5	(43)	
15	-	Move Over Darling	Doris Day	CBS	8		L
16	-	Everything's Alright	Mojos	Decca	6		F L
17	20	Theme For Young Lovers	Shadows	Columbia	6		
18	-	Don't Throw Your Love Away	Searchers	Pye	8	(16)	
19	-	Mockingbird Hill	Migil Five	Pye	6		F L
20	-	Viva Las Vegas	Elvis Presley	RCA	4	(29)	

May 1964

This Mnth	Prev Mnth	Title	Artist	Label	Wks 20	(US Pos)	
1	18	Don't Throw Your Love Away	Searchers	Pye	8	(16)	
2	10	My Boy Lollipop	Millie	Fontana	10	(2)	F L
3	-	Juliet	Four Pennies	Philips	10		F
4	2	I Believe	Bachelors	Decca	11	(33)	
5	4	A World Without Love	Peter & Gordon	Columbia	9	(1)	F
6	-	Don't Let The Sun Catch You Crying	Gerry & The Pacemakers	Columbia	6	(4)	
7	5	I Love You Because	Jim Reeves	RCA	26		
8	-	It's Over	Roy Orbison	London American	14	(9)	
9	-	A Little Loving	Fourmost	Parlophone	8		L
10	-	Walk On By	Dionne Warwick	Pye International	9	(6)	F
11	-	Constantly	Cliff Richard	Columbia	8		
12	-	You're My World	Cilla Black	Parlophone	10	(26)	
13	1	Can't Buy Me Love	Beatles	Parlophone	9	(1)	G
14	15	Move Over Darling	Doris Day	CBS	8		L
15	19	Mockingbird Hill	Migil Five	Pye	6		F L
16	-	Don't Turn Around	Merseybeats	Fontana	5		
17	-	The Rise & Fall Of Flingel Bunt	Shadows	Columbia	8		
18	16	Everything's Alright	Mojos	Decca	6		F L
19	-	I Will	Billy Fury	Decca	6		
20	-	Hubble Bubble Toil And Trouble	Manfred Mann	HMV	4		

June 1964

This Mnth	Prev Mnth	Title	Artist	Label	Wks 20	(US Pos)	
1	12	You're My World	Cilla Black	Parlophone	10	(26)	
2	8	It's Over	Roy Orbison	London American	14	(9)	
3	-	Someone Someone	Brian Poole & The Tremeloes	Decca	11	(97)	
4	-	No Particular Place To Go	Chuck Berry	Pye International	7	(10)	
5	-	Here I Go Again	Hollies	Parlophone	7		
6	-	My Guy	Mary Wells	Stateside	8	(1)	F
7	17	The Rise & Fall Of Flingel Bunt	Shadows	Columbia	8		
8	11	Constantly	Cliff Richard	Columbia	8		
9	3	Juliet	Four Pennies	Philips	10		F
10	-	Shout	Lulu	Decca	7	(94)	F
11	-	Hello, Dolly!	Louis Armstrong	London American	8	(1)	
12	-	Can't You See That She's Mine	Dave Clark Five	Columbia	6	(4)	
13	7	I Love You Because	Jim Reeves	RCA	26		
14	-	Ramona	Bachelors	Decca	8		
15	10	Walk On By	Dionne Warwick	Pye International	9	(6)	F
16	9	A Little Loving	Fourmost	Parlophone	8		L
17	2	My Boy Lollipop	Millie	Fontana	10	(2)	F L
18	-	You're No Good	Swinging Blue Jeans	HMV	8	(97)	L
19	-	Nobody I Know	Peter & Gordon	Columbia	5	(12)	
20	-	Non Ho L'Eta Per Amarti	Gigliola Cinquetti	Decca	4		F

US 1964 APR-JUNE

April 1964

This Mnth	Prev Mnth	Title	Artist	Label	Wks 20	(UK Pos)	
1	-	Can't Buy Me Love	Beatles	Capitol	7	(1)	G
2	10	Twist And Shout	Beatles	Tollie	9	(4)	G
3	19	Suspicion	Terry Stafford	Crusader	9	(31)	F G L
4	11	Hello, Dolly!	Louis Armstrong	Kapp	16	(4)	F G L
5	18	Glad All Over	Dave Clark Five	Epic	9	(1)	F
6	-	Shoop Shoop Song (It's In His Kiss)	Betty Everett	Vee Jay	7	(34)	F
7	2	She Loves You	Beatles	Swan	12	(1)	G
8	-	Don't Let The Rain Come Down (Crooked Little Man)	Serendipity Singers	Philips	9		F L
9	-	Do You Want To Know A Secret	Beatles	Vee Jay	8		G
10	-	The Way You Do The Things You Do	Temptations	Gordy	6		F
11	1	I Want To Hold Your Hand	Beatles	Capitol	13	(1)	F G
12	3	Please Please Me	Beatles	Vee Jay	8	(1)	G
13	-	Needles And Pins	Searchers	Kapp	5	(1)	F
14	-	Dead Man's Curve	Jan & Dean	Liberty	7		
15	-	Bits And Pieces	Dave Clark Five	Epic	7	(2)	
16	17	My Heart Belongs To Only You	Bobby Vinton	Epic	4		
17	-	My Guy	Mary Wells	Motown	11	(5)	G
18	-	You're A Wonderful One	Marvin Gaye	Tamla	5		
19	-	That's The Way Boys Are	Lesley Gore	Mercury	4		
20	14	Hi-Heel Sneakers	Tommy Tucker	Checker	4	(23)	F L

May 1964

This Mnth	Prev Mnth	Title	Artist	Label	Wks 20	(UK Pos)	
1	4	Hello, Dolly!	Louis Armstrong	Kapp	16	(4)	F G L
2	17	My Guy	Mary Wells	Motown	11	(5)	G
3	15	Bits And Pieces	Dave Clark Five	Epic	7	(2)	
4	-	Love Me Do	Beatles	Tollie	9	(27)	G
5	9	Do You Want To Know A Secret	Beatles	Vee Jay	8		G
6	-	Ronnie	Four Seasons	Philips	6		
7	1	Can't Buy Me Love	Beatles	Capitol	7	(1)	G
8	14	Dead Man's Curve	Jan & Dean	Liberty	7		
9	-	It's Over	Roy Orbison	Monument	6	(1)	
10	8	Don't Let The Rain Come Down (Crooked Little Man)	Serendipity Singers	Philips	9		F L
11	-	Chapel Of Love	Dixie Cups	Red Bird	9	(22)	F G
12	-	Love Me With All Your Heart	Ray Charles Singers	Command	8		F L
13	-	(Just Like) Romeo & Juliet	Reflections	Golden World	5		F L
14	-	White On White	Danny Williams	UA	5		F L
15	-	Little Children	Billy J. Kramer & The Dakotas	Imperial	9	(1)	F
16	3	Suspicion	Terry Stafford	Crusader	9	(31)	F G L
17	2	Twist And Shout	Beatles	Tollie	9	(4)	G
18	-	A World Without Love	Peter & Gordon	Capitol	8	(1)	F G
19	-	Shangri-La	Robert Maxwell, His Harp & His Orchestra	Decca	4		F L
20	-	Walk On By	Dionne Warwick	Scepter	8	(9)	

June 1964

This Mnth	Prev Mnth	Title	Artist	Label	Wks 20	(UK Pos)	
1	11	Chapel Of Love	Dixie Cups	Red Bird	9	(22)	F G
2	18	A World Without Love	Peter & Gordon	Capitol	8	(1)	F G
3	12	Love Me With All Your Heart	Ray Charles Singers	Command	8		F L
4	4	Love Me Do	Beatles	Tollie	9	(27)	G
5	20	Walk On By	Dionne Warwick	Scepter	8	(9)	
6	-	I Get Around	Beach Boys	Capitol	12	(7)	G
7	-	People	Barbra Streisand	Columbia	9		F
8	2	My Guy	Mary Wells	Motown	11	(5)	F
9	15	Little Children	Billy J. Kramer & The Dakotas	Imperial	9	(1)	F
10	-	My Boy Lollipop	Millie Small	Smash	7	(2)	F G L
11	1	Hello, Dolly!	Louis Armstrong	Kapp	16	(4)	F G L
12	-	Diane	Bachelors	London	5	(1)	F
13	-	Don't Let The Sun Catch You Crying	Gerry & The Pacemakers	Laurie	7	(6)	F
14	-	Memphis	Johnny Rivers	Imperial	8		F G
15	13	(Just Like) Romeo & Juliet	Reflections	Golden World	5		F L
16	-	Tell Me Why	Bobby Vinton	Epic	4		
17	-	Every Little Bit Hurts	Brenda Holloway	Tamla	4		F L
18	-	Bad To Me	Billy J. Kramer & The Dakotas	Imperial	5	(1)	L
19	-	P.S. I Love You	Beatles	Tollie	4		
20	-	Do You Love Me	Dave Clark Five	Epic	4	(30)	

◆ 'Can't Buy Me Love' by The Beatles amassed record advance orders of over two million and hit the top in a record two weeks (as did **The Beatles Second Album**), giving them the first five places on the chart. At times, they had a record 13 different singles in the Hot 100. **Meet The Beatles** became the biggest selling album to date and was one of three Beatles LPs in the Top 4.

▲ Following in The Beatles' footsteps, The Searchers, Dave Clark Five, Peter & Gordon (above) and the Rolling Stones performed in the USA.

◆ 63-year-old Louis Armstrong finally dethroned The Beatles with 'Hello Dolly'.

UK 1964 JULY-SEPT

◆ The Rolling Stones caused their first fan riots on tour in Britain. The quintet also clocked up their first UK chart topper, 'It's All Over Now', which was recorded in Chicago during their relatively disappointing debut US tour.

◆ The death of US country singer Jim Reeves (the top selling solo artist in Britain in 1964) resulted in a record eight of his albums simultaneously making the Top 20.

▲ As 60s superstars The Kinks (above) and Herman's Hermits debuted on the UK chart, while the High Numbers (Who), Joe Cocker and Rod Stewart released unsuccessful singles.

July 1964

This Mnth	Prev Mnth	Title	Artist	Label	Wks 20	(US Pos)	
1	-	House Of The Rising Sun	Animals	Columbia	7	(1)	F
2	-	Hold Me	P.J. Proby	Decca	8	(70)	F
3	2	It's Over	Roy Orbison	London American	14	(9)	
4	-	It's All Over Now	Rolling Stones	Decca	11	(26)	
5	-	I Won't Forget You	Jim Reeves	RCA	19	(93)	
6	3	Someone Someone	Brian Poole & The Tremeloes	Decca	11	(97)	
7	18	You're No Good	Swinging Blue Jeans	HMV	8	(97)	L
8	14	Ramona	Bachelors	Decca	8		
9	-	A Hard Day's Night	Beatles	Parlophone	11	(1)	
10	11	Hello, Dolly!	Louis Armstrong	London American	8	(1)	
11	-	I Just Don't Know What To Do With Myself	Dusty Springfield	Philips	9		
12	-	On The Beach	Cliff Richard	Columbia	8		
13	-	Kissin' Cousins	Elvis Presley	RCA	6	(12)	
14	6	My Guy	Mary Wells	Stateside	8	(1)	F
15	19	Nobody I Know	Peter & Gordon	Columbia	5	(12)	
16	12	Can't You See That She's Mine	Dave Clark Five	Columbia	6	(4)	
17	1	You're My World	Cilla Black	Parlophone	10	(26)	
18	-	Call Up The Groups	Barron Knights	Columbia	9		F
19	10	Shout	Lulu	Decca	7	(94)	F
20	-	Do Wah Diddy Diddy	Manfred Mann	HMV	10	(1)	

August 1964

This Mnth	Prev Mnth	Title	Artist	Label	Wks 20	(US Pos)	
1	9	A Hard Day's Night	Beatles	Parlophone	11	(1)	
2	20	Do Wah Diddy Diddy	Manfred Mann	HMV	10	(1)	
3	18	Call Up The Groups	Barron Knights	Columbia	9		F
4	4	It's All Over Now	Rolling Stones	Decca	11	(26)	
5	5	I Won't Forget You	Jim Reeves	RCA	19	(93)	
6	-	Tobacco Road	Nashville Teens	Decca	8	(14)	F
7	11	I Just Don't Know What To Do With Myself	Dusty Springfield	Philips	9		
8	-	I Get Around	Beach Boys	Capitol	8	(1)	F
9	12	On The Beach	Cliff Richard	Columbia	8		
10	-	Have I The Right?	Honeycombs	Pye	11	(5)	F
11	-	It's Only Make Believe	Billy Fury	Decca	5		
12	1	House Of The Rising Sun	Animals	Columbia	7	(1)	F
13	-	From A Window	Billy J. Kramer & The Dakotas	Parlophone	4	(23)	
14	-	Someday We're Gonna Love Again	Searchers	Pye	5	(34)	
15	2	Hold Me	P.J. Proby	Decca	8	(70)	F
16	-	It's For You	Cilla Black	Parlophone	6	(79)	
17	-	Wishin' And Hopin'	Merseybeats	Fontana	6		
18	-	You Really Got Me	Kinks	Pye	9	(7)	F
19	-	I Found Out The Hard Way	Four Pennies	Philips	3		
20	3	It's Over	Roy Orbison	London American	14	(9)	

September 1964

This Mnth	Prev Mnth	Title	Artist	Label	Wks 20	(US Pos)	
1	10	Have I The Right?	Honeycombs	Pye	11	(5)	F
2	18	You Really Got Me	Kinks	Pye	9	(7)	F
3	5	I Won't Forget You	Jim Reeves	RCA	19	(93)	
4	-	I Wouldn't Trade You For The World	Bachelors	Decca	11	(69)	
5	-	The Crying Game	Dave Berry	Decca	7		
6	-	I'm Into Something Good	Herman's Hermits	Columbia	10	(13)	F
7	-	Rag Doll	Four Seasons	Philips	9	(1)	
8	2	Do Wah Diddy Diddy	Manfred Mann	HMV	10	(1)	
9	-	As Tears Go By	Marianne Faithfull	Decca	10	(22)	F
10	1	A Hard Day's Night	Beatles	Parlophone	11	(1)	
12	-	Where Did Our Love Go	Supremes	Stateside	10	(1)	F
13	-	She's Not There	Zombies	Decca	6	(2)	F L
14	16	It's For You	Cilla Black	Parlophone	6	(79)	
15	-	Such A Night	Elvis Presley	RCA	5	(16)	
16	-	The Wedding	Julie Rogers	Mercury	13	(10)	F L
17	8	I Get Around	Beach Boys	Capitol	8	(1)	F
18	-	Oh Pretty Woman	Roy Orbison	London American	12	(1)	
19	4	It's All Over Now	Rolling Stones	Decca	11	(26)	
20	-	Everybody Loves Somebody	Dean Martin	Reprise	7	(1)	

July 1964

This Mnth	Prev Mnth	Title	Artist	Label	Wks 20	(UK Pos)	
1	6	I Get Around	Beach Boys	Capitol	12	(7)	G
2	14	Memphis	Johnny Rivers	Imperial	8		F G
3	-	Rag Doll	Four Seasons	Philips	10	(2)	G
4	-	Can't You See That She's Mine	Dave Clark Five	Epic	7	(10)	
5	13	Don't Let The Sun Catch You Crying	Gerry & The Pacemakers	Laurie	7	(6)	F
6	10	My Boy Lollipop	Millie Small	Smash	7	(2)	F G L
7	-	The Girl From Ipanema	Stan Getz/Astrud Gilberto	Verve	7	(29)	L
8	7	People	Barbra Streisand	Columbia	9		F
9	-	The Little Old Lady (From Pasadena)	Jan & Dean	Liberty	7		
10	-	Dang Me	Roger Miller	Smash	6		F
11	-	Good Times	Sam Cooke	RCA	5		
12	2	A World Without Love	Peter & Gordon	Capitol	8	(1)	F G
13	18	Bad To Me	Billy J. Kramer & The Dakotas	Imperial	5	(1)	L
14	-	Keep On Pushing	Impressions	ABC Paramount	5		
15	-	No Particular Place To Go	Chuck Berry	Chess	4	(3)	
16	1	Chapel Of Love	Dixie Cups	Red Bird	9	(22)	F G
17	-	Wishin' And Hopin'	Dusty Springfield	Philips	7		
18	-	A Hard Day's Night	Beatles	Capitol	10	(1)	G
19	-	Everybody Loves Somebody	Dean Martin	Reprise	11	(11)	G
20	-	Try It Baby	Marvin Gaye	Tamla	5		

August 1964

This Mnth	Prev Mnth	Title	Artist	Label	Wks 20	(UK Pos)	
1	-	Where Did Our Love Go	Supremes	Motown	11	(3)	F G
2	18	A Hard Day's Night	Beatles	Capitol	10	(1)	G
3	19	Everybody Loves Somebody	Dean Martin	Reprise	11	(11)	G
4	-	Under The Boardwalk	Drifters	Atlantic	9	(45)	
5	17	Wishin' And Hopin'	Dusty Springfield	Philips	7		
6	3	Rag Doll	Four Seasons	Philips	10	(2)	G
7	9	The Little Old Lady (From Pasadena)	Jan & Dean	Liberty	7		
8	-	C'mon And Swim	Bobby Freeman	Autumn	6		L
9	-	House Of The Rising Sun	Animals	MGM	9	(1)	F G
10	1	I Get Around	Beach Boys	Capitol	12	(7)	G
11	-	I Wanna Love Him So Bad	Jelly Beans	Red Bird	5		F L
12	-	Because	Dave Clark Five	Epic	7		G
13	-	Walk-Don't Run '64	Ventures	Dolton	5		
14	10	Dang Me	Roger Miller	Smash	6		F
15	-	How Do You Do It?	Gerry & The Pacemakers	Laurie	5	(1)	
16	-	People Say	Dixie Cups	Red Bird	5		
17	-	(You Don't Know) How Glad I Am	Nancy Wilson	Capitol	4		F L
18	2	Memphis	Johnny Rivers	Imperial	8		F G
19	-	Nobody I Know	Peter & Gordon	Capitol	4	(10)	
20	4	Can't You See That She's Mine	Dave Clark Five	Epic	7	(10)	

September 1964

This Mnth	Prev Mnth	Title	Artist	Label	Wks 20	(UK Pos)	
1	9	House Of The Rising Sun	Animals	MGM	9	(1)	F G
2	1	Where Did Our Love Go	Supremes	Motown	11	(3)	F G
3	-	Bread And Butter	Newbeats	Hickory	8	(15)	F G
4	-	G.T.O.	Ronny & The Daytonas	Mala	8		F L
5	3	Everybody Loves Somebody	Dean Martin	Reprise	11	(11)	G
6	12	Because	Dave Clark Five	Epic	7		G
7	-	Remember (Walkin' In The Sand)	Shangri-Las	Red Bird	8	(14)	F
8	-	Oh Pretty Woman	Roy Orbison	Monument	11	(1)	G
9	2	A Hard Day's Night	Beatles	Capitol	10	(1)	G
10	8	C'mon And Swim	Bobby Freeman	Autumn	6		L
11	-	Do Wah Diddy Diddy	Manfred Mann	Ascot	10	(1)	F G
12	-	Maybelline	Johnny Rivers	Imperial	4		
13	-	Haunted House	Gene Simmons	Hi	6		F L
14	-	Dancing In The Street	Martha & The Vandellas	Gordy	8	(4)	G
15	4	Under The Boardwalk	Drifters	Atlantic	9	(45)	
16	-	Selfish One	Jackie Ross	Chess	4		F L
17	-	And I Love Her	Beatles	Capitol	4		
18	-	It Hurts To Be In Love	Gene Pitney	Musicor	6	(36)	
19	15	How Do You Do It?	Gerry & The Pacemakers	Laurie	5	(1)	
20	-	Save It For Me	Four Seasons	Philips	4		

◆ The Beatles' second US tour was a tremendous success and the soundtrack album to *A Hard Day's Night* not only sold a million copies in just four days but also gave them No. 1 and No. 2 on the LP chart for the second time.

◆ British group The Animals, whose four minute single 'House Of The Rising Sun' gave them a transatlantic topper, were given the red carpet treatment when they arrived in New York.

◆ British producer Jack Good (of *6-5 Special* and *Oh Boy!* fame) launched US TV show *Shindig*. The initial show featured appearances from Sam Cooke and The Righteous Brothers.

◆ On Independence Day 1964, five of the American Top 10 singles were by British artists.

UK 1964 OCT-DEC

◆ There was an upsurge of interest in "death discs" with Twinkle's self-penned 'Terry' and the US hit 'Leader Of The Pack' by the Shangri-La's (a hit in 1965, 1972 and 1976) both motoring up the chart. However, J. Frank Wilson's ghoulish American smash 'Last Kiss' was a stiff on this side of the Atlantic.

◆ The Beach Boys, who had a successful UK visit, ended the year topping the US album listings with **Beach Boys Concert.**

▲ 'Oh Pretty Woman' by Roy Orbison (above), was the only American record to top the transatlantic charts since 'I Can't Stop Loving You' by Ray Charles in 1962.

October 1964

This Mnth	Prev Mnth	Title	Artist	Label	Wks 20	(US Pos)	
1	17	Oh Pretty Woman	Roy Orbison	London American	12	(1)	
2	11	Where Did Our Love Go	Supremes	Stateside	10	(1)	F
3	6	I'm Into Something Good	Herman's Hermits	Columbia	10	(13)	F
4	15	The Wedding	Julie Rogers	Mercury	13	(10)	F L
5	7	Rag Doll	Four Seasons	Philips	9	(1)	
6	-	When You Walk In The Room	Searchers	Pye	8	(35)	
7	4	I Wouldn't Trade You For The World	Bachelors	Decca	11	(69)	
8	3	I Won't Forget You	Jim Reeves	RCA	19	(93)	
9	-	(There's) Always Something There To Remind Me	Sandie Shaw	Pye	5	(52)	F
10	-	I'm Crying	Animals	Columbia	6	(19)	
11	-	We're Through	Hollies	Parlophone	7		
12	-	Walk Away	Matt Monro	Parlophone	11	(23)	
13	-	Together	P.J. Proby	Decca	6		
14	19	Everybody Loves Somebody	Dean Martin	Reprise	7	(1)	
15	9	As Tears Go By	Marianne Faithfull	Decca	10	(22)	F
16	-	The Twelfth Of Never	Cliff Richard	Columbia	6		
17	1	Have I The Right?	Honeycombs	Pye	11	(5)	F
18	-	How Soon	Henry Mancini & His Orchestra	RCA	4		L
19	-	One Way Love	Cliff Bennett & The Rebel Rousers	Parlophone	4		F
20	2	You Really Got Me	Kinks	Pye	9	(7)	F

November 1964

This Mnth	Prev Mnth	Title	Artist	Label	Wks 20	(US Pos)	
1	-	Baby Love	Supremes	Stateside	10	(1)	
2	1	Oh Pretty Woman	Roy Orbison	London American	12	(1)	
3	-	Sha La La	Manfred Mann	HMV	7	(12)	
4	-	He's In Town	Rockin' Berries	Piccadilly	7		F
5	-	All Day And All Of The Night	Kinks	Pye	9	(7)	
6	12	Walk Away	Matt Monro	Parlophone	11	(23)	
7	-	Um Um Um Um Um Um	Wayne Fontana & The Mindbenders	Fontana	7		F
8	4	The Wedding	Julie Rogers	Mercury	13	(10)	F L
9	6	When You Walk In The Room	Searchers	Pye	8	(35)	
10	-	Tokyo Melody	Helmut Zacharias Orchestra	Polydor	6		F L
11	-	There's A Heartache Following Me	Jim Reeves	RCA	10		
12	16	The Twelfth Of Never	Cliff Richard	Columbia	6		
13	-	Google Eye	Nashville Teens	Decca	3		L
14	-	Don't Bring Me Down	Pretty Things	Fontana	5		F
15	-	I'm Gonna Be Strong	Gene Pitney	Stateside	10	(9)	
16	9	(There's) Always Something There...	Sandie Shaw	Pye	5	(52)	F
17	-	Little Red Rooster	Rolling Stones	Decca	8		
18	2	Where Did Our Love Go	Supremes	Stateside	10	(1)	
19	19	One Way Love	Cliff Bennettt/Rebel Rousers	Parlophone	4		F
20	-	Remember (Walkin' In The Sand)	Shangri-Las	Red Bird	3	(5)	F

December 1964

This Mnth	Prev Mnth	Title	Artist	Label	Wks 20	(US Pos)	
1	-	I Feel Fine	Beatles	Parlophone	10	(1)	G
2	15	I'm Gonna Be Strong	Gene Pitney	Stateside	10	(9)	
3	-	Downtown	Petula Clark	Pye	12	(1)	
4	17	Little Red Rooster	Rolling Stones	Decca	8		
5	-	Walk Tall	Val Doonican	Decca	10		F
6	-	Pretty Paper	Roy Orbison	London American	6	(15)	
7	1	Baby Love	Supremes	Stateside	10	(1)	
8	-	I Understand	Freddie & The Dreamers	Columbia	8	(36)	L
9	11	There's A Heartache Following Me	Jim Reeves	RCA	10		
10	5	All Day And All Of The Night	Kinks	Pye	9	(7)	
11	-	No Arms Could Ever Hold You	Bachelors	Decca	7	(27)	
12	10	Tokyo Melody	Helmut Zacharias Orchestra	Polydor	6		F L
13	-	Losing You	Dusty Springfield	Philips	5	(91)	
14	7	Um Um Um Um Um Um	Wayne Fontana/Mindbenders	Fontana	7		F
15	-	I Could Easily Fall	Cliff Richard	Columbia	8		
16	-	Message To Martha (Kentucky Bluebird)	Adam Faith	Parlophone	6		L
17	4	He's In Town	Rockin' Berries	Piccadilly	7		F
18	-	Somewhere	P.J. Proby	Liberty	8	(91)	
19	-	Blue Christmas	Elvis Presley	RCA	3		
20	-	Terry	Twinkle	Decca	9		F L

October 1964

This Mnth	Prev Mnth	Title	Artist	Label	Wks 20	(UK Pos)	
1	11	Do Wah Diddy Diddy	Manfred Mann	Ascot	10	(1)	F G
2	14	Dancing In The Street	Martha & The Vandellas	Gordy	8	(4)	G
3	8	Oh Pretty Woman	Roy Orbison	Monument	11	(1)	G
4	-	We'll Sing In The Sunshine	Gale Garnett	RCA	9		F L
5	-	Last Kiss	J. Frank Wilson & The Cavaliers	Josie	10		F G L
6	-	A Summer Song	Chad & Jeremy	World Artists	6		F
7	7	Remember (Walkin' In The Sand)	Shangri-Las	Red Bird	8	(14)	F
8	18	It Hurts To Be In Love	Gene Pitney	Musicor	6	(36)	
9	-	Let It Be Me	Jerry Butler & Betty Everett	Vee Jay	7		
10	3	Bread And Butter	Newbeats	Hickory	8	(15)	F G
11	-	Baby Love	Supremes	Motown	10	(1)	G
12	-	When I Grow Up (To Be A Man)	Beach Boys	Capitol	5	(27)	
13	4	G.T.O.	Ronny & The Daytonas	Mala	8		F L
14	-	Little Honda	Hondells	Mercury	5		F L
15	-	Chug-A-Lug	Roger Miller	Smash	5		
16	-	Have I The Right?	Honeycombs	Interphon	7	(1)	F L
17	-	Baby I Need Your Loving	Four Tops	Motown	5		F
18	-	Funny	Joe Hinton	Back Beat	4		F L
19	-	The Door Is Still Open To My Heart	Dean Martin	Reprise	5	(42)	
20	1	House Of The Rising Sun	Animals	MGM	9	(1)	F G

November 1964

This Mnth	Prev Mnth	Title	Artist	Label	Wks 20	(UK Pos)	
1	11	Baby Love	Supremes	Motown	10	(1)	G
2	-	Leader Of The Pack	Shangri-Las	Red Bird	9	(11)	G
3	-	Come A Little Bit Closer	Jay & The Americans	UA	7		
4	5	Last Kiss	J. Frank Wilson & The Cavaliers	Josie	10		F G L
5	16	Have I The Right?	Honeycombs	Interphon	7	(1)	F L
6	-	She's Not There	Zombies	Parrot	9	(12)	F G
7	-	Ringo	Lorne Greene	RCA	9	(22)	F G L
8	19	The Door Is Still Open To My Heart	Dean Martin	Reprise	5	(42)	
9	1	Do Wah Diddy Diddy	Manfred Mann	Ascot	10	(1)	F G
10	-	You Really Got Me	Kinks	Reprise	8	(1)	F
11	9	Let It Be Me	Jerry Butler & Betty Everett	Vee Jay	7		
12	3	Oh Pretty Woman	Roy Orbison	Monument	11	(1)	G
13	-	Time Is On My Side	Rolling Stones	London	8		F
14	-	Mr. Lonely	Bobby Vinton	Epic	11		G
15	-	I'm Gonna Be Strong	Gene Pitney	Musicor	7	(2)	
16	4	We'll Sing In The Sunshine	Gale Garnett	RCA	9		F L
17	15	Chug-A-Lug	Roger Miller	Smash	5		
18	-	Ask Me	Elvis Presley	RCA	4		
19	-	Mountain Of Love	Johnny Rivers	Imperial	6		
20	14	Little Honda	Hondells	Mercury	5		F L

December 1964

This Mnth	Prev Mnth	Title	Artist	Label	Wks 20	(UK Pos)	
1	14	Mr. Lonely	Bobby Vinton	Epic	11		G
2	-	Come See About Me	Supremes	Motown	11	(27)	G
3	6	She's Not There	Zombies	Parrot	9	(12)	F G
4	7	Ringo	Lorne Greene	RCA	9	(22)	F G L
5	13	Time Is On My Side	Rolling Stones	London	8		F
6	-	I Feel Fine	Beatles	Capitol	8	(1)	G
7	-	Dance, Dance, Dance	Beach Boys	Capitol	5	(24)	
8	10	You Really Got Me	Kinks	Reprise	8	(1)	F
9	15	I'm Gonna Be Strong	Gene Pitney	Musicor	7	(2)	
10	-	Goin' Out Of My Head	Little Anthony & The Imperials	DCP	9		
11	19	Mountain Of Love	Johnny Rivers	Imperial	6		
12	1	Baby Love	Supremes	Motown	10	(1)	G
13	2	Leader Of The Pack	Shangri-Las	Red Bird	9	(11)	G
14	-	I'm Into Something Good	Herman's Hermits	MGM	6	(1)	F
15	-	She's A Woman	Beatles	Capitol	6		
16	-	The Jerk	Larks	Money	7		F L
17	-	Sha La La	Manfred Mann	Ascot	7	(3)	
18	18	Ask Me	Elvis Presley	RCA	4		
19	-	The Wedding	Julie Rogers	Mercury	5	(3)	F L
20	-	Love Potion Number Nine	Searchers	Kapp	8		L

◆ 'Hold What You've Got' by Joe Tex was the first of many Top 20 hits recorded in the small Alabama town of Muscle Shoals.

◆ Debuting in the US Top 20 were British acts Chad & Jeremy (who remained virtually unknown in their homeland) and The Rolling Stones, whose appearance on the *Ed Sullivan Show* made Ed Sullivan vow to never have them back (he relented later).

◆ The Beatles achieved a staggering 30 tracks in the US singles chart in 1964 (including six No. 1s). They ended the year topping the transatlantic charts with 'I Feel Fine'.

◆ The Rolling Stones' first American Top 20 hit 'Time Is On My Side' was not released as a single in Britain, and their British chart topper, 'Little Red Rooster', was never an American single. Both songs were covers of US R&B hits.

UK 1965 JAN-MAR

◆ The Who plugged their debut single (under that name), 'I Can't Explain' on TV's *Ready Steady Go*.

◆ Folk rivals Bob Dylan and Donovan debuted on the UK singles chart in the same week. Interestingly, sales of singles were down 25% compared to January 1964.

◆ An all-star Motown package tour played to half empty houses. Incidentally, The Temptations' US chart topper, 'My Girl', finally hit in the UK in 1992. Fellow American, P.J. Proby, who was faring far better, was banned by the BBC, a major theatre chain and American show *Shindig*, after splitting his trousers on stage.

◆ David Bowie's group, The Mannish Boys (named, as were the Rolling Stones, after a Muddy Waters' song), signed to Parlophone and released their debut single, 'I Pity The Fool' (a cover of Bobby Bland's R&B success).

January 1965

This Mnth	Prev Mnth	Title	Artist	Label	Wks 20	(US Pos)	
1	-	Yeh Yeh	Georgie Fame	Columbia	8	(21)	F
2	1	I Feel Fine	Beatles	Parlophone	10	(1)	G
3	20	Terry	Twinkle	Decca	9		F L
4	-	Girl Don't Come	Sandie Shaw	Pye	9	(42)	
5	-	Go Now!	Moody Blues	Decca	9	(10)	F
6	3	Downtown	Petula Clark	Pye	12	(1)	
7	5	Walk Tall	Val Doonican	Decca	10		F
8	18	Somewhere	P.J. Proby	Liberty	8	(91)	
9	15	I Could Easily Fall	Cliff Richard	Columbia	8		
10	2	I'm Gonna Be Strong	Gene Pitney	Stateside	10	(9)	
11	-	Cast Your Fate To The Wind	Sounds Orchestral	Piccadilly	10	(10)	F L
12	-	Ferry Across The Mersey	Gerry & The Pacemakers	Columbia	7	(6)	
13	11	No Arms Could Ever Hold You	Bachelors	Decca	7	(27)	
14	8	I Understand	Freddie & The Dreamers	Columbia	8	(36)	L
15	-	You've Lost That Lovin' Feelin'	Cilla Black	Parlophone	5		
16	-	Come Tomorrow	Manfred Mann	HMV	7	(50)	
17	-	What Have They Done To The Rain	Searchers	Pye	6	(29)	
18	-	Baby Please Don't Go	Them	Decca	6		F
19	16	Message To Martha (Kentucky Bluebird)	Adam Faith	Parlophone	6		L
20	-	You've Lost That Lovin' Feelin'	Righteous Brothers	London American	7	(1)	F

February 1965

This Mnth	Prev Mnth	Title	Artist	Label	Wks 20	(US Pos)	
1	20	You've Lost That Lovin' Feelin'	Righteous Brothers	London American	7	(1)	F
2	-	Tired Of Waiting For You	Kinks	Pye	7	(6)	
3	-	Keep Searchin' (We'll Follow The Sun)	Del Shannon	Stateside	8	(9)	L
4	-	I'll Never Find Another You	Seekers	Columbia	11	(4)	F
5	16	Come Tomorrow	Manfred Mann	HMV	7	(50)	
6	-	The Special Years	Val Doonican	Decca	8		
7	5	Go Now!	Moody Blues	Decca	9	(10)	F
8	-	Game Of Love	Wayne Fontana & The Mindbenders	Fontana	7	(1)	
9	-	Don't Let Me Be Misunderstood	Animals	Columbia	7	(15)	
10	11	Cast Your Fate To The Wind	Sounds Orchestral	Piccadilly	10	(10)	F L
11	15	You've Lost That Lovin' Feelin'	Cilla Black	Parlophone	5		
12	-	Funny How Love Can Be	Ivy League	Piccadilly	6		F
13	18	Baby Please Don't Go	Them	Decca	6		F
14	-	It Hurts So Much	Jim Reeves	RCA	6		
15	12	Ferry Across The Mersey	Gerry & The Pacemakers	Columbia	7	(6)	
16	-	Leader Of The Pack	Shangri-Las	Red Bird	4	(1)	
17	1	Yeh Yeh	Georgie Fame	Columbia	8	(21)	F
18	4	Girl Don't Come	Sandie Shaw	Pye	9	(42)	
19	3	Terry	Twinkle	Decca	9		F L
20	-	Yes I Will	Hollies	Parlophone	7		

March 1965

This Mnth	Prev Mnth	Title	Artist	Label	Wks 20	(US Pos)	
1	-	It's Not Unusual	Tom Jones	Decca	9	(10)	F
2	4	I'll Never Find Another You	Seekers	Columbia	11	(4)	F
3	-	Silhouettes	Herman's Hermits	Columbia	9	(5)	
4	-	Come And Stay With Me	Marianne Faithfull	Decca	7	(26)	
5	-	The Last Time	Rolling Stones	Decca	9	(9)	
6	-	I'll Stop At Nothing	Sandie Shaw	Pye	7	(97)	
7	-	I Must Be Seeing Things	Gene Pitney	Stateside	6	(31)	
8	8	Game Of Love	Wayne Fontana & The Mindbenders	Fontana	7	(1)	
9	9	Don't Let Me Be Misunderstood	Animals	Columbia	7	(15)	
10	20	Yes I Will	Hollies	Parlophone	7		
11	-	Goodbye My Love	Searchers	Pye	5	(52)	
12	6	The Special Years	Val Doonican	Decca	8		
13	12	Funny How Love Can Be	Ivy League	Piccadilly	6		F
14	-	I Apologise	P.J. Proby	Liberty	5		
15	-	Goodnight	Roy Orbison	London American	5	(21)	
16	14	It Hurts So Much	Jim Reeves	RCA	6		
17	2	Tired Of Waiting For You	Kinks	Pye	7	(6)	
18	-	Concrete And Clay	Unit 4 Plus 2	Decca	9	(28)	F
19	-	Honey I Need	Pretty Things	Fontana	3		L
20	-	The Minute You're Gone	Cliff Richard	Columbia	9		

January 1965

This Mnth	Prev Mnth	Title	Artist	Label	Wks 20	(UK Pos)	
1	2	Come See About Me	Supremes	Motown	11	(27)	G
2	6	I Feel Fine	Beatles	Capitol	8	(1)	G
3	20	Love Potion Number Nine	Searchers	Kapp	8		L
4	-	Downtown	Petula Clark	Warner	11	(2)	F G
5	-	You've Lost That Lovin' Feelin'	Righteous Brothers	Philles	12	(1)	F G
6	1	Mr. Lonely	Bobby Vinton	Epic	11		G
7	16	The Jerk	Larks	Money	7		F L
8	10	Goin' Out Of My Head	Little Anthony & The Imperials	DCP	9		
9	-	Keep Searchin' (We'll Follow The Sun)	Del Shannon	Amy	7	(3)	L
10	-	How Sweet It Is To Be Loved By You	Marvin Gaye	Tamla	7	(49)	
11	15	She's A Woman	Beatles	Capitol	6		
12	-	Amen	Impressions	ABC Paramount	5		
13	-	The Name Game	Shirley Ellis	Congress	8		
14	-	Hold What You've Got	Joe Tex	Dial	6		F
15	19	The Wedding	Julie Rogers	Mercury	5	(3)	F L
16	17	Sha La La	Manfred Mann	Ascot	7	(3)	
17	3	She's Not There	Zombies	Parrot	9	(12)	F G
18	-	Thou Shalt Not Steal	Dick & Deedee	Warner	3		L
19	-	Willow Weep For Me	Chad & Jeremy	World Artists	4		
20	-	Any Way You Want It	Dave Clark Five	Epic	6	(25)	

February 1965

This Mnth	Prev Mnth	Title	Artist	Label	Wks 20	(UK Pos)	
1	5	You've Lost That Lovin' Feelin'	Righteous Brothers	Philles	12	(1)	F G
2	-	This Diamond Ring	Gary Lewis & The Playboys	Liberty	9		F G
3	4	Downtown	Petula Clark	Warner	11	(2)	F G
4	-	My Girl	Temptations	Gordy	10	(2)	G
5	13	The Name Game	Shirley Ellis	Congress	8		
6	-	Shake	Sam Cooke	RCA	5		L
7	-	The Jolly Green Giant	Kingsmen	Wand	7		L
8	-	All Day And All Of The Night	Kinks	Reprise	6	(2)	
9	-	I Go To Pieces	Peter & Gordon	Capitol	5		
10	-	Bye, Bye, Baby (Baby Goodbye)	Four Seasons	Philips	5		
11	14	Hold What You've Got	Joe Tex	Dial	6		F
12	-	Tell Her No	Zombies	Parrot	6	(42)	
13	-	The Boy From New York City	Ad Libs	Blue Cat	5		F L
14	-	Let's Lock The Door (And Throw Away The Key)	Jay & The Americans	UA	5		
15	3	Love Potion Number Nine	Searchers	Kapp	8		L
16	-	The "In" Crowd	Dobie Gray	Charger	3	(25)	F
17	-	Twine Time	Alvin Cash & The Crawlers	Mar-V-Lus	5		F L
18	10	How Sweet It Is To Be Loved By You	Marvin Gaye	Tamla	7	(49)	
19	-	King Of The Road	Roger Miller	Smash	9	(1)	G
20	-	Laugh, Laugh	Beau Brummels	Autumn	4		F

March 1965

This Mnth	Prev Mnth	Title	Artist	Label	Wks 20	(UK Pos)	
1	-	Eight Days A Week	Beatles	Capitol	8		G
2	-	Stop! In The Name Of Love	Supremes	Motown	9	(6)	G
3	4	My Girl	Temptations	Gordy	10	(2)	G
4	-	The Birds And The Bees	Jewel Akens	Era	8	(29)	F L
5	19	King Of The Road	Roger Miller	Smash	9	(1)	G
6	2	This Diamond Ring	Gary Lewis & The Playboys	Liberty	9		F G
7	-	Ferry Across The Mersey	Gerry & The Pacemakers	Laurie	7	(8)	L
8	-	Can't You Hear My Heartbeat	Herman's Hermits	MGM	8		G
9	-	Goldfinger	Shirley Bassey	UA	6	(21)	F L
10	7	The Jolly Green Giant	Kingsmen	Wand	7		L
11	-	Red Roses For A Blue Lady	Bert Kaempfert	Decca	7		L
12	1	You've Lost That Lovin' Feelin'	Righteous Brothers	Philles	12	(1)	F G
13	-	Shotgun	Jr. Walker & The All Stars	Soul	8		F
14	-	Hurt So Bad	Little Anthony & The Imperials	DCP	5		
15	12	Tell Her No	Zombies	Parrot	6	(42)	
16	3	Downtown	Petula Clark	Warner	11	(2)	F G
17	13	The Boy From New York City	Ad Libs	Blue Cat	5		F L
18	-	Little Things	Bobby Goldsboro	UA	4		
19	-	Come Home	Dave Clark Five	Epic	3	(16)	
20	-	People Get Ready	Impressions	ABC Paramount	2		

◆ America's first successful answers to the British group invasion were Gary Lewis & The Playboys and The Beau Brummels. Increasing such acts' chances, was the fact that American immigration authorities drastically cut the number of work permits given to UK groups.

◆ Capitol Records' second biggest selling album artist, Nat 'King' Cole, died from cancer as the label's best sellers, The Beatles, held three of the Top 10 LP chart placings and won the Grammy for Best New Act of 1964.

◆ The latest British record to top the transatlantic charts, 'Downtown' by Petula Clark, won the Grammy for Best Rock'n'Roll Record.

◆ Alan Freed, the radio DJ most responsible for the spread of rock'n'roll in the 1950s, died, aged 42, of uremia. He was awaiting a trial for tax evasion.

◆ Bob Dylan concluded a very successful tour of Britain (the subject of the film *Don't Look Back*) where his album **Bringing It All Back Home** followed **Freewheelin'** at No. 1.

◆ The *NME* Poll winner's concert was a Who's Who of British groups including: The Beatles, Rolling Stones, The Kinks, Herman's Hermits, Freddie & The Dreamers, Moody Blues, The Searchers, The Animals and The Mindbenders.

◆ Cliff Richard clocked up his first No. 1 since the start of the beat boom with his Nashville-recorded version of Sonny James's country hit 'The Minute You're Gone'.

◆ Merseybeat pioneers Gerry & The Pacemakers and Billy J. Kramer & The Dakotas enjoyed their last Top 20 entries. From now on The Beatles were Epstein's only hitmaking group.

April 1965

This Mnth	Prev Mnth	Title	Artist	Label	Wks 20	(US Pos)	
1	20	The Minute You're Gone	Cliff Richard	Columbia	9		
2	-	For Your Love	Yardbirds	Columbia	7	(6)	F
3	18	Concrete And Clay	Unit 4 Plus 2	Decca	9	(28)	F
4	-	Catch The Wind	Donovan	Pye	8	(23)	F
5	5	The Last Time	Rolling Stones	Decca	9	(9)	
6	-	Here Comes The Night	Them	Decca	8	(24)	L
7	-	Times They Are A-Changin'	Bob Dylan	CBS	7		F
8	-	I Can't Explain	Who	Brunswick	7	(93)	F
9	-	Stop! In The Name Of Love	Supremes	Tamla Motown	6	(1)	
10	1	It's Not Unusual	Tom Jones	Decca	9	(10)	F
11	3	Silhouettes	Herman's Hermits	Columbia	9	(5)	
12	-	Ticket To Ride	Beatles	Parlophone	9	(1)	
13	11	Goodbye My Love	Searchers	Pye	5	(52)	
14	-	Little Things	Dave Berry	Decca	6		
15	4	Come And Stay With Me	Marianne Faithfull	Decca	7	(26)	
16	-	I'll Be There	Gerry & The Pacemakers	Columbia	4	(14)	L
17	-	You're Breakin' My Heart	Keely Smith	Reprise	5		F L
18	-	Everybody's Gonna Be Happy	Kinks	Pye	3		
19	2	I'll Never Find Another You	Seekers	Columbia	11	(4)	F
20	-	Pop Go The Workers	Barron Knights	Columbia	8		

May 1965

This Mnth	Prev Mnth	Title	Artist	Label	Wks 20	(US Pos)	
1	12	Ticket To Ride	Beatles	Parlophone	9	(1)	
2	-	King Of The Road	Roger Miller	Philips	9	(4)	F
3	-	True Love Ways	Peter & Gordon	Columbia	10	(14)	
4	-	A World Of Our Own	Seekers	Columbia	11	(19)	
5	-	Where Are You Now (My Love)	Jackie Trent	Pye	7		F L
6	20	Pop Go The Workers	Barron Knights	Columbia	8		
7	-	Bring It On Home To Me	Animals	Columbia	8	(32)	
8	6	Here Comes The Night	Them	Decca	8	(24)	L
9	1	The Minute You're Gone	Cliff Richard	Columbia	9		
10	-	Wonderful World	Herman's Hermits	Columbia	7	(4)	
11	-	Oh No Not My Baby	Manfred Mann	HMV	5		
12	-	Subterranean Homesick Blues	Bob Dylan	CBS	6	(39)	
13	-	This Little Bird	Marianne Faithfull	Decca	7	(32)	
14	4	Catch The Wind	Donovan	Pye	8	(23)	F
15	-	Long Live Love	Sandie Shaw	Pye	9		
16	14	Little Things	Dave Berry	Decca	6		
17	9	Stop! In The Name Of Love	Supremes	Tamla Motown	6	(1)	
18	3	Concrete And Clay	Unit 4 Plus 2	Decca	9	(28)	F
19	-	Poor Man's Son	Rockin' Berries	Piccadilly	7		L
20	-	The Clapping Song	Shirley Ellis	London American	8	(8)	F L

June 1965

This Mnth	Prev Mnth	Title	Artist	Label	Wks 20	(US Pos)	
1	15	Long Live Love	Sandie Shaw	Pye	9		
2	-	Crying In The Chapel	Elvis Presley	RCA	11	(3)	
3	-	The Price Of Love	Everly Brothers	Warner	10		
4	-	Trains And Boats And Planes	Burt Bacharach	London American	7		F L
5	19	Poor Man's Son	Rockin' Berries	Piccadilly	7		L
6	4	A World Of Our Own	Seekers	Columbia	11	(19)	
7	20	The Clapping Song	Shirley Ellis	London American	8	(8)	F L
8	-	I'm Alive	Hollies	Parlophone	10		
9	13	This Little Bird	Marianne Faithfull	Decca	7	(32)	
10	-	Marie	Bachelors	Decca	6	(15)	
11	5	Where Are You Now (My Love)	Jackie Trent	Pye	7		F L
12	3	True Love Ways	Peter & Gordon	Columbia	10	(14)	
13	-	Colours	Donovan	Pye	6	(61)	
14	-	Set Me Free	Kinks	Pye	6	(23)	
15	-	You've Never Been In Love Like This Before	Unit 4 Plus 2	Decca	5	(95)	L
16	1	Ticket To Ride	Beatles	Parlophone	9	(1)	
17	-	Anyway Anyhow Anywhere	Who	Brunswick	6		
18	-	Trains And Boats And Planes	Billy J. Kramer & The Dakotas	Parlophone	4	(47)	L
19	2	King Of The Road	Roger Miller	Philips	9	(4)	F
20	-	Looking Through The Eyes Of Love	Gene Pitney	Stateside	8	(28)	

April 1965

This Mnth	Prev Mnth	Title	Artist	Label	Wks 20	(UK Pos)	
1	-	I'm Telling You Now	Freddie & The Dreamers	Tower	7	(3)	F G
2	2	Stop! In The Name Of Love	Supremes	Motown	9	(6)	G
3	13	Shotgun	Jr. Walker & The All Stars	Soul	8		F
4	8	Can't You Hear My Heartbeat	Herman's Hermits	MGM	8		G
5	-	Game Of Love	Wayne Fontana & The Mindbenders	Fontana	8	(2)	F G L
6	-	I Know A Place	Petula Clark	Warner	7	(17)	
7	-	Nowhere To Run	Martha & The Vandellas	Gordy	5	(26)	
8	4	The Birds And The Bees	Jewel Akens	Era	8	(29)	F L
9	-	Tired Of Waiting For You	Kinks	Reprise	6	(1)	
10	5	King Of The Road	Roger Miller	Smash	9	(1)	
11	-	Mrs. Brown You've Got A Lovely Daughter	Herman's Hermits	MGM	10		G
12	1	Eight Days A Week	Beatles	Capitol	8		G
13	-	The Clapping Song	Shirley Ellis	Congress	5	(6)	L
14	-	Go Now!	Moody Blues	London	6	(1)	F
15	-	Red Roses For A Blue Lady	Vic Dana	Dolton	5		F L
16	-	I'll Never Find Another You	Seekers	Capitol	9	(1)	F
17	9	Goldfinger	Shirley Bassey	UA	6	(21)	F L
18	-	Do You Wanna Dance?	Beach Boys	Capitol	4		
19	-	The Race Is On	Jack Jones	Kapp	3		L
20	-	The Last Time	Rolling Stones	London	5	(1)	

May 1965

This Mnth	Prev Mnth	Title	Artist	Label	Wks 20	(UK Pos)	
1	11	Mrs. Brown You've Got A Lovely Daughter	Herman's Hermits	MGM	10		G
2	-	Count Me In	Gary Lewis & The Playboys	Liberty	7		
3	-	Ticket To Ride	Beatles	Capitol	9	(1)	G
4	16	I'll Never Find Another You	Seekers	Capitol	9	(1)	F
5	-	Silhouettes	Herman's Hermits	MGM	9	(3)	
6	6	I Know A Place	Petula Clark	Warner	7	(17)	
7	5	Game Of Love	Wayne Fontana/Mindbenders	Fontana	8	(2)	F G L
8	-	Help Me, Rhonda	Beach Boys	Capitol	8	(27)	G
9	-	Wooly Bully	Sam The Sham & The Pharaohs	MGM	12	(11)	F G
10	-	Just Once In My Life	Righteous Brothers	Philles	7		
11	-	Cast Your Fate To The Wind	Sounds Orchestral	Parkway	6	(5)	F L
12	-	Back In My Arms Again	Supremes	Motown	8	(40)	G
13	-	I'll Be Doggone	Marvin Gaye	Tamla	6		
14	1	I'm Telling You Now	Freddie & The Dreamers	Tower	7	(3)	F G
15	-	Baby The Rain Must Fall	Glenn Yarbrough	RCA	5		F L
16	-	Crying In The Chapel	Elvis Presley	RCA	10	(1)	G
17	20	The Last Time	Rolling Stones	London	5	(1)	
18	9	Tired Of Waiting For You	Kinks	Reprise	6	(1)	
19	-	It's Not Unusual	Tom Jones	Parrot	6	(1)	F
20	-	One Kiss For Old Time's Sake	Ronnie Dove	Diamond	4		

June 1965

This Mnth	Prev Mnth	Title	Artist	Label	Wks 20	(UK Pos)	
1	9	Wooly Bully	Sam The Sham & The Pharaohs	MGM	12	(11)	F G
2	-	I Can't Help Myself	Four Tops	Motown	11	(10)	G
3	16	Crying In The Chapel	Elvis Presley	RCA	10	(1)	G
4	12	Back In My Arms Again	Supremes	Motown	8	(40)	G
5	8	Help Me, Rhonda	Beach Boys	Capitol	8	(27)	G
6	-	Mr. Tambourine Man	Byrds	Columbia	9	(1)	F G
7	-	Wonderful World	Herman's Hermits	MGM	6	(7)	
8	3	Ticket To Ride	Beatles	Capitol	9	(1)	G
9	-	Engine Engine #9	Roger Miller	Smash	4	(33)	
10	-	Just A Little	Beau Brummels	Autumn	6		L
11	-	For Your Love	Yardbirds	Epic	7	(2)	F
12	1	Mrs. Brown You've Got A Lovely Daughter	Herman's Hermits	MGM	10		G
13	-	Hush, Hush Sweet Charlotte	Patti Page	Columbia	5		L
14	19	It's Not Unusual	Tom Jones	Parrot	6	(1)	F
15	-	(I Can't Get No) Satisfaction	Rolling Stones	London	10	(1)	G
16	-	Seventh Son	Johnny Rivers	Imperial	7		
17	-	Last Chance To Turn Around	Gene Pitney	Musicor	4		
18	4	I'll Never Find Another You	Seekers	Capitol	9	(1)	F
19	-	She's About A Mover	Sir Douglas Quintet	Tribe	4	(15)	F L
20	-	A Walk In The Black Forest	Horst Jankowski	Mercury	5	(3)	F L

US 1965

APR-JUNE

◆ Sixteen months after The Beatles first charted in the USA, British-based acts accounted for nine of the Top 10 hits in America.

▲ Manchester bands Herman's Hermits (above), Freddie & The Dreamers and Wayne Fontana & The Mindbenders all topped the chart. Freddie (who at one time had four singles in the Hot 100) reached No. 1 with the two-year-old 'I'm Telling You Now', while the US-only release, 'Mrs Brown You've Got A Lovely Daughter' by Herman's Hermits, accumulated 600,000 advance orders and entered the Hot 100 at a record high position of 12 (in May they had two hits in the Top 5).

UK 1965 JULY-SEPT

◆ The Rolling Stones played the prestigious London Palladium. Supporting them were Steam Packet featuring Rod Stewart.

▲ The Righteous Brothers' revival of 'Unchained Melody' became a transatlantic success. It would repeat that feat in 1990.

◆ Appearing at the National Jazz & Blues Festival at Richmond were such artists as The Spencer Davis Group, Manfred Mann, Rod Stewart, The Who and The Yardbirds.

◆ After a long absence, US groups started to chart again in Britain, with newcomers The Byrds, Sam The Sham & The Pharaohs and The Walker Brothers leading the way.

July 1965

This Mnth	Prev Mnth	Title	Artist	Label	Wks 20	(US Pos)	
1	8	I'm Alive	Hollies	Parlophone	10		
2	-	Heart Full Of Soul	Yardbirds	Columbia	9	(9)	
3	2	Crying In The Chapel	Elvis Presley	RCA	11	(3)	
4	-	Mr. Tambourine Man	Byrds	CBS	9	(1)	F
5	20	Looking Through The Eyes Of Love	Gene Pitney	Stateside	8	(28)	
6	-	To Know You Is To Love You	Peter & Gordon	Columbia	6	(24)	
7	-	Tossing And Turning	Ivy League	Piccadilly	8		L
8	3	The Price Of Love	Everly Brothers	Warner	10		
9	-	Leave A Little Love	Lulu	Decca	5		
10	13	Colours	Donovan	Pye	6	(61)	
11	-	In The Middle Of Nowhere	Dusty Springfield	Philips	6		
12	17	Anyway Anyhow Anywhere	Who	Brunswick	6		
13	-	You've Got Your Troubles	Fortunes	Decca	9	(7)	F
14	-	There But For Fortune	Joan Baez	Fontana	7	(50)	F
15	4	Trains And Boats And Planes	Burt Bacharach	London American	7		F L
16	1	Long Live Love	Sandie Shaw	Pye	9		
17	-	Wooly Bully	Sam The Sham & The Pharaohs	MGM	6	(2)	F L
18	-	On My Word	Cliff Richard	Columbia	5		
19	14	Set Me Free	Kinks	Pye	6	(23)	
20	-	We Gotta Get Out Of This Place	Animals	Columbia	8	(13)	

August 1965

This Mnth	Prev Mnth	Title	Artist	Label	Wks 20	(US Pos)	
1	-	Help!	Beatles	Parlophone	10	(1)	
2	20	We Gotta Get Out Of This Place	Animals	Columbia	8	(13)	
3	13	You've Got Your Troubles	Fortunes	Decca	9	(7)	F
4	4	Mr. Tambourine Man	Byrds	CBS	9	(1)	F
5	-	Catch Us If You Can	Dave Clark Five	Columbia	6	(4)	
6	-	Everyone's Gone To The Moon	Jonathan King	Decca	7	(17)	F
7	-	A Walk In The Black Forest	Horst Jankowski	Mercury	12	(12)	F L
8	7	Tossing And Turning	Ivy League	Piccadilly	8		L
9	14	There But For Fortune	Joan Baez	Fontana	7	(50)	
10	-	I Got You Babe	Sonny & Cher	Atlantic	9	(1)	F
11	-	Zorba's Dance	Marcello Minerbi	Durium	10		F L
12	-	Summer Nights	Marianne Faithfull	Decca	5	(24)	L
13	-	In Thoughts Of You	Billy Fury	Decca	5		L
14	2	Heart Full Of Soul	Yardbirds	Columbia	9	(9)	
15	-	All I Really Want To Do	Byrds	CBS	5	(40)	
16	-	With These Hands	Tom Jones	Decca	4	(27)	
17	17	Wooly Bully	Sam The Sham & The Pharaohs	MGM	6	(2)	F L
18	11	In The Middle Of Nowhere	Dusty Springfield	Philips	6		
19	-	Don't Make My Baby Blue	Shadows	Columbia	5		
20	-	He's Got No Love	Searchers	Pye	5	(79)	

September 1965

This Mnth	Prev Mnth	Title	Artist	Label	Wks 20	(US Pos)	
1	-	(I Can't Get No) Satisfaction	Rolling Stones	Decca	10	(1)	
2	-	Make It Easy On Yourself	Walker Brothers	Philips	10	(16)	
3	10	I Got You Babe	Sonny & Cher	Atlantic	9	(1)	F
4	7	A Walk In The Black Forest	Horst Jankowski	Mercury	12	(12)	F L
5	-	Like A Rolling Stone	Bob Dylan	CBS	8	(2)	
6	1	Help!	Beatles	Parlophone	10	(1)	
7	11	Zorba's Dance	Marcello Minerbi	Durium	10		F L
8	-	Look Through Any Window	Hollies	Parlophone	8	(32)	
9	15	All I Really Want To Do	Byrds	CBS	5	(40)	
10	-	Tears	Ken Dodd	Columbia	21		G
11	-	Laugh At Me	Sonny	Atlantic	6	(10)	F L
12	-	All I Really Want To Do	Cher	Liberty	5	(15)	F
13	-	That's The Way	Honeycombs	Pye	7		L
14	-	What's New Pussycat?	Tom Jones	Decca	5	(3)	
15	6	Everyone's Gone To The Moon	Jonathan King	Decca	7	(17)	F
16	-	Eve Of Destruction	Barry McGuire	RCA	10	(1)	F L
17	-	Unchained Melody	Righteous Brothers	London American	3	(4)	
18	-	See My Friend	Kinks	Pye	4		
19	-	Il Silenzio	Nini Rosso	Durium	7		F L
20	-	Just A Little Bit Better	Herman's Hermits	Columbia	5	(7)	

July 1965

This Mnth	Prev Mnth	Title	Artist	Label	Wks 20	(UK Pos)	
1	15	(I Can't Get No) Satisfaction	Rolling Stones	London	10	(1)	G
2	2	I Can't Help Myself	Four Tops	Motown	11	(10)	G
3	-	Yes, I'm Ready	Barbara Mason	Artic	7		F L
4	-	Cara Mia	Jay & The Americans	UA	8		
5	6	Mr. Tambourine Man	Byrds	Columbia	9	(1)	F G
6	16	Seventh Son	Johnny Rivers	Imperial	7		
7	-	I'm Henry VIII I Am	Herman's Hermits	MGM	8		G
8	-	What The World Needs Now Is Love	Jackie DeShannon	Imperial	7		F
9	-	What's New Pussycat?	Tom Jones	Parrot	8	(11)	
10	-	You Turn Me On	Ian Whitcomb	Tower	6		F L
11	1	Wooly Bully	Sam The Sham & The Pharaohs	MGM	12	(11)	F G
12	7	Wonderful World	Herman's Hermits	MGM	6	(7)	
13	11	For Your Love	Yardbirds	Epic	7	(2)	F
14	-	(Such An) Easy Question	Elvis Presley	RCA	4		
15	20	A Walk In The Black Forest	Horst Jankowski	Mercury	5	(3)	F L
16	-	Save Your Heart For Me	Gary Lewis & The Playboys	Liberty	7		
17	-	I Like It Like That	Dave Clark Five	Epic	4		
18	3	Crying In The Chapel	Elvis Presley	RCA	10	(1)	G
19	-	Too Many Rivers	Brenda Lee	Decca	3	(22)	
20	-	Laurie (Strange Things Happen)	Dickey Lee	TCF Hall	3		L

August 1965

This Mnth	Prev Mnth	Title	Artist	Label	Wks 20	(UK Pos)	
1	-	I Got You Babe	Sonny & Cher	Atco	8	(1)	F G
2	16	Save Your Heart For Me	Gary Lewis & The Playboys	Liberty	7		
3	1	(I Can't Get No) Satisfaction	Rolling Stones	London	10	(1)	G
4	-	Unchained Melody	Righteous Brothers	Philles	8	(14)	
5	7	I'm Henry VIII I Am	Herman's Hermits	MGM	8		G
6	-	It's The Same Old Song	Four Tops	Motown	7	(34)	
7	-	California Girls	Beach Boys	Capitol	7	(26)	
8	9	What's New Pussycat?	Tom Jones	Parrot	8	(11)	
9	-	Help!	Beatles	Capitol	9	(1)	G
10	-	Don't Just Stand There	Patty Duke	UA	5		F L
11	-	Down In The Boondocks	Billy Joe Royal	Columbia	6	(38)	F
12	-	Baby, I'm Yours	Barbara Lewis	Atlantic	5		
13	-	Hold Me Thrill Me Kiss Me	Mel Carter	Imperial	7		F L
14	17	I Like It Like That	Dave Clark Five	Epic	4		
15	-	Like A Rolling Stone	Bob Dylan	Columbia	7	(4)	F G
16	-	Papa's Got A Brand New Bag	James Brown	King	6	(25)	
17	-	I Want Candy	Strangeloves	Bang	4		F L
18	3	Yes, I'm Ready	Barbara Mason	Artic	7		F L
19	4	Cara Mia	Jay & The Americans	UA	8		
20	-	All I Really Want To Do	Cher	Imperial	4	(9)	F

September 1965

This Mnth	Prev Mnth	Title	Artist	Label	Wks 20	(UK Pos)	
1	9	Help!	Beatles	Capitol	9	(1)	G
2	15	Like A Rolling Stone	Bob Dylan	Columbia	7	(4)	F G
3	-	Eve Of Destruction	Barry McGuire	Dunhill	8	(3)	F G L
4	-	You Were On My Mind	We Five	A&M	9		F L
5	4	Unchained Melody	Righteous Brothers	Philles	8	(14)	
6	-	The "In" Crowd	Ramsey Lewis Trio	Argo	8		F
7	-	It Ain't Me Babe	Turtles	White Whale	5		F
8	1	I Got You Babe	Sonny & Cher	Atco	8	(1)	F G
9	-	Hang On Sloopy	McCoys	Bang	9	(5)	F G
10	7	California Girls	Beach Boys	Capitol	7	(26)	
11	-	Catch Us If You Can	Dave Clark Five	Epic	6	(5)	
12	16	Papa's Got A Brand New Bag	James Brown	King	6	(25)	
13	-	Heart Full Of Soul	Yardbirds	Epic	5	(2)	
14	6	It's The Same Old Song	Four Tops	Motown	7	(34)	
15	13	Hold Me Thrill Me Kiss Me	Mel Carter	Imperial	7		F L
16	-	Laugh At Me	Sonny	Atco	5	(9)	F L
17	-	You've Got Your Troubles	Fortunes	Press	6	(2)	F
18	-	Nothing But Heartaches	Supremes	Motown	4		
19	-	Action	Freddy Cannon	Warner	3		L
20	11	Down In The Boondocks	Billy Joe Royal	Columbia	6	(38)	F

US 1965 JULY–SEPT

◆ The Beatles' third US tour was staggeringly successful. Their performance in front of 56,000 fans at the Shea Stadium was filmed for a TV special. During their tour they met Elvis for the only time as, coincidentally, did Herman's Hermits.

◆ With Bob Dylan (whose new electric folk/rock sound was greeted with boos at the Newport Folk Festival) rivalling Lennon & McCartney as the most respected composer, and with Sonny & Cher and The Byrds being the most talked about new acts on both sides of the Atlantic – America was fast regaining the ground it had lost to Britain.

◆ Despite the fact that American acts were reclaiming much of the chart, British artists such as The Dave Clark Five, Herman's Hermits, The Hollies, Tom Jones, The Searchers and The Zombies still attracted large audiences on their American tours.

103

UK 1965 OCT-DEC

◆ Two British records which sold over a million in the UK but failed to even chart Stateside were: 'Tears' by Ken Dodd and 'The Carnival Is Over' by The Seekers.

◆ In a year when rock giants The Beatles, The Rolling Stones and Bob Dylan were the only acts to top the UK album chart, the longest running No. 1 was the MOR soundtrack album **The Sound Of Music**.

◆ As The Stones scored their fifth successive UK No. 1 with 'Get Off Of My Cloud', Motown (America's top label in 1965) act The Supremes notched up their sixth American topper, 'I Hear A Symphony'.

◆ Decca Records released Marc Bolan's debut disc, 'The Wizard'. The label also recorded the first solo tracks by Van Morrison, whose group, Them, had temporarily disbanded.

October 1965

This Mnth	Prev Mnth	Title	Artist	Label	Wks 20	(US Pos)	
1	10	Tears	Ken Dodd	Columbia	21		G
2	-	If You Gotta Go Go Now	Manfred Mann	HMV	8		
3	16	Eve Of Destruction	Barry McGuire	RCA	10	(1)	F L
4	-	Almost There	Andy Williams	CBS	10	(67)	
5	2	Make It Easy On Yourself	Walker Brothers	Philips	10	(16)	
6	-	Hang On Sloopy	McCoys	Immediate	9	(1)	F L
7	8	Look Through Any Window	Hollies	Parlophone	8	(32)	
8	19	Il Silenzio	Nini Rosso	Durium	7		F L
9	1	(I Can't Get No) Satisfaction	Rolling Stones	Decca	10	(1)	
10	-	Message Understood	Sandie Shaw	Pye	5		
11	-	Baby Don't Go	Sonny & Cher	Reprise	5	(8)	
12	4	A Walk In The Black Forest	Horst Jankowski	Mercury	12	(12)	F L
13	-	Some Of Your Lovin'	Dusty Springfield	Philips	6		
14	-	Evil Hearted You/Still I'm Sad	Yardbirds	Columbia	6		
15	5	Like A Rolling Stone	Bob Dylan	CBS	8	(2)	
16	-	It's Good News Week	Hedgehoppers Anonymous	Decca	6	(48)	F L
17	-	In The Midnight Hour	Wilson Pickett	Atlantic	4	(21)	F
18	-	What Cha Gonna Do About It	Small Faces	Decca	5		F
19	-	Yesterday Man	Chris Andrews	Decca	11	(94)	F
20	-	Here It Comes Again	Fortunes	Decca	7	(27)	

November 1965

This Mnth	Prev Mnth	Title	Artist	Label	Wks 20	(US Pos)	
1	-	Get Off Of My Cloud	Rolling Stones	Decca	8	(1)	
2	1	Tears	Ken Dodd	Columbia	21		G
3	19	Yesterday Man	Chris Andrews	Decca	11	(94)	F
4	-	The Carnival Is Over	Seekers	Columbia	14		G
5	20	Here It Comes Again	Fortunes	Decca	7	(27)	
6	14	Evil Hearted You/Still I'm Sad	Yardbirds	Columbia	6		
7	-	It's My Life	Animals	Columbia	6	(23)	
8	16	It's Good News Week	Hedgehoppers Anonymous	Decca	6	(48)	F L
9	-	Yesterday	Matt Monro	Parlophone	7		L
10	-	My Generation	Who	Brunswick	10	(74)	
11	4	Almost There	Andy Williams	CBS	10	(67)	
12	-	1-2-3	Len Barry	Brunswick	11	(2)	F
13	-	Positively 4th Street	Bob Dylan	CBS	9	(7)	
14	-	Love Is Strange	Everly Brothers	Warner	4		L
15	3	Eve Of Destruction	Barry McGuire	RCA	10	(1)	F L
16	-	Wind Me Up (Let Me Go)	Cliff Richard	Columbia	12		
17	-	A Lovers Concerto	Toys	Stateside	9	(2)	F L
18	6	Hang On Sloopy	McCoys	Immediate	9	(1)	F L
19	2	If You Gotta Go Go Now	Manfred Mann	HMV	8		
20	-	Princess In Rags	Gene Pitney	Stateside	8	(37)	

December 1965

This Mnth	Prev Mnth	Title	Artist	Label	Wks 20	(US Pos)	
1	4	The Carnival Is Over	Seekers	Columbia	14		G
2	16	Wind Me Up (Let Me Go)	Cliff Richard	Columbia	12		
3	10	My Generation	Who	Brunswick	10	(74)	
4	12	1-2-3	Len Barry	Brunswick	11	(2)	F
5	-	Day Tripper/We Can Work it Out	Beatles	Parlophone	10	(5)	G
6	2	Tears	Ken Dodd	Columbia	21		G
7	-	The River	Ken Dodd	Columbia	11		
8	17	A Lovers Concerto	Toys	Stateside	9	(2)	F L
9	-	Maria	P.J. Proby	Liberty	6		L
10	20	Princess In Rags	Gene Pitney	Stateside	8	(37)	
11	1	Get Off Of My Cloud	Rolling Stones	Decca	8	(1)	
12	-	My Ship Is Coming In	Walker Brothers	Philips	10	(63)	
13	13	Positively 4th Street	Bob Dylan	CBS	9	(7)	
14	-	Let's Hang On!	Four Seasons	Philips	11	(3)	
15	-	Rescue Me	Fontella Bass	Chess	7	(4)	F L
16	3	Yesterday Man	Chris Andrews	Decca	11	(94)	F
17	-	Don't Bring Me Your Heartaches	Paul & Barry Ryan	Decca	4		F
18	7	It's My Life	Animals	Columbia	6	(23)	
19	-	To Whom It Concerns	Chris Andrews	Decca	5		L
20	-	Tell Me Why	Elvis Presley	RCA	4	(33)	

This Mnth	Prev Mnth	Title	Artist	Label	Wks 20	(UK Pos)	
1	-	Yesterday	Beatles	Capitol	8	(8)	G
2	-	Treat Her Right	Roy Head	Back Beat	7	(30)	F L
3	9	Hang On Sloopy	McCoys	Bang	9	(5)	F G
4	-	Keep On Dancing	Gentrys	MGM	7		F L
5	-	A Lovers Concerto	Toys	Dynovoice	8	(5)	F G
6	6	The "in" Crowd	Ramsey Lewis Trio	Argo	8		F
7	3	Eve Of Destruction	Barry McGuire	Dunhill	8	(3)	F G L
8	-	Just A Little Bit Better	Herman's Hermits	MGM	4	(15)	
9	-	Baby Don't Go	Sonny & Cher	Reprise	5	(11)	
10	-	Get Off Of My Cloud	Rolling Stones	London	9	(1)	
11	-	Do You Believe In Magic	Lovin' Spoonful	Kama Sutra	5		F
12	-	Everybody Loves A Clown	Gary Lewis & The Playboys	Liberty	6		
13	11	Catch Us If You Can	Dave Clark Five	Epic	6	(5)	
14	17	You've Got Your Troubles	Fortunes	Press	6	(2)	F
15	4	You Were On My Mind	We Five	A&M	9		F L
16	-	You're The One	Vogues	Co & Ce	6		F
17	-	I'm Yours	Elvis Presley	RCA	4		
18	-	Positively 4th Street	Bob Dylan	Columbia	5	(8)	
19	-	Liar, Liar	Castaways	Soma	6		F L
20	-	Some Enchanted Evening	Jay & The Americans	UA	5		

1	10	Get Off Of My Cloud	Rolling Stones	London	9	(1)	
2	-	1-2-3	Len Barry	Decca	9	(3)	F L
3	-	I Hear A Symphony	Supremes	Motown	8	(39)	G
4	5	A Lovers Concerto	Toys	Dynovoice	8	(5)	F G
5	-	Rescue Me	Fontella Bass	Checker	8	(11)	F L
6	-	Let's Hang On!	Four Seasons	Philips	12	(4)	
7	-	A Taste Of Honey	Herb Alpert	A&M	8		
8	-	Turn! Turn! Turn!	Byrds	Columbia	10	(26)	G
9	16	You're The One	Vogues	Co & Ce	6		F
10	-	Ain't That Peculiar	Marvin Gaye	Tamla	7		
11	12	Everybody Loves A Clown	Gary Lewis & The Playboys	Liberty	6		
12	1	Yesterday	Beatles	Capitol	8	(8)	G
13	18	Positively 4th Street	Bob Dylan	Columbia	5	(8)	
14	-	Make Me Your Baby	Barbara Lewis	Atlantic	4		L
15	-	You've Got To Hide Your Love Away	Silkie	Fontana	4	(28)	F L
16	4	Keep On Dancing	Gentrys	MGM	7		F L
17	-	I Got You (I Feel Good)	James Brown	King	9	(29)	G
18	-	I Knew You When	Billy Joe Royal	Columbia	4		
19	-	Run, Baby Run (Back Into My Arms)	Newbeats	Hickory	5	(10)	L
20	-	But You're Mine	Sonny & Cher	Atco	4	(17)	

1	8	Turn! Turn! Turn!	Byrds	Columbia	10	(26)	G
2	6	Let's Hang On!	Four Seasons	Philips	12	(4)	G
3	17	I Got You (I Feel Good)	James Brown	King	9	(29)	G
4	-	Over And Over	Dave Clark Five	Epic	8	(45)	
5	3	I Hear A Symphony	Supremes	Motown	8	(39)	G
6	-	I Can Never Go Home Anymore	Shangri-Las	Red Bird	6		L
7	-	Make The World Go Away	Eddy Arnold	RCA	7	(8)	F L
8	2	1-2-3	Len Barry	Decca	9	(3)	F L
9	-	England Swings	Roger Miller	Smash	6	(13)	L
10	-	Fever	McCoys	Bang	7	(44)	L
11	7	A Taste Of Honey	Herb Alpert	A&M	8		
12	-	I Will	Dean Martin	Reprise	5		L
13	5	Rescue Me	Fontella Bass	Checker	8	(11)	F L
14	-	Hang On Sloopy	Ramsey Lewis Trio	Cadet	4		
15	-	The Sounds Of Silence	Simon & Garfunkel	Columbia	8		F G
16	-	Ebb Tide	Righteous Brothers	Philles	6	(48)	
17	-	Don't Think Twice	Wonder Who?	Philips	4		
18	10	Ain't That Peculiar	Marvin Gaye	Tamla	7		
19	1	Get Off Of My Cloud	Rolling Stones	London	9	(1)	
20	-	We Can Work It Out	Beatles	Capitol	9	(1)	G

US
1965
OCT-DEC

◆ The Byrds topped the chart with 'Turn! Turn! Turn!' which contained the oldest lyric ever on a hit (it was taken from a passage in the Book of Ecclesiastes in the Bible). Also heading towards No. 1 were fellow folk-rockers Simon & Garfunkel with 'The Sounds Of Silence', forcing the recently split duo to re-unite.

◆ The Grateful Dead and Jefferson Airplane headlined the first rock show at the Fillmore in San Francisco.

▲ Soul music made its presence felt on both sides of the Atlantic thanks to hits from James Brown (above), Wilson Pickett, Fontella Bass, Marvin Gaye and The Four Tops.

UK 1966 JAN-MAR

◆ Cover versions were still rife with re-treads of recent songs from The Walker Brothers, Cliff Richard, Otis Redding, Crispian St. Peters, The Mindbenders and The Hollies.

◆ A casual remark by John Lennon, which compared the popularity of The Beatles to Jesus, went virtually unnoticed in the UK. However, it caused problems in some American states.

▲ American soul music continued to thrive. Stevie Wonder (above) had his first UK hit, 'Uptight'. James Brown had the whole of *Ready Steady Go* devoted to him, and Wilson Pickett and Mary Wells also had successful appearances on that TV show.

January 1966

This Mnth	Prev Mnth	Title	Artist	Label	Wks 20	(US Pos)	
1	5	Day Tripper/We Can Work it Out	Beatles	Parlophone	10	(1)	G
2	-	Keep On Runnin'	Spencer Davis Group	Fontana	10	(76)	F
3	12	My Ship Is Coming In	Walker Brothers	Philips	10	(63)	
4	2	Wind Me Up (Let Me Go)	Cliff Richard	Columbia	12		
5	7	The River	Ken Dodd	Columbia	11		
6	1	The Carnival Is Over	Seekers	Columbia	14		G
7	14	Let's Hang On!	Four Seasons	Philips	11	(3)	
8	-	Till The End Of The Day	Kinks	Pye	8	(50)	
9	6	Tears	Ken Dodd	Columbia	21		G
10	-	Spanish Flea	Herb Alpert	Pye International	12	(27)	F
11	-	A Must To Avoid	Herman's Hermits	Columbia	7	(8)	
12	4	1-2-3	Len Barry	Brunswick	11	(2)	F
13	-	Merrie Gentle Pops	Barron Knights	Columbia	5		
14	-	Michelle	Overlanders	Pye	6		F L
15	3	My Generation	Who	Brunswick	10	(74)	
16	15	Rescue Me	Fontella Bass	Chess	7	(4)	F L
17	-	My Girl	Otis Redding	Atlantic	7		F
18	-	A Hard Day's Night	Peter Sellers	Parlophone	4		L
19	8	A Lovers Concerto	Toys	Stateside	9	(2)	F L
20	19	To Whom It Concerns	Chris Andrews	Decca	5		L

February 1966

This Mnth	Prev Mnth	Title	Artist	Label	Wks 20	(US Pos)	
1	-	You Were On My Mind	Crispian St. Peters	Decca	8	(36)	F
2	10	Spanish Flea	Herb Alpert	Pye International	12	(27)	F
3	-	These Boots Are Made For Walkin'	Nancy Sinatra	Reprise	10	(1)	F
4	-	Love's Just A Broken Heart	Cilla Black	Parlophone	6		
5	-	A Groovy Kind Of Love	Mindbenders	Fontana	10	(2)	F
6	14	Michelle	Overlanders	Pye	6		F L
7	2	Keep On Runnin'	Spencer Davis Group	Fontana	10	(76)	F
8	-	19th Nervous Breakdown	Rolling Stones	Decca	7	(2)	
9	11	A Must To Avoid	Herman's Hermits	Columbia	7	(8)	
10	-	Mirror Mirror	Pinkerton's Assorted Colours	Decca	4		F L
11	-	Tomorrow	Sandie Shaw	Pye	5		
12	-	Like A Baby	Len Barry	Brunswick	4	(27)	L
13	-	Girl	St. Louis Union	Decca	5		F L
14	-	My Love	Petula Clark	Pye	6	(1)	
15	1	Day Tripper/We Can Work it Out	Beatles	Parlophone	10	(1)	G
16	17	My Girl	Otis Redding	Atlantic	7		F
17	7	Let's Hang On!	Four Seasons	Philips	11	(3)	
18	-	Sha La La La Lee	Small Faces	Decca	8		
19	3	My Ship Is Coming In	Walker Brothers	Philips	10	(63)	
20	-	Michelle	David & Jonathan	Columbia	4	(18)	F

March 1966

This Mnth	Prev Mnth	Title	Artist	Label	Wks 20	(US Pos)	
1	5	A Groovy Kind Of Love	Mindbenders	Fontana	10	(2)	F
2	18	Sha La La La Lee	Small Faces	Decca	8		
3	-	Barbara Ann	Beach Boys	Capitol	8	(2)	
4	3	These Boots Are Made For Walkin'	Nancy Sinatra	Reprise	10	(1)	F
5	-	Backstage	Gene Pitney	Stateside	6	(25)	
6	-	I Can't Let Go	Hollies	Parlophone	6	(42)	
7	-	The Sun Ain't Gonna Shine Anymore	Walker Brothers	Philips	7	(13)	
8	8	19th Nervous Breakdown	Rolling Stones	Decca	7	(2)	
9	14	My Love	Petula Clark	Pye	6	(1)	
10	2	Spanish Flea	Herb Alpert	Pye International	12	(27)	F
11	-	Make The World Go Away	Eddy Arnold	RCA	10	(6)	F L
12	-	Shapes Of Things	Yardbirds	Columbia	7	(11)	
13	-	Lightnin' Strikes	Lou Christie	MGM	5	(1)	F
14	-	Dedicated Follower Of Fashion	Kinks	Pye	8	(36)	
15	-	Inside-Looking Out	Animals	Decca	4	(34)	
16	1	You Were On My Mind	Crispian St. Peters	Decca	8	(36)	F
17	11	Tomorrow	Sandie Shaw	Pye	5		
18	-	What Now My Love	Sonny & Cher	Atlantic	5	(14)	
19	-	Elusive Butterfly	Bob Lind	Fontana	5	(5)	F L
20	-	This Golden Ring	Fortunes	Decca	2	(82)	

January 1966

This Mnth	Prev Mnth	Title	Artist	Label	Wks 20	(UK Pos)	
1	20	We Can Work It Out	Beatles	Capitol	9	(1)	G
2	15	The Sounds Of Silence	Simon & Garfunkel	Columbia	8		F G
3	-	She's Just My Style	Gary Lewis & The Playboys	Liberty	7		
4	-	Five O'Clock World	Vogues	Co & Ce	9		
5	-	Day Tripper	Beatles	Capitol	5	(1)	G
6	16	Ebb Tide	Righteous Brothers	Philles	6	(48)	
7	-	No Matter What Shape (Your Stomach's In)	T-Bones	Liberty	8		F L
8	-	Flowers On The Wall	Statler Brothers	Columbia	5		F L
9	-	As Tears Go By	Rolling Stones	London	5		
10	-	A Must To Avoid	Herman's Hermits	MGM	6	(6)	
11	-	The Men In My Little Girl's Life	Mike Douglas	Epic	5		F L
12	4	Over And Over	Dave Clark Five	Epic	8	(45)	
13	3	I Got You (I Feel Good)	James Brown	King	9	(29)	G
14	1	Turn! Turn! Turn!	Byrds	Columbia	10	(26)	G
15	2	Let's Hang On!	Four Seasons	Philips	12	(4)	
16	10	Fever	McCoys	Bang	7	(44)	L
17	-	You Didn't Have To Be So Nice	Lovin' Spoonful	Kama Sutra	4		
18	-	Barbara Ann	Beach Boys	Capitol	6	(3)	G
19	-	Just Like Me	Paul Revere & The Raiders	Columbia	5		F
20	-	The Duck	Jackie Lee	Mirwood	5		F L

February 1966

This Mnth	Prev Mnth	Title	Artist	Label	Wks 20	(UK Pos)	
1	-	Lightnin' Strikes	Lou Christie	MGM	8	(11)	G
2	-	My Love	Petula Clark	Warner	8	(4)	G
3	-	Uptight (Everything's Alright)	Stevie Wonder	Tamla	6	(14)	G
4	18	Barbara Ann	Beach Boys	Capitol	6	(3)	G
5	-	My World Is Empty Without You	Supremes	Motown	6		
6	-	Crying Time	Ray Charles	ABC Paramount	6	(50)	
7	7	No Matter What Shape (Your Stomach's In)	T-Bones	Liberty	8		F L
8	-	These Boots Are Made For Walkin'	Nancy Sinatra	Reprise	10	(1)	F G
9	1	We Can Work It Out	Beatles	Capitol	9	(1)	G
10	-	Don't Mess With Bill	Marvelettes	Tamla	6		
11	-	Zorba The Greek	Herb Alpert & Tijuana Brass	A&M	4		
12	4	Five O'Clock World	Vogues	Co & Ce	9		
13	-	The Ballad Of The Green Berets	SSgt. Barry Sadler	RCA	11	(24)	F G L
14	-	Going To A Go-Go	Miracles	Tamla	2	(44)	
15	-	A Well Respected Man	Kinks	Reprise	5		
16	11	The Men In My Little Girl's Life	Mike Douglas	Epic	5		F L
17	-	California Dreamin'	Mamas & The Papas	Dunhill	10	(23)	F G
18	-	Working My Way Back To You	Four Seasons	Philips	4	(50)	
19	3	She's Just My Style	Gary Lewis & The Playboys	Liberty	7		
20	-	Jenny Take A Ride!	Mitch Ryder & The Detroit Wheels	New Voice	4	(33)	F

March 1966

This Mnth	Prev Mnth	Title	Artist	Label	Wks 20	(UK Pos)	
1	13	The Ballad Of The Green Berets	SSgt. Barry Sadler	RCA	11	(24)	F G L
2	8	These Boots Are Made For Walkin'	Nancy Sinatra	Reprise	10	(1)	F G
3	-	19th Nervous Breakdown	Rolling Stones	London	8	(2)	G
4	-	Listen People	Herman's Hermits	MGM	6		
5	17	California Dreamin'	Mamas & The Papas	Dunhill	10	(23)	F G
6	-	Elusive Butterfly	Bob Lind	World Pacific	7	(5)	F L
7	-	Nowhere Man	Beatles	Capitol	7		G
8	-	Homeward Bound	Simon & Garfunkel	Columbia	7	(9)	
9	1	Lightnin' Strikes	Lou Christie	MGM	8	(11)	G
10	-	I Fought The Law	Bobby Fuller Four	Mustang	5		F L
11	-	Daydream	Lovin' Spoonful	Kama Sutra	8	(2)	G
12	-	Love Makes The World Go Round	Deon Jackson	Carla	4		F L
13	18	Working My Way Back To You	Four Seasons	Philips	4	(50)	
14	-	The Cheater	Bob Kuban & The In-Men	Musicland	4		F L
15	2	My Love	Petula Clark	Warner	8	(4)	G
16	3	Uptight (Everything's Alright)	Stevie Wonder	Tamla	6	(14)	G
17	-	(You're My) Soul And Inspiration	Righteous Brothers	Verve	10	(15)	G
18	5	My World Is Empty Without You	Supremes	Motown	6		
19	-	634-5789	Wilson Pickett	Atlantic	4	(36)	F
20	-	I'm So Lonesome I Could Cry	B.J. Thomas	Scepter	8		F

◆ Out on the West Coast, the influential group Buffalo Springfield (including Neil Young and Stephen Stills) were formed, Janis Joplin sang with Big Brother & The Holding Company, and Love released their critically acclaimed debut album. Also The Beach Boys started recording **Pet Sounds**, and a virtual Who's Who of surf singers joined them on their revival of The Regents' 1961 hit, 'Barbara Ann'.

◆ At a time when video tape recorders were only rich people's toys, CBS announced they were developing a metal disc containing music and pictures (that could be seen on a TV) for the mass market.

◆ Vietnam veteran, Staff Sergeant Barry Sadler, not only topped the single chart with his patriotic self-composed debut disc, 'The Ballad Of The Green Berets', but also had a No. 1 album with **Ballads Of The Green Berets**.

◆ The Beatles played their last UK date, alongside the Stones and The Who, at the *NME* poll winners' concert. They started their final World tour by returning to Hamburg.

◆ Like their earlier US No. 1s, 'Mrs. Brown You've Got A Lovely Daughter' and 'I'm Henry VIII I Am', Herman's Hermits latest American hit, a revival of George Formby's music hall favourite 'Leaning On The Lamp Post', was not deemed suitable for release in the group's homeland.

◆ American trio The Walker Brothers (who had scored two successive No. 1s) applied to become British Citizens, soon after British duo Chad & Jeremy had requested US citizenship.

◆ Frank Sinatra scored the only solo transatlantic chart topper of his career with Bert Kaempfert's composition 'Strangers In The Night'.

April 1966

This Mnth	Prev Mnth	Title	Artist	Label	Wks 20	(US Pos)	
1	-	Somebody Help Me	Spencer Davis Group	Fontana	7	(47)	
2	-	Hold Tight	Dave Dee, Dozy, Beaky, Mick & Tich	Fontana	10		F
3	-	The Sound Of Silence	Bachelors	Decca	9		
4	-	Elusive Butterfly	Val Doonican	Decca	8		
5	7	The Sun Ain't Gonna Shine Anymore	Walker Brothers	Philips	7	(13)	
6	-	Substitute	Who	Reaction	9		
7	19	Elusive Butterfly	Bob Lind	Fontana	5	(5)	F L
8	-	You Don't Have To Say You Love Me	Dusty Springfield	Philips	10	(4)	
9	14	Dedicated Follower Of Fashion	Kinks	Pye	8	(36)	
10	11	Make The World Go Away	Eddy Arnold	RCA	10	(6)	F L
11	-	Bang Bang (My Baby Shot Me Down)	Cher	Liberty	8	(2)	
12	12	Shapes Of Things	Yardbirds	Columbia	7	(11)	
13	6	I Can't Let Go	Hollies	Parlophone	6	(42)	
14	-	I Put A Spell On You	Alan Price Set	Decca	5	(80)	F
15	-	Alfie	Cilla Black	Parlophone	7	(95)	
16	-	Pied Piper	Crispian St. Peters	Decca	8	(4)	L
17	-	Someday One Day	Seekers	Columbia	6		
18	2	Sha La La La Lee	Small Faces	Decca	8		
19	3	Barbara Ann	Beach Boys	Capitol	8	(2)	
20	-	Pretty Flamingo	Manfred Mann	HMV	7	(29)	

May 1966

This Mnth	Prev Mnth	Title	Artist	Label	Wks 20	(US Pos)	
1	20	Pretty Flamingo	Manfred Mann	HMV	7	(29)	
2	-	Sloop John B	Beach Boys	Capitol	9	(3)	
3	-	Daydream	Lovin' Spoonful	Pye International	8	(2)	F
4	8	You Don't Have To Say You Love Me	Dusty Springfield	Philips	10	(4)	
5	16	Pied Piper	Crispian St. Peters	Decca	8	(4)	L
6	11	Bang Bang (My Baby Shot Me Down)	Cher	Liberty	8	(2)	
7	-	Wild Thing	Troggs	Fontana	8	(1)	F
8	-	Shotgun Wedding	Roy 'C'	Island	6		F
9	2	Hold Tight	Dave Dee, Dozy, Beaky, Mick & Tich	Fontana	10		F
10	-	Sorrow	Merseys	Fontana	8		L
11	-	Paint It, Black	Rolling Stones	Decca	7	(1)	
12	-	Homeward Bound	Simon & Garfunkel	CBS	7	(5)	F
13	3	The Sound Of Silence	Bachelors	Decca	9		
14	-	Strangers In The Night	Frank Sinatra	Reprise	13	(1)	
15	15	Alfie	Cilla Black	Parlophone	7	(95)	
16	-	Rainy Day Women Nos. 12 & 35	Bob Dylan	CBS	5	(2)	
17	-	Monday Monday	Mamas & The Papas	RCA	10	(1)	F
18	-	Hey Girl	Small Faces	Decca	5		
19	-	Promises	Ken Dodd	Columbia	8		
20	1	Somebody Help Me	Spencer Davis Group	Fontana	7	(47)	

June 1966

This Mnth	Prev Mnth	Title	Artist	Label	Wks 20	(US Pos)	
1	14	Strangers In The Night	Frank Sinatra	Reprise	13	(1)	
2	17	Monday Monday	Mamas & The Papas	RCA	10	(1)	F
3	10	Sorrow	Merseys	Fontana	8		L
4	11	Paint It, Black	Rolling Stones	Decca	7	(1)	
5	-	When A Man Loves A Woman	Percy Sledge	Atlantic	9	(1)	F
6	7	Wild Thing	Troggs	Fontana	8	(1)	F
7	-	Don't Bring Me Down	Animals	Decca	6	(12)	
8	19	Promises	Ken Dodd	Columbia	8		
9	2	Sloop John B	Beach Boys	Capitol	9	(3)	
10	-	Paperback Writer	Beatles	Parlophone	7	(1)	
11	16	Rainy Day Women Nos. 12 & 35	Bob Dylan	CBS	5	(2)	
12	-	Over Under Sideways Down	Yardbirds	Columbia	5	(13)	L
13	18	Hey Girl	Small Faces	Decca	5		
14	-	Don't Answer Me	Cilla Black	Parlophone	6		
15	-	Sunny Afternoon	Kinks	Pye	9	(14)	
16	-	Nothing Comes Easy	Sandie Shaw	Pye	4		
17	-	River Deep Mountain High	Ike & Tina Turner	London American	9	(88)	F
18	8	Shotgun Wedding	Roy 'C'	Island	6		F
19	1	Pretty Flamingo	Manfred Mann	HMV	7	(29)	
20	-	Nobody Needs Your Love	Gene Pitney	Stateside	9		

April 1966

This Mnth	Prev Mnth	Title	Artist	Label	Wks 20	(UK Pos)	
1	17	(You're My) Soul And Inspiration	Righteous Brothers	Verve	10	(15)	G
2	11	Daydream	Lovin' Spoonful	Kama Sutra	8	(2)	G
3	-	Bang Bang (My Baby Shot Me Down)	Cher	Imperial	8	(3)	
4	-	Secret Agent Man	Johnny Rivers	Imperial	7		
5	-	Time Won't Let Me	Outsiders	Capitol	7		F
6	3	19th Nervous Breakdown	Rolling Stones	London	8	(2)	G
7	20	I'm So Lonesome I Could Cry	B.J. Thomas	Scepter	8		F
8	1	The Ballad Of The Green Berets	SSgt. Barry Sadler	RCA	11	(24)	F G L
9	-	Good Lovin'	Young Rascals	Atlantic	9		F G
10	7	Nowhere Man	Beatles	Capitol	7		G
11	-	Kicks	Paul Revere & The Raiders	Columbia	9		
12	-	Sloop John B	Beach Boys	Capitol	7	(2)	
13	5	California Dreamin'	Mamas & The Papas	Dunhill	10	(23)	F G
14	-	Sure Gonna Miss Her	Gary Lewis & The Playboys	Liberty	4		
15	-	Monday Monday	Mamas & The Papas	Dunhill	8	(3)	G
16	8	Homeward Bound	Simon & Garfunkel	Columbia	7	(9)	
17	-	A Sign Of The Times	Petula Clark	Warner	3	(49)	
18	-	This Old Heart Of Mine	Isley Brothers	Tamla	4	(3)	
19	2	These Boots Are Made For Walkin'	Nancy Sinatra	Reprise	10	(1)	F G
20	-	Leaning On The Lamp Post	Herman's Hermits	MGM	5		

May 1966

This Mnth	Prev Mnth	Title	Artist	Label	Wks 20	(UK Pos)	
1	15	Monday Monday	Mamas & The Papas	Dunhill	8	(3)	G
2	9	Good Lovin'	Young Rascals	Atlantic	9		F G
3	-	Rainy Day Women #12 & 35	Bob Dylan	Columbia	7	(7)	
4	11	Kicks	Paul Revere & The Raiders	Columbia	9		
5	-	When A Man Loves A Woman	Percy Sledge	Atlantic	8	(4)	F G
6	12	Sloop John B	Beach Boys	Capitol	7	(2)	
7	-	A Groovy Kind Of Love	Mindbenders	Fontana	8	(2)	F G L
8	1	(You're My) Soul And Inspiration	Righteous Brothers	Verve	10	(15)	G
9	-	Message To Michael	Dionne Warwick	Scepter	6		
10	-	How Does That Grab You Darlin'	Nancy Sinatra	Reprise	4	(19)	
11	-	Gloria	Shadows Of Knight	Dunwich	6		F L
12	-	Love Is Like An Itching In My Heart	Supremes	Motown	5		
13	20	Leaning On The Lamp Post	Herman's Hermits	MGM	5		
14	4	Secret Agent Man	Johnny Rivers	Imperial	7		
15	-	Paint It, Black	Rolling Stones	London	9	(1)	G
16	-	I Am A Rock	Simon & Garfunkel	Columbia	8	(17)	
17	-	Did You Ever Have To Make Up Your Mind	Lovin' Spoonful	Kama Sutra	7		
18	-	The Sun Ain't Gonna Shine (Anymore)	Walker Brothers	Smash	4	(1)	F L
19	-	Shapes Of Things	Yardbirds	Epic	4	(3)	
20	-	Eight Miles High	Byrds	Columbia	3	(24)	L

June 1966

This Mnth	Prev Mnth	Title	Artist	Label	Wks 20	(UK Pos)	
1	15	Paint It, Black	Rolling Stones	London	9	(1)	G
2	17	Did You Ever Have To Make Up Your Mind	Lovin' Spoonful	Kama Sutra	7		
3	16	I Am A Rock	Simon & Garfunkel	Columbia	8	(17)	
4	5	When A Man Loves A Woman	Percy Sledge	Atlantic	8	(4)	F G
5	-	Strangers In The Night	Frank Sinatra	Reprise	8	(1)	G
6	7	A Groovy Kind Of Love	Mindbenders	Fontana	8	(2)	F G L
7	-	Barefootin'	Robert Parker	Nola	7	(24)	F L
8	-	Green Grass	Gary Lewis & The Playboys	Liberty	5		
9	-	Sweet Talkin' Guy	Chiffons	Laurie	6	(4)	L
10	-	Cool Jerk	Capitols	Karen	8		F L
11	1	Monday Monday	Mamas & The Papas	Dunhill	8	(3)	G
12	-	It's A Man's Man's Man's World	James Brown	King	5	(13)	
13	-	Red Rubber Ball	Cyrkle	Columbia	8		F G
14	-	Oh How Happy	Shades Of Blue	Impact	6		F L
15	-	Paperback Writer	Beatles	Capitol	8	(1)	G
16	-	You Don't Have To Say You Love Me	Dusty Springfield	Philips	8	(1)	
17	-	Opus 17 (Don't You Worry 'Bout Me)	Four Seasons	Philips	5	(20)	
18	3	Rainy Day Women #12 & 35	Bob Dylan	Columbia	7	(7)	
19	12	Love Is Like An Itching In My Heart	Supremes	Motown	5		
20	-	The More I See You	Chris Montez	A&M	3	(3)	L

US 1966 APR-JUNE

◆ 'Green Grass' gave Gary Lewis & The Playboys a record seventh successive Top 10 entry with their first seven releases. None of Lewis's US hits cracked the UK chart.

▲ Among the most successful new transatlantic artists were trend-setting American acts: The Lovin' Spoonful, Simon & Garfunkel (above) and The Mamas & The Papas.

◆ After losing The Righteous Brothers to MGM, Phil Spector released his most ambitious and expensive ($22,000) production, 'River Deep Mountain High' by Ike & Tina Turner, which was only successful in the UK.

UK 1966

JULY-SEPT

◆ 'They're Coming To Take Me Away Ha-Haaa!' was one of the strangest transatlantic hits of all time. This "madman's monologue" was released by recording engineer-cum-successful MOR songsmith Jerry Samuels under the apt name Napoleon XIV. It cost him $15 to record and sold half a million copies in its first week.

◆ The *NME* announced "The British Beat Boom is over". They pointed out there were now more American records on the US chart than British, and that sales of UK records in America were dropping. *NME* concluded, "Whatever happens, Britain has made her mark upon the world of pop, America now accepts us as a force to be reckoned with – the dark days when British hits in American were regarded as flukes are over."

July 1966

This Mnth	Prev Mnth	Title	Artist	Label	Wks 20	(US Pos)	
1	15	Sunny Afternoon	Kinks	Pye	9	(14)	
2	17	River Deep Mountain High	Ike & Tina Turner	London American	9	(88)	F
3	20	Nobody Needs Your Love	Gene Pitney	Stateside	9		
4	-	Get Away	Georgie Fame	Columbia	7	(70)	
5	1	Strangers In The Night	Frank Sinatra	Reprise	13	(1)	
6	-	Bus Stop	Hollies	Parlophone	7	(5)	
7	10	Paperback Writer	Beatles	Parlophone	7	(1)	
8	-	Out Of Time	Chris Farlowe	Immediate	8		F L
9	-	Black Is Black	Los Bravos	Decca	9	(4)	F
10	-	Hideaway	Dave Dee, Dozy, Beaky, Mick & Tich	Fontana	6		
11	-	I Couldn't Live Without Your Love	Petula Clark	Pye	7	(9)	
12	14	Don't Answer Me	Cilla Black	Parlophone	6		
13	5	When A Man Loves A Woman	Percy Sledge	Atlantic	9	(1)	F
14	-	Love Letters	Elvis Presley	RCA	7	(19)	
15	2	Monday Monday	Mamas & The Papas	RCA	10	(1)	F
16	-	With A Girl Like You	Troggs	Fontana	8	(29)	
17	-	The More I See You	Chris Montez	Pye International	9	(16)	
18	-	Goin' Back	Dusty Springfield	Philips	6		
19	-	Lana	Roy Orbison	London American	5		
20	7	Don't Bring Me Down	Animals	Decca	6	(12)	

August 1966

This Mnth	Prev Mnth	Title	Artist	Label	Wks 20	(US Pos)	
1	16	With A Girl Like You	Troggs	Fontana	8	(29)	
2	9	Black Is Black	Los Bravos	Decca	9	(4)	F
3	17	The More I See You	Chris Montez	Pye International	9	(16)	
4	-	Mama	Dave Berry	Decca	10		L
5	-	God Only Knows	Beach Boys	Capitol	9	(39)	
6	8	Out Of Time	Chris Farlowe	Immediate	8		F L
7	-	Yellow Submarine/Eleanor Rigby	Beatles	Parlophone	9	(2)	
8	-	Visions	Cliff Richard	Columbia	8		
9	-	Summer In The City	Lovin' Spoonful	Kama Sutra	7	(1)	L
10	14	Love Letters	Elvis Presley	RCA	7	(19)	
11	11	I Couldn't Live Without Your Love	Petula Clark	Pye	7	(9)	
12	-	Hi-Lili-Hi-Lo	Alan Price Set	Decca	7		
13	-	They're Coming To Take Me Away Ha-Haaa!	Napoleon XIV	Warner	6	(3)	F L
14	4	Get Away	Georgie Fame	Columbia	7	(70)	
15	1	Sunny Afternoon	Kinks	Pye	9	(14)	
16	18	Goin' Back	Dusty Springfield	Philips	6		
17	-	Lovers Of The World Unite	David & Jonathan	Columbia	7		L
18	-	I Saw Her Again	Mamas & The Papas	RCA	6	(5)	
19	-	I Want You	Bob Dylan	CBS	5	(20)	
20	-	All Or Nothing	Small Faces	Decca	8		

September 1966

This Mnth	Prev Mnth	Title	Artist	Label	Wks 20	(US Pos)	
1	20	All Or Nothing	Small Faces	Decca	8		
2	7	Yellow Submarine/Eleanor Rigby	Beatles	Parlophone	9	(2)	
3	5	God Only Knows	Beach Boys	Capitol	9	(39)	
4	-	Too Soon To Know	Roy Orbison	London American	10	(68)	
5	-	Distant Drums	Jim Reeves	RCA	19	(45)	
6	13	They're Coming To Take Me Away Ha-Haaa!	Napoleon XIV	Warner	6	(3)	F L
7	17	Lovers Of The World Unite	David & Jonathan	Columbia	7		L
8	4	Mama	Dave Berry	Decca	10		L
9	-	Working In The Coal Mine	Lee Dorsey	Stateside	6	(8)	F
10	-	Got To Get You Into My Life	Cliff Bennett & The Rebel Rousers	Parlophone	5		L
11	-	Just Like A Woman	Manfred Mann	Fontana	6		
12	1	With A Girl Like You	Troggs	Fontana	8	(29)	
13	-	I'm A Boy	Who	Reaction	10		
14	8	Visions	Cliff Richard	Columbia	8		
15	-	Little Man	Sonny & Cher	Atlantic	6	(21)	
16	-	You Can't Hurry Love	Supremes	Tamla Motown	8	(1)	
17	18	I Saw Her Again	Mamas & The Papas	RCA	6	(5)	
18	12	Hi-Lili-Hi-Lo	Alan Price Set	Decca	7		
19	9	Summer In The City	Lovin' Spoonful	Kama Sutra	7	(1)	L
20	-	When I Come Home	Spencer Davis Group	Fontana	4		

July 1966

This Mnth	Prev Mnth	Title	Artist	Label	Wks 20	(UK Pos)	
1	-	Hanky Panky	Tommy James & The Shondells	Roulette	8	(38)	F G
2	15	Paperback Writer	Beatles	Capitol	8	(1)	G
3	13	Red Rubber Ball	Cyrkle	Columbia	8		F G
4	-	Wild Thing	Troggs	Fontana/Atco	8	(2)	F G
5	16	You Don't Have To Say You Love Me	Dusty Springfield	Philips	8	(1)	
6	5	Strangers In The Night	Frank Sinatra	Reprise	8	(1)	G
7	-	Lil' Red Riding Hood	Sam The Sham & The Pharaohs	MGM	9	(46)	G L
8	-	Hungry	Paul Revere & The Raiders	Columbia	6		
9	-	Little Girl	Syndicate Of Sound	Bell	4		F L
10	-	The Pied Piper	Crispian St. Peters	Jamie	6	(5)	F L
11	-	I Saw Her Again	Mamas & The Papas	Dunhill	6	(11)	
12	-	Along Comes Mary	Association	Valiant	4		F
13	1	Paint It, Black	Rolling Stones	London	9	(1)	G
14	10	Cool Jerk	Capitols	Karen	8		F L
15	-	Sweet Pea	Tommy Roe	ABC Paramount	7		G
16	-	Dirty Water	Standells	Tower	4		F L
17	-	Ain't Too Proud To Beg	Temptations	Gordy	5	(21)	
18	-	Don't Bring Me Down	Animals	MGM	5	(6)	
19	-	Somewhere, My Love	Ray Conniff & The Singers	Columbia	5		F L
20	3	I Am A Rock	Simon & Garfunkel	Columbia	8	(17)	

August 1966

This Mnth	Prev Mnth	Title	Artist	Label	Wks 20	(UK Pos)	
1	-	Summer In The City	Lovin' Spoonful	Kama Sutra	8	(8)	G
2	7	Lil' Red Riding Hood	Sam The Sham & The Pharaohs	MGM	9	(46)	G L
3	4	Wild Thing	Troggs	Fontana/Atco	8	(2)	F G
4	-	Sunny	Bobby Hebb	Philips	8	(12)	F G L
5	-	They're Coming To Take Me Away Ha-Haaa!	Napoleon XIV	Warner	4	(4)	F L
6	10	The Pied Piper	Crispian St. Peters	Jamie	6	(5)	F L
7	-	See You In September	Happenings	B.T.Puppy	8		F
8	-	Mothers Little Helper	Rolling Stones	London	6		
9	-	I Couldn't Live Without Your Love	Petula Clark	Warner	5	(6)	
10	15	Sweet Pea	Tommy Roe	ABC Paramount	7		G
11	11	I Saw Her Again	Mamas & The Papas	Dunhill	6	(11)	
12	-	Sunshine Superman	Donovan	Epic	9	(2)	F G
13	19	Somewhere, My Love	Ray Conniff & The Singers	Columbia	5		F L
14	-	Blowin' In The Wind	Stevie Wonder	Tamla	5	(36)	
15	-	Over Under Sideways Down	Yardbirds	Epic	4	(10)	L
16	1	Hanky Panky	Tommy James & The Shondells	Roulette	8	(38)	F G
17	-	This Door Swings Both Ways	Herman's Hermits	MGM	4	(18)	
18	-	Sweet Dreams	Tommy McLain	MSL	4		F L
19	-	Summertime	Billy Stewart	Chess	4	(39)	F L
20	-	My Heart's Symphony	Gary Lewis & The Playboys	Liberty	4	(36)	

September 1966

This Mnth	Prev Mnth	Title	Artist	Label	Wks 20	(UK Pos)	
1	-	You Can't Hurry Love	Supremes	Motown	9	(3)	G
2	12	Sunshine Superman	Donovan	Epic	9	(2)	F G
3	-	Yellow Submarine	Beatles	Capitol	7	(1)	G
4	7	See You In September	Happenings	B.T.Puppy	8		F
5	-	Bus Stop	Hollies	Imperial	6	(5)	F
6	-	Wouldn't It Be Nice	Beach Boys	Capitol	5	(58)	
7	-	Cherish	Association	Valiant	8		G
8	-	Land Of 1,000 Dances	Wilson Pickett	Atlantic	5	(22)	
9	4	Sunny	Bobby Hebb	Philips	8	(12)	F G L
10	1	Summer In The City	Lovin' Spoonful	Kama Sutra	8	(8)	G
11	-	Guantanamera	Sandpipers	A&M	5	(7)	F
12	-	Working In The Coal Mine	Lee Dorsey	Amy	5	(8)	L
13	-	Beauty Is Only Skin Deep	Temptations	Gordy	6	(18)	G
14	-	Born A Woman	Sandy Posey	MGM	7	(24)	F
15	19	Summertime	Billy Stewart	Chess	4	(39)	F L
16	-	Black Is Black	Los Bravos	Parrot	6	(2)	F L
17	-	Eleanor Rigby	Beatles	Capitol	3	(1)	
18	14	Blowin' In The Wind	Stevie Wonder	Tamla	5	(36)	
19	-	96 Tears	? (Question Mark) & The Mysterians	Cameo	11	(37)	F G L
20	-	Sunny Afternoon	Kinks	Reprise	4	(1)	

◆ John Lennon's comment that The Beatles were more popular than Jesus resulted in demonstrations during their third and last US tour. Their last ever show was, ironically, in San Francisco – the town that replaced Liverpool and Manchester as rock's trend-setting centre.

▲ You could tell it was summer by the charts, which included such titles as 'Summertime', 'Summer In The City', 'Sunny', 'Sunny Afternoon' and 'Sunshine Superman', the latter introducing British singer/song-writer Donovan (above) to the Top 20.

UK 1966 OCT-DEC

In the year that tape cassettes and tape cartridges were introduced commercially, sales of singles dropped 17% (they had fallen 15% in 1965), and album sales increased by 6%, after a 1965 rise of 13%.

The Beach Boys were mobbed when they arrived for a British tour. They ousted The Beatles as World's Top Group in the *NME* poll, and their transatlantic No. 1, 'Good Vibrations', showed how good pop records could be.

A chart survey showed that the oddly named Dave Dee, Dozy, Beaky, Mick & Tich were the most successful singles act in the UK during 1966. Surprisingly, the group, whose songs and productions were always original and interesting, went almost unnoticed across the Atlantic.

October 1966

This Mnth	Prev Mnth	Title	Artist	Label	Wks 20	(US Pos)	
1	5	Distant Drums	Jim Reeves	RCA	19	(45)	
2	-	Bend It	Dave Dee, Dozy, Beaky, Mick & Tich	Fontana	9		
3	13	I'm A Boy	Who	Reaction	10		
4	-	Winchester Cathedral	New Vaudeville Band	Fontana	9	(1)	F
5	16	You Can't Hurry Love	Supremes	Tamla Motown	8	(1)	
6	-	Have You Seen Your Mother, Baby, Standing In The Shadow	Rolling Stones	Decca	6	(9)	
7	-	Guantanamera	Sandpipers	Pye International	9	(9)	F L
8	15	Little Man	Sonny & Cher	Atlantic	6	(21)	
9	-	All I See Is You	Dusty Springfield	Philips	7	(20)	
10	-	I Can't Control Myself	Troggs	Page One	9	(43)	
11	-	Walk With Me	Seekers	Columbia	6		
12	4	Too Soon To Know	Roy Orbison	London American	10	(68)	
13	-	Reach Out I'll Be There	Four Tops	Tamla Motown	10	(1)	F
14	-	Stop Stop Stop	Hollies	Parlophone	8	(7)	
15	-	Sunny	Georgie Fame	Columbia	4		
16	-	Sunny	Bobby Hebb	Philips	3	(2)	F L
17	1	All Or Nothing	Small Faces	Decca	8		
18	-	Another Tear Falls	Walker Brothers	Philips	3		
19	-	No Milk Today	Herman's Hermits	Columbia	7	(35)	
20	2	Yellow Submarine/Eleanor Rigby	Beatles	Parlophone	9	(2)	

November 1966

This Mnth	Prev Mnth	Title	Artist	Label	Wks 20	(US Pos)	
1	13	Reach Out I'll Be There	Four Tops	Tamla Motown	10	(1)	F
2	14	Stop Stop Stop	Hollies	Parlophone	8	(7)	
3	-	Semi-Detached Suburban Mr.James	Manfred Mann	Fontana	8		
4	-	High Time	Paul Jones	HMV	8		F
5	-	Good Vibrations	Beach Boys	Capitol	11	(1)	
6	10	I Can't Control Myself	Troggs	Page One	9	(43)	
7	1	Distant Drums	Jim Reeves	RCA	19	(45)	
8	-	Gimme Some Loving	Spencer Davis Group	Fontana	7	(7)	
9	-	If I Were A Carpenter	Bobby Darin	Atlantic	7	(8)	L
10	19	No Milk Today	Herman's Hermits	Columbia	7	(35)	
11	4	Winchester Cathedral	New Vaudeville Band	Fontana	9	(1)	F
12	-	Holy Cow	Lee Dorsey	Stateside	8	(23)	L
13	7	Guantanamera	Sandpipers	Pye International	9	(9)	F L
14	-	Green Green Grass Of Home	Tom Jones	Decca	15	(11)	G
15	-	Time Drags By	Cliff Richard	Columbia	4		
16	-	A Fool Am I	Cilla Black	Parlophone	4		
17	2	Bend It	Dave Dee, Dozy, Beaky etc.	Fontana	9		
18	-	What Would I Be	Val Doonican	Decca	11		
19	-	I've Got You Under My Skin	Four Seasons	Philips	5	(9)	
20	-	Help Me Girl	Eric Burdon & The Animals	Decca	4	(29)	

December 1966

This Mnth	Prev Mnth	Title	Artist	Label	Wks 20	(US Pos)	
1	14	Green Green Grass Of Home	Tom Jones	Decca	15	(11)	G
2	18	What Would I Be	Val Doonican	Decca	11		
3	5	Good Vibrations	Beach Boys	Capitol	11	(1)	
4	-	Morningtown Ride	Seekers	Columbia	10	(44)	
5	-	Friday On My Mind	Easybeats	UA	9	(16)	F
6	-	My Mind's Eye	Small Faces	Decca	6		
7	-	Dead End Street	Kinks	Pye	9	(73)	
8	8	Gimme Some Loving	Spencer Davis Group	Fontana	7	(7)	
9	-	What Becomes Of The Brokenhearted	Jimmy Ruffin	Tamla Motown	7	(7)	F
10	3	Semi-Detached Suburban Mr.James	Manfred Mann	Fontana	8		
11	-	Sunshine Superman	Donovan	Pye	7	(1)	
12	12	Holy Cow	Lee Dorsey	Stateside	8	(23)	L
13	-	Just One Smile	Gene Pitney	Stateside	6	(64)	
14	-	You Keep Me Hangin' On	Supremes	Tamla Motown	7	(1)	
15	-	Save Me	Dave Dee, Dozy, Beaky, Mick & Tich	Fontana	7		
16	7	Distant Drums	Jim Reeves	RCA	19	(45)	
17	-	If Every Day Was Like Christmas	Elvis Presley	RCA	4		
18	1	Reach Out I'll Be There	Four Tops	Tamla Motown	10	(1)	F
19	4	High Time	Paul Jones	HMV	8		F
20	-	There Won't Be Many Coming Home	Roy Orbison	London American	3		L

October 1966

This Mnth	Prev Mnth	Title	Artist	Label	Wks 20	(UK Pos)	
1	-	Reach Out I'll Be There	Four Tops	Motown	9	(1)	G
2	19	96 Tears	? (Question Mark) & The Mysterians	Cameo	11	(37)	F G L
3	7	Cherish	Association	Valiant	8		G
4	-	Last Train To Clarksville	Monkees	Colgems	10	(23)	F G
5	-	Psychotic Reaction	Count Five	Double Shot	5		F L
6	-	Walk Away Renee	Left Banke	Smash	7		F
7	-	What Becomes Of The Brokenhearted	Jimmy Ruffin	Soul	9	(8)	F
8	-	Cherry Cherry	Neil Diamond	Bang	6		F
9	1	You Can't Hurry Love	Supremes	Motown	9	(3)	G
10	16	Black Is Black	Los Bravos	Parrot	6	(2)	F L
11	13	Beauty Is Only Skin Deep	Temptations	Gordy	6	(18)	G
12	-	Poor Side Of Town	Johnny Rivers	Imperial	10		G
13	-	I've Got You Under My Skin	Four Seasons	Philips	5	(12)	
14	-	Dandy	Herman's Hermits	MGM	6		
15	-	See See Rider	Eric Burdon & The Animals	MGM	5		
16	-	Hooray For Hazel	Tommy Roe	ABC	7		
17	-	Have You Seen Your Mother Baby Standing In The Shadow?	Rolling Stones	London	5	(5)	
18	-	If I Were A Carpenter	Bobby Darin	Atlantic	7	(9)	L
19	5	Bus Stop	Hollies	Imperial	6	(5)	F
20	2	Sunshine Superman	Donovan	Epic	9	(2)	F G

November 1966

This Mnth	Prev Mnth	Title	Artist	Label	Wks 20	(UK Pos)	
1	4	Last Train To Clarksville	Monkees	Colgems	10	(23)	F G
2	12	Poor Side Of Town	Johnny Rivers	Imperial	10		G
3	2	96 Tears	? (Question Mark)/Mysterians	Cameo	11	(37)	F G L
4	-	Good Vibrations	Beach Boys	Capitol	10	(1)	G
5	-	You Keep Me Hangin' On	Supremes	Motown	8	(8)	G
6	-	Winchester Cathedral	New Vaudeville Band	Fontana	11	(4)	F G L
7	-	I'm Your Puppet	James & Bobby Purify	Bell	7	(12)	F L
8	-	Devil With A Blue Dress On & Good Golly Miss Molly	Mitch Ryder & The Detroit Wheels	New Voice	11		
9	18	If I Were A Carpenter	Bobby Darin	Atlantic	7	(9)	L
10	1	Reach Out I'll Be There	Four Tops	Motown	9	(1)	G
11	14	Dandy	Herman's Hermits	MGM	6		
12	16	Hooray For Hazel	Tommy Roe	ABC	7		
13	-	Love Is A Hurtin' Thing	Lou Rawls	Capitol	5		F
14	-	Born Free	Roger Williams	Kapp	9		L
15	-	Rain On The Roof	Lovin' Spoonful	Kama Sutra	5		
16	6	Walk Away Renee	Left Banke	Smash	7		F
17	-	Lady Godiva	Peter & Gordon	Capitol	6	(16)	
18	7	What Becomes Of The Broken...	Jimmy Ruffin	Soul	9	(8)	F
19	17	Have You Seen Your Mother Baby...	Rolling Stones	London	5	(5)	
20	-	Coming On Strong	Brenda Lee	Decca	5		L

December 1966

This Mnth	Prev Mnth	Title	Artist	Label	Wks 20	(UK Pos)	
1	6	Winchester Cathedral	New Vaudeville Band	Fontana	11	(4)	F G L
2	-	Mellow Yellow	Donovan	Epic	8	(8)	G
3	4	Good Vibrations	Beach Boys	Capitol	10	(1)	G
4	8	Devil With A Blue Dress On &	Mitch Ryder/The Detroit Wheels	New Voice	11		
5	5	You Keep Me Hangin' On	Supremes	Motown	8	(8)	G
6	-	That's Life	Frank Sinatra	Reprise	8	(46)	
7	-	I'm A Believer	Monkees	Colgems	12	(1)	G
8	14	Born Free	Roger Williams	Kapp	9		L
9	-	Sugar Town	Nancy Sinatra	Reprise	8	(8)	G
10	17	Lady Godiva	Peter & Gordon	Capitol	6	(16)	
11	-	A Place In The Sun	Stevie Wonder	Tamla	5	(20)	
12	-	(I Know) I'm Losing You	Temptations	Gordy	6	(19)	
13	-	Snoopy Vs. The Red Baron	Royal Guardsmen	Laurie	9	(8)	F G
14	-	Whispers (Gettin' Louder)	Jackie Wilson	Brunswick	4		
15	-	I'm Ready For Love	Martha & The Vandellas	Gordy	4	(29)	
16	-	Stop Stop Stop	Hollies	Imperial	5	(2)	
17	7	I'm Your Puppet	James & Bobby Purify	Bell	7	(12)	F L
18	-	Tell It Like It Is	Aaron Neville	Par-Lo	9		F G
19	-	A Hazy Shade Of Winter	Simon & Garfunkel	Columbia	4		
20	2	Poor Side Of Town	Johnny Rivers	Imperial	10		G

◆ In 1966 a third of the records sold were LPs. Labels were therefore actively seeking artists with album, as well as single, sales potential.

◆ Light shows and strobes were now part of many West Coast groups' stage shows. LSD was declared dangerous and illegal by the US government who started looking for drug-related hidden meanings in songs.

◆ Hottest new act was The Monkees, a quartet of actors/singers assembled for a Beatles-esque TV series. Their first two singles and debut album topped the chart. Incidentally, fellow chart newcomer, Neil Diamond, penned their hit 'I'm A Believer'.

◆ Over 10,000 records were released in 1966, and the value of record and tape sales in the USA rose to $650 million. Ten years earlier, when rock was starting to roll, 6,000 records were issued with sales totalling $250 million.

UK 1967 JAN-MAR

▲ Tom Jones had his biggest UK hit with 'Green Green Grass Of Home'. Engelbert Humperdinck (above) – who shared Jones's manager – also struck UK gold (and made the US Top 20) with a revival of another US country hit, 'Release Me'.

◆ Pink Floyd, The Jimi Hendrix Experience, Cream and The Monkees debuted on the UK chart. The Monkees' TV show was successful in Britain, catapulting them to the top of the charts.

◆ Acts making their UK stage debuts included Otis Redding and Sam & Dave (on a Stax Records package show) and The Jeff Beck Group with vocalist Rod Stewart.

January 1967

This Mnth	Prev Mnth	Title	Artist	Label	Wks 20	(US Pos)	
1	1	Green Green Grass Of Home	Tom Jones	Decca	15	(11)	G
2	4	Morningtown Ride	Seekers	Columbia	10	(44)	
3	-	Happy Jack	Who	Reaction	7	(24)	
4	11	Sunshine Superman	Donovan	Pye	7	(1)	
5	-	I'm A Believer	Monkees	RCA	10	(1)	F
6	-	In The Country	Cliff Richard	Columbia	6		
7	15	Save Me	Dave Dee, Dozy, Beaky, Mick & Tich	Fontana	7		
8	-	Matthew And Son	Cat Stevens	Deram	7		F
9	-	Any Way That You Want Me	Troggs	Page One	5		
10	-	Night Of Fear	Move	Deram	7		F
11	7	Dead End Street	Kinks	Pye	9	(73)	
12	2	What Would I Be	Val Doonican	Decca	11		
13	-	Sittin' In The Park	Georgie Fame	Columbia	7		
14	14	You Keep Me Hangin' On	Supremes	Tamla Motown	7	(1)	
15	-	Pamela Pamela	Wayne Fontana	Fontana	6		L
16	-	Standing In The Shadows Of Love	Four Tops	Tamla Motown	4	(6)	
17	-	I Feel Free	Cream	Reaction	4		F
18	-	Hey Joe	Jimi Hendrix Experience	Polydor	5		F
19	3	Good Vibrations	Beach Boys	Capitol	11	(1)	
20	5	Friday On My Mind	Easybeats	UA	9	(16)	F

February 1967

This Mnth	Prev Mnth	Title	Artist	Label	Wks 20	(US Pos)	
1	5	I'm A Believer	Monkees	RCA	10	(1)	F
2	-	Let's Spend The Night Together/ Ruby Tuesday	Rolling Stones	Decca	7	(1)	
3	-	I've Been A Bad Bad Boy	Paul Jones	HMV	6		L
4	-	This Is My Song	Petula Clark	Pye	10	(3)	
5	8	Matthew And Son	Cat Stevens	Deram	7		F
6	10	Night Of Fear	Move	Deram	7		F
7	-	Release Me	Engelbert Humperdinck	Decca	15	(4)	F G
8	1	Green Green Grass Of Home	Tom Jones	Decca	15	(11)	G
9	-	Sugar Town	Nancy Sinatra	Reprise	5	(5)	
10	18	Hey Joe	Jimi Hendrix Experience	Polydor	5		F
11	-	Snoopy Vs The Red Baron	Royal Guardsmen	Stateside	8	(2)	F L
12	-	Peek-A-Boo	New Vaudeville Band	Fontana	7	(72)	
13	-	I Won't Come In While He's There	Jim Reeves	RCA	5		
14	-	Here Comes My Baby	Tremeloes	CBS	7	(13)	F
15	16	Standing In The Shadows Of Love	Four Tops	Tamla Motown	4	(6)	
16	-	I'm A Man	Spencer Davis Group	Fontana	3	(10)	L
17	-	Let Me Cry On Your Shoulder	Ken Dodd	Columbia	3		
18	-	Penny Lane/Strawberry Fields Forever	Beatles	Parlophone	8	(1)	
19	-	Mellow Yellow	Donovan	Pye	5	(2)	
20	17	I Feel Free	Cream	Reaction	4		F

March 1967

This Mnth	Prev Mnth	Title	Artist	Label	Wks 20	(US Pos)	
1	7	Release Me	Engelbert Humperdinck	Decca	15	(4)	F G
2	18	Penny Lane/Strawberry Fields...	Beatles	Parlophone	8	(1)	
3	4	This Is My Song	Petula Clark	Pye	10	(3)	
4	-	Edelweiss	Vince Hill	Columbia	11		
5	14	Here Comes My Baby	Tremeloes	CBS	7	(13)	F
6	-	On A Carousel	Hollies	Parlophone	7	(11)	
7	-	There's A Kind Of Hush	Herman's Hermits	Columbia	7	(4)	
8	-	Georgy Girl	Seekers	Columbia	7	(2)	
9	-	Detroit City	Tom Jones	Decca	6	(27)	
10	11	Snoopy Vs The Red Baron	Royal Guardsmen	Stateside	8	(2)	F L
11	19	Mellow Yellow	Donovan	Pye	5	(2)	
12	12	Peek-A-Boo	New Vaudeville Band	Fontana	7	(72)	
13	-	This Is My Song	Harry Secombe	Philips	9		L
14	1	I'm A Believer	Monkees	RCA	10	(1)	F
15	-	Give It To Me	Troggs	Page One	4		
16	-	Simon Smith & His Amazing Dancing Bear	Alan Price Set	Decca	7		
17	-	I Was Kaiser Bill's Batman	Whistling Jack Smith	Deram	7	(20)	F L
18	-	Memories Are Made Of This	Val Doonican	Decca	5		
19	13	I Won't Come In While He's There	Jim Reeves	RCA	5		
20	2	Let's Spend The Night.../Ruby...	Rolling Stones	Decca	7	(1)	

January 1967

This Mnth	Prev Mnth	Title	Artist	Label	Wks 20	(UK Pos)	
1	7	I'm A Believer	Monkees	Colgems	12	(1)	G
2	13	Snoopy Vs. The Red Baron	Royal Guardsmen	Laurie	9	(8)	F G
3	18	Tell It Like It Is	Aaron Neville	Par-Lo	9		F G
4	-	Good Thing	Paul Revere & The Raiders	Columbia	7		
5	-	Words Of Love	Mamas & The Papas	Dunhill	7	(47)	
6	-	Standing In The Shadows Of Love	Four Tops	Motown	7	(6)	G
7	9	Sugar Town	Nancy Sinatra	Reprise	8	(8)	G
8	-	Georgy Girl	Seekers	Capitol	10	(3)	G L
9	1	Winchester Cathedral	New Vaudeville Band	Fontana	11	(4)	F G L
10	-	Tell It To The Rain	Four Seasons	Philips	4	(37)	
11	-	Coming Home Soldier	Bobby Vinton	Epic	6		
12	-	Nashville Cats	Lovin' Spoonful	Kama Sutra	4	(46)	
13	6	That's Life	Frank Sinatra	Reprise	8	(46)	
14	2	Mellow Yellow	Donovan	Epic	8	(8)	G
15	-	(We Ain't Got) Nothin' Yet	Blues Magoos	Mercury	7		F L
16	-	Kind Of A Drag	Buckinghams	USA	9		F G
17	-	98.6	Keith	Mercury	6	(24)	F L
18	-	Single Girl	Sandy Posey	MGM	4	(15)	
19	-	Talk Talk	Music Machine	Original Sound	4		F L
20	4	Devil With A Blue Dress On & Good Golly Miss Molly	Mitch Ryder & The Detroit Wheels	New Voice	11		

February 1967

This Mnth	Prev Mnth	Title	Artist	Label	Wks 20	(UK Pos)	
1	1	I'm A Believer	Monkees	Colgems	12	(1)	G
2	16	Kind Of A Drag	Buckinghams	USA	9		F G
3	8	Georgy Girl	Seekers	Capitol	10	(3)	G L
4	-	Ruby Tuesday	Rolling Stones	London	9	(3)	G
5	15	(We Ain't Got) Nothin' Yet	Blues Magoos	Mercury	7		F L
6	17	98.6	Keith	Mercury	6	(24)	F L
7	-	Love Is Here And Now You're Gone	Supremes	Motown	8	(17)	G
8	3	Tell It Like It Is	Aaron Neville	Par-Lo	9		F G
9	-	The Beat Goes On	Sonny & Cher	Atco	6	(29)	
10	2	Snoopy Vs. The Red Baron	Royal Guardsmen	Laurie	9	(8)	F G
11	-	Green Green Grass Of Home	Tom Jones	Parrot	5	(1)	
12	-	Gimme Some Lovin'	Spencer Davis Group	UA	6	(2)	F
13	-	Then You Can Tell Me Goodbye	Casinos	Fraternity	7	(28)	F L
14	-	Stand By Me	Spyder Turner	MGM	5		F L
15	-	I Had Too Much To Dream (Last Night)	Electric Prunes	Reprise	6		F L
16	5	Words Of Love	Mamas & The Papas	Dunhill	7	(47)	
17	-	Mercy, Mercy, Mercy	Cannonball Adderley	Capitol	4		F L
18	4	Good Thing	Paul Revere & The Raiders	Columbia	7		
19	6	Standing In The Shadows Of Love	Four Tops	Motown	7	(6)	G
20	-	Baby I Need Your Lovin'	Johnny Rivers	Imperial	8		

March 1967

This Mnth	Prev Mnth	Title	Artist	Label	Wks 20	(UK Pos)	
1	20	Baby I Need Your Lovin'	Johnny Rivers	Imperial	8		
2	7	Love Is Here And Now You're Gone	Supremes	Motown	8	(17)	G
3	4	Ruby Tuesday	Rolling Stones	London	9	(3)	G
4	-	Sock It To Me-Baby!	Mitch Ryder & Detroit Wheels	New Voice	7		L
5	-	Penny Lane	Beatles	Capitol	6	(2)	G
6	-	Happy Together	Turtles	White Whale	10	(12)	G
7	13	Then You Can Tell Me Goodbye	Casinos	Fraternity	7	(28)	F L
8	-	Dedicated To The One I Love	Mamas & The Papas	Dunhill	8	(2)	
9	-	My Cup Runneth Over	Ed Ames	RCA	6		F
10	2	Kind Of A Drag	Buckinghams	USA	9		F G
11	-	There's A Kind Of Hush	Herman's Hermits	MGM	6	(7)	G
12	-	For What It's Worth (Stop, Hey What's That Sound)	Buffalo Springfield	Atco	8		F L
13	12	Gimme Some Lovin'	Spencer Davis Group	UA	6	(2)	F
14	-	Strawberry Fields Forever	Beatles	Capitol	5	(2)	G
15	9	The Beat Goes On	Sonny & Cher	Atco	6	(29)	
16	17	Mercy, Mercy, Mercy	Cannonball Adderley	Capitol	4		F L
17	3	Georgy Girl	Seekers	Capitol	10	(3)	G L
18	-	The Hunter Gets Captured By The Game	Marvelettes	Tamla	3		
19	1	I'm A Believer	Monkees	Colgems	12	(1)	G
20	-	I Think We're Alone Now	Tommy James & The Shondells	Roulette	10		

◆ Reprise Records paid $50,000 for the American rights to the Jimi Hendrix Experience, whom they called "The greatest talent since The Rolling Stones".

◆ The first Human Be-In took place in San Francisco. This free festival, whose headliners included Grateful Dead and Jefferson Airplane, attracted 20,000 people.

◆ Top New York DJ Murray The K, who had been known as "The Fifth Beatle" for his support of the mop-tops in their early days, hosted the stage show that introduced new British bands The Who and Cream to American audiences.

◆ Amazingly, Paul Revere & The Raiders and Johnny Rivers, who continued to add to their impressive US hit tallies, never charted across the Atlantic.

UK 1967

APR-JUNE

◆ The Beatles' album **Sergeant Pepper's Lonely Hearts Club Band** was released to much critical acclaim – it helped shape the future of pop and rock music. The group also broke new ground when they sang 'All You Need is Love' on the internationally linked-up TV show, *Our World*.

◆ After coming second on five occasions the UK finally won the Eurovision Song Contest thanks to barefoot Sandie Shaw's bouncy 'Puppet On A String'.

▲ The Monkees, who continued adding to their transatlantic toppers, had a very successful British live debut at Wembley.

April 1967

This Mnth	Prev Mnth	Title	Artist	Label	Wks 20	(US Pos)	
1	-	Somethin' Stupid	Nancy & Frank Sinatra	Reprise	11	(1)	
2	-	Puppet On A String	Sandie Shaw	Pye	13		
3	1	Release Me	Engelbert Humperdinck	Decca	15	(4)	F G
4	13	This Is My Song	Harry Secombe	Philips	9		L
5	-	A Little Bit Me, A Little Bit You	Monkees	RCA	8	(2)	
6	16	Simon Smith & His Amazing Dancing Bear	Alan Price Set	Decca	7		
7	17	I Was Kaiser Bill's Batman	Whistling Jack Smith	Deram	7	(20)	F L
8	-	Ha Ha Said The Clown	Manfred Mann	Fontana	7		
9	4	Edelweiss	Vince Hill	Columbia	11		
10	-	It's All Over	Cliff Richard	Columbia	6		
11	-	Purple Haze	Jimi Hendrix Experience	Track	8	(65)	
12	2	Penny Lane/Strawberry Fields Forever	Beatles	Parlophone	8	(1)	
13	8	Georgy Girl	Seekers	Columbia	7	(2)	
14	-	Bernadette	Four Tops	Tamla Motown	5	(4)	
15	3	This Is My Song	Petula Clark	Pye	10	(3)	
16	-	I'm Gonna Get Me A Gun	Cat Stevens	Deram	5		
17	18	Memories Are Made Of This	Val Doonican	Decca	5		
18	-	Happy Together	Turtles	London American	6	(1)	F
19	-	I Can Hear The Grass Grow	Move	Deram	6		
20	-	Touch Me Touch Me	Dave Dee, Dozy, Beaky, Mick & Tich	Fontana	3		

May 1967

This Mnth	Prev Mnth	Title	Artist	Label	Wks 20	(US Pos)	
1	2	Puppet On A String	Sandie Shaw	Pye	13		
2	-	Dedicated To The One I Love	Mamas & The Papas	RCA	10	(2)	
3	1	Somethin' Stupid	Nancy & Frank Sinatra	Reprise	11	(1)	
4	-	Silence Is Golden	Tremeloes	CBS	10	(11)	
5	-	The Boat That I Row	Lulu	Columbia	6		
6	-	Pictures Of Lily	Who	Track	6	(51)	
7	-	Funny Familiar Forgotten Feeling	Tom Jones	Decca	7	(49)	
8	11	Purple Haze	Jimi Hendrix Experience	Track	8	(65)	
9	-	Seven Drunken Nights	Dubliners	Major Minor	9		F
10	5	A Little Bit Me, A Little Bit You	Monkees	RCA	8	(2)	
11	19	I Can Hear The Grass Grow	Move	Deram	6		
12	-	Waterloo Sunset	Kinks	Pye	7		
13	-	Then I Kissed Her	Beach Boys	Capitol	8		
14	8	Ha Ha Said The Clown	Manfred Mann	Fontana	7		
15	-	Hi-Ho Silver Lining	Jeff Beck	Columbia	5		F
16	16	I'm Gonna Get Me A Gun	Cat Stevens	Deram	5		
17	-	The Wind Cries Mary	Jimi Hendrix Experience	Track	5		
18	3	Release Me	Engelbert Humperdinck	Decca	15	(4)	F G
19	-	New York Mining Disaster 1941	Bee Gees	Polydor	5	(14)	F
20	18	Happy Together	Turtles	London American	6	(1)	F

June 1967

This Mnth	Prev Mnth	Title	Artist	Label	Wks 20	(US Pos)	
1	-	A Whiter Shade Of Pale	Procol Harum	Deram	11	(5)	F
2	4	Silence Is Golden	Tremeloes	CBS	10	(11)	
3	12	Waterloo Sunset	Kinks	Pye	7		
4	-	There Goes My Everything	Engelbert Humperdinck	Decca	13	(20)	
5	-	The Happening	Supremes	Tamla Motown	8	(1)	
6	13	Then I Kissed Her	Beach Boys	Capitol	8		
7	2	Dedicated To The One I Love	Mamas & The Papas	RCA	10	(2)	
8	-	Sweet Soul Music	Arthur Conley	Atlantic	9	(2)	F L
9	-	Carrie-Anne	Hollies	Parlophone	8	(9)	
10	17	The Wind Cries Mary	Jimi Hendrix Experience	Track	5		
11	-	Okay!	Dave Dee, Dozy, Beaky, Mick & Tich	Fontana	6		
12	-	Finchley Central	New Vaudeville Band	Fontana	6		L
13	9	Seven Drunken Nights	Dubliners	Major Minor	9		F
14	6	Pictures Of Lily	Who	Track	6	(51)	
15	-	Paper Sun	Traffic	Island	5	(94)	F
16	1	Puppet On A String	Sandie Shaw	Pye	13		
17	-	Roses Of Picardy	Vince Hill	Columbia	4		
18	-	Groovin'	Young Rascals	Atlantic	7	(1)	F L
19	3	Somethin' Stupid	Nancy & Frank Sinatra	Reprise	11	(1)	
20	19	New York Mining Disaster 1941	Bee Gees	Polydor	5	(14)	

US 1967 APR-JUNE

is Mnth	Prev Mnth	Title	Artist	Label	Wks 20	(UK Pos)	
1	6	Happy Together	Turtles	White Whale	10	(12)	G
2	-	Somethin' Stupid	Nancy & Frank Sinatra	Reprise	10	(1)	G
3	-	This Is My Song	Petula Clark	Warner	7	(1)	
4	-	Bernadette	Four Tops	Motown	6	(8)	
5	-	Western Union	Five Americans	Abnak	6		F L
6	20	I Think We're Alone Now	Tommy James & The Shondells	Roulette	10		
7	-	A Little Bit Me, A Little Bit You	Monkees	Colgems	8	(3)	G
8	8	Dedicated To The One I Love	Mamas & The Papas	Dunhill	8	(2)	
9	-	I Never Loved A Man (The Way I Love You)	Aretha Franklin	Atlantic	7		F G
10	-	Jimmy Mack	Martha & The Vandellas	Gordy	7	(21)	
11	-	Sweet Soul Music	Arthur Conley	Atco	9	(7)	F G
12	5	Penny Lane	Beatles	Capitol	6	(2)	G
13	11	There's A Kind Of Hush	Herman's Hermits	MGM	6	(7)	G
14	12	For What It's Worth (Stop, Hey What's That Sound)	Buffalo Springfield	Atco	8		F L
15	-	The Happening	Supremes	Motown	8	(6)	G
16	-	The 59th Street Bridge Song (Feelin' Groovy)	Harpers Bizarre	Warner	4	(34)	F L
17	14	Strawberry Fields Forever	Beatles	Capitol	5	(2)	G
18	-	I'm A Man	Spencer Davis Group	UA	4	(9)	L
19	-	Don't You Care	Buckinghams	Columbia	6		
20	-	At The Zoo	Simon & Garfunkel	Columbia	3		

May 1967

is Mnth	Prev Mnth	Title	Artist	Label	Wks 20	(UK Pos)	
1	15	The Happening	Supremes	Motown	8	(6)	G
2	11	Sweet Soul Music	Arthur Conley	Atco	9	(7)	F G
3	2	Somethin' Stupid	Nancy & Frank Sinatra	Reprise	10	(1)	G
4	-	Groovin'	Young Rascals	Atlantic	10	(8)	G
5	19	Don't You Care	Buckinghams	Columbia	6		
6	-	I Got Rhythm	Happenings	B.T.Puppy	7	(28)	
7	-	Respect	Aretha Franklin	Atlantic	9	(10)	G
8	-	Close Your Eyes	Peaches & Herb	Date	5		F
9	-	Release Me (And Let Me Love Again)	Engelbert Humperdinck	Parrot	8	(1)	F
10	-	You Got What It Takes	Dave Clark Five	Epic	6	(28)	L
11	-	On A Carousel	Hollies	Imperial	7	(4)	
12	7	A Little Bit Me, A Little Bit You	Monkees	Colgems	8	(3)	G
13	-	Girl, You'll Be A Woman Soon	Neil Diamond	Bang	4		
14	6	I Think We're Alone Now	Tommy James & The Shondells	Roulette	10		
15	1	Happy Together	Turtles	White Whale	10	(12)	G
16	-	Him Or Me - What's It Gonna Be	Paul Revere & The Raiders	Columbia	5		
17	-	Creeque Alley	Mamas & The Papas	Dunhill	4	(9)	
18	8	When I Was Young	Eric Burdon & The Animals	MGM	3	(45)	
19	-	Friday On My Mind	Easybeats	UA	5	(6)	F L
20	18	I'm A Man	Spencer Davis Group	UA	4	(9)	L

June 1967

is Mnth	Prev Mnth	Title	Artist	Label	Wks 20	(UK Pos)	
1	4	Groovin'	Young Rascals	Atlantic	10	(8)	G
2	7	Respect	Aretha Franklin	Atlantic	9	(10)	G
3	9	Release Me (And Let Me Love Again)	Engelbert Humperdinck	Parrot	8	(1)	F
4	-	She'd Rather Be With Me	Turtles	White Whale	6	(4)	
5	-	Somebody To Love	Jefferson Airplane	RCA	6		F
6	6	I Got Rhythm	Happenings	B.T.Puppy	7	(28)	
7	-	Little Bit O' Soul	Music Explosion	Laurie	11		F G L
8	-	Windy	Association	Warner	11		G
9	-	All I Need	Temptations	Gordy	5		
10	16	Him Or Me - What's It Gonna Be	Paul Revere & The Raiders	Columbia	5		
11	-	Mirage	Tommy James & The Shondells	Roulette	5		
12	-	Sunday Will Never Be The Same	Spanky & Our Gang	Mercury	4		F
13	17	Creeque Alley	Mamas & The Papas	Dunhill	4	(9)	
14	-	Can't Take My Eyes Off You	Frankie Valli	Philips	11		F G
15	-	Let's Live For Today	Grass Roots	Dunhill	6		F
16	-	Come On Down To My Boat	Every Mothers' Son	MGM	8		F L
17	-	San Francisco (Be Sure To Wear Flowers In Your Hair)	Scott McKenzie	Ode	8	(1)	F L
18	-	Here Comes My Baby	Tremeloes	Epic	5	(4)	F
19	-	Seven Rooms Of Gloom	Four Tops	Motown	4	(12)	
20	1	The Happening	Supremes	Motown	8	(6)	G

◆ As KMPX in San Francisco launched progressive FM radio, a "cosmic love-in" took place at New York's Village Theatre, shortly renamed Fillmore East.

◆ Atlantic Records paid $250,000 for The Bee Gees' American contract. Their UK label, Polydor, called them, "The most significant talent since The Beatles."

▲ The line up at the Monterey Pop Festival included The Byrds, The Association, The Mamas & The Papas, The Who (above), Jimi Hendrix, Janis Joplin, Otis Redding, Grateful Dead, Jefferson Airplane and Buffalo Springfield.

UK 1967 JULY-SEPT

◆ The UK government banned pirate radio stations and then launched Radio 1 – their own Top 40 station.

◆ Engelbert Humperdinck, one of the few acts not experimenting with psychedelic sounds, earned his second UK million seller of 1967 with 'The Last Waltz'.

◆ Beatles manager Brian Epstein and Bob Dylan's inspiration, folk singer/songwriter Woody Guthrie, died.

▲ Innovative US act The Mothers Of Invention, whose **Freak Out** album was a milestone in rock, made a successful UK debut.

July 1967

This Mnth	Prev Mnth	Title	Artist	Label	Wks 20	(US Pos)	
1	1	A Whiter Shade Of Pale	Procol Harum	Deram	11	(5)	F
2	-	Alternate Title	Monkees	RCA	8		
3	4	There Goes My Everything	Engelbert Humperdinck	Decca	13	(20)	
4	-	She'd Rather Be With Me	Turtles	London American	10	(3)	
5	-	It Must Be Him (Seul Sur Son Etoile)	Vikki Carr	Liberty	10	(3)	F L
6	-	All You Need Is Love	Beatles	Parlophone	10	(1)	
7	9	Carrie-Anne	Hollies	Parlophone	8	(9)	
8	-	See Emily Play	Pink Floyd	Columbia	7		
9	-	If I Were A Rich Man	Topol	CBS	6		F L
10	-	San Francisco (Be Sure To Wear Some Flowers In Your Hair)	Scott McKenzie	CBS	14	(4)	F L
11	18	Groovin'	Young Rascals	Atlantic	7	(1)	F L
12	15	Paper Sun	Traffic	Island	5	(94)	F
13	-	Respect	Aretha Franklin	Atlantic	5	(1)	F
14	11	Okay!	Dave Dee, Dozy, Beaky, Mick & Tich	Fontana	6		
15	-	Here Come The Nice	Small Faces	Immediate	6		
16	8	Sweet Soul Music	Arthur Conley	Atlantic	9	(2)	F L
17	-	Seven Rooms Of Gloom	Four Tops	Tamla Motown	5	(14)	
18	5	The Happening	Supremes	Tamla Motown	8	(1)	
19	-	Don't Sleep In The Subway	Petula Clark	Pye	4	(5)	
20	-	You Only Live Twice/Jackson	Nancy Sinatra	Reprise	5	(44)	

August 1967

This Mnth	Prev Mnth	Title	Artist	Label	Wks 20	(US Pos)	
1	10	San Francisco (Be Sure To Wear Some Flowers In Your Hair)	Scott McKenzie	CBS	14	(4)	F L
2	6	All You Need Is Love	Beatles	Parlophone	10	(1)	
3	-	I'll Never Fall In Love Again	Tom Jones	Decca	10	(6)	
4	-	Death Of A Clown	Dave Davies	Pye	7		F
5	-	I Was Made To Love Her	Stevie Wonder	Tamla Motown	9	(2)	
6	5	It Must Be Him (Seul Sur Son Etoile)	Vikki Carr	Liberty	10	(3)	F L
7	-	Up Up And Away	Johnny Mann Singers	Liberty	7		F L
8	-	Just Loving You	Anita Harris	CBS	15		F L
9	4	She'd Rather Be With Me	Turtles	London American	10	(3)	
10	-	Even The Bad Times Are Good	Tremeloes	CBS	9	(36)	
11	2	Alternate Title	Monkees	RCA	8		
12	-	Creeque Alley	Mamas & The Papas	RCA	6	(5)	L
13	8	See Emily Play	Pink Floyd	Columbia	7		
14	-	The House That Jack Built	Alan Price Set	Decca	7		
15	3	There Goes My Everything	Engelbert Humperdinck	Decca	13	(20)	
16	-	Let's Pretend	Lulu	Columbia	4		
17	-	Gin House Blues	Amen Corner	Deram	5		F
18	1	A Whiter Shade Of Pale	Procol Harum	Deram	11	(5)	F
19	20	You Only Live Twice/Jackson	Nancy Sinatra	Reprise	5	(44)	
20	-	Pleasant Valley Sunday	Monkees	RCA	4	(3)	

September 1967

This Mnth	Prev Mnth	Title	Artist	Label	Wks 20	(US Pos)	
1	-	The Last Waltz	Engelbert Humperdinck	Decca	20	(25)	G
2	3	I'll Never Fall In Love Again	Tom Jones	Decca	10	(6)	
3	1	San Francisco (Be Sure To Wear Some Flowers In Your Hair)	Scott McKenzie	CBS	14	(4)	F L
4	-	Excerpt From A Teenage Opera	Keith West	Parlophone	11		F L
5	-	Itchycoo Park	Small Faces	Immediate	11	(16)	
6	10	Even The Bad Times Are Good	Tremeloes	CBS	9	(36)	
7	-	Let's Go To San Francisco	Flowerpot Men	Deram	7		F L
8	-	We Love You/Dandelion	Rolling Stones	Decca	6	(14)	
9	8	Just Loving You	Anita Harris	CBS	15		F L
10	-	Heroes And Villains	Beach Boys	Capitol	5	(12)	
11	14	The House That Jack Built	Alan Price Set	Decca	7		
12	5	I Was Made To Love Her	Stevie Wonder	Tamla Motown	9	(2)	
13	-	Reflections	Diana Ross & The Supremes	Tamla Motown	8	(2)	
14	-	Flowers In The Rain	Move	Regal Zonophone	10		
15	-	The Day I Met Marie	Cliff Richard	Columbia	8		
16	2	All You Need Is Love	Beatles	Parlophone	10	(1)	
17	-	Hole In My Shoe	Traffic	Island	10		
18	20	Pleasant Valley Sunday	Monkees	RCA	4	(3)	
19	-	There Must Be A Way	Frankie Vaughan	Columbia	14		L
20	4	Death Of A Clown	Dave Davies	Pye	7		F

US 1967 JULY-SEPT

July 1967

This Mnth	Prev Mnth	Title	Artist	Label	Wks 20	(UK Pos)	
1	8	Windy	Association	Warner	11		G
2	7	Little Bit O' Soul	Music Explosion	Laurie	11		F G L
3	14	Can't Take My Eyes Off You	Frankie Valli	Philips	11		F G
4	17	San Francisco (Be Sure To Wear Flowers In Your Hair)	Scott McKenzie	Ode	8	(1)	F L
5	-	Up Up & Away	Fifth Dimension	Soul City	6		
6	-	Light My Fire	Doors	Elektra	12	(49)	F G
7	16	Come On Down To My Boat	Every Mothers' Son	MGM	8		F L
8	-	Don't Sleep In The Subway	Petula Clark	Warner	5	(12)	
9	-	A Whiter Shade Of Pale	Procol Harum	Deram	9	(1)	F
10	-	I Was Made To Love Her	Stevie Wonder	Tamla	9	(5)	G
11	-	C'mon Marianne	Four Seasons	Philips	5		
12	1	Groovin'	Young Rascals	Atlantic	10	(8)	G
13	15	Let's Live For Today	Grass Roots	Dunhill	6		F
14	-	White Rabbit	Jefferson Airplane	RCA	5		
15	-	Mercy, Mercy, Mercy	Buckinghams	Columbia	6		
16	-	The Tracks Of My Tears	Johnny Rivers	Imperial	4		
17	4	She'd Rather Be With Me	Turtles	White Whale	6	(4)	
18	2	Respect	Aretha Franklin	Atlantic	9	(10)	G
19	-	Here We Go Again	Ray Charles	ABC/TRC	4	(38)	L
20	-	Society's Child (Baby I've Been Thinking)	Janis Ian	Verve	3		F

August 1967

This Mnth	Prev Mnth	Title	Artist	Label	Wks 20	(UK Pos)	
1	6	Light My Fire	Doors	Elektra	12	(49)	F G
2	-	All You Need Is Love	Beatles	Capitol	7	(1)	G
3	10	I Was Made To Love Her	Stevie Wonder	Tamla	9	(5)	G
4	-	Pleasant Valley Sunday	Monkees	Colgems	6	(11)	G
5	9	A Whiter Shade Of Pale	Procol Harum	Deram	9	(1)	F
6	15	Mercy, Mercy, Mercy	Buckinghams	Columbia	6		
7	-	Baby I Love You	Aretha Franklin	Atlantic	7	(39)	G
8	-	A Girl Like You	Young Rascals	Atlantic	6	(37)	
9	3	Can't Take My Eyes Off You	Frankie Valli	Philips	11		F G
10	1	Windy	Association	Warner	11		G
11	-	Ode To Billie Joe	Bobbie Gentry	Capitol	10	(13)	F G L
12	-	Silence Is Golden	Tremeloes	Epic	5	(1)	L
13	-	Carrie-Anne	Hollies	Epic	6	(3)	
14	-	Cold Sweat (Part 1)	James Brown	King	6		
15	-	My Mammy	Happenings	B.T.Puppy	4	(34)	L
16	14	White Rabbit	Jefferson Airplane	RCA	5		
17	2	Little Bit O' Soul	Music Explosion	Laurie	11		F G L
18	-	Reflections	Diana Ross & The Supremes	Motown	8	(5)	G
19	-	Jackson	Nancy Sinatra & Lee Hazlewood	Reprise	4	(11)	
20	-	Heroes And Villians	Beach Boys	Brother	3	(8)	

September 1967

This Mnth	Prev Mnth	Title	Artist	Label	Wks 20	(UK Pos)	
1	11	Ode To Billie Joe	Bobbie Gentry	Capitol	10	(13)	F G L
2	18	Reflections	Diana Ross & The Supremes	Motown	8	(5)	G
3	-	Come Back When You Grow Up	Bobby Vee & The Strangers	Liberty	9		G L
4	-	The Letter	Box Tops	Mala	10	(5)	F G
5	-	Apples Peaches Pumpkin Pie	Jay & The Techniques	Smash	9		F
6	-	You're My Everything	Temptations	Gordy	6	(26)	
7	7	Baby I Love You	Aretha Franklin	Atlantic	7	(39)	G
8	2	All You Need Is Love	Beatles	Capitol	7	(1)	G
9	-	Never My Love	Association	Warner	10		G
10	-	Funky Broadway	Wilson Pickett	Atlantic	6	(43)	
11	-	(Your Love Keeps Lifting Me) Higher And Higher	Jackie Wilson	Brunswick	7	(9)	L
12	1	Light My Fire	Doors	Elektra	12	(49)	F G
13	-	Brown Eyed Girl	Van Morrison	Bang	6		F
14	-	You Know What I Mean	Turtles	White Whale	4		
15	-	I Dig Rock And Roll Music	Peter, Paul & Mary	Warner	5		
16	-	San Franciscan Nights	Eric Burdon & The Animals	MGM	3	(7)	
17	-	There Is A Mountain	Donovan	Epic	4	(8)	
18	14	Cold Sweat (Part 1)	James Brown	King	6		
19	4	Pleasant Valley Sunday	Monkees	Colgems	6	(11)	G
20	-	Words	Monkees	Colgems	4		

◆ Among the records forever associated with the "Summer Of Love" are: 'San Francisco (Be Sure To Wear Some Flowers In Your Hair)' by Scott McKenzie, 'Light My Fire' by The Doors and 'Whiter Shade Of Pale' by Procol Harum.

◆ Jimi Hendrix opened the show for The Monkees. Not unexpectedly, Hendrix was soon given his marching orders as his act was considered "too erotic" for young Monkee fans.

◆ At the time only a few people noticed that The Golliwogs had renamed themselves Creedence Clearwater Revival or that Kenny Rogers had left The New Christy Minstrels.

◆ A new noise reduction system for album and tape recording, developed by American technicians Ray and D.W. Dolby, was first used by Elektra Records subsidiary Checkmate Records.

UK 1967 OCT-DEC

◆ The Beatles closed the year with 'Hello Goodbye' topping the transatlantic charts. However, in 1967, they were replaced as the world's most successful act by The Monkees, who, among other achievements, chalked up a (still unbeaten) record of four American chart topping albums in one calendar year.

◆ In the year that US record sales first topped the $1 billion mark and, for the first time, albums outsold singles, the gap between the American and British markets widened, with only 25% of Top 20 hits scoring in both countries. An interesting case was 'To Sir With Love' by Lulu, which topped the US chart but was treated as a B-side in Britain.

◆ Critically acclaimed UK underground band Pink Floyd joined burgeoning teen idols Amen Corner and The Move to support headliner Jimi Hendrix on a UK tour.

October 1967

This Mnth	Prev Mnth	Title	Artist	Label	Wks 20	(US Pos)	
1	-	Massachusetts	Bee Gees	Polydor	10	(11)	
2	1	The Last Waltz	Engelbert Humperdinck	Decca	20	(25)	G
3	17	Hole In My Shoe	Traffic	Island	10		
4	14	Flowers In The Rain	Move	Regal Zonophone	10		
5	-	The Letter	Box Tops	Stateside	8	(1)	F
6	4	Excerpt From A Teenage Opera	Keith West	Parlophone	11		F L
7	13	Reflections	Diana Ross & The Supremes	Tamla Motown	8	(2)	
8	19	There Must Be A Way	Frankie Vaughan	Columbia	14		L
9	-	Homburg	Procol Harum	Regal Zonophone	7	(34)	
10	5	Itchycoo Park	Small Faces	Immediate	11	(16)	
11	-	From The Underworld	Herd	Fontana	8		F
12	-	When Will The Good Apples Fall	Seekers	Columbia	6		L
13	15	The Day I Met Marie	Cliff Richard	Columbia	8		
14	7	Let's Go To San Francisco	Flowerpot Men	Deram	7		F L
15	-	Baby, Now That I Found You	Foundations	Pye	9	(11)	F
16	-	Zabadak	Dave Dee, Dozy, Beaky, Mick & Tich	Fontana	8	(52)	
17	-	Ode To Billie Joe	Bobbie Gentry	Capitol	6	(1)	F
18	9	Just Loving You	Anita Harris	CBS	15		F L
19	-	Black Velvet Band	Dubliners	Major Minor	5		
20	2	I'll Never Fall In Love Again	Tom Jones	Decca	10	(6)	

November 1967

This Mnth	Prev Mnth	Title	Artist	Label	Wks 20	(US Pos)	
1	15	Baby, Now That I Found You	Foundations	Pye	9	(11)	F
2	1	Massachusetts	Bee Gees	Polydor	10	(11)	
3	16	Zabadak	Dave Dee, Dozy, Beaky, Mick & Tich	Fontana	8	(52)	
4	-	Autumn Almanac	Kinks	Pye	7		
5	2	The Last Waltz	Engelbert Humperdinck	Decca	20	(25)	G
6	-	Love Is All Around	Troggs	Page One	7	(7)	L
7	11	From The Underworld	Herd	Fontana	8		F
8	-	San Franciscan Nights	Eric Burdon & The Animals	MGM	5	(9)	
9	9	Homburg	Procol Harum	Regal Zonophone	7	(34)	
10	-	There Is A Mountain	Donovan	Pye	5	(11)	
11	8	There Must Be A Way	Frankie Vaughan	Columbia	14		L
12	-	Let The Heartaches Begin	Long John Baldry	Pye	9	(88)	F
13	3	Hole In My Shoe	Traffic	Island	10		
14	-	If The Whole World Stopped Loving	Val Doonican	Pye	13		
15	-	I Can See For Miles	Who	Track	4	(9)	
16	-	Everybody Knows	Dave Clark Five	Columbia	8	(43)	
17	4	Flowers In The Rain	Move	Regal Zonophone	10		
18	5	The Letter	Box Tops	Stateside	8	(1)	F
19	-	I Feel Love Comin' On	Felice Taylor	President	6		F L
20	12	When Will The Good Apples Fall	Seekers	Columbia	6		L

December 1967

This Mnth	Prev Mnth	Title	Artist	Label	Wks 20	(US Pos)	
1	-	Hello Goodbye	Beatles	Parlophone	10	(1)	
2	14	If The Whole World Stopped Loving	Val Doonican	Pye	13		
3	12	Let The Heartaches Begin	Long John Baldry	Pye	9	(88)	F
4	-	Something's Gotten Hold Of My Heart	Gene Pitney	Stateside	9		
5	-	I'm Comin' Home	Tom Jones	Decca	12	(57)	
6	16	Everybody Knows	Dave Clark Five	Columbia	8	(43)	
7	-	All My Love	Cliff Richard	Columbia	8		
8	-	Careless Hands	Des O'Connor	Columbia	9		F
9	-	Daydream Believer	Monkees	RCA	12	(1)	
10	-	World	Bee Gees	Polydor	10		
11	-	Thank U Very Much	Scaffold	Parlophone	8	(69)	F
12	-	Magical Mystery Tour (Double E.P.)	Beatles	Parlophone	9		
13	6	Love Is All Around	Troggs	Page One	7	(7)	L
14	-	Here We Go Round The Mulberry Bush	Traffic	Island	7		L
15	5	The Last Waltz	Engelbert Humperdinck	Decca	20	(25)	G
16	1	Baby, Now That I Found You	Foundations	Pye	9	(11)	F
17	19	I Feel Love Comin' On	Felice Taylor	President	6		F L
18	-	Kites	Simon Dupree & The Big Sound	Parlophone	8		F L
19	-	Walk Away Renee	Four Tops	Tamla Motown	8	(14)	
20	3	Zabadak	Dave Dee, Dozy, Beaky etc.	Fontana	8	(52)	

October 1967

This Mnth	Prev Mnth	Title	Artist	Label	Wks 20	(UK Pos)	
1	4	The Letter	Box Tops	Mala	10	(5)	F G
2	9	Never My Love	Association	Warner	10		G
3	-	To Sir With Love	Lulu	Epic	11		F G
4	-	How Can I Be Sure	Young Rascals	Atlantic	7		
5	-	Little Ole Man (Uptight-Everything's Alright)	Bill Cosby	Warner	6		F L
6	-	Gimme Little Sign	Brenton Wood	Double Shot	7	(8)	F L
7	-	Expressway To Your Heart	Soul Survivors	Crimson	9		F L
8	1	Ode To Billie Joe	Bobbie Gentry	Capitol	10	(13)	F G L
9	-	Soul Man	Sam & Dave	Stax	10	(24)	F G
10	3	Come Back When You Grow Up	Bobby Vee & The Strangers	Liberty	9		G L
11	11	(Your Love...) Higher And Higher	Jackie Wilson	Brunswick	7	(9)	L
12	-	Your Precious Love	Marvin Gaye & Tammi Terrell	Tamla	7		
13	-	It Must Be Him	Vikki Carr	Liberty	6	(2)	F L
14	-	Get On Up	Esquires	Bunky	6		F L
15	-	Hey Baby (They're Playing Our Song)	Buckinghams	Columbia	5		
16	5	Apples Peaches Pumpkin Pie	Jay & The Techniques	Smash	9		F
17	-	A Natural Woman (You Make Me Feel Like)	Aretha Franklin	Atlantic	6		
18	2	Reflections	Diana Ross & The Supremes	Motown	8	(5)	G
19	-	Incense And Peppermints	Strawberry Alarm Clock	Uni	12		F G L
20	15	I Dig Rock And Roll Music	Peter, Paul & Mary	Warner	5		

November 1967

This Mnth	Prev Mnth	Title	Artist	Label	Wks 20	(UK Pos)	
1	3	To Sir With Love	Lulu	Epic	11		F G
2	9	Soul Man	Sam & Dave	Stax	10	(24)	F G
3	19	Incense And Peppermints	Strawberry Alarm Clock	Uni	12		F G L
4	13	It Must Be Him	Vikki Carr	Liberty	6	(2)	F L
5	-	The Rain, The Park & Other Things	Cowsills	MGM	11		F G
6	12	Your Precious Love	Marvin Gaye & Tammi Terrell	Tamla	7		
7	-	Please Love Me Forever	Bobby Vinton	Epic	9		
8	7	Expressway To Your Heart	Soul Survivors	Crimson	9		F L
9	17	A Natural Woman (You Make Me...)	Aretha Franklin	Atlantic	6		
10	-	I Can See For Miles	Who	Decca	5	(10)	F
11	2	Never My Love	Association	Warner	10		G
12	-	I Say A Little Prayer	Dionne Warwick	Scepter	8		G
13	-	(Loneliness Made Me Realize) It's You That I Need	Temptations	Gordy	5		
14	-	Let It Out (Let It All Hang Out)	Hombres	Verve Forecast	5		F L
15	-	I'm Wondering	Stevie Wonder	Tamla	3	(22)	
16	-	Everlasting Love	Robert Knight	Rising Sons	4	(19)	F L
17	-	Daydream Believer	Monkees	Colgems	10	(5)	G
18	-	Love Is Strange	Peaches & Herb	Date	3		
19	-	Pata Pata	Miriam Makeba	Reprise	4		F L
20	4	How Can I Be Sure	Young Rascals	Atlantic	7		

December 1967

This Mnth	Prev Mnth	Title	Artist	Label	Wks 20	(UK Pos)	
1	17	Daydream Believer	Monkees	Colgems	10	(5)	G
2	-	I Heard It Through The Grapevine	Gladys Knight & The Pips	Soul	11	(47)	
3	5	The Rain, The Park & Other Things	Cowsills	MGM	11		F G
4	-	I Second That Emotion	Smokey Robinson/The Miracles	Tamla	10	(27)	G
5	3	Incense And Peppermints	Strawberry Alarm Clock	Uni	12		F G L
6	-	Hello Goodbye	Beatles	Capitol	9	(1)	G
7	12	I Say A Little Prayer	Dionne Warwick	Scepter	8		G
8	-	Boogaloo Down Broadway	Fantastic Johnny C	Phil L.A. Of Soul	9		F L
9	-	You Better Sit Down Kids	Cher	Imperial	7		
10	-	Woman, Woman	Union Gap Feat. Gary Puckett	Columbia	11	(48)	F G
11	-	In And Out Of Love	Diana Ross & The Supremes	Motown	4	(13)	
12	1	To Sir With Love	Lulu	Epic	11		F G
13	-	Judy In Disguise (With Glasses)	John Fred & His Playboy Band	Paula	11	(3)	F G L
14	-	Skinny Legs And All	Joe Tex	Dial	7		G
15	-	An Open Letter To My Teenage Son	Victor Lundberg	Liberty	3		F L
16	-	(The Lights Went Out In) Massachusetts	Bee Gees	Atco	4	(1)	
17	7	Please Love Me Forever	Bobby Vinton	Epic	9		
18	-	Bend Me, Shape Me	American Breed	Acta	10	(24)	F G L
19	-	Keep The Ball Rollin'	Jay & The Techniques	Smash	4		L
20	10	I Can See For Miles	Who	Decca	5	(10)	F

◆ *Billboard* noted that LPs by "underground" artists such as Cream, Buffalo Springfield, The Mothers Of Invention, The Doors, Canned Heat, Country Joe & The Fish and The Velvet Underground were selling in vast quantities.

◆ Unique soul stylist Otis Redding died in a plane crash. Redding composed 'Respect', a chart topper for 1967's golden girl, Aretha Franklin.

▲ The Steve Miller Band received a record $750,000 to sign with Capitol Records, and Tom Jones (above) signed a $1 million deal for live appearances in Las Vegas.

121

UK 1968

JAN-MAR

◆ Music from *Magical Mystery Tour* kept the Beatles at the top, although the film itself was their first commercial and critical flop. Meanwhile, their previous project, **Sergeant Pepper**, grabbed four Grammies.

◆ Newcomers Love Affair were splashed over the front pages of the tabloids when they admitted that only lead singer Steve Ellis was actually on their chart topping cover of 'Everlasting Love'. This revelation did not stop them being elevated to teen idol status.

◆ Status Quo (who subsequently had more UK chart singles than The Beatles or Stones) debuted on the Top 20. Fellow superstars Genesis released their first single, as did Elton John, described by his label as "1968's greatest new talent".

January 1968

This Mnth	Prev Mnth	Title	Artist	Label	Wks 20	(US Pos)	
1	1	Hello Goodbye	Beatles	Parlophone	10	(1)	
2	12	Magical Mystery Tour (Double E.P.)	Beatles	Parlophone	9		
3	-	Ballad Of Bonnie & Clyde	Georgie Fame	CBS	8	(7)	
4	19	Walk Away Renee	Four Tops	Tamla Motown	8	(14)	
5	9	Daydream Believer	Monkees	RCA	12	(1)	
6	5	I'm Comin' Home	Tom Jones	Decca	12	(57)	
7	11	Thank U Very Much	Scaffold	Parlophone	8	(69)	F
8	-	Everlasting Love	Love Affair	CBS	10		F
9	2	If The Whole World Stopped Loving	Val Doonican	Pye	13		
10	10	World	Bee Gees	Polydor	10		
11	18	Kites	Simon Dupree & The Big Sound	Parlophone	8		F L
12	-	Am I That Easy To Forget	Engelbert Humperdinck	Decca	9	(18)	
13	4	Something's Gotten Hold Of My Heart	Gene Pitney	Stateside	9		
14	-	Tin Soldier	Small Faces	Immediate	8	(73)	
15	14	Here We Go Round The Mulberry Bush	Traffic	Island	7		L
16	-	Judy In Disguise (With Glasses)	John Fred & His Playboy Band	Pye International	7	(1)	F L
17	8	Careless Hands	Des O'Connor	Columbia	9		F
18	-	In And Out Of Love	Diana Ross & The Supremes	Tamla Motown	7	(9)	
19	-	Everything I Am	Plastic Penny	Page One	5		F L
20	-	She Wears My Ring	Solomon King	Columbia	11		F L

February 1968

This Mnth	Prev Mnth	Title	Artist	Label	Wks 20	(US Pos)	
1	8	Everlasting Love	Love Affair	CBS	10		F
2	-	Mighty Quinn	Manfred Mann	Fontana	8	(10)	
3	12	Am I That Easy To Forget	Engelbert Humperdinck	Decca	9	(18)	
4	-	Bend Me Shape Me	Amen Corner	Deram	9		
5	16	Judy In Disguise (With Glasses)	John Fred & His Playboy Band	Pye International	7	(1)	F L
6	20	She Wears My Ring	Solomon King	Columbia	11		F L
7	-	Suddenly You Love Me	Tremeloes	CBS	8	(44)	
8	-	Gimme Little Sign	Brenton Wood	Liberty	7	(9)	F L
9	3	Ballad Of Bonnie & Clyde	Georgie Fame	CBS	8	(7)	
10	-	Pictures Of Matchstick Men	Status Quo	Pye	7	(12)	F
11	19	Everything I Am	Plastic Penny	Page One	5		F L
12	-	I Can Take Or Leave Your Lovin'	Herman's Hermits	Columbia	6	(22)	
13	-	Darlin'	Beach Boys	Capitol	9	(19)	
14	-	Fire Brigade	Move	Regal Zonophone	8		
15	-	Words	Bee Gees	Polydor	7	(15)	
16	-	Cinderella Rockafella	Esther & Abi Ofarim	Philips	9	(68)	F
17	5	Daydream Believer	Monkees	RCA	12	(1)	
18	-	Don't Stop The Carnival	Alan Price Set	Decca	4		
19	14	Tin Soldier	Small Faces	Immediate	8	(73)	
20	2	Magical Mystery Tour (Double E.P.)	Beatles	Parlophone	9		

March 1968

This Mnth	Prev Mnth	Title	Artist	Label	Wks 20	(US Pos)	
1	16	Cinderella Rockafella	Esther & Abi Ofarim	Philips	9	(68)	F
2	-	Legend Of Xanadu	Dave Dee, Dozy, Beaky, Mick & Tich	Fontana	8		
3	14	Fire Brigade	Move	Regal Zonophone	8		
4	-	Rosie	Don Partridge	Columbia	9		F
5	-	Jennifer Juniper	Donovan	Pye	6	(26)	
6	-	Delilah	Tom Jones	Decca	11	(15)	
7	2	Mighty Quinn	Manfred Mann	Fontana	8	(10)	
8	-	(Sittin' On) The Dock Of The Bay	Otis Redding	Stax	8	(1)	
9	-	Green Tambourine	Lemon Pipers	Pye International	6	(1)	F L
10	6	She Wears My Ring	Solomon King	Columbia	11		F L
11	4	Bend Me Shape Me	Amen Corner	Deram	9		
12	10	Pictures Of Matchstick Men	Status Quo	Pye	7	(12)	F
13	15	Words	Bee Gees	Polydor	7	(15)	
14	-	Me The Peaceful Heart	Lulu	Columbia	5	(53)	
15	13	Darlin'	Beach Boys	Capitol	9	(19)	
16	-	Lady Madonna	Beatles	Parlophone	6	(4)	
17	-	What A Wonderful World	Louis Armstrong	HMV	16	(32)	L
18	7	Suddenly You Love Me	Tremeloes	CBS	8	(44)	
19	-	If I Were A Carpenter	Four Tops	Tamla Motown	6	(20)	
20	8	Gimme Little Sign	Brenton Wood	Liberty	7	(9)	F L

January 1968

This Mnth	Prev Mnth	Title	Artist	Label	Wks 20	(UK Pos)	
1	13	Judy In Disguise (With Glasses)	John Fred & His Playboy Band	Paula	11	(3)	F G L
2	6	Hello Goodbye	Beatles	Capitol	9	(1)	G
3	-	Chain Of Fools	Aretha Franklin	Atlantic	9	(43)	G
4	10	Woman, Woman	Union Gap Feat. Gary Puckett	Columbia	11	(48)	F G
5	1	Daydream Believer	Monkees	Colgems	10	(5)	G
6	2	I Heard It Through The Grapevine	Gladys Knight & The Pips	Soul	11	(47)	
7	17	Bend Me, Shape Me	American Breed	Acta	10	(24)	F G L
8	-	Green Tambourine	Lemon Pipers	Buddah	9	(7)	F G L
9	4	I Second That Emotion	Smokey Robinson/The Miracles	Tamla	10	(27)	G
10	-	If I Could Build My Whole World Around You	Marvin Gaye & Tammi Terrell	Tamla	5	(41)	
11	13	Skinny Legs And All	Joe Tex	Dial	7		G
12	-	Honey Chile	Martha & The Vandellas	Gordy	6	(30)	L
13	-	Different Drum	Stone Poneys	Capitol	7		F L
14	8	Boogaloo Down Broadway	Fantastic Johnny C	Phil L.A. Of Soul	9		F L
15	-	Susan	Buckinghams	Columbia	6		L
16	-	Spooky	Classics IV	Imperial	9	(46)	F G
17	-	Nobody But Me	Human Beinz	Capitol	8		F L
18	-	Monterey	Eric Burdon & The Animals	MGM	2		
19	-	Summer Rain	Johnny Rivers	Imperial	5		
20	5	Incense And Peppermints	Strawberry Alarm Clock	Uni	12		F G L

February 1968

This Mnth	Prev Mnth	Title	Artist	Label	Wks 20	(UK Pos)	
1	-	Love Is Blue	Paul Mauriat	Philips	13	(12)	F G L
2	7	Green Tambourine	Lemon Pipers	Buddah	9	(7)	F G L
3	15	Spooky	Classics IV	Imperial	9	(46)	F G
4	20	I Wish It Would Rain	Temptations	Gordy	9	(45)	G
5	1	Judy In Disguise (With Glasses)	John Fred & His Playboy Band	Paula	11	(3)	F G L
6	-	Goin' Out Of My Head/ Can't Take My Eyes Off You	Lettermen	Capitol	6		
7	16	Nobody But Me	Human Beinz	Capitol	8		F L
8	-	(Theme From) Valley Of The Dolls	Dionne Warwick	Scepter	9	(28)	
9	3	Woman, Woman	Union Gap Feat. Gary Puckett	Columbia	11	(48)	F G
10	2	Chain Of Fools	Aretha Franklin	Atlantic	9	(43)	G
11	6	Bend Me, Shape Me	American Breed	Acta	10	(24)	F G L
12	-	Baby Now That I've Found You	Foundations	Uni	8	(1)	F G
13	-	I Wonder What She's Doing Tonight	Tommy Boyce & Bobby Hart	A&M	7		F L
14	-	(Sittin' On) The Dock Of The Bay	Otis Redding	Volt	12	(3)	F G L
15	14	Susan	Buckinghams	Columbia	6		L
16	-	Bottle Of Wine	Fireballs	Atco	6		F L
17	-	Simon Says	1910 Fruitgum Co.	Buddah	9	(2)	F G
18	-	We're A Winner	Impressions	ABC	4		
19	-	Itchycoo Park	Small Faces	Immediate	3	(3)	F L
20	2	Hello Goodbye	Beatles	Capitol	9	(1)	G

March 1968

This Mnth	Prev Mnth	Title	Artist	Label	Wks 20	(UK Pos)	
1	1	Love Is Blue	Paul Mauriat	Philips	13	(12)	F G L
2	13	(Sittin' On) The Dock Of The Bay	Otis Redding	Volt	12	(3)	F G L
3	7	(Theme From) Valley Of The Dolls	Dionne Warwick	Scepter	9	(28)	
4	16	Simon Says	1910 Fruitgum Co.	Buddah	9	(2)	F G
5	-	Just Dropped In (To See What Condition My Condition Was In)	First Edition	Reprise	6		F
6	-	La-La Means I Love You	Delfonics	Philly Groove	9	(19)	F
7	4	I Wish It Would Rain	Temptations	Gordy	9	(45)	G
8	-	Valleri	Monkees	Colgems	6	(12)	G
9	-	(Sweet Sweet Baby) Since You've Been Gone	Aretha Franklin	Atlantic	8		G
10	3	Spooky	Classics IV	Imperial	9	(46)	F G
11	-	I Thank You	Sam & Dave	Stax	5	(34)	L
12	-	Everything That Touches You	Association	Warner	5		L
13	-	The Ballad Of Bonnie And Clyde	Georgie Fame	Epic	9	(1)	F L
14	15	Bottle Of Wine	Fireballs	Atco	6		F L
15	12	I Wonder What She's Doing Tonight	Tommy Boyce & Bobby Hart	A&M	7		F L
16	-	Young Girl	Union Gap Feat. Gary Puckett	Columbia	11	(1)	G
17	-	Dance To The Music	Sly & The Family Stone	Epic	9	(7)	F
18	-	Mighty Quinn	Manfred Mann	Mercury	5	(1)	L
19	11	Baby Now That I've Found You	Foundations	Uni	8	(1)	F G
20	-	The End Of Our Road	Gladys Knight & The Pips	Soul	4		

◆ A daughter, Lisa Marie, was born to Elvis Presley, whose 26th film *Stay Away Joe* was released to little acclaim. It was also announced that Elvis was preparing a 'come-back' TV special.

◆ The first teenage rock hero, Frankie Lymon, died of a drug overdose and fellow fifties R&B teen sensation Little Willie John died in prison.

▲ Fifth Dimension walked away with a handful of awards at the 1967 Grammy presentations. Bobbie Gentry grabbed three and both Glen Campbell and Aretha Franklin (above) received a couple. There was, however, no recognition for the year's best selling act, The Monkees.

UK 1968 APR-JUNE

▲ Pink Floyd (above), Jethro Tull and Tyrannosaurus Rex appeared at the first free concert in London's Hyde Park.

◆ American hits in Britain included: transatlantic No. 1 'Young Girl' by Gary Puckett & The Union Gap, 'Honey ' by Bobby Goldsboro, 'What A Wonderful World' by 66-year-old Louis Armstrong and rock's biggest seller, 'Rock Around The Clock' by Bill Haley.

◆ For a while street busker Don Partridge stopped playing outside theatres and headlined inside, thanks to two successive Top 5 singles, 'Rosie' and 'Blue Eyes'.

April 1968

This Mnth	Prev Mnth	Title	Artist	Label	Wks 20	(US Pos)	
1	-	Congratulations	Cliff Richard	Columbia	9	(99)	
2	17	What A Wonderful World	Louis Armstrong	HMV	16	(32)	L
3	6	Delilah	Tom Jones	Decca	11	(15)	
4	-	If I Only Had Time	John Rowles	MCA	11		F
5	8	(Sittin' On) The Dock Of The Bay	Otis Redding	Stax	8	(1)	
6	16	Lady Madonna	Beatles	Parlophone	6	(4)	
7	-	Simon Says	1910 Fruitgum Co.	Pye International	12	(4)	F L
8	-	Step Inside Love	Cilla Black	Parlophone	5		
9	19	If I Were A Carpenter	Four Tops	Tamla Motown	6	(20)	
10	-	Jennifer Eccles	Hollies	Parlophone	6	(40)	
11	-	Can't Take My Eyes Off You	Andy Williams	CBS	9		
12	1	Cinderella Rockafella	Esther & Abi Ofarim	Philips	9	(68)	F
13	-	I Can't Let Maggie Go	Honeybus	Deram	6		F L
14	-	Captain Of Your Ship	Reperata & The Delrons	Bell	5		F L
15	-	Ain't Nothin' But A Housparty	Showstoppers	Beacon	9		F L
16	-	Valleri	Monkees	RCA	5	(3)	
17	4	Rosie	Don Partridge	Columbia	9		F
18	2	Legend Of Xanadu	Dave Dee, Dozy, Beaky, Mick & Tich	Fontana	8		
19	-	Love Is Blue (L'Amour Est Bleu)	Paul Mauriat	Philips	5	(1)	F L
20	-	Something Here In My Heart (Keeps A-Tellin' Me No)	Paper Dolls	Pye	5		F L

May 1968

This Mnth	Prev Mnth	Title	Artist	Label	Wks 20	(US Pos)	
1	2	What A Wonderful World	Louis Armstrong	HMV	16	(32)	L
2	-	Lazy Sunday	Small Faces	Immediate	7		
3	-	A Man Without Love	Engelbert Humperdinck	Decca	9	(19)	
4	7	Simon Says	1910 Fruitgum Co.	Pye International	12	(4)	F L
5	-	Young Girl	Gary Puckett & The Union Gap	CBS	12	(2)	F
6	11	Can't Take My Eyes Off You	Andy Williams	CBS	9		
7	-	I Don't Want Our Loving To Die	Herd	Fontana	8		L
8	4	If I Only Had Time	John Rowles	MCA	11		F
9	-	Honey	Bobby Goldsboro	UA	11	(1)	F
10	1	Congratulations	Cliff Richard	Columbia	9	(99)	
11	-	White Horses	Jacky	Philips	9		F L
12	10	Jennifer Eccles	Hollies	Parlophone	6	(40)	
13	-	Rainbow Valley	Love Affair	CBS	8		
14	15	Ain't Nothin' But A Housparty	Showstoppers	Beacon	9		F L
15	13	I Can't Let Maggie Go	Honeybus	Deram	6		F L
16	20	Something Here In My Heart (Keeps A-Tellin' Me No)	Paper Dolls	Pye	5		F L
17	3	Delilah	Tom Jones	Decca	11	(15)	
18	-	Sleepy Joe	Herman's Hermits	Columbia	6	(61)	
19	-	Joanna	Scott Walker	Philips	7		F
20	-	Cry Like A Baby	Box Tops	Bell	5	(2)	L

June 1968

This Mnth	Prev Mnth	Title	Artist	Label	Wks 20	(US Pos)	
1	5	Young Girl	Gary Puckett & The Union Gap	CBS	12	(2)	F
2	9	Honey	Bobby Goldsboro	UA	11	(1)	F
3	-	Jumping Jack Flash	Rolling Stones	Decca	9	(3)	
4	3	A Man Without Love	Engelbert Humperdinck	Decca	9	(19)	
5	-	This Wheel's On Fire	Julie Driscoll, Brian Auger & The Trinity	Marmalade	8		F L
6	13	Rainbow Valley	Love Affair	CBS	8		
7	-	Do You Know The Way To San José	Dionne Warwick	Pye International	8	(10)	
8	-	Blue Eyes	Don Partridge	Columbia	8		L
9	-	Hurdy Gurdy Man	Donovan	Pye	7	(5)	
10	7	I Don't Want Our Loving To Die	Herd	Fontana	8		L
11	19	Joanna	Scott Walker	Philips	7		F
12	-	Baby Come Back	Equals	President	12	(32)	F
13	1	What A Wonderful World	Louis Armstrong	HMV	16	(32)	L
14	-	I Pretend	Des O'Connor	Columbia	15		
15	2	Lazy Sunday	Small Faces	Immediate	7		
16	4	Simon Says	1910 Fruitgum Co.	Pye International	12	(4)	F L
17	18	Sleepy Joe	Herman's Hermits	Columbia	6	(61)	
18	-	Lovin' Things	Marmalade	CBS	6		F
19	-	Son Of Hickory Hollers Tramp	O.C. Smith	CBS	9	(40)	F L
20	-	Helule Helule	Tremeloes	CBS	5		

April 1968

This Mnth	Prev Mnth	Title	Artist	Label	Wks 20	(UK Pos)	
1	16	Young Girl	Union Gap Feat. Gary Puckett	Columbia	11	(1)	G
2	-	Honey	Bobby Goldsboro	UA	11	(2)	G
3	-	Cry Like A Baby	Box Tops	Mala	10	(15)	G
4	2	(Sittin' On) The Dock Of The Bay	Otis Redding	Volt	12	(3)	F G L
5	9	(Sweet Sweet Baby) Since You've Been Gone	Aretha Franklin	Atlantic	8		G
6	-	Lady Madonna	Beatles	Capitol	8	(1)	G
7	13	The Ballad Of Bonnie And Clyde	Georgie Fame	Epic	9	(1)	F L
8	6	La-La Means I Love You	Delfonics	Philly Groove	9	(19)	F
9	-	I Got The Feelin'	James Brown	King	9		
10	17	Dance To The Music	Sly & The Family Stone	Epic	9	(7)	F
11	8	Valleri	Monkees	Colgems	6	(12)	G
12	18	Mighty Quinn	Manfred Mann	Mercury	5	(1)	L
13	1	Love Is Blue	Paul Mauriat	Philips	13	(12)	F G L
14	-	If You Can Want	Smokey Robinson & The Miracles	Tamla	6	(50)	
15	-	Scarborough Fair/Canticle	Simon & Garfunkel	Columbia			
16	4	Simon Says	1910 Fruitgum Co.	Buddah	9	(2)	F G
17	-	Cowboys To Girls	Intruders	Gamble	9		F G L
18	-	Tighten Up	Archie Bell & The Drells	Atlantic	10		F G
19	-	Summertime Blues	Blue Cheer	Philips	6		F L
20	-	Playboy	Gene & Debbe	TRX	3		F L

May 1968

This Mnth	Prev Mnth	Title	Artist	Label	Wks 20	(UK Pos)	
1	18	Tighten Up	Archie Bell & The Drells	Atlantic	10		F G
2	2	Honey	Bobby Goldsboro	UA	11	(2)	G
3	-	The Good, The Bad & The Ugly	Hugo Montenegro & Orchestra	RCA	10	(1)	L
4	-	A Beautiful Morning	Rascals	Atlantic	9		G
5	17	Cowboys To Girls	Intruders	Gamble	9		F G L
6	1	Young Girl	Union Gap Feat. Gary Puckett	Columbia	11	(1)	G
7	-	The Unicorn	Irish Rovers	Decca	7		F L
8	-	Mrs. Robinson	Simon & Garfunkel	Columbia	10	(4)	G
9	3	Cry Like A Baby	Box Tops	Mala	10	(15)	G
10	-	Love Is All Around	Troggs	Fontana	5	(5)	L
11	6	Lady Madonna	Beatles	Capitol	8	(1)	G
12	-	Take Time To Know Her	Percy Sledge	Atlantic	5		L
13	9	I Got The Feelin'	James Brown	King	9		
14	-	Shoo-Be-Doo-Be-Doo-Da-Day	Stevie Wonder	Tamla	6	(46)	
15	-	Do You Know The Way To San José	Dionne Warwick	Scepter	4	(8)	
16	-	Ain't Nothing Like The Real Thing	Marvin Gaye & Tammi Terrell	Tamla	5	(34)	
17	19	Summertime Blues	Blue Cheer	Philips	6		F L
18	-	Funky Street	Arthur Conley	Atco	3	(46)	L
19	-	Mony Mony	Tommy James & The Shondells	Roulette	9	(1)	G
20	14	If You Can Want	Smokey Robinson & The Miracles	Tamla	6	(50)	

June 1968

This Mnth	Prev Mnth	Title	Artist	Label	Wks 20	(UK Pos)	
1	-	This Guy's In Love With You	Herb Alpert	A&M	11	(2)	G
2	8	Mrs. Robinson	Simon & Garfunkel	Columbia	10	(4)	G
3	-	Yummy Yummy Yummy	Ohio Express	Buddah	8	(5)	F G
4	1	Tighten Up	Archie Bell & The Drells	Atlantic	10		F G
5	19	Mony Mony	Tommy James & The Shondells	Roulette	9	(1)	G
6	-	MacArthur Park	Richard Harris	Dunhill	8	(4)	F G L
7	-	Think	Aretha Franklin	Atlantic	8	(26)	G
8	3	The Good, The Bad & The Ugly	Hugo Montenegro & Orchestra	RCA	10	(1)	L
9	-	The Look Of Love	Sergio Mendes & Brasil '66	A&M	8		F
10	4	A Beautiful Morning	Rascals	Atlantic	9		G
11	-	Angel Of The Morning	Merrilee Rush	Bell	8		F L
12	2	Honey	Bobby Goldsboro	UA	11	(2)	G
13	16	Ain't Nothing Like The Real Thing	Marvin Gaye & Tammi Terrell	Tamla	5	(34)	
14	-	The Horse	Cliff Nobles & Co.	Phil L.A. of Soul	9		F G L
15	-	Here Comes The Judge	Shorty Long	Soul	7	(30)	F L
16	-	Reach Out Of The Darkness	Friend And Lover	Verve	6		F L
17	5	Cowboys To Girls	Intruders	Gamble	9		F G L
18	-	I Could Never Love Another (After Loving You)	Temptations	Gordy	5	(47)	
19	-	Jumpin' Jack Flash	Rolling Stones	London	9	(1)	G
20	-	I Love You	People	Capitol	6		F L

◆ Archie Bell was still in the army when a re-recording of a track he first cut in 1964, 'Tighten Up' topped the chart. This funky instrumental was originally recorded as a throwaway B-side.

◆ Although they never reached the US Top 100, singles by American acts Reperata & The Delrons, The Showstoppers, Andy Williams and Louis Armstrong were riding high across the Atlantic.

◆ Over half of The Beach Boys' shows with Maharishi Mahesh Yogi were cancelled. Shortly afterwards, The Beatles described their association with the Maharishi as "a public mistake".

◆ Simon & Garfunkel's album **Bookends** replaced **The Graduate** at No. 1, and **Parsley, Sage, Rosemary And Thyme** gave them three in the Top 5!

UK 1968

JULY-SEPT

◆ The Beatles launched their own label, Apple, and released their animated film *Yellow Submarine*. Incidentally, the group's No. 1 rivals of 1967, the Monkees, had their last US Top 20 entry with a Leiber & Stoller song, 'D.W. Washburn'.

◆ Chart topping album act Cream announced they were splitting up, as did The Yardbirds (who later evolved into Led Zeppelin). The Hollies announced they were making solo records, Janis Joplin quit Big Brother & The Holding Company, and ex-Contour Dennis Edwards replaced lead singer David Ruffin in The Temptations.

◆ Robert Plant, who sang with Hobbstweedle, turned down the chance of joining the Alexis Korner Band to be lead vocalist in the New Yardbirds. He then recruited fellow Midlander John Bonham from Band Of Joy.

July 1968

This Mnth	Prev Mnth	Title	Artist	Label	Wks 20	(US Pos)	
1	12	**Baby Come Back**	Equals	President	12	(32)	F
2	14	**I Pretend**	Des O'Connor	Columbia	15		
3	19	**Son Of Hickory Hollers Tramp**	O.C. Smith	CBS	9	(40)	F L
4	-	**Yesterday Has Gone**	Cupid's Inspiration	Nems	7		F L
5	-	**Yummy Yummy Yummy**	Ohio Express	Pye International	9	(4)	F L
6	-	**Mony Mony**	Tommy James & The Shondells	Major Minor	11	(3)	F L
7	3	**Jumping Jack Flash**	Rolling Stones	Decca	9	(3)	
8	-	**My Name Is Jack**	Manfred Mann	Fontana	5		
9	-	**MacArthur Park**	Richard Harris	RCA	7	(2)	F L
10	8	**Blue Eyes**	Don Partridge	Columbia	8		L
11	18	**Lovin' Things**	Marmalade	CBS	6		F
12	9	**Hurdy Gurdy Man**	Donovan	Pye	7	(5)	
13	-	**Hush Not A Word To Mary**	John Rowles	MCA	5		L
14	-	**Fire**	Crazy World Of Arthur Brown	Track	10	(2)	F L
15	-	**One More Dance**	Esther & Abi Ofarim	Philips	4		L
16	1	**Young Girl**	Gary Puckett & The Union Gap	CBS	12	(2)	F
17	-	**This Guy's In Love With You**	Herb Alpert	A&M	11	(1)	
18	-	**Mrs. Robinson**	Simon & Garfunkel	CBS	7	(1)	
19	5	**This Wheel's On Fire**	Julie Driscoll, Brian Auger & The Trinity	Marmalade	8		F L
20	-	**I Close My Eyes And Count To Ten**	Dusty Springfield	Philips	6		

August 1968

This Mnth	Prev Mnth	Title	Artist	Label	Wks 20	(US Pos)	
1	6	**Mony Mony**	Tommy James & The Shondells	Major Minor	11	(3)	F L
2	14	**Fire**	Crazy World Of Arthur Brown	Track	10	(2)	F L
3	17	**This Guy's In Love With You**	Herb Alpert	A&M	11	(1)	
4	2	**I Pretend**	Des O'Connor	Columbia	15		
5	20	**I Close My Eyes And Count To Ten**	Dusty Springfield	Philips	6		
6	-	**Help Yourself**	Tom Jones	Decca	10	(35)	
7	18	**Mrs. Robinson**	Simon & Garfunkel	CBS	7	(1)	
8	-	**Sunshine Girl**	Herman's Hermits	Columbia	8		
9	-	**Dance To The Music**	Sly & The Family Stone	Direction	7	(8)	F
10	-	**Do It Again**	Beach Boys	Capitol	10	(20)	
11	-	**Last Night In Soho**	Dave Dee, Dozy, Beaky, Mick & Tich	Fontana	6		
12	-	**I've Gotta Get A Message To You**	Bee Gees	Polydor	11	(8)	
13	9	**MacArthur Park**	Richard Harris	RCA	7	(2)	F L
14	-	**Keep On**	Bruce Channel	Bell	6		L
15	1	**Baby Come Back**	Equals	President	12	(32)	F
16	-	**High In The Sky**	Amen Corner	Deram	9		
17	-	**Days**	Kinks	Pye	6		
18	5	**Yummy Yummy Yummy**	Ohio Express	Pye International	9	(4)	F L
19	-	**I Say A Little Prayer**	Aretha Franklin	Atlantic	8	(10)	
20	3	**Son Of Hickory Hollers Tramp**	O.C. Smith	CBS	9	(40)	F L

September 1968

This Mnth	Prev Mnth	Title	Artist	Label	Wks 20	(US Pos)	
1	12	**I've Gotta Get A Message To You**	Bee Gees	Polydor	11	(8)	
2	10	**Do It Again**	Beach Boys	Capitol	10	(20)	
3	19	**I Say A Little Prayer**	Aretha Franklin	Atlantic	8	(10)	
4	-	**Hold Me Tight**	Johnny Nash	Regal Zonophone	10	(5)	F
5	-	**Hey Jude**	Beatles	Apple	10	(1)	
6	-	**Those Were The Days**	Mary Hopkin	Apple	14	(2)	F
7	3	**This Guy's In Love With You**	Herb Alpert	A&M	11	(1)	
8	16	**High In The Sky**	Amen Corner	Deram	9		
9	6	**Help Yourself**	Tom Jones	Decca	10	(35)	
10	-	**Jesamine**	Casuals	Decca	11		F L
11	-	**On The Road Again**	Canned Heat	Liberty	7	(16)	F
12	-	**Lady Willpower**	Gary Puckett & The Union Gap	CBS	10	(2)	
13	-	**Dream A Little Dream Of Me**	Mama Cass	RCA	7	(12)	F
14	-	**Little Arrows**	Leapy Lee	MCA	13	(16)	F L
15	1	**Mony Mony**	Tommy James & The Shondells	Major Minor	11	(3)	F L
16	2	**Fire**	Crazy World Of Arthur Brown	Track	10	(2)	F L
17	-	**Hard To Handle**	Otis Redding	Atlantic	6	(51)	L
18	9	**Dance To The Music**	Sly & The Family Stone	Direction	7	(8)	F
19	-	**Classical Gas**	Mason Williams	Warner	8	(2)	F L
20	8	**Sunshine Girl**	Herman's Hermits	Columbia	8		

US 1968
JULY-SEPT

July 1968

This Mnth	Prev Mnth	Title	Artist	Label	Wks 20	(UK Pos)	
1	-	Grazing In The Grass	Hugh Masekela	Uni	9		F G L
2	1	This Guy's In Love With You	Herb Alpert	A&M	11	(2)	G
3	19	Jumpin' Jack Flash	Rolling Stones	London	9	(1)	G
4	-	Lady Willpower	Gary Puckett & The Union Gap	Columbia	10	(5)	G
5	14	The Horse	Cliff Nobles & Co.	Phil L.A. of Soul	9		F G L
6	-	Stoned Soul Picnic	Fifth Dimension	Soul City	9		G
7	9	The Look Of Love	Sergio Mendes & Brasil '66	A&M	8		F
8	15	Here Comes The Judge	Shorty Long	Soul	7	(30)	F L
9	11	Angel Of The Morning	Merrilee Rush	Bell	8		F L
10	16	Reach Out Of The Darkness	Friend And Lover	Verve	6		F L
11	-	Indian Lake	Cowsills	MGM	5		
12	-	Hurdy Gurdy Man	Donovan	Epic	7	(4)	
13	-	Classical Gas	Mason Williams	Warner	8	(9)	F G L
14	-	Hello, I Love You	Doors	Elektra	9	(15)	G
15	6	MacArthur Park	Richard Harris	Dunhill	8	(4)	F G L
16	3	Yummy Yummy Yummy	Ohio Express	Buddah	8	(5)	F G
17	-	Turn Around Look At Me	Vogues	Reprise	9		G
18	5	Mony Mony	Tommy James & The Shondells	Roulette	9	(1)	G
19	2	Mrs. Robinson	Simon & Garfunkel	Columbia	10	(4)	G
20	20	I Love You	People	Capitol	6		F L

August 1968

This Mnth	Prev Mnth	Title	Artist	Label	Wks 20	(UK Pos)	
1	14	Hello, I Love You	Doors	Elektra	9	(15)	G
2	-	People Got To Be Free	Rascals	Atlantic	11		G L
3	13	Classical Gas	Mason Williams	Warner	8	(9)	F G L
4	-	Born To Be Wild	Steppenwolf	Dunhill	9	(30)	F G
5	-	Sunshine Of Your Love	Cream	Atco	8	(25)	F G
6	6	Stoned Soul Picnic	Fifth Dimension	Soul City	9		G
7	17	Turn Around Look At Me	Vogues	Reprise	9		G
8	-	Light My Fire	José Feliciano	RCA	9	(6)	F G L
9	12	Hurdy Gurdy Man	Donovan	Epic	7	(4)	
10	1	Grazing In The Grass	Hugh Masekela	Uni	9		F G L
11	4	Lady Willpower	Gary Puckett & The Union Gap	Columbia	10	(5)	G
12	-	(You Keep Me) Hangin' On	Vanilla Fudge	Atco	7	(18)	F L
13	-	Stay In My Corner	Dells	Cadet	7		
14	3	Jumpin' Jack Flash	Rolling Stones	London	9	(1)	G
15	-	I Can't Stop Dancing	Archie Bell & The Drells	Atlantic	5		L
16	5	The Horse	Cliff Nobles & Co.	Phil L.A. of Soul	9		F G L
17	-	Dream A Little Dream Of Me	Mama Cass	Dunhill	4	(11)	F L
18	-	Journey To The Center Of The Mind	Amboy Dukes	Mainstream	6		F L
19	-	You're All I Need To Get By	Marvin Gaye & Tammi Terrell	Tamla	5	(19)	
20	-	Pictures Of Matchstick Men	Status Quo	Cadet Concept	4	(7)	F L

September 1968

This Mnth	Prev Mnth	Title	Artist	Label	Wks 20	(UK Pos)	
1	2	People Got To Be Free	Rascals	Atlantic	11		G L
2	-	Harper Valley P.T.A.	Jeannie C. Riley	Plantation	11	(12)	F G L
3	-	1 2 3 Red Light	1910 Fruitgum Co.	Buddah	6		G
4	4	Born To Be Wild	Steppenwolf	Dunhill	9	(30)	F G
5	8	Light My Fire	José Feliciano	RCA	9	(6)	F G L
6	-	Hush	Deep Purple	Tetragrammaton	7		F
7	-	Hey Jude	Beatles	Apple	16	(1)	G
8	-	The House That Jack Built	Aretha Franklin	Atlantic	6		
9	-	The Fool On The Hill	Sergio Mendes & Brasil '66	A&M	6		L
10	19	You're All I Need To Get By	Marvin Gaye & Tammi Terrell	Tamla	5	(19)	
11	1	Hello, I Love You	Doors	Elektra	9	(15)	G
12	-	Slip Away	Clarence Carter	Atlantic	7		F G
13	-	I've Gotta Get A Message To You	Bee Gees	Atco	7	(1)	
14	-	Fire	Crazy World Of Arthur Brown	Track	10	(1)	F G L
15	-	I Say A Little Prayer	Aretha Franklin	Atlantic	5	(4)	G
16	-	Girl Watcher	O'Kaysions	ABC	9		F G L
17	-	Time Has Come Today	Chambers Brothers	Columbia	5		F L
18	5	Sunshine Of Your Love	Cream	Atco	8	(25)	F G
19	12	(You Keep Me) Hangin' On	Vanilla Fudge	Atco	7	(18)	F L
20	-	Revolution	Beatles	Capitol	9		G

▲ The Newport Pop Festival was attended by 100,000 fans. Headliners included Sonny & Cher (above), The Byrds, Jefferson Airplane, Grateful Dead, Iron Butterfly, Steppenwolf, Canned Heat and token British band Eric Burdon & The Animals.

◆ Canadian rock group Steppenwolf debuted on the chart with their hard-hitting composition 'Born To Be Wild'. It included the lyric "heavy metal thunder", which is credited as the first reference to the term heavy metal.

◆ The album **Beat Of The Brass** ended a fantastic run of eight consecutive Top 10 LPs for Herb Alpert & The Tijuana Brass.

127

UK 1968 OCT-DEC

◆ John Sebastian left The Lovin' Spoonful, Eric Burdon disbanded The Animals and Graham Nash left The Hollies (to form Crosby, Stills & Nash). Also Mama Cass left The Mamas & The Papas, Peter Tork quit The Monkees and Cream's farewell American tour grossed over $700,000.

◆ Double album, **The Beatles**, topped the charts, and the group's seven minute single, 'Hey Jude', quickly amassed world sales of five million. The first Beatle solo LPs were released by George and John (with Yoko), and a single on their Apple imprint, 'Those Were The Days' by Mary Hopkin, became an international hit.

◆ During a televised *Royal Variety Show* in front of the Queen, Diana Ross (of The Supremes) urged the audience to be more racially tolerant.

◆ For the first time more albums were sold in Britain than singles.

October 1968

This Mnth	Prev Mnth	Title	Artist	Label	Wks 20	(US Pos)	
1	6	Those Were The Days	Mary Hopkin	Apple	14	(2)	F
2	5	Hey Jude	Beatles	Apple	10	(1)	
3	10	Jesamine	Casuals	Decca	11		F L
4	14	Little Arrows	Leapy Lee	MCA	13	(16)	F L
5	12	Lady Willpower	Gary Puckett & The Union Gap	CBS	10	(2)	
6	-	My Little Lady	Tremeloes	CBS	7		
7	-	Red Balloon	Dave Clark Five	Columbia	6		
8	-	A Day Without Love	Love Affair	CBS	7		
9	4	Hold Me Tight	Johnny Nash	Regal Zonophone	10	(5)	F
10	-	Les Bicyclettes De Belsize	Engelbert Humperdinck	Decca	7	(31)	
11	19	Classical Gas	Mason Williams	Warner	8	(2)	F L
12	-	Ice In The Sun	Status Quo	Pye	6	(70)	
13	1	I've Gotta Get A Message To You	Bee Gees	Polydor	11	(8)	
14	-	Light My Fire	José Feliciano	RCA	8	(3)	F L
15	-	The Good, The Bad And The Ugly	Hugo Montenegro & Orchestra	RCA	15	(2)	F L
16	3	I Say A Little Prayer	Aretha Franklin	Atlantic	8	(10)	
17	-	Listen To Me	Hollies	Parlophone	6		
18	-	Hello, I Love You	Doors	Elektra	6	(1)	F
19	8	High In The Sky	Amen Corner	Deram	9		
20	-	Only One Woman	Marbles	Polydor	8		F L

November 1968

This Mnth	Prev Mnth	Title	Artist	Label	Wks 20	(US Pos)	
1	15	The Good, The Bad And The Ugly	Hugo Montenegro & Orchestra	RCA	15	(2)	F L
2	-	With A Little Help From My Friends	Joe Cocker	Regal Zonophone	8	(68)	F
3	-	Eloise	Barry Ryan	MGM	9	(86)	F L
4	1	Those Were The Days	Mary Hopkin	Apple	14	(2)	F
5	-	This Old Heart Of Mine	Isley Brothers	Tamla Motown	10	(12)	
6	20	Only One Woman	Marbles	Polydor	8		F L
7	-	All Along The Watchtower	Jimi Hendrix Experience	Track	6	(20)	
8	14	Light My Fire	Jose Feliciano	RCA	8	(3)	F L
9	-	Breakin' Down The Walls Of Heartache	Johnny Johnson & The Bandwagon	Direction	11		F
10	4	Little Arrows	Leapy Lee	MCA	13	(16)	F L
11	3	Jesamine	Casuals	Decca	11		F L
12	2	Hey Jude	Beatles	Apple	10	(1)	
13	-	Elenore	Turtles	London American	5	(6)	L
14	10	Les Bicyclettes De Belsize	Engelbert Humperdinck	Decca	7	(31)	
15	-	Ain't Got No - I Got Life/ Do What You Gotta Do	Nina Simone	RCA	12	(94)	F
16	-	Lily The Pink	Scaffold	Parlophone	12		
17	17	Listen To Me	Hollies	Parlophone	6		
18	6	My Little Lady	Tremeloes	CBS	7		
19	8	A Day Without Love	Love Affair	CBS	7		
20	-	Mexico	Long John Baldry	Pye	4		L

December 1968

This Mnth	Prev Mnth	Title	Artist	Label	Wks 20	(US Pos)	
1	16	Lily The Pink	Scaffold	Parlophone	12		
2	15	Ain't Got No - I Got Life/ Do What You Gotta Do	Nina Simone	RCA	12	(94)	F
3	1	The Good, The Bad And The Ugly	Hugo Montenegro & Orchestra	RCA	15	(2)	F L
4	-	One Two Three O'Leary	Des O'Connor	Columbia	9		
5	-	Build Me Up Buttercup	Foundations	Pye	9	(3)	
6	-	I'm The Urban Spaceman	Bonzo Dog Doo-Dah Band	Liberty	10		F L
7	5	This Old Heart Of Mine	Isley Brothers	Tamla Motown	10	(12)	F
8	9	Breakin' Down The Walls Of Heartache	Johnny Johnson & The Bandwagon	Direction	11		F
9	-	Race With The Devil	Gun	CBS	7		F L
10	-	I'm A Tiger	Lulu	Columbia	10		
11	-	Sabre Dance	Love Sculpture	Parlophone	8		F L
12	3	Eloise	Barry Ryan	MGM	9	(86)	F L
13	-	May I Have The Next Dream With You	Malcolm Roberts	Major Minor	8		F
14	-	Ob-La-Di Ob-La-Da	Marmalade	CBS	10		
15	-	Harper Valley P.T.A.	Jeannie C. Riley	Polydor	5	(1)	F L
16	13	Elenore	Turtles	London American	5	(6)	L
17	-	Albatross	Fleetwood Mac	Blue Horizon	13		F
18	-	Private Number	Judy Clay & William Bell	Stax	9	(75)	F L
19	-	A Minute Of Your Time	Tom Jones	Decca	7	(48)	
20	7	All Along The Watchtower	Jimi Hendrix Experience	Track	6	(20)	

▲ The Mamas & The Papas were sued by their label Dunhill for disbanding mid-contract, while Motown sued top producer/songwriters Holland, Dozier & Holland for $4 million, for not offering them any recordings in 1968.

◆ Motown Records held the top three places on the US chart for a record four consecutive weeks. The acts concerned were Marvin Gaye, Stevie Wonder, Diana Ross & The Supremes and The Temptations.

◆ Elvis Presley's long awaited TV special was widely considered a commercial and artistic triumph.

US 1968 OCT-DEC

October 1968

This Mnth	Prev Mnth	Title	Artist	Label	Wks 20	(UK Pos)	
1	7	Hey Jude	Beatles	Apple	16	(1)	G
2	14	Fire	Crazy World Of Arthur Brown	Track	10	(1)	F G L
3	-	Little Green Apples	O.C. Smith	Columbia	10		F G L
4	2	Harper Valley P.T.A.	Jeannie C. Riley	Plantation	11	(12)	F G L
5	16	Girl Watcher	O'Kaysions	ABC	9		F G L
6	13	I'vc Gotta Get A Message To You	Bee Gees	Atco	7	(1)	
7	-	Midnight Confessions	Grass Roots	Dunhill	10		G
8	-	My Special Angel	Vogues	Reprise	6		L
9	-	Over You	Gary Puckett & The Union Gap	Columbia	7		G
10	12	Slip Away	Clarence Carter	Atlantic	7		F G
11	-	Say It Loud-I'm Black And I'm Proud	James Brown	King	6		
12	17	Time Has Come Today	Chambers Brothers	Columbia	5		F L
13	-	Those Were The Days	Mary Hopkin	Apple	11	(1)	F G
14	1	People Got To Be Free	Rascals	Atlantic	11		G L
15	20	Revolution	Beatles	Capitol	9		G
16	-	Suzie Q. (Pt. 1)	Creedence Clearwater Revival	Fantasy	6		F
17	-	Elenore	Turtles	White Whale	7	(7)	
18	15	I Say A Little Prayer	Aretha Franklin	Atlantic	5	(4)	G
19	-	Piece Of My Heart	Big Brother & The Holding Company	Columbia	5		F L
20	3	1 2 3 Red Light	1910 Fruitgum Co.	Buddah	6		G

November 1968

This Mnth	Prev Mnth	Title	Artist	Label	Wks 20	(UK Pos)	
1	1	Hey Jude	Beatles	Apple	16	(1)	G
2	13	Those Were The Days	Mary Hopkin	Apple	11	(1)	F G
3	-	Love Child	Diana Ross & The Supremes	Motown	14	(15)	G
4	-	Magic Carpet Ride	Steppenwolf	Dunhill	9		G
5	-	Hold Me Tight	Johnny Nash	Jad	9	(5)	F
6	-	White Room	Cream	Atco	7	(28)	L
7	3	Little Green Apples	O.C. Smith	Columbia	10		F G L
7	1	Elenore	Turtles	White Whale	7	(7)	
9	-	Abraham, Martin And John	Dion	Laurie	10		G L
10	7	Midnight Confessions	Grass Roots	Dunhill	10		G
11	-	Who's Making Love	Johnnie Taylor	Stax	9		F G
12	9	Over You	Gary Puckett & The Union Gap	Columbia	7		G
13	2	Fire	Crazy World Of Arthur Brown	Track	10	(1)	F G L
14	-	For Once In My Life	Stevie Wonder	Tamla	11	(3)	G
15	-	Wichita Lineman	Glen Campbell	Capitol	11	(7)	F G
16	-	Stormy	Classics IV	Imperial	9		
17	16	Suzie Q. (Pt. 1)	Creedence Clearwater Revival	Fantasy	6		F
18	19	Piece Of My Heart	Big Brother & The Holding Company	Columbia	5		F L
19	-	Sweet Blindness	Fifth Dimension	Soul City	2		
20	-	Chewy Chewy	Ohio Express	Buddah	7		G L

December 1968

This Mnth	Prev Mnth	Title	Artist	Label	Wks 20	(UK Pos)	
1	-	I Heard It Through The Grapevine	Marvin Gaye	Tamla	13	(1)	G
2	3	Love Child	Diana Ross & The Supremes	Motown	14	(15)	G
3	14	For Once In My Life	Stevie Wonder	Tamla	11	(3)	G
4	9	Abraham, Martin And John	Dion	Laurie	10		G L
5	15	Wichita Lineman	Glen Campbell	Capitol	11	(7)	F G
6	11	Who's Making Love	Johnnie Taylor	Stax	9		F G
7	16	Stormy	Classics IV	Imperial	9		
8	1	Hey Jude	Beatles	Apple	16	(1)	G
9	-	I Love How You Love Me	Bobby Vinton	Epic	10		G
10	-	Both Sides Now	Judy Collins	Elektra	6	(14)	F
11	4	Magic Carpet Ride	Steppenwolf	Dunhill	9		G
12	-	Cloud Nine	Temptations	Gordy	8	(15)	G
13	-	See Saw	Aretha Franklin	Atlantic	5		G
14	2	Those Were The Days	Mary Hopkin	Apple	11	(1)	F G
15	-	Cinnamon	Derek	Bang	7		L
16	-	I'm Gonna Make You Love Me	Diana Ross & The Supremes & The Temptations	Motown	11	(3)	G
17	20	Chewy Chewy	Ohio Express	Buddah	7		G L
18	-	Bring It On Home To Me	Eddie Floyd	Stax	5		F L
19	5	Hold Me Tight	Johnny Nash	Jad	9	(5)	F
20	-	Scarborough Fair	Sergio Mendes & Brasil '66	A&M	2		

129

UK 1969 JAN-MAR

◆ Martha & The Vandellas' 1964 American hit 'Dancing In The Streets' finally reached the UK Top 20 as did label-mates The Isley Brothers' 1966 recording of 'I Guess I'll Always Love You'.

◆ Led Zeppelin debuted in the US (supported by fellow newcomers Jethro Tull). They would become one of the biggest selling and most influential acts of all time.

▲ Cream's **Goodbye Cream** album was a transatlantic Top 3 entry - although their film of the same name was panned. Meanwhile, ex-Cream members Eric Clapton (above) and Ginger Baker were planning a new group (Blind Faith) with Stevie Winwood.

January 1969

This Mnth	Prev Mnth	Title	Artist	Label	Wks 20	(US Pos)	
1	14	Ob-La-Di Ob-La-Da	Marmalade	CBS	10		
2	1	Lily The Pink	Scaffold	Parlophone	12		
3	17	Albatross	Fleetwood Mac	Blue Horizon	13		F
4	5	Build Me Up Buttercup	Foundations	Pye	9	(3)	
5	6	I'm The Urban Spaceman	Bonzo Dog Doo-Dah Band	Liberty	10		F L
6	-	For Once In My Life	Stevie Wonder	Tamla Motown	10	(2)	
7	11	Sabre Dance	Love Sculpture	Parlophone	8		F L
8	-	Something's Happening	Herman's Hermits	Columbia	8		
9	2	Ain't Got No - I Got Life/ Do What You Gotta Do	Nina Simone	RCA	12	(94)	F
10	-	Son-Of-A Preacher Man	Dusty Springfield	Philips	6	(10)	
11	18	Private Number	Judy Clay & William Bell	Stax	9	(75)	F L
12	4	One Two Three O'Leary	Des O'Connor	Columbia	9		
13	-	Blackberry Way	Move	Regal Zonophone	8		
14	10	I'm A Tiger	Lulu	Columbia	10		
15	-	Fox On The Run	Manfred Mann	Fontana	6	(97)	
16	9	Race With The Devil	Gun	CBS	7		F L
17	3	The Good, The Bad And The Ugly	Hugo Montenegro & Orchestra	RCA	15	(2)	F L
18	-	Love Child	Diana Ross & The Supremes	Tamla Motown	9	(1)	
19	-	Stop Her On Sight (SOS)/ Headline News	Edwin Starr	Polydor	5	(48)	F
20	19	A Minute Of Your Time	Tom Jones	Decca	7	(48)	

February 1969

This Mnth	Prev Mnth	Title	Artist	Label	Wks 20	(US Pos)	
1	3	Albatross	Fleetwood Mac	Blue Horizon	13		F
2	13	Blackberry Way	Move	Regal Zonophone	8		
3	6	For Once In My Life	Stevie Wonder	Tamla Motown	10	(2)	
4	-	Dancing In The Street	Martha & The Vandellas	Tamla Motown	7		F
5	-	You Got Soul	Johnny Nash	Major Minor	6	(58)	
6	-	Please Don't Go	Donald Peers	Columbia	9		F L
7	1	Ob-La-Di Ob-La-Da	Marmalade	CBS	10		
8	-	I'm Gonna Make You Love Me	Diana Ross & The Supremes & The Temptations	Tamla Motown	7	(2)	
9	-	To Love Somebody	Nina Simone	RCA	5		
10	-	(If Paradise Is) Half As Nice	Amen Corner	Immediate	7		
11	15	Fox On The Run	Manfred Mann	Fontana	6	(97)	
12	-	Where Do You Go To My Lovely	Peter Sarstedt	UA	10	(70)	F
13	8	Something's Happening	Herman's Hermits	Columbia	8		
14	-	I Guess I'll Always Love You	Isley Brothers	Tamla Motown	5	(61)	
15	11	Private Number	Judy Clay & William Bell	Stax	9	(75)	F L
16	19	Stop Her On Sight (SOS)/Headline...	Edwin Starr	Polydor	5	(48)	
17	-	The Way It Used To Be	Engelbert Humperdinck	Decca	8	(42)	
18	-	I'll Pick A Rose For My Rose	Marv Johnson	Tamla Motown	6		L
19	2	Lily The Pink	Scaffold	Parlophone	12		
20	-	Mrs. Robinson (E.P.)	Simon & Garfunkel	CBS	1		

March 1969

This Mnth	Prev Mnth	Title	Artist	Label	Wks 20	(US Pos)	
1	12	Where Do You Go To My Lovely	Peter Sarstedt	UA	10	,(70)	F
2	-	Surround Yourself With Sorrow	Cilla Black	Parlophone	9		
3	-	I Heard It Through The Grapevine	Marvin Gaye	Tamla Motown	10	(1)	
4	17	The Way It Used To Be	Engelbert Humperdinck	Decca	8	(42)	
5	6	Please Don't Go	Donald Peers	Columbia	9		F L
6	-	Gentle On My Mind	Dean Martin	Reprise	12		L
7	-	Wichita Lineman	Glen Campbell	Ember	6	(3)	F
8	-	Monsieur Dupont	Sandie Shaw	Pye	8		L
9	10	(If Paradise Is) Half As Nice	Amen Corner	Immediate	7		
10	-	First Of May	Bee Gees	Polydor	6	(37)	
11	8	I'm Gonna Make You Love Me	Diana Ross & The Supremes & The Temptations	Tamla Motown	7	(2)	
12	-	You've Lost That Lovin' Feelin'	Righteous Brothers	London American	6		
13	-	Sorry Suzanne	Hollies	Parlophone	7	(56)	
14	-	If I Can Dream	Elvis Presley	RCA	6	(12)	
15	-	Good Times (Better Times)	Cliff Richard	Columbia	7		
16	4	Dancing In The Street	Martha & The Vandellas	Tamla Motown	7		F
17	18	I'll Pick A Rose For My Rose	Marv Johnson	Tamla Motown	6		L
18	-	Games People Play	Joe South	Capitol	8	(12)	F L
19	2	Blackberry Way	Move	Regal Zonophone	8		
20	1	Albatross	Fleetwood Mac	Blue Horizon	13		F

January 1969

This Mnth	Prev Mnth	Title	Artist	Label	Wks 20	(UK Pos)	
1	1	I Heard It Through The Grapevine	Marvin Gaye	Tamla	13	(1)	G
2	16	I'm Gonna Make You Love Me	Diana Ross & The Supremes & The Temptations	Motown	11	(3)	G
3	-	Soulful Strut	Young-Holt Unlimited	Brunswick	9		F G L
4	-	Hooked On A Feeling	B.J. Thomas	Scepter	7		G
5	5	Wichita Lineman	Glen Campbell	Capitol	11	(7)	F G
6	3	For Once In My Life	Stevie Wonder	Tamla	11	(3)	G
7	-	Crimson & Clover	Tommy James & The Shondells	Roulette	13		G
8	12	Cloud Nine	Temptations	Gordy	8	(15)	G
9	-	Going Up The Country	Canned Heat	Liberty	7	(19)	L
10	-	Son-Of-A Preacher Man	Dusty Springfield	Atlantic	6	(9)	
11	15	Cinnamon	Derek	Bang	7		L
12	2	Love Child	Diana Ross & The Supremes	Motown	14	(15)	G
13	-	Touch Me	Doors	Elektra	10		G
14	-	Worst That Could Happen	Brooklyn Bridge	Buddah	7		F G L
15	9	I Love How You Love Me	Bobby Vinton	Epic	10		G
16	-	Everyday People	Sly & The Family Stone	Epic	11	(36)	G
17	-	Lo Mucho Que Te Quiero (The More I Love You)	Rene & Rene	White Whale	3		F L
18	7	Stormy	Classics IV	Imperial	9		
19	-	I Started A Joke	Bee Gees	Atco	7		
20	6	Who's Making Love	Johnnie Taylor	Stax	9		F G

February 1969

This Mnth	Prev Mnth	Title	Artist	Label	Wks 20	(UK Pos)	
1	16	Everyday People	Sly & The Family Stone	Epic	11	(36)	G
2	7	Crimson & Clover	Tommy James & The Shondells	Roulette	13		G
3	13	Touch Me	Doors	Elektra	10		G
4	14	Worst That Could Happen	Brooklyn Bridge	Buddah	7		F G L
5	-	Build Me Up Buttercup	Foundations	Uni	10	(2)	L
6	-	Can I Change My Mind	Tyrone Davis	Dakar	7		F G
7	1	I Heard It Through The Grapevine	Marvin Gaye	Tamla	13	(1)	G
8	2	I'm Gonna Make You Love Me	Diana Ross & The Supremes & The Temptations	Motown	11	(3)	G
9	19	I Started A Joke	Bee Gees	Atco	7		
10	-	Hang 'Em High	Booker T. & The M.G.'s	Stax	6		
11	-	You Showed Me	Turtles	White Whale	7		L
12	-	This Magic Moment	Jay & The Americans	UA	8		G
13	-	I'm Livin' In Shame	Diana Ross & The Supremes	Motown	4	(14)	
14	4	Hooked On A Feeling	B.J. Thomas	Scepter	7		G
15	-	If I Can Dream	Elvis Presley	RCA	6	(11)	
16	3	Soulful Strut	Young-Holt Unlimited	Brunswick	9		F G L
17	-	Baby, Baby Don't You Cry	Smokey Robinson/The Miracles	Tamla	6		
18	-	Games People Play	Joe South	Capitol	6	(6)	F
19	-	Proud Mary	Creedence Clearwater Revival	Fantasy	9	(8)	G
20	9	Going Up The Country	Canned Heat	Liberty	7	(19)	L

March 1969

This Mnth	Prev Mnth	Title	Artist	Label	Wks 20	(UK Pos)	
1	19	Proud Mary	Creedence Clearwater Revival	Fantasy	9	(8)	G
2	-	Dizzy	Tommy Roe	ABC	10	(1)	G
3	5	Build Me Up Buttercup	Foundations	Uni	10	(2)	L
4	1	Everyday People	Sly & The Family Stone	Epic	11	(36)	G
5	2	Crimson & Clover	Tommy James & The Shondells	Roulette	13		G
6	-	This Girl's In Love With You	Dionne Warwick	Scepter	7		
7	-	Traces	Classics IV	Imperial	9		G
8	-	Indian Giver	1910 Fruitgum Co.	Buddah	7		G L
9	-	Time Of The Season	Zombies	Date	8		G L
10	-	Run Away Child, Running Wild	Temptations	Gordy	8		
11	12	This Magic Moment	Jay & The Americans	UA	8		G
12	17	Baby, Baby Don't You Cry	Smokey Robinson/The Miracles	Tamla	6		
13	3	Touch Me	Doors	Elektra	10		G
14	18	Games People Play	Joe South	Capitol	6	(6)	F
15	-	My Whole World Ended (The Moment You Left Me)	David Ruffin	Motown	5		F
16	-	I've Gotta Be Me	Sammy Davis Jr.	Reprise	7		
17	-	Galveston	Glen Campbell	Capitol	9	(14)	G
18	-	Aquarius/Let The Sunshine In	Fifth Dimension	Soul City	14	(11)	G
19	11	You Showed Me	Turtles	White Whale	7		L
20	6	Can I Change My Mind	Tyrone Davis	Dakar	7		F G

◆ Elvis Presley recorded in Memphis for the first time since 1955. The session produced such hits as 'Suspicious Minds' and 'In The Ghetto'. Incidentally, Dusty Springfield's Memphis-recorded 'Son-Of-A Preacher Man' became her last transatlantic Top 10 solo entry.

◆ As UK police stopped The Beatles last live show on the roof of the Apple building, American officials seized copies of John and Yoko's **Two Virgins** album (which showed them naked). Later, the couple staged a "Bed-In For Peace" at the American Hilton hotel.

◆ Motown Records were riding high again. Their hits included the transatlantic toppers, 'I Heard it Through The Grapevine' by Marvin Gaye (his first British hit, which returned to the Top 10 in 1986) and **TCB,** the second joint album by The Supremes and The Temptations.

131

UK 1969 APR-JUNE

◆ Headliners at the first Country Music Festival in Britain included George Jones, Tammy Wynette, Conway Twitty and Loretta Lynn. Meanwhile, fellow Nashville superstar Johnny Cash appeared on a TV special with Bob Dylan, whose **Nashville Skyline** album was flying high.

◆ Shortly after marrying Bee Gee Maurice Gibb, Lulu won the Eurovision Song Contest (in a four-way tie!) with 'Boom Bang-A-Bang'. The victory did not help her career, as this archetypal entry was her last major UK hit for five years.

◆ Blind Faith's debut show in London's Hyde Park was watched by a crowd of 150,000.

◆ Meanwhile, the first successful rock opera *Tommy* by The Who simultaneously entered the UK and US album charts.

April 1969

This Mnth	Prev Mnth	Title	Artist	Label	Wks 20	(US Pos)	
1	3	I Heard It Through The Grapevine	Marvin Gaye	Tamla Motown	10	(1)	
2	-	Israelites	Desmond Dekker & The Aces	Pyramid	8	(9)	
3	6	Gentle On My Mind	Dean Martin	Reprise	12		L
4	-	Boom Bang-A-Bang	Lulu	Columbia	7		
5	-	Goodbye	Mary Hopkin	Apple	9	(13)	
6	13	Sorry Suzanne	Hollies	Parlophone	7	(56)	
7	-	In The Bad Bad Old Days	Foundations	Pye	7	(51)	L
8	-	Pinball Wizard	Who	Track	8	(19)	
9	18	Games People Play	Joe South	Capitol	8	(12)	F L
10	-	Windmills Of Your Mind	Noel Harrison	Reprise	9		F L
11	8	Monsieur Dupont	Sandie Shaw	Pye	8		L
12	-	I Can Hear Music	Beach Boys	Capitol	7	(24)	
13	2	Surround Yourself With Sorrow	Cilla Black	Parlophone	9		
14	1	Where Do You Go To My Lovely	Peter Sarstedt	UA	10	(70)	F
15	-	Get Back	Beatles with Billy Preston	Apple	10	(1)	
16	-	Come Back And Shake Me	Clodagh Rodgers	RCA	8		F
17	-	Harlem Shuffle	Bob & Earl	Island	7	(44)	F L
18	-	Cupid	Johnny Nash	Major Minor	6	(39)	
19	-	Get Ready	Temptations	Tamla Motown	5	(29)	
20	10	First Of May	Bee Gees	Polydor	6	(37)	

May 1969

This Mnth	Prev Mnth	Title	Artist	Label	Wks 20	(US Pos)	
1	15	Get Back	Beatles with Billy Preston	Apple	10	(1)	
2	-	Man Of The World	Fleetwood Mac	Immediate	9		
3	-	My Sentimental Friend	Herman's Hermits	Columbia	7		
4	5	Goodbye	Mary Hopkin	Apple	9	(13)	
5	16	Come Back And Shake Me	Clodagh Rodgers	RCA	8		F
6	-	My Way	Frank Sinatra	Reprise	9	(27)	
7	-	Behind A Painted Smile	Isley Brothers	Tamla Motown	7		
8	8	Pinball Wizard	Who	Track	8	(19)	
9	2	Israelites	Desmond Dekker & The Aces	Pyramid	8	(9)	
10	-	Dizzy	Tommy Roe	Stateside	10	(1)	L
11	-	The Boxer	Simon & Garfunkel	CBS	7	(7)	
12	-	(I'm A) Road Runner	Jr. Walker & The All Stars	Tamla Motown	6	(20)	F
13	17	Harlem Shuffle	Bob & Earl	Island	7	(44)	F L
14	18	Cupid	Johnny Nash	Major Minor	6	(39)	
15	-	Ragamuffin Man	Manfred Mann	Fontana	6		
16	3	Gentle On My Mind	Dean Martin	Reprise	12		L
17	-	Love Me Tonight	Tom Jones	Decca	6	(13)	
18	10	Windmills Of Your Mind	Noel Harrison	Reprise	9		F L
19	-	Aquarius/Let The Sunshine In (Medley)	Fifth Dimension	Liberty	4	(1)	F
20	-	I'm Living In Shame	Diana Ross & The Supremes	Tamla Motown	3	(10)	

June 1969

This Mnth	Prev Mnth	Title	Artist	Label	Wks 20	(US Pos)	
1	-	Ballad Of John And Yoko	Beatles	Apple	8	(8)	
2	10	Dizzy	Tommy Roe	Stateside	10	(1)	L
3	-	Oh Happy Day	Edwin Hawkins Singers	Buddah	8	(4)	F L
4	-	Time Is Tight	Booker T. & The M.G.'s	Stax	10	(6)	F
5	1	Get Back	Beatles with Nilly Preston	Apple	10	(1)	
6	6	My Way	Frank Sinatra	Reprise	9	(27)	
7	-	Living In The Past	Jethro Tull	Island	6	(11)	F
8	-	The Tracks Of My Tears	Smokey Robinson & The Miracles	Tamla Motown	6		F
9	2	Man Of The World	Fleetwood Mac	Immediate	9		
10	11	The Boxer	Simon & Garfunkel	CBS	7	(7)	
11	-	(Your Love Keeps Lifting Me) Higher And Higher	Jackie Wilson	MCA	6	(6)	
12	-	Big Ship	Cliff Richard	Columbia	5		
13	-	In The Ghetto	Elvis Presley	RCA	11	(3)	
14	15	Ragamuffin Man	Manfred Mann	Fontana	6		
15	17	Love Me Tonight	Tom Jones	Decca	6	(13)	
16	-	Something In The Air	Thunderclap Newman	Track	8	(37)	F L
17	3	My Sentimental Friend	Herman's Hermits	Columbia	7		
18	-	I'd Rather Go Blind	Chicken Shack	Blue Horizon	5		F L
19	-	Galveston	Glen Campbell	Ember	5	(4)	
20	7	Behind A Painted Smile	Isley Brothers	Tamla Motown	7		

April 1969

This Mnth	Prev Mnth	Title	Artist	Label	Wks 20	(UK Pos)	
1	18	Aquarius/Let The Sunshine In	Fifth Dimension	Soul City	14	(11)	G
2	-	You've Made Me So Very Happy	Blood Sweat & Tears	Columbia	8	(35)	F G
3	2	Dizzy	Tommy Roe	ABC	10	(1)	G
4	17	Galveston	Glen Campbell	Capitol	9	(14)	G
5	-	Only The Strong Survive	Jerry Butler	Mercury	8		G
6	-	It's Your Thing	Isley Brothers	T-Neck	10	(30)	G
7	9	Time Of The Season	Zombies	Date	8		G L
8	-	Hair	Cowsills	MGM	10		G L
9	-	Twenty Five Miles	Edwin Starr	Gordy	6	(36)	F
10	10	Run Away Child, Running Wild	Temptations	Gordy	8		
11	-	Rock Me	Steppenwolf	Dunhill	6		L
12	7	Traces	Classics IV	Imperial	9		G
13	-	Sweet Cherry Wine	Tommy James & The Shondells	Roulette	6		
14	1	Proud Mary	Creedence Clearwater Revival	Fantasy	9	(8)	G
15	-	Do Your Thing	Watts 103rd Street Band	Warner	4		F
16	-	Don't Give In To Him	Gary Puckett & The Union Gap	Columbia	4		
17	8	Indian Giver	1910 Fruitgum Co.	Buddah	7		G L
18	-	Gimme Gimme Good Lovin'	Crazy Elephant	Bell	5	(12)	F L
19	-	Time Is Tight	Booker T. & The M.G.'s	Stax	6	(4)	L
20	-	Hot Smoke & Sasafrass	Bubble Puppy	International	3		F L

May 1969

This Mnth	Prev Mnth	Title	Artist	Label	Wks 20	(UK Pos)	
1	1	Aquarius/Let The Sunshine In	Fifth Dimension	Soul City	14	(11)	G
2	8	Hair	Cowsills	MGM	10		G L
3	6	It's Your Thing	Isley Brothers	T-Neck	10	(30)	G
4	-	Get Back	Beatles with Billy Preston	Apple	11	(1)	G
5	-	Love (Can Make You Happy)	Mercy	Sundi	9		F G L
6	-	The Boxer	Simon & Garfunkel	Columbia	8	(6)	
7	-	Hawaii Five-O	Ventures	Liberty	7		L
8	-	Atlantis	Donovan	Epic	8	(23)	L
9	-	These Eyes	Guess Who	RCA	9		F G
10	19	Time Is Tight	Booker T. & The M.G.'s	Stax	6	(4)	L
11	-	Oh Happy Day	Edwin Hawkins Singers	Pavilion	7	(2)	F G
12	2	You've Made Me So Very Happy	Blood Sweat & Tears	Columbia	8	(35)	F G
13	-	Gitarzan	Ray Stevens	Monument	8		G
14	13	Sweet Cherry Wine	Tommy James & The Shondells	Roulette	6		
15	5	Only The Strong Survive	Jerry Butler	Mercury	8		G
16	-	The Chokin' Kind	Joe Simon	Sound Stage 7	5		F G
17	-	Grazin' In The Grass	Friends Of Distinction	RCA	8		F G
18	18	Gimme Gimme Good Lovin'	Crazy Elephant	Bell	5	(12)	F L
19	-	Goodbye	Mary Hopkin	Apple	4	(2)	L
20	-	In The Ghetto	Elvis Presley	RCA	9	(2)	G

June 1969

This Mnth	Prev Mnth	Title	Artist	Label	Wks 20	(UK Pos)	
1	4	Get Back	Beatles with Billy Preston	Apple	11	(1)	G
2	-	Love Theme From Romeo & Juliet	Henry Mancini & His Orchestra	RCA	11		G
3	-	Bad Moon Rising	Creedence Clearwater Revival	Fantasy	10	(1)	G
4	20	In The Ghetto	Elvis Presley	RCA	9	(2)	G
5	5	Love (Can Make You Happy)	Mercy	Sundi	9		F G L
6	17	Grazin' In The Grass	Friends Of Distinction	RCA	8		F G
7	-	Too Busy Thinking About My Baby	Marvin Gaye	Tamla	9	(5)	
8	-	One	Three Dog Night	Dunhill	9		F G
9	11	Oh Happy Day	Edwin Hawkins Singers	Pavilion	7	(2)	F G
10	9	These Eyes	Guess Who	RCA	9		F G
11	1	Aquarius/Let The Sunshine In	Fifth Dimension	Soul City	14	(11)	G
12	-	Good Morning Starshine	Oliver	Jubilee	8	(6)	F
13	-	Spinning Wheel	Blood Sweat & Tears	Columbia	10		G
14	-	The Israelites	Desmond Dekker & The Aces	Uni	5	(1)	F L
15	13	Gitarzan	Ray Stevens	Monument	8		G
16	8	Atlantis	Donovan	Epic	8	(23)	L
17	-	More Today Than Yesterday	Spiral Staircase	Columbia	4		F L
18	-	Ballad Of John And Yoko	Beatles	Apple	6	(1)	G
19	-	Black Pearl	Sonny Charles & The Checkmates, Ltd.	A&M	7		F L
20	-	Love Me Tonight	Tom Jones	Parrot	6	(9)	

◆ With their single 'Get Back', R&B organist Billy Preston became the only act to share label billing with The Beatles.

▲ Headliners at The Newport 69 festival included Jimi Hendrix, Creedence Clearwater Revival, The Rascals, The Byrds, Joe Cocker (above), Ike & Tina Turner, Jethro Tull and Columbia's $300,000 signing Johnny Winter.

◆ The first rock musical, *Hair*, not only topped the album chart for three months, but songs from it, 'Aquarius'/'Let The Sunshine In' and 'Hair' held the top two places on the singles chart in May.

UK 1969
JULY-SEPT

▲ The Rolling Stones (above) attracted 250,000 fans to Hyde Park – during the show they paid tribute to ex-member Brian Jones who had drowned just days before. Other British shows included the Isle of Wight Festival headlined by Bob Dylan, and The National Jazz & Blues Festival featuring The Who, Yes and King Crimson.

◆ Initially Zager & Evans only pressed 1000 copies of their pessimistic peek into the future, 'In The Year 2525'. As in the best fairy tales it sold five million copies and topped the transatlantic charts. Sadly the duo's own future was bleak and they soon returned to obscurity.

July 1969

This Mnth	Prev Mnth	Title	Artist	Label	Wks 20	(US Pos)	
1	16	Something In The Air	Thunderclap Newman	Track	8	(37)	F L
2	13	In The Ghetto	Elvis Presley	RCA	11	(3)	
3	-	Hello Susie	Amen Corner	Immediate	6		L
4	-	Way Of Life	Family Dogg	Bell	8		F L
5	1	Ballad Of John And Yoko	Beatles	Apple	8	(8)	
6	-	Break Away	Beach Boys	Capitol	6	(63)	
7	-	Honky Tonk Women	Rolling Stones	Decca	12	(1)	
8	-	Proud Mary	Creedence Clearwater Revival	Liberty	6	(2)	F
9	7	Living In The Past	Jethro Tull	Island	6	(11)	F
10	-	Give Peace A Chance	Plastic Ono Band	Apple	7	(14)	F
11	-	It Mek	Desmond Dekker & The Aces	Pyramid	5		
12	4	Time Is Tight	Booker T. & The M.G.'s	Stax	10	(6)	F
13	-	Lights Of Cincinatti	Scott Walker	Philips	5		L
14	-	Baby Make It Soon	Marmalade	CBS	7		
15	3	Oh Happy Day	Edwin Hawkins Singers	Buddah	8	(4)	F L
16	-	Frozen Orange Juice	Peter Sarstedt	UA	4		L
17	-	Gimme Gimme Good Lovin'	Crazy Elephant	Major Minor	5	(12)	F L
18	-	Saved By The Bell	Robin Gibb	Polydor	10		F L
19	12	Big Ship	Cliff Richard	Columbia	5		
20	-	That's The Way God Planned It	Billy Preston	Apple	6	(62)	F

August 1969

This Mnth	Prev Mnth	Title	Artist	Label	Wks 20	(US Pos)	
1	7	Honky Tonk Women	Rolling Stones	Decca	12	(1)	
2	18	Saved By The Bell	Robin Gibb	Polydor	10		F L
3	-	Make Me An Island	Joe Dolan	Pye	10		F
4	10	Give Peace A Chance	Plastic Ono Band	Apple	7	(14)	F
5	-	My Cherie Amour	Stevie Wonder	Tamla Motown	9	(4)	
6	-	Goodnight Midnight	Clodagh Rodgers	RCA	8		
7	-	Conversations	Cilla Black	Parlophone	7		
8	2	In The Ghetto	Elvis Presley	RCA	11	(3)	
9	-	In The Year 2525 (Exordium & Terminus)	Zager & Evans	RCA	9	(1)	F L
10	-	Bringing On Back The Good Times	Love Affair	CBS	6		L
11	-	Early In The Morning	Vanity Fare	Page One	6	(12)	
12	-	Too Busy Thinking About My Baby	Marvin Gaye	Tamla Motown	8	(4)	
13	-	Wet Dream	Max Romeo	Unity	6		F L
14	14	Baby Make It Soon	Marmalade	CBS	7		
15	1	Something In The Air	Thunderclap Newman	Track	8	(37)	F L
16	20	That's The Way God Planned It	Billy Preston	Apple	6	(62)	F
17	11	It Mek	Desmond Dekker & The Aces	Pyramid	5		
18	-	Viva Bobbie Joe	Equals	President	8		
19	-	Goo Goo Barabajagal (Love Is Hot)	Donovan & Jeff Beck Group	Pye	4	(36)	L
20	-	Curly	Move	Regal Zonophone	7		

September 1969

This Mnth	Prev Mnth	Title	Artist	Label	Wks 20	(US Pos)	
1	-	Bad Moon Rising	Creedence Clearwater Revival	Liberty	11	(2)	
2	9	In The Year 2525 (Exordium & Terminus)	Zager & Evans	RCA	9	(1)	F L
3	-	Don't Forget To Remember	Bee Gees	Polydor	11	(73)	
4	-	Je T'Aime...Moi Non Plus	Jane Birkin & Serge Gainsbourg	Fontana/ Major Minor	13	(58)	F L
5	-	Natural Born Bugie	Humble Pie	Immediate	7		F L
6	12	Too Busy Thinking About My Baby	Marvin Gaye	Tamla Motown	8	(4)	
7	18	Viva Bobbie Joe	Equals	President	8		
8	5	My Cherie Amour	Stevie Wonder	Tamla Motown	9	(4)	
9	1	Honky Tonk Women	Rolling Stones	Decca	12	(1)	
10	-	Good Morning Starshine	Oliver	CBS	10	(3)	F L
11	-	I'll Never Fall In Love Again	Bobbie Gentry	Capitol	9		
12	2	Saved By The Bell	Robin Gibb	Polydor	10		F L
13	3	Make Me An Island	Joe Dolan	Pye	10		F
14	-	A Boy Named Sue	Johnny Cash	CBS	9	(2)	F
15	20	Curly	Move	Regal Zonophone	7		
16	11	Early In The Morning	Vanity Fare	Page One	6	(12)	
17	-	It's Getting Better	Mama Cass	Stateside	6	(30)	L
18	-	Throw Down A Line	Cliff Richard	Columbia	6		
19	-	I'm A Better Man	Engelbert Humperdinck	Decca	4	(38)	
20	-	Cloud Nine	Temptations	Tamla Motown	3	(6)	

US 1969 JULY-SEPT

July 1969

This Mnth	Prev Mnth	Title	Artist	Label	Wks 20	(UK Pos)	
1	13	Spinning Wheel	Blood Sweat & Tears	Columbia	10		G
2	-	In The Year 2525 (Exordium & Terminus)	Zager & Evans	RCA	10	(1)	F G L
3	-	Crystal Blue Persuasion	Tommy James & The Shondells	Roulette	11		G
4	8	One	Three Dog Night	Dunhill	9		F G
5	2	Love Theme From Romeo & Juliet	Henry Mancini & His Orchestra	RCA	11		G
6	12	Good Morning Starshine	Oliver	Jubilee	8	(6)	F
7	-	What Does It Take To Win Your Love	Jr. Walker & The All Stars	Soul	9	(13)	
8	18	Ballad Of John And Yoko	Beatles	Apple	6	(1)	G
9	3	Bad Moon Rising	Creedence Clearwater Revival	Fantasy	10	(1)	G
10	-	Color Him Father	Winstons	Metromedia	7		F G L
11	-	My Cherie Amour	Stevie Wonder	Tamla	8	(4)	G
12	1	Get Back	Beatles with Billy Preston	Apple	11	(1)	G
13	-	Mother Popcorn (You Got To Have A Mother For Me)	James Brown	King	8		
14	-	Baby I Love You	Andy Kim	Steed	8		F G
15	20	Love Me Tonight	Tom Jones	Parrot	6	(9)	
16	7	Too Busy Thinking About My Baby	Marvin Gaye	Tamla	9	(5)	
17	4	In The Ghetto	Elvis Presley	RCA	9	(2)	G
18	19	Black Pearl	Sonny Charles/Checkmates Ltd.	A&M	7		F L
19	-	Sweet Caroline	Neil Diamond	Uni	9	(8)	G
20	-	Ruby, Don't Take Your Love To Town	Kenny Rogers & First Edition	Reprise	6	(2)	

August 1969

This Mnth	Prev Mnth	Title	Artist	Label	Wks 20	(UK Pos)	
1	-	Honky Tonk Women	Rolling Stones	London	12	(1)	G
2	2	In The Year 2525 (Exordium &...)	Zager & Evans	RCA	10	(1)	F G L
3	3	Crystal Blue Persuasion	Tommy James & The Shondells	Roulette	11		G
4	19	Sweet Caroline	Neil Diamond	Uni	9	(8)	G
5	-	A Boy Named Sue	Johnny Cash	Columbia	10	(4)	G
6	-	Put A Little Love In Your Heart	Jackie DeShannon	Imperial	7		G L
7	20	Ruby, Don't Take Your Love...	Kenny Rogers & First Edition	Reprise	6	(2)	
8	7	What Does It Take To Win Your Love	Jr. Walker & The All Stars	Soul	9	(13)	
9	11	My Cherie Amour	Stevie Wonder	Tamla	8	(4)	G
10	14	Baby I Love You	Andy Kim	Steed	8		F G
11	-	Polk Salad Annie	Tony Joe White	Monument	6		F L
12	1	Spinning Wheel	Blood Sweat & Tears	Columbia	10		G
13	-	Get Together	Youngbloods	RCA	9		F G L
14	-	Green River	Creedence Clearwater Revival	Fantasy	10	(19)	G
15	-	Laughing	Guess Who	RCA	5		G
16	-	Lay Lady Lay	Bob Dylan	Columbia	8	(5)	
17	-	Sugar Sugar	Archies	Calendar	15	(1)	F G
18	13	Mother Popcorn (You GTo Have A...)	James Brown	King	8		
19	-	Quentin's Theme (from TV Series 'Dark Shadows')	Charles Randolph Grean Sounde	Ranwood	5		F L
20	10	Color Him Father	Winstons	Metromedia	7		F G L

September 1969

This Mnth	Prev Mnth	Title	Artist	Label	Wks 20	(UK Pos)	
1	17	Sugar Sugar	Archies	Calendar	15	(1)	F G
2	1	Honky Tonk Women	Rolling Stones	London	12	(1)	G
3	14	Green River	Creedence Clearwater Revival	Fantasy	10	(19)	G
4	5	A Boy Named Sue	Johnny Cash	Columbia	10	(4)	G
5	-	Easy To Be Hard	Three Dog Night	Dunhill	10		
6	13	Get Together	Youngbloods	RCA	9		F G L
7	-	I'll Never Fall In Love Again	Tom Jones	Parrot	11	(2)	G
8	-	I Can't Get Next To You	Temptations	Gordy	13	(13)	G
9	16	Lay Lady Lay	Bob Dylan	Columbia	8	(5)	
10	-	Little Woman	Bobby Sherman	Metromedia	9		F G
11	-	Oh What A Nite	Dells	Cadet	6		L
12	-	Jean	Oliver	Crewe	9		G L
13	6	Put A Little Love In Your Heart	Jackie DeShannon	Imperial	7		G L
14	-	Hurt So Bad	Lettermen	Capitol	6		L
15	4	Sweet Caroline	Neil Diamond	Uni	9	(8)	G
16	-	This Girl Is A Woman Now	Gary Puckett & The Union Gap	Columbia	7		L
17	-	Share Your Love With Me	Aretha Franklin	Atlantic	3		
18	-	I'd Wait A Million Years	Grass Roots	Dunhill	4		
19	-	Hot Fun In The Summertime	Sly & The Family Stone	Epic	8		
20	15	Laughing	Guess Who	RCA	5		G

▲ Important pop festivals took place in Atlanta, Atlantic City, Denver, New Orleans, Newport, Seattle, Texas and Toronto. However, they were all overshadowed by the Woodstock Festival which attracted a crowd of over 400,000 to see acts like Jefferson Airplane, Jimi Hendrix (above), The Who, Creedence Clearwater Revival, Blood, Sweat and Tears and Sly & The Family Stone.

◆ Don Kirshner, the man behind The Monkees, launched cartoon characters The Archies as pop stars. Another successful launch was given by Diana Ross, at a Beverly Hills club, for The Jackson Five.

UK 1969 OCT-DEC

◆ As the year closed, Elton John first collaborated with songwriter Bernie Taupin, Rod Stewart joined The Faces, Jimi Hendrix unveiled his Band Of Gypsies and Isaac Hayes's **Hot Buttered Soul** turned gold.

◆ The Rolling Stones toured the US for the first time in three years. Their record breaking tour was, however, marred by the death of a fan during their set at Altamont. The fateful festival was attended by 300,000 people and also starred Jefferson Airplane, Santana and Grammy winning Crosby, Stills, Nash & Young. Altamont heralded the beginning of the end of the rock festival phenomenon.

◆ The decade's sexiest single 'Je T'Aime . . . Moi Non Plus' by Jane Birkin and Serge Gainsbourg, survived both a BBC ban and being dropped by its original label. The orgasmic ode became the first foreign language record to top the UK chart.

October 1969

This Mnth	Prev Mnth	Title	Artist	Label	Wks 20	(US Pos)	
1	4	Je T'Aime...Moi Non Plus	Jane Birkin & Serge Gainsbourg	Fontana/ Major Minor	13	(58)	F L
2	11	I'll Never Fall In Love Again	Bobbie Gentry	Capitol	9		
3	14	A Boy Named Sue	Johnny Cash	CBS	9	(2)	F
4	-	Lay Lady Lay	Bob Dylan	CBS	7	(7)	
5	1	Bad Moon Rising	Creedence Clearwater Revival	Liberty	11	(2)	
6	-	I'm Gonna Make You Mine	Lou Christie	Buddah	8	(10)	L
7	10	Good Morning Starshine	Oliver	CBS	10	(3)	F L
8	-	Nobody's Child	Karen Young	Major Minor	12		F L
9	3	Don't Forget To Remember	Bee Gees	Polydor	11	(73)	
10	18	Throw Down A Line	Cliff Richard	Columbia	6		
11	17	It's Getting Better	Mama Cass	Stateside	6	(30)	L
12	-	He Ain't Heavy, He's My Brother	Hollies	Parlophone	8	(7)	
13	-	Space Oddity	David Bowie	Philips	8	(15)	F
14	-	Oh Well	Fleetwood Mac	Reprise	10	(55)	
15	-	Sugar Sugar	Archies	RCA	17	(1)	F L
16	-	Hare Krishna	Radha Krishna Temple	Apple	5		F L
17	2	In The Year 2525 (Exordium & Terminus)	Zager & Evans	RCA	9	(1)	F L
18	5	Natural Born Bugie	Humble Pie	Immediate	7		F L
19	-	Do What You Gotta Do	Four Tops	Tamla Motown	1		
20	7	Viva Bobbie Joe	Equals	President	8		

November 1969

This Mnth	Prev Mnth	Title	Artist	Label	Wks 20	(US Pos)	
1	15	Sugar Sugar	Archies	RCA	17	(1)	F L
2	14	Oh Well	Fleetwood Mac	Reprise	10	(55)	
3	-	The Return Of Django	Upsetters	Upsetter	8		F L
4	-	(Call Me) Number One	Tremeloes	CBS	11		
5	12	He Ain't Heavy, He's My Brother	Hollies	Parlophone	8	(7)	
6	8	Nobody's Child	Karen Young	Major Minor	12		F L
7	-	Wonderful World Beautiful People	Jimmy Cliff	Trojan	9	(25)	F
8	6	I'm Gonna Make You Mine	Lou Christie	Buddah	8	(10)	L
9	-	Something/Come Together	Beatles	Apple	8	(1)	
10	-	Love's Been Good To Me	Frank Sinatra	Reprise	7	(75)	
11	13	Space Oddity	David Bowie	Philips	8	(15)	F
12	-	Delta Lady	Joe Cocker	Regal Zonophone	5	(69)	
13	-	Sweet Dream	Jethro Tull	Chrysalis	6		
14	-	Ruby, Don't Take Your Love To Town	Kenny Rogers & First Edition	Reprise	16	(6)	F
15	-	Yester-Me, Yester-You, Yesterday	Stevie Wonder	Tamla Motown	9	(7)	
16	-	What Does It Take To Win Your Love	Jr. Walker & The All Stars	Tamla Motown	5	(4)	
17	3	A Boy Named Sue	Johnny Cash	CBS	9	(2)	
18	-	Cold Turkey	Plastic Ono Band	Apple	5	(30)	
19	1	Je T'Aime...Moi Non Plus	Jane Birkin & Serge Gainsbourg	Fontana/ Major Minor	13	(58)	F L
20	-	Liquidator	Harry J. & The All Stars	Trojan	13		F L

December 1969

This Mnth	Prev Mnth	Title	Artist	Label	Wks 20	(US Pos)	
1	1	Sugar Sugar	Archies	RCA	17	(1)	F L
2	14	Ruby, Don't Take Your Love To...	Kenny Rogers & First Edition	Reprise	16	(6)	F
3	-	Two Little Boys	Rolf Harris	Columbia	16		
4	15	Yester-Me, Yester-You, Yesterday	Stevie Wonder	Tamla Motown	9	(7)	
5	-	Melting Pot	Blue Mink	Philips	10		F
6	4	(Call Me) Number One	Tremeloes	CBS	11		
7	-	Suspicious Minds	Elvis Presley	RCA	11	(1)	
8	-	Winter World Of Love	Engelbert Humperdinck	Decca	9	(16)	
9	20	Liquidator	Harry J. & The All Stars	Trojan	13		F L
10	-	All I Have To Do Is Dream	Bobbie Gentry & Glen Campbell	Capitol	10	(27)	L
11	-	Onion Song	Marvin Gaye & Tammi Terrell	Tamla Motown	8	(50)	
12	9	Something/Come Together	Beatles	Apple	8	(1)	
13	7	Wonderful World Beautiful People	Jimmy Cliff	Trojan	9	(25)	F
14	-	Tracy	Cuff Links	MCA	9	(9)	F
15	-	Love Is All	Malcolm Roberts	Major Minor	6		L
16	-	Durham Town (The Leavin')	Roger Whittaker	Columbia	9		F
17	2	Oh Well	Fleetwood Mac	Reprise	10	(55)	
18	-	Without Love	Tom Jones	Decca	6	(5)	
19	13	Sweet Dream	Jethro Tull	Chrysalis	6		
20	6	Nobody's Child	Karen Young	Major Minor	12		F L

October 1969

This Mnth	Prev Mnth	Title	Artist	Label	Wks 20	(UK Pos)	
1	1	Sugar Sugar	Archies	Calendar	15	(1)	F G
2	8	I Can't Get Next To You	Temptations	Gordy	13	(13)	G
3	12	Jean	Oliver	Crewe	9		G L
4	10	Little Woman	Bobby Sherman	Metromedia	9		F G
5	19	Hot Fun In The Summertime	Sly & The Family Stone	Epic	8		
6	-	Suspicious Minds	Elvis Presley	RCA	11	(2)	G
7	5	Easy To Be Hard	Three Dog Night	Dunhill	10		
8	-	Everybody's Talkin'	Nilsson	RCA	6	(23)	F
9	-	That's The Way Love Is	Marvin Gaye	Tamla	6		
10	2	Honky Tonk Women	Rolling Stones	London	12	(1)	G
11	16	This Girl Is A Woman Now	Gary Puckett & The Union Gap	Columbia	7		L
12	-	I'm Gonna Make You Mine	Lou Christie	Buddah	5	(2)	L
13	3	Green River	Creedence Clearwater Revival	Fantasy	10	(19)	G
14	-	Wedding Bell Blues	Fifth Dimension	Soul City	10	(16)	G
15	-	Baby It's You	Smith	Dunhill	9		F L
16	-	Tracy	Cuff Links	Decca	6	(4)	F L
17	11	Oh What A Nite	Dells	Cadet	6		L
18	7	I'll Never Fall In Love Again	Tom Jones	Parrot	11	(2)	G
19	6	Get Together	Youngbloods	RCA	9		F G L
20	-	Come Together/Something	Beatles	Apple	13	(4)	G

November 1969

This Mnth	Prev Mnth	Title	Artist	Label	Wks 20	(UK Pos)	
1	14	Wedding Bell Blues	Fifth Dimension	Soul City	10	(16)	G
2	20	Come Together/Something	Beatles	Apple	13	(4)	G
3	6	Suspicious Minds	Elvis Presley	RCA	11	(2)	G
4	-	And When I Die	Blood Sweat & Tears	Columbia	10		G
5	15	Baby It's You	Smith	Dunhill	9		F L
6	2	I Can't Get Next To You	Temptations	Gordy	13	(13)	G
7	-	Smile A Little Smile For Me	Flying Machine	Janus	8		F G L
8	1	Sugar Sugar	Archies	Calendar	15	(1)	F G
9	-	Take A Letter Maria	R.B. Greaves	Atco	10		F G L
10	-	Na Na Hey Hey Kiss Him Goodbye	Steam	Fontana	11	(9)	F G L
11	5	Hot Fun In The Summertime	Sly & The Family Stone	Epic	8		
12	16	Tracy	Cuff Links	Decca	6	(4)	F L
13	-	Yester-Me, Yester-You, Yesterday	Stevie Wonder	Tamla	6	(2)	
14	-	Is That All There Is	Peggy Lee	Capitol	5		L
15	-	Down On The Corner/Fortunate Son	Creedence Clearwater Revival	Fantasy	10	(31)	G
16	-	Leaving On A Jet Plane	Peter, Paul & Mary	Warner	12	(2)	G L
17	4	Little Woman	Bobby Sherman	Metromedia	9		F G
18	-	Going In Circles	Friends Of Distinction	RCA	6		G
19	-	Baby, I'm For Real	Originals	Soul	6		F
20	3	Jean	Oliver	Crewe	9		G L

December 1969

This Mnth	Prev Mnth	Title	Artist	Label	Wks 20	(UK Pos)	
1	16	Leaving On A Jet Plane	Peter, Paul & Mary	Warner	12	(2)	G L
2	10	Na Na Hey Hey Kiss Him Goodbye	Steam	Fontana	11	(9)	F G L
3	-	Someday We'll Be Together	Diana Ross & The Supremes	Motown	13	(13)	G
4	15	Down On The Corner/Fortunate Son	Creedence Clearwater Revival	Fantasy	10	(31)	G
5	2	Come Together/Something	Beatles	Apple	13	(4)	G
6	9	Take A Letter Maria	R.B. Greaves	Atco	10		F G L
7	-	Raindrops Keep Fallin' On My Head	B.J. Thomas	Scepter	15	(38)	G
8	13	Yester-Me, Yester-You, Yesterday	Stevie Wonder	Tamla	6	(2)	
9	4	And When I Die	Blood Sweat & Tears	Columbia	10		
10	-	Holly Holy	Neil Diamond	Uni	9		G
11	-	Eli's Coming	Three Dog Night	Dunhill	10		
12	-	Backfield In Motion	Mel & Tim	Bamboo	9		F G
13	1	Wedding Bell Blues	Fifth Dimension	Soul City	10	(16)	G
14	-	Whole Lotta Love	Led Zeppelin	Atlantic	9		F G
15	-	I Want You Back	Jackson Five	Motown	13	(2)	F G
16	-	Midnight Cowboy	Ferrante & Teicher	UA	7		L
17	7	Smile A Little Smile For Me	Flying Machine	Janus	8		F G L
18	-	Cherry Hill Park	Billy Joe Royal	Columbia	5		L
19	-	La La La (If I Had You)	Bobby Sherman	Metromedia	6		G
20	19	Baby, I'm For Real	Originals	Soul	6		F

US 1969
OCT-DEC

◆ Diana Ross's last single with The Supremes, 'Someday We'll be Together', gave the group their twelfth and final No. 1.

◆ Singer/songwriter Laura Nyro had three top hits by other acts 'And When I Die' (Blood Sweat & Tears), 'Eli's Coming' (Three Dog Night) and the No. 1 'Wedding Bell Blues' (Fifth Dimension – their third Nyro-composed Top 20 entry.

▲ On the album front **Led Zeppelin II** gave the group (above) the first of many transatlantic toppers, and the critically un-acclaimed heavy rockers Grand Funk Railroad debuted with **On Time**.

137

UK 1970 JAN-MAR

138

◆ American Ron Dante was the lead vocalist of transatlantic hit makers The Archies and The Cuff Links, while Englishman Tony Burrows sang in three transatlantic hit acts, Edison Lighthouse, White Plains and Brotherhood Of Man.

◆ Davy Jones quit The Monkees, British teen idol Steve Ellis left Love Affair and Joe Cocker split from the Grease Band before joining the *Mad Dogs And Englishmen* tour.

◆ Simon & Garfunkel topped the transatlantic single and album charts with the multi Grammy winning **Bridge Over Troubled Water**. The album headed the UK charts for a record 41 weeks and remained in the Top 10 for 126 weeks!

◆ The new year heralded the introduction of the Minimoog. This instrument, an early synthesizer, was to greatly influence the recording scene over the next decades.

January 1970

This Mnth	Prev Mnth	Title	Artist	Label	Wks 20	(US Pos)	
1	3	Two Little Boys	Rolf Harris	Columbia	16		
2	2	Ruby, Don't Take Your Love To Town	Kenny Rogers & First Edition	Reprise	16	(6)	F
3	10	All I Have To Do Is Dream	Bobbie Gentry & Glen Campbell	Capitol	10	(27)	L
4	7	Suspicious Minds	Elvis Presley	RCA	11	(1)	
5	14	Tracy	Cuff Links	MCA	9	(9)	F
6	1	Sugar Sugar	Archies	RCA	17	(1)	F L
7	5	Melting Pot	Blue Mink	Philips	10		F
8	-	Good Old Rock 'n' Roll	Dave Clark Five	Columbia	8		
9	-	Reflections Of My Life	Marmalade	Decca	7	(10)	
10	-	Come And Get It	Badfinger	Apple	7	(7)	F
11	4	Yester-Me, Yester-You, Yesterday	Stevie Wonder	Tamla Motown	9	(7)	
12	18	Without Love	Tom Jones	Decca	6	(5)	
13	16	Durham Town (The Leavin')	Roger Whittaker	Columbia	9		F
14	9	Liquidator	Harry J. & The All Stars	Trojan	13		F L
15	-	Love Grows (Where My Rosemary Goes)	Edison Lighthouse	Bell	10	(5)	F L
16	-	Friends	Arrival	Decca	5		F
17	8	Winter World Of Love	Engelbert Humperdinck	Decca	9	(16)	
18	11	Onion Song	Marvin Gaye & Tammi Terrell	Tamla Motown	8	(50)	
19	-	Someday We'll Be Together	Diana Ross & The Supremes	Tamla Motown	5	(1)	
20	-	Leavin' On A Jet Plane	Peter, Paul & Mary	Warner	9	(1)	L

February 1970

This Mnth	Prev Mnth	Title	Artist	Label	Wks 20	(US Pos)	
1	15	Love Grows (Where My Rosemary Goes)	Edison Lighthouse	Bell	10	(5)	F L
2	20	Leavin' On A Jet Plane	Peter, Paul & Mary	Warner	9	(1)	L
3	-	Let's Work Together	Canned Heat	Liberty	9	(26)	L
4	-	The Witch's Promise/Teacher	Jethro Tull	Chrysalis	5		
5	-	Temma Harbour	Mary Hopkin	Apple	6	(39)	
6	1	Two Little Boys	Rolf Harris	Columbia	16		
7	-	I Want You Back	Jackson Five	Tamla Motown	9	(1)	F
8	10	Come And Get It	Badfinger	Apple	7	(7)	F
9	9	Reflections Of My Life	Marmalade	Decca	7	(10)	
10	-	Wand'rin' Star	Lee Marvin	Paramount	11		F L
11	-	Venus	Shocking Blue	Penny Farthing	5	(1)	F L
12	-	I'm A Man	Chicago	CBS	6	(49)	F
13	-	Instant Karma	Lennon, Ono & The Plastic Ono Band	Apple	6	(3)	
14	2	Ruby, Don't Take Your Love To...	Kenny Rogers & First Edition	Reprise	16	(6)	F
15	-	I Can't Get Next To You	Temptations	Tamla Motown	5	(1)	
16	16	Friends	Arrival	Decca	5		F
17	-	My Baby Loves Lovin'	White Plains	Deram	5	(13)	F
18	-	Years May Come, Years May Go	Herman's Hermits	Columbia	7		
19	3	All I Have To Do Is Dream	Bobbie Gentry & Glen Campbell	Capitol	10	(27)	L
20	-	United We Stand	Brotherhood Of Man	Deram	6	(13)	F

March 1970

This Mnth	Prev Mnth	Title	Artist	Label	Wks 20	(US Pos)	
1	10	Wand'rin' Star	Lee Marvin	Paramount	11		F L
2	-	Bridge Over Troubled Water	Simon & Garfunkel	CBS	13	(1)	L
3	7	I Want You Back	Jackson Five	Tamla Motown	9	(1)	F
4	-	Let It Be	Beatles	Apple	6	(1)	
5	3	Let's Work Together	Canned Heat	Liberty	9	(26)	L
6	13	Instant Karma	Lennon/Ono/Plastic Ono Band	Apple	6	(3)	
7	-	That Same Old Feeling	Pickettywitch	Pye	8	(67)	F
8	18	Years May Come, Years May Go	Herman's Hermits	Columbia	7		
9	1	Love Grows (Where My Rosemary...)	Edison Lighthouse	Bell	10	(5)	F L
10	-	Na Na Hey Hey Kiss Him Goodbye	Steam	Fontana	6	(1)	F L
11	-	Don't Cry Daddy	Elvis Presley	RCA	7	(6)	
12	-	Can't Help Falling In Love	Andy Williams	CBS	11	(88)	
13	-	Raindrops Keep Fallin' On My Head	Sacha Distel	Warner	5		F L
14	20	United We Stand	Brotherhood Of Man	Deram	6	(13)	F
15	-	Something's Burning	Kenny Rogers & First Edition	Reprise	8	(11)	
16	-	Everybody Get Together	Dave Clark Five	Columbia	5		L
17	2	Leavin' On A Jet Plane	Peter, Paul & Mary	Warner	9	(1)	L
18	17	My Baby Loves Lovin'	White Plains	Deram	5	(13)	F
19	-	Young Gifted And Black	Bob & Marcia	Harry J.	8		F
20	-	Knock Knock Who's There	Mary Hopkin	Apple	7	(92)	

This Mnth	Prev Mnth	Title	Artist	Label	Wks 20	(UK Pos)	
1	7	Raindrops Keep Fallin' On My Head	B.J. Thomas	Scepter	15	(38)	G
2	15	I Want You Back	Jackson Five	Motown	13	(2)	F G
3	-	Venus	Shocking Blue	Colossus	11	(8)	F G L
4	3	Someday We'll Be Together	Diana Ross & The Supremes	Motown	13	(13)	G
5	14	Whole Lotta Love	Led Zeppelin	Atlantic	9		F G
6	1	Leaving On A Jet Plane	Peter, Paul & Mary	Warner	12	(2)	G L
7	-	Don't Cry Daddy/Rubberneckin'	Elvis Presley	RCA	7	(8)	G
8	-	Jam Up Jelly Tight	Tommy Roe	ABC	7		G L
9	4	Down On The Corner/Fortunate Son	Creedence Clearwater Revival	Fantasy	10	(31)	G
10	16	Midnight Cowboy	Ferrante & Teicher	UA	7		L
11	-	Without Love (There Is Nothing)	Tom Jones	Parrot	7	(10)	G
12	19	La La La (If I Had You)	Bobby Sherman	Metromedia	6		G
13	-	Jingle Jangle	Archies	Kirshner	7		G L
14	2	Na Na Hey Hey Kiss Him Goodbye	Steam	Fontana	11	(9)	F G L
15	10	Holly Holy	Neil Diamond	UNI	9		G
16	-	Early In The Morning	Vanity Fare	Page One	6	(8)	F
17	-	I'll Never Fall In Love Again	Dionne Warwick	Scepter	7		
18	-	Thank You (Falettinme Be Mice Elf Agin)/Everybody Is A Star	Sly & The Family Stone	Epic	8		G
19	11	Eli's Coming	Three Dog Night	Dunhill	10		
20	5	Come Together/Something	Beatles	Apple	13	(4)	G

This Mnth	Prev Mnth	Title	Artist	Label	Wks 20	(UK Pos)	
1	18	Thank You (Falettinme Be Mice Elf Agin)/Everybody Is A Star	Sly & The Family Stone	Epic	8		G
2	-	Hey There Lonely Girl	Eddie Holman	ABC	8	(4)	F G L
3	2	I Want You Back	Jackson Five	Motown	13	(2)	F G
4	1	Raindrops Keep Fallin' On My Head	B.J. Thomas	Scepter	15	(38)	G
5	3	Venus	Shocking Blue	Colossus	11	(8)	F G L
6	-	No Time	Guess Who	RCA	7		
7	-	Psychedelic Shack	Temptations	Gordy	7	(33)	
8	-	Travelin' Band/Who'll Stop The Rain	Creedence Clearwater Revival	Fantasy	8	(8)	G
9	-	Bridge Over Troubled Water	Simon & Garfunkel	Columbia	12	(1)	G
10	-	Arizona	Mark Lindsay	Columbia	7		F G L
11	11	Without Love (There Is Nothing)	Tom Jones	Parrot	7	(10)	G
12	17	I'll Never Fall In Love Again	Dionne Warwick	Scepter	7		
13	-	Walk A Mile In My Shoes	Joe South	Capitol	6		L
14	-	Rainy Night In Georgia	Brook Benton	Cotillion	9		G L
15	-	Ma Belle Amie	Tee Set	Colossus	8		F L
16	5	Whole Lotta Love	Led Zeppelin	Atlantic	9		F G
17	-	The Thrill Is Gone	B.B. King	Bluesway	4		F L
18	-	The Rapper	Jaggerz	Kama Sutra	9		F G L
19	13	Jingle Jangle	Archies	Kirshner	7		G L
20	7	Don't Cry Daddy/Rubberneckin'	Elvis Presley	RCA	7	(8)	G

This Mnth	Prev Mnth	Title	Artist	Label	Wks 20	(UK Pos)	
1	9	Bridge Over Troubled Water	Simon & Garfunkel	Columbia	12	(1)	G
2	18	The Rapper	Jaggerz	Kama Sutra	9		F G L
3	-	Give Me Just A Little More Time	Chairmen Of The Board	Invictus	9	(3)	F G
4	14	Rainy Night In Georgia	Brook Benton	Cotillion	9		G L
5	-	He Ain't Heavy, He's My Brother	Hollies	Epic	7	(3)	
6	8	Travelin' Band/Who'll Stop The Rain	Creedence Clearwater Revival	Fantasy	8	(8)	G
7	15	Ma Belle Amie	Tee Set	Colossus	8		F L
8	-	Instant Karma (We All Shine On)	John Lennon/Plastic Ono Band	Apple	10	(5)	G
9	-	Love Grows (Where My Rosemary Goes)	Edison Lighthouse	Bell	9	(1)	F G L
10	-	Let It Be	Beatles	Apple	11	(2)	G
11	-	Evil Ways	Santana	Columbia	6		F
12	1	Thank You (Falettinme Be Mice Elf Agin)/Everybody Is A Star	Sly & The Family Stone	Epic	8		G
13	-	Didn't I (Blow Your Mind This Time)	Delfonics	Philly Groove	6	(22)	G L
14	2	Hey There Lonely Girl	Eddie Holman	ABC	8	(4)	F G L
15	-	ABC	Jackson Five	Motown	11	(8)	G
16	-	Spirit In The Sky	Norman Greenbaum	Reprise	11	(1)	F G L
17	7	Psychedelic Shack	Temptations	Gordy	7	(33)	
18	4	Raindrops Keep Fallin' On My Head	B.J. Thomas	Scepter	15	(38)	G
19	-	House Of The Rising Sun	Frijid Pink	Parrot	7	(4)	F G L
20	-	Easy Come, Easy Go	Bobby Sherman	Metromedia	8		G

US 1970 JAN-MAR

◆ The last newly recorded Beatles single, 'Let It Be', entered the US Hot 100 chart at No. 6 – a record which was not beaten until 1995. John Lennon's latest single offering 'Instant Karma', written with Phil Spector, was also an instant transatlantic hit.

◆ Shocking Blue headed a short-lived mini-invasion of the US charts by Dutch groups. They were followed up the charts by fellow countrymen Tee Set and the George Baker Selection.

◆ The R&B/soul scene mourned the deaths of singers Billy Stewart (car crash), Tammi Terrell (brain tumour), Slim Harpo (heart attack) and James Sheppard (murdered).

◆ As Elvis Presley's last acting film, *Change Of Habit*, was released, his label, RCA, announced that he had sold over 160 million records since bursting onto the scene in 1956.

UK 1970
APR-JUNE

▲ Grateful Dead made their UK debut at the Hollywood Rock Music Festival, where newcomers Mungo Jerry (above, whose 'In The Summertime' would sell seven million world-wide) were the surprise hit. One of several other UK festivals was the Bath Festival Of Blues And Progressive Music, whose headliners included Led Zeppelin, The Byrds, Donovan, Santana, Steppenwolf, Pink Floyd, John Mayall and Frank Zappa.

◆ The first of numerous hits by British football teams quickly shot to the top; it was by England's World Cup Squad (the winners of the previous World Cup) with the stirring 'Back Home'.

April 1970

This Mnth	Prev Mnth	Title	Artist	Label	Wks 20	(US Pos)	
1	2	Bridge Over Troubled Water	Simon & Garfunkel	CBS	13	(1)	L
2	12	Can't Help Falling In Love	Andy Williams	CBS	11	(88)	
3	20	Knock Knock Who's There	Mary Hopkin	Apple	7	(92)	
4	-	All Kinds Of Everything	Dana	Rex	8		F
5	19	Young Gifted And Black	Bob & Marcia	Harry J.	8		F
6	-	Spirit In The Sky	Norman Greenbaum	Reprise	11	(3)	F L
7	1	Wand'rin' Star	Lee Marvin	Paramount	11		F L
8	7	That Same Old Feeling	Pickettywitch	Pye	8	(67)	F
9	-	Gimme Dat Ding	Pipkins	Columbia	6	(9)	F L
10	-	Farewell Is A Lonely Sound	Jimmy Ruffin	Tamla Motown	7		
11	15	Something's Burning	Kenny Rogers & The First Edition	Reprise	8	(11)	
12	-	I Can't Help Myself	Four Tops	Tamla Motown	5	(1)	
13	4	Let It Be	Beatles	Apple	6	(1)	
14	-	Never Had A Dream Come True	Stevie Wonder	Tamla Motown	7	(26)	
15	-	When Julie Comes Around	Cuff Links	MCA	6	(41)	L
16	11	Don't Cry Daddy	Elvis Presley	RCA	7	(6)	
17	16	Everybody Get Together	Dave Clark Five	Columbia	5		L
18	-	Good Morning Freedom	Blue Mink	Philips	4		
19	10	Na Na Hey Hey Kiss Him Goodbye	Steam	Fontana	6	(1)	F L
20	-	You're Such A Good Looking Woman	Joe Dolan	Pye	4		L

May 1970

1	-	Back Home	England World Cup Squad	Pye	9		F
2	6	Spirit In The Sky	Norman Greenbaum	Reprise	11	(3)	F L
3	-	House Of The Rising Sun	Frijid Pink	Deram	8	(7)	F L
4	4	All Kinds Of Everything	Dana	Rex	8		F
5	-	Daughter Of Darkness	Tom Jones	Decca	9	(13)	
6	-	Question	Moody Blues	Threshold	9	(21)	
7	-	Yellow River	Christie	CBS	11	(23)	F
8	1	Bridge Over Troubled Water	Simon & Garfunkel	CBS	13	(1)	L
9	-	Travellin' Band	Creedence Clearwater Revival	Liberty	7	(2)	
10	2	Can't Help Falling In Love	Andy Williams	CBS	11	(88)	
11	-	I Can't Tell The Bottom From The Top	Hollies	Parlophone	5	(82)	
12	-	Brontosaurus	Move	Regal Zonophone	6		
13	14	Never Had A Dream Come True	Stevie Wonder	Tamla Motown	7	(26)	
14	-	I Don't Believe In If Anymore	Roger Whittaker	Columbia	8		
15	15	When Julie Comes Around	Cuff Links	MCA	6	(41)	L
16	9	Gimme Dat Ding	Pipkins	Columbia	6	(9)	F L
17	10	Farewell Is A Lonely Sound	Jimmy Ruffin	Tamla Motown	7		
18	-	Honey Come Back	Glen Campbell	Capitol	10	(19)	
19	18	Good Morning Freedom	Blue Mink	Philips	4		
20	-	Up The Ladder To The Roof	Supremes	Tamla Motown	6	(10)	

June 1970

1	7	Yellow River	Christie	CBS	11	(23)	F
2	-	In The Summertime	Mungo Jerry	Dawn	13	(3)	F
3	-	Groovin' With Mr. Bloe	Mr. Bloe	DJM	10		F L
4	18	Honey Come Back	Glen Campbell	Capitol	10	(19)	
5	1	Back Home	England World Cup Squad	Pye	9		F
6	-	Cottonfields	Beach Boys	Capitol	12		
7	-	Everything Is Beautiful	Ray Stevens	CBS	8	(1)	F
8	6	Question	Moody Blues	Threshold	9	(21)	
9	20	Up The Ladder To The Roof	Supremes	Tamla Motown	6	(10)	
10	-	Sally	Gerry Monroe	Chapter One	9		F
11	-	Abraham Martin & John	Marvin Gaye	Tamla Motown	7		
12	-	All Right Now	Free	Island	11	(4)	F
13	-	The Green Manalishi (With The Two Prong Crown)	Fleetwood Mac	Reprise	9		
14	-	ABC	Jackson Five	Tamla Motown	5	(1)	
15	14	I Don't Believe In If Anymore	Roger Whittaker	Columbia	8		
16	5	Daughter Of Darkness	Tom Jones	Decca	9	(13)	
17	-	Goodbye Sam Hello Samantha	Cliff Richard	Columbia	10		
18	2	Spirit In The Sky	Norman Greenbaum	Reprise	11	(3)	F L
19	-	It's All In The Game	Four Tops	Tamla Motown	9	(24)	
20	-	Down The Dustpipe	Status Quo	Pye	6		

April 1970

This Mnth	Prev Mnth	Title	Artist	Label	Wks 20	(UK Pos)	
1	10	Let It Be	Beatles	Apple	11	(2)	G
2	15	ABC	Jackson Five	Motown	11	(8)	G
3	8	Instant Karma (We All Shine On)	John Lennon	Apple	10	(5)	G
4	16	Spirit In The Sky	Norman Greenbaum	Reprise	11	(1)	F G L
5	1	Bridge Over Troubled Water	Simon & Garfunkel	Columbia	12	(1)	G
6	9	Love Grows (Where My Rosemary...)	Edison Lighthouse	Bell	9	(1)	F G L
7	-	Come And Get It	Badfinger	Apple	7	(4)	F
8	19	House Of The Rising Sun	Frijid Pink	Parrot	7	(4)	F G L
9	20	Easy Come, Easy Go	Bobby Sherman	Metromedia	8		G
10	-	American Woman/No Sugar Tonight	Guess Who	RCA	12	(19)	G
11	-	Up The Ladder To The Roof	Supremes	Motown	6	(6)	
12	-	Love Or Let Me Be Lonely	Friends Of Distinction	RCA	8		L
13	2	The Rapper	Jaggerz	Kama Sutra	9		F G L
14	-	The Bells	Originals	Soul	4		L
15	-	Turn Back The Hands Of Time	Tyrone Davis	Dakar	8		G L
16	-	Call Me	Aretha Franklin	Atlantic	4		
17	3	Give Me Just A Little More Time	Chairmen Of The Board	Invictus	9	(3)	F G
18	-	Something's Burning	Kenny Rogers & First Edition	Reprise	5	(8)	
19	5	He Ain't Heavy, He's My Brother	Hollies	Epic	7	(3)	
20	4	Rainy Night In Georgia	Brook Benton	Cotillion	9		G L

May 1970

This Mnth	Prev Mnth	Title	Artist	Label	Wks 20	(UK Pos)	
1	10	American Woman/No Sugar Tonight	Guess Who	RCA	12	(19)	G
2	1	Let It Be	Beatles	Apple	11	(2)	G
3	-	Vehicle	Ides Of March	Warner	7	(31)	F L
4	2	ABC	Jackson Five	Motown	11	(8)	G
5	-	Everything Is Beautiful	Ray Stevens	Barnaby	9	(6)	G
6	15	Turn Back The Hands Of Time	Tyrone Davis	Dakar	8		G L
7	4	Spirit In The Sky	Norman Greenbaum	Reprise	11	(1)	F G L
8	-	Cecilia	Simon & Garfunkel	Columbia	9		G
9	-	Up Around The Bend/ Run Through The Jungle	Creedence Clearwater Revival	Fantasy	8	(3)	G
10	-	Reflections Of My Life	Marmalade	London	8	(3)	F L
11	-	Love On A Two-Way Street	Moments	Stang	10		F G
12	12	Love Or Let Me Be Lonely	Friends Of Distinction	RCA	8		L
13	-	Woodstock	Crosby, Stills, Nash & Young	Atlantic	7		F
14	-	For The Love Of Him	Bobbi Martin	UA	7		L
15	3	Instant Karma (We All Shine On)	John Lennon/Plastic Ono Band	Apple	10	(5)	G
16	-	Which Way You Goin' Billy	Poppy Family	London	8	(7)	F G L
17	-	Get Ready	Rare Earth	Rare Earth	11		F
18	18	Something's Burning	Kenny Rogers & First Edition	Reprise	5	(8)	
19	-	The Letter	Joe Cocker	A&M	5	(39)	F
20	7	Come And Get It	Badfinger	Apple	7	(4)	F

June 1970

This Mnth	Prev Mnth	Title	Artist	Label	Wks 20	(UK Pos)	
1	-	The Long And Winding Road/ For You Blue	Beatles	Apple	8		G
2	16	Which Way You Goin' Billy	Poppy Family	London	8	(7)	F G L
3	17	Get Ready	Rare Earth	Rare Earth	11		F
4	11	Love On A Two-Way Street	Moments	Stang	10		F G
5	-	The Love You Save	Jackson Five	Motown	11	(7)	G
6	5	Everything Is Beautiful	Ray Stevens	Barnaby	9	(6)	G
7	9	Up Around The Bend/Run Through...	Creedence Clearwater Revival	Fantasy	8	(3)	G
8	-	Lay Down (Candles In The Rain)	Melanie	Buddah	10		F
9	-	Ride Captain Ride	Blues Image	Atco	9		F G L
10	-	Mama Told Me (Not To Come)	Three Dog Night	Dunhill	11	(3)	G
11	-	Ball Of Confusion (That's What The World Is Today)	Temptations	Gordy	11	(7)	G
12	8	Cecilia	Simon & Garfunkel	Columbia	9		G
13	-	Hitchin' A Ride	Vanity Fare	Page One	9	(16)	G L
14	19	The Letter	Joe Cocker	A&M	5	(39)	F
15	-	Make Me Smile	Chicago	Columbia	7		F
16	-	The Wonder Of You/ Mama Liked The Roses	Elvis Presley	RCA	7	(1)	G
17	-	My Baby Loves Lovin'	White Plains	Deram	6	(9)	F L
18	1	American Woman/No Sugar Tonight	Guess Who	RCA	12	(19)	G
19	-	Daughter Of Darkness	Tom Jones	Parrot	4	(5)	
20	-	Band Of Gold	Freda Payne	Invictus	11	(1)	F G

◆ As John, Paul, George and Ringo immersed themselves in solo projects, rumours were rife that The Beatles were to split. The group's final film *Let it Be* was released and, unsurprisingly, its soundtrack topped the charts. In America the album replaced Paul's solo effort, **McCartney,** at the top, and in the same week the group's last official US single, 'The Long And Winding Road', became their 20th and last No. 1.

◆ It may have only been the start of the 1970s, but already there was a 60s revival. Three songs from that decade returned: 'The Letter' (Box Tops/Joe Cocker), 'House Of The Rising Sun' (Animals/Frijid Pink), and 'Get Ready' (Temptations/Rare Earth).

◆ Velvet-voiced soul stylist Brook Benton scored the last of his 16 Top 20 hits with a Tony Joe White song, 'Rainy Night In Georgia'.

UK 1970 JULY-SEPT

142

◆ Just weeks before his untimely death, Jimi Hendrix appeared at the Isle Of Wight Festival which also showcased The Who, The Doors, Chicago, Emerson, Lake & Palmer, The Moody Blues and Free, whose debut hit, 'All Right Now', returned to the UK Top 20 in 1973 and again in 1991.

◆ Pink Floyd packed the crowds into Hyde Park for a free concert with Deep Purple.

◆ One of the most successful British groups of the 1960s, The Dave Clark Five, disbanded after selling over 35 million records.

◆ The *Melody Maker* poll showed Janis Joplin as Top Female Singer and, after eight years, The Beatles were replaced as Top Group by Led Zeppelin. Incidentally, Zeppelin billed their sixth US tour as "The Greatest Live Event Since The Beatles".

July 1970

This Mnth	Prev Mnth	Title	Artist	Label	Wks 20	(US Pos)	
1	2	In The Summertime	Mungo Jerry	Dawn	13	(3)	F
2	12	All Right Now	Free	Island	11	(4)	F
3	-	Up Around The Bend	Creedence Clearwater Revival	Liberty	8	(4)	
4	19	It's All In The Game	Four Tops	Tamla Motown	9	(24)	
5	3	Groovin' With Mr. Bloe	Mr. Bloe	DJM	10		F L
6	6	Cottonfields	Beach Boys	Capitol	12		
7	10	Sally	Gerry Monroe	Chapter One	9		F
8	17	Goodbye Sam Hello Samantha	Cliff Richard	Columbia	10		
9	-	Love Of The Common People	Nicky Thomas	Trojan	7		F L
10	-	Lola	Kinks	Pye	10	(9)	
11	-	Something	Shirley Bassey	UA	12	(55)	
12	13	The Green Manalishi (With The Two Prong Crown)	Fleetwood Mac	Reprise	9		
13	20	Down The Dustpipe	Status Quo	Pye	6		
14	-	The Wonder Of You	Elvis Presley	RCA	16	(9)	
15	1	Yellow River	Christie	CBS	11	(23)	F
16	4	Honey Come Back	Glen Campbell	Capitol	10	(19)	
17	-	Lady D'Arbanville	Cat Stevens	Island	8		
18	11	Abraham Martin & John	Marvin Gaye	Tamla Motown	7		
19	-	Neanderthal Man	Hotlegs	Fontana	9	(22)	F L
20	-	Love Like A Man	Ten Years After	Deram	6	(98)	F L

August 1970

This Mnth	Prev Mnth	Title	Artist	Label	Wks 20	(US Pos)	
1	14	The Wonder Of You	Elvis Presley	RCA	16	(9)	
2	19	Neanderthal Man	Hotlegs	Fontana	9	(22)	F L
3	10	Lola	Kinks	Pye	10	(9)	
4	11	Something	Shirley Bassey	UA	12	(55)	
5	2	All Right Now	Free	Island	11	(4)	F
6	1	In The Summertime	Mungo Jerry	Dawn	13	(3)	F
7	-	Rainbow	Marmalade	Decca	8	(51)	
8	-	I'll Say Forever My Love	Jimmy Ruffin	Tamla Motown	8	(77)	
9	-	Natural Sinner	Fair Weather	RCA	6		F L
10	-	The Tears Of A Clown	Smokey Robinson & The Miracles	Tamla Motown	10	(1)	
11	3	Up Around The Bend	Creedence Clearwater Revival	Liberty	8	(4)	
12	17	Lady D'Arbanville	Cat Stevens	Island	8		
13	4	It's All In The Game	Four Tops	Tamla Motown	9	(24)	
14	20	Love Like A Man	Ten Years After	Deram	6	(98)	F L
15	-	Big Yellow Taxi	Joni Mitchell	Reprise	5	(67)	F L
16	-	The Love You Save	Jackson Five	Tamla Motown	4	(1)	
17	-	25 Or 6 To 4	Chicago	CBS	7	(4)	
18	-	Signed, Sealed, Delivered I'm Yours	Stevie Wonder	Tamla Motown	5	(3)	
19	9	Love Of The Common People	Nicky Thomas	Trojan	7		F L
20	-	Sweet Inspiration	Johnny Johnson & The Bandwagon	Bell	5		

September 1970

This Mnth	Prev Mnth	Title	Artist	Label	Wks 20	(US Pos)	
1	10	The Tears Of A Clown	Smokey Robinson/The Miracles	Tamla Motown	10	(1)	
2	1	The Wonder Of You	Elvis Presley	RCA	16	(9)	
3	-	Give Me Just A Little More Time	Chairmen Of The Board	Invictus	8	(3)	F
4	-	Mama Told Me Not To Come	Three Dog Night	Stateside	8	(1)	F L
5	-	Band Of Gold	Freda Payne	Invictus	11	(3)	F L
6	-	Make It With You	Bread	Elektra	7	(1)	F
7	-	Love Is Life	Hot Chocolate	RAK	8		F
8	-	Wild World	Jimmy Cliff	Island	5		L
9	17	25 Or 6 To 4	Chicago	CBS	7	(4)	
10	7	Rainbow	Marmalade	Decca	8	(51)	
11	-	You Can Get It If You Really Want	Desmond Dekker	Trojan	10		
12	-	Which Way You Goin' Billy	Poppy Family	Decca	7	(2)	F L
13	2	Neanderthal Man	Hotlegs	Fontana	9	(22)	F L
14	4	Something	Shirley Bassey	UA	12	(55)	
15	20	Sweet Inspiration	Johnny Johnson & The Bandwagon	Bell	5		
16	-	Montego Bay	Bobby Bloom	Polydor	8	(8)	F L
17	-	It's So Easy	Andy Williams	CBS	4		
18	9	Natural Sinner	Fair Weather	RCA	6		F L
19	-	Don't Play That Song	Aretha Franklin	Atlantic	5	(11)	
20	-	Black Night	Deep Purple	Harvest	10	(66)	F

US 1970 JULY-SEPT

July 1970

This Mnth	Prev Mnth	Title	Artist	Label	Wks 20	(UK Pos)	
1	10	Mama Told Me (Not To Come)	Three Dog Night	Dunhill	11	(3)	G
2	5	The Love You Save	Jackson Five	Motown	11	(7)	G
3	11	Ball Of Confusion (That's What The World Is Today)	Temptations	Gordy	11	(7)	G
4	20	Band Of Gold	Freda Payne	Invictus	11	(1)	F G
5	9	Ride Captain Ride	Blues Image	Atco	9		F G L
6	-	(They Long To Be) Close To You	Carpenters	A&M	9	(6)	F G
7	8	Lay Down (Candles In The Rain)	Melanie	Buddah	10		F
8	13	Hitchin' A Ride	Vanity Fare	Page One	9	(16)	G L
9	-	Gimme Dat Ding	Pipkins	Capitol	5	(6)	F L
10	-	O-O-O Child	Five Stairsteps	Buddah	8		F G L
11	16	The Wonder Of You/ Mama Liked The Roses	Elvis Presley	RCA	7	(1)	G
12	1	The Long And Winding Road/For...	Beatles	Apple	8		G
13	-	Make It With You	Bread	Elektra	12	(5)	F G
14	-	Tighter, Tighter	Alive & Kicking	Roulette	9		F L
15	3	Get Ready	Rare Earth	Rare Earth	11		F
16	-	A Song Of Joy	Miguel Rios	A&M	5	(16)	F L
17	-	Signed Sealed Delivered I'm Yours	Stevie Wonder	Tamla	10	(15)	G
18	-	United We Stand	Brotherhood Of Man	Deram	4	(10)	F L
19	-	Are You Ready	Pacific Gas & Electric	Columbia	5		F L
20	17	My Baby Loves Lovin'	White Plains	Deram	6	(9)	F L

August 1970

This Mnth	Prev Mnth	Title	Artist	Label	Wks 20	(UK Pos)	
1	6	(They Long To Be) Close To You	Carpenters	A&M	9	(6)	F G
2	13	Make It With You	Bread	Elektra	12	(5)	F G
3	-	Spill The Wine	Eric Burdon & War	MGM	9		F L
4	17	Signed Sealed Delivered I'm Yours	Stevie Wonder	Tamla	10	(15)	G
5	-	War	Edwin Starr	Gordy	11	(3)	G L
6	4	Band Of Gold	Freda Payne	Invictus	11	(1)	F G
7	-	In The Summertime	Mungo Jerry	Janus	8	(1)	F G L
8	14	Tighter, Tighter	Alive & Kicking	Roulette	9		F L
9	1	Mama Told Me (Not To Come)	Three Dog Night	Dunhill	11	(3)	G
10	3	Ball Of Confusion (That's What...)	Temptations	Gordy	11	(7)	G
11	-	I Just Can't Help Believing	B.J. Thomas	Scepter	7		
12	10	O-O-O Child	Five Stairsteps	Buddah	8		F G L
13	-	(If You Let Me Make Love To You Then) Why Can't I Touch You?	Ronnie Dyson	Columbia	5		F L
14	-	Patches	Clarence Carter	Atlantic	9	(2)	L
15	2	The Love You Save	Jackson Five	Motown	11	(7)	G
16	-	Lay A Little Lovin' On Me	Robin McNamara	Steed	5		F L
17	-	25 Or 6 To 4	Chicago	Columbia	8	(7)	
18	-	Ain't No Mountain High Enough	Diana Ross	Motown	11	(6)	F
19	-	Ohio	Crosby, Stills, Nash & Young	Atlantic	3		L
20	5	Ride Captain Ride	Blues Image	Atco	9		F G L

September 1970

This Mnth	Prev Mnth	Title	Artist	Label	Wks 20	(UK Pos)	
1	5	War	Edwin Starr	Gordy	11	(3)	G L
2	18	Ain't No Mountain High Enough	Diana Ross	Motown	11	(6)	F
3	-	Lookin' Out My Back Door/ Long As I Can See The Light	Creedence Clearwater Revival	Fantasy	10	(20)	G
4	14	Patches	Clarence Carter	Atlantic	9	(2)	L
5	17	25 Or 6 To 4	Chicago	Columbia	8	(7)	
6	7	In The Summertime	Mungo Jerry	Janus	8	(1)	F G L
7	-	Julie, Do Ya Love Me	Bobby Sherman	Metromedia	9		G
8	2	Make It With You	Bread	Elektra	12	(5)	F G
9	-	Candida	Dawn	Bell	11	(9)	F G
10	-	Don't Play That Song	Aretha Franklin	Atlantic	5	(13)	G
11	-	Snowbird	Anne Murray	Capitol	8	(23)	F G
12	3	Spill The Wine	Eric Burdon & War	MGM	9		F L
13	-	Cracklin' Rosie	Neil Diamond	UNI	10	(3)	G
14	-	(I Know) I'm Losing You	Rare Earth	Rare Earth	6		
15	-	Signed Sealed Delivered I'm Yours	Stevie Wonder	Tamla	10	(15)	G
16	-	I (Who Have Nothing)	Tom Jones	Parrot	5	(16)	
17	-	Hi-De-Ho	Blood Sweat & Tears	Columbia	4		L
18	-	Groovy Situation	Gene Chandler	Mercury	4		G L
19	13	(If You Let Me Make Love To You...	Ronnie Dyson	Columbia	5		F L
20	-	Rubber Duckie	Ernie	Columbia	3		F L

◆ Over 200,000 fans watched the second Atlanta Pop Festival. Among the headliners were Jimi Hendrix, The Allman Brothers, B.B. King, Mountain, Johnny Winter, Procul Harum and Jethro Tull.

▲ As Motown announced that the Jackson Five (above) had sold 10 million records in just nine months, ex-Motown producers Holland, Dozier & Holland's label Invictus scored a transatlantic smash with 'Band Of Gold' by Freda Payne – the first UK No. 1 by a black American female.

UK 1970
OCT-DEC

◆ Matthews' Southern Comfort's version of 'Woodstock' topped the chart despite the "Summer of Love" being no more than a distant memory.

▲ Double Grammy winners, The Carpenters (above), had their first transatlantic hit , '(They Long To Be) Close To You'. Also debuting on the UK chart were Neil Diamond, Gilbert O' Sullivan and T-Rex, while the US chart welcomed Dawn, James Taylor, and the stars of the latest pop-oriented TV series, The Partridge Family, featuring teen idol David Cassidy.

◆ The price of all record papers in Britain rose to 5p (12c).

October 1970

This Mnth	Prev Mnth	Title	Artist	Label	Wks 20	(US Pos)	
1	5	Band Of Gold	Freda Payne	Invictus	11	(3)	F L
2	20	Black Night	Deep Purple	Harvest	10	(66)	F
3	11	You Can Get It If You Really Want	Desmond Dekker	Trojan	10		
4	-	Paranoid	Black Sabbath	Vertigo	8	(61)	F
5	16	Montego Bay	Bobby Bloom	Polydor	8	(8)	F L
6	-	Me And My Life	Tremeloes	CBS	9		L
7	-	Ain't No Mountain High Enough	Diana Ross	Tamla Motown	7	(1)	F
8	-	(They Long To Be) Close To You	Carpenters	A&M	8	(1)	F
9	12	Which Way You Goin' Billy	Poppy Family	Decca	7	(2)	F L
10	-	Patches	Clarence Carter	Atlantic	8	(4)	F L
11	-	Ball Of Confusion	Temptations	Tamla Motown	7	(3)	
12	-	Woodstock	Matthews Southern Comfort	Uni	8	(23)	F L
13	1	The Tears Of A Clown	Smokey Robinson & The Miracles	Tamla Motown	10	(1)	
14	3	Give Me Just A Little More Time	Chairmen Of The Board	Invictus	8	(3)	F
15	2	The Wonder Of You	Elvis Presley	RCA	16	(9)	
16	-	Strange Band	Family	Reprise	5		F
17	-	Black Pearl	Horace Faith	Trojan	4		F L
18	-	Still Water (Love)	Four Tops	Tamla Motown	6	(11)	
19	7	Love Is Life	Hot Chocolate	RAK	8		F
20	-	Gasoline Alley Bred	Hollies	Parlophone	4		

November 1970

This Mnth	Prev Mnth	Title	Artist	Label	Wks 20	(US Pos)	
1	12	Woodstock	Matthews Southern Comfort	Uni	8	(23)	F L
2	10	Patches	Clarence Carter	Atlantic	8	(4)	F L
3	-	War	Edwin Starr	Tamla Motown	8	(1)	
4	-	Indian Reservation	Don Fardon	Young Blood	11	(20)	F L
5	-	Voodoo Chile	Jimi Hendrix Experience	Track	10		L
6	-	The Witch	Rattles	Decca	5	(79)	F L
7	-	Ruby Tuesday	Melanie	Buddah	7	(52)	F
8	-	San Bernadino	Christie	CBS	6	(100)	L
9	6	Me And My Life	Tremeloes	CBS	9		L
10	2	Black Night	Deep Purple	Harvest	10	(66)	F
11	-	It's Wonderful	Jimmy Ruffin	Tamla Motown	8		
12	1	Band Of Gold	Freda Payne	Invictus	11	(3)	F L
13	11	Ball Of Confusion	Temptations	Tamla Motown	7	(3)	
14	-	Cracklin' Rosie	Neil Diamond	Uni	13	(1)	F
15	-	I Hear You Knocking	Dave Edmunds	MAM	12	(4)	F
16	-	Julie, Do Ya Love Me	White Plains	Deram	9		
17	-	Ride A White Swan	T. Rex	Fly	14	(76)	F
18	4	Paranoid	Black Sabbath	Vertigo	8	(61)	F
19	18	Still Water (Love)	Four Tops	Tamla Motown	6	(11)	
20	-	I've Lost You	Elvis Presley	RCA	8	(32)	

December 1970

This Mnth	Prev Mnth	Title	Artist	Label	Wks 20	(US Pos)	
1	15	I Hear You Knocking	Dave Edmunds	MAM	12	(4)	F
2	-	When I'm Dead And Gone	McGuinness Flint	Capitol	10	(47)	F
3	14	Cracklin' Rosie	Neil Diamond	Uni	13	(1)	F
4	-	It's Only Make Believe	Glen Campbell	Capitol	10	(10)	
5	-	You've Got Me Dangling On A String	Chairmen Of The Board	Invictus	10	(38)	
6	17	Ride A White Swan	T. Rex	Fly	14	(76)	
7	5	Voodoo Chile	Jimi Hendrix Experience	Track	10		L
8	-	I'll Be There	Jackson Five	Tamla Motown	11	(1)	
9	-	Home Lovin' Man	Andy Williams	CBS	9		
10	4	Indian Reservation	Don Fardon	Young Blood	11	(20)	F L
11	-	My Prayer	Gerry Monroe	Chapter One	7		
12	-	Grandad	Clive Dunn	Columbia	14		F L
13	-	Nothing Rhymed	Gilbert O'Sullivan	MAM	7		F
14	20	I've Lost You	Elvis Presley	RCA	8	(32)	
15	16	Julie, Do Ya Love Me	White Plains	Deram	9		
16	-	Lady Barbara	Herman's Hermits	RAK	6		L
17	-	Blame It On The Pony Express	Johnny Johnson & The Bandwagon	Bell	8		L
18	11	It's Wonderful	Jimmy Ruffin	Tamla Motown	8		
19	8	San Bernadino	Christie	CBS	6	(100)	L
20	1	Woodstock	Matthews Southern Comfort	Uni	8	(23)	F L

October 1970

This Mnth	Prev Mnth	Title	Artist	Label	Wks 20	(UK Pos)	
1	-	I'll Be There	Jackson Five	Motown	14	(4)	G
2	13	Cracklin' Rosie	Neil Diamond	Uni	10	(3)	G
3	9	Candida	Dawn	Bell	11	(9)	F G
4	-	All Right Now	Free	Island	10	(2)	F L
5	-	Green Eyed Lady	Sugarloaf	Liberty	10		F
6	2	Ain't No Mountain High Enough	Diana Ross	Motown	11	(6)	F
7	-	We've Only Just Begun	Carpenters	A&M	13	(28)	G
8	7	Julie, Do Ya Love Me	Bobby Sherman	Metromedia	9		G
9	3	Lookin' Out My Back Door/Long As...	Creedence Clearwater Revival	Fantasy	10	(20)	G
10	-	Fire And Rain	James Taylor	Warner	10	(42)	F
11	-	Lola	Kinks	Reprise	6	(2)	
12	-	Express Yourself	Charles Wright & The Watts 103rd Street Rhythm Band	Warner	5		L
13	-	Indiana Wants Me	R. Dean Taylor	Rare Earth	8	(2)	F L
14	11	Snowbird	Anne Murray	Capitol	8	(23)	F G
15	14	(I Know) I'm Losing You	Rare Earth	Rare Earth	6		
16	-	Still Water (Love)	Four Tops	Motown	7	(10)	
17	1	War	Edwin Starr	Gordy	11	(3)	G L
18	-	It's A Shame	Spinners	V.I.P.	3	(20)	F
19	-	Look What They've Done To My Song Ma	New Seekers Featuring Eve Graham	Elektra	4	(44)	F
20	-	It's Only Make Believe	Glen Campbell	Capitol	4	(4)	

November 1970

This Mnth	Prev Mnth	Title	Artist	Label	Wks 20	(UK Pos)	
1	1	I'll Be There	Jackson Five	Motown	14	(4)	G
2	7	We've Only Just Begun	Carpenters	A&M	13	(28)	G
3	-	I Think I Love You	Partridge Family	Bell	14	(18)	F G
4	10	Fire And Rain	James Taylor	Warner	10	(42)	F
5	13	Indiana Wants Me	R. Dean Taylor	Rare Earth	8	(2)	F L
6	-	The Tears Of A Clown	Smokey Robinson/The Miracles	Tamla	12	(1)	G
7	5	Green Eyed Lady	Sugarloaf	Liberty	10		F
8	-	Gypsy Woman	Brian Hyland	Uni	9	(42)	G L
9	-	Montego Bay	Bobby Bloom	L&R/MGM	6	(3)	F L
10	-	Somebody's Been Sleeping	100 Proof Aged In Soul	Hot Wax	6		F G L
11	-	It Don't Matter To Me	Bread	Elektra	5		
12	-	Cry Me A River	Joe Cocker	A&M	5		
13	4	All Right Now	Free	Island	10	(2)	F L
14	2	Cracklin' Rosie	Neil Diamond	Uni	10	(3)	G
15	-	Super Bad (Pts 1 & 2)	James Brown	King	5		
16	-	Heaven Help Us All	Stevie Wonder	Tamla	6	(29)	
17	3	Candida	Dawn	Bell	11	(9)	F G
18	11	Lola	Kinks	Reprise	6	(2)	
19	-	Engine Number 9	Wilson Pickett	Atlantic	4		
20	-	You Don't Have To Say You Love Me/Patch It Up	Elvis Presley	RCA	4	(9)	

December 1970

This Mnth	Prev Mnth	Title	Artist	Label	Wks 20	(UK Pos)	
1	6	The Tears Of A Clown	Smokey Robinson/The Miracles	Tamla	12	(1)	G
2	3	I Think I Love You	Partridge Family	Bell	14	(18)	F G
3	-	One Less Bell To Answer	Fifth Dimension	Bell	12		G
4	-	My Sweet Lord/Isn't It A Pity	George Harrison	Apple	12	(1)	F G
5	8	Gypsy Woman	Brian Hyland	Uni	9	(42)	G L
6	-	Black Magic Woman	Santana	Columbia	9		
7	-	No Matter What	Badfinger	Apple	5	(5)	
8	1	I'll Be There	Jackson Five	Motown	14	(4)	G
9	-	Does Anybody Really Know What Time It Is	Chicago	Columbia	9		
10	2	We've Only Just Begun	Carpenters	A&M	13	(28)	G
11	-	Stoned Love	Supremes	Motown	9	(3)	G
12	-	Knock Three Times	Dawn	Bell	13	(1)	G
13	-	5-10-15-20 (25-30 Years Of Love)	Presidents	Sussex	7		F L
14	-	Share The Land	Guess Who	RCA	5		
15	16	Heaven Help Us All	Stevie Wonder	Tamla	6	(29)	
16	4	Fire And Rain	James Taylor	Warner	10	(42)	F
17	20	You Don't Have To Say.../Patch...	Elvis Presley	RCA	4	(9)	
18	-	Domino	Van Morrison	Warner	4		L
19	9	Montego Bay	Bobby Bloom	L&R/MGM	6	(3)	F L
20	-	See Me, Feel Me	Who	Decca	2		

US 1970
OCT-DEC

◆ Janis Joplin died of a heroin overdose three days after the funeral of Jimi Hendrix. Shortly afterwards President Nixon appealed for the screening of rock lyrics and banning of songs promoting drug use.

◆ In the USA in 1970, 8.5 million tape players were sold. Casey Kasem launched the long running radio show, *American Top 40*, and the majority of the planned 48 Rock Festivals were legally stopped.

◆ After 11 years fronting the successful soul trio The Impressions, influential and innovative singer/songwriter/producer/arranger and label owner Curtis Mayfield went solo.

◆ Jim Morrison played his last shows as lead singer of The Doors. Morrison was also sentenced to eight months hard labour for indecent exposure and profanity on stage in Miami. He was still appealing the sentence when he died in 1971.

UK 1971
JAN-MAR

▲ George Harrison's triple LP, **All Things Must Pass,** topped the American charts, and his single 'My Sweet Lord' was a transatlantic No. 1. Soon afterwards, a court ruled that he had "unconsciously plagiarised" The Chiffons' (with whom The Beatles had toured in 1964) 'He's So Fine' when writing this hit.

◆ Judy Collins's live recording of the ancient hymn 'Amazing Grace' spent an amazing 67 weeks on the chart. Only Frank Sinatra's 'My Way' can claim a longer residence.

◆ Swedish quartet, The Engaged Couples, made their debut at a Gothenburg nightclub. They later changed their name to Abba.

January 1971

This Mnth	Prev Mnth	Title	Artist	Label	Wks 20	(US Pos)	
1	12	Grandad	Clive Dunn	Columbia	14		F L
2	1	I Hear You Knocking	Dave Edmunds	MAM	12	(4)	F
3	6	Ride A White Swan	T. Rex	Fly	14	(76)	F
4	8	I'll Be There	Jackson Five	Tamla Motown	11	(1)	
5	2	When I'm Dead And Gone	McGuinness Flint	Capitol	10	(47)	F
6	3	Cracklin' Rosie	Neil Diamond	Uni	13	(1)	F
7	17	Blame It On The Pony Express	Johnny Johnson & The Bandwagon	Bell	8		L
8	4	It's Only Make Believe	Glen Campbell	Capitol	10	(10)	
9	-	Ape Man	Kinks	Pye	9	(45)	
10	9	Home Lovin' Man	Andy Williams	CBS	9		
11	13	Nothing Rhymed	Gilbert O'Sullivan	MAM	7		F
12	-	My Sweet Lord	George Harrison	Apple	12	(1)	F
13	-	Black Skin Blue Eyed Boys	Equals	President	6		L
14	5	You've Got Me Dangling On A String	Chairmen Of The Board	Invictus	10	(38)	
15	-	Amazing Grace	Judy Collins	Elektra	13	(15)	
16	-	The Pushbike Song	Mixtures	Polydor	13	(44)	F L
17	-	You Don't Have To Say You Love Me	Elvis Presley	RCA	6	(11)	
18	16	Lady Barbara	Herman's Hermits	RAK	6		L
19	11	My Prayer	Gerry Monroe	Chapter One	7		
20	-	You're Ready Now	Frankie Valli	Philips	6		F

February 1971

This Mnth	Prev Mnth	Title	Artist	Label	Wks 20	(US Pos)	
1	12	My Sweet Lord	George Harrison	Apple	12	(1)	F
2	16	The Pushbike Song	Mixtures	Polydor	13	(44)	F L
3	-	Stoned Love	Supremes	Tamla Motown	8	(7)	
4	-	Resurrection Shuffle	Ashton Gardner & Dyke	Capitol	9	(40)	F L
5	15	Amazing Grace	Judy Collins	Elektra	13	(15)	
6	-	No Matter What	Badfinger	Apple	8	(8)	
7	1	Grandad	Clive Dunn	Columbia	14		F L
8	-	Your Song	Elton John	DJM	6	(8)	F
9	-	Candida	Dawn	Bell	6	(3)	F
10	9	Ape Man	Kinks	Pye	9	(45)	
11	-	It's Impossible	Perry Como	RCA	11	(10)	
12	3	Ride A White Swan	T. Rex	Fly	14	(76)	F
13	20	You're Ready Now	Frankie Valli	Philips	6		F
14	-	She's A Lady	Tom Jones	Decca	5	(2)	
15	-	Baby Jump	Mungo Jerry	Dawn	9		
16	4	I'll Be There	Jackson Five	Tamla Motown	11	(1)	
17	-	Rupert	Jackie Lee	Pye	5		F L
18	17	You Don't Have To Say You Love Me	Elvis Presley	RCA	6	(11)	
19	-	(Come 'Round Here) I'm The One You Need	Smokey Robinson & The Miracles	Tamla Motown	4		
20	-	Sweet Caroline	Neil Diamond	Uni	7	(4)	

March 1971

This Mnth	Prev Mnth	Title	Artist	Label	Wks 20	(US Pos)	
1	15	Baby Jump	Mungo Jerry	Dawn	9		
2	-	Another Day	Paul McCartney	Apple	9	(5)	F
3	1	My Sweet Lord	George Harrison	Apple	12	(1)	
4	11	It's Impossible	Perry Como	RCA	11	(10)	
5	-	Rose Garden	Lynn Anderson	CBS	10	(3)	F L
6	-	Hot Love	T. Rex	Fly	12	(72)	
7	2	The Pushbike Song	Mixtures	Polydor	13	(44)	F L
8	20	Sweet Caroline	Neil Diamond	Uni	7	(4)	
9	5	Amazing Grace	Judy Collins	Elektra	13	(15)	
10	4	Resurrection Shuffle	Ashton Gardner & Dyke	Capitol	9	(40)	F L
11	-	Tomorrow Night	Atomic Rooster	B&C	5		F
12	3	Stoned Love	Supremes	Tamla Motown	8	(7)	
13	-	Everything's Tuesday	Chairmen Of The Board	Invictus	5	(38)	
14	-	Bridget The Midget (The Queen Of The Blues)	Ray Stevens	CBS	9	(50)	
15	-	Power To The People	John Lennon & The Plastic Ono Band	Apple	6	(11)	
16	-	Strange Kind Of Woman	Deep Purple	Harvest	5		
17	-	Forget Me Not	Martha & The Vandellas	Tamla Motown	3	(93)	L
18	-	Who Put The Lights Out	Dana	Rex	3		
19	-	Rose Garden	New World	RAK	5		F
20	-	Jack In The Box	Clodagh Rodgers	RCA	6		L

January 1971

This Mnth	Prev Mnth	Title	Artist	Label	Wks 20	(UK Pos)	
1	4	My Sweet Lord/Isn't It A Pity	George Harrison	Apple	12	(1)	F G
2	12	Knock Three Times	Dawn	Bell	13	(1)	G
3	3	One Less Bell To Answer	Fifth Dimension	Bell	12		G
4	6	Black Magic Woman	Santana	Columbia	9		
5	2	I Think I Love You	Partridge Family	Bell	14	(18)	F G
6	-	Lonely Days	Bee Gees	Atco	7	(33)	G
7	11	Stoned Love	Supremes	Motown	9	(3)	G
8	-	Stoney End	Barbra Streisand	Columbia	8	(27)	
9	-	Groove Me	King Floyd	Chimneyville	10		F G L
10	1	The Tears Of A Clown	Smokey Robinson & The Miracles	Tamla	12	(1)	G
11	-	It's Impossible	Perry Como	RCA	9	(4)	L
12	-	Rose Garden	Lynn Anderson	Columbia	10	(3)	F G L
13	-	Your Song	Elton John	Uni	7	(7)	F
14	9	Does Anybody Really Know What Time It Is	Chicago	Columbia	9		
15	-	River Deep-Mountain High	Supremes & Four Tops	Motown	5	(11)	
16	-	Pay To The Piper	Chairmen Of The Board	Invictus	3	(34)	L
17	-	For The Good Times	Ray Price	Columbia	6		F L
18	-	I Hear You Knocking	Dave Edmunds	MAM	7	(1)	F L
19	18	Domino	Van Morrison	Warner	4		L
20	-	If I Were Your Woman	Gladys Knight & The Pips	Soul	5		

February 1971

This Mnth	Prev Mnth	Title	Artist	Label	Wks 20	(UK Pos)	
1	-	One Bad Apple	Osmonds	MGM	10		F G
2	2	Knock Three Times	Dawn	Bell	13	(1)	G
3	12	Rose Garden	Lynn Anderson	Columbia	10	(3)	F G L
4	18	I Hear You Knocking	Dave Edmunds	MAM	7	(1)	F L
5	-	Mama's Pearl	Jackson Five	Motown	7	(25)	G
6	-	If You Could Read My Mind	Gordon Lightfoot	Reprise	8	(30)	F
7	9	Groove Me	King Floyd	Chimneyville	10		F G L
8	6	Lonely Days	Bee Gees	Atco	7	(33)	G
9	1	My Sweet Lord/Isn't It A Pity	George Harrison	Apple	12	(1)	F G
10	-	Watching Scotty Grow	Bobby Goldsboro	UA	5		L
11	-	Mr. Bojangles	Nitty Gritty Dirt Band	Liberty	8		F
12	13	Your Song	Elton John	Uni	7	(7)	F
13	-	Sweet Mary	Wadsworth Mansion	Sussex	5		F L
14	20	If I Were Your Woman	Gladys Knight & The Pips	Soul	5		
15	-	Amos Moses	Jerry Reed	RCA	7		F G
16	3	One Less Bell To Answer	Fifth Dimension	Bell	12		G
17	-	Amazing Grace	Judy Collins	Elektra	5	(5)	
18	8	Stoney End	Barbra Streisand	Columbia	8	(27)	
19	-	Theme From Love Story	Henry Mancini & His Orchestra	RCA	5		L
20	-	Have You Ever Seen The Rain	Creedence Clearwater Revival	Fantasy	6	(36)	G

March 1971

This Mnth	Prev Mnth	Title	Artist	Label	Wks 20	(UK Pos)	
1	-	Me And Bobby McGee	Janis Joplin	Columbia	10		F G L
2	-	Just My Imagination (Running Away With Me)	Temptations	Gordy	11	(8)	G
3	1	One Bad Apple	Osmonds	MGM	10		F G
4	-	She's A Lady	Tom Jones	Parrot	9	(13)	G
5	-	For All We Know	Carpenters	A&M	9	(18)	G
6	-	Proud Mary	Ike & Tina Turner	Liberty	7		G L
7	-	Doesn't Somebody Want To Be Wanted	Partridge Family	Bell	10		G
8	6	If You Could Read My Mind	Gordon Lightfoot	Reprise	8	(30)	F
9	5	Mama's Pearl	Jackson Five	Motown	7	(25)	G
10	15	Amos Moses	Jerry Reed	RCA	7		F G
11	20	Have You Ever Seen The Rain	Creedence Clearwater Revival	Fantasy	6	(36)	G
12	-	Help Me Make It Through The Night	Sammi Smith	Mega	7		F G L
13	-	What's Going On	Marvin Gaye	Tamla	11		G
14	11	Mr. Bojangles	Nitty Gritty Dirt Band	Liberty	8		F
15	-	What Is Life	George Harrison	Apple	6		
16	13	Sweet Mary	Wadsworth Mansion	Sussex	5		F L
17	19	Theme From Love Story	Henry Mancini & His Orchestra	RCA	5		L
18	-	(Where Do I Begin) Love Story	Andy Williams	Columbia	6	(4)	L
19	-	Cried Like A Baby	Bobby Sherman	Metromedia	3		L
20	-	Temptation Eyes	Grass Roots	Dunhill	5		

◆ As the Jackson Five celebrated their fourth successive No. 1, The Osmonds scored their first with the Jackson Five-inspired 'One Bad Apple', which the hitherto MOR-oriented act had recorded in funky Muscle Shoals.

◆ British composers Andrew Lloyd Webber and Tim Rice had their first major American success when **Jesus Christ Superstar**, which featured Murray Head, Ian Gillan and Yvonne Elliman, headed the album charts.

◆ There was a resurgence of interest in country, with Ray Price, Lynn Anderson, Sammi Smith, Jerry Reed and The Nitty Gritty Dirt Band charting. Nashville writer Kris Kristofferson (later a movie star) had two compositions in the Top 20, including chart topper 'Me and Bobby McGee', and black country singer Charley Pride collected three gold albums.

UK 1971 APR-JUNE

◆ **Sticky Fingers,** the Rolling Stones' first album on their own eponymous label, was a transatlantic No. 1, a feat their debut single, 'Brown Sugar', almost equalled.

◆ Photogenic Irish vocalist Clodagh Rodgers had her last hit with the UK's entry to the Eurovision Song Contest, 'Jack In A Box'. The winner 'Un Banc, Un Arbre, Une Rue' by Severine from Monaco also charted.

◆ Ringo Starr had his first solo hit with his composition. 'It Don't Come Easy', which fellow ex-Beatle George Harrison produced.

◆ Eric Clapton won a poll in *NME* for Greatest All-Time Guitarist, with Jimi Hendrix and B.B. King in runner-up positions.

◆ As Free's second major hit, 'My Brother Jake' climbed the chart, the critically acclaimed rock band split up for the first time.

April 1971

This Mnth	Prev Mnth	Title	Artist	Label	Wks 20	(US Pos)	
1	6	Hot Love	T. Rex	Fly	12	(72)	
2	14	Bridget The Midget (The Queen Of The Blues)	Ray Stevens	CBS	9	(50)	
3	5	Rose Garden	Lynn Anderson	CBS	10	(3)	F L
4	20	Jack In The Box	Clodagh Rodgers	RCA	6		L
5	-	There Goes My Everything	Elvis Presley	RCA	6	(21)	
6	-	Walkin'	C.C.S.	RAK	7		
7	2	Another Day	Paul McCartney	Apple	9	(5)	F
8	-	If Not For You	Olivia Newton-John	Pye International	6	(25)	F
9	15	Power To The People	John Lennon	Apple	6	(11)	
10	-	(Where Do I Begin) Love Story	Andy Williams	CBS	8	(9)	
11	-	Double Barrel	Dave & Ansil Collins	Technique	9	(22)	F
12	1	Baby Jump	Mungo Jerry	Dawn	9		
13	4	It's Impossible	Perry Como	RCA	11	(10)	
14	-	Mozart Symphony No. 40 In G Minor	Waldo De Los Rios	A&M	10	(67)	F L
15	16	Strange Kind Of Woman	Deep Purple	Harvest	5		
16	8	Sweet Caroline	Neil Diamond	Uni	7	(4)	
17	-	Funny Funny	Sweet	RCA	6		F
18	3	My Sweet Lord	George Harrison	Apple	12	(1)	F
19	7	The Pushbike Song	Mixtures	Polydor	13	(44)	F L
20	-	Something Old, Something New	Fantastics	Bell	3		F L

May 1971

This Mnth	Prev Mnth	Title	Artist	Label	Wks 20	(US Pos)	
1	-	Knock Three Times	Dawn	Bell	13	(1)	
2	-	Brown Sugar/Bitch/Let It Rock	Rolling Stones	Rolling Stone	9	(1)	
3	11	Double Barrel	Dave & Ansil Collins	Technique	9	(22)	F
4	-	It Don't Come Easy	Ringo Starr	Apple	8	(4)	F
5	14	Mozart Symphony No. 40 In G Minor	Waldo De Los Rios	A&M	10	(67)	F L
6	-	Indiana Wants Me	R. Dean Taylor	Tamla Motown	9	(5)	
7	-	Remember Me	Diana Ross	Tamla Motown	7	(16)	
8	1	Hot Love	T. Rex	Fly	12	(72)	
9	-	Jig A Jig	East Of Eden	Deram	6		F L
10	10	(Where Do I Begin) Love Story	Andy Williams	CBS	8	(9)	
11	-	Heaven Must Have Sent You	Elgins	Tamla Motown	9	(50)	F L
12	-	Malt And Barley Blues	McGuinness Flint	Capitol	7		L
13	-	Un Banc, Un Arbre, Une Rue	Severine	Philips	4		F L
14	2	Bridget The Midget (The Queen Of The Blues)	Ray Stevens	CBS	9	(50)	
15	-	My Brother Jake	Free	Island	7		
16	-	Sugar Sugar	Sakkarin	RCA	5		F L
17	17	Funny Funny	Sweet	RCA	6		F
18	-	It's A Sin To Tell A Lie	Gerry Monroe	Chapter One	5		L
19	-	Rosetta	Fame And Price Together	CBS	5		L
20	20	Something Old, Something New	Fantastics	Bell	3		F L

June 1971

This Mnth	Prev Mnth	Title	Artist	Label	Wks 20	(US Pos)	
1	1	Knock Three Times	Dawn	Bell	13	(1)	
2	-	I Did What I Did For Maria	Tony Christie	MCA	9		F
3	11	Heaven Must Have Sent You	Elgins	Tamla Motown	9	(50)	F L
4	-	I'm Gonna Run Away From You	Tami Lynn	Mojo	8		F L
5	-	I Am ...I Said	Neil Diamond	Uni	8	(4)	
6	6	Indiana Wants Me	R. Dean Taylor	Tamla Motown	9	(5)	
7	-	Lady Rose	Mungo Jerry	Dawn	7		
8	-	Banner Man	Blue Mink	Regal Zonophone	9		
9	15	My Brother Jake	Free	Island	7		
10	-	Chirpy Chirpy Cheep Cheep	Middle Of The Road	RCA	12		F
11	-	Rags To Riches	Elvis Presley	RCA	6	(33)	
12	2	Brown Sugar/Bitch/Let It Rock	Rolling Stones	Rolling Stone	9	(1)	
13	-	He's Gonna Step On You Again	John Kongos	Fly	8	(70)	F
14	12	Malt And Barley Blues	McGuinness Flint	Capitol	7		L
15	-	Oh You Pretty Thing	Peter Noone	Rak	6		F L
16	9	Jig A Jig	East Of Eden	Deram	6		F L
17	-	I Think Of You	Perry Como	RCA	5	(53)	
18	-	Don't Let It Die	Hurricane Smith	Columbia	8		F
19	-	Co-Co	Sweet	RCA	10	(99)	
20	5	Mozart Symphony No. 40 In G Minor	Waldo De Los Rios	A&M	10	(67)	F L

April 1971

This Mnth	Prev Mnth	Title	Artist	Label	Wks 20	(UK Pos)	
1	13	What's Going On	Marvin Gaye	Tamla	11		G
2	2	Just My Imagination (Running Away With Me)	Temptations	Gordy	11	(8)	G
3	-	Joy To The World	Three Dog Night	Dunhill	13	(24)	G
4	1	Me And Bobby McGee	Janis Joplin	Columbia	10		F G L
5	-	Another Day/Oh Woman Oh Why Oh Why	Paul McCartney	Apple	9	(2)	F
6	5	For All We Know	Carpenters	A&M	9	(18)	G
7	4	She's A Lady	Tom Jones	Parrot	9	(13)	G
8	7	Doesn't Somebody Want To Be...	Partridge Family	Bell	10		G
9	-	Put Your Hand In The Hand	Ocean	Kama Sutra	9		F G L
10	6	Proud Mary	Ike & Tina Turner	Liberty	7		G L
11	-	One Toke Over The Line	Brewer And Shipley	Kama Sutra	6		F L
12	-	Never Can Say Goodbye	Jackson Five	Motown	10	(33)	G
13	12	Help Me Make It Through The Night	Sammi Smith	Mega	7		F G L
14	-	Wild World	Cat Stevens	A&M	5		F
15	-	I Am ...I Said	Neil Diamond	Uni	7	(4)	
16	18	(Where Do I Begin) Love Story	Andy Williams	Columbia	6	(4)	L
17	15	What Is Life	George Harrison	Apple	6		
18	-	If	Bread	Elektra	8		
19	-	Stay Awhile	Bells	Polydor	6		F G L
20	-	Oye Como Va	Santana	Columbia	3		

May 1971

This Mnth	Prev Mnth	Title	Artist	Label	Wks 20	(UK Pos)	
1	3	Joy To The World	Three Dog Night	Dunhill	13	(24)	G
2	12	Never Can Say Goodbye	Jackson Five	Motown	10	(33)	G
3	9	Put Your Hand In The Hand	Ocean	Kama Sutra	9		F G L
4	18	If	Bread	Elektra	8		
5	-	Bridge Over Troubled Water/ Brand New Me	Aretha Franklin	Atlantic	8		G
6	-	Brown Sugar	Rolling Stones	Rolling Stone	10	(2)	G
7	-	Me And You And A Dog Named Boo	Lobo	Big Tree	8	(4)	F
8	-	Chick-A-Boom	Daddy Dewdrop	Sunflower	8		F L
9	19	Stay Awhile	Bells	Polydor	6		F G L
10	15	I Am ...I Said	Neil Diamond	Uni	7	(4)	
11	-	Want Ads	Honey Cone	Hot Wax	11		F G
12	1	What's Going On	Marvin Gaye	Tamla	11		G
13	-	Love Her Madly	Doors	Elektra	6		
14	-	It Don't Come Easy	Ringo Starr	Apple	9	(4)	F G
15	-	Sweet And Innocent	Donny Osmond	MGM	9		F G
16	-	Power To The People	John Lennon/Plastic Ono Band	Apple	4	(7)	
17	5	Another Day/Oh Woman Oh Why...	Paul McCartney	Apple	9	(2)	F
18	2	Just My Imagination (Running...)	Temptations	Gordy	11	(8)	G
19	-	Here Comes The Sun	Richie Havens	Stormy Forest	4		F L
20	-	Superstar	Murray Head	Decca	5	(47)	F

June 1971

This Mnth	Prev Mnth	Title	Artist	Label	Wks 20	(UK Pos)	
1	11	Want Ads	Honey Cone	Hot Wax	11		F G
2	-	Rainy Days And Mondays	Carpenters	A&M	10		G
3	6	Brown Sugar	Rolling Stones	Rolling Stone	10	(2)	G
4	-	It's Too Late/I Feel The Earth Move	Carole King	Ode	12	(6)	F G
5	14	It Don't Come Easy	Ringo Starr	Apple	9	(4)	F G
6	1	Joy To The World	Three Dog Night	Dunhill	13	(24)	G
7	-	Treat Her Like A Lady	Cornelius Brothers/Sister Rose	UA	10		F G
8	15	Sweet And Innocent	Donny Osmond	MGM	9		F G
9	-	I'll Meet You Halfway	Partridge Family	Bell	6		
10	-	Indian Reservation (The Lament Of The Cherokee Reservation Indian)	Raiders	Columbia	12		G L
11	5	Bridge Over Troubled Water/Brand...	Aretha Franklin	Atlantic	8		G
12	-	When You're Hot, You're Hot	Jerry Reed	RCA	7		L
13	-	I Don't Know How To Love Him	Helen Reddy	Capitol	5		F
14	7	Me And You And A Dog Named Boo	Lobo	Big Tree	8	(4)	F
15	2	Never Can Say Goodbye	Jackson Five	Motown	10	(33)	G
16	-	Don't Knock My Love (Pt. 1)	Wilson Pickett	Atlantic	5		G L
17	20	Superstar	Murray Head	Decca	5	(47)	F
18	-	Double Lovin'	Osmonds	MGM	4		
19	-	Don't Pull Your Love	Hamilton, Joe Frank & Reynolds	Dunhill	8		F G
20	-	Nathan Jones	Supremes	Motown	4	(5)	

◆ The Beach Boys, The Allman Brothers, Albert King, The J. Geils Band and Mountain appeared on the final bill at the Fillmore East venue. Days later the Fillmore West, too, closed – an era had ended.

◆ Singer/songwriter Carole King's double Grammy wining album, **Tapestry,** hit the top. It would stay on the chart for over 300 weeks!

▲ Ed Sullivan's last TV show aired. Among the guests were Gladys Knight & The Pips.

◆ Grand Funk Railroad sold out Shea Stadium in just three days. Their show broke the venue's box office record set by The Beatles.

UK 1971 JULY-SEPT

▲ Glitter-Rock (aka Glam Rock) was off and running in Britain, thanks to hits from Sweet, T-Rex (above) and chart newcomers Slade.

◆ The Tams' seven-year-old 'Hey Girl Don't Bother Me' was one of several re-issues on the British chart – others came from Tami Lynn, The Elgins and even Elvis, with a coupling of 'Heartbreak Hotel' and 'Hound Dog'.

◆ Cliff Richard, who received an Ivor Novello award for his outstanding services to British music, was heavily promoting newcomer Olivia Newton-John on his weekly TV series.

July 1971

This Mnth	Prev Mnth	Title	Artist	Label	Wks 20	(US Pos)	
1	10	Chirpy Chirpy Cheep Cheep	Middle Of The Road	RCA	12		F
2	19	Co-Co	Sweet	RCA	10	(99)	
3	18	Don't Let It Die	Hurricane Smith	Columbia	8		F
4	8	Banner Man	Blue Mink	Regal Zonophone	9		
5	-	Me And You And A Dog Named Boo	Lobo	Philips	9	(5)	F
6	-	Get It On	T. Rex	Fly	9	(10)	
7	-	Black And White	Greyhound	Trojan	8		F
8	13	He's Gonna Step On You Again	John Kongos	Fly	8	(70)	F
9	-	Just My Imagination (Runnin' Away With Me)	Temptations	Tamla Motown	8	(1)	
10	-	Monkey Spanner	Dave & Ansil Collins	Technique	8		L
11	4	I'm Gonna Run Away From You	Tami Lynn	Mojo	8		F L
12	-	Tom-Tom Turnaround	New World	RAK	10		
13	2	I Did What I Did For Maria	Tony Christie	MCA	9		F
14	-	Pied Piper	Bob & Marcia	Trojan	5		L
15	7	Lady Rose	Mungo Jerry	Dawn	7		
16	-	River Deep-Mountain High	Supremes & Four Tops	Tamla	6	(14)	
17	-	I Don't Blame You At All	Smokey Robinson & The Miracles	Tamla Motown	5	(18)	
18	-	When You Are A King	White Plains	Deram	5		L
19	-	Never Ending Song Of Love	New Seekers	Philips	12		F
20	-	Tonight	Move	Harvest	5		

August 1971

This Mnth	Prev Mnth	Title	Artist	Label	Wks 20	(US Pos)	
1	19	Never Ending Song Of Love	New Seekers	Philips	12		F
2	6	Get It On	T. Rex	Fly	9	(10)	
3	-	I'm Still Waiting	Diana Ross	Tamla Motown	11	(63)	
4	-	Devil's Answer	Atomic Rooster	B&C	7		L
5	-	In My Own Time	Family	Reprise	8		
6	1	Chirpy Chirpy Cheep Cheep	Middle Of The Road	RCA	12		F
7	12	Tom-Tom Turnaround	New World	RAK	10		
8	-	Won't Get Fooled Again	Who	Track	6	(15)	
9	-	What Are You Doing Sunday	Dawn	Bell	7	(39)	
10	5	Me And You And A Dog Named Boo	Lobo	Philips	9	(5)	F
11	2	Co-Co	Sweet	RCA	10	(99)	
12	-	Heartbreak Hotel/Hound Dog	Elvis Presley	RCA	5		
13	-	Leap Up And Down (Wave Your Knickers In The Air)	St. Cecilia	Polydor	7		F L
14	-	Soldier Blue	Buffy Sainte-Marie	RCA	8		F L
15	10	Monkey Spanner	Dave & Ansil Collins	Technique	8		L
16	-	Let Your Yeah Be Yeah	Pioneers	Trojan	6		F L
17	-	Bangla Desh	George Harrison	Apple	4	(23)	
18	7	Black And White	Greyhound	Trojan	8		F
19	-	Get Down And Get With It	Slade	Polydor	4		F
20	-	Hey Girl Don't Bother Me	Tams	Probe	11	(41)	F L

September 1971

This Mnth	Prev Mnth	Title	Artist	Label	Wks 20	(US Pos)	
1	20	Hey Girl Don't Bother Me	Tams	Probe	11	(41)	F L
2	3	I'm Still Waiting	Diana Ross	Tamla Motown	11	(63)	
3	1	Never Ending Song Of Love	New Seekers	Philips	12		F
4	-	Did You Ever	Nancy Sinatra & Lee Hazlewood	Reprise	9		L
5	9	What Are You Doing Sunday	Dawn	Bell	7	(39)	
6	14	Soldier Blue	Buffy Sainte-Marie	RCA	8		F L
7	-	Back Street Luv	Curved Air	Warner	6		F L
8	-	Nathan Jones	Supremes	Tamla Motown	7	(16)	
9	-	It's Too Late	Carole King	A&M	6	(1)	L
10	16	Let Your Yeah Be Yeah	Pioneers	Trojan	6		F L
11	5	In My Own Time	Family	Reprise	8		
12	-	I Believe (In Love)	Hot Chocolate	RAK	6		
13	-	Maggie May	Rod Stewart	Mercury	14	(1)	F
14	-	You've Got A Friend	James Taylor	Warner	9	(1)	F L
15	-	Tweedle Dee Tweedle Dum	Middle Of The Road	RCA	9		
16	-	Cousin Norman	Marmalade	Decca	7		
17	2	Get It On	T. Rex	Fly	9	(10)	
18	17	Bangla Desh	George Harrison	Apple	4	(23)	
19	-	Tap Turns On The Water	C.C.S.	RAK	7		L
20	-	For All We Know	Shirley Bassey	UA	10		

July 1971

This Mnth	Prev Mnth	Title	Artist	Label	Wks 20	(UK Pos)	
1	4	It's Too Late/I Feel The Earth Move	Carole King	Ode	12	(6)	F G
2	10	Indian Reservation (The Lament...)	Raiders	Columbia	12		G L
3	-	You've Got A Friend	James Taylor	Warner	10	(4)	G
4	19	Don't Pull Your Love	Hamilton, Joe Frank & Reynolds	Dunhill	8		F G
5	7	Treat Her Like A Lady	Cornelius Brothers/Sister Rose	UA	10		F G
6	-	Mr. Big Stuff	Jean Knight	Stax	11		F G L
7	2	Rainy Days And Mondays	Carpenters	A&M	10		G
8	-	Draggin' The Line	Tommy James	Roulette	8		F
9	-	How Can You Mend A Broken Heart	Bee Gees	Atco	12		G
10	-	Sooner Or Later	Grass Roots	Dunhill	5		
11	-	That's The Way I've Always Heard It Should Be	Carly Simon	Elektra	6		F
12	-	She's Not Just Another Woman	8th Day	Invictus	6		F G L
13	-	Take Me Home, Country Roads	John Denver	RCA	11		F G
14	12	When You're Hot, You're Hot	Jerry Reed	RCA	7		L
15	1	Want Ads	Honey Cone	Hot Wax	11		F G
16	3	Brown Sugar	Rolling Stones	Rolling Stone	10	(2)	G
17	5	It Don't Come Easy	Ringo Starr	Apple	9	(4)	F G
18	-	Never Ending Song Of Love	Delaney & Bonnie & Friends	Atco	6		F
19	-	Here Comes That Rainy Day Feeling Again	Fortunes	Capitol	5		L
20	-	I Don't Want To Do Wrong	Gladys Knight & The Pips	Soul	5		

August 1971

This Mnth	Prev Mnth	Title	Artist	Label	Wks 20	(UK Pos)	
1	9	How Can You Mend A Broken Heart	Bee Gees	Atco	12		G
2	6	Mr. Big Stuff	Jean Knight	Stax	11		F G L
3	13	Take Me Home, Country Roads	John Denver	RCA	11		F G
4	3	You've Got A Friend	James Taylor	Warner	10	(4)	G
5	-	Mercy Mercy Me (The Ecology)	Marvin Gaye	Tamla	8		
6	-	Beginnings/Colour My World	Chicago	Columbia	8		
7	8	Draggin' The Line	Tommy James	Roulette	8		F
8	-	Signs	Five Man Electrical Band	Lionel	8		F G L
9	2	Indian Reservation (The Lament...)	Raiders	Columbia	12		G L
10	-	Liar	Three Dog Night	Dunhill	7		
11	1	It's Too Late/I Feel The Earth Move	Carole King	Ode	12	(6)	F G
12	-	What The World Need Now Is Love/Abraham, Martin & John	Tom Clay	Mowest	5		F L
13	-	Sweet Hitch-Hiker	Creedence Clearwater Revival	Fantasy	6	(36)	L
14	-	Smiling Faces Sometime	Undisputed Truth	Gordy	9		F G L
15	-	Spanish Harlem	Aretha Franklin	Atlantic	9	(14)	G
16	18	Never Ending Song Of Love	Delaney & Bonnie & Friends	Atco	6		F
17	-	Bring The Boys Home	Freda Payne	Invictus	5		L
18	-	Hot Pants (She Got To Use What She Got To Get What She Wants)	James Brown	People	5		
19	-	Riders On The Storm	Doors	Elektra	4	(68)	L
20	-	Go Away Little Girl	Donny Osmond	MGM	10		G

September 1971

This Mnth	Prev Mnth	Title	Artist	Label	Wks 20	(UK Pos)	
1	20	Go Away Little Girl	Donny Osmond	MGM	10		G
2	15	Spanish Harlem	Aretha Franklin	Atlantic	9	(14)	G
3	-	Ain't No Sunshine	Bill Withers	Sussex	9		F G
4	-	Uncle Albert/Admiral Halsey	Paul & Linda McCartney	Apple	10		G
5	14	Smiling Faces Sometime	Undisputed Truth	Gordy	9		F G L
6	1	How Can You Mend A Broken Heart	Bee Gees	Atco	12		G
7	-	I Just Want To Celebrate	Rare Earth	Rare Earth	6		
8	-	Maggie May/Reason To Believe	Rod Stewart	Mercury	13	(1)	F G
9	-	Whatcha See Is Whatcha Get	Dramatics	Volt	7		F
10	-	Night They Drove Old Dixie Down	Joan Baez	Vanguard	11	(6)	F G L
11	3	Take Me Home, Country Roads	John Denver	RCA	11		F G
12	-	Stick-Up	Honey Cone	Hot Wax	7		G
13	8	Signs	Five Man Electrical Band	Lionel	8		F G L
14	-	Superstar	Carpenters	A&M	11	(18)	G
15	10	Liar	Three Dog Night	Dunhill	7		
16	13	Sweet Hitch-Hiker	Creedence Clearwater Revival	Fantasy	6	(36)	L
17	-	I Woke Up In Love This Morning	Partridge Family	Bell	6		
18	-	Won't Get Fooled Again	Who	Decca	4	(9)	
19	-	Do You Know What I Mean	Lee Michaels	A&M	10		F L
20	5	Mercy Mercy Me (The Ecology)	Marvin Gaye	Tamla	8		

▲ *The Concert For Bangla Desh* took place at Madison Square Garden. George Harrison organized the event which also starred Eric Clapton, Ringo Starr (above), Badfinger and Bob Dylan.

◆ Jim Morrison, leader of The Doors, died of a heart attack on the day the group's 'Riders On The Storm' entered the Hot 100. It became their sixth and last Top 20 entry.

◆ 'Go Away Little Girl' became the first song in the rock era to top the chart on two occasions. Carole King's composition, which originally led the lists in 1963 by Steve Lawrence, now reached the top by 13-year-old Donny Osmond.

UK 1971 OCT-DEC

◆ English comedian Benny Hill topped the chart with the novelty 'Ernie (The Fastest Milkman In The West)', which was loosely based on an earlier record by American humorist Frank Gallup.

◆ Superstars Michael Jackson and Al Green had their first major solo hits with 'Got To Be There' and 'Tired Of Being Alone' respectively. Other chart newcomers included David Cassidy in America and The Bay City Rollers in the UK.

◆ Led Zeppelin's untitled fourth album, which contained the FM classic 'Stairway To Heaven', was released. It spent five years on the American chart and sold eleven million in the US alone.

◆ Slade followed their first No. 1, 'Coz I Luv You', with another four phonetically spelled chart toppers. They were the only act to regularly misspell titles until the late 1980s when Prince and scores of others followed suit.

October 1971

This Mnth	Prev Mnth	Title	Artist	Label	Wks 20	(US Pos)	
1	13	Maggie May	Rod Stewart	Mercury	14	(1)	F
2	15	Tweedle Dee Tweedle Dum	Middle Of The Road	RCA	9		
3	14	You've Got A Friend	James Taylor	Warner	9	(1)	F L
4	1	Hey Girl Don't Bother Me	Tams	Probe	11	(41)	F L
5	4	Did You Ever	Nancy Sinatra & Lee Hazlewood	Reprise	9		L
6	20	For All We Know	Shirley Bassey	UA	10		
7	19	Tap Turns On The Water	C.C.S.	RAK	7		L
8	-	Witch Queen Of New Orleans	Redbone	Epic	8	(21)	F L
9	-	Freedom Come Freedom Go	Fortunes	Capitol	7	(72)	
10	16	Cousin Norman	Marmalade	Decca	7		
11	-	Simple Game	Four Tops	Tamla Motown	8	(90)	
12	-	Sultana	Titanic	CBS	7		F L
13	-	Life Is A Long Song/Up The Pool	Jethro Tull	Chrysalis	5		L
14	8	Nathan Jones	Supremes	Tamla Motown	7	(16)	
15	-	Butterfly	Danyel Gerard	CBS	5	(78)	F L
16	12	I Believe (In Love)	Hot Chocolate	RAK	6		
17	-	Another Time Another Place	Engelbert Humperdinck	Decca	4	(43)	
18	-	You Don't Have To Be In The Army To Fight In The War	Mungo Jerry	Dawn	3		
19	7	Back Street Luv	Curved Air	Warner	6		F L
20	-	Keep On Dancing	Bay City Rollers	Bell	5		F

November 1971

1	-	Coz I Luv You	Slade	Polydor	10		
2	1	Maggie May	Rod Stewart	Mercury	14	(1)	F
3	-	Till	Tom Jones	Decca	10	(41)	
4	-	Tired Of Being Alone	Al Green	London American	6	(11)	F
5	8	Witch Queen Of New Orleans	Redbone	Epic	8	(21)	F L
6	-	Johnny Reggae	Piglets	Bell	7		F L
7	-	I Will Return	Springwater	Polydor	6		F L
8	11	Simple Game	Four Tops	Tamla Motown	8	(90)	
9	-	The Night They Drove Old Dixie Down	Joan Baez	Vanguard	7	(3)	L
10	-	Banks Of The Ohio	Olivia Newton-John	Pye International	8	(94)	
11	-	Gypsys Tramps & Thieves	Cher	MCA	9	(1)	
12	-	Look Around	Vince Hill	Columbia	6		L
13	-	Jeepster	T. Rex	Fly	10		
14	12	Sultana	Titanic	CBS	7		F L
15	-	Brandy	Scott English	Horse	5	(91)	F L
16	-	Ernie (The Fastest Milkman In The West)	Benny Hill	Columbia	10		L
17	6	For All We Know	Shirley Bassey	UA	10		
18	2	Tweedle Dee Tweedle Dum	Middle Of The Road	RCA	9		
19	-	Run, Baby Run (Back Into My Arms)	Newbeats	London American	6		L
20	-	Surrender	Diana Ross	Tamla Motown	5	(38)	

December 1971

1	16	Ernie (The Fastest Milkman In The...)	Benny Hill	Columbia	10		L
2	13	Jeepster	T. Rex	Fly	10		
3	1	Coz I Luv You	Slade	Polydor	10		
4	-	Tokoloshe Man	John Kongos	Fly	7		L
5	11	Gypsys Tramps & Thieves	Cher	MCA	9	(1)	
6	-	Theme From 'Shaft'	Isaac Hayes	Stax	8	(1)	F
7	-	Something Tells Me (Something Is Gonna Happen Tonight)	Cilla Black	Parlophone	8		L
8	10	Banks Of The Ohio	Olivia Newton-John	Pye International	8	(94)	
9	-	No Matter How I Try	Gilbert O'Sullivan	MAM	9		
10	3	Till	Tom Jones	Decca	10	(41)	
11	6	Johnny Reggae	Piglets	Bell	7		F L
12	19	Run, Baby Run (Back Into My Arms)	Newbeats	London American	6		L
13	-	Softly Whispering I Love You	Congregation	Columbia	8	(29)	F L
14	-	Sing A Song Of Freedom	Cliff Richard	Columbia	4		
15	7	I Will Return	Springwater	Polydor	6		F L
16	20	Surrender	Diana Ross	Tamla Motown	5	(38)	
17	-	I'd Like To Teach The World To Sing	New Seekers	Polydor	12	(7)	
18	-	Soley Soley	Middle Of The Road	RCA	8		L
19	-	It Must Be Love	Labi Siffre	Pye International	6		F
20	-	Fireball	Deep Purple	Harvest	6		L

October 1971

This Mnth	Prev Mnth	Title	Artist	Label	Wks 20	(UK Pos)	
1	8	Maggie May/Reason To Believe	Rod Stewart	Mercury	13	(1)	F G
2	14	Superstar	Carpenters	A&M	11	(18)	G
3	-	Yo-Yo	Osmonds	MGM	10		G
4	10	The Night They Drove Old Dixie Down	Joan Baez	Vanguard	11	(6)	F G L
5	19	Do You Know What I Mean	Lee Michaels	A&M	10		F L
6	1	Go Away Little Girl	Donny Osmond	MGM	10		G
7	4	Uncle Albert/Admiral Halsey	Paul & Linda McCartney	Apple	10		G
8	-	If You Really Love Me	Stevie Wonder	Tamla	8	(20)	
9	-	Sweet City Woman	Stampeders	Bell	7		F L
10	-	Gypsys Tramps & Thieves	Cher	Kapp	11	(4)	G
11	3	Ain't No Sunshine	Bill Withers	Sussex	9		F G
12	-	Tired Of Being Alone	Al Green	Hi	10	(4)	F G
13	5	Smiling Faces Sometime	Undisputed Truth	Gordy	9		F G L
14	-	I've Found Someone Of My Own	Free Movement	Decca	7		F L
15	-	Theme From 'Shaft'	Isaac Hayes	Enterprise	10	(4)	F G
16	-	So Far Away/Smackwater Jack	Carole King	Ode	5		
17	2	Spanish Harlem	Aretha Franklin	Atlantic	9	(14)	G
18	-	Trapped By A Thing Called Love	Denise La Salle	Westbound	5		F G L
19	-	Peace Train	Cat Stevens	A&M	8		
20	12	Stick-Up	Honey Cone	Hot Wax	7		G

November 1971

This Mnth	Prev Mnth	Title	Artist	Label	Wks 20	(UK Pos)	
1	10	Gypsys Tramps & Thieves	Cher	Kapp	11	(4)	G
2	15	Theme From 'Shaft'	Isaac Hayes	Enterprise	10	(4)	F G
3	-	Imagine	John Lennon & The Plastic Ono Band	Apple	8	(6)	
4	1	Maggie May/Reason To Believe	Rod Stewart	Mercury	13	(1)	F G
5	19	Peace Train	Cat Stevens	A&M	8		
6	-	Have You Seen Her	Chi-Lites	Brunswick	10	(3)	F
7	3	Yo-Yo	Osmonds	MGM	10		G
8	-	Baby I'm A Want You	Bread	Elektra	7	(14)	G
9	14	I've Found Someone Of My Own	Free Movement	Decca	7		F L
10	-	Got To Be There	Michael Jackson	Motown	11	(5)	F
11	-	Inner City Blues (Makes Me Wanna Holler)	Marvin Gaye	Tamla	4		
12	2	Superstar	Carpenters	A&M	11	(18)	G
13	-	Family Affair	Sly & The Family Stone	Epic	11	(15)	G
14	-	Desiderata	Les Crane	Warner	5	(7)	F L
15	-	Everybody's Everything	Santana	Columbia	4		
16	-	Rock Steady	Aretha Franklin	Atlantic	5		G
17	-	Never My Love	Fifth Dimension	Bell	5		
18	5	Do You Know What I Mean	Lee Michaels	A&M	10		F L
19	12	Tired Of Being Alone	Al Green	Hi	10	(4)	F G
20	-	Easy Loving	Freddie Hart	Capitol	5		F G L

December 1971

This Mnth	Prev Mnth	Title	Artist	Label	Wks 20	(UK Pos)	
1	13	Family Affair	Sly & The Family Stone	Epic	11	(15)	G
2	6	Have You Seen Her	Chi-Lites	Brunswick	10	(3)	F
3	10	Got To Be There	Michael Jackson	Motown	11	(5)	F
4	-	An Old Fashioned Love Song	Three Dog Night	Dunhill	8		G
5	2	Theme From 'Shaft'	Isaac Hayes	Enterprise	10	(4)	F G
6	-	Brand New Key	Melanie	Neighborhood	12	(4)	G L
7	8	Baby I'm A Want You	Bread	Elektra	7	(14)	G
8	-	All I Ever Need Is You	Sonny & Cher	Kapp	7	(8)	
9	-	Cherish	David Cassidy	Bell	8	(2)	F G L
10	1	Gypsys Tramps & Thieves	Cher	Kapp	11	(4)	G
11	-	Scorpio	Dennis Coffey & The Detroit Guitar Band	Sussex	11		F
12	-	American Pie (Pts 1 & 2)	Don McLean	UA	14	(2)	F G
13	-	Respect Yourself	Staple Singers	Stax	6		F
14	14	Desiderata	Les Crane	Warner	5	(7)	F L
15	16	Rock Steady	Aretha Franklin	Atlantic	5		G
16	-	Hey Girl/I Knew You When	Donny Osmond	MGM	7		G
17	3	Imagine	John Lennon/PlasticOno Band	Apple	8	(6)	
18	-	You Are Everything	Stylistics	Avco	10		F G
19	-	Stones	Neil Diamond	Uni	3		
20	-	Where Did Our Love Go	Donnie Elbert	All Platinum	3	(8)	F L

▲ The Faces concert at Madison Square Garden sold out in record time. The group's lead vocalist Rod Stewart (above) topped both the transatlantic single and album charts with his first Top 20 entries, 'Maggie May' and **Every Picture Tells A Story** respectively. John Lennon also hit No. 1 on both sides of the water with his debut solo set, **Imagine.**

◆ US record and tape sales increased to $1.7 billion - 60% being purchased by under 30s.

◆ Their appearances on the new TV series *The Sonny & Cher Comedy Hour* helped return both the duo and Cher to the Top 20 after four years away.

153

UK
1972
JAN-MAR

◆ Pink Floyd pre-viewed their **Dark Side Of The Moon** album at London's new home of rock music, The Rainbow Theatre. The LP, which was released a year later, smashed all records for chart longevity.

◆ As Paul McCartney (& Wings) played his first dates since leaving The Beatles, John Lennon was having problems renewing his US visa. Ringo Starr, meanwhile, was making a film about Britain's latest pop sensations, T-Rex, whose live shows were "creating hysteria not seen since the early days of The Beatles".

◆ 'I'd Like To Teach The World To Sing' by The New Seekers was not the first recording from a TV advertise-ment, but this Coca Cola commercial was the one which proved that major UK hits can come via this route. Since then many more have charted in Britain.

January 1972

This Mnth	Prev Mnth	Title	Artist	Label	Wks 20	(US Pos)	
1	17	I'd Like To Teach The World To Sing	New Seekers	Polydor	12	(7)	
2	13	Softly Whispering I Love You	Congregation	Columbia	8	(29)	F L
3	-	Mother Of Mine	Neil Reid	Decca	14		F L
4	18	Soley Soley	Middle Of The Road	RCA	8		L
5	1	Ernie (The Fastest Milkman In The West)	Benny Hill	Columbia	10		L
6	-	I Just Can't Help Believing	Elvis Presley	RCA	8		
7	7	Something Tells Me (Something Is Gonna Happen Tonight)	Cilla Black	Parlophone	8		L
8	-	Sleepy Shores	Johnny Pearson Orchestra	Penny Farthing	7		F L
9	2	Jeepster	T. Rex	Fly	10		
10	9	No Matter How I Try	Gilbert O'Sullivan	MAM	9		
11	-	Brand New Key	Melanie	Buddah	7	(1)	L
12	-	Horse With No Name	America	Warner	7	(1)	F L
13	6	Theme From 'Shaft'	Isaac Hayes	Stax	8	(1)	F
14	-	Stay With Me	Faces	Warner	5	(17)	F
15	-	Morning Has Broken	Cat Stevens	Island	4	(6)	
16	-	Morning	Val Doonican	Philips	6		L
17	4	Tokoloshe Man	John Kongos	Fly	7		L
18	-	Telegram Sam	T. Rex	T. Rex	7	(67)	
19	-	Where Did Our Love Go	Donnie Elbert	London American	5	(15)	F
20	-	Let's Stay Together	Al Green	London American	7	(1)	

February 1972

This Mnth	Prev Mnth	Title	Artist	Label	Wks 20	(US Pos)	
1	18	Telegram Sam	T. Rex	T. Rex	7	(67)	
2	-	Son Of My Father	Chicory Tip	CBS	9		F
3	3	Mother Of Mine	Neil Reid	Decca	14		F L
4	-	Have You Seen Her	Chi-Lites	MCA	7	(3)	F
5	1	I'd Like To Teach The World To Sing	New Seekers	Polydor	12	(7)	
6	12	Horse With No Name	America	Warner	7	(1)	F L
7	-	Look Wot You Dun	Slade	Polydor	7		
8	20	Let's Stay Together	Al Green	London American	7	(1)	
9	-	American Pie	Don McLean	UA	11	(1)	F
10	11	Brand New Key	Melanie	Buddah	7	(1)	L
11	-	All I Ever Need Is You	Sonny & Cher	MCA	6	(7)	L
12	-	Storm In A Teacup	Fortunes	Capitol	6		L
13	14	Stay With Me	Faces	Warner	5	(17)	F
14	-	Moon River	Greyhound	Trojan	4		
15	19	Where Did Our Love Go	Donnie Elbert	London American	5	(15)	F
16	-	Day After Day	Badfinger	Apple	6	(4)	L
17	-	Without You	Nilsson	RCA	13	(1)	F L
18	6	I Just Can't Help Believing	Elvis Presley	RCA	8		
19	-	Baby I'm A Want You	Bread	Elektra	4	(3)	
20	-	Got To Be There	Michael Jackson	Tamla Motown	6	(4)	F

March 1972

This Mnth	Prev Mnth	Title	Artist	Label	Wks 20	(US Pos)	
1	17	Without You	Nilsson	RCA	13	(1)	F L
2	9	American Pie	Don McLean	UA	11	(1)	F
3	2	Son Of My Father	Chicory Tip	CBS	9		F
4	-	Beg Steal Or Borrow	New Seekers	Polydor	9	(81)	
5	-	Mother & Child Reunion	Paul Simon	CBS	7	(4)	F
6	20	Got To Be There	Michael Jackson	Tamla Motown	6	(4)	F
7	-	Blue Is The Colour	Chelsea F.C.	Penny Farthing	7		F L
8	-	Alone Again (Naturally)	Gilbert O'Sullivan	MAM	7	(1)	
9	7	Look Wot You Dun	Slade	Polydor	7		
10	-	Meet Me On The Corner	Lindisfarne	Charisma	6		F
11	-	Poppa Joe	Sweet	RCA	5		
12	3	Mother Of Mine	Neil Reid	Decca	14		F L
13	12	Storm In A Teacup	Fortunes	Capitol	6		L
14	-	I Can't Help Myself	Donnie Elbert	Avco	5	(22)	
15	16	Day After Day	Badfinger	Apple	6	(4)	L
16	4	Have You Seen Her	Chi-Lites	MCA	7	(3)	F
17	-	Hold Your Head Up	Argent	Epic	7	(5)	F
18	-	Floy Joy	Supremes	Tamla Motown	6	(16)	
19	-	Say You Don't Mind	Colin Blunstone	Epic	3		F L
20	-	Desiderata	Les Crane	Warner	7	(8)	F L

January 1972

This Mnth	Prev Mnth	Title	Artist	Label	Wks 20	(UK Pos)	
1	12	American Pie (Pts 1 & 2)	Don McLean	UA	14	(2)	F G
2	6	Brand New Key	Melanie	Neighborhood	12	(4)	G L
3	-	Let's Stay Together	Al Green	Hi	12	(7)	G
4	-	Sunshine	Jonathan Edwards	Capricorn	10		F G L
5	11	Scorpio	Dennis Coffey & The Detroit Guitar Band	Sussex	11		F
6	1	Family Affair	Sly & The Family Stone	Epic	11	(15)	G
7	-	I'd Like To Teach The World To Sing	New Seekers	Elektra	7	(1)	G L
8	18	You Are Everything	Stylistics	Avco	10		F G
9	3	Got To Be There	Michael Jackson	Motown	11	(5)	F
10	-	Clean Up Woman	Betty Wright	Alston	8		F G L
11	-	Day After Day	Badfinger	Apple	9	(10)	G
12	-	Sugar Daddy	Jackson Five	Motown	5		
13	16	Hey Girl/I Knew You When	Donny Osmond	MGM	7		G
14	-	Drowning In The Sea Of Love	Joe Simon	Spring	7		G
15	-	I'd Like To Teach The World To Sing	Hillside Singers	Metromedia	5		F L
16	9	Cherish	David Cassidy	Bell	8	(2)	F G L
17	-	Never Been To Spain	Three Dog Night	Dunhill	8		
18	4	An Old Fashioned Love Song	Three Dog Night	Dunhill	8		G
19	2	Have You Seen Her	Chi-Lites	Brunswick	10	(3)	F
20	-	One Monkey Don't Stop No Show (Pt. 1)	Honey Cone	Hot Wax	4		L

February 1972

This Mnth	Prev Mnth	Title	Artist	Label	Wks 20	(UK Pos)	
1	3	Let's Stay Together	Al Green	Hi	12	(7)	G
2	-	Without You	Nilsson	RCA	11	(1)	G
3	1	American Pie (Pts 1 & 2)	Don McLean	UA	14	(2)	F G
4	-	Precious And Few	Climax	Carousel	10		F G L
5	-	Hurting Each Other	Carpenters	A&M	8		G
6	17	Never Been To Spain	Three Dog Night	Dunhill	8		
7	-	Down By The Lazy River	Osmonds	MGM	10	(40)	G
8	-	Joy	Apollo 100	Mega	8		F L
9	11	Day After Day	Badfinger	Apple	9	(10)	G
10	2	Brand New Key	Melanie	Neighborhood	12	(4)	G L
11	-	The Lion Sleeps Tonight	Robert John	Atlantic	11		F G
12	-	Sweet Seasons	Carole King	Ode	6		
13	-	Anticipation	Carly Simon	Elektra	6		
14	4	Sunshine	Jonathan Edwards	Capricorn	10		F G L
15	-	Everything I Own	Bread	Elektra	8	(32)	
16	10	Clean Up Woman	Betty Wright	Alston	8		F G L
17	-	Black Dog	Led Zeppelin	Atlantic	2		
18	5	Scorpio	Dennis Coffey & The Detroit Guitar Band	Sussex	11		F
19	-	Don't Say You Don't Remember	Beverly Bremmers	Scepter	5		F L
20	-	Stay With Me	Faces	Warner	4	(6)	F L

March 1972

This Mnth	Prev Mnth	Title	Artist	Label	Wks 20	(UK Pos)	
1	2	Without You	Nilsson	RCA	11	(1)	G
2	-	Heart Of Gold	Neil Young	Reprise	10	(10)	F G L
3	11	The Lion Sleeps Tonight	Robert John	Atlantic	11		F G
4	15	Everything I Own	Bread	Elektra	8	(32)	
5	4	Precious And Few	Climax	Carousel	10		F G L
6	7	Down By The Lazy River	Osmonds	MGM	10	(40)	G
7	-	A Horse With No Name	America	Warner	12	(3)	F G
8	-	The Way Of Love	Cher	Kapp	7		
9	-	Mother And Child Reunion	Paul Simon	Columbia	8	(5)	F
10	5	Hurting Each Other	Carpenters	A&M	8		G
11	-	Puppy Love	Donny Osmond	MGM	8	(1)	G
12	-	Bang A Gong (Get It On)	T. Rex	Fly	6	(1)	F L
13	-	Jungle Fever	Chakachas	Polydor	7	(29)	F G L
14	12	Sweet Seasons	Carole King	Ode	6		
15	-	I Gotcha	Joe Tex	Dial	13		G
16	8	Joy	Apollo 100	Mega	8		F L
17	1	Let's Stay Together	Al Green	Hi	12	(7)	G
18	3	American Pie (Pts 1 & 2)	Don McLean	UA	14	(2)	F G
19	-	In The Rain	Dramatics	Volt	8		L
20	19	Don't Say You Don't Remember	Beverly Bremmers	Scepter	5		F L

◆ Three outstanding black female vocalists died: gutsy blues performer Big Maybelle (Smith), soul stylist Linda Jones and gospel queen Mahalia Jackson (who had 40,000 people file past her coffin at her funeral).

◆ As popular TV group The Partridge Family celebrated their fifth Top 20 entry, family septet The Cowsills, "America's First Family of Music" and allegedly the role models for the TV series, split up and filed for bankruptcy.

▲ Don McLean's (above) 'American Pie' and album of the same title topped the charts. Another singer-songwriter achieving that feat was Neil Young with 'Heart Of Gold' and **Harvest.**

UK 1972
APR-JUNE

◆ Among the record nine re-issued singles in the UK Top 50 were Procol Harum's 'A Whiter Shade of Pale' and tracks by The Chiffons and The Drifters.

◆ Clyde McPhatter, founder of The Drifters and one of the most imitated R&B singers in the 1950s, died of drink related causes.

◆ The Electric Light Orchestra and Roxy Music made their UK debuts, as Slade embarked on their first UK tour (supported by Status Quo). Other firsts included David Bowie's chart album, **The Rise And Fall Of Ziggy Stardust And The Spiders From Mars,** and Bob Marley's first hit as composer of American reggae star Johnny Nash's 'Stir It Up'.

◆ The Rolling Stones played to packed houses on their North American tour as 'Tumbling Dice' became their 11th transatlantic Top 10 entry.

April 1972

This Mnth	Prev Mnth	Title	Artist	Label	Wks 20	(US Pos)	
1	1	Without You	Nilsson	RCA	13	(1)	F L
2	4	Beg Steal Or Borrow	New Seekers	Polydor	9	(81)	
3	-	Amazing Grace	Royal Scots Dragoon Guards	RCA	11	(11)	F
4	-	Sweet Talkin' Guy	Chiffons	London American	8		L
5	17	Hold Your Head Up	Argent	Epic	7	(5)	F
6	-	Back Off Boogaloo	Ringo Starr	Apple	8	(9)	
7	8	Alone Again (Naturally)	Gilbert O'Sullivan	MAM	7	(1)	
8	-	The Young New Mexican Puppeteer	Tom Jones	Decca	7	(80)	
9	20	Desiderata	Les Crane	Warner	7	(8)	F L
10	-	Heart Of Gold	Neil Young	Reprise	5	(1)	F L
11	10	Meet Me On The Corner	Lindisfarne	Charisma	6		F
12	2	American Pie	Don McLean	UA	11	(1)	F
13	18	Floy Joy	Supremes	Tamla Motown	6	(16)	
14	-	Until It's Time For You To Go	Elvis Presley	RCA	6	(40)	
15	-	Debora/One Inch Rock	Tyrannosaurus Rex	Magni Fly	6		
16	-	Run Run Run	Jo Jo Gunne	Asylum	7	(27)	F L
17	-	Crying Laughing Loving Lying	Labi Siffre	Pye International	5		
18	-	It's One Of Those Nights (Yes Love)	Partridge Family	Bell	5	(20)	
19	-	Come What May	Vicky Leandros	Philips	8		F L
20	5	Mother & Child Reunion	Paul Simon	CBS	7	(4)	F

May 1972

This Mnth	Prev Mnth	Title	Artist	Label	Wks 20	(US Pos)	
1	3	Amazing Grace	Royal Scots Dragoon Guards	RCA	11	(11)	F
2	-	Could It Be Forever/Cherish	David Cassidy	Bell	9	(37)	F
3	19	Come What May	Vicky Leandros	Philips	8		F L
4	-	A Thing Called Love	Johnny Cash	CBS	7		L
5	-	Rocket Man	Elton John	DJM	8	(6)	
6	-	Metal Guru	T. Rex	EMI	8		
7	-	Tumbling Dice	Rolling Stones	Rolling Stone	6	(7)	
8	-	Radancer	Marmalade	Decca	6		
9	16	Run Run Run	Jo Jo Gunne	Asylum	7	(27)	F L
10	6	Back Off Boogaloo	Ringo Starr	Apple	8	(9)	
11	4	Sweet Talkin' Guy	Chiffons	London American	8		L
12	-	At The Club/Saturday Night At The Movies	Drifters	Atlantic	9	(43)	
13	15	Debora/One Inch Rock	Tyrannosaurus Rex	Magni Fly	6		
14	-	Oh Babe What Would You Say?	Hurricane Smith	Columbia	7	(3)	L
15	-	Take A Look Around	Temptations	Tamla Motown	5	(30)	
16	-	Leeds United	Leeds United F.C.	Chapter One	5		F L
17	8	The Young New Mexican Puppeteer	Tom Jones	Decca	7	(80)	
18	1	Without You	Nilsson	RCA	13	(1)	F L
19	-	Stir It Up	Johnny Nash	CBS	5	(12)	
20	14	Until It's Time For You To Go	Elvis Presley	RCA	6	(40)	

June 1972

This Mnth	Prev Mnth	Title	Artist	Label	Wks 20	(US Pos)	
1	6	Metal Guru	T. Rex	EMI	8		
2	-	Vincent	Don McLean	UA	9	(12)	
3	12	At The Club/Saturday Night At The Movies	Drifters	Atlantic	9	(43)	
4	-	Lady Eleanor	Lindisfarne	Charisma	6	(82)	
5	14	Oh Babe What Would You Say?	Hurricane Smith	Columbia	7	(3)	L
6	-	California Man	Move	Harvest	8		L
7	5	Rocket Man	Elton John	DJM	8	(6)	
8	-	Rockin' Robin	Michael Jackson	Tamla Motown	7	(2)	
9	-	Take Me Bak 'Ome	Slade	Polydor	9	(97)	
10	-	Sister Jane	New World	RAK	6		L
11	2	Could It Be Forever/Cherish	David Cassidy	Bell	9	(37)	F
12	-	Mary Had A Little Lamb	Wings	Apple	7	(28)	
13	1	Amazing Grace	Royal Scots Dragoon Guards	RCA	11	(11)	F
14	-	Isn't Life Strange	Moody Blues	Threshold	4	(29)	
15	-	Rock & Roll Part 2	Gary Glitter	Bell	10	(7)	F
16	3	Come What May	Vicky Leandros	Philips	8		F L
17	-	Doobedood'ndoobe Doobedood'ndoobe	Diana Ross	Tamla Motown	3		
18	-	A Whiter Shade Of Pale	Procol Harum	Magnifly	4		
19	4	A Thing Called Love	Johnny Cash	CBS	7		L
20	16	Leeds United	Leeds United F.C.	Chapter One	5		F L

April 1972

This Mnth	Prev Mnth	Title	Artist	Label	Wks 20	(UK Pos)	
1	7	A Horse With No Name	America	Warner	12	(3)	F G
2	-	The First Time Ever I Saw Your Face	Roberta Flack	Atlantic	14	(14)	F G
3	15	I Gotcha	Joe Tex	Dial	13		G
4	-	Rockin' Robin	Michael Jackson	Motown	9	(3)	G
5	2	Heart Of Gold	Neil Young	Reprise	10	(10)	F G L
6	19	In The Rain	Dramatics	Volt	8		L
7	11	Puppy Love	Donny Osmond	MGM	8	(1)	G
8	-	Betcha By Golly, Wow	Stylistics	Avco	10	(13)	G
9	-	Day Dreaming	Aretha Franklin	Atlantic	9		G
10	-	A Cowboy's Work Is Never Done	Sonny & Cher	Kapp	8		L
11	9	Mother And Child Reunion	Paul Simon	Columbia	8	(5)	F
12	3	The Lion Sleeps Tonight	Robert John	Atlantic	11		F G
13	13	Jungle Fever	Chakachas	Polydor	7	(29)	F G L
14	-	Doctor My Eyes	Jackson Browne	Asylum	6		F
15	-	Roundabout	Yes	Atlantic	5		F
16	-	Look What You Done For Me	Al Green	Hi	9	(44)	G
17	-	The Family Of Man	Three Dog Night	Dunhill	5		
18	1	Without You	Nilsson	RCA	11	(1)	G
19	-	Baby Blue	Badfinger	Apple	4		L
20	-	Vincent/Castles In The Air	Don McLean	UA	6	(1)	

May 1972

This Mnth	Prev Mnth	Title	Artist	Label	Wks 20	(UK Pos)	
1	2	The First Time Ever I Saw Your Face	Roberta Flack	Atlantic	14	(14)	F G
2	-	I'll Take You There	Staple Singers	Stax	10	(30)	G
3	3	I Gotcha	Joe Tex	Dial	13		G
4	-	Oh Girl	Chi-Lites	Brunswick	11	(14)	G L
5	16	Look What You Done For Me	Al Green	Hi	9	(44)	G
6	8	Betcha By Golly, Wow	Stylistics	Avco	10	(13)	G
7	4	Rockin' Robin	Michael Jackson	Motown	9	(3)	G
8	9	Day Dreaming	Aretha Franklin	Atlantic	9		
9	-	Tumbling Dice	Rolling Stones	Rolling Stone	6	(5)	
10	-	Back Off Boogaloo	Ringo Starr	Apple	5	(2)	
11	-	Morning Has Broken	Cat Stevens	A&M	8	(9)	
12	-	Hot Rod Lincoln	Commander Cody & His Lost Planet Airmen	Paramount	7		F L
13	1	A Horse With No Name	America	Warner	12	(3)	F G
14	-	The Candy Man	Sammy Davis Jr.	MGM	9		G L
15	14	Doctor My Eyes	Jackson Browne	Asylum	6		F
16	20	Vincent/Castles In The Air	Don McLean	UA	6	(1)	
17	-	Sylvia's Mother	Dr. Hook	Columbia	8	(2)	F G
18	-	Little Bitty Pretty One	Jackson Five	Motown	4		
19	17	The Family Of Man	Three Dog Night	Dunhill	5		
20	-	Slippin' Into Darkness	War	UA	4		G

June 1972

This Mnth	Prev Mnth	Title	Artist	Label	Wks 20	(UK Pos)	
1	14	The Candy Man	Sammy Davis Jr.	MGM	9		G L
2	2	I'll Take You There	Staple Singers	Stax	10	(30)	G
3	4	Oh Girl	Chi-Lites	Brunswick	11	(14)	G L
4	-	Song Sung Blue	Neil Diamond	Uni	9	(14)	G
5	-	Nice To Be With You	Gallery	Sussex	7		F G L
6	17	Sylvia's Mother	Dr. Hook	Columbia	8	(2)	F G
7	-	Outa-Space	Billy Preston	A&M	8	(44)	F G
8	-	(Last Night) I Didn't Get To Sleep At All	Fifth Dimension	Bell	7		G
9	1	The First Time Ever I Saw Your Face	Roberta Flack	Atlantic	14	(14)	F G
10	11	Morning Has Broken	Cat Stevens	A&M	8	(9)	
11	-	Troglodyte (Cave Man)	Jimmy Castor Bunch	RCA	7		F G
12	9	Tumbling Dice	Rolling Stones	Rolling Stone	6	(5)	
13	-	Lean On Me	Bill Withers	Sussex	10	(18)	G
14	-	It's Going To Take Some Time	Carpenters	A&M	4		
15	-	Diary	Bread	Elektra	5		
16	-	Walkin' In The Rain With The One I Love	Love Unlimited	Uni	4	(14)	F G L
17	12	Hot Rod Lincoln	Commander Cody & His Lost Planet Airmen	Paramount	7		F L
18	5	Look What You Done For Me	Al Green	Hi	9	(44)	G
19	-	Amazing Grace	Royal Scots Dragoon Guards	RCA	4	(1)	F L
20	-	I Saw The Light	Todd Rundgren	Bearsville	3	(36)	F

◆ One of the era's most unusual transatlantic hits came from the Royal Scots Dragoon Guards. The record that temporarily put the regimental bagpipe band in the pop spotlight was their instrumental interpretation of 'Amazing Grace'.

◆ For the first time, the top eight singles on the US chart (May) were all by African-American artists.

◆ John Hammond, who discovered Bob Dylan, also signed his latest find, Bruce Springsteen, to Columbia Records.

◆ Elvis Presley finally made his live New York debut at Madison Square Garden.

◆ Two songs associated with 1950s hit maker Bobby Day returned to the Top 20. They were 'Rockin' Robin', which hit by Michael Jackson, and Day's composition, 'Little Bitty Pretty One', which was now successful for Michael's group, the Jackson Five.

UK 1972
JULY-SEPT

▲ Wembley Stadium hosted its first pop concert and 45,000 50s fans turned out to watch Bill Haley, Chuck Berry (above), Little Richard, Jerry Lee Lewis and Bo Diddley (filmed as *The London Rock And Roll Show*).

◆ The successful album-oriented TV show, *The Old Grey Whistle Test*, kicked off - it helped launch many less commercial acts in the 1970s.

◆ Making their debuts were Wizzard, formed by ex-Move and Electric Light Orchestra front man Roy Wood, and 10cc, a collection of Manchester's finest, who had evolved from The Mindbenders and Hot Legs.

July 1972

This Mnth	Prev Mnth	Title	Artist	Label	Wks 20	(US Pos)	
1	-	Puppy Love	Donny Osmond	MGM	12	(3)	F
2	15	Rock & Roll Part 2	Gary Glitter	Bell	10	(7)	F
3	9	Take Me Bak 'Ome	Slade	Polydor	9	(97)	
4	-	Little Willie	Sweet	RCA	8	(3)	
5	-	Circles	New Seekers	Polydor	8	(87)	
6	-	Sylvia's Mother	Dr. Hook	CBS	8	(5)	F
7	-	I Can See Clearly Now	Johnny Nash	CBS	9	(1)	
8	-	An American Trilogy	Elvis Presley	RCA	5	(66)	
9	2	Vincent	Don McLean	UA	9	(12)	
10	8	Rockin' Robin	Michael Jackson	Tamla Motown	7	(2)	
11	-	Ooh-Wakka-Doo-Wakka-Day	Gilbert O'Sullivan	MAM	6		
12	-	Breaking Up Is Hard To Do	Partridge Family	Bell	9	(28)	
13	-	Join Together	Who	Track	6	(17)	
14	6	California Man	Move	Harvest	8		L
15	12	Mary Had A Little Lamb	Paul McCartney	Apple	7	(28)	
16	-	Seaside Shuffle	Terry Dactyl & The Dinosaurs	UK	8		F L
17	-	School's Out	Alice Cooper	Warner	9	(7)	F
18	-	Mad About You	Bruce Ruffin	Rhino	5		L
19	-	Walkin' In The Rain With The One I Love	Love Unlimited	Uni	4	(14)	F
20	-	Little Bit Of Love	Free	Island	5		

August 1972

This Mnth	Prev Mnth	Title	Artist	Label	Wks 20	(US Pos)	
1	17	School's Out	Alice Cooper	Warner	9	(7)	F
2	16	Seaside Shuffle	Terry Dactyl & The Dinosaurs	UK	8		F L
3	1	Puppy Love	Donny Osmond	MGM	12	(3)	F
4	-	Silver Machine	Hawkwind	UA	10		F L
5	12	Breaking Up Is Hard To Do	Partridge Family	Bell	9	(28)	
6	-	Popcorn	Hot Butter	Pye International	8	(9)	F L
7	6	Sylvia's Mother	Dr. Hook	CBS	8	(5)	F
8	2	Rock & Roll Part 2	Gary Glitter	Bell	10	(7)	F
9	7	I Can See Clearly Now	Johnny Nash	CBS	9	(1)	
10	-	You Wear It Well	Rod Stewart	Mercury	7	(13)	
11	-	All The Young Dudes	Mott The Hoople	CBS	6	(37)	F
12	5	Circles	New Seekers	Polydor	8	(87)	
13	-	It's Four In The Morning	Faron Young	Mercury	10	(92)	F L
14	-	10538 Overture	Electric Light Orchestra	Harvest	6		F
15	-	Run To Me	Bee Gees	Polydor	5	(16)	
16	-	Automatically Sunshine	Supremes	Tamla Motown	4	(37)	L
17	-	Layla	Derek & The Dominoes	Polydor	5	(10)	F L
18	-	Starman	David Bowie	RCA	6	(65)	
19	18	Mad About You	Bruce Ruffin	Rhino	5		L
20	-	The Loco-Motion	Little Eva	London American	5		L

September 1972

This Mnth	Prev Mnth	Title	Artist	Label	Wks 20	(US Pos)	
1	-	Mama Weer All Crazee Now	Slade	Polydor	7	(76)	
2	10	You Wear It Well	Rod Stewart	Mercury	7	(13)	
3	13	It's Four In The Morning	Faron Young	Mercury	10	(92)	F L
4	-	Sugar Me	Lynsey De Paul	MAM	6		F
5	-	Virginia Plain	Roxy Music	Island	6		F
6	-	Standing In The Road	Blackfoot Sue	Jam	6		F L
7	11	All The Young Dudes	Mott The Hoople	CBS	6	(37)	F
8	-	How Can I Be Sure	David Cassidy	Bell	8	(25)	
9	-	I Get The Sweetest Feeling	Jackie Wilson	MCA	6	(34)	
10	-	Children Of The Revolution	T. Rex	EMI	7		
11	-	Ain't No Sunshine	Michael Jackson	Tamla Motown	6		
12	4	Silver Machine	Hawkwind	UA	10		F L
13	17	Layla	Derek & The Dominoes	Polydor	5	(10)	F L
14	1	School's Out	Alice Cooper	Warner	9	(7)	F
15	-	Too Young	Donny Osmond	MGM	5	(13)	
16	-	Living In Harmony	Cliff Richard	Columbia	4		
17	20	The Loco-Motion	Little Eva	London American	5		L
18	6	Popcorn	Hot Butter	Pye International	8	(9)	F L
19	-	Come On Over To My Place	Drifters	Atlantic	6	(60)	
20	-	Wig Wam Bam	Sweet	RCA	7		

July 1972

This Mnth	Prev Mnth	Title	Artist	Label	Wks 20	(UK Pos)	
1	13	Lean On Me	Bill Withers	Sussex	10	(18)	G
2	-	Too Late To Turn Back Now	Cornelius Brothers & Sister Rose	UA	9		G L
3	-	Daddy Don't You Walk So Fast	Wayne Newton	Chelsea	10		G L
4	-	(If Loving You Is Wrong) I Don't Wanna Be Right	Luther Ingram	Koko	11		F L
5	7	Outa-Space	Billy Preston	A&M	8	(44)	F G
6	4	Song Sung Blue	Neil Diamond	Uni	9	(14)	G
7	-	Brandy (You're A Fine Girl)	Looking Glass	Epic	11		F G L
8	-	Rocket Man	Elton John	Uni	8	(2)	
9	-	Alone Again (Naturally)	Gilbert O'Sullivan	MAM	10	(3)	F G
10	-	How Do You Do?	Mouth & McNeal	Philips	8		F G L
11	-	Where Is The Love	Roberta Flack & Donny Hathaway	Atlantic	8	(29)	G
12	1	The Candy Man	Sammy Davis Jr.	MGM	9		G L
13	-	School's Out	Alice Cooper	Warner	7	(1)	F
14	-	Layla	Derek & The Dominoes	Atco	7	(4)	F L
15	11	Troglodyte (Cave Man)	Jimmy Castor Bunch	RCA	7		F G
16	-	Take It Easy	Eagles	Asylum	6		F
17	-	Too Young	Donny Osmond	MGM	5	(5)	
18	-	I Need You	America	Warner	5		
19	5	Nice To Be With You	Gallery	Sussex	7		F G L
20	-	Long Cool Woman (In A Black Dress)	Hollies	Epic	9	(32)	G

August 1972

This Mnth	Prev Mnth	Title	Artist	Label	Wks 20	(UK Pos)	
1	9	Alone Again (Naturally)	Gilbert O'Sullivan	MAM	10	(3)	F G
2	7	Brandy (You're A Fine Girl)	Looking Glass	Epic	11		F G L
3	4	(If Loving...) I Don't Wanna Be Right	Luther Ingram	Koko	11		F L
4	20	Long Cool Woman (In A Black Dress)	Hollies	Epic	9	(32)	G
5	3	Daddy Don't You Walk So Fast	Wayne Newton	Chelsea	10		G L
6	-	I'm Still In Love With You	Al Green	Hi	8	(35)	G
7	11	Where Is The Love	Roberta Flack/Donny Hathaway	Atlantic	8	(29)	G
8	-	Coconut	Nilsson	RCA	6	(42)	L
9	2	Too Late To Turn Back Now	Cornelius Brothers/Sister Rose	UA	9		G L
10	-	Goodbye To Love	Carpenters	A&M	5	(9)	
11	-	Hold You Head Up	Argent	Epic	6	(5)	F L
12	-	The Happiest Girl In The Whole U.S.A.	Donna Fargo	Dot	5		F G
13	13	School's Out	Alice Cooper	Warner	7	(1)	F
14	10	How Do You Do?	Mouth & McNeal	Philips	8		F G L
15	-	You Don't Mess Around With Jim	Jim Croce	ABC	5		F
16	14	Layla	Derek & The Dominoes	Atco	7	(4)	F L
17	1	Lean On Me	Bill Withers	Sussex	10	(18)	G
18	-	Motorcycle Mama	Sailcat	Elektra	5		F L
19	-	Baby Don't Get Hooked On Me	Mac Davis	Columbia	9	(29)	F G
20	-	Hold Her Tight	Osmonds	MGM	4		

September 1972

This Mnth	Prev Mnth	Title	Artist	Label	Wks 20	(UK Pos)	
1	19	Baby Don't Get Hooked On Me	Mac Davis	Columbia	9	(29)	F G
2	-	Black & White	Three Dog Night	Dunhill	6		G
3	-	Back Stabbers	O'Jays	Philly International	8	(14)	F G
4	-	Saturday In The Park	Chicago	Columbia	7		G
5	4	Long Cool Woman (In A Black Dress)	Hollies	Epic	9	(32)	G
6	-	Rock And Roll Part 2	Gary Glitter	Bell	5	(2)	F L
7	6	I'm Still In Love With You	Al Green	Hi	8	(35)	G
8	2	Brandy (You're A Fine Girl)	Looking Glass	Epic	11		F G L
9	-	Go All The Way	Raspberries	Capitol	8		F G
10	1	Alone Again (Naturally)	Gilbert O'Sullivan	MAM	10	(3)	F G
11	-	Ben	Michael Jackson	Motown	9	(7)	G
12	-	Honky Cat	Elton John	Uni	4	(31)	
13	-	Everybody Plays The Fool	Main Ingredient	RCA	8		F G
14	-	Power Of Love	Joe Simon	Spring	4		G
15	-	Guitar Man	Bread	Elektra	5	(16)	
16	15	You Don't Mess Around With Jim	Jim Croce	ABC	5		F
17	11	Hold You Head Up	Argent	Epic	6	(5)	F L
18	-	Use Me	Bill Withers	Sussex	8		G L
19	-	Play Me	Neil Diamond	Uni	6		
20	10	Goodbye To Love	Carpenters	A&M	5	(9)	

◆ Both the Pocono International Raceway Festival (Emerson, Lake & Palmer, Humble Pie, J. Geils Band, etc.), and the Bull Island Festival (Canned Heat, Black Oak Arkansas, Brownsville Station, etc.) attracted 200,000 fans. However, the first charity festival, *The Festival Of Hope*, (Jefferson Airplane, Stephen Stills, James Brown, etc.) lost money.

◆ Britain's Elton John scored the first of many US No. 1 albums with **Honky Chateau**, as one of the decade's top selling UK acts, Gary Glitter, had his only American hit, 'Rock And Roll Part 2'.

◆ New names on the chart included The Eagles, Jim Croce and Alice Cooper, while Derek & The Dominoes introduced the world to 'Layla' and veteran R&B group The O'Jays gave new label Philly International their first hit.

UK 1972 OCT-DEC

Compilation albums of 1950s hits held the top spot for 14 consecutive weeks, and re-issues of earlier hits continued to clog the charts, the latest coming from Americans Neil Sedaka, The Shangri-Las, Chris Montez and Roy C.

◆ With Osmond-mania at its height in the UK, nine-year-old Little Jimmy's minor US hit, 'Long Haired Lover From Liverpool', became the biggest British seller by any of the family.

◆ The Moody Blues' US tour was a resounding success. The group, who had a transatlantic hit with the five-year-old, 'Nights in White Satin', topped the album chart with **Seventh Sojourn.**

◆ American band The New York Dolls made an impressive if not highly publicized UK debut. Although not hitmakers themselves, the group greatly influenced late 1970s UK punk music.

October 1972

This Mnth	Prev Mnth	Title	Artist	Label	Wks 20	(US Pos)	
1	-	Mouldy Old Dough	Lieutenant Pigeon	Decca	11		F
2	8	How Can I Be Sure	David Cassidy	Bell	8	(25)	
3	-	You're A Lady	Peter Skellern	Decca	7	(50)	F
4	-	I Didn't Know I Loved You (Till I Saw You Rock 'n' Roll)	Gary Glitter	Bell	7	(35)	
5	20	Wig Wam Bam	Sweet	RCA	7		
6	-	Donna	10cc	UK	9		F
7	10	Children Of The Revolution	T. Rex	EMI	7		
8	-	Burning Love	Elvis Presley	RCA	6	(2)	
9	-	In A Broken Dream	Python Lee Jackson	Youngblood	7	(56)	F L
10	15	Too Young	Donny Osmond	MGM	5	(13)	
11	-	Big Six	Judge Dread	Big Shot	8		F
12	-	Elected	Alice Cooper	Warner	7	(26)	
13	-	John I'm Only Dancing	David Bowie	RCA	5		
14	-	There Are More Questions Than Answers	Johnny Nash	CBS	6		
15	-	Clair	Gilbert O'Sullivan	MAM	8	(2)	
16	19	Come On Over To My Place	Drifters	Atlantic	6	(60)	
17	3	It's Four In The Morning	Faron Young	Mercury	10	(92)	F L
18	1	Mama Weer All Crazee Now	Slade	Polydor	7	(76)	
19	-	Suzanne Beware Of The Devil	Dandy Livingstone	Horse	5		F L
20	-	Goodbye To Love/I Won't Last A Day Without You	Carpenters	A&M	6	(7)	

November 1972

This Mnth	Prev Mnth	Title	Artist	Label	Wks 20	(US Pos)	
1	15	Clair	Gilbert O'Sullivan	MAM	8	(2)	
2	1	Mouldy Old Dough	Lieutenant Pigeon	Decca	11		F
3	-	Leader Of The Pack	Shangri-Las	Kama Sutra	6		
4	-	Loop Di Love	Shag	UK	7		F L
5	-	My Ding-A-Ling	Chuck Berry	Chess	10	(1)	
6	6	Donna	10cc	UK	9		F
7	12	Elected	Alice Cooper	Warner	7	(26)	
8	9	In A Broken Dream	Python Lee Jackson	Youngblood	7	(56)	F L
9	20	Goodbye To Love/I Won't Last A...	Carpenters	A&M	6	(7)	
10	-	Crazy Horses	Osmonds	MGM	12	(14)	F
11	-	Why	Donny Osmond	MGM	9	(13)	
12	-	Crocodile Rock	Elton John	DJM	10	(1)	
13	-	Let's Dance	Chris Montez	London American	5		L
14	-	Hallelujah Freedom	Junior Campbell	Deram	5		F
15	-	I'm Stone In Love With You	Stylistics	Avco	5	(10)	
16	-	Here I Go Again	Archie Bell & The Drells	Atlantic	3		F
17	14	There Are More Questions Than...	Johnny Nash	CBS	6		
18	-	Burlesque	Family	Reprise	5		L
19	8	Burning Love	Elvis Presley	RCA	6	(2)	
20	3	You're A Lady	Peter Skellern	Decca	7	(50)	F

December 1972

This Mnth	Prev Mnth	Title	Artist	Label	Wks 20	(US Pos)	
1	5	My Ding-A-Ling	Chuck Berry	Chess	10	(1)	
2	10	Crazy Horses	Osmonds	MGM	12	(14)	F
3	-	Gudbuy T'Jane	Slade	Polydor	9	(68)	
4	11	Why	Donny Osmond	MGM	9	(13)	
5	-	Long Haired Lover From Liverpool	Little Jimmy Osmond	MGM	14	(38)	F
6	-	Solid Gold Easy Action	T. Rex	EMI	8		
7	12	Crocodile Rock	Elton John	DJM	10	(1)	
8	-	Ben	Michael Jackson	Tamla Motown	8	(1)	
9	-	Angel/What Made Milwaukee Famous	Rod Stewart	Mercury	5	(40)	
10	-	Happy Xmas (War Is Over)	John & Yoko/Plastic Ono Band	Apple	5		
11	-	Stay With Me	Blue Mink	Regal Zonophone	5		
12	-	Shotgun Wedding	Roy 'C'	UK	7		L
13	-	Lookin' Through The Windows	Jackson Five	Tamla Motown	6	(16)	
14	-	Rock Me Baby	David Cassidy	Bell	5	(38)	
15	-	Nights In White Satin	Moody Blues	Deram	6	(2)	
16	-	Lay Down	Strawbs	A&M	4		F
17	1	Clair	Gilbert O'Sullivan	MAM	8	(2)	
18	-	Help Me Make It Through The Night	Gladys Knight & The Pips	Tamla Motown	7	(33)	
19	15	I'm Stone In Love With You	Stylistics	Avco	5	(10)	
20	-	Little Drummer Boy	Royal Scots Dragoon Guards	RCA	4		L

October 1972

This Mnth	Prev Mnth	Title	Artist	Label	Wks 20	(UK Pos)	
1	18	Use Me	Bill Withers	Sussex	8		G L
2	-	Burning Love	Elvis Presley	RCA	9	(7)	G
3	11	Ben	Michael Jackson	Motown	9	(7)	G
4	-	My Ding-A-Ling	Chuck Berry	Chess	9	(1)	G L
5	13	Everybody Plays The Fool	Main Ingredient	RCA	8		F G
6	-	Nights In White Satin	Moody Blues	Deram	12	(19)	G
7	9	Go All The Way	Raspberries	Capitol	8		F G
8	-	Garden Party	Rick Nelson	Decca	8	(41)	G L
9	-	Popcorn	Hot Butter	Musicor	6	(5)	F L
10	-	Tight Rope	Leon Russell	Shelter	5		F
11	3	Back Stabbers	O'Jays	Philly International	8	(14)	F G
12	19	Play Me	Neil Diamond	Uni	6		
13	1	Baby Don't Get Hooked On Me	Mac Davis	Columbia	9	(29)	F G
14	-	Freddie's Dead	Curtis Mayfield	Curtom	7		F G
15	-	Why/Lonely Boy	Donny Osmond	MGM	4	(3)	
16	-	Goodtime Charlie's Got The Blues	Danny O'Keefe	Signpost	5		F L
17	-	You Wear It Well	Rod Stewart	Mercury	3	(1)	
18	-	Speak To The Sky	Rick Springfield	Capitol	5		F
19	-	I Can See Clearly Now	Johnny Nash	Epic	10	(5)	G
20	2	Black & White	Three Dog Night	Dunhill	6		G

November 1972

This Mnth	Prev Mnth	Title	Artist	Label	Wks 20	(UK Pos)	
1	19	I Can See Clearly Now	Johnny Nash	Epic	10	(5)	G
2	-	I'd Love You To Want Me	Lobo	Big Tree	7	(5)	G
3	6	Nights In White Satin	Moody Blues	Deram	12	(19)	G
4	-	I'll Be Around	Spinners	Atlantic	7		G
5	14	Freddie's Dead	Curtis Mayfield	Curtom	7		F G
6	-	I Am Woman	Helen Reddy	Capitol	11		G
7	-	Papa Was A Rollin' Stone	Temptations	Gordy	9	(14)	G
8	4	My Ding-A-Ling	Chuck Berry	Chess	9	(1)	G L
9	8	Garden Party	Rick Nelson	Decca	8	(41)	G L
10	-	If I Could Reach You	Fifth Dimension	Bell	6		L
11	-	Convention '72	Delegates	Mainstream	3		F L
12	-	Witchy Woman	Eagles	Asylum	5		
13	-	Summer Breeze	Seals & Crofts	Warner	6		F
14	2	Burning Love	Elvis Presley	RCA	9	(7)	G
15	-	Listen To The Music	Doobie Brothers	Warner	5	(29)	F
16	-	If You Don't Know Me By Now	Harold Melvin & The Blue Notes	Philly International	8	(9)	F G
17	-	You Ought To Be With Me	Al Green	Hi	8		G
18	16	Goodtime Charlie's Got The Blues	Danny O'Keefe	Signpost	5		F L
19	3	Ben	Michael Jackson	Motown	9	(7)	G
20	-	Ventura Highway	America	Warner	6	(43)	

December 1972

This Mnth	Prev Mnth	Title	Artist	Label	Wks 20	(UK Pos)	
1	6	I Am Woman	Helen Reddy	Capitol	11		G
2	-	Me And Mrs. Jones	Billy Paul	Philly International	11	(12)	F G L
3	17	You Ought To Be With Me	Al Green	Hi	8		G
4	-	It Never Rains In Southern California	Albert Hammond	Mums	8		F G L
5	7	Papa Was A Rollin' Stone	Temptations	Gordy	9	(14)	G
6	-	Clair	Gilbert O'Sullivan	MAM	10	(1)	G
7	16	If You Don't Know Me By Now	Harold Melvin & The Blue Notes	Philly International	8	(9)	F G
8	1	I Can See Clearly Now	Johnny Nash	Epic	10	(5)	G
9	-	Funny Face	Donna Fargo	Dot	9		G L
10	-	Rockin' Pneumonia & The Boogie Woogie Flu	Johnny Rivers	UA	10		G
11	20	Ventura Highway	America	Warner	6	(43)	
12	-	Something's Wrong With Me	Austin Roberts	Chelsea	7		F
13	-	I'm Stone In Love With You	Stylistics	Avco	5	(9)	G
14	-	You're So Vain	Carly Simon	Elektra	12	(3)	G
15	13	Summer Breeze	Seals & Crofts	Warner	6		F
16	-	Superfly	Curtis Mayfield	Curtom	8		G L
17	2	I'd Love You To Want Me	Lobo	Big Tree	7	(5)	G
18	-	Keeper Of The Castle	Four Tops	Dunhill	6	(18)	
19	-	Crazy Horses	Osmonds	MGM	4	(2)	
20	-	Your Mama Don't Dance	Loggins & Messina	Columbia	8		F G

◆ "The Woodstock of the West" festival, starring The Eagles, Bee Gees, Stevie Wonder and Sly & The Family Stone, attracted only 32,000 people to the 100,000 seater LA Coliseum.

◆ Chuck Berry scored his biggest hit with the double-entendre transatlantic No. 1, 'My Ding-A-Ling'. Coincidentally, in October, 50s favourites Chuck, Rick Nelson and Elvis simultaneously had their last Top 10 entries.

▲ Don Kirshner launched the TV series *In Concert*. Initial guests included Alice Cooper (above), The Allman Brothers, Blood, Sweat & Tears and Chuck Berry.

UK 1973 JAN-MAR

▲ Local glam rock greats, Sweet, Gary Glitter, T-Rex, David Bowie and Slade vied for the affection of British teeny boppers with American superstars The Osmonds and David Cassidy (above).

◆ Pink Floyd's album **Dark Side Of The Moon** entered the US chart, where it has remained for a record smashing 17 years (selling over 12 million copies)!

◆ Reluctant guitar hero Eric Clapton made his live comeback after two years with a performance at London's Rainbow Theatre. Pete Townshend organized the show which also featured Steve Winwood, Ron Wood and Jim Capaldi.

January 1973

This Mnth	Prev Mnth	Title	Artist	Label	Wks 20	(US Pos)	
1	5	Long Haired Lover From Liverpool	Little Jimmy Osmond	MGM	14	(38)	F
2	-	The Jean Genie	David Bowie	RCA	8	(71)	
3	-	Hi Hi Hi/C Moon	Wings	Apple	6	(10)	
4	6	Solid Gold Easy Action	T. Rex	EMI	8		
5	2	Crazy Horses	Osmonds	MGM	12	(14)	F
6	-	Ball Park Incident	Wizzard	Harvest	6		F
7	-	You're So Vain	Carly Simon	Elektra	8	(1)	F
8	-	Blockbuster	Sweet	RCA	10	(73)	
9	-	Big Seven	Judge Dread	Big Shot	7		
10	-	Always On My Mind	Elvis Presley	RCA	5		
11	3	Gudbuy T'Jane	Slade	Polydor	9	(68)	
12	12	Shotgun Wedding	Roy 'C'	UK	7		L
13	15	Nights In White Satin	Moody Blues	Deram	6	(2)	
14	10	Happy Xmas (War Is Over)	John & Yoko & The Plastic Ono Band	Apple	5		
15	1	My Ding-A-Ling	Chuck Berry	Chess	10	(1)	
16	18	Help Me Make It Through The Night	Gladys Knight & The Pips	Tamla Motown	7	(33)	
17	8	Ben	Michael Jackson	Tamla Motown	8	(1)	
18	-	Do You Wanna Touch Me (Oh Yeah)	Gary Glitter	Bell	7		
19	-	Wishing Well	Free	Island	5		
20	-	Can't Keep It In	Cat Stevens	Island	4		

February 1973

This Mnth	Prev Mnth	Title	Artist	Label	Wks 20	(US Pos)	
1	8	Blockbuster	Sweet	RCA	10	(73)	
2	18	Do You Wanna Touch Me (Oh Yeah)	Gary Glitter	Bell	7		
3	-	Part Of The Union	Strawbs	A&M	9		L
4	-	Daniel	Elton John	DJM	6	(2)	
5	7	You're So Vain	Carly Simon	Elektra	8	(1)	F
6	1	Long Haired Lover From Liverpool	Little Jimmy Osmond	MGM	14	(38)	F
7	-	Sylvia	Focus	Polydor	6	(89)	L
8	-	Roll Over Beethoven	Electric Light Orchestra	Harvest	5	(42)	
9	-	Paper Plane	Status Quo	Vertigo	5		
10	19	Wishing Well	Free	Island	5		
11	-	Whiskey In The Jar	Thin Lizzy	Decca	6		F
12	-	If You Don't Know Me By Now	Harold Melvin & The Blue Notes	CBS	4	(3)	F
13	2	The Jean Genie	David Bowie	RCA	8	(71)	
14	-	Superstition	Stevie Wonder	Tamla Motown	5	(1)	
15	-	Me And Mrs. Jones	Billy Paul	Epic	4	(1)	F L
16	-	Cindy Incidentally	Faces	Warner	7	(48)	
17	-	Baby I Love You	Dave Edmunds	Rockfield	6		
18	-	Lookin' Through The Eyes Of Love	Partridge Family	Bell	5	(39)	
19	6	Ball Park Incident	Wizzard	Harvest	6		F
20	20	Can't Keep It In	Cat Stevens	Island	4		

March 1973

This Mnth	Prev Mnth	Title	Artist	Label	Wks 20	(US Pos)	
1	-	Cum On Feel The Noize	Slade	Polydor	7	(98)	
2	-	Feel The Need In Me	Detroit Emeralds	Janus	7	(90)	F
3	-	20th Century Boy	T. Rex	EMI	6		
4	16	Cindy Incidentally	Faces	Warner	7	(48)	
5	-	The Twelfth Of Never	Donny Osmond	MGM	9	(8)	
6	-	Killing Me Softly With His Song	Roberta Flack	Atlantic	8	(1)	
7	-	Hello Hurray	Alice Cooper	Warner	8	(35)	
8	3	Part Of The Union	Strawbs	A&M	9		L
9	-	Power To All Our Friends	Cliff Richard	EMI	7		
10	1	Blockbuster	Sweet	RCA	10	(73)	
11	-	Gonna Make You An Offer You Can't Refuse	Jimmy Helms	Cube	5		F L
12	7	Sylvia	Focus	Polydor	6	(89)	L
13	-	Doctor My Eyes	Jackson Five	Tamla Motown	5		
14	17	Baby I Love You	Dave Edmunds	Rockfield	6		
15	-	Get Down	Gilbert O'Sullivan	MAM	8	(7)	
16	11	Whiskey In The Jar	Thin Lizzy	Decca	6		F
17	2	Do You Wanna Touch Me (Oh Yeah)	Gary Glitter	Bell	7		
18	18	Lookin' Through The Eyes Of Love	Partridge Family	Bell	5	(39)	
19	-	Never Never Never	Shirley Bassey	UA	8	(48)	L
20	-	Heart Of Stone	Kenny	RAK	6		F L

January 1973

This Mnth	Prev Mnth	Title	Artist	Label	Wks 20	(UK Pos)	
1	14	You're So Vain	Carly Simon	Elektra	12	(3)	G
2	-	Superstition	Stevie Wonder	Tamla	9	(11)	G
3	2	Me And Mrs. Jones	Billy Paul	Philly International	11	(12)	F G L
4	20	Your Mama Don't Dance	Loggins & Messina	Columbia	8		F G
5	6	Clair	Gilbert O'Sullivan	MAM	10	(1)	G
6	-	Crocodile Rock	Elton John	MCA	12	(5)	G
7	10	Rockin' Pneumonia & The Boogie...	Johnny Rivers	UA	10		G
8	16	Superfly	Curtis Mayfield	Curtom	8		G L
9	9	Funny Face	Donna Fargo	Dot	9		G L
10	-	Why Can't We Live Together	Timmy Thomas	Glades	8	(12)	F L
11	-	Oh Babe What Would You Say	Hurricane Smith	Capitol	8	(4)	F L
12	18	Keeper Of The Castle	Four Tops	Dunhill	6	(18)	
13	-	Don't Let Me Be Lonely Tonight	James Taylor	Warner	4		
14	-	Trouble Man	Marvin Gaye	Tamla	6		
15	4	It Never Rains In Southern California	Albert Hammond	Mums	8		F G L
16	-	Hi, Hi, Hi	Wings	Apple	5	(5)	
17	-	Living In The Past	Jethro Tull	Chrysalis	6	(3)	F
18	-	The World Is A Ghetto	War	UA	6		G
19	3	You Ought To Be With Me	Al Green	Hi	8		G
20	-	Do It Again	Steely Dan	ABC	7	(39)	F

February 1973

This Mnth	Prev Mnth	Title	Artist	Label	Wks 20	(UK Pos)	
1	6	Crocodile Rock	Elton John	MCA	12	(5)	G
2	1	You're So Vain	Carly Simon	Elektra	12	(3)	G
3	11	Oh Babe What Would You Say	Hurricane Smith	Capitol	8	(4)	F L
4	20	Do It Again	Steely Dan	ABC	7	(39)	F
5	10	Why Can't We Live Together	Timmy Thomas	Glades	8	(12)	F L
6	-	Dueling Banjos	Eric Weissberg & Steve Mandell	Warner	10	(17)	F G L
7	-	Could It Be I'm Falling In Love	Spinners	Atlantic	8	(11)	G
8	2	Superstition	Stevie Wonder	Tamla	9	(11)	G
9	-	Don't Expect Me To Be Your Friend	Lobo	Big Tree	7		L
10	-	Killing Me Softly With His Song	Roberta Flack	Atlantic	12	(6)	G
11	18	The World Is A Ghetto	War	UA	6		G
12	-	Rocky Mountain High	John Denver	RCA	7		
13	14	Trouble Man	Marvin Gaye	Tamla	6		
14	-	Dancing In The Moonlight	King Harvest	Perception	7		F L
15	4	Your Mama Don't Dance	Loggins & Messina	Columbia	8		F G
16	-	Last Song	Edward Bear	Capitol	9		F L
17	-	Love Train	O'Jays	Philly International	9	(9)	G
18	-	Daddy's Home	Jermaine Jackson	Motown	7		F
19	16	Hi, Hi, Hi	Wings	Apple	5	(5)	
20	3	Me And Mrs. Jones	Billy Paul	Philly International	11	(12)	F G L

March 1973

This Mnth	Prev Mnth	Title	Artist	Label	Wks 20	(UK Pos)	
1	10	Killing Me Softly With His Song	Roberta Flack	Atlantic	12	(6)	G
2	17	Love Train	O'Jays	Philly International	9	(9)	G
3	-	Also Sprach Zarathustra (2001)	Deodata	CTI	8	(7)	F L
4	16	Last Song	Edward Bear	Capitol	9		F L
5	6	Dueling Banjos	Eric Weissberg & Steve Mandell	Warner	10	(17)	F G L
6	-	The Cover Of 'Rolling Stone'	Dr. Hook	Columbia	7		G
7	7	Could It Be I'm Falling In Love	Spinners	Atlantic	8	(11)	G
8	-	Neither One Of Us (Wants To Be The First To Say Goodbye)	Gladys Knight & The Pips	Soul	9	(31)	
9	-	Danny's Song	Anne Murray	Capitol	9		
10	-	Break Up To Make Up	Stylistics	Avco	7	(34)	G
11	1	Crocodile Rock	Elton John	MCA	12	(5)	G
12	-	Ain't No Woman (Like The One I've Got)	Four Tops	Dunhill	9		G
13	18	Daddy's Home	Jermaine Jackson	Motown	7		F
14	12	Rocky Mountain High	John Denver	RCA	7		
15	-	I'm Just A Singer (In A Rock 'n' Roll Band)	Moody Blues	Threshold	4	(36)	
16	2	You're So Vain	Carly Simon	Elektra	12	(3)	G
17	-	Sing	Carpenters	A&M	9		G
18	-	Call Me (Come Back Home)	Al Green	Hi	6		G
19	9	Don't Expect Me To Be Your Friend	Lobo	Big Tree	7		L
20	-	The Night The Lights Went Out In Georgia	Vicki Lawrence	Bell	10		F G L

US
1973
JAN-MAR

◆ Columbia Records showcased Bruce Springsteen at the trendy Max's Kansas City club in New York to promote his debut LP, **Greetings From Asbury Park, N.J.** , which initially sold few copies.

◆ TV series *Midnight Special* was launched as a more MOR-slanted rival to the successful *In Concert*.

◆ Recently wed Carly Simon's transatlantic hit, 'You're So Vain', turned gold at the same time as husband James Taylor's album **One Man Dog.**

◆ A survey showed that underground radio was replacing Top 40 as the breeding ground for new acts and recent examples of this trend included Steely Dan and Loggins & Messina. Solid gold radio was also shown to be very popular, proving that many people still loved the "oldies".

UK 1973
APR-JUNE

◆ As John Lennon denied that The Beatles would re-unite, the group's compilation album **1967-1970** was replaced at the top of the US chart by **Red Rose Speedway** from Paul McCartney & Wings. This in turn was followed by George Harrison's **Living In The Material World**. For the record, Paul, who starred in the TV special *James Paul McCartney*, was enjoying his biggest US solo hit, 'My Love'.

▲ Fleetwood Mac's re-issued instrumental 'Albatross' peaked at No. 2, narrowly failing to become the first record to top the UK chart on two separate occasions.

April 1973

This Mnth	Prev Mnth	Title	Artist	Label	Wks 20	(US Pos)	
1	-	Tie A Yellow Ribbon Round The Old Oak Tree	Dawn	Bell	17	(1)	
2	15	Get Down	Gilbert O'Sullivan	MAM	8	(7)	
3	-	I'm A Clown/Some Kind Of A Summer	David Cassidy	Bell	8		
4	5	The Twelfth Of Never	Donny Osmond	MGM	9	(8)	
5	-	Tweedle Dee	Little Jimmy Osmond	MGM	7	(59)	
6	-	Hello Hello I'm Back Again	Gary Glitter	Bell	10		
7	9	Power To All Our Friends	Cliff Richard	EMI	7		
8	19	Never Never Never	Shirley Bassey	UA	8	(48)	L
9	-	Love Train	O'Jays	CBS	6	(1)	
10	-	Pyjamarama	Roxy Music	Island	6		
11	-	All Because Of You	Geordie	EMI	6		F
12	-	Drive-In Saturday	David Bowie	RCA	7		
13	-	Crazy	Mud	RAK	5		F
14	20	Heart Of Stone	Kenny	RAK	6		F L
15	-	My Love	Paul McCartney & Wings	Apple	6	(1)	
16	-	Amanda	Stuart Gillies	Philips	5		F L
17	6	Killing Me Softly With His Song	Roberta Flack	Atlantic	8	(1)	
18	2	Feel The Need In Me	Detroit Emeralds	Janus	7	(90)	F
19	-	Why Can't We Live Together	Timmy Thomas	Mojo	4	(3)	F L
20	1	Cum On Feel The Noize	Slade	Polydor	7	(98)	

May 1973

This Mnth	Prev Mnth	Title	Artist	Label	Wks 20	(US Pos)	
1	1	Tie A Yellow Ribbon Round The Old Oak Tree	Dawn	Bell	17	(1)	
2	-	Hell Raiser	Sweet	RCA	6		
3	-	See My Baby Jive	Wizzard	Harvest	10		
4	6	Hello Hello I'm Back Again	Gary Glitter	Bell	10		
5	12	Drive-In Saturday	David Bowie	RCA	7		
6	-	Giving It All Away	Roger Daltrey	Track	6	(83)	F
7	-	Brother Louie	Hot Chocolate	RAK	6		
8	-	And I Love You So	Perry Como	RCA	12	(29)	
9	15	My Love	Paul McCartney & Wings	Apple	6	(1)	
10	-	No More Mr. Nice Guy	Alice Cooper	Warner	4	(25)	
11	11	All Because Of You	Geordie	EMI	6		F
12	-	Also Sprach Zarathustra (2001)	Deodata	CTI	5	(2)	F L
13	-	Wonderful Dream	Ann-Marie David	Epic	4		F L
14	5	Tweedle Dee	Little Jimmy Osmond	MGM	7	(59)	
15	-	One And One Is One	Medicine Head	Polydor	7		F
16	2	Get Down	Gilbert O'Sullivan	MAM	8	(7)	
17	3	I'm A Clown/Some Kind Of A...	David Cassidy	Bell	8		
18	-	Big Eight	Judge Dread	Big Shot	5		
19	-	Can The Can	Suzi Quatro	RAK	7	(56)	F
20	-	Broken Down Angel	Nazareth	Mooncrest	5		F

June 1973

This Mnth	Prev Mnth	Title	Artist	Label	Wks 20	(US Pos)	
1	19	Can The Can	Suzi Quatro	RAK	7	(56)	F
2	-	Rubber Bullets	10cc	UK	9	(73)	
3	3	See My Baby Jive	Wizzard	Harvest	10		
4	15	One And One Is One	Medicine Head	Polydor	7		F
5	-	Albatross	Fleetwood Mac	CBS	8		
6	8	And I Love You So	Perry Como	RCA	12	(29)	
7	-	The Groover	T. Rex	EMI	5		
8	-	Stuck In The Middle With You	Stealer's Wheel	A&M	6	(6)	F L
9	1	Tie A Yellow Ribbon Round The..	Dawn	Bell	17	(1)	
10	-	Walking In The Rain	Partridge Family	Bell	5		L
11	-	You Are The Sunshine Of My Life	Stevie Wonder	Tamla Motown	5	(1)	
12	-	Welcome Home	Peters & Lee	Philips	15		F
13	-	Snoopy Vs. The Red Baron	Hotshots	Mooncrest	8		F L
14	-	Give Me Love (Give Me Peace On Earth)	George Harrison	Apple	6	(1)	
15	2	Hell Raiser	Sweet	RCA	6		
16	-	Walk On The Wild Side	Lou Reed	RCA	4	(16)	F L
17	-	Live And Let Die	Wings	Apple	7	(2)	
18	20	Broken Down Angel	Nazareth	Mooncrest	5		F
19	-	Skweeze Me Pleeze Me	Slade	Polydor	6		
20	12	Also Sprach Zarathustra (2001)	Deodata	CTI	5	(2)	F L

April 1973

This Mnth	Prev Mnth	Title	Artist	Label	Wks 20	(UK Pos)	
1	20	The Night The Lights Went Out In Georgia	Vicki Lawrence	Bell	10		F G L
2	-	Tie A Yellow Ribbon Round The Old Oak Tree	Dawn	Bell	14	(1)	G
3	17	Sing	Carpenters	A&M	9		G
4	8	Neither One Of Us (Wants To Be...)	Gladys Knight & The Pips	Soul	9	(31)	
5	-	The Cisco Kid	War	UA	7		G
6	12	Ain't No Woman (Like The One...)	Four Tops	Dunhill	9		G
7	-	Masterpiece	Temptations	Gordy	6		L
8	9	Danny's Song	Anne Murray	Capitol	9		
9	-	Little Willy	Sweet	Bell	9	(4)	F G
10	1	Killing Me Softly With His Song	Roberta Flack	Atlantic	12	(6)	G
11	10	Break Up To Make Up	Stylistics	Avco	7	(34)	G
12	-	The Twelfth Of Never	Donny Osmond	MGM	6	(1)	G
13	-	Stir It Up	Johnny Nash	Epic	5	(13)	L
14	-	You Are The Sunshine Of My Life	Stevie Wonder	Tamla	10	(7)	G
15	18	Call Me (Come Back Home)	Al Green	Hi	6		G
16	-	Stuck In The Middle With You	Stealer's Wheel	A&M	9	(8)	F L
17	3	Also Sprach Zarathustra (2001)	Deodata	CTI	8	(7)	F L
18	-	Drift Away	Dobie Gray	Decca	9		G L
19	2	Love Train	O'Jays	Philly International	9	(9)	G
20	-	Peaceful	Helen Reddy	Capitol	4		

May 1973

This	Prev	Title	Artist	Label	Wks 20	(UK Pos)	
1	2	Tie A Yellow Ribbon Round The...	Dawn	Bell	14	(1)	G
2	14	You Are The Sunshine Of My Life	Stevie Wonder	Tamla	10	(7)	G
3	9	Little Willy	Sweet	Bell	9	(4)	F G
4	-	Frankenstein	Edgar Winter Group	Epic	10	(18)	F G
5	18	Drift Away	Dobie Gray	Decca	9		G L
6	-	Daniel	Elton John	MCA	9	(4)	G
7	16	Stuck In The Middle With You	Stealer's Wheel	A&M	9	(8)	F L
8	1	The Night The Lights Went Out In...	Vicki Lawrence	Bell	10		F G L
9	-	My Love	Paul McCartney & Wings	Apple	10	(9)	G
10	5	The Cisco Kid	War	UA	7		G
11	-	Wildflower	Skylark	Capitol	9		F L
12	-	Reeling In The Years	Steely Dan	ABC	6		
13	-	Pillow Talk	Sylvia	Vibration	11	(14)	F G
14	12	The Twelfth Of Never	Donny Osmond	MGM	6	(1)	G
15	-	Hocus Pocus	Focus	Sire	7	(20)	F L
16	3	Sing	Carpenters	A&M	9		G
17	-	Daisy A Day	Jud Strunk	MGM	4		F L
18	-	Funky Worm	Ohio Players	Westbound	3		F G
19	7	Masterpiece	Temptations	Gordy	6		L
20	-	I'm Gonna Love You Just A Little More Baby	Barry White	20th Century	9	(23)	F G

June 1973

This	Prev	Title	Artist	Label	Wks 20	(UK Pos)	
1	9	My Love	Paul McCartney & Wings	Apple	10	(9)	G
2	13	Pillow Talk	Sylvia	Vibration	11	(14)	F G
3	20	I'm Gonna Love You Just A Little...	Barry White	20th Century	9	(23)	G
4	-	Playground In My Mind	Clint Holmes	Epic	10		F G L
5	6	Daniel	Elton John	MCA	9	(4)	G
6	4	Frankenstein	Edgar Winter Group	Epic	10	(18)	F G
7	-	Give Me Love (Give Me Peace On Earth)	George Harrison	Apple	9	(8)	G
8	-	Will It Go Round In Circles	Billy Preston	A&M	11		G
9	-	Right Place Wrong Time	Dr. John	Atco	8		F L
10	-	Kodachrome	Paul Simon	Columbia	8		
11	-	Long Train Running	Doobie Brothers	Warner	7		
12	1	Tie A Yellow Ribbon Round The...	Dawn	Bell	14	(1)	G
13	-	One Of A Kind (Love Affair)	Spinners	Atlantic	5		G
14	2	You Are The Sunshine Of My Life	Stevie Wonder	Tamla	10	(7)	G
15	15	Hocus Pocus	Focus	Sire	7	(20)	F L
16	-	Shambala	Three Dog Night	Dunhill	11		G
17	5	Drift Away	Dobie Gray	Decca	9		G L
18	-	Bad, Bad Leroy Brown	Jim Croce	ABC	12		G
19	11	Wildflower	Skylark	Capitol	9		F L
20	3	Little Willy	Sweet	Bell	9	(4)	F G

◆ Led Zeppelin set off on a US tour modestly labelled, "The biggest and most profitable rock & roll tour in the history of the United States" – which, at the time, it probably was.

◆ Attracting big audiences were Paul Simon's and the Electric Light Orchestra's first tours, Bread's last and Carole King's free concert in Central Park. Also drawing the crowds was a British Re-Invasion show featuring Herman's Hermits, Gerry & The Pacemakers, The Searchers and Wayne Fontana & The Mindbenders.

◆ Astoundingly, The Doobie Brothers, who were one of America's biggest selling acts of the 1970s, had to wait until 1993 to crack the UK Top 20 singles chart with a dance remix of their current US hit 'Long Train Running'.

UK
1973
JULY-SEPT

◆ 'Monster Mash' by Bobby 'Boris' Pickett & The Crypt Kickers, which had topped the US chart in 1962, not only returned to the Top 10 but also hit in re-issue-mad Britain for the first time.

◆ David Bowie and Jethro Tull (who topped the US LP chart with **A Passion Play**) announced that their touring days were over. The Everly Brothers split up and Ray Davis quit The Kinks. More permanent, however, were the dissolution of The Doors and Eno's departure from Roxy Music.

◆ Soon after Freddie Mercury's debut single 'I Can Hear Music' (as Larry Lurex) failed to click, his group Queen's first 45, 'Keep Yourself Alive' also fell by the wayside. Despite this disappointing chart start, they went on to become one of the biggest selling and most influential British acts of all time.

July 1973

This Mnth	Prev Mnth	Title	Artist	Label	Wks 20	(US Pos)	
1	12	Welcome Home	Peters & Lee	Philips	15		F
2	19	Skweeze Me Pleeze Me	Slade	Polydor	6		
3	-	Life On Mars	David Bowie	RCA	8		
4	-	Born To Be With You	Dave Edmunds	Rockfield	7		
5	13	Snoopy Vs. The Red Baron	Hotshots	Mooncrest	8		F L
6	-	Take Me To The Mardi Gras	Paul Simon	CBS	5		
7	2	Rubber Bullets	10cc	UK	9	(73)	
8	-	Saturday Night's Alright For Fighting	Elton John	DJM	5	(12)	
9	-	I'm The Leader Of The Gang (I Am)	Gary Glitter	Bell	8		
10	5	Albatross	Fleetwood Mac	CBS	8		
11	-	Going Home	Osmonds	MGM	6	(36)	
12	-	Alright Alright Alright	Mungo Jerry	Dawn	6		
13	-	Randy	Blue Mink	EMI	5		L
14	17	Live And Let Die	Wings	Apple	7	(2)	
15	-	Gaye	Clifford T. Ward	Charisma	5		F L
16	14	Give Me Love (Give Me Peace On Earth)	George Harrison	Apple	6	(1)	
17	-	Honaloochie Boogie	Mott The Hoople	CBS	3		
18	7	The Groover	T. Rex	EMI	5		
19	-	Can You Do It	Geordie	EMI	4		L
20	-	Step By Step	Joe Simon	Mojo	3	(37)	F L

August 1973

1	9	I'm The Leader Of The Gang (I Am)	Gary Glitter	Bell	8		
2	1	Welcome Home	Peters & Lee	Philips	15		F
3	-	Yesterday Once More	Carpenters	A&M	8	(2)	
4	-	48 Crash	Suzi Quatro	RAK	5		
5	12	Alright Alright Alright	Mungo Jerry	Dawn	6		
6	-	Spanish Eyes	Al Martino	Capitol	13		L
7	11	Going Home	Osmonds	MGM	6	(36)	
8	-	You Can Do Magic	Limmie & The Family Cookin'	Avco	7	(84)	F
9	3	Life On Mars	David Bowie	RCA	8		
10	-	Touch Me In The Morning	Diana Ross	Tamla Motown	6	(1)	
11	-	Ying Tong Song	Goons	Decca	4		L
12	-	Bad Bad Boy	Nazareth	Mooncrest	5		
13	-	(Dancing) On A Saturday Night	Barry Blue	Bell	9		F
14	-	Young Love	Donny Osmond	MGM	7	(25)	
15	-	Smarty Pants	First Choice	Bell	5	(56)	L
16	13	Randy	Blue Mink	EMI	5		L
17	15	Gaye	Clifford T. Ward	Charisma	5		F L
18	-	All Right Now	Free	Island	3		
19	-	Rising Sun	Medicine Head	Polydor	5		L
20	-	Summer (The First Time)	Bobby Goldsboro	UA	5	(21)	

September 1973

1	-	Angel Fingers	Wizzard	Harvest	8		
2	14	Young Love	Donny Osmond	MGM	7	(25)	
3	-	Rock On	David Essex	CBS	7	(5)	F
4	13	(Dancing) On A Saturday Night	Barry Blue	Bell	9		F
5	6	Spanish Eyes	Al Martino	Capitol	13		L
6	-	Angie	Rolling Stones	Rolling Stone	5	(1)	
7	8	You Can Do Magic	Limmie & The Family Cookin'	Avco	7	(84)	F
8	-	Oh No Not My Baby	Rod Stewart	Mercury	5	(59)	
9	-	Say, Has Anybody Seen My Sweet Gypsy Rose	Dawn	Bell	5	(3)	L
10	-	Like Sister And Brother	Drifters	Bell	6		
11	3	Yesterday Once More	Carpenters	A&M	8	(2)	
12	-	Ballroom Blitz	Sweet	RCA	6	(5)	
13	-	Pick Up The Pieces	Hudson-Ford	A&M	4		F
14	-	Monster Mash	Bobby 'Boris' Pickett & The Crypt Kickers	London American	6	(10)	F L
15	-	The Dean And I	10cc	UK	4		
16	20	Summer (The First Time)	Bobby Goldsboro	UA	5	(21)	
17	-	Eye Level	Simon Park Orchestra	Columbia	10		F G L
18	2	Welcome Home	Peters & Lee	Philips	15		F
19	-	For The Good Times	Perry Como	RCA	10		L
20	1	I'm The Leader Of The Gang (I Am)	Gary Glitter	Bell	8		

July 1973

This Mnth	Prev Mnth	Title	Artist	Label	Wks 20	(UK Pos)	
1	8	Will It Go Round In Circles	Billy Preston	A&M	11		G
2	18	Bad, Bad Leroy Brown	Jim Croce	ABC	12		G
3	10	Kodachrome	Paul Simon	Columbia	8		
4	16	Shambala	Three Dog Night	Dunhill	11		G
5	-	Yesterday Once More	Carpenters	A&M	9	(2)	G
6	7	Give Me Love (Give Me Peace On...)	George Harrison	Apple	9	(8)	G
7	-	Smoke On The Water	Deep Purple	Warner	9	(21)	G L
8	4	Playground In My Mind	Clint Holmes	Epic	10		F G L
9	-	Boogie Woogie Bugle Boy	Bette Midler	Atlantic	6		
10	-	Diamond Girl	Seals & Crofts	Warner	7		
11	-	Natural High	Bloodstone	London	6	(40)	F G L
12	9	Right Place Wrong Time	Dr. John	Atco	8		F L
13	1	My Love	Paul McCartney & Wings	Apple	10	(9)	G
14	11	Long Train Running	Doobie Brothers	Warner	7		
15	-	Money	Pink Floyd	Harvest	5		F
16	3	I'm Gonna Love You Just A Little...	Barry White	20th Century	9	(23)	F G
17	-	Monster Mash	Bobby 'Boris' Pickett & The Crypt Kickers	Parrott	7	(3)	F L
18	-	Touch Me In The Morning	Diana Ross	Motown	12	(9)	
19	-	Behind Closed Doors	Charlie Rich	Epic	4	(16)	F G
20	-	The Morning After (Song From The Poseidon Adventure)	Maureen McGovern	20th Century	9		F G

August 1973

This Mnth	Prev Mnth	Title	Artist	Label	Wks 20	(UK Pos)	
1	-	Live And Let Die	Paul McCartney & Wings	Apple	8	(9)	G
2	20	The Morning After (Song From...)	Maureen McGovern	20th Century	9		F G
3	-	Brother Louie	Stories	Kama Sutra	11		F G L
4	18	Touch Me In The Morning	Diana Ross	Motown	12	(9)	
5	2	Bad, Bad Leroy Brown	Jim Croce	ABC	12		G
6	-	Let's Get It On	Marvin Gaye	Tamla	15	(31)	G
7	-	Get Down	Gilbert O'Sullivan	MAM	8	(1)	G L
8	-	Uneasy Rider	Charlie Daniels Band	Kama Sutra	5		F
9	7	Smoke On The Water	Deep Purple	Warner	9	(21)	G L
10	-	Feelin' Stronger Every Day	Chicago	Columbia	9		
11	17	Monster Mash	Bobby 'Boris' Pickett & Crypt...	Parrott	7	(3)	F L
12	-	I Believe In You (You Believe In Me)	Johnnie Taylor	Stax	8		G
13	5	Yesterday Once More	Carpenters	A&M	9	(2)	G
14	-	Delta Dawn	Helen Reddy	Capitol	10		G
15	10	Diamond Girl	Seals & Crofts	Warner	7		
16	-	Say, Has Anybody Seen My Sweet Gypsy Rose	Dawn Featuring Tony Orlando	Bell	9	(12)	G
17	4	Shambala	Three Dog Night	Dunhill	11		G
18	-	Here I Am (Come And Take Me)	Al Green	Hi	8		G
19	-	If You Want Me To Stay	Sly & The Family Stone	Epic	8		G L
20	1	Will It Go Round In Circles	Billy Preston	A&M	11		G

September 1973

This Mnth	Prev Mnth	Title	Artist	Label	Wks 20	(UK Pos)	
1	6	Let's Get It On	Marvin Gaye	Tamla	15	(31)	G
2	14	Delta Dawn	Helen Reddy	Capitol	10		G
3	16	Say, Has Anybody Seen My Sweet...	Dawn Featuring Tony Orlando	Bell	9	(12)	G
4	3	Brother Louie	Stories	Kama Sutra	11		F G L
5	-	We're An American Band	Grand Funk	Capitol	10		F G
6	-	Loves Me Like A Rock	Paul Simon	Columbia	10	(39)	G
7	4	Touch Me In The Morning	Diana Ross	Motown	12	(9)	
8	1	Live And Let Die	Paul McCartney & Wings	Apple	8	(9)	G
9	-	Half-Breed	Cher	MCA	11		G
10	-	Higher Ground	Stevie Wonder	Tamla	9	(29)	
11	-	Gypsy Man	War	UA	6		
12	-	That Lady	Isley Brothers	T-Neck	10	(14)	G
13	18	Here I Am (Come And Take Me)	Al Green	Hi	8		G
14	-	Saturday Night's Alright For Fighting	Elton John	MCA	6	(7)	
15	-	My Maria	B.W. Stevenson	RCA	7		F L
16	2	The Morning After (Song From...)	Maureen McGovern	20th Century	9		F G
17	7	Get Down	Gilbert O'Sullivan	MAM	8	(1)	G L
18	19	If You Want Me To Stay	Sly & The Family Stone	Epic	8		G L
19	10	Feelin' Stronger Every Day	Chicago	Columbia	9		
20	-	Ramblin' Man	Allman Brothers Band	Capricorn	9		F L

▲ The best attended Rock Festival of the era was the Summer Jam Festival at Watkins Glen (New York), where 600,000 saw the Grateful Dead (above), The Band and The Allman Brothers.

◆ Jim Croce, whose course was set for superstardom, died in a plane crash. Ex-Byrds Clarence White and Gram Parsons (whose role in rock was acknowledged posthumously) also met untimely ends.

◆ Among the American acts faring better on the other side of the Atlantic were The Drifters, Suzi Quatro, First Choice, Perry Como and teen idols Donny Osmond, The Osmonds and David Cassidy.

UK 1973 OCT-DEC

◆ It was announced that David Bowie had sold over eight million units in Britain in two years, making him the biggest seller since The Beatles.

▲ Hottest producer/ songwriters in Britain in 1973 were Nicky Chinn & Mike Chapman, who were responsible for hits from Sweet, (above), American rocker Suzi Quatro and new teen idols Mud.

◆ John Rostill of The Shadows was electro- cuted in his studio. His death came days after his song 'Let Me Be There' gave Olivia Newton-John her first American pop hit and days before her record became the first UK recording to crack the US country Top 10.

October 1973

This Mnth	Prev Mnth	Title	Artist	Label	Wks 20	(US Pos)	
1	17	Eye Level	Simon Park Orchestra	Columbia	10		F G L
2	-	My Friend Stan	Slade	Polydor	6		
3	-	Nutbush City Limits	Ike & Tina Turner	UA	7	(22)	L
4	12	Ballroom Blitz	Sweet	RCA	6	(5)	
5	14	Monster Mash	Bobby 'Boris' Pickett & The Crypt Kickers	London American	6	(10)	F L
6	-	The Laughing Gnome	David Bowie	Deram	6		
7	19	For The Good Times	Perry Como	RCA	10		L
8	-	Daydreamer/The Puppy Song	David Cassidy	Bell	8		
9	-	Caroline	Status Quo	Vertigo	8		
10	-	Goodbye Yellow Brick Road	Elton John	DJM	7	(2)	
11	1	Angel Fingers	Wizzard	Harvest	8		
12	-	Joybringer	Manfred Mann's Earth Band	Vertigo	5		L
13	-	A Hard Rain's Gonna Fall	Bryan Ferry	Island	5		F
14	-	Sorrow	David Bowie	RCA	8		
15	-	Ghetto Child	Detroit Spinners	Atlantic	6	(29)	
16	8	Oh No Not My Baby	Rod Stewart	Mercury	5	(59)	
17	5	Spanish Eyes	Al Martino	Capitol	13		L
18	-	All The Way From Memphis	Mott The Hoople	CBS	4		
19	-	Showdown	Electric Light Orchestra	Harvest	5	(53)	
20	-	That Lady (Pt. 1)	Isley Brothers	Epic	2	(6)	

November 1973

This Mnth	Prev Mnth	Title	Artist	Label	Wks 20	(US Pos)	
1	-	Let Me In	Osmonds	MGM	9	(36)	
2	14	Sorrow	David Bowie	RCA	8		
3	8	Daydreamer/The Puppy Song	David Cassidy	Bell	8		
4	-	Top Of The World	Carpenters	A&M	8	(1)	
5	-	Dyna-Mite	Mud	RAK	7		
6	1	Eye Level	Simon Park Orchestra	Columbia	10		F G L
7	-	I Love You Love Me Love	Gary Glitter	Bell	12		G
8	15	Ghetto Child	Detroit Spinners	Atlantic	6	(29)	
9	7	For The Good Times	Perry Como	RCA	10		L
10	-	Photograph	Ringo Starr	Apple	5	(1)	
11	-	This Flight Tonight	Nazareth	Mooncrest	5		
12	9	Caroline	Status Quo	Vertigo	8		
13	-	When I Fall In Love	Donny Osmond	MGM	9	(14)	
14	10	Goodbye Yellow Brick Road	Elton John	DJM	7	(2)	
15	-	Do You Wanna Dance	Barry Blue	Bell	6		
16	19	Showdown	Electric Light Orchestra	Harvest	5	(53)	
17	-	Deck Of Cards	Max Bygraves	Pye	5		L
18	-	Paper Roses	Marie Osmond	MGM	11	(5)	F L
19	2	My Friend Stan	Slade	Polydor	6		
20	-	Won't Somebody Dance With Me	Lynsey De Paul	MAM	5		

December 1973

This Mnth	Prev Mnth	Title	Artist	Label	Wks 20	(US Pos)	
1	7	I Love You Love Me Love	Gary Glitter	Bell	12		G
2	-	My Coo-Ca-Choo	Alvin Stardust	Magnet	12		F
3	-	You Won't Find Another Fool Like Me	New Seekers	Polydor	12		
4	18	Paper Roses	Marie Osmond	MGM	11	(5)	F L
5	-	Lamplight	David Essex	CBS	11	(71)	
6	-	Merry Xmas Everybody	Slade	Polydor	7		G
7	-	Why Oh Why Oh Why	Gilbert O'Sullivan	MAM	10		
8	-	Roll Away The Stone	Mott The Hoople	CBS	9		
9	-	I Wish It Could Be Christmas Everyday	Wizzard	Harvest	7		
10	-	Street Life	Roxy Music	Island	8		
11	13	When I Fall In Love	Donny Osmond	MGM	9	(14)	
12	5	Dyna-Mite	Mud	RAK	7		
13	1	Let Me In	Osmonds	MGM	9	(36)	
14	-	Truck On (Tyke)	T. Rex	EMI	7		
15	-	The Show Must Go On	Leo Sayer	Chrysalis	9		F
16	15	Do You Wanna Dance	Barry Blue	Bell	6		
17	-	Helen Wheels	Paul McCartney & Wings	Apple	9	(10)	
18	-	Forever	Roy Wood	Harvest	9		
19	-	Loving And Free/Amoureuse	Kiki Dee	Rocket	5		F
20	10	Photograph	Ringo Starr	Apple	5	(1)	

This Mnth	Prev Mnth	Title	Artist	Label	Wks 20	(UK Pos)	
1	9	Half-Breed	Cher	MCA	11		G
2	-	Angie	Rolling Stones	Rolling Stone	10	(5)	G
3	20	Ramblin' Man	Allman Brothers Band	Capricorn	9		F L
4	1	Let's Get It On	Marvin Gaye	Tamla	15	(31)	G
5	-	Midnight Train To Georgia	Gladys Knight & The Pips	Buddah	12	(10)	G
6	10	Higher Ground	Stevie Wonder	Tamla	9	(29)	
7	12	That Lady	Isley Brothers	T-Neck	10	(14)	G
8	-	Keep On Truckin' (Pt 1)	Eddie Kendricks	Tamla	13	(18)	F G
9	6	Loves Me Like A Rock	Paul Simon	Columbia	10	(39)	G
10	5	We're An American Band	Grand Funk	Capitol	10		F G
11	-	Yes We Can Can	Pointer Sisters	Blue Thumb	7		F
12	-	Heartbeat - It's A Lovebeat	DeFranco Family	20th Century	9		F G
13	-	Paper Roses	Marie Osmond	MGM	9	(2)	F G L
14	-	All I Know	Garfunkel	Columbia	7		F
15	15	My Maria	B.W. Stevenson	RCA	7		F L
16	2	Delta Dawn	Helen Reddy	Capitol	10		G
17	-	Knockin' On Heaven's Door	Bob Dylan	Columbia	6	(14)	L
18	-	Free Ride	Edgar Winter Group	Epic	4		L
19	-	Basketball Jones Feat. Tyrone Shoelaces	Cheech & Chong	Ode	4		F
20	-	China Grove	Doobie Brothers	Warner	4		

This Mnth	Prev Mnth	Title	Artist	Label	Wks 20	(UK Pos)	
1	8	Keep On Truckin' (Pt 1)	Eddie Kendricks	Tamla	13	(18)	F G
2	5	Midnight Train To Georgia	Gladys Knight & The Pips	Buddah	12	(10)	G
3	12	Heartbeat - It's A Lovebeat	DeFranco Family	20th Century	9		F G
4	-	Photograph	Ringo Starr	Apple	9	(8)	G
5	2	Angie	Rolling Stones	Rolling Stone	10	(5)	G
6	13	Paper Roses	Marie Osmond	MGM	9	(2)	F G L
7	-	Space Race	Billy Preston	A&M	9		G
8	-	Top Of The World	Carpenters	A&M	11	(5)	G
9	1	Half-Breed	Cher	MCA	11		G
10	-	Just You 'n' Me	Chicago	Columbia	9		G
11	14	All I Know	Garfunkel	Columbia	7		F
12	-	I Got A Name	Jim Croce	ABC	6		
13	3	Ramblin' Man	Allman Brothers Band	Capricorn	9		F L
14	-	You're A Special Part Of Me	Marvin Gaye & Diana Ross	Motown	5		
15	-	The Love I Lost (Part 1)	Harold Melvin & The Blue Notes	Philly International	7	(21)	G
16	-	Goodbye Yellow Brick Road	Elton John	MCA	9	(6)	G
17	17	Knockin' On Heaven's Door	Bob Dylan	Columbia	6	(14)	L
18	4	Let's Get It On	Marvin Gaye	Tamla	15	(31)	G
19	-	Why Me	Kris Kristofferson	Monument	3		F G L
20	-	The Most Beautiful Girl	Charlie Rich	Epic	11	(2)	G

This Mnth	Prev Mnth	Title	Artist	Label	Wks 20	(UK Pos)	
1	16	Goodbye Yellow Brick Road	Elton John	MCA	9	(6)	G
2	20	The Most Beautiful Girl	Charlie Rich	Epic	11	(2)	G
3	8	Top Of The World	Carpenters	A&M	11	(5)	G
4	10	Just You 'n' Me	Chicago	Columbia	9		G
5	-	Hello It's Me	Todd Rundgren	Bearsville	8		L
6	-	Leave Me Alone (Ruby Red Dress)	Helen Reddy	Capitol	8		G
7	-	Time In A Bottle	Jim Croce	ABC	11		G
8	4	Photograph	Ringo Starr	Apple	9	(8)	G
9	-	The Joker	Steve Miller Band	Capitol	11		F G
10	-	If You're Ready Come Go With Me	Staple Singers	Stax	6	(34)	G
11	7	Space Race	Billy Preston	A&M	9		G
12	15	The Love I Lost (Part 1)	Harold Melvin & The Blue Notes	Philly International	7	(21)	G
13	1	Keep On Truckin' (Pt 1)	Eddie Kendricks	Tamla	13	(18)	F G
14	-	Never, Never Gonna Give Ya Up	Barry White	20th Century	11	(14)	G
15	2	Midnight Train To Georgia	Gladys Knight & The Pips	Buddah	12	(10)	G
16	-	Show And Tell	Al Wilson	Rocky Road	11		F G L
17	-	Smokin' In The Boys Room	Brownsville Station	Big Tree	8	(27)	F G L
18	3	Heartbeat - It's A Lovebeat	DeFranco Family	20th Century	9		F G
19	-	Living For The City	Stevie Wonder	Tamla	9	(15)	
20	-	Rockin' Roll Baby	Stylistics	Avco	4	(6)	

US 1973 OCT-DEC

◆ In 1973, rock continued to fragment and progressive FM radio no longer seemed to be breaking new acts. *Rolling Stone* added politics and art to the magazine's musical content and wondered if, "rock had run out of new things to say."

◆ In the year when 75% of new albums failed to break even, Virgin released its successful debut LP, **Tubular Bells** by Mike Oldfield. It was a year when soul was supreme, southern rock was on the rise and female vocalists accounted for a record nine US No. 1s.

◆ When The Isley Brothers originally released their hit 'That Lady' under the title 'Who's That Lady' it went nowhere. Similarly, when Charlie Rich's hit 'The Most Beautiful Girl In The World' was first released as simply 'Hey Mister', it was also a non-starter.

UK 1974 JAN-MAR

▲ Newcomers who were creating interest included: Queen, Leo Sayer (above), Alvin Stardust, Bad Company, The Wombles, and a new-look Bay City Rollers.

◆ The main winners in the *NME* poll were David Bowie (Top Male), Diana Ross (Top Female) and Yes (Top Group). Incidentally, Yes, who quickly sold out their Madison Square Garden shows, scored their first UK chart topper with the LP **Tales From Topographic Oceans**.

◆ Soon after Elvis and Priscilla ended their marriage, Cher filed for divorce from Sonny and John Lennon and Yoko Ono temporarily separated.

January 1974

This Mnth	Prev Mnth	Title	Artist	Label	Wks 20	(US Pos)	
1	3	You Won't Find Another Fool Like Me	New Seekers	Polydor	12		
2	15	The Show Must Go On	Leo Sayer	Chrysalis	9		F
3	6	Merry Xmas Everybody	Slade	Polydor	7		G
4	2	My Coo-Ca-Choo	Alvin Stardust	Magnet	12		
5	-	Dance With The Devil	Cozy Powell	RAK	10	(49)	F
6	1	I Love You Love Me Love	Gary Glitter	Bell	12		G
7	18	Forever	Roy Wood	Harvest	9		
8	4	Paper Roses	Marie Osmond	MGM	11	(5)	F L
9	-	Radar Love	Golden Earring	Track	6	(13)	F L
10	9	I Wish It Could Be Christmas Everyday	Wizzard	Harvest	7		
11	-	Pool Hall Richard/I Wish It Would Rain	Faces	Warner	7		
12	-	Love On A Mountain Top	Robert Knight	Monument	10		F
13	5	Lamplight	David Essex	CBS	11	(71)	
14	-	Teenage Rampage	Sweet	RCA	6		
15	-	Tiger Feet	Mud	RAK	8		
16	8	Roll Away The Stone	Mott The Hoople	CBS	9		
17	-	Solitaire	Andy Williams	CBS	8		L
18	10	Street Life	Roxy Music	Island	8		
19	7	Why Oh Why Oh Why	Gilbert O'Sullivan	MAM	10		
20	14	Truck On (Tyke)	T. Rex	EMI	7		

February 1974

This Mnth	Prev Mnth	Title	Artist	Label	Wks 20	(US Pos)	
1	15	Tiger Feet	Mud	RAK	8		
2	14	Teenage Rampage	Sweet	RCA	6		
3	17	Solitaire	Andy Williams	CBS	8		L
4	-	The Man Who Sold The World	Lulu	Polydor	6		
5	5	Dance With The Devil	Cozy Powell	RAK	10	(49)	F
6	-	Devil Gate Drive	Suzi Quatro	RAK	7		
7	-	Rockin' Roll Baby	Stylistics	Avco	6	(14)	
8	-	All Of My Life	Diana Ross	Tamla Motown	6		
9	2	The Show Must Go On	Leo Sayer	Chrysalis	9		F
10	-	The Wombling Song	Wombles	CBS	7		F
11	1	You Won't Find Another Fool Like Me	New Seekers	Polydor	12		
12	-	How Come	Ronnie Lane	GM	4		F L
13	9	Radar Love	Golden Earring	Track	6	(13)	F L
14	7	Forever	Roy Wood	Harvest	9		
15	12	Love On A Mountain Top	Robert Knight	Monument	10		F
16	-	Jealous Mind	Alvin Stardust	Magnet	6		
17	4	My Coo-Ca-Choo	Alvin Stardust	Magnet	12		F
18	-	Teenage Lament '74	Alice Cooper	Warner	3	(48)	L
19	-	Teenage Dream	Marc Bolan & T. Rex	EMI	3		
20	-	Rebel Rebel	David Bowie	RCA	5	(64)	

March 1974

This Mnth	Prev Mnth	Title	Artist	Label	Wks 20	(US Pos)	
1	-	The Air That I Breathe	Hollies	Polydor	7	(6)	
2	-	Billy, Don't Be A Hero	Paper Lace	Bus Stop	9	(96)	F
3	16	Jealous Mind	Alvin Stardust	Magnet	6		
4	-	You're Sixteen	Ringo Starr	Apple	7	(1)	L
5	-	The Most Beautiful Girl	Charlie Rich	CBS	9	(1)	F
6	6	Devil Gate Drive	Suzi Quatro	RAK	7		
7	-	Remember (Sha-La-La)	Bay City Rollers	Bell	6		
8	-	Jet	Paul McCartney & Wings	Apple	6	(7)	
9	10	The Wombling Song	Wombles	CBS	7		F
10	-	It's You	Freddie Starr	Tiffany	6		F L
11	20	Rebel Rebel	David Bowie	RCA	5	(64)	
12	-	I Get A Little Sentimental Over You	New Seekers	Polydor	6		L
13	-	Candle In The Wind	Elton John	DJM	6		
14	-	Ma He's Making Eyes At Me	Lena Zavaroni	Philips	6	(91)	F L
15	-	Emma	Hot Chocolate	RAK	7	(8)	
16	-	School Love	Barry Blue	Bell	5		
17	1	Tiger Feet	Mud	Rak	8		
18	-	Seasons In The Sun	Terry Jacks	Bell	9	(1)	F
19	-	Never, Never Gonna Give Ya Up	Barry White	Pye International	4	(7)	F
20	-	Love's Theme	Love Unlimited Orchestra	Pye	6	(1)	F L

170

January 1974

This Mnth	Prev Mnth	Title	Artist	Label	Wks 20	(UK Pos)	
1	9	The Joker	Steve Miller Band	Capitol	11		F G
2	16	Show And Tell	Al Wilson	Rocky Road	11		F G L
3	7	Time In A Bottle	Jim Croce	ABC	11		G
4	17	Smokin' In The Boys Room	Brownsville Station	Big Tree	8	(27)	F G L
5	-	I've Got To Use My Imagination	Gladys Knight & The Pips	Buddah	9		G
6	-	You're Sixteen	Ringo Starr	Apple	10	(4)	G
7	-	The Way We Were	Barbra Streisand	Columbia	12	(31)	G
8	19	Living For The City	Stevie Wonder	Tamla	9	(15)	
9	14	Never, Never Gonna Give Ya Up	Barry White	20th Century	11	(14)	G
10	-	Let Me Be There	Olivia Newton-John	MCA	10		F G
11	-	Love's Theme	Love Unlimited Orchestra	20th Century	11	(10)	F G L
12	-	Helen Wheels	Paul McCartney & Wings	Apple	7	(12)	
13	2	The Most Beautiful Girl	Charlie Rich	Epic	11	(2)	G
14	6	Leave Me Alone (Ruby Red Dress)	Helen Reddy	Capitol	8		G
15	-	Until You Come Back To Me (That's What I'm Gonna Do)	Aretha Franklin	Atlantic	12	(26)	G
16	-	When I Fall In Love	Donny Osmond	MGM	4	(4)	L
17	-	Me And Baby Brother	War	UA	5	(21)	
18	1	Goodbye Yellow Brick Road	Elton John	MCA	9	(6)	G
19	-	Americans	Byron MacGregor	Westbound	6		F G L
20	3	Top Of The World	Carpenters	A&M	11	(5)	G

February 1974

This Mnth	Prev Mnth	Title	Artist	Label	Wks 20	(UK Pos)	
1	7	The Way We Were	Barbra Streisand	Columbia	12	(31)	G
2	11	Love's Theme	Love Unlimited Orchestra	20th Century	11	(10)	F G L
3	6	You're Sixteen	Ringo Starr	Apple	10	(4)	G
4	15	Until You Come Back To Me (That's What I'm Gonna Do)	Aretha Franklin	Atlantic	12	(26)	G
5	-	Spiders & Snakes	Jim Stafford	MGM	9	(14)	F
6	19	Americans	Byron MacGregor	Westbound	6		F G L
7	10	Let Me Be There	Olivia Newton-John	MCA	10		F G
8	-	Jungle Boogie	Kool & The Gang	De-Lite	11		F G
9	2	Show And Tell	Al Wilson	Rocky Road	11		F G L
10	-	Rock On	David Essex	Columbia	10	(3)	F G L
11	-	Boogie Down	Eddie Kendricks	Tamla	10	(39)	G
12	5	I've Got To Use My Imagination	Gladys Knight & The Pips	Buddah	9		G
13	-	Seasons In The Sun	Terry Jacks	Bell	10	(1)	F G L
14	-	Put Your Hands Together	O'Jays	Philly International	6		
15	1	The Joker	Steve Miller Band	Capitol	11	(1)	F G
16	4	Smokin' In The Boys Room	Brownsville Station	Big Tree	8	(27)	F G L
17	-	I Love	Tom T. Hall	Mercury	5		F L
18	-	Doo Doo Doo Doo Doo (Heartbreaker)	Rolling Stones	Rolling Stone	3		
19	8	Living For The City	Stevie Wonder	Tamla	9	(15)	
20	3	Time In A Bottle	Jim Croce	ABC	11		G

March 1974

This Mnth	Prev Mnth	Title	Artist	Label	Wks 20	(UK Pos)	
1	13	Seasons In The Sun	Terry Jacks	Bell	10	(1)	F G L
2	11	Boogie Down	Eddie Kendricks	Tamla	10	(39)	G
3	-	Dark Lady	Cher	MCA	8	(36)	G
4	-	Sunshine On My Shoulders	John Denver	RCA	10		G
5	-	Mockingbird	Carly Simon & James Taylor	Elektra	8	(34)	G
6	8	Jungle Boogie	Kool & The Gang	De-Lite	11		F G
7	1	The Way We Were	Barbra Streisand	Columbia	12	(31)	G
8	10	Rock On	David Essex	Columbia	10	(3)	F G L
9	-	Jet	Paul McCartney & Wings	Apple	7	(7)	
10	-	Eres Tu (Touch The Wind)	Mocedades	Tara	7		F L
11	5	Spiders & Snakes	Jim Stafford	MGM	9	(14)	F
12	-	Bennie And The Jets	Elton John	MCA	11	(37)	G
13	-	Hooked On A Feeling	Blue Swede	EMI	9		F G
14	-	Come And Get Your Love	Redbone	Epic	10		F G L
15	2	Love's Theme	Love Unlimited Orchestra	20th Century	11	(10)	F G L
16	4	Until You Come Back To Me (That's What I'm Gonna Do)	Aretha Franklin	Atlantic	12	(26)	G
17	-	The Lord's Prayer	Sister Janet Mead	A&M	7		F G L
18	-	Trying To Hold On To My Woman	Lamont Dozier	ABC	4		F L
19	14	Put Your Hands Together	O'Jays	Philly International	6		
20	-	A Love Song	Anne Murray	Capitol	4		

◆ Many new faces appeared as the new year started: Jefferson Starship evolved from Jefferson Airplane, debut LPs from Billy Joel and Kiss were on release, and Olivia Newton-John, Kool & The Gang and The Steve Miller Band (whose 'The Joker' was a UK chart topper in 1990), made their Top 20 debuts.

◆ Ringo Starr became the third member of The Beatles to clock up two US No. 1s as a solo artist. Surprisingly the only ex-Beatle yet to reach the summit was John Lennon.

◆ Dick Clark launched the American Music Awards. Twenty years later, the AMA are still running second only to the Grammys.

◆ In January, the late Jim Croce had the top two albums and a No. 1 single, 'Time In A Bottle'. No other rock performer (Elvis included) has equalled this posthumous achievement.

◆ Rick Wakeman quit Yes and his solo album **Journey To The Centre Of The Earth** reached the transatlantic Top 3. Also stretching their wings were Bill Wyman, who became the first Rolling Stone to release a solo album, and The Who's Roger Daltrey, who staged his first solo concert.

◆ *NME* writers selected **Sergeant Pepper** (The Beatles), **Blonde On Blonde** (Bob Dylan) and **Pet Sounds** (Beach Boys) as the three greatest albums ever recorded.

◆ Bill Haley & The Comets' original 1954 recording of 'Rock Around The Clock' returned to the chart; it was the fifth separate visit to the UK Top 20 for the single which had sold over 20 million copies worldwide.

◆ As Blue Swede put Sweden on the US musical map, Abba gave Scandinavia its biggest British hit, with their Eurovision Song Contest winner, 'Waterloo'.

April 1974

This Mnth	Prev Mnth	Title	Artist	Label	Wks 20	(US Pos)	
1	18	Seasons In The Sun	Terry Jacks	Bell	9	(1)	F
2	-	Angel Face	Glitter Band	Bell	7		F
3	-	Everyday	Slade	Polydor	5		
4	-	Remember Me This Way	Gary Glitter	Bell	6		
5	-	You Are Everything	Diana Ross	Tamla Motown	7		
6	2	Billy, Don't Be A Hero	Paper Lace	Bus Stop	9	(96)	F
7	15	Emma	Hot Chocolate	RAK	7	(8)	
8	-	The Cat Crept In	Mud	RAK	6		
9	-	Doctor's Orders	Sunny	CBS	5		F L
10	-	Seven Seas Of Rhye	Queen	EMI	6		F
11	-	Remember You're A Womble	Wombles	CBS	9		
12	5	The Most Beautiful Girl	Charlie Rich	CBS	9	(1)	F
13	12	I Get A Little Sentimental Over You	New Seekers	Polydor	6		L
14	-	I'm Gonna Knock On Your Door	Little Jimmy Osmond	MGM	4		L
15	-	Waterloo	Abba	Epic	7	(6)	F
16	-	Homely Girl	Chi-Lites	Brunswick	6	(54)	
17	-	Rock Around The Clock	Bill Haley & His Comets	MCA	5		L
18	-	A Walkin' Miracle	Limmie & The Family Cookin'	Avco	5		L
19	-	Long Live Love	Olivia Newton-John	Pye International	4		
20	-	Jambalaya	Carpenters	A&M	5		

May 1974

This Mnth	Prev Mnth	Title	Artist	Label	Wks 20	(US Pos)	
1	15	Waterloo	Abba	Epic	7	(6)	F
2	-	Don't Stay Away Too Long	Peters & Lee	Philips	8		
3	-	Shang-A-Lang	Bay City Rollers	Bell	6		
4	-	Sugar Baby Love	Rubettes	Polydor	7	(37)	F
5	11	Remember You're A Womble	Wombles	CBS	9		
6	-	Rock 'n' Roll Winter	Wizzard	Warner	4		
7	16	Homely Girl	Chi-Lites	Brunswick	6	(54)	
8	-	The Night Chicago Died	Paper Lace	Bus Stop	6	(1)	
9	18	A Walkin' Miracle	Limmie & The Family Cookin'	Avco	5		L
10	-	Red Dress	Alvin Stardust	Magnet	5		
11	8	The Cat Crept In	Mud	RAK	6		
12	1	Seasons In The Sun	Terry Jacks	Bell	9	(1)	F
13	-	This Town Ain't Big Enough For Both Of Us	Sparks	Island	6		F
14	-	He's Misstra Know It All	Stevie Wonder	Tamla Motown	5		
15	-	I Can't Stop	Osmonds	MCA	5	(96)	
16	5	You Are Everything	Diana Ross	Tamla Motown	7		
17	9	Doctor's Orders	Sunny	CBS	5		F L
18	-	Long Legged Woman Dressed In Black	Mungo Jerry	Dawn	5		L
19	-	Spiders & Snakes	Jim Stafford	MGM	4	(3)	F
20	-	Break The Rules	Status Quo	Vertigo	4		

June 1974

This Mnth	Prev Mnth	Title	Artist	Label	Wks 20	(US Pos)	
1	-	Hey Rock And Roll	Showaddywaddy	Bell	8		F
2	-	There's A Ghost In My House	R. Dean Taylor	Tamla Motown	7		L
3	-	The Streak	Ray Stevens	Janus	7	(1)	
4	13	This Town Ain't Big Enough For Both Of Us	Sparks	Island	6		F
5	4	Sugar Baby Love	Rubettes	Polydor	7	(37)	F
6	-	Judy Teen	Cockney Rebel	EMI	6		F
7	-	Always Yours	Gary Glitter	Bell	6		
8	-	Jarrow Song	Alan Price	Warner	5		L
9	8	The Night Chicago Died	Paper Lace	Bus Stop	6	(1)	
10	-	A Touch Too Much	Arrows	RAK	5		F L
11	-	I See A Star	Mouth & McNeal	Decca	5		F L
12	-	Go (Before You Break My Heart)	Gigliola Cinquetti	CBS	4		
13	-	She	Charles Aznavour	Barclay	8		F L
14	-	If I Didn't Care	David Cassidy	Bell	4		
15	2	Don't Stay Away Too Long	Peters & Lee	Philips	8		
16	-	Liverpool Lou	Scaffold	Warner	4		L
17	-	I'd Love You To Want Me	Lobo	UK	6	(2)	L
18	-	One Man Band	Leo Sayer	Chrysalis	5	(96)	
19	-	The In Crowd	Bryan Ferry	Island	4		
20	3	Shang-A-Lang	Bay City Rollers	Bell	6		

US 1974 APR-JUNE

April 1974

This Mnth	Prev Mnth	Title	Artist	Label	Wks 20	(UK Pos)	
1	12	Bennie And The Jets	Elton John	MCA	11	(37)	G
2	13	Hooked On A Feeling	Blue Swede	EMI	9		F G
3	-	TSOP (The Sound Of Philadelphia)	MFSB Featuring The Three Degrees	Philly International	10	(22)	F G L
4	14	Come And Get Your Love	Redbone	Epic	10		F G L
5	-	Best Thing That Ever Happened To Me	Gladys Knight & The Pips	Buddah	9	(7)	G
6	4	Sunshine On My Shoulders	John Denver	RCA	10		G
7	-	Oh My My	Ringo Starr	Apple	7		
8	17	The Lord's Prayer	Sister Janet Mead	A&M	7		F G L
9	1	Seasons In The Sun	Terry Jacks	Bell	10	(1)	F G L
10	-	Lookin' For A Love	Bobby Womack	UA	6		F G L
11	-	The Loco-Motion	Grand Funk	Capitol	10		G
12	-	I'll Have To Say I Love You In A Song	Jim Croce	ABC	5		L
13	-	A Very Special Love Song	Charlie Rich	Epic	4		
14	5	Mockingbird	Carly Simon & James Taylor	Elektra	8	(34)	G
15	-	Dancing Machine	Jackson Five	Motown	13		G
16	-	Just Don't Want To Be Lonely	Main Ingredient	RCA	7	(27)	G L
17	3	Dark Lady	Cher	MCA	8	(36)	G
18	9	Jet	Paul McCartney & Wings	Apple	7	(7)	
19	-	Tubular Bells	Mike Oldfield	Virgin	6	(31)	F L
20	-	The Show Must Go On	Three Dog Night	Dunhill	9		G

May 1974

This Mnth	Prev Mnth	Title	Artist	Label	Wks 20	(UK Pos)	
1	-	The Streak	Ray Stevens	Barnaby	11	(1)	G
2	15	Dancing Machine	Jackson Five	Motown	13		G
3	11	The Loco-Motion	Grand Funk	Capitol	10		G
4	-	The Entertainer	Marvin Hamlisch	MCA	9	(25)	F G L
5	20	The Show Must Go On	Three Dog Night	Dunhill	9		G
6	1	Bennie And The Jets	Elton John	MCA	11	(37)	G
7	-	(I've Been) Searchin' So Long	Chicago	Columbia	7		
8	3	TSOP (The Sound Of Philadelphia)	MFSB Feat The Three Degrees	Philly International	10	(22)	F G L
9	-	Midnight At The Oasis	Maria Muldaur	Reprise	8	(21)	F
10	-	You Make Me Feel Brand New	Stylistics	Avco	11	(2)	G
11	-	Band On The Run	Paul McCartney & Wings	Apple	10	(3)	G
12	19	Tubular Bells	Mike Oldfield	Virgin	6	(31)	F L
13	5	Best Thing That Ever Happened To Me	Gladys Knight & The Pips	Buddah	9	(7)	G
14	-	I Won't Last A Day Without You	Carpenters	A&M	6	(32)	
15	2	Hooked On A Feeling	Blue Swede	EMI	9		F G
16	-	Help Me	Joni Mitchell	Asylum	6		F L
17	16	Just Don't Want To Be Lonely	Main Ingredient	RCA	7	(27)	G L
18	-	Oh Very Young	Cat Stevens	A&M	6		
19	7	Oh My My	Ringo Starr	Apple	7		
20	4	Come And Get Your Love	Redbone	Epic	10		F G L

June 1974

This Mnth	Prev Mnth	Title	Artist	Label	Wks 20	(UK Pos)	
1	10	You Make Me Feel Brand New	Stylistics	Avco	11	(2)	G
2	-	Billy, Don't Be A Hero	Bo Donaldson & The Heywoods	ABC	9		F G L
3	-	Sundown	Gordon Lightfoot	Reprise	10	(33)	G
4	11	Band On The Run	Paul McCartney & Wings	Apple	10	(3)	G
5	1	The Streak	Ray Stevens	Barnaby	11	(1)	G
6	2	Dancing Machine	Jackson Five	Motown	13		G
7	-	Be Thankful For What You Got	William DeVaughn	Roxbury	7		F G L
8	4	The Entertainer	Marvin Hamlisch	MCA	9	(25)	F G L
9	9	Midnight At The Oasis	Maria Muldaur	Reprise	8	(21)	F
10	-	If You Love Me (Let Me Know)	Olivia Newton-John	MCA	8		G
11	-	For The Love Of Money	O'Jays	Philly International	6		G
12	-	Hollywood Swinging	Kool & The Gang	De-Lite	6		G
13	16	Help Me	Joni Mitchell	Asylum	6		F L
14	-	My Girl Bill	Jim Stafford	MGM	4	(20)	
15	-	Rock The Boat	Hues Corporation	RCA	7	(6)	F G
16	18	Oh Very Young	Cat Stevens	A&M	6		
17	3	The Loco-Motion	Grand Funk	Capitol	10		G
18	-	Rock Your Baby	George McCrae	TK	7	(1)	F G L
19	-	You Won't See Me	Anne Murray	Capitol	7		
20	5	The Show Must Go On	Three Dog Night	Dunhill	9		G

▲ The California Jam Festival was seen by 200,000, and was taped for TV. Among the headliners were The Eagles (above), Emerson, Lake & Palmer, Black Sabbath and Deep Purple.

◆ Grand Funk Railroad scored their biggest hit with a revival of 'The Loco-Motion' and Three Dog Night collected their last Top 10 entry with a cover of Leo Sayer's 'The Show Must Go On'. Although both acts were enormously successful in their homeland, they had little UK success.

◆ While The Who were filming *Tommy* they heard that the 80,000 tickets for their Madison Square Garden gig had sold out in just eight hours.

173

UK
1974
JULY-SEPT

◆ American oldies on the UK chart included Gary Puckett's 'Young Girl', 'Baby Love' by The Supremes and Jimmy Ruffin's 'What Becomes Of The Broken Hearted'.

◆ The Moody Blues opened the world's first quadrophonic (a system with four separate soundtracks as compared to stereo's two) recording studio in West London. One of the first projects recorded there was **Blue Jays,** a transatlantic Top 20 album by Moody members Justin Hayward & John Lodge.

◆ Mama Cass, of The Mamas & The Papas, was found dead in Nilsson's London apartment. Four years later, The Who's extrovert drummer Keith Moon was to die in the same Park Street flat.

◆ Elton John re-signed with MCA Records. The five album deal netted him a record $8 million.

July 1974

This Mnth	Prev Mnth	Title	Artist	Label	Wks 20	(US Pos)	
1	13	She	Charles Aznavour	Barclay	8		F L
2	-	Kissin' In The Back Row Of The Movies	Drifters	Bell	8		
3	-	Bangin' Man	Slade	Polydor	5		
4	-	Rock Your Baby	George McCrae	Jayboy	9	(1)	F
5	17	I'd Love You To Want Me	Lobo	UK	6	(2)	L
6	-	Young Girl	Gary Puckett & The Union Gap	CBS	6		L
7	-	Band On The Run	Paul McCartney & Wings	Apple	6	(1)	
8	7	Always Yours	Gary Glitter	Bell	6		
9	-	Banana Rock	Wombles	CBS	5		
10	-	Wall Street Shuffle	10cc	UK	5		
11	1	Hey Rock And Roll	Showaddywaddy	Bell	8		F
12	18	One Man Band	Leo Sayer	Chrysalis	5	(96)	
13	-	Born With A Smile On My Face	Stephanie De Sykes	Bradley's	6		F
14	-	The Six Teens	Sweet	RCA	5		
15	-	If You Go Away	Terry Jacks	Bell	4	(68)	L
16	3	The Streak	Ray Stevens	Janus	7	(1)	
17	-	When Will I See You Again	Three Degrees	Philly International	10	(2)	
18	-	Guilty	Pearls	Bell	4		F L
19	-	Beach Baby	First Class	UK	4	(4)	F L
20	-	Going Down The Road	Roy Wood	Harvest	3		

August 1974

This	Prev	Title	Artist	Label	Wks	(US Pos)	
1	17	When Will I See You Again	Three Degrees	Philly International	10	(2)	
2	-	You Make Me Feel Brand New	Stylistics	Avco	9	(2)	
3	4	Rock Your Baby	George McCrae	Jayboy	9	(1)	F
4	-	Summerlove Sensation	Bay City Rollers	Bell	7		
5	13	Born With A Smile On My Face	Stephanie De Sykes	Bradley's	6		F
6	-	Rocket	Mud	RAK	5		
7	-	Rock The Boat	Hues Corporation	RCA	5	(1)	F L
8	-	What Becomes Of The Brokenhearted	Jimmy Ruffin	Tamla Motown	8		
9	-	Amateur Hour	Sparks	Island	5		
10	7	Band On The Run	Paul McCartney & Wings	Apple	6	(1)	
11	-	I'm Leaving It (All) Up To You	Donny & Marie Osmond	MGM	8	(4)	F
12	-	I Shot The Sheriff	Eric Clapton	RSO	4	(1)	F
13	-	It's Only Rock 'n Roll (But I Like It)	Rolling Stones	Rolling Stone	4	(16)	
14	-	Tonight	Rubettes	Polydor	5		
15	2	Kissin' In The Back Row Of The...	Drifters	Bell	8		
16	-	Love Me For A Reason	Osmonds	MGM	7	(10)	
17	-	Mr. Soft	Cockney Rebel	EMI	5		
18	6	Young Girl	Gary Puckett & The Union Gap	CBS	6		L
19	-	Honey Honey	Sweet Dreams	Bradley's	6	(68)	F L
20	-	Just For You	Glitter Band	Bell	4		

September 1974

		Title	Artist	Label			
1	-	Kung Fu Fighting	Carl Douglas	Pye	8	(1)	F L
2	16	Love Me For A Reason	Osmonds	MGM	7	(10)	
3	-	Annie's Song	John Denver	RCA	9	(1)	F L
4	-	Y Viva Espana	Sylvia	Sonet	8		L
5	11	I'm Leaving It (All) Up To You	Donny & Marie Osmond	MGM	8	(4)	F
6	-	Hang On In There Baby	Johnny Bristol	MGM	7	(8)	F L
7	-	You You You	Alvin Stardust	Magnet	6		
8	1	When Will I See You Again	Three Degrees	Philly International	10	(2)	
9	8	What Becomes Of The Brokenhearted	Jimmy Ruffin	Tamla Motown	8		
10	-	Queen Of Clubs	KC & The Sunshine Band	Jayboy	6	(66)	F
11	-	Na Na Na	Cozy Powell	RAK	6		
12	-	Can't Get Enough Of Your Love, Babe	Barry White	Pye International	6	(1)	
13	19	Honey Honey	Sweet Dreams	Bradley's	6	(68)	F L
14	2	You Make Me Feel Brand New	Stylistics	Avco	9	(2)	
15	17	Mr. Soft	Cockney Rebel	EMI	5		
16	-	The Black Eyed Boys	Paper Lace	Bus Stop	4	(41)	
17	-	Baby Love	Diana Ross & The Supremes	Tamla Motown	3		L
18	-	Rock 'n' Roll Lady	Showaddywaddy	Bell	4		
19	-	Rock Me Gently	Andy Kim	Capitol	5	(1)	F L
20	-	Long Tall Glasses	Leo Sayer	Chrysalis	5	(9)	

July 1974

This Mnth	Prev Mnth	Title	Artist	Label	Wks 20	(UK Pos)	
1	18	Rock Your Baby	George McCrae	TK	7	(1)	F G L
2	-	Annie's Song	John Denver	RCA	8	(1)	G
3	15	Rock The Boat	Hues Corporation	RCA	7	(6)	F G
4	-	Rock And Roll Heaven	Righteous Brothers	Haven	7		
5	-	On And On	Gladys Knight & The Pips	Buddah	7		G
6	-	Don't Let The Sun Go Down On Me	Elton John	MCA	6	(16)	G
7	-	The Air That I Breathe	Hollies	Epic	7	(2)	G L
8	-	Rikki Don't Lose That Number	Steely Dan	ABC	7	(58)	
9	3	Sundown	Gordon Lightfoot	Reprise	10	(33)	G
10	2	Billy, Don't Be A Hero	Bo Donaldson & The Heywoods	ABC	9		F G L
11	19	You Won't See Me	Anne Murray	Capitol	7		
12	10	If You Love Me (Let Me Know)	Olivia Newton-John	MCA	8		G
13	-	Sideshow	Blue Magic	Atco	10		F G L
14	-	One Hell Of A Woman	Mac Davis	Columbia	6		
15	-	Feel Like Makin' Love	Roberta Flack	Atlantic	8	(34)	G
16	-	Radar Love	Golden Earring	Track	5	(7)	F
17	12	Hollywood Swinging	Kool & The Gang	De-Lite	6		G
18	1	You Make Me Feel Brand New	Stylistics	Avco	11	(2)	G
19	-	Please Come To Boston	Dave Loggins	Epic	7		F L
20	-	Waterloo	Abba	Atlantic	7	(1)	F

August 1974

This Mnth	Prev Mnth	Title	Artist	Label	Wks 20	(UK Pos)	
1	-	The Night Chicago Died	Paper Lace	Mercury	8	(3)	F G L
2	15	Feel Like Makin' Love	Roberta Flack	Atlantic	8	(34)	G
3	-	(You're) Having My Baby	Paul Anka & Odia Coates	UA	8	(6)	G
4	-	Tell Me Something Good	Rufus	ABC	7		F G
5	-	Wildwood Weed	Jim Stafford	MGM	7		L
6	19	Please Come To Boston	Dave Loggins	Epic	7		F L
7	20	Waterloo	Abba	Atlantic	7	(1)	F
8	13	Sideshow	Blue Magic	Atco	10		F G L
9	-	I Shot The Sheriff	Eric Clapton	RSO	7	(9)	G
10	-	Call On Me	Chicago	Columbia	5		
11	-	I'm Leaving It (All) Up To You	Donny & Marie Osmond	MGM	7	(2)	F G
12	2	Annie's Song	John Denver	RCA	8	(1)	G
13	6	Don't Let The Sun Go Down On Me	Elton John	MCA	6	(16)	G
14	-	Keep On Smilin'	Wet Willie	Capricorn	5		F L
15	-	Rock Me Gently	Andy Kim	Capitol	9	(2)	G L
16	-	You And Me Against The World	Helen Reddy	Capitol	6		
17	8	Rikki Don't Lose That Number	Steely Dan	ABC	7	(58)	
18	-	Takin' Care Of Business	Bachman-Turner Overdrive	Mercury	5		F
19	4	Rock And Roll Heaven	Righteous Brothers	Haven	7		
20	-	Shinin' On	Grand Funk	Capitol	4		

September 1974

This Mnth	Prev Mnth	Title	Artist	Label	Wks 20	(UK Pos)	
1	15	Rock Me Gently	Andy Kim	Capitol	9	(2)	G L
2	-	Nothing From Nothing	Billy Preston	A&M	10		G
3	9	I Shot The Sheriff	Eric Clapton	RSO	7	(9)	G
4	3	(You're) Having My Baby	Paul Anka & Odia Coates	UA	8	(6)	G
5	-	Can't Get Enough Of Your Love, Babe	Barry White	20th Century	6	(8)	G
6	-	Then Came You	Dionne Warwick	Warner	11	(29)	G
7	-	I Honestly Love You	Olivia Newton-John	MCA	8	(22)	G
8	-	Clap For The Wolfman	Guess Who	RCA	7		L
9	-	You Haven't Done Nothin	Stevie Wonder	Tamla	12	(30)	G
10	11	I'm Leaving It (All) Up To You	Donny & Marie Osmond	MGM	7	(2)	F G
11	-	Hang On In There Baby	Johnny Bristol	MGM	7	(3)	F L
12	4	Tell Me Something Good	Rufus	ABC	7		F G
13	-	Beach Baby	First Class	UK	6	(13)	F L
14	-	Another Saturday Night	Cat Stevens	A&M	5	(19)	L
15	16	You And Me Against The World	Helen Reddy	Capitol	6		
16	-	Sweet Home Alabama	Lynyrd Skynyrd	MCA	9		F
17	1	The Night Chicago Died	Paper Lace	Mercury	8	(3)	F G L
18	-	Who Do You Think You Are	Bo Donaldson & The Heywoods	ABC	3		F L
19	-	It's Only Rock 'n' Roll (But I Like It)	Rolling Stones	Rolling Stone	3	(10)	
20	-	Earache My Eye - Feat. Alice Bowie	Cheech & Chong	Ode	4		L

US 1974
JULY-SEPT

◆ Bob Marley first came to the attention of US rock fans when Eric Clapton's recording of his 'I Shot The Sheriff' bulleted to the top as did its parent LP, **461 Ocean Boulevard**.

◆ Dance hits from George McCrae, The Hues Corporation, Barry White, Johnny Bristol and KC & The Sunshine Band laid the foundations for the forthcoming world-wide disco craze. For the record, Bristol also penned The Osmonds transatlantic Top 10 hit, 'Love Me For A Reason'.

▲ Surprisingly, British-born, Australian-raised Olivia Newton-John was voted No. 1 female country singer (tied with Dolly Parton) in the *Billboard* Awards.

UK 1974 OCT-DEC

◆ British soul singers were making their mark. In the UK teenage Manchester group Sweet Sensation topped the chart with their debut 'Sad Sweet Dreamer' and in the USA Carl Douglas repeated his UK success by reaching No. 1 with 'Kung Fu Fighting'.

▲ The Drifters, who started as a trend-setting R&B act in 1953, were now resident in Britain and scored their third successive UK-written Top 10 hit, 'Down On The Beach Tonight'. Another American R&B group who would soon follow in their footsteps were female Philadelphian trio The Three Degrees (above).

October 1974

This Mnth	Prev Mnth	Title	Artist	Label	Wks 20	(US Pos)	
1	-	Sad Sweet Dreamer	Sweet Sensation	Pye	7	(14)	F
2	3	Annie's Song	John Denver	RCA	9	(1)	F L
3	-	Gee Baby	Peter Shelley	Magnet	6	(81)	F
4	19	Rock Me Gently	Andy Kim	Capitol	5	(1)	F L
5	-	Everything I Own	Ken Boothe	Trojan	9		F
6	20	Long Tall Glasses	Leo Sayer	Chrysalis	5	(9)	
7	1	Kung Fu Fighting	Carl Douglas	Pye	8	(1)	F L
8	6	Hang On In There Baby	Johnny Bristol	MGM	7	(8)	F L
9	-	Far Far Away	Slade	Polydor	5		
10	-	I Get A Kick Out Of You	Gary Shearston	Charisma	5		F L
11	-	Farewell/Bring It On Home To Me	Rod Stewart	Mercury	4		
12	-	Reggae Tune	Andy Fairweather-Low	A&M	4		F
13	-	(You're) Having My Baby	Paul Anka & Odia Coates	UA	6	(1)	L
14	-	All Of Me Loves All Of You	Bay City Rollers	Bell	6		
15	7	You You You	Alvin Stardust	Magnet	6		
16	12	Can't Get Enough Of Your Love...	Barry White	Pye International	6	(1)	
17	-	I Can't Leave You Alone	George McCrae	Jayboy	5	(50)	
18	-	Knock On Wood	David Bowie	RCA	4		
19	10	Queen Of Clubs	KC & The Sunshine Band	Jayboy	6	(66)	F
20	-	Gonna Make You A Star	David Essex	CBS	9		

November 1974

This Mnth	Prev Mnth	Title	Artist	Label	Wks 20	(US Pos)	
1	20	Gonna Make You A Star	David Essex	CBS	9		
2	-	Killer Queen	Queen	EMI	6	(12)	
3	5	Everything I Own	Ken Boothe	Trojan	9		F
4	-	(Hey There) Lonely Girl	Eddie Holman	ABC	7		F L
5	14	All Of Me Loves All Of You	Bay City Rollers	Bell	6		
6	-	You're The First, The Last, My Everything	Barry White	20th Century	9	(2)	
7	9	Far Far Away	Slade	Polydor	5		
8	-	Down On The Beach Tonight	Drifters	Bell	5		
9	-	Let's Put It All Together	Stylistics	Avco	5	(18)	
10	-	Let's Get Together Again	Glitter Band	Bell	5		
11	-	Pepper Box	Peppers	Spark	5		F L
12	13	(You're) Having My Baby	Paul Anka & Odia Coates	UA	6	(1)	L
13	-	Juke Box Jive	Rubettes	Polydor	9		
14	17	I Can't Leave You Alone	George McCrae	Jayboy	5	(50)	
15	-	The Wild One	Suzi Quatro	RAK	5		
16	-	All I Want Is You	Roxy Music	Island	6		
17	-	Oh Yes! You're Beautiful	Gary Glitter	Bell	7		
18	-	No Honestly	Lynsey De Paul	Jet	4		
19	-	Never Turn Your Back On Mother Earth	Sparks	Island	4		
20	-	Magic	Pilot	EMI	5	(5)	F

December 1974

This Mnth	Prev Mnth	Title	Artist	Label	Wks 20	(US Pos)	
1	6	You're The First, The Last, My...	Barry White	20th Century	9	(2)	
2	-	You Ain't Seen Nothin' Yet	Bachman-Turner Overdrive	Mercury	9	(1)	F L
3	13	Juke Box Jive	Rubettes	Polydor	9		
4	17	Oh Yes! You're Beautiful	Gary Glitter	Bell	7		
5	-	Lonely This Christmas	Mud	RAK	8		
6	-	My Boy	Elvis Presley	RCA	9	(20)	
7	-	Tell Him	Hello	Bell	6		F
8	-	Get Dancing	Disco Tex & The Sex-O-Lettes	Chelsea	8	(10)	F
9	-	Streets Of London	Ralph McTell	Reprise	9		F L
10	-	Ire Feelings (Skanga)	Rupie Edwards	Cactus	6		F L
11	-	Lucy In The Sky With Diamonds	Elton John	DJM	8	(1)	
12	1	Gonna Make You A Star	David Essex	CBS	9		
13	-	Wombling Merry Christmas	Wombles	CBS	5		
14	20	Magic	Pilot	EMI	5	(5)	F
15	-	You Can Make Me Dance Sing Or Anything	Rod Stewart & The Faces	Warner	4		L
16	-	The In Betweenies/Father Christmas Do Not Touch Me	Goodies	Bradley's	6		F
17	-	Too Good To Be Forgotten	Chi-Lites	Brunswick	4		
18	4	(Hey There) Lonely Girl	Eddie Holman	ABC	7		F L
19	-	Down Down	Status Quo	Vertigo	8		
20	2	Killer Queen	Queen	EMI	6	(12)	

October 1974

This Mnth	Prev Mnth	Title	Artist	Label	Wks 20	(UK Pos)	
1	6	Then Came You	Dionne Warwick	Warner	11	(29)	G
2	9	You Haven't Done Nothin	Stevie Wonder	Tamla	12	(30)	G
3	2	Nothing From Nothing	Billy Preston	A&M	10		G
4	7	I Honestly Love You	Olivia Newton-John	MCA	8	(22)	G
5	-	Can't Get Enough	Bad Company	Swan Song	8	(15)	F
6	-	The Bitch Is Back	Elton John	MCA	7	(15)	
7	-	Steppin' Out (Gonna Boogie Tonight)	Tony Orlando & Dawn	Bell	6		
8	-	Jazzman	Carole King	Ode	8		
9	-	Stop And Smell The Roses	Mac Davis	Columbia	6		
10	-	Never My Love	Blue Swede	EMI	4		L
11	13	Beach Baby	First Class	UK	6	(13)	F L
12	16	Sweet Home Alabama	Lynyrd Skynyrd	MCA	9		F
13	14	Another Saturday Night	Cat Stevens	A&M	5	(19)	L
14	11	Hang On In There Baby	Johnny Bristol	MGM	7	(3)	F L
15	-	Love Me For A Reason	Osmonds	MGM	3	(1)	L
16	20	Earache My Eye - Feat. Alice Bowie	Cheech & Chong	Ode	4		L
17	-	You Little Trustmaker	Tymes	RCA	4	(18)	L
18	-	You Ain't Seen Nothin' Yet	Bachman-Turner Overdrive	Mercury	8	(2)	G
19	-	Do It Baby	Miracles	Tamla	5		
20	-	Skin Tight	Ohio Players	Mercury	3		G

November 1974

This Mnth	Prev Mnth	Title	Artist	Label	Wks 20	(UK Pos)	
1	-	Do It ('Til You're Satisfied)	B.T. Express	Roadshow	9	(52)	F G
2	18	You Ain't Seen Nothin' Yet	Bachman-Turner Overdrive	Mercury	8	(2)	G
3	-	Tin Man	America	Warner	7		
4	-	My Melody Of Love	Bobby Vinton	ABC	7		G L
5	-	Whatever Gets You Thru The Night	John Lennon & The Plastic Ono Nuclear Band	Apple	6	(36)	
6	-	I Can Help	Billy Swan	Monument	7	(6)	F G L
7	-	Back Home Again	John Denver	RCA	7		G
8	-	Longfellow Serenade	Neil Diamond	Columbia	5		
9	-	Everlasting Love	Carl Carlton	ABC	6		F L
10	2	You Haven't Done Nothin	Stevie Wonder	Tamla	12	(30)	G
11	8	Jazzman	Carole King	Ode	8		
12	-	Life Is A Rock (But The Radio Rolled Me)	Reunion	RCA	5	(33)	F L
13	-	When Will I See You Again	Three Degrees	Philly International	9	(1)	G L
14	6	The Bitch Is Back	Elton John	MCA	7	(15)	
15	-	Kung Fu Fighting	Carl Douglas	20th Century	9	(1)	F G L
16	-	Carefree Highway	Gordon Lightfoot	Reprise	4		
17	-	The Need To Be	Jim Weatherly	Buddah	4		F L
18	-	Cat's In The Cradle	Harry Chapin	Elektra	7		F G L
19	-	I've Got The Music In Me	Kiki Dee	Rocket	5	(19)	F L
20	5	Can't Get Enough	Bad Company	Swan Song	8	(15)	F

December 1974

This Mnth	Prev Mnth	Title	Artist	Label	Wks 20	(UK Pos)	
1	15	Kung Fu Fighting	Carl Douglas	20th Century	9	(1)	F G L
2	-	Angie Baby	Helen Reddy	Capitol	9	(5)	G
3	18	Cat's In The Cradle	Harry Chapin	Elektra	7		F G L
4	13	When Will I See You Again	Three Degrees	Philly International	9	(1)	G L
5	-	You're The First, The Last, My Everything	Barry White	20th Century	9	(1)	G
6	6	I Can Help	Billy Swan	Monument	7	(6)	F G L
7	-	Junior's Farm /Sally G	Paul McCartney & Wings	Apple	9	(16)	
8	-	Lucy In The Sky With Diamonds	Elton John	MCA	8	(10)	G
9	-	Sha-La-La (Make Me Happy)	Al Green	Hi	7	(20)	G
10	1	Do It ('Til You're Satisfied)	B.T. Express	Roadshow	9	(52)	F G
11	-	You Got The Love	Rufus Featuring Chaka Khan	ABC	6		
12	-	Laughter In The Rain	Neil Sedaka	Rocket	11	(15)	
13	-	Only You	Ringo Starr	Apple	6	(28)	
14	-	Boogie On Reggae Woman	Stevie Wonder	Tamla	9	(12)	G
15	4	My Melody Of Love	Bobby Vinton	ABC	7		G L
16	-	Please Mr. Postman	Carpenters	A&M	8	(2)	G
17	-	Wishing You Were Here	Chicago	Columbia	5		
18	-	Must Of Got Lost	J. Geils Band	Atlantic	4		F
19	-	Fairytale	Pointer Sisters	Blue Thumb	3		
20	-	Mandy	Barry Manilow	Bell	8	(11)	F G

US
1974
OCT-DEC

◆ George Harrison was the first ex-Beatle to tour America - he did so to half-empty houses. John Lennon fared better; he had his first solo No. 1, 'Whatever Gets You Thru The Night', from the chart topping **Walls And Bridges** album. To celebrate, Lennon appeared on stage with Elton John at Madison Square Garden. Elton ended 1974 with his **Greatest Hits** topping the transatlantic charts.

◆ Comparative veterans scoring Top 20 hits included Bobby Vinton, Neil Sedaka, The Three Degrees, Billy Swann and The J. Geils Band.

◆ Folk-rock singer/songwriter Harry Chapin had the biggest hit of his career with 'Cats In The Cradle'. Chapin's charity work was legendary and possibly inspired later projects like *Live Aid*, which came after his untimely death in a car accident in 1981.

UK 1975 JAN-MAR

◆ Status Quo, who have put more singles in the UK charts than any other group, went up to the top for the only time in their long career with 'Down Down'.

◆ American acts whose current records were faring far better in Britain included: *Kojak* actor Telly Savalas, The Tymes, The Moments & The Whatnauts, Johnny Mathis and Love Unlimited.

▲ Disco was taking over, with hits by Gloria Gaynor, Disco Tex, Barry White (above), Shirley & Co., Labelle and B. T. Express. Another type of dance music selling well in the UK was northern soul – the biggest hit from obscure Canadian band Wigan's Chosen Few.

January 1975

This Mnth	Prev Mnth	Title	Artist	Label	Wks 20	(US Pos)	
1	9	Streets Of London	Ralph McTell	Reprise	9		F L
2	19	Down Down	Status Quo	Vertigo	8		
3	5	Lonely This Christmas	Mud	RAK	8		
4	-	The Bump	Kenny	RAK	6		F
5	-	Never Can Say Goodbye	Gloria Gaynor	MGM	5	(9)	F
6	-	Ms Grace	Tymes	RCA	5	(91)	L
7	8	Get Dancing	Disco Tex & The Sex-O-Lettes	Chelsea	8	(10)	F
8	-	I Can Help	Billy Swan	Monument	7	(1)	F L
9	13	Wombling Merry Christmas	Wombles	CBS	5		
10	6	My Boy	Elvis Presley	RCA	9	(20)	
11	16	The In Betweenies/Father Christmas Do Not Touch Me	Goodies	Bradley's	6		F
12	3	Juke Box Jive	Rubettes	Polydor	9		
13	-	Stardust	David Essex	CBS	4		
14	-	Are You Ready To Rock	Wizzard	Warner	5		L
15	2	You Ain't Seen Nothin' Yet	Bachman-Turner Overdrive	Mercury	9	(1)	F L
16	-	Help Me Make It Through The Night	John Holt	Trojan	6		F L
17	-	Crying Over You	Ken Boothe	Trojan	4		L
18	-	Morning Side Of The Mountain	Donny & Marie Osmond	MGM	5	(8)	
19	1	You're The First, The Last, My...	Barry White	20th Century	9	(2)	
20	11	Lucy In The Sky With Diamonds	Elton John	DJM	8	(1)	

February 1975

This Mnth	Prev Mnth	Title	Artist	Label	Wks 20	(US Pos)	
1	-	January	Pilot	EMI	6	(87)	L
2	-	Goodbye My Love	Glitter Band	Bell	6		
3	-	Sugar Candy Kisses	Mac & Katie Kissoon	Polydor	5		F
4	-	Please Mr. Postman	Carpenters	A&M	7	(1)	
5	4	The Bump	Kenny	RAK	6		F
6	18	Morning Side Of The Mountain	Donny & Marie Osmond	MGM	5	(8)	
7	-	Angie Baby	Helen Reddy	Capitol	6	(1)	F L
8	6	Ms Grace	Tymes	RCA	5	(91)	L
9	5	Never Can Say Goodbye	Gloria Gaynor	MGM	5	(9)	F
10	-	Make Me Smile (Come Up And See Me)	Steve Harley & Cockney Rebel	EMI	6	(96)	
11	-	Black Superman (Muhammad Ali)	Johnny Wakelin & The Kinshasa Band	Pye	4	(21)	F
12	-	Promised Land	Elvis Presley	RCA	5	(14)	
13	16	Help Me Make It Through The Night	John Holt	Trojan	6		F L
14	-	Footsee	Wigan's Chosen Few	Disco Demand	5		F L
15	-	Now I'm Here	Queen	EMI	5		
16	-	Shame, Shame, Shame	Shirley And Company	All Platinum	5	(12)	F L
17	-	Purely By Coincidence	Sweet Sensation	Pye	4		L
18	-	Star On A TV Show	Stylistics	Avco	4	(47)	
19	-	Boogie On Reggae Woman	Stevie Wonder	Tamla Motown	3	(3)	
20	-	The Secrets That You Keep	Mud	RAK	5		

March 1975

This Mnth	Prev Mnth	Title	Artist	Label	Wks 20	(US Pos)	
1	-	If	Telly Savalas	MCA	7		F L
2	-	Only You Can	Fox	GTO	7	(53)	F
3	-	Bye Bye Baby	Bay City Rollers	Bell	11		
4	10	Make Me Smile (Come Up And See...)	Steve Harley & Cockney Rebel	EMI	6	(96)	
5	20	The Secrets That You Keep	Mud	RAK	5		
6	-	My Eyes Adored You	Frankie Valli	Private Stock	5	(1)	
7	-	Pick Up The Pieces	Average White Band	Atlantic	5	(1)	F
8	-	There's A Whole Lot Of Loving	Guys & Dolls	Magnet	7		F
9	4	Please Mr. Postman	Carpenters	A&M	7	(1)	
10	-	What Am I Gonna Do With You	Barry White	20th Century	6	(8)	
11	16	Shame, Shame, Shame	Shirley And Company	All Platinum	5	(12)	F L
12	-	Girls	Moments And Whatnauts	All Platinum	6		F
13	-	Please Tell Him I Said Hello	Dana	GTO	6		
14	-	Fancy Pants	Kenny	RAK	6		
15	-	Mandy	Barry Manilow	Arista	4	(1)	F
16	-	I'm Stone In Love With You	Johnny Mathis	CBS	6		
17	-	I Can Do It	Rubettes	State	6		
18	-	Dreamer	Supertramp	A&M	4	(15)	F
19	14	Footsee	Wigan's Chosen Few	Disco Demand	5		F L
20	-	It May Be Winter Outside (But In My Heart It's Spring)	Love Unlimited	20th Century	4	(83)	L

January 1975

This Mnth	Prev Mnth	Title	Artist	Label	Wks 20	(UK Pos)	
1	12	Laughter In The Rain	Neil Sedaka	Rocket	11	(15)	
2	8	Lucy In The Sky With Diamonds	Elton John	MCA	8	(10)	G
3	20	Mandy	Barry Manilow	Bell	8	(11)	F G
4	16	Please Mr. Postman	Carpenters	A&M	8	(2)	G
5	5	You're The First, The Last, My Everything	Barry White	20th Century	9	(1)	G
6	14	Boogie On Reggae Woman	Stevie Wonder	Tamla	9	(12)	G
7	7	Junior's Farm/Sally G	Paul McCartney & Wings	Apple	9	(16)	
8	-	One Man Woman/One Woman Man	Paul Anka & Odia Coates	UA	7		
9	-	Morning Side Of The Mountain	Donny & Marie Osmond	MGM	7	(5)	
10	13	Only You	Ringo Starr	Apple	6	(28)	
11	-	Fire	Ohio Players	Mercury	8		G
12	-	Never Can Say Goodbye	Gloria Gaynor	MGM	7	(2)	F
13	1	Kung Fu Fighting	Carl Douglas	20th Century	9	(1)	F G L
14	2	Angie Baby	Helen Reddy	Capitol	9	(5)	G
15	-	Pick Up The Pieces	Average White Band	Atlantic	9	(6)	F G
16	-	Doctor's Orders	Carol Douglas	Midland Int.	6		F L
17	-	Bungle In The Jungle	Jethro Tull	Chrysalis	5		L
18	-	Some Kind Of Wonderful	Grand Funk	Capitol	8		
19	-	You're No Good	Linda Ronstadt	Capitol	6		F G
20	-	Get Dancin'	Disco Tex & The Sex-O-Lettes	Chelsea	5	(8)	F L

February 1975

This Mnth	Prev Mnth	Title	Artist	Label	Wks 20	(UK Pos)	
1	15	Pick Up The Pieces	Average White Band	Atlantic	9	(6)	F G
2	19	You're No Good	Linda Ronstadt	Capitol	6		F G
3	-	Best Of My Love	Eagles	Asylum	10		G
4	11	Fire	Ohio Players	Mercury	8		G
5	18	Some Kind Of Wonderful	Grand Funk	Capitol	8		
6	-	Black Water	Doobie Brothers	Warner	10		
7	6	Boogie On Reggae Woman	Stevie Wonder	Tamla	9	(12)	G
8	-	Lonely People	America	Warner	6		
9	1	Laughter In The Rain	Neil Sedaka	Rocket	11	(15)	
10	-	My Eyes Adored You	Frankie Valli	Private Stock	9	(5)	G
11	-	#9 Dream	John Lennon	Apple	5	(23)	
12	-	Look In My Eyes Pretty Woman	Tony Orlando & Dawn	Bell	4		
13	20	Get Dancin'	Disco Tex & The Sex-O-Lettes	Chelsea	5	(8)	F L
14	16	Doctor's Orders	Carol Douglas	Midland Int.	6		F L
15	4	Please Mr. Postman	Carpenters	A&M	8	(2)	G
16	-	Sweet Surrender	John Denver	RCA	3		
17	-	Have You Never Been Mellow	Olivia Newton-John	MCA	9		G
18	3	Mandy	Barry Manilow	Bell	8	(11)	F G
19	-	Nightingale	Carole King	Ode	4		
20	9	Morning Side Of The Mountain	Donny & Marie Osmond	MGM	7	(5)	

March 1975

This Mnth	Prev Mnth	Title	Artist	Label	Wks 20	(UK Pos)	
1	10	My Eyes Adored You	Frankie Valli	Private Stock	9	(5)	G
2	-	Lady Marmalade (Voulez-Vous Coucher Avec Moi)	Labelle	Epic	9	(17)	F G L
3	17	Have You Never Been Mellow	Olivia Newton-John	MCA	9		G
4	6	Black Water	Doobie Brothers	Warner	10		G
5	-	Lovin' You	Minnie Riperton	Epic	9	(2)	F G L
6	-	Express	B.T. Express	Roadshow	9	(34)	G L
7	-	Lady	Styx	Wooden Nickel	6		F
8	-	Don't Call Us We'll Call You	Sugarloaf/Jerry Corbetta	Claridge	6		L
9	-	Poetry Man	Phoebe Snow	Shelter	7		F L
10	8	Lonely People	America	Warner	6		
11	3	Best Of My Love	Eagles	Asylum	10		G
12	-	You Are So Beautiful	Joe Cocker	A&M	6		
13	-	Can't Get It Out Of My Head	Electric Light Orchestra	UA	6		F
14	-	No No Song/Snookeroo	Ringo Starr	Apple	6		
15	-	Philadelphia Freedom	Elton John	MCA	14	(12)	G
16	1	Pick Up The Pieces	Average White Band	Atlantic	9	(6)	F G
17	-	Shame Shame Shame	Shirley And Company	Vibration	3	(6)	F L
18	-	I'm A Woman	Maria Muldaur	Reprise	4		L
19	-	Sad Sweet Dreamer	Sweet Sensation	Pye	3	(1)	F
20	5	Some Kind Of Wonderful	Grand Funk	Capitol	8		

◆ In just four hours, Led Zeppelin sold the 60,000 seats for their Madison Square Garden appearances. All their six albums were simultaneously situated in the US chart (a record), including the group's first Swan Song LP, **Physical Graffiti**, which topped the transatlantic charts.

◆ Influential performers and forefathers of r'n'r', Louis Jordan and T-Bone Walker both died. Early rockers Bill Haley and Chuck Berry both owed much to Jordan, and Walker's influence can be heard in many rock and R&B guitar stars' work.

◆ Bette Midler's ex-pianist, Barry Manilow, made his American chart debut with 'Mandy'. The song had been a British hit in 1971 for its composer, American-born Scott English, under the title 'Brandy'.

UK 1975 APR-JUNE

▲ A 12 city American tour by The Beach Boys and Chicago (whose **Chicago VIII** was a chart topper) was seen by 700,000, who paid over $7 million. The Beach Boys then joined Elton John (above), Rufus and The Eagles, playing to 80,000 at London's Wembley Stadium. For the record books, Elton's **Captain Fantastic And The Brown Dirt Cowboy** became the first album to enter the US LP charts at No. 1.

◆ Groundbreaking German group Kraftwerk had a transatlantic Top 40 hit with 'Autobahn'. Their electro-pop sound was a blueprint for many later dance acts.

April 1975

This Mnth	Prev Mnth	Title	Artist	Label	Wks 20	(US Pos)	
1	3	Bye Bye Baby	Bay City Rollers	Bell	11		
2	-	Fox On The Run	Sweet	RCA	6	(5)	
3	-	Swing Your Daddy	Jim Gilstrap	Chelsea	7	(55)	F L
4	-	Love Me Love My Dog	Peter Shelley	Magnet	6		L
5	-	Funky Gibbon/Sick Man Blues	Goodies	Bradley's	6	(79)	
6	8	There's A Whole Lot Of Loving	Guys & Dolls	Magnet	7		F
7	12	Girls	Moments And Whatnauts	All Platinum	6		F
8	14	Fancy Pants	Kenny	RAK	6		
9	17	I Can Do It	Rubettes	State	6		
10	-	Honey	Bobby Goldsboro	UA	6		L
11	-	Play Me Like You Play Your Guitar	Duane Eddy & Rebelettes	GTO	5		
12	-	The Ugly Duckling	Mike Reid	Pye	4		F L
13	10	What Am I Gonna Do With You	Barry White	20th Century	6	(8)	
14	-	Let Me Be The One	Shadows	EMI	3		
15	-	Philadelphia Freedom	Elton John	DJM	6	(1)	
16	-	Skiing In The Snow	Wigan's Ovation	Spark	4		F L
17	-	Life Is A Minestone	10cc	Mercury	5		
18	-	Oh Boy	Mud	RAK	6		
19	-	Reach Out I'll Be There	Gloria Gaynor	MGM	4	(60)	
20	-	Loving You	Minnie Riperton	Epic	6	(1)	F L

May 1975

This Mnth	Prev Mnth	Title	Artist	Label	Wks 20	(US Pos)	
1	18	Oh Boy	Mud	RAK	6		
2	20	Loving You	Minnie Riperton	Epic	6	(1)	F L
3	-	Stand By Your Man	Tammy Wynette	Epic	8		F
4	-	Hurt So Good	Susan Cadogan	Magnet	6		F L
5	-	Let Me Try Again	Tammy Jones	Epic	6		F L
6	10	Honey	Bobby Goldsboro	UA	6		L
7	-	I Wanna Dance Wit Choo'	Disco Tex & The Sex-O-Lettes	Chelsea	5	(23)	L
8	-	The Way We Were/Try To Remember (Medley)	Gladys Knight & The Pips	Buddah	7	(11)	
9	-	Sing Baby Sing	Stylistics	Avco	7		
10	-	Only Yesterday	Carpenters	A&M	5	(4)	
11	-	The Night	Frankie Valli & Four Seasons	Mowest	5		
12	-	Whispering Grass	Windsor Davies & Don Estelle	EMI	9		F L
13	1	Bye Bye Baby	Bay City Rollers	Bell	11		
14	-	Thanks For The Memory (Wham Bam Thank You Mam)	Slade	Polydor	5		
15	-	Take Good Care Of Yourself	Three Degrees	Philly Int.	4		
16	-	A Little Love And Understanding	Gilbert Becaud	Decca	5		F L
17	-	The Tears I Cried	Glitter Band	Bell	5		
18	-	Don't Do It Baby	Mac & Katie Kissoon	State	4		
19	-	Three Steps To Heaven	Showaddywaddy	Bell	8		
20	-	Send In The Clowns	Judy Collins	Elektra	5	(19)	L

June 1975

This Mnth	Prev Mnth	Title	Artist	Label	Wks 20	(US Pos)	
1	12	Whispering Grass	Windsor Davies & Don Estelle	EMI	9		F L
2	19	Three Steps To Heaven	Showaddywaddy	Bell	8		
3	-	I'm Not In Love	10cc	Mercury	8	(2)	
4	-	The Proud One	Osmonds	MGM	6	(22)	L
5	3	Stand By Your Man	Tammy Wynette	Epic	8		F
6	9	Sing Baby Sing	Stylistics	Avco	7		
7	-	The Hustle	Van McCoy	Avco	8	(1)	F
8	8	The Way We Were/Try To Remember (Medley)	Gladys Knight & The Pips	Buddah	7	(11)	
9	-	Listen To What The Man Said	Wings	Capitol	5	(1)	
10	20	Send In The Clowns	Judy Collins	Elektra	5	(19)	L
11	-	Disco Stomp	Hamilton Bohannon	Brunswick	7		F L
12	-	Disco Queen	Hot Chocolate	RAK	4	(28)	
13	-	Autobahn	Kraftwerk	Vertigo	5	(25)	F
14	-	Tears On My Pillow	Johnny Nash	CBS	9		L
15	-	Roll Over Lay Down	Status Quo	Vertigo	5		
16	-	The Israelites	Desmond Dekker & The Aces	Cactus	5		
17	-	Oh What A Shame	Roy Wood	Jet	4		L
18	-	Doing Alright With The Boys	Gary Glitter	Bell	4		L
19	-	Baby I Love You, OK	Kenny	RAK	4		
20	14	Thanks For The Memory (Wham Bam Thank You Mam)	Slade	Polydor	5		

April 1975

This Mnth	Prev Mnth	Title	Artist	Label	Wks 20	(UK Pos)	
1	15	Philadelphia Freedom	Elton John	MCA	14	(12)	G
2	5	Lovin' You	Minnie Riperton	Epic	9	(2)	F G L
3	-	(Hey Won't You Play) Another Somebody Done Somebody Wrong Song	B.J. Thomas	ABC	10		G
4	14	No No Song/Snookeroo	Ringo Starr	Apple	6		L
5	-	Chevy Van	Sammy Johns	GRC	8		F G L
6	-	Supernatural Thing Part 1	Ben E. King	Atlantic	5		
7	-	What Am I Gonna Do With You	Barry White	20th Century	4	(5)	
8	-	Emma	Hot Chocolate	Big Tree	6	(3)	F
9	2	Lady Marmalade (Voulez-Vous Coucher Avec Moi)	Labelle	Epic	9	(17)	F G L
10	6	Express	B.T. Express	Roadshow	9	(34)	G L
11	-	Before The Next Teardrop Falls	Freddy Fender	ABC/Dot	11		F G
12	-	He Don't Love You (Like I Love You)	Tony Orlando & Dawn	Elektra	7		G
13	9	Poetry Man	Phoebe Snow	Shelter	7		F L
14	-	Walking In Rhythm	Blackbyrds	Fantasy	8	(23)	F
15	-	Once You Get Started	Rufus	ABC	5		
16	-	L-O-V-E (Love)	Al Green	Hi	5	(24)	
17	-	Shining Star	Earth, Wind & Fire	Columbia	11		F G
18	12	You Are So Beautiful	Joe Cocker	A&M	6		
19	-	Long Tall Glasses (I Can Dance)	Leo Sayer	Warner	6	(4)	F
20	-	Harry Truman	Chicago	Columbia	3		

May 1975

This Mnth	Prev Mnth	Title	Artist	Label	Wks 20	(UK Pos)	
1	11	Before The Next Teardrop Falls	Freddy Fender	ABC/Dot	11		F G
2	17	Shining Star	Earth, Wind & Fire	Columbia	11		F G
3	12	He Don't Love You (Like I Love You)	Tony Orlando & Dawn	Elektra	7		G
4	-	Only Yesterday	Carpenters	A&M	6	(7)	
5	-	Jackie Blue	Ozark Mountain Daredevils	A&M	7		F L
6	-	How Long	Ace	Anchor	8	(20)	F L
7	-	Thank God I'm A Country Boy	John Denver	RCA	8		G
8	-	I Don't Like To Sleep Alone	Paul Anka & Odia Coates	UA	7		
9	1	Philadelphia Freedom	Elton John	MCA	14	(12)	G
10	3	(Hey...) Another Somebody Done...	B.J. Thomas	ABC	10		G
11	14	Walking In Rhythm	Blackbyrds	Fantasy	8	(23)	F
12	-	Sister Golden Hair	America	Warner	8		G
13	-	Bad Time	Grand Funk	Capitol	7		L
14	-	Old Days	Chicago	Columbia	7		
15	-	Killer Queen	Queen	Elektra	5	(2)	F
16	19	Long Tall Glasses (I Can Dance)	Leo Sayer	Warner	6	(4)	F
17	-	When Will I Be Loved	Linda Ronstadt	Capitol	10		
18	-	Love Won't Let Me Wait	Major Harris	Atlantic	9	(37)	F G L
19	5	Chevy Van	Sammy Johns	GRC	8		F G L
20	-	It's A Miracle	Barry Manilow	Arista	3		

June 1975

This Mnth	Prev Mnth	Title	Artist	Label	Wks 20	(UK Pos)	
1	17	When Will I Be Loved	Linda Ronstadt	Capitol	10		
2	-	Love Will Keep Us Together	Captain & Tennille	A&M	13	(32)	F G
3	12	Sister Golden Hair	America	Warner	8		G
4	-	I'm Not Lisa	Jessi Colter	Capitol	7		F L
5	18	Love Won't Let Me Wait	Major Harris	Atlantic	9	(37)	F G L
6	-	Wildfire	Michael Murphey	Epic	7		F G
7	-	Get Down, Get Down (Get On The Floor)	Joe Simon	Spring	5		L
8	-	Cut The Cake	Average White Band	Atlantic	6	(31)	L
9	13	Bad Time	Grand Funk	Capitol	7		L
10	7	Thank God I'm A Country Boy	John Denver	RCA	8		G
11	14	Old Days	Chicago	Columbia	7		
12	-	Only Women	Alice Cooper	Atlantic	6		
13	-	The Hustle	Van McCoy	Avco	8	(3)	F G L
14	-	Take Me In Your Arms (Rock Me)	Doobie Brothers	Warner	4		
15	-	Listen To What The Man Said	Wings	Capitol	9	(6)	G
16	9	Philadelphia Freedom	Elton John	MCA	14	(12)	G
17	-	Magic	Pilot	EMI	7	(11)	F G L
18	6	How Long	Ace	Anchor	8	(20)	F L
19	1	Before The Next Teardrop Falls	Freddy Fender	ABC/Dot	11		F G
20	-	Bad Luck (Pt. 1)	Harold Melvin & The Blue Notes	Philly Int.	3		

◆ Even though their popularity was waning in their homeland, American soul group The Stylistics topped the UK LP chart with a collection of hits. Other US acts with UK-only hits were The Moments, The Whatnauts, The Three Degrees, Hamilton Bohannon, Johnny Nash and top 1950s star Duane Eddy with his "twangy" guitar.

◆ Highly respected record executives Clive Davis (Columbia/ Arista) and Kenny Gamble and Leon Huff (Philly International) were indicted on payola charges.

◆ Jefferson Starship attracted 60,000 to Central Park, Stevie Wonder played to 125,000 at the Washington Monument, and The Rolling Stones started their first US tour with guitarist Ron Wood, which grossed over $13 million.

UK 1975
JULY-SEPT

◆ Paul McCartney, who had yet to score a solo No. 1 single in his homeland, notched up his fourth American chart topping single, 'Listen To What The Man Said', and another transatlantic album topper, **Venus And Mars.**

◆ Soon after David Bowie announced "rock'n'roll is dead", he had his biggest American hit with 'Fame', co-written with John Lennon.

◆ Shortly before his group The Faces finally called it a day, lead singer Rod Stewart had the biggest British hit of his long and successful career with 'Sailing'. The single, which failed to make the American Top 40, returned to the Top 3 the following year, after its use as the theme to the BBC TV documentary *Sailor*, and was also a minor hit in 1987, with royalties being donated to the Zeebrugge Ferry Disaster Fund.

July 1975

This Mnth	Prev Mnth	Title	Artist	Label	Wks 20	(US Pos)	
1	14	Tears On My Pillow	Johnny Nash	CBS	9		L
2	-	Misty	Ray Stevens	Janus	7	(14)	L
3	7	The Hustle	Van McCoy	Avco	8	(1)	F
4	-	Have You Seen Her/Oh Girl	Chi-Lites	Brunswick	5		
5	3	I'm Not In Love	10cc	Mercury	8	(2)	
6	-	Give A Little Love	Bay City Rollers	Bell	7		
7	11	Disco Stomp	Hamilton Bohannon	Brunswick	7		F L
8	-	Eighteen With A Bullet	Pete Wingfield	Island	5	(15)	F L
9	-	Barbados	Typically Tropical	Gull	9		F L
10	1	Whispering Grass	Windsor Davies & Don Estelle	EMI	9		F L
11	18	Doing Alright With The Boys	Gary Glitter	Bell	4		L
12	-	Moonshine Sally	Mud	RAK	4		
13	-	Rollin' Stone	David Essex	CBS	4		
14	-	Je T'Aime (Moi Non Plus)	Judge Dread	Cactus	6		
15	2	Three Steps To Heaven	Showaddywaddy	Bell	8		
16	-	Jive Talkin'	Bee Gees	RSO	7	(1)	
17	-	Sealed With A Kiss	Brian Hyland	ABC	8		L
18	-	D.I.V.O.R.C.E.	Tammy Wynette	Epic	4	(63)	
19	-	My White Bicycle	Nazareth	Mooncrest	4		
20	19	Baby I Love You, OK	Kenny	RAK	4		

August 1975

This Mnth	Prev Mnth	Title	Artist	Label	Wks 20	(US Pos)	
1	9	Barbados	Typically Tropical	Gull	9		F L
2	-	Can't Give You Anything (But My Love)	Stylistics	Avco	8	(51)	
3	-	If You Think You Know How To Love Me	Smokey	RAK	7	(96)	F
4	6	Give A Little Love	Bay City Rollers	Bell	7		
5	16	Jive Talkin'	Bee Gees	RSO	7	(1)	
6	-	The Last Farewell	Roger Whittaker	EMI	9	(19)	
7	-	It's Been So Long	George McCrae	Jayboy	7		
8	17	Sealed With A Kiss	Brian Hyland	ABC	8		L
9	-	It's In His Kiss	Linda Lewis	Arista	5		L
10	-	Blanket On The Ground	Billie Jo Spears	UA	6	(78)	F
11	-	Delilah	Sensational Alex Harvey Band	Vertigo	5		F
12	-	Sailing	Rod Stewart	Warner	9	(58)	
13	1	Tears On My Pillow	Johnny Nash	CBS	9		L
14	-	Sherry	Adrian Baker	Magnet	4		F L
15	-	Dolly My Love	Moments	All Platinum	5		L
16	-	That's The Way (I Like It)	KC & The Sunshine Band	Jayboy	6	(1)	
17	14	Je T'Aime (Moi Non Plus)	Judge Dread	Cactus	6		
18	-	The Best Thing That Ever Happened	Gladys Knight & The Pips	Buddah	6	(3)	
19	2	Misty	Ray Stevens	Janus	7	(14)	L
20	-	El Bimbo	Bimbo Jet	EMI	4	(43)	F L

September 1975

This Mnth	Prev Mnth	Title	Artist	Label	Wks 20	(US Pos)	
1	12	Sailing	Rod Stewart	Warner	9	(58)	
2	6	The Last Farewell	Roger Whittaker	EMI	9	(19)	
3	-	Moonlighting	Leo Sayer	Chrysalis	6		
4	-	Summertime City	Mike Batt	Epic	5		F L
5	-	Funky Moped/Magic Roundabout	Jasper Carrott	DJM	10		F L
6	-	A Child's Prayer	Hot Chocolate	RAK	5		
7	2	Can't Give You Anything (But My Love)	Stylistics	Avco	8	(51)	
8	16	That's The Way (I Like It)	KC & The Sunshine Band	Jayboy	6	(1)	
9	-	I'm On Fire	5000 Volts	Philips	6	(26)	F
10	-	Heartbeat	Showaddywaddy	Bell	5		
11	-	Julie Ann	Kenny	RAK	5		L
12	7	It's Been So Long	George McCrae	Jayboy	7		
13	-	Hold Me Close	David Essex	CBS	8		
14	18	The Best Thing That Ever Happened	Gladys Knight & The Pips	Buddah	6	(3)	
15	10	Blanket On The Ground	Billie Jo Spears	UA	6	(78)	F
16	-	There Goes My First Love	Drifters	Bell	8		
17	-	Motor Biking	Chris Spedding	RAK	4		F L
18	-	Fattie Bum-Bum	Carl Malcolm	UK	5		F L
19	-	Love In The Sun	Glitter Band	Bell	4		
20	-	I Only Have Eyes For You	Art Garfunkel	CBS	8	(18)	F

July 1975

This Mnth	Prev Mnth	Title	Artist	Label	Wks 20	(UK Pos)	
1	13	The Hustle	Van McCoy	Avco	8	(3)	F G L
2	15	Listen To What The Man Said	Wings	Capitol	9	(6)	G
3	2	Love Will Keep Us Together	Captain & Tennille	A&M	13	(32)	F G
4	-	One Of These Nights	Eagles	Asylum	11	(23)	
5	-	Please Mr. Please	Olivia Newton-John	MCA	9		G
6	-	I'm Not In Love	10cc	Mercury	8	(1)	F
7	-	Swearin' To God	Frankie Valli	Private Stock	5	(31)	
8	17	Magic	Pilot	EMI	7	(11)	F G L
9	-	Rockin' Chair	Gwen McCrae	Cat	5		F L
10	6	Wildfire	Michael Murphey	Epic	7		F G
11	-	Midnight Blue	Melissa Manchester	Arista	8		F
12	-	The Way We Were/Try To Remember (Medley)	Gladys Knight & The Pips	Buddah	6	(4)	
13	-	Jive Talkin'	Bee Gees	RSO	9	(5)	G
14	5	Love Won't Let Me Wait	Major Harris	Atlantic	9	(37)	F G L
15	1	When Will I Be Loved	Linda Ronstadt	Capitol	10		
16	-	Dynomite	Bazuka	A&M	6		F L
17	-	Someone Saved My Life Tonight	Elton John	MCA	8	(22)	G
18	-	Misty	Ray Stevens	Barnaby	4	(2)	L
19	4	I'm Not Lisa	Jessi Colter	Capitol	7		F L
20	-	Why Can't We Be Friends?	War	UA	9		G

August 1975

This Mnth	Prev Mnth	Title	Artist	Label	Wks 20	(UK Pos)	
1	4	One Of These Nights	Eagles	Asylum	11	(23)	
2	13	Jive Talkin'	Bee Gees	RSO	9	(5)	G
3	17	Someone Saved My Life Tonight	Elton John	MCA	8	(22)	G
4	-	Rhinestone Cowboy	Glen Campbell	Capitol	14	(4)	G
5	5	Please Mr. Please	Olivia Newton-John	MCA	9		G
6	20	Why Can't We Be Friends?	War	UA	9		G
7	-	Fallin' In Love	Hamilton, Joe Frank & Reynolds	Playboy	8		G L
8	-	How Sweet It Is (To Be Loved By You)	James Taylor	Warner	9		
9	11	Midnight Blue	Melissa Manchester	Arista	8		F
10	-	Get Down Tonight	KC & The Sunshine Band	TK	6	(21)	F G
11	6	I'm Not In Love	10cc	Mercury	8	(1)	F
12	-	At Seventeen	Janis Ian	Columbia	8		L
13	-	Fight The Power Pt. 1	Isley Brothers	T-Neck	8		G L
14	-	The Rockford Files	Mike Post	MGM	5		F
15	1	The Hustle	Van McCoy	Avco	8	(3)	F G L
16	2	Listen To What The Man Said	Wings	Capitol	9	(6)	G
17	3	Love Will Keep Us Together	Captain & Tennille	A&M	13	(32)	F G
18	16	Dynomite	Bazuka	A&M	6		F L
19	-	Could It Be Magic	Barry Manilow	Arista	8	(25)	
20	-	Mornin' Beautiful	Tony Orlando & Dawn	Elektra	4		L

September 1975

This Mnth	Prev Mnth	Title	Artist	Label	Wks 20	(UK Pos)	
1	4	Rhinestone Cowboy	Glen Campbell	Capitol	14	(4)	G
2	-	Fame	David Bowie	RCA	8	(17)	G
3	12	At Seventeen	Janis Ian	Columbia	8		L
4	13	Fight The Power Pt. 1	Isley Brothers	T-Neck	8		G L
5	-	I'm Sorry/Calypso	John Denver	RCA	12		G
6	19	Could It Be Magic	Barry Manilow	Arista	8	(25)	
7	7	Fallin' In Love	Hamilton, Joe Frank & Reynolds	Playboy	8		G L
8	-	Wasted Days And Wasted Nights	Freddy Fender	ABC/Dot	9		G
9	-	Run Joey Run	David Geddes	Big Tree	6		F
10	10	Get Down Tonight	KC & The Sunshine Band	TK	6	(21)	F G
11	-	Feel Like Makin' Love	Bad Company	Swan Song	6	(20)	
12	-	Ballroom Blitz	Sweet	Capitol	10	(2)	
13	-	That's The Way Of The World	Earth, Wind & Fire	Columbia	6		
14	-	Ain't No Way To Treat A Lady	Helen Reddy	Capitol	6		
15	8	How Sweet It Is (To Be Loved By You)	James Taylor	Warner	9		
16	2	Jive Talkin'	Bee Gees	RSO	9	(5)	G
17	-	Third Rate Romance	Amazing Rhythm Aces	ABC	4		F L
18	-	Dance With Me	Orleans	Asylum	7		F
19	1	One Of These Nights	Eagles	Asylum	11	(23)	
20	-	I Believe There's Nothing Stronger Than Our Love	Paul Anka & Odia Coates	UA	4		

▲ As the Grand Ole Opry celebrated its 50th birthday, country singer Glen Campbell (above) topped the pop chart with 'Rhinestone Cowboy', and the death was announced of legendary performer Lefty Frizzell.

◆ Other news included Peter Gabriel leaving Genesis, with drummer Phil Collins taking over vocals, and Stevie Wonder re-signing with Motown for a record $13 million.

◆ 'Get Down Tonight' was the first of four self-composed chart toppers in less than two years for the multi-racial Miami-based disco group KC & The Sunshine Band.

183

▲ Queen's 'Bohemian Rhapsody' topped the chart and sold over a million. In 1991, after Freddie Mercury's death, it returned and repeated the feat.

◆ The latest oldies to chart included Chubby Checker's 'Let's Twist Again' from 1961, David Bowie's 'Space Oddity' from 1969 and Laurel & Hardy's 1937 recording 'The Trail Of The Lonesome Pine'.

◆ Elton John's US tour closed with a spectacular show at the Dodger Stadium in L.A., and **Rock Of The Westies** became his second LP to enter the US chart at No. 1.

◆ The Faces played their last show together and The Sex Pistols played their first.

October 1975

This Mnth	Prev Mnth	Title	Artist	Label	Wks 20	(US Pos)	
1	13	Hold Me Close	David Essex	CBS	8		
2	20	I Only Have Eyes For You	Art Garfunkel	CBS	8	(18)	F
3	16	There Goes My First Love	Drifters	Bell	8		
4	-	It's Time For Love	Chi-Lites	Brunswick	5	(94)	
5	-	Una Paloma Blanca	Jonathan King	UK	6		L
6	-	Who Loves You	Four Seasons	Warner	5	(3)	
7	-	S.O.S.	Abba	Epic	6	(15)	
8	-	Scotch On The Rocks	Band Of The Black Watch	Spark	7		F L
9	-	Feelings	Morris Albert	Decca	6	(6)	F L
10	5	Funky Moped/Magic Roundabout	Jasper Carrott	DJM	10		F L
11	-	Paloma Blanca	George Baker Selection	Warner	4	(26)	F L
12	18	Fattie Bum-Bum	Carl Malcolm	UK	5		F L
13	9	I'm On Fire	5000 Volts	Philips	6	(26)	F
14	1	Sailing	Rod Stewart	Warner	9	(58)	
15	-	Space Oddity	David Bowie	RCA	8	(15)	
16	-	L-L-Lucy	Mud	Private Stock	4		
17	-	Don't Play Your Rock 'n' Roll To Me	Smokey	RAK	4		
18	3	Moonlighting	Leo Sayer	Chrysalis	6		
19	10	Heartbeat	Showaddywaddy	Bell	5		
20	-	Big Ten	Judge Dread	Cactus	4		

November 1975

This Mnth	Prev Mnth	Title	Artist	Label	Wks 20	(US Pos)	
1	15	Space Oddity	David Bowie	RCA	8	(15)	
2	-	Love Is The Drug	Roxy Music	Island	6	(30)	
3	-	D.I.V.O.R.C.E.	Billy Connolly	Polydor	6		F L
4	-	Rhinestone Cowboy	Glen Campbell	Capitol	6	(1)	L
5	-	Love Hurts	Jim Capaldi	Island	6	(97)	F L
6	-	You Sexy Thing	Hot Chocolate	RAK	9	(3)	
7	2	I Only Have Eyes For You	Art Garfunkel	CBS	8	(18)	F
8	-	Imagine	John Lennon	Apple	5		G
9	-	Hold Back The Night	Trammps	Buddah	5	(35)	F
10	-	Blue Guitar	Justin Hayward & John Lodge	Threshold	5	(94)	F
11	-	What A Diff'rence A Day Makes	Esther Phillips	Kudu	5	(20)	F L
12	-	Bohemian Rhapsody	Queen	EMI	14	(9)	G
13	9	Feelings	Morris Albert	Decca	6	(6)	F L
14	-	New York Groove	Hello	Bell	4		L
15	-	Sky High	Jigsaw	Splash	5	(3)	F L
16	7	S.O.S.	Abba	Epic	6	(15)	
17	3	There Goes My First Love	Drifters	Bell	8		
18	-	This Old Heart Of Mine	Rod Stewart	Riva	5		
19	-	Right Back Where We Started From	Maxine Nightingale	UA	5	(2)	F
20	-	Money Honey	Bay City Rollers	Bell	8	(9)	

December 1975

This Mnth	Prev Mnth	Title	Artist	Label	Wks 20	(US Pos)	
1	12	Bohemian Rhapsody	Queen	EMI	14	(9)	G
2	6	You Sexy Thing	Hot Chocolate	RAK	9	(3)	
3	-	The Trail Of The Lonesome Pine	Laurel & Hardy With The Avalon Boys	UA	7		F L
4	-	Na Na Is The Saddest Word	Stylistics	Avco	7		
5	20	Money Honey	Bay City Rollers	Bell	8	(9)	
6	-	Let's Twist Again	Chubby Checker	London American	8		
7	-	All Around My Hat	Steeleye Span	Chrysalis	7		L
8	-	I Believe In Father Christmas	Greg Lake	Manticore	6	(95)	F L
9	-	Happy To Be On An Island In The Sun	Demis Roussos	Philips	7		F
10	-	Show Me You're A Woman	Mud	Private Stock	6		
11	18	This Old Heart Of Mine	Rod Stewart	Riva	5		
12	-	Golden Years	David Bowie	RCA	7	(10)	
13	5	Love Hurts	Jim Capaldi	Island	6	(97)	F L
14	8	Imagine	John Lennon	Apple	5		G
15	-	Renta Santa	Chris Hill	Philips	3		F
16	-	It's Gonna Be A Cold Cold Christmas	Dana	GTO	5		
17	15	Sky High	Jigsaw	Splash	5	(3)	F L
18	3	D.I.V.O.R.C.E.	Billy Connolly	Polydor	6		F L
19	-	In For A Penny	Slade	Polydor	3		
20	-	Wide Eyed And Legless	Andy Fairweather-Low	A&M	7		L

US 1975 OCT-DEC

October 1975

This Mnth	Prev Mnth	Title	Artist	Label	Wks 20	(UK Pos)	
1	5	I'm Sorry/Calypso	John Denver	RCA	12		G
2	-	Bad Blood	Neil Sedaka	Rocket	6		G
3	12	Ballroom Blitz	Sweet	Capitol	10	(2)	
4	-	Miracles	Jefferson Starship	Grunt	7		
5	18	Dance With Me	Orleans	Asylum	7		F
6	-	Lyin' Eyes	Eagles	Asylum	8	(23)	
7	-	Feelings	Morris Albert	RCA	11	(4)	F G L
8	2	Fame	David Bowie	RCA	8	(17)	G
9	-	They Just Can't Stop It The (Games People Play)	Spinners	Atlantic	9		G
10	-	Mr. Jaws	Dickie Goodman	Cash	5		F G L
11	14	Ain't No Way To Treat A Lady	Helen Reddy	Capitol	6		
12	-	It Only Takes A Minute	Tavares	Capitol	6	(46)	F
13	-	Who Loves You	Four Seasons	Warner	9	(6)	
14	-	Rocky	Austin Roberts	Private Stock	3	(22)	L
15	-	Brazil	Ritchie Family	20th Century	5	(41)	F
16	1	Rhinestone Cowboy	Glen Campbell	Capitol	14	(4)	G
17	9	Run Joey Run	David Geddes	Big Tree	6		F
18	-	Heat Wave/Love Is A Rose	Linda Ronstadt	Asylum	8		
19	-	Island Girl	Elton John	MCA	9	(14)	G
20	-	Something Better To Do	Olivia Newton-John	MCA	6		

November 1975

This Mnth	Prev Mnth	Title	Artist	Label	Wks 20	(UK Pos)	
1	19	Island Girl	Elton John	MCA	9	(14)	G
2	13	Who Loves You	Four Seasons	Warner	9	(6)	
3	-	This Will Be	Natalie Cole	Capitol	7	(32)	F
4	6	Lyin' Eyes	Eagles	Asylum	8	(23)	
5	-	The Way I Want To Touch You	Captain & Tennille	A&M	9	(28)	G
6	7	Feelings	Morris Albert	RCA	11	(4)	F G L
7	4	Miracles	Jefferson Starship	Grunt	7		
8	-	That's The Way (I Like It)	KC & The Sunshine Band	TK	10	(4)	G
9	18	Heat Wave/Love Is A Rose	Linda Ronstadt	Asylum	8		
10	-	Low Rider	War	UA	8	(12)	
11	9	They Just Can't Stop It The (Games People Play)	Spinners	Atlantic	9		G
12	1	I'm Sorry/Calypso	John Denver	RCA	12		G
13	-	Fly Robin Fly	Silver Convention	Midland Int.	8	(28)	F G
14	-	Sky High	Jigsaw	Chelsea	10	(9)	F L
15	-	Nights On Broadway	Bee Gees	RSO	8		
16	-	Let's Do It Again	Staple Singers	Curtom	8		G L
17	-	Do It Any Way You Wanna	Peoples Choice	TSOP	5	(36)	F G L
18	20	Something Better To Do	Olivia Newton-John	MCA	6		
19	2	Bad Blood	Neil Sedaka	Rocket	6		G
20	-	My Little Town	Simon & Garfunkel	Columbia	6		L

December 1975

This Mnth	Prev Mnth	Title	Artist	Label	Wks 20	(UK Pos)	
1	16	Let's Do It Again	Staple Singers	Curtom	8		G L
2	8	That's The Way (I Like It)	KC & The Sunshine Band	TK	10	(4)	G
3	13	Fly Robin Fly	Silver Convention	Midland Int.	8	(28)	F G
4	-	Saturday Night	Bay City Rollers	Arista	9		F G
5	14	Sky High	Jigsaw	Chelsea	10	(9)	F L
6	-	Love Rollercoaster	Ohio Players	Mercury	12		G
7	-	Theme From Mahogany (Do You Know Where You're Going To)	Diana Ross	Motown	10	(5)	
8	-	I Write The Songs	Barry Manilow	Arista	13		G
9	15	Nights On Broadway	Bee Gees	RSO	8		
10	-	Fox On The Run	Sweet	Capitol	8	(2)	G
11	-	Our Day Will Come	Frankie Valli	Private Stock	5		
12	20	My Little Town	Simon & Garfunkel	Columbia	6		L
13	-	I Love Music (Pt. 1)	O'Jays	Philly Int.	10	(13)	G
14	1	Island Girl	Elton John	MCA	9	(14)	G
15	5	The Way I Want To Touch You	Captain & Tennille	A&M	9	(28)	G
16	-	Convoy	C.W. McCall	MGM	9	(2)	F G L
17	10	Low Rider	War	UA	8	(12)	
18	-	Venus And Mars Rock Show	Wings	Capitol	3		
19	-	I Want'a Do Something Freaky To You	Leon Haywood	20th Century	4		F L
20	-	Times Of Your Life	Paul Anka	UA	8		L

◆ A record 35 singles topped the US chart in 1975 and sales of records and tapes rose to $2.36 billion.

◆ Bruce Springsteen simultaneously made the front cover of *Time* and *Newsweek*, and soon after made his debut in the Top 40 with 'Born To Run'.

◆ *Saturday Night Live* bowed in on NBC. The first show included Grammy winning Janis Ian, whose **Between The Lines** topped the LP chart. Simon & Garfunkel briefly re-united the following week to plug 'My Little Town'. For the record, Simon's **Still Crazy After All These Years** headed the US album charts and Garfunkel's Flamingos-cloned 'I Only Have Eyes For You' topped the UK singles chart.

◆ After being seen on TV's *Saturday Night Variety Show*, UK teen idols The Bay City Rollers' debut US hit, 'Saturday Night', went to the top.

UK 1976

JAN-MAR

◆ Thirteen years after taking the US charts by storm, The Four Seasons had their only transatlantic No. 1, 'December '63 (Oh What A Night)'.

◆ In Britain, album chart toppers included 1950s star Slim Whitman and 1960s chart regular Roy Orbison, whilst 1940s favourite Glenn Miller returned to the singles chart!

◆ Despite minimal British success Fleetwood Mac (with new members Stevie Nicks and Lindsey Buckingham) headed up the US LP chart with their eponymous album – it took 58 weeks to reach No. 1!

◆ The chart topper 'Save Your Kisses For Me' from mixed quartet Brotherhood Of Man went on to win the Eurovision Song Contest and sold over a million copies. Unlike all the earlier British entries this catchy single reached the US Top 40.

January 1976

This Mnth	Prev Mnth	Title	Artist	Label	Wks 20	(US Pos)	
1	1	Bohemian Rhapsody	Queen	EMI	14	(9)	G
2	-	Glass Of Champagne	Sailor	Epic	8		F
3	-	Mamma Mia	Abba	Epic	8	(32)	
4	6	Let's Twist Again	Chubby Checker	London American	8		
5	20	Wide Eyed And Legless	Andy Fairweather-Low	A&M	7		L
6	3	The Trail Of The Lonesome Pine	Laurel & Hardy/Avalon Boys	UA	7		F L
7	-	In Dulce Jubilo/On Horseback	Mike Oldfield	Virgin	4		F
8	-	King Of The Cops	Billy Howard	Penny Farthing	6		F L
9	8	I Believe In Father Christmas	Greg Lake	Manticore	6	(95)	F L
10	-	Love Machine	Miracles	Tamla Motown	7	(1)	L
11	12	Golden Years	David Bowie	RCA	7	(10)	
12	16	It's Gonna Be A Cold Cold...	Dana	GTO	5		
13	-	We Do It	R & J Stone	RCA	7		F L
14	-	Forever & Ever	Slik	Bell	7		F L
15	-	Itchycoo Park	Small Faces	Immediate	5		L
16	-	Let The Music Play	Barry White	20th Century	4	(32)	
17	-	Can I Take You Home Little Girl	Drifters	Bell	5		
18	9	Happy To Be On An Island In The Sun	Demis Roussos	Philips	7		F
19	2	You Sexy Thing	Hot Chocolate	RAK	9	(3)	
20	-	If I Could	David Essex	CBS	4		

February 1976

This Mnth	Prev Mnth	Title	Artist	Label	Wks 20	(US Pos)	
1	14	Forever & Ever	Slik	Bell	7		F L
2	-	December '63 (Oh What A Night)	Four Seasons	Warner	8	(1)	
3	3	Mamma Mia	Abba	Epic	8	(32)	
4	-	Love To Love You Baby	Donna Summer	GTO	6	(2)	F
5	10	Love Machine	Miracles	Tamla Motown	7	(1)	L
6	-	Rodrigo's Guitar Concerto De Aranjuez	Manuel & His Music Of The Mountains	EMI	6		F L
7	13	We Do It	R & J Stone	RCA	7		F L
8	-	No Regrets	Walker Brothers	GTO	5		L
9	-	I Love To Love (But My Baby Loves To Dance)	Tina Charles	CBS	7		F
10	-	Convoy	C.W. McCall	MGM	7	(1)	F L
11	-	Dat	Pluto Shervington	Opal	5		F
12	-	Moonlight Serenade/Little Brown Jug/In The Mood	Glenn Miller	RCA	5		L
13	-	It Should Have Been Me	Yvonne Fair	Tamla Motown	5	(85)	F L
14	-	Low Rider	War	UA	5	(7)	F
15	1	Bohemian Rhapsody	Queen	EMI	14	(9)	G
16	-	Evil Woman	Electric Light Orchestra	Jet	4	(10)	
17	-	Squeeze Box	Who	Polydor	6	(16)	
18	-	Walk Away From Love	David Ruffin	Tamla	4	(9)	F L
19	-	Midnight Rider	Paul Davidson	Tropical	4		F L
20	-	Rain	Status Quo	Vertigo	5		

March 1976

This Mnth	Prev Mnth	Title	Artist	Label	Wks 20	(US Pos)	
1	9	I Love To Love (But My Baby...)	Tina Charles	CBS	7		F
2	10	Convoy	C.W. McCall	MGM	7	(1)	F L
3	-	Love Really Hurts Without You	Billy Ocean	GTO	8	(22)	F
4	2	December '63 (Oh What A Night)	Four Seasons	Warner	5	(1)	
5	-	You Don't Have To Say You Love Me	Guys & Dolls	Magnet	5		L
6	-	People Like You And People Like Me	Glitter Band	Bell	6		L
7	-	Save Your Kisses For Me	Brotherhood Of Man	Pye	13	(27)	G
8	13	It Should Have Been Me	Yvonne Fair	Tamla Motown	5	(85)	F L
9	6	Rodrigo's Guitar Concerto...	Manuel/Music Of The Moutains	EMI	6		F L
10	-	You See The Trouble With Me	Barry White	20th Century	7		
11	-	I Wanna Stay With You	Gallagher & Lyle	A&M	6	(49)	
12	-	(Do The) Spanish Hustle	Fatback Band	Polydor	4		
13	20	Rain	Status Quo	Vertigo	5		
14	11	Dat	Pluto Shervington	Opal	5		F
15	-	Funky Weekend	Stylistics	Avco	4	(76)	
16	-	Falling Apart At The Seams	Marmalade	Target	6	(49)	
17	-	Miss You Nights	Cliff Richard	EMI	6		
18	-	Yesterday	Beatles	Apple	6		
19	17	Squeeze Box	Who	Polydor	6	(16)	
20	-	I Love Music	O'Jays	Philly International	4	(5)	

January 1976

This Mnth	Prev Mnth	Title	Artist	Label	Wks 20	(UK Pos)	
1	8	I Write The Songs	Barry Manilow	Arista	13		G
2	6	Love Rollercoaster	Ohio Players	Mercury	12		G
3	7	Theme From Mahogany (Do You Know Where You're Going To)	Diana Ross	Motown	10	(5)	
4	16	Convoy	C.W. McCall	MGM	9	(2)	F G L
5	13	I Love Music (Pt. 1)	O'Jays	Philly Int.	10	(13)	G
6	-	Love To Love You Baby	Donna Summer	Oasis	11	(4)	F G
7	20	Times Of Your Life	Paul Anka	UA	8		L
8	-	You Sexy Thing	Hot Chocolate	Big Tree	12	(2)	G
9	-	Walk Away From Love	David Ruffin	Motown	6	(10)	L
10	10	Fox On The Run	Sweet	Capitol	8	(2)	G
11	-	Sing A Song	Earth, Wind & Fire	Columbia	8		G
12	4	Saturday Night	Bay City Rollers	Arista	9		F G
13	-	Country Boy (You Got Your Feet In L.A.)	Glen Campbell	Capitol	6		
14	-	Rock And Roll All Nite (Live Version)	Kiss	Casablanca	5		F
15	-	Fly Away	John Denver	RCA	5		L
16	-	50 Ways To Leave Your Lover	Paul Simon	Columbia	10	(23)	G
17	2	That's The Way (I Like It)	KC & The Sunshine Band	TK	10	(4)	G
18	-	Evil Woman	Electric Light Orchestra	UA	8	(10)	
19	1	Let's Do It Again	Staple Singers	Curtom	8		G L
20	-	Love Machine	Miracles	Tamla	11	(3)	G L

February 1976

This Mnth	Prev Mnth	Title	Artist	Label	Wks 20	(UK Pos)	
1	16	50 Ways To Leave Your Lover	Paul Simon	Columbia	10	(23)	G
2	-	Theme From S.W.A.T.	Rhythm Heritage	ABC	8		F G
3	8	You Sexy Thing	Hot Chocolate	Big Tree	12	(2)	G
4	6	Love To Love You Baby	Donna Summer	Oasis	11	(4)	F G
5	20	Love Machine	Miracles	Tamla	11	(3)	G L
6	1	I Write The Songs	Barry Manilow	Arista	13		G
7	-	Breaking Up Is Hard To Do	Neil Sedaka	Rocket	8		
8	-	All By Myself	Eric Carmen	Arista	10	(12)	F G
9	-	Take It To The Limit	Eagles	Asylum	9	(12)	
10	-	Love Hurts	Nazareth	A&M	9		F G L
11	11	Sing A Song	Earth, Wind & Fire	Columbia	8		G
12	18	Evil Woman	Electric Light Orchestra	UA	8	(10)	
13	2	Love Rollercoaster	Ohio Players	Mercury	12		G
14	-	December '63 (Oh What A Night)	Four Seasons	Warner	12	(1)	G L
15	-	Wake Up Everybody (Pt. 1)	Harold Melvin & The Blue Notes	Philly Int.	6	(23)	L
16	4	Convoy	C.W. McCall	MGM	9	(2)	F G L
17	-	Lonely Night (Angel Face)	Captain & Tennille	A&M	10		G
18	-	Grow Some Funk Of Your Own/ I Feel Like A Bullet	Elton John	MCA	3		
19	-	Dream Weaver	Gary Wright	Warner	10		F G
20	7	Times Of Your Life	Paul Anka	UA	8		L

March 1976

This Mnth	Prev Mnth	Title	Artist	Label	Wks 20	(UK Pos)	
1	14	December '63 (Oh What A Night)	Four Seasons	Warner	12	(1)	G L
2	8	All By Myself	Eric Carmen	Arista	10	(12)	F G
3	19	Dream Weaver	Gary Wright	Warner	10		F G
4	17	Lonely Night (Angel Face)	Captain & Tennille	A&M	10		G
5	9	Take It To The Limit	Eagles	Asylum	9	(12)	
6	5	Love Machine	Miracles	Tamla	11	(3)	G L
7	-	Sweet Thing	Rufus Featuring Chaka Khan	ABC	9		G L
8	-	Disco Lady	Johnnie Taylor	Columbia	10	(25)	P L
9	-	Dream On	Aerosmith	Columbia	8		F
10	-	Junk Food Junkie	Larry Groce	Warner	5		F L
11	2	Theme From S.W.A.T.	Rhythm Heritage	ABC	8		F G
12	-	Fanny (Be Tender With My Love)	Bee Gees	RSO	6		
13	-	Money Honey	Bay City Rollers	Arista	6	(3)	
14	10	Love Hurts	Nazareth	A&M	9		F G L
15	-	Golden Years	David Bowie	RCA	8	(8)	
16	1	50 Ways To Leave Your Lover	Paul Simon	Columbia	10	(23)	G
17	-	Right Back Where We Started From	Maxine Nightingale	UA	12	(8)	F G
18	-	Let Your Love Flow	Bellamy Brothers	Warner	9	(7)	F L
19	3	You Sexy Thing	Hot Chocolate	Big Tree	12	(2)	G
20	-	Deep Purple	Donny & Marie Osmond	MGM	6	(25)	L

US 1976 JAN-MAR

◆ Rockers Kiss and Aerosmith, who were among the decade's top album sellers, had their first single hits with 'Rock And Roll All Nite' and 'Dream On' respectively.

◆ A new award, the platinum album, was introduced for albums selling over one million copies. First recipient was **Eagles/Their Greatest Hits 1971-1974** - which went on to sell 14 million copies!

▲ German based producer/composer Giorgio Moroder's latest discovery, American disco diva Donna Summer, had the first of her numerous hits with a controversial heavy breathing opus, 'Love To Love You Baby'.

UK 1976 APR-JUNE

▲ The Rolling Stones, whose **Black And Blue** headed the American LP listings, played six nights at Earl's Court in London as part of their eight-week European tour. Other major UK events included The Who at Charlton Athletic Football Club and David Bowie (above) at Wembley. Also gigging were The Sex Pistols, America's Patti Smith, The Stranglers, The Damned and AC/DC.

◆ A harbinger of the forthcoming British rockabilly revival was the success of 'Jungle Rock' by Hank Mizell. The old time rock'n'roll hit sold few copies in the USA when first released in 1957 but gave the 52-year-old sales manager a surprise European hit in 1976.

April 1976

This Mnth	Prev Mnth	Title	Artist	Label	Wks 20	(US Pos)	
1	7	Save Your Kisses For Me	Brotherhood Of Man	Pye	13	(27)	G
2	-	Music	John Miles	Decca	7	(88)	
3	10	You See The Trouble With Me	Barry White	20th Century	7		
4	-	Fernando	Abba	Epic	12	(13)	
5	-	I'm Mandy Fly Me	10cc	Mercury	6	(60)	
6	-	Jungle Rock	Hank Mizell	Charly	9		F L
7	-	Pinball Wizard	Elton John	DJM	4		
8	-	Theme From Mahogany (Do You Know Where You're Going To)	Diana Ross	Tamla Motown	5	(1)	
9	3	Love Really Hurts Without You	Billy Ocean	GTO	8	(22)	F
10	18	Yesterday	Beatles	Apple	6		
11	-	Girls Girls Girls	Sailor	Epic	5		L
12	11	I Wanna Stay With You	Gallagher & Lyle	A&M	6	(49)	F
13	16	Falling Apart At The Seams	Marmalade	Target	6	(49)	L
14	-	Hello Happiness	Drifters	Bell	5		
15	-	Love Me Like I Love You	Bay City Rollers	Bell	5		
16	-	Don't Stop It Now	Hot Chocolate	RAK	5	(42)	
17	-	Hey Jude	Beatles	Apple	4		
18	6	People Like You And People Like Me	Glitter Band	Bell	6		L
19	1	I Love To Love (But My Baby Loves To Dance)	Tina Charles	CBS	7		F
20	-	S-S-S-Single Bed	Fox	GTO	7		L

May 1976

This Mnth	Prev Mnth	Title	Artist	Label	Wks 20	(US Pos)	
1	4	Fernando	Abba	Epic	12	(13)	
2	1	Save Your Kisses For Me	Brotherhood Of Man	Pye	13	(27)	G
3	6	Jungle Rock	Hank Mizell	Charly	9		F L
4	20	S-S-S-Single Bed	Fox	GTO	7		L
5	-	Silver Star	Four Seasons	Warner	5	(38)	L
6	-	More, More, More	Andrea True Connection	Buddah	7	(4)	F L
7	-	Arms Of Mary	Sutherland Brothers And Quiver	CBS	5	(81)	F L
8	-	Get Up And Boogie (That's Right)	Silver Convention	Magnet	6	(2)	F L
9	-	No Charge	J.J. Barrie	Power Exchange	7		F L
10	-	Convoy GB	Laurie Lingo & The Dipsticks	State	5		F L
11	-	Can't Help Falling In Love	Stylistics	Avco	6		
12	-	Fool To Cry	Rolling Stones	Rolling Stone	6	(10)	
13	-	Life Is Too Short Girl	Sheer Elegance	Pye International	6		L
14	8	Theme From Mahogany (Do You Know Where You're Going To)	Diana Ross	Tamla Motown	5	(1)	
15	-	My Resistance Is Low	Robin Sarstedt	Decca	5		F L
16	-	Combine Harvester (Brand New Key)	Wurzels	EMI	7		F
17	-	Love Hangover	Diana Ross	Tamla Motown	6	(1)	
18	-	Disco Connection	Isaac Hayes	ABC	5		L
19	11	Girls Girls Girls	Sailor	Epic	5		L
20	15	Love Me Like I Love You	Bay City Rollers	Bell	5		

June 1976

This Mnth	Prev Mnth	Title	Artist	Label	Wks 20	(US Pos)	
1	16	Combine Harvester (Brand New Key)	Wurzels	EMI	7		F
2	-	Silly Love Songs	Wings	Parlophone	8	(1)	
3	9	No Charge	J.J. Barrie	Power Exchange	7		F L
4	-	You To Me Are Everything	Real Thing	Pye International	8	(64)	F
5	15	My Resistance Is Low	Robin Sarstedt	Decca	5		F L
6	-	You Just Might See Me Cry	Our Kid	Polydor	7		F L
7	-	Let Your Love Flow	Bellamy Brothers	Warner	8	(1)	F
8	12	Fool To Cry	Rolling Stones	Rolling Stone	6	(10)	
9	1	Fernando	Abba	Epic	12	(13)	
10	-	Tonight's The Night (Gonna Be Alright)	Rod Stewart	Riva	7	(1)	
11	-	Jolene	Dolly Parton	RCA	6	(60)	F
12	-	Heart On My Sleeve	Gallagher & Lyle	A&M	7	(67)	L
13	-	Show Me The Way	Peter Frampton	A&M	5	(6)	F L
14	-	Devil Woman	Cliff Richard	EMI	4	(6)	
15	-	Midnight Train To Georgia	Gladys Knight & The Pips	Buddah	4	(1)	
16	-	This Is It	Melba Moore	Buddah	4	(91)	F
17	-	Young Hearts Run Free	Candi Staton	Warner	9	(20)	F
18	17	Love Hangover	Diana Ross	Tamla Motown	6	(1)	
19	-	Shake It Down	Mud	Private Stock	2		
20	-	Let's Stick Together	Bryan Ferry	Island	7		

April 1976

This Mnth	Prev Mnth	Title	Artist	Label	Wks 20	(UK Pos)	
1	8	Disco Lady	Johnnie Taylor	Columbia	10	(25)	P L
2	18	Let Your Love Flow	Bellamy Brothers	Warner	9	(7)	F L
3	17	Right Back Where We Started From	Maxine Nightingale	UA	12	(8)	F G
4	4	Lonely Night (Angel Face)	Captain & Tennille	A&M	10		G
5	3	Dream Weaver	Gary Wright	Warner	10		F G
6	-	On!y Sixteen	Dr. Hook	Capitol	7		G
7	-	Boogie Fever	Sylvers	Capitol	11		F G
8	-	Sweet Love	Commodores	Motown	6	(32)	
9	-	Show Me The Way	Peter Frampton	A&M	10	(10)	F
10	9	Dream On	Aerosmith	Columbia	8		F
11	-	Bohemian Rhapsody	Queen	Elektra	9	(1)	G
12	7	Sweet Thing	Rufus Featuring Chaka Khan	ABC	9		G L
13	1	December '63 (Oh What A Night)	Four Seasons	Warner	12	(1)	G L
14	-	There's A Kind Of Hush (All Over The World)	Carpenters	A&M	4	(22)	
15	15	Golden Years	David Bowie	RCA	8	(8)	
16	-	Welcome Back	John Sebastian	Reprise	10		F G L
17	-	Fooled Around And Fell In Love	Elvin Bishop	Capricorn	9	(34)	F G L
18	13	Money Honey	Bay City Rollers	Arista	6	(3)	
19	20	Deep Purple	Donny & Marie Osmond	MGM	6	(25)	L
20	-	I Do, I Do, I Do, I Do, I Do	Abba	Atlantic	3	(38)	

May 1976

This Mnth	Prev Mnth	Title	Artist	Label	Wks 20	(UK Pos)	
1	16	Welcome Back	John Sebastian	Reprise	10		F G L
2	17	Fooled Around And Fell In Love	Elvin Bishop	Capricorn	9	(34)	F G L
3	-	Silly Love Songs	Wings	Capitol	12	(2)	G
4	7	Boogie Fever	Sylvers	Capitol	11		F G
5	-	Love Hangover	Diana Ross	Motown	10	(10)	
6	-	Get Up And Boogie	Silver Convention	Midland Int.	11	(7)	G L
7	3	Right Back Where We Started From	Maxine Nightingale	UA	12	(8)	F G
8	-	Shannon	Henry Gross	Lifesong	9		F G L
9	9	Show Me The Way	Peter Frampton	A&M	10	(10)	F
10	-	Tryin' To Get The Feeling Again	Barry Manilow	Arista	7		
11	-	Happy Days	Pratt & McClain	Reprise	7	(31)	F L
12	-	Sara Smile	Daryl Hall & John Oates	RCA	11		F G
13	-	Misty Blue	Dorothy Moore	Malaco	11	(5)	F L
14	2	Let Your Love Flow	Bellamy Brothers	Warner	9	(7)	F L
15	1	Disco Lady	Johnnie Taylor	Columbia	10	(25)	P L
16	-	Fool To Cry	Rolling Stones	Rolling Stone	6	(6)	
17	-	Rhiannon (Will You Ever Win)	Fleetwood Mac	Reprise	6	(46)	
18	11	Bohemian Rhapsody	Queen	Elektra	9	(1)	G
19	-	Strange Magic	Electric Light Orchestra	UA	5	(38)	
20	8	Sweet Love	Commodores	Motown	6	(32)	

June 1976

This Mnth	Prev Mnth	Title	Artist	Label	Wks 20	(UK Pos)	
1	3	Silly Love Songs	Wings	Capitol	12	(2)	G
2	6	Get Up And Boogie	Silver Convention	Midland Int.	11	(7)	G L
3	13	Misty Blue	Dorothy Moore	Malaco	11	(5)	F L
4	5	Love Hangover	Diana Ross	Motown	10	(10)	
5	12	Sara Smile	Daryl Hall & John Oates	RCA	11		F G
6	-	Shop Around	Captain & Tennille	A&M	10		G
7	-	More, More, More (Pt. 1)	Andrea True Connection	Buddah	10	(5)	F G L
8	8	Shannon	Henry Gross	Lifesong	9		F G L
9	11	Happy Days	Pratt & McClain	Reprise	7	(31)	F L
10	-	I'll Be Good To You	Brothers Johnson	A&M	8		F G
11	-	Love Is Alive	Gary Wright	Warner	14		
12	-	Afternoon Delight	Starland Vocal Band	Windsong	10	(18)	F G L
13	1	Welcome Back	John Sebastian	Reprise	10		F G L
14	16	Fool To Cry	Rolling Stones	Rolling Stone	6	(6)	
15	-	Kiss And Say Goodbye	Manhattans	Columbia	11	(4)	F G
16	17	Rhiannon (Will You Ever Win)	Fleetwood Mac	Reprise	6	(46)	
17	-	Takin' It To The Streets	Doobie Brothers	Warner	3		
18	-	Movin'	Brass Construction	UA	4	(23)	F L
19	-	Never Gonna Fall In Love Again	Eric Carmen	Arista	6		
20	-	I Want You	Marvin Gaye	Tamla	4		

US
1976
APR-JUNE

◆ Paul McCartney & Wings played to a record indoor crowd of 67,000 in Seattle, during their debut US tour. They topped the charts with 'Silly Love Songs' and their LP, **Wings At The Speed of Sound** (which stopped The Beatles' **Rock'n'Roll Music** hitting No. 1).

◆ Johnnie Taylor's US-only hit, 'Disco Lady', became the first certified platinum single (two million sales). Meanwhile, disco ladies Diana Ross, Silver Convention and The Andrea True Connection were scoring transatlantic Top 20 hits.

◆ Motown finalized a record breaking $13 million advance to re-sign Stevie Wonder whose last LP, **Fulfillingness' First Finale**, was voted album of the year at the 1974 Grammy awards.

◆ Eddy Arnold's 'Cowboy' made him the first artist to have had 100 singles on the country charts.

UK 1976 JULY-SEPT

◆ A UK visit by The Ramones helped to heighten interest in punk. The Sex Pistols appeared on TV, and The Clash, The Buzzcocks and Siouxsie & The Banshees made their live debuts. Stiff Records was launched, and the first issue of fanzine *Sniffin' Glue* hit the streets.

◆ The Rolling Stones, Lynyrd Skynyrd, and 10cc attracted 200,000 to the Knebworth Festival, while 60,000 attended Queen's Hyde Park concert and Grateful Dead and Santana packed the crowds into Wembley.

◆ Britain's top solo artist, Cliff Richard, finally cracked the US Top 10 with 'Devil Woman'. His 20 date Russian tour was also a great success.

◆ Sid Bernstein, who had promoted The Beatles' famous Shea Stadium gig, reportedly offered the group $200 million to reform and tour for him.

July 1976

This Mnth	Prev Mnth	Title	Artist	Label	Wks 20	(US Pos)	
1	17	Young Hearts Run Free	Candi Staton	Warner	9	(20)	F
2	-	The Roussos Phenomenon E.P.	Demis Roussos	Philips	9		
3	-	A Little Bit More	Dr. Hook	Capitol	11	(11)	
4	-	Kiss And Say Goodbye	Manhattans	CBS	8	(1)	F
5	4	You To Me Are Everything	Real Thing	Pye International	8	(64)	F
6	-	Don't Go Breaking My Heart	Elton John & Kiki Dee	Rocket	11	(1)	
7	20	Let's Stick Together	Bryan Ferry	Island	7		
8	6	You Just Might See Me Cry	Our Kid	Polydor	7		F L
9	-	Misty Blue	Dorothy Moore	Contempo	9	(3)	F
10	-	You're My Best Friend	Queen	EMI	5	(16)	
11	10	Tonight's The Night (Gonna Be Alright)	Rod Stewart	Riva	7	(1)	
12	-	Leader Of The Pack	Shangri-Las	Charly/Contempo	5		L
13	-	It Only Takes A Minute	One Hundred Ton & A Feather	UK	5		F L
14	-	The Boys Are Back In Town	Thin Lizzy	Vertigo	5	(12)	
15	-	You Are My Love	Liverpool Express	Warner	6		F
16	-	Heaven Must Be Missing An Angel	Tavares	Capitol	7	(15)	F
17	12	Heart On My Sleeve	Gallagher & Lyle	A&M	7	(67)	L
18	2	Silly Love Songs	Wings	Parlophone	8	(1)	
19	-	I Love To Boogie	T. Rex	EMI	5		
20	-	Man To Man	Hot Chocolate	RAK	4		

August 1976

This Mnth	Prev Mnth	Title	Artist	Label	Wks 20	(US Pos)	
1	6	Don't Go Breaking My Heart	Elton John & Kiki Dee	Rocket	11	(1)	
2	3	A Little Bit More	Dr. Hook	Capitol	11	(11)	
3	-	Jeans On	David Dundas	Air	6	(17)	F L
4	16	Heaven Must Be Missing An Angel	Tavares	Capitol	7	(15)	F
5	-	In Zaire	Johnny Wakelin	Pye	6		L
6	-	Now Is The Time	Jimmy James & The Vagabonds	Pye	6		F L
7	-	Dr Kiss Kiss	5000 Volts	Philips	6		L
8	-	Let 'Em In	Wings	Parlophone	8	(3)	
9	9	Misty Blue	Dorothy Moore	Contempo	9	(3)	F
10	-	You Should Be Dancing	Bee Gees	RSO	7	(1)	
11	2	The Roussos Phenomenon E.P.	Demis Roussos	Philips	9		
12	-	Mystery Song	Status Quo	Vertigo	5		
13	-	Harvest For The World	Isley Brothers	Epic	4	(63)	
14	4	Kiss And Say Goodbye	Manhattans	CBS	8	(1)	F
15	-	Here Comes The Sun	Steve Harley	EMI	4		
16	-	You Don't Have To Go	Chi-Lites	Brunswick	7		L
17	-	Extended Play (E.P.)	Bryan Ferry	Island	6		
18	-	What I've Got In Mind	Billie Jo Spears	UA	5		L
19	1	Young Hearts Run Free	Candi Staton	Warner	9	(20)	F
20	-	You'll Never Find Another Love Like Mine	Lou Rawls	Philly International	4	(2)	F L

September 1976

This Mnth	Prev Mnth	Title	Artist	Label	Wks 20	(US Pos)	
1	-	Dancing Queen	Abba	Epic	12	(1)	
2	8	Let 'Em In	Wings	Parlophone	8	(3)	
3	-	The Killing Of Georgie	Rod Stewart	Riva	7	(30)	
4	16	You Don't Have To Go	Chi-Lites	Brunswick	7		L
5	-	(Light Of Experience) Doina De Jale	Georghe Zamfir	Epic	6		F L
6	-	Can't Get By Without You	Real Thing	Pye	8		
7	-	16 Bars	Stylistics	H & L	7		L
8	1	Don't Go Breaking My Heart	Elton John & Kiki Dee	Rocket	11	(1)	
9	18	What I've Got In Mind	Billie Jo Spears	UA	5		L
10	-	Aria	Acker Bilk	Pye	6		L
11	-	Blinded By The Light	Manfred Mann's Earth Band	Bronze	6	(1)	F
12	-	I Am A Cider Drinker (Paloma Blanca)	Wurzels	EMI	5		L
13	-	I Only Wanna Be With You	Bay City Rollers	Bell	6	(12)	
14	17	Extended Play (E.P.)	Bryan Ferry	Island	6		
15	10	You Should Be Dancing	Bee Gees	RSO	7	(1)	
16	-	Mississippi	Pussycat	Sonet	13		F L
17	2	A Little Bit More	Dr. Hook	Capitol	11	(11)	
18	-	Dance Little Lady Dance	Tina Charles	CBS	6		
19	20	You'll Never Find Another Love Like Mine	Lou Rawls	Philly International	4	(2)	F L
20	5	In Zaire	Johnny Wakelin	Pye	6		L

July 1976

This Mnth	Prev Mnth	Title	Artist	Label	Wks 20	(UK Pos)	
1	12	Afternoon Delight	Starland Vocal Band	Windsong	10	(18)	F G L
2	15	Kiss And Say Goodbye	Manhattans	Columbia	11	(4)	F G
3	10	I'll Be Good To You	Brothers Johnson	A&M	8		F G
4	11	Love Is Alive	Gary Wright	Warner	14		
5	-	Moonlight Feels Right	Starbuck	Private Stock	9		F L
6	-	Got To Get You Into My Life	Beatles	Capitol	8		
7	6	Shop Around	Captain & Tennille	A&M	10		G
8	7	More, More, More (Pt. 1)	Andrea True Connection	Buddah	10	(5)	F G L
9	1	Silly Love Songs	Wings	Capitol	12	(2)	G
10	9	Rock And Roll Music	Beach Boys	Brother	10	(36)	
11	-	Let Her In	John Travolta	Midland Int.	5		F
12	-	Get Closer	Seals & Crofts	Warner	6		
13	3	Misty Blue	Dorothy Moore	Malaco	11	(5)	F L
14	-	Take The Money And Run	Steve Miller Band	Capitol	6		
15	-	If You Know What I Mean	Neil Diamond	Columbia	6	(35)	
16	5	Sara Smile	Daryl Hall & John Oates	RCA	11		F G
17	-	Don't Go Breaking My Heart	Elton John & Kiki Dee	Rocket	9	(1)	G
18	-	The Boys Are Back In Town	Thin Lizzy	Mercury	5	(8)	F L
19	19	Never Gonna Fall In Love Again	Eric Carmen	Arista	6		
20	2	Get Up And Boogie	Silver Convention	Midland Int.	11	(7)	G L

August 1976

This Mnth	Prev Mnth	Title	Artist	Label	Wks 20	(UK Pos)	
1	17	Don't Go Breaking My Heart	Elton John & Kiki Dee	Rocket	9	(1)	G
2	-	You Should Be Dancing	Bee Gees	RSO	10	(5)	G
3	-	Let 'Em In	Wings	Capitol	8	(2)	G
4	-	You'll Never Find Another Love Like Mine	Lou Rawls	Philly Int.	9	(10)	G L
5	4	Love Is Alive	Gary Wright	Warner	14		
6	-	I'd Really Love To See You Tonight	England Dan & John Ford Coley	Big Tree	11		F G
7	10	Rock And Roll Music	Beach Boys	Brother	10	(36)	
8	2	Kiss And Say Goodbye	Manhattans	Columbia	11	(4)	F G
9	-	(Shake, Shake, Shake) Shake Your Booty	KC & The Sunshine Band	TK	12	(22)	G
10	-	This Masquerade	George Benson	Warner	7		F
11	-	Turn The Beat Around	Vicki Sue Robinson	RCA	6		F L
12	-	Play That Funky Music	Wild Cherry	Epic	13	(7)	F G L
13	-	A Fifth Of Beethoven	Walter Murphy/Big Apple Band	Private Stock	14	(28)	F G L
14	-	Baby, I Love Your Way	Peter Frampton	A&M	5	(43)	
15	1	Afternoon Delight	Starland Vocal Band	Windsong	10	(18)	F G L
16	5	Moonlight Feels Right	Starbuck	Private Stock	9		F L
17	6	Got To Get You Into My Life	Beatles	Capitol	8		
18	-	Say You Love Me	Fleetwood Mac	Reprise	9	(40)	
19	-	I'm Easy	Keith Carradine	ABC	4		F L
20	15	If You Know What I Mean	Neil Diamond	Columbia	6	(35)	

September 1976

This Mnth	Prev Mnth	Title	Artist	Label	Wks 20	(UK Pos)	
1	12	Play That Funky Music	Wild Cherry	Epic	13	(7)	F G L
2	9	(Shake, Shake, Shake) Shake Your Booty	KC & The Sunshine Band	TK	12	(22)	G
3	6	I'd Really Love To See You Tonight	England Dan & John Ford Coley	Big Tree	11		F G
4	4	You'll Never Find Another Love Like Mine	Lou Rawls	Philly Int.	9	(10)	G L
5	13	A Fifth Of Beethoven	Walter Murphy/Big Apple Band	Private Stock	14	(28)	F G L
6	-	Lowdown	Boz Scaggs	Columbia	9	(28)	F G
7	-	Summer	War	UA	6		G L
8	2	You Should Be Dancing	Bee Gees	RSO	10	(5)	G
9	-	Devil Woman	Cliff Richard	Rocket	9	(9)	F G
10	-	If You Leave Me Now	Chicago	Columbia	12	(1)	G
11	18	Say You Love Me	Fleetwood Mac	Reprise	9	(40)	
12	1	Don't Go Breaking My Heart	Elton John & Kiki Dee	Rocket	9	(1)	G
13	3	Let 'Em In	Paul McCartney	Capitol	8	(2)	G
14	-	With Your Love	Jefferson Starship	Grunt	6		
15	-	Disco Duck	Rick Dees & His Cast Of Idiots	RSO	12	(6)	F G L
16	-	A Little Bit More	Dr. Hook	Capitol	7	(2)	
17	-	Still The One	Orleans	Asylum	8		
18	10	This Masquerade	George Benson	Warner	7		F
19	-	Getaway	Earth, Wind & Fire	Columbia	6		G
20	-	Heaven Must Be Missing An Angel	Tavares	Capitol	4	(4)	G L

◆ Fleetwood Mac, whose earlier US hits had sold only modestly in America, now topped the US LP chart with a self-titled set, which failed to crack the Top 20 in their homeland. The addition of American members Stevie Nicks and Lindsey Buckingham was seen as the group's turning point.

▲ Joining the droves of disco artists in the charts were soulful singers Lou Rawls, The Isley Brothers, The Manhattans, Dorothy Moore (above) and Candi Staton.

◆ Deep Purple and The Allman Brothers disbanded, and Loggins and Messina split up.

UK 1976 OCT-DEC

▲ 'New Rose' by The Damned, widely accepted as the first British punk single, was released. The Sex Pistols' (above) debut disc 'Anarchy In The UK' charted, but EMI, offended by their "disgraceful... aggressive behaviour", withdrew the record, paid them off with £40,000 ($100,000) and dropped them!

◆ One of the leading exponents of the current British craze Pub Rock, Dr. Feelgood (named after an earlier US R&B singer), took their R&B-styled live album **Stupidity** to the top without the benefit of a hit single.

October 1976

This Mnth	Prev Mnth	Title	Artist	Label	Wks 20	(US Pos)	
1	16	Mississippi	Pussycat	Sonet	13		F L
2	1	Dancing Queen	Abba	Epic	12	(1)	
3	-	Sailing	Rod Stewart	Warner	8	(58)	
4	6	Can't Get By Without You	Real Thing	Pye	8		
5	-	When Forever Has Gone	Demis Roussos	Philips	7		L
6	-	Disco Duck	Rick Dees & His Cast Of Idiots	RSO	6	(1)	F L
7	-	Howzat	Sherbet	Epic	7	(61)	F L
8	-	Girl Of My Best Friend	Elvis Presley	RCA	6		
9	18	Dance Little Lady Dance	Tina Charles	CBS	6		
10	13	I Only Wanna Be With You	Bay City Rollers	Bell	6	(12)	
11	-	Hurt	Manhattans	CBS	8	(97)	L
12	-	If You Leave Me Now	Chicago	CBS	12	(1)	
13	-	The Best Disco In Town	Ritchie Family	Polydor	5	(17)	F L
14	12	I Am A Cider Drinker (Paloma Blanca)	Wurzels	EMI	5		L
15	-	Summer Of My Life	Simon May	Pye	6		F L
16	-	Don't Take Away The Music	Tavares	Capitol	7	(34)	
17	10	Aria	Acker Bilk	Pye	6		L
18	11	Blinded By The Light	Manfred Mann's Earth Band	Bronze	6	(1)	F
19	-	I'll Meet You At Midnight	Smokie	RAK	5		
20	-	Loving And Free/Amoureuse	Kiki Dee	Rocket	5		

November 1976

This Mnth	Prev Mnth	Title	Artist	Label	Wks 20	(US Pos)	
1	12	If You Leave Me Now	Chicago	CBS	12	(1)	
2	1	Mississippi	Pussycat	Sonet	13		F L
3	-	You Make Me Feel Like Dancing	Leo Sayer	Chrysalis	7	(1)	
4	16	Don't Take Away The Music	Tavares	Capitol	7	(34)	
5	-	Play That Funky Music	Wild Cherry	Epic	7	(1)	F L
6	11	Hurt	Manhattans	CBS	8	(97)	L
7	5	When Forever Has Gone	Demis Roussos	Philips	7		L
8	-	If Not You	Dr. Hook	Capitol	6	(55)	
9	-	Under The Moon Of Love	Showaddywaddy	Bell	12		
10	-	Couldn't Get It Right	Climax Blues Band	BTM	6	(3)	F L
11	7	Howzat	Sherbet	Epic	7	(61)	F L
12	15	Summer Of My Life	Simon May	Pye	6		F L
13	-	Dancing With The Captain	Paul Nicholas	RSO	5		
14	-	Substitute	Who	Polydor	5		
15	-	Love And Affection	Joan Armatrading	A&M	5		F
16	-	Beautiful Noise	Neil Diamond	CBS	4		
17	-	Lost In France	Bonnie Tyler	RCA	5		F
18	-	Somebody To Love	Queen	EMI	8	(13)	
19	-	Jaws	Lalo Schifrin	CTI	4		F L
20	3	Sailing	Rod Stewart	Warner	8	(58)	

December 1976

This Mnth	Prev Mnth	Title	Artist	Label	Wks 20	(US Pos)	
1	9	Under The Moon Of Love	Showaddywaddy	Bell	12		
2	18	Somebody To Love	Queen	EMI	8	(13)	
3	-	Money Money Money	Abba	Epic	10	(56)	
4	-	Livin' Thing	Electric Light Orchestra	Jet	8	(13)	
5	-	When A Child Is Born (Soleado)	Johnny Mathis	CBS	8		
6	-	Love Me	Yvonne Elliman	RSO	8	(14)	F
7	1	If You Leave Me Now	Chicago	CBS	12	(1)	
8	3	You Make Me Feel Like Dancing	Leo Sayer	Chrysalis	7	(1)	
9	-	Lean On Me	Mud	Private Stock	7		L
10	-	Portsmouth	Mike Oldfield	Virgin	9		
11	-	Get Back	Rod Stewart	Riva	6		
12	17	Lost In France	Bonnie Tyler	RCA	5		F
13	8	If Not You	Dr. Hook	Capitol	6	(55)	
14	-	Sorry Seems To Be The Hardest Word	Elton John	Rocket	3	(6)	
15	-	Living Next Door To Alice	Smokie	RAK	7	(25)	
16	-	Bionic Santa	Chris Hill	Philips	5		L
17	-	Little Does She Know	Kursaal Flyers	CBS	6		F L
18	-	Dr. Love	Tina Charles	CBS	8		L
19	-	Stop Me (If You've Heard It All Before)	Billy Ocean	GTO	4		
20	-	Rock'n Me	Steve Miller Band	Mercury	4	(1)	F

October 1976

This Mnth	Prev Mnth	Title	Artist	Label	Wks 20	(UK Pos)	Flags
1	15	Disco Duck	Rick Dees & His Cast Of Idiots	RSO	12	(6)	F G L
2	5	A Fifth Of Beethoven	Walter Murphy/Big Apple Band	Private Stock	14	(28)	F G L
3	10	If You Leave Me Now	Chicago	Columbia	12	(1)	G
4	1	Play That Funky Music	Wild Cherry	Epic	13	(7)	F G L
5	6	Lowdown	Boz Scaggs	Columbia	9	(28)	F G
6	2	(Shake, Shake...) Shake Your Booty	KC & The Sunshine Band	TK	12	(22)	G
7	17	Still The One	Orleans	Asylum	8		
8	-	She's Gone	Daryl Hall & John Oates	Atlantic	9	(42)	
9	9	Devil Woman	Cliff Richard	Rocket	9	(9)	F G
10	-	Rock'n Me	Steve Miller Band	Capitol	9	(11)	
11	3	I'd Really Love To See You Tonight	England Dan & John Ford Coley	Big Tree	11		F G
12	-	That'll Be The Day	Linda Ronstadt	Asylum	6		
13	-	Love So Right	Bee Gees	RSO	9	(41)	G
14	-	Magic Man	Heart	Mushroom	7		F
15	-	I Only Want To Be With You	Bay City Rollers	Arista	5	(4)	
16	-	Wreck Of The Edmund Fitzgerald	Gordon Lightfoot	Reprise	9	(40)	L
17	16	A Little Bit More	Dr. Hook	Capitol	7	(2)	
18	19	Getaway	Earth, Wind & Fire	Columbia	6		G
19	-	(Don't Fear) The Reaper	Blue Oyster Cult	Columbia	7	(16)	F L
20	11	Say You Love Me	Fleetwood Mac	Reprise	9	(40)	

November 1976

This Mnth	Prev Mnth	Title	Artist	Label	Wks 20	(UK Pos)	Flags
1	16	Wreck Of The Edmund Fitzgerald	Gordon Lightfoot	Reprise	9	(40)	L
2	-	Tonight's The Night (Gonna Be Alright)	Rod Stewart	Warner	12	(5)	G
3	1	Disco Duck	Rick Dees & His Cast Of Idiots	RSO	12	(6)	F G L
4	13	Love So Right	Bee Gees	RSO	9	(41)	G
5	-	Muskrat Love	Captain & Tennille	A&M	11		G
6	10	Rock'n Me	Steve Miller Band	Capitol	9	(11)	
7	-	Just To Be Close To You	Commodores	Motown	6		
8	-	The Rubberband Man	Spinners	Atlantic	11	(16)	G
9	-	Beth	Kiss	Casablanca	10		G
10	-	Do You Feel Like We Do	Peter Frampton	A&M	4	(39)	
11	3	If You Leave Me Now	Chicago	Columbia	12	(1)	G
12	-	Nadia's Theme (The Young & The Restless)	Barry DeVorzon & Perry Botkin	A&M	11		F G L
13	-	More Than A Feeling	Boston	Epic	11	(22)	F
14	-	You Are The Woman	Firefall	Atlantic	8		F
15	19	(Don't Fear) The Reaper	Blue Oyster Cult	Columbia	7	(16)	F L
16	-	Fernando	Abba	Atlantic	5	(1)	
17	8	She's Gone	Daryl Hall & John Oates	Atlantic	9	(42)	
18	-	Nights Are Forever Without You	England Dan & John Ford Coley	Big Tree	8		
19	14	Magic Man	Heart	Mushroom	7		F
20	-	I Never Cry	Alice Cooper	Warner	8		G

December 1976

This Mnth	Prev Mnth	Title	Artist	Label	Wks 20	(UK Pos)	Flags
1	2	Tonight's The Night (Gonna Be...)	Rod Stewart	Warner	12	(5)	G
2	8	The Rubberband Man	Spinners	Atlantic	11	(16)	G
3	-	You Don't Have To Be A Star (To Be In My Show)	Marilyn McCoo & Billy Davis Jr	ABC	11	(7)	F G
4	13	More Than A Feeling	Boston	Epic	11	(22)	F
5	-	You Make Me Feel Like Dancing	Leo Sayer	Warner	13	(2)	G
6	5	Muskrat Love	Captain & Tennille	A&M	11		G
7	-	Sorry Seems To Be The Hardest Word	Elton John	MCA/Rocket	8	(11)	G
8	12	Nadia's Theme (Young & Restless)	Barry DeVorzon & Perry Botkin	A&M	11		F G L
9	4	Love So Right	Bee Gees	RSO	9	(41)	G
10	14	You Are The Woman	Firefall	Atlantic	8		F
11	18	Nights Are Forever Without You	England Dan & John Ford Coley	Big Tree	8		
12	-	After The Lovin'	Engelbert Humperdinck	Epic	9		G L
13	20	I Never Cry	Alice Cooper	Warner	8		G
14	-	Dazz	Brick	Bang	11	(36)	F
15	-	Stand Tall	Burton Cummings	Portrait	8		F G L
16	9	Beth	Kiss	Casablanca	10		G
17	1	Wreck Of The Edmund Fitzgerald	Gordon Lightfoot	Reprise	9	(40)	L
18	-	Hot Line	Sylvers	Capitol	10		G
19	-	Love Me	Yvonne Elliman	RSO	7	(6)	F
20	-	I Wish	Stevie Wonder	Tamla	12	(5)	G

◆ Record and tape sales for the year went up to $2.74 billion, thanks partly to disco, whose rhythms were also being heard in rock and jazz.

◆ The death was reported of Freddie King and Leonard Lee (Shirley & Lee), and fellow R&B star Ike Turner split up acrimoniously with his wife Tina.

◆ Noteworthy rock acts enjoying their first Top 20 singles included Heart, England Dan & John Ford Coley, Firefall, Blue Oyster Cult and Boston, whose eponymous album became the fastest selling debut LP.

◆ Stevie Wonder's long-awaited album, **Songs In The Key Of Life,** headed the US charts for 14 weeks and earned Stevie a couple of Grammies.

UK 1977 JAN-MAR

◆ American actor David Soul's version of the British-written 'Don't Give Up On Us', topped the transatlantic charts and sold a million copies in the UK alone. Interestingly, teen-heartthrob Soul had previously recorded unsuccessfully in 1966 as The Covered Man (advertisements showed him with a bag on his head)!

◆ Punk was making the headlines, and most major labels quickly clambered onto the fast moving bandwagon. United Artists signed The Stranglers, Polydor nabbed The Jam and A&M briefly inked The Sex Pistols.

◆ Two American acts faring better in Britain were Manhattan Transfer with the chart-topping single 'Chanson D'Amour', and 53-year-old country singer Slim Whitman, who had a No. 1 album, **Red River Valley –** neither record charted Stateside.

January 1977

This Mnth	Prev Mnth	Title	Artist	Label	Wks 20	(US Pos)	
1	-	Don't Give Up On Us	David Soul	Private Stock	12	(1)	F G
2	1	Under The Moon Of Love	Showaddywaddy	Bell	12		
3	3	Money Money Money	Abba	Epic	10	(56)	
4	5	When A Child Is Born (Soleado)	Johnny Mathis	CBS	8		
5	18	Dr. Love	Tina Charles	CBS	8		L
6	10	Portsmouth	Mike Oldfield	Virgin	9		
7	15	Living Next Door To Alice	Smokie	RAK	7	(25)	
8	-	Things We Do For Love	10cc	Mercury	8	(5)	
9	-	Side Show	Barry Biggs	Dynamic	9		F L
10	-	Don't Cry For Me Argentina	Julie Covington	MCA	10		F
11	-	Wild Side Of Life	Status Quo	Vertigo	9		
12	-	I Wish	Stevie Wonder	Tamla Motown	6	(1)	
13	2	Somebody To Love	Queen	EMI	8	(13)	
14	-	Grandma's Party	Paul Nicholas	RSO	8		L
15	-	You're More Than A Number In My Little Red Book	Drifters	Arista	6		L
16	9	Lean On Me	Mud	Private Stock	7		L
17	-	Isn't She Lovely	David Parton	Pye	7		F L
18	4	Livin' Thing	Electric Light Orchestra	Jet	8	(13)	
19	-	Fairytale	Dana	GTO	6		L
20	16	Bionic Santa	Chris Hill	Philips	5		L

February 1977

This Mnth	Prev Mnth	Title	Artist	Label	Wks 20	(US Pos)	
1	10	Don't Cry For Me Argentina	Julie Covington	MCA	10		F
2	1	Don't Give Up On Us	David Soul	Private Stock	12	(1)	F G
3	-	When I Need You	Leo Sayer	Chrysalis	9	(1)	
4	9	Side Show	Barry Biggs	Dynamic	9		F L
5	17	Isn't She Lovely	David Parton	Pye	7		F L
6	-	Don't Leave Me This Way	Harold Melvin & The Blue Notes	Philly Int.	7		L
7	-	Daddy Cool	Boney M	Atlantic	6	(65)	F
8	-	Jack In The Box	Moments	All Platinum	6		L
9	-	Boogie Nights	Heatwave	GTO	10	(2)	F
10	-	Car Wash	Rose Royce	MCA	6	(1)	F
11	-	Suspicion	Elvis Presley	RCA	6		
12	15	You're More Than A Number In My Little Red Book	Drifters	Arista	6		L
13	-	Chanson D'Amour	Manhattan Transfer	Atlantic	11		F
14	-	Sing Me	Brothers	Bus Stop	6		F L
15	-	Don't Believe A Word	Thin Lizzy	Vertigo	4		
16	8	Things We Do For Love	10cc	Mercury	8	(5)	
17	11	Wild Side Of Life	Status Quo	Vertigo	9		
18	-	This Is Tomorrow	Bryan Ferry	Polydor	6		
19	-	Romeo	Mr. Big	EMI	7	(87)	F L
20	12	I Wish	Stevie Wonder	Tamla Motown	6	(1)	

March 1977

This Mnth	Prev Mnth	Title	Artist	Label	Wks 20	(US Pos)	
1	13	Chanson D'Amour	Manhattan Transfer	Atlantic	11		F
2	9	Boogie Nights	Heatwave	GTO	10	(2)	F
3	3	When I Need You	Leo Sayer	Chrysalis	9	(1)	
4	19	Romeo	Mr. Big	EMI	7	(87)	F L
5	-	Knowing Me Knowing You	Abba	Epic	11	(14)	
6	-	Sound And Vision	David Bowie	RCA	9	(69)	
7	-	Torn Between Two Lovers	Mary MacGregor	Ariola America	8	(1)	F L
8	1	Don't Cry For Me Argentina	Julie Covington	MCA	10		F
9	-	When	Showaddywaddy	Arista	8		
10	18	This Is Tomorrow	Bryan Ferry	Polydor	6		
11	-	Baby I Know	Rubettes	State	7		L
12	-	Rockaria	Electric Light Orchestra	Jet	5		
13	-	What Can I Say	Boz Scaggs	CBS	5	(42)	F
14	6	Don't Leave Me This Way	Harold Melvin & The Blue Notes	Philly Int.	7		L
15	14	Sing Me	Brothers	Bus Stop	6		F L
16	2	Don't Give Up On Us	David Soul	Private Stock	12	(1)	F G
17	-	Moody Blue	Elvis Presley	RCA	5	(31)	
18	-	Don't Leave Me This Way	Thelma Houston	Motown	4	(1)	F L
19	8	Jack In The Box	Moments	All Platinum	6		L
20	-	Going In With My Eyes Open	David Soul	Private Stock	6	(54)	

January 1977

This Mnth	Prev Mnth	Title	Artist	Label	Wks 20	(UK Pos)	
1	5	You Make Me Feel Like Dancing	Leo Sayer	Warner	13	(2)	G
2	20	I Wish	Stevie Wonder	Tamla	12	(5)	G
3	-	Car Wash	Rose Royce	MCA	12	(9)	F G
4	14	Dazz	Brick	Bang	11	(36)	F
5	3	You Don't Have To Be A Star (To Be In My Show)	Marilyn McCoo & Billy Davis Jr	ABC	11	(7)	F G
6	1	Tonight's The Night (Gonna Be Alright)	Rod Stewart	Warner	12	(5)	G
7	18	Hot Line	Sylvers	Capitol	10		G
8	12	After The Lovin'	Engelbert Humperdinck	Epic	9		G L
9	-	New Kid In Town	Eagles	Asylum	12	(20)	
10	7	Sorry Seems To Be The Hardest Word	Elton John	MCA/Rocket	8	(11)	G
11	2	The Rubberband Man	Spinners	Atlantic	11	(16)	G
12	15	Stand Tall	Burton Cummings	Portrait	8		F G L
13	-	Walk This Way	Aerosmith	Columbia	6		
14	-	Somebody To Love	Queen	Elektra	7	(2)	
15	-	Blinded By The Light	Manfred Mann's Earth Band	Warner	10	(6)	F G L
16	-	Torn Between Two Lovers	Mary MacGregor	Ariola America	12	(4)	F G L
17	-	Livin' Thing	Electric Light Orchestra	UA	6	(4)	
18	-	Lost Without You Love	Bread	Elektra	8	(27)	L
19	4	More Than A Feeling	Boston	Epic	11	(22)	F
20	-	Enjoy Yourself	Jacksons	Epic	9	(42)	G

February 1977

This Mnth	Prev Mnth	Title	Artist	Label	Wks 20	(UK Pos)	
1	9	New Kid In Town	Eagles	Asylum	12	(20)	G
2	16	Torn Between Two Lovers	Mary MacGregor	Ariola America	12	(4)	F G L
3	15	Blinded By The Light	Manfred Mann's Earth Band	Warner	10	(6)	F G L
4	-	Evergreen (Love Theme From 'A Star Is Born')	Barbra Streisand	Columbia	15	(3)	G
5	3	Car Wash	Rose Royce	MCA	12	(9)	F G
6	20	Enjoy Yourself	Jacksons	Epic	9	(42)	G
7	-	I Like Dreamin'	Kenny Nolan	20th Century	12		F G
8	-	Fly Like An Eagle	Steve Miller Band	Capitol	12		G
9	2	I Wish	Stevie Wonder	Tamla	12	(5)	G
10	4	Dazz	Brick	Bang	11	(36)	F
11	-	Weekend In New England	Barry Manilow	Arista	7		
12	18	Lost Without You Love	Bread	Elektra	8	(27)	L
13	-	Night Moves	Bob Seger & Silver Bullet Band	Capitol	8		
14	-	Dancing Queen	Abba	Atlantic	12	(1)	G
15	7	Hot Line	Sylvers	Capitol	10		G
16	-	Year Of The Cat	Al Stewart	Janus	6	(31)	F
17	-	Hard Luck Woman	Kiss	Casablanca	5		
18	13	Walk This Way	Aerosmith	Columbia	6		
19	-	Go Your Own Way	Fleetwood Mac	Warner	5	(38)	
20	1	You Make Me Feel Like Dancing	Leo Sayer	Warner	13	(2)	G

March 1977

This Mnth	Prev Mnth	Title	Artist	Label	Wks 20	(UK Pos)	
1	4	Evergreen (From 'A Star Is Born')	Barbra Streisand	Columbia	15	(3)	G
2	8	Fly Like An Eagle	Steve Miller Band	Capitol	12		G
3	14	Dancing Queen	Abba	Atlantic	12	(1)	G
4	13	Night Moves	Bob Seger & Silver Bullet Band	Capitol	8		
5	7	I Like Dreamin'	Kenny Nolan	20th Century	12		F G
6	-	Rich Girl	Daryl Hall & John Oates	RCA	10		G
7	2	Torn Between Two Lovers	Mary MacGregor	Ariola America	12	(4)	F G L
8	-	Don't Leave Me This Way	Thelma Houston	Tamla	12	(13)	F G L
9	-	Things We Do For Love	10cc	Mercury	10	(6)	G L
10	3	Blinded By The Light	Manfred Mann's Earth Band	Warner	10	(6)	F G L
11	-	Don't Give Up On Us	David Soul	Private Stock	9	(1)	F G L
12	1	New Kid In Town	Eagles	Asylum	12	(20)	G
13	16	Year Of The Cat	Al Stewart	Janus	6	(31)	F
14	-	Boogie Child	Bee Gees	RSO	6		
15	-	Maybe I'm Amazed	Wings	Capitol	7	(28)	
16	-	Carry On Wayward Son	Kansas	Kirshner	7	(51)	F
17	19	Go Your Own Way	Fleetwood Mac	Warner	5	(38)	
18	-	I've Got Love On My Mind	Natalie Cole	Capitol	10		G
19	11	Weekend In New England	Barry Manilow	Arista	7		
20	-	So In To You	Atlanta Rhythm Section	Polydor	10		F

US 1977 JAN-MAR

▲ *American Bandstand* celebrated its 25th birthday. Chuck Berry, Johnny Rivers, Seals & Crofts, Jr. Walker and The Pointer Sisters (above) joined the party.

◆ Paul McCartney notched up his fifth successive US No. 1 LP with the live triple album **Wings Over America**. The set, which contained Wings' versions of five old Beatles songs, turned gold in just three days.

◆ Progressive rockers Kansas, who sold millions of LPs in the 1970s, made their Top 20 single debut with 'Carry on Wayward Son'.

◆ The Sex Pistols topped some charts with 'God Save The Queen'. The Clash and The Stranglers had hit albums and newcomers The Boomtown Rats and Adam & The Ants attracted media acclaim.

◆ US cult heroes Blondie, Television, Talking Heads and The Ramones toured the UK, and The Damned became the first UK punk act to perform at CBGB's in New York.

▲ Debuting in the UK Top 20 were Genesis (above) with 'Spot The Pigeon' and their former lead singer, Peter Gabriel, with 'Solsbury Hill'.

April 1977

This Mnth	Prev Mnth	Title	Artist	Label	Wks 20	(US Pos)	
1	5	Knowing Me Knowing You	Abba	Epic	11	(14)	
2	20	Going In With My Eyes Open	David Soul	Private Stock	6	(54)	
3	-	I Don't Want To Put A Hold On You	Berni Flint	EMI	8		F L
4	-	Red Light Spells Danger	Billy Ocean	GTO	9		
5	9	When	Showaddywaddy	Arista	8		
6	-	Sunny	Boney M	Atlantic	6		
7	6	Sound And Vision	David Bowie	RCA	9	(69)	
8	-	Oh Boy	Brotherhood Of Man	Pye	7		
9	1	Chanson D'Amour	Manhattan Transfer	Atlantic	11		F
10	-	You Don't Have To Be A Star (To Be In My Show)	Marilyn McCoo & Billy Davis Jr	ABC	5	(1)	F L
11	17	Moody Blue	Elvis Presley	RCA	5	(31)	
12	-	Free	Deniece Williams	CBS	9	(25)	F
13	-	Have I The Right?	Dead End Kids	CBS	7		F L
14	-	Sir Duke	Stevie Wonder	Motown	7	(1)	
15	-	Lay Back In The Arms Of Someone	Smokie	RAK	6		
16	-	Love Hit Me	Maxine Nightingale	UA	3		L
17	-	Gimme Some	Brendon	Magnet	5		F L
18	7	Torn Between Two Lovers	Mary MacGregor	Ariola America	8	(1)	F L
19	-	Pearl's A Singer	Elkie Brooks	A&M	6		F
20	2	Boogie Nights	Heatwave	GTO	10	(2)	F

May 1977

This Mnth	Prev Mnth	Title	Artist	Label	Wks 20	(US Pos)	
1	-	I Don't Want To Talk About It/First Cut Is The Deepest	Rod Stewart	Riva	10	(46)	
2	12	Free	Deniece Williams	CBS	9	(25)	F
3	-	Ain't Gonna Bump No More (With No Big Fat Woman)	Joe Tex	Epic	8	(12)	F L
4	14	Sir Duke	Stevie Wonder	Motown	7	(1)	
5	-	The Shuffle	Van McCoy	H & L	8		L
6	-	Whodunit	Tavares	Capitol	7	(22)	
7	-	Evergreen (From 'A Star Is Born')	Barbra Streisand	CBS	12	(1)	
8	-	Hotel California	Eagles	Asylum	5	(1)	L
9	-	Good Morning Judge	10cc	Mercury	7	(69)	
10	-	Lucille	Kenny Rogers	UA	10	(5)	
11	13	Have I The Right?	Dead End Kids	CBS	7		F L
12	4	Red Light Spells Danger	Billy Ocean	GTO	9		
13	-	Mah Na Mah Na	Piero Umiliani	EMI International	5	(55)	F L
14	19	Pearl's A Singer	Elkie Brooks	A&M	6		F
15	-	Solsbury Hill	Peter Gabriel	Charisma	5	(68)	F
16	1	Knowing Me Knowing You	Abba	Epic	11	(14)	
17	-	Got To Give It Up	Marvin Gaye	Motown	6	(1)	
18	-	How Much Love	Leo Sayer	Chrysalis	5	(17)	
19	-	Lonely Boy	Andrew Gold	Asylum	5	(7)	F
20	3	I Don't Want To Put A Hold On You	Berni Flint	EMI	8		F L

June 1977

This Mnth	Prev Mnth	Title	Artist	Label	Wks 20	(US Pos)	
1	10	Lucille	Kenny Rogers	UA	10	(5)	
2	1	I Don't Want To Talk About It/First...	Rod Stewart	Riva	10	(46)	
3	7	Evergreen (From 'A Star Is Born')	Barbra Streisand	CBS	12	(1)	
4	-	God Save The Queen	Sex Pistols	Virgin	6		F
5	3	Ain't Gonna Bump No More (With...)	Joe Tex	Epic	8	(12)	F L
6	-	Show You The Way To Go	Jacksons	Epic	7	(28)	
7	-	You're Moving Out Today	Carole Bayer Sager	Elektra	7	(69)	F L
8	-	Halfway Down The Stairs	Muppets	Pye	6		F
9	5	The Shuffle	Van McCoy	H & L	8		L
10	17	Got To Give It Up	Marvin Gaye	Motown	6	(1)	
11	9	Good Morning Judge	10cc	Mercury	7	(69)	
12	-	Telephone Line	Electric Light Orchestra	Jet	7	(7)	
13	-	Lido Shuffle	Boz Scaggs	CBS	7	(11)	L
14	-	O.K.	Rock Follies	Polydor	4		F L
15	-	Baby Don't Change Your Mind	Gladys Knight & The Pips	Buddah	7	(52)	
16	-	So You Win Again	Hot Chocolate	RAK	10	(31)	
17	-	Too Hot To Handle/Slip Your Disc To This	Heatwave	GTO	7		
18	-	Fanfare For The Common Man	Emerson, Lake & Palmer	Atlantic	10		F L
19	13	Mah Na Mah Na	Piero Umiliani	EMI International	5	(55)	F L
20	-	Spot The Pigeon (E.P.)	Genesis	Charisma	2		F

April 1977

This Mnth	Prev Mnth	Title	Artist	Label	Wks 20	(UK Pos)	
1	8	Don't Leave Me This Way	Thelma Houston	Tamla	12	(13)	F G L
2	11	Don't Give Up On Us	David Soul	Private Stock	9	(1)	F G L
3	-	Southern Nights	Glen Campbell	Capitol	11	(28)	G L
4	-	Hotel California	Eagles	Asylum	13	(8)	G
5	18	I've Got Love On My Mind	Natalie Cole	Capitol	10		G
6	9	Things We Do For Love	10cc	Mercury	10	(6)	G L
7	6	Rich Girl	Daryl Hall & John Oates	RCA	10		G
8	1	Evergreen (Love Theme From 'A Star Is Born')	Barbra Streisand	Columbia	15	(3)	G
9	20	So In To You	Atlanta Rhythm Section	Polydor	10		F
10	3	Dancing Queen	Abba	Atlantic	12	(1)	G
11	-	Right Time Of The Night	Jennifer Warnes	Arista	9		F
12	-	When I Need You	Leo Sayer	Warner	10	(1)	G
13	-	Tryin' To Love Two	William Bell	Mercury	5		F G L
14	-	I Wanna Get Next To You	Rose Royce	MCA	6	(14)	L
15	16	Carry On Wayward Son	Kansas	Kirshner	7	(51)	F
16	15	Maybe I'm Amazed	Wings	Capitol	7	(28)	
17	-	Couldn't Get It Right	Climax Blues Band	Sire	9	(10)	F
18	-	Lido Shuffle	Boz Scaggs	Columbia	7	(13)	
19	2	Fly Like An Eagle	Steve Miller Band	Capitol	12		G
20	-	Sir Duke	Stevie Wonder	Tamla	5	(2)	G

May 1977

This Mnth	Prev Mnth	Title	Artist	Label	Wks 20	(UK Pos)	
1	12	When I Need You	Leo Sayer	Warner	10	(1)	G
2	4	Hotel California	Eagles	Asylum	13	(8)	G
3	17	Couldn't Get It Right	Climax Blues Band	Sire	9	(10)	F
4	-	I'm Your Boogie Man	KC & The Sunshine Band	TK	11	(41)	
5	20	Sir Duke	Stevie Wonder	Tamla	5	(2)	G
6	3	Southern Nights	Glen Campbell	Capitol	11	(28)	G L
7	-	Got To Give It Up (Pt.1)	Marvin Gaye	Tamla	12	(7)	G
8	11	Right Time Of The Night	Jennifer Warnes	Arista	9		F
9	-	Dreams	Fleetwood Mac	Warner	9	(24)	G
10	-	Lucille	Kenny Rogers	UA	9	(1)	G
11	9	So In To You	Atlanta Rhythm Section	Polydor	10		F
12	18	Lido Shuffle	Boz Scaggs	Columbia	7	(13)	
13	-	Gonna Fly Now (Theme From 'Rocky')	Bill Conti	UA	10		F G L
14	-	Lonely Boy	Andrew Gold	Asylum	9	(11)	F L
15	14	I Wanna Get Next To You	Rose Royce	MCA	6	(14)	L
16	-	Feels Like The First Time	Foreigner	Atlantic	8	(39)	F
17	-	Hello Stranger	Yvonne Elliman	RSO	5	(26)	
18	1	Don't Leave Me This Way	Thelma Houston	Tamla	12	(13)	F G L
19	5	I've Got Love On My Mind	Natalie Cole	Capitol	10		G
20	-	Can't Stop Dancin'	Captain & Tennille	A&M	5		

June 1977

This Mnth	Prev Mnth	Title	Artist	Label	Wks 20	(UK Pos)	
1	7	Got To Give It Up (Pt.1)	Marvin Gaye	Tamla	12	(7)	G
2	9	Dreams	Fleetwood Mac	Warner	9	(24)	G
3	13	Gonna Fly Now (Theme From 'Rocky')	Bill Conti	UA	10		F G L
4	16	Feels Like The First Time	Foreigner	Atlantic	8	(39)	F
5	10	Lucille	Kenny Rogers	UA	9	(1)	G
6	-	Undercover Angel	Alan O'Day	Pacific	13	(43)	F G L
7	14	Lonely Boy	Andrew Gold	Asylum	9	(11)	F L
8	4	I'm Your Boogie Man	KC & The Sunshine Band	TK	11	(41)	
9	-	Angel In Your Arms	Hot	Big Tree	12		F G L
10	-	Jet Airliner	Steve Miller Band	Capitol	9		
11	3	Couldn't Get It Right	Climax Blues Band	Sire	9	(10)	F
12	-	Life In The Fast Lane	Eagles	Asylum	5		
13	-	Ain't Gonna Bump No More (With No Big Fat Woman)	Joe Tex	Epic	5	(2)	G L
14	-	Heard It In A Love Song	Marshall Tucker Band	Capricorn	5		F L
15	-	Da Doo Ron Ron	Shaun Cassidy	Warner	10		F G
16	-	Looks Like We Made It	Barry Manilow	Arista	11		G
17	1	When I Need You	Leo Sayer	Warner	10	(1)	G
18	-	Margaritaville	Jimmy Buffett	ABC	9		F L
19	2	Hotel California	Eagles	Asylum	13	(8)	G
20	-	My Heart Belongs To Me	Barbra Streisand	Columbia	9		

◆ New heavy rock band Foreigner had their first of 14 US Top 20 singles with the aptly titled 'Feels Like The First Time'. It came from their four million-selling eponymous debut album. Surprisingly, this platinum-plated Anglo-American outfit were far less successful in the UK.

◆ Led Zeppelin broke the attendance record for a single act show when 76,000 saw them perform at the Silverdrome in Pontiac, Michigan.

◆ Elvis Presley made his last appearance at the Market Square Arena, Indianapolis.

◆ Fleetwood Mac's **Rumours** (which went on to sell 14 million copies!) topped the album chart for 31 weeks. It stopped The Beatles scoring their last No. 1 with **The Beatles At The Hollywood Bowl**.

UK 1977 JULY-SEPT

◆ As one of the era's top female singers Debbie Harry, and her group Blondie, signed with Chrysalis, an earlier teen queen, Connie Francis, was the first woman to top the UK LP chart.

▲ The Bay City Rollers (above), whose star had already waned in the UK, scored their last American Top 20 entry, as new teen idols Shaun Cassidy (David's brother) and Andy Gibb (Brother of the Bee Gees) debuted on the chart.

◆ Marc Bolan, front man of the highly successful glam rock duo T-Rex, died in a car crash. He was a major figure in British rock music.

July 1977

This Mnth	Prev Mnth	Title	Artist	Label	Wks 20	(US Pos)	
1	16	So You Win Again	Hot Chocolate	RAK	10	(31)	
2	18	Fanfare For The Common Man	Emerson, Lake & Palmer	Atlantic	10		F L
3	15	Baby Don't Change Your Mind	Gladys Knight & The Pips	Buddah	7	(52)	
4	-	Ma Baker	Boney M	Atlantic	10	(96)	
5	-	I Feel Love	Donna Summer	GTO	9	(6)	
6	6	Show You The Way To Go	Jacksons	Epic	7	(28)	
7	-	Sam	Olivia Newton-John	EMI	7	(20)	
8	-	Peaches/Go Buddy Go	Stranglers	UA	7		F
9	-	Angelo	Brotherhood Of Man	Pye	11		
10	-	Pretty Vacant	Sex Pistols	Virgin	5		
11	-	Oh Lori	Alessi	A&M	8		F L
12	7	You're Moving Out Today	Carole Bayer Sager	Elektra	7	(69)	F L
13	1	Lucille	Kenny Rogers	UA	10	(5)	
14	3	Evergreen (Love Theme From 'A Star Is Born')	Barbra Streisand	CBS	12	(1)	
15	-	Slow Down	John Miles	Decca	6	(34)	L
16	-	You're Gonna Get Next To Me	Bo Kirkland & Ruth Davis	EMI International	5		F L
17	-	Feel The Need In Me	Detroit Emeralds	Atlantic	8	(90)	L
18	-	Do What You Wanna Do	T-Connection	TK	3	(46)	F
19	12	Telephone Line	Electric Light Orchestra	Jet	7	(7)	
20	8	Halfway Down The Stairs	Muppets	Pye	6		F

August 1977

This Mnth	Prev Mnth	Title	Artist	Label	Wks 20	(US Pos)	
1	9	Angelo	Brotherhood Of Man	Pye	11		
2	5	I Feel Love	Donna Summer	GTO	9	(6)	
3	-	You Got What It Takes	Showaddywaddy	Arista	8		
4	-	Float On	Floaters	ABC	9	(2)	F L
5	4	Ma Baker	Boney M	Atlantic	10	(96)	
6	-	We're All Alone	Rita Coolidge	A&M	8	(7)	F L
7	-	The Crunch	Rah Band	Good Earth	8		F
8	-	It's Your Life	Smokie	RAK	6		
9	-	Easy	Commodores	Motown	6	(4)	
10	-	Something Better Change/ Straighten Out	Stranglers	UA	5		
11	2	Fanfare For The Common Man	Emerson, Lake & Palmer	Atlantic	10		F L
12	1	So You Win Again	Hot Chocolate	RAK	10	(31)	
13	-	That's What Friends Are For	Deniece Williams	CBS	7		
14	-	Roadrunner	Jonathan Richman & The Modern Lovers	Berserkley	3		F
15	10	Pretty Vacant	Sex Pistols	Virgin	5		
16	-	Nights On Broadway	Candi Staton	Warner	8		
17	11	Oh Lori	Alessi	A&M	8		F L
18	-	Nobody Does It Better	Carly Simon	Elektra	8	(2)	
19	-	Way Down	Elvis Presley	RCA	10	(18)	
20	17	Feel The Need In Me	Detroit Emeralds	Atlantic	8	(90)	L

September 1977

This Mnth	Prev Mnth	Title	Artist	Label	Wks 20	(US Pos)	
1	19	Way Down	Elvis Presley	RCA	10	(18)	
2	-	Magic Fly	Space	Pye International	8		F L
3	-	Silver Lady	David Soul	Private Stock	11	(52)	
4	-	Oxygene Part IV	Jean-Michel Jarre	Polydor	7		F L
5	4	Float On	Floaters	ABC	9	(2)	F L
6	-	Deep Down Inside	Donna Summer	Casablanca	7		
7	16	Nights On Broadway	Candi Staton	Warner	8		
8	18	Nobody Does It Better	Carly Simon	Elektra	8	(2)	
9	1	Angelo	Brotherhood Of Man	Pye	11		
10	13	That's What Friends Are For	Deniece Williams	CBS	7		
11	3	You Got What It Takes	Showaddywaddy	Arista	8		
12	-	Telephone Man	Meri Wilson	Pye International	7	(18)	F L
13	7	The Crunch	Rah Band	Good Earth	8		F
14	-	Do Anything You Wanna Do	Rods	Island	7		F L
15	-	Tulane	Steve Gibbons Band	Polydor	4		F L
16	-	Dancin' In The Moonlight (It's Caught Me In The Spotlight)	Thin Lizzy	Vertigo	4		
17	-	Looking After Number One	Boomtown Rats	Ensign	5		F
18	-	Best Of My Love	Emotions	CBS	7	(1)	F
19	2	I Feel Love	Donna Summer	GTO	9	(6)	
20	-	Wonderous Stories	Yes	Atlantic	7		F L

July 1977

This Mnth	Prev Mnth	Title	Artist	Label	Wks 20	(UK Pos)	
1	16	Looks Like We Made It	Barry Manilow	Arista	11		G
2	15	Da Doo Ron Ron	Shaun Cassidy	Warner	10		F G
3	-	I Just Want To Be Your Everything	Andy Gibb	RSO	18	(26)	F G
4	6	Undercover Angel	Alan O'Day	Pacific	13	(43)	F G L
5	-	I'm In You	Peter Frampton	A&M	10	(41)	
6	20	My Heart Belongs To Me	Barbra Streisand	Columbia	9		
7	9	Angel In Your Arms	Hot	Big Tree	12		F G L
8	18	Margaritaville	Jimmy Buffett	ABC	9		F L
9	-	Do You Wanna Make Love	Peter McCann	20th Century	10		F G L
10	3	Gonna Fly Now (Theme From 'Rocky')	Bill Conti	UA	10		F G L
11	10	Jet Airliner	Steve Miller Band	Capitol	9		
12	-	Best Of My Love	Emotions	Columbia	15	(4)	F G
13	-	(Your Love Has Lifted Me) Higher And Higher	Rita Coolidge	A&M	13	(48)	F G
14	1	Got To Give It Up (Pt.1)	Marvin Gaye	Tamla	12	(7)	G
15	-	Whatcha Gonna Do	Pablo Cruise	A&M	10		F
16	-	You And Me	Alice Cooper	Warner	7		
17	2	Dreams	Fleetwood Mac	Warner	9	(24)	G
18	-	Knowing Me Knowing You	Abba	Atlantic	5	(1)	
19	-	You Made Me Believe In Magic	Bay City Rollers	Arista	6	(34)	L
20	-	Easy	Commodores	Motown	9	(9)	G

August 1977

This Mnth	Prev Mnth	Title	Artist	Label	Wks 20	(UK Pos)	
1	3	I Just Want To Be Your Everything	Andy Gibb	RSO	18	(26)	F G
2	12	Best Of My Love	Emotions	Columbia	15	(4)	F G
3	13	(Your Love Has Lifted Me) Higher And Higher	Rita Coolidge	A&M	13	(48)	F G
4	5	I'm In You	Peter Frampton	A&M	10	(41)	
5	20	Easy	Commodores	Motown	9	(9)	G
6	15	Whatcha Gonna Do	Pablo Cruise	A&M	10		F
7	9	Do You Wanna Make Love	Peter McCann	20th Century	10		F G L
8	-	Just A Song Before I Go	Crosby, Stills & Nash	Atlantic	7		
9	-	Handy Man	James Taylor	Columbia	9		
10	-	Don't Stop	Fleetwood Mac	Warner	10	(32)	
11	16	You And Me	Alice Cooper	Warner	7		
12	6	My Heart Belongs To Me	Barbra Streisand	Columbia	9		
13	19	You Made Me Believe In Magic	Bay City Rollers	Arista	6	(34)	L
14	2	Da Doo Ron Ron	Shaun Cassidy	Warner	10		F G
15	-	Barracuda	Heart	Portrait	7		
16	-	Float On	Floaters	ABC	7	(1)	F G L
17	1	Looks Like We Made It	Barry Manilow	Arista	11		G
18	-	Smoke From A Distant Fire	Sanford/Townsend Band	Warner	6		F L
19	-	Telephone Line	Electric Light Orchestra	UA	10	(8)	G
20	-	Strawberry Letter 23	Brothers Johnson	A&M	7	(35)	G

September 1977

This Mnth	Prev Mnth	Title	Artist	Label	Wks 20	(UK Pos)	
1	2	Best Of My Love	Emotions	Columbia	15	(4)	F G
2	1	I Just Want To Be Your Everything	Andy Gibb	RSO	18	(26)	F G
3	16	Float On	Floaters	ABC	7	(1)	F G L
4	10	Don't Stop	Fleetwood Mac	Warner	10	(32)	
5	9	Handy Man	James Taylor	Columbia	9		
6	20	Strawberry Letter 23	Brothers Johnson	A&M	7	(35)	G
7	19	Telephone Line	Electric Light Orchestra	UA	10	(8)	G
8	3	(Your Love Has Lifted Me) Higher And Higher	Rita Coolidge	A&M	13	(48)	F G
9	-	Keep It Comin' Love	KC & The Sunshine Band	TK	9	(31)	
10	5	Easy	Commodores	Motown	9	(9)	G
11	18	Smoke From A Distant Fire	Sanford/Townsend Band	Warner	6		F L
12	-	Cold As Ice	Foreigner	Atlantic	11	(24)	
13	-	Star Wars (Main Title)	London Symphony Orchestra	20th Century	4		F
14	-	Star Wars Theme/Cantina Band	Meco	Millenium	10	(7)	F G
15	8	Just A Song Before I Go	Crosby, Stills & Nash	Atlantic	7		
16	-	That's Rock 'n' Roll	Shaun Cassidy	Warner	11		G
17	-	On And On	Stephen Bishop	ABC	7		F L
18	15	Barracuda	Heart	Portrait	7		
19	-	Swayin' To The Music (Slow Dancin')	Johnny Rivers	Big Tree	9		G L
20	-	Nobody Does It Better	Carly Simon	Elektra	11	(7)	G

◆ Elvis Presley, the most important and influential artist of the rock era, died, and was mourned world-wide. In America, the demand for Presley product far out-stripped the quantities that RCA (at full stretch) could produce. In Britain he had nine singles simultaneously in the UK chart and a staggering 27 albums in the Top 100! Some estimates say that 20 million Elvis records were sold world-wide the day after his death!

◆ America's top single of 1977, 'Float On', gave Detroit quartet The Floaters a transatlantic No. 1. The group joined Zager & Evans as the only acts who failed to chart again in either country after topping both the US and UK charts with their debut hit.

◆ The Commodores (who included singer/songwriter Lionel Richie) started a 70-city American tour which grossed over $6 million.

UK 1977
OCT-DEC

Bing Crosby died. The well-loved singer, who had amassed 299 American Top 20 hits, found himself back in the British Top 10 with the evergreen 'White Christmas'.

Noted punk venue The Vortex opened. Among the early headliners were Adam & The Ants, controversial girl group The Slits and Siouxsie & The Banshees.

▲ Understandably, British punk had few initial takers Stateside. However the Sex Pistols' chart topping UK debut LP **Never Mind the Bollocks** and Elvis Costello's (above) **My Aim Is True** (which included musical contributions from Huey Lewis) were minor US successes.

October 1977

This Mnth	Prev Mnth	Title	Artist	Label	Wks 20	(US Pos)	
1	3	Silver Lady	David Soul	Private Stock	11	(52)	
2	-	Black Is Black	La Belle Epoque	Harvest	9		F L
3	18	Best Of My Love	Emotions	CBS	7	(1)	F
4	-	I Remember Elvis Presley (The King Is Dead)	Danny Mirror	Sonet	6		F L
5	1	Way Down	Elvis Presley	RCA	10	(18)	
6	-	Yes Sir I Can Boogie	Baccara	RCA	9		F
7	-	You're In My Heart	Rod Stewart	Riva	8	(4)	
8	-	From New York To L.A.	Patsy Gallant	EMI	5		F L
9	2	Magic Fly	Space	Pye International	8		F L
10	-	Black Betty	Ram Jam	Epic	8	(18)	F
11	-	No More Heroes	Stranglers	UA	6		
12	12	Telephone Man	Meri Wilson	Pye International	7	(18)	F L
13	20	Wonderous Stories	Yes	Atlantic	7		F L
14	6	Deep Down Inside	Donna Summer	Casablanca	7		
15	-	Star Wars Theme - Cantina Band	Meco	RCA	5	(1)	F L
16	4	Oxygene Part IV	Jean-Michel Jarre	Polydor	7		F L
17	-	Rockin' All Over The World	Status Quo	Vertigo	10		
18	-	Sunshine After The Rain	Elkie Brooks	A&M	4		
19	-	I Remember Yesterday	Donna Summer	GTO	5		
20	-	Holidays In The Sun	Sex Pistols	Virgin	5		

November 1977

This Mnth	Prev Mnth	Title	Artist	Label	Wks 20	(US Pos)	
1	-	The Name Of The Game	Abba	Epic	9	(12)	
2	17	Rockin' All Over The World	Status Quo	Vertigo	10		
3	-	We Are The Champions	Queen	EMI	8	(4)	
4	6	Yes Sir I Can Boogie	Baccara	RCA	9		F
5	7	You're In My Heart	Rod Stewart	Riva	8	(4)	
6	-	2-4-6-8 Motorway	Tom Robinson Band	EMI	6		F
7	2	Black Is Black	La Belle Epoque	Harvest	9		F L
8	-	Calling Occupants Of Interplanetary Craft	Carpenters	A&M	6	(32)	L
9	-	How Deep Is Your Love	Bee Gees	RSO	11	(1)	
10	-	Needles And Pins	Smokie	RAK	6	(68)	
11	-	Dancin' Party	Showaddywaddy	Arista	9		
12	-	Live In Trouble	Barron Knights	Epic	5		
13	-	Virginia Plain	Roxy Music	Polydor	5		
14	10	Black Betty	Ram Jam	Epic	8	(18)	F
15	20	Holidays In The Sun	Sex Pistols	Virgin	5		
16	-	Daddy Cool/The Girl Can't Help It	Darts	Magnet	10		F
17	1	Silver Lady	David Soul	Private Stock	11	(52)	
18	-	She's Not There	Santana	CBS	5	(27)	F L
19	-	Mull Of Kintyre/Girls' School	Wings	Capitol	13	(33)	P
20	-	Hot Track E.P.	Nazareth	Mountain	4		L

December 1977

This Mnth	Prev Mnth	Title	Artist	Label	Wks 20	(US Pos)	
1	19	Mull Of Kintyre/Girls' School	Wings	Capitol	13	(33)	P
2	-	The Floral Dance	Brighouse & Rastrick Brass Band	Transatlantic	10		F L
3	9	How Deep Is Your Love	Bee Gees	RSO	11	(1)	
4	-	I Will	Ruby Winters	Creole	9		F
5	16	Daddy Cool/The Girl Can't Help It	Darts	Magnet	10		F
6	11	Dancin' Party	Showaddywaddy	Arista	9		
7	-	Egyptian Reggae	Jonathan Richman & The Modern Lovers	Berserkley	6		L
8	-	Belfast	Boney M	Atlantic	7		
9	3	We Are The Champions	Queen	EMI	8	(4)	
10	-	Love's Unkind	Donna Summer	GTO	10		
11	2	Rockin' All Over The World	Status Quo	Vertigo	10		
12	-	White Christmas	Bing Crosby	MCA	4		G
13	-	It's A Heartache	Bonnie Tyler	RCA	9	(3)	
14	-	Love Of My Life	Dooleys	GTO	5		
15	-	Put Your Love In Me	Hot Chocolate	RAK	6		
16	1	The Name Of The Game	Abba	Epic	9	(12)	
17	-	Mary Of The Fourth Form	Boomtown Rats	Ensign	5		
18	-	Watching The Detectives	Elvis Costello	Stiff	5		F
19	-	My Way	Elvis Presley	RCA	6	(22)	
20	12	Live In Trouble	Barron Knights	Epic	5		

October 1977

This Mnth	Prev Mnth	Title	Artist	Label	Wks 20	(UK Pos)	
1	9	Keep It Comin' Love	KC & The Sunshine Band	TK	9	(31)	
2	20	Nobody Does It Better	Carly Simon	Elektra	11	(7)	G
3	-	You Light Up My Life	Debby Boone	Warner	16	(48)	F P L
4	16	That's Rock 'n' Roll	Shaun Cassidy	Warner	11		G
5	14	Star Wars Theme/Cantina Band	Meco	Millenium	10	(7)	F G
6	-	Boogie Nights	Heatwave	Epic	13	(2)	F P
7	12	Cold As Ice	Foreigner	Atlantic	11	(24)	
8	-	Brick House	Commodores	Motown	9	(32)	
9	-	I Feel Love	Donna Summer	Casablanca	10	(1)	G
10	19	Swayin' To The Music (Slow Dancin')	Johnny Rivers	Big Tree	9		G L
11	2	I Just Want To Be Your Everything	Andy Gibb	RSO	18	(26)	F G
12	1	Best Of My Love	Emotions	Columbia	15	(4)	F G
13	-	It's Ecstasy When You Lay Down Next To Me	Barry White	20th Century	9	(40)	G
14	-	Don't It Make My Brown Eyes Blue	Crystal Gayle	UA	14	(5)	F G
15	17	On And On	Stephen Bishop	ABC	7		F L
16	-	The King Is Gone	Ronnie McDowell	Scorpion	5		F G L
17	4	Don't Stop	Fleetwood Mac	Warner	10	(32)	
18	7	Telephone Line	Electric Light Orchestra	UA	10	(8)	G
19	6	Strawberry Letter 23	Brothers Johnson	A&M	7	(35)	G
20	-	Heaven On The 7th Floor	Paul Nicholas	RSO	9	(40)	F G L

November 1977

This Mnth	Prev Mnth	Title	Artist	Label	Wks 20	(UK Pos)	
1	3	You Light Up My Life	Debby Boone	Warner	16	(48)	F P L
2	6	Boogie Nights	Heatwave	Epic	13	(2)	F P
3	14	Don't It Make My Brown Eyes Blue	Crystal Gayle	UA	14	(5)	F G
4	13	It's Ecstasy When You Lay Down Next To Me	Barry White	20th Century	9	(40)	G
5	-	Baby What A Big Surprise	Chicago	Columbia	9	(41)	
6	-	How Deep Is Your Love	Bee Gees	RSO	21	(3)	G
7	2	Nobody Does It Better	Carly Simon	Elektra	11	(7)	G
8	20	Heaven On The 7th Floor	Paul Nicholas	RSO	9	(40)	F G L
9	-	We're All Alone	Rita Coolidge	A&M	10	(6)	
10	9	I Feel Love	Donna Summer	Casablanca	10	(1)	G
11	-	Blue Bayou	Linda Ronstadt	Asylum	11	(35)	G
12	4	That's Rock 'n' Roll	Shaun Cassidy	Warner	11		G
13	-	Just Remember I Love You	Firefall	Atlantic	5		
14	8	Brick House	Commodores	Motown	9	(32)	
15	-	Help Is On Its Way	Little River Band	Harvest	4		F
16	-	You Make Lovin' Fun	Fleetwood Mac	Warner	6	(45)	
17	-	It's So Easy	Linda Ronstadt	Asylum	8		
18	5	Star Wars Theme/Cantina Band	Meco	Millenium	10	(7)	F G
19	-	We Just Disagree	Dave Mason	Columbia	4		F L
20	-	Back In Love Again	L.T.D.	A&M	10		G L

December 1977

This Mnth	Prev Mnth	Title	Artist	Label	Wks 20	(UK Pos)	
1	1	You Light Up My Life	Debby Boone	Warner	16	(48)	F P L
2	6	How Deep Is Your Love	Bee Gees	RSO	21	(3)	G
3	11	Blue Bayou	Linda Ronstadt	Asylum	11	(35)	G
4	3	Don't It Make My Brown Eyes Blue	Crystal Gayle	UA	14	(5)	F G
5	17	It's So Easy	Linda Ronstadt	Asylum	8		
6	20	Back In Love Again	L.T.D.	A&M	10		G L
7	-	Baby Come Back	Player	RSO	14	(32)	F G
8	9	We're All Alone	Rita Coolidge	A&M	10	(6)	
9	-	Here You Come Again	Dolly Parton	RCA	9	(75)	F G
10	-	Sentimental Lady	Bob Welch	Capitol	8		F
11	-	Isn't It Time	Babys	Chrysalis	6	(45)	F
12	-	Slip Slidin' Away	Paul Simon	Columbia	10	(36)	
13	5	Baby What A Big Surprise	Chicago	Columbia	9	(41)	
14	16	You Make Lovin' Fun	Fleetwood Mac	Warner	6	(45)	
15	8	Heaven On The 7th Floor	Paul Nicholas	RSO	9	(40)	F G L
16	-	You Can't Turn Me Off (In The Middle Of Turning Me On)	High Inergy	Gordy	7		F L
17	-	You're In My Heart	Rod Stewart	Warner	12	(3)	G
18	-	Come Sail Away	Styx	A&M	9		
19	2	Boogie Nights	Heatwave	Epic	13	(2)	F P
20	-	Hey Deanie	Shaun Cassidy	Warner	9		G L

◆ American sales of records (including the new twelve inch disco singles) and tapes zoomed to $3.5 billion, with the latter accounting for nearly a quarter of all business.

◆ 'How Deep Is Your Love' by The Bee Gees gave RSO Records the first of a record six consecutive No. 1 singles.

In America, Pat Boone's daughter, Debbie, topped the chart for a record 10 weeks with the award winning 'You Light Up My Life'. In Britain, Paul McCartney & Wings' (above) 'Mull Of Kintyre' sold over two million copies to become Britain's biggest selling single. Neither single was a hit in the other country.

UK 1978 JAN-MAR

◆ British acts working the USA included Genesis, David Bowie, The Stranglers, The Jam and The Sex Pistols, whose leader, Johnny Rotten, announced at the end of their short and controversial tour, that they were disbanding. Fellow punk pioneers, The Damned, also called it a day (re-uniting later) and *Sniffin' Glue* ceased publication. Punk had peaked and its more widely acceptable, close relative "new wave" was now "in".

◆ Pink Floyd's Dave Gilmour helped Kate Bush get a record deal with EMI. The multi-talented teenager's first single 'Wuthering Heights' shot her to instant stardom in Britain. Meanwhile, in Ireland, U2 won a record audition in a major local talent competition.

◆ For the third time in the 1970s, Free's recording of 'All Right Now' reached the UK Top 20. This time it was on the 'Free EP'.

January 1978

This Mnth	Prev Mnth	Title	Artist	Label	Wks 20	(US Pos)	
1	1	Mull Of Kintyre/Girls' School	Wings	Capitol	13	(33)	P
2	10	Love's Unkind	Donna Summer	GTO	10		
3	13	It's A Heartache	Bonnie Tyler	RCA	9	(3)	
4	2	The Floral Dance	Brighouse & Rastrick Brass Band	Transatlantic	10		F L
5	-	Don't It Make My Brown Eyes Blue	Crystal Gayle	UA	8	(2)	F
6	-	Dance Dance Dance (Yowsah Yowsah Yowsah)	Chic	Atlantic	8	(6)	F
7	-	Uptown Top Ranking	Althia And Donna	Lightning	8		F L
8	3	How Deep Is Your Love	Bee Gees	RSO	11	(1)	
9	-	Let's Have A Quiet Night In	David Soul	Private Stock	7		
10	4	I Will	Ruby Winters	Creole	9		F
11	-	Native New Yorker	Odyssey	RCA	7	(21)	F
12	-	Who Pays The Ferryman	Yannis Markopoulos	BBC	4		F L
13	5	Daddy Cool/The Girl Can't Help It	Darts	Magnet	10		F
14	-	Figaro	Brotherhood Of Man	Pye	9		
15	-	Jamming/Punky Reggae Party	Bob Marley & The Wailers	Island	5		
16	-	Only Women Bleed	Julie Covington	Virgin	4		L
17	-	I Love You	Donna Summer	Casablanca	3	(37)	
18	19	My Way	Elvis Presley	RCA	6	(22)	
19	-	Lovely Day	Bill Withers	CBS	6	(30)	
20	-	If I Had Words	Scott Fitzgerald & Yvonne Keeley	Pepper	7		F L

February 1978

This Mnth	Prev Mnth	Title	Artist	Label	Wks 20	(US Pos)	
1	14	Figaro	Brotherhood Of Man	Pye	9		
2	-	Take A Chance On Me	Abba	Epic	10	(3)	
3	20	If I Had Words	Scott Fitzgerald/Yvonne Keeley	Pepper	7		F L
4	7	Uptown Top Ranking	Althia And Donna	Lightning	8		F L
5	-	Come Back My Love	Darts	Magnet	10		
6	-	Sorry I'm A Lady	Baccara	RCA	5		L
7	1	Mull Of Kintyre/Girls' School	Wings	Capitol	13	(33)	P
8	11	Native New Yorker	Odyssey	RCA	7	(21)	F
9	19	Lovely Day	Bill Withers	CBS	6	(30)	
10	-	Wishing On A Star	Rose Royce	Warner	8		
11	-	Hotlegs/I Was Only Joking	Rod Stewart	Riva	6	(28)	
12	-	Mr. Blue Sky	Electric Light Orchestra	Jet	8	(35)	
13	2	Love's Unkind	Donna Summer	GTO	10		
14	-	Love Is Like Oxygen	Sweet	Polydor	5	(8)	L
15	-	The Groove Line	Heatwave	GTO	5	(7)	
16	15	Jamming/Punky Reggae Party	Bob Marley & The Wailers	Island	5		
17	-	Drummer Man	Tonight	Target	3		F L
18	-	Just One More Night	Yellow Dog	Virgin	5		F L
19	3	It's A Heartache	Bonnie Tyler	RCA	9	(3)	
20	6	Dance Dance Dance (Yowsah...)	Chic	Atlantic	8	(6)	F

March 1978

This Mnth	Prev Mnth	Title	Artist	Label	Wks 20	(US Pos)	
1	-	Wuthering Heights	Kate Bush	EMI	9		F
2	2	Take A Chance On Me	Abba	Epic	10	(3)	
3	5	Come Back My Love	Darts	Magnet	10		
4	10	Wishing On A Star	Rose Royce	Warner	8		
5	-	Denis	Blondie	Chrysalis	9		F
6	-	Stayin' Alive	Bee Gees	RSO	7	(1)	
7	-	Baker Street	Gerry Rafferty	UA	10	(2)	F
8	-	I Can't Stand The Rain	Eruption	Atlantic	8	(18)	F
9	12	Mr. Blue Sky	Electric Light Orchestra	Jet	8	(35)	
10	-	Matchstalk Men And Matchstalk Cats And Dogs	Brian & Michael	Pye	11		F L
11	-	Is This Love	Bob Marley & The Wailers	Island	6		
12	18	Just One More Night	Yellow Dog	Virgin	5		F L
13	-	Emotions	Samantha Sang	Private Stock	8	(3)	F L
14	1	Figaro	Brotherhood Of Man	Pye	9		
15	-	Free (E.P.)	Free	Island	4		L
16	-	Fantasy	Earth, Wind & Fire	CBS	4	(32)	
17	14	Love Is Like Oxygen	Sweet	Polydor	5	(8)	L
18	3	If I Had Words	Scott Fitzgerald/Yvonne Keeley	Pepper	7		F L
19	-	Ally's Tartan Army	Andy Cameron	Klub	5		F L
20	-	I Love The Sound Of Breaking Glass	Nick Lowe & His Cowboy Outfit	Radar	4		F

January 1978

This Mnth	Prev Mnth	Title	Artist	Label	Wks 20	(UK Pos)	
1	7	Baby Come Back	Player	RSO	14	(32)	F G
2	2	How Deep Is Your Love	Bee Gees	RSO	21	(3)	G
3	17	You're In My Heart	Rod Stewart	Warner	12	(3)	G
4	9	Here You Come Again	Dolly Parton	RCA	9	(75)	F G
5	12	Slip Slidin' Away	Paul Simon	Columbia	10	(36)	
6	20	Hey Deanie	Shaun Cassidy	Warner	9		G L
7	-	We Are The Champions	Queen	Elektra	11	(2)	G
8	18	Come Sail Away	Styx	A&M	9		
9	-	Short People	Randy Newman	Warner	11		F G L
10	6	Back In Love Again	L.T.D.	A&M	10		G L
11	-	Stayin' Alive	Bee Gees	RSO	16	(4)	P
12	-	Just The Way You Are	Billy Joel	Columbia	13	(19)	F G
13	10	Sentimental Lady	Bob Welch	Capitol	8		F
14	3	Blue Bayou	Linda Ronstadt	Asylum	11	(35)	G
15	1	You Light Up My Life	Debby Boone	Warner	16	(48)	F P L
16	-	Runaround Sue	Leif Garrett	Atlantic	5		
17	-	(Love Is) Thicker Than Water	Andy Gibb	RSO	14		G
18	16	You Can't Turn Me Off (In The Middle Of Turning Me On)	High Inergy	Gordy	7		F L
19	-	Sometimes When We Touch	Dan Hill	20th Century	10	(13)	F G
20	-	Turn To Stone	Electric Light Orchestra	Jet	5	(18)	

February 1978

This Mnth	Prev Mnth	Title	Artist	Label	Wks 20	(UK Pos)	
1	11	Stayin' Alive	Bee Gees	RSO	16	(4)	P
2	17	(Love Is) Thicker Than Water	Andy Gibb	RSO	14		G
3	12	Just The Way You Are	Billy Joel	Columbia	13	(19)	F G
4	7	We Are The Champions	Queen	Elektra	11	(2)	G
5	19	Sometimes When We Touch	Dan Hill	20th Century	10	(13)	F G
6	9	Short People	Randy Newman	Warner	11		F G L
7	-	Emotion	Samantha Sang	Private Stock	12	(11)	F P L
8	-	Dance, Dance, Dance (Yowsah, Yowsah, Yowsah)	Chic	Atlantic	10	(6)	F G
9	1	Baby Come Back	Player	RSO	14	(32)	F G
10	2	How Deep Is Your Love	Bee Gees	RSO	21	(3)	G
11	-	I Go Crazy	Paul Davis	Bang	11		F
12	3	You're In My Heart	Rod Stewart	Warner	12	(3)	G
13	-	Lay Down Sally	Eric Clapton	RSO	14	(39)	G
14	-	Peg	Steely Dan	ABC	6		
15	6	Hey Deanie	Shaun Cassidy	Warner	9		G L
16	-	Night Fever	Bee Gees	RSO	15	(1)	P
17	-	Theme From 'Close Encounters Of The Third Kind'	John Williams	Arista	4		L
18	-	Serpentine Fire	Earth, Wind & Fire	Columbia	6		
19	-	Don't Let Me Be Misunderstood	Santa Esmeralda	Casablanca	3	(41)	F L
20	-	Desiree	Neil Diamond	Columbia	3	(39)	

March 1978

This Mnth	Prev Mnth	Title	Artist	Label	Wks 20	(UK Pos)	
1	16	Night Fever	Bee Gees	RSO	15	(1)	P
2	1	Stayin' Alive	Bee Gees	RSO	16	(4)	P
3	2	(Love Is) Thicker Than Water	Andy Gibb	RSO	14		G
4	7	Emotion	Samantha Sang	Private Stock	12	(11)	F P L
5	13	Lay Down Sally	Eric Clapton	RSO	14	(39)	G
6	5	Sometimes When We Touch	Dan Hill	20th Century	10	(13)	F G
7	11	I Go Crazy	Paul Davis	Bang	11		F
8	8	Dance, Dance, Dance (Yowsah...)	Chic	Atlantic	10	(6)	F G
9	-	Can't Smile Without You	Barry Manilow	Arista	12	(43)	G
10	3	Just The Way You Are	Billy Joel	Columbia	13	(19)	F G
11	-	Thunder Island	Jay Ferguson	Asylum	8		F L
12	-	The Name Of The Game	Abba	Atlantic	4	(1)	
13	-	What's Your Name	Lynyrd Skynyrd	MCA	6		L
14	-	If I Can't Have You	Yvonne Elliman	RSO	12	(4)	G L
15	14	Peg	Steely Dan	ABC	6		
16	10	How Deep Is Your Love	Bee Gees	RSO	21	(3)	G
17	-	Falling	Leblanc & Carr	Big Tree	4		F L
18	-	Happy Anniversary	Little River Band	Harvest	4		
19	-	Wonderful World	Art Garfunkel, James Taylor & Paul Simon	Columbia	4		L
20	4	We Are The Champions	Queen	Elektra	11	(2)	G

▲ Not only did The Bee Gees have the top two singles in March, they also composed and produced the top four – an unprecedented achievement.

◆ The film *Saturday Night Fever* took disco to even greater heights - the soundtrack (heavily featuring The Bee Gees) topped the charts for six months, and sold 11 million in America, 25 million worldwide.

◆ Despite its success, disco music received little critical acclaim. Chic, however, could not be accused of being unoriginal or talentless. Their records had class, and members Nile Rodgers and Bernard Edwards went on to become successful producers and songwriters.

UK
1978
APR-JUNE

◆ As The Bee Gees scored their only transatlantic topper of the 1970s with the Grammy winning 'Night Fever', its parent album, **Saturday Night Fever,** started an 18 week run (a record for the decade) at the top in Britain.

▲ Boney M's double-sided chart topper, 'Rivers Of Babylon'/ 'Brown Girl In The Ring', which sold over two million in Britain, was the only American Top 40 entry for these regular European hit makers.

◆ Dire Straits' debut single 'Sultans Of Swing' was released. It caused little interest until 1979 when it first charted in the USA.

April 1978

This Mnth	Prev Mnth	Title	Artist	Label	Wks 20	(US Pos)	
1	10	Matchstalk Men And Matchstalk...	Brian & Michael	Pye	11		F L
2	-	I Wonder Why	Showaddywaddy	Arista	7		
3	7	Baker Street	Gerry Rafferty	UA	10	(2)	F
4	-	If You Can't Give Me Love	Suzi Quatro	RAK	8	(45)	
5	5	Denis	Blondie	Chrysalis	9		F
6	1	Wuthering Heights	Kate Bush	EMI	9		F
7	-	Follow You Follow Me	Genesis	Charisma	7	(23)	
8	-	Never Let Her Slip Away	Andrew Gold	Asylum	8	(67)	
9	-	With A Little Luck	Wings	Parlophone	5	(1)	
10	-	Night Fever	Bee Gees	RSO	12	(1)	
11	8	I Can't Stand The Rain	Eruption	Atlantic	8	(18)	F
12	-	Too Much, Too Little, Too Late	Johnny Mathis/Deniece Williams	CBS	9	(1)	
13	20	I Love The Sound Of Breaking Glass	Nick Lowe & His Cowboy Outfit	Radar	4		F
14	19	Ally's Tartan Army	Andy Cameron	Klub	5		F L
15	-	Walk In Love	Manhattan Transfer	Atlantic	5		
16	-	Every 1's A Winner	Hot Chocolate	RAK	6	(6)	
17	-	Singin' In The Rain (Pt. 1)	Sheila B. Devotion	Carrere	4		F
18	-	Sometimes When We Touch	Dan Hill	20th Century	5	(3)	F L
19	11	Is This Love	Bob Marley & The Wailers	Island	6		
20	-	More Like The Movies	Dr. Hook	Capitol	5		

May 1978

This Mnth	Prev Mnth	Title	Artist	Label	Wks 20	(US Pos)	
1	-	Rivers Of Babylon/Brown Girl In The Ring	Boney M	Atlantic/Hansa	22	(30)	P
2	10	Night Fever	Bee Gees	RSO	12	(1)	
3	12	Too Much, Too Little, Too Late	Johnny Mathis/Deniece Williams	CBS	9	(1)	
4	-	Automatic Lover	Dee D. Jackson	Mercury	5		F L
5	8	Never Let Her Slip Away	Andrew Gold	Asylum	8	(67)	
6	-	Boy From New York City	Darts	Magnet	8		
7	-	Because The Night	Patti Smith Group	Arista	6	(13)	F L
8	-	Let's All Chant	Michael Zager Band	Private Stock	6	(36)	F L
9	1	Matchstalk Men And Matchstalk...	Brian & Michael	Pye	11		F L
10	-	Jack And Jill	Raydio	Arista	5	(8)	F
11	-	If I Can't Have You	Yvonne Elliman	RSO	7	(1)	L
12	-	Love Is In The Air	John Paul Young	Ariola	6	(7)	F L
13	-	She's So Modern	Boomtown Rats	Ensign	6		
14	-	Do It Again	Raffaella Carra	Epic	5		F L
15	4	If You Can't Give Me Love	Suzi Quatro	RAK	8	(45)	
16	-	More Than A Woman	Tavares	Capitol	6	(32)	
17	-	Everybody Dance	Chic	Atlantic	5	(38)	
18	2	I Wonder Why	Showaddywaddy	Arista	7		
19	-	Bad Old Days	Co-Co	Ariola/Hansa	3		F L
20	-	(I'm Always Touched By Your) Presence Dear	Blondie	Chrysalis	5		

June 1978

This Mnth	Prev Mnth	Title	Artist	Label	Wks 20	(US Pos)	
1	1	Rivers Of Babylon/Brown Girl In...	Boney M	Atlantic/Hansa	22	(30)	P
2	-	You're The One That I Want	John Travolta & Olivia Newton-John	RSO	17	(1)	F P
3	6	Boy From New York City	Darts	Magnet	8		
4	11	If I Can't Have You	Yvonne Elliman	RSO	7	(1)	L
5	2	Night Fever	Bee Gees	RSO	12	(1)	
6	-	Ca Plane Pour Moi	Plastic Bertrand	Sire	7		F L
7	-	Oh Carol	Smokie	RAK	6		
8	12	Love Is In The Air	John Paul Young	Ariola	6	(7)	F L
9	-	Davy's On The Road Again	Manfred Mann's Earth Band	Bronze	5		L
10	-	Annie's Song	James Galway	RCA Red Seal	8		F L
11	16	More Than A Woman	Tavares	Capitol	6	(32)	
12	-	Miss You	Rolling Stones	Rolling Stone	6	(1)	
13	7	Because The Night	Patti Smith Group	Arista	6	(13)	F L
14	-	The Smurf Song	Father Abraham & The Smurfs	Decca	11		F
15	-	Ole Ola (Muhler Brasileira)	Rod Stewart	Riva	3		
16	-	What A Waste	Ian Dury & The Blockheads	Stiff	4		F
17	-	Making Up Again	Goldie	Bronze	5		F L
18	-	Hi Tension	Hi Tension	Island	3		F
19	-	It Sure Brings Out The Love In Your Eyes	David Soul	Private Stock	4		L
20	-	Come To Me	Ruby Winters	Creole	4		L

US 1978 APR-JUNE

April 1978

This Mnth	Prev Mnth	Title	Artist	Label	Wks 20	(UK Pos)	
1	1	Night Fever	Bee Gees	RSO	15	(1)	P
2	9	Can't Smile Without You	Barry Manilow	Arista	12	(43)	G
3	5	Lay Down Sally	Eric Clapton	RSO	14	(39)	G
4	14	If I Can't Have You	Yvonne Elliman	RSO	12	(4)	G L
5	2	Stayin' Alive	Bee Gees	RSO	16	(4)	P
6	-	Dust In The Wind	Kansas	Kirshner	8		G
7	-	The Closer I Get To You	Roberta Flack/Donny Hathaway	Atlantic	11	(42)	G
8	-	Jack And Jill	Raydio	Arista	8	(11)	F G
9	-	Our Love	Natalie Cole	Capitol	8		G
10	-	With A Little Luck	Wings	Capitol	11	(5)	
11	4	Emotion	Samantha Sang	Private Stock	12	(11)	F P L
12	-	We'll Never Have To Say Goodbye Again	England Dan/John Ford Coley	Big Tree	5		
13	-	Runnin' On Empty	Jackson Browne	Asylum	6		
14	3	(Love Is) Thicker Than Water	Andy Gibb	RSO	14		G
15	-	You're The One That I Want	John Travolta & Olivia Newton-John	RSO	13	(1)	P
16	11	Thunder Island	Jay Ferguson	Asylum	8		F L
17	-	Count On Me	Jefferson Starship	Grunt	8		
18	-	Ebony Eyes	Bob Welch	Capitol	4		
19	-	Goodbye Girl	David Gates	Elektra	4		F L
20	7	I Go Crazy	Paul Davis	Bang	11		F

May 1978

This Mnth	Prev Mnth	Title	Artist	Label	Wks 20	(UK Pos)	
1	10	With A Little Luck	Wings	Capitol	11	(5)	
2	7	The Closer I Get To You	Roberta Flack/Donny Hathaway	Atlantic	11	(42)	G
3	4	If I Can't Have You	Yvonne Elliman	RSO	12	(4)	G L
4	-	Too Much, Too Little, Too Late	Johnny Mathis/Deniece Williams	Columbia	11	(3)	G L
5	15	You're The One That I Want	John Travolta & Olivia Newton-John	RSO	13	(1)	P
6	1	Night Fever	Bee Gees	RSO	15	(1)	P
7	-	Shadow Dancing	Andy Gibb	RSO	15	(42)	G
8	17	Count On Me	Jefferson Starship	Grunt	8		
9	-	Feels So Good	Chuck Mangione	A&M	10		F
10	-	Imaginary Lover	Atlanta Rhythm Section	Polydor	7		
11	2	Can't Smile Without You	Barry Manilow	Arista	12	(43)	G
12	-	Disco Inferno	Trammps	Atlantic	6	(16)	F L
13	-	This Time I'm In It For Love	Player	RSO	7		L
14	-	On Broadway	George Benson	Warner	7		
15	6	Dust In The Wind	Kansas	Kirshner	8		G
16	3	Lay Down Sally	Eric Clapton	RSO	14	(39)	G
17	-	Baby Hold On	Eddie Money	Columbia	5		F
18	-	Love Is Like Oxygen	Sweet	Capitol	9	(9)	L
19	-	Take A Chance On Me	Abba	Atlantic	11	(1)	G
20	8	Jack And Jill	Raydio	Arista	8	(11)	F G

June 1978

This Mnth	Prev Mnth	Title	Artist	Label	Wks 20	(UK Pos)	
1	7	Shadow Dancing	Andy Gibb	RSO	15	(42)	G
2	5	You're The One That I Want	John Travolta & Olivia Newton-John	RSO	13	(1)	P
3	4	Too Much, Too Little, Too Late	Johnny Mathis/Deniece Williams	Columbia	11	(3)	G L
4	-	Baker Street	Gerry Rafferty	UA	12	(3)	F G
5	-	It's A Heartache	Bonnie Tyler	RCA	11	(4)	F G
6	19	Take A Chance On Me	Abba	Atlantic	11	(1)	G
7	9	Feels So Good	Chuck Mangione	A&M	10		F
8	18	Love Is Like Oxygen	Sweet	Capitol	9	(9)	L
9	14	On Broadway	George Benson	Warner	7		
10	-	You Belong To Me	Carly Simon	Elektra	7		
11	-	Dance With Me	Peter Brown	Drive	9	(57)	L
12	1	With A Little Luck	Wings	Capitol	11	(5)	
13	-	Use Ta Be My Girl	O'Jays	Philly Int.	9	(12)	G L
14	-	The Groove Line	Heatwave	Epic	9	(12)	G L
15	2	The Closer I Get To You	Roberta Flack/Donny Hathaway	Atlantic	11	(42)	G
16	13	This Time I'm In It For Love	Player	RSO	7		L
17	-	Two Out Of Three Ain't Bad	Meat Loaf	Epic	7	(69)	F G
18	17	Baby Hold On	Eddie Money	Columbia	5		F
19	-	Still The Same	Bob Seger & Silver Bullet Band	Capitol	8		
20	-	Because The Night	Patti Smith Group	Arista	5	(5)	F L

◆ The record breaking Bee Gees wrote four successive No. 1 singles and produced three of them. A few weeks later, their younger brother, Andy Gibb, scored his third successive chart topper with his third release, 'Shadow Dancing'.

◆ Rick James, who had been in an earlier group with Neil Young, was the latest sensation in the R&B arena. As the Motown act's debut "punk-funk" hit 'You And I' headed to the top, Warner Brothers prepared to launch their own multi-talented, multi-faceted R&B-based artist, Prince.

◆ Meat Loaf made his Top 20 debut with 'Two Out Of Three Ain't Bad', as his album **Bat Out Of Hell** climbed the transatlantic charts. The LP went on to sell over 25 million world-wide.

UK 1978
JULY–SEPT

▲ The soundtrack album to John Travolta's latest box office smash *Grease* topped the American album chart for three months and it repeated that feat in Britain. It contained the transatlantic smash duets, 'You're The One That I Want' and 'Summer Nights' by Travolta and Olivia Newton-John (both selling over a million in the UK alone), as well as the chart topping title song by Frankie Valli.

◆ Soon after The Who's original manager Pete Meaden committed suicide, the group's colourful and extrovert drummer Keith Moon died from drug and drink-related causes.

July 1978

This Mnth	Prev Mnth	Title	Artist	Label	Wks 20	(US Pos)	
1	2	You're The One That I Want	John Travolta & Olivia Newton-John	RSO	17	(1)	F P
2	14	The Smurf Song	Father Abraham & The Smurfs	Decca	11		F
3	-	Dancing In The City	Marshall Hain	Harvest	9	(43)	F L
4	-	Airport	Motors	Virgin	7		F
5	10	Annie's Song	James Galway	RCA Red Seal	8		F L
6	-	Like Clockwork	Boomtown Rats	Ensign	7		
7	-	Man With The Child In His Eyes	Kate Bush	EMI	6	(85)	
8	-	A Little Bit Of Soap	Showaddywaddy	Arista	6		
9	12	Miss You	Rolling Stones	Rolling Stone	6	(1)	
10	-	Substitute	Clout	Carrere	9	(67)	F L
11	-	Boogie Oogie Oogie	Taste Of Honey	Capitol	8	(1)	F L
12	-	No One Is Innocent/My Way	Sex Pistols	Virgin	5		
13	1	Rivers Of Babylon/Brown Girl In...	Boney M	Atlantic/Hansa	22	(30)	P
14	-	Mind Blowing Decisions	Heatwave	GTO	4		
15	-	Used Ta Be My Girl	O'Jays	Philly International	5	(4)	L
16	-	Wild West Hero	Electric Light Orchestra	Jet	6		
17	-	Run For Home	Lindisfarne	Mercury	5	(33)	
18	17	Making Up Again	Goldie	Bronze	5		F L
19	9	Davy's On The Road Again	Manfred Mann's Earth Band	Bronze	5		L
20	-	Argentine Melody (Cancion De Argentina)	San Jose	MCA	3		F L

August 1978

This Mnth	Prev Mnth	Title	Artist	Label	Wks 20	(US Pos)	
1	1	You're The One That I Want	John Travolta & Olivia Newton-John	RSO	17	(1)	F P
2	10	Substitute	Clout	Carrere	9	(67)	F L
3	11	Boogie Oogie Oogie	Taste Of Honey	Capitol	8	(1)	F L
4	13	Rivers Of Babylon/Brown Girl In...	Boney M	Atlantic/Hansa	22	(30)	P
5	-	Three Times A Lady	Commodores	Motown	10	(1)	
6	-	Forever Autumn	Justin Hayward	CBS	6	(47)	L
7	2	The Smurf Song	Father Abraham & The Smurfs	Decca	11		F
8	-	5-7-0-5	City Boy	Vertigo	5	(27)	F L
9	-	If The Kids Are United	Sham 69	Polydor	5		
10	-	It's Raining	Darts	Magnet	8		
11	3	Dancing In The City	Marshall Hain	Harvest	9	(43)	F L
12	-	Northern Lights	Renaissance	Warner	5		F L
13	16	Wild West Hero	Electric Light Orchestra	Jet	6		
14	-	Supernature	Cerrone	Atlantic	5	(70)	F L
15	8	A Little Bit Of Soap	Showaddywaddy	Arista	6		
16	6	Like Clockwork	Boomtown Rats	Ensign	7		
17	-	Dreadlock Holiday	10cc	Mercury	9	(44)	L
18	-	Come Back And Finish What You Started	Gladys Knight & The Pips	Buddah	5		
19	-	Stay	Jackson Browne	Asylum	4	(20)	F L
20	-	Baby Stop Crying	Bob Dylan	CBS	5		L

September 1978

This Mnth	Prev Mnth	Title	Artist	Label	Wks 20	(US Pos)	
1	5	Three Times A Lady	Commodores	Motown	10	(1)	
2	17	Dreadlock Holiday	10cc	Mercury	9	(44)	L
3	4	Rivers Of Babylon/Brown Girl In...	Boney M	Atlantic/Hansa	22	(30)	P
4	-	Oh What A Circus	David Essex	Mercury	8		
5	-	Jilted John	Jilted John	EMI International	7		F L
6	10	It's Raining	Darts	Magnet	8		
7	1	You're The One That I Want	John Travolta/O. Newton-John	RSO	17	(1)	F P
8	-	Kiss You All Over	Exile	RAK	6	(1)	F L
9	-	British Hustle/Peace On Earth	Hi Tension	Island	5		L
10	-	Hong Kong Garden	Siouxsie & The Banshees	Polydor	5		F
11	14	Supernature	Cerrone	Atlantic	5	(70)	F L
12	-	Grease	Frankie Valli	RSO	6	(1)	L
13	-	Picture This	Blondie	Chrysalis	6		
14	-	Summer Nights	John Travolta/O. Newton-John	RSO	11	(5)	G
15	-	An Everlasting Love	Andy Gibb	RSO	5	(5)	F L
16	-	Summer Night City	Abba	Epic	5		
17	-	It's Only Make Believe	Child	Ariola Hansa	5		F L
18	-	Forget About You	Motors	Virgin	4		L
19	-	Again And Again	Status Quo	Vertigo	4		
20	-	Love Don't Live Here Anymore	Rose Royce	Whitfield	7	(32)	

July 1978

This Mnth	Prev Mnth	Title	Artist	Label	Wks 20	(UK Pos)	
1	1	Shadow Dancing	Andy Gibb	RSO	15	(42)	G
2	4	Baker Street	Gerry Rafferty	UA	12	(3)	F G
3	19	Still The Same	Bob Seger & The Silver Bullet Band	Capitol	8		
4	13	Use Ta Be My Girl	O'Jays	Philly Int.	9	(12)	G L
5	-	Miss You	Rolling Stones	Rolling Stone	12	(3)	G
6	6	Take A Chance On Me	Abba	Atlantic	11	(1)	G
7	14	The Groove Line	Heatwave	Epic	9	(12)	G L
8	5	It's A Heartache	Bonnie Tyler	RCA	11	(4)	F G
9	-	Last Dance	Donna Summer	Casablanca	11	(51)	G
10	-	Grease	Frankie Valli	RSO	11	(3)	P L
11	11	Dance With Me	Peter Brown	Drive	9	(57)	L
12	-	Love Will Find A Way	Pablo Cruise	A&M	8		
13	17	Two Out Of Three Ain't Bad	Meat Loaf	Epic	7	(69)	F G
14	-	Three Times A Lady	Commodores	Motown	12	(1)	G
15	10	You Belong To Me	Carly Simon	Elektra	7		
16	-	Bluer Than Blue	Michael Johnson	EMI America	6		F
17	-	Runaway	Jefferson Starship	Grunt	4		
18	8	Love Is Like Oxygen	Sweet	Capitol	9	(9)	L
19	-	Hot Blooded	Foreigner	Atlantic	12	(42)	G
20	-	Copacabana (At The Copa)	Barry Manilow	Arista	7	(42)	G

August 1978

This Mnth	Prev Mnth	Title	Artist	Label	Wks 20	(UK Pos)	
1	14	Three Times A Lady	Commodores	Motown	12	(1)	G
2	10	Grease	Frankie Valli	RSO	11	(3)	P L
3	5	Miss You	Rolling Stones	Rolling Stone	12	(3)	G
4	9	Last Dance	Donna Summer	Casablanca	11	(51)	G
5	19	Hot Blooded	Foreigner	Atlantic	12	(42)	G
6	12	Love Will Find A Way	Pablo Cruise	A&M	8		
7	-	Boogie Oogie Oogie	Taste Of Honey	Capitol	14	(3)	F P
8	-	Magnet And Steel	Walter Egan	Columbia	8		F G L
9	20	Copacabana (At The Copa)	Barry Manilow	Arista	7	(42)	G
10	-	An Everlasting Love	Andy Gibb	RSO	10	(10)	G
11	-	Hopelessly Devoted To You	Olivia Newton-John	RSO	12	(2)	G
12	-	Life's Been Good	Joe Walsh	Asylum	7	(14)	F
13	-	My Angel Baby	Toby Beau	RCA	7		F L
14	1	Shadow Dancing	Andy Gibb	RSO	15	(42)	G
15	2	Baker Street	Gerry Rafferty	UA	12	(3)	F G
16	-	I'm Not Gonna Let It Bother Me Tonight	Atlanta Rhythm Section	Polydor	4		
17	-	Kiss You All Over	Exile	Warner	15	(6)	F G L
18	-	Shame	Evelyn 'Champagne' King	RCA	7	(39)	F G
19	4	Use Ta Be My Girl	O'Jays	Philly Int.	9	(12)	G L
20	3	Still The Same	Bob Seger & Silver Bullet Band	Capitol	8		

September 1978

This Mnth	Prev Mnth	Title	Artist	Label	Wks 20	(UK Pos)	
1	7	Boogie Oogie Oogie	Taste Of Honey	Capitol	14	(3)	F P
2	1	Three Times A Lady	Commodores	Motown	12	(1)	G
3	11	Hopelessly Devoted To You	Olivia Newton-John	RSO	12	(2)	G
4	17	Kiss You All Over	Exile	Warner	15	(6)	F G L
5	5	Hot Blooded	Foreigner	Atlantic	12	(42)	G
6	10	An Everlasting Love	Andy Gibb	RSO	10	(10)	G
7	-	Summer Nights	John Travolta & Olivia Newton-John	RSO	9	(1)	G L
8	-	Hot Child In The City	Nick Gilder	Chrysalis	14		F P L
9	-	Don't Look Back	Boston	Epic	9	(43)	
10	-	Love Is In The Air	John Paul Young	Scotti Bros	11	(5)	F L
11	2	Grease	Frankie Valli	RSO	11	(3)	P L
12	-	Got To Get You Into My Life	Earth, Wind & Fire	Columbia	6	(33)	G
13	-	Fool (If You Think It's Over)	Chris Rea	UA	7	(30)	F L
14	18	Shame	Evelyn 'Champagne' King	RCA	7	(39)	F G
15	-	Reminiscing	Little River Band	Harvest	10		
16	-	You And I	Rick James	Gordy	6	(46)	F
17	-	You Needed Me	Anne Murray	Capitol	13	(22)	G
18	3	Miss You	Rolling Stones	Rolling Stone	12	(3)	G
19	-	Hollywood Nights	Bob Seger & The Silver Bullet Band	Capitol	6	(42)	
20	-	Whenever I Call You 'Friend'	Kenny Loggins	Columbia	10		F

◆ Newcomers on the transatlantic charts included Grammy winning R&B duo A Taste Of Honey, Scotand's Gerry Rafferty (whose LP **City To City** was a US No. 1) and future country stars Exile whose debut hit 'Kiss You All Over' was written and produced by the successful British team of Chinn & Chapman.

◆ Despite the involvement of The Bee Gees, the film *Sergeant Pepper's Lonely Hearts Club Band* was a resounding miss.

◆ Steve Miller and The Eagles drew 65,000 to a gig in Bloomington, and both Bob Dylan's and Fleetwood Mac's US tours were sell-outs. Other successful live events included Canada Jam, with headliners The Doobie Brothers, Kansas and The Commodores, and Grateful Dead's performance at the Egyptian pyramids.

UK 1978
OCT-DEC

◆ It was reported that The Rolling Stones' US tour had grossed a record-breaking $6 million.

◆ The film *Grease* continued to spawn hits, with three songs, 'Summer Nights', 'Sandy' and 'Hopelessly Devoted To You', taking slots in the British Top 4 in November.

▲ The Cars , who were voted Best New Band in *Rolling Stone*, started a European tour. Their debut hit, 'My Best Friend's Girl', was the first picture disc to be successfully marketed in Britain.

◆ Sex Pistol Sid Vicious was charged in New York with the murder of his girlfriend Nancy Spungen.

October 1978

This Mnth	Prev Mnth	Title	Artist	Label	Wks 20	(US Pos)	
1	14	Summer Nights	John Travolta & Olivia Newton-John	RSO	11	(5)	G
2	-	Rasputin	Boney M	Atlantic/Hansa	7		
3	20	Love Don't Live Here Anymore	Rose Royce	Whitfield	7	(32)	
4	-	Lucky Stars	Dean Friedman	Lifesong	6		F L
5	-	I Can't Stop Lovin' You (Though I Try)	Leo Sayer	Chrysalis	6		
6	-	Sandy	John Travolta	Polydor	7		
7	-	Sweet Talkin' Woman	Electric Light Orchestra	Jet	7	(17)	
8	12	Grease	Frankie Valli	RSO	6	(1)	L
9	-	You Make Me Feel (Mighty Real)	Sylvester	Fantasy	5	(36)	F L
10	-	Now That We've Found Love	Third World	Island	4	(47)	F
11	-	Talking In Your Sleep	Crystal Gayle	UA	5	(18)	L
12	-	Blame It On The Boogie	Jacksons	Epic	7	(54)	
13	16	Summer Night City	Abba	Epic	5		
14	-	Rat Trap	Boomtown Rats	Ensign	9		
15	-	Macarthur Park	Donna Summer	Casablanca	6	(1)	
16	2	Dreadlock Holiday	10cc	Mercury	9	(44)	L
17	-	A Rose Has To Die	Dooleys	GTO	4		
18	8	Kiss You All Over	Exile	RAK	6	(1)	F L
19	1	Three Times A Lady	Commodores	Motown	10	(1)	
20	4	Oh What A Circus	David Essex	Mercury	8		

November 1978

This Mnth	Prev Mnth	Title	Artist	Label	Wks 20	(US Pos)	
1	14	Rat Trap	Boomtown Rats	Ensign	9		
2	1	Summer Nights	John Travolta/O. Newton-John	RSO	11	(5)	G
3	6	Sandy	John Travolta	Polydor	7		
4	-	Hopelessly Devoted To You	Olivia Newton-John	RSO	5	(3)	
5	-	Darlin'	Frankie Miller	Chrysalis	7		F L
6	15	Macarthur Park	Donna Summer	Casablanca	6	(1)	
7	-	My Best Friend's Girl	Cars	Elektra	5	(35)	F
8	12	Blame It On The Boogie	Jacksons	Epic	7	(54)	
9	2	Rasputin	Boney M	Atlantic/Hansa	7		
10	-	Pretty Little Angel Eyes	Showaddywaddy	Arista	6		
11	7	Sweet Talkin' Woman	Electric Light Orchestra	Jet	7	(17)	
12	-	Instant Replay	Dan Hartman	Sky	6	(29)	F
13	-	Givin' Up Givin' In	Three Degrees	Ariola	5		
14	-	Public Image	Public Image Ltd.	Virgin	4		F
15	-	Bicycle Race/Fat Bottomed Girls	Queen	EMI	4	(24)	
16	-	Da Ya Think I'm Sexy	Rod Stewart	Riva	9	(1)	
17	4	Lucky Stars	Dean Friedman	Lifesong	6		F L
18	-	Dippety Day	Father Abraham & The Smurfs	Decca	5		
19	-	Hurry Up Harry	Sham 69	Polydor	5		
20	-	Hanging On The Telephone	Blondie	Chrysalis	7		

December 1978

This Mnth	Prev Mnth	Title	Artist	Label	Wks 20	(US Pos)	
1	-	Mary's Boy Child-Oh My Lord	Boney M	Atlantic/Hansa	7	(85)	G
2	16	Da Ya Think I'm Sexy	Rod Stewart	Riva	9	(1)	
3	-	Too Much Heaven	Bee Gees	RSO	9	(1)	
4	-	A Taste Of Aggro	Barron Knights	Epic	8		
5	-	I Lost My Heart To A Starship Trooper	Sarah Brightman & Hot Gossip	Ariola	8		F
6	-	Y.M.C.A.	Village People	Mercury	10	(2)	F G
7	-	Le Freak	Chic	Atlantic	10	(1)	
8	-	Always And Forever/Mind Blowing Decisions	Heatwave	GTO	9	(18)	
9	20	Hanging On The Telephone	Blondie	Chrysalis	7		
10	-	You Don't Bring Me Flowers	Barbra & Neil	Columbia	6	(1)	
11	1	Rat Trap	Boomtown Rats	Ensign	9		
12	-	Lay Your Love On Me	Racey	RAK	9		F
13	-	Don't Cry Out Loud	Elkie Brooks	A&M	5		
14	4	Hopelessly Devoted To You	Olivia Newton-John	RSO	5	(3)	
15	10	Pretty Little Angel Eyes	Showaddywaddy	Arista	6		
16	7	My Best Friend's Girl	Cars	Elektra	5	(35)	
17	-	Greased Lightning	John Travolta	Polydor	5	(47)	
18	-	Song For Guy	Elton John	Rocket	6		
19	12	Instant Replay	Dan Hartman	Sky	6	(29)	F
20	-	In The Bush	Musique	CBS	5	(58)	F L

208

This Mnth	Prev Mnth	Title	Artist	Label	Wks 20	(UK Pos)	
1	8	Hot Child In The City	Nick Gilder	Chrysalis	14		F P L
2	4	Kiss You All Over	Exile	Warner	15	(6)	F G L
3	1	Boogie Oogie Oogie	Taste Of Honey	Capitol	14	(3)	F P
4	15	Reminiscing	Little River Band	Harvest	10		
5	17	You Needed Me	Anne Murray	Capitol	13	(22)	G
6	20	Whenever I Call You 'Friend'	Kenny Loggins	Columbia	10		F
7	10	Love Is In The Air	John Paul Young	Scotti Bros	11	(5)	F L
8	7	Summer Nights	John Travolta & Olivia Newton-John	RSO	9	(1)	G L
9	9	Don't Look Back	Boston	Epic	9	(43)	
10	-	MacArthur Park	Donna Summer	Casablanca	12	(5)	G
11	-	How Much I Feel	Ambrosia	Warner	11		
12	-	Right Down The Line	Gerry Rafferty	UA	6		
13	3	Hopelessly Devoted To You	Olivia Newton-John	RSO	12	(2)	G
14	-	Get Off	Foxy	Dash	7		F L
15	-	Double Vision	Foreigner	Atlantic	9		G
16	19	Hollywood Nights	Bob Seger & The Silver Bullet Band	Capitol	6	(42)	
17	-	You Never Done It Like That	Captain & Tennille	A&M	8	(63)	
18	-	Back In The U.S.A.	Linda Ronstadt	Asylum	4		
19	2	Three Times A Lady	Commodores	Motown	12	(1)	G
20	-	Beast Of Burden	Rolling Stones	Rolling Stone	4		

This Mnth	Prev Mnth	Title	Artist	Label	Wks 20	(UK Pos)	
1	10	MacArthur Park	Donna Summer	Casablanca	12	(5)	G
2	15	Double Vision	Foreigner	Atlantic	9		G
3	5	You Needed Me	Anne Murray	Capitol	13	(22)	G
4	11	How Much I Feel	Ambrosia	Warner	11		
5	1	Hot Child In The City	Nick Gilder	Chrysalis	14		F P L
6	2	Kiss You All Over	Exile	Warner	15	(6)	F G L
7	-	I Just Wanna Stop	Gino Vannelli	A&M	9		F
8	6	Whenever I Call You 'Friend'	Kenny Loggins	Columbia	10		F
9	17	You Never Done It Like That	Captain & Tennille	A&M	8	(63)	
10	-	You Don't Bring Me Flowers	Barbra & Neil	Columbia	12	(5)	G
11	-	Ready To Take A Chance Again	Barry Manilow	Arista	5		
12	-	I Love The Night Life (Disco 'Round)	Alicia Bridges	Polydor	12	(32)	F G L
13	20	Beast Of Burden	Rolling Stones	Rolling Stone	4		
14	4	Reminiscing	Little River Band	Harvest	10		
15	-	Time Passages	Al Stewart	Arista	9		L
16	14	Get Off	Foxy	Dash	7		F L
17	-	(Our Love) Don't Throw It All Away	Andy Gibb	RSO	10	(32)	G
18	-	Sharing The Night Together	Dr. Hook	Capitol	10	(43)	G
19	-	Le Freak	Chic	Atlantic	17	(7)	P
20	-	Who Are You	Who	Decca	5	(18)	

This Mnth	Prev Mnth	Title	Artist	Label	Wks 20	(UK Pos)	
1	19	Le Freak	Chic	Atlantic	17	(7)	P
2	10	You Don't Bring Me Flowers	Barbra & Neil	Columbia	12	(5)	G
3	7	I Just Wanna Stop	Gino Vannelli	A&M	9		F
4	12	I Love The Night Life (Disco 'Round)	Alicia Bridges	Polydor	12	(32)	F G L
5	-	My Life	Billy Joel	Columbia	12	(12)	G
6	-	Too Much Heaven	Bee Gees	RSO	11	(3)	P
7	18	Sharing The Night Together	Dr. Hook	Capitol	10	(43)	G
8	1	MacArthur Park	Donna Summer	Casablanca	12	(5)	G
9	17	(Our Love) Don't Throw It All Away	Andy Gibb	RSO	10	(32)	G
10	15	Time Passages	Al Stewart	Arista	9		L
11	-	Y.M.C.A.	Village People	Casablanca	17	(1)	F P
12	4	How Much I Feel	Ambrosia	Warner	11		
13	-	Hold The Line	Toto	Columbia	10	(14)	F G
14	-	Strange Way	Firefall	Atlantic	7		L
15	-	How You Gonna See Me Now	Alice Cooper	Warner	6	(61)	
16	-	Ooh Baby Baby	Linda Ronstadt	Asylum	7		
17	2	Double Vision	Foreigner	Atlantic	9		G
18	-	Promises	Eric Clapton	RSO	6	(37)	
19	-	Alive Again	Chicago	Columbia	6		
20	-	Straight On	Heart	Portrait	4		

US 1978 OCT-DEC

◆ American record and tape sales topped $4 billion for the first time in 1978. Disco remained supreme, pop prospered, funk fared well, new wave caused more than a ripple of interest and rock ruled on the album chart - there was room for many styles to be simultaneously successful.

◆ Solo albums by the four members of Kiss (who were now also stars of a regular cartoon series) all shipped gold.

◆ CBS Records became the first label to hike their album prices up a dollar to $8.98.

◆ Singer, songwriter and pianist Billy Joel, whose single 'Just The Way You Are' won the 1978 Grammy awards for Record Of The Year and Song Of The Year, topped the chart for the last two months of the year with **52nd Street**. The LP went on to win the Album Of The Year award the following year.

UK 1979
JAN-MAR

◆ British single sales continued to amaze, with hits from the Village People ('Y.M.C.A'.) and Blondie ('Heart Of Glass') selling over a million and Ian Dury's new wave disco track, 'Hit Me With Your Rhythm Stick', only narrowly missing.

▲ British success for local groups Dire Straits and Police (above) only came after their respective singles 'Sultans Of Swing' and 'Roxanne' charted in America.

◆ The biggest transatlantic hits of the period were Gloria Gaynor's smash 'I Will Survive' and Rod Stewart's disco-oriented 'Da Ya Think I'm Sexy'.

January 1979

This Mnth	Prev Mnth	Title	Artist	Label	Wks 20	(US Pos)	
1	6	Y.M.C.A.	Village People	Mercury	10	(2)	F G
2	-	Hit Me With Your Rhythm Stick	Ian Dury & The Blockheads	Stiff	10		
3	12	Lay Your Love On Me	Racey	RAK	9		F
4	-	September	Earth, Wind & Fire	CBS	7	(8)	
5	18	Song For Guy	Elton John	Rocket	6		
6	7	Le Freak	Chic	Atlantic	10	(1)	
7	-	A Little More Love	Olivia Newton-John	EMI	6	(3)	
8	4	A Taste Of Aggro	Barron Knights	Epic	8		
9	-	Hello This Is Joannie (Telephone Answering Machine Song)	Paul Evans	Spring	5		F L
10	10	You Don't Bring Me Flowers	Barbra & Neil	Columbia	6	(1)	
11	1	Mary's Boy Child-Oh My Lord	Boney M	Atlantic/Hansa	7	(85)	G
12	3	Too Much Heaven	Bee Gees	RSO	9	(1)	
13	-	I'm Every Woman	Chaka Khan	Warner	7	(21)	F
14	5	I Lost My Heart To A Starship Trooper	Sarah Brightman & Hot Gossip	Ariola	8		F
15	-	One Nation Under A Groove (Pt. 1)	Funkadelic	Warner	4	(28)	F L
16	-	Car 67	Driver 67	Logo	5		F L
17	-	I'll Put You Together Again	Hot Chocolate	RAK	4		
18	-	Women In Love	Three Degrees	Ariola	8		
19	-	Heart Of Glass	Blondie	Chrysalis	8	(1)	G
20	8	Always And Forever/Mind Blowing Decisions	Heatwave	GTO	9	(18)	

February 1979

This Mnth	Prev Mnth	Title	Artist	Label	Wks 20	(US Pos)	
1	19	Heart Of Glass	Blondie	Chrysalis	8	(1)	G
2	18	Women In Love	Three Degrees	Ariola	8		
3	-	Chiquitita	Abba	Epic	7	(29)	
4	-	Don't Cry For Me Argentina	Shadows	EMI	6		
5	2	Hit Me With Your Rhythm Stick	Ian Dury & The Blockheads	Stiff	10		
6	-	I Was Made For Dancin'	Leif Garrett	Scotti Bros	5	(10)	F L
7	-	Contact	Edwin Starr	20th Century	6	(65)	
8	16	Car 67	Driver 67	Logo	5		F L
9	4	September	Earth, Wind & Fire	CBS	7	(8)	
10	-	Milk And Alcohol	Dr. Feelgood	UA	5		F L
11	-	Tragedy	Bee Gees	RSO	7	(1)	
12	1	Y.M.C.A.	Village People	Mercury	10	(2)	F G
13	7	A Little More Love	Olivia Newton-John	EMI	6	(3)	
14	-	My Life	Billy Joel	CBS	4	(3)	
15	-	Oliver's Army	Elvis Costello	Radar	9		
16	-	King Rocker	Generation X	Chrysalis	4		F L
17	-	Just The Way You Are	Barry White	20th Century	5		
18	9	Hello This Is Joannie (Telephone...)	Paul Evans	Spring	5		F L
19	-	I Will Survive	Gloria Gaynor	Polydor	9	(1)	
20	3	Lay Your Love On Me	Racey	RAK	9		F

March 1979

This Mnth	Prev Mnth	Title	Artist	Label	Wks 20	(US Pos)	
1	19	I Will Survive	Gloria Gaynor	Polydor	9	(1)	
2	15	Oliver's Army	Elvis Costello	Radar	9		
3	11	Tragedy	Bee Gees	RSO	7	(1)	
4	-	Lucky Number	Lene Lovich	Stiff	7		F
5	-	Can You Feel The Force	Real Thing	Pye	7		
6	-	Something Else/Friggin' In The Riggin'	Sex Pistols	Virgin	7		
7	-	I Want Your Love	Chic	Atlantic	7	(7)	
8	1	Heart Of Glass	Blondie	Chrysalis	8	(1)	G
9	-	Keep On Dancin'	Gary's Gang	CBS	5	(41)	F L
10	7	Contact	Edwin Starr	20th Century	5	(65)	
11	-	Get Down	Gene Chandler	20th Century	5	(53)	F L
12	-	Into The Valley	Skids	Virgin	6		F
13	3	Chiquitita	Abba	Epic	7	(29)	
14	-	Painter Man	Boney M	Atlantic/Hansa	3		
15	-	Get It	Darts	Magnet	4		
16	-	Waiting For An Alibi	Thin Lizzy	Vertigo	4		
17	-	In The Navy	Village People	Mercury	6	(3)	
18	-	Don't Stop Me Now	Queen	EMI	4	(86)	
19	-	Sound Of The Suburbs	Members	Virgin	4		F L
20	6	I Was Made For Dancin'	Leif Garrett	Scotti Bros	5	(10)	F L

January 1979

This Mnth	Prev Mnth	Title	Artist	Label	Wks 20	(UK Pos)	
1	1	Le Freak	Chic	Atlantic	17	(7)	P
2	6	Too Much Heaven	Bee Gees	RSO	11	(3)	P
3	5	My Life	Billy Joel	Columbia	12	(12)	G
4	11	Y.M.C.A.	Village People	Casablanca	17	(1)	F P
5	2	You Don't Bring Me Flowers	Barbra & Neil	Columbia	12	(5)	G
6	13	Hold The Line	Toto	Columbia	10	(14)	F G
7	16	Ooh Baby Baby	Linda Ronstadt	Asylum	7		
8	-	A Little More Love	Olivia Newton-John	MCA	15	(4)	G
9	-	Every 1's A Winner	Hot Chocolate	Infinity	7	(12)	G L
10	18	Promises	Eric Clapton	RSO	6	(37)	
11	-	September	Earth, Wind & Fire	Arc	9	(3)	G
12	7	Sharing The Night Together	Dr. Hook	Capitol	10	(43)	G
13	-	Da Ya Think I'm Sexy	Rod Stewart	Warner	13	(1)	G
14	9	(Our Love) Don't Throw It All Away	Andy Gibb	RSO	10	(32)	G
15	-	Lotta Love	Nicolette Larson	Warner	10		F L
16	-	We've Got Tonite	Bob Seger & The Silver Bullet Band	Capitol	5	(41)	
17	-	Fire	Pointer Sisters	Planet	13	(34)	G
18	15	How You Gonna See Me Now	Alice Cooper	Warner	6	(61)	
19	-	New York Groove	Ace Frehley	Casablanca	6		F L
20	4	I Love The Night Life (Disco 'Round)	Alicia Bridges	Polydor	12	(32)	F G L

February 1979

This Mnth	Prev Mnth	Title	Artist	Label	Wks 20	(UK Pos)	
1	13	Da Ya Think I'm Sexy	Rod Stewart	Warner	13	(1)	G
2	4	Y.M.C.A.	Village People	Casablanca	17	(1)	F P
3	8	A Little More Love	Olivia Newton-John	MCA	15	(4)	G
4	1	Le Freak	Chic	Atlantic	17	(7)	P
5	17	Fire	Pointer Sisters	Planet	13	(34)	G
6	-	I Will Survive	Gloria Gaynor	Polydor	15	(1)	G L
7	15	Lotta Love	Nicolette Larson	Warner	10		F L
8	9	Every 1's A Winner	Hot Chocolate	Infinity	7	(12)	G L
9	-	Somewhere In The Night	Barry Manilow	Arista	6	(42)	
10	-	I Was Made For Dancin'	Leif Garrett	Scotti Bros	7	(4)	L
11	11	September	Earth, Wind & Fire	Arc	9	(3)	G
12	-	Got To Be Real	Cheryl Lynn	Columbia	7		F G L
13	2	Too Much Heaven	Bee Gees	RSO	11	(3)	P
14	-	Shake It	Ian Matthews	Mushroom	6		F L
15	-	Heaven Knows	Donna Summer	Casablanca	10	(34)	G
16	-	Soul Man	Blues Brothers	Atlantic	5		F
17	-	Tragedy	Bee Gees	RSO	11	(1)	P
18	19	New York Groove	Ace Frehley	Casablanca	6		F L
19	-	No Tell Lover	Chicago	Columbia	5		
20	3	My Life	Billy Joel	Columbia	12	(12)	G

March 1979

This Mnth	Prev Mnth	Title	Artist	Label	Wks 20	(UK Pos)	
1	6	I Will Survive	Gloria Gaynor	Polydor	15	(1)	G L
2	17	Tragedy	Bee Gees	RSO	11	(1)	P
3	1	Da Ya Think I'm Sexy	Rod Stewart	Warner	13	(1)	G
4	15	Heaven Knows	Donna Summer	Casablanca	10	(34)	G
5	-	What A Fool Believes	Doobie Brothers	Warner	10	(31)	G
6	-	Shake Your Groove Thing	Peaches & Herb	Polydor	8	(26)	G
7	5	Fire	Pointer Sisters	Planet	13	(34)	G
8	-	Sultans Of Swing	Dire Straits	Warner	9	(8)	F
9	3	A Little More Love	Olivia Newton-John	MCA	15	(4)	G
10	-	What You Won't Do For Love	Bobby Caldwell	Clouds	6		F L
11	-	Don't Cry Out Loud	Melissa Manchester	Arista	7		
12	2	Y.M.C.A.	Village People	Casablanca	17	(1)	F P
13	4	Le Freak	Chic	Atlantic	17	(7)	P
14	-	Lady	Little River Band	Harvest	7		
15	-	Knock On Wood	Amii Stewart	Ariola	10	(6)	F G L
16	-	Every Time I Think Of You	Babys	Chrysalis	4		L
17	7	Lotta Love	Nicolette Larson	Warner	10		F L
18	-	Big Shot	Billy Joel	Columbia	3		
19	12	Got To Be Real	Cheryl Lynn	Columbia	7		F G L
20	-	I Just Fall In Love Again	Anne Murray	Capitol	7	(58)	

US 1979 JAN–MAR

◆ A UNICEF benefit concert in New York starred The Bee Gees, Olivia Newton-John, Abba, Linda Ronstadt, Rod Stewart, Donna Summer, John Denver and Earth Wind & Fire.

◆ Sid Vicious died of a heroin overdose before his murder trial. Soul star Donny Hathaway leapt to his death, and 1966 No. 1 chart–topper SSgt. Barry Sadler was arrested for killing a songwriter.

◆ Almost 20 years after his three successive US Top 20 hits, New Yorker Paul Evans debuted in the UK Top 20 with 'Hello This Is Joanie (The Telephone Answering Machine Song)', a genuine message song that sold few copies in the USA.

◆ Stephen Stills became the first rock artist to record digitally. Digital recording was the biggest advance since stereo. Instead of recording on tape, sounds are sampled 40-50,000 times a second, and the information stored in binary numbers.

211

UK 1979
APR-JUNE

◆ The film *Quadrophenia*, based on The Who album, and featuring Sting and Toyah, premiered in London, on the night of The Who's first gig with new drummer Kenny Jones (Keith Moon having died in September 1978). Soon afterwards, The Who's movie *The Kids Are Alright* premiered in New York.

◆ As the Sex Pistols clicked with Eddie Cochran's 'Something Else', German-based Eruption charted with a revival of another lesser known late 1950s song, Neil Sedaka's 'One Way Ticket'.

◆ Art Garfunkel's 'Bright Eyes', from the animated film *Watership Down*, topped the UK chart, selling over a million copies. Surprisingly it failed to chart in his homeland.

◆ For the first time in 16 years The Shadows had two successive Top 10 hits, 'Don't Cry For Me Argentina' and 'Theme From The Deer Hunter'.

April 1979

This Mnth	Prev Mnth	Title	Artist	Label	Wks 20	(US Pos)	
1	-	Bright Eyes	Art Garfunkel	CBS	11		G L
2	-	Cool For Cats	Squeeze	A&M	7		
3	-	Some Girls	Racey	RAK	7		
4	17	In The Navy	Village People	Mercury	6	(3)	
5	1	I Will Survive	Gloria Gaynor	Polydor	9	(1)	
6	-	Shake Your Body (Down To The Ground)	Jacksons	Epic	6	(7)	
7	-	Sultans Of Swing	Dire Straits	Vertigo	5	(4)	F
8	-	He's The Greatest Dancer	Sister Sledge	Atlantic/Cotillion	5	(9)	
9	-	Silly Thing/Who Killed Bambi	Sex Pistols	Virgin	4		
10	-	The Runner	Three Degrees	Ariola	4		
11	7	I Want Your Love	Chic	Atlantic	7	(7)	
12	-	Hallelujah	Milk & Honey	Polydor	4		F L
13	6	Something Else/Friggin' In The Riggin'	Sex Pistols	Virgin	7		
14	-	Pop Muzik	M	MCA	9	(1)	F
15	-	Wow	Kate Bush	EMI	4		
16	-	Turn The Music Up	Players Association	Vanguard	4		F L
17	-	I Don't Wanna Lose You	Kandidate	RAK	5		F L
18	4	Lucky Number	Lene Lovich	Stiff	7		F
19	2	Oliver's Army	Elvis Costello	Radar	9		
20	-	The Logical Song	Supertramp	A&M	5	(6)	

May 1979

This Mnth	Prev Mnth	Title	Artist	Label	Wks 20	(US Pos)	
1	1	Bright Eyes	Art Garfunkel	CBS	11		G L
2	14	Pop Muzik	M	MCA	9	(1)	F
3	-	Hooray Hooray It's A Holi-Holiday	Boney M	Atlantic/Hansa	6		
4	-	Does Your Mother Know	Abba	Epic	6	(19)	
5	-	Knock On Wood	Amii Stewart	Atlantic/Hansa	6	(1)	F
6	-	Reunited	Peaches & Herb	CBS	7	(1)	F L
7	3	Some Girls	Racey	RAK	7		
8	-	Goodnight Tonight	Wings	Parlophone	5	(5)	
9	20	The Logical Song	Supertramp	A&M	5	(6)	
10	-	Dance Away	Roxy Music	Polydor	10	(44)	
11	-	One Way Ticket	Eruption	Atlantic/Hansa	6		L
12	-	Sunday Girl	Blondie	Chrysalis	8		
13	-	Banana Splits (Tra La La Song)	Dickies	A&M	3		F L
14	6	Shake Your Body (Down To The...)	Jacksons	Epic	6	(7)	
15	-	Parisienne Walkways	Gary Moore	MCA	5		F
16	12	Hallelujah	Milk & Honey	Polydor	4		F L
17	-	Love You Inside Out	Bee Gees	RSO	3	(1)	
18	-	Boys Keep Swingin'	David Bowie	RCA	6		
19	-	Roxanne	Police	A&M	5	(32)	F
20	2	Cool For Cats	Squeeze	A&M	7		

June 1979

This Mnth	Prev Mnth	Title	Artist	Label	Wks 20	(US Pos)	
1	10	Dance Away	Roxy Music	Polydor	10	(44)	
2	12	Sunday Girl	Blondie	Chrysalis	8		
3	-	Boogie Wonderland	Earth, Wind & Fire With The Emotions	CBS	7	(6)	
4	-	Ring My Bell	Anita Ward	TK	7	(1)	F L
5	-	Ain't No Stoppin' Us Now	McFadden & Whitehead	Philly Int.	6	(13)	F L
6	-	Theme From The Deer Hunter (Cavatina)	Shadows	EMI	6		
7	-	Are 'Friends' Electric	Tubeway Army	Beggars Banquet	10		F L
8	-	Shine A Little Love	Electric Light Orchestra	Jet	6	(8)	
9	6	Reunited	Peaches & Herb	CBS	7	(1)	F L
10	-	Up The Junction	Squeeze	A&M	6		
11	-	We Are Family	Sister Sledge	Atlantic	4	(2)	
12	2	Pop Muzik	M	MCA	9	(1)	F
13	-	The Lone Ranger	Quantum Jump	Electric	5		F L
14	-	Hot Stuff	Donna Summer	Casablanca	4	(1)	
15	18	Boys Keep Swingin'	David Bowie	RCA	6		
16	-	H.A.P.P.Y. Radio	Edwin Starr	RCA	5	(79)	L
17	4	Does Your Mother Know	Abba	Epic	6	(19)	
18	-	Masquerade	Skids	Virgin	4		
19	15	Parisienne Walkways	Gary Moore	MCA	5		F
20	-	Night Owl	Gerry Rafferty	UA	5		L

April 1979

This Mnth	Prev Mnth	Title	Artist	Label	Wks 20	(UK Pos)	
1	1	I Will Survive	Gloria Gaynor	Polydor	15	(1)	G L
2	15	Knock On Wood	Amii Stewart	Ariola	10	(6)	F G L
3	5	What A Fool Believes	Doobie Brothers	Warner	10	(31)	G
4	-	Music Box Dancer	Frank Mills	Polydor	8		F G L
5	-	Heart Of Glass	Blondie	Chrysalis	10	(1)	F G
6	-	Reunited	Peaches & Herb	Polydor	13	(4)	P
7	2	Tragedy	Bee Gees	RSO	11	(1)	P
8	8	Sultans Of Swing	Dire Straits	Warner	9	(8)	F
9	-	Stumblin' In	Suzi Quatro & Chris Norman	RSO	10	(41)	F G L
10	-	I Want Your Love	Chic	Atlantic	8	(4)	G
11	-	Goodnight Tonight	Wings	Columbia	11	(5)	G
12	-	In The Navy	Village People	Casablanca	9	(2)	G L
13	14	Lady	Little River Band	Harvest	7		
14	-	He's The Greatest Dancer	Sister Sledge	Cotillion	8	(6)	F
15	-	Take Me Home	Cher	Casablanca	7		G
16	20	I Just Fall In Love Again	Anne Murray	Capitol	7	(58)	
17	6	Shake Your Groove Thing	Peaches & Herb	Polydor	8	(26)	G
18	3	Da Ya Think I'm Sexy	Rod Stewart	Warner	13	(1)	G
19	-	Livin' It Up (Friday Night)	Bell & James	A&M	3	(59)	F G L
20	-	Shake Your Body (Down To The Ground)	Jacksons	Epic	11	(4)	G

May 1979

This Mnth	Prev Mnth	Title	Artist	Label	Wks 20	(UK Pos)	
1	6	Reunited	Peaches & Herb	Polydor	13	(4)	P
2	12	In The Navy	Village People	Casablanca	9	(2)	G L
3	9	Stumblin' In	Suzi Quatro & Chris Norman	RSO	10	(41)	F G L
4	11	Goodnight Tonight	Wings	Columbia	11	(5)	G
5	-	Hot Stuff	Donna Summer	Casablanca	16	(11)	G
6	5	Heart Of Glass	Blondie	Chrysalis	10	(1)	F G
7	20	Shake Your Body (Down To The Ground)	Jacksons	Epic	11	(4)	G
8	-	Love You Inside Out	Bee Gees	RSO	10	(13)	G
9	2	Knock On Wood	Amii Stewart	Ariola	10	(6)	F G L
10	14	He's The Greatest Dancer	Sister Sledge	Cotillion	8	(6)	F
11	15	Take Me Home	Cher	Casablanca	7		G
12	-	Love Is The Answer	England Dan/John Ford Coley	Big Tree	7		L
13	10	I Want Your Love	Chic	Atlantic	8	(4)	G
14	-	Love Takes Time	Orleans	Infinity	5		L
15	4	Music Box Dancer	Frank Mills	Polydor	8		F G L
16	-	We Are Family	Sister Sledge	Cotillion	9	(8)	G L
17	-	Just When I Needed You Most	Randy Vanwarmer	Bearsville	9	(8)	F G L
18	-	The Logical Song	Supertramp	A&M	10	(7)	
19	-	Disco Nights (Rock Freak)	G.Q.	Arista	6	(42)	F G
20	3	What A Fool Believes	Doobie Brothers	Warner	10	(31)	G

June 1979

This Mnth	Prev Mnth	Title	Artist	Label	Wks 20	(UK Pos)	
1	5	Hot Stuff	Donna Summer	Casablanca	16	(11)	G
2	16	We Are Family	Sister Sledge	Cotillion	9	(8)	G L
3	17	Just When I Needed You Most	Randy Vanwarmer	Bearsville	9	(8)	F G L
4	8	Love You Inside Out	Bee Gees	RSO	10	(13)	G
5	-	Ring My Bell	Anita Ward	Juana	13	(1)	F G L
6	18	The Logical Song	Supertramp	A&M	10	(7)	
7	-	Chuck E.'s In Love	Rickie Lee Jones	Warner	9	(18)	F L
8	1	Reunited	Peaches & Herb	Polydor	13	(4)	P
9	-	She Believes In Me	Kenny Rogers	UA	9	(42)	G
10	-	Bad Girls	Donna Summer	Casablanca	12	(14)	G
11	-	You Take My Breath Away	Rex Smith	Columbia	7		F G L
12	-	Boogie Wonderland	Earth, Wind & Fire With The Emotions	Arc	9	(4)	
13	7	Shake Your Body (Down To The Ground)	Jacksons	Epic	11	(4)	G
14	4	Goodnight Tonight	Wings	Columbia	11	(5)	G
15	-	Rock 'n' Roll Fantasy	Bad Company	Swan Song	6		
16	19	Disco Nights (Rock Freak)	G.Q.	Arista	6	(42)	F G
17	-	Minute By Minute	Doobie Brothers	Warner	5	(47)	
18	-	Deeper Than The Night	Olivia Newton-John	MCA	4	(64)	
19	-	Makin' It	David Naughton	RSO	11		F G L
20	2	In The Navy	Village People	Casablanca	9	(2)	G L

▲ African-Americans with top transatlantic hits included Earth Wind & Fire (above), with The Emotions, Peaches & Herb, Anita Ward, McFadden & Whitehead, Donna Summer, Amii Stewart and The Jacksons.

◆ Donna Summer was not the only American who had to re-locate to Europe to find success at home. Amii Stewart, Suzi Quatro and Blondie all achieved US fame after they based themselves in the UK.

◆ Lowell George, the well-respected leader of recently disbanded rock group Little Feat, died of drug-related causes.

UK 1979 JULY-SEPT

July 1979

This Mnth	Prev Mnth	Title	Artist	Label	Wks 20	(US Pos)	
1	7	Are 'Friends' Electric	Tubeway Army	Beggars Banquet	10		F L
2	-	Silly Games	Janet Kay	Scope	6		F L
3	-	C'mon Everybody	Sex Pistols	Virgin	5		L
4	-	Light My Fire/137 Disco Heaven (Medley)	Amii Stewart	Atlantic	5	(69)	
5	10	Up The Junction	Squeeze	A&M	6		
6	20	Night Owl	Gerry Rafferty	UA	5		L
7	-	Lady Lynda	Beach Boys	Caribou	4		
8	-	Good Times	Chic	Atlantic	5	(1)	
9	-	Wanted	Dooleys	GTO	7		
10	-	Girls Talk	Dave Edmunds	Swansong	5	(65)	
11	4	Ring My Bell	Anita Ward	TK	7	(1)	F L
12	-	Babylon's Burning	Ruts	Virgin	4		F L
13	-	I Don't Like Mondays	Boomtown Rats	Ensign	9	(73)	
14	13	The Lone Ranger	Quantum Jump	Electric	5		F L
15	1	Dance Away	Roxy Music	Polydor	10	(44)	
16	-	Living On The Front Line	Eddy Grant	Ensign	4		F
17	-	Breakfast In America	Supertramp	A&M	4	(62)	L
18	-	Maybe	Thom Pace	RSO	4		F L
19	-	Born To Be Alive	Patrick Hernandez	Gem	5	(16)	F L
20	-	My Sharona	Knack	Capitol	3	(1)	F L

August 1979

This Mnth	Prev Mnth	Title	Artist	Label	Wks 20	(US Pos)	
1	13	I Don't Like Mondays	Boomtown Rats	Ensign	9	(73)	
2	-	We Don't Talk Anymore	Cliff Richard	EMI	10	(7)	
3	-	Angel Eyes/Voulez Vous	Abba	Epic	6	(64)	
4	-	Can't Stand Losing You	Police	A&M	6		
5	9	Wanted	Dooleys	GTO	7		
6	-	Reasons To Be Cheerful (Pt 3)	Ian Dury & The Blockheads	Stiff	5		L
7	-	Hersham Boys	Sham 69	Polydor	4		L
8	-	After The Love Has Gone	Earth, Wind & Fire	CBS	6	(2)	
9	-	The Diary Of Horace Wimp	Electric Light Orchestra	Jet	5		
10	-	Beat The Clock	Sparks	Virgin	4		L
11	10	Girls Talk	Dave Edmunds	Swansong	5	(65)	
12	-	Duke Of Earl	Darts	Magnet	6		
13	-	Bang Bang	B.A. Robertson	Asylum	7		F
14	19	Born To Be Alive	Patrick Hernandez	Gem	5	(16)	F L
15	20	My Sharona	Knack	Capitol	3	(1)	F L
16	-	Gangsters	Specials	2 Tone	6		F
17	17	Breakfast In America	Supertramp	A&M	4	(62)	L
18	-	Angel Eyes	Roxy Music	Polydor	7		
19	2	Silly Games	Janet Kay	Scope	6		F L
20	1	Are 'Friends' Electric	Tubeway Army	Beggars Banquet	10		F L

September 1979

This Mnth	Prev Mnth	Title	Artist	Label	Wks 20	(US Pos)	
1	2	We Don't Talk Anymore	Cliff Richard	EMI	10	(7)	
2	-	Cars	Gary Numan	Beggars Banquet	8	(9)	F
3	13	Bang Bang	B.A. Robertson	Asylum	7		F
4	-	Street Life	Crusaders	MCA	6	(36)	F L
5	-	Don't Bring Me Down	Electric Light Orchestra	Jet	6	(4)	
6	18	Angel Eyes	Roxy Music	Polydor	7		
7	-	If I Said You Had A Beautiful Body, Would You Hold It Against Me	Bellamy Brothers	Warner	7	(39)	L
8	-	Just When I Needed You Most	Randy Vanwarmer	Bearsville	5	(4)	F L
9	-	Love's Gotta Hold On Me	Dollar	Carrere	6		
10	-	Money	Flying Lizards	Virgin	5	(50)	F L
11	16	Gangsters	Specials	2 Tone	6		F
12	1	I Don't Like Mondays	Boomtown Rats	Ensign	9	(73)	
13	-	Message In A Bottle	Police	A&M	7	(74)	
14	8	After The Love Has Gone	Earth, Wind & Fire	CBS	6	(2)	
15	-	Gotta Go Home/El Lute	Boney M	Atlantic/Hansa	4		L
16	-	Ooh! What A Life	Gibson Brothers	Island	5		F
17	-	Strut Your Funky Stuff	Frantique	Philly Int.	4		F L
18	-	Sail On	Commodores	Motown	4	(4)	
19	12	Duke Of Earl	Darts	Magnet	6		
20	-	Reggae For It Now	Bill Lovelady	Charisma	4		F L

▲ West Indian sounds continued to gain popularity thanks in part to ska-based 2-Tone music, whose foremost purveyors, The Specials and Madness (above), debuted on the British chart.

◆ *Rolling Stone* called videotapes "The newest selling tool in rock", citing David Bowie's 'Boys Keep Swinging' and Queen's 'Bohemian Rhapsody' as good examples.

◆ Disco performer Patrick Hernandez had his sole transatlantic Top 20 entry with his composition 'Born To Be Alive'. Among the Frenchman's backing vocalists in the early 1980s was a certain Madonna Ciccone.

July 1979

This Mnth	Prev Mnth	Title	Artist	Label	Wks 20	(UK Pos)	
1	10	Bad Girls	Donna Summer	Casablanca	12	(14)	G
2	5	Ring My Bell	Anita Ward	Juana	13	(1)	F G L
3	1	Hot Stuff	Donna Summer	Casablanca	16	(11)	G
4	19	Makin' It	David Naughton	RSO	11		F G L
5	12	Boogie Wonderland	Earth, Wind & Fire With The Emotions	Arc	9	(4)	
6	-	I Want You To Want Me	Cheap Trick	Epic	9	(29)	F G
7	-	Gold	John Stewart	RSO	9	(43)	F L
8	9	She Believes In Me	Kenny Rogers	UA	9	(42)	G
9	-	Shine A Little Love	Electric Light Orchestra	Jet	9	(6)	
10	-	Good Times	Chic	Atlantic	11	(5)	G L
11	7	Chuck E.'s In Love	Rickie Lee Jones	Warner	9	(18)	F L
12	-	When You're In Love With A Beautiful Woman	Dr. Hook	Capitol	10	(1)	G
13	6	The Logical Song	Supertramp	A&M	10	(7)	
14	-	Ain't No Stoppin' Us Now	McFadden & Whitehead	Philly Int.	7	(5)	F P L
15	2	We Are Family	Sister Sledge	Cotillion	9	(8)	G L
16	-	I Can't Stand It No More	Peter Frampton	A&M	4		L
17	-	You Can't Change That	Raydio	Arista	7		
18	-	The Main Event/Fight	Barbra Streisand	Columbia	9		G
19	-	Dance The Night Away	Van Halen	Warner	4		F
20	4	Love You Inside Out	Bee Gees	RSO	10	(13)	G

August 1979

This Mnth	Prev Mnth	Title	Artist	Label	Wks 20	(UK Pos)	
1	10	Good Times	Chic	Atlantic	11	(5)	G L
2	1	Bad Girls	Donna Summer	Casablanca	12	(14)	G
3	-	My Sharona	Knack	Capitol	14	(6)	F G
4	18	The Main Event/Fight	Barbra Streisand	Columbia	9		G
5	2	Ring My Bell	Anita Ward	Juana	13	(1)	F G L
6	12	When You're In Love With A Beautiful Woman	Dr. Hook	Capitol	10	(1)	G
7	-	Mama Can't Buy You Love	Elton John	MCA	8		G
8	17	You Can't Change That	Raydio	Arista	7		
9	-	After The Love Has Gone	Earth, Wind & Fire	Arc	10	(4)	G
10	7	Gold	John Stewart	RSO	9	(43)	F L
11	4	Makin' It	David Naughton	RSO	11		F G L
12	-	Sad Eyes	Robert John	EMI America	13	(31)	G L
13	-	I Was Made For Lovin' You	Kiss	Casablanca	6	(50)	G
14	-	Lead Me On	Maxine Nightingale	Windsong	9		G L
15	-	The Devil Went Down To Georgia	Charlie Daniels Band	Epic	8	(14)	G
16	3	Hot Stuff	Donna Summer	Casablanca	16	(11)	G
17	-	Don't Bring Me Down	Electric Light Orchestra	Jet	10	(3)	G
18	6	I Want You To Want Me	Cheap Trick	Epic	9	(29)	F G
19	-	I'll Never Love This Way Again	Dionne Warwick	Arista	14		G
20	14	Ain't No Stoppin' Us Now	McFadden & Whitehead	Philly Int.	7	(5)	F P L

September 1979

This Mnth	Prev Mnth	Title	Artist	Label	Wks 20	(UK Pos)	
1	3	My Sharona	Knack	Capitol	14	(6)	F G
2	9	After The Love Has Gone	Earth, Wind & Fire	Arc	10	(4)	G
3	15	The Devil Went Down To Georgia	Charlie Daniels Band	Epic	8	(14)	G
4	12	Sad Eyes	Robert John	EMI America	13	(31)	G L
5	17	Don't Bring Me Down	Electric Light Orchestra	Jet	10	(3)	G
6	14	Lead Me On	Maxine Nightingale	Windsong	9		G L
7	-	Lonesome Loser	Little River Band	Capitol	9		
8	19	I'll Never Love This Way Again	Dionne Warwick	Arista	14		G
9	1	Good Times	Chic	Atlantic	11	(5)	G L
10	-	Sail On	Commodores	Motown	10	(8)	
11	-	Rise	Herb Alpert	A&M	13	(13)	G
12	7	Mama Can't Buy You Love	Elton John	MCA	8		G
13	-	Don't Stop Till You Get Enough	Michael Jackson	Epic	9	(3)	G
14	4	The Main Event/Fight	Barbra Streisand	Columbia	9		G
15	-	Heaven Must Have Sent You	Bonnie Pointer	Motown	8		F L
16	-	Let's Go	Cars	Elektra	4	(51)	F
17	-	Bad Case Of Loving You (Doctor, Doctor)	Robert Palmer	Island	5	(61)	
18	-	Cruel To Be Kind	Nick Lowe	Columbia	4	(12)	F L
19	-	Goodbye Stranger	Supertramp	A&M	5	(57)	
20	-	Pop Muzik	M	Sire	13	(2)	F G L

US 1979

JULY–SEPT

◆ Michael Jackson had his first Top 20 solo single for over seven years with 'Don't Stop Till You Get Enough' and Herb Alpert came back after an 11 year absence, with 'Rise'.

◆ Recent hit makers Van McCoy ('The Hustle') and Minnie Ripperton ('Loving You') died, as did Norrie Paramor, arguably Britain's most successful record producer.

◆ The *No Nukes* shows at Madison Square Garden featured such headliners as Bruce Springsteen, James Taylor, The Doobie Brothers and Crosby, Stills & Nash. Other successful live shows included The Cars in Central Park, The Who (plus AC/DC and The Stranglers) at Wembley, and Led Zeppelin's first UK date for four years at Knebworth. Zeppelin, incidentally, scored their eighth and last successive UK No. 1 LP with **In Through The Out Door.**

UK
1979
OCT-DEC

◆ Almost overnight The Police became teen idols. They had two consecutive chart toppers, 'Message in A Bottle' and 'Walking on The Moon', and the first of five successive No. 1 LPs, **Regatta De Blanc**.

▲ Among the year's top record deals were Paul McCartney signing to Columbia for $20 million, and Paul Simon's (above) seven album deal with Warner, which was reportedly worth $14 million.

◆ As the 1970s ended Annie Lennox first charted with The Tourists, 16-year-olds George Michael and Andrew Ridgeley formed a group, and we were warned by The Buggles that 'Video Killed The Radio Star'.

October 1979

This Mnth	Prev Mnth	Title	Artist	Label	Wks 20	(US Pos)	
1	-	Video Killed The Radio Star	Buggles	Island	6	(40)	F
2	13	Message In A Bottle	Police	A&M	7	(74)	
3	-	Don't Stop Till You Get Enough	Michael Jackson	Epic	7	(1)	
4	-	Dreaming	Blondie	Cnrysalis	6	(27)	
5	-	Whatever You Want	Status Quo	Vertigo	6		
6	-	Since You've Been Gone	Rainbow	Polydor	6	(57)	F
7	-	One Day At A Time	Lena Martell	Pye	8		F L
8	-	Every Day Hurts	Sad Café	RCA	6		F
9	2	Cars	Gary Numan	Beggars Banquet	8	(9)	F
10	7	If I Said You Had A Beautiful Body...	Bellamy Brothers	Warner	7	(39)	L
11	-	When You're In Love With A Beautiful Woman	Dr. Hook	Capitol	9	(6)	
12	-	The Chosen Few	Dooleys	GTO	5		L
13	-	Kate Bush On Stage E.P.	Kate Bush	EMI	3		
14	9	Love's Gotta Hold On Me	Dollar	Carrere	6		
15	-	Queen Of Hearts	Dave Edmunds	Swansong	5		L
16	-	O.K. Fred	Erroll Dunkley	Scope	5		F L
17	-	Cruel To Be Kind	Nick Lowe	Radar	5	(12)	L
18	18	Sail On	Commodores	Motown	4	(4)	
19	-	Gimme Gimme Gimme (A Man After Midnight)	Abba	Epic	6		
20	-	Tusk	Fleetwood Mac	Warner	5	(8)	

November 1979

This Mnth	Prev Mnth	Title	Artist	Label	Wks 20	(US Pos)	
1	11	When You're In Love With A...	Dr. Hook	Capitol	9	(6)	
2	7	One Day At A Time	Lena Martell	Pye	8		F L
3	-	Crazy Little Thing Called Love	Queen	EMI	7	(1)	
4	19	Gimme Gimme Gimme (A Man...)	Abba	Epic	6		
5	-	The Eton Rifles	Jam	Polydor	5		
6	8	Every Day Hurts	Sad Café	RCA	6		F
7	-	Still	Commodores	Motown	6	(1)	
8	20	Tusk	Fleetwood Mac	Warner	5	(8)	
9	-	Gonna Get Along Without You Now	Viola Wills	Ariola/Hansa	5		F L
10	-	On My Radio	Selecter	2 Tone	3		F
11	-	She's In Love With You	Suzi Quatro	RAK	4	(41)	L
12	1	Video Killed The Radio Star	Buggles	Island	6	(40)	F
13	-	The Sparrow	Ramblers	Decca	5		F L
14	-	No More Tears (Enough Is Enough)	Barbra Streisand & Donna Summer	Casablanca/CBS	8	(1)	
15	-	A Message To You Rudy/Nite Klub	Specials	2 Tone	4		
16	12	The Chosen Few	Dooleys	GTO	5		L
17	3	Don't Stop Till You Get Enough	Michael Jackson	Epic	7	(1)	
18	16	O.K. Fred	Erroll Dunkley	Scope	5		F L
19	-	Knocked It Off	B.A. Robertson	Asylum	4		
20	-	Ladies Night	Kool & The Gang	Mercury	4	(8)	F

December 1979

This Mnth	Prev Mnth	Title	Artist	Label	Wks 20	(US Pos)	
1	-	Walking On The Moon	Police	A&M	7		
2	-	Another Brick In The Wall (Pt. 2)	Pink Floyd	Harvest	8	(1)	G L
3	14	No More Tears (Enough Is Enough)	Barbra Streisand & D. Summer	Casablanca/CBS	8	(1)	
4	-	Que Sera Mi Vida (If You Should Go)	Gibson Brothers	Island	8		
5	-	I Only Want To Be With You	Tourists	Logo	7	(83)	F
6	-	Rapper's Delight	Sugarhill Gang	Sugarhill	7	(36)	F L
7	1	When You're In Love With A...	Dr. Hook	Capitol	9	(6)	
8	-	Confusion/Last Train To London	Electric Light Orchestra	Jet	6	(37)	
9	3	Crazy Little Thing Called Love	Queen	EMI	7	(1)	
10	-	One Step Beyond	Madness	Stiff	6		
11	-	I Have A Dream	Abba	Epic	6		
12	-	My Simple Heart	Three Degrees	Ariola	6		L
13	-	Day Trip To Bangor (Didn't We Have A Lovely Time)	Fiddler's Dram	Dingles	5		F L
14	-	Complex	Gary Numan	Beggars Banquet	4		
15	-	Off The Wall	Michael Jackson	Epic	4	(10)	
16	7	Still	Commodores	Motown	6	(1)	
17	-	Wonderful Christmastime	Paul McCartney	Parlophone	5		
18	-	Union City Blue	Blondie	Chrysalis	5		
19	-	Brass In Pocket	Pretenders	Real	9	(14)	F
20	5	The Eton Rifles	Jam	Polydor	5		

This Mnth	Prev Mnth	Title	Artist	Label	Wks 20	(UK Pos)	
1	11	Rise	Herb Alpert	A&M	13	(13)	G G
2	13	Don't Stop Till You Get Enough	Michael Jackson	Epic	9	(3)	G
3	10	Sail On	Commodores	Motown	10	(8)	
4	20	Pop Muzik	M	Sire	13	(2)	F G L
5	4	Sad Eyes	Robert John	EMI America	13	(31)	G L
6	8	I'll Never Love This Way Again	Dionne Warwick	Arista	14		G
7	-	Dim All The Lights	Donna Summer	Casablanca	11	(29)	G
8	1	My Sharona	Knack	Capitol	14	(6)	F G
9	7	Lonesome Loser	Little River Band	Capitol	9		
10	-	Heartache Tonight	Eagles	Asylum	12	(40)	G
11	15	Heaven Must Have Sent You	Bonnie Pointer	Motown	8		F L
12	-	You Decorated My Life	Kenny Rogers	UA	8		
13	-	Still	Commodores	Motown	13	(4)	G
14	2	After The Love Has Gone	Earth, Wind & Fire	Arc	10	(4)	G
15	-	Dirty White Boy	Foreigner	Atlantic	5		
16	-	Tusk	Fleetwood Mac	Warner	7	(6)	
17	5	Don't Bring Me Down	Electric Light Orchestra	Jet	10	(3)	G
18	18	Cruel To Be Kind	Nick Lowe	Columbia	4	(12)	F L
19	-	Please Don't Go	KC & The Sunshine Band	TK	15	(3)	
20	-	Born To Be Alive	Patrick Hernandez	Columbia	5	(10)	F G L

This Mnth	Prev Mnth	Title	Artist	Label	Wks 20	(UK Pos)	
1	7	Dim All The Lights	Donna Summer	Casablanca	11	(29)	G
2	13	Still	Commodores	Motown	13	(4)	G
3	10	Heartache Tonight	Eagles	Asylum	12	(40)	G
4	-	Babe	Styx	A&M	12	(6)	G
5	-	No More Tears (Enough Is Enough)	Barbra Streisand & Donna Summer	Casablanca/CBS	9	(3)	G
6	4	Pop Muzik	M	Sire	13	(2)	F G L
7	1	Rise	Herb Alpert	A&M	13	(13)	G
8	12	You Decorated My Life	Kenny Rogers	UA	8		
9	16	Tusk	Fleetwood Mac	Warner	7	(6)	
10	19	Please Don't Go	KC & The Sunshine Band	TK	15	(3)	
11	-	Ships	Barry Manilow	Arista	8		
12	2	Don't Stop Till You Get Enough	Michael Jackson	Epic	9	(3)	G
13	-	Good Girls Don't	Knack	Capitol	5	(66)	L
14	-	Send One Your Love	Stevie Wonder	Tamla	12	(52)	
15	15	Dirty White Boy	Foreigner	Atlantic	5		
16	6	I'll Never Love This Way Again	Dionne Warwick	Arista	14		G
17	-	Broken Hearted Me	Anne Murray	Capitol	5		
18	-	Come To Me	France Joli	Prelude	4		F L
19	-	You're Only Lonely	J.D. Souther	Columbia	8		F
20	-	Take The Long Way Home	Supertramp	A&M	7		

This Mnth	Prev Mnth	Title	Artist	Label	Wks 20	(UK Pos)	
1	4	Babe	Styx	A&M	12	(6)	G
2	10	Please Don't Go	KC & The Sunshine Band	TK	15	(3)	
3	-	Escape (The Pina Colada Song)	Rupert Holmes	Infinity	12	(23)	F G
4	2	Still	Commodores	Motown	13	(4)	G
5	5	No More Tears (Enough Is Enough)	Barbra Streisand & Donna Summer	Casablanca/CBS	9	(3)	G
6	14	Send One Your Love	Stevie Wonder	Tamla	12	(52)	
7	19	You're Only Lonely	J.D. Souther	Columbia	8		F
8	-	Do That To Me One More Time	Captain & Tennille	Casablanca	17	(7)	G L
9	20	Take The Long Way Home	Supertramp	A&M	7		
10	-	Ladies Night	Kool & The Gang	De-Lite	10	(9)	G
11	3	Heartache Tonight	Eagles	Asylum	12	(40)	G
12	-	Cool Change	Little River Band	Capitol	9		
13	-	Rock With You	Michael Jackson	Epic	13	(7)	G
14	11	Ships	Barry Manilow	Arista	8		
15	-	We Don't Talk Anymore	Cliff Richard	EMI America	10	(1)	
16	-	Head Games	Foreigner	Atlantic	6		
17	6	Pop Muzik	M	Sire	13	(2)	F G L
18	17	Broken Hearted Me	Anne Murray	Capitol	5		
19	1	Dim All The Lights	Donna Summer	Casablanca	11	(29)	G
20	-	Better Love Next Time	Dr. Hook	Capitol	8	(8)	

US 1979 OCT-DEC

◆ In 1979, the value of record sales in the USA dropped 11% to $3.7 billion (albums accounting for 90% of the total), and platinum and gold record awards plummeted by almost 50%. The decrease in disco sales and increase in home taping were thought to be the main causes.

◆ A survey showed that 50% of the highest rated American radio stations were broadcasting on FM.

◆ Eleven fans were crushed to death in the rush for good seats at a Who concert in Cincinatti.

◆ Merging with rock and new wave kept disco music alive for a little longer, but a "disco sucks" campaign was beginning to gain momentum.

◆ Rap, which previously was a New York-only craze, had its first hit, 'Rapper's Delight' by The Sugarhill Gang.

UK 1980 JAN-MAR

◆ In the week that he was awarded an OBE by the Queen, Cliff Richard had the second US Top 10 entry of his long career with 'We Don't Talk Anymore'.

◆ Among the past hit makers who died as the decade dawned were Mantovani (the most successful British act in the US before The Beatles), R&B legends Amos Milburn and Professor Longhair, early rocker Larry Williams and million selling 1950s British balladeer David Whitfield.

▲ The first indie LP chart in the UK showed **Dirk Wears White Sox** by Adam & The Ants at No. 1.

January 1980

This Mnth	Prev Mnth	Title	Artist	Label	Wks 20	(US Pos)	
1	19	Brass In Pocket	Pretenders	Real	9	(14)	F
2	2	Another Brick In The Wall (Pt. 2)	Pink Floyd	Harvest	8	(1)	G L
3	11	I Have A Dream	Abba	Epic	6		
4	-	Please Don't Go	KC & The Sunshine Band	TK	6	(1)	
5	-	With You I'm Born Again	Billy Preston & Syreeta	Motown	5	(4)	L
6	13	Day Trip To Bangor (Didn't We Have A Lovely Time)	Fiddler's Dram	Dingles	5		F L
7	5	I Only Want To Be With You	Tourists	Logo	7	(83)	F
8	-	My Girl	Madness	Stiff	6		
9	-	Tears Of A Clown/Ranking Full Stop	Beat	2 Tone	7		F
10	-	I'm In The Mood For Dancing	Nolans	Epic	8		F
11	6	Rapper's Delight	Sugarhill Gang	Sugarhill	7	(36)	F L
12	12	My Simple Heart	Three Degrees	Ariola	6		L
13	1	Walking On The Moon	Police	A&M	7		
14	-	Is It Love You're After	Rose Royce	Whitfield	6		
15	-	Green Onions	Booker T. & The M.G.'s	Atlantic	4		L
16	-	London Calling	Clash	CBS	3		
17	-	John I'm Only Danncing (Again)	David Bowie	RCA	5		
18	-	Better Love Next Time	Dr. Hook	Capitol	4	(12)	
19	-	Babe	Styx	A&M	6	(1)	F L
20	17	Wonderful Christmastime	Paul McCartney	Parlophone	5		

February 1980

This Mnth	Prev Mnth	Title	Artist	Label	Wks 20	(US Pos)	
1	-	Too Much Too Young E.P. (Special AKA Live!)	Specials	2 Tone	6		
2	-	Coward Of The County	Kenny Rogers	UA	8	(3)	
3	10	I'm In The Mood For Dancing	Nolans	Epic	8		F
4	-	Someone's Looking At You	Boomtown Rats	Ensign	5		
5	-	It's Different For Girls	Joe Jackson	A&M	5		
6	8	My Girl	Madness	Stiff	6		
7	19	Babe	Styx	A&M	6	(1)	F L
8	-	Captain Beaky/Wilfred The Weasel	Keith Michel	Polydor	5		F L
9	-	And The Beat Goes On	Whispers	Solar	7	(19)	F
10	-	I Hear You Now	Jon & Vangelis	Polydor	6	(58)	F
11	1	Brass In Pocket	Pretenders	Real	9	(14)	F
12	-	7 Teen	Regents	Rialto	4		F L
13	5	With You I'm Born Again	Billy Preston & Syreeta	Motown	5	(4)	L
14	-	Carrie	Cliff Richard	EMI	6	(34)	
15	15	Green Onions	Booker T. & The M.G.'s	Atlantic	4		L
16	4	Please Don't Go	KC & The Sunshine Band	TK	6	(1)	
17	-	Atomic	Blondie	Chrysalis	6	(39)	
18	-	Rock With You	Michael Jackson	Epic	5	(1)	
19	-	I Can't Stand Up For Falling Down	Elvis Costello	F. Beat	5		
20	-	Living By Numbers	New Muzik	GTO	3		F L

March 1980

This Mnth	Prev Mnth	Title	Artist	Label	Wks 20	(US Pos)	
1	-	Together We Are Beautiful	Fern Kinney	WEA	7		F L
2	-	Take That Look Off Your Face	Marti Webb	Polydor	6		F
3	17	Atomic	Blondie	Chrysalis	6	(39)	
4	-	Games Without Frontiers	Peter Gabriel	Charisma	5	(48)	
5	-	All Night Long	Rainbow	Polydor	6		
6	-	Turning Japanese	Vapors	UA	7	(36)	F L
7	9	And The Beat Goes On	Whispers	Solar	7	(19)	F
8	2	Coward Of The County	Kenny Rogers	UA	8	(3)	
9	14	Carrie	Cliff Richard	EMI	6	(34)	
10	19	I Can't Stand Up For Falling Down	Elvis Costello	F. Beat	5		
11	-	So Lonely	Police	A&M	5		
12	-	Going Underground/Dreams Of Children	Jam	Polydor	6		
13	-	Dance Yourself Dizzy	Liquid Gold	Polo	8		F
14	-	Do That To Me One More Time	Captain & Tennille	Casablanca	4	(1)	F L
15	18	Rock With You	Michael Jackson	Epic	5	(1)	
16	-	Hands Off-She's Mine	Beat	Go Feet	4		
17	-	Working My Way Back To You-Forgive Me, Girl (Medley)	Detroit Spinners	Atlantic	9	(2)	
18	-	So Good To Be Back Home Again	Tourists	Logo	5		L
19	-	Riders In The Sky	Shadows	EMI	4		L
20	-	Cuba/Better Do It Salsa	Gibson Brothers	Island	3	(81)	

January 1980

This Mnth	Prev Mnth	Title	Artist	Label	Wks 20	(UK Pos)	
1	13	Rock With You	Michael Jackson	Epic	13	(7)	G
2	3	Escape (The Pina Colada Song)	Rupert Holmes	Infinity	12	(23)	F G
3	8	Do That To Me One More Time	Captain & Tennille	Casablanca	17	(7)	G L
4	6	Send One Your Love	Stevie Wonder	Tamla	12	(52)	
5	-	Coward Of The County	Kenny Rogers	UA	8	(1)	G
6	15	We Don't Talk Anymore	Cliff Richard	EMI America	10	(1)	
7	2	Please Don't Go	KC & The Sunshine Band	TK	15	(3)	
8	-	Cruisin'	Smokey Robinson	Tamla	12		F
9	10	Ladies Night	Kool & The Gang	De-Lite	10	(9)	G
10	-	The Long Run	Eagles	Asylum	10	(66)	
11	12	Cool Change	Little River Band	Capitol	9		
12	20	Better Love Next Time	Dr. Hook	Capitol	8	(8)	
13	4	Still	Commodores	Motown	13	(4)	G
14	-	I Wanna Be Your Lover	Prince	Warner	6	(41)	F G
15	1	Babe	Styx	A&M	12	(6)	G
16	-	Sara	Fleetwood Mac	Warner	7	(37)	
17	-	Jane	Jefferson Starship	Grunt	6	(21)	L
18	-	This Is It	Kenny Loggins	Columbia	8		
19	-	Crazy Little Thing Called Love	Queen	Elektra	14	(2)	
20	-	Don't Do Me Like That	Tom Petty & The Heartbreakers	Backstreet	6		F

February 1980

This Mnth	Prev Mnth	Title	Artist	Label	Wks 20	(UK Pos)	
1	3	Do That To Me One More Time	Captain & Tennille	Casablanca	17	(7)	G L
2	1	Rock With You	Michael Jackson	Epic	13	(7)	G
3	19	Crazy Little Thing Called Love	Queen	Elektra	14	(2)	
4	8	Cruisin'	Smokey Robinson	Tamla	12		F
5	5	Coward Of The County	Kenny Rogers	UA	8	(1)	G
6	-	Yes, I'm Ready	Teri DeSario With K.C.	Casablanca	9		F G L
7	16	Sara	Fleetwood Mac	Warner	7	(37)	
8	-	Longer	Dan Fogelberg	Full Moon	9	(59)	F
9	-	On The Radio	Donna Summer	Casablanca	9	(32)	G
10	18	This Is It	Kenny Loggins	Columbia	8		
11	-	Desire	Andy Gibb	RSO	10		
12	10	The Long Run	Eagles	Asylum	10	(66)	
13	20	Don't Do Me Like That	Tom Petty & The Heartbreakers	Backstreet	6		F
14	2	Escape (The Pina Colada Song)	Rupert Holmes	Infinity	12	(23)	F G
15	-	Romeo's Tune	Steve Forbert	Nemperor	5		F L
16	-	Daydream Believer	Anne Murray	Capitol	7	(61)	L
17	-	An American Dream	Nitty Gritty Dirt Band	UA	5		L
18	-	Working My Way Back To You/ Forgive Me, Girl	Spinners	Atlantic	12	(1)	G
19	-	Deja Vu	Dionne Warwick	Arista	3		
20	14	I Wanna Be Your Lover	Prince	Warner	6	(41)	F G

March 1980

This Mnth	Prev Mnth	Title	Artist	Label	Wks 20	(UK Pos)	
1	3	Crazy Little Thing Called Love	Queen	Elektra	14	(2)	
2	-	Another Brick In The Wall	Pink Floyd	Columbia	15	(1)	G L
3	11	Desire	Andy Gibb	RSO	10		
4	8	Longer	Dan Fogelberg	Full Moon	9	(59)	F
5	18	Working My Way Back To You/ Forgive Me, Girl	Spinners	Atlantic	12	(1)	G
6	9	On The Radio	Donna Summer	Casablanca	9	(32)	G
7	6	Yes I'm Ready	Teri DeSario With K.C.	Casablanca	9		F G L
8	-	Him	Rupert Holmes	MCA	7	(31)	L
9	-	The Second Time Around	Shalamar	Solar	9	(45)	F
10	-	Too Hot	Kool & The Gang	De-Lite	10	(23)	
11	1	Do That To Me One More Time	Captain & Tennille	Casablanca	17	(7)	G L
12	-	How Do I Make You	Linda Ronstadt	Asylum	9		
13	-	Call Me	Blondie	Chrysalis	16	(1)	G
14	-	Special Lady	Ray, Goodman & Brown	Polydor	9		F G L
15	-	Ride Like The Wind	Christopher Cross	Warner	11	(69)	F
16	16	Daydream Believer	Anne Murray	Capitol	7	(61)	L
17	4	Cruisin'	Smokey Robinson	Tamla	12		F
18	2	Rock With You	Michael Jackson	Epic	13	(7)	G
19	-	Refugee	Tom Petty & The Heartbreakers	Backstreet	4		
20	-	I Can't Tell You Why	Eagles	Asylum	9		L

◆ Pink Floyd, who were touring America, headed the LP chart for 15 weeks with **The Wall**, and their single 'Another Brick In The Wall' was a transatlantic million seller. Also Floyd's **Dark Side Of The Moon** broke the longevity record on the album chart, which previously stood at 302 weeks.

◆ 'Rock With You' gave Michael Jackson his second successive No. 1, and his first solo album for six years, **Off The Wall**, hit the Transatlantic Top 5 and went platinum.

◆ AC/DC's lead singer Bon Scott died of drink- related causes, as the Australian act earned their first platinum album, **Highway To Hell.**

◆ Christopher Cross made his chart debut with 'Ride Like The Wind'. The Texan born singer/songwriter went on to win a record five Grammy awards including that for Best New Artist.

UK 1980 APR-JUNE

◆ 'Mirror In The Bathroom' by 2-Tone act The Beat, was the UK's first digitally recorded hit. Another first was The Police's 'Six Pack' – six separate singles sold as a package – which reached the Top 20.

◆ American records creating much more interest in Britain included dance tracks from Crown Heights Affair and Teena Marie, a soulful duet by Robert Flack & the late Donny Hathaway, and the chart topping ten-year-old theme to the TV series M*A*S*H.

◆ Two of the 1980s' most successful acts made their Top 20 debuts. UB40 scored with 'King' (a tribute to Martin Luther King) and Orchestral Manoeuvres In The Dark charted with 'Messages'.

◆ The Jam's 'Going Underground' became the first record to enter the chart at No. 1 since 1973. The trio were also voted Top Group in the *NME* Poll.

April 1980

This Mnth	Prev Mnth	Title	Artist	Label	Wks 20	(US Pos)	
1	17	Working My Way Back To You...	Detroit Spinners	Atlantic	9	(2)	
2	13	Dance Yourself Dizzy	Liquid Gold	Polo	8		F
3	-	King/Food For Thought	UB40	Graduate	7		F
4	-	Sexy Eyes	Dr. Hook	Capitol	6	(5)	L
5	12	Going Underground/Dreams Of...	Jam	Polydor	6		
6	-	Work Rest & Play (E.P.)	Madness	Stiff	5		
7	-	Poison Ivy	Lambrettas	Rocket	5		F
8	-	Call Me	Blondie	Chrysalis	5	(1)	
9	-	Turn It On Again	Genesis	Charisma	4	(58)	
10	-	January February	Barbara Dickson	Epic	6		
11	6	Turning Japanese	Vapors	UA	7	(36)	F L
12	-	Stomp!	Brothers Johnson	A&M	5	(7)	F L
13	-	Talk Of The Town	Pretenders	Real	4		
14	-	Silver Dream Machine (Pt. 1)	David Essex	Mercury	7		
15	-	Geno	Dexy's Midnight Runners	Late Night Feelings	8		F
16	1	Together We Are Beautiful	Fern Kinney	WEA	7		F L
17	-	Living After Midnight	Judas Priest	CBS	4		
18	-	Don't Push It, Don't Force It	Leon Haywood	20th Century	6	(49)	F L
19	-	Echo Beach	Martha & The Muffins	Dindisc	4		F L
20	-	Coming Up	Paul McCartney	Parlophone	5	(1)	

May 1980

This Mnth	Prev Mnth	Title	Artist	Label	Wks 20	(US Pos)	
1	15	Geno	Dexy's Midnight Runners	Late Night...	8		F
2	-	What's Another Year	Johnny Logan	Epic	6		F
3	-	No Doubt About It	Hot Chocolate	RAK	8		
4	20	Coming Up	Paul McCartney	Parlophone	5	(1)	
5	-	Mirror In The Bathroom	Beat	Go Feet	5		
6	-	She's Out Of My Life	Michael Jackson	Epic	5	(10)	
7	14	Silver Dream Machine (Pt. 1)	David Essex	Mercury	7		
8	-	Hold On To My Love	Jimmy Ruffin	RSO	5	(10)	L
9	8	Call Me	Blondie	Chrysalis	5	(1)	
10	-	I Shoulda Loved Ya	Narada Michael Walden	Atlantic	5	(66)	F
11	-	The Groove	Rodney Franklin	CBS	4		F L
12	-	Toccata	Sky	Ariola	4		F L
13	-	Theme From M*A*S*H (Suicide Is Painless)	Mash	CBS	7		F L
14	-	My Perfect Cousin	Undertones	Sire	3		
15	-	Over You	Roxy Music	Polydor	7	(80)	
16	-	Don't Make Waves	Nolans	Epic	4		
17	-	We Are Glass	Gary Numan	Beggars Banquet	5		
18	-	Check Out The Groove	Bobby Thurston	Epic	3		F L
19	3	King/Food For Thought	UB40	Graduate	7		F
20	-	The Golden Years (E.P.)	Motorhead	Bronze	3		F

June 1980

This Mnth	Prev Mnth	Title	Artist	Label	Wks 20	(US Pos)	
1	-	Crying	Don McLean	EMI	9	(5)	
2	13	Theme From M*A*S*H (Suicide...)	Mash	CBS	7		F L
3	-	Funkytown	Lipps Inc.	Casablanca	8	(1)	F L
4	3	No Doubt About It	Hot Chocolate	Rak	8		
5	-	Back Together Again	Roberta Flack/Donny Hathaway	Atlantic	7	(56)	
6	-	Rat Race/Rude Buoys Outa Jail	Specials	2 Tone	6		
7	-	Let's Get Serious	Jermaine Jackson	Motown	5	(9)	F
8	15	Over You	Roxy Music	Polydor	7	(80)	
9	-	You Gave Me Love	Crown Heights Affair	De-Lite	6		F L
10	-	Everybody's Got To Learn Sometime	Korgis	Rialto	6	(18)	L
11	-	Behind The Groove	Teena Marie	Motown	5		F L
12	17	We Are Glass	Gary Numan	Beggars Banquet	5		
13	6	She's Out Of My Life	Michael Jackson	Epic	5	(10)	
14	-	Messages	Orchestral Manoeuvres In The Dark	Dindisc	4		F
15	-	Midnite Dynamos	Matchbox	Magnet	5		
16	-	Substitute	Liquid Gold	Polo	4		L
17	-	Let's Go Round Again Pt. 1	Average White Band	RCA	5	(53)	L
18	-	Breaking The Law	Judas Priest	CBS	3		L
19	-	D-a-a-ance	Lambrettas	Rocket	3		L
20	-	Simon Templar/Two Pints Of Lager And A Packet Of Crisps Please	Splodgenessabounds	Deram	4		F L

April 1980

This Mnth	Prev Mnth	Title	Artist	Label	Wks 20	(UK Pos)	
1	13	Call Me	Blondie	Chrysalis	16	(1)	G
2	2	Another Brick In The Wall	Pink Floyd	Columbia	15	(1)	G L
3	15	Ride Like The Wind	Christopher Cross	Warner	11	(69)	F
4	14	Special Lady	Ray, Goodman & Brown	Polydor	9		F G L
5	5	Working My Way Back To You/ Forgive Me, Girl	Spinners	Atlantic	12	(1)	G
6	-	With You I'm Born Again	Billy Preston & Syreeta	Motown	8	(2)	L
7	10	Too Hot	Kool & The Gang	De-Lite	10	(23)	
8	20	I Can't Tell You Why	Eagles	Asylum	9		L
9	-	Fire Lake	Bob Seger & The Silver Bullet Band	Capitol	8		
10	-	Lost In Love	Air Supply	Arista	12		F
11	1	Crazy Little Thing Called Love	Queen	Elektra	14	(2)	
12	-	Off The Wall	Michael Jackson	Epic	7	(7)	G
13	-	You May Be Right	Billy Joel	Columbia	7		
14	-	Sexy Eyes	Dr. Hook	Capitol	11	(4)	G L
15	8	Him	Rupert Holmes	MCA	7	(31)	L
16	-	Hold On To My Love	Jimmy Ruffin	RSO	6	(7)	L
17	12	How Do I Make You	Linda Ronstadt	Asylum	9		
18	3	Desire	Andy Gibb	RSO	10		
19	-	Don't Fall In Love With A Dreamer	Kenny Rogers & Kim Carnes	UA	11		
20	9	The Second Time Around	Shalamar	Solar	9	(45)	F

May 1980

This Mnth	Prev Mnth	Title	Artist	Label	Wks 20	(UK Pos)	
1	1	Call Me	Blondie	Chrysalis	16	(1)	G
2	10	Lost In Love	Air Supply	Arista	12		F
3	14	Sexy Eyes	Dr. Hook	Capitol	11	(4)	G L
4	3	Ride Like The Wind	Christopher Cross	Warner	11	(69)	F
5	19	Don't Fall In Love With A Dreamer	Kenny Rogers & Kim Carnes	UA	11		
6	-	Funkytown	Lipps Inc.	Casablanca	11	(2)	F P L
7	-	Biggest Part Of Me	Ambrosia	Warner	12		
8	-	Hurt So Bad	Linda Ronstadt	Asylum	9		
9	6	With You I'm Born Again	Billy Preston & Syreeta	Motown	8	(2)	L
10	2	Another Brick In The Wall	Pink Floyd	Columbia	15	(1)	G L
11	13	You May Be Right	Billy Joel	Columbia	7		
12	-	Cars	Gary Numan	Atco	10	(1)	F L
13	-	I Can't Help It	Andy Gibb & Olivia Newton-John	RSO	5		
14	-	Stomp!	Brothers Johnson	A&M	7	(6)	L
15	9	Fire Lake	Bob Seger & Silver Bullet Band	Capitol	8		
16	-	Coming Up (Live At Glasgow)	Paul McCartney	Columbia	14	(2)	G
17	-	Against The Wind	Bob Seger & Silver Bullet Band	Capitol	9		
18	-	Breakdown Dead Ahead	Boz Scaggs	Columbia	5		
19	-	Pilot Of The Airwaves	Charlie Dore	Island	5	(66)	F L
20	16	Hold On To My Love	Jimmy Ruffin	RSO	6	(7)	L

June 1980

This Mnth	Prev Mnth	Title	Artist	Label	Wks 20	(UK Pos)	
1	6	Funkytown	Lipps Inc.	Casablanca	11	(2)	F P L
2	16	Coming Up (Live At Glasgow)	Paul McCartney	Columbia	14	(2)	G
3	-	The Rose	Bette Midler	Atlantic	12		G
4	7	Biggest Part Of Me	Ambrosia	Warner	12		
5	17	Against The Wind	Bob Seger & Silver Bullet Band	Capitol	9		
6	-	It's Still Rock And Roll To Me	Billy Joel	Columbia	14	(14)	G
7	-	Little Jeannie	Elton John	MCA	13	(33)	G
8	1	Call Me	Blondie	Chrysalis	16	(1)	G
9	-	Steal Away	Robbie Dupree	Elektra	11		F
10	12	Cars	Gary Numan	Atco	10	(1)	F L
11	-	She's Out Of My Life	Michael Jackson	Epic	7	(3)	G
12	-	Cupid/I've Loved You For A Long Time	Spinners	Atlantic	12	(4)	L
13	5	Don't Fall In Love With A Dreamer	Kenny Rogers & Kim Carnes	UA	11		
14	-	Let's Get Serious	Jermaine Jackson	Motown	8	(8)	
15	8	Hurt So Bad	Linda Ronstadt	Asylum	9		
16	-	Let Me Love You Tonight	Pure Prairie League	Casablanca	8		F L
17	-	Brass In Pocket	Pretenders	Sire	7	(1)	F
18	-	Shining Star	Manhattans	Columbia	10	(45)	G L
19	14	Stomp!	Brothers Johnson	A&M	7	(6)	L
20	3	Sexy Eyes	Dr. Hook	Capitol	11	(4)	G L

◆ The live version of Paul McCartney's 'Coming Up' was an American No. 1, while the studio version of the same song became a major UK success.

▲ The combination of top German disco producer Giorgio Moroder and Blondie resulted in the group's second successive transatlantic topper, 'Call Me'. It happened in the month that top disco, Club 54, closed its doors.

◆ The 1950s rock'n'roll musical Grease closed after a record 3,883 performances on Broadway – that's more nights than there were in the whole of the 1950s!

UK 1980
JULY-SEPT

◆ Critically acclaimed Manchester group Joy Division's 'Love Will Tear Us Apart' reached the Top 20 shortly after the group's leader Ian Curtis had committed suicide.

▲ Scottish singer Sheena Easton found herself with two singles in the Top 10 after being the subject of the TV series *The Big Time*. She went on to win the Grammy for Best New Artist of 1981.

◆ On the album charts **Emotional Rescue** gave The Rolling Stones their only transatlantic No. 1 of the decade and singer/songwriter Kate Bush's **Never For Ever** became the first LP by a female British singer to head the UK charts.

July 1980

This Mnth	Prev Mnth	Title	Artist	Label	Wks 20	(US Pos)	
1	-	Xanadu	Olivia Newton-John/ Electric Light Orchestra	Jet	8	(8)	
2	-	Jump To The Beat	Stacy Lattisaw	Atlantic	7		F L
3	-	Use It Up And Wear It Out	Odyssey	RCA	8		
4	1	Crying	Don McLean	EMI	9	(5)	
5	-	Cupid-I've Loved You For A Long Time (Medley)	Detroit Spinners	Atlantic	6	(4)	L
6	-	My Way Of Thinking/I Think It's Going To Rain	UB40	Graduate	6		
7	-	Could You Be Loved	Bob Marley & The Wailers	Island	6		
8	3	Funkytown	Lipps Inc.	Casablanca	8	(1)	F L
9	-	Waterfalls	Paul McCartney	Parlophone	5		
10	10	Everybody's Got To Learn Sometime	Korgis	Rialto	6	(18)	L
11	-	Babooshka	Kate Bush	EMI	6		
12	20	Simon Templar/Two Pints Of Lager...	Splodgenessabounds	Deram	4		F L
13	-	To Be Or Not To Be	B.A. Robertson	Asylum	3		
14	-	More Than I Can Say	Leo Sayer	Chrysalis	6	(2)	
15	5	Back Together Again	Roberta Flack/Donny Hathaway	Atlantic	7	(56)	
16	-	747 (Strangers In The Night)	Saxon	Carrere	4		
17	11	Behind The Groove	Teena Marie	Motown	5		F L
18	-	Emotional Rescue	Rolling Stones	Rolling Stone	5	(3)	
19	-	Let's Hang On	Darts	Magnet	4		L
20	-	Love Will Tear Us Apart	Joy Division	Factory	4		F

August 1980

This Mnth	Prev Mnth	Title	Artist	Label	Wks 20	(US Pos)	
1	-	The Winner Takes It All	Abba	Epic	7	(8)	
2	-	Upside Down	Diana Ross	Motown	7	(1)	
3	-	9 to 5 (a.k.a. Morning Train)	Sheena Easton	EMI	9	(1)	F
4	-	Oops Upside Your Head	Gap Band	Mercury	8		F
5	-	Ashes To Ashes	David Bowie	RCA	7		
6	14	More Than I Can Say	Leo Sayer	Chrysalis	6	(2)	
7	3	Use It Up And Wear It Out	Odyssey	RCA	8		
8	-	Oh Yeah (On The Radio)	Roxy Music	Polydor	5		
9	-	Give Me The Night	George Benson	Warner	5	(4)	F
10	11	Babooshka	Kate Bush	EMI	6		
11	-	Start	Jam	Polydor	6		
12	7	Could You Be Loved	Bob Marley & The Wailers	Island	6		
13	-	Tom Hark	Piranhas	Sire	6		F
14	-	Feels Like I'm In Love	Kelly Marie	Calibre	9		F L
15	-	Funkin' For Jamaica (N.Y.)	Tom Browne	Arista	4		F L
16	1	Xanadu	Olivia Newton-John/E.L.O.	Jet	8	(8)	
17	-	There There My Dear	Dexy's Midnight Runners	Late Night Feelings	5		
18	-	Mariana	Gibson Brothers	Island	3		L
19	-	Lip Up Fatty	Bad Manners	Magnet	4		F
20	-	Sunshine Of Your Smile	Mike Berry	Polydor	6		L

September 1980

This Mnth	Prev Mnth	Title	Artist	Label	Wks 20	(US Pos)	
1	14	Feels Like I'm In Love	Kelly Marie	Calibre	9		F L
2	11	Start	Jam	Polydor	6		
3	-	Eighth Day	Hazel O'Connor	A&M	6		F
4	5	Ashes To Ashes	David Bowie	RCA	7		
5	-	One Day I'll Fly Away	Randy Crawford	Warner	6		F
6	-	It's Only Love/Beyond The Reef	Elvis Presley	RCA	6	(51)	L
7	3	9 to 5	Sheena Easton	EMI	9	(1)	F
8	-	Dreaming	Cliff Richard	EMI	6	(10)	
9	-	Modern Girl	Sheena Easton	EMI	6	(18)	
10	-	Master Blaster (Jammin')	Stevie Wonder	Motown	6	(5)	
11	20	Sunshine Of Your Smile	Mike Berry	Polydor	6		L
12	13	Tom Hark	Piranhas	Sire	6		F
13	-	Another One Bites The Dust	Queen	EMI	5	(1)	
14	-	I Die: You Die	Gary Numan	Beggars Banquet	4		
15	-	Can't Stop The Music	Village People	Mercury	4		L
16	-	Bank Robber	Clash	CBS	4		
17	-	Don't Stand So Close To Me	Police	A&M	7	(10)	
18	-	It's Still Rock And Roll To Me	Billy Joel	CBS	6	(1)	
19	1	The Winner Takes It All	Abba	Epic	7	(8)	
20	-	Baggy Trousers	Madness	Stiff	7		

This Mnth	Prev Mnth	Title	Artist	Label	Wks 20	(UK Pos)	
1	6	It's Still Rock And Roll To Me	Billy Joel	Columbia	14	(14)	G
2	2	Coming Up (Live At Glasgow)	Paul McCartney	Columbia	14	(2)	G
3	7	Little Jeannie	Elton John	MCA	13	(33)	G
4	12	Cupid/I've Loved You For A Long Time	Spinners	Atlantic	12	(4)	L
5	3	The Rose	Bette Midler	Atlantic	12		G
6	9	Steal Away	Robbie Dupree	Elektra	11		F
7	-	Magic	Olivia Newton-John	MCA	12	(32)	G
8	18	Shining Star	Manhattans	Columbia	10	(45)	G L
9	16	Let Me Love You Tonight	Pure Prairie League	Casablanca	8		F L
10	-	Tired Of Toein' The Line	Rocky Burnette	EMI America	8	(58)	F L
11	14	Let's Get Serious	Jermaine Jackson	Motown	8	(8)	
12	1	Funkytown	Lipps Inc.	Casablanca	11	(2)	F P L
13	-	One Fine Day	Carole King	Capitol	7		L
14	5	Against The Wind	Bob Seger & The Silver Bullet Band	Capitol	9		
15	-	Take Your Time (Do It Right) (Pt. 1)	S.O.S. Band	Tabu	9	(51)	F G L
16	-	In America	Charlie Daniels Band	Epic	5		L
17	-	More Love	Kim Carnes	EMI America	9		
18	4	Biggest Part Of Me	Ambrosia	Warner	12		
19	-	Emotional Rescue	Rolling Stones	Rolling Stone	10	(9)	
20	-	I'm Alive	Electric Light Orchestra	MCA	3	(20)	G

August 1980

This Mnth	Prev Mnth	Title	Artist	Label	Wks 20	(UK Pos)	
1	7	Magic	Olivia Newton-John	MCA	12	(32)	G
2	-	Sailing	Christopher Cross	Warner	9	(48)	
3	15	Take Your Time (Do It Right) (Pt. 1)	S.O.S. Band	Tabu	9	(51)	F G L
4	19	Emotional Rescue	Rolling Stones	Rolling Stone	10	(9)	
5	1	It's Still Rock And Roll To Me	Billy Joel	Columbia	14	(14)	G
6	-	Upside Down	Diana Ross	Motown	14	(2)	G
7	8	Shining Star	Manhattans	Columbia	10	(45)	G L
8	17	More Love	Kim Carnes	EMI America	9		
9	3	Little Jeannie	Elton John	MCA	13	(33)	G
10	-	Fame	Irene Cara	RSO	10	(1)	F
11	4	Cupid/I've Loved You For A Long Time	Spinners	Atlantic	12	(4)	L
12	-	Let My Love Open The Door	Pete Townshend	Atco	5	(46)	F L
13	2	Coming Up (Live At Glasgow)	Paul McCartney	Columbia	14	(2)	G
14	-	Give Me The Night	George Benson	Warner	10	(7)	
15	-	All Out Of Love	Air Supply	Arista	12	(11)	G
16	-	Misunderstanding	Genesis	Atlantic	4	(42)	F
17	10	Tired Of Toein' The Line	Rocky Burnette	EMI America	8	(58)	F L
18	-	Into The Night	Benny Mardones	Polydor	6		F
19	-	Late In The Evening	Paul Simon	Warner	10	(58)	L
20	-	Take A Little Rhythm	Ali Thomson	A&M	3		F L

September 1980

This Mnth	Prev Mnth	Title	Artist	Label	Wks 20	(UK Pos)	
1	6	Upside Down	Diana Ross	Motown	14	(2)	G
2	15	All Out Of Love	Air Supply	Arista	12	(11)	G
3	10	Fame	Irene Cara	RSO	10	(1)	F
4	14	Give Me The Night	George Benson	Warner	10	(7)	
5	-	Lookin' For Love	Johnny Lee	Full Moon	8		F G L
6	19	Late In The Evening	Paul Simon	Warner	10	(58)	L
7	-	Another One Bites The Dust	Queen	Elektra	18	(7)	G
8	4	Emotional Rescue	Rolling Stones	Rolling Stone	10	(9)	
9	-	Drivin' My Life Away	Eddie Rabbitt	Elektra	10		G
10	2	Sailing	Christopher Cross	Warner	9	(48)	
11	-	One In A Million You	Larry Graham	Warner	4		F G L
12	-	I'm Alright	Kenny Loggins	Columbia	8		
13	-	You're The Only Woman (You & I)	Ambrosia	Warner	6		L
14	1	Magic	Olivia Newton-John	MCA	12	(32)	G
15	-	Xanadu	Olivia Newton-John/ Electric Light Orchestra	MCA	7	(1)	
16	-	You'll Accomp'ny Me	Bob Seger & Silver Bullet Band	Capitol	5		
17	18	Into The Night	Benny Mardones	Polydor	6		F
18	-	All Over The World	Electric Light Orchestra	MCA	5	(11)	
19	3	Take Your Time (Do It Right) (Pt. 1)	S.O.S. Band	Tabu	9	(51)	F G L
20	-	Woman In Love	Barbra Streisand	Columbia	13	(1)	G

US 1980 JULY-SEPT

◆ A crowd of 400,000 flocked to Central Park to see Elton John, and half a million thronged to a Beach Boys concert in Washington.

◆ John Bonham, the drummer of Led Zeppelin, died after a heavy drinking bout. The platinum-selling group cancelled their planned US tour and disbanded.

◆ In America, British acts Elton John, Genesis, Pete Townshend, Ali Thomson and Olivia Newton-John hit with records that had missed the UK Top 40. In Britain, American artists Stacy Lattisaw, Odyssey, Tom Browne, The Village People and Randy Crawford charted with US pop flops.

◆ Despite the fact that the film *Xanadu* was a relative box office failure, the soundtrack album sold two million, and three tracks taken from it reached the Top 20 including the chart-topping 'Magic'.

UK 1980

OCT-DEC

◆ The Police had the year's top UK single and album with the Grammy winning 'Don't Stand So Close To Me' and **Zenyatta Mondatta,** both of which entered at No. 1.

◆ Abba's 'Super Trooper' gave them their ninth and last chart topper, as the album of the same name chalked up over a million British advance orders.

◆ Fleetwood Mac followed the record breaking **Rumours** album with **Tusk,**which reportedly cost over $1 million to record

◆ Queen notched up their second US chart topper of the year when 'Another One Bites The Dust' followed in the footsteps of their retro-rockabilly track 'Crazy Little Thing Called Love'.

◆ Paul McCartney received a rhodium plated record from *The Guinness Book Of Records* for being the most successful songwriter of all time.

October 1980

This Mnth	Prev Mnth	Title	Artist	Label	Wks 20	(US Pos)	
1	17	Don't Stand So Close To Me	Police	A&M	7	(10)	
2	-	D.I.S.C.O.	Ottawan	Carrere	7		F
3	20	Baggy Trousers	Madness	Stiff	7		
4	10	Master Blaster (Jammin')	Stevie Wonder	Motown	6	(5)	
5	-	My Old Piano	Diana Ross	Motown	5		
6	-	If You're Lookin' For A Way Out	Odyssey	RCA	8		
7	-	Et Les Oiseaux Chantaient (And The Birds Were Singing)	Sweet People	Polydor	4		F L
8	-	Amigo	Black Slate	Ensign	4		F L
9	-	What You're Proposing	Status Quo	Vertigo	4		
10	-	Woman In Love	Barbra Streisand	CBS	8	(1)	
11	-	When You Ask About Love	Matchbox	Magnet	7		
12	5	One Day I'll Fly Away	Randy Crawford	Warner	6		F
13	-	Killer On The Loose	Thin Lizzy	Vertigo	4		
14	1	Feels Like I'm In Love	Kelly Marie	Calibre	9		F L
15	-	Searching	Change	WEA	3		
16	-	Gotta Pull Myself Together	Nolans	Epic	5		
17	13	Another One Bites The Dust	Queen	EMI	5	(1)	
18	-	Casanova	Coffee	De-Lite	4		F L
19	-	Stereotype/International Jet Set	Specials	2 Tone	1		
20	6	It's Only Love/Beyond The Reef	Elvis Presley	RCA	6	(51)	L

November 1980

This Mnth	Prev Mnth	Title	Artist	Label	Wks 20	(US Pos)	
1	10	Woman In Love	Barbra Streisand	CBS	8	(1)	
2	-	The Tide Is High	Blondie	Chrysalis	9	(1)	
3	-	Special Brew	Bad Manners	Magnet	6		
4	-	Fashion	David Bowie	RCA	6	(70)	
5	-	Enola Gay	Orchestral Manoeuvres In The Dark	Dindisc	7		
6	-	I Could Be So Good For You	Dennis Waterman	EMI	6		F L
7	-	Dog Eat Dog	Adam & The Ants	CBS	6		F
8	-	Super Trouper	Abba	Epic	9	(45)	
9	-	Never Knew Love Like This Before	Stephanie Mills	20th Century	7	(6)	F L
10	11	When You Ask About Love	Matchbox	Magnet	7		
11	6	If You're Lookin' For A Way Out	Odyssey	RCA	8		
12	9	What You're Proposing	Status Quo	Vertigo	4		
13	2	D.I.S.C.O.	Ottawan	Carrere	7		F
14	-	The Earth Dies Screaming/ Dream A Lie	UB40	Graduate	5		
15	16	Gotta Pull Myself Together	Nolans	Epic	5		
16	-	Celebration	Kool & The Gang	De-Lite	5	(1)	
17	3	Baggy Trousers	Madness	Stiff	7		
18	-	(Just Like) Starting Over	John Lennon	Geffen	10	(1)	
19	-	All Out Of Love	Air Supply	Arista	4	(2)	F L
20	-	The Same Old Scene	Roxy Music	Polydor	3		

December 1980

This Mnth	Prev Mnth	Title	Artist	Label	Wks 20	(US Pos)	
1	8	Super Trouper	Abba	Epic	9	(45)	
2	-	There's No One Quite Like Grandma	St. Winifred's School Choir	MFP	6		F L
3	-	Embarrassment	Madness	Stiff	8		
4	-	Stop The Cavalry	Jona Lewie	Stiff	8		L
5	-	Banana Republic	Boomtown Rats	Ensign	7		L
6	18	(Just Like) Starting Over	John Lennon	Geffen	10	(1)	
7	-	To Cut A Long Story Short	Spandau Ballet	Reformation	8		F
8	-	De Do Do Do, De Da Da Da	Police	A&M	6	(10)	
9	2	The Tide Is High	Blondie	Chrysalis	9	(1)	
10	-	Do You Feel My Love	Eddy Grant	Ensign	6		
11	-	Runaway Boys	Stray Cats	Arista	6		F
12	-	Antmusic	Adam & The Ants	CBS	12		
13	16	Celebration	Kool & The Gang	De-Lite	5	(1)	
14	-	Lady	Kenny Rogers	UA	5	(1)	
15	9	Never Knew Love Like This Before	Stephanie Mills	20th Century	7	(6)	F L
16	6	I Could Be So Good For You	Dennis Waterman	EMI	6		F L
17	-	Lies/Don't Drive My Car	Status Quo	Vertigo	6		
18	-	Happy Xmas (War Is Over)	John & Yoko & The Plastic Ono Band	Apple	5		
19	-	Flash	Queen	EMI	8	(42)	
20	-	Rock 'n' Roll Ain't Noise Pollution	AC/DC	Atlantic	3		F

October 1980

This Mnth	Prev Mnth	Title	Artist	Label	Wks 20	(UK Pos)	
1	7	Another One Bites The Dust	Queen	Elektra	18	(7)	G
2	20	Woman In Love	Barbra Streisand	Columbia	13	(1)	G
3	1	Upside Down	Diana Ross	Motown	14	(2)	G
4	2	All Out Of Love	Air Supply	Arista	12	(11)	G
5	-	Real Love	Doobie Brothers	Warner	8		
6	12	I'm Alright	Kenny Loggins	Columbia	8		
7	9	Drivin' My Life Away	Eddie Rabbitt	Elektra	10		G
8	-	He's So Shy	Pointer Sisters	Planet	11		G
9	6	Late In The Evening	Paul Simon	Warner	10	(58)	L
10	15	Xanadu	Olivia Newton-John/ Electric Light Orchestra	MCA	7	(1)	
11	4	Give Me The Night	George Benson	Warner	10	(7)	
12	-	Never Knew Love Like This Before	Stephanie Mills	20th Century	10	(4)	F G L
13	-	The Wanderer	Donna Summer	Geffen	9	(48)	G
14	-	Jesse	Carly Simon	Warner	6		G
15	5	Lookin' For Love	Johnny Lee	Full Moon	8		F G L
16	-	Lady	Kenny Rogers	Liberty	16	(12)	
17	-	Look What You've Done To Me	Boz Scaggs	Columbia	5		
18	-	Hot Rod Hearts	Robbie Dupree	Elektra	6		L
19	18	All Over The World	Electric Light Orchestra	MCA	5	(11)	
20	-	I'm Comin' Out	Diana Ross	Motown	9	(13)	

November 1980

This Mnth	Prev Mnth	Title	Artist	Label	Wks 20	(UK Pos)	
1	2	Woman In Love	Barbra Streisand	Columbia	13	(1)	G
2	16	Lady	Kenny Rogers	Liberty	16	(12)	
3	1	Another One Bites The Dust	Queen	Elektra	18	(7)	G
4	13	The Wanderer	Donna Summer	Geffen	9	(48)	G
5	20	I'm Comin' Out	Diana Ross	Motown	9	(13)	
6	-	Master Blaster (Jammin')	Stevie Wonder	Tamla	13	(2)	
7	12	Never Knew Love Like This Before	Stephanie Mills	20th Century	10	(4)	F G L
8	8	He's So Shy	Pointer Sisters	Planet	11		G
9	-	Dreaming	Cliff Richard	EMI America	8	(8)	
10	-	More Than I Can Say	Leo Sayer	Warner	12	(2)	G L
11	-	(Just Like) Starting Over	John Lennon	Geffen	16	(1)	G
12	-	Lovely One	Jacksons	Epic	5	(29)	
13	5	Real Love	Doobie Brothers	Warner	8		
14	-	You've Lost That Lovin' Feeling	Daryl Hall & John Oates	RCA	7	(55)	
15	-	Love On The Rocks	Neil Diamond	Columbia	13	(17)	
16	3	Upside Down	Diana Ross	Motown	14	(2)	G
17	-	Whip It	Devo	Warner	7	(51)	F G L
18	-	Hit Me With Your Best Shot	Pat Benatar	Chrysalis	11		F G
19	14	Jesse	Carly Simon	Warner	6		G
20	-	Dreamer	Supertramp	A&M	4	(13)	

December 1980

This Mnth	Prev Mnth	Title	Artist	Label	Wks 20	(UK Pos)	
1	2	Lady	Kenny Rogers	Liberty	16	(12)	
2	10	More Than I Can Say	Leo Sayer	Warner	12	(2)	G L
3	11	(Just Like) Starting Over	John Lennon	Geffen	16	(1)	G
4	15	Love On The Rocks	Neil Diamond	Columbia	13	(17)	
5	-	Hungry Heart	Bruce Springsteen	Columbia	10	(44)	F
6	3	Another One Bites The Dust	Queen	Elektra	18	(7)	G
7	6	Master Blaster (Jammin')	Stevie Wonder	Tamla	13	(2)	
8	-	Guilty	Barbra Streisand & Barry Gibb	Columbia	11	(34)	G
9	18	Hit Me With Your Best Shot	Pat Benatar	Chrysalis	11		F G
10	-	Every Woman In The World	Air Supply	Arista	13		
11	1	Woman In Love	Barbra Streisand	Columbia	13	(1)	G
12	-	Tell It Like It Is	Heart	Epic	8		
13	-	The Tide Is High	Blondie	Chrysalis	14	(1)	G
14	14	You've Lost That Lovin' Feeling	Daryl Hall & John Oates	RCA	7	(55)	
15	-	De Do Do Do, De Da Da Da	Police	A&M	8	(5)	F
16	5	I'm Comin' Out	Diana Ross	Motown	9	(13)	
17	-	Passion	Rod Stewart	Warner	12	(17)	
18	-	It's My Turn	Diana Ross	RCA	10	(16)	
19	-	Never Be The Same	Christopher Cross	Warner	5		
20	9	Dreaming	Cliff Richard	EMI America	8	(8)	

US
1980
OCT-DEC

▲ John Lennon's murder shook the world, as Elvis Presley's death had in 1977. Lennon's comeback album, **Double Fantasy,** and its debut single, '(Just Like) Starting Over', shot to the top, as sales of all his (and The Beatles') earlier records increased dramatically.

◆ In the year that video discs were introduced, the sale of pre-recorded audio tapes now accounted for 39% of all album sales. However, the total sales of records and tapes continued to drop, with 34 million fewer units being sold than in 1979.

◆ Country music was in the midst of a sales revival thanks in part to the success of the John Travolta film *Urban Cowboy.*

UK 1981

JAN-MAR

◆ In January, the late John Lennon held three of the Top 4 places in the UK chart. His recordings of 'Woman' and the re-released 'Imagine' hit the top, as did Roxy Music's interpretation of his composition 'Jealous Guy'.

◆ The rockabilly revival continued with American trio The Stray Cats and Welsh rocker Shakin' Stevens leading the way. Interest was also growing in Brit-funk, thanks to Freeez and Beggar & Co.

▲ Major new artists on the UK charts included Phil Collins (whose first solo album **Face Value** entered at No. 1), 'new romantics' Spandau Ballet and Duran Duran (above), Kim Wilde and influential bands New Order and Ultravox.

January 1981

This Mnth	Prev Mnth	Title	Artist	Label	Wks 20	(US Pos)	
1	-	Imagine	John Lennon	Apple	9		
2	12	Antmusic	Adam & The Ants	CBS	12		
3	18	Happy Xmas (War Is Over)	John & Yoko & The Plastic Ono Band	Apple	5		
4	6	(Just Like) Starting Over	John Lennon	Geffen	10	(1)	
5	4	Stop The Cavalry	Jona Lewie	Stiff	8		L
6	-	Do Nothing/Maggie's Farm	Specials	2 Tone	5		
7	19	Flash	Queen	EMI	8	(42)	
8	8	De Do Do Do, De Da Da Da	Police	A&M	6	(10)	
9	-	Woman	John Lennon	Geffen	7	(2)	
10	-	Too Nice To Talk To	Beat	Go Feet	4		
11	2	There's No One Quite Like Grandma	St. Winifred's School Choir	MFP	6		F L
12	-	In The Air Tonight	Phil Collins	Virgin	6	(19)	F
13	-	I Am The Beat	Look	MCA	5		F L
14	-	Rabbit	Chas & Dave	Rockney	6		
15	3	Embarrassment	Madness	Stiff	8		
16	1	Super Trouper	Abba	Epic	9	(45)	
17	-	Don't Stop The Music	Yarbrough & Peoples	Mercury	6	(19)	F L
18	17	Lies/Don't Drive My Car	Status Quo	Vertigo	6		
19	11	Runaway Boys	Stray Cats	Arista	6		F
20	-	I Ain't Gonna Stand For It	Stevie Wonder	Motown	4	(11)	

February 1981

This Mnth	Prev Mnth	Title	Artist	Label	Wks 20	(US Pos)	
1	9	Woman	John Lennon	Geffen	7	(2)	
2	-	Vienna	Ultravox	Chrysalis	10		F
3	12	In The Air Tonight	Phil Collins	Virgin	6	(19)	F
4	-	I Surrender	Rainbow	Polydor	6		
5	-	Shaddup You Face	Joe Dolce Music Theatre	Epic	6	(53)	F L
6	-	Return Of The Los Palmas 7	Madness	Stiff	7		
7	-	Oldest Swinger In Town	Fred Wedlock	Rocket	5		F L
8	-	Romeo And Juliet	Dire Straits	Vertigo	6		
9	-	Rapture	Blondie	Chrysalis	5	(1)	
10	1	Imagine	John Lennon	Apple	9		
11	-	Fade To Grey	Visage	Polydor	5		F
12	2	Antmusic	Adam & The Ants	CBS	12		
13	-	Rock This Town	Stray Cats	Arista	5	(9)	
14	17	Don't Stop The Music	Yarbrough & Peoples	Mercury	6	(19)	F L
15	-	We'll Bring The House Down	Slade	Cheapskate	4		
16	-	St. Valentine's Day Massacre E.P.	Motorhead & Girlschool	Bronze	5		
17	-	(Do) The Hucklebuck	Coast To Coast	Polydor	8		F L
18	-	Young Parisians	Adam & The Ants	Decca	4		
19	-	Message Of Love	Pretenders	Real	3		
20	-	Jealous Guy	Roxy Music	EG	7		

March 1981

This Mnth	Prev Mnth	Title	Artist	Label	Wks 20	(US Pos)	
1	20	Jealous Guy	Roxy Music	EG	7		
2	-	Kings Of The Wild Frontier	Adam & The Ants	CBS	6		
3	17	(Do) The Hucklebuck	Coast To Coast	Polydor	8		F L
4	2	Vienna	Ultravox	Chrysalis	10		F
5	-	Kids In America	Kim Wilde	RAK	8	(25)	F
6	-	This Ole House	Shakin' Stevens	Epic	9		
7	5	Shaddup You Face	Joe Dolce Music Theatre	Epic	6	(53)	F L
8	-	Four From Toyah E.P.	Toyah	Safari	7		F
9	-	Reward	Teardrop Explodes	Vertigo	4		F
10	-	Southern Freeez	Freeez	Beggars Banquet	4		F
11	16	St. Valentine's Day Massacre E.P.	Motorhead & Girlschool	Bronze	5		
12	-	Something 'Bout You Baby I Like	Status Quo	Vertigo	4		
13	-	You Better You Bet	Who	Polydor	4	(18)	L
14	4	I Surrender	Rainbow	Polydor	6		
15	-	Once In A Lifetime	Talking Heads	Sire	3	(91)	F
16	-	Lately	Stevie Wonder	Motown	7	(64)	
17	-	Star	Kiki Dee	Ariola	4		L
18	6	Return Of The Los Palmas 7	Madness	Stiff	7		
19	-	(Somebody) Help Me Out	Beggar & Co	Ensign	3		F L
20	-	I Missed Again	Phil Collins	Virgin	3	(19)	

January 1981

This Mnth	Prev Mnth	Title	Artist	Label	Wks 20	(UK Pos)	
1	3	(Just Like) Starting Over	John Lennon	Geffen	16	(1)	G
2	4	Love On The Rocks	Neil Diamond	Columbia	13	(17)	
3	13	The Tide Is High	Blondie	Chrysalis	14	(1)	G
4	10	Every Woman In The World	Air Supply	Arista	13		
5	8	Guilty	Barbra Streisand & Barry Gibb	Columbia	11	(34)	G
6	17	Passion	Rod Stewart	Warner	12	(17)	
7	5	Hungry Heart	Bruce Springsteen	Columbia	10	(44)	F
8	18	It's My Turn	Diana Ross	RCA	10	(16)	
9	-	I Love A Rainy Night	Eddie Rabbitt	Elektra	14	(53)	G
10	12	Tell It Like It Is	Heart	Epic	8		
11	-	Celebration	Kool & The Gang	De-Lite	16	(7)	P
12	1	Lady	Kenny Rogers	Liberty	16	(12)	
13	-	I Made It Through The Rain	Barry Manilow	Arista	6	(37)	
14	15	De Do Do Do, De Da Da Da	Police	A&M	8	(5)	F
15	2	More Than I Can Say	Leo Sayer	Warner	12	(2)	G L
16	-	Hey Nineteen	Steely Dan	MCA	10		L
17	9	Hit Me With Your Best Shot	Pat Benatar	Chrysalis	11		F G
18	-	Giving It Up For Your Love	Delbert McClinton	Capitol	9		F L
19	-	Time Is Time	Andy Gibb	RSO	4		L
20	-	9 To 5	Dolly Parton	RCA	12	(47)	G

February 1981

This Mnth	Prev Mnth	Title	Artist	Label	Wks 20	(UK Pos)	
1	9	I Love A Rainy Night	Eddie Rabbitt	Elektra	14	(53)	G
2	20	9 To 5	Dolly Parton	RCA	12	(47)	G
3	11	Celebration	Kool & The Gang	De-Lite	16	(7)	P
4	3	The Tide Is High	Blondie	Chrysalis	14	(1)	G
5	-	Woman	John Lennon	Geffen	13	(1)	G
6	-	Keep On Loving You	REO Speedwagon	Epic	13	(7)	F P
7	6	Passion	Rod Stewart	Warner	12	(17)	
8	18	Giving It Up For Your Love	Delbert McClinton	Capitol	9		F L
9	-	Same Old Lang Syne	Dan Fogelberg	Full Moon	7		
10	1	(Just Like) Starting Over	John Lennon	Geffen	16	(1)	G
11	-	The Best Of Times	Styx	A&M	12	(42)	
12	16	Hey Nineteen	Steely Dan	MCA	10		L
13	-	The Winner Takes It All	Abba	Atlantic	11	(1)	L
14	4	Every Woman In The World	Air Supply	Arista	13		
15	-	I Ain't Gonna Stand For It	Stevie Wonder	Tamla	7	(10)	
16	-	Crying	Don McLean	Millenium	12	(1)	L
17	8	It's My Turn	Diana Ross	RCA	10	(16)	
18	-	Miss Sun	Boz Scaggs	Columbia	5		L
19	-	Hello Again	Neil Diamond	Capitol	10	(51)	
20	-	Together	Tierra	Boardwalk	5		F L

March 1981

This Mnth	Prev Mnth	Title	Artist	Label	Wks 20	(UK Pos)	
1	5	Woman	John Lennon	Geffen	13	(1)	G
2	6	Keep On Loving You	REO Speedwagon	Epic	13	(7)	F P
3	2	9 To 5	Dolly Parton	RCA	12	(47)	G
4	11	The Best Of Times	Styx	A&M	12	(42)	
5	16	Crying	Don McLean	Millenium	12	(1)	L
6	-	Rapture	Blondie	Chrysalis	12	(5)	G L
7	1	I Love A Rainy Night	Eddie Rabbitt	Elektra	14	(53)	G
8	19	Hello Again	Neil Diamond	Capitol	10	(51)	
9	13	The Winner Takes It All	Abba	Atlantic	11	(1)	L
10	3	Celebration	Kool & The Gang	De-Lite	16	(7)	P
11	-	What Kind Of Fool	Barbra Streisand & Barry Gibb	Columbia	7		
12	-	Kiss On My List	Daryl Hall & John Oates	RCA	12	(33)	G
13	15	I Ain't Gonna Stand For It	Stevie Wonder	Tamla	7	(10)	
14	8	Giving It Up For Your Love	Delbert McClinton	Capitol	9		F L
15	-	While You See A Chance	Steve Winwood	Island	8	(45)	F
16	4	The Tide Is High	Blondie	Chrysalis	14	(1)	G
17	-	Don't Stand So Close To Me	Police	A&M	7	(1)	
18	-	Just The Two Of Us	Grover Washington Jr.	Elektra	12	(34)	F L
19	-	Games People Play	Alan Parsons Project	Arista	3		F
20	-	A Little In Love	Cliff Richard	EMI America	5	(15)	L

◆ Bill Haley died. The performer, widely acknowledged as the first rock'n'roll star, had sold over 25 million copies of 'Rock Around The Clock' – the biggest selling single in the rock era.

◆ AOR rock pioneers, REO Speedwagon, whose 'Keep On Loving You' introduced them to the Top 20, replaced John Lennon at the peak of the LP chart with **Hi Infidelity.** The album was on top 15 weeks, selling over seven million copies.

◆ Blondie's transatlantic hit 'Rapture', one of the first rap releases by a white artist, brought rap back to the forefront of pop music.

◆ For the first time in pop music history, one country record replaced another at the top, when Dolly Parton's '9 To 5' dethroned Eddie Rabbitt's 'I Love A Rainy Night'.

UK 1981

APR-JUNE

◆ The first demonstration of the compact disc took place in Europe. The revolutionary digital playback system for music, which utilised laser beam technology, eventually replaced vinyl as the most popular system of carrying recorded sound.

◆ A re-issue of his 1975 recording 'One Day In Your Life', which had previously failed to take Michael Jackson into the US Top 40, gave him his first British chart topper.

◆ Toni Basil's **Word of Mouth** (which included the future No. 1 'Mickey') claimed to be the first album to be simultaneously released on record and video.

◆ The first US shows by Britain's hottest act Adam & The Ants were successful, but American sales were minimal. In the UK their seventh chart entry in nine months, 'Stand And Deliver', came in at No. 1.

April 1981

This Mnth	Prev Mnth	Title	Artist	Label	Wks 20	(US Pos)	
1	6	This Ole House	Shakin' Stevens	Epic	9		
2	-	Making Your Mind Up	Bucks Fizz	RCA	8		F
3	16	Lately	Stevie Wonder	Motown	7	(64)	
4	-	Einstein A Go-Go	Landscape	RCA	7		F L
5	5	Kids In America	Kim Wilde	RAK	8	(25)	F
6	-	Intuition	Linx	Chrysalis	6		
7	-	It's A Love Thing	Whispers	Solar	7	(28)	L
8	-	Chi Mai (Theme From 'The Life And Times Of David Lloyd George')	Ennio Morricone	BBC	8		F L
9	-	Good Thing Going (We've Got A Good Thing Going)	Sugar Minott	RCA	6		F L
10	-	Capstick Comes Home/The Sheffield Grinder	Tony Capstick	Dingles	4		F L
11	-	Night Games	Graham Bonnett	Vertigo	5		F L
12	-	Can You Feel It	Jacksons	Epic	6	(77)	
13	-	D-Days	Hazel O'Connor	Albion	5		
14	8	Four From Toyah E.P.	Toyah	Safari	7		F
15	-	Attention To Me	Nolans	Epic	7		
16	1	Jealous Guy	Roxy Music	EG	7		
17	3	(Do) The Hucklebuck	Coast To Coast	Polydor	8		F L
18	-	Just A Feeling	Bad Manners	Magnet	5		
19	-	Mind Of A Toy	Visage	Polydor	3		
20	-	And The Bands Played On	Saxon	Carrere	4		

May 1981

This Mnth	Prev Mnth	Title	Artist	Label	Wks 20	(US Pos)	
1	-	Stars On 45	Starsound	CBS	8	(1)	F
2	-	Stand And Deliver	Adam & The Ants	CBS	8		
3	-	You Drive Me Crazy	Shakin' Stevens	Epic	8		
4	-	Grey Day	Madness	Stiff	6		
5	8	Chi Mai (Theme From...)	Ennio Morricone	BBC	8		F L
6	2	Making Your Mind Up	Bucks Fizz	RCA	8		F
7	-	Chequered Love	Kim Wilde	Rak	5		
8	-	Ossie's Dream (Spurs Are On Their Way To Wembley)	Tottenham Hotspur F.A. Cup Final Squad	Rockney	4		F
9	-	Swords Of A Thousand Men	Ten Pole Tudor	Stiff	6		F
10	-	Keep On Loving You	REO Speedwagon	Epic	5	(1)	F
11	9	Good Thing Going (We've Got A...)	Sugar Minott	RCA	6		F L
12	12	Can You Feel It	Jacksons	Epic	6	(77)	
13	15	Attention To Me	Nolans	Epic	7		
14	-	Musclebound/Glow	Spandau Ballet	Reformation	5		
15	-	Stray Cat Strut	Stray Cats	Arista	4	(3)	L
16	-	Only Crying	Keith Marshall	Arrival	4		F L
17	11	Night Games	Graham Bonnett	Vertigo	5		F L
18	-	Bette Davis Eyes	Kim Carnes	EMI America	5	(1)	F L
19	-	I Want To Be Free	Toyah	Safari	6		
20	7	It's A Love Thing	Whispers	Solar	7	(28)	L

June 1981

This Mnth	Prev Mnth	Title	Artist	Label	Wks 20	(US Pos)	
1	-	Being With You	Smokey Robinson	Motown	7	(2)	F L
2	-	One Day In Your Life	Michael Jackson	Motown	8	(55)	
3	-	More Than In Love	Kate Robbins & Beyond	RCA	6		F L
4	-	How 'Bout Us	Champaign	CBS	7	(12)	F L
5	2	Stand And Deliver	Adam & The Ants	CBS	8		
6	3	You Drive Me Crazy	Shakin' Stevens	Epic	8		
7	-	Will You	Hazel O'Connor	A&M	5		L
8	-	Going Back To My Roots	Odyssey	RCA	7		
9	-	Funeral Pyre	Jam	Polydor	3		
10	19	I Want To Be Free	Toyah	Safari	6		
11	-	Teddy Bear	Red Sovine	Starday	4	(40)	F L
12	-	All Stood Still	Ultravox	Chrysalis	5		
13	-	Ain't No Stoppin'	Enigma	Creole	5		F
14	1	Stars On 45	Starsound	CBS	8	(1)	F
15	9	Swords Of A Thousand Men	Ten Pole Tudor	Stiff	6		F
16	7	Chequered Love	Kim Wilde	RAK	5		
17	-	Memory	Elaine Paige	Polydor	6		F
18	-	Chariots Of Fire - Titles	Vangelis	Polydor	3	(1)	F L
19	18	Bette Davis Eyes	Kim Carnes	EMI America	5	(1)	F L
20	-	Ghost Town	Specials	2 Tone	8		

April 1981

This Mnth	Prev Mnth	Title	Artist	Label	Wks 20	(UK Pos)	
1	12	Kiss On My List	Daryl Hall & John Oates	RCA	12	(33)	G
2	6	Rapture	Blondie	Chrysalis	12	(5)	G L
3	18	Just The Two Of Us	Grover Washington Jr.	Elektra	12	(34)	F L
4	-	Morning Train (9 To 5)	Sheena Easton	EMI America	9	(3)	F G
5	4	The Best Of Times	Styx	A&M	12	(42)	
6	15	While You See A Chance	Steve Winwood	Island	8	(45)	F
7	1	Woman	John Lennon	Geffen	13	(1)	G
8	-	Angel Of The Morning	Juice Newton	Capitol	11	(43)	F G
9	5	Crying	Don McLean	Millenium	12	(1)	L
10	17	Don't Stand So Close To Me	Police	A&M	7	(1)	
11	2	Keep On Loving You	REO Speedwagon	Epic	13	(7)	F P
12	-	Being With You	Smokey Robinson	Tamla	13	(1)	G
13	-	I Can't Stand It	Eric Clapton	RSO	8		
14	8	Hello Again	Neil Diamond	Capitol	10	(51)	
15	-	Her Town Too	James Taylor & J. D. Souther	Columbia	6		L
16	-	Somebody's Knockin'	Terri Gibbs	MCA	5		F L
17	11	What Kind Of Fool	Barbra Streisand & Barry Gibb	Columbia	7		
18	3	9 To 5	Dolly Parton	RCA	12	(47)	G
19	9	The Winner Takes It All	Abba	Atlantic	11	(1)	L
20	-	Living Inside Myself	Gino Vannelli	Arista	11		L

May 1981

This Mnth	Prev Mnth	Title	Artist	Label	Wks 20	(UK Pos)	
1	12	Being With You	Smokey Robinson	Tamla	13	(1)	G
2	-	Bette Davis Eyes	Kim Carnes	EMI America	16	(10)	G
3	3	Just The Two Of Us	Grover Washington Jr.	Elektra	12	(34)	F L
4	8	Angel Of The Morning	Juice Newton	Capitol	11	(43)	F G
5	-	Take It On The Run	REO Speedwagon	Epic	11	(19)	G
6	20	Living Inside Myself	Gino Vannelli	Arista	11		L
7	4	Morning Train (9 To 5)	Sheena Easton	EMI America	9	(3)	F G
8	-	Sukiyaki	Taste Of Honey	Capitol	11		G L
9	-	Too Much Time On My Hands	Styx	A&M	8		
10	1	Kiss On My List	Daryl Hall & John Oates	RCA	12	(33)	G
11	-	Watching The Wheels	John Lennon	Geffen	6	(30)	
12	-	Stars On 45 (Medley)	Stars On 45	Radio	11	(2)	F G L
13	-	Sweetheart	Franke & The Knockouts	Millennium	8		F L
14	13	I Can't Stand It	Eric Clapton	RSO	8		
15	-	A Woman Needs Love (Just Like You Do)	Ray Parker Jr. & Raydio	Arista	12		
16	2	Rapture	Blondie	Chrysalis	12	(5)	G L
17	-	How 'Bout Us	Champaign	Columbia	6	(5)	F L
18	15	Her Town Too	James Taylor & J. D. Souther	Columbia	6		L
19	6	While You See A Chance	Steve Winwood	Island	8	(45)	F
20	-	America	Neil Diamond	Capitol	10		

June 1981

This Mnth	Prev Mnth	Title	Artist	Label	Wks 20	(UK Pos)	
1	2	Bette Davis Eyes	Kim Carnes	EMI America	16	(10)	G
2	12	Stars On 45 (Medley)	Stars On 45	Radio	11	(2)	F G L
3	8	Sukiyaki	Taste Of Honey	Capitol	11		G L
4	15	A Woman Needs Love (Just Like You Do)	Ray Parker Jr. & Raydio	Arista	12		
5	-	All Those Years Ago	George Harrison	Dark Horse	9	(13)	
6	1	Being With You	Smokey Robinson	Tamla	13	(1)	G
7	20	America	Neil Diamond	Capitol	10		
8	6	Living Inside Myself	Gino Vannelli	Arista	11		L
9	5	Take It On The Run	REO Speedwagon	Epic	11	(19)	G
10	-	The One That You Love	Air Supply	Arista	11		G
11	-	This Little Girl	Gary U.S. Bonds	EMI America	8	(43)	L
12	-	You Make My Dreams	Daryl Hall & John Oates	RCA	10		
13	13	Sweetheart	Franke & The Knockouts	Millennium	8		F L
14	-	I Love You	Climax Blues Band	Warner	6		L
15	-	Jessie's Girl	Rick Springfield	RCA	16	(43)	G
16	-	What Are We Doin' In Love	Dottie West & Kenny Rogers	Liberty	6		F L
17	3	Just The Two Of Us	Grover Washington Jr.	Elektra	12	(34)	F L
18	17	How 'Bout Us	Champaign	Columbia	6	(5)	F L
19	-	Elvira	Oak Ridge Boys	MCA	10		F G
20	-	Theme From 'Greatest American Hero' (Believe It Or Not)	Joey Scarbury	Elektra	14		F G L

◆ A Dutch session group called Starsound in Britain, and known as both as Stars On 45 and Stars On Long Play in America, started a world-wide medley craze with their smash, 'Stars On 45'.

◆ Bob Marley, the world's best known and most successful reggae artist, died of cancer. He was given a states-man's funeral in Jamaica.

▲ Daryl Hall & John Oates, who became the most successful duo in the rock era, scored the first of their five No. 1 singles with 'Kiss On My List'.

◆ 1960s star Jackie DeShannon penned Kim Carnes's nine week chart topper 'Bette Davis Eyes'.

UK 1981 JULY-SEPT

◆ When Soft Cell's revival of the northern soul favourite 'Tainted Love' was re-issued it became Britain's Top Single of 1981. It also went on to spend a record 43 weeks in the US Hot 100.

◆ Meat Loaf's long-awaited album, **Dead Ringer,** was the first LP by an American artist to enter the British chart at No. 1.

◆ The most successful purveyors of 2-Tone music, The Specials, topped the chart with their last single, 'Ghost Town'. It was their seventh Top 10 entry in two years.

◆ The medley craze was at its height; artists scoring in this vein were Tight Fit, Gidea Park, Royal Philharmonic Orchestra and genre pioneers Starsound, who scored a second successive hit. Meanwhile in the USA, a segue single of past hits by The Beach Boys was riding high.

July 1981

This Mnth	Prev Mnth	Title	Artist	Label	Wks 20	(US Pos)	
1	20	Ghost Town	Specials	2 Tone	8		
2	-	Can Can	Bad Manners	Magnet	8		
3	2	One Day In Your Life	Michael Jackson	Motown	8	(55)	
4	-	Body Talk	Imagination	R&B	9		F
5	-	Stars On 45 (Vol 2)	Starsound	CBS	6		
6	8	Going Back To My Roots	Odyssey	RCA	7		
7	-	Wordy Rappinghood	Tom Tom Club	Island	5		F L
8	-	No Woman No Cry	Bob Marley & The Wailers	Island	6		
9	17	Memory	Elaine Paige	Polydor	6		F
10	-	Motorhead Live	Motorhead	Bronze	4		L
11	-	You Might Need Somebody	Randy Crawford	Warner	5		
12	1	Being With You	Smokey Robinson	Motown	7	(2)	F L
13	-	Dancing On The Floor (Hooked On Love)	Third World	CBS	6		L
14	-	Razzamatazz	Quincy Jones	A&M	3		L
15	-	Chant No. 1 (I Don't Need This Pressure On)	Spandau Ballet	Reformation	7		
16	-	Piece Of The Action	Bucks Fizz	RCA	5		
17	-	Lay All Your Love On Me	Abba	Epic	4		
18	3	More Than In Love	Kate Robbins & Beyond	RCA	6		F L
19	-	Sat In Your Lap	Kate Bush	EMI	4		
20	11	Teddy Bear	Red Sovine	Starday	4	(40)	F L

August 1981

This Mnth	Prev Mnth	Title	Artist	Label	Wks 20	(US Pos)	
1	-	Green Door	Shakin' Stevens	Epic	6		
2	-	Hooked On Classics	Royal Philharmonic Orchestra	RCA	7	(10)	F L
3	-	Happy Birthday	Stevie Wonder	Motown	7		
4	15	Chant No. 1 (I Don't Need This Pressure On)	Spandau Ballet	Reformation	7		
5	-	Back To The Sixties	Tight Fit	Jive	6	(89)	F
6	-	Girls On Film	Duran Duran	EMI	6		
7	-	Love Action (I Believe In Love)	Human League	Virgin	7		
8	-	Hold On Tight	Electric Light Orchestra	Jet	9	(10)	
9	1	Ghost Town	Specials	2 Tone	8		
10	-	For Your Eyes Only	Sheena Easton	EMI	5	(4)	
11	-	Japanese Boy	Aneka	Hansa	7		F L
12	-	Walk Right Now	Jacksons	Epic	5	(73)	
13	2	Can Can	Bad Manners	Magnet	8		
14	-	Tainted Love	Soft Cell	Some Bizzare	9	(8)	F
15	-	Caribbean Disco	Lobo	Polydor	5		F L
16	-	Water On Glass/Boys	Kim Wilde	RAK	4		
17	5	Stars On 45 (Vol 2)	Starsound	CBS	6		
18	-	New Life	Depeche Mode	Mute	6		F
19	-	Beach Boy Gold	Gidea Park	Sonet	4		F L
20	13	Dancing On The Floor (Hooked...)	Third World	CBS	6		L

September 1981

This Mnth	Prev Mnth	Title	Artist	Label	Wks 20	(US Pos)	
1	14	Tainted Love	Soft Cell	Some Bizzare	9	(8)	F
2	11	Japanese Boy	Aneka	Hansa	7		F L
3	-	Prince Charming	Adam & The Ants	CBS	7		
4	-	Wired For Sound	Cliff Richard	EMI	6	(71)	
5	8	Hold On Tight	Electric Light Orchestra	Jet	9	(10)	
6	7	Love Action (I Believe In Love)	Human League	Virgin	7		
7	-	Souvenir	Orchestral Manoeuvres In The Dark	Dindisc	6		
8	-	Hands Up (Give Me Your Heart)	Ottawan	Carrere	8		L
9	-	Start Me Up	Rolling Stones	Rolling Stone	4	(2)	
10	-	One In Ten	UB40	Dep International	5		
11	-	She's Got Claws	Gary Numan	Beggars Banquet	4		
12	-	Pretend	Alvin Stardust	Stiff	6		
13	-	Slow Hand	Pointer Sisters	Planet	5	(2)	F
14	-	Abacab	Genesis	Charisma	4	(26)	
15	2	Hooked On Classics	Royal Philharmonic Orchestra	RCA	7	(10)	F L
16	-	Endless Love	Diana Ross & Lionel Richie	Motown	6	(1)	
17	-	Everybody Salsa	Modern Romance	WEA	3		F
18	-	The Thin Wall	Ultravox	Chrysalis	4		
19	15	Caribbean Disco	Lobo	Polydor	5		F L
20	1	Green Door	Shakin' Stevens	Epic	6		

US 1981 JULY-SEPT

July 1981

This Mnth	Prev Mnth	Title	Artist	Label	Wks 20	(UK Pos)	
1	1	Bette Davis Eyes	Kim Carnes	EMI America	16	(10)	G
2	10	The One That You Love	Air Supply	Arista	11		G
3	15	Jessie's Girl	Rick Springfield	RCA	16	(43)	G
4	5	All Those Years Ago	George Harrison	Dark Horse	9	(13)	
5	19	Elvira	Oak Ridge Boys	MCA	10		F G
6	12	You Make My Dreams	Daryl Hall & John Oates	RCA	10		
7	20	Theme From 'Greatest American Hero' (Believe It Or Not)	Joey Scarbury	Elektra	14		F G L
8	-	I Don't Need You	Kenny Rogers	Liberty	11		
9	2	Stars On 45 (Medley)	Stars On 45	Radio	11	(2)	F G L
10	-	Slow Hand	Pointer Sisters	Planet	13	(10)	G
11	4	A Woman Needs Love (Just Like...)	Ray Parker Jr. & Raydio	Arista	12		
12	-	Hearts	Marty Balin	EMI America	11		F L
13	-	The Boy From New York City	Manhattan Transfer	Atlantic	10		F L
14	-	Gemini Dream	Moody Blues	Threshold	6		
15	11	This Little Girl	Gary U.S. Bonds	EMI America	8	(43)	L
16	7	America	Neil Diamond	Capitol	10		
17	3	Sukiyaki	Taste Of Honey	Capitol	11		G L
18	-	Queen Of Hearts	Juice Newton	Capitol	13		G
19	-	Winning	Santana	Columbia	3		
20	-	Modern Girl	Sheena Easton	EMI America	3	(8)	

August 1981

This Mnth	Prev Mnth	Title	Artist	Label	Wks 20	(UK Pos)	
1	7	Theme From 'Greatest American...'	Joey Scarbury	Elektra	14		F G L
2	3	Jessie's Girl	Rick Springfield	RCA	16	(43)	G
3	-	Endless Love	Diana Ross & Lionel Richie	Motown	15	(7)	G
4	10	Slow Hand	Pointer Sisters	Planet	13	(10)	G
5	8	I Don't Need You	Kenny Rogers	Liberty	11		
6	13	The Boy From New York City	Manhattan Transfer	Atlantic	10		F L
7	5	Elvira	Oak Ridge Boys	MCA	10		F G
8	18	Queen Of Hearts	Juice Newton	Capitol	13		G
9	-	(There's) No Gettin' Over Me	Ronnie Milsap	RCA	11		
10	12	Hearts	Marty Balin	EMI America	11		F L
11	-	Lady You Bring Me Up	Commodores	Motown	10	(56)	
12	2	The One That You Love	Air Supply	Arista	11		G
13	-	Stop Draggin' My Heart Around	Stevie Nicks With Tom Petty & The Heartbreakers	Modern	10	(50)	F
14	-	Who's Crying Now	Journey	Columbia	11	(46)	
15	1	Bette Davis Eyes	Kim Carnes	EMI America	16	(10)	G
16	-	Urgent	Foreigner	Atlantic	11	(54)	
17	-	It's Now Or Never	John Schneider	Scotti Bros	5		F L
18	-	Touch Me When We're Dancing	Carpenters	A&M	5		L
19	6	You Make My Dreams	Daryl Hall & John Oates	RCA	10		
20	-	Time	Alan Parsons Project	Arista	6		

September 1981

This Mnth	Prev Mnth	Title	Artist	Label	Wks 20	(UK Pos)	
1	3	Endless Love	Diana Ross & Lionel Richie	Motown	15	(7)	G
2	13	Stop Draggin' My Heart Around	S. Nicks/T. Petty/Heartbreakers	Modern	10	(50)	F
3	8	Queen Of Hearts	Juice Newton	Capitol	13		G
4	16	Urgent	Foreigner	Atlantic	11	(54)	
5	9	(There's) No Gettin' Over Me	Ronnie Milsap	RCA	11		
6	4	Slow Hand	Pointer Sisters	Planet	13	(10)	G
7	14	Who's Crying Now	Journey	Columbia	11	(46)	
8	11	Lady You Bring Me Up	Commodores	Motown	10	(56)	
9	-	Step By Step	Eddie Rabbitt	Elektra	10		
10	-	Arthur's Theme (Best That You Can Do)	Christopher Cross	Warner	13	(7)	G
11	2	Jessie's Girl	Rick Springfield	RCA	16	(43)	G
12	-	Hold On Tight	Electric Light Orchestra	Jet	7	(4)	
13	1	Theme From 'Greatest American...'	Joey Scarbury	Elektra	14		F G L
14	-	Start Me Up	Rolling Stones	Rolling Stone	13	(7)	
15	-	Cool Love	Pablo Cruise	A&M	6		
16	-	The Beach Boys Medley	Beach Boys	Capitol	5	(47)	
17	-	The Breakup Song (They Don't Write 'Em)	Greg Kihn Band	Beserkley	5		F
18	5	I Don't Need You	Kenny Rogers	Liberty	11		
19	-	Really Wanna Know You	Gary Wright	Warner	3		L
20	-	For Your Eyes Only	Sheena Easton	Liberty	9	(8)	

◆ Scotland's Sheena Easton, the recent subject of a UK TV documentary about a singer trying to make the big time, had four US Top 20 singles in 1981 and won the Grammy for Best New Artist.

▲ Lionel Richie was the first person to produce the top pop, R&B and country records in the same week. Also, his duet with Diana Ross (above), 'Endless Love', a nine week chart topper, became Motown's biggest ever seller.

◆ Newsworthy shows included Simon & Garfunkel's re-union in front of 500,000 in Central Park, and a 36-city tour by The Jacksons, which grossed $5.5 million.

231

UK 1981 OCT-DEC

◆ The Rolling Stones' American tour grossed a record $35 million, with each Stone supposedly pocketing $4 million.

▲ The Human League's 'Don't You Want Me' sold almost 1.5 million in the UK alone. Six months later it topped the American chart and opened the doors there to other British synth bands. Incidentally, the group's **Dare** album also reached No. 1 in Britain.

◆ Early rock songs enjoying a return to favour included 'Why Do Fools Fall In Love' by Diana Ross, 'It's My Party' by Dave Stewart & Barbara Gaskin and Cliff Richard's revival of 'Daddy's Home'.

October 1981

This Mnth	Prev Mnth	Title	Artist	Label	Wks 20	(US Pos)	
1	-	The Birdie Song (Birdie Dance)	Tweets	PRT	8		F L
2	-	It's My Party	Dave Stewart & Barbara Gaskin	Broken	8	(72)	L
3	-	Under Your Thumb	Godley & Creme	Polydor	6		F
4	3	Prince Charming	Adam & The Ants	CBS	7		
5	8	Hands Up (Give Me Your Heart)	Ottawan	Carrere	8		L
6	-	Thunder In Mountains	Toyah	Safari	5		
7	-	Invisible Sun	Police	A&M	4		
8	-	Just Can't Get Enough	Depeche Mode	Mute	5		
9	-	Shut Up	Madness	Stiff	5		
10	-	Happy Birthday	Altered Images	Epic	7		F
11	-	O Superman	Laurie Anderson	Warner	4		F L
12	-	Open Your Heart	Human League	Virgin	5		
13	12	Pretend	Alvin Stardust	Stiff	6		
14	16	Endless Love	Diana Ross & Lionel Richie	Motown	6	(1)	
15	-	A Good Year For The Roses	Elvis Costello	F. Beat	6		L
16	-	It's Raining	Shakin' Stevens	Epic	5		
17	-	Absolute Beginners	Jam	Polydor	4		
18	7	Souvenir	Orchestral Manoeuvres In The Dark	Dindisc	6		
19	-	Walkin' In The Sunshine	Bad Manners	Magnet	5		
20	1	Tainted Love	Soft Cell	Some Bizzare	9	(8)	F

November 1981

This Mnth	Prev Mnth	Title	Artist	Label	Wks 20	(US Pos)	
1	-	Every Little Thing She Does Is Magic	Police	A&M	6	(3)	
2	-	Joan Of Arc	Orchestral Manoeuvres In The Dark	Dindisc	5		
3	-	When She Was My Girl	Four Tops	Casablanca	5	(11)	
4	-	Under Pressure	Queen & David Bowie	EMI	6	(29)	
5	10	Happy Birthday	Altered Images	Epic	7		F
6	-	Begin The Beguine (Volver A Empezar)	Julio Iglesias	CBS	8		F
7	-	Labelled With Love	Squeeze	A&M	6		
8	-	Favourite Shirts (Boy Meets Girl)	Haircut 100	Arista	5		F
9	-	Tonight I'm Yours (Don't Hurt Me)	Rod Stewart	Riva	6	(20)	
10	2	It's My Party	Dave Stewart & Barbara Gaskin	Broken	8	(72)	L
11	-	Physical	Olivia Newton-John	EMI	6	(1)	
12	-	Let's Groove	Earth, Wind & Fire	CBS	6	(3)	L
13	15	A Good Year For The Roses	Elvis Costello	F. Beat	6		L
14	-	Bed Sitter	Soft Cell	Some Bizzare	7		
15	-	I Go To Sleep	Pretenders	Real	5		
16	-	Hold Me	B.A. Robertson & Maggie Bell	Swansong	5		L
17	-	When You Were Sweet Sixteen	Fureys & Davey Arthur	Ritz	4		F L
18	1	The Birdie Song (Birdie Dance)	Tweets	PRT	8		F L
19	12	Open Your Heart	Human League	Virgin	5		
20	12	Why Do Fools Fall In Love	Diana Ross	Capitol	8	(7)	

December 1981

This Mnth	Prev Mnth	Title	Artist	Label	Wks 20	(US Pos)	
1	-	Don't You Want Me	Human League	Virgin	9	(1)	G
2	-	Daddy's Home	Cliff Richard	EMI	8	(23)	
3	6	Begin The Beguine (Volver A...)	Julio Iglesias	CBS	8		F
4	20	Why Do Fools Fall In Love	Diana Ross	Capitol	8	(7)	
5	14	Bed Sitter	Soft Cell	Some Bizzare	7		
6	-	One Of Us	Abba	Epic	7		L
7	-	Ant Rap	Adam & The Ants	CBS	7		
8	-	It Must Be Love	Madness	Stiff	7	(33)	
9	12	Let's Groove	Earth, Wind & Fire	CBS	6	(3)	L
10	-	Wedding Bells	Godley & Creme	Polydor	6		
11	4	Under Pressure	Queen & David Bowie	EMI	6	(29)	
12	-	Land Of Make Believe	Bucks Fizz	RCA	10		
13	15	I Go To Sleep	Pretenders	Real	5		
14	-	Rock 'n' Roll	Status Quo	Vertigo	6		
15	-	Cambodia	Kim Wilde	RAK	6		
16	-	Ay Ay Ay Ay Moosey	Modern Romance	WEA	4		
17	-	Spirits In The Material World	Police	A&M	5	(11)	
18	-	Mirror Mirror (Mon Amour)	Dollar	WEA	8		
19	-	Four More From Toyah E.P.	Toyah	Safari	2		L
20	8	Favourite Shirts (Boy Meets Girl)	Haircut 100	Arista	5		F

232

US 1981 OCT-DEC

◆ In 1981, the CD was first demonstrated, home video games took off and home taping increased. Also, MTV first appeared on the screen, Top 40 radio audiences decreased, and Sony sold 1.5 million of their new portable Walkman cassette players.

◆ Several major record labels upped the price of singles to $1.99 (30 months earlier they had been just $1.29).

◆ Fleetwood Mac's Stevie Nicks and Lindsey Buckingham (the pair had earlier appeared together in Fritz and Buckingham Nicks) scored simultaneous solo hits with 'Leather And Lace' and 'Trouble'.

◆ In November a record three Australian acts were in the Top 10: Little River Band, Air Supply and Rick Springfield, as Australian-raised Olivia Newton-John headed for a 10-week residency at the top with 'Physical'.

October 1981

This Mnth	Prev Mnth	Title	Artist	Label	Wks 20	(UK Pos)	
1	10	Arthur's Theme (Best That You Can Do)	Christopher Cross	Warner	13	(7)	G
2	1	Endless Love	Diana Ross & Lionel Richie	Motown	15	(7)	G
3	14	Start Me Up	Rolling Stones	Rolling Stone	13	(7)	
4	20	For Your Eyes Only	Sheena Easton	Liberty	9	(8)	
5	9	Step By Step	Eddie Rabbitt	Elektra	10		
6	-	Private Eyes	Daryl Hall & John Oates	RCA	12	(32)	G
7	2	Stop Draggin' My Heart Around	Stevie Nicks With Tom Petty & The Heartbreakers	Modern	10	(50)	F
8	7	Who's Crying Now	Journey	Columbia	11	(46)	
9	-	The Night Owls	Little River Band	Capitol	11		
10	-	Hard To Say	Dan Fogelberg	Full Moon	7		
11	-	I've Done Everything For You	Rick Springfield	RCA	7		
12	4	Urgent	Foreigner	Atlantic	11	(54)	
13	-	Tryin' To Live My Life Without You	Bob Seger & Silver Bullet Band	Capitol	7		
14	12	Hold On Tight	Electric Light Orchestra	Jet	7	(4)	
15	-	Share Your Love	Kenny Rogers	Liberty	6		
16	3	Queen Of Hearts	Juice Newton	Capitol	13		G
17	-	When She Was My Girl	Four Tops	Casablanca	6	(3)	L
18	5	(There's) No Gettin' Over Me	Ronnie Milsap	RCA	11		
19	-	Here I Am (Just When You Thought I Was Over You)	Air Supply	Arista	9		
20	-	Super Freak (Pt. 1)	Rick James	Gordy	4		L

November 1981

This Mnth	Prev Mnth	Title	Artist	Label	Wks 20	(UK Pos)	
1	6	Private Eyes	Daryl Hall & John Oates	RCA	12	(32)	G
2	3	Start Me Up	Rolling Stones	Rolling Stone	13	(7)	
3	-	Physical	Olivia Newton-John	MCA	17	(7)	P
4	-	Waiting For A Girl Like You	Foreigner	Atlantic	16	(8)	G
5	13	Tryin' To Live My Life Without You	Bob Seger & Silver Bullet Band	Capitol	7		
6	19	Here I Am (Just When You...)	Air Supply	Arista	9		
7	1	Arthur's Theme (Best That You...)	Christopher Cross	Warner	13	(7)	G
8	9	The Night Owls	Little River Band	Capitol	11		
9	-	Every Little Thing She Does Is Magic	Police	A&M	9	(1)	
10	-	Oh No	Commodores	Motown	10	(44)	
11	-	The Theme From Hill Street Blues	Mike Post Feat. Larry Carlton	Elektra	6	(25)	L
12	11	I've Done Everything For You	Rick Springfield	RCA	7		
13	-	Why Do Fools Fall In Love	Diana Ross	RCA	9	(4)	
14	17	When She Was My Girl	Four Tops	Casablanca	6	(3)	L
15	4	For Your Eyes Only	Sheena Easton	Liberty	9	(8)	
16	-	Young Turks	Rod Stewart	Warner	10	(11)	
17	10	Hard To Say	Dan Fogelberg	Full Moon	7		
18	-	The Old Songs	Barry Manilow	Arista	5	(48)	
19	-	Let's Groove	Earth, Wind & Fire	Arc	12	(3)	G
20	-	We're In This Love Together	Al Jarreau	Warner	7	(55)	F L

December 1981

This Mnth	Prev Mnth	Title	Artist	Label	Wks 20	(UK Pos)	
1	3	Physical	Olivia Newton-John	MCA	17	(7)	G
2	4	Waiting For A Girl Like You	Foreigner	Atlantic	16	(8)	G
3	19	Let's Groove	Earth, Wind & Fire	Arc	12	(3)	G
4	16	Young Turks	Rod Stewart	Warner	10	(11)	
5	10	Oh No	Commodores	Motown	10	(44)	
6	13	Why Do Fools Fall In Love	Diana Ross	RCA	9	(4)	
7	-	Harden My Heart	Quarterflash	Geffen	15	(49)	F
8	9	Every Little Thing She Does Is Magic	Police	A&M	9	(1)	
9	-	Don't Stop Believing	Journey	Columbia	7	(62)	
10	-	I Can't Go For That (No Can Do)	Daryl Hall & John Oates	RCA	15	(8)	G
11	-	Leather And Lace	Stevie Nicks	Modern	12		
12	-	Trouble	Lindsey Buckingham	Asylum	10	(31)	F L
13	6	Here I Am (Just When You...)	Air Supply	Arista	9		
14	-	Yesterday's Songs	Neil Diamond	Columbia	7		
15	-	Comin' In And Out Of Your Life	Barbra Streisand	Columbia	10	(66)	L
16	1	Private Eyes	Daryl Hall & John Oates	RCA	12	(32)	G
17	-	Turn Your Love Around	George Benson	Warner	11	(29)	L
18	-	The Sweetest Thing (I've Ever Known)	Juice Newton	Capitol	13		
19	2	Start Me Up	Rolling Stones	Rolling Stone	13	(7)	
20	-	Centerfold	J. Geils Band	EMI America	15	(3)	G

UK 1982 JAN-MAR

◆ Retro rock'n'roller Shakin' Stevens scored his third No. 1 with 'Oh Julie' (covered in America by Barry Manilow). The Jam had their third chart topping single with 'Town Called Malice' and their only No. 1 LP, **The Gift**.

▲ UB40's new record deal with Dep International was described as "The best since Paul McCartney signed with Columbia".

◆ Few pundits at the time would have prophesied that Bananarama, who made their chart debut alongside The Specials' off-shoot Fun Boy Three, would go on to amass more UK and US hits than any other female British group.

January 1982

This Mnth	Prev Mnth	Title	Artist	Label	Wks 20	(US Pos)	
1	12	Land Of Make Believe	Bucks Fizz	RCA	10		
2	1	Don't You Want Me	Human League	Virgin	9	(1)	G
3	-	Get Down On It	Kool & The Gang	De-Lite	7	(10)	
4	18	Mirror Mirror (Mon Amour)	Dollar	WEA	8		
5	-	I'll Find My Way Home	Jon & Vangelis	Polydor	8	(51)	L
6	7	Ant Rap	Adam & The Ants	CBS	7		
7	6	One Of Us	Abba	Epic	7		L
8	8	It Must Be Love	Madness	Stiff	7	(33)	
9	-	The Model/Computer Love	Kraftwerk	EMI	7		
10	-	Oh Julie	Shakin' Stevens	Epic	7		
11	-	I Could Be Happy	Altered Images	Epic	7		
12	-	Waiting For A Girl Like You	Foreigner	Atlantic	8	(2)	F
13	2	Daddy's Home	Cliff Richard	EMI	8	(23)	
14	-	Being Boiled	Human League	Virgin	5		
15	10	Wedding Bells	Godley & Creme	Polydor	6		
16	14	Rock 'n' Roll	Status Quo	Vertigo	6		
17	-	Dead Ringer For Love	Meat Loaf	Epic	6		
18	-	Young Turks	Rod Stewart	Riva	4	(5)	
19	-	Golden Brown	Stranglers	Liberty	7		
20	17	Spirits In The Material World	Police	A&M	5	(11)	

February 1982

This Mnth	Prev Mnth	Title	Artist	Label	Wks 20	(US Pos)	
1	19	Golden Brown	Stranglers	Liberty	7		
2	9	The Model/Computer Love	Kraftwerk	EMI	7		
3	-	Maid Of Orleans (The Waltz Joan Of Arc)	Orchestral Manoeuvres In The Dark	Dindisc	7		
4	-	Town Called Malice/Precious	Jam	Polydor	6		
5	10	Oh Julie	Shakin' Stevens	Epic	7		
6	17	Dead Ringer For Love	Meat Loaf	Epic	6		
7	-	Arthur's Theme (Best That You Can Do)	Christopher Cross	Warner	6	(1)	F L
8	-	The Lion Sleeps Tonight	Tight Fit	Jive	9		
9	-	Say Hello Wave Goodbye	Soft Cell	Some Bizzare	6		
10	-	Love Plus One	Haircut 100	Arista	7	(37)	
11	-	I Can't Go For That (No Can Do)	Daryl Hall & John Oates	RCA	5	(1)	F
12	1	Land Of Make Believe	Bucks Fizz	RCA	10		
13	-	Drowning In Berlin	Mobiles	Rialto	5		F L
14	-	Senses Working Overtime	XTC	Virgin	5		L
15	-	Easier Said Than Done	Shakatak	Polydor	4		F
16	-	Centrefold	J. Geils Band	EMI America	6	(1)	F L
17	3	Get Down On It	Kool & The Gang	De-Lite	7	(10)	
18	14	Bein' Boiled	Human League	Virgin	5		
19	-	Let's Get It Up	AC/DC	Atlantic	2	(44)	
20	12	Waiting For A Girl Like You	Foreigner	Atlantic	8	(2)	F

March 1982

This Mnth	Prev Mnth	Title	Artist	Label	Wks 20	(US Pos)	
1	8	The Lion Sleeps Tonight	Tight Fit	Jive	9		
2	-	Mickey	Toni Basil	Radialchoice	6	(1)	F L
3	10	Love Plus One	Haircut 100	Arista	7	(37)	
4	-	It Ain't What You Do It's The Way That You Do It	Fun Boy Three & Bananarama	Chrysalis	5		
5	-	Seven Tears	Goombay Dance Band	Epic	7		F L
6	16	Centrefold	J. Geils Band	EMI America	6	(1)	F L
7	-	Poison Arrow	ABC	Neutron	6	(25)	
8	-	See You	Depeche Mode	Mute	5		
9	-	Go Wild In The Country	Bow Wow Wow	RCA	5		F
10	-	Run To The Hills	Iron Maiden	EMI	5		F
11	-	Classic	Adrian Gurvitz	RAK	5		F L
12	-	Just An Illusion	Imagination	R&B	7		
13	4	Town Called Malice/Precious	Jam	Polydor	6		
14	-	Quiereme Mucho (Yours)	Julio Iglesias	CBS	4		
15	-	Cardiac Arrest	Madness	Stiff	4		
16	-	Layla	Derek & The Dominoes	RSO	5		F L
17	9	Say Hello Wave Goodbye	Soft Cell	Some Bizzare	6		
18	-	Party Fears Two	Associates	Associates	3		F
19	-	Deutscher Girls	Adam & The Ants	Ego	4		
20	3	Maid Of Orleans (The Waltz Joan Of Arc)	Orchestral Manoeuvres In The Dark	Dindisc	7		

January 1982

This Mnth	Prev Mnth	Title	Artist	Label	Wks 20	(UK Pos)	
1	1	Physical	Olivia Newton-John	MCA	17	(7)	P
2	2	Waiting For A Girl Like You	Foreigner	Atlantic	16	(8)	G
3	10	I Can't Go For That (No Can Do)	Daryl Hall & John Oates	RCA	15	(8)	G
4	3	Let's Groove	Earth, Wind & Fire	Arc	12	(3)	G
5	7	Harden My Heart	Quarterflash	Geffen	15	(49)	F
6	20	Centerfold	J. Geils Band	EMI America	15	(3)	G
7	11	Leather And Lace	Stevie Nicks	Modern	12		
8	17	Turn Your Love Around	George Benson	Warner	11	(29)	L
9	18	The Sweetest Thing (I've Ever Known)	Juice Newton	Capitol	13		
10	12	Trouble	Lindsey Buckingham	Asylum	10	(31)	F L
11	15	Comin' In And Out Of Your Life	Barbra Streisand	Columbia	10	(66)	L
12	-	Hooked On Classics	Royal Philharmonic Orchestra	RCA	8	(2)	F L
13	4	Young Turks	Rod Stewart	Warner	10	(11)	
14		Cool Night	Paul Davis	Arista	9		
15	6	Why Do Fools Fall In Love	Diana Ross	RCA	9	(4)	
16	14	Yesterday's Songs	Neil Diamond	Columbia	7		
17	-	Someone Could Lose A Heart Tonight	Eddie Rabbitt	Elektra	4		
18	-	Shake It Up	Cars	Elektra	11		
19	-	Waiting On A Friend	Rolling Stones	Rolling Stone	7	(50)	
20	9	Don't Stop Believing	Journey	Columbia	7	(62)	

February 1982

This Mnth	Prev Mnth	Title	Artist	Label	Wks 20	(UK Pos)	
1	6	Centerfold	J. Geils Band	EMI America	15	(3)	G
2	3	I Can't Go For That (No Can Do)	Daryl Hall & John Oates	RCA	15	(8)	G
3	5	Harden My Heart	Quarterflash	Geffen	15	(49)	F
4	18	Shake It Up	Cars	Elektra	11		
5	-	Open Arms	Journey	Columbia	11		
6	9	The Sweetest Thing (I've Ever Known)	Juice Newton	Capitol	13		
7	-	Sweet Dreams	Air Supply	Arista	11		
8	1	Physical	Olivia Newton-John	MCA	17	(7)	P
9	8	Turn Your Love Around	George Benson	Warner	11	(29)	L
10	-	Leader Of The Band	Dan Fogelberg	Full Moon	10		
11	-	That Girl	Stevie Wonder	Tamla	9	(39)	
12	-	Take It Easy On Me	Little River Band	Capitol	9		
13	2	Waiting For A Girl Like You	Foreigner	Atlantic	16	(8)	G
14	19	Waiting On A Friend	Rolling Stones	Rolling Stone	7	(50)	
15	7	Leather And Lace	Stevie Nicks	Modern	12		
16	14	Cool Night	Paul Davis	Arista	9		
17	-	Mirror Mirror	Diana Ross	RCA	6	(36)	
18	-	You Could Have Been With Me	Sheena Easton	EMI America	5	(54)	
19	12	Hooked On Classics	Royal Philharmonic Orchestra	RCA	8	(2)	F L
20	-	I Love Rock 'n' Roll	Joan Jett & The Blackhearts	Boardwalk	14	(4)	F G

March 1982

This Mnth	Prev Mnth	Title	Artist	Label	Wks 20	(UK Pos)	
1	20	I Love Rock 'n' Roll	Joan Jett & The Blackhearts	Boardwalk	14	(4)	F G
2	5	Open Arms	Journey	Columbia	11		
3	1	Centerfold	J. Geils Band	EMI America	15	(3)	G
4	11	That Girl	Stevie Wonder	Tamla	9	(39)	
5	7	Sweet Dreams	Air Supply	Arista	11		
6	-	We Got The Beat	Go-Go's	IRS	12		G
7	4	Shake It Up	Cars	Elektra	11		
8	17	Mirror Mirror	Diana Ross	RCA	6	(36)	
9	-	Pac-Man Fever	Buckner & Garcia	Columbia	7		F G L
10	-	Make A Move On Me	Olivia Newton-John	MCA	8	(43)	
11	10	Leader Of The Band	Dan Fogelberg	Full Moon	10		
12	-	Bobbie Sue	Oak Ridge Boys	MCA	4		L
13	-	Spirits In The Material World	Police	A&M	5	(12)	
14	12	Take It Easy On Me	Little River Band	Capitol	9		
15	-	Key Largo	Bertie Higgins	Kat Family	10		F L
16	-	Chariots Of Fire - Titles	Vangelis	Polydor	12	(12)	F L
17	-	Through The Years	Kenny Rogers	Liberty	5		
18	2	I Can't Go For That (No Can Do)	Daryl Hall & John Oates	RCA	15	(8)	G
19	-	Freeze-Frame	J. Geils Band	EMI America	10	(27)	G L
20	-	Should I Do It	Pointer Sisters	Planet	5	(50)	

◆ Anglo-American rockers Foreigner scored their first British Top 10 hit with, 'Waiting For A Girl Like You'. This single, their 10th major US hit, spent a record 10 weeks at No. 2 in the USA. It came from the album **4**, which spent 10 weeks at No. 1.

◆ Oddly, two top transatlantic hits had been originally recorded unsuccessfully on producer Mickie Most's RAK label; America's No. 1 'I Love Rock 'n' Roll' by Joan Jett (first released by The Arrows) and 'Mickey' by Toni Basil (previously by Racey).

◆ With a decade of hits behind them, The Doobie Brothers decided to go their separate ways – their farewell tour was recorded for a live album.

◆ Soul star Teddy Pendergrass (ex-lead singer of Harold Melvin & The Blue Notes) was left partially paralysed after an auto accident.

UK 1982 APR-JUNE

▲ In their homeland, British supergroup Asia's eponymous album, which headed the US chart for nine weeks, failed to make the Top 10.

◆ Adam & The Ants split, and Adam's first solo effort, 'Goody Two Shoes', topped the UK listings and became his first US Top 20 entry.

◆ The Rolling Stones made their first British appearance in six years. Their two shows at Wembley attracted 140,000 fans.

◆ The UK's 500th No. 1 was Eurovision Song Contest winner 'A Little Peace' by 17-year-old German Nicole (Hohloch). It entered at No. 8 – a record for a new artist.

April 1982

This Mnth	Prev Mnth	Title	Artist	Label	Wks 20	(US Pos)
1	-	My Camera Never Lies	Bucks Fizz	RCA	5	
2	-	Ain't No Pleasing You	Chas & Dave	Rockney	6	
3	5	Seven Tears	Goombay Dance Band	Epic	7	F L
4	12	Just An Illusion	Imagination	R&B	7	
5	-	Give Me Back My Heart	Dollar	WEA	6	
6	-	Ghosts	Japan	Virgin	5	
7	-	More Than This	Roxy Music	EG	5	
8	-	Ebony And Ivory	Paul McCartney & Stevie Wonder	Parlophone	7	(1)
9	16	Layla	Derek & The Dominoes	RSO	5	F L
10	14	Quiereme Mucho (Yours)	Julio Iglesias	CBS	4	
11	-	Papa's Got A Brand New Pigbag	Pigbag	Y	5	F L
12	-	Have You Ever Been In Love	Leo Sayer	Chrysalis	3	
13	-	Dear John	Status Quo	Vertigo	4	
14	-	Is It A Dream	Classix Nouveaux	Liberty	3	F L
15	-	Night Birds	Shakatak	Polydor	4	
16	-	One Step Further	Bardo	Epic	4	F L
17	-	See Those Eyes	Altered Images	Epic	4	
18	7	Poison Arrow	ABC	Neutron	6	(25)
19	-	Damned Don't Cry	Visage	Polydor	3	
20	-	Blue Eyes	Elton John	Rocket	4	(12)

May 1982

This Mnth	Prev Mnth	Title	Artist	Label	Wks 20	(US Pos)
1	-	I Won't Let You Down	PhD	WEA	7	F L
2	8	Ebony And Ivory	Paul McCartney & Stevie Wonder	Parlophone	7	(1)
3	-	A Little Peace	Nicole	CBS	6	F L
4	-	I Love Rock 'n' Roll	Joan Jett & The Blackhearts	Epic	6	(1) F L
5	-	Only You	Yazoo	Mute	7	(67) F
6	-	Really Saying Something	Bananarama With Funboy Three	Deram	5	
7	-	This Time (We'll Get It Right)/ England We'll Fly The Flag	England World Cup Squad	England	5	
8	-	We Have A Dream	Scotland World Cup Squad	WEA	5	L
9	-	Girl Crazy	Hot Chocolate	RAK	6	
10	11	Papa's Got A Brand New Pigbag	Pigbag	Y	5	F L
11	-	Goody Two Shoes	Adam Ant	CBS	7	(12)
12	16	One Step Further	Bardo	Epic	4	F L
13	-	Forget Me Nots	Patrice Rushen	Elektra	5	(23) F L
14	-	House Of Fun	Madness	Stiff	6	
15	-	Fantasy Island	Tight Fit	Jive	7	L
16	-	I Can Make You Feel Good	Shalamar	Solar	5	
17	-	Fantastic Day	Haircut 100	Arista	5	
18	-	Shirley	Shakin' Stevens	Epic	2	
19	-	The Look Of Love (Part 1)	ABC	Neutron	7	(18)
20	-	Instinction	Spandau Ballet	Chrysalis	4	

June 1982

This Mnth	Prev Mnth	Title	Artist	Label	Wks 20	(US Pos)
1	11	Goody Two Shoes	Adam Ant	CBS	7	(12)
2	-	Torch	Soft Cell	Some Bizzare	6	
3	19	The Look Of Love (Part 1)	ABC	Neutron	7	(18)
4	14	House Of Fun	Madness	Stiff	6	
5	-	Hungry Like The Wolf	Duran Duran	EMI	8	(3)
6	-	I've Never Been To Me	Charlene	Motown	6	(3) F L
7	15	Fantasy Island	Tight Fit	Jive	7	L
8	-	Mama Used To Say	Junior	Mercury	7	(30) F
9	5	Only You	Yazoo	Mute	7	(67) F
10	-	I'm A Wonderful Thing (Baby)	Kid Creole & The Coconuts	Ze	5	F
11	-	I Want Candy	Bow Wow Wow	RCA	4	(62) L
12	-	Work That Body	Diana Ross	Capitol	5	(44)
13	-	3 X 3 (E.P.)	Genesis	Charisma	4	(32)
14	-	We Take Mystery (To Bed)	Gary Numan	Beggars Banquet	2	
15	-	Island Of Lost Souls	Blondie	Chrysalis	4	(37)
16	-	Club Country	Associates	Associates	4	
17	13	Forget Me Nots	Patrice Rushen	Elektra	5	(23) F L
18	1	I Won't Let You Down	PhD	WEA	7	F L
19	-	Inside Out	Odyssey	RCA	7	L
20	-	Do I Do	Stevie Wonder	Motown	3	(13)

April 1982

This Mnth	Prev Mnth	Title	Artist	Label	Wks 20	(UK Pos)	
1	1	I Love Rock 'n' Roll	Joan Jett & The Blackhearts	Boardwalk	14	(4)	F G
2	6	We Got The Beat	Go-Go's	IRS	12		G
3	16	Chariots Of Fire - Titles	Vangelis	Polydor	12	(12)	F L
4	19	Freeze-Frame	J. Geils Band	EMI America	10	(27)	G L
5	-	Don't Talk To Strangers	Rick Springfield	RCA	14		
6	10	Make A Move On Me	Olivia Newton-John	MCA	8	(43)	
7	15	Key Largo	Bertie Higgins	Kat Family	10		F L
8	-	Do You Believe In Love	Huey Lewis & The News	Chrysalis	7	(9)	F
9	2	Open Arms	Journey	Columbia	11		
10	4	That Girl	Stevie Wonder	Tamla	9	(39)	
11	-	Edge Of Seventeen (Just Like The White Winged Dove)	Stevie Nicks	Modern	6		
12	-	(Oh) Pretty Woman	Van Halen	Warner	6		
13	-	'65 Love Affair	Paul Davis	Arista	11		L
14	9	Pac-Man Fever	Buckner & Garcia	Columbia	7		F G L
15	-	867-5309/Jenny	Tommy Tutone	Columbia	10		F L
16	-	One Hundred Ways	Quincy Jones/James Ingram	A&M	3		L
17	20	Should I Do It	Pointer Sisters	Planet	5	(50)	
18	-	Ebony And Ivory	Paul McCartney & Stevie Wonder	Columbia	12	(1)	G
19	5	Sweet Dreams	Air Supply	Arista	11		
20	-	Find Another Fool	Quarterflash	Geffen	4		

May 1982

This Mnth	Prev Mnth	Title	Artist	Label	Wks 20	(UK Pos)	
1	18	Ebony And Ivory	Paul McCartney & Stevie Wonder	Columbia	12	(1)	G
2	5	Don't Talk To Strangers	Rick Springfield	RCA	14		
3	15	867-5309/Jenny	Tommy Tutone	Columbia	10		F L
4	-	I've Never Been To Me	Charlene	Motown	9	(1)	F G L
5	3	Chariots Of Fire	Vangelis	Polydor	12	(12)	F L
6	13	'65 Love Affair	Paul Davis	Arista	11		L
7	1	I Love Rock 'n' Roll	Joan Jett & The Blackhearts	Boardwalk	14	(4)	F G
8	-	The Other Woman	Ray Parker Jr.	Arista	10		
9	-	Did It In A Minute	Daryl Hall & John Oates	RCA	8		
10	4	Freeze-Frame	J. Geils Band	EMI America	10	(27)	G L
11	-	Get Down On It	Kool & The Gang	De-Lite	7	(3)	
12	-	Always On My Mind	Willie Nelson	Columbia	11	(49)	G
13	2	We Got The Beat	Go-Go's	IRS	12		G
14	-	Don't You Want Me	Human League	A&M	15	(1)	F G
15	-	The Beatles Movie Medley	Beatles	Capitol	6	(10)	
16	-	Heat Of The Moment	Asia	Geffen	11	(46)	F
17	-	Empty Garden (Hey Hey Johnny)	Elton John	Geffen	6	(51)	
18	8	Do You Believe In Love	Huey Lewis & The News	Chrysalis	7	(9)	F
19	-	Man On Your Mind	Little River Band	Capitol	6		
20	-	Goin' Down	Greg Guidry	Columbia	5		F L

June 1982

This Mnth	Prev Mnth	Title	Artist	Label	Wks 20	(UK Pos)	
1	1	Ebony And Ivory	Paul McCartney & Stevie Wonder	Columbia	12	(1)	G
2	14	Don't You Want Me	Human League	A&M	15	(1)	F G
3	12	Always On My Mind	Willie Nelson	Columbia	11	(49)	G
4	-	Rosanna	Toto	Columbia	15	(12)	
5	8	The Other Woman	Ray Parker Jr.	Arista	10		
6	16	Heat Of The Moment	Asia	Geffen	11	(60)	F
7	-	Crimson And Clover	Joan Jett & The Blackhearts	Boardwalk	6		
8	2	Don't Talk To Strangers	Rick Springfield	RCA	14		
9	-	It's Gonna Take A Miracle	Deniece Williams	Arc/Columbia	6		
10	3	867-5309/Jenny	Tommy Tutone	Columbia	10		F L
11	-	Let It Whip	Dazz Band	Motown	11		F L
12	-	Body Language	Queen	Elektra	4	(25)	
13	-	Hurts So Good	John Cougar	Riva	19		G
14	4	I've Never Been To Me	Charlene	Motown	9	(1)	F G L
15	-	Love's Been A Little Bit Hard On Me	Juice Newton	Capitol	10		
16	-	Making Love	Roberta Flack	Atlantic	5		
17	19	Man On Your Mind	Little River Band	Capitol	6		
18	6	'65 Love Affair	Paul Davis	Arista	11		L
19	-	Caught Up In You	38 Special	A&M	8		F
20	-	Tainted Love	Soft Cell	Sire	9	(1)	F L

◆ **Tug of War,** Paul McCartney's last transatlantic No. 1 album, contained the duet 'Ebony And Ivory', which gave vocal partner Stevie Wonder his first British No. 1. McCartney also became the first songwriter with two compositions simultaneously on both the American soul and country charts.

◆ Joan Weber, whose 'Let Me Go Lover' was a No. 1 in 1955, died aged 45.

◆ A medley of Beatles movie songs gave the fab four their last US Top 20 hit until 'Free As A Bird' in 1995.

◆ Peace Sunday at California's Rose Bowl attracted 85,000 to watch the likes of Bob Dylan, Stevie Wonder, Linda Ronstadt, Tom Petty and Stevie Nicks, while over a million attended the New York Peace Rally starring James Taylor, Jackson Browne (with Bruce Springsteen) and Gary 'U.S.' Bonds.

◆ 'Come On Eileen', by Dexy's Midnight Runners, which sold over a million in the UK, was Britain's top single of 1982 and went on to top the American charts too.

◆ Thanks to the TV series *Fame* (based on the 1980 film), Irene Cara's 'Fame' headed the British listings, two years after reaching the US Top 5. The film's soundtrack album also hit No. 1, being replaced by the million selling **Kids From Fame** from the TV series. This American series spawned five UK hit albums and four singles – none of which were successful in the act's homeland.

◆ Survivor become the first US rock group to top the British charts in six years with their American No. 1, 'Eye of The Tiger'. The Steve Miller Band had nearly accomplished this feat just weeks earlier with 'Abracadabra'.

July 1982

This Mnth	Prev Mnth	Title	Artist	Label	Wks 20	(US Pos)	
1	-	Abracadabra	Steve Miller Band	Mercury	7	(1)	
2	-	Fame	Irene Cara	RSO	10	(4)	F
3	19	Inside Out	Odyssey	RCA	7		L
4	-	Happy Talk	Captain Sensible	A&M	4		F
5	-	A Night To Remember	Shalamar	Solar	6	(44)	
6	-	Music And Lights	Imagination	R&B	5		L
7	-	Da Da Da	Trio	Mobile Suit	5		F L
8	-	Shy Boy	Bananarama	London	7	(83)	
9	-	Now Those Days Are Gone	Bucks Fizz	RCA	5		
10	-	It Started With A Kiss	Hot Chocolate	RAK	8		
11	-	Don't Go	Yazoo	Mute	6		
12	-	No Regrets	Midge Ure	Chrysalis	5		F
13	6	I've Never Been To Me	Charlene	Motown	6	(3)	F L
14	-	Iko Iko	Natasha	Towerbell	5		F L
15	-	Driving In My Car	Madness	Stiff	6		
16	-	Come On Eileen	Dexy's Midnight Runners	Mercury	11	(1)	G
17	12	Work That Body	Diana Ross	Capitol	5	(44)	
18	-	Just Who Is The Five O'Clock Hero	Jam	Polydor	3		
19	-	Beatles Movie Medley	Beatles	Parlophone	4	(12)	
20	-	Night Train	Visage	Polydor	4		L

August 1982

This Mnth	Prev Mnth	Title	Artist	Label	Wks 20	(US Pos)	
1	16	Come On Eileen	Dexy's Midnight Runners	Mercury	11	(1)	G
2	2	Fame	Irene Cara	RSO	10	(4)	F
3	11	Don't Go	Yazoo	Mute	6		
4	10	It Started With A Kiss	Hot Chocolate	RAK	8		
5	-	Eye Of The Tiger	Survivor	Scotti Brothers	10	(1)	F
6	15	Driving My Car	Madness	Stiff	6		
7	-	Strange Little Girl	Stranglers	Liberty	5		
8	-	Stool Pigeon	Kid Creole & The Coconuts	Ze	5		
9	-	Can't Take My Eyes Off You	Boystown Gang	ERC	6		F L
10	-	My Girl Lollipop (My Boy Lollipop)	Bad Manners	Magnet	3		L
11	8	Shy Boy	Bananarama	London	7	(83)	
12	-	What	Soft Cell	Some Bizzare	5		
13	-	The Clapping Song	Belle Stars	Stiff	4		F
14	7	Da Da Da	Trio	Mobile Suit	5		F L
15	-	I Second That Emotion	Japan	Hansa	6		L
16	-	I Eat Cannibals Pt. 1	Toto Coelo	Radialchoice	5	(66)	F L
17	-	The Only Way Out	Cliff Richard	EMI	4	(64)	
18	-	Save A Prayer	Duran Duran	EMI	6	(16)	
19	-	Arthur Daley ('E's Alright)	Firm	Bark	3		F
20	-	John Wayne Is Big Leggy	Haysi Fantayzee	Regard	4		F

September 1982

This Mnth	Prev Mnth	Title	Artist	Label	Wks 20	(US Pos)	
1	5	Eye Of The Tiger	Survivor	Scotti Brothers	10	(1)	F
2	18	Save A Prayer	Duran Duran	EMI	6	(16)	
3	-	Walking On Sunshine	Rocker's Revenge	London	8		F L
4	-	Private Investigations	Dire Straits	Vertigo	6		
5	1	Come On Eileen	Dexy's Midnight Runners	Mercury	11	(1)	G
6	-	Hi-Fidelity	Kids From 'Fame' (Featuring Valerie Landsberg)	RCA	6		F
7	-	All Of My Heart	ABC	Neutron	5		
8	-	Give Me Your Heart Tonight	Shakin' Stevens	Epic	4		
9	12	What	Soft Cell	Some Bizzare	5		
10	-	The Message	Grandmaster Flash, Melle Mel & The Furious Five	Sugar Hill	4	(62)	F
11	-	The Bitterest Pill (I Ever Had To Swallow)	Jam	Polydor	5		
12	16	I Eat Cannibals Pt. 1	Toto Coelo	Radialchoice	5	(66)	F L
13	-	There It Is	Shalamar	Solar	7		
14	9	Can't Take My Eyes Off You	Boystown Gang	ERC	6		F L
15	-	Nobody's Fool	Haircut 100	Arista	4		L
16	-	Today	Talk Talk	EMI	4		F
17	-	Saddle Up	David Christie	KR	5		F L
18	20	John Wayne Is Big Leggy	Haysi Fantayzee	Regard	4		F
19	-	Why	Carly Simon	WEA	5	(74)	F
20	2	Fame	Irene Cara	RSO	10	(4)	F

July 1982

This Mnth	Prev Mnth	Title	Artist	Label	Wks 20	(UK Pos)	
1	4	Rosanna	Toto	Columbia	15	(12)	
2	2	Don't You Want Me	Human League	A&M	15	(1)	F G
3	13	Hurts So Good	John Cougar	Riva	19		G
4	-	Eye Of The Tiger	Survivor	Scotti Brothers	18	(1)	F P
5	11	Let It Whip	Dazz Band	Motown	11		F L
6	-	Hold Me	Fleetwood Mac	Warner	11		
7	15	Love's Been A Little Bit Hard On Me	Juice Newton	Capitol	10		
8	20	Tainted Love	Soft Cell	Sire	9	(1)	F L
9	-	Only The Lonely	Motels	Capitol	12		F
10	-	Abracadabra	Steve Miller Band	Capitol	17	(2)	G L
11	19	Caught Up In You	38 Special	A&M	8		F
12	-	Keep The Fire Burnin'	REO Speedwagon	Epic	10		
13	6	Heat Of The Moment	Asia	Geffen	11	(46)	F
14	-	Do I Do	Stevie Wonder	Tamla	6	(10)	
15	1	Ebony And Ivory	Paul McCartney & Stevie Wonder	Columbia	12	(1)	G
16	-	Hard To Say I'm Sorry	Chicago	Full Moon	15	(4)	G
17	-	Even The Nights Are Better	Air Supply	Arista	10	(44)	
18	-	Any Day Now	Ronnie Milsap	RCA	5		L
19	3	Always On My Mind	Willie Nelson	Columbia	11	(49)	G
20	-	Wasted On The Way	Crosby, Stills & Nash	Atlantic	10		

August 1982

This Mnth	Prev Mnth	Title	Artist	Label	Wks 20	(UK Pos)	
1	4	Eye Of The Tiger	Survivor	Scotti Brothers	18	(1)	F P
2	3	Hurts So Good	John Cougar	Riva	19		G
3	10	Abracadabra	Steve Miller Band	Capitol	17	(2)	G L
4	6	Hold Me	Fleetwood Mac	Warner	11		
5	16	Hard To Say I'm Sorry	Chicago	Full Moon	15	(4)	G
6	17	Even The Nights Are Better	Air Supply	Arista	10	(44)	
7	12	Keep The Fire Burnin'	REO Speedwagon	Epic	10		
8	-	Vacation	Go-Go's	IRS	7		
9	20	Wasted On The Way	Crosby, Stills & Nash	Atlantic	10		
10	-	Take It Away	Paul McCartney	Columbia	9	(15)	
11	1	Rosanna	Toto	Columbia	15	(12)	
12	-	You Should Hear How She Talks About You	Melissa Manchester	Arista	10		L
13	9	Only The Lonely	Motels	Capitol	12		F
14	-	Love Is In Control (Finger On The Trigger)	Donna Summer	Warner	8	(18)	
15	-	Love Will Turn You Around	Kenny Rogers	Liberty	7		
16	2	Don't You Want Me	Human League	A&M	15	(1)	F G
17	5	Let It Whip	Dazz Band	Motown	11		F L
18	-	Jack & Diane	John Cougar	Riva	14	(25)	G
19	-	Eye In The Sky	Alan Parsons Project	Arista	13		
20	-	American Music	Pointer Sisters	Planet	5		

September 1982

This Mnth	Prev Mnth	Title	Artist	Label	Wks 20	(UK Pos)	
1	3	Abracadabra	Steve Miller Band	Capitol	17	(2)	G L
2	5	Hard To Say I'm Sorry	Chicago	Full Moon	15	(4)	G
3	1	Eye Of The Tiger	Survivor	Scotti Brothers	18	(1)	F P
4	18	Jack & Diane	John Cougar	Riva	14	(25)	G
5	12	You Should Hear How She Talks About You	Melissa Manchester	Arista	10		L
6	2	Hurts So Good	John Cougar	Riva	19		G
7	6	Even The Nights Are Better	Air Supply	Arista	10	(44)	
8	4	Hold Me	Fleetwood Mac	Warner	11		
9	10	Take It Away	Paul McCartney	Columbia	9	(15)	
10	19	Eye In The Sky	Alan Parsons Project	Arista	13		
11	14	Love Is In Control (Finger On The...)	Donna Summer	Warner	8	(18)	
12	-	Who Can It Be Now?	Men At Work	Columbia	14	(45)	F
13	15	Love Will Turn You Around	Kenny Rogers	Liberty	7		
14	9	Wasted On The Way	Crosby, Stills & Nash	Atlantic	10		
15	8	Vacation	Go-Go's	IRS	7		
16	-	You Can Do Magic	America	Capitol	11	(59)	L
17	-	Think I'm In Love	Eddie Money	Columbia	7		
18	-	Somebody's Baby	Jackson Browne	Asylum	9		
19	-	Blue Eyes	Elton John	Geffen	5	(8)	
20	20	American Music	Pointer Sisters	Planet	5		

▲ 'The Message' by Grandmaster Flash (above) was the first successful rap record to address social problems in America, and showed what could be achieved through that medium. Another equally important black music recording was 'Planet Rock' by Afrika Bambaataa, which helped lay the foundations of hip-hop.

◆ John Cougar (Mellencamp) wrote and produced his singles 'Jack And Diane' and 'Hurts So Good', which were both in the Top 10 as his LP **American Fool** moved into the top slot.

UK 1982 OCT-DEC

▲ Big American hits from the first British invasion, 'Love Me Do' by The Beatles and 'House Of The Rising Sun' by The Animals returned to the UK chart. Debuting on that chart were Culture Club, Wham! (above) and Tears for Fears – artists who would help lead the second UK invasion.

◆ Shortly after Musical Youth (featuring 11-year-old Kelvin Grant) became the youngest group to top the chart, David Bowie & the late Bing Crosby became the oldest duo to reach the Top 5.

◆ The 1980s' most influential British pop TV show, *The Tube*, was launched.

October 1982

This Mnth	Prev Mnth	Title	Artist	Label	Wks 20	(US Pos)	
1	-	Pass The Dutchie	Musical Youth	MCA	6	(10)	F
2	-	Zoom	Fat Larry's Band	Virgin	7		F L
3	-	Do You Really Want To Hurt Me	Culture Club	Virgin	9	(2)	F
4	-	Hard To Say I'm Sorry	Chicago	Full Moon	6	(1)	
5	-	Starmaker	Kids From 'Fame'	RCA	7		
6	-	Love Come Down	Evelyn King	EMI	7	(17)	F L
7	-	Jackie Wilson Said	Dexy's Midnight Runners	Mercury	4		
8	13	There It Is	Shalamar	Solar	7		
9	-	Love Me Do	Beatles	Parlophone	5		L
10	-	Just What I Always Wanted	Mari Wilson	Compact	5		F L
11	-	Lifeline	Spandau Ballet	Chrysalis	5		
12	-	Annie I'm Not Your Daddy	Kid Creole & The Coconuts	Ze	5		L
13	11	The Bitterest Pill (I Ever Had To Swallow)	Jam	Polydor	5		
14	-	Friend Or Foe	Adam Ant	CBS	4		
15	1	Eye Of The Tiger	Survivor	Scotti Brothers	10	(1)	F
16	3	Walking On Sunshine	Rocker's Revenge	London	8		F L
17	19	Why	Carly Simon	WEA	5	(74)	
18	-	House Of The Rising Sun	Animals	RAK	4		L
19	-	Danger Games	Pinkees	Creole	2		F L
20	-	Mad World	Tears For Fears	Mercury	7		F

November 1982

This Mnth	Prev Mnth	Title	Artist	Label	Wks 20	(US Pos)	
1	-	I Don't Wanna Dance	Eddy Grant	Ice	7	(53)	
2	-	Heartbreaker	Dionne Warwick	Arista	6	(10)	
3	20	Mad World	Tears For Fears	Mercury	7		F
4	3	Do You Really Want To Hurt Me	Culture Club	Virgin	9	(2)	F
5	-	(Sexual) Healing	Marvin Gaye	CBS	6	(3)	
6	-	Theme From Harry's Game	Clannad	RCA	4		F
7	-	Maneater	Daryl Hall & John Oates	RCA	4	(1)	
8	-	Ooh La La La (Let's Go Dancing)	Kool & The Gang	De-Lite	4	(30)	
9	-	The Girl Is Mine	Michael Jackson & Paul McCartney	Epic	3	(2)	
10	5	Starmaker	Kids From 'Fame'	RCA	7		
11	-	Mirror Man	Human League	Virgin	8	(30)	
12	-	I Wanna Do It With You	Barry Manilow	Arista	5		
13	-	Young Guns (Go For It)	Wham!	Innervision	9		F
14	-	Living On The Ceiling	Blancmange	London	6		F
15	12	Annie I'm Not Your Daddy	Kid Creole & The Coconuts	Ze	5		L
16	9	Love Me Do	Beatles	Parlophone	5		
17	-	I'll Be Satisfied	Shakin' Stevens	Epic	4		
18	-	Caroline (Live At The N.E.C.)	Status Quo	Vertigo	3		
19	-	Rio	Duran Duran	EMI	5	(14)	
20	11	Lifeline	Spandau Ballet	Chrysalis	5		

December 1982

This Mnth	Prev Mnth	Title	Artist	Label	Wks 20	(US Pos)	
1	-	Save Your Love	Renee And Renato	Hollywood	10		F L
2	-	Beat Surrender	Jam	Polydor	6		L
3	-	Time (Clock Of The Heart)	Culture Club	Virgin	8	(2)	
4	11	Mirror Man	Human League	Virgin	8	(30)	
5	-	Truly	Lionel Richie	Motown	7	(1)	
6	13	Young Guns (Go For It)	Wham!	Innervision	9		F
7	-	Our House	Madness	Stiff	8	(7)	
8	14	Living On The Ceiling	Blancmange	London	6		F
9	-	Best Years Of Our Lives	Modern Romance	WEA	8		
10	-	The Shakin' Stevens E.P.	Shakin' Stevens	Epic	4		
11	1	I Don't Wanna Dance	Eddy Grant	Ice	7	(53)	
12	19	Rio	Duran Duran	EMI	5	(14)	
13	-	Peace On Earth/Little Drummer Boy	David Bowie & Bing Crosby	RCA	4		
14	-	Wishing (If I Had A Photograph Of You)	Flock Of Seagulls	Jive	4	(26)	F L
15	-	Hymn	Ultravox	Chrysalis	8		
16	-	The Other Side Of Love	Yazoo	Mute	4		
17	-	You Can't Hurry Love	Phil Collins	Virgin	10	(10)	
18	2	Heartbreaker	Dionne Warwick	Arista	6	(10)	
19	-	Friends	Shalamar	Solar	6		
20	-	A Winter's Tale	David Essex	Mercury	6		

October 1982

This Mnth	Prev Mnth	Title	Artist	Label	Wks 20	(UK Pos)	
1	4	Jack & Diane	John Cougar	Riva	14	(25)	G
2	12	Who Can It Be Now?	Men At Work	Columbia	14	(45)	F
3	10	Eye In The Sky	Alan Parsons Project	Arista	13		
4	-	I Keep Forgettin' (Everytime You're Near)	Michael McDonald	Warner	8	(43)	F
5	18	Somebody's Baby	Jackson Browne	Asylum	9		
6	1	Abracadabra	Steve Miller Band	Capitol	17	(2)	G L
7	16	You Can Do Magic	America	Capitol	11	(59)	L
8	-	Heart Attack	Olivia Newton-John	MCA	11	(46)	
9	2	Hard To Say I'm Sorry	Chicago	Full Moon	15	(4)	G
10	-	I Ran (So Far Away)	Flock Of Seagulls	Jive/Arista	6	(43)	F L
11	-	Up Where We Belong	Joe Cocker & Jennifer Warnes	Island	11	(7)	G
12	3	Eye Of The Tiger	Survivor	Scotti Brothers	18	(1)	F P
13	-	Break It To Me Gently	Juice Newton	Capitol	6		L
14	19	Blue Eyes	Elton John	Geffen	5	(8)	
15	-	Gypsy	Fleetwood Mac	Warner	4	(46)	
16	-	Hold On	Santana	Columbia	6		L
17	5	You Should Hear How She Talks About You	Melissa Manchester	Arista	10		L
18	-	Heartlight	Neil Diamond	Columbia	9	(47)	L
19	-	Gloria	Laura Branigan	Atlantic	16	(6)	F G
20	6	Hurts So Good	John Cougar	Riva	19		G

November 1982

This Mnth	Prev Mnth	Title	Artist	Label	Wks 20	(UK Pos)	
1	11	Up Where We Belong	Joe Cocker & Jennifer Warnes	Island	11	(7)	G
2	8	Heart Attack	Olivia Newton-John	MCA	11	(46)	
3	-	Truly	Lionel Richie	Motown	11	(6)	G
4	19	Gloria	Laura Branigan	Atlantic	16	(6)	F G
5	18	Heartlight	Neil Diamond	Columbia	9	(47)	L
6	2	Who Can It Be Now?	Men At Work	Columbia	14	(45)	F
7	1	Jack & Diane	John Cougar	Riva	14	(25)	G
8	-	Muscles	Diana Ross	RCA	8	(15)	
9	-	Mickey	Toni Basil	Chrysalis	12	(2)	F G L
10	-	Maneater	Daryl Hall & John Oates	RCA	14	(6)	G
11	-	Steppin' Out	Joe Jackson	A&M	10	(6)	F
12	4	I Keep Forgettin' (Everytime...)	Michael McDonald	Warner	8	(43)	F
13	7	You Can Do Magic	America	Capitol	11	(59)	L
14	3	Eye In The Sky	Alan Parsons Project	Arista	13		
15	-	The Girl Is Mine	Paul McCartney & Michael Jackson	Epic	12	(8)	G
16	-	Dirty Laundry	Don Henley	Asylum	12	(59)	F G
17	-	Rock This Town	Stray Cats	EMI America	8	(9)	F
18	-	Nobody	Sylvia	RCA	4		G L
19	-	You Don't Want Me Anymore	Steel Breeze	RCA	3		F L
20	-	The One You Love	Glenn Frey	Asylum	4		F

December 1982

This Mnth	Prev Mnth	Title	Artist	Label	Wks 20	(UK Pos)	
1	9	Mickey	Toni Basil	Chrysalis	12	(2)	F G L
2	10	Maneater	Daryl Hall & John Oates	RCA	14	(6)	G
3	4	Gloria	Laura Branigan	Atlantic	16	(6)	F G
4	3	Truly	Lionel Richie	Motown	11	(6)	G
5	15	The Girl Is Mine	Paul McCartney & Michael Jackson	Epic	12	(8)	G
6	11	Steppin' Out	Joe Jackson	A&M	10	(6)	F
7	16	Dirty Laundry	Don Henley	Asylum	12	(59)	F G
8	-	Sexual Healing	Marvin Gaye	Columbia	13	(4)	G L
9	17	Rock This Town	Stray Cats	EMI America	8	(9)	F
10	-	It's Raining Again	Supertramp	A&M	7	(26)	L
11	8	Muscles	Diana Ross	RCA	8	(15)	
12	-	Down Under	Men At Work	Columbia	15	(1)	G
13	-	Shadows Of The Night	Pat Benatar	Chrysalis	6	(50)	
14	1	Up Where We Belong	Joe Cocker & Jennifer Warnes	Island	11	(7)	G
15	-	Heartbreaker	Dionne Warwick	Arista	9	(2)	
16	5	Heartlight	Neil Diamond	Columbia	9	(47)	L
17	-	Africa	Toto	Columbia	12	(3)	
18	-	Rock The Casbah	Clash	Epic	10	(15)	F L
19	2	Heart Attack	Olivia Newton-John	MCA	11	(46)	
20	-	You And I	Eddie Rabbitt	Elektra	12		L

◆ Rock videos came of age in 1982, as MTV gained importance and many clubs added video screens. It was a year when AOR rockers ruled the American album charts, rap showed it had teeth and synth-rock started to thrive. Nonetheless, record and tape sales dropped (by 3%) for the fourth consecutive year, to $3.59 billion.

◆ After five years of virtual vinyl silence Marvin Gaye returned with his last major hit 'Sexual Healing' which had "modesty" brackets added around "Sexual" in the UK.

▲ Stars at the Jamaican World Music Festival included Rick James, Gladys Knight, Aretha Franklin and Joe Jackson (above).

UK 1983 JAN-MAR

▲ Noteworthy new-comers on the UK chart included future transat-lantic stars U2 (above, whose album **War** entered at No. 1), The Eurythmics and the Thompson Twins.

◆ Shortly after dis-banding, The Jam had a record 15 singles in the UK Top 100, and lead singer Paul Weller signed a £250,000 deal for his new act Style Council.

◆ CDs (which stored sounds digitally, thus eliminating most distor-tion) went on sale for the first time.

◆ Billy Fury, one of Britain's first home grown rock stars, died from heart problems, aged 41.

January 1983

This Mnth	Prev Mnth	Title	Artist	Label	Wks 20	(US Pos)	
1	17	You Can't Hurry Love	Phil Collins	Virgin	10	(10)	
2	20	A Winter's Tale	David Essex	Mercury	6		
3	1	Save Your Love	Renee And Renato	Hollywood	10		F L
4	-	Orville's Song	Keith Harris & Orville	BBC	5		F L
5	-	Down Under	Men At Work	Epic	7	(1)	F L
6	9	Best Years Of Our Lives	Modern Romance	WEA	8		
7	7	Our House	Madness	Stiff	8	(7)	
8	-	The Story Of The Blues	Wah!	Eternal	6		F
9	3	Time (Clock Of The Heart)	Culture Club	Virgin	8	(2)	
10	-	Buffalo Gals	Malcolm McLaren & The World's Famous Supreme Team	Charisma	7		F
11	15	Hymn	Ultravox	Chrysalis	8		
12	-	Electric Avenue	Eddy Grant	Ice	5	(2)	
13	-	Heartache Avenue	Maisonettes	Ready Steady Go!	4		F L
14	10	The Shakin' Stevens E.P.	Shakin' Stevens	Epic	4		
15	-	All The Love In The World	Dionne Warwick	Arista	5		
16	13	Peace On Earth/Little Drummer Boy	David Bowie & Bing Crosby	RCA	4		
17	-	Steppin' Out	Joe Jackson	A&M	5	(6)	L
18	-	Cacharpaya (Andes Pumpsa Daesi)	Incantation	Beggars Banquet	4		F L
19	-	European Female	Stranglers	Epic	3		
20	-	If You Can't Stand The Heat	Bucks Fizz	RCA	6		

February 1983

This Mnth	Prev Mnth	Title	Artist	Label	Wks 20	(US Pos)	
1	-	Too Shy	Kajagoogoo	EMI	8	(5)	F
2	5	Down Under	Men At Work	Epic	7	(1)	F L
3	-	Sign Of The Times	Belle Stars	Stiff	7	(75)	L
4	-	Change	Tears For Fears	Mercury	6	(73)	
5	-	Up Where We Belong	Joe Cocker & Jennifer Warnes	Island	6	(1)	
6	12	Electric Avenue	Eddy Grant	Ice	5	(2)	
7	-	Wham Rap	Wham!	Innervision	5		
8	-	Gloria	Laura Branigan	Atlantic	6	(2)	F
9	-	Billie Jean	Michael Jackson	Epic	10	(1)	
10	-	Oh Diane	Fleetwood Mac	Warner	5		
11	1	You Can't Hurry Love	Phil Collins	Virgin	10	(10)	
12	-	Africa	Toto	CBS	6	(1)	
13	-	The Cutter	Echo & The Bunnymen	Korova	4		
14	8	The Story Of The Blues	Wah!	Eternal	6		F
15	-	Last Night A D.J. Saved My Life	Indeep	Sound Of New York	4		F L
16	-	New Year's Day	U2	Island	3	(53)	F
17	-	Never Gonna Give You Up	Musical Youth	MCA	5		L
18	-	Christian	China Crisis	Virgin	3		F
19	17	Steppin' Out	Joe Jackson	A&M	5	(6)	L
20	-	The Tunnel Of Love	Fun Boy Three	Chrysalis	5		

March 1983

This Mnth	Prev Mnth	Title	Artist	Label	Wks 20	(US Pos)	
1	-	Total Eclipse Of The Heart	Bonnie Tyler	CBS	8	(1)	
2	-	Sweet Dreams (Are Made Of This)	Eurythmics	RCA	7	(1)	F
3	9	Billie Jean	Michael Jackson	Epic	10	(1)	
4	-	Rock The Boat	Forrest	CBS	6		F
5	12	Africa	Toto	CBS	6	(1)	
6	-	Na Na Hey Hey Kiss Him Goodbye	Bananarama	London	5		
7	1	Too Shy	Kajagoogoo	EMI	8	(5)	F
8	-	Love On Your Side	Thompson Twins	Arista	5	(45)	F
9	-	Speak Like A Child	Style Council	Polydor	5		F
10	-	Tomorrow's (Just Another Day)/ Madness (Is All In The Mind)	Madness	Stiff	4		
11	17	Never Gonna Give You Up	Musical Youth	MCA	5		L
12	-	High Life	Modern Romance	WEA	3		
13	-	She Means Nothing To Me	Phil Everly & Cliff Richard	Capitol	4		F
14	-	Baby, Come To Me	Patti Austin & James Ingram	Qwest	5	(1)	F L
15	-	Communication	Spandau Ballet	Reformation	4	(59)	
16	-	Rip It Up	Orange Juice	Polydor	5		F L
17	20	The Tunnel Of Love	Fun Boy Three	Chrysalis	5		
18	-	Is There Something I Should Know	Duran Duran	EMI	5	(4)	
19	4	Change	Tears For Fears	Mercury	6	(73)	
20	-	Let's Dance	David Bowie	EMI America	8	(1)	

January 1983

This Mnth	Prev Mnth	Title	Artist	Label	Wks 20	(UK Pos)	
1	5	The Girl Is Mine	Paul McCartney & Michael Jackson	Epic	12	(8)	G
2	12	Down Under	Men At Work	Columbia	15	(1)	G
3	7	Dirty Laundry	Don Henley	Asylum	12	(59)	F G
4	2	Maneater	Daryl Hall & John Oates	RCA	14	(6)	G
5	8	Sexual Healing	Marvin Gaye	Columbia	13	(4)	G L
6	1	Mickey	Toni Basil	Chrysalis	12	(2)	F P L
7	17	Africa	Toto	Columbia	12	(3)	
8	-	Baby Come To Me	Patti Austin With James Ingram	Qwest	13	(11)	F G L
9	18	Rock The Casbah	Clash	Epic	10	(15)	F L
10	3	Gloria	Laura Branigan	Atlantic	16	(6)	F G
11	20	You And I	Eddie Rabbitt	Elektra	12		L
12	15	Heartbreaker	Dionne Warwick	Arista	9	(2)	
13	6	Steppin' Out	Joe Jackson	A&M	10	(6)	F
14	-	The Other Guy	Little River Band	Capitol	9		L
15	-	You Can't Hurry Love	Phil Collins	Atlantic	9	(1)	
16	-	Shame On The Moon	Bob Seger & The Silver Bullet Band	Capitol	13		
17	9	Rock This Town	Stray Cats	EMI America	8	(9)	F
18	4	Truly	Lionel Richie	Motown	11	(6)	G
19	-	Heart To Heart	Kenny Loggins	Columbia	8		
20	-	Goody Two Shoes	Adam Ant	Epic	7	(1)	F L

February 1983

This Mnth	Prev Mnth	Title	Artist	Label	Wks 20	(UK Pos)	
1	8	Baby Come To Me	Patti Austin With James Ingram	Qwest	13	(11)	F G L
2	2	Down Under	Men At Work	Columbia	15	(1)	G
3	16	Shame On The Moon	Bob Seger & The Silver Bullet Band	Capitol	13		
4	-	Stray Cat Strut	Stray Cats	EMI America	8	(11)	
5	7	Africa	Toto	Columbia	12	(3)	
6	11	You And I	Eddie Rabbitt	Elektra	12		L
7	5	Sexual Healing	Marvin Gaye	Columbia	13	(4)	G L
8	20	Goody Two Shoes	Adam Ant	Epic	7	(1)	F L
9	-	Pass The Dutchie	Musical Youth	MCA	6	(1)	F L
10	15	You Can't Hurry Love	Phil Collins	Atlantic	9	(1)	
11	-	Billie Jean	Michael Jackson	Epic	12	(1)	G
12	-	Do You Really Want To Hurt Me	Culture Club	Epic	12	(1)	F
13	4	Maneater	Daryl Hall & John Oates	RCA	14	(6)	G
14	14	The Other Guy	Little River Band	Capitol	9		L
15	-	Hungry Like The Wolf	Duran Duran	Harvest	12	(5)	F
16	9	Rock The Casbah	Clash	Epic	10	(15)	F L
17	-	Your Love Is Driving Me Crazy	Sammy Hagar	Geffen	5		F L
18	19	Heart To Heart	Kenny Loggins	Columbia	8		
19	-	All Right	Christopher Cross	Warner	9	(51)	
20	-	Allentown	Billy Joel	Columbia	8		

March 1983

This Mnth	Prev Mnth	Title	Artist	Label	Wks 20	(UK Pos)	
1	11	Billie Jean	Michael Jackson	Epic	12	(1)	G
2	12	Do You Really Want To Hurt Me	Culture Club	Epic	12	(1)	F
3	15	Hungry Like The Wolf	Duran Duran	Harvest	12	(5)	F
4	3	Shame On The Moon	Bob Seger & The Silver Bullet Band	Capitol	13		
5	-	Back On The Chain Gang	Pretenders	Sire	9	(17)	
6	-	You Are	Lionel Richie	Motown	11	(43)	
7	-	We've Got Tonight	Kenny Rogers/Sheena Easton	Liberty	9	(28)	
8	4	Stray Cat Strut	Stray Cats	EMI America	8	(11)	
9	-	Separate Ways (Worlds Apart)	Journey	Columbia	10		
10	-	One On One	Daryl Hall & John Oates	RCA	9	(63)	
11	-	Mr. Roboto	Styx	A&M	11		G
12	-	Twilight Zone	Golden Earring	21	8		L
13	19	All Right	Christopher Cross	Warner	9	(51)	
14	1	Baby Come To Me	Patti Austin/James Ingram	Qwest	13	(11)	F G L
15	-	I Know There's Something Going On	Frida	Atlantic	7	(43)	F L
16	-	Come On Eileen	Dexy's Midnight Runners	Mercury	11	(1)	F L
17	6	You And I	Eddie Rabbitt	Elektra	12		L
18	2	Down Under	Men At Work	Columbia	15	(1)	G
19	-	Jeopardy	Greg Kihn Band	Beserkley	11	(63)	L
20	9	Pass The Dutchie	Musical Youth	MCA	6	(1)	F L

◆ Michael Jackson's Grammy winning **Thriller** album (which eventually sold a record 40 million copies worldwide) started a stunning 37 weeks run at the top. Incidentally, 'Billie Jean', the first single spawned from it, became a No. 1 on both sides of the Atlantic, as did 'Down Under' by Australia's Men At Work and 'Total Eclipse Of The Heart' by Welsh songstress Bonnie Tyler.

◆ 'Baby Come To Me' by Patti Austin took a record 23 weeks to reach No. 1. It was produced by her godfather Quincy Jones.

◆ Toto, scoring their biggest hit with 'Africa', collected a record five Grammy Awards.

◆ Karen Carpenter, the voice that sold fifty million albums by The Carpenters, died of heartbeat irregularities brought about by anorexia nevosa.

◆ Led Zeppelin earned their tenth successive gold award for **Coda**.

UK 1983 APR-JUNE

◆ Police scored the last of their five UK No. 1 singles and albums with 'Every Breath You Take' and **Synchronicity**. Both records also topped the US chart, with the latter holding sway for 17 weeks.

◆ David Bowie signed a $10 million deal with EMI, and the first release 'Let's Dance' (co-produced with Nile Rodgers) became his biggest transatlantic hit. He also launched his *Serious Moonlight* tour, which would be seen by over 2.5 million people around the world.

◆ Youthful British hard rockers Def Leppard first tasted fame Stateside when 'Photograph' reached the Top 20 and their album **Pyromania** narrowly missed the No. 1 spot.

◆ 'Blue Monday', the 12-inch only release from New Order, was released. It became the UK's biggest selling single on that particular format and spent nearly a year on the chart.

April 1983

This Mnth	Prev Mnth	Title	Artist	Label	Wks 20	(US Pos)	
1	20	Let's Dance	David Bowie	EMI America	8	(1)	
2	18	Is There Something I Should Know	Duran Duran	EMI	5	(4)	
3	-	Church Of The Poison Mind	Culture Club	Virgin	6	(10)	
4	-	Boxer Beat	Joboxers	RCA	5		F
5	-	Breakaway	Tracey Ullman	Stiff	6	(70)	F
6	-	Beat It	Michael Jackson	Epic	6	(1)	
7	-	Words	F.R. David	Carrere	7	(62)	F L
8	-	Ooh To Be Ah	Kajagoogoo	EMI	5		
9	9	Speak Like A Child	Style Council	Polydor	5		F
10	2	Sweet Dreams (Are Made Of This)	Eurythmics	RCA	7	(1)	F
11	1	Total Eclipse Of The Heart	Bonnie Tyler	CBS	8	(1)	
12	-	Blue Monday	New Order	Factory	8		F
13	-	Fields Of Fire (400 Miles)	Big Country	Mercury	4	(52)	F
14	-	True	Spandau Ballet	Reformation	8	(4)	
15	-	Snot Rap	Kenny Everett	RCA	3		F L
16	-	Love Is A Stranger	Eurythmics	RCA	4	(23)	
17	-	Don't Talk To Me About Love	Altered Images	Epic	4		L
18	-	The House That Jack Built	Tracie	Respond	3		F L
19	16	Rip It Up	Orange Juice	Polydor	5		F L
20	-	Whistle Down The Wind	Nick Heyward	Arista	4		F

May 1983

This Mnth	Prev Mnth	Title	Artist	Label	Wks 20	(US Pos)	
1	14	True	Spandau Ballet	Reformation	8	(4)	
2	-	Temptation	Heaven 17	Virgin	7		F
3	-	Dancing Tight	Galaxy Featuring Phil Fearon	Ensign	6		F
4	-	(Keep Feeling) Fascination	Human League	Virgin	6	(8)	
5	-	Candy Girl	New Edition	London	6	(46)	F
6	7	Words	F.R. David	Carrere	7	(62)	F L
7	-	Pale Shelter	Tears For Fears	Mercury	4		
8	-	Can't Get Used To Losing You	Beat	Go Feet	5		L
9	-	Our Lips Are Sealed	Fun Boy Three	Chrysalis	5		L
10	-	We Are Detective	Thompson Twins	Arista	4		
11	6	Beat It	Michael Jackson	Epic	6	(1)	
12	-	Blind Vision	Blancmange	London	4		
13	-	Bad Boys	Wham!	Innervision	8	(60)	
14	1	Let's Dance	David Bowie	EMI America	8	(1)	
15	-	What Kinda Boy You Looking For (Girl)	Hot Chocolate	RAK	4		
16	-	True Love Ways	Cliff Richard	EMI	4		
17	-	Friday Night (Live Version)	Kids From 'Fame'	RCA	4		L
18	3	Church Of The Poison Mind	Culture Club	Virgin	6	(10)	
19	-	Every Breath You Take	Police	A&M	8	(1)	
20	-	Nobody's Diary	Yazoo	Mute	7		

June 1983

This Mnth	Prev Mnth	Title	Artist	Label	Wks 20	(US Pos)	
1	19	Every Breath You Take	Police	A&M	8	(1)	
2	13	Bad Boys	Wham!	Innervision	8	(60)	
3	20	Nobody's Diary	Yazoo	Mute	7		
4	-	Buffalo Soldier	Bob Marley & The Wailers	Island	6		
5	-	China Girl	David Bowie	EMI America	5	(10)	
6	-	Love Town	Booker Newberry III	Polydor	5		F L
7	-	Flashdance....What A Feeling	Irene Cara	Casablanca	9	(1)	L
8	5	Candy Girl	New Edition	London	6	(46)	F
9	-	Just Got Lucky	Joboxers	RCA	4	(36)	L
10	-	Baby Jane	Rod Stewart	Warner	9	(14)	
11	-	Lady Love Me (One More Time)	George Benson	Warner	5	(30)	
12	-	Waiting For A Train	Flash And The Pan	Ensign	5		F L
13	-	I Guess That's Why They Call It The Blues	Elton John	Rocket	6	(4)	
14	8	Can't Get Used To Losing You	Beat	Go Feet	5		L
15	-	Wanna Be Startin' Something	Michael Jackson	Epic	3	(5)	
16	2	Temptation	Heaven 17	Virgin	7		F
17	-	Money Go Round (Pt.1)	Style Council	Polydor	3		
18	-	Hang On Now	Kajagoogoo	EMI	3	(78)	
19	1	True	Spandau Ballet	Reformation	8	(4)	
20	-	Dark Is The Night	Shakatak	Polydor	2		

April 1983

This Mnth	Prev Mnth	Title	Artist	Label	Wks 20	(UK Pos)	
1	1	Billie Jean	Michael Jackson	Epic	12	(1)	G
2	16	Come On Eileen	Dexy's Midnight Runners	Mercury	11	(1)	F L
3	11	Mr. Roboto	Styx	A&M	11		G
4	-	Beat It	Michael Jackson	Epic	15	(3)	G
5	19	Jeopardy	Greg Kihn Band	Beserkley	11	(63)	L
6	3	Hungry Like The Wolf	Duran Duran	Harvest	12	(5)	F
7	9	Separate Ways (Worlds Apart)	Journey	Columbia	10		
8	10	One On One	Daryl Hall & John Oates	RCA	9	(63)	
9	2	Do You Really Want To Hurt Me	Culture Club	Epic	12	(1)	F
10	-	Der Kommissar	After The Fire	Epic	11	(47)	F L
11	7	We've Got Tonight	Kenny Rogers/Sheena Easton	Liberty	9	(28)	
12	6	You Are	Lionel Richie	Motown	11	(43)	
13	-	She Blinded Me With Science	Thomas Dolby	Capitol	11	(49)	F L
14	-	Let's Dance	David Bowie	EMI America	12	(1)	G
15	5	Back On The Chain Gang	Pretenders	Sire	9	(17)	
16	-	Little Red Corvette	Prince & The Revolution	Warner	10	(2)	
17	15	I Know There's Something Going On	Frida	Atlantic	7	(43)	F L
18	-	Even Now	Bob Seger & The Silver Bullet Band	Capitol	5	(73)	
19	-	Overkill	Men At Work	Columbia	11	(21)	
20	12	Twilight Zone	Golden Earring	21	8		L

May 1983

This Mnth	Prev Mnth	Title	Artist	Label	Wks 20	(UK Pos)	
1	4	Beat It	Michael Jackson	Epic	15	(3)	G
2	14	Let's Dance	David Bowie	EMI America	12	(1)	G
3	19	Overkill	Men At Work	Columbia	11	(21)	
4	13	She Blinded Me With Science	Thomas Dolby	Capitol	11	(49)	F L
5	-	Flashdance....What A Feeling	Irene Cara	Casablanca	16	(2)	G
6	5	Jeopardy	Greg Kihn Band	Beserkley	11	(63)	L
7	16	Little Red Corvette	Prince & The Revolution	Warner	10	(2)	
8	-	Solitaire	Laura Branigan	Atlantic	8		
9	10	Der Kommissar	After The Fire	Epic	11	(47)	F L
10	-	My Love	Lionel Richie	Motown	8	(70)	
11	2	Come On Eileen	Dexy's Midnight Runners	Mercury	11	(1)	F L
12	-	Time (Clock Of The Heart)	Culture Club	Epic	11	(3)	
13	-	I Won't Hold You Back	Toto	Columbia	7	(37)	
14	-	Straight From The Heart	Bryan Adams	A&M	5	(51)	F
15	-	Photograph	Def Leppard	Mercury	6	(66)	F
16	-	Rio	Duran Duran	Capitol	4	(9)	
17	3	Mr. Roboto	Styx	A&M	11		G
18	-	Affair Of The Night	Rick Springfield	RCA	9		
19	-	There's Always Something There To Remind Me	Naked Eyes	EMI America	7	(59)	F
20	18	Even Now	Bob Seger & The Silver Bullet Band	Capitol	5	(73)	

June 1983

This Mnth	Prev Mnth	Title	Artist	Label	Wks 20	(UK Pos)	
1	5	Flashdance....What A Feeling	Irene Cara	Casablanca	16	(2)	G
2	12	Time (Clock Of The Heart)	Culture Club	Epic	11	(3)	
3	2	Let's Dance	David Bowie	EMI America	12	(1)	G
4	3	Overkill	Men At Work	Columbia	11	(21)	
5	-	Electric Avenue	Eddy Grant	Portrait	12	(2)	F G L
6	1	Beat It	Michael Jackson	Epic	15	(3)	G
7	-	Don't Let It End	Styx	A&M	9	(56)	
8	10	My Love	Lionel Richie	Motown	8	(70)	
9	18	Affair Of The Night	Rick Springfield	RCA	9		
10	19	There's Always Something There To Remind Me	Naked Eyes	EMI America	7	(59)	F
11	-	Family Man	Daryl Hall & John Oates	RCA	7	(15)	
12	-	Faithfully	Journey	Columbia	7		
13	4	She Blinded Me With Science	Thomas Dolby	Capitol	11	(49)	F L
14	-	Never Gonna Let You Go	Sergio Mendes	A&M	12	(45)	L
15	-	Every Breath You Take	Police	A&M	16	(1)	G
16	-	Too Shy	Kajagoogoo	EMI America	8	(1)	F L
17	7	Little Red Corvette	Prince & The Revolution	Warner	10	(2)	
18	-	She's A Beauty	Tubes	Capitol	7		F L
19	8	Solitaire	Laura Branigan	Atlantic	8		
20	-	Wanna Be Startin' Something	Michael Jackson	Epic	10	(8)	

◆ For the first time ever, over 60% of the Hot 100 were recorded by non-American artists – the majority being British!

▲ Michael Jackson's 'Beat It' video, with its 150 extras, cost a then record $70,000. The Grammy winning single soon joined its predecessor, 'Billie Jean', in the Top 5.

◆ The US '83 Festival, which only attracted half the estimated 600,000 crowd, lost $10 million. Headliners David Bowie and Van Halen received $1 million each.

◆ All Motown's major acts appeared on the TV special *Motown 25* along with guests including Adam Ant and Linda Ronstadt.

UK 1983
JULY-SEPT

◆ David Bowie had ten albums in the British Top 100 (a feat bettered only by Elvis Presley), including the transatlantic Top 5 hit, **Let's Dance.**

▲ Stars of the Castle Donnington Rock Festival included ZZ Top (above), Meat Loaf, Twisted Sister and Whitesnake. Other successful live shows included Barry Manilow at Blenheim Palace, and The Prince's Trust Gala which included Duran Duran and Dire Straits.

◆ As 'Wings Of A Dove' gave Madness their 16th successive Top 20 hit, 'Our House' became their only US Top 20 entry.

July 1983

This Mnth	Prev Mnth	Title	Artist	Label	Wks 20	(US Pos)	
1	10	Baby Jane	Rod Stewart	Warner	9	(14)	
2	-	Wherever I Lay My Hat (That's My Home)	Paul Young	CBS	9	(70)	F
3	-	I.O.U.	Freeez	Beggars Banquet	9		L
4	-	Moonlight Shadow	Mike Oldfield	Virgin	9		
5	7	Flashdance....What A Feeling	Irene Cara	Casablanca	9	(1)	L
6	-	Come Live With Me	Heaven 17	Virgin	7		
7	-	War Baby	Tom Robinson	Panic	5		L
8	-	Who's That Girl	Eurythmics	RCA	6	(21)	
9	-	Double Dutch	Malcolm McLaren	Charisma	9		
10	-	It's Over	Funk Masters	Master Funk	4		F L
11	-	Dead Giveaway	Shalamar	Solar	5	(22)	
12	13	I Guess That's Why They Call It The Blues	Elton John	Rocket	6	(4)	
13	1	Every Breath You Take	Police	A&M	8	(1)	
14	-	Rock 'n' Roll Is King	Electric Light Orchestra	Jet	4	(19)	L
15	-	Take That Situation	Nick Heyward	Arista	3		
16	-	Cruel Summer	Bananarama	London	5	(9)	
17	-	Wrapped Around Your Finger	Police	A&M	4	(8)	
18	-	The Trooper	Iron Maiden	EMI	3		
19	5	China Girl	David Bowie	EMI America	5	(10)	
20	-	When We Were Young	Bucks Fizz	RCA	3		

August 1983

This Mnth	Prev Mnth	Title	Artist	Label	Wks 20	(US Pos)	
1	-	Give It Up	KC & The Sunshine Band	Epic	9	(18)	L
2	-	Club Tropicana	Wham!	Innervision	7		
3	9	Double Dutch	Malcolm McLaren	Charisma	9		
4	3	I.O.U.	Freeez	Beggars Banquet	9		L
5	2	Wherever I Lay My Hat (That's My Home)	Paul Young	CBS	9	(70)	F
6	-	Long Hot Summer	Style Council	Polydor	5		
7	-	Gold	Spandau Ballet	Reformation	6	(29)	
8	-	I'm Still Standing	Elton John	Rocket	6	(12)	
9	-	Everything Counts	Depeche Mode	Mute	5		
10	-	The Crown	Gary Byrd & The GB Experience	Motown	5		F L
11	8	Who's That Girl	Eurythmics	RCA	6	(21)	
12	-	Rockit	Herbie Hancock	CBS	5	(71)	L
13	-	Big Log	Robert Plant	WEA	4	(20)	F L
14	16	Cruel Summer	Bananarama	London	5	(9)	
15	-	Wings Of A Dove	Madness	Stiff	6		
16	17	Wrapped Around Your Finger	Police	A&M	4	(8)	
17	-	It's Late	Shakin' Stevens	Epic	3		
18	4	Moonlight Shadow	Mike Oldfield	Virgin	9		
19	-	Watching You Watching Me	David Grant	Chrysalis	5		
20	6	Come Live With Me	Heaven 17	Virgin	7		

September 1983

This Mnth	Prev Mnth	Title	Artist	Label	Wks 20	(US Pos)	
1	-	Red Red Wine	UB40	Dep International	10	(34)	
2	15	Wings Of A Dove	Madness	Stiff	6		
3	-	Tonight I Celebrate My Love	Peabo Bryson & Roberta Flack	Capitol	7	(16)	F
4	-	What Am I Gonna Do	Rod Stewart	Warner	5	(35)	
5	-	Mama	Genesis	Virgin/Charisma	7	(73)	
6	-	Walking In The Rain	Modern Romance	WEA	6		L
7	1	Give It Up	KC & The Sunshine Band	Epic	9	(18)	F
8	-	The Sun Goes Down (Living It Up)	Level 42	Polydor	5		F
9	-	Karma Chameleon	Culture Club	Virgin	11	(1)	G
10	7	Gold	Spandau Ballet	Reformation	6	(29)	
11	8	I'm Still Standing	Elton John	Rocket	6	(12)	
12	-	Come Back And Stay	Paul Young	CBS	5	(22)	
13	-	Dolce Vita	Ryan Paris	Carrere	5		F L
14	2	Club Tropicana	Wham!	Innervision	7		
15	-	Chance	Big Country	Mercury	5		
16	6	Long Hot Summer	Style Council	Polydor	5		
17	-	Ol' Rag Blues	Status Quo	Vertigo	4		
18	19	Watching You Watching Me	David Grant	Chrysalis	5		
19	-	Confusion	New Order	Factory	3		
20	-	Modern Love	David Bowie	EMI America	6	(14)	

US 1983 JULY-SEPT

This Mnth	Prev Mnth	Title	Artist	Label	Wks 20	(UK Pos)	
1	15	Every Breath You Take	Police	A&M	16	(1)	G
2	5	Electric Avenue	Eddy Grant	Portrait	12	(2)	F G L
3	1	Flashdance....What A Feeling	Irene Cara	Casablanca	16	(2)	G
4	14	Never Gonna Let You Go	Sergio Mendes	A&M	12	(45)	L
5	20	Wanna Be Startin' Something	Michael Jackson	Epic	10	(8)	
6	-	Come Dancing	Kinks	Arista	8	(12)	L
7	-	Our House	Madness	Geffen	7	(5)	F L
8	-	Is There Something I Should Know	Duran Duran	Capitol	9	(1)	
9	16	Too Shy	Kajagoogoo	EMI America	8	(1)	F L
10	-	Stand Back	Stevie Nicks	Modern	10		
11	2	Time (Clock Of The Heart)	Culture Club	Epic	11	(3)	
12	-	She Works Hard For The Money	Donna Summer	Mercury	11	(25)	
13	-	Sweet Dreams (Are Made Of This)	Eurythmics	RCA	13	(2)	F G
14	-	1999	Prince & The Revolution	Warner	6	(2)	
15	7	Don't Let It End	Styx	A&M	9	(56)	
16	-	I'm Still Standing	Elton John	Geffen	6	(4)	
17	11	Family Man	Daryl Hall & John Oates	RCA	7	(15)	
18	-	Baby Jane	Rod Stewart	Warner	4	(1)	
19	-	Maniac	Michael Sembello	Casablanca	13	(43)	F L
20	18	She's A Beauty	Tubes	Capitol	7		F L

This Mnth	Prev Mnth	Title	Artist	Label	Wks 20	(UK Pos)	
1	1	Every Breath You Take	Police	A&M	16	(1)	G
2	13	Sweet Dreams (Are Made Of This)	Eurythmics	RCA	13	(2)	F G
3	12	She Works Hard For The Money	Donna Summer	Mercury	11	(25)	
4	19	Maniac	Michael Sembello	Casablanca	13	(43)	F L
5	10	Stand Back	Stevie Nicks	Modern	10		
6	8	Is There Something I Should Know	Duran Duran	Capitol	9	(1)	
7	-	It's A Mistake	Men At Work	Columbia	8	(33)	L
8	-	(Keep Feeling) Fascination	Human League	A&M	9	(2)	
9	3	Flashdance....What A Feeling	Irene Cara	Casablanca	16	(2)	G
10	-	Puttin' On The Ritz	Taco	RCA	9		F G L
11	4	Never Gonna Let You Go	Sergio Mendes	A&M	12	(45)	L
12	-	I'll Tumble 4 Ya	Culture Club	Epic	8		
13	-	China Girl	David Bowie	EMI America	6	(2)	
14	-	Hot Girls In Love	Loverboy	Columbia	6		F
15	2	Electric Avenue	Eddy Grant	Portrait	12	(2)	F G L
16	5	Wanna Be Startin' Something	Michael Jackson	Epic	10	(8)	
17	-	Human Nature	Michael Jackson	Epic	7		
18	-	The Safety Dance	Men Without Hats	Backstreet	11	(6)	F
19	-	Take Me To Heart	Quarterflash	Geffen	4		L
20	-	Lawyers In Love	Jackson Browne	Asylum	6		

This Mnth	Prev Mnth	Title	Artist	Label	Wks 20	(UK Pos)	
1	4	Maniac	Michael Sembello	Casablanca	13	(43)	F L
2	2	Sweet Dreams (Are Made Of This)	Eurythmics	RCA	13	(2)	F G
3	-	Tell Her About It	Billy Joel	Columbia	9	(4)	
4	18	The Safety Dance	Men Without Hats	Backstreet	11	(6)	F
5	10	Puttin' On The Ritz	Taco	RCA	9		F G L
6	-	Total Eclipse Of The Heart	Bonnie Tyler	Columbia	14	(1)	G L
7	1	Every Breath You Take	Police	A&M	16	(1)	G
8	17	Human Nature	Michael Jackson	Epic	7		
9	-	Don't Cry	Asia	Geffen	7	(33)	L
10	-	Making Love Out Of Nothing At All	Air Supply	Arista	13		G
11	-	(She's) Sexy + 17	Stray Cats	EMI America	8	(29)	L
12	3	She Works Hard For The Money	Donna Summer	Mercury	11	(25)	
13	12	I'll Tumble 4 Ya	Culture Club	Epic	8		
14	20	Lawyers In Love	Jackson Browne	Asylum	6		
15	8	(Keep Feeling) Fascination	Human League	A&M	9	(2)	
16	-	Far From Over	Frank Stallone	RSO	6	(68)	F L
17	7	It's A Mistake	Men At Work	Columbia	8	(33)	L
18	-	King Of Pain	Police	A&M	9	(17)	
19	-	Promises, Promises	Naked Eyes	EMI America	6		L
20	-	True	Spandau Ballet	Chrysalis	9	(1)	F L

◆ In April half the American Top 30 singles were by British artists, and in June, British acts had their best ever showing on the US Hot 100. Included among the hit makers were veterans of the first British Invasion, The Kinks and The Hollies.

◆ In Britain, UB40 had their first No. 1, with a revival of Neil Diamond's 'Red Red Wine', while in America, Canadian quintet Sheriff had a minor hit with 'When I'm With You'. Both records returned to top the US charts in the late 1980s.

◆ Producers Phil Ramone and Jim Steinman both had Top 10 singles in September. Ramone registered with tracks by Billy Joel and Michael Sembello while Steinman scored with hits from Bonnie Tyler and Air Supply.

UK 1983

OCT-DEC

▲ Culture Club's only transatlantic chart topper, 'Karma Chameleon', was Britain's top single in 1983, selling nearly 1.5 million.

◆ In 1983, Michael Jackson not only had the biggest album, **Thriller,** he also earned the first platinum music video for *The Making Of Thriller*, and amassed seven US Top 10 singles –. the best yearly performance since The Beatles in 1964!

◆ Britain's most successful chart year in the US since 1964 ended with legendary hitmakers The Who splitting and chart regulars ELO starting a long sabbatical.

October 1983

This Mnth	Prev Mnth	Title	Artist	Label	Wks 20	(US Pos)	
1	9	Karma Chameleon	Culture Club	Virgin	11	(1)	G
2	20	Modern Love	David Bowie	EMI America	6	(14)	
3	-	They Don't Know	Tracey Ullman	Stiff	6	(8)	
4	-	Dear Prudence	Siouxsie & The Banshees	Wonderland	6		
5	-	New Song	Howard Jones	WEA	6	(27)	F
6	1	Red Red Wine	UB40	Dep International	10	(34)	
7	-	This Is Not A Love Song	Public Image Ltd.	Virgin	5		
8	-	Blue Monday	New Order	Factory	7		
9	-	In Your Eyes	George Benson	Warner	6		
10	-	All Night Long (All Night)	Lionel Richie	Motown	8	(1)	
11	-	(Hey You) The Rocksteady Crew	Rocksteady Crew	Virgin	6		F L
12	12	Come Back And Stay	Paul Young	CBS	5	(22)	
13	3	Tonight I Celebrate My Love	Peabo Bryson & Roberta Flack	Capitol	7	(16)	F
14	-	Superman (Gioca Jouer)	Black Lace	Flair	5		F
15	-	Tahiti (From Mutiny On The Bounty)	David Essex	Mercury	5		L
16	5	Mama	Genesis	Virgin/Charisma	7	(73)	
17	-	Big Apple	Kajagoogoo	EMI	4		L
18	-	The Safety Dance	Men Without Hats	Statik	6	(3)	F L
19	13	Dolce Vita	Ryan Paris	Carrere	5		F L
20	15	Chance	Big Country	Mercury	5		

November 1983

This Mnth	Prev Mnth	Title	Artist	Label	Wks 20	(US Pos)	
1	-	Uptown Girl	Billy Joel	CBS	12	(3)	
2	10	All Night Long (All Night)	Lionel Richie	Motown	8	(1)	
3	-	Say Say Say	Paul McCartney & Michael Jackson	Parlophone	9	(1)	
4	-	Cry Just A Little Bit	Shakin' Stevens	Epic	7	(67)	
5	-	Puss 'n Boots	Adam Ant	CBS	4		
6	-	The Love Cats	Cure	Fiction	5		
7	1	Karma Chameleon	Culture Club	Virgin	11	(1)	G
8	18	The Safety Dance	Men Without Hats	Statik	6	(3)	F L
9	-	The Sun And The Rain	Madness	Stiff	4	(72)	
10	-	Union Of The Snake	Duran Duran	EMI	4	(3)	
11	-	Never Never	Assembly	Mute	4		F L
12	-	Please Don't Make Me Cry	UB40	Dep International	5		
13	11	(Hey You) The Rocksteady Crew	Rocksteady Crew	Virgin	6		F L
14	3	They Don't Know	Tracey Ullman	Stiff	6	(8)	
15	5	New Song	Howard Jones	WEA	6	(27)	F
16	-	Love Of The Common People	Paul Young	CBS	10	(45)	
17	-	Solid Bond In Your Heart	Style Council	Polydor	3		
18	-	Undercover Of The Night	Rolling Stones	Rolling Stone	3	(9)	
19	-	Calling Your Name	Marilyn	Mercury	4		F L
20	-	Unconditional Love	Donna Summer	Mercury	2	(43)	

December 1983

This Mnth	Prev Mnth	Title	Artist	Label	Wks 20	(US Pos)	
1	-	Only You	Flying Pickets	10	7		F
2	16	Love Of The Common People	Paul Young	CBS	10	(45)	
3	-	Hold Me Now	Thompson Twins	Arista	9	(3)	
4	-	My Oh My	Slade	RCA	7	(37)	
5	-	Let's Stay Together	Tina Turner	Capitol	8	(26)	F
6	1	Uptown Girl	Billy Joel	CBS	12	(3)	
7	-	Victims	Culture Club	Virgin	6		
8	-	Please Don't Fall In Love	Cliff Richard	EMI	6		
9	-	Move Over Darling	Tracey Ullman	Stiff	5		
10	-	Islands In The Stream	Kenny Rogers & Dolly Parton	RCA	7	(1)	L
11	-	Tell Her About It	Billy Joel	CBS	7	(1)	
12	-	Thriller	Michael Jackson	Epic	9	(4)	
13	19	Calling Your Name	Marilyn	Mercury	4		F L
14	-	Marguerita Time	Status Quo	Vertigo	6		
15	3	Say Say Say	Paul McCartney & Michael Jackson	Parlophone	9	(1)	
16	-	What Is Love	Howard Jones	WEA	8	(33)	
17	11	Never Never	Assembly	Mute	4		F L
18	4	Cry Just A Little Bit	Shakin' Stevens	Epic	7	(67)	
19	-	Right By Your Side	Eurythmics	RCA	4	(29)	
20	-	That's All!	Genesis	Charisma/virgin	4	(6)	

October 1983

This Mnth	Prev Mnth	Title	Artist	Label	Wks 20	(UK Pos)	
1	6	Total Eclipse Of The Heart	Bonnie Tyler	Columbia	14	(1)	G L
2	10	Making Love Out Of Nothing At All	Air Supply	Arista	13		G
3	20	True	Spandau Ballet	Chrysalis	9	(1)	F L
4	-	Islands In The Stream	Kenny Rogers & Dolly Parton	RCA	15	(7)	G
5	18	King Of Pain	Police	A&M	9	(17)	
6	-	One Thing Leads To Another	Fixx	MCA	9		
7	4	The Safety Dance	Men Without Hats	Backstreet	11	(6)	F
8	-	All Night Long (All Night)	Lionel Richie	Motown	15	(2)	G
9	3	Tell Her About It	Billy Joel	Columbia	9	(4)	
10	11	(She's) Sexy + 17	Stray Cats	EMI America	8	(29)	L
11	-	Telefone (Long Distance Love Affair)	Sheena Easton	EMI America	9		
12	-	Delirious	Prince & The Revolution	Warner	8		
13	-	Burning Down The House	Talking Heads	Sire	5		F L
14	16	Far From Over	Frank Stallone	RSO	6	(68)	F L
15	19	Promises, Promises	Naked Eyes	EMI America	6		L
16	-	Suddenly Last Summer	Motels	Capitol	8		L
17	-	How Am I Supposed To Live Without You	Laura Branigan	Atlantic	6		
18	1	Maniac	Michael Sembello	Casablanca	13	(43)	F L
19	-	Uptown Girl	Billy Joel	Columbia	13	(1)	G
20	-	If Anyone Falls	Stevie Nicks	Modern	4		

November 1983

This Mnth	Prev Mnth	Title	Artist	Label	Wks 20	(UK Pos)	
1	8	All Night Long (All Night)	Lionel Richie	Motown	15	(2)	G
2	4	Islands In The Stream	Kenny Rogers & Dolly Parton	RCA	15	(7)	G
3	-	Say Say Say	Paul McCartney & Michael Jackson	Columbia	16	(2)	G
4	19	Uptown Girl	Billy Joel	Columbia	13	(1)	G
5	1	Total Eclipse Of The Heart	Bonnie Tyler	Columbia	14	(1)	G L
6	-	Cum On Feel The Noize	Quiet Riot	Pasha	11	(45)	F G L
7	6	One Thing Leads To Another	Fixx	MCA	9		
8	-	Love Is A Battlefield	Pat Benatar	Chrysalis	12	(17)	
9	16	Suddenly Last Summer	Motels	Capitol	8		L
10	12	Delirious	Prince & The Revolution	Warner	8		
11	2	Making Love Out Of Nothing At All	Air Supply	Arista	13		G
12	11	Telefone (Long Distance Love Affair)	Sheena Easton	EMI America	9		
13	-	Say It Isn't So	Daryl Hall & John Oates	RCA	13	(69)	
14	-	Heart And Soul	Huey Lewis & The News	Chrysalis	7		
15	-	P.Y.T. (Pretty Young Thing)	Michael Jackson	Epic	6	(11)	L
16	-	Crumblin' Down	John Cougar Mellencamp	Riva	6		
17	3	True	Spandau Ballet	Chrysalis	9	(1)	F L
18	-	Modern Love	David Bowie	EMI America	5	(2)	
19	-	Tonight I Celebrate My Love	Peabo Bryson & Roberta Flack	Capitol	8	(2)	F
20	-	Church Of The Poison Mind	Culture Club	Epic	8	(2)	

December 1983

This Mnth	Prev Mnth	Title	Artist	Label	Wks 20	(UK Pos)	
1	3	Say Say Say	Paul McCartney & Michael Jackson	Columbia	16	(2)	G
2	13	Say It Isn't So	Daryl Hall & John Oates	RCA	13	(69)	
3	1	All Night Long (All Night)	Lionel Richie	Motown	15	(2)	G
4	4	Uptown Girl	Billy Joel	Columbia	13	(1)	G
5	-	Union Of The Snake	Duran Duran	Capitol	10	(3)	
6	8	Love Is A Battlefield	Pat Benatar	Chrysalis	12	(17)	
7	-	Owner Of A Lonely Heart	Yes	Atco	13	(28)	L
8	-	Twist Of Fate	Olivia Newton-John	MCA	10	(57)	
9	2	Islands In The Stream	Kenny Rogers & Dolly Parton	RCA	15	(7)	G
10	20	Church Of The Poison Mind	Culture Club	Epic	8	(2)	
11	6	Cum On Feel The Noize	Quiet Riot	Pasha	11	(45)	F G L
12	-	Undercover Of The Night	Rolling Stones	Rolling Stone	8	(11)	
13	16	Crumblin' Down	John Cougar Mellencamp	Riva	6		
14	-	Why Me?	Irene Cara	Geffen/Network	7		
15	-	Break My Stride	Matthew Wilder	Private I	11	(4)	F L
16	-	Major Tom (Coming Home)	Peter Schilling	Elektra	7	(42)	F L
17	-	I Guess That's Why They Call It The Blues	Elton John	Geffen	10	(5)	
18	-	Synchronicity II	Police	A&M	6	(17)	
19	14	Heart And Soul	Huey Lewis & The News	Chrysalis	7		
20	-	Talking In Your Sleep	Romantics	Nemperor	12		F L

◆ Total record and tape sales in 1983 went up 3% to $3.7 billion, with tapes outselling records for the first time.

◆ The success of MTV, and videos in general, meant an act's image was now almost as important as their sound. This situation not only benefited the British invaders, it boosted heavy metal sales and helped Michael Jackson and Prince crossover to the pop market (they were among the very few black artists seen on MTV).

◆ Country music video channel TNN (The Nashville Network) was launched and the genre's leading group, Alabama, collected three more platinum albums.

◆ Winners of the first *Billboard* Video Awards included Michael Jackson, ZZ Top, Duran Duran and Eurythmics.

UK 1984
JAN-MAR

◆ As 'Nobody Told Me' gave John Lennon his last transatlantic Top 20 hit, Paul McCartney scored his only British No. 1 of the 1980s, 'Pipes Of Peace', which, oddly, failed to chart Stateside.

◆ Despite being banned by the BBC, 'Relax' by Frankie Goes To Hollywood became one of Britain's biggest ever sellers.

◆ The *NME* Poll showed New Order as Best Group, their 'Blue Monday' as Top Record, and fellow Mancunians The Smiths as Best New Group. Incidentally, in January, The Smiths' first three releases held the top three rungs on the Independent chart.

◆ The Beatles City Exhibition Centre opened in Liverpool, and Yoko Ono presented a cheque for £250,000 ($375,000) to Liverpool's Strawberry Fields old people's home (immortalized in The Beatles song 'Strawberry Fields Forever').

January 1984

This Mnth	Prev Mnth	Title	Artist	Label	Wks 20	(US Pos)	
1	-	Pipes Of Peace	Paul McCartney	Parlophone	6		
2	16	What Is Love	Howard Jones	WEA	8	(33)	
3	-	Relax	Frankie Goes To Hollywood	ZTT	25	(10)	F G
4	14	Marguerita Time	Status Quo	Vertigo	6		
5	11	Tell Her About It	Billy Joel	CBS	7	(1)	
6	2	Love Of The Common People	Paul Young	CBS	10	(45)	
7	-	A Rockin' Good Way	Shaky & Bonnie	CBS	5		
8	-	That's Living (Alright)	Joe Fagin	Towerbell	7		F L
9	10	Islands In The Stream	Kenny Rogers & Dolly Parton	RCA	7	(1)	L
10	3	Hold Me Now	Thompson Twins	Arista	9	(3)	
11	1	Only You	Flying Pickets	10	7		F
12	7	Victims	Culture Club	Virgin	6		
13	-	Bird Of Paradise	Snowy White	Towerbell	4		F L
14	4	My Oh My	Slade	RCA	7	(37)	
15	-	Nobody Told Me	John Lennon	Ono/Polydor	3	(5)	L
16	12	Thriller	Michael Jackson	Epic	9	(4)	
17	-	Wonderland	Big Country	Mercury	4	(86)	
18	-	Running With The Night	Lionel Richie	Motown	2	(7)	
19	-	Wishful Thinking	China Crisis	Virgin	4		
20	5	Let's Stay Together	Tina Turner	Capitol	8	(26)	F

February 1984

This Mnth	Prev Mnth	Title	Artist	Label	Wks 20	(US Pos)	
1	3	Relax	Frankie Goes To Hollywood	ZTT	25	(10)	F G
2	-	Radio Ga Ga	Queen	EMI	6	(16)	
3	-	Girls Just Want To Have Fun	Cyndi Lauper	Portrait	7	(2)	F
4	-	Break My Stride	Matthew Wilder	Epic	7	(5)	F L
5	-	Doctor Doctor	Thompson Twins	Arista	7	(11)	
6	8	That's Living (Alright)	Joe Fagin	Towerbell	7		F L
7	-	Holiday	Madonna	Sire	5	(16)	F
8	-	New Moon On Monday	Duran Duran	EMI	4	(10)	
9	-	(Feels Like) Heaven	Fiction Factory	CBS	4		F L
10	-	99 Red Balloons	Nena	Epic	8	(2)	F L
11	-	My Ever Changing Moods	Style Council	Polydor	4		
12	-	Here Comes The Rain Again	Eurythmics	RCA	5	(4)	
13	-	The Killing Moon	Echo & The Bunnymen	Korova	3		
14	-	What Difference Does It Make	Smiths	Rough Trade	4		F
15	-	Somebody's Watching Me	Rockwell	Motown	6	(2)	F L
16	-	Love Theme From 'The Thorn Birds'	Juan Martin	WEA	2		F L
17	-	Wouldn't It Be Good	Nik Kershaw	MCA	7	(46)	F
18	17	Wonderland	Big Country	Mercury	4	(86)	
19	-	Michael Caine	Madness	Stiff	3		
20	1	Pipes Of Peace	Paul McCartney	Parlophone	6		

March 1984

This Mnth	Prev Mnth	Title	Artist	Label	Wks 20	(US Pos)	
1	10	99 Red Balloons	Nena	Epic	8	(2)	F L
2	-	Joanna/Tonight	Kool & The Gang	De-Lite	7	(2)	
3	-	Street Dance	Break Machine	Record Shack	8		F
4	17	Wouldn't It Be Good	Nik Kershaw	MCA	7	(46)	F
5	1	Relax	Frankie Goes To Hollywood	ZTT	25	(10)	F G
6	-	Hello	Lionel Richie	Motown	10	(1)	
7	-	An Innocent Man	Billy Joel	CBS	7	(10)	
8	15	Somebody's Watching Me	Rockwell	Motown	6	(2)	F L
9	-	It's Raining Men	Weather Girls	CBS	6	(46)	F L
10	-	Jump	Van Halen	Warner	5	(1)	F
11	-	What Do I Do	Phil Fearon & Galaxy	Ensign	5		
12	-	The Music Of Torvill & Dean EP	Richard Hartley/ Michael Reed Orchestra	Safari	5		F L
13	-	Run Runaway	Slade	RCA	5	(20)	
14	-	Robert De Niro's Waiting	Bananarama	London	5	(95)	
15	5	Doctor Doctor	Thompson Twins	Arista	7	(11)	
16	-	Your Love Is King	Sade	Epic	5	(54)	F
17	-	Hide And Seek	Howard Jones	WEA	5		
18	-	It's A Miracle	Culture Club	Virgin	5	(13)	
19	2	Radio Ga Ga	Queen	EMI	6	(16)	
20	11	My Ever Changing Moods	Style Council	Polydor	4		

250

January 1984

This Mnth	Prev Mnth	Title	Artist	Label	Wks 20	(UK Pos)	
1	7	Owner Of A Lonely Heart	Yes	Atco	13	(28)	L
2	1	Say Say Say	Paul McCartney & Michael Jackson	Columbia	16	(2)	G
3	20	Talking In Your Sleep	Romantics	Nemperor	12		F L
4	15	Break My Stride	Matthew Wilder	Private I	11	(4)	F L
5	17	I Guess That's Why They Call It The Blues	Elton John	Geffen	10	(5)	
6	8	Twist Of Fate	Olivia Newton-John	MCA	10	(57)	
7	-	Karma Chameleon	Culture Club	Virgin	13	(1)	G
8	2	Say It Isn't So	Daryl Hall & John Oates	RCA	13	(69)	
9	5	Union Of The Snake	Duran Duran	Capitol	10	(3)	
10	-	Running With The Night	Lionel Richie	Motown	8	(9)	
11	-	Joanna	Kool & The Gang	De-Lite	10	(2)	
12	-	That's All!	Genesis	Atlantic	8	(16)	
13	12	Undercover Of The Night	Rolling Stones	Rolling Stone	8	(11)	
14	3	All Night Long (All Night)	Lionel Richie	Motown	15	(2)	G
15	4	Uptown Girl	Billy Joel	Columbia	13	(1)	G
16	-	Think Of Laura	Christopher Cross	Warner	6		L
17	-	Pink Houses	John Cougar Mellencamp	Riva	5		
18	6	Love Is A Battlefield	Pat Benatar	Chrysalis	12	(17)	
19	-	The Curly Shuffle	Jump 'N The Saddle	Atlantic	3		F L
20	-	I Still Can't Get Over You	Ray Parker Jr.	Arista	5		

February 1984

This Mnth	Prev Mnth	Title	Artist	Label	Wks 20	(UK Pos)	
1	7	Karma Chameleon	Culture Club	Virgin	13	(1)	G
2	11	Joanna	Kool & The Gang	De-Lite	10	(2)	
3	-	Jump	Van Halen	Warner	13	(7)	G
4	3	Talking In Your Sleep	Romantics	Nemperor	12		F L
5	12	That's All!	Genesis	Atlantic	8	(16)	
6	1	Owner Of A Lonely Heart	Yes	Atco	13	(28)	L
7	-	99 Luftballons	Nena	Epic	10	(1)	F G L
8	10	Running With The Night	Lionel Richie	Motown	8	(9)	
9	-	Let The Music Play	Shannon	Mirage	8	(14)	F G L
10	-	Girls Just Want To Have Fun	Cyndi Lauper	Portrait	10	(2)	F G
11	16	Think Of Laura	Christopher Cross	Warner	6		L
12	-	An Innocent Man	Billy Joel	Columbia	7	(8)	
13	-	Thriller	Michael Jackson	Epic	8	(10)	G
14	4	Break My Stride	Matthew Wilder	Private I	11	(4)	F L
15	5	I Guess That's Why They Call It The Blues	Elton John	Geffen	10	(5)	
16	17	Pink Houses	John Cougar Mellencamp	Riva	5		
17	-	Nobody Told Me	John Lennon	Polydor	7	(6)	L
18	-	Wrapped Around Your Finger	Police	A&M	7	(7)	L
19	20	I Still Can't Get Over You	Ray Parker Jr.	Arista	5		
20	-	Somebody's Watching Me	Rockwell	Motown	10	(6)	F G L

March 1984

This Mnth	Prev Mnth	Title	Artist	Label	Wks 20	(UK Pos)	
1	3	Jump	Van Halen	Warner	13	(7)	G
2	20	Somebody's Watching Me	Rockwell	Motown	10	(6)	F G L
3	10	Girls Just Want To Have Fun	Cyndi Lauper	Portrait	10	(2)	F G
4	7	99 Luftballons	Nena	Epic	10	(1)	F G L
5	-	Footloose	Kenny Loggins	Columbia	12	(6)	G
6	-	Here Comes The Rain Again	Eurythmics	RCA	10	(8)	
7	-	I Want A New Drug	Huey Lewis & The News	Chrysalis	8		
8	13	Thriller	Michael Jackson	Epic	8	(10)	G
9	17	Nobody Told Me	John Lennon	Polydor	7	(6)	L
10	-	Automatic	Pointer Sisters	Planet	9	(2)	
11	-	Got A Hold On Me	Christine McVie	Warner	6		F L
12	-	Adult Education	Daryl Hall & John Oates	RCA	8	(63)	
13	-	New Moon On Monday	Duran Duran	Capitol	6	(9)	
14	1	Karma Chameleon	Culture Club	Virgin	13	(1)	G
15	18	Wrapped Around Your Finger	Police	A&M	7	(7)	L
16	-	The Language Of Love	Dan Fogelberg	Full Moon	5		L
17	-	Against All Odds (Take A Look At Me Now)	Phil Collins	Atlantic	10	(2)	G
18	9	Let The Music Play	Shannon	Mirage	8	(14)	F G L
19	-	Miss Me Blind	Culture Club	Virgin	8		
20	-	Hold Me Now	Thompson Twins	Arista	11	(4)	F

◆ Michael Jackson's **Thriller,** with world sales of 30 million, became the biggest selling record ever. Jackson also received a record eight Grammy Awards and seven American Music Awards.

◆ Six years after making their chart debut, platinum sellers Van Halen had their first Top 10 single with the self-composed 'Jump'.

▲ Two new American women creating a stir were Cyndi Lauper (above), who won Best New Act in the Grammy Awards, and Madonna.

◆ Jackie Wilson, one of the all-time greats of soul music, died after spending over eight years in a coma.

UK 1984
APR-JUNE

◆ The Beatles, who had recently had streets named after them in Liverpool, were made Freemen of that city – its highest honour.

◆ The late Bob Marley's **Legend** entered the LP chart at No. 1 and held that spot for three months.

◆ Frankie Goes To Hollywood's second single, 'Two Tribes', entered at No. 1 and spent nine weeks at the summit. Soon afterwards 'Relax' moved back up to No. 2. Both sold over a million.

▲ Elton John (above), Kool & The Gang and Brits winner Paul Young (whose **No Parlez** album sold over a million) performed in front of 72,000 at Wembley Stadium.

April 1984

This Mnth	Prev Mnth	Title	Artist	Label	Wks 20	(US Pos)	
1	6	Hello	Lionel Richie	Motown	10	(1)	
2	-	You Take Me Up	Thompson Twins	Arista	6	(44)	
3	-	A Love Worth Waiting For	Shakin' Stevens	Epic	6		
4	-	People Are People	Depeche Mode	Mute	6	(13)	
5	-	Glad It's All Over/Damned On 45	Captain Sensible	A&M	5		L
6	-	Against All Odds (Take A Look At Me Now)	Phil Collins	Virgin	8	(1)	
7	14	Robert De Niro's Waiting	Bananarama	London	5	(95)	
8	-	I Want To Break Free	Queen	EMI	9	(45)	
9	-	Nelson Mandela	Special AKA	2 Tone	4		L
10	18	It's A Miracle	Culture Club	Virgin	5	(13)	
11	-	Ain't Nobody	Rufus & Chaka Khan	Warner	6	(22)	F
12	9	It's Raining Men	Weather Girls	CBS	6	(46)	F L
13	-	(When You Say You Love Somebody) In The Heart	Kool & The Gang	De-Lite	4		
14	11	What Do I Do	Phil Fearon & Galaxy	Ensign	5		
15	-	Wood Beez (Pray Like Aretha Franklin)	Scritti Politti	Virgin	3	(91)	F
16	-	P.Y.T. (Pretty Young Thing)	Michael Jackson	Epic	3	(10)	
17	16	Your Love Is King	Sade	Epic	5	(54)	F
18	-	The Reflex	Duran Duran	EMI	8	(1)	
19	-	Don't Tell Me	Blancmange	London	6		L
20	-	Cherry Oh Baby	UB40	Dep International	3		

May 1984

This Mnth	Prev Mnth	Title	Artist	Label	Wks 20	(US Pos)	
1	18	The Reflex	Duran Duran	EMI	8	(1)	
2	-	Automatic	Pointer Sisters	Planet	7	(5)	
3	6	Against All Odds (Take A Look At...)	Phil Collins	Virgin	8	(1)	
4	8	I Want To Break Free	Queen	EMI	9	(45)	
5	-	One Love/People Get Ready	Bob Marley & The Wailers	Island	5		L
6	-	Locomotion	O.M.D.	Virgin	7		
7	-	When You're Young And In Love	Flying Pickets	10	5		L
8	19	Don't Tell Me	Blancmange	London	6		L
9	-	Footloose	Kenny Loggins	CBS	4	(1)	F L
10	-	Let's Hear It For The Boy	Deniece Williams	CBS	7	(1)	L
11	1	Hello	Lionel Richie	Motown	10	(1)	
12	-	Dancing Girls	Nik Kershaw	MCA	3		
13	-	The Lebanon	Human League	Virgin	3	(64)	
14	-	I'm Falling	Bluebells	London	4		F
15	-	Love Games	Belle & The Devotions	CBS	2		F L
16	-	Wake Me Up Before You Go Go	Wham!	Epic	8	(1)	
17	-	Break Dance Party	Break Machine	Record Shack	4		L
18	13	(When You Say You...) In The Heart	Kool & The Gang	De-Lite	4		
19	-	Somebody Else's Guy	Jocelyn Brown	4th & Broadway	3	(75)	F
20	2	You Take Me Up	Thompson Twins	Arista	6	(44)	

June 1984

This Mnth	Prev Mnth	Title	Artist	Label	Wks 20	(US Pos)	
1	16	Wake Me Up Before You Go Go	Wham!	Epic	8	(1)	
2	-	Two Tribes	Frankie Goes To Hollywood	ZTT	14	(43)	G
3	-	Smalltown Boy	Bronski Beat	Forbidden Fruit	7	(48)	F
4	-	High Energy	Evelyn Thomas	Record Shack	5	(85)	F L
5	10	Let's Hear It For The Boy	Deniece Williams	CBS	7	(1)	L
6	-	Dancing With Tears In My Eyes	Ultravox	Chrysalis	5		
7	-	Only When You Leave	Spandau Ballet	Reformation	4	(34)	
8	-	Relax	Frankie Goes To Hollywood	ZTT	25	(10)	F G
9	-	Sad Songs (Say So Much)	Elton John	Rocket	5	(5)	
10	-	Pearl In The Shell	Howard Jones	WEA	4		
11	-	Searchin' (I Gotta Find A Man)	Hazell Dean	Proto	5		F
12	-	Groovin' (You're The Best Thing)/Big Boss Groove	Style Council	Polydor	5		
13	-	I Won't Let The Sun Go Down On Me	Nik Kershaw	MCA	8		
14	1	The Reflex	Duran Duran	EMI	8	(1)	
15	-	Farewell My Summer Love	Michael Jackson	Motown	6	(38)	
16	-	Heaven Knows I'm Miserable Now	Smiths	Rough Trade	5		
17	-	I Feel Like Buddy Holly	Alvin Stardust	Stiff	5		
18	-	Thinking Of You	Sister Sledge	Cotillion/Atlantic	6		
19	2	Automatic	Pointer Sisters	Planet	7	(5)	
20	4	I Want To Break Free	Queen	EMI	9	(45)	

April 1984

This Mnth	Prev Mnth	Title	Artist	Label	Wks 20	(UK Pos)	
1	5	Footloose	Kenny Loggins	Columbia	12	(6)	G
2	17	Against All Odds (Take A Look At Me Now)	Phil Collins	Atlantic	10	(2)	G
3	-	Hello	Lionel Richie	Motown	14	(1)	G
4	2	Somebody's Watching Me	Rockwell	Motown	10	(6)	F G L
5	19	Miss Me Blind	Culture Club	Virgin	8		
6	10	Automatic	Pointer Sisters	Planet	9	(2)	
7	20	Hold Me Now	Thompson Twins	Arista	11	(4)	F
8	6	Here Comes The Rain Again	Eurythmics	RCA	10	(8)	
9	12	Adult Education	Daryl Hall & John Oates	RCA	8	(63)	
10	-	Love Somebody	Rick Springfield	RCA	8		
11	-	They Don't Know	Tracey Ullman	MCA	7	(2)	F L
12	1	Jump	Van Halen	Warner	13	(7)	G
13	-	You Might Think	Cars	Elektra	8		
14	-	Eat It	Weird Al Yankovic	Rock 'n' Roll	5	(36)	F L
15	-	To All The Girls I've Loved Before	Julio Iglesias & Willie Nelson	Columbia	9	(17)	F G
16	3	Girls Just Want To Have Fun	Cyndi Lauper	Portrait	10	(2)	F G
17	7	I Want A New Drug	Huey Lewis & The News	Chrysalis	8		
18	-	Girls	Dwight Twilley	EMI America	4		L
19	-	Tonight	Kool & The Gang	De-Lite	6	(2)	
20	-	Let's Hear It For The Boy	Deniece Williams	Columbia	11	(2)	G L

May 1984

This Mnth	Prev Mnth	Title	Artist	Label	Wks 20	(UK Pos)	
1	3	Hello	Lionel Richie	Motown	14	(1)	G
2	20	Let's Hear It For The Boy	Deniece Williams	Columbia	11	(2)	G L
3	7	Hold Me Now	Thompson Twins	Arista	11	(4)	F
4	15	To All The Girls I've Loved Before	Julio Iglesias & Willie Nelson	Columbia	9	(17)	F G
5	2	Against All Odds (Take A Look At Me Now)	Phil Collins	Atlantic	10	(2)	G
6	10	Love Somebody	Rick Springfield	RCA	8		
7	-	Time After Time	Cyndi Lauper	Portrait	11	(3)	
8	-	Oh, Sherrie	Steve Perry	Columbia	11		
9	13	You Might Think	Cars	Elektra	8		
10	1	Footloose	Kenny Loggins	Columbia	12	(6)	G
11	-	Head Over Heels	Go-Go's	IRS	7		L
12	-	Breakdance	Irene Cara	Geffen	8		L
13	11	They Don't Know	Tracey Ullman	MCA	7	(2)	F L
14	-	The Reflex	Duran Duran	Capitol	11	(1)	
15	-	The Longest Time	Billy Joel	Columbia	5	(25)	
16	-	Sister Christian	Night Ranger	MCA	8		F
17	19	Tonight	Kool & The Gang	De-Lite	6	(2)	
18	-	Authority Song	John Cougar Mellencamp	Riva	4		
19	5	Miss Me Blind	Culture Club	Virgin	8		
20	-	The Heart Of Rock 'n' Roll	Huey Lewis & The News	Chrysalis	9		

June 1984

This Mnth	Prev Mnth	Title	Artist	Label	Wks 20	(UK Pos)	
1	7	Time After Time	Cyndi Lauper	Portrait	11	(3)	
2	14	The Reflex	Duran Duran	Capitol	11	(1)	
3	2	Let's Hear It For The Boy	Deniece Williams	Columbia	11	(2)	G L
4	8	Oh, Sherrie	Steve Perry	Columbia	11		
5	20	The Heart Of Rock 'n' Roll	Huey Lewis & The News	Chrysalis	9		
6	-	Self Control	Laura Branigan	Atlantic	10	(5)	
7	-	Jump (For My Love)	Pointer Sisters	Planet	11	(6)	
8	-	Dancing In The Dark	Bruce Springsteen	Columbia	13	(4)	G
9	16	Sister Christian	Night Ranger	MCA	8		F
10	-	Borderline	Madonna	Sire	8	(2)	
11	1	Hello	Lionel Richie	Motown	14	(1)	G
12	12	Breakdance	Irene Cara	Geffen	8		L
13	-	Eyes Without A Face	Billy Idol	Chrysalis	10	(18)	F
14	-	When Doves Cry	Prince	Warner	14	(4)	P
15	-	It's A Miracle	Culture Club	Virgin	6	(4)	
16	-	Almost Paradise...Love Theme From Footloose	Mike Reno & Ann Wilson	Columbia	9		F L
17	-	I'll Wait	Van Halen	Warner	5		
18	4	To All The Girls I've Loved Before	Julio Iglesias & Willie Nelson	Columbia	9	(17)	F G
19	-	You Can't Get What You Want (Till You Know What You Want)	Joe Jackson	A&M	4		L
20	-	Stay The Night	Chicago	Full Moon	3		

◆ British artists held a record forty places on the Hot 100.

◆ Transatlantic toppers included 'Wake Me Up Before You Go Go' by Wham!, 'The Reflex' by Duran Duran (remixed by Nile Rodgers) and Lionel Richie's 'Hello'. Richie was on a 50-date American tour with Tina Turner.

◆ Among the hit makers who died were soul superstar Marvin Gaye, Ral Donner, R&B great Z.Z. Hill and top tunesmiths Meredith Wilson and Jimmy Kennedy.

◆ Pink Floyd's album **Dark Side Of The Moon** celebrated its tenth year on the American chart. It broke the longevity record previously held by **Johnny's** (Mathis) **Greatest Hits**, and was still on the US Catalog LP chart in 1996.

UK 1984 JULY–SEPT

Stevie Wonder's 36th British hit 'I Just Called To Say I Love You' was not only his first solo No. 1, but also Motown's first UK million seller. It was the third British million seller in a row to head the chart (following 'Two Tribes' and 'Careless Whisper') – a record unlikely to be broken.

▲ After Billy Joel's successful Wembley show was screened on TV, the singer/songwriter found himself with six albums in the British chart.

◆ Soon after releasing a duet with Cliff Richard, 'Two To The Power', Michael Jackson's 18-year-old sister Janet eloped with El Debarge, from the group Debarge.

July 1984

This Mnth	Prev Mnth	Title	Artist	Label	Wks 20	(US Pos)	
1	2	Two Tribes	Frankie Goes To Hollywood	ZTT	14	(43)	G
2	-	Relax	Frankie Goes To Hollywood	ZTT	25	(10)	F G
3	-	Time After Time	Cyndi Lauper	Portrait	7	(1)	
4	13	I Won't Let The Sun Go Down On Me	Nik Kershaw	MCA	8		
5	-	Hole In My Shoe	neil	WEA	6		F L
6	-	Jump (For My Love)	Pointer Sisters	Planet	5	(3)	
7	-	White Lines (Don't Don't Do It)	Grandmaster Flash, Melle Mel & The Furious Five	Sugar Hill	12		L
8	-	When Doves Cry	Prince	Warner	8	(1)	F
9	-	Breakin'...There's No Stopping Us	Ollie & Jerry	Polydor	5	(9)	F L
10	-	What's Love Got To Do With It	Tina Turner	Capitol	10	(1)	
11	-	Love Resurrection	Alison Moyet	CBS	5	(82)	F
12	-	Young At Heart	Bluebells	London	6		
13	-	Sister Of Mercy	Thompson Twins	Arista	3		
14	3	Smalltown Boy	Bronski Beat	Forbidden	7	(48)	F
15	-	Talking Loud And Clear	Orchestral Manoeuvres In The Dark	Virgin	4		
16	15	Farewell My Summer Love	Michael Jackson	Motown	6	(38)	
17	-	Stuck On You	Lionel Richie	Motown	4	(3)	
18	1	Wake Me Up Before You Go Go	Wham!	Epic	8	(1)	
19	-	Everybody's Laughing	Phil Fearon & Galaxy	Ensign	5		
20	18	Thinking Of You	Sister Sledge	Cotillion/Atlantic	6		

August 1984

This Mnth	Prev Mnth	Title	Artist	Label	Wks 20	(US Pos)	
1	1	Two Tribes	Frankie Goes To Hollywood	ZTT	14	(43)	G
2	-	Careless Whisper	George Michael	Epic	12	(1)	F G
3	10	What's Love Got To Do With It	Tina Turner	Capitol	10	(1)	
4	-	Agadoo	Black Lace	Flair	10		
5	-	Relax	Frankie Goes To Hollywood	ZTT	25	(10)	F G
6	8	When Doves Cry	Prince	Warner	8	(1)	F
7	-	Whatever I Do (Wherever I Go)	Hazell Dean	Proto	7		
8	5	Hole In My Shoe	neil	WEA	6		F L
9	-	It's A Hard Life	Queen	EMI	4	(72)	
10	-	Self Control	Laura Branigan	Atlantic	7	(4)	L
11	7	White Lines (Don't Don't Do It)	Grandmaster Flash, Melle Mel & The Furious Five	Sugar Hill	12		L
12	-	Like To Get To Know You Well	Howard Jones	WEA	7	(49)	
13	19	Everybody's Laughing	Phil Fearon & Galaxy	Ensign	5		
14	-	On The Wings Of Love	Jeffrey Osborne	A&M	5	(29)	L
15	-	Down On The Street	Shakatak	Polydor	4		L
16	-	Closest Thing To Heaven	Kane Gang	Kitchenware	5		F L
17	-	I Just Called To Say I Love You	Stevie Wonder	Motown	13	(1)	G
18	3	Time After Time	Cyndi Lauper	Portrait	7	(1)	
19	-	Stuck On You	Trevor Walters	Sanity	4		F L
20	12	Young At Heart	Bluebells	London	6		

September 1984

This Mnth	Prev Mnth	Title	Artist	Label	Wks 20	(US Pos)	
1	16	I Just Called To Say I Love You	Stevie Wonder	Motown	13	(1)	G
2	2	Careless Whisper	George Michael	Epic	12	(1)	F G
3	4	Agadoo	Black Lace	Flair	10		
4	-	Ghostbusters	Ray Parker Jr.	Arista	17	(1)	
5	-	Dr. Beat	Miami Sound Machine	Epic	7		F
6	11	Like To Get To Know You Well	Howard Jones	WEA	7	(49)	
7	-	Passengers	Elton John	Rocket	5		
8	-	Pride (In The Name Of Love)	U2	Island	7	(33)	
9	9	Self Control	Laura Branigan	Atlantic	7	(4)	L
10	-	Big In Japan	Alphaville	WEA International	5	(66)	F L
11	-	Lost In Music	Sister Sledge	Cotillion/Atlantic	6		
12	-	Master And Servant	Depeche Mode	Mute	4	(87)	
13	-	I'll Fly For You	Spandau Ballet	Reformation	4		
14	6	Whatever I Do (Wherever I Go)	Hazell Dean	Proto	7		
15	-	Madame Butterfly	Malcolm McLaren	Charisma	4		L
16	1	Two Tribes	Frankie Goes To Hollywood	ZTT	14	(43)	G
17	10	White Lines (Don't Don't Do It)	Grandmaster Flash, Melle Mel & The Furious Five	Sugar Hill	12		L
18	-	A Letter To You	Shakin' Stevens	Epic	4		
19	-	Blue Jean	David Bowie	EMI America	4	(8)	
20	18	Stuck On You	Trevor Walters	Sanity	4		F L

This Mnth	Prev Mnth	Title	Artist	Label	Wks 20	(UK Pos)	
1	14	When Doves Cry	Prince	Warner	14	(4)	P
2	8	Dancing In The Dark	Bruce Springsteen	Columbia	13	(4)	G
3	13	Eyes Without A Face	Billy Idol	Chrysalis	10	(18)	F
4	7	Jump (For My Love)	Pointer Sisters	Planet	11	(6)	
5	-	Ghostbusters	Ray Parker Jr.	Arista	13	(2)	G
6	16	Almost Paradise...Love Theme From Footloose	Mike Reno & Ann Wilson	Columbia	9		F L
7	-	Legs	ZZ Top	Warner	8	(16)	
8	-	Infatuation	Rod Stewart	Warner	8	(27)	
9	6	Self Control	Laura Branigan	Atlantic	10	(5)	
10	2	The Reflex	Duran Duran	Capitol	11	(1)	
11	-	State Of Shock	Jacksons	Epic	8	(14)	G
12	-	Sad Songs (Say So Much)	Elton John	Geffen	9	(7)	
13	-	Doctor! Doctor!	Thompson Twins	Arista	6	(3)	
14	-	Magic	Cars	Elektra	7		
15	5	The Heart Of Rock 'n' Roll	Huey Lewis & The News	Chrysalis	9		
16	-	Breakin'...There's No Stopping Us	Ollie & Jerry	Polydor	6	(5)	F L
17	1	Time After Time	Cyndi Lauper	Portrait	11	(3)	
18	-	What's Love Got To Do With It	Tina Turner	Capitol	13	(3)	F G
19	-	I Can Dream About You	Dan Hartman	MCA	8	(12)	F L
20	3	Let's Hear It For The Boy	Deniece Williams	Columbia	11	(2)	G L

1	5	Ghostbusters	Ray Parker Jr.	Arista	13	(2)	G
2	1	When Doves Cry	Prince	Warner	14	(4)	P
3	18	What's Love Got To Do With It	Tina Turner	Capitol	13	(3)	F G
4	11	State Of Shock	Jacksons	Epic	8	(14)	G
5	-	Stuck On You	Lionel Richie	Motown	11	(12)	
6	19	I Can Dream About You	Dan Hartman	MCA	8	(12)	F L
7	12	Sad Songs (Say So Much)	Elton John	Geffen	9	(7)	
8	2	Dancing In The Dark	Bruce Springsteen	Columbia	13	(4)	G
9	-	Sunglasses At Night	Corey Hart	EMI America	9		F
10	-	Missing You	John Waite	EMI America	11	(9)	F L
11	8	Infatuation	Rod Stewart	Warner	8	(27)	
12	-	If Ever You're In My Arms Again	Peabo Bryson	Elektra	7		
13	16	Breakin'...There's No Stopping Us	Ollie & Jerry	Polydor	6	(5)	F L
14	-	Round And Round	Ratt	Atlantic	6		F L
15	-	She Bop	Cyndi Lauper	Portrait	11	(46)	
16	-	Panama	Van Halen	Warner	4	(61)	
17	-	If This Is It	Huey Lewis & The News	Chrysalis	10	(39)	
18	7	Legs	ZZ Top	Warner	8	(16)	
19	3	Eyes Without A Face	Billy Idol	Chrysalis	10	(18)	F
20	-	The Warrior	Scandal Featuring Patty Smyth	Columbia	9		F L

1	10	Missing You	John Waite	EMI America	11	(9)	F L
2	3	What's Love Got To Do With It	Tina Turner	Capitol	13	(3)	F G
3	15	She Bop	Cyndi Lauper	Portrait	11	(46)	
4	-	Let's Go Crazy	Prince & The Revolution	Warner	11	(7)	G
5	-	Drive	Cars	Elektra	10	(5)	
6	17	If This Is It	Huey Lewis & The News	Chrysalis	10	(39)	
7	20	The Warrior	Scandal Featuring Patty Smyth	Columbia	9		F L
8	5	Stuck On You	Lionel Richie	Motown	11	(12)	
9	1	Ghostbusters	Ray Parker Jr.	Arista	13	(2)	G
10	-	The Glamorous Life	Sheila E	Warner	8		F
11	9	Sunglasses At Night	Corey Hart	EMI America	9		F
12	-	Cruel Summer	Bananarama	London	6	(8)	F
13	-	Cover Me	Bruce Springsteen	Columbia	8	(16)	
14	-	I Just Called To Say I Love You	Stevie Wonder	Motown	12	(1)	G
15	2	When Doves Cry	Prince & The Revolution	Warner	14	(4)	P
16	-	Lights Out	Peter Wolf	EMI America	6		F
17	-	Dynamite	Jermaine Jackson	Arista	5		
18	12	If Ever You're In My Arms Again	Peabo Bryson	Elektra	7		
19	-	Hard Habit To Break	Chicago	Full Moon	11	(8)	
20	-	Rock Me Tonite	Billy Squier	Capitol	5		L

US 1984
JULY–SEPT

◆ The Jacksons' *Victory* tour was the year's top road show. Their three days at New Jersey's Giant's Stadium alone grossed $4.5 million. Michael Jackson reportedly gave the $5 million he made from the tour to charity.

▲ The soundtrack to Prince's film *Purple Rain* sold a million in its first week. It led the lists for 24 weeks. The first two singles from it, 'When Doves Cry' and 'Let's Go Crazy', also hit the top.

◆ The deaths were announced of Big Mama Thornton (who first cut 'Hound Dog'), country legend Ernest Tubb, and Norman Petty, who co-wrote and produced many of Buddy Holly's hits.

UK 1984 OCT-DEC

◆ Bob Geldof and Midge Ure organized an all-star group, Band Aid, whose 'Do They Know It's Christmas' not only raised a fortune for the starving in Ethiopia but also became Britain's biggest ever seller (over 3.5 million).

▲ 'The Power Of Love' gave the year's most successful UK act, Frankie Goes To Hollywood, their third consecutive No. 1 with their first three hits, equalling a record set by fellow Liverpudlians Gerry & The Pacemakers.

◆ U2's first Top 5 entry 'Pride (In The Name Of Love)' was dedicated to Martin Luther King.

October 1984

This Mnth	Prev Mnth	Title	Artist	Label	Wks 20	(US Pos)	
1	1	I Just Called To Say I Love You	Stevie Wonder	Motown	13	(1)	G
2	-	The War Song	Culture Club	Virgin	5	(17)	
3	-	Freedom	Wham!	Epic	8	(3)	
4	4	Ghostbusters	Ray Parker Jr.	Arista	17	(1)	
5	-	No More Lonely Nights (Ballad)	Paul McCartney	Parlophone	6	(6)	
6	-	Drive	Cars	Elektra	6	(3)	
7	-	Together In Electric Dreams	Giorgio Moroder & Phil Oakey	Virgin	6		L
8	-	Why?	Bronski Beat	Forbidden Fruit	5		
9	8	Pride (In The Name Of Love)	U2	Island	7	(33)	
10	-	Shout To The Top	Style Council	Polydor	4		
11	-	Purple Rain	Prince & The Revolution	Warner	4	(2)	
12	11	Lost In Music	Sister Sledge	Cotillion/Atlantic	6		
13	-	Missing You	John Waite	EMI	6	(1)	F L
14	-	If It Happens Again	UB40	Dep International	4		
15	-	I'm Gonna Tear Your Playhouse Down	Paul Young	CBS	3	(13)	
16	-	All Cried Out	Alison Moyet	CBS	6		
17	-	Love Kills	Freddie Mercury	CBS	4	(69)	F
18	19	Blue Jean	David Bowie	Emi America	4	(8)	
19	-	I Feel For You	Chaka Khan	Warner	8	(3)	
20	2	Careless Whisper	George Michael	Epic	12	(1)	F G

November 1984

This Mnth	Prev Mnth	Title	Artist	Label	Wks 20	(US Pos)	
1	19	I Feel For You	Chaka Khan	Warner	8	(3)	
2	-	The Wild Boys	Duran Duran	Parlophone	6	(2)	
3	3	Freedom	Wham!	Epic	8	(3)	
4	-	The Wanderer	Status Quo	Vertigo	5		
5	-	Caribbean Queen (No More Love On The Run)	Billy Ocean	Jive	6	(1)	
6	16	All Cried Out	Alison Moyet	CBS	6		
7	-	I Should Have Known Better	Jim Diamond	A&M	8		F
8	-	Never Ending Story	Limahl	EMI	7	(17)	L
9	-	Too Late For Goodbyes	Julian Lennon	Charisma	5	(5)	F
10	5	No More Lonely Nights (Ballad)	Paul McCartney	Parlophone	6	(6)	
11	7	Together In Electric Dreams	Giorgio Moroder & Phil Oakey	Virgin	6		L
12	-	Gimme All Your Lovin'	ZZ Top	Warner	4	(37)	F
13	-	Love's Great Adventure	Ultravox	Chrysalis	5		
14	-	Hard Habit To Break	Chicago	Full Moon	4	(3)	
15	-	I'm So Excited	Pointer Sisters	Planet	4	(9)	
16	1	I Just Called To Say I Love You	Stevie Wonder	Motown	13	(1)	G
17	-	The Riddle	Nik Kershaw	MCA	9		
18	13	Missing You	John Waite	EMI	6	(1)	F L
19	-	Sexcrime (Nineteen Eighty Four)	Eurythmics	Virgin	7	(81)	
20	6	Drive	Cars	Elektra	6	(3)	

December 1984

This Mnth	Prev Mnth	Title	Artist	Label	Wks 20	(US Pos)	
1	-	The Power Of Love	Frankie Goes To Hollywood	ZTT	8		
2	18	The Riddle	Nik Kershaw	MCA	9		
3	-	We All Stand Together	Paul McCartney	Parlophone	7		
4	-	Like A Virgin	Madonna	Sire	10	(1)	
5	-	Do They Know It's Christmas	Band Aid	Mercury	8	(13)	F P
6	-	Teardrops	Shakin' Stevens	Epic	6		
7	7	I Should Have Known Better	Jim Diamond	A&M	8		F
8	-	Last Christmas/Everything She Wants	Wham!	Epic	8	(1)	G
9	20	Sexcrime (Nineteen Eighty Four)	Eurythmics	Virgin	7	(81)	
10	-	I Won't Run Away	Alvin Stardust	Chrysalis	6		L
11	1	I Feel For You	Chaka Khan	Warner	8	(3)	
12	-	Fresh	Kool & The Gang	De-Lite	7	(9)	
13	-	Nellie The Elephant	Toy Dolls	Volume	6		F L
14	-	Do The Conga	Black Lace	Flair	6		L
15	-	One Night In Bangkok	Murray Head	RCA	7	(3)	F L
16	8	Never Ending Story	Limahl	EMI	7	(17)	L
17	-	Everything Must Change	Paul Young	CBS	7	(56)	
18	-	Another Rock And Roll Christmas	Gary Glitter	Arista	3		L
19	15	Hard Habit To Break	Chicago	Full Moon	4	(3)	
20	-	Shout	Tears For Fears	Mercury	9	(1)	

October 1984

This Mnth	Prev Mnth	Title	Artist	Label	Wks 20	(UK Pos)	
1	14	I Just Called To Say I Love You	Stevie Wonder	Motown	12	(1)	G
2	4	Let's Go Crazy	Prince & The Revolution	Warner	11	(7)	G
3	19	Hard Habit To Break	Chicago	Full Moon	11	(8)	
4	-	Caribbean Queen (No More Love On The Run)	Billy Ocean	Jive	11	(6)	F G
5	-	Lucky Star	Madonna	Sire	8	(14)	
6	5	Drive	Cars	Elektra	10	(5)	
7	13	Cover Me	Bruce Springsteen	Columbia	8	(16)	
8	-	On The Dark Side	John Cafferty & The Beaver Brown Band	Scotti Brothers	6		F
9	1	Missing You	John Waite	EMI America	11	(9)	F L
10	-	I'm So Excited	Pointer Sisters	Planet	6	(11)	
11	10	The Glamorous Life	Sheila E	Warner	8		F
12	-	Purple Rain	Prince & The Revolution	Warner	9	(8)	G
13	3	She Bop	Cyndi Lauper	Portrait	11	(46)	
14	-	Wake Me Up Before You Go-Go	Wham!	Columbia	11	(1)	F G
15	7	The Warrior	Scandal Featuring Patty Smyth	Columbia	9		F L
16	-	Some Guys Have All The Luck	Rod Stewart	Warner	5	(15)	
17	12	Cruel Summer	Bananarama	London	6	(8)	F
18	-	Blue Jean	David Bowie	EMI America	7	(6)	
19	2	What's Love Got To Do With It	Tina Turner	Capitol	13	(3)	F G
20	-	Are We Ourselves?	Fixx	MCA	3		

November 1984

This Mnth	Prev Mnth	Title	Artist	Label	Wks 20	(UK Pos)	
1	12	Purple Rain	Prince & The Revolution	Warner	9	(8)	G
2	14	Wake Me Up Before You Go-Go	Wham!	Columbia	11	(1)	F G
3	4	Caribbean Queen (No More Love On The Run)	Billy Ocean	Jive	11	(6)	F G
4	1	I Just Called To Say I Love You	Stevie Wonder	Motown	12	(1)	G
5	-	Out Of Touch	Daryl Hall & John Oates	RCA	12	(48)	
6	-	Better Be Good To Me	Tina Turner	Capitol	8	(45)	
7	-	I Feel For You	Chaka Khan	Warner	11	(1)	F G L
8	-	Strut	Sheena Easton	EMI America	8		
9	18	Blue Jean	David Bowie	EMI America	7	(6)	
10	3	Hard Habit To Break	Chicago	Full Moon	11	(8)	
11	-	Desert Moon	Dennis Deyoung	A&M	7		F L
12	-	All Through The Night	Cyndi Lauper	Portrait	9	(64)	
13	-	Penny Lover	Lionel Richie	Motown	9	(18)	
14	8	On The Dark Side	John Cafferty & The Beaver Brown Band	Scotti Brothers	6		F
15	5	Lucky Star	Madonna	Sire	8	(14)	
16	-	No More Lonely Nights	Paul McCartney	Columbia	9	(2)	
17	10	I'm So Excited	Pointer Sisters	Planet	6	(11)	
18	-	Cool It Now	New Edition	MCA	11		F G
19	16	Some Guys Have All The Luck	Rod Stewart	Warner	5	(15)	
20	-	The Wild Boys	Duran Duran	Capitol	11	(2)	

December 1984

This Mnth	Prev Mnth	Title	Artist	Label	Wks 20	(UK Pos)	
1	5	Out Of Touch	Daryl Hall & John Oates	RCA	12	(48)	
2	20	The Wild Boys	Duran Duran	Capitol	11	(2)	
3	7	I Feel For You	Chaka Khan	Warner	11	(1)	F G L
4	-	Sea Of Love	Honeydrippers	Es Paranza	10	(56)	F L
5	2	Wake Me Up Before You Go-Go	Wham!	Columbia	11	(1)	F G
6	-	Like A Virgin	Madonna	Sire	11	(3)	G
7	16	No More Lonely Nights	Paul McCartney	Columbia	9	(2)	
8	18	Cool It Now	New Edition	MCA	11		F G
9	-	We Belong	Pat Benatar	Chrysalis	10	(22)	
10	12	All Through The Night	Cyndi Lauper	Portrait	9	(64)	
11	13	Penny Lover	Lionel Richie	Motown	9	(18)	
12	-	Valotte	Julian Lennon	Atlantic	8	(55)	F
13	-	All I Need	Jack Wagner	Qwest	9		F L
14	-	I Can't Hold Back	Survivor	Scotti Brothers	7		
15	6	Better Be Good To Me	Tina Turner	Capitol	8	(45)	
16	1	Purple Rain	Prince & The Revolution	Warner	9	(8)	G
17	8	Strut	Sheena Easton	EMI America	8		
18	-	Run To You	Bryan Adams	A&M	8	(11)	
19	-	Born In The U.S.A.	Bruce Springsteen	Columbia	7	(5)	
20	-	You're The Inspiration	Chicago	Full Moon	10	(14)	

◆ American record and tape sales in 1984 shot up 17% to $4.46 billion, 8% higher than the industry's previous best year (1978). In the year that cassette singles were introduced, pre-recorded cassette sales rocketed by 100%, and the fledgling CD accounted for $4.2 million, with the industry predicting that they would replace vinyl by 1992.

◆ It was the year the British invaded the singles chart and Prince was king of the albums. Also enjoying a good year were Hall & Oates, who scored their sixth and last No. 1 with 'Out of Touch', and Bruce Springsteen, whose 11-country *Born In The USA* tour was seen by 4.7 million in 61 cities.

◆ Billy Ocean's chart topping 'Caribbean Queen' had originally been released unsuccessfully as both 'European Queen' and 'African Queen'. The single made him the undisputed king of UK R&B and started his string of US hits.

UK 1985 JAN-MAR

◆ Bruce Springsteen's 12 million selling **Born In The USA** topped the transatlantic charts as 'Dancing In The Dark' gave him his first major British hit. Also debuting in the Top 20 were the production team of Stock, Aitken & Waterman with 'You Spin Me Round' by Dead Or Alive, which took a record 15 weeks on the chart to reach the top.

◆ Wham! were voted British Group of the Year at the Brits, and George Michael became the youngest person to win the Songwriter of the Year trophy at the Ivor Novello Awards, where the transatlantic chart topper 'Careless Whisper' was named Most Performed Song of the Year.

◆ Queen, Rod Stewart, Yes, Iron Maiden, AC/DC, Whitesnake, The Scorpions and Ozzy Osbourne were among the headliners at the massive *Rock In Rio* festival.

January 1985

This Mnth	Prev Mnth	Title	Artist	Label	Wks 20	(US Pos)	
1	5	Do They Know It's Christmas	Band Aid	Mercury	8	(13)	F P
2	8	Last Christmas/Everything She Wants	Wham!	Epic	8	(1)	G
3	-	I Want To Know What Love Is	Foreigner	Atlantic	9	(1)	
4	4	Like A Virgin	Madonna	Sire	10	(1)	
5	4	Ghostbusters	Ray Parker Jr.	Arista	17	(1)	
6	20	Shout	Tears For Fears	Mercury	9	(1)	
7	3	We All Stand Together	Paul McCartney	Parlophone	7		
8	18	Everything Must Change	Paul Young	CBS	7	(56)	
9	13	Nellie The Elephant	Toy Dolls	Volume	6		F L
10	-	I Know Him So Well	Elaine Paige & Barbara Dickson	RCA	10		L
11	-	Step Off (Pt. 1)	Grandmaster Melle Mel & The Furious Five	Sugar Hill	4		F L
12	-	1999/Little Red Corvette	Prince & The Revolution	Warner	7	(12)	
13	-	Since Yesterday	Strawberry Switchblade	Korova	5		F L
14	1	The Power Of Love	Frankie Goes To Hollywood	ZTT	8		
15	-	Police Officer	Smiley Culture	Fashion	3		F L
16	2	The Riddle	Nik Kershaw	MCA	9		
17	12	Fresh	Kool & The Gang	De-Lite	7	(9)	
18	-	Love & Pride	King	CBS	8	(55)	F
19	-	Atmosphere	Russ Abbot	Spirit	7		F
20	-	Friends	Amii Stewart	RCA	4		

February 1985

This Mnth	Prev Mnth	Title	Artist	Label	Wks 20	(US Pos)	
1	9	I Know Him So Well	Elaine Paige & Barbara Dickson	RCA	10		L
2	17	Love & Pride	King	CBS	8	(55)	F
3	-	Solid	Ashford & Simpson	Capitol	8	(12)	F L
4	3	I Want To Know What Love Is	Foreigner	Atlantic	9	(1)	L
5	11	1999/Little Red Corvette	Prince & The Revolution	Warner	7	(12)	
6	-	Dancing In The Dark	Bruce Springsteen	CBS	9	(2)	F
7	18	Atmosphere	Russ Abbot	Spirit	7		F
8	-	Close (To The Edit)	Art Of Noise	ZTT	4		F
9	5	Shout	Tears For Fears	Mercury	9	(1)	
10	-	A New England	Kirsty MacColl	Stiff	5		
11	-	Run To You	Bryan Adams	A&M	6	(6)	F
12	-	Things Can Only Get Better	Howard Jones	WEA	6	(5)	
13	12	Since Yesterday	Strawberry Switchblade	Korova	5		F L
14	-	Sussudio	Phil Collins	Virgin	4	(1)	
15	-	Loverboy	Billy Ocean	Jive	5	(2)	
16	-	Thinking Of You	Colour Field	Chrysalis	4		F L
17	-	You Spin Me Round (Like A Record)	Dead Or Alive	Epic	8	(11)	F
18	-	Nightshift	Commodores	Motown	8	(3)	
19	4	Like A Virgin	Madonna	Sire	10	(1)	
20	-	Yah Mo B There	James Ingram & Michael McDonald	A&M	2	(19)	

March 1985

This Mnth	Prev Mnth	Title	Artist	Label	Wks 20	(US Pos)	
1	17	You Spin Me Round (Like A Record)	Dead Or Alive	Epic	8	(11)	F
2	-	Material Girl	Madonna	Sire	6	(2)	
3	1	I Know Him So Well	Elaine Paige & Barbara Dickson	RCA	10		L
4	18	Nightshift	Commodores	Motown	8	(3)	
5	-	Kiss Me	Stephen 'Tin Tin' Duffy	10	6		F
6	-	Easy Lover	Philip Bailey & Phil Collins	CBS	9	(2)	F L
7	-	That Ole Devil Called Love	Alison Moyet	CBS	6		
8	-	The Last Kiss	David Cassidy	Arista	5		L
9	-	Everytime You Go Away	Paul Young	CBS	6	(1)	
10	-	Do What You Do	Jermaine Jackson	Arista	6	(13)	L
11	6	Dancing In The Dark	Bruce Springsteen	CBS	9	(2)	F
12	-	Let's Go Crazy/Take Me With You	Prince & The Revolution	Warner	4	(1)	
13	3	Solid	Ashford & Simpson	Capitol	8	(12)	F L
14	2	Love & Pride	King	CBS	8	(55)	F
15	-	We Close Our Eyes	Go West	Chrysalis	8	(41)	F
16	12	Things Can Only Get Better	Howard Jones	WEA	6	(5)	
17	-	Wide Boy	Nik Kershaw	MCA	6		
18	-	Pie Jesu	Sarah Brightman & Paul Miles-Kingston	HMV	5		
19	10	A New England	Kirsty MacColl	Stiff	5		
20	-	The Boys Of Summer	Don Henley	Geffen	3	(5)	F L

January 1985

This Mnth	Prev Mnth	Title	Artist	Label	Wks 20	(UK Pos)	
1	6	Like A Virgin	Madonna	Sire	11	(3)	G
2	13	All I Need	Jack Wagner	Qwest	9		F L
3	20	You're The Inspiration	Chicago	Full Moon	10	(14)	
4	2	The Wild Boys	Duran Duran	Capitol	11	(2)	
5	18	Run To You	Bryan Adams	A&M	8	(11)	
6	-	I Want To Know What Love Is	Foreigner	Atlantic	11	(1)	G
7	9	We Belong	Pat Benatar	Chrysalis	10	(22)	
8	-	Easy Lover	Philip Bailey & Phil Collins	Columbia	10	(1)	F G L
9	4	Sea Of Love	Honeydrippers	Es Paranza	10	(56)	F L
10	19	Born In The U.S.A.	Bruce Springsteen	Columbia	7	(5)	
11	8	Cool It Now	New Edition	MCA	11		F G
12	-	The Boys Of Summer	Don Henley	Geffen	8	(12)	
13	-	Careless Whisper	Wham! Feat. George Michael	Columbia	12	(1)	F G
14	12	Valotte	Julian Lennon	Atlantic	8	(55)	F
15	1	Out Of Touch	Daryl Hall & John Oates	RCA	12	(48)	
16	-	I Would Die 4 U	Prince & The Revolution	Warner	6	(58)	
17	-	Do What You Do	Jermaine Jackson	Arista	7	(6)	
18	-	Do They Know It's Christmas	Band Aid	Columbia	4	(1)	F G L
19	-	Loverboy	Billy Ocean	Jive	9	(15)	
20	-	Jamie	Ray Parker Jr.	Arista	5		L

February 1985

This Mnth	Prev Mnth	Title	Artist	Label	Wks 20	(UK Pos)	
1	13	Careless Whisper	Wham! Feat.George Michael	Columbia	12	(1)	F G
2	6	I Want To Know What Love Is	Foreigner	Atlantic	11	(1)	G
3	8	Easy Lover	Philip Bailey & Phil Collins	Columbia	10	(1)	F G L
4	19	Loverboy	Billy Ocean	Jive	9	(15)	
5	-	Method Of Modern Love	Daryl Hall & John Oates	RCA	7	(21)	
6	-	Neutron Dance	Pointer Sisters	Planet	9	(31)	
7	12	The Boys Of Summer	Don Henley	Geffen	8	(12)	
8	-	The Heat Is On	Glenn Frey	MCA	10	(12)	
9	3	You're The Inspiration	Chicago	Full Moon	10	(14)	
10	-	Can't Fight This Feeling	REO Speedwagon	Epic	10	(16)	G
11	-	California Girls	David Lee Roth	Warner	7	(68)	F
12	-	Solid	Ashford & Simpson	Capitol	5	(3)	F L
13	1	Like A Virgin	Madonna	Sire	11	(3)	G
14	-	Sugar Walls	Sheena Easton	EMI America	7		
15	16	I Would Die 4 U	Prince & The Revolution	Warner	6	(58)	
16	-	The Old Man Down The Road	John Fogerty	Warner	6		F
17	-	Mr. Telephone Man	New Edition	MCA	4	(19)	
18	-	Misled	Kool & The Gang	De-Lite	6	(28)	
19	-	Call To The Heart	Giuffria	MCA	2		F L
20	2	All I Need	Jack Wagner	Qwest	9		F L

March 1985

This Mnth	Prev Mnth	Title	Artist	Label	Wks 20	(UK Pos)	
1	10	Can't Fight This Feeling	REO Speedwagon	Epic	10	(16)	G
2	8	The Heat Is On	Glenn Frey	MCA	10	(12)	
3	-	Material Girl	Madonna	Sire	8	(3)	
4	-	Too Late For Goodbyes	Julian Lennon	Atlantic	8	(6)	L
5	1	Careless Whisper	Wham! Feat. George Michael	Columbia	12	(1)	F G
6	11	California Girls	David Lee Roth	Warner	7	(68)	F
7	-	One More Night	Phil Collins	Atlantic	9	(4)	
8	-	Lovergirl	Teena Marie	Epic	9		F L
9	-	Private Dancer	Tina Turner	Capitol	7	(26)	
10	6	Neutron Dance	Pointer Sisters	Planet	9	(31)	
11	2	I Want To Know What Love Is	Foreigner	Atlantic	11	(1)	G
12	-	High On You	Survivor	Scotti Brothers	5		
13	-	Only The Young	Journey	Geffen	5		
14	-	Relax	Frankie Goes To Hollywood	Island	5	(1)	F L
15	14	Sugar Walls	Sheena Easton	EMI America	7		
16	4	Loverboy	Billy Ocean	Jive	9	(15)	
17	18	Misled	Kool & The Gang	De-Lite	6	(28)	
18	16	The Old Man Down The Road	John Fogerty	Warner	6		F
19	-	Just Another Night	Mick Jagger	Columbia	5	(32)	F
20	3	Easy Lover	Philip Bailey & Phil Collins	Columbia	10	(1)	F G L

US 1985 JAN-MAR

▲ Madonna's 'Like A Virgin' single and album simultaneously topped the chart. This was not the reason why the first female to accomplish this feat, The Singing Nun, committed suicide soon afterwards.

◆ Tina Turner picked up four Grammy Awards, Prince received a record 10 American Music Award nominations, and Brits winners included Prince, Paul Young, Alison Moyet and Wham!

◆ To commemorate what would have been his 50th birthday, Elvis Presley's likeness appeared on a US stamp. Over the years the US postage services have sold a record breaking 500 million Elvis stamps.

UK 1985
APR-JUNE

▲ Few Chinese noticed as Wham! became the first western pop group to play in China and to have records released there. In contrast, few Britons could have been unaware of Bruce Springsteen's (above) UK tour. He was an unqualified success, and all his seven albums returned to the chart.

◆ Paul Hardcastle, ex-keyboard player with Brit-funk band Direct Drive, took sampling to new heights with his groundbreaking transatlantic hit '19'. Its success helped make him the most in-demand remixer of the time.

April 1985

This Mnth	Prev Mnth	Title	Artist	Label	Wks 20	(US Pos)	
1	-	Everybody Wants To Rule The World	Tears For Fears	Mercury	9	(1)	
2	6	Easy Lover	Philip Bailey & Phil Collins	CBS	9	(2)	F L
3	-	Welcome To The Pleasure Dome	Frankie Goes To Hollywood	ZTT	5	(48)	
4	15	We Close Our Eyes	Go West	Chrysalis	8	(41)	F
5	-	Move Closer	Phyllis Nelson	Carrere	11		F L
6	-	We Are The World	USA For Africa	CBS	6	(1)	F L
7	-	Could It Be I'm Falling In Love	David Grant & Jaki Graham	Chrysalis	6		
8	18	Pie Jesu	Sarah Brightman & Paul Miles-Kingston	HMV	5		
9	7	That Ole Devil Called Love	Alison Moyet	CBS	6		
10	9	Everytime You Go Away	Paul Young	CBS	6	(1)	
11	-	One More Night	Phil Collins	Virgin	5	(1)	
12	-	Clouds Across The Moon	Rah Band	RCA	5		L
13	-	Spend The Night	Coolnotes	Abstract Dance	4		F
14	17	Wide Boy	Nik Kershaw	MCA	6		
15	-	The Heat Is On	Glenn Frey	MCA	4	(2)	F L
16	10	Do What You Do	Jermaine Jackson	Arista	6	(13)	L
17	5	Kiss Me	Stephen 'Tin Tin' Duffy	10	6		F
18	2	Material Girl	Madonna	Sire	6	(2)	
19	-	I Feel Love	Bronski Beat & Marc Almond	Forbidden Fruit	7		
20	-	Don't You (Forget About Me)	Simple Minds	Virgin	5	(1)	

May 1985

This Mnth	Prev Mnth	Title	Artist	Label	Wks 20	(US Pos)	
1	-	19	Paul Hardcastle	Chrysalis	9	(15)	F
2	5	Move Closer	Phyllis Nelson	Carrere	11		F L
3	19	I Feel Love	Bronski Beat & Marc Almond	Forbidden Fruit	7		
4	1	Everybody Wants To Rule The World	Tears For Fears	Mercury	9	(1)	
5	-	Feel So Real	Steve Arrington	Atlantic	7		F L
6	-	Rhythm Of The Night	DeBarge	Gordy	6	(3)	F L
7	20	Don't You (Forget About Me)	Simple Minds	Virgin	5	(1)	
8	6	We Are The World	USA For Africa	CBS	6	(1)	F L
9	-	The Unforgettable Fire	U2	Island	3		
10	-	I Was Born To Love You	Freddie Mercury	CBS	5	(76)	
11	-	Walls Come Tumbling Down!	Style Council	Polydor	4		
12	-	A View To Kill	Duran Duran	Parlophone	7	(1)	
13	-	Love Don't Live Here Anymore	Jimmy Nail	Virgin	6		F
14	11	One More Night	Phil Collins	Virgin	5	(1)	
15	12	Clouds Across The Moon	Rah Band	RCA	5		L
16	-	Kayleigh	Marillion	EMI	9		
17	7	Could It Be I'm Falling In Love	David Grant & Jaki Graham	Chrysalis	6		
18	-	Slave To Love	Bryan Ferry	EG	4		
19	-	Lover Come Back To Me	Dead Or Alive	Epic	3	(75)	
20	-	I Want Your Lovin' (Just A Little Bit)	Curtis Hairston	London	2		F L

June 1985

This Mnth	Prev Mnth	Title	Artist	Label	Wks 20	(US Pos)	
1	16	Kayleigh	Marillion	EMI	9		
2	-	You'll Never Walk Alone	The Crowd	Spartan	6		F L
3	1	19	Paul Hardcastle	Chrysalis	9	(15)	F
4	12	A View To Kill	Duran Duran	Parlophone	7	(1)	
5	-	Suddenly	Billy Ocean	Jive	8	(4)	
6	-	Obsession	Animotion	Mercury	6	(6)	F L
7	-	The Word Girl	Scritti Politti Feat. Ranking Ann	Virgin	6		
8	-	Frankie	Sister Sledge	Atlantic	10	(75)	
9	-	Crazy For You	Madonna	Geffen	10	(1)	
10	-	Out In The Fields	Gary Moore & Phil Lynott	10	6		
11	-	History	Mai Tai	Virgin	7		F
12	-	Cherish	Kool & The Gang	De-Lite	12	(2)	L
13	-	Walking On Sunshine	Katrina & The Waves	Capitol	5	(9)	F L
14	13	Love Don't Live Here Anymore	Jimmy Nail	Virgin	6		F
15	-	Axel F	Harold Faltermeyer	MCA	9	(3)	F L
16	6	Rhythm Of The Night	DeBarge	Gordy	6	(3)	F L
17	-	Ben	Marti Webb	Starblend	6		
18	-	Call Me	Go West	Chrysalis	3	(54)	
19	3	I Feel Love	Bronski Beat & Marc Almond	Forbidden Fruit	7		
20	-	Johnny Come Home	Fine Young Cannibals	London	7	(76)	F

April 1985

This Mnth	Prev Mnth	Title	Artist	Label	Wks 20	(UK Pos)	
1	-	We Are The World	USA For Africa	Columbia	9	(1)	F P L
2	-	Crazy For You	Madonna	Geffen	11	(2)	G
3	7	One More Night	Phil Collins	Atlantic	9	(4)	
4	-	Nightshift	Commodores	Motown	8	(3)	L
5	-	Rhythm Of The Night	DeBarge	Gordy	9	(4)	
6	-	I'm On Fire	Bruce Springsteen	Columbia	7	(5)	
7	-	Obsession	Animotion	Mercury	8	(5)	F
8	3	Material Girl	Madonna	Sire	8	(3)	
9	-	Don't You (Forget About Me)	Simple Minds	A&M	11	(7)	F
10	-	One Night In Bangkok	Murray Head	RCA	9	(12)	L
11	-	Missing You	Diana Ross	RCA	6		L
12	8	Lovergirl	Teena Marie	Epic	9		F L
13	-	All She Wants To Do Is Dance	Don Henley	Geffen	7		
14	-	Some Like It Hot	Power Station	Capitol	8	(14)	F
15	1	Can't Fight This Feeling	REO Speedwagon	Epic	10	(16)	G
16	-	Somebody	Bryan Adams	A&M	5	(35)	
17	-	Along Comes A Woman	Chicago	Full Moon	3		
18	-	Smooth Operator	Sade	Portrait	8	(19)	F
19	19	Just Another Night	Mick Jagger	Columbia	5	(32)	F
20	4	Too Late For Goodbyes	Julian Lennon	Atlantic	8	(6)	L

May 1985

This Mnth	Prev Mnth	Title	Artist	Label	Wks 20	(UK Pos)	
1	9	Don't You (Forget About Me)	Simple Minds	A&M	11	(7)	F
2	2	Crazy For You	Madonna	Geffen	11	(2)	G
3	10	One Night In Bangkok	Murray Head	RCA	9	(12)	L
4	-	Everything She Wants	Wham!	Columbia	10	(2)	
5	1	We Are The World	USA For Africa	Columbia	9	(1)	F P L
6	18	Smooth Operator	Sade	Portrait	8	(19)	F
7	14	Some Like It Hot	Power Station	Capitol	8	(14)	F
8	5	Rhythm Of The Night	DeBarge	Gordy	9	(4)	
9	-	Everybody Wants To Rule The World	Tears For Fears	Mercury	11	(2)	F
10	-	Axel F	Harold Faltermeyer	MCA	8	(2)	F L
11	7	Obsession	Animotion	Mercury	8	(5)	F
12	-	Suddenly	Billy Ocean	Jive	9	(4)	
13	13	All She Wants To Do Is Dance	Don Henley	Geffen	7		
14	-	Don't Come Around Here No More	Tom Petty & The Heartbreakers	MCA	6	(50)	
15	4	Nightshift	Commodores	Motown	8	(3)	L
16	-	Things Can Only Get Better	Howard Jones	Elektra	9	(6)	F
17	-	Fresh	Kool & The Gang	De-Lite	7	(11)	
18	-	That Was Yesterday	Foreigner	Atlantic	4	(28)	
19	-	In My House	Mary Jane Girls	Gordy	9		F L
20	-	Heaven	Bryan Adams	A&M	10	(38)	

June 1985

This Mnth	Prev Mnth	Title	Artist	Label	Wks 20	(UK Pos)	
1	9	Everybody Wants To Rule The World	Tears For Fears	Mercury	11	(2)	F
2	20	Heaven	Bryan Adams	A&M	10	(38)	
3	16	Things Can Only Get Better	Howard Jones	Elektra	9	(6)	F
4	-	Sussudio	Phil Collins	Atlantic	9	(12)	
5	19	In My House	Mary Jane Girls	Gordy	9		F L
6	12	Suddenly	Billy Ocean	Jive	9	(4)	
7	4	Everything She Wants	Wham!	Columbia	10	(2)	
8	10	Axel F	Harold Faltermeyer	MCA	8	(2)	F L
9	-	Angel	Madonna	Sire	8	(5)	G
10	-	Walking On Sunshine	Katrina & The Waves	Capitol	7	(8)	F
11	-	A View To Kill	Duran Duran	Capitol	10	(2)	
12	-	Raspberry Beret	Prince & The Revolution	Paisley Park	9	(25)	
13	-	The Search Is Over	Survivor	Scotti Brothers	8		
14	1	Don't You (Forget About Me)	Simple Minds	A&M	11	(7)	F
15	17	Fresh	Kool & The Gang	De-Lite	7	(11)	
16	-	Smuggler's Blues	Glenn Frey	MCA	6	(22)	
17	-	Would I Lie To You?	Eurythmics	RCA	8	(17)	
18	6	Smooth Operator	Sade	Portrait	8	(19)	F
19	-	Voices Carry	Til Tuesday	Epic	7		F L
20	-	You Give Good Love	Whitney Houston	Arista	10		F

◆ A galaxy of top American artists recorded Michael Jackson & Lionel Richie's song 'We Are The World' under the name USA For Africa. The Grammy winning single, inspired by Britain's Band Aid, hit No. 1 in just four weeks and sold over four million copies – making it the fastest mover and biggest seller of the decade. The **We Are The World** album hit the summit in two weeks and went triple platinum.

◆ Arista Records were very excited about new signing Whitney Houston, who made her chart debut with 'You Give Good Love'. Incidentally, the B-side, 'The Greatest Love Of All', reached No. 1 in its own right a year later.

◆ At the end of May, Madonna was the only all-American act in the US Top 10 – seven of the others being British and one, The Power Station, being Anglo-American.

UK 1985
JULY-SEPT

◆ 'Dancing In The Street' by David Bowie & Mick Jagger, entered at No. 1. Proceeds from the hit helped the starving in Ethiopia.

◆ In September, a record nine re-issued singles were simultaneously in the UK Top 40, including re-mixes of Amii Stewart's 1979 'Knock On Wood' and 'Light My Fire' – the earliest of dozens of dance re-mixes to chart in Britain.

◆ Dire Straits scored simultaneous US chart-toppers with **Brothers In Arms** (which eventually sold six million in America, nearly four million in the UK and topped the chart in 22 countries!), and the Grammy winning 'Money For Nothing' on which co-writer Sting apeared.

◆ Madonna became the first female to simultaneously hold the top 2 places, thanks to 'Into The Groove' (which only appeared on the 12" version of 'Angel' in the US) and a re-issue of 'Holiday'.

July 1985

This Mnth	Prev Mnth	Title	Artist	Label	Wks 20	(US Pos)	
1	8	Frankie	Sister Sledge	Atlantic	10	(75)	
2	15	Axel F	Harold Faltermeyer	MCA	9	(3)	F L
3	9	Crazy For You	Madonna	Geffen	10	(1)	
4	12	Cherish	Kool & The Gang	De-Lite	12	(2)	L
5	-	I'm On Fire/Born In The U.S.A.	Bruce Springsteen	CBS	7	(6)	
6	-	There Must Be An Angel (Playing With My Heart)	Eurythmics	RCA	8	(22)	
7	-	My Toot Toot	Denise La Salle	Epic	6		F L
8	17	Ben	Marti Webb	Starblend	6		
9	20	Johnny Come Home	Fine Young Cannibals	London	7	(76)	F
10	-	Live Is Life	Opus	Polydor	7	(32)	F L
11	11	History	Mai Tai	Virgin	7		F
12	5	Suddenly	Billy Ocean	Jive	8	(4)	
13	-	Head Over Heels	Tears For Fears	Mercury	4	(3)	
14	-	Round And Round	Jaki Graham	EMI	4		
15	1	Kayleigh	Marillion	EMI	9		
16	-	Into The Groove	Madonna	Sire	10		
17	2	You'll Never Walk Alone	The Crowd	Spartan	6		F L
18	-	Turn It Up	Conway Brothers	10	3		F L
19	-	Money's Too Tight (To Mention)	Simply Red	Elektra	3	(28)	F
20	-	Living On Video	Trans-X	Boiling Point	5	(61)	F L

August 1985

This Mnth	Prev Mnth	Title	Artist	Label	Wks 20	(US Pos)	
1	16	Into The Groove	Madonna	Sire	10		
2	-	We Don't Need Another Hero (Thunderdome)	Tina Turner	Capitol	7	(2)	
3	-	Money For Nothing	Dire Straits	Vertigo	8	(1)	
4	6	There Must Be An Angel (Playing With My Heart)	Eurythmics	RCA	8	(22)	
5	-	I Got You Babe	UB40 Feat Chrissie Hynde	Dep International	8	(28)	
6	-	Holiday	Madonna	Sire	5		
7	-	White Wedding	Billy Idol	Chrysalis	8	(36)	
8	-	Running Up That Hill	Kate Bush	EMI	6	(30)	
9	-	Drive	Cars	Elektra	7		L
10	10	Live Is Life	Opus	Polydor	7	(32)	F L
11	4	Cherish	Kool & The Gang	De-Lite	12	(2)	L
12	-	Say I'm Your No. 1	Princess	Supreme	6		F
13	1	Frankie	Sister Sledge	Atlantic	10	(75)	
14	2	Axel F	Harold Faltermeyer	MCA	9	(3)	F L
15	-	Don Quixote	Nik Kershaw	MCA	3		L
16	-	Tarzan Boy	Baltimora	Columbia	7	(13)	F L
17	-	Excitable	Amazulu	Island	3		F
18	20	Living On Video	Trans-X	Boiling Point	5	(61)	F L
19	-	Alone Without You	King	CBS	5		
20	14	Round And Round	Jaki Graham	EMI	4		

September 1985

This Mnth	Prev Mnth	Title	Artist	Label	Wks 20	(US Pos)	
1	-	Dancing In The Street	David Bowie & Mick Jagger	EMI America	7	(7)	
2	-	Holding Out For A Hero	Bonnie Tyler	CBS	8	(34)	L
3	16	Tarzan Boy	Baltimora	Columbia	7	(13)	F L
4	5	I Got You Babe	UB40 Feat. Chrissie Hynde	Dep International	8	(28)	
5	-	Part Time Lover	Stevie Wonder	Motown	5	(1)	
6	-	Body And Soul	Mai Tai	Virgin	6		L
7	1	Into The Groove	Madonna	Sire	10		
8	-	Knock On Wood/Light My Fire	Amii Stewart	Sedition	5		L
9	9	Drive	Cars	Elektra	7		L
10	-	Lavender	Marillion	EMI	5		
11	8	Running Up That Hill	Kate Bush	EMI	6	(30)	
12	12	Say I'm Your No. 1	Princess	Supreme	6		F
13	-	If I Was	Midge Ure	Chrysalis	7		
14	-	Angel	Madonna	Sire	5	(5)	
15	19	Alone Without You	King	CBS	5		
16	-	The Power Of Love	Huey Lewis & The News	Chrysalis	5	(1)	
17	3	Money For Nothing	Dire Straits	Vertigo	8	(1)	
18	-	Lean On Me (Ah-Li-Ayo)	Red Box	Sire	8		F
19	-	Body Rock	Maria Vidal	EMI America	5	(48)	F L
20	-	I Can Dream About You	Dan Hartman	MCA	3	(6)	L

262

US 1985 JULY-SEPT

July 1985

This Mnth	Prev Mnth	Title	Artist	Label	Wks 20	(UK Pos)	
1	11	A View To Kill	Duran Duran	Capitol	10	(2)	
2	12	Raspberry Beret	Prince & The Revolution	Paisley Park	9	(25)	
3	-	Everytime You Go Away	Paul Young	Columbia	11	(4)	F
4	4	Sussudio	Phil Collins	Atlantic	9	(12)	
5	20	You Give Good Love	Whitney Houston	Arista	10		F
6	13	The Search Is Over	Survivor	Scotti Brothers	8		
7	-	Glory Days	Bruce Springsteen	Columbia	8	(17)	
8	-	If You Love Somebody Set Them Free	Sting	A&M	10	(26)	F
9	17	Would I Lie To You?	Eurythmics	RCA	8	(17)	
10	19	Voices Carry	Til Tuesday	Epic	7		F L
11	-	Shout	Tears For Fears	Mercury	9	(4)	
12	-	Sentimental Street	Night Ranger	MCA/Camel	7		
13	2	Heaven	Bryan Adams	A&M	10	(38)	
14	-	The Goonies 'R' Good Enough	Cyndi Lauper	Portrait	5		
15	-	Never Surrender	Corey Hart	EMI America	9		
16	-	Get It On (Bang A Gong)	Power Station	Capitol	6	(22)	L
17	-	19	Paul Hardcastle	Chrysalis	4	(1)	F L
18	9	Angel	Madonna	Sire	8	(5)	G
19	-	Who's Holding Donna Now	DeBarge	Gordy	6		L
20	-	Crazy In The Night (Barking At Airplanes)	Kim Carnes	EMI America	2		L

August 1985

This Mnth	Prev Mnth	Title	Artist	Label	Wks 20	(UK Pos)	
1	11	Shout	Tears For Fears	Mercury	9	(4)	
2	-	The Power Of Love	Huey Lewis & The News	Chrysalis	10	(9)	
3	15	Never Surrender	Corey Hart	EMI America	9		
4	-	Freeway Of Love	Aretha Franklin	Arista	9	(68)	F
5	8	If You Love Somebody Set Them...	Sting	A&M	10	(26)	F
6	3	Everytime You Go Away	Paul Young	Columbia	11	(4)	F
7	-	St. Elmo's Fire (Man In Motion)	John Parr	Atlantic	10	(6)	F L
8	-	Summer Of '69	Bryan Adams	A&M	7	(42)	
9	-	We Don't Need Another Hero (Thunderdome)	Tina Turner	Capitol	9	(3)	
10	19	Who's Holding Donna Now	DeBarge	Gordy	6		L
11	7	Glory Days	Bruce Springsteen	Columbia	8	(17)	
12	-	What About Love?	Heart	Capitol	6	(14)	
13	16	Get It On (Bang A Gong)	Power Station	Capitol	6	(22)	L
14	5	You Give Good Love	Whitney Houston	Arista	10		F
15	-	Cherish	Kool & The Gang	De-Lite	10	(4)	
16	-	You Spin Me Round (Like A Record)	Dead Or Alive	Epic	5	(1)	F
17	-	You're Only Human (Second Wind)	Billy Joel	Columbia	7		
18	-	People Are People	Depeche Mode	Sire	5	(4)	F
19	-	Don't Lose My Number	Phil Collins	Atlantic	9		
20	-	Invincible (Theme From The Legend Of Billie Jean)	Pat Benatar	Chrysalis	6	(53)	

September 1985

This Mnth	Prev Mnth	Title	Artist	Label	Wks 20	(UK Pos)	
1	-	Money For Nothing	Dire Straits	Warner	10	(4)	
2	7	St. Elmo's Fire (Man In Motion)	John Parr	Atlantic	10	(6)	F L
3	15	Cherish	Kool & The Gang	De-Lite	10	(4)	
4	9	We Don't Need Another Hero (...)	Tina Turner	Capitol	9	(3)	
5	19	Don't Lose My Number	Phil Collins	Atlantic	9		
6	-	Freedom	Wham!	Columbia	8	(1)	
7	2	The Power Of Love	Huey Lewis & The News	Chrysalis	10	(9)	
8	-	Pop Life	Prince & The Revolution	Paisley Park	6	(60)	
9	-	Oh Sheila	Ready For The World	MCA	10	(50)	F
10	-	Dress You Up	Madonna	Sire	7	(5)	
11	4	Freeway Of Love	Aretha Franklin	Arista	9	(68)	
12	-	Dare Me	Pointer Sisters	RCA	7	(17)	L
13	20	Invincible (From The Legend Of...)	Pat Benatar	Chrysalis	6	(53)	
14	8	Summer Of '69	Bryan Adams	A&M	7	(42)	
15	-	Take On Me	A-Ha	Warner	10	(2)	F
16	17	You're Only Human (Second Wind)	Billy Joel	Columbia	7		
17	-	Saving All My Love For You	Whitney Houston	Arista	10	(1)	
18	-	Lonely Ol' Night	John Cougar Mellencamp	Riva	8		
19	-	Dancing In The Street	Mick Jagger & David Bowie	EMI America	6	(1)	L
20	-	Smokin' In The Boys Room	Motley Crue	Elektra	4	(71)	F

◆ Rock music's greatest live show, *Live Aid* (which included over two dozen top rock acts), was staged in both London and Philadelphia. A TV audience of approximately 1.6 billion people in 170 countries watched the show, which raised $80 million (£50 million) for famine relief in Africa.

▲ A record eight consecutive US chart-toppers were by non-American acts. Among the seven UK No. 1s were two by Tears For Fears, whose **Songs From The Big Chair** headed the LP chart.

◆ Farm Aid raised $10 million. Headliners included Bob Dylan, Tom Petty, Kenny Rogers and Billy Joel.

UK 1985 OCT-DEC

▲ It was claimed that Dire Straits' 'Brothers In Arms' was the first commercially successful CD single.

◆ American Jennifer Rush topped the chart with 'The Power Of Love'. It became the first UK million seller by a female artist. In her homeland it failed to reach the Top 40. The song, however, became an American No. 1 by French-Canadian Celine Dion in 1994.

◆ NME writers chose The Jesus & Mary Chain's 'Never Understood' and **Psychocandy** as the Top Single and Album of the Year respectively.

October 1985

This Mnth	Prev Mnth	Title	Artist	Label	Wks 20	(US Pos)	
1	-	The Power Of Love	Jennifer Rush	CBS	11	(57)	F G
2	13	If I Was	Midge Ure	Chrysalis	7		
3	-	Trapped	Colonel Abrams	MCA	10		F L
4	18	Lean On Me (Ah-Li-Ayo)	Red Box	Sire	8		F
5	-	Rebel Yell	Billy Idol	Chrysalis	6	(46)	
6	-	Take On Me	A-Ha	Warner	8	(1)	F
7	-	St. Elmo's Fire (Man In Motion)	John Parr	London	6	(1)	F L
8	1	Dancing In The Street	David Bowie & Mick Jagger	EMI America	7	(7)	
9	2	Holding Out For A Hero	Bonnie Tyler	CBS	8	(34)	L
10	-	Alive And Kicking	Simple Minds	Virgin	6	(3)	
11	14	Angel	Madonna	Sire	5	(5)	
12	-	Gambler	Madonna	Geffen	6		
13	-	Miami Vice Theme	Jan Hammer	MCA	4	(1)	F
14	10	Lavender	Marillion	EMI	5		
15	19	Body Rock	Maria Vidal	EMI America	5	(48)	F L
16	16	The Power Of Love	Huey Lewis & The News	Chrysalis	5	(1)	F
17	-	Slave To The Rhythm	Grace Jones	ZTT	4		
18	-	Nikita	Elton John	Rocket	7	(7)	
19	-	Single Life	Cameo	Club	3		F
20	-	The Lodgers	Style Council	Polydor	3		

November 1985

This Mnth	Prev Mnth	Title	Artist	Label	Wks 20	(US Pos)	
1	1	The Power Of Love	Jennifer Rush	CBS	11	(57)	F G
2	-	A Good Heart	Feargal Sharkey	Virgin	10	(67)	F
3	6	Take On Me	A-Ha	Warner	8	(1)	F
4	18	Nikita	Elton John	Rocket	7	(7)	
5	-	Don't Break My Heart	UB40	Dep International	8		
6	-	Something About You	Level 42	Polydor	6	(7)	
7	3	Trapped	Colonel Abrams	MCA	10		F L
8	-	I'm Your Man	Wham!	Epic	8	(3)	
9	-	Road To Nowhere	Talking Heads	EMI	6		
10	-	One Vision	Queen	EMI	4	(61)	
11	12	Gambler	Madonna	Geffen	6		
12	-	Sisters Are Doin' It For Themselves	Eurythmics & Aretha Franklin	RCA	5	(18)	
13	-	Stairway To Heaven	Far Corporation	Arista	4	(89)	F L
14	7	St. Elmo's Fire (Man In Motion)	John Parr	London	6	(1)	F L
15	-	The Show	Doug E. Fresh & The Get Fresh Crew	Cooltempo	6		F L
16	-	The Taste Of Your Tears	King	CBS	5		L
17	-	Election Day	Arcadia	Odeon	4	(6)	F L
18	10	Alive And Kicking	Simple Minds	Virgin	6	(3)	
19	-	See The Day	Dee C. Lee	CBS	8		F L
20	13	Miami Vice Theme	Jan Hammer	MCA	4	(1)	F

December 1985

This Mnth	Prev Mnth	Title	Artist	Label	Wks 20	(US Pos)	
1	-	Saving All My Love For You	Whitney Houston	Arista	9	(1)	F
2	8	I'm Your Man	Wham!	Epic	8	(3)	
3	19	See The Day	Dee C. Lee	CBS	8		F L
4	-	Separate Lives	Phil Collins & Marilyn Martin	Virgin	8	(1)	
5	-	Do They Know It's Christmas	Band Aid	Mercury	5		P L
6	-	Merry Christmas Everyone	Shakin' Stevens	Epic	6		
7	-	Dress You Up	Madonna	Sire	6	(5)	
8	-	West End Girls	Pet Shop Boys	Parlophone	8	(1)	F
9	2	A Good Heart	Feargal Sharkey	Virgin	10	(67)	F
10	-	Say You, Say Me	Lionel Richie	Motown	7	(1)	
11	15	The Show	Doug E. Fresh & The Get Fresh Crew	Cooltempo	6		F L
12	-	We Built This City	Starship	RCA	6	(1)	F
13	-	Last Christmas	Wham!	Epic	4		
14	-	Santa Claus Is Comin' To Town/ My Home Town	Bruce Springsteen	Epic	4		
15	5	Don't Break My Heart	UB40	Dep International	8		
16	-	Don't Look Down-The Sequel	Go West	Chrysalis	6	(39)	
17	-	Walking In The Air	Aled Jones	HMV	5		F L
18	9	Road To Nowhere	Talking Heads	EMI	6		
19	-	Spies Like Us	Paul McCartney	Parlophone	6	(7)	
20	-	Hit That Perfect Beat	Bronski Beat	Forbidden Fruit	7		

October 1985

This Mnth	Prev Mnth	Title	Artist	Label	Wks 20	(UK Pos)	
1	15	Take On Me	A-Ha	Warner	10	(2)	F
2	17	Saving All My Love For You	Whitney Houston	Arista	10	(1)	
3	9	Oh Sheila	Ready For The World	MCA	10	(50)	F
4	-	Part Time Lover	Stevie Wonder	Tamla	10	(3)	
5	1	Money For Nothing	Dire Straits	Warner	10	(4)	
6	18	Lonely Ol' Night	John Cougar Mellencamp	Riva	8		
7	-	Miami Vice Theme	Jan Hammer	MCA	9	(5)	F L
8	19	Dancing In The Street	Mick Jagger & David Bowie	EMI America	6	(1)	L
9	-	Fortress Around Your Heart	Sting	A&M	7	(49)	
10	3	Cherish	Kool & The Gang	De-Lite	10	(4)	
11	-	I'm Goin' Down	Bruce Springsteen	Columbia	6		
12	-	Head Over Heels	Tears For Fears	Mercury	9	(12)	
13	10	Dress You Up	Madonna	Sire	7	(5)	
14	-	Lovin' Every Minute Of It	Loverboy	Columbia	7		
15	6	Freedom	Wham!	Columbia	8	(1)	
16	-	You Belong To The City	Glenn Frey	MCA	9		
17	5	Don't Lose My Number	Phil Collins	Atlantic	9		
18	-	I'm Gonna Tear Your Playhouse Down	Paul Young	Columbia	5	(9)	
19	-	We Built This City	Starship	Grunt	10	(12)	F
20	-	Cry	Godley & Creme	Polydor	5	(19)	F L

November 1985

This Mnth	Prev Mnth	Title	Artist	Label	Wks 20	(UK Pos)	
1	19	We Built This City	Starship	Grunt	10	(12)	F
2	16	You Belong To The City	Glenn Frey	MCA	9		
3	7	Miami Vice Theme	Jan Hammer	MCA	9	(5)	F L
4	-	Separate Lives	Phil Collins & Marilyn Martin	Atlantic	13	(4)	
5	12	Head Over Heels	Tears For Fears	Mercury	9	(12)	
6	4	Part Time Lover	Stevie Wonder	Tamla	10	(3)	
7	-	Broken Wings	Mr. Mister	RCA	11	(4)	F
8	-	Never	Heart	Capitol	8	(8)	
9	-	Lay Your Hands On Me	Thompson Twins	Arista	8	(13)	
10	-	Be Near Me	ABC	Mercury	7	(26)	
11	-	Who's Zoomin' Who	Aretha Franklin	Arista	7	(11)	
12	2	Saving All My Love For You	Whitney Houston	Arista	10	(1)	
13	1	Take On Me	A-Ha	Warner	10	(2)	F
14	-	You Are My Lady	Freddie Jackson	Capitol	6	(49)	L
15	-	Election Day	Arcadia	Capitol	10	(7)	F L
16	-	Sleeping Bag	ZZ Top	Warner	8	(27)	L
17	-	One Night Love Affair	Bryan Adams	A&M	5		
18	14	Lovin' Every Minute Of It	Loverboy	Columbia	7		
19	9	Fortress Around Your Heart	Sting	A&M	7	(49)	
20	-	Party All The Time	Eddie Murphy	Columbia	11		F G L

December 1985

This Mnth	Prev Mnth	Title	Artist	Label	Wks 20	(UK Pos)	
1	-	Say You, Say Me	Lionel Richie	Motown	12	(8)	G
2	7	Broken Wings	Mr. Mister	RCA	11	(4)	F
3	4	Separate Lives	Phil Collins & Marilyn Martin	Atlantic	13	(4)	
4	20	Party All The Time	Eddie Murphy	Columbia	11		F G L
5	-	Alive & Kicking	Simple Minds	A&M	10	(7)	
6	15	Election Day	Arcadia	Capitol	10	(7)	F L
7	-	I Miss You	Klymaxx	MCA/Constell.	11		F
8	16	Sleeping Bag	ZZ Top	Warner	8	(27)	L
9	-	Small Town	John Cougar Mellencamp	Riva	8	(53)	
10	-	That's What Friends Are For	Dionne Warwick & Friends	Arista	13	(16)	G
11	8	Never	Heart	Capitol	8	(8)	
12	1	We Built This City	Starship	Grunt	10	(12)	F
13	-	Perfect Way	Scritti Politti	Warner	6	(48)	F L
14	-	Tonight She Comes	Cars	Elektra	8		
15	11	Who's Zoomin' Who	Aretha Franklin	Arista	7	(11)	
16	-	Walk Of Life	Dire Straits	Warner	10	(2)	
17	2	You Belong To The City	Glenn Frey	MCA	9		
18	-	Talk To Me	Stevie Nicks	Modern	10	(68)	
19	9	Lay Your Hands On Me	Thompson Twins	Arista	8	(13)	
20	-	Burning Heart	Survivor	Scotti Brothers	11	(5)	

◆ 1985 was the year many stars actively became involved in charity work, helping to raise much money for deserving causes. Apart from helping bring the famine in Africa to the public's attention, recording artists alerted many to such serious issues as AIDS and environmental damage.

◆ Total record and tape sales held steady in the USA, where compact discs now accounted for 21 million of the 643 million units sold (a rise of 250%!). In Britain cassette albums outsold records for the first time in 1985.

◆ 18 years after the Grace Slick-fronted Jefferson Airplane made their US chart debut, the act's latest incarnation, Starship, gave Slick her first No. 1 single, 'We Built This City'. The Bernie Taupin composition also became her first UK Top 20 entry.

UK 1986 JAN-MAR

◆ An *NME* survey showed that Madonna was the UK's Top Singles Artist in 1985 and that Bruce Springsteen was Top Album Artist.

◆ Annie Lennox again collected the Best Female Artist trophy at the Brit Awards. Other winners included Phil Collins (Best Male), Dire Straits (Best Group), Go West (Best Newcomer), Bruce Springsteen (Best International Artist) and Huey Lewis & The News (Best International Group).

◆ After a Dire Straits concert was shown on TV, all the group's previous five albums joined the record-breaking **Brothers In Arms** in the chart.

◆ Among the American re-releases hitting the heights were 'Borderline' by Madonna, 'The Power of Love' by Huey Lewis & The News and, perhaps most surprisingly, 'Theme From New York New York' by Frank Sinatra.

January 1986

This Mnth	Prev Mnth	Title	Artist	Label	Wks 20	(US Pos)	
1	8	West End Girls	Pet Shop Boys	Parlophone	8	(1)	F
2	20	Hit That Perfect Beat	Bronski Beat	Forbidden Fruit	7		
3	-	The Sun Always Shines On T.V.	A-Ha	Warner	7	(20)	
4	1	Saving All My Love For You	Whitney Houston	Arista	9	(1)	F
5	-	Saturday Love	Cherelle & Alexander O'Neal	Tabu	5	(26)	F L
6	-	Girlie Girlie	Sophia George	Winner	5		F L
7	6	Merry Christmas Everyone	Shakin' Stevens	Epic	6		
8	-	Walk Of Life	Dire Straits	Vertigo	6	(7)	L
9	17	Walking In The Air	Aled Jones	HMV	5		F L
10	-	You Little Thief	Feargal Sharkey	Virgin	4		
11	-	Broken Wings	Mr Mister	RCA	4	(1)	F
12	7	Dress You Up	Madonna	Sire	6	(5)	
13	5	Do They Know It's Christmas	Band Aid	Mercury	5		P L
14	2	I'm Your Man	Wham!	Epic	8	(3)	
15	4	Separate Lives	Phil Collins & Marilyn Martin	Virgin	8	(1)	
16	-	Alice I Want You Just For Me	Full Force	CBS	3		F L
17	13	Last Christmas	Wham!	Epic	4		
18	-	Who's Zoomin' Who	Aretha Franklin	Arista	3	(7)	
19	-	Russians	Sting	A&M	3	(16)	
20	-	It's Alright (Baby's Coming Back)	Eurythmics	RCA	4	(78)	

February 1986

This Mnth	Prev Mnth	Title	Artist	Label	Wks 20	(US Pos)	
1	-	When The Going Gets Tough, The Tough Get Going	Billy Ocean	Jive	8	(2)	
2	-	Borderline	Madonna	Sire	6	(10)	
3	3	The Sun Always Shines On T.V.	A-Ha	Warner	7	(20)	
4	-	Only Love	Nana Mouskouri	Philips	6		F L
5	-	System Addict	Five Star	Tent	6		
6	8	Walk Of Life	Dire Straits	Vertigo	6	(7)	L
7	-	Living In America	James Brown	Scotti Bros	6	(4)	
8	-	Eloise	Damned	MCA	6		L
9	-	The Phantom Of The Opera	Sarah Brightman/Steve Harley	Polydor	4		
10	-	Starting Together	Su Pollard	Rainbow	5		F L
11	-	The Captain Of Her Heart	Double	Polydor	4	(16)	F L
12	-	How Will I Know	Whitney Houston	Arista	6	(1)	
13	-	Suspicious Minds	Fine Young Cannibals	London	5		
14	11	Broken Wings	Mr Mister	RCA	4	(1)	F
15	-	Chain Reaction	Diana Ross	Capitol	10	(66)	
16	5	Saturday Love	Cherrelle & Alexander O'Neal	Tabu	5	(26)	F L
17	-	Rise	Public Image Ltd.	Virgin	5		L
18	-	Pull Up To The Bumper/La Vie En Rose	Grace Jones	Island	4		L
19	-	Burning Heart	Survivor	Scotti Brothers	5	(2)	L
20	-	Sanctify Yourself	Simple Minds	Virgin	3	(14)	

March 1986

This Mnth	Prev Mnth	Title	Artist	Label	Wks 20	(US Pos)	
1	15	Chain Reaction	Diana Ross	Capitol	10	(66)	
2	-	Manic Monday	Bangles	CBS	6	(2)	F
3	1	When The Going Gets Tough, The Tough Get Going	Billy Ocean	Jive	8	(2)	
4	-	Love Missile F1-11	Sigue Sigue Sputnik	Parlophone	4		F
5	-	Absolute Beginners	David Bowie	Virgin	5	(53)	
6	-	Hi Ho Silver	Jim Diamond	A&M	7		L
7	10	Starting Together	Su Pollard	Rainbow	5		F L
8	19	Burning Heart	Survivor	Scotti Brothers	5	(2)	L
9	-	Theme From New York New York	Frank Sinatra	Reprise	3	(32)	L
10	-	(Nothin' Serious) Just Buggin'	Whistle	Champion	4		F L
11	12	How Will I Know	Whitney Houston	Arista	6	(1)	
12	-	Living Doll	Cliff Richard & The Young Ones	WEA	7		
13	-	Kiss	Prince & The Revolution	Paisley Park	4	(1)	
14	-	The Power Of Love/Do You Believe In Love	Huey Lewis & The News	Chrysalis	4		
15	8	Eloise	Damned	MCA	6		L
16	-	Don't Waste My Time	Paul Hardcastle	Chrysalis	4		
17	-	Move Away	Culture Club	Virgin	4	(12)	L
18	-	Kyrie	Mr. Mister	RCA	5	(1)	L
19	-	Digging Your Scene	Blow Monkeys	RCA	4	(14)	F
20	-	Touch Me (I Want Your Body)	Samantha Fox	Jive	6	(4)	F

US 1986 JAN-MAR

January 1986

This Mnth	Prev Mnth	Title	Artist	Label	Wks 20	(UK Pos)	
1	1	Say You, Say Me	Lionel Richie	Motown	12	(8)	G
2	10	That's What Friends Are For	Dionne Warwick & Friends	Arista	13	(16)	G
3	4	Party All The Time	Eddie Murphy	Columbia	11		F G L
4	5	Alive & Kicking	Simple Minds	A&M	10	(7)	
5	7	I Miss You	Klymaxx	MCA/Constell.	11		F
6	18	Talk To Me	Stevie Nicks	Modern	10	(68)	
7	9	Small Town	John Cougar Mellencamp	Riva	8	(53)	
8	20	Burning Heart	Survivor	Scotti Brothers	11	(5)	
9	16	Walk Of Life	Dire Straits	Warner	10	(2)	
10	14	Tonight She Comes	Cars	Elektra	8		
11	-	My Hometown	Bruce Springsteen	Columbia	7	(9)	
12	-	I'm Your Man	Wham!	Columbia	8	(1)	
13	6	Election Day	Arcadia	Capitol	10	(7)	F L
14	2	Broken Wings	Mr. Mister	RCA	11	(4)	F
15	3	Separate Lives	Phil Collins & Marilyn Martin	Atlantic	13	(4)	
16	-	Spies Like Us	Paul McCartney	Columbia	6	(16)	L
17	-	Go Home	Stevie Wonder	Tamla	6	(67)	
18	-	It's Only Love	Bryan Adams & Tina Turner	A&M	5	(29)	
19	-	When The Going Gets Tough, The Tough Get Going	Billy Ocean	Jive	8	(1)	
20	-	Conga	Miami Sound Machine	Epic	8		F

February 1986

This Mnth	Prev Mnth	Title	Artist	Label	Wks 20	(UK Pos)	
1	8	Burning Heart	Survivor	Scotti Brothers	11	(5)	
2	19	When The Going Gets Tough, The Tough Get Going	Billy Ocean	Jive	8	(1)	
3	2	That's What Friends Are For	Dionne Warwick & Friends	Arista	13	(16)	G
4	-	How Will I Know	Whitney Houston	Arista	10	(5)	
5	-	Kyrie	Mr. Mister	RCA	9	(11)	
6	-	Living In America	James Brown	Scotti Bros	7	(5)	L
7	-	The Sweetest Taboo	Sade	Portrait	7	(31)	
8	12	I'm Your Man	Wham!	Columbia	8	(1)	
9	20	Conga	Miami Sound Machine	Epic	8		F
10	-	Sara	Starship	Grunt	9	(66)	
11	16	Spies Like Us	Paul McCartney	Columbia	6	(16)	L
12	6	Talk To Me	Stevie Nicks	Modern	10	(68)	
13	-	Life In A Northern Town	Dream Academy	Warner	7	(15)	F L
14	17	Go Home	Stevie Wonder	Tamla	6	(67)	
15	-	Silent Running (On Dangerous Ground)	Mike + The Mechanics	Atlantic	7	(21)	F
16	1	Say You, Say Me	Lionel Richie	Motown	12	(8)	G
17	11	My Hometown	Bruce Springsteen	Columbia	7	(9)	
18	-	A Love Bizarre	Sheila E	Paisley Park	4		L
19	9	Walk Of Life	Dire Straits	Warner	10	(2)	
20	-	Secret Lovers	Atlantic Starr	A&M	10	(10)	F

March 1986

This Mnth	Prev Mnth	Title	Artist	Label	Wks 20	(UK Pos)	
1	10	Sara	Starship	Grunt	9	(66)	
2	-	These Dreams	Heart	Capitol	9	(8)	
3	20	Secret Lovers	Atlantic Starr	A&M	10	(10)	F
4	5	Kyrie	Mr. Mister	RCA	9	(11)	
5	4	How Will I Know	Whitney Houston	Arista	10	(5)	
6	-	R.O.C.K In The U.S.A. (A Salute To '60s Rock)	John Cougar Mellencamp	Riva	8	(67)	
7	-	Rock Me Amadeus	Falco	A&M	9	(1)	F
8	-	King For A Day	Thompson Twins	Arista	7	(22)	L
9	-	Nikita	Elton John	Geffen	5	(3)	
10	15	Silent Running (On Dangerous...)	Mike + The Mechanics	Atlantic	7	(21)	F
11	-	What You Need	INXS	Atlantic	9	(51)	F
12	7	The Sweetest Taboo	Sade	Portrait	7	(31)	
13	6	Living In America	James Brown	Scotti Bros	7	(5)	L
14	-	Kiss	Prince & The Revolution	Paisley Park	10	(6)	G
15	-	This Could Be The Night	Loverboy	Columbia	5		
16	13	Life In A Northern Town	Dream Academy	Warner	7	(15)	F L
17	-	Let's Go All The Way	Sly Fox	Capitol	8	(3)	F L
18	2	When The Going Gets Tough, The...	Billy Ocean	Jive	8	(1)	
19	-	Sanctify Yourself	Simple Minds	A&M	4	(10)	L
20	-	Manic Monday	Bangles	Columbia	9	(2)	F

◆ The deaths were reported of Phil Lynott (Thin Lizzy), Dick James (publisher of The Beatles and Elton John), O'Kelly Isley (Isley Brothers), Richard Manuel (The Band), Neil Sedaka's writing partner Howard Greenfield and Mark Dinning whose "death disc" 'Earth Angel' was a No. 1 hit in 1960.

▲ In March a record four of the Top 5 and 13 of the Top 40 albums featured female singers, one of whom, Sade, won the Grammy for Best New Act.

◆ Lionel Richie's 'Say You, Say Me' gave him a record nine successful years when (at least) one of his compositions had reached No. 1.

UK 1986

APR-JUNE

◆ Bob Geldof received an honorary knighthood from the Queen for his charity work. Among the current charity hits were 'Everybody Wants To Run the World' (the theme to Sports Aid's *Race Against Time*) by Tears For Fears and an update of 'Living Doll' by Cliff Richard & The Young Ones (for Comic Relief).

◆ Sam Cooke's 'Wonderful World' (from 1960) and Marvin Gaye's 'I Heard it Through The Grapevine' (from 1968), were the first of many oldies that hit after being heard in Levis' jeans advertisements.

◆ Shortly before his last gig with Wham!, George Michael's 'A Different Corner' became the first British No. 1 sung, written, produced, arranged and played (all instruments!) by the same person.

◆ Michael Jackson signed a sponsorship deal with Pepsi, reportedly for an unprecedented $15 million.

April 1986

This Mnth	Prev Mnth	Title	Artist	Label	Wks 20	(US Pos)	
1	12	Living Doll	Cliff Richard & The Young Ones	WEA	7		
2	-	A Different Corner	George Michael	Epic	7	(7)	
3	-	Rock Me Amadeus	Falco	A&M	9	(1)	F
4	20	Touch Me (I Want Your Body)	Samantha Fox	Jive	6	(4)	F
5	-	A Kind Of Magic	Queen	EMI	8	(42)	
6	-	Wonderful World	Sam Cooke	RCA	6		L
7	-	You To Me Are Everything	Real Thing	PRT	7		
8	-	Peter Gunn	Art Of Noise & Duane Eddy	China	4	(50)	
9	-	Secret Lovers	Atlantic Starr	A&M	6	(3)	F
10	-	Train Of Thought	A-Ha	Warner	3		
11	-	Look Away	Big Country	Mercury	5		
12	-	All The Things She Said	Simple Minds	Virgin	5	(28)	
13	1	Chain Reaction	Diana Ross	Capitol	10	(66)	
14	5	Absolute Beginners	David Bowie	Virgin	5	(53)	
15	-	E=MC^2	Big Audio Dynamite	CBS	4		F L
16	-	What Have You Done For Me Lately	Janet Jackson	A&M	6	(4)	F
17	-	Can't Wait Another Minute	Five Star	Tent	7	(41)	
18	-	Just Say No	Grange Hill Cast	BBC	3		F L
19	6	Hi Ho Silver	Jim Diamond	A&M	7		L
20	18	Kyrie	Mr. Mister	RCA	5	(1)	L

May 1986

This Mnth	Prev Mnth	Title	Artist	Label	Wks 20	(US Pos)	
1	-	Lessons In Love	Level 42	Polydor	7	(12)	
2	3	Rock Me Amadeus	Falco	A&M	9	(1)	F
3	-	On My Own	Patti Labelle/Michael McDonald	MCA	8	(1)	F L
4	-	The Chicken Song	Spitting Image	Virgin	6		F L
5	-	Live To Tell	Madonna	Sire	6	(1)	
6	16	What Have You Done For Me Lately	Janet Jackson	A&M	6	(4)	F
7	-	Sledgehammer	Peter Gabriel	Virgin	8	(1)	
8	17	Can't Wait Another Minute	Five Star	Tent	7	(41)	
9	-	Greatest Love Of All	Whitney Houston	Arista	5	(1)	
10	2	A Different Corner	George Michael	Epic	7	(7)	
11	-	Snooker Loopy	Matchroom Mob With Chas & Dave	Rockney	4		F L
12	-	Spirit In The Sky	Doctor & The Medics	IRS	9	(69)	F L
13	-	I Heard It Through The Grapevine	Marvin Gaye	Tamla Motown	4		L
14	-	Why Can't This Be Love	Van Halen	Warner	4	(3)	L
15	5	A Kind Of Magic	Queen	EMI	8	(42)	
16	18	Just Say No	Grange Hill Cast	BBC	3		F L
17	-	There'll Be Sad Songs (To Make You Cry)	Billy Ocean	Jive	4	(1)	
18	-	Rolling Home	Status Quo	Vertigo	3		
19	11	Look Away	Big Country	Mercury	5		
20	-	You And Me Tonight	Aurra	10	4		F L

June 1986

This Mnth	Prev Mnth	Title	Artist	Label	Wks 20	(US Pos)	
1	12	Spirit In The Sky	Doctor & The Medics	IRS	9	(69)	F L
2	-	Holding Back The Years	Simply Red	WEA	8	(1)	
3	-	I Can't Wait	Nu Shooz	Atlantic	7	(3)	F L
4	-	Addicted To Love	Robert Palmer	Island	7	(1)	
5	7	Sledgehammer	Peter Gabriel	Virgin	8	(1)	
6	-	Can't Get By Without You	Real Thing	PRT	6		L
7	-	The Edge Of Heaven/Where Did Your Heart Go	Wham!	Epic	6	(10)	L
8	-	Hunting High And Low	A-Ha	Warner	5		
9	-	Set Me Free	Jaki Graham	EMI	5		
10	-	Everybody Wants To Run The World	Tears For Fears	Mercury	3		
11	-	Too Good To Be Forgotten	Amazulu	Island	6		
12	-	Vienna Calling	Falco	A&M	4	(18)	L
13	4	The Chicken Song	Spitting Image	Virgin	6		F L
14	-	Happy Hour	Housemartins	Go! Discs	7		F
15	3	On My Own	Patti Labelle/Michael McDonald	MCA	8	(1)	F L
16	-	New Beginning (Mamba Seyra)	Bucks Fizz	Polydor	5		L
17	1	Lessons In Love	Level 42	Polydor	7	(12)	
18	-	My Favourite Waste Of Time	Owen Paul	Epic	7		F L
19	-	Opportunities (Let's Make Lots Of Money)	Pet Shop Boys	Parlophone	4	(10)	
20	-	Amityville (The House On The Hill)	Lovebug Starski	Epic	4		F L

US 1986
APR-JUNE

April 1986

This Mnth	Prev Mnth	Title	Artist	Label	Wks 20	(UK Pos)	
1	14	Kiss	Prince & The Revolution	Paisley Park	10	(6)	G
2	7	Rock Me Amadeus	Falco	A&M	9	(1)	F
3	20	Manic Monday	Bangles	Columbia	9	(2)	F
4	-	Addicted To Love	Robert Palmer	Island	10	(5)	
5	-	West End Girls	Pet Shop Boys	EMI America	11	(1)	F
6	11	What You Need	INXS	Atlantic	9	(51)	F
7	-	Harlem Shuffle	Rolling Stones	Rolling Stone	8	(13)	
8	17	Let's Go All The Way	Sly Fox	Capitol	8	(3)	F L
9	6	R.O.C.K In The U.S.A. (A Salute To '60s Rock)	John Cougar Mellencamp	Riva	8	(67)	
10	-	Why Can't This Be Love	Van Halen	Warner	8	(8)	
11	-	Tender Love	Force M.D's	Warner	6	(23)	F L
12	3	Secret Lovers	Atlantic Starr	A&M	10	(10)	F
13	-	What Have You Done For Me Lately	Janet Jackson	A&M	9	(3)	F
14	-	Your Love	Outfield	Columbia	8		F
15	2	These Dreams	Heart	Capitol	9	(8)	
16	-	Take Me Home	Phil Collins	Atlantic	8	(19)	
17	-	American Storm	Bob Seger & Silver Bullet Band	Capitol	5		
18	-	I Can't Wait	Stevie Nicks	Modern	3	(54)	
19	-	I Think It's Love	Jermaine Jackson	Arista	3		L
20	-	Bad Boy	Miami Sound Machine	Epic	7	(16)	

May 1986

This Mnth	Prev Mnth	Title	Artist	Label	Wks 20	(UK Pos)	
1	-	Greatest Love Of All	Whitney Houston	Arista	9	(8)	
2	5	West End Girls	Pet Shop Boys	EMI America	11	(1)	F
3	13	What Have You Done For Me Lately	Janet Jackson	A&M	9	(3)	F
4	-	Live To Tell	Madonna	Sire	10	(2)	
5	-	If You Leave	Orchestral Manoeuvres In The Dark	A&M	9	(48)	F
6	10	Why Can't This Be Love	Van Halen	Warner	8	(8)	
7	-	On My Own	Patti Labelle/Michael McDonald	MCA	11	(2)	G L
8	16	Take Me Home	Phil Collins	Atlantic	8	(19)	
9	4	Addicted To Love	Robert Palmer	Island	10	(5)	
10	20	Bad Boy	Miami Sound Machine	Epic	7	(16)	
11	14	Your Love	Outfield	Columbia	8		F
12	-	I Can't Wait	Nu Shooz	Atlantic	9	(2)	F L
13	-	Something About You	Level 42	Polydor	9	(6)	F
14	-	All I Need Is A Miracle	Mike + The Mechanics	Atlantic	7	(53)	
15	1	Kiss	Prince & The Revolution	Paisley Park	10	(6)	G
16	7	Harlem Shuffle	Rolling Stones	Rolling Stone	8	(13)	
17	-	Is It Love	Mr. Mister	RCA	6		L
18	-	Be Good To Yourself	Journey	Columbia	6		
19	-	Move Away	Culture Club	Virgin	5	(7)	L
20	3	Manic Monday	Bangles	Columbia	9	(2)	F

June 1986

This Mnth	Prev Mnth	Title	Artist	Label	Wks 20	(UK Pos)	
1	7	On My Own	Patti Labelle/Michael McDonald	MCA	11	(2)	G L
2	-	There'll Be Sad Songs (To Make You Cry)	Billy Ocean	Jive	10	(12)	
3	4	Live To Tell	Madonna	Sire	10	(2)	
4	-	Crush On You	Jets	MCA	8	(5)	F
5	12	I Can't Wait	Nu Shooz	Atlantic	9	(2)	F L
6	-	A Different Corner	George Michael	Columbia	6	(1)	
7	-	No One Is To Blame	Howard Jones	Elektra	8	(16)	
8	-	Holding Back The Years	Simply Red	Elektra	8	(2)	F
9	1	Greatest Love Of All	Whitney Houston	Arista	9	(8)	
10	-	Who's Johnny	El DeBarge	Gordy	8		F L
11	13	Something About You	Level 42	Polydor	9	(6)	F
12	-	Nothin' At All	Heart	Capitol	6	(38)	
13	14	All I Need Is A Miracle	Mike + The Mechanics	Atlantic	7	(53)	
14	-	I Wanna Be A Cowboy	Boys Don't Cry	Profile	5		F L
15	5	If You Leave	Orchestral Manoeuvres In The Dark	A&M	9	(48)	F
16	-	Nasty	Janet Jackson	A&M	8	(19)	
17	-	Invisible Touch	Genesis	Atlantic	8	(15)	
18	-	Sledgehammer	Peter Gabriel	Geffen	10	(4)	F
19	18	Be Good To Yourself	Journey	Columbia	6		
20	17	Is It Love	Mr. Mister	RCA	6		L

◆ When Prince's self-composed 'Kiss' was at No. 1, 'Manic Monday', which he had written for The Bangles, held the runner-up position. 'Kiss' accomplished a rare treble by also topping the dance music and R&B lists.

▲ In June, Whitney Houston, Patti Labelle and Janet Jackson (above) held the Top 3 positions on the album chart. It was the first time that either females or black artists had achieved this feat. Whitney also became the first female to score three successive No. 1 singles.

◆ A record 20 British artists were simultaneously resident in the Top 40 in June.

◆ Madonna's self-penned and produced 'Papa Don't Preach' was a transatlantic topper, as was her album **True Blue,** the first LP by an American female to enter the UK chart at the summit.

◆ Chicago club DJ Farley 'Jackmaster' Funk's 'Love Can't Turn You Around' is generally regarded as the earliest "house music" hit.

◆ Frankie Goes To Hollywood announced they were to disband, septet Madness shrunk to a quartet and Stiff Records closed – it was the end of another era in British pop.

◆ Irish singer/songwriter Chris De Burgh, who had sold 10 million albums globally, gained his first UK Top 40 single with his 24th release, the chart topping 'The Lady In Red'. It was also his only US Top 20 entry.

July 1986

This Mnth	Prev Mnth	Title	Artist	Label	Wks 20	(US Pos)	
1	-	Papa Don't Preach	Madonna	Sire	9	(1)	
2	18	My Favourite Waste Of Time	Owen Paul	Epic	7		F L
3	7	The Edge Of Heaven/Where Did Your Heart Go	Wham!	Epic	6	(10)	L
4	14	Happy Hour	Housemartins	Go! Discs	7		F
5	-	Let's Go All The Way	Sly Fox	Capitol	6	(7)	F L
6	-	Venus	Bananarama	London	5	(1)	
7	11	Too Good To Be Forgotten	Amazulu	Island	6		
8	-	Every Beat Of My Heart	Rod Stewart	Warner	6	(83)	
9	3	I Can't Wait	Nu Shooz	Atlantic	7	(3)	F L
10	-	Sing Our Own Song	UB40	Dep International	4		
11	-	The Lady In Red	Chris De Burgh	A&M	9	(3)	F
12	16	New Beginning (Mamba Seyra)	Bucks Fizz	Polydor	5		L
13	-	Bang Zoom (Let's Go Go)	Real Roxanne With Hitman Howie Tee	Cooltempo	4		F L
14	-	Do Ya Do Ya (Wanna Please Me)	Samantha Fox	Jive	3	(87)	
15	8	Hunting High And Low	A-Ha	Warner	5		
16	-	Paranoimia	Art Of Noise	China	3	(34)	
17	-	Camouflage	Stan Ridgway	IRS	6		F L
18	1	Spirit In The Sky	Doctor & The Medics	IRS	9	(69)	F L
19	-	It's 'Orrible Being In Love (When You're 8½)	Claire & Friends	BBC	3		F L
20	-	Higher Love	Steve Winwood	Island	3	(1)	F

August 1986

This Mnth	Prev Mnth	Title	Artist	Label	Wks 20	(US Pos)	
1	11	The Lady In Red	Chris De Burgh	A&M	9	(3)	F
2	-	So Macho/Cruising	Sinitta	Fanfare	9		F
3	-	I Want To Wake Up With You	Boris Gardiner	Revue	9		
4	17	Camouflage	Stan Ridgway	IRS	6		F L
5	-	Ain't Nothing Goin' On But The Rent	Gwen Guthrie	Boiling Point	7	(42)	F L
6	1	Papa Don't Preach	Madonna	Sire	9	(1)	
7	-	Anyone Can Fall In Love	Anita Dobson	BBC	4		F L
8	5	Let's Go All The Way	Sly Fox	Capitol	6	(7)	F L
9	-	Find The Time	Five Star	Tent	4		
10	-	Calling All The Heroes	It Bites	Virgin	5		F L
11	8	Every Beat Of My Heart	Rod Stewart	Warner	6	(83)	
12	-	What's The Colour Of Money?	Hollywood Beyond	WEA	5		F L
13	-	Shout	Lulu	Jive/Decca	4		
14	-	Panic	Smiths	Rough Trade	4		
15	-	I Didn't Mean To Turn You On	Robert Palmer	Island	4	(2)	
16	-	Dancing On The Ceiling	Lionel Richie	Motown	4	(2)	
17	-	Brother Louie	Modern Talking	RCA	6		F L
18	-	I Can Prove It	Phil Fearon	Ensign	4		L
19	-	We Don't Have To ...	Jermaine Stewart	10	9	(5)	F
20	10	Sing Our Own Song	UB40	Dep International	4		

September 1986

This Mnth	Prev Mnth	Title	Artist	Label	Wks 20	(US Pos)	
1	-	Don't Leave Me This Way	Communards	London	9	(40)	F
2	19	We Don't Have To ...	Jermaine Stewart	10	9	(5)	F
3	3	I Want To Wake Up With You	Boris Gardiner	Revue	9		
4	-	Glory Of Love	Peter Cetera	Full Moon	7	(1)	F L
5	-	(I Just) Died In Your Arms	Cutting Crew	Siren	6	(1)	F L
6	-	Rage Hard	Frankie Goes To Hollywood	ZTT	4		
7	17	Brother Louie	Modern Talking	RCA	6		F L
8	-	Word Up	Cameo	Club	7	(6)	
9	-	Holiday Rap	M.C. Miker 'G' & Deejay Sven	Debut	3		F L
10	-	Love Can't Turn Around	Farley 'Jackmaster' Funk	D.J. International	6		F L
11	2	So Macho/Cruising	Sinitta	Fanfare	9		F
12	-	Walk This Way	Run D.M.C.	London	6	(4)	F
13	-	Thorn In My Side	Eurythmics	RCA	7	(68)	
14	-	Human	Human League	Virgin	5	(1)	
15	-	Rain Or Shine	Five Star	Tent	7		
16	-	When I Think Of You	Janet Jackson	A&M	4	(1)	
17	1	The Lady In Red	Chris De Burgh	A&M	9	(3)	F
18	-	You Give Love A Bad Name	Bon Jovi	Vertigo	3	(1)	F
19	-	Sweet Freedom	Michael McDonald	MCA	3	(7)	L
20	5	Ain't Nothing Goin' On But The Rent	Gwen Guthrie	Boiling Point	7	(42)	F L

July 1986

This Mnth	Prev Mnth	Title	Artist	Label	Wks 20	(UK Pos)	
1	17	Invisible Touch	Genesis	Atlantic	8	(15)	
2	16	Nasty	Janet Jackson	A&M	8	(19)	
3	8	Holding Back The Years	Simply Red	Elektra	8	(2)	F
4	18	Sledgehammer	Peter Gabriel	Geffen	10	(4)	F
5	-	Danger Zone	Kenny Loggins	Columbia	8	(45)	
6	2	There'll Be Sad Songs (To Make You Cry)	Billy Ocean	Jive	10	(12)	
7	10	Who's Johnny	El DeBarge	Gordy	8		F L
8	-	Glory Of Love	Peter Cetera	Full Moon	10	(3)	F
9	-	Your Wildest Dreams	Moody Blues	Threshold	6		L
10	7	No One Is To Blame	Howard Jones	Elektra	8	(16)	
11	-	Love Touch	Rod Stewart	Warner	7	(27)	
12	-	Mad About You	Belinda Carlisle	IRS	9	(67)	F
13	-	Opportunities (Let's Make Lots Of Money)	Pet Shop Boys	EMI America	6	(11)	
14	-	Papa Don't Preach	Madonna	Sire	9	(1)	
15	-	When The Heart Rules The Mind	GTR	Arista	4		F L
16	-	Tuff Enuff	Fabulous Thunderbirds	CBS Associated	6		F L
17	-	Like A Rock	Bob Seger & Silver Bullet Band	Capitol	5		
18	1	On My Own	Patti Labelle/Michael McDonald	MCA	11	(2)	G L
19	4	Crush On You	Jets	MCA	8	(5)	F
20	-	Modern Woman	Billy Joel	Epic	5		

August 1986

This	Prev	Title	Artist	Label	Wks 20	(UK Pos)	
1	14	Papa Don't Preach	Madonna	Sire	9	(1)	
2	8	Glory Of Love	Peter Cetera	Full Moon	10	(3)	F
3	12	Mad About You	Belinda Carlisle	IRS	9	(67)	F
4	-	Higher Love	Steve Winwood	Island	9	(13)	
5	-	Venus	Bananarama	London	9	(8)	
6	-	We Don't Have To Take Our Clothes Off	Jermaine Stewart	Arista	7	(2)	F L
7	-	Rumors	Timex Social Club	Jay	8	(13)	F L
8	-	Dancing On The Ceiling	Lionel Richie	Motown	11	(7)	
9	4	Sledgehammer	Peter Gabriel	Geffen	10	(4)	F
10	-	Take My Breath Away	Berlin	Columbia	9	(1)	F L
11	11	Love Touch	Rod Stewart	Warner	7	(27)	
12	-	Sweet Freedom	Michael McDonald	MCA	8	(12)	L
13	-	The Edge Of Heaven	Wham!	Columbia	5	(1)	L
14	5	Danger Zone	Kenny Loggins	Columbia	8	(45)	
15	-	Friends And Lovers	Gloria Loring & Carl Anderson	USA Carrere	10		F L
16	1	Invisible Touch	Genesis	Atlantic	8	(15)	
17	-	You Should Be Mine (The Woo Woo Song)	Jeffrey Osborne	A&M	4		F
18	2	Nasty	Janet Jackson	A&M	8	(19)	
19	-	Stuck With You	Huey Lewis & The News	Chrysalis	9	(12)	
20	-	Baby Love	Regina	Atlantic	7	(50)	F L

September 1986

This	Prev	Title	Artist	Label	Wks 20	(UK Pos)	
1	19	Stuck With You	Huey Lewis & The News	Chrysalis	9	(12)	
2	8	Dancing On The Ceiling	Lionel Richie	Motown	11	(7)	
3	15	Friends And Lovers	Gloria Loring & Carl Anderson	USA Carrere	10		F L
4	10	Take My Breath Away	Berlin	Columbia	9	(1)	F L
5	-	Walk This Way	Run D.M.C.	Profile	8	(8)	F L
6	5	Venus	Bananarama	London	9	(8)	
7	-	Words Get In The Way	Miami Sound Machine	Epic	8		
8	-	Don't Forget Me (When I'm Gone)	Glass Tiger	Manhattan	9	(29)	F
9	-	Dreamtime	Daryl Hall	RCA	7	(28)	F L
10	4	Higher Love	Steve Winwood	Island	9	(13)	
11	20	Baby Love	Regina	Atlantic	7	(50)	F L
12	12	Sweet Freedom	Michael McDonald	MCA	8	(12)	L
13	-	Love Zone	Billy Ocean	Jive	6	(49)	
14	-	When I Think Of You	Janet Jackson	A&M	9	(10)	
15	-	Two Of Hearts	Stacey Q	Atlantic	7		F L
16	1	Papa Don't Preach	Madonna	Sire	9	(1)	
17	-	The Captain Of Her Heart	Double	A&M	4	(8)	F L
18	-	Throwing It All Away	Genesis	Atlantic	8	(22)	
19	7	Rumors	Timex Social Club	Jay	8	(13)	F L
20	-	Man Size Love	Klymaxx	MCA	3		

▲ Run DMC's *Raising Hell* tour (including fellow rappers L.L. Cool J, Whodini and The Beastie Boys) sparked off mini-riots at several venues. Run DMC's **Raising Hell** LP was the first platinum rap album, and 'Walk This Way' (featuring Aerosmith's Steve Tyler) (above) was the earliest hit to combine the rap and rock genres.

◆ Janet Jackson became the youngest singer to top the album charts since Little Stevie Wonder in 1963.

◆ New kids on the block included the teenage act of that name, who were supporting The Four Tops on tour, and Guns N' Roses, who started recording their first album for Geffen.

271

UK 1986 OCT-DEC

◆ Status Quo scored their 20th Top 10 hit, 'In The Army Now'. The Beatles and The Rolling Stones were the only other groups to achieve this feat.

◆ 'Take My Breath Away' (from the five million selling **Top Gun** soundtrack) gave Berlin a transatlantic chart-topper. It also returned to the British Top 3 in 1990.

▲ In October, for the first time, the top three US singles were by different solo female singers, Janet Jackson, Tina Turner (above) and Cyndi Lauper. A month later female vocalists held a record Top 5 slots on the UK chart.

October 1986

This Mnth	Prev Mnth	Title	Artist	Label	Wks 20	(US Pos)	
1	-	True Blue	Madonna	Sire	7	(3)	
2	15	Rain Or Shine	Five Star	Tent	7		
3	1	Don't Leave Me This Way	Communards	London	9	(40)	F
4	-	You Can Call Me Al	Paul Simon	Warner	6	(23)	
5	-	Every Loser Wins	Nick Berry	BBC	6		F
6	-	In The Army Now	Status Quo	Vertigo	7		
7	8	Word Up	Cameo	Club	7	(6)	
8	13	Thorn In My Side	Eurythmics	RCA	7	(68)	
9	-	Suburbia	Pet Shop Boys	Parlophone	5	(70)	
10	-	I've Been Losing You	A-Ha	Warner	4		
11	-	All I Ask Of You	Cliff Richard & Sarah Brightman	Polydor	8		
12	-	Walk Like An Egyptian	Bangles	CBS	8	(1)	
13	2	We Don't Have To ...	Jermaine Stewart	10	9	(5)	F
14	-	(Forever) Live And Die	Orchestral Manoeuvres In The Dark	Virgin	5	(19)	
15	-	Always There	Marti Webb	BBC	5		L
16	12	Walk This Way	Run D.M.C.	London	6	(4)	F
17	5	(I Just) Died In Your Arms	Cutting Crew	Siren	6	(1)	F L
18	-	True Colors	Cyndi Lauper	Portrait	5	(1)	
19	-	Stuck With You	Huey Lewis & The News	Chrysalis	4	(1)	L
20	-	Montego Bay	Amazulu	Island	3	(90)	L

November 1986

This Mnth	Prev Mnth	Title	Artist	Label	Wks 20	(US Pos)	
1	-	Take My Breath Away	Berlin	CBS	11	(1)	F
2	-	You Keep Me Hangin' On	Kim Wilde	MCA	7	(1)	
3	12	Walk Like An Egyptian	Bangles	CBS	8	(1)	
4	-	Showing Out (Get Fresh At The Weekend)	Mel & Kim	Supreme	6	(78)	F
5	6	In The Army Now	Status Quo	Vertigo	7		
6	5	Every Loser Wins	Nick Berry	BBC	6		F
7	-	Breakout	Swing Out Sister	Mercury	7	(6)	F
8	11	All I Ask Of You	Cliff Richard & Sarah Brightman	Polydor	8		
9	-	Livin' On A Prayer	Bon Jovi	Vertigo	10	(1)	
10	-	The Final Countdown	Europe	Epic	10	(8)	F
11	-	Through The Barricades	Spandau Ballet	Reformation	5		L
12	-	Don't Give Up	Peter Gabriel & Kate Bush	Virgin	4	(72)	
13	-	Notorious	Duran Duran	EMI	4	(2)	
14	-	For America	Red Box	Sire	5		L
15	-	Midas Touch	Midnight Star	Solar	4	(42)	L
16	1	True Blue	Madonna	Sire	7	(3)	
17	-	Don't Get Me Wrong	Pretenders	Real	4	(10)	
18	4	You Can Call Me Al	Paul Simon	Warner	6	(23)	
19	-	Each Time You Break My Heart	Nick Kamen	WEA	5		F
20	-	French Kissin' In The USA	Debbie Harry	Chrysalis	7	(57)	F L

December 1986

This Mnth	Prev Mnth	Title	Artist	Label	Wks 20	(US Pos)	
1	10	The Final Countdown	Europe	Epic	10	(8)	F
2	-	Sometimes	Erasure	Mute	10		F
3	-	Caravan Of Love	Housemartins	Go! Discs	6		
4	-	The Rain	Oran 'Juice' Jones	Def Jam	8	(9)	F L
5	9	Livin' On A Prayer	Bon Jovi	Vertigo	10	(1)	
6	1	Take My Breath Away	Berlin	CBS	11	(1)	F
7	-	Open Your Heart	Madonna	Sire	6	(1)	
8	-	Shake You Down	Gregory Abbott	CBS	7	(1)	F L
9	-	Reet Petite	Jackie Wilson	SMP	9		
10	-	So Cold The Night	Communards	London	6		
11	19	Each Time You Break My Heart	Nick Kamen	WEA	5		F
12	20	French Kissin' In The USA	Debbie Harry	Chrysalis	7	(57)	F L
13	-	Cry Wolf	A-Ha	Warner	6	(50)	
14	7	Breakout	Swing Out Sister	Mercury	7	(6)	F
15	-	The Skye Boat Song	Roger Whittaker & Des O'Connor	Tembo	5		L
16	-	Is This Love	Alison Moyet	CBS	9		
17	2	You Keep Me Hangin' On	Kim Wilde	MCA	7	(1)	
18	4	Showing Out (Get Fesh At The Weekend)	Mel & Kim	Supreme	6	(78)	F
19	-	Big Fun	Gap Band	Total Experience	8		
20	-	Land Of Confusion	Genesis	Virgin	7	(4)	

This Mnth	Prev Mnth	Title	Artist	Label	Wks 20	(UK Pos)	
1	14	When I Think Of You	Janet Jackson	A&M	9	(10)	
2	-	Typical Male	Tina Turner	Capitol	9	(33)	
3	18	Throwing It All Away	Genesis	Atlantic	8	(22)	
4	15	Two Of Hearts	Stacey Q	Atlantic	7		F L
5	-	True Colors	Cyndi Lauper	Portrait	8	(12)	
6	8	Don't Forget Me (When I'm Gone)	Glass Tiger	Manhattan	9	(29)	F
7	-	Heartbeat	Don Johnson	Epic	7	(46)	F L
8	1	Stuck With You	Huey Lewis & The News	Chrysalis	9	(12)	
9	-	All Cried Out	Lisa Lisa & Cult Jam With Full Force	Columbia	7		F
10	-	I Didn't Mean To Turn You On	Robert Palmer	Island	8	(9)	
11	3	Friends And Lovers	Gloria Loring & Carl Anderson	USA Carrere	10		F L
12	9	Dreamtime	Daryl Hall	RCA	7	(28)	F L
13	-	A Matter Of Trust	Billy Joel	Columbia	5	(52)	
14	-	Sweet Love	Anita Baker	Elektra	6	(13)	F
15	-	Heaven In Your Eyes	Loverboy	Columbia	5		L
16	-	Amanda	Boston	MCA	8		
17	-	Human	Human League	A&M	10	(8)	L
18	5	Walk This Way	Run D.M.C.	Profile	8	(8)	F L
19	-	Missionary Man	Eurythmics	RCA	5	(31)	L
20	13	Love Zone	Billy Ocean	Jive	6	(49)	

This Mnth	Prev Mnth	Title	Artist	Label	Wks 20	(UK Pos)	
1	17	Human	Human League	A&M	10	(8)	L
2	16	Amanda	Boston	MCA	8		
3	-	True Blue	Madonna	Sire	8	(1)	
4	-	You Give Love A Bad Name	Bon Jovi	Mercury	9	(14)	F
5	-	Take Me Home Tonight	Eddie Money	Columbia	8		
6	-	Word Up	Cameo	Atlanta Artists	8	(3)	F L
7	10	I Didn't Mean To Turn You On	Robert Palmer	Island	8	(9)	
8	-	The Next Time I Fall	Peter Cetera & Amy Grant	Full Moon	8		
9	5	True Colors	Cyndi Lauper	Portrait	8	(12)	
10	-	Hip To Be Square	Huey Lewis & The News	Chrysalis	9	(41)	
11	-	The Rain	Oran 'Juice' Jones	Def Jam	6	(4)	F L
12	-	Love Will Conquer All	Lionel Richie	Motown	7	(45)	
13	-	I'll Be Over You	Toto	Columbia	5		L
14	-	The Way It Is	Bruce Hornsby & The Range	RCA	11	(15)	F
15	2	Typical Male	Tina Turner	Capitol	9	(33)	
16	14	Sweet Love	Anita Baker	Elektra	6	(13)	F
17	-	Everybody Have Fun Tonight	Wang Chung	Geffen	10		
18	-	To Be A Lover	Billy Idol	Chrysalis	9	(22)	
19	1	When I Think Of You	Janet Jackson	A&M	9	(10)	
20	-	Walk Like An Egyptian	Bangles	Columbia	11	(3)	G

This Mnth	Prev Mnth	Title	Artist	Label	Wks 20	(UK Pos)	
1	20	Walk Like An Egyptian	Bangles	Columbia	11	(3)	G
2	14	The Way It Is	Bruce Hornsby & The Range	RCA	11	(15)	F
3	17	Everybody Have Fun Tonight	Wang Chung	Geffen	10		
4	-	Notorious	Duran Duran	Capitol	9	(7)	
5	10	Hip To Be Square	Huey Lewis & The News	Chrysalis	9	(41)	
6	-	Shake You Down	Gregory Abbott	Columbia	11	(6)	F G L
7	18	To Be A Lover	Billy Idol	Chrysalis	9	(22)	
8	8	The Next Time I Fall	Peter Cetera & Amy Grant	Full Moon	8		
9	-	Stand By Me	Ben E. King	Atlantic	9	(1)	L
10	4	You Give Love A Bad Name	Bon Jovi	Mercury	9	(14)	F
11	-	C'Est La Vie	Robbie Nevil	Manhattan/EMI	10	(3)	F
12	-	Don't Get Me Wrong	Pretenders	Sire	7	(10)	L
13	-	War	Bruce Springsteen	Columbia	7	(18)	
14	-	Control	Janet Jackson	A&M	9	(42)	
15	6	Word Up	Cameo	Atlanta Artists	8	(3)	F L
16	12	Love Will Conquer All	Lionel Richie	Motown	7	(45)	
17	1	Human	Human League	A&M	10	(8)	L
18	-	Is This Love	Survivor	Scotti Brothers	8		L
19	-	Land Of Confusion	Genesis	Atlantic	10	(14)	
20	-	Victory	Kool & The Gang	Mercury	7	(30)	

US
1986
OCT-DEC

◆ American record and tape shipments rose 6% to $4.65 billion, with CD sales up 139% to $930 million. Singles sales, however, were down 22%.

◆ The five album box set **Bruce Springsteen & The E Street Band Live/1975-85** entered at No. 1. Springsteen was only the third artist to accomplish this feat – Elton John and Stevie Wonder had previously done so, but with single albums.

◆ In 1986, the *Rock And Roll Hall Of Fame* chose Cleveland as its home. The initial artists inducted were Chuck Berry, James Brown, Sam Cooke, Fats Domino, The Everly Brothers, Alan Freed, Buddy Holly, Jerry Lee Lewis, Little Richard, Sun Records owner Sam Phillips and Elvis Presley.

◆ R&B producers Jimmy Jam and Terry Lewis scored their sixth Top 10 of the year with 'Human' by UK synth band The Human League.

UK 1987

JAN-MAR

◆ Ben E. King's 25-year-old 'Stand By Me' was a transatlantic Top 10 hit, while in Britain Percy Sledge's 1966 smash, 'When A Man Loves A Woman', scored again. Jackie Wilson's 29-year-old 'Reet Petite' hit the top and half the Top 10 in March were re-issues.

▲ *Record Mirror's* readers poll showed Prince as Top Male, Madonna as Top Female and The Smiths (above) as Top Group.

◆ Kate Bush, who was voted Best Female Artist at the Brit Awards, became the first British female to chalk up three No. 1 LPs when **The Whole Story** completed her hat-trick.

January 1987

This Mnth	Prev Mnth	Title	Artist	Label	Wks 20	(US Pos)	
1	9	Reet Petite	Jackie Wilson	SMP	9		
2	16	Is This Love	Alison Moyet	CBS	9		
3	19	Big Fun	Gap Band	Total Experience	8		
4	-	Jack Your Body	Steve 'Silk' Hurley	DJ International	7		F L
5	-	No More The Fool	Elkie Brooks	Legend	8		L
6	3	Caravan Of Love	Housemartins	Go! Discs	6		
7	-	C'est La Vie	Robbie Nevil	Manhattan	5	(2)	F L
8	2	Sometimes	Erasure	Mute	10		F
9	1	The Final Countdown	Europe	Epic	10	(8)	F
10	7	Open Your Heart	Madonna	Sire	6	(1)	
11	4	The Rain	Oran 'Juice' Jones	Def Jam	8	(9)	F L
12	13	Cry Wolf	A-Ha	Warner	6	(50)	
13	-	Surrender	Swing Out Sister	Mercury	4		L
14	-	Hymn To Her	Pretenders	Real	5		
15	8	Shake You Down	Gregory Abbott	CBS	7	(1)	F L
16	-	It Didn't Matter	Style Council	Polydor	3		
17	-	I Knew You Were Waiting (For Me)	Aretha Franklin & George Michael	Epic	6	(1)	
18	-	Down To Earth	Curiosity Killed The Cat	Mercury	8		F
19	5	Livin' On A Prayer	Bon Jovi	Vertigo	10	(1)	
20	10	So Cold The Night	Communards	London	6		

February 1987

This Mnth	Prev Mnth	Title	Artist	Label	Wks 20	(US Pos)	
1	17	I Knew You Were Waiting (For Me)	Aretha Franklin & George Michael	Epic	6	(1)	
2	-	Heartache	Pepsi & Shirlie	Polydor	6	(78)	F
3	18	Down To Earth	Curiosity Killed The Cat	Mercury	8		F
4	-	Almaz	Randy Crawford	Warner	5		L
5	-	It Doesn't Have To Be That Way	Blow Monkeys	RCA	4		L
6	-	Male Stripper	Man 2 Man Meet Man Parrish	Bolts	7		F L
7	-	Stand By Me	Ben E. King	Atlantic	7	(9)	F L
8	-	I Love My Radio	Taffy	Transglobal	4		F L
9	-	When A Man Loves A Woman	Percy Sledge	Atlantic	6		L
10	4	Jack Your Body	Steve 'Silk' Hurley	Dj International	7		F L
11	-	Stay Out Of My Life	Five Star	Tent	4		
12	-	The Music Of The Night/Wishing You Were Somehow Here Again	Michael Crawford/ Sarah Brightman	Polydor	4		F L
13	-	Running In The Family	Level 42	Polydor	6	(83)	
14	-	You Sexy Thing	Hot Chocolate	EMI	4		L
15	5	No More The Fool	Elkie Brooks	Legend	8		L
16	7	C'est La Vie	Robbie Nevil	Manhattan	5	(2)	F L
17	-	Coming Around Again	Carly Simon	Arista	5	(18)	L
18	-	Shoplifters Of The World Unite	Smiths	Rough Trade	2		
19	2	Is This Love	Alison Moyet	CBS	9		
20	-	Once Bitten Twice Shy	Vesta Williams	A&M	3		F L

March 1987

This Mnth	Prev Mnth	Title	Artist	Label	Wks 20	(US Pos)	
1	-	Everything I Own	Boy George	Virgin	6		F
2	-	I Get The Sweetest Feeling	Jackie Wilson	SMP	6		
3	-	Live It Up	Mental As Anything	Epic	7		F L
4	-	The Great Pretender	Freddie Mercury	Parlophone	6		
5	7	Stand By Me	Ben E. King	Atlantic	7	(9)	F L
6	-	Respectable	Mel & Kim	Supreme	9		
7	9	When A Man Loves A Woman	Percy Sledge	Atlantic	6		L
8	-	Crush On You	Jets	MCA	6	(3)	F L
9	6	Male Stripper	Man 2 Man Meet Man Parrish	Bolts	7		F L
10	13	Running In The Family	Level 42	Polydor	6	(83)	
11	-	Weak In The Presence Of Beauty	Alison Moyet	CBS	6		
12	-	Moonlighting ('Theme')	Al Jarreau	WEA	4	(23)	F L
13	-	Respect Yourself	Bruce Willis	Motown	4	(5)	F
14	-	The Right Thing	Simply Red	WEA	4	(27)	
15	-	It Doesn't Have To Be	Erasure	Mute	5		
16	3	Down To Earth	Curiosity Killed The Cat	Mercury	8		F
17	17	Coming Around Again	Carly Simon	Arista	5	(18)	L
18	-	With Or Without You	U2	Island	6	(1)	
19	-	Sign 'O' The Times	Prince	Paisley Park	5	(3)	
20	-	(You Gotta) Fight For Your Right (To Party)	Beastie Boys	Def Jam	3	(7)	F

US 1987 JAN-MAR

January 1987

This Mnth	Prev Mnth	Title	Artist	Label	Wks 20	(UK Pos)	
1	11	C'Est La Vie	Robbie Nevil	Manhattan/EMI	10	(3)	F
2	6	Shake You Down	Gregory Abbott	Columbia	11	(6)	F G L
3	4	Notorious	Duran Duran	Capitol	10	(7)	
4	14	Control	Janet Jackson	A&M	9	(42)	
5	-	At This Moment	Billy Vera & The Beaters	Rhino	9		F G L
6	1	Walk Like An Egyptian	Bangles	Columbia	11	(3)	G
7	19	Land Of Confusion	Genesis	Atlantic	10	(14)	
8	-	Open Your Heart	Madonna	Sire	8	(4)	
9	18	Is This Love	Survivor	Scotti Brothers	8		L
10	3	Everybody Have Fun Tonight	Wang Chung	Geffen	10		
11	-	Someday	Glass Tiger	Manhattan	8	(66)	L
12	20	Victory	Kool & The Gang	Mercury	7	(30)	
13	-	Change Of Heart	Cyndi Lauper	Portrait	6	(67)	
14	2	The Way It Is	Bruce Hornsby & The Range	RCA	11	(15)	F
15	13	War	Bruce Springsteen	Columbia	7	(18)	
16	-	Touch Me (I Want Your Body)	Samantha Fox	Jive	7	(3)	F
17	9	Stand By Me	Ben E. King	Atlantic	9	(1)	L
18	-	Livin' On A Prayer	Bon Jovi	Mercury	10	(4)	
19	12	Don't Get Me Wrong	Pretenders	Sire	7	(10)	L
20	-	Keep Your Hands To Yourself	Georgia Satellites	Elektra	9	(69)	F L

February 1987

This Mnth	Prev Mnth	Title	Artist	Label	Wks 20	(UK Pos)	
1	18	Livin' On A Prayer	Bon Jovi	Mercury	10	(4)	
2	20	Keep Your Hands To Yourself	Georgia Satellites	Elektra	9	(69)	F L
3	-	Will You Still Love Me	Chicago	Warner	8		
4	16	Touch Me (I Want Your Body)	Samantha Fox	Jive	7	(3)	F
5	-	Jacob's Ladder	Huey Lewis & The News	Chrysalis	8		
6	8	Open Your Heart	Madonna	Sire	8	(4)	
7	13	Change Of Heart	Cyndi Lauper	Portrait	6	(67)	
8	-	You Got It All	Jets	MCA	8		
9	-	Ballerina Girl	Lionel Richie	Motown	7	(17)	
10	5	At This Moment	Billy Vera & The Beaters	Rhino	9		F G L
11	-	Love You Down	Ready For The World	MCA	6	(60)	L
12	-	Somewhere Out There	Linda Ronstadt/James Ingram	MCA	8	(8)	
13	-	Respect Yourself	Bruce Willis	Motown	7	(7)	F L
14	-	Big Time	Peter Gabriel	Geffen	7	(13)	L
15	-	(You Gotta) Fight For Your Right (To Party)	Beastie Boys	Def Jam	6	(11)	F L
16	-	We're Ready	Boston	Epic	5		
17	-	Nobody's Fool	Cinderella	Mercury	4		F
18	7	Land Of Confusion	Genesis	Atlantic	10	(14)	
19	11	Someday	Glass Tiger	Manhattan	8	(66)	L
20	-	Stop To Love	Luther Vandross	Epic	4	(24)	F

March 1987

This Mnth	Prev Mnth	Title	Artist	Label	Wks 20	(UK Pos)	
1	12	Somewhere Out There	Linda Ronstadt/James Ingram	MCA	8	(8)	
2	-	Let's Wait Awhile	Janet Jackson	A&M	7	(3)	
3	-	Lean On Me	Club Nouveau	Warner	8	(3)	F G L
4	5	Jacob's Ladder	Huey Lewis & The News	Chrysalis	8		
5	-	Mandolin Rain	Bruce Hornsby & The Range	RCA	8	(70)	
6	-	Nothing's Gonna Stop Us Now	Starship	Grunt	10	(1)	
7	1	Livin' On A Prayer	Bon Jovi	Mercury	10	(4)	
8	-	Tonight Tonight Tonight	Genesis	Atlantic	7	(18)	
9	13	Respect Yourself	Bruce Willis	Motown	7	(7)	F L
10	14	Big Time	Peter Gabriel	Geffen	7	(13)	L
11	8	You Got It All	Jets	MCA	8		
12	-	Come Go With Me	Expose	Arista	8		F
13	15	(You Gotta) Fight For Your Right (To Party)	Beastie Boys	Def Jam	6	(11)	F L
14	-	The Final Countdown	Europe	Epic	6	(1)	F
15	2	Keep Your Hands To Yourself	Georgia Satellites	Elektra	9	(69)	F L
16	-	Don't Dream It's Over	Crowded House	Capitol	10	(27)	F
17	-	I Knew You Were Waiting (For Me)	Aretha Franklin & George Michael	Arista	8	(1)	
18	-	Let's Go	Wang Chung	Geffen	5		L
19	-	I Wanna Go Back	Eddie Money	Columbia	4		
20	-	Brand New Lover	Dead Or Alive	Epic	4	(31)	L

◆ Aretha Franklin's duet with George Michael, 'I Knew You Were Waiting', was the Queen of Soul's only transatlantic No. 1.

◆ The Beastie Boys' **Licensed To Ill** became the first rap album to top the chart. The white trio's first single '(You Gotta) Fight For Your Right (To Party)' was also a transatlantic hit.

▲ Huey Lewis & The News scored their third and last American No. 1 with 'Jacob's Ladder'. It was one of five Top 10 hits from their chart-topping **Fore** album.

◆ Paul Simon picked up a Grammy for Album Of The Year for **Graceland** and the Brit Award for Best International Solo Artist.

UK 1987
APR-JUNE

◆ This year's Prince's Trust Gala starred Eric Clapton, Bryan Adams, Ben E. King, Alison Moyet and new teeny bop idols Curiosity Killed The Cat. Acts enjoying sell out shows at Wembley included Americans Lionel Richie, Luther Vandross and Tina Turner and UK-based Duran Duran, David Bowie, U2 and The Pretenders.

◆ Headliners at Switzerland's Montreux Rock Festival included Whitney Houston, Cameo, Duran Duran, Spandau Ballet, Run DMC and The Beastie Boys. The latter two then toured Britain where The Beasties received a hammering from the British press for their alleged anti-social behaviour.

◆ The influx of old songs onto the chart continued and even classic old recordings such as Tom Jones's debut hit single 'It's Not Unusual' and The Beatles' **Sergeant Pepper** album returned to the Top 20.

April 1987

This Mnth	Prev Mnth	Title	Artist	Label	Wks 20	(US Pos)	
1	-	Let It Be	Ferry Aid	The Sun	5		F L
2	-	La Isla Bonita	Madonna	Sire	8	(4)	
3	6	Respectable	Mel & Kim	Supreme	9		
4	-	Lean On Me	Club Nouveau	King Jay	7	(1)	F L
5	-	Let's Wait Awhile	Janet Jackson	Breakout	6	(2)	
6	18	With Or Without You	U2	Island	6	(1)	
7	-	If You Let Me Stay	Terence Trent D'Arby	CBS	7	(68)	F
8	-	Can't Be With You Tonight	Judy Boucher	Orbitone	9		F
9	-	Ever Fallen In Love	Fine Young Cannibals	London	6		
10	11	Weak In The Presence Of Beauty	Alison Moyet	CBS	6		
11	-	Living In A Box	Living In A Box	Chrysalis	8	(17)	F
12	-	The Irish Rover	Pogues & The Dubliners	Stiff	3		
13	1	Everything I Own	Boy George	Virgin	6		F
14	2	I Get The Sweetest Feeling	Jackie Wilson	SMP	6		
15	-	Ordinary Day	Curiosity Killed The Cat	Mercury	3		
16	-	The Slightest Touch	Five Star	Tent	6		
17	-	Wanted Dead Or Alive	Bon Jovi	Vertigo	4	(7)	
18	19	Sign 'O' The Times	Prince	Paisley Park	5	(3)	
19	13	Respect Yourself	Bruce Willis	Motown	4	(5)	F
20	-	Big Time	Peter Gabriel	Charisma	3	(8)	

May 1987

This Mnth	Prev Mnth	Title	Artist	Label	Wks 20	(US Pos)	
1	-	Nothing's Gonna Stop Us Now	Starship	RCA	11	(1)	L
2	8	Can't Be With You Tonight	Judy Boucher	Orbitone	9		F
3	-	A Boy From Nowhere	Tom Jones	Epic	8		
4	11	Living In A Box	Living In A Box	Chrysalis	8	(17)	F
5	-	(Something Inside) So Strong	Labi Siffre	China	7		L
6	2	La Isla Bonita	Madonna	Sire	8	(4)	
7	-	Another Step (Closer To You)	Kim Wilde & Junior	MCA	7		
8	16	The Slightest Touch	Five Star	Tent	6		
9	-	Big Love	Fleetwood Mac	Warner	5	(5)	
10	-	Shattered Dreams	Johnny Hates Jazz	Virgin	6	(2)	F
11	-	Back And Forth	Cameo	Club	5	(50)	L
12	-	I Wanna Dance With Somebody (Who Loves Me)	Whitney Houston	Arista	10	(1)	
13	4	Lean On Me	Club Nouveau	King Jay	7	(1)	F L
14	-	Incommunicado	Marillion	EMI	3		
15	-	April Skies	Jesus And Mary Chain	Blanco	3		
16	-	To Be With You Again	Level 42	Polydor	3		
17	7	If You Let Me Stay	Terence Trent D'Arby	CBS	7	(68)	F
18	-	Lil' Devil	Cult	Beggars Banquet	4		
19	-	Boops (Here To Go)	Sly And Robbie	4th & Broadway	3		F L
20	-	Hold Me Now	Johnny Logan	Epic	7		L

June 1987

This Mnth	Prev Mnth	Title	Artist	Label	Wks 20	(US Pos)	
1	12	I Wanna Dance With Somebody (Who Loves Me)	Whitney Houston	Arista	10	(1)	
2	20	Hold Me Now	Johnny Logan	Epic	7		L
3	1	Nothing's Gonna Stop Us Now	Starship	RCA	11	(1)	L
4	-	I Want Your Sex	George Michael	Epic	5	(2)	
5	-	Star Trekkin'	Firm	Bark	7		L
6	-	I Still Haven't Found What I'm Looking For	U2	Island	4	(1)	
7	-	Jack Mix II	Mirage	Debut	5		F
8	-	Victim Of Love	Erasure	Mute	4		
9	-	Nothing's Gonna Stop Me Now	Samantha Fox	Jive	5	(80)	
10	-	Under The Boardwalk	Bruce Willis	Motown	10	(59)	L
11	-	Goodbye Stranger	Pepsi & Shirlie	Polydor	4		L
12	10	Shattered Dreams	Johnny Hates Jazz	Virgin	6	(2)	F
13	-	Wishing I Was Lucky	Wet Wet Wet	Precious	5	(58)	F
14	-	You're The Voice	John Farnham	Wheatley	6	(82)	F L
15	-	Serious	Donna Allen	Portrait	3	(21)	F
16	-	It's A Sin	Pet Shop Boys	Parlophone	8	(9)	
17	-	When Smokey Sings	ABC	Neutron	4	(5)	L
18	-	Looking For A New Love	Jody Watley	MCA	3	(2)	F L
19	-	Is This Love	Whitesnake	EMI	5	(2)	
20	-	No Sleep Till Brooklyn	Beastie Boys	Def Jam	3		

April 1987

This Mnth	Prev Mnth	Title	Artist	Label	Wks 20	(UK Pos)	
1	6	Nothing's Gonna Stop Us Now	Starship	Grunt	10	(1)	
2	17	I Knew You Were Waiting (For Me)	Aretha Franklin/George Michael	Arista	8	(1)	
3	16	Don't Dream It's Over	Crowded House	Capitol	10	(27)	F
4	3	Lean On Me	Club Nouveau	Warner	8	(3)	F G L
5	-	Sign 'O' The Times	Prince	Paisley Park	8	(10)	
6	-	Midnight Blue	Lou Gramm	Atlantic	7		F
7	12	Come Go With Me	Expose	Arista	8		F
8	-	Looking For A New Love	Jody Watley	MCA	10	(13)	F
9	-	The Finer Things	Steve Winwood	Island	8		
10	8	Tonight Tonight Tonight	Genesis	Atlantic	7	(18)	
11	-	(I Just) Died In Your Arms	Cutting Crew	Virgin	8	(4)	F
12	-	Walking Down Your Street	Bangles	Columbia	5	(16)	
13	18	Let's Go	Wang Chung	Geffen	5		L
14	-	La Isla Bonita	Madonna	Sire	8	(1)	
15	2	Let's Wait Awhile	Janet Jackson	A&M	7	(3)	
16	14	The Final Countdown	Europe	Epic	6	(1)	F
17	-	With Or Without You	U2	Island	10	(4)	F
18	-	Stone Love	Kool & The Gang	Mercury	6	(45)	L
19	5	Mandolin Rain	Bruce Hornsby & The Range	RCA	8	(70)	
20	-	What You Get Is What You See	Tina Turner	Capitol	3	(30)	

May 1987

This Mnth	Prev Mnth	Title	Artist	Label	Wks 20	(UK Pos)	
1	17	With Or Without You	U2	Island	10	(4)	F
2	8	Looking For A New Love	Jody Watley	MCA	10	(13)	F
3	11	(I Just) Died In Your Arms	Cutting Crew	Virgin	8	(4)	F
4	-	Lady In Red	Chris De Burgh	A&M	9	(1)	F L
5	14	La Isla Bonita	Madonna	Sire	8	(1)	
6	-	Heat Of The Night	Bryan Adams	A&M	7	(50)	
7	-	Big Love	Fleetwood Mac	Warner	7	(9)	
8	-	You Keep Me Hangin' On	Kim Wilde	MCA	8	(2)	F L
9	-	Always	Atlantic Starr	Warner	10	(3)	
10	-	Right On Track	Breakfast Club	MCA	7	(54)	F L
11	3	Don't Dream It's Over	Crowded House	Capitol	10	(27)	F
12	5	Sign 'O' The Times	Prince	Paisley Park	8	(10)	
13	-	Talk Dirty To Me	Poison	Enigma	4	(67)	F
14	-	I Know What I Like	Huey Lewis & The News	Chrysalis	5		
15	-	Nothing's Gonna Change My Love For You	Glenn Medeiros	Amherst	6	(1)	F
16	2	I Knew You Were Waiting (For Me)	Aretha Franklin/George Michael	Arista	8	(1)	
17	-	Wanted Dead Or Alive	Bon Jovi	Mercury	8	(13)	
18	9	The Finer Things	Steve Winwood	Island	8		
19	-	Head To Toe	Lisa Lisa & Cult Jam	Columbia	10		
20	-	What's Going On	Cyndi Lauper	Portrait	5	(57)	

June 1987

This Mnth	Prev Mnth	Title	Artist	Label	Wks 20	(UK Pos)	
1	19	Head To Toe	Lisa Lisa & Cult Jam	Columbia	10		
2	9	Always	Atlantic Starr	Warner	10	(3)	
3	-	In Too Deep	Genesis	Atlantic	8	(19)	
4	-	I Wanna Dance With Somebody (Who Loves Me)	Whitney Houston	Arista	11	(1)	G
5	8	You Keep Me Hangin' On	Kim Wilde	MCA	8	(2)	F L
6	-	Diamonds	Herb Alpert	A&M	7	(27)	L
7	17	Wanted Dead Or Alive	Bon Jovi	Mercury	8	(13)	
8	-	Alone	Heart	Capitol	11	(3)	
9	-	Just To See Her	Smokey Robinson	Tamla	7	(52)	
10	-	Songbird	Kenny G	Arista	8	(22)	F
11	4	Lady In Red	Chris De Burgh	A&M	9	(1)	F L
12	-	Meet Me Half Way	Kenny Loggins	Columbia	6		
13	1	With Or Without You	U2	Island	10	(4)	F
14	-	Shakedown	Bob Seger & The Silver Bullet Band	MCA	10		L
15	-	Lessons In Love	Level 42	Polydor	4	(3)	L
16	-	Don't Disturb The Groove	System	Atlantic	7		F L
17	7	Big Love	Fleetwood Mac	Warner	7	(9)	
18	15	Nothing's Gonna Change My Love For You	Glenn Medeiros	Amherst	6	(1)	F
19	10	Right On Track	Breakfast Club	MCA	7	(54)	F L
20	-	Point Of No Return	Expose	Arista	7		

US
1987
APR-JUNE

◆ U2's transatlantic No. 1 album **The Joshua Tree,** which had sold 250,000 in its first week in the UK, shipped over two million in America in just six weeks.

◆ Madonna scored her 11th consecutive Top 5 hit with 'La Isla Bonita' – a feat bettered only by Elvis and The Beatles. In Britain, it was her 14th Top 10 entry and her fourth No. 1 – both records for a female artist.

◆ **Whitney,** became the first album to enter both the US and UK charts at No. 1. For the record, Miss Houston's Grammy winning 'I Wanna Dance With Somebody' was produced by Narada Michael Walden, who was also responsible for another transatlantic topper, 'Nothing's Gonna Stop Us Now' by Starship.

◆ Janet Jackson sang on 'Diamonds', the track that returned Herb Alpert to the Top 20 after an eight year absence.

UK 1987 JULY-SEPT

◆ The video for Peter Gabriel's 'Sledgehammer' won a record 10 MTV awards.

◆ Cliff Richard scored his 50th British Top 10 hit, 'My Pretty One', and Bananarama collected their 13th chart entry – a record for a British female group.

▲ Rick Astley had Britain's biggest selling single of 1987, 'Never Gonna Give You Up'.

◆ **Introducing The Hardline According To Terence Trent D'Arby** was the first debut album by an American act to enter the UK chart at No. 1. In his homeland it spent 26 weeks on the chart before reaching the Top 10.

July 1987

This Mnth	Prev Mnth	Title	Artist	Label	Wks 20	(US Pos)	
1	16	It's A Sin	Pet Shop Boys	Parlophone	8	(9)	
2	10	Under The Boardwalk	Bruce Willis	Motown	10	(59)	L
3	-	Wishing Well	Terence Trent D'Arby	CBS	6	(1)	
4	5	Star Trekkin'	Firm	Bark	7		L
5	-	Always	Atlantic Starr	Warner	8	(1)	L
6	-	The Living Daylights	A-Ha	Warner	5		
7	1	I Wanna Dance With Somebody (Who Loves Me)	Whitney Houston	Arista	10	(1)	
8	-	My Pretty One	Cliff Richard	EMI	4		
9	-	Who's That Girl	Madonna	Sire	7	(1)	
10	-	Sweetest Smile	Black	A&M	4		F
11	-	Alone	Heart	Capitol	7	(1)	F
12	-	F.L.M.	Mel & Kim	Supreme	5		
13	14	You're The Voice	John Farnham	Wheatley	6	(82)	F L
14	-	Misfit	Curiosity Killed The Cat	Mercury	4	(42)	
15	19	Is This Love	Whitesnake	EMI	5	(2)	
16	-	Higher And Higher	Jackie Wilson	SMP	2		L
17	-	Jive Talkin'	Boogie Box High	Hardback	5		F L
18	-	Let's Dance	Chris Rea	Magnet	4	(81)	F
19	17	When Smokey Sings	ABC	Neutron	4	(5)	L
20	-	La Bamba	Los Lobos	Slash	6	(1)	F

August 1987

This Mnth	Prev Mnth	Title	Artist	Label	Wks 20	(US Pos)	
1	20	La Bamba	Los Lobos	Slash	6	(1)	F
2	-	I Just Can't Stop Loving You	Michael Jackso	Epic	6	(1)	
3	-	Call Me	Spagna	CBS	6		F L
4	-	True Faith	New Order	Factory	6		
5	9	Who's That Girl	Madonna	Sire	7	(1)	
6	11	Alone	Heart	Capitol	7	(1)	F
7	5	Always	Atlantic Starr	Warner	8	(1)	L
8	-	Labour Of Love	Hue & Cry	Circa	6		F
9	-	Never Gonna Give You Up	Rick Astley	RCA	10	(1)	F
10	-	Toy Boy	Sinitta	Fanfare	8		
11	-	Animal	Def Leppard	Bludgeon Riffola	5	(19)	F
12	-	Sweet Little Mystery	Wet Wet Wet	Precious	6		
13	-	Somewhere Out There	Linda Ronstadt/James Ingram	MCA	4	(2)	F
14	-	What Have I Done To Deserve This	Pet Shop Boys & Dusty Springfield	Parlophone	6	(2)	
15	17	Jive Talkin'	Boogie Box High	Hardback	5		F L
16	1	It's A Sin	Pet Shop Boys	Parlophone	8	(9)	
17	-	Just Don't Want To Be Lonely	Freddie McGregor	Germain	4		F L
18	-	She's On It	Beastie Boys	Def Jam	4		
19	2	Under The Boardwalk	Bruce Willis	Motown	10	(59)	L
20	-	Funky Town	Pseudo Echo	RCA	4	(6)	F L

September 1987

This Mnth	Prev Mnth	Title	Artist	Label	Wks 20	(US Pos)	
1	9	Never Gonna Give You Up	Rick Astley	RCA	10	(1)	F
2	-	Wipeout	Fat Boys & Beach Boys	Urban	7	(12)	F
3	-	Heart And Soul	T'Pau	Siren	6	(4)	F
4	14	What Have I Done To Deserve This	Pet Shop Boys & Dusty Springfield	Parlophone	6	(2)	
5	-	Some People	Cliff Richard	EMI	7		
6	10	Toy Boy	Sinitta	Fanfare	8		
7	-	Pump Up The Volume	M/A/R/R/S	4AD	8	(13)	F L
8	-	Where The Streets Have No Name	U2	Island	3	(13)	
9	-	Wonderful Life	Black	A&M	5		L
10	12	Sweet Little Mystery	Wet Wet Wet	Precious	6		
11	-	Casanova	Levert	Atlantic	5	(5)	F L
12	-	Causing A Commotion	Madonna	Sire	5	(2)	
13	-	Bridge To Your Heart	Wax	RCA	5		F L
14	3	Call Me	Spagna	CBS	6		F L
15	-	House Nation	House Master Boyz & The Rude Boy Of House	Magnetic Dance	4		F L
16	-	It's Over	Level 42	Polydor	4		
17	2	I Just Can't Stop Loving You	Michael Jackson	Epic	6	(1)	
18	-	I Don't Want To Be A Hero	Johnny Hates Jazz	Virgin	5	(31)	
19	-	U Got The Look	Prince	Paisley Park	4	(2)	
20	-	Bad	Michael Jackson	Epic	5	(1)	

This Mnth	Prev Mnth	Title	Artist	Label	Wks 20	(UK Pos)	
1	8	Alone	Heart	Capitol	11	(3)	
2	4	I Wanna Dance With Somebody (...)	Whitney Houston	Arista	11	(1)	G
3	14	Shakedown	Bob Seger & Silver Bullet Band	MCA	10		L
4	16	Don't Disturb The Groove	System	Atlantic	7		F L
5	20	Point Of No Return	Expose	Arista	7		
6	-	Funky Town	Pseudo Echo	RCA	6	(8)	F L
7	-	Something So Strong	Crowded House	Capitol	7		L
8	-	I Still Haven't Found What I'm Looking For	U2	Island	9	(6)	
9	10	Songbird	Kenny G	Arista	8	(22)	F
10	-	I Want Your Sex	George Michael	Columbia	9	(3)	G
11	-	Rhythm Is Gonna Get You	Gloria Estefan & The Miami Sound Machine	Epic	7	(16)	
12	1	Head To Toe	Lisa Lisa & Cult Jam	Columbia	10		
13	-	Heart And Soul	T'Pau	Virgin	9	(4)	F L
14	-	Girls Girls Girls	Motley Crue	Elektra	6	(26)	
15	3	In Too Deep	Genesis	Atlantic	8	(19)	
16	9	Just To See Her	Smokey Robinson	Tamla	7	(52)	
17	-	Kiss Him Goodbye	Nylons	Open Air	5		F L
18	-	Every Little Kiss	Bruce Hornsby & The Range	RCA	4		
19	-	Cross My Broken Heart	Jets	MCA	6		
20	2	Always	Atlantic Starr	Warner	10	(3)	

August 1987

This Mnth	Prev Mnth	Title	Artist	Label	Wks 20	(UK Pos)	
1	8	I Still Haven't Found What I'm...	U2	Island	9	(6)	
2	-	Who's That Girl?	Madonna	Sire	8	(1)	
3	-	Luka	Suzanne Vega	A&M	7	(23)	F L
4	10	I Want Your Sex	George Michael	Columbia	9	(3)	G
5	-	La Bamba	Los Lobos	Slash	9	(1)	F L
6	-	Don't Mean Nothing	Richard Marx	Manhattan	7		F
7	13	Heart And Soul	T'Pau	Virgin	9	(4)	F L
8	-	Only In My Dreams	Debbie Gibson	Atlantic	8	(11)	F
9	-	Rock Steady	Whispers	Solar	7	(38)	L
10	3	Shakedown	Bob Seger & Silver Bullet Band	MCA	10		L
11	19	Cross My Broken Heart	Jets	MCA	6		
12	11	Rhythm Is Gonna Get You	Gloria Estefan/Miami Sound...	Epic	7	(16)	
13	1	Alone	Heart	Capitol	11	(3)	
14	-	I Just Can't Stop Loving You	Michael Jackson	Epic	8	(1)	G
15	-	It's Not Over ('Til It's Over)	Starship	Grunt	5		
16	-	Wot's It To Ya	Robbie Nevil	Manhattan	4	(43)	L
17	-	Love Power	Dionne Warwick & Jeffrey Osborne	Arista	5	(63)	L
18	-	Can't We Try	Dan Hill (with Vonda Shepard)	Columbia	7		L
19	-	Back In The High Life Again	Steve Winwood	Island	3	(53)	
20	-	Didn't We Almost Have It All	Whitney Houston	Arista	9	(14)	

September 1987

This Mnth	Prev Mnth	Title	Artist	Label	Wks 20	(UK Pos)	
1	14	I Just Can't Stop Loving You	Michael Jackson	Epic	8	(1)	G
2	20	Didn't We Almost Have It All	Whitney Houston	Arista	9	(14)	
3	5	La Bamba	Los Lobos	Slash	9	(1)	F L
4	-	Here I Go Again	Whitesnake	Geffen	11	(9)	F
5	-	When Smokey Sings	ABC	Mercury	8	(11)	L
6	-	Doing It All For My Baby	Huey Lewis & The News	Chrysalis	6		
7	18	Can't We Try	Dan Hill (with Vonda Shepard)	Columbia	7		L
8	-	I Heard A Rumour	Bananarama	London	7	(14)	L
9	8	Only In My Dreams	Debbie Gibson	Atlantic	8	(11)	F
10	-	Touch Of Grey	Grateful Dead	Arista	6		F L
11	-	Lost In Emotion	Lisa Lisa & Cult Jam	Columbia	8	(58)	L
12	2	Who's That Girl?	Madonna	Sire	8	(1)	
13	-	Wipeout	Fat Boys & Beach Boys	Tin Pan Apple	6	(2)	F
14	-	Carrie	Europe	Epic	8	(22)	L
15	6	Don't Mean Nothing	Richard Marx	Manhattan	7		F
16	-	I Need Love	L.L. Cool J	Def Jam	4	(8)	F
17	-	U Got The Look	Prince	Paisley Park	9	(11)	
18	9	Rock Steady	Whispers	Solar	7	(38)	L
19	17	Love Power	Dionne Warwick & Jeffrey Osborne	Arista	5	(63)	L
20	-	Who Will You Run To	Heart	Capitol	6	(30)	

US 1987

JULY-SEPT

◆ 'Who's That Girl?' (Madonna), 'La Bamba' (Los Lobos) and 'I Just Can't Stop Loving You' (Michael Jackson) followed each other in the No. 1 spot in both the USA and Britain. Siedah Garrett, who sang with Jackson on his 11th No. 1, also sang on Madonna's chart-topper.

◆ Michael Jackson's first album since 1982, **Bad,** shipped a record 2.25 million copies in America, and sold a record 380,000 in its first week in the UK.

◆ Old hits 'Kiss Him Goodbye' (Steam), 'La Bamba' (Ritchie Valens), 'Funky Town' (Lipps Inc) and 'Wipeout' (Surfaris) returned by The Nylons, Los Lobos, Pseudo Echo and The Fat Boys & The Beach Boys respectively.

◆ Legendary band The Grateful Dead's first Top 40 singles entry 'Touch Of Grey' occured 20 years after their chart debut.

UK
1987
OCT-DEC

◆ Half the songs on December's UK chart were oldies. Among them were re-issues of 'When I Fall In Love' by Nat 'King' Cole (1957) and 'My Baby Just Cares For Me' by Nina Simone (1959).

◆ 1987 was the year when "sampling" surfaced, three inch CDs were unsuccessfully launched, Japanese company Sony bought CBS Records and MTV debuted in Europe.

◆ Performers inducted into the *Rock And Roll Hall Of Fame* in 1987 were The Coasters, Eddie Cochran, Bo Diddley, Aretha Franklin, Marvin Gaye, Bill Haley, B.B. King, Clyde McPhatter, Rick Nelson, Roy Orbison, Carl Perkins, Smokey Robinson, Joe Turner, Muddy Waters and Jackie Wilson.

◆ The boundary breaking single 'Pump Up The Volume' by M/A/R/R/S was the first record to top the indie, dance and pop charts.

October 1987

This Mnth	Prev Mnth	Title	Artist	Label	Wks 20	(US Pos)	
1	-	Crockett's Theme	Jan Hammer	MCA	8		L
2	-	Full Metal Jacket (I Wanna Be Your Drill Instructor)	Abigail Mead & Nigel Goulding	Warner	6		F L
3	7	Pump Up The Volume	M/A/R/R/S	4AD	8	(13)	F L
4	-	You Win Again	Bee Gees	Warner	8	(75)	
5	-	Crazy Crazy Nights	Kiss	Vertigo	5	(65)	F
6	20	Bad	Michael Jackson	Epic	5	(1)	
7	1	Never Gonna Give You Up	Rick Astley	RCA	10	(1)	F
8	-	I Need Love	L.L. Cool J	CBS	5	(14)	F L
9	-	The Circus	Erasure	Mute	5		
10	5	Some People	Cliff Richard	EMI	7		
11	-	I Found Lovin'	Fatback Band	Master Mix	4		L
12	-	Love In The First Degree/Mr. Sleaze	Bananarama/S.A.W.	London	6	(48)	
13	12	Causing A Commotion	Madonna	Sire	5	(2)	
14	-	This Corrosion	Sisters Of Mercy	Merciful Release	3		F
15	-	Mony Mony	Billy Idol	Chrysalis	6	(1)	
16	-	Faith	George Michael	Epic	5	(1)	
17	-	Little Lies	Fleetwood Mac	Warner	5	(4)	
18	-	The Real Thing	Jellybean Feat.\ Steven Dante	Chrysalis	4	(82)	F
19	15	House Nation	House Master Boyz/Rude Boy...	Magnetic Dance	4		F L
20	-	Walk The Dinosaur	Was (Not Was)	Fontana	5	(7)	F

November 1987

This Mnth	Prev Mnth	Title	Artist	Label	Wks 20	(US Pos)	
1	-	China In Your Hand	T'Pau	Siren	11		
2	-	Got My Mind Set On You	George Harrison	Dark Horse	9	(1)	L
3	-	Whenever You Need Somebody	Rick Astley	RCA	6		
4	4	You Win Again	Bee Gees	Warner	8	(75)	
5	-	Never Can Say Goodbye	Communards	London	7	(51)	
6	16	Faith	George Michael	Epic	5	(1)	
7	12	Love In The First Degree/Mr. Sleaze	Bananarama/S.A.W.	London	6	(48)	
8	-	(I've Had) The Time Of My Life	Bill Medley & Jennifer Warnes	RCA	4	(1)	F
9	-	My Baby Just Cares For Me	Nina Simone	Charly	4		L
10	-	Barcelona	Freddie Mercury/M. Caballé	Polydor	4		
11	-	Here I Go Again	Whitesnake	EMI	5	(1)	
12	17	Little Lies	Fleetwood Mac	Warner	5	(4)	
13	-	Jack Mix IV	Mirage	Debut	4		L
14	-	So Emotional	Whitney Houston	Arista	6	(1)	
15	15	Mony Mony	Billy Idol	Chrysalis	6	(1)	
16	-	Criticize	Alexander O'Neal	Tabu	8	(70)	
17	1	Crockett's Theme	Jan Hammer	MCA	8		L
18	20	Walk The Dinosaur	Was (Not Was)	Fontana	5	(7)	F
19	-	I Don't Think That Man Should Sleep Alone	Ray Parker Jr.	Geffen	3	(68)	L
20	9	The Circus	Erasure	Mute	5		

December 1987

This Mnth	Prev Mnth	Title	Artist	Label	Wks 20	(US Pos)	
1	1	China In Your Hand	T'Pau	Siren	11		
2	-	Always On My Mind	Pet Shop Boys	Parlophone	8	(4)	
3	-	The Way You Make Me Feel	Michael Jackson	Epic	7	(1)	
4	-	When I Fall In Love/My Arms Keep Missing You	Rick Astley	RCA	6		
5	-	What Do You Want To Make Those Eyes At Me For	Shakin' Stevens	Epic	5		
6	-	Letter From America	Proclaimers	Chrysalis	6		F
7	-	Love Letters	Alison Moyet	CBS	6		
8	2	Got My Mind Set On You	George Harrison	Dark Horse	9	(1)	L
9	16	Criticize	Alexander O'Neal	Tabu	8	(70)	
10	-	Rockin' Around The Christmas Tree	Mel & Kim (Smith & Wilde)	10	5		
11	-	Fairytale Of New York	Pogues Feat. Kirsty MacColl	Pogue Mahone	6		F
12	-	Who Found Who	Jellybean Featuring Elisa Fiorillo	Chrysalis	6	(16)	
13	14	So Emotional	Whitney Houston	Arista	6	(1)	
14	5	Never Can Say Goodbye	Communards	London	7	(51)	
15	-	The Look Of Love	Madonna	Sire	5		
16	-	Once Upon A Long Ago	Paul McCartney	Parlophone	3		
17	-	When I Fall In Love	Nat 'King' Cole	Capitol	4		L
18	-	Heaven Is A Place On Earth	Belinda Carlisle	Virgin	10	(1)	F
19	-	Ev'ry Time We Say Goodbye	Simply Red	Elektra	3		
20	-	Some Guys Have All The Luck	Maxi Priest	10	4		F

October 1987

This Mnth	Prev Mnth	Title	Artist	Label	Wks 20	(UK Pos)	
1	11	Lost In Emotion	Lisa Lisa & Cult Jam	Columbia	8	(58)	L
2	17	U Got The Look	Prince	Paisley Park	9	(11)	
3	-	Bad	Michael Jackson	Epic	7	(3)	
4	-	Causing A Commotion	Madonna	Sire	8	(4)	
5	4	Here I Go Again	Whitesnake	Geffen	11	(9)	F
6	-	Casanova	Levert	Atlantic	7	(9)	F L
7	14	Carrie	Europe	Epic	8	(22)	L
8	-	Let Me Be The One	Expose	Arista	7		
9	20	Who Will You Run To	Heart	Capitol	6	(30)	
10	-	I Think We're Alone Now	Tiffany	MCA	9	(1)	F
11	8	I Heard A Rumour	Bananarama	London	7	(14)	L
12	-	Paper In Fire	John Cougar Mellencamp	Mercury	6		
13	-	Mony Mony	Billy Idol	Chrysalis	9	(7)	
14	-	Little Lies	Fleetwood Mac	Warner	8	(5)	
15	2	Didn't We Almost Have It All	Whitney Houston	Arista	9	(14)	
16	-	Breakout	Swing Out Sister	Mercury	8	(4)	F L
17	-	Jump Start	Natalie Cole	EMI Manhattan	4	(36)	
18	-	One Heartbeat	Smokey Robinson	Tamla	4		L
19	-	It's A Sin	Pet Shop Boys	EMI Manhattan	6	(1)	
20	-	Brilliant Disguise	Bruce Springsteen	Columbia	7	(20)	

November 1987

This Mnth	Prev Mnth	Title	Artist	Label	Wks 20	(UK Pos)	
1	13	Mony Mony	Billy Idol	Chrysalis	9	(7)	
2	-	(I've Had) The Time Of My Life	Bill Medley & Jennifer Warnes	RCA	9	(6)	F L
3	10	I Think We're Alone Now	Tiffany	MCA	9	(1)	F
4	-	Heaven Is A Place On Earth	Belinda Carlisle	MCA	11	(1)	
5	20	Brilliant Disguise	Bruce Springsteen	Columbia	7	(20)	
6	16	Breakout	Swing Out Sister	Mercury	8	(4)	F L
7	-	Should've Known Better	Richard Marx	EMI Manhattan	8	(50)	
8	14	Little Lies	Fleetwood Mac	Warner	8	(5)	
9	-	I've Been In Love Before	Cutting Crew	Virgin	5	(24)	L
10	4	Causing A Commotion	Madonna	Sire	8	(4)	
11	-	Faith	George Michael	Columbia	10	(2)	
12	19	It's A Sin	Pet Shop Boys	EMI Manhattan	6	(1)	
13	-	We'll Be Together	Sting	A&M	7	(41)	
14	-	The One I Love	R.E.M.	IRS	6	(16)	F
15	3	Bad	Michael Jackson	Epic	7	(3)	
16	-	I Won't Forget You	Poison	Enigma	4		
17	-	Shake Your Love	Debbie Gibson	Atlantic	10	(7)	
18	8	Let Me Be The One	Expose	Arista	7		
19	-	Where The Streets Have No Name	U2	Island	4	(4)	
20	-	Is This Love	Whitesnake	Geffen	10	(9)	L

December 1987

This Mnth	Prev Mnth	Title	Artist	Label	Wks 20	(UK Pos)	
1	11	Faith	George Michael	Columbia	10	(2)	
2	20	Is This Love	Whitesnake	Geffen	10	(9)	L
3	-	So Emotional	Whitney Houston	Arista	11	(5)	
4	17	Shake Your Love	Debbie Gibson	Atlantic	10	(7)	
5	4	Heaven Is A Place On Earth	Belinda Carlisle	MCA	11	(1)	
6	-	Got My Mind Set On You	George Harrison	Dark Horse	11	(2)	L
7	-	Don't You Want Me	Jody Watley	MCA	9	(55)	
8	-	Catch Me I'm Falling	Pretty Poison	Virgin	8		F L
9	7	Should've Known Better	Richard Marx	EMI Manhattan	8	(50)	
10	2	(I've Had) The Time Of My Life	Bill Medley & Jennifer Warnes	RCA	9	(6)	F L
11	13	We'll Be Together	Sting	A&M	7	(41)	
12	-	Valerie	Steve Winwood	Island	7	(19)	
13	-	The Way You Make Me Feel	Michael Jackson	Epic	9	(3)	
14	-	Cherry Bomb	John Cougar Mellencamp	Mercury	7		
15	-	Dude (Looks Like A Lady)	Aerosmith	Geffen	6	(20)	
16	14	The One I Love	R.E.M.	IRS	6	(16)	F
17	-	Tell It To My Heart	Taylor Dayne	Arista	9	(3)	F
18	-	Need You Tonight	INXS	Atlantic	11	(2)	
19	-	Candle In The Wind (Live)	Elton John	MCA	7	(5)	
20	1	Mony Mony	Billy Idol	Chrysalis	9	(7)	

US 1987

OCT-DEC

◆ American record and tape shipments were up 19.7% to $5.56 billion, with CD sales up 93% to 100 million.

◆ The **Dirty Dancing** soundtrack topped the US chart for 19 weeks. It contained the Grammy and Academy Award-winning No. 1 '(I've Had) The Time Of My Life' by Bill Medley & Jennifer Warnes.

▲ Revivals of two hits by Tommy James & The Shondells followed each other at the top: 'I Think We're Alone Now' by Tiffany and 'Mony Mony' by Billy Idol (above).

UK 1988 JAN-MAR

▲ Female artists scored a record three successive No. 1s when Australian soap star Kylie Minogue followed transatlantic toppers Belinda Carlisle (above) and Tiffany to the top spot.

◆ A survey showed that the richest people in the music business in Britain were Virgin Records' head Richard Branson followed by Paul McCartney and Elton John.

◆ Expose became the first group to have four American Top 10 singles on their debut LP. Surprisingly, the female trio, whose next three singles also graced the Top 10, never had a major UK hit.

January 1988

This Mnth	Prev Mnth	Title	Artist	Label	Wks 20	(US Pos)	
1	18	Heaven Is A Place On Earth	Belinda Carlisle	Virgin	10	(1)	F
2	2	Always On My Mind	Pet Shop Boys	Parlophone	8	(4)	
3	-	House Arrest	Krush	Club	7		F L
4	-	Stutter Rap (No Sleep 'Til Bedtime)	Morris Minor & The Majors	10/Virgin	5		F L
5	-	Angel Eyes (Home And Away)	Wet Wet Wet	Precious	6		
6	-	I Found Someone	Cher	Geffen	4	(10)	
7	-	Sign Your Name	Terence Trent D'Arby	CBS	6	(4)	
8	-	I Think We're Alone Now	Tiffany	MCA	9	(1)	F
9	-	Come Into My Life	Joyce Sims	London	5		L
10	11	Fairytale Of New York	Pogues Feat. Kirsty MacColl	Pogue Mahone	6		F
11	-	All Day And All Of The Night	Stranglers	Epic	4		
12	3	The Way You Make Me Feel	Michael Jackson	Epic	7	(1)	
13	7	Love Letters	Alison Moyet	CBS	6		
14	-	Rise To The Occasion	Climie Fisher	EMI	4		F
15	4	When I Fall In Love/My Arms Keep Missing You	Rick Astley	RCA	6		
16	10	Rockin' Around The Christmas Tree	Mel & Kim (Smith & Wilde)	10	5		
17	17	When I Fall In Love	Nat 'King' Cole	Capitol	4		
18	-	Heatseeker	AC/DC	Atlantic	3		
19	-	When Will I Be Famous	Bros	CBS	6	(83)	F
20	-	Rok Da House	Beatmasters Feat. Cookie Crew	Rhythm King	5		F

February 1988

This Mnth	Prev Mnth	Title	Artist	Label	Wks 20	(US Pos)	
1	8	I Think We're Alone Now	Tiffany	MCA	9	(1)	F
2	-	Tell It To My Heart	Taylor Dayne	Arista	6	(7)	F
3	-	I Should Be So Lucky	Kylie Minogue	PWL	10	(28)	F
4	19	When Will I Be Famous	Bros	CBS	6	(83)	F
5	-	Get Outta My Dreams Get Into My Car	Billy Ocean	Jive	6	(1)	L
6	-	Candle In The Wind (Live)	Elton John	Rocket	5	(6)	
7	-	Shake Your Love	Debbie Gibson	Atlantic	5	(4)	F
8	-	Say It Again	Jermaine Stewart	10	5	(27)	
9	-	The Jack That House Built	Jack 'n' Chill	Oval	5		F L
10	-	Beat Dis	Bomb The Bass	Mister-Ron	5		F
11	20	Rok Da House	Beatmasters Feat. Cookie Crew	Rhythm King	5		F
12	7	Sign Your Name	Terence Trent D'Arby	CBS	6	(4)	
13	1	Heaven Is A Place On Earth	Belinda Carlisle	Virgin	10	(1)	F
14	-	O L'Amour	Dollar	London	5		L
15	-	Valentine	T'Pau	Siren	4		
16	-	Gimme Hope Jo'anna	Eddy Grant	Ice	5		L
17	3	House Arrest	Krush	Club	7		F L
18	-	Hot In The City	Billy Idol	Chrysalis	4	(23)	L
19	-	Tower Of Strength	Mission	Mercury	4		
20	-	Suedehead	Morrissey	HMV	3		F

March 1988

This Mnth	Prev Mnth	Title	Artist	Label	Wks 20	(US Pos)	
1	3	I Should Be So Lucky	Kylie Minogue	PWL	10	(28)	F
2	-	Together Forever	Rick Astley	RCA	5	(1)	
3	-	Joe Le Taxi	Vanessa Paradis	FA Prods	6		F
4	10	Beat Dis	Bomb The Bass	Mister-Ron	5		F
5	-	Crash	Primitives	Lazy	5		F L
6	5	Get Outta My Dreams Get Into My Car	Billy Ocean	Jive	6	(1)	L
7	-	Doctorin' The House	Coldcut Featuring Yazz & The Plastic Population	Ahead Of Our Time	5		F
8	-	Don't Turn Around	Aswad	Mango	5		F
9	-	Ship Of Fools	Erasure	Mute	5		
10	16	Gimme Hope Jo'anna	Eddy Grant	Ice	5		L
11	-	I Get Weak	Belinda Carlisle	Virgin	5	(2)	
12	20	Suedehead	Morrissey	HMV	3		F
13	-	Love Is Contagious	Taja Sevelle	Paisley	3		F L
14	-	Drop The Boy	Bros	CBS	7		
15	-	Never/These Dreams	Heart	Capitol	5	(4)	
16	2	Tell It To My Heart	Taylor Dayne	Arista	6	(7)	F
17	-	That's The Way It Is	Mel & Kim	Supreme	3		L
18	-	Hazy Shade Of Winter	Bangles	Def Jam	3	(2)	
19	-	Can I Play With Madness	Iron Maiden	EMI	4		
20	-	Could've Been	Tiffany	MCA	5	(1)	

US 1988 JAN-MAR

January 1988

This Mnth	Prev Mnth	Title	Artist	Label	Wks 20	(UK Pos)	
1	6	Got My Mind Set On You	George Harrison	Dark Horse	11	(2)	L
2	13	The Way You Make Me Feel	Michael Jackson	Epic	9	(3)	
3	18	Need You Tonight	INXS	Atlantic	11	(2)	
4	3	So Emotional	Whitney Houston	Arista	11	(5)	
5	-	Could've Been	Tiffany	MCA	10	(4)	
6	-	Hazy Shade Of Winter	Bangles	Def Jam	10	(11)	
7	19	Candle In The Wind (Live)	Elton John	MCA	7	(5)	
8	17	Tell It To My Heart	Taylor Dayne	Arista	9	(3)	F
9	2	Is This Love	Whitesnake	Geffen	10	(9)	L
10	-	Seasons Change	Expose	Arista	11		
11	4	Shake Your Love	Debbie Gibson	Atlantic	10	(7)	
12	1	Faith	George Michael	Columbia	10	(2)	
13	14	Cherry Bomb	John Cougar Mellencamp	Mercury	7		
14	-	I Want To Be Your Man	Roger	Reprise	7	(61)	F L
15	7	Don't You Want Me	Jody Watley	MCA	9	(55)	
16	-	Hungry Eyes	Eric Carmen	RCA	9		
17	-	There's The Girl	Heart	Capitol	6	(34)	
18	-	I Could Never Take The Place Of Your Man	Prince	Paisley Park	5	(29)	
19	8	Catch Me I'm Falling	Pretty Poison	Virgin	8		F L
20	12	Valerie	Steve Winwood	Island	7	(19)	

February 1988

This Mnth	Prev Mnth	Title	Artist	Label	Wks 20	(UK Pos)	
1	10	Seasons Change	Expose	Arista	11		
2	5	Could've Been	Tiffany	MCA	10	(4)	
3	-	What Have I Done To Deserve This	Pet Shop Boys/Dusty Springfield	EMI Manhattan	8	(2)	
4	16	Hungry Eyes	Eric Carmen	RCA	9		
5	-	Say You Will	Foreigner	Atlantic	7	(71)	
6	14	I Want To Be Your Man	Roger	Reprise	7	(61)	F L
7	-	She's Like The Wind	Patrick Swayze (With Wendy Fraser)	RCA	8	(17)	F L
8	-	Father Figure	George Michael	Columbia	9	(11)	
9	-	Don't Shed A Tear	Paul Carrack	Chrysalis	6	(60)	F L
10	-	Never Gonna Give You Up	Rick Astley	RCA	10	(1)	F
11	3	Need You Tonight	INXS	Atlantic	11	(2)	
12	6	Hazy Shade Of Winter	Bangles	Def Jam	10	(11)	
13	-	Can't Stay Away From You	Gloria Estefan & The Miami Sound Machine	Epic	5	(7)	
14	-	I Get Weak	Belinda Carlisle	MCA	8	(10)	
15	-	Pump Up The Volume	M/A/R/R/S	4th & Broadway	5	(1)	F G L
16	-	Tunnel Of Love	Bruce Springsteen	Columbia	4	(45)	
17	-	Everywhere	Fleetwood Mac	Warner	4	(4)	L
18	-	I Live For Your Love	Natalie Cole	EMI Manhattan	4	(23)	
19	-	I Found Someone	Cher	Geffen	6	(5)	
20	-	Just Like Paradise	David Lee Roth	Warner	6	(27)	L

March 1988

This Mnth	Prev Mnth	Title	Artist	Label	Wks 20	(UK Pos)	
1	10	Never Gonna Give You Up	Rick Astley	RCA	10	(1)	F
2	8	Father Figure	George Michael	Columbia	9	(11)	
3	14	I Get Weak	Belinda Carlisle	MCA	8	(10)	
4	-	Endless Summer Nights	Richard Marx	EMI Manhattan	9	(50)	
5	-	Man In The Mirror	Michael Jackson	Epic	10	(21)	
6	7	She's Like The Wind	Patrick Swayz/Wendy Fraser	RCA	8	(17)	F L
7	-	Out Of The Blue	Debbie Gibson	Atlantic	9	(19)	
8	20	Just Like Paradise	David Lee Roth	Warner	6	(27)	L
9	-	I Want Her	Keith Sweat	Vintertainment	8	(26)	F
10	-	Get Outta My Dreams Get Into My Car	Billy Ocean	Jive	10	(3)	
11	-	Hysteria	Def Leppard	Mercury	5	(26)	
12	13	Can't Stay Away From You	Gloria Estefan/Miami Sound...	Epic	5	(7)	
13	-	Rocket 2 U	Jets	MCA	7	(69)	
14	19	I Found Someone	Cher	Geffen	6	(5)	
15	-	(Sittin' On) The Dock Of The Bay	Michael Bolton	Columbia	5		
16	3	What Have I Done To Deserve This	Pet Shop Boys/Dusty Springfield	EMI Manhattan	8	(2)	
17	-	Girlfriend	Pebbles	MCA	9	(8)	F
18	-	Devil Inside	INXS	Atlantic	8	(47)	
19	-	Be Still My Beating Heart	Sting	A&M	3		
20	-	Love Overboard	Gladys Knight & The Pips	MCA	3	(42)	L

◆ Louis Armstrong's 1968 UK No. 1, 'What A Wonderful World', debuted in the US Top 40. That week's chart topper Tiffany was not even born at the time of Armstrong's death 17 years earlier.

◆ Gripes at the Grammies included the fact that there were no awards for rap, hard rock or heavy metal and that the Best Female Rock award had been dropped. The year's winners included U2, Sting, Paul Simon and Jody Watley.

◆ George Michael's first solo album, **Faith,** headed the US chart for 12 weeks (a record for a British male singer) and 'Father Figure' gave him his sixth No. 1 single.

◆ Andy Gibb died aged 30. He was the only singer to place his first three singles in the top slot in the USA.

UK 1988 APR-JUNE

◆ Nelson Mandela's 70th birthday show was the most star-studded event since 'Live Aid'. Appearing were such notables as Bryan Adams, The Bee Gees, Natalie Cole, Phil Collins, Dire Straits, Eurythmics, Al Green, Whitney Houston, George Michael, Salt-N-Pepa, Sting and Stevie Wonder. The suprise hit of the show was Grammy winning American newcomer Tracy Chapman.

◆ Bros, whose UK tour incited mass hysteria among Britain's teeny-boppers, topped the chart with a re-issue of their first single 'I Owe You Nothing'.

◆ Indie-dance act The Justified Ancients Of Mu Mu were convinced they knew the formula to get a UK No. 1 single. Their made-to-measure track 'Doctorin' The Tardis', released under the name The Timelords, not only reached the top, it also spent three months on the US chart.

April 1988

This Mnth	Prev Mnth	Title	Artist	Label	Wks 20	(US Pos)	
1	-	Heart	Pet Shop Boys	Parlophone	7		
2	-	Love Changes (Everything)	Climie Fisher	EMI	6	(23)	L
3	14	Drop The Boy	Bros	CBS	7		
4	20	Could've Been	Tiffany	MCA	5	(1)	
5	-	Everywhere	Fleetwood Mac	Warner	5	(14)	L
6	8	Don't Turn Around	Aswad	Mango	5		F
7	-	Cross My Broken Heart	Sinitta	Fanfare	5		
8	-	Who's Leaving Who	Hazell Dean	EMI	7		
9	-	Pink Cadillac	Natalie Cole	Manhattan	6	(5)	F
10	-	I'm Not Scared	Eighth Wonder	CBS	6		F
11	-	Theme From S'Express	S'Express	Rhythm King	7	(91)	F
12	19	Can I Play With Madness	Iron Maiden	EMI	4		
13	-	I Want You Back	Bananarama	London	6		
14	-	Stay On These Roads	A-Ha	Warner	4		
15	-	Prove Your Love	Taylor Dayne	Arista	4	(7)	L
16	-	Girlfriend	Pebbles	MCA	3	(5)	F L
17	-	Mary's Prayer	Danny Wilson	Virgin	6	(23)	F L
18	1	I Should Be So Lucky	Kylie Minogue	PWL	10	(28)	F
19	-	I Want You Back '88	Michael Jackson With The Jackson Five	Epic	5	(1)	
20	-	Only In My Dreams	Debbie Gibson	Atlantic	3	(4)	

May 1988

This Mnth	Prev Mnth	Title	Artist	Label	Wks 20	(US Pos)	
1	-	Perfect	Fairground Attraction	RCA	8	(80)	F
2	11	Theme From S'express	S'express	Rhythm King	7	(91)	F
3	-	Blue Monday 1988	New Order	Factory	6	(68)	
4	-	With A Little Help From My Friends/ She's Leaving Home	Wet Wet Wet/ Billy Bragg & Cara Tivey	Childline	7		
5	-	Loadsamoney (Doin' Up The House)	Harry Enfield	Mercury	4		F L
6	17	Mary's Prayer	Danny Wilson	Virgin	6	(23)	F L
7	-	Anfield Rap (Red Machine In Full Effect)	Liverpool F.C.	Virgin	4		L
8	13	I Want You Back	Bananarama	London	6		
9	-	Got To Be Certain	Kylie Minogue	PWL	8		
10	8	Who's Leaving Who	Hazell Dean	EMI	7		
11	9	Pink Cadillac	Natalie Cole	Manhattan	6	(5)	F
12	-	Divine Emotions	Narada	Reprise	4		L
13	19	I Want You Back '88	Michael Jackson/Jackson Five	Epic	5	(1)	
14	-	Alphabet Street	Prince	Paisley Park	3	(8)	
15	-	Circle In The Sand	Belinda Carlisle	Virgin	5	(7)	
16	-	The King Of Rock 'n' Roll	Prefab Sprout	Kitchenware	4		F L
17	1	Heart	Pet Shop Boys	Parlophone	7		
18	-	Somewhere In My Heart	Aztec Camera	WEA	6		
19	-	Let's All Chant	Mick And Pat	PWL	4		F L
20	-	Pump Up The Bitter	Star Turn On 45 Pints	Pacific	2		F L

June 1988

This Mnth	Prev Mnth	Title	Artist	Label	Wks 20	(US Pos)	
1	4	With A Little Help From My Friends/ She's Leaving Home	Wet Wet Wet/ Billy Bragg & Cara Tivey	Childline	7		
2	9	Got To Be Certain	Kylie Minogue	PWL	8		
3	-	Doctorin' The Tardis	Timelords	KLF Comms.	5	(66)	F L
4	18	Somewhere In My Heart	Aztec Camera	WEA	6		
5	-	Voyage Voyage	Desireless	CBS	6		F L
6	15	Circle In The Sand	Belinda Carlisle	Virgin	5	(7)	
7	-	I Owe You Nothing	Bros	CBS	7		
8	-	My One Temptation	Mica Paris	4th & Broadway	5	(97)	F
9	-	Wild World	Maxi Priest	10	6	(25)	
10	-	Boys (Summertime Love)	Sabrina	CBS	6		F L
11	1	Perfect	Fairground Attraction	RCA	8	(80)	F
12	-	Check This Out	L.A. Mix	Breakout	4		F L
13	-	I Saw Him Standing There	Tiffany	MCA	3	(7)	
14	-	Everyday Is Like Sunday	Morrissey	HMV	3		
15	16	The King Of Rock 'n' Roll	Prefab Sprout	Kitchenware	4		F L
16	-	Chains Of Love	Erasure	Mute	4	(12)	
17	-	Tribute (Right On)	Pasadenas	CBS	7	(52)	F
18	-	Give A Little Love	Aswad	Mango	3		
19	-	The Twist (Yo, Twist)	Fat Boys/Chubby Checker	Urban	7	(16)	L
20	-	Love Will Save The Day	Whitney Houston	Arista	2	(9)	

April 1988

This Mnth	Prev Mnth	Title	Artist	Label	Wks 20	(UK Pos)	
1	10	Get Outta My Dreams Get Into My Car	Billy Ocean	Jive	10	(3)	
2	18	Devil Inside	INXS	Atlantic	8	(47)	
3	-	Where Do Broken Hearts Go	Whitney Houston	Arista	10	(14)	
4	-	Wishing Well	Terence Trent D'Arby	Columbia	10	(4)	F
5	5	Man In The Mirror	Michael Jackson	Epic	10	(21)	
6	17	Girlfriend	Pebbles	MCA	9	(8)	F
7	-	Angel	Aerosmith	Geffen	9	(69)	
8	-	I Saw Him Standing There	Tiffany	MCA	6	(8)	
9	13	Rocket 2 U	Jets	MCA	7	(69)	
10	7	Out Of The Blue	Debbie Gibson	Atlantic	9	(19)	
11	-	Pink Cadillac	Natalie Cole	EMI Manhattan	7	(5)	
12	4	Endless Summer Nights	Richard Marx	EMI Manhattan	9	(50)	
13	-	Prove Your Love	Taylor Dayne	Arista	7	(8)	
14	-	Anything For You	Gloria Estefan & The Miami Sound Machine	Epic	10	(10)	
15	-	Some Kind Of Lover	Jody Watley	MCA	6		
16	9	I Want Her	Keith Sweat	Vintertainment	8	(26)	F
17	-	One Step Up	Bruce Springsteen	Columbia	5		
18	-	Electric Blue	Icehouse	Chrysalis	7	(53)	L
19	15	(Sittin' On) The Dock Of The Bay	Michael Bolton	Columbia	5		
20	1	Never Gonna Give You Up	Rick Astley	RCA	10	(1)	F

May 1988

This Mnth	Prev Mnth	Title	Artist	Label	Wks 20	(UK Pos)	
1	14	Anything For You	Gloria Estefan & The Miami Sound Machine	Epic	10	(10)	
2	-	Shattered Dreams	Johnny Hates Jazz	Virgin	9	(5)	F L
3	-	One More Try	George Michael	Columbia	9	(8)	
4	-	Always On My Mind	Pet Shop Boys	EMI Manhattan	7	(1)	
5	-	Naughty Girls (Need Love Too)	Samantha Fox	Jive	7	(31)	
6	-	I Don't Want To Live Without You	Foreigner	Atlantic	7		L
7	4	Wishing Well	Terence Trent D'Arby	Columbia	10	(4)	F
8	18	Electric Blue	Icehouse	Chrysalis	7	(53)	L
9	-	Wait	White Lion	Atlantic	6		F
10	11	Pink Cadillac	Natalie Cole	EMI Manhattan	7	(5)	
11	7	Angel	Aerosmith	Geffen	9	(69)	
12	-	Two Occasions	Deele	Solar	5		F L
13	-	Everything Your Heart Desires	Daryl Hall & John Oates	Arista	7		
14	-	Piano In The Dark	Brenda Russell & Joe Esposito	A&M	6	(23)	F L
15	3	Where Do Broken Hearts Go	Whitney Houston	Arista	10	(14)	
16	-	Together Forever	Rick Astley	RCA	9	(2)	
17	13	Prove Your Love	Taylor Dayne	Arista	7	(8)	
18	-	Dreaming	Orchestral Manoeuvres In The Dark	A&M	3	(50)	L
19	-	Make It Real	Jets	MCA	9		L
20	-	Circle In The Sand	Belinda Carlisle	MCA	6	(4)	

June 1988

This Mnth	Prev Mnth	Title	Artist	Label	Wks 20	(UK Pos)	
1	3	One More Try	George Michael	Columbia	9	(8)	
2	16	Together Forever	Rick Astley	RCA	9	(2)	
3	-	Foolish Beat	Debbie Gibson	Atlantic	8	(9)	
4	19	Make It Real	Jets	MCA	9		L
5	-	Dirty Diana	Michael Jackson	Epic	8	(4)	
6	13	Everything Your Heart Desires	Daryl Hall & John Oates	Arista	7		
7	-	The Valley Road	Bruce Hornsby & The Range	RCA	8	(44)	
8	20	Circle In The Sand	Belinda Carlisle	MCA	6	(4)	
9	2	Shattered Dreams	Johnny Hates Jazz	Virgin	9	(5)	F L
10	-	Alphabet Street	Prince	Paisley Park	6	(9)	
11	-	The Flame	Cheap Trick	Epic	9		
12	5	Naughty Girls (Need Love Too)	Samantha Fox	Jive	9	(31)	
13	14	Piano In The Dark	Brenda Russell & Joe Esposito	A&M	6	(23)	F L
14	-	Kiss Me Deadly	Lita Ford	RCA	6	(75)	F
15	-	Mercedes Boy	Pebbles	MCA	8	(42)	
16	-	I Still Believe	Brenda K. Starr	MCA	7		F L
17	-	Nothin' But A Good Time	Poison	Enigma	6	(48)	
18	-	We All Sleep Alone	Cher	Geffen	4	(47)	
19	-	Pour Some Sugar On Me	Def Leppard	Mercury	9	(18)	
20	6	I Don't Want To Live Without You	Foreigner	Atlantic	7		L

US 1988 APR–JUNE

▲ Whitney Houston became the first artist in history to score seven successive No. 1 singles, and, with 'Foolish Beat', 17-year-old Debbie Gibson (above) became the first teenager to write, produce and sing on a US No. 1.

◆ Velvet voiced early 1960s hitmaker Brook Benton died, as did Dave Prater of Sam & Dave and fellow soul singer Carolyn Franklin.

◆ George Michael's **Faith** became the first LP by a white British artist to top the US R&B charts.

◆ Pink Floyd's **Dark Side Of The Moon** exited the Top 200 albums after a record-shattering 725 weeks.

UK
1988
JULY-SEPT

◆ Two fans died at the *Monsters Of Rock* festival at Castle Donnington. Headlining were Iron Maiden, Kiss, Guns N' Roses, Megadeth and David Lee Roth. Britain's biggest crowd for years, 125,000, watched Michael Jackson in Liverpool. Jackson, who had six albums charting, also attracted 500,000 to his seven Wembley dates.

◆ The Hollies' 19-year-old 'He Ain't Heavy, He's My Brother' hit the top. Other oldies returning included 'Lovely Day' by Bill Withers, 'Easy' by The Commodores and 'Reach Out I'll Be There' by The Four Tops. In America the 1962 hit 'Do You Love Me' by The Contours re-charted.

◆ Even though it sold few copies in their homeland, 'Jackie' by Blue Zone charted in America. It featured vocalist Lisa Stansfield.

◆ The Proclaimers' current hit 'I'm Gonna Be', reached the US Top 20 five years later.

July 1988

This Mnth	Prev Mnth	Title	Artist	Label	Wks 20	(US Pos)	
1	-	Nothing's Gonna Change My Love For You	Glenn Medeiros	London	8	(12)	F
2	-	Push It/Tramp	Salt 'n' Pepa	Champion/ffrr	8	(19)	F
3	19	The Twist (Yo, Twist)	Fat Boys/Chubby Checker	Urban	7	(16)	L
4	7	I Owe You Nothing	Bros	CBS	7		
5	-	Fast Car	Tracy Chapman	Elektra	6	(6)	F L
6	-	Breakfast In Bed	UB40 Featuring Chrissie Hynde	Dep International	6		
7	10	Boys (Summertime Love)	Sabrina	CBS	6		F L
8	-	I Don't Want To Talk About It	Everything But The Girl	Blanco Y Negro	6		F
9	-	In The Air Tonight	Phil Collins	Virgin	5		
10	-	Roses Are Red	Mac Band Featuring The McCampbell Brothers	MCA	7		F L
11	17	Tribute (Right On)	Pasadenas	CBS	7	(52)	F
12	-	Dirty Diana	Michael Jackson	Epic	5	(1)	
13	-	I Want Your Love	Transvision Vamp	MCA	6		F
14	-	Don't Blame It On That Girl/ Wap Bam Boogie	Matt Bianco	WEA	6		L
15	9	Wild World	Maxi Priest	10	6	(25)	
16	-	Foolish Beat	Debbie Gibson	Atlantic	5	(1)	
17	3	Doctorin' The Tardis	Timelords	KLF	5	(66)	F L
18	-	You Came	Kim Wilde	MCA	7	(41)	
19	-	Love Bites	Def Leppard	Bludgeon Riffola	4	(1)	
20	-	Tougher Than The Rest	Bruce Springsteen	CBS	3		

August 1988

This Mnth	Prev Mnth	Title	Artist	Label	Wks 20	(US Pos)	
1	-	The Only Way Is Up	Yazz & The Plastic Population	Big Life	9	(96)	
2	-	The Loco-Motion	Kylie Minogue	PWL	7	(3)	
3	18	You Came	Kim Wilde	MCA	7	(41)	
4	-	I Need You	B.V.S.M.P.	Debut	6		F L
5	-	Superfly Guy	S'Express	Rhythm King	6		
6	-	Find My Love	Fairground Attraction	RCA	6		L
7	-	The Evil That Men Do	Iron Maiden	EMI	3		
8	1	Nothing's Gonna Change My Love...	Glenn Medeiros	London	8	(12)	F
9	-	Reach Out I'll Be There	Four Tops	Motown	5		
10	-	Hands To Heaven	Breathe	Siren	6	(2)	F L
11	2	Push It/Tramp	Salt 'n' Pepa	Champion/ffrr	8	(19)	F
12	-	The Harder I Try	Brother Beyond	Parlophone	6		F
13	13	I Want Your Love	Transvision Vamp	MCA	6		F
14	-	Martha's Harbour	All About Eve	Mercury	3		F L
15	8	I Don't Want To Talk About It	Everything But The Girl	Blanco Y Negro	6		F
16	-	Hustle! (To The Music...)	Funky Worm	Fon	4		F L
17	10	Roses Are Red	Mac Band/McCampbell Brothers	MCA	7		F L
18	-	My Love	Julio Iglesias (featuring Stevie Wonder)	CBS	5	(80)	L
19	-	Good Tradition	Tanita Tikaram	WEA	4		F L
20	12	Dirty Diana	Michael Jackson	Epic	5	(1)	

September 1988

This Mnth	Prev Mnth	Title	Artist	Label	Wks 20	(US Pos)	
1	-	Groovy Kind Of Love	Phil Collins	Virgin	10	(1)	
2	-	Teardrops	Womack & Womack	4th & Broadway	11		
3	12	The Harder I Try	Brother Beyond	Parlophone	6		F
4	1	The Only Way Is Up	Yazz & The Plastic Population	Big Life	9	(96)	
5	-	He Ain't Heavy, He's My Brother	Hollies	EMI	7		L
6	-	Megablast/Don't Make Me Wait	Bomb The Bass	Mister-Ron	5		
7	-	The Race	Yello	Mercury	6		F L
8	18	My Love	Julio Iglesias/Stevie Wonder	CBS	5	(80)	L
9	2	The Loco-Motion	Kylie Minogue	PWL	7	(3)	
10	10	Hands To Heaven	Breathe	Siren	6	(2)	F L
11	-	Lovely Day	Bill Withers	CBS	5		L
12	-	I Quit	Bros	CBS	3		
13	-	Anything For You	Gloria Estefan/Miami Sound...	Epic	6	(1)	
14	-	Rush Hour	Jane Wiedlin	Manhattan	4	(9)	F L
15	-	Nothing Can Divide Us	Jason Donovan	PWL	7		F
16	-	Touchy!	A-Ha	Warner	3		
17	4	I Need You	B.V.S.M.P.	Debut	6		F L
18	-	I'm Gonna Be	Proclaimers	Chrysalis	5		
19	-	Big Fun	Inner City	10	7		F
20	6	Find My Love	Fairground Attraction	RCA	6		L

July 1988

This Mnth	Prev Mnth	Title	Artist	Label	Wks 20	(UK Pos)	
1	19	Pour Some Sugar On Me	Def Leppard	Mercury	9	(18)	
2	11	The Flame	Cheap Trick	Epic	9		
3	-	New Sensation	INXS	Atlantic	7	(25)	
4	-	Hold On To The Nights	Richard Marx	EMI Manhattan	9	(60)	
5	15	Mercedes Boy	Pebbles	MCA	8	(42)	
6	-	Roll With It	Steve Winwood	Virgin	9	(53)	
7	-	Hands To Heaven	Breathe	A&M	10	(4)	F
8	-	Make Me Lose Control	Eric Carmen	Arista	8		L
9	-	Nite And Day	Al B. Sure!	Warner	7	(44)	F L
10	5	Dirty Diana	Michael Jackson	Epic	8	(4)	
11	3	Foolish Beat	Debbie Gibson	Atlantic	8	(9)	
12	-	Rush Hour	Jane Wiedlin	EMI Manhattan	6	(12)	F L
13	17	Nothin' But A Good Time	Poison	Enigma	6	(48)	
14	-	Sign Your Name	Terence Trent D'Arby	Columbia	8	(2)	L
15	7	The Valley Road	Bruce Hornsby & The Range	RCA	8	(44)	
16	4	Make It Real	Jets	MCA	9		L
17	-	1-2-3	Gloria Estefan & The Miami Sound Machine	Epic	8	(9)	
18	-	Lost In You	Rod Stewart	Warner	5	(21)	
19	-	Parents Just Don't Understand	D.J. Jazzy Jeff & Fresh Prince	Jive	5		F
20	16	I Still Believe	Brenda K. Starr	MCA	7		F L

August 1988

This Mnth	Prev Mnth	Title	Artist	Label	Wks 20	(UK Pos)	
1	6	Roll With It	Steve Winwood	Virgin	9	(53)	
2	-	I Don't Wanna Go On With You Like That	Elton John	MCA	8	(30)	
3	-	Monkey	George Michael	Columbia	8	(13)	
4	7	Hands To Heaven	Breathe	A&M	10	(4)	F
5	8	Make Me Lose Control	Eric Carmen	Arista	8		L
6	-	I Don't Wanna Live Without Your Love	Chicago	Reprise	8		
7	17	1-2-3	Gloria Estefan & The Miami Sound Machine	Epic	8	(9)	
8	14	Sign Your Name	Terence Trent D'Arby	Columbia	8	(2)	L
9	-	Fast Car	Tracy Chapman	Elektra	8	(5)	F L
10	-	Sweet Child O' Mine	Guns N' Roses	Geffen	10	(6)	F
11	-	Love Will Save The Day	Whitney Houston	Arista	5	(10)	
12	4	Hold On To The Nights	Richard Marx	EMI Manhattan	9	(60)	
13	-	Simply Irresistible	Robert Palmer	EMI Manhattan	9	(44)	
14	-	Just Got Paid	Johnny Kemp	Columbia	5	(68)	F L
15	-	Perfect World	Huey Lewis & The News	Chrysalis	7	(48)	
16	-	Do You Love Me	Contours	Motown	4		L
17	1	Pour Some Sugar On Me	Def Leppard	Mercury	9	(18)	
18	-	When It's Love	Van Halen	Warner	6	(28)	
19	-	The Twist (Yo, Twist)	Fat Boys With Chubby Checker	Tin Pan Apple	3	(2)	L
20	19	Parents Just Don't Understand	D.J. Jazzy Jeff & Fresh Prince	Jive	5		F

September 1988

This Mnth	Prev Mnth	Title	Artist	Label	Wks 20	(UK Pos)	
1	10	Sweet Child O' Mine	Guns N' Roses	Geffen	10	(6)	F
2	13	Simply Irresistible	Robert Palmer	EMI Manhattan	9	(44)	
3	15	Perfect World	Huey Lewis & The News	Chrysalis	7	(48)	
4	-	I'll Always Love You	Taylor Dayne	Arista	10	(41)	
5	-	Don't Worry Be Happy	Bobby McFerrin	EMI Manhattan	9	(2)	F L
6	-	If It Isn't Love	New Edition	MCA	8		L
7	18	When It's Love	Van Halen	Warner	6	(28)	
8	3	Monkey	George Michael	Columbia	8	(13)	
9	-	Nobody's Fool	Kenny Loggins	Columbia	6		L
10	-	Another Part Of Me	Michael Jackson	Epic	6	(15)	
11	-	It Would Take A Strong Strong Man	Rick Astley	RCA	6		
12	-	One Good Woman	Peter Cetera	Full Moon	7		
13	9	Fast Car	Tracy Chapman	Elektra	8	(5)	F L
14	-	Love Bites	Def Leppard	Mercury	8	(11)	
15	2	I Don't Wanna Go On With You...	Elton John	MCA	8	(30)	
16	6	I Don't Wanna Live Without Your...	Chicago	Reprise	8		
17	-	Don't Be Cruel	Cheap Trick	Epic	8		
18	-	I Hate Myself For Loving You	Joan Jett & The Blackhearts	Blackheart	6	(46)	
19	-	A Nightmare On My Street	D.J. Jazzy Jeff & Fresh Prince	Jive	4		
20	11	Love Will Save The Day	Whitney Houston	Arista	5	(10)	

US 1988
JULY-SEPT

◆ Grateful Dead's nine days at Madison Square Gardens broke the box office record set by Neil Diamond.

▲ For the first time three heavy metal albums held the top rungs. The acts concerned were Van Halen, Def Leppard and Guns N' Roses (above). Def Leppard's multi-platinum **Hysteria** was also the first heavy metal album to spawn four Top 10 hit singles.

◆ Chubby Checker took 'The Twist' into the Top 20 for a record third time (it had reached No. 1 twice previously). On this recording he was joined by heavyweight rap trio The Fat Boys.

UK 1988 OCT-DEC

◆ U2's film *Rattle And Hum* premiered: the double album soundtrack sold a record one million copies in its first week in America and 300,000 in Britain.

▲ Britain's fastest selling single of 1988 was 'Mistletoe And Wine', which gave Cliff Richard his 100th chart record and his 55th Top 10 hit (equalling Elvis Presley's record).

◆ Australian Kylie Minogue became the first female singer in the UK to have her first four singles sell over 250,000 copies each.

◆ Stock, Aitken & Waterman wrote and produced a record six singles in the Top 30 in October.

October 1988

This Mnth	Prev Mnth	Title	Artist	Label	Wks 20	(US Pos)	
1	-	One Moment In Time	Whitney Houston	Arista	8	(5)	
2	2	Teardrops	Womack & Womack	4th & Broadway	11		
3	5	He Ain't Heavy, He's My Brother	Hollies	EMI	7		L
4	-	Don't Worry Be Happy	Bobby McFerrin	Manhattan	5	(1)	F L
5	-	Desire	U2	Island	4	(3)	
6	-	She Wants To Dance With Me	Rick Astley	RCA	7	(6)	
7	1	Groovy Kind Of Love	Phil Collins	Virgin	10	(1)	
8	-	A Little Respect	Erasure	Mute	8	(14)	
9	15	Nothing Can Divide Us	Jason Donovan	PWL	7		F
10	-	Wee Rule	Wee Papa Girl Rappers	Jive	6		F L
11	19	Big Fun	Inner City	10	7		F
12	-	Orinoco Flow	Enya	WEA	6	(24)	F
13	-	We Call It Acieed	D. Mob Feat. Gary Haisman	ffrr	6		F
14	11	Lovely Day	Bill Withers	CBS	5		L
15	-	Domino Dancing	Pet Shop Boys	Parlophone	4	(18)	
16	-	Never Trust A Stranger	Kim Wilde	MCA	5		
17	-	Je Ne Sais Pas Pourquoi	Kylie Minogue	PWL	6		
18	-	Riding On A Train	Pasadenas	CBS	5		
19	-	Harvest For The World	Christians	Island	4		
20	-	Burn It Up	Beatmasters With P.P. Arnold	Rhythm King	4		

November 1988

This Mnth	Prev Mnth	Title	Artist	Label	Wks 20	(US Pos)	
1	-	Stand Up For Your Love Rights	Yazz	Big Life	6		
2	17	Je Ne Sais Pas Pourquoi	Kylie Minogue	PWL	6		
3	12	Orinoco Flow	Enya	WEA	6	(24)	F
4	-	The First Time	Robin Beck	Mercury	9		F L
5	-	Girl You Know It's True	Milli Vanilli	Cooltempo	6	(2)	F
6	-	She Makes My Day	Robert Palmer	EMI	5		
7	-	Real Gone Kid	Deacon Blue	CBS	5		F
8	-	He Ain't No Competiition	Brother Beyond	Parlophone	4		
9	-	Need You Tonight	INXS	Mercury	5	(1)	F
10	-	Missing You	Chris De Burgh	A&M	6		L
11	-	Kiss	Art Of Noise & Tom Jones	China	4	(31)	L
12	-	1-2-3	Gloria Estefan & The Miami Sound Machine	Epic	3	(3)	
13	13	We Call It Acieed	D. Mob Feat. Gary Haisman	ffrr	6		F
14	-	Twist And Shout	Salt 'n' Pepa	ffrr	4		
15	1	One Moment In Time	Whitney Houston	Arista	8	(5)	
16	-	The Clairvoyant	Iron Maiden	EMI	3		
17	8	A Little Respect	Erasure	Mute	8	(14)	
18	-	Let's Stick Together	Bryan Ferry	EG	2		
19	19	Harvest For The World	Christians	Island	4		
20	-	Left To My Own Devices	Pet Shop Boys	Parlophone	4	(84)	

December 1988

This Mnth	Prev Mnth	Title	Artist	Label	Wks 20	(US Pos)	
1	-	Mistletoe And Wine	Cliff Richard	EMI	7		
2	-	Cat Among The Pigeons/Silent Night	Bros	CBS	6		
3	-	Especially For You	Kylie Minogue/Jason Donovan	PWL	10		
4	-	Suddenly	Angry Anderson	Food For Thought	8		F L
5	-	Two Hearts	Phil Collins	Virgin	8	(1)	
6	-	Crackers International (E.P.)	Erasure	Mute	10		
7	4	The First Time	Robin Beck	Mercury	9		F L
8	-	Smooth Criminal	Michael Jackson	Epic	8	(7)	
9	-	Take Me To Your Heart	Rick Astley	RCA	7		
10	-	Good Life	Inner City	10	8	(73)	
11	-	Burning Bridges (On And Off And On Again)	Status Quo	Vertigo	6		
12	10	Missing You	Chris De Burgh	A&M	6		L
13	-	Angel Of Harlem	U2	Island	4	(14)	
14	-	Say A Little Prayer	Bomb The Bass	Rhythm King	5		
15	20	Left To My Own Devices	Pet Shop Boys	Parlophone	4	(84)	
16	-	Downtown '88	Petula Clark	PRT	4		L
17	9	Need You Tonight	INXS	Mercury	5	(1)	F
18	-	Buffalo Stance	Neneh Cherry	Circa	7	(3)	F
19	-	Fine Time	New Order	Factory	4		
20	-	Loco In Acapulco	Four Tops	Arista	5		L

October 1988

This Mnth	Prev Mnth	Title	Artist	Label	Wks 20	(UK Pos)	
1	-	Red Red Wine	UB40	A&M	9		F
2	14	Love Bites	Def Leppard	Mercury	8	(11)	
3	-	Groovy Kind Of Love	Phil Collins	Atlantic	8	(1)	
4	5	Don't Worry Be Happy	Bobby McFerrin	EMI Manhattan	9	(2)	F L
5	-	What's On Your Mind (Pure Energy)	Information Society	Tommy Boy	8		F
6	17	Don't Be Cruel	Cheap Trick	Epic	8		
7	-	Don't You Know What The Night Can Do	Steve Winwood	Virgin	7		
8	-	Don't Be Cruel	Bobby Brown	MCA	8	(13)	FG
9	-	Wild Wild West	Escape Club	Atlantic	10		F
10	12	One Good Woman	Peter Cetera	Full Moon	7		
11	4	I'll Always Love You	Taylor Dayne	Arista	10	(41)	
12	-	Kokomo	Beach Boys	Elektra	8	(25)	G L
13	18	I Hate Myself For Loving You	Joan Jett & The Blackhearts	Blackheart	6	(46)	
14	-	Never Tear Us Apart	INXS	Atlantic	6	(24)	
15	-	The Loco-Motion	Kylie Minogue	Geffen	9	(2)	F L
16	-	Forever Young	Rod Stewart	Warner	4	(57)	
17	-	True Love	Glenn Frey	MCA	5		L
18	-	One Moment In Time	Whitney Houston	Arista	7	(1)	
19	-	Please Don't Go Girl	New Kids On The Block	Columbia	5		F
20	1	Sweet Child O' Mine	Guns N' Roses	Geffen	10	(6)	F

November 1988

This Mnth	Prev Mnth	Title	Artist	Label	Wks 20	(UK Pos)	
1	-	Bad Medicine	Bon Jovi	Mercury	8	(17)	
2	9	Wild Wild West	Escape Club	Atlantic	10		F
3	12	Kokomo	Beach Boys	Elektra	8	(25)	G L
4	15	The Loco-Motion	Kylie Minogue	Geffen	9	(2)	F L
5	-	Desire	U2	Island	8	(1)	
6	-	Baby I Love Your Way/ Freebird Medley	Will To Power	Epic	9	(6)	F
7	-	How Can I Fall	Breathe	A&M	10	(48)	
8	-	Kissing A Fool	George Michael	Columbia	6	(18)	
9	18	One Moment In Time	Whitney Houston	Arista	7	(1)	
10	-	Look Away	Chicago	Reprise	11		
11	3	Groovy Kind Of Love	Phil Collins	Atlantic	8	(1)	
12	-	I Don't Want Your Love	Duran Duran	Capitol	9	(14)	
13	-	Don't Know What You Got (Till It's Gone)	Cinderella	Mercury	5	(54)	
14	14	Never Tear Us Apart	INXS	Atlantic	6	(24)	
15	-	Giving You The Best That I Got	Anita Baker	Elektra	10	(55)	
16	-	Another Lover	Giant Steps	A&M	6		F L
17	-	Waiting For A Star To Fall	Boy Meets Girl	RCA	10	(9)	F L
18	5	What's On Your Mind (Pure Energy)	Information Society	Tommy Boy	8		F
19	1	Red Red Wine	UB40	A&M	9	(1)	F
20	7	Don't You Know What The Night...	Steve Winwood	Virgin	7		

December 1988

This Mnth	Prev Mnth	Title	Artist	Label	Wks 20	(UK Pos)	
1	10	Look Away	Chicago	Reprise	11		
2	-	Every Rose Has Its Thorn	Poison	Enigma	10	(13)	
3	15	Giving You The Best That I Got	Anita Baker	Elektra	10	(55)	
4	-	My Prerogative	Bobby Brown	MCA	10	(6)	
5	17	Waiting For A Star To Fall	Boy Meets Girl	RCA	10	(9)	F L
6	6	Baby I Love Your Way/ Freebird Medley	Will To Power	Epic	9	(6)	F
7	-	Welcome To The Jungle	Guns N' Roses	Geffen	8	(24)	
8	12	I Don't Want Your Love	Duran Duran	Capitol	9	(14)	
9	7	How Can I Fall	Breathe	A&M	10	(48)	
10	-	Walk On Water	Eddie Money	Columbia	8		
11	-	Two Hearts	Phil Collins	Atlantic	9	(6)	
12	-	In Your Room	Bangles	Columbia	8	(35)	
13	-	The Promise	When In Rome	Virgin	7	(58)	F L
14	-	Don't Rush Me	Taylor Dayne	Arista	9		
15	5	Desire	U2	Island	8	(1)	
16	-	Finish What Ya Started	Van Halen	Warner	5		L
17	1	Bad Medicine	Bon Jovi	Mercury	8	(17)	
18	-	Armageddon It	Def Leppard	Mercury	8	(20)	
19	-	I Remember Holding You	Boys Club	MCA	6		F L
20	8	Kissing A Fool	George Michael	Columbia	6	(18)	

US 1988
OCT-DEC

◆ American record and tape shipments reached a new high of $6.25 billion, with CD business increasing 47%. It was also a record year in Britain, with sales of over $1 billion, and CDs showing a 60% increase.

▲ Among the acts enjoying their first Top 20 entries were future superstars Bobby Brown (above), Guns N' Roses and New Kids On The Block.

◆ 'Kokomo' was the Beach Boys' first No. 1 hit since 1966. It was co-written by two other 1960s stalwarts, John Phillips of The Mamas & The Papas and Scott McKenzie, who is best remembered for the hit 'San Francisco (Be Sure To Wear Flowers In Your Hair)'.

UK 1989

JAN-MAR

◆ A new album chart was introduced which contained only multi-artist albums, leaving the main chart for solo artist sets.

◆ American producers L.A. & Babyface had five singles simultaneously in the US Top 40. In Britain, Stock, Aitken & Waterman scored their 80th UK Top 75 hit in less than five years, and in March produced three of the Top 4 singles.

◆ The quasi-religious video for Madonna's transatlantic topper, 'Like A Prayer', caused a major controversy, resulting in Pepsi dropping an $8 million advertising campaign.

◆ 1960s superstar Gene Pitney had his only No. 1 with a revival of his last Top 10 entry (from 1967), 'Something's Gotten Hold Of My Heart'. He shared billing on this re-recording with Marc Almond.

◆ TV's *Top Of The Pops* celebrated its 25th birthday.

January 1989

This Mnth	Prev Mnth	Title	Artist	Label	Wks 20	(US Pos)	
1	3	Especially For You	Kylie Minogue/Jason Donovan	PWL	10		
2	6	Crackers International (E.P.)	Erasure	Mute	10		
3	18	Buffalo Stance	Neneh Cherry	Circa	7	(3)	F
4	10	Good Life	Inner City	10	8	(73)	
5	-	She Drives Me Crazy	Fine Young Cannibals	London	6	(1)	
6	-	The Living Years	Mike + The Mechanics	WEA	7	(1)	F
7	4	Suddenly	Angry Anderson	Food For Thought	8		F L
8	-	Four Letter Word	Kim Wilde	MCA	6		
9	-	Baby I Love Your Way/Freebird	Will To Power	Epic	5	(1)	F L
10	20	Loco In Acapulco	Four Tops	Arista	5		L
11	-	Something's Gotten Hold Of My Heart	Marc Almond Featuring Gene Pitney	Parlophone	9		
12	-	You Got It	Roy Orbison	Virgin	6	(9)	
13	-	Waiting For A Star To Fall	Boy Meets Girl	RCA	4	(5)	F L
14	-	Cuddly Toy	Roachford	CBS	5		F L
15	11	Burning Bridges (On And Off...)	Status Quo	Vertigo	6		
16	-	All She Wants Is	Duran Duran	EMI	2	(22)	
17	1	Mistletoe And Wine	Cliff Richard	EMI	7		
18	-	Keeping The Dream Alive	Freiheit	CBS	4		F L
19	5	Two Hearts	Phil Collins	Virgin	8	(1)	
20	-	You Are The One	A-Ha	Warner	5		

February 1989

This Mnth	Prev Mnth	Title	Artist	Label	Wks 20	(US Pos)	
1	11	Something's Gotten Hold Of My...	Marc Almond Feat. Gene Pitney	Parlophone	9		
2	6	The Living Years	Mike + The Mechanics	WEA	7	(1)	F
3	-	Love Train	Holly Johnson	MCA	6	(65)	F
4	12	You Got It	Roy Orbison	Virgin	6	(9)	
5	-	Love Changes Everything	Michael Ball	Really Useful	8		F L
6	-	My Prerogative	Bobby Brown	MCA	6	(1)	F
7	14	Cuddly Toy	Roachford	CBS	5		F L
8	-	Wait	Robert Howard & Kym Mazelle	RCA	5		F L
9	-	Belfast Child	Simple Minds	Virgin	5		
10	-	That's The Way Love Is	Ten City	Atlantic	5		F L
11	-	Fine Time	Yazz	Big Life	4		
12	5	She Drives Me Crazy	Fine Young Cannibals	London	6	(1)	
13	-	Last Of The Famous International Playboys	Morrissey	HMV	2		
14	-	Hold Me In Your Arms	Rick Astley	RCA	4		
15	-	Stop	Sam Brown	A&M	7	(65)	F
16	1	Especially For You	Kylie Minogue/Jason Donovan	PWL	10		
17	-	Leave Me Alone	Michael Jackson	Epic	6		
18	2	Crackers International (E.P.)	Erasure	Mute	10		
19	-	It's Only Love	Simply Red	Elektra	2	(57)	
20	-	Big Area	Then Jerico	London	2		L

March 1989

This Mnth	Prev Mnth	Title	Artist	Label	Wks 20	(US Pos)	
1	-	Too Many Broken Hearts	Jason Donovan	PWL	9		
2	-	Help	Bananarama/La Na Nee Nee Noo Nioo	London	6		
3	15	Stop	Sam Brown	A&M	7	(65)	F
4	5	Love Changes Everything	Michael Ball	Really Useful	8		F L
5	-	Can't Stay Away From You	Gloria Estefan & The Miami Sound Machine	Epic	6	(6)	
6	17	Leave Me Alone	Michael Jackson	Epic	6		
7	-	Hey Music Lover	S'Express	Rhythm King	5		L
8	-	This Time I Know It's For Real	Donna Summer	Warner	8	(7)	
9	9	Belfast Child	Simple Minds	Virgin	5		
10	-	Like A Prayer	Madonna	Sire	7	(1)	
11	-	Straight Up	Paula Abdul	Siren	9	(1)	F
12	-	I Don't Want A Lover	Texas	Mercury	5	(77)	F
13	-	Blow The House Down	Living In A Box	Chrysalis	4		
14	-	I'd Rather Jack	Reynolds Girls	PWL	6		F L
15	-	Keep On Movin'	Soul II Soul Feat. Caron Wheeler	10	6	(11)	F
16	6	My Prerogative	Bobby Brown	MCA	6	(1)	F
17	-	Turn Up The Bass	Tyree Feat. Kool Rock Steady	ffrr	3		F L
18	-	Every Rose Has Its Thorn	Poison	Enigma	4	(1)	F
19	-	Paradise City	Guns N' Roses	Geffen	5	(5)	F
20	14	Hold Me In Your Arms	Rick Astley	RCA	4		

January 1989

This Mnth	Prev Mnth	Title	Artist	Label	Wks 20	(UK Pos)	
1	11	Two Hearts	Phil Collins	Atlantic	9	(6)	
2	14	Don't Rush Me	Taylor Dayne	Arista	9		
3	4	My Prerogative	Bobby Brown	MCA	10	(6)	
4	18	Armageddon It	Def Leppard	Mercury	8	(20)	
5	2	Every Rose Has Its Thorn	Poison	Enigma	10	(13)	
6	-	When I'm With You	Sheriff	Capitol	8		F L
7	-	Smooth Criminal	Michael Jackson	Epic	7	(8)	
8	-	The Way You Love Me	Karyn White	Warner	6	(42)	F
9	-	When The Children Cry	White Lion	Atlantic	7		L
10	-	Born To Be My Baby	Bon Jovi	Mercury	9	(22)	
11	-	Put A Little Love In Your Heart	Annie Lennox & Al Green	A&M	6	(28)	F
12	12	In Your Room	Bangles	Columbia	8	(35)	
13	19	I Remember Holding You	Boys Club	MCA	6		F L
14	-	All This Time	Tiffany	MCA	7	(47)	
15	5	Waiting For A Star To Fall	Boy Meets Girl	RCA	10	(9)	F L
16	-	Straight Up	Paula Abdul	Virgin	9	(3)	F G
17	3	Giving You The Best That I Got	Anita Baker	Elektra	10	(55)	
18	-	Wild Thing	Tone Loc	Delicious Vinyl	8	(21)	F P
19	-	Holding On	Steve Winwood	Virgin	4		
20	1	Look Away	Chicago	Reprise	11		

February 1989

This Mnth	Prev Mnth	Title	Artist	Label	Wks 20	(UK Pos)	
1	16	Straight Up	Paula Abdul	Virgin	9	(3)	F G
2	18	Wild Thing	Tone Loc	Delicious Vinyl	8	(21)	F P
3	10	Born To Be My Baby	Bon Jovi	Mercury	9	(22)	
4	6	When I'm With You	Sheriff	Capitol	8		F L
5	-	The Lover In Me	Sheena Easton	MCA	8	(15)	
6	-	She Wants To Dance With Me	Rick Astley	RCA	6	(6)	
7	-	Lost In Your Eyes	Debbie Gibson	Atlantic	9	(34)	
8	9	When The Children Cry	White Lion	Atlantic	7		L
9	-	What I Am	Edie Brickell & New Bohemians	Geffen	7	(31)	F L
10	-	Walking Away	Information Society	Tommy Boy	5		L
11	-	You Got It (The Right Stuff)	New Kids On The Block	Columbia	8	(1)	
12	-	I Wanna Have Some Fun	Samantha Fox	Jive	6	(63)	L
13	14	All This Time	Tiffany	MCA	7	(47)	L
14	-	Surrender To Me	Ann Wilson & Robin Zander	Capitol	7		L
15	8	The Way You Love Me	Karyn White	Warner	6	(42)	F
16	-	Dial My Heart	Boys	Motown	5	(61)	F L
17	4	Armageddon It	Def Leppard	Mercury	8	(20)	
18	-	Angel Of Harlem	U2	Island	3	(9)	
19	-	The Living Years	Mike + The Mechanics	Atlantic	8	(2)	L
20	2	Don't Rush Me	Taylor Dayne	Arista	9		

March 1989

This Mnth	Prev Mnth	Title	Artist	Label	Wks 20	(UK Pos)	
1	7	Lost In Your Eyes	Debbie Gibson	Atlantic	9	(34)	
2	19	The Living Years	Mike + The Mechanics	Atlantic	8	(2)	L
3	-	Roni	Bobby Brown	MCA	6	(21)	
4	-	Girl You Know It's True	Milli Vanilli	Arista	9	(3)	F G
5	-	Paradise City	Guns N' Roses	Geffen	6	(6)	
6	-	My Heart Can't Tell You No	Rod Stewart	Warner	8	(49)	
7	11	You Got It (The Right Stuff)	New Kids On The Block	Columbia	8	(1)	
8	-	Eternal Flame	Bangles	Columbia	8	(1)	L
9	-	The Look	Roxette	EMI	8	(7)	F
10	1	Straight Up	Paula Abdul	Virgin	9	(3)	F G
11	-	Don't Tell Me Lies	Breathe	A&M	5	(45)	L
12	5	The Lover In Me	Sheena Easton	MCA	8	(15)	
13	14	Surrender To Me	Ann Wilson & Robin Zander	Capitol	7		L
14	-	You're Not Alone	Chicago	Reprise	4		
15	-	Walk The Dinosaur	Was (Not Was)	Chrysalis	5	(10)	L
16	-	She Drives Me Crazy	Fine Young Cannibals	IRS	9	(5)	F
17	9	What I Am	Edie Brickell & New Bohemians	Geffen	7	(31)	F L
18	-	Dreamin'	Vanessa Williams	Wing	7	(74)	F
19	2	Wild Thing	Tone Loc	Delicious Vinyl	8	(21)	F P
20	-	I Beg Your Pardon	Kon Kan	Atlantic	4	(5)	F L

◆ Due to the drop in singles sales, the qualification for an American gold record was halved to 500,000, and a platinum to 1 million, while in Britain sales of 600,000 earned a platinum record and 400,000 a gold.

◆ *Rock And Roll Hall Of Fame* inductees for 1988/89 were The Beach Boys, The Beatles, Dion, The Drifters, Bob Dylan, Otis Redding, Rolling Stones, The Supremes, The Temptations and Stevie Wonder.

◆ The first CDs to sell a million were U2's **The Joshua Tree,** the **Dirty Dancing** soundtrack, Def Leppard's **Hysteria** and George Michael's **Faith.**

◆ Debbie Gibson became the first teenager to simultaneously top the singles and albums chart since Little Stevie Wonder in 1963. Also, Guns N' Roses became the first act to have two albums in the Top 5 since Jim Croce in 1974.

UK 1989
APR-JUNE

◆ Wembley crowd-pullers included The Bee Gees, Bobby Brown, Bob Dylan, Elton John, R.E.M., Diana Ross and Stevie Wonder.

▲ Stock, Aitken & Waterman scored a record three successive No. 1s with singles by Kylie Minogue (above), Jason Donovan and an all star group featuring Gerry (& The Pacemakers) Marsden, whose re-recording of 'Ferry Cross The Mersey' was the eighth charity chart topper in five years, and the fourth to enter at No. 1.

◆ Cliff Richard released his 100th single, 'The Best Of Me'. It coincided with the 100th anniversary of the first commercially released record.

April 1989

This Mnth	Prev Mnth	Title	Artist	Label	Wks 20	(US Pos)	
1	-	Eternal Flame	Bangles	CBS	9	(1)	L
2	10	Like A Prayer	Madonna	Sire	7	(1)	
3	11	Straight Up	Paula Abdul	Siren	9	(1)	F
4	-	I Beg Your Pardon	Kon Kan	Atlantic	7	(15)	F L
5	1	Too Many Broken Hearts	Jason Donovan	PWL	9		
6	8	This Time I Know It's For Real	Donna Summer	Warner	8	(7)	
7	-	If You Don't Know Me By Now	Simply Red	Elektra	7	(1)	
8	-	Baby I Don't Care	Transvision Vamp	MCA	8		
9	-	Americanos	Holly Johnson	MCA	7		
10	15	Keep On Movin'	Soul II Soul Feat. Caron Wheeler	10	6	(11)	F
11	19	Paradise City	Guns N' Roses	Geffen	5	(5)	F
12	-	When Love Comes To Town	U2 With B.B. King	Island	3	(68)	
13	-	People Hold On	Coldcut Feat. Lisa Stansfield	Ahead Of Our Time	4		L
14	-	Good Thing	Fine Young Cannibals	London	5	(1)	
15	14	I'd Rather Jack	Reynolds Girls	PWL	6		F L
16	-	Lullaby	Cure	Fiction	3	(74)	
17	-	I Haven't Stopped Dancing Yet	Pat & Mick	PWL	3		F L
18	-	International Rescue	Fuzzbox	WEA	4		F
19	-	Don't Be Cruel	Bobby Brown	MCA	3	(8)	
20	5	Can't Stay Away From You	Gloria Estefa/Miami Sound...	Epic	6	(6)	

May 1989

This Mnth	Prev Mnth	Title	Artist	Label	Wks 20	(US Pos)	
1	-	Hand On Your Heart	Kylie Minogue	PWL	7		
2	-	Requiem	London Boys	WEA	7		F
3	-	Miss You Like Crazy	Natalie Cole	EMI	8	(7)	
4	1	Eternal Flame	Bangles	CBS	9	(1)	L
5	-	I Want It All	Queen	Parlophone	4	(50)	
6	-	Bring Me Edelweiss	Edelweiss	WEA	5		F L
7	-	Beds Are Burning	Midnight Oil	CBS/Sprint	5	(17)	F L
8	-	Ferry 'Cross The Mersey	Christians/Holly Johnson/Paul McCartney/Gerry Marsden & Stock Aitken Waterman	PWL	5		F L
9	8	Baby I Don't Care	Transvision Vamp	MCA	8		
10	-	I'm Every Woman	Chaka Khan	Warner	4		L
11	9	Americanos	Holly Johnson	MCA	7		
12	7	If You Don't Know Me By Now	Simply Red	Elektra	7	(1)	
13	-	The Look	Roxette	EMI	4	(1)	F
14	-	Who's In The House	Beatmasters	Rhythm King	4		
15	-	Electric Youth	Debbie Gibson	Atlantic	3	(11)	
16	-	Every Little Step	Bobby Brown	MCA	4	(3)	
17	-	Your Mama Don't Dance	Poison	Capitol	3	(10)	
18	14	Good Thing	Fine Young Cannibals	London	5	(1)	
19	-	Manchild	Neneh Cherry	Circa	5		
20	-	Where Has All The Love Gone	Yazz	Big Life	3		

June 1989

This Mnth	Prev Mnth	Title	Artist	Label	Wks 20	(US Pos)	
1	-	Sealed With A Kiss	Jason Donovan	PWL	5		
2	3	Miss You Like Crazy	Natalie Cole	EMI	8	(7)	
3	-	Express Yourself	Madonna	Sire	5	(2)	
4	-	The Best Of Me	Cliff Richard	EMI	4		
5	-	Right Back Where We Started From	Sinitta	Fanfare	7	(84)	
6	-	Back To Life (However Do You Want Me)	Soul II Soul Featuring Caron Wheeler	10	10	(4)	
7	-	Sweet Child O' Mine	Guns N' Roses	Geffen	6	(1)	
8	8	Ferry 'Cross The Mersey	Christians, Holly Johnson etc.	PWL	5		F L
9	19	Manchild	Neneh Cherry	Circa	5		
10	-	I Don't Wanna Get Hurt	Donna Summer	Warner	5		
11	-	On The Inside (Theme 'Prisoner- Cell Block H')	Lynne Hamilton	A1	4		F L
12	-	I Drove All Night	Cyndi Lauper	Epic	6	(6)	
13	1	Hand On Your Heart	Kylie Minogue	PWL	7		
14	2	Requiem	London Boys	WEA	7		F
15	-	Song For Whoever	Beautiful South	Go! Discs	7		F
16	-	It Is Time To Get Funky	D. Mob Featuring LRS	London	5		
17	6	Bring Me Edelweiss	Edelweiss	WEA	5		F L
18	16	Every Little Step	Bobby Brown	MCA	4	(3)	
19	-	Batdance	Prince	Warner	5	(1)	
20	-	Just Keep Rockin'	Double Trouble & Rebel M.C.	Desire	7		F

US 1989
APR-JUNE

April 1989

This Mnth	Prev Mnth	Title	Artist	Label	Wks 20	(UK Pos)	
1	9	The Look	Roxette	EMI	8	(7)	F
2	16	She Drives Me Crazy	Fine Young Cannibals	IRS	9	(5)	F
3	-	Like A Prayer	Madonna	Sire	9	(1)	G
4	8	Eternal Flame	Bangles	Columbia	8	(1)	L
5	4	Girl You Know It's True	Milli Vanilli	Arista	9	(3)	F G
6	-	Funky Cold Medina	Tone Loc	Delicious	7	(13)	G L
7	-	Stand	R.E.M.	Warner	6	(48)	
8	-	I'll Be There For You	Bon Jovi	Mercury	10	(18)	
9	-	Heaven Help Me	Deon Estus	Mika/Polydor	6	(41)	F L
10	6	My Heart Can't Tell You No	Rod Stewart	Warner	8	(49)	
11	-	Second Chance	Thirty Eight Special	A&M	8		L
12	-	Your Mama Don't Dance	Poison	Enigma	5	(13)	
13	18	Dreamin'	Vanessa Williams	Wing	7	(74)	F
14	-	Superwoman	Karyn White	Warner	5	(11)	
15	-	You Got It	Roy Orbison	Virgin	6	(3)	L
16	15	Walk The Dinosaur	Was (Not Was)	Chrysalis	5	(10)	L
17	-	Room To Move	Animotion	Polydor	5		L
18	-	Rocket	Def Leppard	Mercury	4	(15)	
19	2	The Living Years	Mike + The Mechanics	Atlantic	8	(2)	L
20	-	Real Love	Jody Watley	MCA	8	(31)	

May 1989

This Mnth	Prev Mnth	Title	Artist	Label	Wks 20	(UK Pos)	
1	20	Real Love	Jody Watley	MCA	8	(31)	
2	-	Forever Your Girl	Paula Abdul	Virgin	9	(24)	
3	8	I'll Be There For You	Bon Jovi	Mercury	10	(18)	
4	-	Soldier Of Love	Donny Osmond	Capitol	8	(29)	
5	-	Rock On	Michael Damian	Cypress	8		F L
6	3	Like A Prayer	Madonna	Sire	9	(1)	G
7	-	Patience	Guns N' Roses	Geffen	7	(10)	
8	-	After All	Cher & Peter Cetera	Geffen	7		
9	-	Wind Beneath My Wings	Bette Midler	Atlantic	10	(5)	G
10	11	Second Chance	Thirty Eight Special	A&M	8		L
11	-	Electric Youth	Debbie Gibson	Atlantic	5	(14)	
12	-	Every Little Step	Bobby Brown	MCA	9	(6)	
13	-	I'll Be Loving You (Forever)	New Kids On The Block	Columbia	8	(5)	
14	6	Funky Cold Medina	Tone Loc	Delicious	7	(13)	G L
15	-	Thinking Of You	Sa-Fire	Polydor/Cutting	6		F L
16	-	Cult Of Personality	Living Colour	Epic	4	(67)	F L
17	-	Close My Eyes Forever	Lita Ford (& Ozzy Osbourne)	RCA	7	(47)	L
18	-	Everlasting Love	Howard Jones	Elektra	5	(62)	L
19	-	Iko Iko	Belle Stars	Capitol	4	(35)	F L
20	2	She Drives Me Crazy	Fine Young Cannibals	IRS	9	(5)	F

June 1989

This Mnth	Prev Mnth	Title	Artist	Label	Wks 20	(UK Pos)	
1	13	I'll Be Loving You (Forever)	New Kids On The Block	Columbia	8	(5)	
2	9	Wind Beneath My Wings	Bette Midler	Atlantic	10	(5)	G
3	12	Every Little Step	Bobby Brown	MCA	9	(6)	
4	-	Buffalo Stance	Neneh Cherry	Virgin	9	(3)	F
5	-	Satisfied	Richard Marx	EMI	8	(52)	
6	5	Rock On	Michael Damian	Cypress	8		F L
7	-	Baby Don't Forget My Number	Milli Vanilli	Arista	9	(16)	
8	7	Patience	Guns N' Roses	Geffen	7	(10)	
9	17	Close My Eyes Forever	Lita Ford (& Ozzy Osbourne)	RCA	7	(47)	L
10	-	Good Thing	Fine Young Cannibals	I.R.S.	9	(7)	
11	-	This Time I Know It's For Real	Donna Summer	Atlantic	6	(3)	L
12	-	Cry	Waterfront	Polydor	6	(17)	F L
13	4	Soldier Of Love	Donny Osmond	Capitol	8	(29)	
14	2	Forever Your Girl	Paula Abdul	Virgin	9	(24)	
15	-	Miss You Like Crazy	Natalie Cole	EMI	8	(2)	
16	-	Where Are You Now	Jimmy Harnen With Synch	WTG	5		F L
17	-	I Drove All Night	Cyndi Lauper	Epic	6	(7)	L
18	1	Real Love	Jody Watley	MCA	8	(31)	
19	-	If You Don't Know Me By Now	Simply Red	Elektra	9	(2)	L
20	18	Everlasting Love	Howard Jones	Elektra	5	(62)	L

◆ For the first time, over half the Top 10 black albums were by rap artists. *Billboard* introduced an all-rap chart, and MTV banned NWA's 'Straight Outta Compton' video for being too "pro-gang".

◆ As veteran rockers The Who (they earned $30 million from their shows) and The Beach Boys started successful US tours, old singles by The Belle Stars, Jimmy Harnen & Synch, Benny Mardones and Real Life climbed the Hot 100.

◆ German-based duo Milli Vanilli's debut hit, 'Girl You Know It's True', was the first of five Top 3 singles to be extracted from their six million selling debut LP of the same name. It was a great start to a career that would soon come to an abrupt end.

UK 1989 JULY-SEPT

◆ Madonna scored a record 16th successive Top 5 single in the USA with 'Cherish'. In the UK Kylie Minogue's 'Wouldn't Change A Thing' was the fourth of her six singles to enter in runner-up position (surprisingly she never had a record enter at No. 1).

◆ Paul McCartney started his first world tour for 13 years in Sweden, and The Pet Shop Boys, who chalked up their 12th Top 20 hit with 'It's Alright', toured the UK for the first time.

◆ In September, Italian records held the top three places in the UK dance chart with the chart topping 'Ride On Time' by Black Box outselling all other singles in 1989.

◆ Phonogram bought Island Records for $480 (£300) million with shareholders U2 making $48 (£30) million from the deal.

July 1989

This Mnth	Prev Mnth	Title	Artist	Label	Wks 20	(US Pos)	
1	6	Back To Life (However Do You Want Me)	Soul II Soul Featuring Caron Wheeler	10	10	(4)	
2	-	London Nights	London Boys	Teldec/WEA	7		
3	15	Song For Whoever	Beautiful South	Go! Discs	7		F
4	-	You'll Never Stop Me From Loving You	Sonia	Chrysalis	8		F
5	-	Licence To Kill	Gladys Knight	MCA	7		L
6	-	It's Alright	Pet Shop Boys	Parlophone	4		
7	19	Batdance	Prince	Warner	5	(1)	
8	-	Ain't Nobody	Rufus & Chaka Khan	Warner	7	(22)	L
9	-	On Our Own	Bobby Brown	MCA	6	(2)	
10	-	Wind Beneath My Wings	Bette Midler	Atlantic	6	(1)	F L
11	12	I Drove All Night	Cyndi Lauper	Epic	6	(6)	
12	-	All I Want Is You	U2	Island	3	(83)	
13	-	Breakthru'	Queen	Parlophone	3		
14	-	Superwoman	Karyn White	Warner	4	(8)	F L
15	-	Don't Wanna Lose You	Gloria Estefan	Epic	6	(1)	
16	20	Just Keep Rockin'	Double Trouble & Rebel M.C.	Desire	7		F
17	5	Right Back Where We Started From	Sinitta	Fanfare	7	(84)	
18	-	Voodoo Ray (EP)	A Guy Called Gerald	Rham!	4		F L
19	1	Sealed With A Kiss	Jason Donovan	PWL	5		
20	-	Patience	Guns N' Roses	Geffen	3	(4)	

August 1989

This Mnth	Prev Mnth	Title	Artist	Label	Wks 20	(US Pos)	
1	-	Swing The Mood	Jive Bunny & The Mastermixers	Music Factory	10	(11)	F
2	-	Wouldn't Change A Thing	Kylie Minogue	PWL	6		
3	-	French Kiss	Lil Louis	ffrr	7	(50)	F
4	-	Poison	Alice Cooper	Epic	7	(7)	L
5	4	You'll Never Stop Me From Loving...	Sonia	Chrysalis	8		F
6	15	Don't Wanna Lose You	Gloria Estefan	Epic	6	(1)	
7	-	Toy Soldiers	Martika	CBS	6	(1)	F
8	-	Too Much	Bros	CBS	4		
9	9	On Our Own	Bobby Brown	MCA	6	(2)	
10	-	You're History	Shakespear's Sister	ffrr	4		F
11	-	Losing My Mind	Liza Minnelli	Epic	3		F L
12	-	Ride On Time	Black Box	De Construction	14		F
13	-	Blame It On The Boogie	Big Fun	Jive	6		F
14	8	Ain't Nobody	Rufus & Chaka Khan	Warner	7	(22)	L
15	10	Wind Beneath My Wings	Bette Midler	Atlantic	6	(1)	F L
16	2	London Nights	London Boys	Teldec/WEA	7		
17	-	Hey D.J. I Can't Dance To That Music You're Playing/Ska Train	Beatmasters Featuring Betty Boo	Rhythm King	6		L
18	-	Days	Kirsty MacColl	Virgin	4		L
19	-	Do The Right Thing	Redhead Kingpin & The FBI	10	3		F L
20	1	Back To Life (However Do You ...)	Soul II Soul Feat. Caron Wheeler	10	10	(4)	

September 1989

This Mnth	Prev Mnth	Title	Artist	Label	Wks 20	(US Pos)	
1	12	Ride On Time	Black Box	De Construction	14		F
2	1	Swing The Mood	Jive Bunny & The Mastermixers	Music Factory	10	(11)	F
3	-	Sowing The Seeds Of Love	Tears For Fears	Fontana	5	(2)	
4	-	Right Here Waiting	Richard Marx	EMI	7	(1)	F
5	13	Blame It On The Boogie	Big Fun	Jive	6		F
6	-	Every Day (I Love You More)	Jason Donovan	PWL	4		
7	-	I Need Your Lovin'	Alyson Williams	Def Jam	7		L
8	-	The Time Warp	Damian	Jive	5		F L
9	-	The Best	Tina Turner	Capitol	7	(15)	
10	-	I Just Don't Have The Heart	Cliff Richard	EMI	5		
11	-	Numero Uno	Starlight	City Beat	6		F L
12	17	Hey D.J. I Can't Dance To That Music You're Playing/Ska Train	Beatmasters Featuring Betty Boo	Rhythm King	6		L
13	-	Pump Up The Jam	Technotronic Featuring Felly	Swanyard	9	(2)	F
14	-	Cherish	Madonna	Sire	5	(2)	
15	4	Poison	Alice Cooper	Epic	7	(7)	L
16	-	If Only I Could	Sydney Youngblood	Circa	9		F
17	7	Toy Soldiers	Martika	CBS	6	(1)	F
18	3	French Kiss	Lil Louis	ffrr	7	(50)	F
19	2	Wouldn't Change A Thing	Kylie Minogue	PWL	6		
20	-	Personal Jesus	Depeche Mode	Mute	3	(28)	

July 1989

This Mnth	Prev Mnth	Title	Artist	Label	Wks 20	(UK Pos)	
1	-	Express Yourself	Madonna	Sire	7	(5)	
2	19	If You Don't Know Me By Now	Simply Red	Elektra	9	(2)	L
3	-	Toy Soldiers	Martika	Columbia	9	(5)	
4	10	Good Thing	Fine Young Cannibals	I.R.S.	9	(7)	
5	7	Baby Don't Forget My Number	Milli Vanilli	Arista	9	(16)	
6	15	Miss You Like Crazy	Natalie Cole	EMI	8	(2)	
7	-	Batdance	Prince	Warner	8	(2)	G
8	-	What You Don't Know	Expose	Arista	6		
9	-	So Alive	Love And Rockets	RCA	8		F L
10	-	On Our Own	Bobby Brown	MCA	10	(4)	G
11	-	Lay Your Hands On Me	Bon Jovi	Mercury	7	(18)	
12	5	Satisfied	Richard Marx	EMI	8	(52)	
13	17	I Drove All Night	Cyndi Lauper	Epic	6	(7)	L
14	-	The Doctor	Doobie Brothers	Capitol	5	(73)	L
15	4	Buffalo Stance	Neneh Cherry	Virgin	9	(3)	F
16	-	Once Bitten Twice Shy	Great White	Capitol	9		F L
17	-	Crazy About Her	Rod Stewart	Warner	5		
18	-	I Like It	Dino	4th & Broadway	8		F
19	11	This Time I Know It's For Real	Donna Summer	Atlantic	6	(3)	L
20	-	I Won't Back Down	Tom Petty	MCA	5	(28)	

August 1989

This Mnth	Prev Mnth	Title	Artist	Label	Wks 20	(UK Pos)	
1	-	Right Here Waiting	Richard Marx	EMI	10	(2)	G
2	10	On Our Own	Bobby Brown	MCA	10	(4)	G
3	-	Cold Hearted	Paula Abdul	Virgin	11	(46)	
4	16	Once Bitten Twice Shy	Great White	Capitol	9		F L
5	7	Batdance	Prince	Warner	8	(2)	G
6	-	Don't Wanna Lose You	Gloria Estefan	Epic	9	(6)	
7	18	I Like It	Dino	4th & Broadway	8		F
8	-	Hangin' Tough	New Kids On The Block	Columbia	8	(1)	G
9	9	So Alive	Love And Rockets	RCA	8		F L
10	-	Secret Rendezvous	Karyn White	Warner	8	(22)	
11	3	Toy Soldiers	Martika	Columbia	9	(5)	
12	-	Friends	Jody Watley With Eric B & Rakim	MCA	6	(21)	L
13	11	Lay Your Hands On Me	Bon Jovi	Mercury	7	(18)	
14	-	The End Of The Innocence	Don Henley	Geffen	5	(48)	L
15	-	Angel Eyes	Jeff Healey Band	Arista	7		F L
16	2	If You Don't Know Me By Now	Simply Red	Elektra	9	(2)	L
17	-	Sacred Emotion	Donny Osmond	Capitol	4		L
18	-	Shower Me With Your Love	Surface	Columbia	7		
19	-	Keep On Movin'	Soul Ii Soul	Virgin	6	(5)	F G
20	-	I'm That Type Of Guy	L.L. Cool J	Def Jam	3	(43)	

September 1989

This Mnth	Prev Mnth	Title	Artist	Label	Wks 20	(UK Pos)	
1	-	Heaven	Warrant	Columbia	9		F
2	-	Girl I'm Gonna Miss You	Milli Vanilli	Arista	9	(2)	
3	6	Don't Wanna Lose You	Gloria Estefan	Epic	9	(6)	
4	-	If I Could Turn Back Time	Cher	Geffen	9	(6)	
5	3	Cold Hearted	Paula Abdul	Virgin	11	(46)	
6	8	Hangin' Tough	New Kids On The Block	Columbia	8	(1)	G
7	-	18 And Life	Skid Row	Atlantic	9	(12)	F
8	18	Shower Me With Your Love	Surface	Columbia	7		
9	-	Cherish	Madonna	Sire	8	(3)	
10	1	Right Here Waiting	Richard Marx	EMI	10	(2)	G
11	15	Angel Eyes	Jeff Healey Band	Arista	7		F L
12	-	One	Bee Gees	Warner	5	(71)	L
13	-	Miss You Much	Janet Jackson	A&M	10	(22)	G
14	19	Keep On Movin'	Soul II Soul	Virgin	6	(5)	FG
15	-	Kisses On The Wind	Neneh Cherry	Virgin	4	(20)	L
16	10	Secret Rendezvous	Karyn White	Warner	8	(22)	
17	14	The End Of The Innocence	Don Henley	Geffen	5	(48)	L
18	12	Friends	Jody Watley With Eric B & Rakim	MCA	6	(21)	L
19	-	Love Song	Cure	Elektra	6	(18)	F
20	-	Don't Look Back	Fine Young Cannibals	IRS	5	(34)	L

◆ New Kids On The Block, America's hottest new act, simultaneously headed the single and album chart with 'Hangin' Tough'. Other successful new artists included hard rockers Warrant, Skid Row and Great White.

◆ Producer/songwriters L.A. & Babyface scored their twelfth No. 1 black hit in two years with Babyface's own single 'It's No Crime'.

▲ The Moscow Peace Festival starred Bon Jovi (above), Motley Crue, Ozzy Osbourne, The Scorpions, Skid Row and Cinderella.

◆ WEA announced they were phasing out production of seven inch vinyl records in 1990.

UK 1989 OCT-DEC

▲ Richard Marx's debut UK Top 20 entry, 'Right Here Waiting', had been his sixth successive US Top 3 entry.

◆ Jive Bunny & The Mastermixers scored a third successive No. 1 with their third release 'Let's Party', equalling the record set by Gerry & The Pacemakers and Frankie Goes To Hollywood.

◆ Stock, Aitken & Waterman produced a record breaking 11 of the year's Top 40 British singles.

◆ The decade ended with Band Aid II (a collection of current UK stars) topping the chart with an update of 'Do They Know It's Christmas'.

October 1989

This Mnth	Prev Mnth	Title	Artist	Label	Wks 20	(US Pos)	
1	1	Ride On Time	Black Box	De Construction	14		F
2	13	Pump Up The Jam	Technotronic Featuring Felly	Swanyard	9	(2)	F
3	16	If Only I Could	Sydney Youngblood	Circa	9		F
4	-	Street Tuff	Rebel MC/Double Trouble	Desire	8		
5	-	That's What I Like	Jive Bunny & The Mastermixers	Music Factory	8	(69)	
6	-	We Didn't Start The Fire	Billy Joel	CBS	6	(1)	
7	-	Girl I'm Gonna Miss You	Milli Vanilli	Cooltempo	8	(1)	L
8	-	Sweet Surrender	Wet Wet Wet	Precious	5		
9	-	Drama!	Erasure	Mute	4		
10	-	If I Could Turn Back Time	Cher	Geffen	7	(3)	
11	-	Leave A Light On	Belinda Carlisle	Virgin	6	(11)	
12	-	You Keep It All In	Beautiful South	Go! Discs	5		
13	4	Right Here Waiting	Richard Marx	EMI	7	(1)	F
14	-	Room In Your Heart	Living In A Box	Chrysalis	7		L
15	9	The Best	Tina Turner	Capitol	7	(15)	
16	-	Wishing On A Star	Fresh 4 Featuring Lizz E	10	3		F L
17	-	Chocolate Box	Bros	CBS	2		
18	-	Name And Number	Curiosity Killed The Cat	Mercury	3		
19	-	The Road To Hell (Pt. 2)	Chris Rea	WEA	5		
20	14	Cherish	Madonna	Sire	5	(2)	

November 1989

This Mnth	Prev Mnth	Title	Artist	Label	Wks 20	(US Pos)	
1	-	All Around The World	Lisa Stansfield	Arista	7	(3)	
2	7	Girl I'm Gonna Miss You	Milli Vanilli	Cooltempo	8	(1)	L
3	5	That's What I Like	Jive Bunny & The Mastermixers	Music Factory	8	(69)	L
4	-	Never Too Late	Kylie Minogue	PWL	5		
5	-	Another Day In Paradise	Phil Collins	Virgin	5	(1)	
6	4	Street Tuff	Rebel MC/Double Trouble	Desire	8		L
7	-	I Feel The Earth Move	Martika	CBS	6	(25)	
8	14	Room In Your Heart	Living In A Box	Chrysalis	7		L
9	-	You Got It (The Right Stuff)	New Kids On The Block	CBS	8	(3)	F
10	11	Leave A Light On	Belinda Carlisle	Virgin	6	(11)	
11	-	Don't Know Much	Linda Ronstadt (featuring Aaron Neville)	Elektra	7	(2)	L
12	-	Grand Piano	Mixmaster	BCM	4		F L
13	10	If I Could Turn Back Time	Cher	Geffen	7	(3)	
14	19	The Road To Hell (Pt. 2)	Chris Rea	WEA	5		
15	-	Infinite Dreams	Iron Maiden	EMI	2		
16	1	Ride On Time	Black Box	De Construction	14		F
17	-	I Want That Man	Deborah Harry	Chrysalis	4		L
18	-	Never Too Much (89 Remix)	Luther Vandross	Epic	3	(33)	
19	-	C'mon And Get My Love	D. Mob Featuring Cathy Dennis	Ffrr	4	(10)	
20	3	If Only I Could	Sydney Youngblood	Circa	9		F

December 1989

This Mnth	Prev Mnth	Title	Artist	Label	Wks 20	(US Pos)	
1	11	Don't Know Much	Linda Ronstadt (featuring Aaron Neville)	Elektra	7	(2)	L
2	9	You Got It (The Right Stuff)	New Kids On The Block	CBS	8	(3)	F
3	-	Lambada	Kaoma	CBS	9	(46)	F L
4	-	When You Come Back To Me	Jason Donovan	PWL	8		
5	-	Get A Life	Soul II Soul	10	8	(54)	
6	-	Eve Of The War	Jeff Wayne	CBS	6		F L
7	-	Let's Party	Jive Bunny & The Mastermixers	Music Factory	5		
8	-	I Don't Wanna Lose You	Tina Turner	Capitol	5	(9)	
9	-	Donald Where's Your Troosers	Andy Stewart	Stone	5	(77)	F L
10	-	Dear Jessie	Madonna	Sire	6		
11	-	Do They Know It's Christmas?	Band Aid II	PWL/Polydor	4		F L
12	-	Homely Girl	UB40	Dep International	4		
13	-	Can't Shake The Feeling	Big Fun	Jive	5		
14	-	Got To Get	Rob 'n' Raz Featuring Leila K	Arista	9		F L
15	1	All Around The World	Lisa Stansfield	Arista	7	(3)	
16	-	Fool's Gold/What The World Is Waiting For	Stone Roses	Silvertone	4		F
17	5	Another Day In Paradise	Phil Collins	Virgin	5	(1)	
18	-	In Private	Dusty Springfield	Parlophone	4		L
19	-	Sister	Bros	CBS	3		
20	-	Pacific	808 State	ZTT	4		F

October 1989

This Mnth	Prev Mnth	Title	Artist	Label	Wks 20	(UK Pos)	
1	13	Miss You Much	Janet Jackson	A&M	10	(22)	G
2	-	Sowing The Seeds Of Love	Tears For Fears	Fontana	8	(5)	L
3	19	Love Song	Cure	Elektra	6	(18)	F
4	-	Listen To Your Heart	Roxette	EMI	8	(6)	
5	-	Bust A Move	Young M.C.	Delicious Vinyl	11	(73)	F G L
6	-	Mixed Emotions	Rolling Stones	Columbia	6	(36)	L
7	-	It's No Crime	Babyface	Solar	6		F
8	9	Cherish	Madonna	Sire	8	(3)	
9	-	Love In An Elevator	Aerosmith	Geffen	6	(13)	
10	2	Girl I'm Gonna Miss You	Milli Vanilli	Arista	9	(2)	
11	-	Cover Girl	New Kids On The Block	Columbia	7	(4)	
12	-	Dr. Feelgood	Motley Crue	Elektra	6	(50)	
13	1	Heaven	Warrant	Columbia	9		F
14	-	When I Looked At Him	Expose	Arista	5		
15	4	If I Could Turn Back Time	Cher	Geffen	9	(6)	
16	-	Rock Wit'cha	Bobby Brown	MCA	7	(33)	
17	-	When I See You Smile	Bad English	Epic	8	(61)	F
18	-	Healing Hands	Elton John	MCA	4	(1)	
19	7	18 And Life	Skid Row	Atlantic	9	(12)	F
20	-	It's Not Enough	Starship	RCA	5		L

November 1989

This Mnth	Prev Mnth	Title	Artist	Label	Wks 20	(UK Pos)	
1	17	When I See You Smile	Bad English	Epic	8	(61)	F
2	-	Blame It On The Rain	Milli Vanilli	Arista	10	(53)	G
3	4	Listen To Your Heart	Roxette	EMI	8	(6)	
4	-	Love Shack	B-52's	Reprise	8	(2)	F
5	-	(It's Just) The Way You Love Me	Paula Abdul	Virgin	8	(74)	
6	11	Cover Girl	New Kids On The Block	Columbia	7	(4)	
7	-	Angelia	Richard Marx	EMI	7	(45)	
8	1	Miss You Much	Janet Jackson	A&M	10	(22)	G
9	-	We Didn't Start The Fire	Billy Joel	Columbia	10	(7)	
10	-	Poison	Alice Cooper	Epic	6	(2)	L
11	2	Sowing The Seeds Of Love	Tears For Fears	Fontana	8	(5)	L
12	-	Didn't I (Blow Your Mind)	New Kids On The Block	Columbia	6	(8)	
13	-	Back To Life	Soul II Soul Feat. Caron Wheeler	Virgin	11	(1)	G L
14	16	Rock Wit'cha	Bobby Brown	MCA	7	(33)	
15	5	Bust A Move	Young M.C.	Delicious Vinyl	11	(73)	F G L
16	9	Love In An Elevator	Aerosmith	Geffen	6	(13)	
17	-	Don't Know Much	Linda Ronstadt (featuring Aaron Neville)	Elektra	11	(2)	
18	-	Get On Your Feet	Gloria Estefan	Epic	4	(23)	
19	-	Don't Close You Eyes	Kix	Atlantic	6		F L
20	12	Dr. Feelgood	Motley Crue	Eiektra	6	(50)	

December 1989

This Mnth	Prev Mnth	Title	Artist	Label	Wks 20	(UK Pos)	
1	9	We Didn't Start The Fire	Billy Joel	Columbia	10	(7)	
2	-	Another Day In Paradise	Phil Collins	Atlantic	10	(2)	
3	17	Don't Know Much	Linda Ronstadt (feat uring Aaron Neville)	Elektra	11	(2)	
4	13	Back To Life	Soul II Soul Feat. Caron Wheeler	Virgin	11	(1)	G L
5	-	With Every Beat Of My Heart	Taylor Dayne	Arista	9	(53)	
6	2	Blame It On The Rain	Milli Vanilli	Arista	10	(53)	G
7	-	Rhythm Nation	Janet Jackson	A&M	9	(23)	
8	-	Pump Up The Jam	Technotronic Featuring Felly	SBK	12	(2)	F G
9	-	Living In Sin	Bon Jovi	Mercury	7	(35)	
10	5	(It's Just) The Way You Love Me	Paula Abdul	Virgin	8	(74)	
11	-	Just Like Jesse James	Cher	Geffen	8	(11)	
12	7	Angelia	Richard Marx	EMI	7	(45)	
13	4	Love Shack	B-52's	Reprise	8	(2)	F
14	-	This One's For The Children	New Kids On The Block	Columbia	6	(9)	
15	19	Don't Close You Eyes	Kix	Atlantic	6		F L
16	-	Everything	Jody Watley	MCA	10	(74)	
17	-	How Am I Supposed To Live Without You	Michael Bolton	Columbia	10	(3)	
18	-	Leave A Light On	Belinda Carlisle	MCA	5	(4)	L
19	1	When I See You Smile	Bad English	Epic	8	(61)	F
20	10	Poison	Alice Cooper	Epic	6	(2)	L

◆ The year's singles sales decreased 35% and vinyl LPs dropped 59%. However, CD sales rose 24%, cassette singles increased by 240%, and total sales increased to $6.46 billion. In Britain, CDs now outsold vinyl.

◆ In the last year of the decade, Dick Clark left *American Bandstand*, relatively few British artists scored Stateside, Michael Jackson's *Bad* tour (seen by 4.4 million in 15 countries) grossed $125 million, and The Rolling Stones and The Who were America's top live attractions.

◆ Janet Jackson and her ex-choreographer, Paula Abdul, topped the album chart. Jackson with **Rhythm Nation 1814,** crammed full of future Top 5 hits, and Abdul's **Forever Your Girl** which became the first debut LP to include four No. 1s.

◆ Elton John became the first act to headline 30 times at Madison Square Garden.

UK 1990 JAN-MAR

◆ Ruby Turner became the first female British singer to top the US black music chart. A month later Lisa Stansfield followed in her footsteps.

◆ In February female-fronted singles held the top five places. Chart topper Sinead O'Connor also became the first Irish woman to top the LP chart.

▲ Phil Collins's **...But Seriously** sold a million in Britain in a record five weeks, topping the charts for 15 weeks. Oddly, for a week in February, Collins's 'I Wish It Would Rain Down' was the only male vocal record in the UK Top 10!

January 1990

This Mnth	Prev Mnth	Title	Artist	Label	Wks 20	(US Pos)	
1	-	Hangin' Tough	New Kids On The Block	CBS	6	(1)	
2	5	Get A Life	Soul II Soul	10	8	(54)	
3	4	When You Come Back To Me	Jason Donovan	PWL	8		
4	-	Touch Me	49ers	4th & Broadway	7		F
5	14	Got To Get	Rob 'n' Raz Featuring Leila K	Arista	9		F L
6	-	Got To Have Your Love	Mantronix Featuring Wondress	Capitol	7	(82)	F
7	-	Tears On My Pillow	Kylie Minogue	PWL	6		
8	-	The Magic Number/Buddy	De La Soul	Big Life	5		
9	11	Do They Know It's Christmas?	Band Aid II	PWL/Polydor	4		F L
10	10	Dear Jessie	Madonna	Sire	6		
11	3	Lambada	Kaoma	CBS	9	(46)	F L
12	-	Put Your Hands Together	D. Mob Featuring Nuff Juice	London	4		L
13	-	You Make Me Feel (Mighty Real)	Jimmy Somerville	London	4	(87)	
14	-	Going Back To My Roots/Rich In Paradise	FPI Project	Rumour	4		F L
15	-	Deep Heat '89	Latino Rave	Deep Heat	6		F L
16	-	Could Have Told You So	Halo James	Epic	5		F L
17	7	Let's Party	Jive Bunny & The Mastermixers	Music Factory	5		
18	-	Listen To Your Heart	Sonia	Chrysalis	3		
19	-	Nothing Compares 2 U	Sinead O'Connor	Ensign	10	(1)	F L
20	9	Donald Where's Your Troosers	Andy Stewart	Stone	5	(77)	F L

February 1990

This Mnth	Prev Mnth	Title	Artist	Label	Wks 20	(US Pos)	
1	19	Nothing Compares 2 U	Sinead O'Connor	Ensign	10	(1)	F L
2	-	Get Up (Before The Night Is Over)	Technotronic Feat. Ya Kid K	Swanyard	7	(7)	
3	-	Happenin' All Over Again	Lonnie Gordon	Supreme	6		F L
4	7	Tears On My Pillow	Kylie Minogue	PWL	6		
5	6	Got To Have Your Love	Mantronix Featuring Wondress	Capitol	7	(82)	F
6	-	I Wish It Would Rain Down	Phil Collins	Virgin	5	(3)	
7	-	Dub Be Good To Me	Beats International Featuring Lindy Layton	Go Beat	10	(76)	F
8	4	Touch Me	49ers	4th & Broadway	7		F
9	-	Walk On By	Sybil	PWL	5	(74)	
10	-	Instant Replay	Yell!	Fanfare	4		F L
11	-	I Don't Know Anybody Else	Black Box	Deconstruction	5	(23)	
12	16	Could Have Told You So	Halo James	Epic	5		F L
13	-	Live Together	Lisa Stansfield	Arista	3		
14	-	Nothing Ever Happens	Del Amitri	A&M	4		F
15	1	Hangin' Tough	New Kids On The Block	CBS	6	(1)	
16	-	Enjoy The Silence	Depeche Mode	Mute	6	(8)	
17	-	Just Like Jesse James	Cher	Geffen	4	(8)	
18	13	You Make Me Feel (Mighty Real)	Jimmy Somerville	London	4	(87)	
19	-	18 And Life	Skid Row	Atlantic	2	(4)	F
20	-	How Am I Supposed To Live Without You	Michael Bolton	CBS	6	(1)	F

March 1990

This Mnth	Prev Mnth	Title	Artist	Label	Wks 20	(US Pos)	
1	7	Dub Be Good To Me	Beats International/Lindy Layton	Go Beat	10	(76)	F
2	20	How Am I Supposed To Live...	Michael Bolton	CBS	6	(1)	F
3	-	The Brits 1990	Various Artists	RCA	5		F L
4	-	Infinity	Guru Josh	Deconstruction	5		F L
5	-	Love Shack	B-52's	Reprise	8	(3)	
6	1	Nothing Compares 2 U	Sinead O'Connor	Ensign	10	(1)	F
7	-	Blue Savannah	Erasure	Mute	7		
8	-	That Sounds Good To Me	Jive Bunny & The Mastermixers	Music Factory	3		
9	-	Moments In Soul	Jt And The Big Family	Champion	4		F L
10	-	Lily Was Here	David A. Stewart Featuring Candy Dulfer	Anxious	7	(11)	F L
11	-	I'll Be Loving You (Forever)	New Kids On The Block	CBS	4	(1)	
12	16	Enjoy The Silence	Depeche Mode	Mute	6	(8)	
13	11	I Don't Know Anybody Else	Black Box	Deconstruction	5	(23)	
14	-	Strawberry Fields Forever	Candy Flip	Debut	7		F L
15	2	Get Up (Before The Night Is Over)	Technotronic Feat. Ya Kid K	Swanyard	7	(7)	
16	-	The Power	Snap	Arista	10	(2)	F
17	-	Elephant Stone	Stone Roses	Silvertone	2		
18	-	Downtown Train	Rod Stewart	Warner	4	(3)	
19	-	Black Betty	Ram Jam	Epic	3		L
20	-	Birdhouse In Your Soul	They Might Be Giants	Elektra	6		F L

January 1990

This Mnth	Prev Mnth	Title	Artist	Label	Wks 20	(UK Pos)	
1	8	Pump Up The Jam	Technotronic Featuring Felly	SBK	12	(2)	F G
2	17	How Am I Supposed To Live Without You	Michael Bolton	Columbia	10	(3)	
3	2	Another Day In Paradise	Phil Collins	Atlantic	10	(2)	
4	16	Everything	Jody Watley	MCA	10	(74)	
5	7	Rhythm Nation	Janet Jackson	A&M	9	(23)	
6	-	Downtown Train	Rod Stewart	Warner	10	(10)	
7	-	Just Between You And Me	Lou Gramm	Atlantic	7		L
8	-	Free Fallin'	Tom Petty	MCA	8	(64)k	
9	3	Don't Know Much	Linda Ronstadt (Featuring Aaron Neville)	Elektra	11	(2)	
10	-	Two To Make It Right	Seduction	Vendetta	11		F
11	-	Love Song	Tesla	Geffen	9		F
12	14	This One's For The Children	New Kids On The Block	Columbia	6	(9)	
13	5	With Every Beat Of My Heart	Taylor Dayne	Arista	9	(53)	
14	11	Just Like Jesse James	Cher	Geffen	8	(11)	
15	-	Swing The Mood	Jive Bunny & The Mastermixers	Atco	6	(1)	F L
16	-	When The Night Comes	Joe Cocker	Capitol	6	(65)	L
17	-	I Remember You	Skid Row	Atlantic	6	(36)	L
18	-	Opposites Attract	Paula Abdul (duet with The Wild Pair)	Virgin	9	(2)	
19	-	Janie's Got A Gun	Aerosmith	Geffen	7		
20	1	We Didn't Start The Fire	Billy Joel	Columbia	10	(7)	

February 1990

This Mnth	Prev Mnth	Title	Artist	Label	Wks 20	(UK Pos)	
1	18	Opposites Attract	Paula Abdul (with The Wild Pair)	Virgin	9	(2)	
2	10	Two To Make It Right	Seduction	Vendetta	11		F
3	-	Dangerous	Roxette	EMI	8	(6)	
4	19	Janie's Got A Gun	Aerosmith	Geffen	7		
5	-	What Kind Of Man Would I Be?	Chicago	Reprise	6		L
6	-	Escapade	Janet Jackson	A&M	10	(17)	
7	6	Downtown Train	Rod Stewart	Warner	10	(10)	
8	-	All Or Nothing	Milli Vanilli	Arista	6	(74)	L
9	2	How Am I Supposed To Live Without You	Michael Bolton	Columbia	10	(3)	
10	-	We Can't Go Wrong	Cover Girls	Capitol	6		F
11	17	I Remember You	Skid Row	Atlantic	6	(36)	L
12	-	Here We Are	Gloria Estefan	Epic	6	(23)	
13	-	Roam	B-52's	Reprise	9	(17)	L
14	-	Tell Me Why	Expose	Arista	5		
15	-	Price Of Love	Bad English	Epic	7		L
16	8	Free Fallin'	Tom Petty	MCA	8	(64)	
17	-	Peace In Our Time	Eddie Money	Columbia	4		L
18	-	No More Lies	Michel'le	Ruthless	7		F L
19	1	Pump Up The Jam	Technotronic Featuring Felly	SBK	12	(2)	F G
20	4	Everything	Jody Watley	MCA	10	(74)	

March 1990

This Mnth	Prev Mnth	Title	Artist	Label	Wks 20	(UK Pos)	
1	6	Escapade	Janet Jackson	A&M	10	(17)	
2	-	Black Velvet	Alannah Myles	Atlantic	10	(2)	F L
3	13	Roam	B-52's	Reprise	9	(17)	L
4	-	Love Will Lead You Back	Taylor Dayne	Arista	9	(69)	
5	-	I Wish It Would Rain Down	Phil Collins	Atlantic	8	(7)	
6	-	I Go To Extremes	Billy Joel	Columbia	7	(70)	
7	3	Dangerous	Roxette	EMI	8	(6)	
8	15	Price Of Love	Bad English	Epic	7		L
9	18	No More Lies	Michel'le	Ruthless	7		F L
10	-	All Around The World	Lisa Stansfield	Arista	10	(1)	F G
11	-	C'mon And Get My Love	D. Mob	Ffrr	7	(15)	F L
12	-	I'll Be Your Everything	Tommy Page	Sire	7	(53)	F L
13	1	Opposites Attract	Paula Abdul (with The Wild Pair)	Virgin	9	(2)	
14	-	Keep It Together	Madonna	Sire	5		
15	-	Just A Friend	Biz Markie	Cold Chillin'	5	(55)	F G L
16	-	Get Up! (Before The Night Is Over)	Technotronic	SBK	7	(2)	
17	12	Here We Are	Gloria Estefan	Epic	6	(23)	
18	-	Too Late To Say Goodbye	Richard Marx	EMI	5	(38)	
19	-	Don't Wanna Fall In Love	Jane Child	Warner	9	(22)	F L
20	-	No Myth	Michael Penn	RCA	5		F L

◆ New Kids On The Block's **Hangin' Tough** became the first music video to sell a million copies and the title song also gave them a No. 1 in the UK.

◆ Michael Jackson received an award for selling over 110 million records in the 1980s, and Gloria Estefan was presented with a Golden Globe for sales of over five million albums outside the United States.

◆ For the first time three girl groups were simultaneously situated in the Top 10, The Cover Girls, Seduction and Expose. The latter, also equalled a 23-year-old record set by The Supremes, by scoring their seventh Top 10 single in two years.

◆ German-based duo Milli Vanilli won the Grammy for Best New Artist, which they had to return later, when it was revealed that they had not sung on their award winning records.

UK 1990
APR–JUNE

◆ The biggest recorded audience for a one act pop show was broken by Paul McCartney who attracted 184,000 to the Maracana Stadium in Brazil.

◆ Stars at a Wembley show, celebrating the release of Nelson Mandela from a South African prison, included Tracy Chapman, Peter Gabriel, Patti Labelle, Simple Minds and Neil Young. An all-star John Lennon tribute show in Liverpool featured Natalie Cole, Terence Trent D'Arby, Roberta Flack, Hall & Oates, Cyndi Lauper, Kylie Minogue and Wet Wet Wet. Headliners at a huge charity show at Knebworth included Phil Collins, Paul McCartney, Pink Floyd and Status Quo.

◆ Between February and April, Iron Maiden had 10 different twin pack twelve inch records enter the album Top 20. They were re-issues of their earlier singles and were ineligible for the singles chart.

April 1990

This Mnth	Prev Mnth	Title	Artist	Label	Wks 20	(US Pos)	
1	-	Vogue	Madonna	Sire	10	(1)	
2	16	The Power	Snap	Arista	10	(2)	F
3	-	Black Velvet	Alannah Myles	Atlantic	8	(1)	F L
4	-	Kingston Town	UB40	Dep International	8		
5	-	Don't Miss The Partyline	Bizz Nizz	Cooltempo	5		F L
6	5	Love Shack	B-52's	Reprise	8	(3)	
7	-	Step On	Happy Mondays	Factory	7	(57)	
8	-	Hang On To Your Love	Jason Donovan	PWL	4		
9	-	All I Wanna Do Is Make Love To You	Heart	Capitol	8	(2)	
10	14	Strawberry Fields Forever	Candy Flip	Debut	7		F L
11	20	Birdhouse In Your Soul	They Might Be Giants	Elektra	6		F L
12	-	Opposites Attract	Paula Abdul (with The Wild Pair)	Siren	9	(1)	
13	-	Ghetto Heaven	Family Stand	Atlantic	8		F L
14	10	Lily Was Here	David A. Stewart/Candy Dulfer	Anxious	7	(11)	F L
15	7	Blue Savannah	Erasure	Mute	7		
16	-	This Beat Is Technotronic	Technotronic Feat. MC Eric	Swanyard	3		
17	-	Killer	Adamski	MCA	13		
18	-	Mamma Gave Birth To The Soul Children	Queen Latifah & De La Soul	Tommy Boy	4		F L
19	1	Dub Be Good To Me	Beats International/Lindy Layton	Go Beat	10	(76)	F
20	-	Everybody Needs Somebody To Love	Blues Brothers	Atlantic	3		F L

May 1990

This Mnth	Prev Mnth	Title	Artist	Label	Wks 20	(US Pos)	
1	17	Killer	Adamski	MCA	13		
2	-	Dirty Cash	Adventures Of Stevie V	Mercury	9	(25)	F L
3	12	Opposites Attract	Paula Abdul (with The Wild Pair)	Siren	9	(1)	
4	1	Vogue	Madonna	Sire	10	(1)	
5	-	Better The Devil You Know	Kylie Minogue	PWL	6		
6	3	Black Velvet	Alannah Myles	Atlantic	8	(1)	F L
7	-	Cover Girl	New Kids On The Block	CBS	5	(2)	
8	-	A Dream's A Dream	Soul II Soul	Virgin	4	(85)	
9	4	Kingston Town	UB40	Dep International	8		
10	-	Hold On	En Vogue	Atlantic	6	(2)	F L
11	2	The Power	Snap	Arista	10	(2)	F
12	9	All I Wanna Do Is Make Love To You	Heart	Capitol	8	(2)	
13	-	Won't Talk About It	Beats International	Go Beat	5	(76)	L
14	13	Ghetto Heaven	Family Stand	Atlantic	8		F L
15	-	Take Your Time	Mantronix Featuring Wondress	Capitol	4		L
16	7	Step On	Happy Mondays	Factory	7	(57)	
17	-	I Still Haven't Found What I'm Looking For	Chimes	CBS	5		F L
18	-	How Can We Be Lovers	Michael Bolton	CBS	4	(3)	
19	-	November Spawned A Monster	Morrissey	HMV	2		
20	-	Something Happened On The Way To Heaven	Phil Collins	Virgin	3	(4)	

June 1990

This Mnth	Prev Mnth	Title	Artist	Label	Wks 20	(US Pos)	
1	-	World In Motion	Englandneworder	Factory	9		L
2	1	Killer	Adamski	MCA	13		
3	-	Hear The Drummer (Get Wicked)	Chad Jackson	Big Wave	6		F L
4	-	Doin' The Doo	Betty Boo	Rhythm King	7		F
5	-	Sacrifice/Healing Hands	Elton John	Rocket	10	(18)	
6	-	Venus	Don Pablo's Animals	Rumour	6		F L
7	-	It Must Have Been Love	Roxette	EMI	9	(1)	
8	2	Dirty Cash	Adventures Of Stevie V	Mercury	9	(25)	F L
9	-	Step By Step	New Kids On The Block	CBS	3	(1)	
10	-	The Only One I Know	Charlatans	Situation Two	5		F
11	5	Better The Devil You Know	Kylie Minogue	PWL	6		
12	-	Oops Up	Snap	Arista	8	(35)	
13	-	Hold On	Wilson Phillips	SBK	7	(1)	F
14	-	Nessun Dorma	Luciano Pavarotti	Decca	6		F
15	10	Hold On	En Vogue	Atlantic	6	(2)	F L
16	17	I Still Haven't Found What I'm...	Chimes	CBS	5		F L
17	-	Star	Erasure	Mute	4		
18	-	The Only Rhyme That Bites	MC Tunes Versus 808 State	ZTT	6		F
19	-	Papa Was A Rolling Stone	Was (Not Was)	Fontana	3		
20	7	Cover Girl	New Kids On The Block	CBS	5	(2)	

US 1990
APR–JUNE

April 1990

This Mnth	Prev Mnth	Title	Artist	Label	Wks 20	(UK Pos)	
1	19	Don't Wanna Fall In Love	Jane Child	Warner	9	(22)	F L
2	10	All Around The World	Lisa Stansfield	Arista	10	(1)	F G
3	-	Nothing Compares 2 U	Sinead O'Connor	Chrysalis	12	(1)	F G L
4	12	I'll Be Your Everything	Tommy Page	Sire	7	(53)	F L
5	-	I Wanna Be Rich	Calloway	Solar	10		F L
6	-	Here And Now	Luther Vandross	Epic	7	(43)	
7	4	Love Will Lead You Back	Taylor Dayne	Arista	9	(69)	
8	-	How Can We Be Lovers	Michael Bolton	Columbia	8	(10)	
9	-	Whole Wide World	A'me Lorain	RCA	6		F L
10	-	Forever	Kiss	Mercury	6	(65)	L
11	-	Without You	Motley Crue	Elektra	6	(39)	
12	2	Black Velvet	Alannah Myles	Atlantic	10	(2)	F L
13	-	Whip Appeal	Babyface	Solar	6		
14	16	Get Up! (Before The Night Is Over)	Technotronic	SBK	7	(2)	
15	5	I Wish It Would Rain Down	Phil Collins	Atlantic	8	(7)	
16	-	What It Takes	Aerosmith	Geffen	7		
17	-	Heartbeat	Seduction	Vendetta	5	(75)	
18	-	All I Wanna Do Is Make Love To You	Heart	Capitol	10	(8)	
19	-	All My Life	Linda Ronstadt (Featuring Aaron Neville)	Elektra	4		L
20	-	Sending All My Love	Linear	Atlantic	11		F L

May 1990

This Mnth	Prev Mnth	Title	Artist	Label	Wks 20	(UK Pos)	
1	3	Nothing Compares 2 U	Sinead O'Connor	Chrysalis	12	(1)	F G L
2	-	Vogue	Madonna	Sire	11	(1)	G
3	18	All I Wanna Do Is Make Love To You	Heart	Capitol	10	(8)	
4	5	I Wanna Be Rich	Calloway	Solar	10		F L
5	-	Hold On	Wilson Phillips	SBK	13	(6)	F
6	-	Alright	Janet Jackson	A&M	9	(20)	
7	20	Sending All My Love	Linear	Atlantic	11		F L
8	8	How Can We Be Lovers	Michael Bolton	Columbia	8	(10)	
9	-	Poison	Bell Biv Devoe	MCA	12	(19)	F G
10	16	What It Takes	Aerosmith	Geffen	7		
11	-	This Old Heart Of Mine	Rod Stewart With Ronald Isley	Warner	6	(51)	
12	-	It Must Have Been Love	Roxette	EMI	12	(3)	
13	-	Love Child	Sweet Sensation	Atco	5		
14	1	Don't Wanna Fall In Love	Jane Child	Warner	9	(22)	F L
15	13	Whip Appeal	Babyface	Solar	6		
16	2	All Around The World	Lisa Stansfield	Arista	10	(1)	F G
17	-	U Can't Touch This	M.C. Hammer	Capitol	9	(3)	F
18	-	The Humpty Dance	Digital Underground	Tommy Boy	8		F G L
19	-	Ooh La La (I Can't Get Over You)	Perfect Gentlemen	Columbia	4		F L
20	-	Room At The Top	Adam Ant	MCA	3	(13)	F L

June 1990

This Mnth	Prev Mnth	Title	Artist	Label	Wks 20	(UK Pos)	
1	12	It Must Have Been Love	Roxette	EMI	12	(3)	
2	5	Hold On	Wilson Phillips	SBK	13	(6)	F
3	9	Poison	Bell Biv Devoe	MCA	12	(19)	F G
4	2	Vogue	Madonna	Sire	11	(1)	G
5	-	Step By Step	New Kids On The Block	Columbia	9	(2)	G
6	3	All I Wanna Do Is Make Love To You	Heart	Capitol	10	(8)	
7	-	Ready Or Not	After 7	Virgin	9		F
8	17	U Can't Touch This	M.C. Hammer	Capitol	9	(3)	F
9	-	Do You Remember?	Phil Collins	Atlantic	7	(57)	
10	-	Hold On	En Vogue	Atlantic	12	(5)	F G
11	6	Alright	Janet Jackson	A&M	9	(20)	
12	7	Sending All My Love	Linear	Atlantic	11		F L
13	18	The Humpty Dance	Digital Underground	Tommy Boy	8		F G L
14	-	I'll Be Your Shelter	Taylor Dayne	Arista	7	(43)	
15	1	Nothing Compares 2 U	Sinead O'Connor	Chrysalis	12	(1)	F G L
16	-	She Ain't Worth It	Glenn Medeiros (Featuring Bobby Brown)	MCA	10	(12)	L
17	-	Children Of The Night	Richard Marx	EMI	4	(54)	
18	19	Ooh La La (I Can't Get Over You)	Perfect Gentlemen	Columbia	4		F L
19	-	Rub You The Right Way	Johnny Gill	Motown	10		F
20	-	Baby, It's Tonight	Jude Cole	Reprise	5		F L

◆ Two different songs with the same title, 'Hold On', introduced the world to two of the early 1990s' top acts, En Vogue and Wilson Phillips.

▲ Paula Abdul (above) broke Connie Francis's 28-year-old record when she clocked up 68 consecutive weeks in the US Top 40.

◆ For the first time, female singers held the top three rungs in April with their first hits. Simultaneously a record four female singers held the top spots on the album chart: Bonnie Raitt, Sinead O'Connor, Janet Jackson and Paula Abdul.

UK 1990
JULY-SEPT

▲ Pink Floyd's *The Wall* show in Berlin drew 200,000 people and an estimated one billion saw it on TV. Among those appearing were Bryan Adams, The Band, Van Morrison, Sinead O'Connor (above) and The Scorpions.

◆ Elton John's 'Sacrifice'/'Healing Hands' not only helped him equal Elvis Presley's American record of (at least) one Top 40 hit a year for 21 years, it also gave him his first British solo chart topper.

◆ Steve Miller's 1974 US No. 1, 'The Joker', finally repeated that feat in the UK after it was heard in a TV advertisement for Levi jeans.

July 1990

This Mnth	Prev Mnth	Title	Artist	Label	Wks 20	(US Pos)	
1	5	Sacrifice/Healing Hands	Elton John	Rocket	10	(18)	
2	-	Mona	Craig McLachlan & Check 1-2	Epic	8		F
3	7	It Must Have Been Love	Roxette	EMI	9	(1)	
4	14	Nessun Dorma	Luciano Pavarotti	Decca	6		F
5	-	U Can't Touch This	M.C. Hammer	Capitol	11	(8)	F
6	-	Thunderbirds Are Go	FAB Featuring MC Parker	Brothers Org.	5		F L
7	12	Oops Up	Snap	Arista	8	(35)	
8	1	World In Motion	Englandneworder	Factory	9		L
9	-	Close To You	Maxi Priest	10	6	(1)	
10	-	Turtle Power	Partners In Kryme	SBK	8	(13)	F L
11	-	One Love	Stone Roses	Silvertone	4		
12	13	Hold On	Wilson Phillips	SBK	7	(1)	F
13	-	She Ain't Worth It	Glenn Medeiros Featuring Bobby Brown	London	4	(1)	L
14	-	Hanky Panky	Madonna	Sire	6	(10)	
15	18	The Only Rhyme That Bites	MC Tunes Versus 808 State	ZTT	6		F
16	-	I'm Free	Soup Dragons	Raw TV/Big Life	8	(79)	F L
17	-	Rockin' Over The Beat	Technotronic Featuring Ya Kid K	Swanyard	5	(95)	
18	-	Naked In The Rain	Blue Pearl	W.A.U.!Mr.Modo	9		F
19	-	Thinking Of You	Maureen	Urban	4		F L
20	4	Doin' The Doo	Betty Boo	Rhythm King	7		F

August 1990

This Mnth	Prev Mnth	Title	Artist	Label	Wks 20	(US Pos)	
1	10	Turtle Power	Partners In Kryme	SBK	8	(13)	F L
2	-	Tom's Diner	DNA Featuring Suzanne Vega	A&M	7	(5)	F
3	18	Naked In The Rain	Blue Pearl	W.A.U.!Mr.Modo	9		F
4	5	U Can't Touch This	M.C. Hammer	Capitol	11	(8)	F
5	16	I'm Free	Soup Dragons	Raw TV/Big Life	8	(79)	F L
6	14	Hanky Panky	Madonna	Sire	6	(10)	
7	-	Tonight	New Kids On The Block	CBS	8	(7)	
8	-	Itsy Bitsy Teeny Weeny Yellow Polka Dot Bikini	Bombalurina	Carpet	8		F
9	1	Sacrifice/Healing Hands	Elton John	Rocket	10	(18)	
10	-	Thieves In The Temple	Prince	Paisley Park	3	(6)	
11	17	Rockin' Over The Beat	Technotronic Feat. Ya Kid K	Swanyard	5	(95)	
12	-	Listen To Your Heart/Dangerous	Roxette	EMI	5	(1)	
13	2	Mona	Craig McLachlan & Check 1-2	Epic	8		F
14	-	Hardcore Uproar	Together	Ffrr	4		F L
15	-	LFO	LFO	Warp	3		F L
16	-	Where Are You Baby?	Betty Boo	Rhythm King	6		
17	-	California Dreamin'/Carry The Blame	River City People	EMI	5		F L
18	-	Blaze Of Glory	Jon Bon Jovi	Vertigo	3	(1)	F L
19	3	It Must Have Been Love	Roxette	EMI	9	(1)	
20	-	Tricky Disco	Tricky Disco	Warp	3		F L

September 1990

This Mnth	Prev Mnth	Title	Artist	Label	Wks 20	(US Pos)	
1	-	The Joker	Steve Miller Band	Capitol	7		L
2	-	Groove Is In The Heart	Deee-Lite	Elektra	8	(4)	F L
3	-	Four Bacharach & David Songs (EP)	Deacon Blue	CBS	6		
4	8	Itsy Bitsy Teeny Weeny Yellow Polka Dot Bikini	Bombalurina	Carpet	8		F
5	-	What Time Is Love	KLF/Children Of The Revolution	KLF Comms.	7	(57)	F
6	16	Where Are You Baby?	Betty Boo	Rhythm King	6		
7	7	Tonight	New Kids On The Block	CBS	8	(7)	
8	-	Vision Of Love	Mariah Carey	CBS	5	(1)	F
9	-	The Space Jungle	Adamski	MCA	4		L
10	-	Show Me Heaven	Maria McKee	Epic	9		F L
11	-	Groovy Train	Farm	Produce	5	(41)	F
12	-	Praying For Time	George Michael	Epic	4	(1)	
13	-	Holy Smoke	Iron Maiden	EMI	2		
14	3	Naked In The Rain	Blue Pearl	W.A.U.!Mr.Modo	9		F
15	-	I've Been Thinking About You	Londonbeat	Anxious	7	(1)	L
16	12	Listen To Your Heart/Dangerous	Roxette	EMI	5	(1)	
17	-	Can Can You Party	Jive Bunny & The Mastermixers	Music Factory	3		
18	-	Rhythm Of The Rain	Jason Donovan	PWL	2		
19	2	Tom's Diner	DNA Featuring Suzanne Vega	A&M	7	(5)	F
20	-	Silhouettes	Cliff Richard	EMI	4		

302

This Mnth	Prev Mnth	Title	Artist	Label	Wks 20	(UK Pos)	
1	16	She Ain't Worth It	Glenn Medeiros Featuring Bobby Brown	MCA	10	(12)	L
2	10	Hold On	En Vogue	Atlantic	12	(5)	F G
3	-	Cradle Of Love	Billy Idol	Chrysalis	11	(34)	L
4	5	Step By Step	New Kids On The Block	Columbia	9	(2)	G
5	19	Rub You The Right Way	Johnny Gill	Motown	10		F
6	-	The Power	Snap	Arista	10	(1)	F G
7	1	It Must Have Been Love	Roxette	EMI	12	(3)	
8	-	Enjoy The Silence	Depeche Mode	Sire	7	(6)	
9	-	Vision Of Love	Mariah Carey	Columbia	12	(9)	F
10	-	Girls Nite Out	Tyler Collins	RCA	7		F L
11	14	I'll Be Your Shelter	Taylor Dayne	Arista	7	(43)	
12	-	When I'm Back On My Feet Again	Michael Bolton	Columbia	6	(44)	
13	3	Poison	Bell Biv Devoe	MCA	12	(19)	F G
14	9	Do You Remember?	Phil Collins	Atlantic	7	(57)	
15	2	Hold On	Wilson Phillips	SBK	13	(6)	F
16	6	King Of Wishful Thinking	Go West	EMI	7	(18)	F
17	-	Mentirosa	Mellow Man Ace	Capitol	4		F L
18	-	You Can't Deny It	Lisa Stansfield	Arista	3		L
19	-	Hanky Panky	Madonna	Sire	3	(2)	
20	-	If Wishes Came True	Sweet Sensation	Atco	10		L

This Mnth	Prev Mnth	Title	Artist	Label	Wks 20	(UK Pos)	
1	9	Vision Of Love	Mariah Carey	Columbia	12	(9)	F
2	20	If Wishes Came True	Sweet Sensation	Atco	10		L
3	-	Come Back To Me	Janet Jackson	A&M	8	(20)	
4	6	The Power	Snap	Arista	10	(1)	F G
5	-	Unskinny Bop	Poison	Enigma	10	(15)	
6	3	Cradle Of Love	Billy Idol	Chrysalis	11	(34)	L
7	-	Do Me	Bell Biv Devoe	MCA	11	(56)	L
8	5	Rub You The Right Way	Johnny Gill	Motown	10		F
9	-	Blaze Of Glory	Jon Bon Jovi	Mercury	10	(13)	F G
10	-	Have You Seen Her	M.C. Hammer	Capitol	9	(8)	
11	16	King Of Wishful Thinking	Go West	EMI	7	(18)	F
12	-	Jerk Out	Time	Paisley Park	6		L
13	1	She Ain't Worth It	Glenn Medeiros Featuring Bobby Brown	MCA	10	(12)	L
14	-	Epic	Faith No More	Slash	7	(25)	F L
15	-	Release Me	Wilson Phillips	SBK	10	(36)	
16	-	Could This Be Love	Seduction	A&M	5		L
17	-	Make You Sweat	Keith Sweat	Vintertainment	8		
18	10	Girls Nite Out	Tyler Collins	RCA	7		F L
19	12	When I'm Back On My Feet Again	Michael Bolton	Columbia	6	(44)	
20	2	Hold On	En Vogue	Atlantic	12	(5)	F G

This Mnth	Prev Mnth	Title	Artist	Label	Wks 20	(UK Pos)	
1	15	Release Me	Wilson Phillips	SBK	10	(36)	
2	9	Blaze Of Glory	Jon Bon Jovi	Mercury	10	(13)	F G
3	7	Do Me	Bell Biv Devoe	MCA	11	(56)	L
4	-	(Can't Live Without Your) Love And Affection	Nelson	DGC	10	(54)	F
5	5	Unskinny Bop	Poison	Enigma	10	(15)	
6	10	Have You Seen Her	M.C. Hammer	Capitol	9	(8)	
7	-	Thieves In The Temple	Prince	Paisley Park	6	(7)	
8	-	Close To You	Maxi Priest	Charisma	11	(7)	F
9	2	If Wishes Came True	Sweet Sensation	Atco	10		L
10	-	Something Happened On The Way To Heaven	Phil Collins	Atlantic	7	(15)	L
11	-	Tonight	New Kids On The Block	Columbia	5	(3)	
12	3	Come Back To Me	Janet Jackson	A&M	8	(20)	
13	-	Praying For Time	George Michael	Columbia	8	(6)	
14	1	Vision Of Love	Mariah Carey	Columbia	12	(9)	F
15	-	Oh Girl	Paul Young	Columbia	6	(25)	L
16	14	Epic	Faith No More	Slash	7	(25)	F L
17	-	My, My, My	Johnny Gill	Motown	6		L
18	-	Can't Stop Falling Into Love	Cheap Trick	Epic	3		L
19	12	Jerk Out	Time	Paisley Park	6		L
20	-	Heart Of Stone	Taylor Dayne	Arista	4		

US 1990

JULY-SEPT

◆ M.C. Hammer's **Please Hammer Don't Hurt 'Em** topped the album chart for 21 weeks (spending a record 32 consecutive weeks in the Top 2), selling over 10 million copies.

◆ New Kids On The Block, who had three of the Top 4 US music videos, signed a $10 million sponsorship deal with McDonalds. Incidentally, in July, Maurice Starr, the group's producer/manager, had discovered three of the top four singles artists, the others being Bell Biv Devoe and Bobby Brown.

◆ Columbia Records were very excited about newcomer Mariah Carey whose debut single 'Vision Of Love' was the first of her five successive No. 1s.

◆ Guitar hero Stevie Ray Vaughan died in a helicopter crash and soul giant Curtis Mayfield was paralysed after a lighting rack fell on him during a show.

◆ Bobby Vinton's 1963 US chart topper, 'Blue Velvet', hit in Britain as Berlin's 'Take My Breath Away' returned. The Righteous Brothers' 'You've Lost That Lovin' Feeling' spent a record third time in the Top 10, and the duo's 25-year-old 'Unchained Melody' became the year's top seller.

◆ In October, for the first time since March 1986, there were no Stock Aitken & Waterman records in the Top 40. They had produced over 100 Top 75 entries.

◆ New Kids On The Block scored their seventh Top 10 single in 1990 equalling Bill Haley & The Comets' 1956 record. NKOTB reportedly earned $115 million in 1990.

◆ Queen, who had not graced the American Top 20 since 1984, signed a $10 million deal with the Walt Disney-owned Hollywood label.

October 1990

This Mnth	Prev Mnth	Title	Artist	Label	Wks 20	(US Pos)	
1	10	Show Me Heaven	Maria McKee	Epic	9		F L
2	-	Blue Velvet	Bobby Vinton	Epic	8		L
3	-	The Anniversary Waltz - Part 1	Status Quo	Vertigo	6		
4	15	I've Been Thinking About You	Londonbeat	Anxious	7	(1)	L
5	-	I Can't Stand It	Twenty 4 Seven Featuring Captain Hollywood	BCM	6		F
6	-	Megamix	Technotronic	Swanyard	5		L
7	-	A Little Time	Beautiful South	Go! Discs	8		
8	-	So Hard	Pet Shop Boys	Parlophone	3	(62)	
9	-	Have You Seen Her	M.C. Hammer	Capitol	4	(4)	
10	-	Fascinating Rhythm	Bass-O-Matic	Virgin	5		F L
11	2	Groove Is In The Heart	Deee-Lite	Elektra	8	(4)	F L
12	1	The Joker	Steve Miller Band	Capitol	7		L
13	-	It's A Shame (My Sister)	Monie Love Feat. True Image	Cooltempo	4	(26)	
14	-	Let's Try Again/Didn't I Blow Your Mind	New Kids On The Block	CBS	3	(53)	
15	-	I'm Your Baby Tonight	Whitney Houston	Arista	6	(1)	
16	11	Groovy Train	Farm	Produce	5	(41)	F
17	-	Unchained Melody	Righteous Brothers	Verve	11	(13)	
18	-	Kinky Afro	Happy Mondays	Factory	4		
19	-	From A Distance	Cliff Richard	EMI	3		
20	-	Cult Of Snap	Snap	Arista	3		

November 1990

This Mnth	Prev Mnth	Title	Artist	Label	Wks 20	(US Pos)	
1	17	Unchained Melody	Righteous Brothers	Verve	11	(13)	
2	7	A Little Time	Beautiful South	Go! Discs	8		
3	-	Don't Worry	Kim Appleby	Parlophone	8		F
4	-	Take My Breath Away	Berlin	CBS	6		L
5	-	Step Back In Time	Kylie Minogue	PWL	4		
6	-	(We Want) The Same Thing	Belinda Carlisle	MCA	5		
7	-	Fog On The Tyne (Revisited)	Gazza And Lindisfarne	Best	4		F L
8	-	Fantasy	Black Box	De Construction	6		
9	15	I'm Your Baby Tonight	Whitney Houston	Arista	6	(1)	
10	-	I'll Be Your Baby Tonight	Robert Palmer And UB40	EMI	6		
11	1	Show Me Heaven	Maria McKee	Epic	9		F L
12	-	Unbelievable	EMF	Parlophone	8	(1)	F
13	-	To Love Somebody	Jimmy Somerville	London	4		
14	-	Working Man	Rita McNeil	Polydor	4		F L
15	18	Kinky Afro	Happy Mondays	Factory	4		
16	-	Cubik/Olympic	808 State	ZTT	3		
17	-	Ice Ice Baby	Vanilla Ice	SBK	10	(1)	F
18	3	The Anniversary Waltz - Part 1	Status Quo	Vertigo	6		
19	-	Close To Me	Cure	Elektra	3	(97)	
20	2	Blue Velvet	Bobby Vinton	Epic	8		L

December 1990

This Mnth	Prev Mnth	Title	Artist	Label	Wks 20	(US Pos)	
1	17	Ice Ice Baby	Vanilla Ice	SBK	10	(1)	F
2	12	Unbelievable	EMF	Parlophone	8	(1)	F
3	1	Unchained Melody	Righteous Brothers	Verve	11	(13)	
4	-	Saviour's Day	Cliff Richard	EMI	6		
5	-	Justify My Love	Madonna	Sire	6	(1)	
6	-	All Together Now	Farm	Produce	8		
7	3	Don't Worry	Kim Appleby	Parlophone	8		F
8	-	You've Lost That Lovin' Feeling/Ebb Tide	Righteous Brothers	Verve	6		L
9	-	Kinky Boots	Patrick MacNee & Honor Blackman	Deram	4		F L
10	-	Wicked Game	Chris Isaak	London	5	(6)	F
11	-	Mary Had A Little Boy	Snap	Arista	6		
12	-	Pray	M.C. Hammer	Capitol	7	(2)	
13	-	Sadness Part 1	Enigma	Virgin Int.	9	(5)	
14	-	It Takes Two	Rod Stewart & Tina Turner	Warner	4		
15	-	Falling	Julee Cruise	Warner	4		F L
16	-	This One's For The Children	New Kids On The Block	CBS	4	(7)	
17	8	Fantasy	Black Box	De Construction	6		
18	-	The Grease Megamix	John Travolta/O. Newton-John	Polydor	6		L
19	-	Just This Side Of Love	Malandra Burrows	YTV	4		F L
20	-	King Of The Road (EP)	Proclaimers	Chrysalis	3		L

This Mnth	Prev Mnth	Title	Artist	Label	Wks 20	(UK Pos)	
1	-	I Don't Have The Heart	James Ingram	Warner	10		L
2	13	Praying For Time	George Michael	Columbia	8	(6)	
3	8	Close To You	Maxi Priest	Charisma	11	(7)	F
4	-	Ice Ice Baby	Vanilla Ice	SBK	11	(1)	F G
5	-	Black Cat	Janet Jackson	A&M	7	(15)	
6	4	(Can't Live Without Your) Love And Affection	Nelson	DGC	10	(54)	F
7	-	Romeo	Dino	Island	6		L
8	-	Giving You The Benefit	Pebbles	MCA	7	(73)	
9	-	Can't Stop	After 7	Virgin	8	(54)	
10	-	Everybody Everybody	Black Box	RCA	7	(16)	F
11	10	Something Happened On The Way To Heaven	Phil Collins	Atlantic	7	(15)	L
12	-	Suicide Blonde	INXS	Atlantic	5	(11)	
13	-	Love Takes Time	Mariah Carey	Columbia	14	(37)	
14	15	Oh Girl	Paul Young	Columbia	6	(25)	L
15	-	Unchained Melody	Righteous Brothers	Verve	6	(1)	G
16	2	Blaze Of Glory	Jon Bon Jovi	Mercury	10	(13)	F G
17	3	Do Me	Bell Biv Devoe	MCA	11	(56)	L
18	17	My, My, My	Johnny Gill	Motown	6		L
19	-	Pray	M.C. Hammer	Capitol	7	(8)	
20	1	Release Me	Wilson Phillips	SBK	10	(36)	

1	13	Love Takes Time	Mariah Carey	Columbia	14	(37)	
2	19	Pray	M.C. Hammer	Capitol	7	(8)	
3	-	More Than Words Can Say	Alias	EMI	8		F
4	4	Ice Ice Baby	Vanilla Ice	SBK	11	(1)	F G
5	-	Groove Is In The Heart	Deee-Lite	Elektra	10	(2)	F L
6	1	I Don't Have The Heart	James Ingram	Warner	10		L
7	-	I'm Your Baby Tonight	Whitney Houston	Arista	12	(5)	
8	-	Something To Believe In	Poison	Enigma	11	(35)	L
9	-	Knockin' Boots	Candyman	Epic	5		F G L
10	8	Giving You The Benefit	Pebbles	MCA	7	(73)	
11	5	Black Cat	Janet Jackson	A&M	7	(15)	
12	-	Feels Good	Tony! Toni! Tone!	Wing	9		F
13	-	Because I Love You (The Postman Song)	Stevie B	LMR	12	(6)	L
14	-	From A Distance	Bette Midler	Atlantic	12	(45)	G L
15	-	Cherry Pie	Warrant	Columbia	5	(35)	
16	9	Can't Stop	After 7	Virgin	8	(54)	
17	-	So Close	Daryl Hall John Oates	Arista	5	(69)	L
18	-	Hippychick	Soho	Atco	4	(8)	F L
19	12	Suicide Blonde	INXS	Atlantic	5	(11)	
20	3	Close To You	Maxi Priest	Charisma	11	(7)	F

1	13	Because I Love You (The Postman Song)	Stevie B	LMR	12	(6)	L
2	14	From A Distance	Bette Midler	Atlantic	12	(45)	G L
3	7	I'm Your Baby Tonight	Whitney Houston	Arista	12	(5)	
4	-	Impulsive	Wilson Phillips	SBK	10	(42)	
5	-	Tom's Diner	DNA Featuring Suzanne Vega	A&M	10	(2)	F L
6	-	Justify My Love	Madonna	Sire	10	(2)	G
7	-	The Way You Do The Things You Do	UB40	Virgin	10	(49)	
8	8	Something To Believe In	Poison	Enigma	11	(35)	L
9	1	Love Takes Time	Mariah Carey	Columbia	14	(37)	
10	-	High Enough	Damn Yankees	Warner	13		F
11	5	Groove Is In The Heart	Deee-Lite	Elektra	10	(2)	F L
12	-	Freedom	George Michael	Columbia	8	(28)	
13	-	Miracle	Jon Bon Jovi	Mercury	6	(29)	L
14	-	Sensitivity	Ralph Tresvant	MCA	11	(18)	F L
15	-	Love Will Never Do (Without You)	Janet Jackson	A&M	11	(34)	
16	12	Feels Good	Tony! Toni! Tone!	Wing	9		F
17	3	More Than Words Can Say	Alias	EMI	8		F
18	-	Stranded	Heart	Capitol	5	(60)	L
19	17	So Close	Daryl Hall John Oates	Arista	5	(69)	L
20	-	Wiggle It	2 In A Room	Cutting	5	(3)	F L

US
1990
OCT-DEC

◆ Record and tape sales in 1990 increased 14% with total shipments of $7.5 billion. Vinyl albums were down 60% and CD sales up 33%.

▲ 1990 closed with Vanilla Ice's 'Ice Ice Baby' becoming rap's first No. 1 and with Taylor Dayne's run of seven successive Top 10 hits ending.

◆ Matsushita bought MCA Records for $3 billion and CBS Records changed their name to Sony.

◆ The deaths were reported of *West Side Story* composer Leonard Bernstein, previous hitmakers Dee Clark and Ronnie Dyson and rock'n'roll pioneer/writer Jesse Stone.

UK 1991 JAN-MAR

◆ Another spate of re-entries hit the UK Top 20 including records by Bill Medley & Jennifer Warnes, The Clash, Madonna, John Travolta & Olivia Newton-John and Free, while Patsy Cline's 1961 American hit, 'Crazy' made its UK debut.

◆ Eric Clapton played a record 24 nights at London's prestigious Royal Albert Hall.

◆ Michael Jackson, whose **Bad** album had now passed the 25 million sales mark globally, signed the world's biggest record deal (reportedly worth somewhere between $50 million and a billion!) with Sony.

◆ Despite the fact that The Simpsons cartoon TV series was only seen by a minority of the British public who had satellite or cable TV, the single, 'Do The Bartman', took the quirky quintet to the top.

January 1991

This Mnth	Prev Mnth	Title	Artist	Label	Wks 20	(US Pos)	
1	13	Sadness Part 1	Enigma	Virgin Int.	9	(5)	
2	-	Crazy	Seal	ZTT	9	(8)	F
3	18	The Grease Megamix	John Travolta/O. Newton-John	Polydor	6		L
4	1	Ice Ice Baby	Vanilla Ice	SBK	10	(1)	F
5	-	Bring Your Daughter...To The Slaughter	Iron Maiden	EMI	3		
6	6	All Together Now	Farm	Produce	8		
7	-	Gonna Make You Sweat	C&C Music Factory/F. Williams	CBS	6	(1)	F
8	-	3 A.M. Eternal	KLF/Children Of The Revolution	KLF Comms.	8	(5)	
9	-	(I've Had) The Time Of My Life	Bill Medley & Jennifer Warnes	RCA	4		L
10	8	You've Lost That Lovin' Feeling	Righteous Brothers	Verve	6		L
11	12	Pray	M.C. Hammer	Capitol	7	(2)	
12	11	Mary Had A Little Boy	Snap	Arista	6		
13	-	International Bright Young Thing	Jesus Jones	Food	3		F L
14	-	I Can't Take The Power	Off-Shore	CBS	4		F L
15	5	Justify My Love	Madonna	Sire	6	(1)	
16	-	Mercy Mercy Me - I Want You	Robert Palmer	EMI	4	(16)	L
17	-	Innuendo	Queen	Parlophone	3		
18	4	Saviour's Day	Cliff Richard	EMI	6		
19	-	The Total Mix	Black Box	De Construction	4		
20	-	All The Man That I Need	Whitney Houston	Arista	3	(1)	

February 1991

This Mnth	Prev Mnth	Title	Artist	Label	Wks 20	(US Pos)	
1	-	Do The Bartman	Simpsons	Geffen	10		F
2	8	3 A.M. Eternal	KLF/Children Of The Revolution	KLF Comms.	8	(5)	
3	-	Wiggle It	2 In A Room	Big Life	6	(15)	F L
4	-	(I Wanna Give You) Devotion	Nomad/MC Mikee Freedom	Rumour	8		F
5	-	What Do I Have To Do	Kylie Minogue	PWL	5		
6	-	Only You	Praise	Epic	5		F L
7	-	I Believe	EMF	Parlophone	4		
8	-	Hippychick	Soho	S&M/Savage	5	(14)	F L
9	-	Get Here	Oleta Adams	Fontana	7	(5)	F L
10	-	Cry For Help	Rick Astley	RCA	5	(7)	L
11	2	Crazy	Seal	ZTT	9	(8)	F
12	-	Play That Funky Music	Vanilla Ice	SBK	4	(4)	L
13	17	Innuendo	Queen	Parlophone	3		
14	1	Sadness Part 1	Enigma	Virgin Int.	9	(5)	
15	-	You Got The Love	Source Featuring Candi Staton	Truelove	7		F L
16	-	G.L.A.D.	Kim Appleby	Parlophone	3		
17	7	Gonna Make You Sweat	C&C Music Factory/F. Williams	CBS	6	(1)	F
18	-	In Yer Face	808 State	ZTT	4		
19	-	All Right Now	Free	Island	5		L
20	16	Mercy Mercy Me - I Want You	Robert Palmer	EMI	4	(16)	L

March 1991

This Mnth	Prev Mnth	Title	Artist	Label	Wks 20	(US Pos)	
1	-	Should I Stay Or Should I Go	Clash	CBS	6		
2	15	You Got The Love	Source Featuring Candi Staton	Truelove	7		F L
3	1	Do The Bartman	Simpsons	Geffen	10		F
4	-	The Stonk	Hale & Pace & The Stonkers	London	5		F L
5	-	Crazy For You	Madonna	Sire	4		
6	-	Because I Love You (Postman Song)	Stevie B	LMR	6	(1)	F L
7	-	Move Your Body (Elevation)	Xpansions	Optimism	5		F L
8	-	Joyride	Roxette	EMI	7	(1)	
9	4	(I Wanna Give You) Devotion	Nomad/MC Mikee Freedom	Rumour	8		F
10	-	The One And Only	Chesney Hawkes	Chrysalis	6	(10)	F L
11	-	It's Too Late	Quartz Introducing Dina Carroll	Mercury	6		F L
12	-	Rhythm Of My Heart	Rod Stewart	Warner	8		
13	19	All Right Now	Free	Island	5		L
14	9	Get Here	Oleta Adams	Fontana	7	(5)	F L
15	-	Where The Streets Have No Name-Can't Take My Eyes Off You/How Can You Expect To Be Taken Seriously	Pet Shop Boys	EMI	4	(72)	
16	-	Love Rears It's Ugly Head	Living Colour	Epic	5		F L
17	2	3 A.M. Eternal	KLF/Children Of The Revolution	KLF Comms.	8	(5)	
18	-	Let There Be Love	Simple Minds	Virgin	4		
19	18	In Yer Face	808 State	ZTT	4		
20	-	Secret Love	Bee Gees	Warner	5		

US 1991 JAN-MAR

January 1991

This Mnth	Prev Mnth	Title	Artist	Label	Wks 20	(UK Pos)	
1	6	Justify My Love	Madonna	Sire	10	(2)	G
2	15	Love Will Never Do (Without You)	Janet Jackson	A&M	11	(34)	
3	10	High Enough	Damn Yankees	Warner	13		F
4	-	The First Time	Surface	Columbia	12	(60)	
5	14	Sensitivity	Ralph Tresvant	MCA	11	(18)	F L
6	1	Because I Love You (The Postman Song)	Stevie B	LMR	12	(6)	L
7	-	Gonna Make You Sweat	C&C Music Factory Featuring Freedom Williams	Columbia	11	(3)	F G
8	2	From A Distance	Bette Midler	Atlantic	12	(45)	G L
9	5	Tom's Diner	DNA Featuring Suzanne Vega	A&M	10	(2)	F L
10	-	Play That Funky Music	Vanilla Ice	SBK	8	(10)	L
11	-	After The Rain	Nelson	DGC	9		
12	4	Impulsive	Wilson Phillips	SBK	10	(42)	
13	-	I'm Not In Love	Will To Power	Epic	6	(29)	L
14	-	Miles Away	Winger	Atlantic	7	(56)	L
15	3	I'm Your Baby Tonight	Whitney Houston	Arista	12	(5)	
16	-	Just Another Dream	Cathy Dennis	Polydor	5	(13)	F
17	7	The Way You Do The Things You Do	UB40	Virgin	10	(49)	
18	-	I'll Give All My Love To You	Keith Sweat	Vintertainment	6		
19	12	Freedom	George Michael	Columbia	8	(28)	
20	-	All The Man That I Need	Whitney Houston	Arista	10	(13)	

February 1991

This Mnth	Prev Mnth	Title	Artist	Label	Wks 20	(UK Pos)	
1	7	Gonna Make You Sweat	C&C Music Factory Featuring Freedom Williams	Columbia	11	(3)	F G
2	4	The First Time	Surface	Columbia	12	(60)	
3	20	All The Man That I Need	Whitney Houston	Arista	10	(13)	
4	-	One More Try	Timmy T	Quality	12		F G L
5	-	Where Does My Heart Beat Now	Celine Dion	Epic	9	(73)	F
6	10	Play That Funky Music	Vanilla Ice	SBK	8	(10)	L
7	18	I'll Give All My Love To You	Keith Sweat	Vintertainment	6		
8	2	Love Will Never Do (Without You)	Janet Jackson	A&M	11	(34)	
9	-	Someday	Mariah Carey	Columbia	10	(38)	
10	-	Disappear	INXS	Atlantic	6	(21)	L
11	5	Sensitivity	Ralph Tresvant	MCA	11	(18)	F L
12	11	After The Rain	Nelson	DGC	9		
13	-	I Saw Red	Warrant	Columbia	6		L
14	-	Wicked Game	Chris Isaak	Reprise	6	(10)	F L
15	13	I'm Not In Love	Will To Power	Epic	6	(29)	L
16	1	Justify My Love	Madonna	Sire	10	(2)	G
17	-	Love Makes Things Happen	Pebbles	MCA	4		L
18	16	Just Another Dream	Cathy Dennis	Polydor	5	(13)	F
19	-	Around The Way Girl	L.L. Cool J	Def Jam	8	(36)	
20	3	High Enough	Damn Yankees	Warner	13		F

March 1991

This Mnth	Prev Mnth	Title	Artist	Label	Wks 20	(UK Pos)	
1	4	One More Try	Timmy T	Quality	12		F G L
2	9	Someday	Mariah Carey	Columbia	10	(38)	
3	-	Coming Out Of The Dark	Gloria Estefan	Epic	9	(25)	
4	-	This House	Tracie Spencer	Capitol	8	(65)	F L
5	-	Get Here	Oleta Adams	Fontana	7	(4)	F L
6	3	All The Man That I Need	Whitney Houston	Arista	10	(13)	
7	-	Show Me The Way	Styx	A&M	6		L
8	-	Hold You Tight	Tara Kemp	Giant	10	(69)	F
9	-	All This Time	Sting	A&M	6	(22)	
10	5	Where Does My Heart Beat Now	Celine Dion	Epic	9	(73)	F
11	-	Rescue Me	Madonna	Sire	5	(3)	
12	-	I've Been Thinking About You	Londonbeat	Radioactive	10	(2)	F
13	-	You're In Love	Wilson Phillips	SBK	10	(29)	
14	1	Gonna Make You Sweat	C&C Music Factory Featuring Freedom Williams	Columbia	11	(3)	F G
15	-	Signs	Tesla	Geffen	8	(70)	L
16	19	Around The Way Girl	L.L. Cool J	Def Jam	8	(36)	
17	-	Iesha	Another Bad Creation	Motown	9		F
18	14	Wicked Game	Chris Isaak	Reprise	6	(10)	F L
19	-	Sadeness Part 1	Enigma	Charisma	8	(1)	F
20	-	Waiting For Love	Alias	EMI	3		L

◆ R&B legends The Impressions, Ike & Tina Turner, John Lee Hooker, Wilson Pickett, "Little Miss Sharecropper" Lavern Baker and the late Jimmy Reed and Howlin' Wolf were all inducted into the Rock And Roll Hall Of Fame.

▲ As Whitney Houston (above) equalled Madonna's (female) record of nine No. 1s, it was reported that the latter had sold 54 million albums and 26 million singles worldwide.

◆ Vanilla Ice's **To The Extreme** sold five million in 12 weeks. It was the first No. 1 not available on vinyl.

◆ Janet Jackson signed a $50 million record deal with Virgin.

UK 1991
APR-JUNE

▲ New Kids On The Block ended their European tour at Wembley. They had played 31 dates and grossed $8.8 million.

◆ As sister Dannii scored her second successive hit, Kylie Minogue became the first artist to see her first 13 hit singles all go into the Top 10.

◆ Small Faces' singer Steve Marriott died in a fire, and ex-Temptation David Ruffin died of drug-related causes.

◆ For the first time three consecutive No. 1s came from films. 'The One And Only' (*Buddy's Song*), 'The Shoop Shoop Song' (*Mermaids*) and 'I Wanna Sex You Up' (*New Jack City*).

April 1991

This Mnth	Prev Mnth	Title	Artist	Label	Wks 20	(US Pos)	
1	-	Sit Down	James	Fontana	8		F
2	-	The Whole Of The Moon	Waterboys	Ensign	6		F L
3	10	The One And Only	Chesney Hawkes	Chrysalis	6	(10)	F L
4	12	Rhythm Of My Heart	Rod Stewart	Warner	8		
5	-	Rescue Me	Madonna	Sire	5	(9)	
6	-	The Size Of A Cow	Wonder Stuff	Polydor	5		
7	8	Joyride	Roxette	EMI	7	(1)	
8	-	Deep, Deep Trouble	Simpsons Feat. Bart & Homer	Geffen	5	(69)	L
9	-	Love & Kisses	Dannii Minogue	MCA	5		F
10	-	Human Nature	Gary Clail On-U Sound System	Perfecto	5		F L
11	-	Anthem	N-Joi	Deconstruction	5		F
12	20	Secret Love	Bee Gees	Warner	5		
13	-	I've Got News For You	Feargal Sharkey	Virgin	4		L
14	11	It's Too Late	Quartz Introducing Dina Carroll	Mercury	6		F L
15	18	Let There Be Love	Simple Minds	Virgin	4		
16	-	The Shoop Shoop Song (It's In His Kiss)	Cher	Geffen	11	(33)	
17	15	Where The Streets Have No Name...	Pet Shop Boys	EMI	4	(72)	
18	-	Snap Mega Mix	Snap	Arista	3		
19	-	Sailing On The Seven Seas	OMD	Virgin	8		
20	4	The Stonk	Hale & Pace & The Stonkers	London	5		F L

May 1991

This Mnth	Prev Mnth	Title	Artist	Label	Wks 20	(US Pos)	
1	16	The Shoop Shoop Song (It's In His...)	Cher	Geffen	11	(33)	
2	-	Last Train To Trancentral	KLF	KLF Comms.	7		
3	19	Sailing On The Seven Seas	OMD	Virgin	8		
4	-	Senza Una Donna (Without A Woman)	Zucchero & Paul Young	London	6		F
5	-	Touch Me (All Night Long)	Cathy Dennis	Polydor	6	(2)	
6	-	Promise Me	Beverley Craven	Epic	8		F L
7	-	There's No Other Way	Blur	Food	5	(82)	F
8	-	Gypsy Woman (La Da Dee)	Crystal Waters	A&M	6	(8)	F
9	-	Get The Message	Electronic	Factory	4		
10	-	Born Free	Vic Reeves & The Roman Numerals	Sense	4		F
11	1	Sit Down	James	Fontana	8		F
12	-	Tainted Love	Soft Cell/Marc Almond	Mercury	5		L
13	-	Ring Ring Ring (Ha Ha Hey)	De La Soul	Big Life	4		L
14	2	The Whole Of The Moon	Waterboys	Ensign	6		F L
15	-	Future Love (EP)	Seal	ZTT	3		
16	-	Fading Like A Flower (Every Time You Leave)	Roxette	EMI	3	(2)	
17	-	I Wanna Sex You Up	Color Me Badd	Giant	9	(2)	F
18	-	Quadrophonia	Quadrophonia	ARS	2		F L
19	-	Anasthasia	T99	Citybeat	2		F L
20	-	Baby Baby	Amy Grant	A&M	7	(1)	F

June 1991

This Mnth	Prev Mnth	Title	Artist	Label	Wks 20	(US Pos)	
1	17	I Wanna Sex You Up	Color Me Badd	Giant	9	(2)	F
2	1	The Shoop Shoop Song (It's In His...)	Cher	Geffen	11	(33)	
3	20	Baby Baby	Amy Grant	A&M	7	(1)	F
4	6	Promise Me	Beverley Craven	Epic	8		F L
5	-	Shiny Happy People	R.E.M.	Warner	6	(10)	
6	8	Gypsy Woman (La Da Dee)	Crystal Waters	A&M	6	(8)	F
7	-	Thinking About Your Love	Kenny Thomas	Cooltempo	8		
8	-	Shocked	Kylie Minogue	PWL	4		
9	-	Any Dream Will Do	Jason Donovan	Really Useful	9		
10	-	Do You Want Me	Salt-N-Pepa	ffrr	6	(21)	
11	12	Tainted Love	Soft Cell/Marc Almond	Mercury	5		L
12	-	Light My Fire	Doors	Elektra	3		L
13	-	Only Fools (Never Fall In Love)	Sonia	IQ	5		
14	-	Holiday	Madonna	Sire	3		
15	2	Last Train To Trancentral	KLF	KLF Comms.	7		
16	5	Touch Me (All Night Long)	Cathy Dennis	Polydor	6	(2)	
17	-	Move That Body	Technotronic Featuring Reggie	ARS	3		
18	-	The Motown Song	Rod Stewart	Warner	4	(10)	
19	-	Success	Dannii Minogue	MCA	3		
20	-	Chorus	Erasure	Mute	6		

April 1991

This Mnth	Prev Mnth	Title	Artist	Label	Wks 20	(UK Pos)	
1	13	You're In Love	Wilson Phillips	SBK	10	(29)	
2	12	I've Been Thinking About You	Londonbeat	Radioactive	10	(2)	F
3	-	Baby Baby	Amy Grant	A&M	11	(2)	
4	8	Hold You Tight	Tara Kemp	Giant	10	(69)	F
5	-	Joyride	Roxette	EMI	9	(4)	
6	19	Sadeness Part 1	Enigma	Charisma	8	(1)	F
7	-	Rico Suave	Gerardo	Interscope	6		F
8	-	Cry For Help	Rick Astley	RCA	7	(7)	L
9	-	I Like The Way (The Kissing Game)	Hi-Five	Jive	12	(43)	F
10	3	Coming Out Of The Dark	Gloria Estefan	Epic	9	(25)	
11	17	Iesha	Another Bad Creation	Motown	9		F
12	-	Here We Go	C&C Music Factory Featuring Freedom Williams & Zelma Davis	Columbia	9	(20)	
13	-	Touch Me (All Night Long)	Cathy Dennis	Polydor	10	(5)	
14	15	Signs	Tesla	Geffen	8	(70)	L
15	-	I Touch Myself	Divinyls	Virgin	8	(10)	F L
16	1	One More Try	Timmy T	Quality	12		F G L
17	-	Voices That Care	Voices That Care	Giant	6		F L
18	-	Round And Round	Tevin Campbell	Qwest	5		F
19	-	Rhythm Of My Heart	Rod Stewart	Warner	8		
20	4	This House	Tracie Spencer	Capitol	8	(65)	F L

May 1991

This Mnth	Prev Mnth	Title	Artist	Label	Wks 20	(UK Pos)	
1	9	I Like The Way (The Kissing Game)	Hi-Five	Jive	12	(43)	F
2	13	Touch Me (All Night Long)	Cathy Dennis	Polydor	10	(5)	
3	12	Here We Go	C&C Music Factory/Freedom Williams/Zelma Davis	Columbia	9	(20)	
4	3	Baby Baby	Amy Grant	A&M	11	(2)	
5	15	I Touch Myself	Divinyls	Virgin	8	(10)	F L
6	5	Joyride	Roxette	EMI	9	(4)	
7	19	Rhythm Of My Heart	Rod Stewart	Warner	8		
8	-	I Don't Wanna Cry	Mariah Carey	Columbia	10		
9	-	More Than Words	Extreme	A&M	11	(2)	F
10	-	Silent Lucidity	Queensryche	EMI	7	(18)	F L
11	-	I Wanna Sex You Up	Color Me Badd	Giant	13	(1)	F P
12	8	Cry For Help	Rick Astley	RCA	7	(7)	L
13	-	Love Is A Wonderful Thing	Michael Bolton	Columbia	8	(23)	
14	-	Losing My Religion	R.E.M.	Warner	9	(19)	
15	17	Voices That Care	Voices That Care	Giant	6		F L
16	-	You Don't Have To Go Home Tonight	Triplets	Mercury	4		F L
17	-	More Than Ever	Nelson	DGC	4		L
18	1	You're In Love	Wilson Phillips	SBK	10	(29)	
19	-	Save Some Love	Keedy	Arista	4		F L
20	2	I've Been Thinking About You	Londonbeat	Radioactive	10	(2)	F

June 1991

This Mnth	Prev Mnth	Title	Artist	Label	Wks 20	(UK Pos)	
1	-	Rush Rush	Paula Abdul	Virgin	11	(6)	
2	11	I Wanna Sex You Up	Color Me Badd	Giant	13	(1)	F P
3	9	More Than Words	Extreme	A&M	11	(2)	F
4	13	Love Is A Wonderful Thing	Michael Bolton	Columbia	8	(23)	
5	14	Losing My Religion	R.E.M.	Warner	9	(19)	
6	8	I Don't Wanna Cry	Mariah Carey	Columbia	10		
7	-	Unbelievable	EMF	EMI	12	(3)	F
8	-	Power Of Love-Love Power	Luther Vandross	Epic	8	(46)	
9	-	Strike It Up	Black Box	RCA	5	(16)	L
10	1	I Like The Way (The Kissing Game)	Hi-Five	Jive	12	(43)	F
11	-	Playground	Another Bad Creation	Motown	5		L
12	-	Right Here, Right Now	Jesus Jones	SBK	10	(31)	F
13	-	Miracle	Whitney Houston	Arista	5		
14	-	Couple Days Off	Huey Lewis & The News	EMI	4		L
15	-	Here I Am (Come And Take Me)	UB40	Virgin	7	(46)	
16	2	Touch Me (All Night Long)	Cathy Dennis	Polydor	10	(5)	
17	10	Silent Lucidity	Queensryche	EMI	7	(18)	F L
18	-	How Can I Ease The Pain	Lisa Fischer	Elektra	5		F L
19	7	Rhythm Of My Heart	Rod Stewart	Warner	8		
20	-	Gypsy Woman (She's Homeless)	Crystal Waters	Mercury	6	(2)	F

US
1991
APR-JUNE

◆ When *Billboard* changed their method of calculating album charts, country and rap records fared much better. Also, records entering at No. 1 were no longer rare.

◆ NWA's album **Efil4zaggin** was the first No. 1 LP since Led Zeppelin's **Presence**, in 1976, which did not contain a hit single.

◆ Session singer Yvette Marine claimed she had sung lead on some Paula Abdul tracks. This did not seem to affect Abdul's sales as 'Rush Rush' and **Spellbound** hit the top.

◆ Almost 100 recording stars gave their support to the troops in the Gulf by singing on the hit 'Voices That Care'. Among them were Paul Anka, Michael Bolton, Garth Brooks, Bobby Brown, Celine Dion, Fresh Prince, Little Richard, Donny Osmond, Kenny Rogers and Luther Vandross.

UK 1991

JULY-SEPT

▲ Bryan Adams's recording of '(Everything I Do) I Do It For You' was the world's top selling single in 1991. It sold over three million in America, and became the first million seller for six years in Britain, where it spent a record 16 successive weeks at the top.

◆ Of the current wave of new UK chart makers only EMF, Jesus Jones, The KLF, Cathy Dennis and Seal were selling well in the USA.

◆ Opera singer Luciano Pavarotti topped the LP chart with **Essential Pavarotti II**. In America his **In Concert** album completed a year at the helm of the classical chart.

July 1991

This Mnth	Prev Mnth	Title	Artist	Label	Wks 20	(US Pos)	
1	-	(Everything I Do) I Do It For You	Bryan Adams	A&M	22	(1)	G
2	9	Any Dream Will Do	Jason Donovan	Really Useful	9		
3	20	Chorus	Erasure	Mute	6		
4	-	Rush Rush	Paula Abdul	Virgin	7	(1)	
5	7	Thinking About Your Love	Kenny Thomas	Cooltempo	8		
6	-	You Could Be Mine	Guns N' Roses	Geffen	7	(29)	
7	-	Now That We've Found Love	Heavy D. & The Boyz	MCA	8	(11)	F L
8	-	Always There	Incognito Featuring Jocelyn Brown	Talkin Loud	5		F
9	1	I Wanna Sex You Up	Color Me Badd	Giant	9	(2)	F
10	10	Do You Want Me	Salt-N-Pepa	ffrr	6	(21)	
11	-	Things That Make You Go Hmmmm....	C&C Music Factory Featuring Freedom Williams	Columbia	7	(4)	L
12	-	7 Ways To Love	Cola Boy	Arista	4		F L
13	-	Pandora's Box	OMD	Virgin	5		L
14	-	Are You Mine?	Bros	Columbia	3		L
15	-	It Ain't Over 'Til It's Over	Lenny Kravitz	Virgin America	4	(2)	F
16	-	Love And Understanding	Cher	Geffen	5	(17)	
17	-	I Touch Myself	Divinyls	Virgin America	5	(4)	F L
18	-	More Than Words	Extreme	A&M	8	(1)	
19	18	The Motown Song	Rod Stewart	Warner	4	(10)	
20	-	Move Any Mountain	Shamen	One Little Indian	7	(38)	F

August 1991

This Mnth	Prev Mnth	Title	Artist	Label	Wks 20	(US Pos)	
1	1	(Everything I Do) I Do It For You	Bryan Adams	A&M	22	(1)	G
2	18	More Than Words	Extreme	A&M	8	(1)	
3	-	I'm Too Sexy	Right Said Fred	Tug	11	(1)	F
4	20	Move Any Mountain	Shamen	One Little Indian	7	(38)	F
5	7	Now That We've Found Love	Heavy D. & The Boyz	MCA	8	(11)	F L
6	-	All For Love	Color Me Badd	Giant	6	(1)	L
7	-	Winter In July	Bomb The Bass	Rhythm King	5		L
8	-	Set Adrift On Memory Bliss	P.M. Dawn	Gee Street	5	(1)	F
9	11	Things That Make You Go Hmmmm....	C&C Music Factory Featuring Freedom Williams	Columbia	7	(4)	L
10	-	Summertime	D.J. Jazzy Jeff & Fresh Prince	Jive	5	(4)	F
11	-	Twist & Shout	Deacon Blue	Columbia	4		
12	13	Pandora's Box	OMD	Virgin	5		L
13	2	Any Dream Will Do	Jason Donovan	Really Useful	9		
14	-	Charly	Prodigy	XL	7		F
15	-	Enter Sandman	Metallica	Vertigo	2	(16)	
16	6	You Could Be Mine	Guns N' Roses	Geffen	7	(29)	
17	-	Sunshine On A Rainy Day	Zoe	M&G	9		F L
18	-	Jump To The Beat	Dannii Minogue	MCA	3		
19	-	Happy Together	Jason Donovan	PWL	4		
20	16	Love And Understanding	Cher	Geffen	5	(17)	

September 1991

This Mnth	Prev Mnth	Title	Artist	Label	Wks 20	(US Pos)	
1	1	(Everything I Do) I Do It For You	Bryan Adams	A&M	22	(1)	G
2	3	I'm Too Sexy	Right Said Fred	Tug	11	(1)	F
3	-	Insanity	Oceanic	Dead Dead Good	11		F
4	14	Charly	Prodigy	XL	7		F
5	17	Sunshine On A Rainy Day	Zoe	M&G	9		F L
6	-	Let's Talk About Sex	Salt-N-Pepa	ffrr	9	(13)	
7	-	Gett Off	Prince/New Power Generation	Paisley Park	5	(21)	
8	-	What Can You Do For Me	Utah Saints	ffrr	7		F
9	-	I'll Be Back	Arnee & The Terminaters	Epic	4		F L
10	-	Love...Thy Will Be Done	Martika	Columbia	5	(10)	
11	-	Love To Hate You	Erasure	Mute	6		
12	-	Peace	Sabrina Johnson	East West	6		F L
13	8	Set Adrift On Memory Bliss	P.M. Dawn	Gee Street	5	(1)	F
14	-	Everybody's Free (To Feel Good)	Rozalla	Pulse 8	6	(37)	F
15	6	All For Love	Color Me Badd	Giant	6	(1)	L
16	-	20th Century Boy	Marc Bolan & T. Rex	Marc On Wax	4		L
17	-	Don't Cry	Guns N' Roses	Geffen	2	(10)	
18	2	More Than Words	Extreme	A&M	8	(1)	
19	-	Good Vibrations	Marky Mark & The Funky Bunch Featuring Loleatta Holloway	Interscope	3	(1)	F L
20	-	Something Got Me Started	Simply Red	East West	4	(23)	

July 1991

This Mnth	Prev Mnth	Title	Artist	Label	Wks 20	(UK Pos)	
1	7	Unbelievable	EMF	EMI	12	(3)	F
2	1	Rush Rush	Paula Abdul	Virgin	11	(6)	
3	12	Right Here, Right Now	Jesus Jones	SBK	10	(31)	F
4	2	I Wanna Sex You Up	Color Me Badd	Giant	13	(1)	F P
5	-	Place In This World	Michael W. Smith	Reunion	7		F L
6	-	P.A.S.S.I.O.N.	Rythm Syndicate	Impact	9	(58)	F
7	-	Piece Of My Heart	Tara Kemp	Giant	6		L
8	-	(Everything I Do) I Do It For You	Bryan Adams	A&M	13	(1)	P
9	15	Here I Am (Come And Take Me)	UB40	Virgin	7	(46)	
10	-	Summertime	D.J. Jazzy Jeff & Fresh Prince	Jive	9	(8)	G
11	8	Power Of Love/Love Power	Luther Vandross	Epic	8	(46)	
12	-	Lily Was Here	David A. Stewart Introducing Candy Dulfer	Anxious	5	(6)	F L
13	20	Gypsy Woman (She's Homeless)	Crystal Waters	Mercury	6	(2)	F
14	-	Every Heartbeat	Amy Grant	A&M	10	(25)	
15	-	It Ain't Over 'Til It's Over	Lenny Kravitz	Virgin America	9	(11)	F L
16	3	More Than Words	Extreme	A&M	11	(2)	F
17	-	The Dream Is Still Alive	Wilson Phillips	SBK	5		
18	-	Temptation	Corina	Cutting	7		F L
19	-	Walking In Memphis	Marc Cohn	Atlantic	5	(22)	F L
20	-	Fading Like A Flower (Every Time You Leave)	Roxette	EMI	8	(12)	L

August 1991

This Mnth	Prev Mnth	Title	Artist	Label	Wks 20	(UK Pos)	
1	8	(Everything I Do) I Do It For You	Bryan Adams	A&M	13	(1)	P
2	14	Every Heartbeat	Amy Grant	A&M	10	(25)	
3	15	It Ain't Over 'Til It's Over	Lenny Kravitz	Virgin America	9	(11)	F L
4	20	Fading Like A Flower (Every Time...)	Roxette	EMI	8	(12)	L
5	10	Summertime	D.J. Jazzy Jeff & Fresh Prince	Jive	9	(8)	G
6	-	Wind Of Change	Scorpions	Mercury	10	(2)	F L
7	18	Temptation	Corina	Cutting	7		F L
8	6	P.A.S.S.I.O.N.	Rythm Syndicate	Impact	9	(58)	F
9	-	3 A.M. Eternal	KLF	Arista	7	(1)	F
10	-	I Can't Wait Another Minute	Hi-Five	Jive	10		
11	-	The Promise Of A New Day	Paula Abdul	Captive/Virgin	9	(52)	
12	-	Motownphilly	Boyz II Men	Motown	12	(23)	F G
13	3	Right Here, Right Now	Jesus Jones	SBK	10	(31)	F
14	-	Crazy	Seal	Sire	7	(2)	F
15	-	I'll Be There	Escape Club	Atlantic	5		L
16	-	Things That Make You Go Hmmmm....	C&C Music Factory Featuring Freedom Williams	Columbia	9	(4)	L
17	1	Unbelievable	EMF	EMI	12	(3)	F
18	-	Unforgettable	Natalie Cole	Elektra	6	(19)	L
19	-	Time, Love And Tenderness	Michael Bolton	Columbia	8	(28)	
20	-	Too Many Walls	Cathy Dennis	Polydor	9	(17)	L

September 1991

This Mnth	Prev Mnth	Title	Artist	Label	Wks 20	(UK Pos)	
1	-	I Adore Mi Amor	Color Me Badd	Giant	10	(44)	
2	12	Motownphilly	Boyz II Men	Motown	12	(23)	F G
3	16	Things That Make You Go	C&C Music Factory/F. Williams	Columbia	9	(4)	L
4	-	Good Vibrations	Marky Mark & The Funky Bunch Loleatta Holloway	Interscope	9	(14)	F
5	1	(Everything I Do) I Do It For You	Bryan Adams	A&M	13	(1)	P
6	11	The Promise Of A New Day	Paula Abdul	Captive/Virgin	9	(52)	
7	19	Time, Love And Tenderness	Michael Bolton	Columbia	8	(28)	
8	20	Too Many Walls	Cathy Dennis	Polydor	9	(17)	L
9	-	Love Of A Lifetime	Firehouse	Epic	7		
10	-	Emotions	Mariah Carey	Columbia	11	(17)	
11	-	The Motown Song	Rod Stewart	Warner	6	(10)	
12	-	Now That We Found Love	Heavy D. & The Boyz	Uptown	7	(2)	F
13	9	3 A.M. Eternal	KLF	Arista	7	(1)	F
14	10	I Can't Wait Another Minute	Hi-Five	Jive	10		
15	-	Shiny Happy People	R.E.M.	Warner	5	(6)	
16	-	Something To Talk About	Bonnie Raitt	Capitol	8		F
17	6	Wind Of Change	Scorpions	Mercury	10	(2)	F L
18	-	Do Anything	Natural Selection	East West	12	(69)	F L
19	14	Crazy	Seal	Sire	7	(2)	F
20	2	Every Heartbeat	Amy Grant	A&M	10	(25)	

◆ **Ropin' the Wind** by Garth Brooks, which shipped 2.6 million in its first week, was the first country album ever to enter in pole position. It remained at the top for 18 weeks, and sold over nine million copies. At times Brooks held the top 3 places on the country chart.

◆ Over 750,000 people saw Paul Simon's free Central Park concerts.

▲ R.E.M. snared a record six MTV awards including Best Video for 'Losing My Religion'.

◆ AMA award winners Aerosmith signed a $40 million deal with Columbia, and Motley Crue re-signed to Elektra for a similar amount.

UK 1991 OCT-DEC

◆ In 1991, more singles charted than ever. Records tended to enter higher and have shorter chart life spans.

◆ At times the Top 6 all came from different countries: Ireland, England, Holland, Canada, New Zealand and Germany.

◆ The Rolling Stones signed to Virgin for a $40 million advance, while Madonna's new deal guaranteed her at least $5 million per album.

▲ Freddie Mercury died. His group Queen ended the year as Britain's top album act and top singles group, and their **Greatest Hits** album was certified as a three million seller.

October 1991

This Mnth	Prev Mnth	Title	Artist	Label	Wks 20	(US Pos)	
1	1	(Everything I Do) I Do It For You	Bryan Adams	A&M	22	(1)	G
2	-	Wind Of Change	Scorpions	Mercury	7	(4)	F L
3	3	Insanity	Oceanic	Dead Dead Good	11		F
4	6	Let's Talk About Sex	Salt-N-Pepa	ffrr	9	(13)	
5	-	Saltwater	Julian Lennon	Virgin	6		L
6	11	Love To Hate You	Erasure	Mute	6		
7	14	Everybody's Free (To Feel Good)	Rozalla	Pulse 8	6	(37)	F
8	-	Always Look On The Bright Side Of Life	Monty Python	Virgin	5		F L
9	-	World In Union	Kiri Te Kanawa	Columbia	7		F L
10	-	Get Ready For This	2 Unlimited	PWL Continental	8	(76)	
11	12	Peace	Sabrina Johnson	East West	6		F L
12	5	Sunshine On A Rainy Day	Zoe	M&G	9		F L
13	2	I'm Too Sexy	Right Said Fred	Tug	11	(1)	F
14	-	Best Of You	Kenny Thomas	Cooltempo	3		
15	-	Such A Feeling	Bizarre Inc	Vinyl Solution	5		F
16	-	Change	Lisa Stansfield	Arista	4	(30)	
17	-	Live Your Life Be Free	Belinda Carlisle	Virgin	3		
18	-	Dizzy	Vic Reeves & The Wonder Stuff	Sense	8		
19	20	Something Got Me Started	Simply Red	East West	4	(23)	
20	-	Baby Love	Dannii Minogue	MCA	2		

November 1991

This Mnth	Prev Mnth	Title	Artist	Label	Wks 20	(US Pos)	
1	18	Dizzy	Vic Reeves & The Wonder Stuff	Sense	8		
2	10	Get Ready For This	2 Unlimited	PWL Continental	8	(76)	F
3	1	(Everything I Do) I Do It For You	Bryan Adams	A&M	22	(1)	G
4	-	Rhythm Is A Mystery	K-Klass	De Construction	4		F
5	-	The Fly	U2	Island	3	(58)	
6	-	If You Were Here With Me Now	Kylie Minogue/Keith Washington	PWL	5		
7	9	World In Union	Kiri Te Kanawa	Columbia	7		F L
8	-	Activ 8 (Come With Me)	Altern 8	Network	5		F
9	-	Is There Anybody Out There?	Bassheads	De Construction	4		F
10	-	Black Or White	Michael Jackson	Epic	9	(1)	
11	-	No Son Of Mine	Genesis	Virgin	3	(12)	
12	-	Playing With Knives	Bizarre Inc	Vinyl Solution	3		
13	2	Wind Of Change	Scorpions	Mercury	7	(4)	F L
14	8	Always Look On The Bright Side Of Life	Monty Python	Virgin	5		F L
15	-	American Pie	Don McLean	Liberty	4		L
16	-	Killer (EP)	Seal	ZTT	3	(100)	
17	-	When A Man Loves A Woman	Michael Bolton	Columbia	3	(1)	
18	-	Go	Moby	Outer-Rhythm	4		F L
19	3	Insanity	Oceanic	Dead Dead Good	11		F
20	-	DJs Take Control/Way In My Brain	SL2	XL	2		F

December 1991

This Mnth	Prev Mnth	Title	Artist	Label	Wks 20	(US Pos)	
1	-	Don't Let The Sun Go Down On Me	George Michael & Elton John	Epic	6	(1)	
2	-	When You Tell Me That You Love Me	Diana Ross	EMI	9		
3	-	Justified And Ancient	KLF Feat. Tammy Wynette	KLF Comms.	9	(11)	
4	10	Black Or White	Michael Jackson	Epic	9	(1)	
5	-	Driven By You	Brian May	Parlophone	6		F
6	-	Ride Like The Wind	East Side Beat	ffrr	6		F L
7	-	Too Blind To See It	Kym Sims	Atco	8	(38)	F
8	-	Stars	Simply Red	East West	6	(44)	
9	-	Bohemian Rhapsody/These Are The Days Of Our Lives	Queen	Parlophone	10	(2)	P
10	-	Don't Talk Just Kiss	Right Said Fred/Jocelyn Brown	Tug	7	(76)	
11	-	Live And Let Die	Guns N' Roses	Geffen	4	(33)	
12	8	Activ 8 (Come With Me)	Altern 8	Network	5		F
13	-	Smells Like Teen Spirit	Nirvana	DGC	3	(6)	F
14	-	We Should Be Together	Cliff Richard	EMI	3		
15	-	Rocket Man (I Think It's Going To Be A Long Long Time)	Kate Bush	Mercury	4		
16	1	Dizzy	Vic Reeves & The Wonder Stuff	Sense	8		
17	-	If You Go Away	New Kids On The Block	Columbia	2		L
18	-	Addams Groove	Hammer	Capitol	7	(7)	
19	-	Sound	James	Fontana	3		
20	-	The Bare Necessities Megamix	UK Mixmasters	Connect	4		F L

This Mnth	Prev Mnth	Title	Artist	Label	Wks 20	(UK Pos)	
1	10	Emotions	Mariah Carey	Columbia	11	(17)	
2	18	Do Anything	Natural Selection	East West	12	(69)	F L
3	-	Romantic	Karyn White	Warner	11	(23)	
4	4	Good Vibrations	Marky Mark & The Funky Bunch Featuring Loleatta Holloway	Interscope	9	(14)	F
5	-	Hole Hearted	Extreme	A&M	9	(12)	L
6	1	I Adore Mi Amor	Color Me Badd	Giant	10	(44)	
7	16	Something To Talk About	Bonnie Raitt	Capitol	8		F
8	-	Can't Stop This Thing We Started	Bryan Adams	A&M	11	(12)	
9	-	Everybody Plays The Fool	Aaron Neville	A&M	5		L
10	9	Love Of A Lifetime	Firehouse	Epic	7		
11	-	Real Real Real	Jesus Jones	SBK	6	(19)	L
12	-	Love...Thy Will Be Done	Martika	Columbia	5	(9)	L
13	2	Motownphilly	Boyz II Men	Motown	12	(23)	F G
14	-	Cream	Prince & The New Power Generation.	Paisley Park	12	(15)	
15	-	Don't Want To Be A Fool	Luther Vandross	Epic	5		
16	15	Shiny Happy People	R.E.M.	Warner	5	(6)	
17	-	O.P.P.	Naughty By Nature	Tommy Boy	14	(35)	F P
18	12	Now That We Found Love	Heavy D. & The Boyz	Uptown	7	(2)	F
19	-	Enter Sandman	Metallica	Elektra	3	(5)	F L
20	5	(Everything I Do) I Do It For You	Bryan Adams	A&M	13	(1)	P

This Mnth	Prev Mnth	Title	Artist	Label	Wks 20	(UK Pos)	
1	14	Cream	Prince/New Power Generation	Paisley Park	12	(15)	
2	8	Can't Stop This Thing We Started	Bryan Adams	A&M	11	(12)	
3	-	When A Man Loves A Woman	Michael Bolton	Columbia	12	(8)	
4	-	It's So Hard To Say Goodbye To Yesterday	Boyz II Men	Motown	14		
5	17	O.P.P.	Naughty By Nature	Tommy Boy	14	(35)	F P
6	3	Romantic	Karyn White	Warner	11	(23)	
7	-	Set Adrift On Memory Bliss	P.M. Dawn	Gee Street/Island	13	(3)	F
8	-	Set The Night To Music	Roberta Flack With Maxi Priest	Atlantic	8		L
9	2	Do Anything	Natural Selection	East West	12	(69)	F L
10	-	Don't Cry	Guns N' Roses	Geffen	12	(8)	
11	1	Emotions	Mariah Carey	Columbia	11	(17)	
12	-	That's What Love Is For	Amy Grant	A&M	11	(60)	
13	-	The One And Only	Chesney Hawkes	Chrysalis	7	(1)	F L
14	-	Blowing Kisses In The Wind	Paula Abdul	Captive	10		
15	11	Real Real Real	Jesus Jones	SBK	6	(19)	L
16	-	I Wonder Why	Curtis Stigers	Arista	4	(5)	F L
17	5	Hole Hearted	Extreme	A&M	9	(12)	L
18	-	Let's Talk About Sex	Salt-N-Pepa	Next Plateau	8	(2)	
19	-	Black Or White	Michael Jackson	Epic	12	(1)	G
20	15	Don't Want To Be A Fool	Luther Vandross	Epic	5		

This Mnth	Prev Mnth	Title	Artist	Label	Wks 20	(UK Pos)	
1	19	Black Or White	Michael Jackson	Epic	12	(1)	G
2	4	It's So Hard To Say Goodbye To Yesterday	Boyz II Men	Motown	14		
3	7	Set Adrift On Memory Bliss	P.M. Dawn	Gee Street/Island	13	(3)	F
4	3	When A Man Loves A Woman	Michael Bolton	Columbia	12	(8)	
5	-	All 4 Love	Color Me Badd	Giant	15	(5)	
6	14	Blowing Kisses In The Wind	Paula Abdul	Captive	10		
7	-	Can't Let Go	Mariah Carey	Columbia	14	(20)	
8	-	Finally	Ce Ce Peniston	A&M	14	(2)	F
9	12	That's What Love Is For	Amy Grant	A&M	11	(60)	
10	-	Wildside	Marky Mark & The Funky Bunch	Intercope	8	(42)	L
11	-	2 Legit 2 Quit	Hammer	Capitol	13	(60)	G L
12	1	Cream	Prince/New Power Generation	Paisley Park	12	(15)	
13	-	Keep Coming Back	Richard Marx	Capitol	7	(55)	
14	5	O.P.P.	Naughty By Nature	Tommy Boy	14	(35)	F P
15	18	Let's Talk About Sex	Salt-N-Pepa	Next Plateau	8	(2)	
16	-	No Son Of Mine	Genesis	Atlantic	9	(6)	
17	10	Don't Cry	Guns N' Roses	Geffen	12	(8)	
18	2	Can't Stop This Thing We Started	Bryan Adams	A&M	11	(12)	
19	8	Set The Night To Music	Roberta Flack With Maxi Priest	Atlantic	8		L
20	-	Smells Like Teen Spirit	Nirvana	Geffen	13	(7)	F G L

US 1991
OCT-DEC

◆ Thanks to CDs, the value of America's music sales in 1991 went up 3.8% to $7.8 billion.

◆ Michael Jackson's album **Dangerous** entered the transatlantic charts at No. 1. It shipped four million in America, and sold a record 200,000 in three days in the UK. Its lead-off single, 'Black Or White', was the first American record to enter the UK chart at No. 1 since 1960.

◆ Guns N' Roses' albums **Use Your Illusion I** and **II** entered the American and UK charts in the top two rungs (bettering a record set by The Beatles).

◆ Interest in record breaking white rapper Vanilla Ice cooled quickly and his debut film *Cool As Ice* was out on video just 13 days after its unsuccessful cinema launch.

313

UK 1992 JAN-MAR

◆ Following Freddie Mercury's death, Queen had the top 4 music videos and 'Bohemian Rhapsody' became the first record ever to top the charts twice (selling over a million on both occasions). Its double A-side, 'These Are The Days Of Our Lives', was voted Record of The Year at the Brit Awards.

◆ Inducted into the *Rock And Roll Hall Of Fame* between 1989 and 1992 were The Four Tops, Eric Clapton, Jimi Hendrix, The Impressions, John Lee Hooker, The Kinks, Jimmy Page, Simon & Garfunkel, Ike & Tina Tuner and The Who.

◆ The KLF announced they were quitting the music business, on stage at the Brit Awards where they were voted Best British Group. Their 'Justified And Ancient' gave guest vocalist Tammy Wynette the highest placed US pop hit of her career.

January 1992

This Mnth	Prev Mnth	Title	Artist	Label	Wks 20	(US Pos)	
1	9	Bohemian Rhapsody/These Are The Days Of Our Lives	Queen	Parlophone	10	(2)	P
2	3	Justified And Ancient	KLF Feat. Tammy Wynette	KLF Comms.	9	(11)	
3	7	Too Blind To See It	Kym Sims	Atco	8	(38)	F
4	18	Addams Groove	Hammer	Capitol	7	(7)	
5	10	Don't Talk Just Kiss	Right Said Fred/Jocelyn Brown	Tug	7	(76)	
6	-	Goodnight Girl	Wet Wet Wet	Precious	9		
7	-	Everybody In The Place (EP)	Prodigy	XL	5		
8	2	When You Tell Me That You Love Me	Diana Ross	EMI	9		
9	-	We Got A Love Thang	Ce Ce Peniston	A&M	5	(20)	F
10	1	Don't Let The Sun Go Down On Me	George Michael & Elton John	Epic	6	(1)	
11	-	God Gave Rock & Roll To You Ii	Kiss	Interscope	5		L
12	11	Live And Let Die	Guns N' Roses	Geffen	4	(33)	
13	-	I Can't Dance	Genesis	Virgin	5	(7)	
14	5	Driven By You	Brian May	Parlophone	6		F
15	4	Black Or White	Michael Jackson	Epic	9	(1)	
16	-	Give Me Just A Little More Time	Kylie Minogue	PWL	5		
17	-	Different Strokes	Isotonik	Ffrreedom	2		F L
18	-	Feel So High	Des'ree	Dusted Sound	4		F
19	-	(Can You) Feel The Passion	Blue Pearl	Big Life	3		L
20	-	Twilight Zone	2 Unlimited	PWL Continental	7	(49)	

February 1992

This Mnth	Prev Mnth	Title	Artist	Label	Wks 20	(US Pos)	
1	6	Goodnight Girl	Wet Wet Wet	Precious	9		
2	-	Stay	Shakespears Sister	London	14	(4)	
3	20	Twilight Zone	2 Unlimited	PWL Continental	7	(49)	
4	-	I'm Doing Fine Now	Pasadenas	Columbia	7		
5	-	I Wonder Why	Curtis Stigers	Arista	6	(9)	F
6	16	Give Me Just A Little More Time	Kylie Minogue	PWL	5		
7	-	Remember The Time/Come Together	Michael Jackson	Epic	4	(3)	
8	-	My Girl	Temptations	Epic	8		L
9	1	Bohemian Rhapsody/These Are The Days Of Our Lives	Queen	Parlophone	10	(2)	P
10	-	The Bouncer	Kicks Like A Mule	Tribal Bass	4		F L
11	-	For Your Babies	Simply Red	East West	5		
12	11	God Gave Rock & Roll To You Ii	Kiss	Interscope	5		L
13	-	I Love Your Smile	Shanice	Motown	7	(2)	F L
14	13	I Can't Dance	Genesis	Virgin	5	(7)	
15	-	It's A Fine Day	Opus III	PWL Int.	5		F L
16	7	Everybody In The Place (EP)	Prodigy	XL	5		
17	-	Thought I'd Died And Gone To Heaven	Bryan Adams	A&M	4	(13)	
18	-	Welcome To The Cheap Seats (EP)	Wonder Stuff	Polydor	3		
19	-	Dixie-Narco (EP)	Primal Scream	Creation	2		
20	-	It Must Be Love	Madness	Virgin	5		L

March 1992

This Mnth	Prev Mnth	Title	Artist	Label	Wks 20	(US Pos)	
1	2	Stay	Shakespears Sister	London	14	(4)	
2	13	I Love Your Smile	Shanice	Motown	7	(2)	F L
3	8	My Girl	Temptations	Epic	8		L
4	-	America: What Time Is Love?	KLF	KLF Comms.	4	(57)	L
5	-	Weather With You	Crowded House	Capitol	5		
6	15	It's A Fine Day	Opus III	PWL Int.	5		F L
7	-	November Rain	Guns N' Roses	Geffen	3	(3)	
8	-	Tears In Heaven	Eric Clapton	Reprise	5	(2)	
9	-	Finally	Ce Ce Peniston	A&M	6	(5)	
10	-	To Be With You	Mr. Big	Atlantic	7	(1)	F L
11	20	It Must Be Love	Madness	Virgin	5		L
12	4	I'm Doing Fine Now	Pasadenas	Columbia	7		
13	-	Deeply Dippy	Right Said Fred	Tug	10		
14	-	Come As You Are	Nirvana	DGC	2	(32)	
15	-	Human Touch	Bruce Springsteen	Columbia	2	(16)	
16	-	I Know	New Atlantic	3 Beat	4		F L
17	17	Thought I'd Died And Gone To Heaven	Bryan Adams	A&M	4	(13)	
18	-	Let's Get Rocked	Def Leppard	Bludgeon Riffola	4	(15)	
19	-	Dragging Me Down	Inspiral Carpets	Cow	3		
20	-	Rave Generator	Toxic Two	PWL Int.	3		F L

January 1992

This Mnth	Prev Mnth	Title	Artist	Label	Wks 20	(UK Pos)	
1	1	Black Or White	Michael Jackson	Epic	12	(1)	G
2	5	All 4 Love	Color Me Badd	Giant	15	(5)	
3	7	Can't Let Go	Mariah Carey	Columbia	14	(20)	
4	8	Finally	Ce Ce Peniston	A&M	14	(2)	F
5	-	Don't Let The Sun Go Down On Me	George Michael & Elton John	Columbia	13	(1)	
6	2	It's So Hard To Say Goodbye To Yesterday	Boyz II Men	Motown	14		
7	11	2 Legit 2 Quit	Hammer	Capitol	13	(60)	G L
8	20	Smells Like Teen Spirit	Nirvana	Geffen	13	(7)	F G L
9	-	I Love Your Smile	Shanice	Motown	14	(2)	F
10	-	Diamonds And Pearls	Prince & The New Power Generation	Paisley Park	12	(25)	
11	-	Addams Groove	Hammer	Capitol	8	(4)	
12	3	Set Adrift On Memory Bliss	P.M. Dawn	Gee Street/Island	13	(3)	F
13	10	Wildside	Marky Mark & The Funky Bunch	Intercope	8	(42)	L
14	16	No Son Of Mine	Genesis	Atlantic	9	(6)	
15	4	When A Man Loves A Woman	Michael Bolton	Columbia	12	(8)	
16	6	Blowing Kisses In The Wind	Paula Abdul	Captive	10		
17	-	Mysterious Ways	U2	Island	8	(13)	
18	-	Tell Me What You Want Me To Do	Tevin Campbell	Qwest	12	(63)	
19	-	I'm Too Sexy	Right Said Fred	Charisma	13	(2)	F G L
20	-	The Way I Feel About You	Karyn White	Warner	7	(65)	L

February 1992

This Mnth	Prev Mnth	Title	Artist	Label	Wks 20	(UK Pos)	
1	19	I'm Too Sexy	Right Said Fred	Charisma	13	(2)	F G L
2	9	I Love Your Smile	Shanice	Motown	14	(2)	F
3	10	Diamonds And Pearls	Prince/New Power Generation	Paisley Park	12	(25)	
4	5	Don't Let The Sun Go Down On Me	George Michael & Elton John	Columbia	13	(1)	
5	-	To Be With You	Mr. Big	Atlantic	13	(3)	F
6	2	All 4 Love	Color Me Badd	Giant	15	(5)	
7	8	Smells Like Teen Spirit	Nirvana	Geffen	13	(7)	F G L
8	18	Tell Me What You Want Me To Do	Tevin Campbell	Qwest	12	(63)	
9	-	Remember The Time	Michael Jackson	Epic	13	(3)	
10	4	Finally	Ce Ce Peniston	A&M	14	(2)	F
11	3	Can't Let Go	Mariah Carey	Columbia	14	(20)	
12	20	The Way I Feel About You	Karyn White	Warner	7	(65)	L
13	17	Mysterious Ways	U2	Island	8	(13)	
14	-	Good For Me	Amy Grant	A&M	10	(60)	
15	7	2 Legit 2 Quit	Hammer	Capitol	13	(60)	G L
16	-	Masterpiece	Atlantic Starr	Warner	14		L
17	1	Black Or White	Michael Jackson	Epic	12	(1)	G
18	-	Vibeology	Paula Abdul	Captive	5	(19)	
19	-	Save The Best For Last	Vanessa Williams	Wing	17	(3)	
20	-	Tears In Heaven	Eric Clapton	Duck	16	(5)	G

March 1992

This Mnth	Prev Mnth	Title	Artist	Label	Wks 20	(UK Pos)	
1	5	To Be With You	Mr. Big	Atlantic	13	(3)	F
2	19	Save The Best For Last	Vanessa Williams	Wing	17	(3)	
3	9	Remember The Time	Michael Jackson	Epic	13	(3)	
4	1	I'm Too Sexy	Right Said Fred	Charisma	13	(2)	F G L
5	20	Tears In Heaven	Eric Clapton	Duck	16	(5)	G
6	2	I Love Your Smile	Shanice	Motown	14	(2)	F
7	16	Masterpiece	Atlantic Starr	Warner	14		L
8	14	Good For Me	Amy Grant	A&M	10	(60)	
9	-	I Can't Dance	Genesis	Virgin	9	(7)	
10	8	Tell Me What You Want Me To Do	Tevin Campbell	Qwest	12	(63)	
11	-	Breakin' My Heart (Pretty Brown Eyes)	Mint Condition	Perspective	9		F L
12	-	Missing You Now	Michael Bolton	Columbia	7	(28)	
13	3	Diamonds And Pearls	Prince/New Power Geneartion	Paisley Park	12	(25)	
14	-	Justified And Ancient	KLF Feat. Tammy Wynette	Arista	5	(2)	L
15	-	Make It Happen	Mariah Carey	Columbia	11	(17)	
16	-	Beauty And The Beast	Celine Dion & Peabo Bryson	Epic	9	(9)	
17	-	If You Go Away	NKOTB (New Kids On The Block)	Columbia	3		L
18	4	Don't Let The Sun Go Down On Me	George Michael & Elton John	Columbia	13	(1)	
19	-	Uhh Ahh	Boyz II Men	Motown	6		
20	7	Smells Like Teen Spirit	Nirvana	Geffen	13	(7)	F G L

US 1992
JAN-MAR

◆ Garth Brooks became the first artist since Herb Alpert in 1966 to have two albums in the Top 3 simultaneously. He also had a further LP in the Top 20 and his total sales were approaching 16 million.

▲ The royalties earned by George Michael (above) and Elton John's transatlantic top-per, 'Don't Let The Sun Go Down On Me', went to a variety of AIDS charities.

◆ Alternative rock band Nirvana's album **Nevermind** topped the chart and their single 'Smells Like Teen Spirit' was a transatlantic Top 20 entry. To celebrate, singer Kurt Cobain wed Hole's lead vocalist Courtney Love.

UK
1992
APR-JUNE

◆ Bruce Springsteen's albums **Human Touch** and **Lucky Town** entered the UK chart in positions 1 and 2 (Nos. 2 and 3 in the USA) - the feat is more remarkable considering only three days' sales were taken into account - the albums were released on a Thursday rather than Monday as is usual in the UK.

◆ Stars appearing in a successful tribute show for Freddie Mercury at Wembley included David Bowie, Def Leppard, Guns N' Roses, Elton John, Metallica, George Michael, Liza Minnelli, Robert Plant, Queen, Lisa Stansfield and U2.

◆ U2, who at times had seven albums on the UK chart, signed a £10 ($15) million publishing deal with Phonogram.

◆ Erasure's 17th Top 20 entry, the Abba tribute 'Abba-Esque', was their first chart topper. It also headed the list in Abba's homeland, Sweden.

April 1992

This Mnth	Prev Mnth	Title	Artist	Label	Wks 20	(US Pos)	
1	13	Deeply Dippy	Right Said Fred	Tug	10		
2	1	Stay	Shakespears Sister	London	14	(4)	
3	10	To Be With You	Mr. Big	Atlantic	7	(1)	F L
4	-	Save The Best For Last	Vanessa Williams	Polydor	7	(1)	F L
5	-	Joy	Soul II Soul	Ten	4		
6	9	Finally	Ce Ce Peniston	A&M	6	(5)	
7	-	Why	Annie Lennox	RCA	5	(34)	F
8	18	Let's Get Rocked	Def Leppard	Bludgeon Riffola	4	(15)	
9	-	Evapor 8	Altern 8	Network	3		
10	-	On A Ragga Tip	SL2	XL	9		L
11	-	You're All That Matters To Me	Curtis Stigers	Arista	7	(98)	L
12	-	Breath Of Life	Erasure	Mute	4		
13	-	Viva Las Vegas	ZZ Top	Warner	4		
14	8	Tears In Heaven	Eric Clapton	Reprise	5	(2)	
15	-	You	Ten Sharp	Columbia	7		F L
16	-	Be Quick Or Be Dead	Iron Maiden	EMI	2		
17	-	(I Want To Be) Elected	Mr. Bean & Smear Campaign	London	3		F L
18	-	Take My Advice	Kym Sims	Atco	2	(86)	L
19	-	Time To Make You Mine	Lisa Stansfield	Arista	4		
20	-	The Only Living Boy In New Cross	Carter-Unstoppable Sex Machine	Big Cat	3		

May 1992

This Mnth	Prev Mnth	Title	Artist	Label	Wks 20	(US Pos)	
1	-	Please Don't Go	KWS	Network	12	(6)	F
2	10	On A Ragga Tip	SL2	XL	9		L
3	-	Hang On In There Baby	Curiosity	RCA	6		L
4	1	Deeply Dippy	Right Said Fred	Tug	10		
5	-	The Days Of Pearly Spencer	Marc Almond	Some Bizzare	4		L
6	-	Workaholic	2 Unlimited	PWL Continental	4		
7	-	My Lovin'	En Vogue	East West America	5	(2)	
8	11	You're All That Matters To Me	Curtis Stigers	Arista	7	(98)	L
9	-	Everything About You	Ugly Kid Joe	Mercury	7	(9)	F
10	-	Nothing Else Matters	Metallica	Vertigo	3	(35)	
11	-	Knockin' On Heaven's Door	Guns N' Roses	Geffen	6		
12	-	Temple Of Love (1992)	Sisters Of Mercy	Merciful Release	3		
13	15	You	Ten Sharp	Columbia	7		F L
14	-	I Don't Care	Shakespears Sister	London	4	(55)	
15	-	In The Closet	Michael Jackson	Epic	3	(6)	
16	4	Save The Best For Last	Vanessa Williams	Polydor	7	(1)	F L
17	-	Beauty And The Beast	Celine Dion & Peabo Bryson	Epic	3	(9)	F
18	-	Keep On Walkin'	Ce Ce Peniston	A&M	3	(15)	
19	-	Song For Love	Extreme	A&M	3		
20	20	The Only Living Boy In New Cross	Carter-Unstoppable Sex Machine	Big Cat	3		

June 1992

This Mnth	Prev Mnth	Title	Artist	Label	Wks 20	(US Pos)	
1	1	Please Don't Go	KWS	Network	12	(6)	F
2	-	Hazard	Richard Marx	Capitol	10	(9)	
3	-	Jump	Kris Kross	Ruffhouse	6	(1)	F
4	-	Abba-Esque (EP)	Erasure	Mute	8		
5	-	Something Good	Utah Saints	ffrr	7	(98)	
6	-	Heartbeat	Nick Berry	Columbia	5		L
7	-	Toofunky	George Michael	Epic	5	(10)	
8	9	Everything About You	Ugly Kid Joe	Mercury	7	(9)	F
9	-	It Only Takes A Minute	Take That	RCA	6		F
10	11	Knockin' On Heaven's Door	Guns N' Roses	Geffen	6		
11	-	The One	Elton John	Rocket	5	(9)	
12	-	Friday, I'm In Love	Cure	Fiction	4	(18)	L
13	-	Blue Room	Orb	Big Life	3		F
14	2	On A Ragga Tip	SL2	XL	9		L
15	7	My Lovin'	En Vogue	East West America	5	(2)	
16	-	Midlife Crisis	Faith No More	Slash	2		F
17	-	Even Better Than The Real Thing	U2	Island	6	(32)	
18	-	Ain't 2 Proud 2 Beg	TLC	Arista	3	(6)	F
19	-	I'll Be There	Mariah Carey	Columbia	6	(1)	
20	14	I Don't Care	Shakespears Sister	London	4	(55)	

April 1992

This Mnth	Prev Mnth	Title	Artist	Label	Wks 20	(UK Pos)	
1	2	Save The Best For Last	Vanessa Williams	Wing	17	(3)	
2	5	Tears In Heaven	Eric Clapton	Duck	16	(5)	G
3	7	Masterpiece	Atlantic Starr	Warner	14		L
4	15	Make It Happen	Mariah Carey	Columbia	11	(17)	
5	3	Remember The Time	Michael Jackson	Epic	13	(3)	
6	11	Breakin' My Heart (Pretty Brown Eyes)	Mint Condition	Perspective	9		F L
7	-	Ain't Too Proud 2 Beg	TLC	Laface	12	(13)	F G
8	-	Jump	Kris Kross	Ruffhouse	15	(2)	F P
9	-	Bohemian Rhapsody	Queen	Hollywood	9	(1)	L
10	16	Beauty And The Beast	Celine Dion & Peabo Bryson	Epic	9	(9)	
11	9	I Can't Dance	Genesis	Virgin	9	(7)	
12	-	My Lovin' (You're Never Gonna Get It)	En Vogue	Atlantic	16	(4)	
13	-	Hazard	Richard Marx	Capitol	9	(3)	
14	4	I'm Too Sexy	Right Said Fred	Charisma	13	(2)	F G L
15	1	To Be With You	Mr. Big	Atlantic	13	(3)	F
16	-	Live And Learn	Joe Public	Columbia	13	(43)	F L
17	-	Everything Changes	Kathy Troccoli	Reunion	6		F L
18	-	Human Touch/Better Days	Bruce Springsteen	Columbia	7	(11)	
19	8	Good For Me	Amy Grant	A&M	10	(60)	
20	14	Justified And Ancient	KLF Feat. Tammy Wynette	Arista	5	(2)	L

May 1992

This Mnth	Prev Mnth	Title	Artist	Label	Wks 20	(UK Pos)	
1	8	Jump	Kris Kross	Ruffhouse	15	(2)	F P
2	12	My Lovin' (You're Never Gonna Get It)	En Vogue	Atlantic	16	(4)	
3	9	Bohemian Rhapsody	Queen	Hollywood	9	(1)	L
4	1	Save The Best For Last	Vanessa Williams	Wing	17	(3)	
5	16	Live And Learn	Joe Public	Columbia	13	(43)	F L
6	2	Tears In Heaven	Eric Clapton	Duck	16	(5)	G
7	-	Under The Bridge	Red Hot Chili Peppers	Warner	15	(26)	F L
8	7	Ain't Too Proud 2 Beg	TLC	Laface	12	(13)	F G
9	-	Everything About You	Ugly Kid Joe	Star Dog	7	(3)	F
10	-	One	U2	Island	8		
11	-	In The Closet	Michael Jackson	Epic	8	(8)	
12	4	Make It Happen	Mariah Carey	Columbia	11	(17)	
13	13	Hazard	Richard Marx	Capitol	9	(3)	
14	-	Thought I'd Died And Gone To Heaven	Bryan Adams	A&M	7	(8)	
15	-	Baby Got Back	Sir Mix-A-Lot	Def American	20	(56)	F P
16	-	Damn I Wish I Was Your Lover	Sophie B. Hawkins	Columbia	11	(14)	F
17	-	Let's Get Rocked	Def Leppard	Mercury	8	(2)	
18	3	Masterpiece	Atlantic Starr	Warner	14		L
19	-	If You Asked Me To	Celine Dion	Epic	12	(60)	
20	10	Beauty And The Beast	Celine Dion & Peabo Bryson	Epic	9	(9)	

June 1992

This Mnth	Prev Mnth	Title	Artist	Label	Wks 20	(UK Pos)	
1	-	I'll Be There	Mariah Carey	Columbia	11	(2)	
2	1	Jump	Kris Kross	Ruffhouse	15	(2)	F P
3	7	Under The Bridge	Red Hot Chili Peppers	Warner	15	(26)	F L
4	15	Baby Got Back	Sir Mix-A-Lot	Def American	20	(56)	F P
5	2	My Lovin' (You're Never Gonna...)	En Vogue	Atlantic	16	(4)	
6	16	Damn I Wish I Was Your Lover	Sophie B. Hawkins	Columbia	11	(14)	F
7	19	If You Asked Me To	Celine Dion	Epic	12	(60)	
8	5	Live And Learn	Joe Public	Columbia	13	(43)	F L
9	-	Achy Breaky Heart	Billy Ray Cyrus	Mercury	16	(3)	F G L
10	-	Tennessee	Arrested Development	Chrysalis	11	(18)	F
11	11	In The Closet	Michael Jackson	Epic	8	(8)	
12	-	The Best Things In Life Are Free	Luther Vandross/Janet Jackson	Perspective	12	(2)	
13	-	Hold On My Heart	Genesis	Atlantic	8	(16)	L
14	8	Ain't Too Proud 2 Beg	TLC	Laface	12	(13)	F G
15	-	Wishing On A Star	Cover Girls	Epic	10	(38)	L
16	-	Just Another Day	Jon Secada	SBK	18	(5)	F
17	6	Tears In Heaven	Eric Clapton	Duck	16	(5)	G
18	4	Save The Best For Last	Vanessa Williams	Wing	17	(3)	
19	-	Come & Talk To Me	Jodeci	Uptown/MCA	13		F
20	-	Just Take My Heart	Mr. Big	Atlantic	2	(26)	L

▲ Schoolboy rap duo Kris Kross (above) topped both the single and album charts with their debut releases, 'Jump' and **Totally Krossed Out.** Other noteworthy chart new-comers included Arrested Development, TLC, Red Hot Chili Peppers, Jodeci and Jon Secada.

◆ The soundtrack to *Wayne's World* hit the top, launching Queen's 'Bohemian Rhapsody' back into the Top 10. Queen also had America's top music video and four albums climbing the chart.

◆ Rap acts continued to attract bad publicity with regular stories about their lewd stage acts, anti-social lyrics or involvement in crime.

UK 1992
JULY-SEPT

▲ Elton John overtook The Beatles when he collected his 50th US Top 40 entry with 'The One'. Madonna's (above) 'This Used To Be My Playground', not only gave her a (female) record 10th American No. 1, but also meant she had more UK Top 10 hits than The Beatles. Morrissey sold out the Hollywood Bowl in 23 minutes breaking another record set by The Beatles.

◆ Elvis Presley's estate received 110 gold and platinum records which went on display at Graceland.

◆ Motown hitmaker Mary Wells, reggae star Jackie Edwards and Tony Williams, the voice of The Platters, all died.

July 1992

This Mnth	Prev Mnth	Title	Artist	Label	Wks 20	(US Pos)	
1	4	Abba-Esque (EP)	Erasure	Mute	8		
2	19	I'll Be There	Mariah Carey	Columbia	6	(1)	
3	-	Rhythm Is A Dancer	Snap	Arista	16	(5)	
4	-	Ain't No Doubt	Jimmy Nail	East West	9		
5	-	Sesame's Treet	Smart E's	Suburban Base	6	(60)	F L
6	2	Hazard	Richard Marx	Capitol	10	(9)	
7	-	A Trip To Trumpton	Urban Hype	Faze	5		F L
8	5	Something Good	Utah Saints	ffrr	7	(98)	
9	17	Even Better Than The Real Thing	U2	Island	6	(32)	
10	-	One Shining Moment	Diana Ross	EMI	6		
11	-	Sexy MF/Strollin'	Prince/New Power Generation	Paisley Park	4	(66)	
12	6	Heartbeat	Nick Berry	Columbia	5		L
13	-	I Drove All Night	Roy Orbison	MCA	6		
14	-	Disappointed	Electronic	Parlophone	2		L
15	-	L.S.I.	Shamen	One Little Indian	6		
16	1	Please Don't Go	KWS	Network	12	(6)	F L
17	7	Toofunky	George Michael	Epic	5	(10)	
18	-	Shake Your Head	Was (Not Was)	Fontana	8		L
19	-	This Used To Be My Playground	Madonna	Sire	6	(1)	
20	9	It Only Takes A Minute	Take That	RCA	6		F

August 1992

This Mnth	Prev Mnth	Title	Artist	Label	Wks 20	(US Pos)	
1	3	Rhythm Is A Dancer	Snap	Arista	16	(5)	
2	4	Ain't No Doubt	Jimmy Nail	East West	9		
3	-	Achy Breaky Heart	Billy Ray Cyrus	Mercury	8	(4)	F L
4	-	Barcelona	Freddie Mercury & Montserrat Caballe	Polydor	5		
5	19	This Used To Be My Playground	Madonna	Sire	6	(1)	
6	18	Shake Your Head	Was (Not Was)	Fontana	8		L
7	-	Just Another Day	Jon Secada	SBK	10	(5)	F L
8	-	The Best Things In Life Are Free	Luther Vandross/Janet Jackson	Epic	10	(10)	L
9	-	Don't You Want Me	Felix	Deconstruction	8		F
10	15	L.S.I.	Shamen	One Little Indian	6		
11	5	Sesame's Treet	Smart E's	Suburban Base	6	(60)	F L
12	13	I Drove All Night	Roy Orbison	MCA	6		
13	-	Baker Street	Undercover	PWL Int.	11		F
14	-	This Charming Man	Smiths	WEA	2		
15	-	Book Of Days	Enya	WEA	3		
16	-	Who Is It	Michael Jackson	Epic	4	(14)	
17	-	Rock Your Baby	KWS	Network	4		L
18	-	How Do You Do!	Roxette	EMI	4	(58)	
19	-	Magic Friend	2 Unlimited	PWL Continental	4		
20	7	A Trip To Trumpton	Urban Hype	Faze	5		F L

September 1992

This Mnth	Prev Mnth	Title	Artist	Label	Wks 20	(US Pos)	
1	1	Rhythm Is A Dancer	Snap	Arista	16	(5)	
2	-	Ebeneezer Goode	Shamen	One Little Indian	8		
3	13	Baker Street	Undercover	PWL Int.	11		F
4	8	The Best Things In Life Are Free	Luther Vandross/Janet Jackson	Epic	10	(10)	
5	-	Too Much Love Will Kill You	Brian May	Parlophone	6		
6	7	Just Another Day	Jon Secada	SBK	10	(5)	F L
7	-	It's My Life	Dr. Alban	Arista	9	(88)	F
8	-	My Destiny	Lionel Richie	Motown	9		L
9	3	Achy Breaky Heart	Billy Ray Cyrus	Mercury	8	(4)	F L
10	-	Walking On Broken Glass	Annie Lennox	RCA	5	(14)	
11	9	Don't You Want Me	Felix	Deconstruction	8		F
12	-	House Of Love	East 17	London	4		F
13	-	Theme From M*A*S*H (Suicide Is Painless)/(Everything I Do) I Do It For You	Manic Street Preachers/ Fatima Mansions	Columbia	4		
14	-	Iron Lion Zion	Bob Marley & The Wailers	Tuff Gong	5		
15	17	Rock Your Baby	KWS	Network	4		L
16	-	Jam	Michael Jackson	Epic	2	(26)	
17	-	Take This Heart	Richard Marx	Capitol	2	(20)	
18	4	Barcelona	Freddie Mercury & Montserrat Caballe	Polydor	5		
19	-	Fire/Jericho	Prodigy	XL	2		
20	-	Rest In Peace	Extreme	A&M	2	(96)	

July 1992

This Mnth	Prev Mnth	Title	Artist	Label	Wks 20	(UK Pos)	
1	4	Baby Got Back	Sir Mix-A-Lot	Def American	20	(56)	F P
2	1	I'll Be There	Mariah Carey	Columbia	11	(2)	
3	3	Under The Bridge	Red Hot Chili Peppers	Warner	15	(26)	F L
4	9	Achy Breaky Heart	Billy Ray Cyrus	Mercury	16	(3)	F G L
5	7	If You Asked Me To	Celine Dion	Epic	12	(60)	
6	10	Tennessee	Arrested Development	Chrysalis	11	(18)	F
7	15	Wishing On A Star	Cover Girls	Epic	10	(38)	L
8	-	Baby-Baby-Baby	TLC	Laface	18	(55)	G
9	6	Damn I Wish I Was Your Lover	Sophie B. Hawkins	Columbia	11	(14)	F
10	16	Just Another Day	Jon Secada	SBK	18	(5)	F
11	-	Life Is A Highway	Tom Cochrane	Capitol	15	(62)	F L
12	-	This Used To Be My Playground	Madonna	Sire	11	(3)	
13	2	Jump	Kris Kross	Ruffhouse	15	(2)	F P
14	-	Toofunky	George Michael	Columbia	9	(4)	
15	12	The Best Things In Life Are Free	Luther Vandross & Janet Jackson	Perspective	12	(2)	
16	5	My Lovin' (You're Never Gonna Get It)	En Vogue	Atlantic	16	(4)	
17	-	November Rain	Guns N' Roses	Geffen	14	(4)	L
18	19	Come & Talk To Me	Jodeci	Uptown/MCA	13		F
19	-	Warm It Up	Kris Kross	Columbia	7	(16)	
20	13	Hold On My Heart	Genesis	Atlantic	8	(16)	L

August 1992

This Mnth	Prev Mnth	Title	Artist	Label	Wks 20	(UK Pos)	
1	8	Baby-Baby-Baby	TLC	Laface	18	(55)	G
2	12	This Used To Be My Playground	Madonna	Sire	11	(3)	
3	-	End Of The Road	Boyz II Men	Motown	21	(1)	G
4	1	Baby Got Back	Sir Mix-A-Lot	Def American	20	(56)	F P
5	17	November Rain	Guns N' Roses	Geffen	14	(4)	L
6	10	Just Another Day	Jon Secada	SBK	18	(5)	F
7	11	Life Is A Highway	Tom Cochrane	Capitol	15	(62)	F L
8	4	Achy Breaky Heart	Billy Ray Cyrus	Mercury	16	(3)	F G L
9	-	Giving Him Something He Can Feel	En Vogue	Atco	11	(44)	
10	18	Come & Talk To Me	Jodeci	Uptown/MCA	13		F
11	-	Move This	Technotronic Featuring Ya Kid K	SBK	8		L
12	-	Humpin' Around	Bobby Brown	MCA	11	(19)	
13	-	Stay	Shakespears Sister	London	9	(1)	F L
14	19	Warm It Up	Kris Kross	Columbia	7	(16)	
15	14	Toofunky	George Michael	Columbia	9	(4)	
16	-	The One	Elton John	MCA	10	(10)	
17	7	Wishing On A Star	Cover Girls	Epic	10	(38)	L
18	-	Keep On Walkin'	Ce Ce Peniston	A&M	4	(10)	L
19	2	I'll Be There	Mariah Carey	Columbia	11	(2)	
20	5	If You Asked Me To	Celine Dion	Epic	12	(60)	

September 1992

This Mnth	Prev Mnth	Title	Artist	Label	Wks 20	(UK Pos)	
1	3	End Of The Road	Boyz II Men	Motown	21	(1)	G
2	1	Baby-Baby-Baby	TLC	Laface	18	(55)	G
3	12	Humpin' Around	Bobby Brown	MCA	11	(19)	
4	5	November Rain	Guns N' Roses	Geffen	14	(4)	L
5	13	Stay	Shakespears Sister	London	9	(1)	F L
6	-	Sometimes Love Just Ain't Enough	Patty Smyth With Don Henley	MCA	16	(22)	F L
7	-	Jump Around	House Of Pain	Tommy Boy	16	(8)	F G L
8	6	Just Another Day	Jon Secada	SBK	18	(5)	F
9	9	Giving Him Something He Can Feel	En Vogue	Atco	11	(44)	
10	11	Move This	Technotronic Featuring Ya Kid K	SBK	8		L
11	16	The One	Elton John	MCA	10	(10)	
12	2	This Used To Be My Playground	Madonna	Sire	11	(3)	
13	4	Baby Got Back	Sir Mix-A-Lot	Def American	20	(56)	F P
14	-	She's Playing Hard To Get	Hi-Five	Jive	12	(55)	L
15	-	Please Don't Go	KWS	Next Plateau	9	(1)	F L
16	7	Life Is A Highway	Tom Cochrane	Capitol	15	(62)	F L
17	-	All I Want	Toad The Wet Sprocket	Columbia	7		F
18	-	Do I Have To Say The Words?	Bryan Adams	A&M	7	(30)	
19	-	People Everyday	Arrested Development	Chrysalis	10	(2)	
20	10	Come & Talk To Me	Jodeci	Uptown/MCA	13		F

◆ **Some Gave All** by Billy Ray Cyrus became the first debut album to top the chart in two weeks and the first to hold the top spot for 17 weeks. Cyrus's transatlantic hit, 'Achy Breaky Heart', was the first million selling country single since 'Islands In The Stream' by Kenny Rogers and Dolly Parton in 1983.

◆ The Lollapalooza '92 tour kicked off in San Francisco. Headliners included The Red Hot Chili Peppers, Ice-T, Ice Cube and Britain's Jesus & Mary Chain.

◆ Richard Marx scored his twelfth successive Top 20 entry with 'Take This Heart', and Michael Jackson missed the Top 20 for the first time since 1979 with 'Jam'. For the record, Jackson's **Dangerous** album had now sold over 15 million globally in just 10 months.

◆ Gloria Estefan, The Bee Gees and Paul Simon attracted 53,000 people to a Hurricane Relief show in Miami.

UK 1992 OCT–DEC

◆ American shows by Elton John, George Michael, Lionel Richie, Madonna and Billy Idol raised over $7 million for AIDS research. At the same time, Elton signed his publishing to Warner for a world record $26 million.

▲ U2 (above) grossed $64 million from their 1992 US tour. Barbra Streisand's new record contract with Columbia was slated to earn her a similar figure.

◆ Soon after the launch of her book, *Sex*, Madonna's equally controversial 'Erotica' single rocketed to No. 3 on both sides of the Atlantic and her album of the same name reached runner-up spot in the UK and USA.

October 1992

This Mnth	Prev Mnth	Title	Artist	Label	Wks 20	(US Pos)	
1	-	Sleeping Satellite	Tasmin Archer	EMI	9	(32)	F
2	-	End Of The Road	Boyz II Men	Motown	12	(1)	F
3	7	It's My Life	Dr. Alban	Arista	9	(88)	F
4	2	Ebeneezer Goode	Shamen	One Little Indian	8		
5	-	I'm Gonna Get You	Bizarre Inc Feat. Angie Brown	Vinyl Solution	8	(47)	
6	-	Erotica	Madonna	Maverick	5	(3)	
7	3	Baker Street	Undercover	PWL Int.	11		F
8	-	A Million Love Songs (EP)	Take That	RCA	5		
9	-	Tetris	Doctor Spin	Carpet	5		F L
10	14	Iron Lion Zion	Bob Marley & The Wailers	Tuff Gong	5		
11	8	My Destiny	Lionel Richie	Motown	9		L
12	-	Love Song/Alive And Kicking	Simple Minds	Virgin	3		
13	-	Keep The Faith	Bon Jovi	Jambco	4	(29)	
14	-	My Name Is Prince	Prince/New Power Generation	Paisley Park	3	(36)	
15	-	People Everyday	Arrested Development	Cooltempo	8	(8)	F
16	-	Sentinel	Mike Oldfield	WEA	3		L
17	1	Rhythm Is A Dancer	Snap	Arista	16	(5)	
18	4	The Best Things In Life Are Free	Luther Vandross/Janet Jackson	Epic	10	(10)	
19	5	Too Much Love Will Kill You	Brian May	Parlophone	6		
20	13	Theme From M*A*S*H.../(...) I Do It...	Manic St. Preachers/Fatima...	Columbia	4		

November 1992

This Mnth	Prev Mnth	Title	Artist	Label	Wks 20	(US Pos)	
1	2	End Of The Road	Boyz II Men	Motown	12	(1)	F
2	15	People Everyday	Arrested Development	Cooltempo	8	(8)	F
3	-	Would I Lie To You?	Charles & Eddie	Capitol	12	(13)	F L
4	-	Boss Drum	Shamen	One Little Indian	5		
5	-	Never Let Her Slip Away	Undercover	PWL Int.	5		L
6	-	Run To You	Rage	Pulse 8	5		F L
7	-	I Will Always Love You	Whitney Houston	Arista	17	(1)	G
8	-	Be My Baby	Vanessa Paradis	Remark	6		L
9	-	Supermarioland	Ambassadors Of Funk/MC Mario	Living Beat	5		F L
10	5	I'm Gonna Get You	Bizarre Inc Feat Angie Brown	Vinyl Solution	8	(47)	
11	-	Temptation	Heaven 17	Virgin	8		L
12	1	Sleeping Satellite	Tasmin Archer	EMI	9	(32)	F
13	-	Invisible Touch (Live)	Genesis	Virgin	2		L
14	-	Who Needs Love (Like That)	Erasure	Mute	3		
15	-	Out Of Space/Ruff In The Jungle Bizness	Prodigy	XL	9		
16	-	Yesterdays/November Rain	Guns N' Roses	Geffen	3	(3)	
17	-	Montreux EP	Simply Red	East West	7		
18	13	Keep The Faith	Bon Jovi	Jambco	4	(29)	
19	-	Hello (Turn Your Radio On)	Shakespears Sister	London	2		L
20	-	Free Your Mind/Giving Him Something He Can Feel	En Vogue	East West America	3	(8)	L

December 1992

This Mnth	Prev Mnth	Title	Artist	Label	Wks 20	(US Pos)	
1	6	I Will Always Love You	Whitney Houston	Arista	17	(1)	G
2	-	Heal The World	Michael Jackson	Epic	8	(27)	
3	3	Would I Lie To You?	Charles & Eddie	Capitol	12	(13)	F L
4	-	Tom Traubert's Blues (Waltzing Matilda)	Rod Stewart	Warner	5		
5	-	Slam Jam	WWF Superstars	Arista	5		F
6	14	Out Of Space/Ruff In The Jungle...	Prodigy	XI	9		
7	-	Could It Be Magic	Take That	RCA	9		
8	10	Temptation	Heaven 17	Virgin	8		L
9	-	I Still Believe In You	Cliff Richard	EMI	4		
10	-	Deeper And Deeper	Madonna	Maverick	5	(7)	
11	-	Boney M Megamix	Boney M	Arista	5		L
12	-	In My Defence	Freddie Mercury	Parlophone	4		L
13	-	Phorever People	Shamen	One Little Indian	7		
14	16	Montreux EP	Simply Red	East West	7		L
15	-	Step It Up	Stereo MCs	4th & Broadway	7		
16	-	If We Hold On Together	Diana Ross	EMI	6		
17	1	End Of The Road	Boyz II Men	Motown	12	(1)	F
18	-	Miami Hit Mix/Christmas Through Your Eyes	Gloria Estefan	Epic	5		
19	2	People Everyday	Arrested Development	Cooltempo	8	(8)	F
20	5	Never Let Her Slip Away	Undercover	PWL Int.	5		L

US 1992 OCT–DEC

October 1992

This Mnth	Prev Mnth	Title	Artist	Label	Wks 20	(UK Pos)	
1	1	End Of The Road	Boyz II Men	Motown	21	(1)	G
2	6	Sometimes Love Just Ain't Enough	Patty Smyth With Don Henley	MCA	16	(22)	F L
3	7	Jump Around	House Of Pain	Tommy Boy	16	(8)	F G L
4	14	She's Playing Hard To Get	Hi-Five	Jive	12	(55)	L
5	-	I'd Die Without You	P.M. Dawn	Laface	19	(30)	
6	15	Please Don't Go	KWS	Next Plateau	9	(1)	F L
7	19	People Everyday	Arrested Development	Chrysalis	10	(2)	
8	-	When I Look Into Your Eyes	Firehouse	Epic	8	(65)	L
9	2	Baby-Baby-Baby	TLC	Laface	18	(55)	G
10	3	Humpin' Around	Bobby Brown	MCA	11	(19)	
11	-	Erotica	Madonna	Maverick	7	(3)	
12	-	How Do You Talk To An Angel	Heights	Capitol	13		F L
13	-	Free Your Mind	En Vogue	Atco	8	(16)	
14	-	Have You Ever Needed Someone So Bad	Def Leppard	Mercury	9	(16)	L
15	-	Rhythm Is A Dancer	Snap	Arista	20	(1)	L
16	4	November Rain	Guns N' Roses	Geffen	14	(4)	L
17	18	Do I Have To Say The Words?	Bryan Adams	A&M	7	(30)	
18	-	Real Love	Mary J. Blige	Uptown	16	(26)	F
19	-	Forever Love	Color Me Badd	Giant	4		L
20	5	Stay	Shakespears Sister	London	9	(1)	F L

November 1992

This Mnth	Prev Mnth	Title	Artist	Label	Wks 20	(UK Pos)	
1	12	How Do You Talk To An Angel	Heights	Capitol	13		F L
2	1	End Of The Road	Boyz II Men	Motown	21	(1)	G
3	5	I'd Die Without You	P.M. Dawn	Laface	19	(30)	
4	-	If I Ever Fall In Love	Shai	Gasoline Alley	18	(36)	F G
5	-	Rump Shaker	Wreckx-N-Effect	MCA	17	(24)	F P L
6	15	Rhythm Is A Dancer	Snap	Arista	20	(1)	L
7	2	Sometimes Love Just Ain't Enough	Patty Smyth With Don Henley	MCA	16	(22)	F L
8	-	What About Your Friends	TLC	Laface	16	(59)	
9	18	Real Love	Mary J. Blige	Uptown	16	(26)	F
10	3	Jump Around	House Of Pain	Tommy Boy	16	(8)	F G L
11	11	Erotica	Madonna	Maverick/Sire	7	(3)	
12	-	Good Enough	Bobby Brown	MCA	15	(41)	
13	-	I Will Always Love You	Whitney Houston	Arista	19	(1)	P
14	13	Free Your Mind	En Vogue	Atco East West	8	(16)	
15	-	Layla	Eric Clapton	Duck	8	(45)	L
16	-	Walking On Broken Glass	Annie Lennox	Arista	8	(8)	L
17	14	Have You Ever Needed Someone So Bad	Def Leppard	Mercury	9	(16)	L
18	-	Would I Lie To You?	Charles & Eddie	Capitol	7	(1)	F L
19	-	Love Is On The Way	Saigon Kick	Third Stone	10		F L
20	7	People Everyday	Arrested Development	Chrysalis	10	(2)	

December 1992

This Mnth	Prev Mnth	Title	Artist	Label	Wks 20	(UK Pos)	
1	13	I Will Always Love You	Whitney Houston	Arista	19	(1)	P
2	4	If I Ever Fall In Love	Shai	Gasoline Alley	18	(36)	F G
3	5	Rump Shaker	Wreckx-N-Effect	MCA	17	(24)	F P L
4	3	I'd Die Without You	P.M. Dawn	Laface	19	(30)	
5	-	In The Still Of The Night (I'll Remember)	Boyz II Men	Motown	14	(27)	G
6	1	How Do You Talk To An Angel	Heights	Capitol	13		F L
7	6	Rhythm Is A Dancer	Snap	Arista	20	(1)	L
8	12	Good Enough	Bobby Brown	MCA	15	(41)	
9	9	Real Love	Mary J. Blige	Uptown	16	(26)	F
10	8	What About Your Friends	TLC	Laface	16	(59)	
11	-	To Love Somebody	Michael Bolton	Columbia	9	(16)	
12	-	Saving Forever For You	Shanice	Motown	14	(42)	L
13	19	Love Is On The Way	Saigon Kick	Third Stone	10		F L
14	15	Layla	Eric Clapton	Duck	8	(45)	L
15	-	Do You Believe In Us	Jon Secada	SBK	9	(30)	
16	2	End Of The Road	Boyz II Men	Motown	21	(1)	G
17	-	Deeper And Deeper	Madonna	Maverick	9	(6)	
18	16	Walking On Broken Glass	Annie Lennox	Arista	8	(8)	L
19	7	Sometimes Love Just Ain't Enough	Patty Smyth With Don Henley	MCA	16	(22)	F L
20	-	Little Miss Can't Be Wrong	Spin Doctors	Epic	5	(23)	F

◆ With CDs now outselling cassettes, shipments of recorded music in America jumped 15.2% to over $9 billion.

◆ In October, Garth Brooks had four albums in the Top 20, and his LP **The Chase** was the first album to be certified quintuple platinum in its first month. By November, a record-shattering 40% of the Top 25 albums were by country artists!

◆ Boyz II Men's transatlantic topper, 'End Of The Road', spent an unprecedented 13 weeks at No. 1. They were one of a record nine black vocalists in the Top 10 of December.

◆ Cuban-born Jon Secada broke a record set by The Bee Gees' 1971 chart topper 'How Deep Is Your Love', when his debut hit 'Just Another Day', spent its 30th consecutive week in the Top 40.

UK 1993 JAN-MAR

◆ Revivals enjoyed a revival with updated hits from such diverse acts as Take That, Faith No More, West End, Whitney Houston, Shaggy and Ugly Kid Joe, plus veterans Rolf Harris and Rod Stewart.

◆ Thirty-four years after his death, Buddy Holly's album **Words of Love** topped the UK chart.

▲ At the end of March, for the first time, reggae records held the top three places on the UK chart. They were 'Oh Carolina' by Shaggy, 'Informer' by Snow (above) and 'Mr. Loverman' by Shabba Ranks.

January 1993

This Mnth	Prev Mnth	Title	Artist	Label	Wks 20	(US Pos)	
1	1	I Will Always Love You	Whitney Houston	Arista	17	(1)	G
2	7	Could It Be Magic	Take That	RCA	9		
3	-	Exterminate!	Snap Featuring Niki Haris	Arista	8		
4	2	Heal The World	Michael Jackson	Epic	8	(27)	
5	13	Phorever People	Shamen	One Little Indian	7		
6	-	Mr. Wendal/Revolution	Arrested Development	Cooltempo	5	(6)	
7	3	Would I Lie To You?	Charles & Eddie	Capitol	12	(13)	F L
8	-	I'm Easy/Be Aggressive	Faith No More	Slash	5	(58)	
9	-	The Love I Lost	West End Featuring Sybil	PWL Sanctuary	9		F L
10	5	Slam Jam	WWF Superstars	Arista	5		F
11	-	We Are Family	Sister Sledge	Atlantic	4		
12	-	Open Your Mind	Usura	Deconstruction	5		F L
13	18	Miami Hit Mix/Christmas Through Your Eyes	Gloria Estefan	Epic	5		
14	-	Sweet Harmony	Beloved	East West	5		L
15	-	After All	Frank And Walters	Setanta	3		F L
16	11	Boney M Megamix	Boney M	Arista	5		L
17	6	Out Of Space/Ruff In The Jungle Bizness	Prodigy	XL	9		
18	-	Someday (I'm Coming Back)	Lisa Stansfield	Arista	5		
19	-	Steam	Peter Gabriel	Realworld	3	(32)	L
20	-	No Limit	2 Unlimited	PWL Continental	13		

February 1993

This Mnth	Prev Mnth	Title	Artist	Label	Wks 20	(US Pos)	
1	20	No Limit	2 Unlimited	PWL Continental	13		
2	1	I Will Always Love You	Whitney Houston	Arista	17	(1)	G
3	-	Deep	East 17	London	8		
4	9	The Love I Lost	West End Featuring Sybil	PWL Sanctuary	9		F L
5	-	Little Bird/Love Song For A Vampire	Annie Lennox	RCA	8	(49)	
6	-	Ordinary World	Duran Duran	Parlophone	6	(3)	
7	3	Exterminate!	Snap Featuring Niki Haris	Arista	8		
8	-	How Can I Love You More?	M People	Deconstruction	4		F
9	-	Why Can't I Wake Up With You?	Take That	RCA	4		
10	-	I'm Every Woman	Whitney Houston	Arista	6	(4)	
11	-	Stairway To Heaven	Rolf Harris	Vertigo	3		L
12	14	Sweet Harmony	Beloved	East West	5		L
13	12	Open Your Mind	Usura	Deconstruction	5		F L
14	-	Are You Gonna Go My Way	Lenny Kravitz	Virgin America	7		
15	11	We Are Family	Sister Sledge	Atlantic	4		
16	-	Independence	Lulu	Dome	3		
17	-	Give In To Me	Michael Jackson	Epic	6		
18	-	You're In A Bad Way	Saint Etienne	Heavenly	2		F
19	-	Ruby Tuesday	Rod Stewart	Warner	3		
20	-	I Feel You	Depeche Mode	Mute	2	(37)	

March 1993

This Mnth	Prev Mnth	Title	Artist	Label	Wks 20	(US Pos)	
1	1	No Limit	2 Unlimited	PWL Continental	13		
2	-	Oh Carolina	Shaggy	Greensleeves	12	(59)	F
3	17	Give In To Me	Michael Jackson	Epic	6		
4	5	Little Bird/Love Song For A Vampire	Annie Lennox	RCA	8	(49)	
5	14	Are You Gonna Go My Way	Lenny Kravitz	Virgin America	7		
6	-	Mr. Loverman	Shabba Ranks	Epic	8	(40)	
7	-	Stick It Out	Right Said Fred & Friends	Tug	5		L
8	10	I'm Every Woman	Whitney Houston	Arista	6	(4)	
9	-	Animal Nitrate	Suede	Nude	3		
10	-	Informer	Snow	East West America	11	(1)	F L
11	3	Deep	East 17	London	8		
12	-	Too Young To Die	Jamiroquai	Sony S^2	3		F
13	-	Cat's In The Cradle	Ugly Kid Joe	Mercury	6	(6)	L
14	-	Shortsharpshock (EP)	Therapy?	A&M	2		F
15	-	Bad Girl	Madonna	Maverick	3	(36)	
16	9	Why Can't I Wake Up With You?	Take That	RCA	4		
17	-	Looking Through Patient Eyes	P.M. Dawn	Gee Street	4	(6)	L
18	-	Young At Heart	Bluebells	London	8		L
19	-	Fear Of The Dark (Live)	Iron Maiden	EMI	2		
20	-	Peace In Our Time	Cliff Richard	EMI	2		

January 1993

This Mnth	Prev Mnth	Title	Artist	Label	Wks 20	(UK Pos)	
1	1	I Will Always Love You	Whitney Houston	Arista	19	(1)	P
2	2	If I Ever Fall In Love	Shai	Gasoline Alley	18	(36)	F G
3	3	Rump Shaker	Wreckx-N-Effect	MCA	17	(24)	F P L
4	5	In The Still Of The Night (I'll Remember)	Boyz II Men	Motown	14	(27)	G
5	12	Saving Forever For You	Shanice	Motown	14	(42)	L
6	7	Rhythm Is A Dancer	Snap	Arista	20	(1)	L
7	8	Good Enough	Bobby Brown	MCA	15	(41)	
8	4	I'd Die Without You	P.M. Dawn	Laface	19	(30)	
9	17	Deeper And Deeper	Madonna	Maverick	9	(6)	
10	9	Real Love	Mary J. Blige	Uptown	16	(26)	F
11	10	What About Your Friends	TLC	Laface	16	(59)	
12	-	A Whole New World (Aladdin's Theme)	Peabo Bryson & Regina Belle	Columbia	15	(12)	L
13	-	When She Cries	Restless Heart	RCA	8		F L
14	11	To Love Somebody	Michael Bolton	Columbia	9	(16)	
15	-	7	Prince/New Power Generation	Paisley Park	11	(27)	
16	-	Faithful	Go West	EMI	6	(13)	L
17	13	Love Is On The Way	Saigon Kick	Third Stone	10		F L
18	-	Mr. Wendal	Arrested Development	Chrysalis	15	(4)	L
19	6	How Do You Talk To An Angel	Heights	Capitol	13		F L
20	-	Flex	Mad Cobra	Columbia	2		F L

February 1993

This Mnth	Prev Mnth	Title	Artist	Label	Wks 20	(UK Pos)	
1	1	I Will Always Love You	Whitney Houston	Arista	19	(1)	P
2	12	A Whole New World (Aladdin's Theme)	Peabo Bryson & Regina Belle	Columbia	15	(12)	L
3	-	Ordinary World	Duran Duran	Capitol	12	(6)	
4	5	Saving Forever For You	Shanice	Motown	14	(42)	L
5	2	If I Ever Fall In Love	Shai	Gasoline Alley	18	(36)	F G
6	18	Mr. Wendal	Arrested Development	Chrysalis	15	(4)	L
7	15	7	Prince/New Power Generation	Paisley Park	11	(27)	
8	-	I'm Every Woman	Whitney Houston	Arista	11	(4)	
9	4	In The Still Of The Night (I'll Remember)	Boyz II Men	Motown	14	(27)	G
10	-	Here We Go Again!	Portrait	Capitol	9	(37)	F L
11	3	Rump Shaker	Wreckx-N-Effect	MCA	17	(24)	F P L
12	-	Nuthin' But A "G" Thang	Dr. Dre	Death Row	19		F G
13	-	Hip Hop Hurray	Naughty By Nature	Tommy Boy	14	(20)	G
14	6	Rhythm Is A Dancer	Snap	Arista	20	(1)	L
15	-	Don't Walk Away	Jade	Giant	19	(7)	
16	9	Deeper And Deeper	Madonna	Maverick	9	(6)	
17	-	Informer	Snow	Atco	15	(2)	F
18	13	When She Cries	Restless Heart	RCA	8		F L
19	-	Get Away	Bobby Brown	MCA	5		L
20	7	Good Enough	Bobby Brown	MCA	15	(41)	

March 1993

This Mnth	Prev Mnth	Title	Artist	Label	Wks 20	(UK Pos)	
1	17	Informer	Snow	Atco	15	(2)	F
2	12	Nuthin' But A "G" Thang	Dr. Dre	Death Row	19		F G
3	2	A Whole New World (Aladdin's...)	Peabo Bryson & Regina Belle	Columbia	15	(12)	L
4	3	Ordinary World	Duran Duran	Capitol	12	(6)	
5	8	I'm Every Woman	Whitney Houston	Arista	11	(4)	
6	15	Don't Walk Away	Jade	Giant	19	(7)	
7	-	Freak Me	Silk	Keia	18	(46)	F G L
8	6	Mr. Wendal	Arrested Development	Chrysalis	15	(4)	L
9	1	I Will Always Love You	Whitney Houston	Arista	19	(1)	P
10	-	Bed Of Roses	Bon Jovi	Jambco	10	(13)	
11	13	Hip Hop Hurray	Naughty By Nature	Tommy Boy	14	(20)	G
12	-	I Have Nothing	Whitney Houston	Arista	13	(3)	
13	-	Comforter	Shai	Gasoline Alley	13		
14	-	Two Princes	Spin Doctors	Epic	14	(3)	L
15	7	7	Prince/New Power Generation	Paisley Park	11	(27)	
16	-	I Got A Man	Positive K	Island	8	(43)	F L
17	10	Here We Go Again!	Portrait	Capitol	9	(37)	F L
18	-	The Right Kind Of Love	Jeremy Jordan	Giant	5		F L
19	-	Cat's In The Cradle	Ugly Kid Joe	Stardog	8	(7)	L
20	19	Get Away	Bobby Brown	MCA	5		L

◆ Whitney Houston's soundtrack album **The Bodyguard** sold a record six million copies in just eight weeks. Her transatlantic topper, 'I Will Always Love You', became the top selling single ever by a female vocalist in Britain. It also headed the US chart for a record 14 weeks, selling over three million in two months.

◆ Madonna's string of 27 consecutive Top 20 hits ended when 'Bad Girl' missed the mark.

◆ Eric Clapton picked up six Grammy Awards including Best Male Vocalist and Best Record and Song of The Year for 'Tears In Heaven', while **Unplugged,** voted Album Of The Year, moved to the top.

◆ Only three different singles headed the US chart between August 15 and February 27, 1993. The acts involved were Boyz II Men, TV group The Heights and Whitney Houston.

UK
1993
APR-JUNE

▲ Depeche Mode, whose 'Walking in My Shoes' was their 21st Top 20 entry, entered the transatlantic charts at No. 1 with their album **Songs Of Faith & Devotion.**

◆ In April, nine of the British Top 10 were dance records, and at times only five of the Top 20 records were by British artists - two more firsts.

◆ Over 180,000 people saw France's top selling rock artist Johnny Halliday at the Parc Des Princes Stadium in Paris. To celebrate his 50th birthday a 40 CD box set was released – the biggest ever by a solo artist.

April 1993

This Mnth	Prev Mnth	Title	Artist	Label	Wks 20	(US Pos)	
1	18	Young At Heart	Bluebells	London	8		L
2	10	Informer	Snow	East West America	11	(1)	F L
3	2	Oh Carolina	Shaggy	Greensleeves	12	(59)	F
4	-	When I'm Good And Ready	Sybil	PWL Int.	8		L
5	6	Mr. Loverman	Shabba Ranks	Epic	8	(40)	
6	-	Show Me Love	Robin S.	Champion	6	(5)	F
7	-	Don't Walk Away	Jade	Giant	6	(4)	F
8	-	Ain't No Love (Ain't No Use)	Sub Sub Featuring Melanie Williams	Rob's	8		F L
9	1	No Limit	2 Unlimited	PWL Continental	13		
10	-	U Got 2 Know	Cappella	Internal	7		
11	13	Cat's In The Cradle	Ugly Kid Joe	Mercury	6	(6)	L
12	-	Fever	Madonna	Maverick	3		
13	-	Regret	New Order	London	3	(28)	
14	-	Go Away	Gloria Estefan	Epic	4		
15	-	Wind It Up (Rewound)	Prodigy	XL	3		
16	-	Come Undone	Duran Duran	Parlophone	4	(7)	
17	-	Wrestlemania	WWF Superstars	Arista	3		L
18	-	Slow It Down	East 17	London	3		
19	-	I Have Nothing	Whitney Houston	Arista	6	(4)	
20	-	Jump They Say	David Bowie	Arista	2		L

May 1993

This Mnth	Prev Mnth	Title	Artist	Label	Wks 20	(US Pos)	
1	-	Five Live (EP)	George Michael & Queen	Parlophone	7		
2	-	All That She Wants	Ace Of Base	London	12	(2)	F
3	-	Sweat (A La La La La Long)	Inner Circle	Magnet	8	(16)	F
4	-	That's The Way Love Goes	Janet Jackson	Virgin	6	(1)	
5	-	Tribal Dance	2 Unlimited	PWL Continental	7		
6	19	I Have Nothing	Whitney Houston	Arista	6	(4)	
7	-	Everybody Hurts	REM	Warner	8	(29)	
8	8	Ain't No Love (Ain't No Use)	Sub Sub Feat. Melanie Williams	Rob's	8		F L
9	2	Informer	Snow	East West	11	(1)	F L
10	1	Young At Heart	Bluebells	London	8		L
11	-	Housecall	Shabba Ranks Feat. Maxi Priest	Epic	5	(37)	
12	-	(I Can't Help) Falling In Love With You	UB40	Dep International	12	(1)	
13	10	U Got 2 Know	Cappella	Internal	7		
14	-	Believe In Me	Utah Saints	ffrr	3		L
15	4	When I'm Good And Ready	Sybil	PWL Int.	8		L
16	-	In These Arms	Bon Jovi	Jambco	3	(28)	
17	-	I Don't Wanna Fight	Tina Turner	Parlophone	5	(9)	
18	-	Jump Around	House Of Pain	Ruffness	4	(3)	F
19	6	Show Me Love	Robin S.	Champion	6	(5)	F
20	-	Express	Dina Carroll	A&M	3		

June 1993

This Mnth	Prev Mnth	Title	Artist	Label	Wks 20	(US Pos)	
1	12	(I Can't Help) Falling In Love With You	UB40	Dep International	12	(1)	
2	2	All That She Wants	Ace Of Base	London	12	(2)	F
3	-	Two Princes	Spin Doctors	Epic	10	(7)	F L
4	-	What Is Love	Haddaway	Arista	12	(11)	F
5	-	Three Little Pigs	Green Jelly	Zoo	5	(17)	F L
6	3	Sweat (A La La La La Long)	Inner Circle	Magnet	8	(16)	F
7	-	In All The Right Places	Lisa Stansfield	Arista	7		
8	-	Dreams	Gabrielle	Go.Beat	11	(32)	F
9	-	Shout	Louchie Lou & Michie One	ffrr	5		F L
10	-	Tease Me	Chaka Demus & Pliers	Mango	13		F
11	-	Can You Forgive Her?	Pet Shop Boys	Parlophone	3		
12	-	Do You See The Light (Looking For)	Snap Featuring Niki Haris	Arista	4		
13	5	Tribal Dance	2 Unlimited	PWL Continental	7		
14	-	Blow Your Mind	Jamiroquai	Sony S²	3		
15	17	I Don't Wanna Fight	Tina Turner	Parlophone	5	(9)	
16	1	Five Live (EP)	George Michael & Queen	Parlophone	7		
17	18	Jump Around	House Of Pain	Ruffness	4	(3)	F
18	4	That's The Way Love Goes	Janet Jackson	Virgin	6	(1)	
19	-	Have I Told You Lately	Rod Stewart	Warner	5	(5)	
20	-	One Night In Heaven	M People	Deconstruction	8		

US 1993 APR–JUNE

April 1993

This Mnth	Prev Mnth	Title	Artist	Label	Wks 20	(UK Pos)	
1	1	Informer	Snow	Atco	15	(2)	F
2	7	Freak Me	Silk	Keia	18	(46)	F G L
3	2	Nuthin' But A "G" Thang	Dr. Dre	Death Row	19		F G
4	12	I Have Nothing	Whitney Houston	Arista	13	(3)	
5	6	Don't Walk Away	Jade	Giant	19	(7)	
6	19	Cat's In The Cradle	Ugly Kid Joe	Stardog	8	(7)	L
7	14	Two Princes	Spin Doctors	Epic	14	(3)	L
8	-	Love Is	Vanessa Williams & Brian McKnight	Giant	14		L
9	13	Comforter	Shai	Gasoline Alley	13		
10	10	Bed Of Roses	Bon Jovi	Jambco	10	(13)	
11	-	I'm So Into You	SWV	RCA	15	(17)	F
12	4	Ordinary World	Duran Duran	Capitol	12	(6)	
13	8	Mr. Wendal	Arrested Development	Chrysalis	15	(4)	L
14	11	Hip Hop Hurray	Naughty By Nature	Tommy Boy	14	(20)	G
15	-	Ditty	Paperboy	Next Plateau	12		F G L
16	5	I'm Every Woman	Whitney Houston	Arista	11	(4)	
17	-	Looking Through Patient Eyes	P.M. Dawn	Gee Street	14	(11)	L
18	16	I Got A Man	Positive K	Island	8	(43)	F L
19	3	A Whole New World (Aladdin's Theme)	Peabo Bryson & Regina Belle	Columbia	15	(12)	L
20	-	It Was A Good Day	Ice Cube	Priority	5	(27)	F

May 1993

This Mnth	Prev Mnth	Title	Artist	Label	Wks 20	(UK Pos)	
1	2	Freak Me	Silk	Keia	18	(46)	F G L
2	-	That's The Way Love Goes	Janet Jackson	Virgin	16	(2)	G
3	8	Love Is	Vanessa Williams/B. McKnight	Giant	14		
4	3	Nuthin' But A "G" Thang	Dr. Dre	Death Row	19		F G
5	4	I Have Nothing	Whitney Houston	Arista	13	(3)	
6	1	Informer	Snow	Atco	15	(2)	F
7	11	I'm So Into You	SWV	RCA	15	(17)	F
8	17	Looking Through Patient Eyes	P.M. Dawn	Gee Street	14	(11)	L
9	5	Don't Walk Away	Jade	Giant	19	(7)	
10	-	Knockin' Da Boots	H-Town	Luke	15		F G L
11	15	Ditty	Paperboy	Next Plateau	12		F G L
12	7	Two Princes	Spin Doctors	Epic	14	(3)	L
13	-	Weak	SWV	RCA	17	(33)	G
14	-	Who Is It	Michael Jackson	Epic	5	(10)	
15	9	Comforter	Shai	Gasoline Alley	13		
16	14	Hip Hop Hurray	Naughty By Nature	Tommy Boy	14	(20)	G
17	20	It Was A Good Day	Ice Cube	Priority	5	(27)	F
18	-	Have I Told You Lately	Rod Stewart	Warner	13	(5)	
19	-	The Crying Game	Boy George	SBK	4	(22)	F L
20	6	Cat's In The Cradle	Ugly Kid Joe	Stardog	8	(7)	L

June 1993

This Mnth	Prev Mnth	Title	Artist	Label	Wks 20	(UK Pos)	
1	2	That's The Way Love Goes	Janet Jackson	Virgin	16	(2)	G
2	1	Freak Me	Silk	Keia	18	(46)	F G L
3	13	Weak	SWV	RCA	17	(33)	G
4	10	Knockin' Da Boots	H-Town	Luke	15		F G L
5	-	Show Me Love	Robin S.	Big Beat	13	(6)	F L
6	18	Have I Told You Lately	Rod Stewart	Warner	13	(5)	
7	8	Looking Through Patient Eyes	P.M. Dawn	Gee Street	14	(11)	L
8	-	Come Undone	Duran Duran	Capitol	11	(13)	L
9	-	Bad Boys	Inner Circle	Big Beat	8	(52)	F
10	7	I'm So Into You	SWV	RCA	15	(17)	F
11	3	Love Is	Vanessa Williams/B. McKnight	Giant	14		
12	-	Dre Day	Dr. Dre	Death Row	10		
13	-	I'll Never Get Over You (Getting Over Me)	Expose	Arista	12	(75)	L
14	4	Nuthin' But A "G" Thang	Dr. Dre	Death Row	19		F G
15	-	Whoomp! (There It Is)	Tag Team	Life/Bellmark	28		F P L
16	9	Don't Walk Away	Jade	Giant	19	(7)	
17	11	Ditty	Paperboy	Next Plateau	12		F G L
18	-	(I Can't Help) Falling In Love With You	UB40	Virgin	19	(1)	G L
19	-	Dazzey Duks	Duice	TMR/Bellmark	11		F G L
20	-	More And More	Captain Hollywood Project	Imago	6	(23)	F L

◆ The only UK acts charting Stateside were stalwarts Rod Stewart, UB40, Duran Duran and Boy George whose 'The Crying Game' had been a British hit for Dave Berry in 1964.

◆ As rap lifestyles and lyrics made the head-lines, rappers charting included Dr Dre, Arrested Development, Paperboy, Naughty By Nature, Positive K and Ice Cube. Also hitting were the Tag Team (whose 'Whoomp! (There It Is')' spent a record 24 weeks in the Top 10) and Duice (whose 'Dazzey Duks' was on the sales chart for over a year).

◆ Soul stars Arthur Alexander and Marv Johnson died, as did Conway Twitty, who had amassed a record 40 country No. 1 hits.

◆ Barbra Streisand's **Back To Broadway** had a million advance orders and Billy Ray Cyrus's sophomore album, **It Won't Be The Last,** collected 1.5 million orders.

UK 1993

JULY-SEPT

◆ Several disco classics from the 1970s returned: 'If I Can't Have You' (Yvonne Elliman/Kim Wilde), 'This Is It' (Melba Moore/Dannii Minogue), 'Go West' (Village People/Pet Shop Boys), 'Disco Inferno' (Trammps/Tina Turner) and a remix of Gloria Gaynor's 'I Will Survive'.

◆ European music conglomerate Polygram bought Motown Records' 30,000 masters for $325 million, as the label re-signed Boyz II Men in a deal that could earn the act $30 million.

◆ British acts Cream, Elton John, The Animals, John Lennon, Van Morrison and Rod Stewart joined other 1993 *Rock And Roll Hall Of Fame* inductees The Band, Ruth Brown, Creedence Clearwater Revival, The Doors, Duane Eddy, Grateful Dead, Etta James, Frankie Lymon & The Teenagers, Bob Marley and Sly & The Family Stone.

July 1993

This Mnth	Prev Mnth	Title	Artist	Label	Wks 20	(US Pos)	
1	8	Dreams	Gabrielle	Go.Beat	11	(32)	F
2	4	What Is Love	Haddaway	Arista	12	(11)	F
3	10	Tease Me	Chaka Demus & Pliers	Mango	13		F
4	20	One Night In Heaven	M People	Deconstruction	8		
5	-	What's Up	4 Non Blondes	Interscope	11	(16)	F L
6	1	(I Can't Help) Falling In Love With You	UB40	Dep International	12	(1)	
7	-	I Will Survive	Gloria Gaynor	Polydor	6		L
8	-	Pray	Take That	RCA	7		
9	19	Have I Told You Lately	Rod Stewart	Warner	5	(5)	
10	3	Two Princes	Spin Doctors	Epic	10	(7)	F L
11	-	Will You Be There	Michael Jackson	Epic	4	(7)	
12	2	All That She Wants	Ace Of Base	London	12	(2)	F
13	-	If I Can't Have You	Kim Wilde	MCA	4		L
14	-	Almost Unreal	Roxette	EMI	5	(94)	
15	-	This Is It	Dannii Minogue	MCA	5		L
16	7	In All The Right Places	Lisa Stansfield	Arista	7		
17	-	Living On My Own	Freddie Mercury	Parlophone	9		L
18	-	Nothin' My Love Can't Fix	Joey Lawrence	EMI	3	(19)	F L
19	-	I Wanna Love You	Jade	Giant	3	(16)	
20	-	Can't Get Enough Of Your Love	Taylor Dayne	Arista	3	(20)	L

August 1993

This Mnth	Prev Mnth	Title	Artist	Label	Wks 20	(US Pos)	
1	17	Living On My Own	Freddie Mercury	Parlophone	9		L
2	-	The Key The Secret	Urban Cookie Collective	Pulse 8	10		F
3	5	What's Up	4 Non Blondes	Interscope	11	(16)	F L
4	-	The River Of Dreams	Billy Joel	Columbia	9	(3)	L
5	8	Pray	Take That	RCA	7		
6	-	It Keeps Rainin' (Tears From My Eyes)	Bitty McLean	Brilliant	9		F
7	3	Tease Me	Chaka Demus & Pliers	Mango	13		F
8	-	Mr. Vain	Culture Beat	Epic	11	(20)	F
9	-	Nuff Vibes (EP)	Apache Indian	Island	6		L
10	1	Dreams	Gabrielle	Go.Beat	11	(32)	F
11	-	Rain	Madonna	Maverick	4	(14)	
12	-	Looking Up	Michelle Gayle	RCA	4		F L
13	14	Almost Unreal	Roxette	EMI	5	(94)	
14	-	Higher Ground	UB40	Dep International	5	(46)	
15	-	Luv 4 Luv	Robin S.	Champion	4		L
16	-	I Will Always Love You	Sarah Washington	Almighty	4		F L
17	2	What Is Love	Haddaway	Arista	12	(11)	F
18	-	Dreamlover	Mariah Carey	Columbia	6	(1)	
19	15	This Is It	Dannii Minogue	MCA	5		L
20	-	Right Here	SWV	RCA	8	(2)	

September 1993

This Mnth	Prev Mnth	Title	Artist	Label	Wks 20	(US Pos)	
1	8	Mr. Vain	Culture Beat	Epic	11	(20)	F
2	6	It Keeps Rainin' (Tears From My Eyes)	Bitty McLean	Brilliant	9		F
3	20	Right Here	SWV	RCA	8	(2)	
4	4	The River Of Dreams	Billy Joel	Columbia	9	(3)	L
5	-	Boom! Shake The Room	Jazzy Jeff & Fresh Prince	Jive	10	(13)	F L
6	1	Living On My Own	Freddie Mercury	Parlophone	9		L
7	-	Faces	2 Unlimited	PWL Continental	4		
8	18	Dreamlover	Mariah Carey	Columbia	6	(1)	
9	-	Go West	Pet Shop Boys	Parlophone	6		
10	2	The Key The Secret	Urban Cookie Collective	Pulse 8	10		F
11	9	Nuff Vibes (EP)	Apache Indian	Island	6		L
12	14	Higher Ground	UB40	Dep International	5	(46)	
13	-	Heart-Shaped Box	Nirvana	Geffen	2		L
14	-	Creep	Radiohead	Parlophone	3	(34)	F
15	-	Slave To The Vibe	Aftershock	Virgin	5		F L
16	-	She Don't Let Nobody	Chaka Demus & Pliers	Mango	7		
17	-	Moving On Up	M People	Deconstruction	7		
18	-	Rubberband Girl	Kate Bush	EMI	2	(88)	
19	-	Disco Inferno	Tina Turner	Parlophone	3		
20	-	It Must Have Been Love	Roxette	EMI	4		

This Mnth	Prev Mnth	Title	Artist	Label	Wks 20	(UK Pos)	
1	3	Weak	SWV	RCA	17	(33)	G
2	18	(I Can't Help) Falling In Love With You	UB40	Virgin	19	(1)	G L
3	15	Whoomp! (There It Is)	Tag Team	Life/Bellmark	28		F P L
4	1	That's The Way Love Goes	Janet Jackson	Virgin	16	(2)	G
5	4	Knockin' Da Boots	H-Town	Luke	15		F G L
6	5	Show Me Love	Robin S.	Big Beat	13	(6)	F L
7	6	Have I Told You Lately	Rod Stewart	Warner	13	(5)	
8	13	I'll Never Get Over You (Getting Over Me)	Expose	Arista	12	(75)	L
9	-	Lately	Jodeci	Uptown/MCA	15		
10	12	Dre Day	Dr. Dre	Death Row	10		
11	-	Slam	Onyx	Ral/Chaos	10	(31)	F G L
12	-	I'm Gonna Be (500 Miles)	Proclaimers	Chrysalis	12		F L
13	19	Dazzey Duks	Duice	TMR/Bellmark	11		F G L
14	8	Come Undone	Duran Duran	Capitol	11	(13)	L
15	-	Whoot, There It Is	95 South	Wrap	10		F G L
16	-	What's Up	4 Non Blondes	Interscope	9	(2)	F L
17	-	I Don't Wanna Fight	Tina Turner	Virgin	11	(7)	L
18	-	If I Had No Loot	Tony! Toni! Tone!	Wing	11	(44)	
19	9	Bad Boys	Inner Circle	Big Beat	8	(52)	F
20	2	Freak Me	Silk	Keia	18	(46)	F G L

This Mnth	Prev Mnth	Title	Artist	Label	Wks 20	(UK Pos)	
1	2	(I Can't Help) Falling In Love With You	UB40	Virgin	19	(1)	G L
2	3	Whoomp! (There It Is)	Tag Team	Life/Bellmark	28		F P L
3	12	I'm Gonna Be (500 Miles)	Proclaimers	Chrysalis	12		F L
4	9	Lately	Jodeci	Uptown/MCA	15		
5	11	Slam	Onyx	Ral/Chaos	10	(31)	F G L
6	18	If I Had No Loot	Tony! Toni! Tone!	Wing	11	(44)	
7	1	Weak	SWV	RCA	17	(33)	G
8	-	Runaway Train	Soul Asylum	Columbia	12	(7)	F
9	-	If	Janet Jackson	Virgin	16	(14)	
10	17	I Don't Wanna Fight	Tina Turner	Virgin	11	(7)	L
11	-	Dreamlover	Mariah Carey	Columbia	19	(9)	G
12	15	Whoot, There It Is	95 South	Wrap	10		F G L
13	6	Show Me Love	Robin S.	Big Beat	13	(6)	F L
14	-	Right Here (Human Nature)	SWV	RCA	14	(3)	
15	4	That's The Way Love Goes	Janet Jackson	Virgin	16	(2)	G
16	8	I'll Never Get Over You (Getting Over Me)	Expose	Arista	12	(75)	L
17	-	Will You Be There	Michael Jackson	Epic	9	(9)	
18	13	Dazzey Duks	Duice	TMR/Bellmark	11		F G L
19	16	What's Up	4 Non Blondes	Interscope	9	(2)	F L
20	5	Knockin' Da Boots	H-Town	Luke	15		F G L

This Mnth	Prev Mnth	Title	Artist	Label	Wks 20	(UK Pos)	
1	11	Dreamlover	Mariah Carey	Columbia	19	(9)	G
2	1	(I Can't Help) Falling In Love With...	UB40	Virgin	19	(1)	G L
3	2	Whoomp! (There It Is)	Tag Team	Life/Bellmark	28		F P L
4	9	If	Janet Jackson	Virgin	16	(14)	
5	14	Right Here (Human Nature)	SWV	RCA	14	(3)	
6	8	Runaway Train	Soul Asylum	Columbia	12	(7)	F
7	4	Lately	Jodeci	Uptown/MCA	15		
8	17	Will You Be There	Michael Jackson	Epic	9	(9)	
9	-	The River Of Dreams	Billy Joel	Columbia	14	(3)	L
10	-	Baby I'm Yours	Shai	Gasoline Alley	9		L
11	6	If I Had No Loot	Tony! Toni! Tone!	Wing	11	(44)	
12	3	I'm Gonna Be (500 Miles)	Proclaimers	Chrysalis	12		F L
13	-	One Last Cry	Brian McKnight	Giant	7		L
14	-	I Get Around	2Pac	Interscope	8		F
15	-	Rain	Madonna	Maverick	6	(7)	
16	-	Another Sad Love Song	Toni Braxton	Laface	11	(51)	F
17	5	Slam	Onyx	Ral/Chaos	10	(31)	F G L
18	10	I Don't Wanna Fight	Tina Turner	Virgin	11	(7)	L
19	-	Boom! Shake The Room	Jazzy Jeff & Fresh Prince	Jive	4	(1)	L
20	-	Cryin'	Aerosmith	Geffen	9	(17)	

US

1993

JULY-SEPT

▲ Rapper Snoop Doggy Dogg gave himself up on a murder charge (immediately after presenting En Vogue with an MTV award). He was released on a $1 million bail and was acquitted in 1996.

◆ Patsy Cline's **Greatest Hits** completed a record two years at the top of the country catalog charts. It was still at No. 1 in 1996 with total sales of over six million.

◆ Garth Brooks, who had a record four albums in the country Top 5, sold out 200,000 tickets for three shows at the Texas Stadium in a record-crushing 305 minutes!

UK 1993
OCT-DEC

◆ In America, only 10 different singles made No. 1 in 1993 (a record low), and records, in general, stayed on the charts longer. In contrast, in Britain, more records than ever charted and a hit's life-span was shorter than ever. 1993 was the year of the American rock act, and the worst year for British artists in the US charts since the British Invasion in 1964.

◆ British teen idols Take That became the first act to have three successive singles enter at No. 1. They also had three of the country's Top 4 videos.

◆ Chaka Demus & Pliers, the first reggae act to have three successive Top 5 entries, took the song 'Twist And Shout' into the Top 10 for the fourth time.

◆ The year ended with the death of one of rock's true originals, Frank Zappa.

October 1993

This Mnth	Prev Mnth	Title	Artist	Label	Wks 20	(US Pos)	
1	5	Boom! Shake The Room	Jazzy Jeff & Fresh Prince	Jive	10	(13)	F L
2	17	Moving On Up	M People	Deconstruction	7		
3	16	She Don't Let Nobody	Chaka Demus & Pliers	Mango	7		
4	-	I'd Do Anything For Love (But I Won't Do That)	Meat Loaf	Virgin	12	(1)	
5	-	Relight My Fire	Take That Featuring Lulu	RCA	5		
6	-	Stay	Eternal	EMI	6		F
7	-	Relax	Frankie Goes To Hollywood	ZTT	5		
8	-	Life	Haddaway	Logic	5	(83)	
9	9	Go West	Pet Shop Boys	Parlophone	6		
10	1	Mr. Vain	Culture Beat	Epic	11	(20)	F
11	-	U Got 2 Let The Music	Cappella	Internal	6		
12	-	One Love	Prodigy	XL	4		
13	-	Going Nowhere	Gabrielle	Go.Beat	4		
14	-	Don't Be A Stranger	Dina Carroll	A&M	11		L
15	3	Right Here	SWV	RCA	8	(2)	
16	-	Here We Go	Stakka Bo	Polydor	4		F L
17	-	Please Forgive Me	Bryan Adams	A&M	9	(7)	
18	-	Play Dead	Bjork & David Arnold	Island	4		F
19	20	It Must Have Been Love	Roxette	EMI	4		
20	-	Both Sides Of The Story	Phil Collins	Virgin	2	(25)	

November 1993

This Mnth	Prev Mnth	Title	Artist	Label	Wks 20	(US Pos)	
1	4	I'd Do Anything For Love (But I Won't Do That)	Meat Loaf	Virgin	12	(1)	
2	17	Please Forgive Me	Bryan Adams	A&M	9	(7)	
3	14	Don't Be A Stranger	Dina Carroll	A&M	11		
4	-	Got To Get It	Culture Beat	Epic	5		
5	11	U Got 2 Let The Music	Cappella	Internal	6		
6	-	Hero	Mariah Carey	Columbia	8	(1)	
7	-	Feels Like Heaven	Urban Cookie Collective	Pulse 8	4		
8	-	Runaway Train	Soul Asylum	Columbia	5	(5)	F L
9	-	True Love	Elton John & Kiki Dee	Rocket	6	(56)	
10	-	Real Love '93	Time Frequency	Internal Affairs	3		L
11	-	Again	Janet Jackson	Virgin	6	(1)	
12	-	Feel Like Making Love	Pauline Henry	Sony S²	4		F L
13	-	Ain't It Fun	Guns N' Roses	Geffen	2		
14	-	Little Fluffy Clouds	Orb	Big Life	2		
15	1	Boom! Shake The Room	Jazzy Jeff & Fresh Prince	Jive	10	(13)	F L
16	6	Stay	Eternal	EMI	6		F
17	-	Queen Of The Night	Whitney Houston	Arista	2		
18	-	Long Train Runnin'	Doobie Brothers	Warner	4		F L
19	20	Both Sides Of The Story	Phil Collins	Virgin	2	(25)	
20	-	Said I Love You....But I Lied	Michael Bolton	Columbia	2	(10)	

December 1993

This Mnth	Prev Mnth	Title	Artist	Label	Wks 20	(US Pos)	
1	-	Mr. Blobby	Mr. Blobby	Destiny Music	4		F L
2	1	I'd Do Anything For Love (But I...)	Meat Loaf	Virgin	12	(1)	
3	9	True Love	Elton John & Kiki Dee	Rocket	6	(56)	
4	-	For Whom The Bell Tolls	Bee Gees	Polydor	4		
5	2	Please Forgive Me	Bryan Adams	A&M	9	(7)	
6	-	It's Alright	East 17	London	4		
7	-	Babe	Take That	RCA	2		
8	-	Stay (Faraway, So Close)	U2	Island	3	(66)	
9	-	Don't Look Any Further	M People	Deconstruction	4		
10	-	Twist And Shout	Chaka Demus & Pliers Featuring Jack Radics & Taxi Gang	Mango	2		
11	11	Again	Janet Jackson	Virgin	6	(1)	
12	-	The Perfect Year	Dina Carroll	A&M	3		
13	3	Don't Be A Stranger	Dina Carroll	A&M	11		
14	18	Long Train Runnin'	Doobie Brothers	Warner	4		F L
15	-	Bat Out Of Hell	Meat Loaf	Epic	2		
16	-	Controversy	Prince	Paisley Park	2		
17	-	The Power Of Love	Frankie Goes To Hollywood	ZTT	2		
18	-	Y.M.C.A.	Village People	Bell	2		L
19	6	Hero	Mariah Carey	Columbia	8	(1)	
20	-	I Wouldn't Normally Do This Kind Of Thing	Pet Shop Boys	Parlophone	3		

October 1993

This Mnth	Prev Mnth	Title	Artist	Label	Wks 20	(UK Pos)	
1	1	Dreamlover	Mariah Carey	Columbia	19	(9)	G
2	5	Right Here (Human Nature)	SWV	RCA	14	(3)	
3	9	The River Of Dreams	Billy Joel	Columbia	14	(3)	L
4	3	Whoomp! (There It Is)	Tag Team	Life/Bellmark	28		F P L
5	4	If	Janet Jackson	Virgin	16	(14)	
6	-	I'd Do Anything For Love (But I Won't Do That)	Meat Loaf	MCA	12	(1)	G
7	-	Just Kickin' It	Xscape	Columbia	12	(49)	F G
8	16	Another Sad Love Song	Toni Braxton	Laface	11	(51)	F
9	-	Hey Mr. D.J.	Zhane	Flavor Unit	13	(26)	F
10	-	All That She Wants	Ace Of Base	Arista	11	(1)	F G
11	2	(I Can't Help) Falling In Love With...	UB40	Virgin	19	(1)	G L
12	14	I Get Around	2Pac	Interscope	8		F
13	20	Cryin'	Aerosmith	Geffen	9	(17)	
14	-	Two Steps Behind	Def Leppard	Mercury	7	(32)	L
15	8	Will You Be There	Michael Jackson	Epic	9	(9)	
16	-	Anniversary	Tony! Toni! Tone!	Wing	9		L
17	6	Runaway Train	Soul Asylum	Columbia	12	(7)	F
18	-	Sweat (A La La La La Long)	Inner Circle	Big Beat	7	(3)	L
19	-	What Is Love	Haddaway	Arista	10	(2)	F L
20	-	Again	Janet Jackson	Virgin	8	(6)	G

November 1993

This Mnth	Prev Mnth	Title	Artist	Label	Wks 20	(UK Pos)	
1	6	I'd Do Anything For Love (But I Won't Do That)	Meat Loaf	MCA	12	(1)	G
2	10	All That She Wants	Ace Of Base	Arista	11	(1)	F G
3	20	Again	Janet Jackson	Virgin	8	(6)	G
4	7	Just Kickin' It	Xscape	Columbia	12	(49)	F G
5	-	Gangsta Lean	DRS	Capitol	8		F G L
6	-	Shoop	Salt-N-Pepa	Next Plateau	9	(29)	
7	9	Hey Mr. D.J.	Zhane	Flavor Unit	13	(26)	F
8	4	Whomp! (There It Is)	Tag Team	Life/Bellmark	28		F P L
9	1	Dreamlover	Mariah Carey	Columbia	19	(9)	G
10	-	Hero	Mariah Carey	Columbia	7	(7)	G
11	16	Anniversary	Tony! Toni! Tone!	Wing	9		L
12	-	Breathe Again	Toni Braxton	Laface	8		
13	19	What Is Love	Haddaway	Arista	10	(2)	F L
14	3	The River Of Dreams	Billy Joel	Columbia	14	(3)	L
15	-	Please Forgive Me	Bryan Adams	A&M	6	(2)	
16	-	Can We Talk	Tevin Campbell	Qwest	8		
17	8	Another Sad Love Song	Toni Braxton	Laface	11	(51)	F
18	2	Right Here (Human Nature)	SWV	RCA	14	(3)	
19	-	Keep Ya Head Up	2Pac	Interscope	6		
20	-	Said I Love You....But I Lied	Michael Bolton	Columbia	6	(15)	

December 1993

This Mnth	Prev Mnth	Title	Artist	Label	Wks 20	(UK Pos)	
1	3	Again	Janet Jackson	Virgin	8	(6)	G
2	1	I'd Do Anything For Love (But I Won't Do That)	Meat Loaf	MCA	12	(1)	G
3	2	All That She Wants	Ace Of Base	Arista	11	(1)	F G
4	10	Hero	Mariah Carey	Columbia	7	(7)	G
5	6	Shoop	Salt-N-Pepa	Next Plateau	9	(29)	
6	5	Gangsta Lean	DRS	Capitol	8		F G L
7	12	Breathe Again	Toni Braxton	Laface	8		
8	15	Please Forgive Me	Bryan Adams	A&M	6	(2)	
9	-	All For Love	Bryan Adams/Rod Stewart/Sting	A&M	4		G
10	4	Just Kickin' It	Xscape	Columbia	12	(49)	F G
11	20	Said I Love You....But I Lied	Michael Bolton	Columbia	6	(15)	
12	16	Can We Talk	Tevin Campbell	Qwest	8		
13	8	Whoomp! (There It Is)	Tag Team	Life/Bellmark	28		F P L
14	19	Keep Ya Head Up	2Pac	Interscope	6		
15	7	Hey Mr. D.J.	Zhane	Flavor Unit	13	(26)	F
16	9	Dreamlover	Mariah Carey	Columbia	19	(9)	G
17	-	What's My Name?	Snoop Doggy Dogg	Death Row/Interscope	2	(20)	F
18	13	What Is Love	Haddaway	Arista	10	(2)	F L
19	-	Linger	Cranberries	Island	3	(74)	F L
20	-	Come Baby Come	K7	Tommy Boy	3	(13)	F L

◆ CDs now clearly outsold cassettes and vinyl on both sides of the Atlantic, with total sales in recession-hit Britain up by 13.5%. The MiniDisc and the Digital Compact Cassette enjoyed their first year on the market.

◆ 77-year-old Frank Sinatra's **Duets** shipped 1.3 million copies. He joined fellow veterans Nat 'King' Cole, Jimmy Durante and Louis Armstrong in the LP Top 40 (they were on the *Sleepless in Seattle* soundtrack).

▲ Mariah Carey became the only artist in history to reach the Top 5 with her first 10 singles (nine of them made the Top 2!).

UK 1994 JAN-MAR

◆ Jamaican reggae performers Chaka Demus & Pliers became the fourth act to take 'Twist And Shout' into the Top 10 and their recording was also the 700th different single to head the UK chart.

◆ The classic ballad 'Without You' returned to the top, this time by Mariah Carey. Her transatlantic No. 1 was the first single by a female artist to enter the UK lists in pole position.

◆ Among the Brit Award winners were Sting, Dina Caroll, the Stereo MCs, M People and Take That.

◆ A record number of European artists reached the chart this quarter and for the first time since the late 1950s, 7 vinyl singles accounted for less than 10% of the market.

January 1994

This Mnth	Prev Mnth	Title	Artist	Label	Wks 20	(US Pos)	
1	11	Twist And Shout	Chaka Demus & Pliers Feat. Jack Radics & Taxi Gang	Mango	9		
2	-	Things Can Only Get Better	D:ream	FXU/Magnet	11		
3	-	Come Baby Come	K7	Tommy Boy/Big Life	10	(18)	F
4	7	It's Alright	East 17	London	10		
5	1	Mr. Blobby	Mr. Blobby	Destiny Music	7		F L
6	-	All For Love	Bryan Adams/Rod Stewart/Sting	A&M	9	(1)	
7	8	Babe	Take That	RCA	5		
8	4	For Whom The Bell Tolls	Bee Gees	Polydor	9		L
9	13	The Perfect Year	Dina Carroll	A&M	7		L
10	-	Anything	Culture Beat	Epic	5		
11	-	Cornflake Girl	Tori Amos	East West	4		
12	-	I Miss You	Haddaway	Logic/Arista	8		
13	2	I'll Do Anything For Love (But I Won't Do That)	Meat Loaf	Virgin	15	(1)	
14	-	Save Our Love	Eternal	EMI	4		
15	15	Bat Out Of Hell	Meat Loaf	Epic	5		
16	-	Breathe Again	Toni Braxton	Laface/Arista	9	(3)	F
17	-	In Your Room	Depeche Mode	Mute	2		L
18	-	Here I Stand	Bitty McLean	Brilliant	3		
19	-	A Whole New World (Aladdin's Theme)	Peabo Bryson & Regina Belle	Columbia	5	(1)	L
20	-	Return To Innocence	Enigma	Virgin	11	(4)	L

February 1994

This Mnth	Prev Mnth	Title	Artist	Label	Wks 20	(US Pos)	
1	2	Things Can Only Get Better	D:ream	FXU/Magnet	11		
2	16	Breathe Again	Toni Braxton	Laface/Arista	9	(3)	F
3	20	Return To Innocence	Enigma	Virgin	11	(4)	L
4	6	All For Love	Bryan Adams/Rod Stewart/Sting	A&M	9	(1)	
5	-	The Power Of Love	Celine Dion	550 Music	6	(1)	
6	-	Without You	Mariah Carey	Columbia	9	(3)	
7	3	Come Baby Come	K7	Tommy Boy/Big Life	10	(18)	F
8	-	A Deeper Love	Aretha Franklin	Arista	3	(63)	
9	-	Stay Together	Suede	Nude	3		
10	-	Come In Out Of The Rain	Wendy Moten	EMI USA	4		F L
11	11	Cornflake Girl	Tori Amos	East West	4		
12	-	Move On Baby	Cappella	Internal	4		
13	-	I Like To Move It	Reel 2 Real/The Mad Stuntman	Positiva	15	(89)	F
14	-	Let The Beat Control Your Body	2 Unlimited	PWL Continental	5		
15	10	Anything	Culture Beat	Epic	5		
16	-	The Sign	Ace Of Base	Arista	10	(1)	
17	-	Give It Away	Red Hot Chili Peppers	Warner	2	(73)	F
18	-	Sweet Lullaby	Deep Forest	Columbia	3	(78)	F
19	12	I Miss You	Haddaway	Logic/Arista	8		
20	1	Twist And Shout	Chaka Demus & Pliers Feat. Jack Radics & Taxi Gang	Mango	9		

March 1994

This Mnth	Prev Mnth	Title	Artist	Label	Wks 20	(US Pos)	
1	6	Without You	Mariah Carey	Columbia	9	(3)	
2	16	The Sign	Ace Of Base	Arista	10	(1)	
3	-	Doop	Doop	Citybeat	7		F L
4	3	Return To Innocence	Enigma	Virgin	11	(4	L
5	2	Breathe Again	Toni Braxton	Laface/Arista	9	(3)	F
6	-	Streets Of Philadelphia	Bruce Springsteen	Columbia	8	(9)	L
7	-	Renaissance	M People	Deconstruction	3		
8	13	I Like To Move It	Reel 2 Real/The Mad Stuntman	Positiva	15	(89)	F
9	-	Girls And Boys	Blur	Food	4	(59)	
10	14	Let The Beat Control Your Body	2 Unlimited	PWL Continental	5		
11	1	Things Can Only Get Better	D:ream	FXU/Magnet	11		
12	-	U R The Best Thing	D:ream	FXU/Magnet	5		
13	-	Don't Go Breaking My Heart	Elton John & RuPaul	Rocket	3		
14	-	Rocks/Funky Jam	Primal Scream	Creation	2		L
15	12	Move On Baby	Cappella	Internal	4		
16	-	Whatta Man	Salt-N-Pepa Featuring En Vogue	Next Plateau	6	(3)	
17	-	Pretty Good Year	Tori Amos	East West	1		
18	-	Shine On	Degrees Of Motion	ffrr	5		F L
19	-	The More You Ignore Me, The Closer I Get	Morrissey	Parlophone	1	(46)	L
20	4	All For Love	Bryan Adams/Rod Stewart/Sting	A&M	9	(1)	

This Mnth	Prev Mnth	Title	Artist	Label	Wks 20	(UK Pos)	
1	4	Hero	Mariah Carey	Columbia	20	(7)	G
2	9	All For Love	Bryan Adams/Rod Stewart/Sting	A&M	17	(2)	G
3	1	Again	Janet Jackson	Virgin	17	(6)	G
4	3	All That She Wants	Ace Of Base	Arista	20	(1)	F G
5	7	Breathe Again	Toni Braxton	Laface	26	(2)	
6	11	Said I Love You....But I Lied	Michael Bolton	Columbia	15	(15)	L
7	6	Gangsta Lean	DRS	Capitol	13		F G L
8	8	Please Forgive Me	Bryan Adams	A&M	15	(2)	
9	5	Shoop	Salt-N-Pepa	Next Plateau	16	(13)	
10	-	The Power Of Love	Celine Dion	550 Music	22	(4)	
11	12	Can We Talk	Tevin Campbell	Qwest	16		
12	2	I'd Do Anything For Love (But I Won't Do That)	Meat Loaf	MCA	15	(1)	G
13	13	Whoomp! (There It Is)	Tag Team	Life/Bellmark	33	(34)	F G L
14	17	What's My Name	Snoop Doggy Dogg	Death Row/ Interscope	6	(20)	F
15	-	Getto Jam	Domino	Outburst/Ral	10	(33)	F L
16	19	Linger	Cranberries	Island	11	(14)	F L
17	14	Keep Ya Head Up	2Pac	Interscope	9		
18	-	Because The Night	10,000 Maniacs	Elektra	10	(65)	F L
19	-	Understanding	Xscape	So So Def	9		
20	10	Just Kickin' It	Xscape	Columbia	15	(49)	F G L

This Mnth	Prev Mnth	Title	Artist	Label	Wks 20	(UK Pos)	
1	10	The Power Of Love	Celine Dion	550 Music	22	(4)	
2	2	All For Love	Bryan Adams/Rod Stewart/Sting	A&M	17	(2)	G
3	-	The Sign	Ace Of Base	Arista	26	(2)	
4	1	Hero	Mariah Carey	Columbia	20	(7)	G
5	5	Breathe Again	Toni Braxton	Laface	26	(2)	
6	-	Whatta Man	Salt-N-Pepa Feat. En Vogue	Next Plateau	15	(7)	L
7	15	Getto Jam	Domino	Outburst/Ral	10	(33)	F L
8	-	Without You/Never Forget You	Mariah Carey	Columbia	17	(1)	
9	19	Understanding	Xscape	So So Def	9		
10	4	All That She Wants	Ace Of Base	Arista	20	(1)	F G
11	6	Said I Love You....But I Lied	Michael Bolton	Columbia	15	(15)	L
12	8	Please Forgive Me	Bryan Adams	A&M	15	(2	
13	-	So Much In Love	All-4-One	Blitzz	14	(60)	F L
14	16	Linger	Cranberries	Island	11	(14)	F L
15	3	Again	Janet Jackson	Virgin	17	(6)	G
16	18	Because The Night	10,000 Maniacs	Elektra	10	(65)	F L
17	9	Shoop	Salt-N-Pepa	Next Plateau	16	(13)	
18	-	Now And Forever	Richard Marx	Capitol	16	(13)	
19	-	Because Of Love	Janet Jackson	Virgin	12	(19)	
20	-	Cantaloop (Flip Fantasia)	Us3	Blue Note/Capitol	11	(23)	F L

This Mnth	Prev Mnth	Title	Artist	Label	Wks 20	(UK Pos)	
1	3	The Sign	Ace Of Base	Arista	26	(2)	
2	1	The Power Of Love	Celine Dion	550 Music	22	(4)	
3	8	Without You/Never Forget You	Mariah Carey	Columbia	17	(1)	
4	6	Whatta Man	Salt-N-Pepa feat. En Vogue	Next Plateau	15	(7)	L
5	-	Bump N' Grind	R. Kelly	Jive	17	(8)	G
6	13	So Much In Love	All-4-One	Blitzz	14	(60)	F L
7	5	Breathe Again	Toni Braxton	Laface	26	(2)	
8	18	Now And Forever	Richard Marx	Capitol	16	(13)	
9	2	All For Love	Bryan Adams/Rod Stewart/Sting	A&M	17	(2)	G
10	20	Cantaloop (Flip Fantasia)	Us3	Blue Note/Capitol	11	(23)	F L
11	-	Gin And Juice	Snoop Doggy Dogg	Death Row/ Interscope	11	(39)	L
12	19	Because Of Love	Janet Jackson	Virgin	12	(19)	
13	4	Hero	Mariah Carey	Columbia	20	(7)	G
14	-	Rock And Roll Dreams Come Through	Meat Loaf	MCA	6	(11)	L
15	-	Mmm Mmm Mmm Mmm	Crash Test Dummies	Arista	12	(2)	F L
16	9	Understanding	Xscape	So So Def	9		
17	-	Mary Jane's Last Dance	Tom Petty & The Heartbreakers	MCA	5	(52)	
18	-	The Most Beautiful Girl In The World	TAFKAP	NPG/Bellmark	16	(1)	
19	-	Streets Of Philadelphia	Bruce Springsteen	Columbia	11	(2)	L
20	-	Groove Thang	Zhane	Motown	5	(34)	L

US 1994 JAN-MAR

▲ At the end of March, for the first time, reggae records held the top three places on the UK chart. They were 'Oh Carolina' by Shaggy, 'Informer' by Snow (above) and 'Mr. Loverman' by Shabba Ranks.

◆ Janet Jackson became the second female singer to amass 13 gold singles, and brother Michael collected his twelfth - among male singers, only his future father-in-law, Elvis Presley, had more.

◆ The multi-talented artists Nilsson and Dan Hartman died, as did veteran superstar Dinah Shore.

◆ Whitney Houston scooped eight American Music Awards.

331

UK 1994 APR-JUNE

▲ 'Everything Changes' gave Take That a record fourth entry at No. 1; the single had logged up 300,000 advance orders. They were the first act since The Beatles to take four successive singles to the top. Also, group member Gary Barlow was named Songwriter of the Year at the Ivor Novello Awards.

◆ Prince changed his name to a symbol, and released his first single away from Warner Brothers. The record, 'The Most Beautiful Girl In The World', gave him his first British No. 1.

April 1994

This Mnth	Prev Mnth	Title	Artist	Label	Wks 20	(US Pos)	
1	6	Streets Of Philadelphia	Bruce Springsteen	Columbia	8	(9)	L
2	-	The Most Beautiful Girl In The World	TAFKAP	NPG/Bellmark	9	(3)	
3	-	Everything Changes	Take That	RCA	5		
4	3	Doop	Doop	Citybeat	7		F L
5	8	I Like To Move It	Reel 2 Real/The Mad Stuntman	Positiva	15	(89)	F
6	2	The Sign	Ace Of Base	Arista	10	(1)	
7	-	The Real Thing	Tony Di Bart	Cleveland City	8		F L
8	12	U R The Best Thing	D:ream	FXU/Magnet	5		
9	-	Mmm Mmm Mmm Mmm	Crash Test Dummies	Arista	6	(4)	F L
10	16	Whatta Man	Salt-N-Pepa Featuring En Vogue	Next Plateau	6	(3)	
11	-	Dedicated To The One I Love	Bitty McLean	Brilliant	6		L
12	-	I'll Remember	Madonna	Maverick/Sire	4	(2)	
13	-	Rock My Heart	Haddaway	Logic/Arista	5		
14	1	Without You/Never Forget You	Mariah Carey	Columbia	9	(3)	
15	-	Sweets For My Sweet	CJ Lewis	Black Market	8		F
16	18	Shine On	Degrees Of Motion	ffrr	5		F L
17	-	Dry County	Bon Jovi	Vertigo	2		
18	-	I'll Stand By You	Pretenders	WEA	4	(16)	L
19	-	Light My Fire	Clubhouse Featuring Carl	PWL International	5		L
20	-	Hung Up	Paul Weller	Go! Discs	1		

May 1994

This Mnth	Prev Mnth	Title	Artist	Label	Wks 20	(US Pos)	
1	-	Come On You Reds	Manchester United Football Squad	Polygram TV	10		
2	-	Inside	Stiltskin	White Water	8		F L
3	7	The Real Thing	Tony Di Bart	Cleveland City	8		F L
4	15	Sweets For My Sweet	CJ Lewis	Black Market	8		F
5	2	The Most Beautiful Girl In The World	TAFKAP	NPG/Bellmark	9	(3)	
6	9	Mmm Mmm Mmm Mmm	Crash Test Dummies	Arista	6	(4)	F L
7	-	Around The World	East 17	London	7		
8	-	Love Is All Around	Wet Wet Wet	Precious	21	(45)	G
9	-	Just A Step From Heaven	Eternal	EMI	6		
10	19	Light My Fire	Clubhouse Featuring Carl	PWL International	5		L
11	-	Always	Erasure	Mute	5	(20)	L
12	-	Get-A-Way	Maxx	Pulse 8	7		F
13	-	The Real Thing	2 Unlimited	PWL	4		
14	-	More To This World	Bad Boys Inc	A&M	4		
15	11	Dedicated To The One I Love	Bitty McLean	Brilliant	6		L
16	5	I Like To Move It	Reel 2 Real/The Mad Stuntman	Positiva	15	(89)	F
17	-	No Good (Start The Dance)	Prodigy	XL	8		
18	18	I'll Stand By You	Pretenders	WEA	4	(16)	L
19	-	Carry Me Home	Gloworm	Go! Discs	6		L
20	-	Under The Bridge	Red Hot Chili Peppers	Warner	3	(2)	L

June 1994

This Mnth	Prev Mnth	Title	Artist	Label	Wks 20	(US Pos)	
1	8	Love Is All Around	Wet Wet Wet	Precious	21	(45)	G
2	-	Baby I Love Your Way	Big Mountain	RCA	10	(6)	F L
3	1	Come On You Reds	Manchester United Football Squad	Polygram TV	10		
4	17	No Good (Start The Dance)	Prodigy	XL	8		
5	12	Get-A-Way	Maxx	Pulse 8	7		F
6	7	Around The World	East 17	London	7		
7	-	You Don't Love Me (No, No, No)	Dawn Penn	Big Beat/Atlantic	7	(58)	F L
8	-	Swamp Thing	Grid	Deconstruction/RCA	12		F
9	-	Don't Turn Around	Ace Of Base	Arista	7	(4)	
10	-	Absolutely Fabulous	Absolutely Fabulous	Spaghetti/Parlophone	3		F L
11	2	Inside	Stiltskin	White Water	8		F L
12	-	Anytime You Need A Friend	Mariah Carey	Columbia	3	(12)	
13	-	I Swear	All-4-One	Blitzz	14	(1)	F L
14	19	Carry Me Home	Gloworm	Go! Discs	6		L
15	4	Sweets For My Sweet	CJ Lewis	Black Market	8		F
16	-	Since I Don't Have You	Guns N' Roses	Geffen	2	(69)	
17	-	Everybody's Talkin'	Beautiful South	Go! Discs	4		
18	13	The Real Thing	2 Unlimited	PWL	4		
19	-	No More Tears (Enough Is Enough)	Kym Mazelle & Jocelyn Brown	Bell/Arista	3		L
20	14	More To This World	Bad Boys Inc	A&M	4		

April 1994

This Mnth	Prev Mnth	Title	Artist	Label	Wks 20	(UK Pos)	
1	5	Bump N' Grind	R. Kelly	Jive	17	(8)	G
2	1	The Sign	Ace Of Base	Arista	26	(2)	
3	3	Without You/Never Forget You	Mariah Carey	Columbia	17	(1)	
4	2	The Power Of Love	Celine Dion	550 Music	22	(4)	
5	15	Mmm Mmm Mmm Mmm	Crash Test Dummies	Arista	12	(2)	F L
6	18	The Most Beautiful Girl In The World	TAFKAP	NPG/Bellmark	16	(1)	
7	6	So Much In Love	All-4-One	Blitzz	14	(60)	F L
8	4	Whatta Man	Salt-N-Pepa Featuring En Vogue	Next Plateau	15	(7)	L
9	8	Now And Forever	Richard Marx	Capitol	16	(13)	
10	19	Streets Of Philadelphia	Bruce Springsteen	Columbia	11	(2)	L
11	11	Gin And Juice	Snoop Doggy Dogg	Death Row/Interscope	11	(39)	L
12	10	Cantaloop (Flip Fantasia)	Us3	Blue Note/Capitol	11	(23)	F L
13	-	Baby I Love Your Way	Big Mountain	RCA	18	(2)	F L
14	-	Loser	Beck	DGC	8	(15)	F L
15	-	Return To Innocence	Enigma	Virgin	13	(3)	L
16	12	Because Of Love	Janet Jackson	Virgin	12	(19)	
17	-	I'm Ready	Tevin Campbell	Qwest	12		
18	-	I'll Remember	Madonna	Maverick/Sire	19	(7)	
19	7	Breathe Again	Toni Braxton	Laface	26	(2)	
20	-	Indian Outlaw	Tim McGraw	Curb	6		F

May 1994

This Mnth	Prev Mnth	Title	Artist	Label	Wks 20	(UK Pos)	
1	2	The Sign	Ace Of Base	Arista	26	(2)	
2	18	I'll Remember	Madonna	Maverick/Sire	19	(7)	
3	1	Bump N' Grind	R. Kelly	Jive	17	(8)	G
4	6	The Most Beautiful Girl In The World	TAFKAP	NPG/Bellmark	16	(1)	
5	-	I Swear	All-4-One	Blitzz	21	(2)	G L
6	15	Return To Innocence	Enigma	Virgin	13	(3)	L
7	13	Baby I Love Your Way	Big Mountain	RCA	18	(2)	F L
8	5	Mmm Mmm Mmm Mmm	Crash Test Dummies	Arista	12	(2)	F L
9	3	Without You/Never Forget You	Mariah Carey	Columbia	17	(1)	
10	-	You Mean The World To Me	Toni Braxton	Laface	19	(30)	L
11	17	I'm Ready	Tevin Campbell	Qwest	12		
12	4	The Power Of Love	Celine Dion	550 Music	22	(4)	
13	9	Now And Forever	Richard Marx	Capitol	16	(13)	
14	14	Loser	Beck	DGC	8	(15)	F L
15	-	Back & Forth	Aaliyah	Jive	17	(16)	F
16	-	Regulate	Warren G & Nate Dogg	Death Row/Interscope	16	(5)	F G L
17	-	Don't Turn Around	Ace Of Base	Arista	22	(5)	
18	7	So Much In Love	All-4-One	Blitzz	14	(60)	F L
19	10	Streets Of Philadelphia	Bruce Springsteen	Columbia	11	(2)	L
20	8	Whatta Man	Salt-N-Pepa Feat. En Vogue	Next Plateau	15	(7)	L

June 1994

This Mnth	Prev Mnth	Title	Artist	Label	Wks 20	(UK Pos)	
1	5	I Swear	All-4-One	Blitzz	21	(2)	G L
2	2	I'll Remember	Madonna	Maverick/Sire	19	(7)	
3	-	Any Time, Any Place/And On And On	Janet Jackson	Virgin	15	(13)	
4	16	Regulate	Warren G & Nate Dogg	Death Row/Interscope	16	(5)	F G L
5	1	The Sign	Ace Of Base	Arista	26	(2)	
6	17	Don't Turn Around	Ace Of Base	Arista	22	(5)	
7	4	The Most Beautiful Girl In The World	TAFKAP	NPG/Bellmark	16	(1)	
8	7	Baby I Love Your Way	Big Mountain	RCA	18	(2)	F L
9	6	Return To Innocence	Enigma	Virgin	13	(3)	L
10	15	Back & Forth	Aaliyah	Jive	17	(16)	F
11	10	You Mean The World To Me	Toni Braxton	Laface	19	(30)	L
12	-	If You Go	Jon Secada	SBK	18	(39)	L
13	-	Stay	Lisa Loeb & Nine Stories	RCA	20	(6)	F L
14	-	Your Body's Callin'	R. Kelly	Jive	10	(19)	L
15	11	I'm Ready	Tevin Campbell	Qwest	12		
16	3	Bump N' Grind	R. Kelly	Jive	17	(8)	G
17	-	Anytime You Need A Friend	Mariah Carey	Columbia	13	(8)	
18	-	Can You Feel The Love Tonight	Elton John	Hollywood	17	(14)	
19	-	Don't Take The Girl	Tim McGraw	Curb	4		L
20	13	Now And Forever	Richard Marx	Capitol	16	(13)	

◆ Veteran act Pink Floyd broke box office records on their US tour. Not only did their previous albums sell like new releases but **The Division Bell** entered both the US and UK chart at No. 1. Other 'oldies' packing them in included Frank Sinatra and Barbra Streisand, who grossed record amounts on both sides of the Atlantic.

◆ Kurt Cobain, the charismatic leader of Nirvana, committed suicide a week after the press reported he had lost interest in performing live.

◆ R. Kelly's million selling 'Bump N Grind' led the R&B lists for 12 weeks, a feat unequalled since 1958. It was one of three simultaneous Top 10 entries that he had both written and produced.

UK 1994
JULY-SEPT

◆ Danish-born Whigfield became the first artists to make their UK chart debut at No. 1. 'Saturday Night', one of Europe's biggest summertime hits, sold over half a million in just three weeks.

◆ Sweden's latest hit making machine, Ace Of Base, reached the Top 5 in 30 countries with their album **The Sign (aka Happy Nation).** Their current transatlantic hit ,'Don't Turn Around' was one of a record seven reggae-styled tracks in the UK Top 30.

In Britain, Wet Wet Wet held the top rung for a staggering 15 weeks with a revival of The Troggs' 'Love Is All Around', whilst in the USA 'I'll Make Love To You' by Boyz II Men hogged the No. 1 position for an unprecedented 14 weeks.

July 1994

This Mnth	Prev Mnth	Title	Artist	Label	Wks 20	(US Pos)	
1	1	Love Is All Around	Wet Wet Wet	Precious	21	(45)	G
2	13	I Swear	All-4-One	Blitzz	14	(1)	
3	8	Swamp Thing	Grid	Deconstruction/RCA	12		F
4	-	(Meet) The Flintstones	BC-52s	MCA	9	(33)	L
5	2	Baby I Love Your Way	Big Mountain	RCA	10	(6)	F L
6	-	Love Ain't Here Anymore	Take That	RCA	4		
7	-	Shine	Aswad	Bubblin'	9		L
8	-	Crazy For You	Let Loose	Mercury	13		F
9	7	You Don't Love Me (No, No, No)	Dawn Penn	Big Beat/Atlantic	7	(58)	F L
10	-	Go On Move	Reel 2 Real/Mad Stuntman	Positiva	4		
11	9	Don't Turn Around	Ace Of Base	Arista	7	(4)	
12	-	Everybody Gonfi Gon	Two Cowboys	3 Beat/ffrreedom	5		F L
13	-	Regulate	Warren G & Nate Dogg	Death Row/Interscope	10	(2)	F L
14	-	Word Up	Gun	A&M	4		F
15	4	No Good (Start The Dance)	Prodigy	XL	8		
16	-	Run To The Sun	Erasure	Mute	2		
17	-	Searching	China Black	Wild Card	10		F
18	-	U & Me	Cappella	Internal	3		
19	-	Everything Is Alright (Uptight)	CJ Lewis	Black Market/MCA	4		
20	-	Shakermaker	Oasis	Creation	2		F

August 1994

This Mnth	Prev Mnth	Title	Artist	Label	Wks 20	(US Pos)	
1	1	Love Is All Around	Wet Wet Wet	Precious	21	(45)	G
2	8	Crazy For You	Let Loose	Mercury	13		F
3	2	I Swear	All-4-One	Blitzz	14	(1)	F L
4	17	Searching	China Black	Wild Card	10		F
5	-	Compliments On Your Kiss	Red Dragon With Brian & Tony Gold	Mango	9		F L
6	4	(Meet) The Flintstones	BC-52s	MCA	9	(33)	L
7	13	Regulate	Warren G & Nate Dogg	Death Row/Interscope	10	(2)	F L
8	-	7 Seconds	Youssou N'dour/Neneh Cherry	Columbia	9	(98)	F L
9	-	What's Up	DJ Miko	Systematic	6		F L
10	-	No More (I Can't Stand It)	Maxx	Pulse 8	4		L
11	-	Let's Get Ready To Rumble	PJ And Duncan	XSrhythm/Telstar	7		F
12	7	Shine	Aswad	Bubblin'	9		L
13	-	Trouble	Shampoo	Food/Parlophone	7		F L
14	3	Swamp Thing	Grid	Deconstruction/RCA	12		F
15	-	Eighteen Strings	Tinman	ffrr	4		F L
16	-	Live Forever	Oasis	Creation	3		
17	19	Everything Is Alright (Uptight)	CJ Lewis	Black Market/MCA	4		
18	-	Black Hole Sun	Soundgarden	A&M	2		L
19	-	Midnight At The Oasis	Brand New Heavies	Acid Jazz	3		L
20	-	So Good	Eternal	EMI	3		

September 1994

This Mnth	Prev Mnth	Title	Artist	Label	Wks 20	(US Pos)	
1	1	Love Is All Around	Wet Wet Wet	Precious	21	(45)	G
2	8	7 Seconds	Youssou N'dour/Neneh Cherry	Columbia	9	(98)	F L
3	5	Compliments On Your Kiss	Red Dragon With Brian & Tony Gold	Mango	9		F L
4	-	Confide In Me	Kylie Minogue	Deconstruction/RCA	4		
5	-	I'll Make Love To You	Boyz II Men	Motown	7	(1)	
6	-	The Rhythm Of The Night	Corona	WEA	8	(11)	F
7	-	Saturday Night	Whigfield	Systematic	12		F G
8	2	Crazy For You	Let Loose	Mercury	13		F
9	-	Endless Love	Luther Vandross/Mariah Carey	Columbia	5	(2)	
10	4	Searching	China Black	Wild Card	10		F
11	7	Regulate	Warren G & Nate Dogg	Death Row/Interscope	10	(2)	F L
12	3	I Swear	All-4-One	Blitzz	14	(1)	F L
13	-	Incredible	M-Beat feat General Levy	Renk	5		F
14	-	Always	Bon Jovi	Mercury	12	(4)	
15	9	What's Up	DJ Miko	Systematic	6		F L
16	-	What's The Frequency, Kenneth?	REM	Warner	3	(21)	
17	-	Parklife	Blur	Food	3		
18	-	Hey Now (Girls Just Want To Have Fun)	Cyndi Lauper	Epic	9	(87)	L
19	-	Right Beside You	Sophie B. Hawkins	Columbia	6	(56)	L
20	15	Eighteen Strings	Tinman	ffrr	4		F L

July 1994

This Mnth	Prev Mnth	Title	Artist	Label	Wks 20	(UK Pos)	
1	1	I Swear	All-4-One	Blitzz	21	(2)	G L
2	4	Regulate	Warren G & Nate Dogg	Death Row/Interscope	16	(5)	F G L
3	13	Stay	Lisa Loeb & Nine Stories	RCA	20	(6)	F L
4	3	Any Time, Any Place/And On And On	Janet Jackson	Virgin	15	(13)	
5	6	Don't Turn Around	Ace Of Base	Arista	22	(5)	
6	10	Back & Forth	Aaliyah	Jive	17	(16)	F
7	-	Fantastic Voyage	Coolio	Tommy Boy	15	(41)	F G L
8	18	Can You Feel The Love Tonight	Elton John	Hollywood	17	(14)	
9	2	I'll Remember	Madonna	Maverick/Sire	19	(7)	
10	11	You Mean The World To Me	Toni Braxton	Laface	19	(30)	L
11	-	Funkdafied	Da Brat	So So Def/Chaos	14	(65)	F G L
12	12	If You Go	Jon Secada	SBK	18	(39)	L
13	-	Wild Night	John Mellencamp & Me'shell Ndegeocello	Mercury	19	(34)	L
14	17	Anytime You Need A Friend	Mariah Carey	Columbia	13	(8)	
15	8	Baby I Love Your Way	Big Mountain	RCA	18	(2)	F L
16	-	Shine	Collective Soul	Atlantic	17		F
17	14	Your Body's Callin'	R. Kelly	Jive	10	(19)	L
18	5	The Sign	Ace Of Base	Arista	26	(2)	
19	-	I Miss You	Aaron Hall	Silas	10		F L
20	7	The Most Beautiful Girl In The World	TAFKAP	NPG/Bellmark	16	(1)	

August 1994

This Mnth	Prev Mnth	Title	Artist	Label	Wks 20	(UK Pos)	
1	3	Stay	Lisa Loeb & Nine Stories	RCA	20	(6)	F L
2	1	I Swear	All-4-One	Blitzz	21	(2)	G L
3	7	Fantastic Voyage	Coolio	Tommy Boy	15	(41)	F G L
4	13	Wild Night	John Mellencamp & Me'shell Ndegeocello	Mercury	19	(34)	L
5	8	Can You Feel The Love Tonight	Elton John	Hollywood	17	(14)	
6	-	I'll Make Love To You	Boyz II Men	Motown	24	(5)	G
7	5	Don't Turn Around	Ace Of Base	Arista	22	(5)	
8	11	Funkdafied	Da Brat	So So Def/Chaos	14	(65)	F G L
9	4	Any Time, Any Place/And On And On	Janet Jackson	Virgin	15	(13)	
10	2	Regulate	Warren G & Nate Dogg	Death Row/Interscope	16	(5)	F G L
11	-	When Can I See You	Babyface	Epic	17	(35)	
12	6	Back & Forth	Aaliyah	Jive	17	(16)	F
13	16	Shine	Collective Soul	Atlantic	17		F
14	12	If You Go	Jon Secada	SBK	18	(39)	L
15	-	This D.J.	Warren G	Violator/Ral	10	(12)	F L
16	-	Stroke You Up	Changing Faces	Spoiled Rotten	12	(43)	F G L
17	19	I Miss You	Aaron Hall	Silas	10		F L
18	10	You Mean The World To Me	Toni Braxton	Laface	19	(30)	L
19	14	Anytime You Need A Friend	Mariah Carey	Columbia	13	(8)	
20	9	I'll Remember	Madonna	Maverick/Sire	19	(7)	

September 1994

This Mnth	Prev Mnth	Title	Artist	Label	Wks 20	(UK Pos)	
1	6	I'll Make Love To You	Boyz II Men	Motown	24	(5)	G
2	1	Stay	Lisa Loeb & Nine Stories	RCA	20	(6)	F L
3	4	Wild Night	John Mellencamp & Me'shell Ndegeocello	Mercury	19	(34)	L
4	16	Stroke You Up	Changing Faces	Spoiled Rotten	12	(43)	F G L
5	11	When Can I See You	Babyface	Epic	17	(35)	
6	3	Fantastic Voyage	Coolio	Tommy Boy	15	(41)	F G L
7	5	Can You Feel The Love Tonight	Elton John	Hollywood	17	(14)	
8	-	Endless Love	Luther Vandross & Mariah Carey	Columbia	10	(3)	L
9	2	I Swear	All-4-One	Blitzz	21	(2)	G L
10	-	All I Wanna Do	Sheryl Crow	A&M	21	(4)	F L
11	15	This D.J.	Warren G	Violator/Ral	10	(12)	F L
12	7	Don't Turn Around	Ace Of Base	Arista	22	(5)	
13	8	Funkdafied	Da Brat	So So Def/Chaos	14	(65)	F G L
14	13	Shine	Collective Soul	Atlantic	17		F
15	-	At Your Best (You Are Love)	Aaliyah	Blackground/Jive	10	(27)	L
16	14	If You Go	Jon Secada	SBK	18	(39)	L
17	9	Any Time, Any Place/And On And On	Janet Jackson	Virgin	15	(13)	
18	-	100% Pure Love	Crystal Waters	Mercury	16	(15)	L
19	-	Tootsie Roll	69 Boyz	Down Low/Rip-It	21		F G L
20	-	Never Lie	Immature	MCA	15		F L

▲ Woodstock 94 attracted as many of the top names of the era as Woodstock had 25 years earlier. Alongside today's top acts such as Nine Inch Nails, Red Hot Chili Peppers, Candlebox, Metallica and Green Day were sixties stars Crosby, Stills & Nash, Bob Dylan and Joe Cocker.

◆ The biggest money earners on the road were long-time favorites The Rolling Stones, Eagles, Grateful Dead, the re-formed Traffic and the singer/song-writer dream team of Elton John and Billy Joel.

◆ At times multi-talented R&B artist Babyface had seven records that he had both produced and written simultaneously on the Top 100.

UK 1994 OCT-DEC

◆ Record piracy rocketed to new heights, sales were up 17% in the UK and 20% in the USA. Interestingly, there had been only nine US No. 1 singles in 1994, fewer than any year since 1955.

◆ In a year when the remaining members of Led Zeppelin reportedly refused $100 million to reform, tours by fellow UK veterans The Rolling Stones and Pink Floyd both surpassed $100 million in ticket sales alone.

◆ As the ground breaking ceremony took place for the National Black Music Hall Of Fame in New Orleans, a survey pointed out that black American artists were seven times more likely to get a British hit than white ones.

◆ 1994 was a year of unrest for major superstars with George Michael, Prince and Metallica taking legal action against their record companies.

October 1994

This Mnth	Prev Mnth	Title	Artist	Label	Wks 20	(US Pos)	
1	7	Saturday Night	Whigfield	Systematic	12		F G
2	14	Always	Bon Jovi	Mercury	12	(4)	
3	-	Baby Come Back	Pato Banton	Virgin	15		F
4	18	Hey Now (Girls Just Want To Have Fun)	Cyndi Lauper	Epic	9	(87)	L
5	6	The Rhythm Of The Night	Corona	WEA	8	(11)	F
6	-	Sure	Take That	RCA	4		
7	-	Sweetness	Michelle Gayle	Ist Avenue/RCA	10		
8	-	Stay	Lisa Loeb & Nine Stories	RCA	9	(1)	F L
9	9	Endless Love	Luther Vandross & Mariah Carey	Columbia	5	(2)	
10	-	Secret	Madonna	Maverick/Sire	5	(3)	
11	-	Steam	East 17	London	4		
12	-	Welcome To Tomorrow	Snap Featuring Summer	Arista	7		
13	-	She's Got That Vibe	R. Kelly	Jive	6	(59)	
14	-	Cigarettes & Alcohol	Oasis	Creation	2		
15	-	Circle Of Life	Elton John	Rocket	6	(18)	
16	5	I'll Make Love To You	Boyz II Men	Motown	7	(1)	
17	1	Love Is All Around	Wet Wet Wet	Precious	21	(45)	G
18	13	Incredible	M-Beat Featuring General Levy	Renk	5		F
19	-	When We Dance	Sting	A&M	3	(38)	
20	-	Seventeen	Let Loose	Mercury	3		

November 1994

This Mnth	Prev Mnth	Title	Artist	Label	Wks 20	(US Pos)	
1	3	Baby Come Back	Pato Banton	Virgin	15		F
2	2	Always	Bon Jovi	Mercury	12	(4)	
3	-	Another Night	(MC Sar &) the Real McCoy	Arista	10	(3)	F
4	13	She's Got That Vibe	R. Kelly	Jive	6	(59)	
5	-	Oh Baby I	Eternal	EMI	7		
6	1	Saturday Night	Whigfield	Systematic	12		F G
7	-	All I Wanna Do	Sheryl Crow	A&M	6	(2)	F L
8	-	Let Me Be Your Fantasy	Baby D	Systematic	9		F
9	7	Sweetness	Michelle Gayle	Ist Avenue/RCA	10		
10	12	Welcome To Tomorrow	Snap Featuring Summer	Arista	7		
11	-	We Have All The Time In The World	Louis Armstrong	EMI	7		L
12	-	Sight For Sore Eyes	M People	Deconstruction	5		
13	-	Some Girls	Ultimate Kaos	Wild Card	5		F
14	4	Hey Now (Girls Just Want To Have Fun)	Cyndi Lauper	Epic	9	(87	L
15	-	True Faith - 94	New Order	Centredate Co/ London	3		
16	-	Crocodile Shoes	Jimmy Nail	East West	8		
17	-	If I Only Knew	Tom Jones	ZTT/Atlantic	3		L
18	8	Stay	Lisa Loeb & Nine Stories	RCA	9	(1)	F L
19	-	Spin The Black Circle	Pearl Jam	Epic	1	(18)	L
20	-	This D.J.	Warren G	Violator/Ral	2	(9)	F L

December 1994

This Mnth	Prev Mnth	Title	Artist	Label	Wks 20	(US Pos)	
1	-	Stay Another Day	East 17	London	9		
2	-	All I Want For Christmas Is You	Mariah Carey	Columbia	5		L
3	8	Let Me Be Your Fantasy	Baby D	Systematic	9		F
4	11	We Have All The Time In The World	Louis Armstrong	EMI	7		L
5	16	Crocodile Shoes	Jimmy Nail	East West	8		
6	-	Love Me For A Reason	Boyzone	Polydor	9		F
7	-	Think Twice	Celine Dion	Epic	20	(95)	G
8	-	Power Rangers	Mighty Morph'n Power Rangers	RCA	5		F L
9	3	Another Night	(MC Sar &) the Real McCoy	Arista	10	(3)	F
10	-	Love Spreads	Stone Roses	Geffen	2		
11	1	Baby Come Back	Pato Banton	Virgin	15		F
12	-	Cotton Eye Joe	Rednex	Internal Affairs	12	(25)	F
13	-	Please Come Home For Christmas	Bon Jovi	Jambco	4		
14	-	Whatever	Oasis	Creation	6		
15	-	Hold Me, Thrill Me, Kiss Me	Gloria Estefan	Epic	6		
16	-	Another Day	Whigfield	Systematic	6		
17	-	Them Girls Them Girls	Zig And Zag	RCA	5		F L
18	7	All I Wanna Do	Sheryl Crow	A&M	6	(2)	F L
19	-	Eternal Love	PJ And Duncan	XSrhythm/Telstar	6		
20	12	Sight For Sore Eyes	M People	Deconstruction	5		

US
1994
OCT-DEC

This Mnth	Prev Mnth	Title	Artist	Label	Wks 20	(UK Pos)	
1	1	I'll Make Love To You	Boyz II Men	Motown	24	(5)	G
2	10	All I Wanna Do	Sheryl Crow	A&M	21	(4)	F L
3	8	Endless Love	Luther Vandross & Mariah Carey	Columbia	10	(3)	L
4	5	When Can I See You	Babyface	Epic	17	(35)	
5	20	Never Lie	Immature	MCA	15		F L
6	15	At Your Best (You Are Love)	Aaliyah	Blackground/Jive	10	(27)	L
7	3	Wild Night	John Mellencamp & Me'shell Ndegeocello	Mercury	19	(34)	L
8	4	Stroke You Up	Changing Faces	Spoiled Rotten	12	(43)	F G L
9	-	Another Night	Real McCoy	Arista	28	(2)	F G
10	2	Stay	Lisa Loeb & Nine Stories	RCA	20	(6)	F L
11	-	Secret	Madonna	Maverick/Sire	15	(5)	
12	18	100% Pure Love	Crystal Waters	Mercury	16	(15)	L
13	-	Always	Bon Jovi	Mercury	23	(2)	G
14	11	This D.J.	Warren G	Violator/Ral	10	(12)	F L
15	12	Don't Turn Around	Ace Of Base	Arista	22	(5)	
16	-	I Wanna Be Down	Brandy	Atlantic	18	(36)	F
17	19	Tootsie Roll	69 Boyz	Down Low/Rip-It	21		F G L
18	-	Here Comes The Hotstepper	Ini Kamoze	Columbia	18	(4)	F G L
19	6	Fantastic Voyage	Coolio	Tommy Boy	15	(41)	F G L
20	-	December 1963 (Oh, What A Night)	Four Seasons	Curb	9		L

November 1994

This Mnth	Prev Mnth	Title	Artist	Label	Wks 20	(UK Pos)	
1	1	I'll Make Love To You	Boyz II Men	Motown	24	(5)	G
2	18	Here Comes The Hotstepper	Ini Kamoze	Columbia	18	(4)	F G L
3	2	All I Wanna Do	Sheryl Crow	A&M	21	(4)	F L
4	9	Another Night	Real McCoy	Arista	28	(2)	F G
5	11	Secret	Madonna	Maverick/Sire	15	(5)	
6	13	Always	Bon Jovi	Mercury	23	(2)	G
7	16	I Wanna Be Down	Brandy	Atlantic	18	(36)	F
8	5	Never Lie	Immature	MCA	15		F L
9	-	On Bended Knee	Boyz II Men	Motown	20	(20)	G
10	-	You Want This/70's Love Groove	Janet Jackson	Virgin	14	(14)	
11	3	Endless Love	Luther Vandross & Mariah Carey	Columbia	10	(3)	L
12	-	I'm The Only One	Melissa Etheridge	Island	20		F
13	6	At Your Best (You Are Love)	Aaliyah	Blackground/Jive	10	(27)	L
14	12	100% Pure Love	Crystal Waters	Mercury	16	(15)	L
15	4	When Can I See You	Babyface	Epic	17	(35)	
16	17	Tootsie Roll	69 Boyz	Down Low/Rip-It	21		F G L
17	-	Turn The Beat Around	Gloria Estefan	Crescent Moon	11	(21)	L
18	-	Creep	TLC	Laface	24	(22)	G
19	20	December 1963 (Oh, What A Night)	Four Seasons	Curb	9		L
20	8	Stroke You Up	Changing Faces	Spoiled Rotten	12	(43)	F G L

December 1994

This Mnth	Prev Mnth	Title	Artist	Label	Wks 20	(UK Pos)	
1	9	On Bended Knee	Boyz II Men	Motown	20	(20)	G
2	2	Here Comes The Hotstepper	Ini Kamoze	Columbia	18	(4)	F G L
3	4	Another Night	Real McCoy	Arista	28	(2)	F G
4	6	Always	Bon Jovi	Mercury	23	(2)	G
5	1	I'll Make Love To You	Boyz II Men	Motown	24	(5)	G
6	18	Creep	TLC	Laface	24	(22)	G
7	7	I Wanna Be Down	Brandy	Atlantic	18	(36)	F
8	5	Secret	Madonna	Maverick/Sire	15	(5)	
9	3	All I Wanna Do	Sheryl Crow	A&M	21	(4)	F L
10	10	You Want This/70's Love Groove	Janet Jackson	Virgin	14	(14)	
11	12	I'm The Only One	Melissa Etheridge	Island	20		F
12	-	Before I Let You Go	Blackstreet	Interscope	13		F L
13	16	Tootsie Roll	69 Boyz	Down Low/Rip-It	21		F G L
14	17	Turn The Beat Around	Gloria Estefan	Crescent Moon	11	(21)	L
15	-	Sukiyaki	4 P.M.	Next Plateau	15		F L
16	8	Never Lie	Immature	MCA	15		F L
17	14	100% Pure Love	Crystal Waters	Mercury	16	(15)	L
18	-	Take A Bow	Madonna	Maverick/Sire	21	(16)	L
19	-	Short Dick Man	20 Fingers Featuring Gilette	DJ World	4	(11)	F L
20	-	You Gotta Be	Des'ree	550 Music	20	(14)	F L

▲ When On Bended Knee dethroned 'I'll Make Love To You' at No. 1, Boyz II Men joined Elvis and The Beatles as the only acts ever to replace themselves at No. 1.

◆ A report showed that four times as many people were listening to Modern Rock radio than three years ago.

◆ A remix of the Four Seasons' 1975 chart topper 'December, 1963 (Oh, What A Night)' revisited the Top 20, and made it the first single to spend over a year on the Top 100.

UK 1995 JAN-MAR

A survey of 1994 showed that for the first time there were more European than American artists among the UK's Top 100 singles acts. British acts were having their worst spell on the US charts since the start of the Beat Boom, 32 years earlier.

▲ Celine Dion's minor US hit 'Think Twice' was one of the year's biggest sellers in Britain. Canadian Dion held the top single and album positions for five consecutive weeks, a feat last performed by The Beatles.

◆ At times, re-mixes of singles that flopped when first released hogged half of the UK Top 10.

January 1995

This Mnth	Prev Mnth	Title	Artist	Label	Wks 20	(US Pos)	
1	12	Cotton Eye Joe	Rednex	Internal Affairs	12	(25)	F
2	7	Think Twice	Celine Dion	Epic	20	(95)	G
3	6	Love Me For A Reason	Boyzone	Polydor	9		F
4	1	Stay Another Day	East 17	London	9		
5	-	Here Comes The Hotstepper	Ini Kamoze	Columbia	11	(1)	F L
6	-	Set You Free	N-Trance	All Around The World	10		F
7	-	Tell Me When	Human League	East West	6	(31)	
8	14	Whatever	Oasis	Creation	6		
9	-	Total Eclipse Of The Heart	Nicki French	Bags of Fun	8	(2)	F L
10	17	Them Girls Them Girls	Zig And Zag	RCA	5		F L
11	16	Another Day	Whigfield	Systematic	6		
12	-	Bump N' Grind	R. Kelly	Jive	6	(1)	L
13	-	Basket Case	Green Day	Reprise	3		
14	-	Sympathy For The Devil	Guns N' Roses	Geffen	2	(55)	L
15	5	Crocodile Shoes	Jimmy Nail	East West	8		
16	2	All I Want For Christmas Is You	Mariah Carey	Columbia	5		L
17	-	Riverdance	Bill Whelan	Son	9		F L
18	-	She's A River	Simple Minds	Virgin	2	(52)	
19	-	Glory Box	Portishead	Go Beat	3		F
20	8	Power Rangers	Mighty Morph'n Power Rangers	RCA	5		F L

February 1995

		Title	Artist	Label			
1	2	Think Twice	Celine Dion	Epic	20	(95)	G
2	6	Set You Free	N-Trance	All Around The World	10		F
3	1	Cotton Eye Joe	Rednex	Internal Affairs	12	(25)	F
4	-	I've Got A Little Something For You	MN8	Columbia	8		F
5	5	Here Comes The Hotstepper	Ini Kamoze	Columbia	11	(1)	F L
6	9	Total Eclipse Of The Heart	Nicki French	Bags of Fun	8	(2)	F L
7	-	No More 'I Love You's	Annie Lennox	RCA	5	(23)	
8	-	Run Away	Real McCoy	Arista	7	(3)	
9	-	Reach Up (Papa's Got A Brand New Pig Bag)	Perfecto Allstarz	Perfecto/East West	7		F L
10	-	Don't Give Me Your Life	Alex Party	Systematic	9		F L
11	-	Bedtime Story	Madonna	Maverick/Sire	2	(42)	
12	17	Riverdance	Bill Whelan	Son	9		F L
13	-	Open Your Heart	M People	Deconstruction	3		L
14	13	Basket Case	Green Day	Reprise	3		
15	-	Call It Love	Deuce	London	5		F
16	-	Independent Love Song	Scarlet	WEA	7		F L
17	-	Someday I'll Be Saturday Night	Bon Jovi	Jambco	3		
18	7	Tell Me When	Human League	East West	6	(31)	
19	12	Bump N' Grind	R. Kelly	Jive	6	(1)	L
20	-	One Night Stand	Let Loose	Mercury	3		

March 1995

		Title	Artist	Label			
1	1	Think Twice	Celine Dion	Epic	20	(95)	G
2	10	Don't Give Me Your Life	Alex Party	Systematic	9		F L
3	-	Push The Feeling On	Nightcrawlers	ffrr	7		F
4	4	I've Got A Little Something For You	MN8	Columbia	8		F
5	-	Love Can Build A Bridge	Cher/Chrissie Hynde/ Neneh Cherry/Eric Clapton	London	5		
6	-	The Bomb! (These Sounds Fall Into My Mind)	Bucketheads	Positiva	9	(49)	F L
7	7	No More 'I Love You's	Annie Lennox	RCA	5	(23)	
8	-	Don't Stop (Wiggle Wiggle)	Outhere Brothers	Eternal	11		F
9	-	Turn On, Tune In, Cop Out	Freak Power	4th & Broadway	5		F L
10	-	Axel F/Keep Pushin'	Clock	Media/MCA	5		F
11	9	Reach Up (Papa's Got A Brand New Pig Bag)	Perfecto Allstarz	Perfecto/East West	7		F L
12	2	Set You Free	N-Trance	All Around The World	10		F
13	-	Julia Says	Wet Wet Wet	Precious	5		
14	-	Wake Up Boo!	Boo Radleys	Creation	3		F L
15	17	Someday I'll Be Saturday Night	Bon Jovi	Jambco	3		
16	-	Whoops Now/What'll I Do	Janet Jackson	Virgin	4		
17	5	Here Comes The Hotstepper	Ini Kamoze	Columbia	11	(1)	F L
18	11	Bedtime Story	Madonna	Maverick/Sire	2	(42)	
19	-	Over My Shoulder	Mike + The Mechanics	Virgin	3		L
20	3	Cotton Eye Joe	Rednex	Internal Affairs	12	(25)	F

January 1995

This Mnth	Prev Mnth	Title	Artist	Label	Wks 20	(UK Pos)	
1	1	On Bended Knee	Boyz II Men	Motown	20	(20)	G
2	6	Creep	TLC	Laface	24	(22)	G
3	3	Another Night	Real McCoy	Arista	28	(2)	F G
4	2	Here Comes The Hotstepper	Ini Kamoze	Columbia	18	(4)	F G L
5	4	Always	Bon Jovi	Mercury	23	(2)	G
6	18	Take A Bow	Madonna	Maverick/Sire	21	(16)	L
7	7	I Wanna Be Down	Brandy	Atlantic	18	(36)	F
8	12	Before I Let You Go	Blackstreet	Interscope	13		F L
9	11	I'm The Only One	Melissa Etheridge	Island	20		F
10	20	You Gotta Be	Des'ree	550 Music	20	(14)	F L
11	15	Sukiyaki	4 P.M.	Next Plateau	15		F L
12	13	Tootsie Roll	69 Boyz	Down Low/Rip-It	21		F G L
13	5	I'll Make Love To You	Boyz II Men	Motown	24	(5)	G
14	10	You Want This/70's Love Groove	Janet Jackson	Virgin	14	(14)	
15	-	The Rhythm Of The Night	Corona	East West	8	(2)	F L
16	19	Short Dick Man	20 Fingers Featuring Gillette	DJ World	4	(11)	F L
17	-	Hold My Hand	Hootie & The Blowfish	Atlantic	17	(50)	F
18	8	Secret	Madonna	Maverick/Sire	15	(5)	
19	9	All I Wanna Do	Sheryl Crow	A&M	21	(4)	F L
20	-	You Don't Know How It Feels	Tom Petty	Warner	8		L

February 1995

This Mnth	Prev Mnth	Title	Artist	Label	Wks 20	(UK Pos)	
1	2	Creep	TLC	Laface	24	(22)	G
2	6	Take A Bow	Madonna	Maverick/Sire	21	(16)	L
3	1	On Bended Knee	Boyz II Men	Motown	20	(20)	G
4	3	Another Night	Real McCoy	Arista	28	(2)	F G
5	10	You Gotta Be	Des'ree	550 Music	20	(14)	F L
6	5	Always	Bon Jovi	Mercury	23	(2)	G
7	-	Baby	Brandy	Atlantic	13		G L
8	-	Candy Rain	Soul For Real	Uptown	16	(23)	F
9	11	Sukiyaki	4 P.M.	Next Plateau	15		F L
10	8	Before I Let You Go	Blackstreet	Interscope	13		F L
11	18	Hold My Hand	Hootie & The Blowfish	Atlantic	17	(50)	F
12	-	If You Love Me	Brownstone	MJJ	13	(8)	F L
13	9	I'm The Only One	Melissa Etheridge	Island	20		F
14	15	The Rhythm Of The Night	Corona	East West	8	(2)	F L
15	4	Here Comes The Hotstepper	Ini Kamoze	Columbia	18	(4)	F G L
16	20	You Don't Know How It Feels	Tom Petty	Warner	8		L
17	-	Strong Enough	Sheryl Crow	A&M	16	(33)	L
18	-	Big Poppa/Warning	Notorious B.I.G.	Bad Boy	13	(63)	F G
19	7	I Wanna Be Down	Brandy	Atlantic	18	(36)	F
20	-	Constantly	Immature	MCA	6		L

March 1995

This Mnth	Prev Mnth	Title	Artist	Label	Wks 20	(UK Pos)	
1	2	Take A Bow	Madonna	Maverick/Sire	21	(16)	L
2	1	Creep	TLC	Laface	24	(22)	G
3	8	Candy Rain	Soul For Real	Uptown	16	(23)	F
4	7	Baby	Brandy	Atlantic	13		G
5	3	On Bended Knee	Boyz II Men	Motown	20	(20)	G
6	5	You Gotta Be	Des'ree	550 Music	20	(14)	F L
7	17	Strong Enough	Sheryl Crow	A&M	16	(33)	L
8	4	Another Night	Real McCoy	Arista	28	(2)	F G
9	18	Big Poppa/Warning	Notorious B.I.G.	Bad Boy	13	(63)	F G
10	-	Red Light Special	TLC	Laface	15	(18)	
11	12	If You Love Me	Brownstone	MJJ	13	(8)	F L
12	11	Hold My Hand	Hootie & The Blowfish	Atlantic	17	(50)	F
13	-	I Know	Dionne Farris	Columbia	20	(47)	F L
14	6	Always	Bon Jovi	Mercury	23	(2)	G
15	9	Sukiyaki	4 P.M.	Next Plateau	15		F L
16	-	Run Away	Real McCoy	Arista	13	(6)	
17	-	Freak Like Me	Adina Howard	Mecca Don/East West	20	(33)	F G L
18	16	You Don't Know How It Feels	Tom Petty	Warner	8		L
19	-	If I Wanted To/Like The Way I Do	Melissa Etheridge	Island	5		L
20	-	This Is How We Do It	Montell Jordan	PPM/Ral	18	(11)	F G L

◆ Among the acts joining the Rock And Roll Hall Of Fame were The Allman Brothers, Janis Joplin, Led Zeppelin, Neil Young and Frank Zappa. R&B greats inducted included Martha & The Vandellas, Al Green and The Orioles.

◆ Influential rapper Eazy-E (ex NWA) and David Cole, mastermind behind the C&C Music Factory, both died from Aids-related illnesses.

◆ Madonna scored her 11th chart topper and her 23rd Top 5 entry with 'Take A Bow' — both records for a female artist. She also replaced Carole King as the female who had written the most No. 1s.

UK 1995

APR-JUNE

▲ TV actors Robson Green & Jerome Flynn became the first UK act to make their chart debut at No. 1. Their version of the oft-recorded 'Unchained Melody' sold a million in three weeks!

◆ Take That's 'Back For Good' sold half a million in two weeks and their LP **Nobody Else** went double platinum in three days. These successes led to a $1 million US deal with Arista.

◆ Soon after Blur won a record four Brit Awards, arch rivals Oasis clocked up their first chart topper, 'Some Might Say' and five of their previous singles re-charted.

April 1995

This Mnth	Prev Mnth	Title	Artist	Label	Wks 20	(US Pos)	
1	8	Don't Stop (Wiggle Wiggle)	Outhere Brothers	Eternal	11		F
2	-	Back For Good	Take That	Arista	8	(7)	
3	-	Two Can Play The Game	Bobby Brown	MCA	8		
4	-	U Sure Do	Strike	Fresh	5		F L
5	13	Julia Says	Wet Wet Wet	Precious	5		
6	-	Baby Baby	Corona	Eternal/WEA	5	(57)	
7	5	Love Can Build A Bridge	Cher/Chrissie Hynde/ Neneh Cherry/Eric Clapton	London	5		L
8	-	Not Over Yet	Grace	Perfecto/East West	4		F L
9	-	Have You Ever Really Loved A Woman?	Bryan Adams	A&M	4	(1)	L
10	1	Think Twice	Celine Dion	Epic	20	(95)	G
11	-	If You Love Me	Brownstone	MJJ	6	(8)	F
12	-	Chains	Tina Arena	Columbia	8	(38)	F L
13	-	Key To My Life	Boyzone	Polydor	4		
14	6	The Bomb! (These Sounds Fall Into My Mind)	Bucketheads	Positiva	9	(49)	F L
15	2	Don't Give Me Your Life	Alex Party	Systematic	9		F L
16	-	Baby It's You	Beatles	Apple	2	(67)	L
17	-	If You Only Let Me In	MN8	Columbia	3		
18	9	Turn On, Tune In, Cop Out	Freak Power	4th & Broadway	5		F L
19	-	Best In Me	Let Loose	Mercury	2		L
20	-	Let It Rain	East 17	London	3		

May 1995

This Mnth	Prev Mnth	Title	Artist	Label	Wks 20	(US Pos)	
1	-	Guaglione	Perez 'Prez' Prado	RCA	8		L
2	-	Some Might Say	Oasis	Creation	4		
3	-	Dreamer	Livin' Joy	Undiscovered/MCA	5	(72)	L
4	2	Back For Good	Take That	Arista	8	(7)	
5	-	Scatman (Ski-Ba-Bop-Ba-Dop-Bop)	Scatman John	RCA	8	(60)	F
6	-	Unchained Melody/ White Cliffs ...	Robson Green/Jerome Flynn	RCA	11		F G L
7	13	Key To My Life	Boyzone	Polydor	4		
8	12	Chains	Tina Arena	Columbia	8	(38)	F L
9	3	Two Can Play The Game	Bobby Brown	MCA	8		
10	1	Don't Stop (Wiggle Wiggle)	Outhere Brothers	Eternal	11		F
11	-	We're Gonna Do It Again	Manchester United FC	Polygram TV	3		L
12	-	Love City Groove	Love City Groove	Planet3	6		F L
13	-	That Look In Your Eye	Ali Campbell	Kuff	6		F L
14	-	Your Loving Arms	Billie Ray Martin	Magnet	6		F L
15	-	Only One Road	Celine Dion	Epic	3	(93)	
16	17	If You Only Let Me In	MN8	Columbia	3		
17	-	Surrender Your Love	Nightcrawlers/John Reid	Final Vinyl/Arista	4		
18	-	The Changingman	Paul Weller	Go! Discs	1		
19	9	Have You Ever Really Loved A Woman?	Bryan Adams	A&M	4	(1)	L
20	-	This Is How We Do It	Montell Jordan	Def Jam	5	(1)	F

June 1995

This Mnth	Prev Mnth	Title	Artist	Label	Wks 20	(US Pos)	
1	6	Unchained Melody/White Cliffs ...	Robson Green/Jerome Flynn	RCA	11		F G L
2	-	Common People	Pulp	Island	7		
3-	-	(Everybody's Got To Learn Sometime) I Need Your Loving	Baby D	Systematic	6		L
4	1	Guaglione	Perez 'Prez' Prado	RCA	8		L
5	-	Scream	Michael & Janet Jackson	Epic	5	(5)	
6	5	Scatman (Ski-Ba-Bop-Ba-Dop-Bop)	Scatman John	RCA	8	(60)	F
7	-	Hold Me, Thrill Me, Kiss Me, Kill Me	U2	Island	10	(16)	L
8	13	That Look In Your Eye	Ali Campbell	Kuff	6		F L
9	-	This Ain't A Love Song	Bon Jovi	Mercury	3	(14)	
10	-	Think Of You	Whigfield	Systematic	6		
11	-	Boom Boom Boom	Outhere Brothers	Eternal	11	(65)	
12	-	Don't Want To Forgive Me Now	Wet Wet Wet	Precious	3		
13	14	Your Loving Arms	Billie Ray Martin	Magnet	6		F L
14	17	Surrender Your Love	Nightcrawlers/John Reid	Final Vinyl/Arista	4		
15	-	Yes	McAlmont & Butler	Hut	3		F
16	-	Right In The Night (Fall In Love With Music)	Jam & Spoon Feat Plavka	Epic	5		F L
17	-	A Girl Like You	Edwyn Collins	Setanta	9	(32)	F L
18	-	Reverend Black Grape	Black Grape	Radioactive	1		F
19	-	Search For The Hero	M People	Deconstruction	3		L
20	3	Dreamer	Livin' Joy	Undiscovered/MCA	5	(72)	L

April 1995

This Mnth	Prev Mnth	Title	Artist	Label	Wks 20	(UK Pos)	Flags
1	20	This Is How We Do It	Montell Jordan	PPM/Ral	18	(11)	F G L
2	3	Candy Rain	Soul For Real	Uptown	16	(23)	F
3	10	Red Light Special	TLC	Laface	15	(18)	
4	1	Take A Bow	Madonna	Maverick/Sire	21	(16)	L
5	16	Run Away	Real McCoy	Arista	13	(6)	
6	17	Freak Like Me	Adina Howard	Mecca Don/East West	20	(33)	F G L
7	7	Strong Enough	Sheryl Crow	A&M	16	(33)	L
8	2	Creep	TLC	Laface	24	(22)	G
9	13	I Know	Dionne Farris	Columbia	20	(47)	F L
10	9	Big Poppa/Warning	Notorious B.I.G.	Bad Boy	13	(63)	F G
11	4	Baby	Brandy	Atlantic	13		G
12	6	You Gotta Be	Des'ree	550 Music	20	(14)	F L
13	-	Dear Mama/Old School	2Pac	Interscope	11		G L
14	-	Keep Their Heads Ringin'	Dr. Dre	Priority	13	(25)	L
15	-	I Believe	Blessid Union Of Souls	EMI	13	(29)	F L
16	11	If You Love Me	Brownstone	MJJ	13	(8)	F L
17	12	Hold My Hand	Hootie & The Blowfish	Atlantic	17	(50)	F
18	-	Believe	Elton John	Rocket	10	(15)	L
19	-	This Lil' Game We Play	Subway (featuring 702)	Biv/Motown	8		F L
20	8	Another Night	Real McCoy	Arista	28	(2)	F G

May 1995

This Mnth	Prev Mnth	Title	Artist	Label	Wks 20	(UK Pos)	Flags
1	1	This Is How We Do It	Montell Jordan	PPM/Ral	18	(11)	F G L
2	6	Freak Like Me	Adina Howard	Mecca Don/East West	20	(33)	F G L
3	-	Have You Ever Really Loved A Woman?	Bryan Adams	A&M	15	(4)	L
4	3	Red Light Special	TLC	Laface	15	(18)	
5	9	I Know	Dionne Farris	Columbia	20	(47)	F L
6	-	Water Runs Dry	Boyz II Men	Motown	19	(24)	L
7	5	Run Away	Real McCoy	Arista	13	(6)	
8	-	I'll Be There For You/You're All I Need To Get By	Method Man/Mary J. Blige	Def Jam/Ral	11	(10)	F G
9	15	I Believe	Blessid Union Of Souls	EMI	13	(29)	F L
10	7	Strong Enough	Sheryl Crow	A&M	16	(33)	L
11	2	Candy Rain	Soul For Real	Uptown	16	(23)	F
12	-	Total Eclipse Of The Heart	Nicki French	Critique	15	(5)	F L
13	13	Dear Mama/Old School	2Pac	Interscope	11	18	
14	18	Believe	Elton John	Rocket	10	(15)	L
15	4	Take A Bow	Madonna	Maverick/Sire	21	(16)	L
16	-	Don't Take It Personal (Just One Of Dem Days)	Monica	Rowdy	18	(32)	F G L
17	-	Let Her Cry	Hootie & The Blowfish	Atlantic	15	(75)	L
18	-	In The House Of Stone And Light	Martin Page	Mercury	10		F L
19	10	Big Poppa/Warning	Notorious B.I.G.	Bad Boy	13	(63)	F G
20	14	Keep Their Heads Ringin'	Dr. Dre	Priority	13	(25)	L

June 1995

This Mnth	Prev Mnth	Title	Artist	Label	Wks 20	(UK Pos)	Flags
1	3	Have You Ever Really Loved A Woman?	Bryan Adams	A&M	15	(4)	L
2	12	Total Eclipse Of The Heart	Nicki French	Critique	15	(5)	F L
3	6	Water Runs Dry	Boyz II Men	Motown	19	(24)	L
4	1	This Is How We Do It	Montell Jordan	PPM/Ral	18	(11)	F G L
5	16	Don't Take It Personal (Just One Of Dem Days)	Monica	Rowdy	18	(32)	F G L
6	8	I'll Be There For You/You're All I Need To Get By	Method Man/Mary J. Blige	Def Jam/Ral	11	(10)	F G
7	2	Freak Like Me	Adina Howard	Mecca Don/East West	20	(33)	F G L
8	9	I Believe	Blessid Union Of Souls	EMI	13	(29)	F L
9	5	I Know	Dionne Farris	Columbia	20	(47)	F L
10	-	Scream/Childhood	Michael & Janet Jackson	Epic	7	(3)	G
11	17	Let Her Cry	Hootie & The Blowfish	Atlantic	15	(75)	L
12	-	One More Chance/Stay With Me	Notorious B.I.G.	Bad Boy	14	(34)	G L
13	-	Waterfalls	TLC	Laface	22	(4)	G L
14	4	Red Light Special	TLC	Laface	15	(18)	
15	20	Keep Their Heads Ringin'	Dr. Dre	Priority	13	(25)	L
16	-	Can't You See	Total/The Notorious B.I.G.	Tommy Boy	6	(43)	F L
17	13	Dear Mama/Old School	2Pac	Interscope	11		G L
18	-	Someone To Love	Jon B. Featuring Babyface	Yab Yum	13		F L
19	-	Run-Around	Blues Traveler	A&M	23		F L
20	7	Run Away	Real McCoy	Arista	13	(6)	

◆ Michael and Janet Jackson teamed on 'Scream' which became the first single ever to enter the Top 100 in the Top 5. The record with its $6 million video launched Jackson's **History** album, which sold over six million world-wide in the first two weeks.

◆ After up-and-coming Latin American artist Selena was murdered by her fan club secretary, five of her albums debuted on the pop chart and took the top 5 rungs on the US Latin American hit list.

◆ As Garth Brooks was given a star on the prestigious Hollywood Walk Of Fame, it was announced that he had sold a staggering 50 million albums in the USA in the 1990s.

341

UK 1995

JULY-SEPT

▲ For the first time in years, a battle for the top of the charts made the national press, when Oasis and Blur released new singles simultaneously. Blur's 'Country House' came in at No. 1 and 'Roll With It' by Oasis entered in runner-up position.

◆ Records were spending less time on the UK Top 20 than ever before. It was now quite normal for singles to peak in their first chart week and to spend less than three weeks on the Top 20. Interestingly, almost twice as many singles were entering the UK Top 20 than the equivalent US chart.

July 1995

This Mnth	Prev Mnth	Title	Artist	Label	Wks 20	(US Pos)	
1	11	Boom Boom Boom	Outhere Brothers	Eternal	11	(65)	
2	1	Unchained Melody/ White Cliffs Of Dover	Robson Green/Jerome Flynn	RCA	11		F G L
3	-	Shy Guy	Diana King	Work	9	(13)	F
4	7	Hold Me, Thrill Me, Kiss Me, Kill Me	U2	Island	10	(16)	L
5	17	A Girl Like You	Edwyn Collins	Setanta	9	(32)	F L
6	-	Alright/Time	Supergrass	Parlophone	7		L
7	-	Whoomph! (There It Is)	Clock	Media	5		
8	-	In The Summertime	Shaggy Featuring Rayvon	Virgin	7	(3)	
9	-	I'm A Believer	EMF/Reeves And Mortimer	Parlophone	3		L
10	-	Kiss From A Rose	Seal	ZTT/Sire	9	(1)	L
11	10	Think Of You	Whigfield	Systematic	6		
12	3	(Everybody's Got To Learn Sometime) I Need Your Loving	Baby D	Systematic	6		L
13	-	This Is A Call	Foo Fighters	Roswell	1		F
14	-	Shoot Me With Your Love	D:ream	FXU/Magnet	2		
15	-	Humpin' Around	Bobby Brown	MCA	2		
16	-	3 Is Family	Dana Dawson	EMI	4		F L
17	-	Try Me Out	Corona	Eternal/WEA	8		L
18	-	Happy	MN8	Columbia	3		L
19	5	Scream	Michael Jackson/Janet Jackson	Epic	5	(5)	
20	-	Stillness In Time	Jamiroquai	Sony	2		L

August 1995

1	-	Never Forget	Take That	RCA	6		L
2	10	Kiss From A Rose	Seal	ZTT/Sire	9	(1)	L
3	3	Shy Guy	Diana King	Work	9	(13)	F
4	1	Boom Boom Boom	Outhere Brothers	Eternal	11	(65)	
5	-	Waterfalls	TLC	Laface	10	(1)	
6	17	Try Me Out	Corona	Eternal/WEA	8		L
7	-	I Luv U Baby	Original	Ore	5		F L
8	-	So Good	Boyzone	Polydor	3		L
9	6	Alright/Time	Supergrass	Parlophone	7		L
10	-	Country House	Blur	Food/Parlophone	6		
11	-	Roll With It	Oasis	Creation	4		L
12	-	Son Of A Gun	JX	Ffrreedom	3		L
13	-	I'm Only Sleeping/Off On Holiday	Suggs	WEA	3		F
14	4	Hold Me, Thrill Me, Kiss Me, Kill Me	U2	Island	10	(16)	L
15	-	Everybody	Clock	Media	3		L
16	-	In The Name Of The Father	Black Grape	Radioactive	2		
17	8	In The Summertime	Shaggy Featuring Rayvon	Virgin	7	(3)	
18	-	Human Nature	Madonna	Maverick/Sire	1		
19	-	Don't You Want Me	Felix	Deconstruction	2		L
20	5	A Girl Like You	Edwyn Collins	Setanta	9	(32)	F L

September 1995

1	-	You Are Not Alone	Michael Jackson	Epic	10	(1)	L
2	-	I'll Be There For You	Rembrandts	East West	8	(17)	F L
3	10	Country House	Blur	Food/Parlophone	6		
4	-	The Sunshine After The Rain	Berri	Ffrreedom	6		F
5	-	Stayin' Alive	N-Trance Featuring Ricardo Da Force	All Around The World	6		L
6	11	Roll With It	Oasis	Creation	4		L
7	-	Boombastic	Shaggy	Virgin	8	(3)	L
8	7	I Luv U Baby	Original	Ore	5		F L
9	-	Who The F**k Is Alice?	Smokie/Roy Chubby Brown	Now	10		L
10	5	Waterfalls	TLC	Laface	10	(1)	
11	-	Fantasy	Mariah Carey	Columbia	7	(1)	L
12	-	Fairground	Simply Red	East West	9		L
13	-	Can I Touch You...There?	Michael Bolton	Columbia	4	(27)	L
14	-	Hideaway	De'lacy	Slip'n'slide	4		F L
15	-	Runaway	Janet Jackson	Epic	3	(3)	
16	-	Tu M'Aimes Encore (To Love Me Again)	Celine Dion	Epic	3		
17	-	La La La Hey Hey	Outhere Brothers	Eternal	3		L
18	-	Scatman's World	Scatman John	RCA	4		L
19	1	Never Forget	Take That	RCA	6		L
20	-	I Feel Love	Donna Summer	Manifesto/Mercury	2		L

July 1995

This Mnth	Prev Mnth	Title	Artist	Label	Wks 20	(UK Pos)	
1	13	Waterfalls	TLC	Laface	22	(4)	G L
2	12	One More Chance/Stay With Me	Notorious B.I.G.	Bad Boy	14	(34)	G L
3	5	Don't Take It Personal (Just One Of Dem Days)	Monica	Rowdy	18	(32)	F G L
4	1	Have You Ever Really Loved A Woman?	Bryan Adams	A&M	15	(4)	L
5	3	Water Runs Dry	Boyz II Men	Motown	19	(24)	L
6	2	Total Eclipse Of The Heart	Nicki French	Critique	15	(5)	F L
7	10	Scream/Childhood	Michael & Janet Jackson	Epic	7	(3)	G
8	-	I Can Love You Like That	All-4-One	Blitzz	22	(33)	L
9	-	Boombastic/In The Summertime	Shaggy	Virgin	16	(1)	F G L
10	11	Let Her Cry	Hootie & The Blowfish	Atlantic	15	(75)	L
11	19	Run-Around	Blues Traveler	A&M	23		F L
12	4	Kiss From A Rose	Seal	ZTT/Sire	21	(20)	L
13	6	I'll Be There For You/ You're All I Need To Get By	Method Man/ Mary J. Blige	Def Jam/Ral	11	(10)	F G
14	18	Someone To Love	Jon B. Featuring Babyface	Yab Yum	13		F L
15	7	Freak Like Me	Adina Howard	Mecca Don/East West	20	(33)	F G L
16	4	This Is How We Do It	Montell Jordan	PPM/Ral	18	(11)	F G L
17	-	Colors Of The Wind	Vanessa Williams	Hollywood	11	(21)	L
18	-	Shy Guy	Diana King	Work	10	(2)	F L
19	8	I Believe	Blessid Union Of Souls	EMI	13	(29)	F L
20	-	Freek'n You	Jodeci	Uptown/MCA	8	(17)	L

August 1995

This Mnth	Prev Mnth	Title	Artist	Label	Wks 20	(UK Pos)	
1	1	Waterfalls	TLC	Laface	22	(4)	G L
2	12	Kiss From A Rose	Seal	ZTT/Sire	21	(20)	L
3	9	Boombastic/In The Summertime	Shaggy	Virgin	16	(1)	F G L
4	3	Don't Take It Personal (Just One Of Dem Days)	Monica	Rowdy	18	(32)	F G L
5	2	One More Chance/Stay With Me	Notorious B.I.G.	Bad Boy	14	(34)	G L
6	17	Colors Of The Wind	Vanessa Williams	Hollywood	11	(21)	L
7	8	I Can Love You Like That	All-4-One	Blitzz	22	(33)	L
8	11	Run-Around	Blues Traveler	A&M	23		F L
9	-	He's Mine	Mokenstef	Outburst/Ral	12	(70)	F L
10	5	Water Runs Dry	Boyz II Men	Motown	19	(24)	L
11	14	Someone To Love	Jon B. Featuring Babyface	Yab Yum	13		F L
12	-	Gangsta's Paradise	Coolio Featuring L.V.	MCA	24	(1)	P
6	13	Total Eclipse Of The Heart	Nicki French	Critique	15	(5)	F L
14	-	I Got 5 On It	Luniz	Noo Trybe	12	(3)	F G L
15	-	Player's Anthem	Junior M.A.F.I.A.	Undeas/Big Beat	6		F L
16	-	Only Wanna Be With You	Hootie & The Blowfish	Atlantic	18		L
17	4	Have You Ever Really Loved A Woman?	Bryan Adams	A&M	15	(4)	L
18	20	Freek'n You	Jodeci	Uptown/MCA	8	(17)	L
19	-	I Wish	Skee-Lo	Sunshine	6	(15)	F L
20	-	This Ain't A Love Song	Bon Jovi	Mercury	4	(6)	L

September 1995

This Mnth	Prev Mnth	Title	Artist	Label	Wks 20	(UK Pos)	
1	12	Gangsta's Paradise	Coolio Featuring L.V.	MCA	24	(1)	P
2	-	You Are Not Alone	Michael Jackson	Epic	12	(1)	G L
3	2	Kiss From A Rose	Seal	ZTT/Sire	21	(20)	L
4	1	Waterfalls	TLC	Laface	22	(4)	G L
5	3	Boombastic/In The Summertime	Shaggy	Virgin	16	(1)	F G L
6	7	I Can Love You Like That	All-4-One	Blitzz	22	(33)	L
7	16	Only Wanna Be With You	Hootie & The Blowfish	Atlantic	18		L
8	-	Runaway	Janet Jackson	Epic	19	(6)	L
9	6	Colors Of The Wind	Vanessa Williams	Hollywood	11	(21)	L
10	14	I Got 5 On It	Luniz	Noo Trybe	12	(3)	F G L
11	8	Run-Around	Blues Traveler	A&M	23		F L
12	-	Fantasy	Mariah Carey	Columbia	19	(4)	P L
13	9	He's Mine	Mokenstef	Outburst/Ral	12	(70)	F L
14	-	As I Lay Me Down	Sophie B. Hawkins	Columbia	19	(24)	L
15	4	Don't Take It Personal (Just One Of Dem Days)	Monica	Rowdy	18	(32)	F G L
16	19	I Wish	Skee-Lo	Sunshine	6	(15)	F L
17	-	1st Of Tha Month	Bone Thugs-N-Harmony	Ruthless/Relativity	5	(32)	F L
18	-	How High	Redman/Method Man	Def Jam/Ral	3		F L
19	5	One More Chance/Stay With Me	Notorious B.I.G.	Bad Boy	14	(34)	G L
20	-	I Hate U	TAFKAP	NPG/Warner	3	(20)	L

◆ 'You Are Not Alone' by Michael Jackson became the first single in history to enter the US chart at No. 1.

◆ As their single 'Waterfalls' headed the chart, female R&B trio TLC filed for bankruptcy with reported debts of $3.5 million. Simultaneously, their record company head, producer/songwriter Babyface, notched up his 50th US Top 40 entry with After 7's 'Til You Do Me Right'.

◆ Two rock legends died: Jerry Garcia of the Grateful Dead and pioneer DJ Wolfman Jack. Soon afterwards seven Grateful Dead albums re-appeared on the US chart. Other deaths included past hit-makers Phil Harris, Jerry Lordan, Big Dee Irwin, Charlie Rich and Phyllis Hyman.

◆ The Beatles' 'Free As A Bird' just failed to give them their 18th UK No. 1, which would have topped Elvis Presley's total. Their **Anthology I** double album sold an unprecedented 500,000 on its first day in America, and the first *Beatles Anthology* TV show attracted 47 million US viewers, double the amount of its nearest competitor.

◆ In Christmas week, a record-shattering 10.6 million albums were sold in the UK. The biggest seller was Robson & Jerome's eponymous debut LP which sold a record-breaking 2 million copies in just seven weeks. The duo also clocked up their second No. I single, 'I Believe', which had amassed 600,000 advance orders.

October 1995

This Mnth	Prev Mnth	Title	Artist	Label	Wks 20	(US Pos)	
1	12	Fairground	Simply Red	East West	9		L
2	7	Boombastic	Shaggy	Virgin	8	(3)	L
3	9	Who The F**k Is Alice?	Smokie/Roy Chubby Brown	Now	10		L
4	-	Mis-Shapes/Sorted For Es & Wizz	Pulp	Island	4		
5	1	You Are Not Alone	Michael Jackson	Epic	10	(1)	L
6	-	When Love & Hate Collide	Def Leppard	Bludgeon Riffola	6		L
7	11	Fantasy	Mariah Carey	Columbia	7	(1)	L
8	-	Gangsta's Paradise	Coolio Featuring L.V.	Tommy Boy	17	(1)	G L
9	-	I'd Lie For You (And That's The Truth)	Meat Loaf	MCA	5	(13)	L
10	-	Power Of A Woman	Eternal	EMI	4		L
11	-	Light Of My Life	Louise	EMI	4		F L
12	-	Somewhere Somehow	Wet Wet Wet	Precious	4		
13	5	Stayin' Alive	N-Trance Featuring Ricardo Da Force	All Around The World	6		L
14	-	Higher State Of Consciousness	Josh Wink	Manifesto	3		F L
15	2	I'll Be There For You	Rembrandts	East West	8	(17)	F L
16	-	Something For The Pain	Bon Jovi	Mercury	3		
17	-	Missing	Everything But The Girl	Blanco Y Negro	16	(2)	L
18	-	Man On The Edge	Iron Maiden	EMI	1		L
19	-	Renegade Master	Wildchild	Hi-Life/Polydor	2		F L
20	-	Walking In Memphis	Cher	WEA	2		L

November 1995

This Mnth	Prev Mnth	Title	Artist	Label	Wks 20	(US Pos)	
1	8	Gangsta's Paradise	Coolio Featuring L.V.	Tommy Boy	17	(1)	G L
2	-	I Believe/Up On The Roof	Robson Green & Jerome Flynn	RCA	10		G L
3	17	Missing	Everything But The Girl	Blanco Y Negro	16	(2)	L
4	-	Wonderwall	Oasis	Creation	13	(8)	L
5	-	Heaven For Everyone	Queen	Parlophone	4		
6	-	Thunder	East 17	London	8		L
7	9	I'd Lie For You (And That's The Truth)	Meat Loaf	MCA	5	(13)	L
8	-	You'll See	Madonna	Maverick/Sire	8	(8)	
9	-	Fairground	Simply Red	East West	9		L
10	6	When Love & Hate Collide	Def Leppard	Bludgeon Riffola	6		L
11	-	The Universal	Blur	Food/Parlophone	3		L
12	-	Anywhere Is	Enya	WEA	7		L
13	-	I Believe	Happy Clappers	Shindig/PWL	2		F L
14	3	Who The F**k Is Alice?	Smokie/Roy Chubby Brown	Now	10		L
15	-	Father And Son	Boyzone	Polydor	11		L
16	10	Power Of A Woman	Eternal	EMI	4		
17	-	It's Oh So Quiet	Bjork	One Little Indian	9		L
18	2	Boombastic	Shaggy	Virgin	8	(3)	
19	-	Goldeneye	Tina Turner	Parlophone	2		L
20	-	He's On The Phone	Saint Etienne	Heavenly	2		

December 1995

This Mnth	Prev Mnth	Title	Artist	Label	Wks 20	(US Pos)	
1	15	Father And Son	Boyzone	Polydor	11		L
2	-	Earth Song	Michael Jackson	Epic	11		G L
3	2	I Believe/Up On The Roof	Robson Green/Jerome Flynn	RCA	10		G L
4	1	Gangsta's Paradise	Coolio Featuring L.V.	Tommy Boy	17	(1)	G L
5	3	Missing	Everything But The Girl	Blanco Y Negro	16	(2)	L
6	17	It's Oh So Quiet	Bjork	One Little Indian	9		L
7	4	Wonderwall	Oasis	Creation	13	(8)	L
8	-	Free As A Bird	Beatles	Apple	4	(6)	L
9	-	One Sweet Day	Mariah Carey & Boyz II Men	Columbia	6	(1)	L
10	12	Anywhere Is	Enya	WEA	7		L
11	-	Wonderwall	Mike Flowers Pops	London	3		F L
12	-	Disco 2000	Pulp	Island	6		L
13	-	Miss Sarajevo	Passengers	Island	3		F L
14	-	A Winter's Tale	Queen	Parlophone	2		L
15	-	The Gift Of Christmas	Childliners	London	4		F L
16	-	I Am Blessed	Eternal	EMI	7		L
17	-	The Best Things In Life Are Free	Luther Vandross/Janet Jackson	A&M	3		F L
18	8	You'll See	Madonna	Maverick/Sire	8	(8)	
19	-	Gold	TAFKAP	Warner	5		L
20	-	Lie To Me	Bon Jovi	Mercury	2		L

October 1995

This Mnth	Prev Mnth	Title	Artist	Label	Wks 20	(UK Pos)	
1	12	**Fantasy**	Mariah Carey	Columbia	19	(4)	P L
2	1	**Gangsta's Paradise**	Coolio Featuring L.V.	MCA	24	(1)	P L
3	8	**Runaway**	Janet Jackson	Epic	19	(6)	L
4	2	**You Are Not Alone**	Michael Jackson	Epic	12	(1)	G L
5	3	**Kiss From A Rose**	Seal	ZTT/Sire	21	(20)	L
6	7	**Only Wanna Be With You**	Hootie & The Blowfish	Atlantic	18		L
7	14	**As I Lay Me Down**	Sophie B. Hawkins	Columbia	19	(24)	L
8	4	**Waterfalls**	TLC	Laface	22	(4)	G L
9	-	**Brokenhearted**	Brandy	Atlantic	9		L
10	6	**I Can Love You Like That**	All-4-One	Blitzz	22	(33)	L
11	-	**Tell Me**	Groove Theory	Epic	18		F L
12	-	**Carnival**	Natalie Merchant	Elektra	11		F L
13	-	**Back For Good**	Take That	Arista	13	(1)	F L
14	10	**I Got 5 On It**	Luniz	Noo Trybe	12	(3)	F G L
15	-	**Roll To Me**	Del Amitri	A&M	12	(22)	F L
16	11	**Run-Around**	Blues Traveler	A&M	23		F L
17	20	**I Hate U**	TAFKAP	NPG/Warner	3	(20)	L
18	5	**Boombastic/In The Summertime**	Shaggy	Virgin	16	(1)	F G L
19	-	**Who Can I Run To**	Xscape	So So Def	8		L
20	-	**I'll Be There For You/ This House Is Not A Home**	Rembrandts	East West	5		L

November 1995

This Mnth	Prev Mnth	Title	Artist	Label	Wks 20	(UK Pos)	
1	1	**Fantasy**	Mariah Carey	Columbia	19	(4)	P L
2	2	**Gangsta's Paradise**	Coolio Featuring L.V.	MCA	24	(1	P L
3	3	**Runaway**	Janet Jackson	Epic	19	(6)	L
4	5	**Kiss From A Rose**	Seal	ZTT/Sire	21	(20)	L
5	11	**Tell Me**	Groove Theory	Epic	18		F L
6	7	**As I Lay Me Down**	Sophie B. Hawkins	Columbia	19	(24)	L
7.	13	**Back For Good**	Take That	Arista	13	(1)	F L
8	-	**You Remind Me Of Something**	R. Kelly	Jive	9	(24)	G L
9	-	**Exhale (Shoop Shoop)**	Whitney Houston	Arista	18	(11)	G L
10	6	**Only Wanna Be With You**	Hootie & The Blowfish	Atlantic	18		L
11	19	**Who Can I Run To**	Xscape	So So Def	8		L
12	-	**Name**	Goo Goo Dolls	Metal Blade	22		F L
13	-	**Hey Lover**	LL Cool J	Def Jam	17		G L
14	4	**You Are Not Alone**	Michael Jackson	Epic	12	(1)	G L
15	15	**Roll To Me**	Del Amitri	A&M	12	(22)	F L
16	-	**Diggin' On You**	TLC	Laface	13		L
17	12	**Carnival**	Natalie Merchant	Elektra	11		F L
18	-	**I'd Lie For You (And That's The Truth)**	Meat Loaf	MCA	7	(2)	L
19	9	**Brokenhearted**	Brandy	Atlantic	9		L
20	10	**I Can Love You Like That**	All-4-One	Blitzz	22	(33)	L

December 1995

This Mnth	Prev Mnth	Title	Artist	Label	Wks 20	(UK Pos)	
1	-	**One Sweet Day**	Mariah Carey & Boyz II Men	Columbia	22	(6)	P L
2	9	**Exhale (Shoop Shoop)**	Whitney Houston	Arista	18	(11)	G L
3	13	**Hey Lover**	LL Cool J	Def Jam	17		G L
4	2	**Gangsta's Paradise**	Coolio Featuring L.V.	MCA	24	(1)	P L
5	1	**Fantasy**	Mariah Carey	Columbia	19	(4)	P L
6	16	**Diggin' On You**	TLC	Laface	13		L
7	8	**You Remind Me Of Something**	R. Kelly	Jive	9	(24)	G L
8	12	**Name**	Goo Goo Dolls	Metal Blade	22		F L
9.	-	**You'll See**	Madonna	Maverick/Sire	11	(5)	L
10	3	**Runaway**	Janet Jackson	Epic	19	(6)	L
11	-	**Breakfast At Tiffany's**	Deep Blue Something	Rainmaker/ Interscope	16		F L
12	-	**Before You Walk Out Of My Life/ Like This And Like That**	Monica	Rowdy	19		L
13	5	**Tell Me**	Groove Theory	Epic	18		F L
14	-	**I Got ID/Long Road**	Pearl Jam	Epic	4		L
15	7	**Back For Good**	Take That	Arista	13	(1)	F L
16	-	**Missing**	Everything But The Girl	Atlantic	23	(3)	F L
17	-	**Free As A Bird**	Beatles	Apple	3	(2)	L
18	18	**I'd Lie For You (And That's The Truth)**	Meat Loaf	MCA	7	(2)	L
19	4	**Kiss From A Rose**	Seal	ZTT/Sire	21	(20)	L
20	6	**As I Lay Me Down**	Sophie B. Hawkins	Columbia	19	(24)	L

▲ The video of 'Waterfalls' by TLC picked up the top trophy at both the MTV and Billboard awards. The trio were also the Top Pop and Top R&B Act in Billboard's survey of 1995.

◆ America's top single of 1995, 'Gangsta's Paradise' by Coolio featuring LV., was also a massive international hit. In the US, it sold over three million and in the UK moved 650,000 in a month.

◆ After a poor sales year, UK acts (Take That, Del Amitri, Seal, Everything But The Girl and The Beatles) were making their mark again in the USA.

UK 1996 JAN-MAR

▲ The Brit Awards attracted massive media coverage when Jarvis Cocker of Pulp semi-sabotaged Michael Jackson's performance of 'Earth Song'.

◆ The Beatles, whose **Anthology I** passed the 10 million mark world-wide, ended this last quarter with **Anthology 2** at the top.

◆ Take That, Britain's top act of the 1990s, disbanded. Their final single, 'How Deep Is Your Love' giving them eight No.1s from their last nine releases.

◆ Eighteen years after they split, controversial punk pioneers the Sex Pistols reformed for a world tour.

◆ Ten successive singles entered at No. 1.

January 1996

This Mnth	Prev Mnth	Title	Artist	Label	Wks 20	(US Pos)	
1	2	**Earth Song**	Michael Jackson	Epic	11		G L
2	1	**Father And Son**	Boyzone	Polydor	11		L
3	5	**Missing**	Everything But The Girl	Blanco Y Negro	16	(2)	L
4	7	**Wonderwall**	Oasis	Creation	13	(8)	L
5	-	**Jesus To A Child**	George Michael	Virgin	4	(7)	L
6	-	**So Pure**	Baby D	Systematic	4		L
7	-	**Spaceman**	Babylon Zoo	EMI	7		G L
8	6	**It's Oh So Quiet**	Bjork	One Little Indian	9		
9	11	**Wonderwall**	Mike Flowers Pops	London	3		F L
10	4	**Gangsta's Paradise**	Coolio Featuring L.V.	Tommy Boy	17	(1)	F
11	16	**I Am Blessed**	Eternal	EMI	7		
12	-	**Whole Lotta Love**	Goldbug	Make Dust/ Acid Jazz	3		F L
13	-	**Creep '96**	TLC	Laface	3		L
14	-	**Anything**	3T	MJJ	9	(15)	F L
15	-	**One By One**	Cher	WEA	5		L
16	-	**If You Wanna Party**	Molella Featuring The Outhere Brothers	Eternal	6		F L
17	-	**Sandstorm**	Cast	Polydor	2		L
18	3	**I Believe/Up On The Roof**	Robson Green/ Jerome Flynn	RCA	10		G L
19	-	**Too Hot**	Coolio	Tommy Boy	2		L
20	-	**Why You Treat Me So Bad**	Shaggy Featuring Grand Puba	Virgin	2		L

February 1996

This Mnth	Prev Mnth	Title	Artist	Label	Wks 20	(US Pos)	
1	7	**Spaceman**	Babylon Zoo	EMI	7		G L
2	14	**Anything**	3T	MJJ	9		F L
3	-	**Slight Return**	Bluetones	Superior Quality	4		L
4	-	**Lifted**	Lighthouse Family	Wild Card	6		F L
5	-	**I Got 5 On It**	Luniz	Noo Trybe	7	(8)	F L
6	6	**I Just Want To Make Love To You**	Etta James	Chess/MCA	4		F L
7	-	**One Of Us**	Joan Osborne	Blue Gorilla/ Mercury	4	(4)	F L
8	5	**Jesus To A Child**	George Michael	Virgin	4	(7)Q	L
9	-	**I Wanna Be A Hippy**	Technohead	Mokum	9		F L
10	-	**Children**	Robert Miles	Deconstruction	13	(54)	F L
11	-	**Do U Still?**	East 17	London	3		L
12	-	**Open Arms**	Mariah Carey	Columbia	2		L
13	-	**Not A Dry Eye In The House**	Meat Loaf	Virgin	3		
14	15	**One By One**	Cher	WEA	5		L
15	-	**Street Spirit (Fade Out)**	Radiohead	Parlophone	1		L
16	12	**Whole Lotta Love**	Goldbug	Make Dust/ Acid Jazz	3		F L
17	-	**Stereotypes**	Blur	Food/Parlophone	2		L
18	-	**No Fronts - The Remixes**	Dog Eat Dog	Roadrunner	2		F
19	-	**Hyperballad**	Bjork	One Little Indian	1		L
20	-	**Change Your Mind**	Upside Down	World	3		F L

March 1996

This Mnth	Prev Mnth	Title	Artist	Label	Wks 20	(US Pos)	
1	10	**Children**	Robert Miles	Deconstruction	13	(54)	F L
2	-	**Don't Look Back In Anger**	Oasis	Creation	8		L
3	-	**How Deep Is Your Love**	Take That	RCA	7		L
4	-	**Coming Home Now**	Boyzone	Polydor	4		L
5	-	**Give Me A Little More Time**	Gabrielle	Go!discs	10		L
6	9	**I Wanna Be A Hippy**	Technohead	Mokum	9		F L
7	2	**Anything**	3T	MJJ	9		F L
8	-	**Return Of The Mack**	Mark Morrison	WEA	*10		L
9	-	**I Got 5 On It**	Luniz	Noo Trybe	7	(8)	F L
10	-	**Firestarter**	Prodigy	XL	6		L
11	-	**Real Love**	Beatles	Apple	2	(11)	L
12	-	**Stupid Girl**	Garbage	Mushroom	2		L
13	-	**The X Files**	Mark Snow	Warner	6		F L
14	-	**Passion**	Gat Decor	Way Of Life	3		F L
15	-	**Spaceman**	Babylon Zoo	EMI	7		G L
16	-	**Going Out**	Supergrass	Parlophone	3		L
17	-	**Falling Into You**	Celine Dion	Epic	5		L
18	-	**Perseverance**	Terrorvision	Total Vegas	1		F L
19	-	**These Days**	Bon Jovi	Mercury	2		L
20	4	**Lifted**	Lighthouse Family	Wild Card	6		F L

January 1996

This Mnth	Prev Mnth	Title	Artist	Label	Wks 20	(UK Pos)	
1	1	One Sweet Day	Mariah Carey & Boyz II Men	Columbia	22	(6)	P L
2	2	Exhale (Shoop Shoop)	Whitney Houston	Arista	18	(11)	G L
3	3	Hey Lover	LL Cool J	Def Jam	17		G L
4	16	Missing	Everything But The Girl	Atlantic	*23	(3)	F L
5	11	Breakfast At Tiffany's	Deep Blue Something	Rainmaker/Interscope	16		F L
6	4	Gangsta's Paradise	Coolio Featuring L.V.	MCA	24	(1)	P L
7	6	Diggin' On You	TLC	Laface	13		L
8	8	Name	Goo Goo Dolls	Metal Blade	22		F L
9	-	One Of Us	Joan Osborne	Blue Gorilla/Mercury	17	(6)	F L
10	5	Fantasy	Mariah Carey	Columbia	19	(4)	P L
11	12	Before You Walk Out Of My Life/ Like This And Like That	Monica	Rowdy	19		L
12	9	You'll See	Madonna	Maverick/Sire	11	(5)	L
13	17	Free As A Bird	Beatles	Apple	3	(2)	
14	-	Be My Lover	La Bouche	RCA	14		F L
15	10	Runaway	Janet Jackson	Epic	19	(6)	L
16	13	Tell Me	Groove Theory	Epic	18		F L
17	-	Nobody Knows	Tony Rich Project	Laface	*17	(10)	F L
18	7	You Remind Me Of Something	R. Kelly	Jive	9	(24)	G L
19	-	Time	Hootie & The Blowfish	Atlantic	9		L
20	14	I Got ID/Long Road	Pearl Jam	Epic	4		L

February 1996

This Mnth	Prev Mnth	Title	Artist	Label	Wks 20	(UK Pos)	
1	1	One Sweet Day	Mariah Carey & Boyz II Men	Columbia	22	(6)	P L
2	4	Missing	Everything But The Girl	Atlantic	*23	(3)	F L
3	2	Exhale (Shoop Shoop)	Whitney Houston	Arista	18	(11)	G L
4	-	Not Gon' Cry	Mary J. Blige	Arista	13		L
5	9	One Of Us	Joan Osborne	Blue Gorilla/ Mercury	17	(6)	F L
6	17	Nobody Knows	Tony Rich Project	Laface	*17	(10)	F L
7	3	Hey Lover	LL Cool J	Def Jam	17		G L
8	14	Be My Lover	La Bouche	RCA	14		F L
9	-	Sittin' Up In My Room	Brandy	Atlantic	*17		L
10	8	Name	Goo Goo Dolls	Metal Blade	22		F L
11	5	Breakfast At Tiffany's	Deep Blue Something	Rainmaker/Interscope	16		F L
12	11	Before You Walk Out Of My Life/ Like This And Like That	Monica	Rowdy	19		L
13	-	Jesus To A Child	George Michael	Dreamworks	4	(1)	L
14	-	Till I Hear It From You/ Follow You Down	Gin Blossoms	A&M	*15	(30)	F L
15	-	Tonite's Tha Night	Kris Kross	Ruffhouse	9		L
16	-	Wonderwall	Oasis	Epic	9	(2)	F L
17	12	You'll See	Madonna	Maverick/Sire	11	(5)	L
18	19	Time	Hootie & The Blowfish	Atlantic	9		L
19	7	Diggin' On You	TLC	Laface	13		L
20	-	Anything	3T	MJJ	14	(2)	F L

March 1996

This Mnth	Prev Mnth	Title	Artist	Label	Wks 20	(UK Pos)	
1	1	One Sweet Day	Mariah Carey & Boyz II Men	Columbia	22		P L
2	9	Sittin' Up In My Room	Brandy	Atlantic	*17		L
3	6	Nobody Knows	Tony Rich Project	Laface	*17		F L
4	4	Not Gon' Cry	Mary J. Blige	Arista	13		L
5	2	Missing	Everything But The Girl	Atlantic	*23		F L
6	-	Because You Loved Me	Celine Dion	550 Music	*10		L
7	-	Down Low (Nobody Has To Know)	R. Kelly/Ronald Isley	Jive	*11		L
8	8	Be My Lover	La Bouche	RCA	14		F L
9	5	One Of Us	Joan Osborne	Blue Gorilla/Mercury	17	(6)	F L
10	14	Till I Hear It From You/ Follow You Down	Gin Blossoms	A&M	*15	(30)	F L
11	-	Ironic	Alanis Morisette	Maverick	*10	(11)	F L
12	16	Wonderwall	Oasis	Epic	9	(2)	F L
13	3	Exhale (Shoop Shoop)	Whitney Houston	Arista	18		G L
14	13	Jesus To A Child	George Michael	Dreamworks	4	(1)	L
15	-	1979	Smashing Pumpkins	Virgin	12	(16)	F L
16	-	Lady	D'Angelo	EMI	9		F L
17	7	Hey Lover	LL Cool J	Def Jam	17		G L
18	-	All The Things (Your Man Won't Do)	Joe	Island	8	(34)	F L
19	-	Real Love	Beatles	Apple	1	(4)	L
20	10	Name	Goo Goo Dolls	Metal Blade	22		F LP

◆ Regular 1990s chart toppers Mariah Carey & Boyz II Men headed the US list for a record 16 weeks with 'One Sweet Day'. Only Elvis Presley and The Beatles have spent longer at No. 1 in the rock era than these two acts.

◆ Garth Brooks refused the American Music Award for Favorite Artist of the Year, saying that it should have gone to Grammy winners Hootie & The Blowfish.

◆ Days after being acquitted of murder, 2 Pac's double album **All Eyez On Me** entered the charts at No. 1.

◆ George Michael's first solo single for almost four years, 'Jesus To A Child', reached the transatlantic Top 10 and gave him his tenth UK No. 1.

Denotes singles still charting at time of going to press.

April 1996

This Mnth	Prev Mnth	Title	Artist	Label	Wks 20	(US Pos)	
1	8	Return Of The Mack	Mark Morrison	WEA	14	(2)	
2	10	Firestarter	The Prodigy	XL	6	(30)	
3	-	Ooh Aah...Just A Little Bit	Gina G	Eternal/WEA	11	(12)	F
4	13	The X Files	Mark Snow	Warner	6		F L
5	1	Children	Robert Miles	Deconstruction	14	(21)	F
6	5	Give Me A Little More Time	Gabrielle	Go!Discs	10		
7	-	They Don't Care About Us	Michael Jackson	Epic	5	(30)	
8	-	A Design For Life	Manic Street Preachers	Epic	5		
9	-	California Love	2 Pac feat. Dr Dre	Death Row/Island	3	(1)	F
10	-	Cecilia	Suggs	WEA	8		L
11	-	X-Files	DJ Dado	ZYX	3		F L
12	-	Walking Wounded	Everything But The Girl	Virgin	2		
13	-	Goldfinger	Ash	Infectious	2		
14	-	Peaches	Presidents Of The United States	Columbia	3	(29)	
15	3	How Deep Is Your Love	Take That	RCA	7		L
16	-	You've Got It Bad	Ocean Colour Scene	MCA	2		
17	-	Keep On Jumpin'	Lisa Marie Experience	3 Beat/ffrr	4		F L
18	-	Bulls On Parade	Rage Against The Machine	Epic	1		L
19	2	Don't Look Back In Anger	Oasis	Creation	8	(55)	
20	-	Something Changed	Pulp	Island	1		

May 1996

This Mnth	Prev Mnth	Title	Artist	Label	Wks 20	(US Pos)	
1	-	Fastlove	George Michael	Virgin	7	(8)	
2	3	Ooh Aah...Just A Little Bit	Gina G	Eternal	11	(12)	F
3	1	Return Of The Mack	Mark Morrison	WEA	14	(2)	
4	10	Cecilia	Suggs	WEA	8		L
5	-	Move Move Move (The Red Tribe)	Manchester United FA Cup Squad	Music Collection	5		L
6	8	A Design For Life	Manic Street Preachers	Epic	5		
7	-	There's Nothing I Won't Do	JX	Ffrreedom	8		
8	-	Charmless Man	Blur	Food/Parlophone	3		
9	-	Pass & Move (It's The Liverpool Groove)	Liverpool FC & The Boot Room Boys	Telstar	2		L
10	-	Nobody Knows	Tony Rich Project	Lafac	10	(2)	F L
11	7	They Don't Care About Us	Michael Jackson	Epic	5	(30)	
12	-	Tonight, Tonight	Smashing Pumpkins	Virgin	2	(36)	
13	-	Cut Some Rug/Castle Rock	Bluetones	Superior Quality	1		
14	-	Before	Pet Shop Boys	Parlophone	1		
15	-	Woo-Hah!! Got You All In Check	Busta Rhymes	Elektra	2	(8)	F
16	17	Keep On Jumpin'	Lisa Marie Experience	ffrr	4		F L
17	-	Klubbhopping	Klubbheads	AM:PM	3		F L
18	-	24/7	3T	MJJ	3		
19	-	Blue Moon/Only You	John Alford	Love This	2		L
20	-	Sale Of The Century	Sleeper	Indolent	2		

June 1996

This Mnth	Prev Mnth	Title	Artist	Label	Wks 20	(US Pos)	
1	-	Three Lions (Official Song Of The England Team)	Baddiel & Skinner & Lightning Seeds	Epic	10		F L
2	-	Mysterious Girl	Peter Andre feat. Bubbler Ranx	Mushroom	13		
3	-	Killing Me Softly	Fugees	Columbia	12		F G
4	-	Because You Loved Me	Celine Dion	Epic	10	(1)	
5	10	Nobody Knows	Tony Rich Project	Laface/Arista	10	(2)	F L
6	2	Ooh Aah...Just A Little Bit	Gina G	Eternal/WEA	11	(12)	F
7	-	Don't Stop Movin'	Livin' Joy	Undiscovered/MCA	9	(67)	
8	-	The Day We Caught The Train	Ocean Colour Scene	MCA	5		
9	-	Always Be My Baby	Mariah Carey	Columbia	5	(1)	
10	7	There's Nothing I Won't Do	JX	Ffrreedom	8		
11	-	Blurred	Pianoman	Ffrreedom	4		F L
12	-	Naked	Louise	1st Avenue/EMI	3		
13	-	Until It Sleeps	Metallica	Vertigo	2	(10)	
14	1	Fastlove	George Michael	Virgin	7	(8)	
15	-	The Only Thing That Looks Good On Me Is You	Bryan Adams	A&M	2	(52)	
16	-	Fable	Robert Miles	Deconstruction	2		
17	-	Theme From 'Mission: Impossible'	Adam Clayton & Larry Mullen	Mother	7	(7)	F L
18	-	Make It With You	Let Loose	Mercury	2		L
19	-	England's Irie	Black Grape	Radioactive	2		L
20	3	Return Of The Mack	Mark Morrison	WEA	14	(2)	

◆ Genesis frontman and drummer Phil Collins quits the band to concentrate on his multi-platinum solo career. He is eventually replaced by former Stiltskin singer Ray Wilson.

◆ Punk legends The Sex Pistols – including original bassist Glen Matlock – reunite after 18 years for the appropriately named Filthy Lucre Tour. Each member receives an estimated £1,000,000.

▲ England may have lost to Germany on penalties – again – but Euro 96 also gives us the most popular football song of all time, 'Three Lions On A Shirt' by Baddiel & Skinner with The Lightning Seeds.

This Mnth	Prev Mnth	Title	Artist	Label	Wks 20	(UK Pos)	
1	6	Because You Loved Me	Celine Dion	550 Music	10		G
2	-	Always Be My Baby	Mariah Carey	Columbia	20	(4)	G
3	3	Nobody Knows	The Tony Rich Project	Laface	17		FGL
4	11	Ironic	Alanis Morissette	Maverick	10	(11)	F
5	7	Down Low (Nobody Has To Know)	R Kelly feat. Ronald Isley	Jive	11		G
6	-	1,2,3,4 (Sumpin' New)	Coolio	Tommy Boy	10	(13)	
7	2	Sittin' Up In My Room	Brandy	A&M	17		G
8	4	No Gon' Cry	Mary J Blige	Arista	13		
9	-	Woo-Hah!! Got You All In Check/Everything Remains Raw	Busta Rhymes	Elektra	9	(8)	G
10	-	Doin It	LL Cool J	Def Jam	9	(15)	
11	10	Follow You Down/Til I Hear It From...	Gin Blossoms	A&M	15	(30)	FL
12	5	Missing	Everything But The Girl	Atlantic	23	(3)	FL
13	-	Count On Me	Whitney Houston & Ce Ce Winans	Arista	11	(12)	
14	-	18 And The Things (Your Man Won't Do)	Joe	Island	8	(34)	F
15	16	Lady	D'Angelo	EMI	9		F
16	-	You're The One	SWV	RCA	13	(13)	
17	1	One Sweet Day	Mariah Carey & Boyz II Men	Columbia	22	(6)	P
18	15	1979	Smashing Pumpkins	Virgin	12	(16)	F
19	8	Be My Lover	La Bouche	RCA	14		F
20	-	Closer To Free	Bodeans	Slash	1		FL

This Mnth	Prev Mnth	Title	Artist	Label	Wks 20	(UK Pos)	
1	2	Always Be My Baby	Mariah Carey	Columbia	20	(4)	G
2	-	Tha Crossroads	Bone Thugs-N-Harmony	Ruthless	13	(8)	P
3	1	Because You Loved Me	Celine Dion	550 Music	10		G
4	3	Nobody Knows	The Tony Rich Project	Laface	17		FGL
5	4	Ironic	Alanis Morissette	Maverick	10	(11)	F
6	16	You're The One	SWV	RCA	13	(13)	
7	6	1,2,3,4 (Sumpin' New)	Coolio	Tommy Boy	10	(13)	
8	13	Count On Me	Whitney Houston & Ce Winans	Arista	11	(12)	
9	5	Down Low (Nobody Has To Know)	R Kelly feat. Ronald Isley	Jive	11		G
10	-	Give Me One Reason	Tracy Chapman	Elektra	24		GL
11	11	Follow You Down/Til I Hear It From...	Gin Blossoms	A&M	15	(30)	FL
12	7	Sittin' Up In My Room	Brandy	A&M	17		G
13	9	Woo-Hah!! Got You All...	Busta Rhymes	Elektra	9	(8)	G
14	-	Keep On, Keepin' On	MC Lyte/Xscape	Flavor Unit/east west	5	(39)	F
15	12	Missing	Everything But The Girl	Atlantic	23	(3)	FL
16	10	Doin It	LL Cool J	Def Jam	9	(15)	
17	-	Old Man & Me (When I Get...)	Hootie & The Blowfish	Atlantic	6		L
18	-	Insensitive	Jann Arden	A&M	19	(40)	FL
19	14	All The Things (Your Man Won't Do)	Joe	Island	8	(34)	F
20	20	Closer To Free	Bodeans	Slash		(4)	FL

This Mnth	Prev Mnth	Title	Artist	Label	Wks 20	(UK Pos)	
1	2	Tha Crossroads	Bone Thugs-N-Harmony	Ruthless	13	(8)	P
2	1	Always Be My Baby	Mariah Carey	Columbia	20	(4)	G
3	10	Give Me One Reason	Tracy Chapman	Elektra	24		GL
4	3	Because You Loved Me	Celine Dion	550 Music	24		G
5	4	Nobody Knows	The Tony Rich Project	Laface	17		FGL
6	-	You're Makin Me High/Let It Flow	Toni Braxton	Laface	23	(7)	G
7	6	You're The One	SWV	RCA	13	(13)	
8	5	Ironic	Alanis Morissette	Maverick	10	(11)	F
9	-	Fastlove	George Michael	Dreamworks	5	(1)	L
10	-	Theme From Mission:Impossible	Adam Clayton & Larry Mullen	Mother	6	(7)	FL
11	18	Insensitive	Jann Arden	A&M	19	(40)	FL
12	-	How Do U Want It/California Love	2 Pac/KC And California Love	Death Row	18	(6)	P
13	-	Macarena (Bayside Boys Remix)	Los Del Rio	RCA	34		LP
14	-	Why I Love You So Much/ Much/Ain't Nobody	Monica	Arista	12		
15	-	Until It Sleeps	Metallica	Elektra	3	(5)	L
16	-	Sweet Dreams	La Bouche	RCA	7	(44)	L
17	11	Follow You Down/Til I Hear It From You	Gin Blossoms	A&M	15	(30)	FL
18	-	Touch Me Tease Me	Case/Foxy Brown	Spoiled Rotten/Def..	4	(26)	F
19	17	Old Man & Me (When I Get...)	Hootie & The Blowfish	Atlantic	8		L
20	8	Count On Me	Whitney Houston & Ce Ce Winans	Arista	11	(12)	

US 1996

APR-JUNE

◆ The world mourns the loss of one of pop culture's greatest characters, Timothy Leary. The self-styled acid prophet and the man who coined the phrase "Turn on, tune in and drop out" lost a long battle against prostate cancer.

◆ Singer-songwriter Tracy Chapman – remember 'Fast Car' – returns from commercial exile with the Top 10 single 'Give Me One Reason'. Her new album is cunningly titled *New Beginning*.

◆ And talking of, er, new beginnings, those rock'n'roll old-timers Kiss decide to get all theatrical for their first full make-up show in 17 years. Fans are treated to blood, sweat, explosions and even the odd song or two.

◆ Over 100,000 punters – plus the likes of the Beastie Boys, Red Hot Chili Peppers and the Fugees – flock to San Francisco's Golden Gate Park for the biggest benefit show since Live Aid, the Tibetan Freedom Concert.

UK 1996

JULY-SEPT

◆ Newcomers the Spice Girls notched up the first of a record-shattering six successive Number 1 singles with 'Wannabe'. The record goes on to top the charts in more than 30 countries and becomes the biggest-selling debut record by a British act.

◆ England is gripped by *Trainspotting* fever and fills the air with cries of "Lager Lager Lager" as Underworld score their first ever hit single with 'Born Slippy', taken from the film's best-selling soundtrack album.

◆ Veteran Spanish duo Los Del Rio enjoy a big UK hit with the infectious and annoying 'Macarena'. The record also spends a record-breaking 60 weeks in the US Hot 100 Chart.

◆ Former teen star Robbie Williams takes his first shot at solo stardom with a cover of George Michael's 'Freedom'. Whatever happened to young Robbie, eh?

July 1996

This Mnth	Prev Mnth	Title	Artist	Label	Wks 20	(US Pos)	
1	3	Killing Me Softly	Fugees	Columbia	12		F G
2	1	Three Lions (Official Song Of The England Team)	Baddiel & Skinner & Lightning Seeds	Epic	10		F L
3	2	Mysterious Girl	Peter Andre feat. Bubbler Ranx	Mushroom	13		
4	-	Born Slippy	Underworld	Junior Boy's Own	10		F L
5	4	Because You Loved Me	Celine Dion	Epic	10	(1)	
6	-	Wannabe	Spice Girls	Virgin	13	(1)	F
7	-	Forever Love	Gary Barlow	RCA	4		F
8	7	Don't Stop Movin'	Livin' Joy	Undiscovered	9	(67)	
9	-	Tattva	Kula Shaker	Columbia	3		F
10	-	You're Makin' Me High	Toni Braxton	Laface	4	(1)	
11	-	In Too Deep	Belinda Carlisle	Chrysalis	2		
12	-	Jazz It Up	Reel 2 Real	Positiva	3		L
13	-	Oh Yeah	Ash	Infectious	2		
14	-	Crazy	Mark Morrison	WEA	3		
15	-	Macarena (Bayside Boys Mix)	Los Del Rio	RCA	11	(1)	F L
16	-	Keep On Jumpin'	Todd Terry featuring Martha Wash & Jocelyn Brown	Manifesto	3		F
17	-	Higher State Of Consciousness '96	Wink	Manifesto	5		F L
18	-	Where Love Lies	Alison Limerick	Arista	2		L
19	9	Always Be My Baby	Mariah Carey	Columbia	5	(1)	
20	-	Bad Actress	Terrorvision	Total Vegas	1		

August 1996

This Mnth	Prev Mnth	Title	Artist	Label	Wks 20	(US Pos)	
1	6	Wannabe	Spice Girls	Virgin	13	(1)	F
2	15	Macarena (Bayside Boys Mix)	Los Del Rio	RCA	11	(1)	F L
3	1	Killing Me Softly	Fugees	Columbia	12		F G
4	-	Why	3T featuring Michael Jackson	MJJ	3		
5	-	Good Enough	Dodgy	A&M	5		
6	-	Freedom	Robbie Williams	RCA	3		F
7	3	Mysterious Girl	Peter Andre feat. Bubbler Ranx	Mushroom	13		
8	-	How Bizarre	OMC	Polydor	10		F L
9	4	Born Slippy	Underworld	Junior Boy's Own	10		F L
10	-	We've Got It Goin' On	Backstreet Boys	Jive	4	(69)	
11	-	Someday	Eternal	EMI	3		
12	-	Trash	Suede	Nude	2		
13	-	Spinning The Wheel	George Michael	Virgin	4		
14	-	Tha Crossroads	Bone Thugs-N-Harmony	Epic	5	(1)	F
15	-	Virtual Insanity	Jamiroquai	Sony S^2	7		
16	-	E-Bow The Letter	REM	Warner Bros.	2	(49)	
17	17	Higher State Of Consciousness '96	Wink	Manifesto	5		F L
18	-	Everything Must Go	Manic Street Preachers	Epic	2		
19	-	Undivided Love	Louise	EMI	3		
20	-	Peacock Suite	Paul Weller	Go! Discs	1		

September 1996

This Mnth	Prev Mnth	Title	Artist	Label	Wks 20	(US Pos)	
1	1	Wannabe	Spice Girls	Virgin	13	(1)	F G
2	-	Ready Or Not	Fugees	Columbia	7		
3	-	Flava	Peter Andre	Mushroom	5		
4	-	I've Got A Little Puppy	Smurfs	EMI TV	5		
5	15	Virtual Insanity	Jamiroquai	Sony S^2	7		
6	-	Hey Dude	Kula Shaker	Columbia	3		
7	-	Breakfast At Tiffany's	Deep Blue Something	Interscope	8	(5)	F L
8	-	One To Another	Charlatans	Beggars Banquet	2		
9	-	I'm Alive	Stretch & Vern Present Maddog	ffrr	4		F L
10	8	How Bizarre	OMC	Polydor	10		F L
11	2	Macarena	Los Del Rio	RCA	11	(1)	F L
12	-	Escaping	Dina Carroll	A&M	4		L
13	13	Spinning The Wheel	George Michael	Virgin	4		
14	-	Seven Days And One Week	BBE	Positiva	5		F
15	-	The Circle	Ocean Colour Scene	MCA	2		
16	-	I Love You Always Forever	Donna Lewis	Atlantic	9	(2)	F L
17	-	Marblehead Johnson	Bluetones	Superior Quality	2		
18	-	Me And You Versus The World	Space	Gut	3		
19	-	Always Breaking My Heart	Belinda Carlisle	Chrysalis	2		
20	-	Oh What A Night	Clock	MCA	7		

July 1996

This Mnth	Prev Mnth	Title	Artist	Label	Wks 20	(UK Pos)	
1	12	How Do U Want It/California Love	2 Pac/KC And JoJo	Death Row	18	(6)	P
2	6	You're Makin Me High/Let It Flow	Toni Braxton	Laface	23	(7)	G
3	1	Tha Crossroads	Bone Thugs-N-Harmony	Ruthless	13	(8)	P
4	3	Give Me One Reason	Tracy Chapman	Elektra	24		GL
5	13	Macarena (Bayside Boys Remix)	Los Del Rio	RCA	34	(2)	PL
6	-	Twisted	Keith Sweat	Elektra	24	(39)	G
7	4	Because You Loved Me	Celine Dion	550 Music	24		G
8	2	Always Be My Baby	Mariah Carey	Columbia	20		G
9	-	C'Mon N' Ride It (The Train)	Quad City DJ's	Quadrasound/	23		FGL
10	14	Why I Love You So Much/Ain't...	Monica	Arista	12		
11	-	I Can't Sleep Baby (If I)	R Kelly	Jive	15		G
12	-	Who Will Save Your Soul	Jewel	Atlantic	17	(52)	F
13	-	Kissin' You	Total	Bad Boy	11	(29)	
14	5	Nobody Knows	The Tony Rich	Laface Project	17		FGL
15	-	Change The World	Eric Clapton	Reprise	21	(18)	L
16	8	Ironic	Alanis Morissette	Maverick	10	(11)	F
17	10	Theme From Mission:Impossible	Adam Clayton & Larry Mullen	Mother	6	(7)	FL
18	11	Insensitive	Jann Arden	A&M	19	(40)	FL
19	-	You Learn/You Oughta Know	Alanis Morissette	Maverick	15	(24)	
20	-	Loungin	LL Cool J	Def Jam	15	(7)	G

August 1996

This Mnth	Prev Mnth	Title	Artist	Label	Wks 20	(UK Pos)	
1	5	Macarena (Bayside Boys Remix)	Los Del Rio	RCA	34	(2)	LP
2	6	Twisted	Keith Sweat	Elektra	24	(39)	G
3	2	You're Makin Me High/Let It Flow	Toni Braxton	Laface	23	(7)	G
4	9	C'Mon N' Ride It (The Train)	Quad City DJs	Quadrasound	23		FGL
5	15	Change The World	Eric Clapton	Reprise	21	(18)	L
6	20	Loungin	LL Cool J	Def Jam	15	(7)	G
7	1	How Do U Want It/California Love	2 Pac/KC And JoJo	Death Row	18	(6)	P
8	11	I Can't Sleep Baby (If I)	R Kelly	Jive	15		G
9	-	I Love You Always Forever	Donna Lewis	Atlantic	27	(5)	FL
10	4	Give Me One Reason	Tracy Chapman	Elektra	24		GL
11	19	You Learn/You Oughta Know	Alanis Morissette	Maverick	15	(24)	
12	12	Who Will Save Your Soul	Jewel	Atlantic	17	(52)	F
13	-	Elevators (Me & You)	Outkast	Arista	9		FL
14	18	Insensitive	Jann Arden	A&M	19	(40)	FL
15	-	Only You	112/The Notorious B.I.G.	Bad Boy	13		F
16	-	Hit Me Off	New Edition	MCA	5	(20)	
17	-	Counting Blue Cars	Dishwalla	A&M	11		FL
18	7	Because You Loved Me	Celine Dion	550 Music	10		G
19	13	Kissin' You	Total	Bad Boy	11	(29)	
20	-	It's All Coming Back To Me Now	Celine Dion	550 Music	26	(3)	G

September 1996

This Mnth	Prev Mnth	Title	Artist	Label	Wks 20	(UK Pos)	
1	1	Macarena (Bayside Boys Remix)	Los Del Rio	RCA	34	(2)	FLP
2	9	I Love You Always Forever	Donna Lewis	Atlantic	27	(5)	FL
3	2	Twisted	Keith Sweat	Elektra	24	(39)	G
4	4	C'Mon N' Ride It (The Train)	Quad City DJ's	Quadrasound/	23		FGL
5	6	Loungin	LL Cool J	Def Jam	15	(7)	G
6	5	Change The World	Eric Clapton	Reprise	21	(18)	L
7	20	It's All Coming Back To Me Now	Celine Dion	550 Music	26	(3)	G
8	3	You're Makin Me High/Let It Flow	Toni Braxton	Laface	23	(7)	G
9	11	You Learn/You Oughta Know	Alanis Morissette	Maverick	15	(24)	
10	8	I Can't Sleep Baby (If I)	R Kelly	Jive	15		G
11	10	Give Me One Reason	Tracy Chapman	Elektra	24		GL
12	-	Where Do You Go	No Mercy	Arista	27	(2)	FL
13	16	Hit Me Off	New Edition	MCA	5	(20)	
14	15	Only You	112/The Notorious B.I.G.	Bad Boy	13		F
15	12	Who Will Save Your Soul	Jewel	Atlantic	17	(52)	F
16	7	How Do U Want It/California Love	2 Pac/KC And JoJo	Death Row	18	(6)	P
17	17	Counting Blue Cars	Dishwalla	A&M	11		FL
18	-	If Your Girl Only Knew	Aaliyah	Blackground	10	(15)	
19	13	Elevators (Me & You)	Outkast	Arista	9		FL
20	-	Last Night	Az Yet	Laface	21	(21)	F

◆ Summer sizzled and so does the critically acclaimed Smokin' Grooves Tour featuring the likes of Cypress Hill, Nas and the Fugees.

◆ Alanis Morissette's *Jagged Little Pill* becomes the best-selling debut album of the decade and – eventually – the best-selling album by a female artist ever. Can 30 million listeners be wrong?

◆ Rap superstar Tupac Shakur – aka 2 Pac – is gunned down in a drive-by shooting in Las Vegas, the most violent act in what many feel is an ever-escalating US rap war being fought by the East and West coast bands.

◆ He's back! Vocalist Dave Lee Roth rejoins his old mates in Van Halen at the MTV Video Music Awards. Later, news stories circulate that the band have actually hired ex-Extreme frontman Gary Cherone.

UK 1996 OCT-DEC

◆ Crossover is the name of the game as one of the UK's biggest 'dance' acts the Chemical Brothers are joined by Oasis' Noel Gallagher on vocals for their chart-topping single 'Setting Sun'.

▲ The debut album by the Spice Girls goes platinum after just five days in the shops. It becomes the biggest and fastest selling debut album ever by a British act. They also grab the Christmas Number One spot with '2 Become 1' – the fastest selling single since Band Aid.

◆ The Stones' Mick Jagger is back in the tabloid spotlight as rumours emerge that his wife Jerry is consulting Princess Di's divorce lawyer, Anthony Julius.

October 1996

This Mnth	Prev Mnth	Title	Artist	Label	Wks 20	(US Pos)	
1	7	Breakfast At Tiffany's	Deep Blue Something	Interscope	8	(5)	F L
2	-	It's All Coming Back To Me Now	Celine Dion	Epic	7	(2)	
3	-	Setting Sun	Chemical Brothers	Virgin	3		
4	16	I Love You Always Forever	Donna Lewis	Atlantic	9	(2)	F L
5	14	Seven Days And One Week	BBE	Positiva	5		F
6	-	You're Gorgeous	Baby Bird	Echo	8		F
7	-	Words	Boyzone	Polydor	6		
8	2	Ready Or Not	Fugees	Columbia	7		
9	-	Rotterdam	Beautiful South	Go! Discs	4		
10	12	Escaping	Dina Carroll	A&M	4		L
11	-	Say You'll Be There	Spice Girls	Virgin	11	(3)	
12	-	Insomnia	Faithless	Cheeky	6		F
13	-	Loungin'	LL Cool J	Def Jam	4	(3)	
14	-	Flying	Cast	Polydor	2		
15	-	Trippin'	Mark Morrison	WEA	2		
16	3	Flava	Peter Andre	Mushroom	5		
17	-	No Diggity	Blackstreet feat. Dr Dre	Interscope	3	(1)	F
18	-	Beautiful Ones	Suede	Nude	2		
19	-	Dance Into The Light	Phil Collins	Face Value	2	(45)	L
20	-	Kevin Carter	Manic Street Preachers	Epic	1		

November 1996

This Mnth	Prev Mnth	Title	Artist	Label	Wks 20	(US Pos)	
1	11	Say You'll Be There	Spice Girls	Virgin	11	(3)	
2	-	If You Ever	East 17 featuring Gabrielle	London	10		
3	-	What Becomes Of The Broken Hearted	Robson Green & Jerome Flynn	RCA	6		L
4	-	Un-Break My Heart	Toni Braxton	Laface	14	(1)	
5	-	Breathe	Prodigy	XL	10		
6	-	What's Love Got To Do With It	Warren G feat. Adina Howard	Interscope	6		
7	7	Words	Boyzone	Polydor	6		
8	12	Insomnia (remix)	Faithless	Cheeky	6		F
9	-	Hillbilly Rock Hillbilly Roll	Woolpackers	RCA	9		F L
10	6	You're Gorgeous	Baby Bird	Echo	8		F
11	-	One & One	Robert Miles feat. Maria Nayler	Deconstruction	10	(54)	
12	-	Stranger In Moscow	Michael Jackson	Epic	3	(91)	
13	-	No Woman No Cry	Fugees	Columbia	3		
14	-	Angel	Simply Red	East West	2		
15	-	Child	Mark Owen	RCA	3		F
16	-	I Belong To You	Gina G	Eternal/WEA	3		
17	-	Place Your Hands	Reef	Sony	3		
18	2	It's All Coming Back To Me Now	Celine Dion	Epic	7	(2)	
19	-	Govinda	Kula Shaker	Columbia	3		
20	-	I'll Never Break Your Heart	Backstreet Boys	Jive	2		

December 1996

This Mnth	Prev Mnth	Title	Artist	Label	Wks 20	(US Pos)	
1	4	Un-Break My Heart	Toni Braxton	Laface	14	(1)	
2	5	Breathe	Prodigy	XL	10		
3	11	One & One	Robert Miles	Deconstruction	10	(54)	
4	-	A Different Beat	Boyzone	Polydor	5		
5	-	Knockin' On Heaven's Door/ Throw These Guns Away	Dunblane	BMG	4		F L
6	-	I Feel You	Peter Andre	Mushroom	3		
7	-	I Need You	3T	Epic	6		
8	-	2 Becomes 1	Spice Girls	Virgin	9	(4)	
9	-	Forever	Damage	Big Life	5		
10	-	Horny	Mark Morrison	WEA	5		
11	-	Don't Cry For Me Argentina	Madonna	Warner Bros.	6	(8)	
12	-	All By Myself	Celine Dion	Epic	4	(4)	
13	-	Don't Marry Her	Beautiful South	Go! Discs	5		L
14	-	Cosmic Girl	Jamiroquai	Sony S²	6		
15	6	What's Love Got To Do With It	Warren G	Interscope	6		
16	9	Hillbilly Rock Hillbilly Roll	Woolpackers	RCA	9		F L
17	-	Your Christmas Wish	Smurfs	EMI TV	3		L
18	2	If You Ever	East 17 feat. Gabrielle	London	10		
19	-	Australia	Manic Street Preachers	Epic	1		L
20	13	No Woman No Cry	Fugees	Columbia	3		

October 1996

This Mnth	Prev Mnth	Title	Artist	Label	Wks 20	(UK Pos)	
1	1	Macarena (Bayside Boys Remix)	Los Del Rio	RCA	34	(2)	FLP
2	2	I Love You Always Forever	Donna Lewis	Atlantic	27	(5)	FL
3	7	It's All Coming Back To Me Now	Celine Dion	550 Music	26	(3)	G
4	3	Twisted	Keith Sweat	Elektra	24	(39)	G
5	12	Where Do You Go	No Mercy	Arista	27	(2)	FL
6	6	Change The World	Eric Clapton	Reprise	21	(18)	L
7	4	C'Mon N' Ride It (The Train)	Quad City DJs	Quadrasound	23		FGL
8	8	You're Makin Me High/Let It Flow	Toni Braxton	Laface	23	(7)	G
9	5	Loungin	LL Cool J	Def Jam	15	(7)	G
10	-	No Diggity	Blackstreet/Dr Dre	Interscope	21	(9)	G
11	18	If Your Girl Only Knew	Aaliyah	Blackground	10	(15)	
12	20	Last Night	Az Yet	Laface	21	(21)	F
13	9	You Learn/You Oughta Know	Alanis Morissette	Maverick	15	(24)	
14	-	Key West Intermezzo (I Saw...	John Mellencamp	Mercury	9		L
15	16	How Do U Want It/California Love	2 Pac/KC And JoJo	Death Row	18	(6)	P
16	-	Mouth	Merril Bainbridge	Universal	21	(51)	FL
17	-	Nobody	Keith Sweat/Athena Cage	Elektra	25	(30)	G
18	-	This Is For The Lover	Babyface/LL Cool J/H Hewett/J Watley & J Daniels	Epic	9	(12)	
19	-	If It Makes You Happy	Sheryl Crow	A&M	19	(9)	
20	11	Give Me One Reason	Tracy Chapman	Elektra	24		GL

November 1996

This Mnth	Prev Mnth	Title	Artist	Label	Wks 20	(UK Pos)	
1	10	No Diggity	Blackstreet/Dr Dre	Interscope	21	(9)	G
2	3	It's All Coming Back To Me Now	Celine Dion	550 Music	26	(3)	G
3	1	Macarena (Bayside Boys Remix)	Los Del Rio	RCA	34	(2)	FLP
4	-	Un-Break My Heart	Toni Braxton	Laface	28	(2)	G
5	2	I Love You Always Forever	Donna Lewis	Atlantic	27	(5)	FL
6	16	Mouth	Merril Bainbridge	Universal	21	(51)	FL
7	17	Nobody	Keith Sweat/Athena Cage	Elektra	25	(30)	G
8	5	Where Do You Go	No Mercy	Arista	27	(2)	FL
9	-	Pony	Ginuwine	550 Music	13	(16)	GL
10	18	This Is For The Lover In You	Babyface/LL Cool J/H Hewett/J Watley & J Daniels	Epic	9	(12)	
11	4	Twisted	Keith Sweat	Elektra	24	(39)	G
12	19	If It Makes You Happy	Sheryl Crow	A&M	19	(9)	
13	-	When You Love A Woman	JourneyColumbia		17		L
14	12	Last Night	Az Yet	Laface	21	(21)	F
15	-	I'm Still In Love With You	New Edition	MCA	17		L
16	-	Don't Let Go (Love)	En Vogue	east west	23	(5)	G
17	6	Change The World	Eric Clapton	Reprise	21	(18)	L
18	7	C'Mon N' Ride It (The Train)	Quad City DJs	Quadrasound/	23		FGL
19	-	I Finally Found Someone	Barbra Streisand/Bryan Adams	Columbia	9	(10)	L
20	14	Key West Intermezzo (I Saw...	John Mellencamp	Mercury	9		L

December 1996

This Mnth	Prev Mnth	Title	Artist	Label	Wks 20	(UK Pos)	
1	4	Un-Break My Heart	Toni Braxton	Laface	28	(2)	G
2	1	No Diggity	Blackstreet/Dr Dre	Interscope	21	(9)	G
3	16	Don't Let Go (Love)	En Vogue	east west	23	(5)	G
4	7	Nobody	Keith Sweat/Athena Cage	Elektra	25	(30)	G
5	6	Mouth	Merril Bainbridge	Universal	21	(51)	FL
6	2	It's All Coming Back To Me Now	Celine Dion	550 Music	26	(3)	G
7	9	Pony	Ginuwine	550 Music	13	(16)	GL
8	19	I Finally Found Someone	Barbra Streisand/Bryan Adams	Columbia	9	(10)	L
9	15	I'm Still In Love With You	New Edition	MCA	14		L
10	8	Where Do You Go	No Mercy	Arista	27	(2)	FL
11	-	I Believe I Can Fly	R Kelly	Warner Sunset/Atlantic	19	(1)	G
12	3	Macarena (Bayside Boys Remix)	Los Del Rio	RCA	34	(2)	FLP
13	12	If It Makes You Happy	Sheryl Crow	A&M	19	(9)	
14	13	When You Love A Woman	Journey	Columbia	17		L
15	5	I Love You Always Forever	Donna Lewis	Atlantic	27	(5)	FL
16	14	Last Night	Az Yet	Laface	21	(21)	F
17	-	I Believe In You And Me	Whitney Houston	Arista	11	(16)	G
18	-	What Kind Of Man Would I Be	Mint Condition	Perspective	7	(38)	L
19	-	Fly Like An Eagle	Seal	ZTT/Warner Sunset	7	(13)	L
20	-	Falling	Montell Jordan	Def Jam		(5)	

◆ After countless image changes and style tinkering, Madonna dons her jogging pants and sweatshirt for what has to be the year's most public pregnancy. She decides to call her baby Lourdes and is already talking about sending her to school in Europe.

◆ The surviving members of Nirvana give Kurt's fans something to cheer about as they put together a live retrospective album called *From The Muddy Banks Of The Wishkah*.

◆ In case you'd forgotten about her, Madonna pops up again in the cinematic remake of the stage musical *Evita*. Pundits are predicting Oscar success, but Courtney Love has other plans as she turns in a sterling performance opposite Woody Harrelson in *The People vs Larry Flint*.

UK 1997 JAN-MAR

▲ Remember Texas? After years without a hit, the Scots rockers find themselves back in the Top 10 with 'Say What You Want', ending the year as one of the UK's biggest selling bands.

◆ Former Beatle Paul McCartney is called to Buckingham Palace to receive a Knighthood. Sir Paul reckons it's one of the best days of his life. What…even better than writing 'Mull Of Kintyre'?

◆ Jyoti Mishra – aka White Town – confounds all the pundits by taking a song he recorded in his bedroom in Derby to the UK's top spot. Did somebody say one-hit wonder!

January 1997

This Mnth	Prev Mnth	Title	Artist	Label	Wks 20	(US Pos)	
1	8	2 Become 1	Spice Girls	Virgin	9	(4)	
2	-	Professional Widow (It's Got To Be Big)	Tori Amos	East West	5		L
3	1	Un-Break My Heart	Toni Braxton	Laface/Arista	14	(1)	
4	11	Don't Cry For Me Argentina	Madonna	Warner Bros.	6	(8)	
5	-	Quit Playing Games (With My Heart)	Backstreet Boys	Jive	6	(2)	
6	3	One & One	Robert Miles feat. Maria Nayler	Deconstruction	10	(54)	
7	-	Say What You Want	Texas	Mercury	6		
8	-	Don't Let Go (Love)	En Vogue	East West America	10	(2)	
9	-	Your Woman	White Town	Chrysalis	5	(23)	F L
10	-	Satan	Orbital	Internal	2		
11	5	Knockin' On Heaven's Door-Throw These Guns Away	Dunblane	BMG	4		F L
12	-	Hey Child	East 17	London	2		L
13	-	People Hold On (The Bootleg Mixes)	Lisa Stansfield Vs The Dirty Rotten Scoundrels	Arista	2		
14	2	Breathe	Prodigy	XL	10		
15	-	Where Do You Go	No Mercy	Arista	12	(5)	F
16	10	Horny	Mark Morrison	WEA	5		
17	4	A Different Beat	Boyzone	Polydor	5		
18	-	Saturday Night	Suede	Nude	1		
19	-	I Can Make You Feel Good	Kavana	Nemesis	3		F
20	-	Come Back Brighter	Reef	Sony	2		

February 1997

This Mnth	Prev Mnth	Title	Artist	Label	Wks 20	(US Pos)	
1	15	Where Do You Go	No Mercy	Arista	12	(5)	F
2	9	Your Woman	White Town	Chrysalis	5	(23)	F L
3	-	Ain't Nobody	LL Cool J	Geffen	4	(46)	
4	8	Don't Let Go (Love)	En Vogue	East West America	10	(2)	
5	-	Discotheque	U2	Island	3	(10)	
6	-	Beetlebum	Blur	Food	2		
7	7	Say What You Want	Texas	Mercury	6		
8	-	Don't Speak	No Doubt	Interscope	11		F
9	-	Older/I Can't Make You Love Me	George Michael	Virgin	2		
10	-	Nancy Boy	Placebo	Elevator Music	3		F
11	-	Clementine	Mark Owen	RCA	3		L
12	-	Remember Me	Blue Boy	Pharm	8		F L
13	-	I Shot The Sheriff	Warren G	Def Jam	3	(20)	
14	-	Toxygene	Orb	Island	2		
15	-	The Day We Find Love	911	Ginga	2		
16	-	Barrel Of A Gun	Depeche Mode	Mute	1		
17	-	Do You Know	Michelle Gayle	RCA	2		
18	-	Walk On By	Gabrielle	Go. Beat	2		L
19	-	Ain't Talkin' 'Bout Dub	Apollo Four Forty	Stealth Sonic	3		F L
20	-	Da Funk/Musique	Daft Punk	Virgin	2	(61)	F

March 1997

This Mnth	Prev Mnth	Title	Artist	Label	Wks 20	(US Pos)	
1	8	Don't Speak	No Doubt	Interscope	11		F
2	-	Encore Une Fois	Sash!	Multiply	10		F
3	-	Mama/Who Do You Think...	Spice Girls	Virgin	7		
4	1	Where Do You Go	No Mercy	Arista	12	(5)	F
5	-	Alone	Bee Gees	Polydor	5	(28)	
6	-	Hush	Kula Shaker	Columbia	3		L
7	-	Rumble In The Jungle	Fugees	Mercury	4		L
8	-	You Got The Love	Source featuring Candi Staton	React	3		L
9	-	Don't You Love Me	Eternal	EMI	3		
10	-	Isn't It A Wonder	Boyzone	Polydor	3		
11	-	If I Never See You Again	Wet Wet Wet	Precious Org.	3		
12	-	I Believe I Can Fly	R Kelly	Jive	11	(2)	
13	4	Don't Let Go (Love)	En Vogue	East West America	10	(2)	
14	-	Fresh	Gina G	Eternal	3		
15	-	Anywhere For You	Backstreet Boys	Jive	2		
16	12	Remember Me	Blue Boy	Pharm	8		F L
17	-	Flash	BBE	Positiva	2		L
18	-	Natural	Peter Andre	Mushroom	2		
19	-	Swallowed	Bush	Interscope	2		F L
20	-	Love Guaranteed	Damage	Big Life	2		

US 1997 JAN-MAR

January 1997

This Mnth	Prev Mnth	Title	Artist	Label	Wks 20	(UK Pos)	
1	1	Un-Break My Heart	Toni Braxton	Laface	28	(2)	GL
2	3	Don't Let Go (Love)	En Vogue	east west	23	(5)	G
3	11	I Believe I Can Fly	R Kelly	Warner Sunset/Atlantic	19	(1)	G
4	4	Nobody	Keith Sweat/Athena Cage	Elektra Athena Cage	25	(30)	G
5	17	I Believe In You And Me	Whitney Houston	Arista	11	(16)	G
6	2	No Diggity	Blackstreet/Dr Dre	Interscope	21	(9)	G
7	5	Mouth	Merril Bainbridge	Universal	21	(51)	FL
8	9	I'm Still In Love With You	New Edition	MCA	17		L
9	6	It's All Coming Back To Me Now	Celine Dion	550 Music	26	(3)	G
10	19	Fly Like An Eagle	Seal	ZTT/Warner Sunset	7	(13)	L
11	13	If It Makes You Happy	Sheryl Crow	A&M		(19)	9
12	14	When You Love A Woman	Journey	Columbia	17		L
13	10	Where Do You Go	No Mercy	Arista	27	(2)	FL
14	8	I Finally Found Someone	Barbra Streisand/Bryan Adams	Columbia	9	(10)	L
15	16	Last Night	Az Yet	Laface	21	(21)	F
16	12	Macarena (Bayside Boys Remix)	Los Del Rio	RCA	34	(2)	FLP
17	7	Pony	Ginuwine	550 Music	13	(17)	GL
18	15	I Love You Always Forever	Donna Lewis	Atlantic	27	(5)	FL
19	-	No Time	Lil' Kim/Puff Daddy	Undeas/Big Beat	5	(45)	F
20	-	Wannabe	Spice Girls	Virgin	18	(1)	FG

February 1997

This Mnth	Prev Mnth	Title	Artist	Label	Wks 20	(UK Pos)	
1	1	Un-Break My Heart	Toni Braxton	Laface	28	(2)	GL
2	20	Wannabe	Spice Girls	Virgin	18	(1)	FG
3	2	Don't Let Go (Love)	En Vogue	east west	23	(5)	G
4	3	I Believe I Can Fly	R Kelly	Warner Sunset/Atlantic	19	(1)	G
5	5	I Believe In You And Me	Whitney Houston	Arista	11	(16)	G
6	-	Can't Nobody Hold Me Down	Puff Daddy/Mase	Bad Boy	23	(19)	FP
7	4	Nobody	Keith Sweat/Athena Cage	Elektra	25	(30)	G
8	-	You Were Meant For Me	Jewel	Atlantic	31	(53)	G
9	6	No Diggity	Blackstreet/Dr Dre	Interscope	21	(9)	G
10	8	I'm Still In Love With You	New Edition	MCA	17		L
11	-	Everytime I Close My Eyes	Babyface	Epic	16	(13)	L
12	-	Cold Rock A Party	MC Lyte	east west	8	(15)	L
13	-	Ooh Aah... Just A Little Bit	Gina G	Warner Bros	9	(1)	FL
14	7	Mouth	Merril Bainbridge	Universal	21	(51)	FL
15	-	In My Bed	Dru Hill	Island	13	(16)	G
16	-	On & On	Erykah Badu	Kedar	5	(12)	FL
17	13	Where Do You Go	No Mercy	Arista	27		
18	9	It's All Coming Back To Me Now	Celine Dion	550 Music	26	(3)	G
19	11	If It Makes You Happy	Sheryl Crow	A&M	19	(9)	
20	-	Discotheque	U2	Island	3	(1)	L

March 1997

This Mnth	Prev Mnth	Title	Artist	Label	Wks 20	(UK Pos)	
1	2	Wannabe	Spice Girls	Virgin	18	(1)	FG
2	6	Can't Nobody Hold Me Down	Puff Daddy/Mase	Bad Boy	23	(19)	FP
3	1	Un-Break My Heart	Toni Braxton	Laface	28	(2)	GL
4	8	You Were Meant For Me	Jewel	Atlantic	31	(53)	G
5	15	In My Bed	Dru Hill	Island	13	(16)	G
6	4	I Believe I Can Fly	R Kelly	Warner Sunset/Atlantic	19	(1)	G
7	11	Everytime I Close My Eyes	Babyface	Epic	16	(13)	L
8	3	Don't Let Go (Love)	En Vogue	east west	23	(5)	G
9	-	Don't Cry For Me Argentina	Madonna	Warner Bros	5	(3)	
10	7	Nobody	Keith Sweat/Athena Cage	Elektra	25	(30)	G
11	-	Get It Together	702	BIV 10		(9)	L
12	-	For You I Will	Monica	Rowdy/Warner Sunset	19	(27)	G
13	-	Hard To Say I'm Sorry	Az Yet/Peter Cetera	Laface	21	(7)	GL
14	5	I Believe In You And Me	Whitney Houston	Arista	11	(16)	G
15	13	Ooh Aah...Just A Little Bit	Gina G	Warner Bros.	9	(1)	FL
16	12	Cold Rock A Party	MC Lyte	east west	8	(15)	L
17	-	I Want You	Savage Garden	Columbia	18	(11)	
18	-	I'll Be	Foxy Brown/ Def	Violator/Jay-Z	9	(9)	L
19	-	All By Myself	Celine Dion	550 Music	7	(6)	
20	16	On & On	Erykah Badu	Kedar	5	(12)	FL

◆ David Bowie's 50th birthday bash is held in New York's Madison Square Gardens. Among the guests are relative newcomers like the Smashing Pumpkins' Billy Corgan, Frank Black and the Foo Fighters.

◆ The Spice Girls grab their first ever US Number One. 'Wannabe' takes the top spot, just as it did in the UK – and most other countries on Earth.

◆ The rap world suffers yet another huge set-back in March when the Notorious B.I.G. is gunned down in LA. The 24-year-old's death comes just six months after the murder of Tupac Shakur.

◆ Elvis' manager Col Tom Parker dies from stroke complications. He is 87. Parker worked with Elvis until his death in 1977 and was actually sued for fraud and mismanagement in 1981, a move that forced him to relinquish any claims to the Presley estate.

UK 1997 APR-JUNE

◆ Teenage girls have something new to shout about as Hanson release 'Mmmbop'. The fresh-faced US trio offer something new to the teen market though – they play and write all their own songs. Cor!

▲ After an acrimonious split a couple of years earlier, The Verve return with the excellent 'Bitter Sweet Symphony'. The band's comeback album establishes them as one of the UK's best bands. They eventually split again in 1999.

◆ Among the first quarter's top selling albums is Radiohead's *OK Computer*. The UK album chart also enjoys its first ever Number One hardcore rap album – the Wu-Tang Clan's *Wu-Tang Forever*.

April 1997

This Mnth	Prev Mnth	Title	Artist	Label	Wks 20	(US Pos)	
1	12	I Believe I Can Fly	R Kelly	Jive	11	(2)	
2	1	Don't Speak	No Doubt	Interscope	11		F
3	-	Belissima	DJ Quicksilver	Positiva	12		F
4	3	Mama/Who Do You Think You Are	Spice Girls	Virgin	7		
5	-	Block Rockin' Beats	Chemical Brothers	Virgin	3		
6	-	Richard III	Supergrass	Parlophone	2		
7	-	Song 2	Blur	Food	2		
8	-	The Saint	Orbital	ffrr	2		L
9	-	Underwater Love	Smoke City	Jive	3		F L
10	-	Old Before I Die	Robbie Williams	RCA	3		
11	-	North Country Boy	Charlatans	Beggars Banquet	2		
12	-	Ready Or Not	Course	The Brothers	4		F
13	-	Staring At The Sun	U2	Island	2	(26)	
14	-	It's No Good	Depeche Mode	Mute	2	(38)	L
15	2	Encore Une Fois	Sash!	Multiply	10		F
16	-	You Might Need Somebody	Shola Ama	WEA	8		F
17	-	Around The World	Daft Punk	Virgin	2	(61)	L
18	-	Don't Leave Me	Blackstreet	Interscope	5		
19	-	Free Me	Cast	Polydor	2		
20	-	Hit 'Em High (The Monstars' Anthem)	B Real/Busta Rhymes/ Coolio/LL Cool J/M. Man	Atlantic	2		F L

May 1997

This Mnth	Prev Mnth	Title	Artist	Label	Wks 20	(US Pos)	
1	-	Lovefool	Cardigans	Stockholm	7		F L
2	1	I Believe I Can Fly	R Kelly	Jive	11	(2)	
3	16	You Might Need Somebody	Shola Ama	WEA	8		F
4	-	You Are Not Alone	Olive	RCA	6	(56)	F
5	3	Belissima	DJ Quicksilver	Positiva	12		F
6	-	Love Won't Wait	Gary Barlow	RCA	3		
7	-	Wonderful Tonight	Damage	Big Life	4		L
8	-	Time To Say Goodbye (Con Te Partiro)	Sarah Brightman & Andrea Bocelli	Coalition	8		L
9	-	Blood On The Dance Floor	Michael Jackson	Epic	2	(42)	
10	-	Love Shine A Light	Katrina & The Waves	Eternal	4		L
11	-	Bodyshakin'	911	Virgin	4		
12	-	Star People '97	George Michael	Virgin	2		
13	-	I Wanna Be The Only One	Eternal featuring Bebe Winans	EMI	10		
14	-	Love Is The Law	Seahorses	Geffen	2		F
15	-	Please Don't Go	No Mercy	Arista	3	(21)	
16	-	I'll Be There For You	Rembrandts	east west	5	(17)	L
17	-	Closer Than Close	Rosie Gaines	Big Bang	7		F L
18	-	I'm A Man Not A Boy	North & South	RCA	3		F
19	-	Alright	Jamiroquai	Sony S^2	2	(78)	
20	18	Don't Leave Me	Blackstreet	Interscope	5		

June 1997

This Mnth	Prev Mnth	Title	Artist	Label	Wks 20	(US Pos)	
1	-	Mmmbop	Hanson	Mercury	8	(1)	F
2	13	I Wanna Be The Only One	Eternal featuring Bebe Winans	EMI	10		
3	8	Time To Say Goodbye (Con Te Partiro)	Sarah Brightman & Andrea Bocelli	Coalition	8		L
4	17	Closer Than Close	Rosie Gaines	Big Bang	7		F L
5	-	Free	Ultra Naté	AM:PM	12	(75)	F
6	-	Paranoid Android	Radiohead	Parlophone	2		
7	-	I'll Be Missing You	Puff Daddy & Faith Evans	Puff Daddy	15	(1)	G
8	-	Bitter Sweet Symphony	Verve	Hut	7	(12)	F
9	-	Midnight In Chelsea	Jon Bon Jovi	Mercury	2		
10	-	Coco Jamboo	Mr President	WEA	6	(21)	F L
11	16	I'll Be There For You	Rembrandts	east west	5	(17)	L
12	-	Hundred Mile High City	Ocean Colour Scene	MCA	3		
13	4	You Are Not Alone	Olive	RCA	6	(56)	F
14	-	On Your Own	Blur	Food	1		
15	-	Love Rollercoaster	Red Hot Chili Peppers	Geffen	3		L
16	-	How High	Charlatans	Beggars Banquet	1		
17	-	Hard To Say I'm Sorry	Az Yet	Laface	2	(8)	F L
18	1	Lovefool	Cardigans	Stockholm	7		F L
19	-	Nothing Lasts Forever	Echo & The Bunnymen	London	3		L
20	-	I'll Be	Foxy Brown featuring Jay Z	Def Jam	1	(7)	

April 1997

This Mnth	Prev Mnth	Title	Artist	Label	Wks 20	(UK Pos)	
1	2	Can't Nobody Hold Me Down	Puff Daddy/Mase	Bad Boy	23	(19)	FP
2	4	You Were Meant For Me	Jewel	Atlantic	31	(53)	G
3	1	Wannabe	Spice Girls	Virgin	18	(1)	FG
4	19	All By Myself	Celine Dion	550 Music	7	(6)	
5	12	For You I Will	Monica	Rowdy/WarnerSunset	19	(27)	G
6	5	In My Bed	Dru Hill	Island	13	(16)	G
7	18	I'll Be	Foxy Brown/Jay Z	Violator/Def Jam	9	(9)	L
8	17	I Want You	Savage Garden	Columbia	18	(11)	
9	7	Every Time I Close My Eyes	Babyface	Epic	16	(13)	L
10	3	Un-Break My Heart	Toni Braxton	Laface	28	(2)	GL
11	13	Hard To Say I'm Sorry	Az Yet/Peter Cetera	Laface	21	(7)	GL
12	6	I Believe I Can Fly	R Kelly	Warner Sunset/ Atlantic	19	(1)	G
13	-	Everyday Is A Winding Road	Sheryl Crow	A&M	6	(12)	
14	-	Return Of The Mack	Mark Morrison	Atlantic	23	(1)	FGL
15	11	Get It Together	702	BIV 10	9		L
16	-	Where Have All The Cowboys Gone?	Paula Cole	Imago	12	(15)	F
17	-	Hypnotize	The Notorious B.I.G.	Bad Boy	10	(10)	G
18	8	Don't Let Go (Love)	En Vogue	east west	23	(5)	G
19	-	Big Daddy	Heavy D	Uptown	6		L
20	-	Barely Breathing	Duncan Sheik	Atlantic	16		FL

May 1997

This Mnth	Prev Mnth	Title	Artist	Label	Wks 20	(UK Pos)	
1	17	Hypnotize	The Notorious B.I.G.	Bad Boy	10	(10)	G
2	-	Mmmbop	Hanson	Mercury	15	(1)	FG
3	2	You Were Meant For Me	Jewel	Atlantic	31	(53)	G
4	14	Return Of The Mack	Mark Morrison	Atlantic	23	(1)	FGL
5	5	For You I Will	Monica	Rowdy/Warner Sunset	19	(27)	G
6	8	I Want You	Savage Garden	Columbia	18	(11)	
7	1	Can't Nobody Hold Me Down	Puff Daddy/Mase	Bad Boy	23	(19)	FP
8	16	Where Have All The Cowboys Gone?	Paula Cole	Imago	12	(15)	F
9	11	Hard To Say I'm Sorry	Az Yet/Peter Cetera	Laface	21	(7)	GL
10	-	I Belong To You (Every Time I See Your Face)	Rome	RCA	14		FGL
11	-	My Baby Daddy Bizz	B-Rock & The Laface	Tony Mercedes/	7		FL
12	-	The Freshmen	The Verve Pipe	RCA	17		FL
13	3	Wannabe	Spice Girls	Virgin	18	(1)	FG
14	-	Say You'll Be There	Spice Girls	Virgin	13	(1)	
15	-	Cupid	112	Bad Boy	11		G
16	-	G.H.E.T.T.O.U.T.	Changing Faces	Big Beat	16	(10)	GL
17	-	Da' Pip	Freak Nasty	Hard Hood/Power	8		FGL
18	7	I'll Be	Foxy Brown/Jay Z	Violator/Def Jam	9	(9)	L
19	20	Barely Breathing	Duncan Sheik	Atlantic	16		FL
20	4	All By Myself	Celine Dion	550 Music	7	(6)	

June 1997

This Mnth	Prev Mnth	Title	Artist	Label	Wks 20	(UK Pos)	
1	-	I'll Be Missing You	Puff Daddy/Faith Evans	Bad Boy	21	(1)	P
2	2	Mmmbop	Hanson	Mercury	15	(1)	FG
3	4	Return Of The Mack	Mark Morrison	Atlantic	23	(1)	FGL
4	14	Say You'll Be There	Spice Girls	Virgin	13	(1)	
5	10	I Belong To You (Every Time I...	Rome	RCA	14		FGL
6	12	The Freshmen	The Verve Pipe	RCA	17		FL
7	1	Hypnotize	The Notorious	Bad Boy	10	(10)	G
8	-	It's Your Love	Tim McGraw/Faith Hill	Curb	9		GL
9	-	Bitch	Meredith Brooks	Capital	17	(6)	FL
10	16	G.H.E.T.T.O.U.T.	Changing Faces	Big Beat	16	(10)	GL
11	3	You Were Meant For Me	Jewel	Atlantic	31	(53)	G
12	9	Hard To Say I'm Sorry	Az Yet/Peter Cetera	Laface	21	(7)	GL
13	6	I Want You	Savage Garden	Columbia	18	(11)	
14	-	Look Into My Eyes	Bone Thugs-N-Harmony	Ruthless	9	(16)	
15	5	For You I Will	Monica	Rowdy/WarnerSunset	19	(27)	G
16	8	Where Have All The Cowboys...	Paula Cole	Imago	12	(15)	F
17	15	Cupid	112	Bad Boy	11		G
18	7	Can't Nobody Hold Me Down	Puff Daddy/Mase	Bad Boy	23	(19)	FP
19	17	Da' Pip	Freak Nasty	Hard Hood/Power	8		FGL
20	-	Do You Know (What It Takes)	Robyn	RCA	15	(26)	F

US 1997

APR-JUNE

◆ For the first time ever, the Rock'N'Roll Hall Of Fame Ceremony is held in Cleveland. Among those honoured are disco heroes The Bee Gees, The Jackson 5, Joni Mitchell and George Clinton's Parliament-Funkadelic.

◆ The Second Tibetan Freedom Concert is held in New York and draws a star-studded line-up that includes U2, Radiohead, Alanis Morissette and organisers the Beastie Boys.

◆ Jeff Buckley, son of late folk legend Tim, drowns in Memphis. He first appeared at a New York tribute to his father in 1991 and was soon signed to Columbia Records. Buckley only met his father once.

◆ Rap tearaways the Insane Clown Posse are dropped after their Disney-backed label Hollywood Records decides their lyrics are, ahem, inappropriate. What did they expect with a singer called Violent J?

357

UK 1997 JULY-SEPT

◆ Oasis unveil the first single from their third album, *Be Here Now*. Although a Number One hit, 'Right Here Right Now' is only given a cautious welcome by the critics. The backlash has started.

◆ Do anarcho-punks from Leeds still have hit singles? Well, Chumbawamba certainly think so. The bleached and pierced collective's 'Tubthumping' single is a big seller in both the US and UK markets.

◆ Elton John's tribute to the late Princess Di, 'Candle In The Wind' is Number One in just about every country you could mention – it only recently left the Canadian Top Five! The song eventually becomes the best-selling single of all time, beating the record set by Bing Crosby's 'White Christmas'.

July 1997

This Mnth	Prev Mnth	Title	Artist	Label	Wks 20	(US Pos)	
1	7	I'll Be Missing You	Puff Daddy & Faith Evans	Puff Daddy	15	(1)	G
2	-	Ecuador	Sash! featuring Rodriguez	Multiply	7		
3	5	Free	Ultra Naté	AM:PM	12	(75)	F
4	-	D'You Know What I Mean?	Oasis	Creation	6		
5	8	Bitter Sweet Symphony	Verve	Virgin	7	(12)	F
6	1	Mmmbop	Hanson	Mercury	8	(1)	F
7	-	Freed From Desire	Gala	Big Life	10		F
8	-	C U When U Get There	Coolio featuring 40 Thevz	Tommy Boy	7	(12)	
9	-	Just A Girl	No Doubt	Interscope	3	(23)	
10	-	The Journey	911	Virgin	2		
11	-	Something Goin' On	Todd Terry	Manifesto	5		
12	-	History/Ghosts	Michael Jackson	Epic	3		L
13	2	I Wanna Be The Only One	Eternal featuring Bebe Winans	EMI	10		
14	-	Piece Of My Heart	Shaggy featuring Marsha	Virgin	3	(72)	L
15	-	Ain't Nobody	Course	The Brothers	2		L
16	-	Blinded By The Sun	Seahorses	Geffen	2		
17	-	Gotham City	R Kelly	Jive	3	(9)	L
18	10	Coco Jamboo	Mr President	WEA	6	(21)	F L
19	-	A Change Would Do You Good	Sheryl Crow	A&M	1		
20	-	Lazy Days	Robbie Williams	Chrysalis	1		

August 1997

This Mnth	Prev Mnth	Title	Artist	Label	Wks 20	(US Pos)	
1	1	I'll Be Missing You	Puff Daddy & Faith Evans	Puff Daddy	15	(1)	G
2	7	Freed From Desire	Gala	Big Life	10		F
3	-	Everybody (Backstreet's Back)	Backstreet Boys	Jive	7	(8)	
4	-	Men In Black	Will Smith	Columbia	11		F L
5	-	Picture Of You	Boyzone	Polydor	5		
6	-	Bitch	Meredith Brooks	Capitol	6	(2)	F L
7	-	Mo Money Mo Problems	Notorious B.I.G. featuring Puff Daddy & Mase	Puff Daddy	5	(1)	L
8	-	Tubthumping	Chumbawamba	EMI	14	(6)	F L
9	8	C U When U Get There	Coolio featuring 40 Thevz	Tommy Boy	7	(12)	
10	-	All About Us	Peter Andre	Mushroom	3		
11	-	All I Wanna Do	Dannii Minogue	Eternal	4		
12	4	D'You Know What I Mean?	Oasis	Creation	6		
13	-	Yesterday	Wet Wet Wet	Precious Org.	3		L
14	-	Everything	Mary J Blige	MCA	3	(24)	
15	-	You're The One I Love	Shola Ama	WEA	3		
16	3	Free	Ultra Naté	AM:PM	12	(75)	F
17	-	Black Eyed Boy	Texas	Mercury	3		
18	-	California Dreamin	Mamas & The Papas	MCA	3		L
19	-	Never Gonna Let You Go	Tina Moore	Delirious	9		F
20	-	Filmstar	Suede	Nude	1		L

September 1997

This Mnth	Prev Mnth	Title	Artist	Label	Wks 20	(US Pos)	
1	4	Men In Black	Will Smith	Columbia	11		F L
2	8	Tubthumping	Chumbawamba	EMI	14	(6)	F L
3	-	The Drugs Don't Work	Verve	Hut	7		
4	-	Candle In The Wind 1997/Something About The...	Elton John	Rocket	17	(1)	P L
5	-	I Know Where It's At	All Saints	London	4	(36)	F L
6	1	I'll Be Missing You	Puff Daddy & Faith Evans	Puff Daddy	15	(1)	G
7	-	Honey	Mariah Carey	Columbia	4	(1)	L
8	-	You Have Been Loved/The Strangest Thing '97	George Michael	Virgin	3		L
9	-	Where's The Love	Hanson	Mercury	4		
10	-	Sunchyme	Dario G	Eternal	8		F L
11	19	Never Gonna Let You Go	Tina Moore	Delirious	9		F
12	-	(Un, Dos, Tres) Maria	Ricky Martin	Virgin	3		F L
13	-	Travellers Tune	Ocean Colour Scene	MCA	2		
14	-	Free	DJ Quicksilver	Positiva	2		L
15	-	Fix	Blackstreet	Interscope	2	(58)	
16	-	Live The Dream	Cast	Polydor	1		
17	2	Freed From Desire	Gala	Big Life	10		F
18	-	Samba De Janeiro	Bellini	Virgin	3		F L
19	-	Karma Police	Radiohead	Parlophone	1		
20	-	All Mine	Portishead	Go Beat	1		L

July 1997

This Mnth	Prev Mnth	Title	Artist	Label	Wks 20	(UK Pos)	
1	1	I'll Be Missing You	Puff Daddy/Faith Evans	Bad Boy	21	(1)	P
2	9	Bitch	Meredith Brooks	Capital	17	(6)	FL
3	2	Mmmbop	Hanson	Mercury	15	(1)	FG
4	3	Return Of The Mack	Mark Morrison	Atlantic	23	(1)	FGL
5	14	Look Into My Eyes	Bone Thugs-N-Harmony	Ruthless	9	(16)	
6	-	Quit Playing Games (With My Heart)	Backstreet Boys	Jive	24		G
7	4	Say You'll Be There	Spice Girls	Virgin	13	(1)	
8	20	Do You Know (What It Takes)	Robyn	RCA	15	(26)	F
9	10	G.H.E.T.T.O.U.T.	Changing Faces	Big Beat	16	(10)	GL
10	-	Sunny Came Home	Shawn Colvin	Columbia	13	(29)	FL
11	5	I Belong To You (Every Time I See Your Face)	Rome	RCA	14		FGL
12	-	Semi-Charmed Life	Third Eye Blind	Elektra	23	(37)	F
13	8	It's Your Love	Tim McGraw/Faith Hill	Curb	9		GL
14	-	Smile	Scarface/2 Pac/Johnny P	Rap-A-Lot/Noo Trybe	5		FL
15	6	The Freshmen	The Verve Pipe	RCA	17		FL
16	11	You Were Meant For Me	Jewel	Atlantic	31	(53)	G
17	12	Hard To Say I'm Sorry	Az Yet/Peter Cetera	Laface	21	(7)	GL
18	-	Gotham City	R Kelly	Jive	6	(9)	
19	15	For You I Will	Monica	Rowdy/WarnerSunset	19	(27)	G
20	-	Whatever	En Vogue	east west	3	(14)	L

August 1997

This	Prev	Title	Artist	Label	Wks 20	(UK Pos)	
1	1	I'll Be Missing You	Puff Daddy/Faith Evans	Bad Boy	21	(1)	P
2	-	Mo Money Mo Problems	The Notorious B.I.G/Puff Daddy	Bad Boy	15	(6)	G
3	6	Quit Playing Games...	Backstreet Boys	Jive	24		G
4	12	Semi-Charmed Life	Third Eye Blind	Elektra	23	(37)	F
5	2	Bitch	Meredith Brooks	Capital	17	(6)	FL
6	8	Do You Know (What It Takes)	Robyn	RCA	15	(26)	F
7	-	How Do I Live	LeAnn Rimes	Curb	37		FP
8	10	Sunny Came Home	Shawn Colvin	Columbia	13	(27)	FL
9	-	Not Tonight	Lil Kim/Da Brat/Left Eye/Missy Elliott/Angie Martinez	Undeas/Atlantic	9	(11)	
10	-	Never Make A Promise	Dru Hill	Island	9		
11	-	2 Become 1	Spice Girls	Virgin	12	(1)	
12	4	Return Of The Mack	Mark Morrison	Atlantic	23	(1)	FGL
13	-	C U When U Get There	Coolio/40 Theyv	Tommy Boy	7	(3)	
14	-	All For You	Sister Hazel	Universal	17		FL
15	9	G.H.E.T.T.O.U.T.	Changing Faces	Big Beat	16	(10)	GL
16	5	Look Into My Eyes	Bone Thugs-N-Harmony	Ruthless 13	9	(16)	
17	7	Say You'll Be There	Spice Girls	Virgin	10	(1)	
18	-	Invisible Man	98 Degrees	Motown	15	(66)	F
19	3	Mmmbop	Hanson	Mercury	9	(1)	FG
20	13	It's Your Love	Tim McGraw/Faith Hill	Curb			GL

September 1997

This	Prev	Title	Artist	Label	Wks 20	(UK Pos)	
1	-	Honey	Mariah Carey	Columbia	10	(3)	G
2	2	Mo Money Mo Problems	The Notorious B.I.G/Puff Daddy/Mase	Bad Boy	15	(6)	G
3	3	Quit Playing Games (With My...	Backstreet Boys	Jive	24		G
4	7	How Do I Live	LeAnn Rimes	Curb	37	(7)	FP
5	-	You Make Me Wanna...	Usher	Laface	28	(1)	FG
6	4	Semi-Charmed Life	Third Eye Blind	Elektra	23	(37)	F
7	1	I'll Be Missing You	Puff Daddy/Faith Evans	Bad Boy	21	(1)	P
8	11	2 Become 1	Spice Girls	Virgin	12	(1)	
9	-	Barbie Girl	Aqua	MCA	5	(1)	FL
10	14	All For You	Sister Hazel	Universal	17		FL
11	10	Never Make A Promise	Dru Hill	Island	9		
12	18	Invisible Man	98 Degrees	Motown	10	(66)	F
13	-	Foolish Games/You Were Meant For Me	Jewel	Atlantic	15	(32)	G
14	9	Not Tonight	Lil Kim/Da Brat/Left Eye/Missy	Undeas/Atlantic	9	(11)	
15	-	Up Jumps Da Boogie	Magoo And Timbaland	Blackground	8		FL
16	-	4 Seasons Of Loneliness	Boyz II Men	Motown	13	(10)	G
17	-	Building A Mystery	Sarah McLachlan	Nettwerk	11		F
18	6	Do You Know (What It Takes)	Robyn	RCA	15	(26)	F
19	8	Sunny Came Home	Shawn Colvin	Columbia	13	(29)	FL
20	-	All Cried Out	Allure/112	Track Masters	16	(12)	FL

▲ American critics brace themselves for an electronica explosion as the Prodigy's third LP, *Fat Of The Land*, makes the US Number One spot, selling over 200,000 copies in its first week of release. Also enjoying US success are the Chemical Brothers.

◆ Bob Dylan is back on the road after a spell in hospital earlier in the year with a viral infection. The veteran singer-songwriter also delivers what many consider to be his best album in years – *Time Out Of Mind*.

◆ One of the surprise underground hits in the US is 'When I Was Born For The 7th Time', by the UK's Anglo-Asian indie groovers Cornershop.

UK 1997 OCT-DEC

▲ "I'm a Barbie girl/In a Barbie world." Never a truer word was spoken as Denmark's Aqua drive music lovers bonkers with their teen techno anthem. The record eventually notches up huge successes in the Far East and the US, too.

◆ And if that isn't bad enough, the Christmas chart also gets a severe thrashing by four Day-Glo aliens called the Tellytubbies. They apparently like to say "Eh-Oh".

◆ Another bunch of newcomers is All Saints. Initially billed as the new Spice Girls, the London-based quartet scores a big hit with their debut single, the very funky 'I Know Where It's At'.

October 1997

This Mnth	Prev Mnth	Title	Artist	Label	Wks 20	(US Pos)	
1	4	Candle In The Wind 1997/ Something About The...	Elton John	Rocket	17	(1)	P L
2	10	Sunchyme	Dario G	Eternal	8		F L
3	-	As Long As You Love Me	Backstreet Boys	Jive	9		L
4	2	Tubthumping	Chumbawamba	EMI	14	(6)	F L
5	-	Stand By Me	Oasis	Creation	3		
6	-	Angel Of Mine	Eternal	EMI	6		L
7	-	Stay	Sash! featuring La Trec	Multiply	6		
8	-	Got 'Til It's Gone	Janet feat. Q-Tip And Joni Mitchell	Virgin	4		L
9	-	Arms Around The World	Louise	EMI	3		
10	-	Spice Up Your Life	Spice Girls	Virgin	6	(18)	
11	-	Barbie Girl	Aqua	Universal	13	(7)	F G L
12	-	Raincloud	Lighthouse Family	Wild Card	3		L
13	1	Men In Black	Will Smith	Columbia	11		F L
14	-	On Her Majesty's Secret Service	Propellerheads/David Arnold	east west	2		F
15	-	Just For You	M People	M People	3		L
16	-	Please	U2	Island	1		
17	-	You've Got A Friend	Brand New Heavies	London	4		L
18	11	Never Gonna Let You Go	Tina Moore	Delirious	9		F
19	3	The Drugs Don't Work	Verve	Hut	7		
20	-	U Sexy Thing	Clock	Media	5		

November 1997

This Mnth	Prev Mnth	Title	Artist	Label	Wks 20	(US Pos)	
1	11	Barbie Girl	Aqua	Universal	13	(7)	F G
2	-	Torn	Natalie Imbruglia	RCA	13		F
3	1	Candle In The Wind 1997/ Something About The...	Elton John	Rocket	17	(1)	P L
4	10	Spice Up Your Life	Spice Girls	Virgin	6	(18)	
5	-	Tell Him	Barbra Streisand & Celine Dion	Epic	8		L
6	7	Stay	Sash! featuring La Trec	Multiply	6		
7	3	As Long As You Love Me	Backstreet Boys	Jive	9		L
8	-	Never Ever	All Saints	London	17		G L
9	-	Perfect Day	Various	Chrysalis	11		F G L
10	-	Do Ya Think I'm Sexy?	N-Trance featuring Rod Stewart	All Around The World	4		L
11	2	Sunchyme	Dario G	Eternal	8		F L
12	-	Wind Beneath My Wings	Steven Houghton	RCA	7		F L
13	-	Choose Life	PF Project feat. Ewan McGregor	Positiva	4		F L
14	-	Party People...Friday Night	911	Ginga	2		L
15	-	I Will Come To You	Hanson	Mercury	2	(9)	L
16	-	You Sexy Thing	Hot Chocolate	EMI	3		L
17	-	Ain't That Just The Way	Lutricia McNeal	Wildstar	7	(63)	F L
18	-	Lonely	Peter Andre	Mushroom	1		
19	-	Open Road	Gary Barlow	RCA	2		L
20	-	James Bond Theme	Moby	Mute	2		L

December 1997

This Mnth	Prev Mnth	Title	Artist	Label	Wks 20	(US Pos)	
1	9	Perfect Day	Various	Chrysalis	11		F G L
2	1	Barbie Girl	Aqua	Universal	13	(7)	F G
3	-	Teletubbies Say Eh-Oh!	Teletubbies	BBC Worldwide	6		F G L
4	-	Baby Can I Hold You/Shooting Star	Boyzone	Polydor	8		L
5	8	Never Ever	All Saints	London	17		L G
6	12	Wind Beneath My Wings	Steven Houghton	RCA	7		F L
7	2	Torn	Natalie Imbruglia	RCA	13		F
8	-	Together Again	Janet Jackson	Virgin	13	(1)	
9	-	Angels	Robbie Williams	Chrysalis	14		
10	-	Too Much	Spice Girls	Virgin	5	(9)	
11	5	Tell Him	Barbra Streisand & Celine Dion	Epic	8		L
12	3	Candle In The Wind 1997/ Something About The...	Elton John	Rocket	17	(1)	P L
13	17	Ain't That Just The Way	Lutricia McNeal	Wildstar	7	(63)	F L
14	-	Lucky Man	Verve	Hut	1		L
15	-	Slam Dunk (Da Funk)	5ive	RCA	5		F L
16	-	Sing Up For The Champions	Reds United	Music Collection	5		F L
17	-	Feel So Good	Mase	Puff Daddy	3	(5)	L
18	-	The Reason	Celine Dion	Epic	3		
19	-	Let A Boy Cry	Gala	Big Life	1		L
20	-	If God Will Send His Angels	U2	Island	1		L

This Mnth	Prev Mnth	Title	Artist	Label	Wks 20	(UK Pos)	
1	-	Candle In The Wind/1997	Elton John	Rocket	19	(1)	LP
2	16	4 Seasons Of Loneliness	Boyz II Men	Motown	13	(10)	G
3	5	You Make Me Wanna…	Usher	Laface	28	(1)	FG
4	4	How Do I Live	LeAnn Rimes	Curb	37	(7)	FP
5	1	Honey	Mariah Carey	Columbia	10	(3)	G
6	3	Quit Playing Games (With My…	Backstreet Boys	Jive	24		G
7	6	Semi-Charmed Life	Third Eye Blind	Elektra	23	(37)	F
8	20	All Cried Out	Allure/112	Track Masters	16	(12)	FL
9	2	Mo Money Mo Problems	The Notorious B.I.G/Puff Daddy	Bad Boy	15	(6)	G
10	13	Foolish Games/You Were Meant For Me	Jewel	Atlantic	15	(32)	G
11	8	2 Become 1	Spice Girls	Virgin	12	(1)	
12	7	I'll Be Missing You	Puff Daddy/Faith Evans	Bad Boy	21	(1)	P
13	17	Building A Mystery	Sarah McLachlan	Nettwerk	11		F
14	-	My Love Is The Shhh!	Somethin' For The People/Trina & Tamara	Warner Bros	16	(64)	FGL
15	10	All For You	Sister Hazel	Universal	17		FL
16	12	Invisible Man	98 Degrees	Motown	10	(66)	F
17	-	You Should Be… (Don't Waste…	Brian McKnight/Mase	Mercury	5	(36)	L
18	-	The One I Gave My Heart Too	Aaliyah	Blackground	15	(30)	L
19	-	Tubthumping	Chumbawamba	Republic	19	(2)	FL
20	15	Up Jumps Da Boogie	Magoo And Timbaland	Blackground	8		FL

November 1997

This Mnth	Prev Mnth	Title	Artist	Label	Wks 20	(UK Pos)	
1	1	Candle In The Wind/1997	Elton John	Rocket	19	(1)	LP
2	3	You Make Me Wanna…	Usher	Laface	28	(1)	FG
3	4	How Do I Live	LeAnn Rimes	Curb	37	(7)	FP
4	2	4 Seasons Of Loneliness	Boyz II Men	Motown	13	(10)	G
5	8	All Cried Out	Allure/112	Track Masters	16	(12)	FL
6	14	My Love Is The Shhh!	Somethin' For The People/Trina & Tamara	Warner Bros	16	(64)	FGL
7	19	Tubthumping	Chumbawamba	Republic	19	(2)	FL
8	10	Foolish Games/You Were Meant For Me	Jewel	Atlantic	15	(32)	G
9	-	My Body	LSG	east west	15	(21)	FGL
10	18	The One I Gave My Heart Too	Aaliyah	Blackground	15	(30)	L
11	6	Quit Playing Games (With My…	Backstreet Boys	Jive	24		G
12	-	Feels So Good	Mase	Bad Boy	13	(10)	G
13	7	Semi-Charmed Life	Third Eye Blind	Elektra	23	(37)	F
14	-	I Don't Want To Wait	Paula Cole	Imago	19	(43)	L
15	-	Sock It 2 Me "Misdemeanor"	Missy Elliott/Da Brat	east west	10	(33)	
16	5	Honey	Mariah Carey	Columbia	10	(3)	G
17	-	Show Me Love	Robyn	RCA	14	(8)	L
18	-	What About Us	Total	Laface	9		
19	13	Building A Mystery	Sarah McLachlan	Nettwerk	11		F
20	-	Butta Love	Next	Arista	9		F

December 1997

This Mnth	Prev Mnth	Title	Artist	Label	Wks 20	(UK Pos)	
1	1	Candle In The Wind 1997	Elton John	Rocket	19	(1)	LP
2	3	How Do I Live	LeAnn Rimes	Curb	37	(7)	FP
3	2	You Make Me Wanna…	Usher	Laface	28	(1)	FG
4	9	My Body	LSG	east west	15	(21)	FGL
5	12	Feels So Good	Mase	Bad Boy	13	(10)	G
6	6	My Love Is The Shhh!	Somethin' For The People/Trina & Tamara	Warner Bros	16	(64)	FGL
7	7	Tubthumping	Chumbawamba	Republic	19	(2)	FL
8	17	Show Me Love	Robyn	RCA	14	(8)	L
9	-	I Will Come To You	Hanson	Mercury	8	(5)	L
10	-	It's All About The Benjamins	Puff Daddy & The Family	Bad Boy	14	(18)	G
11	5	All Cried Out	Allure/112	Track Masters	16	(12)	FL
12	14	I Don't Want To Wait	Paula Cole	Imago	19	(43)	L
13	-	Together Again	Janet	Virgin	18	(4)	
14	-	Truly Madly Deeply	Savage Garden	Columbia	36	(4)	
15	10	The One I Gave My Heart Too	Aaliyah	Blackground	15		
16	4	4 Seasons Of Loneliness	Boyz II Men	Motown	13	(10)	G
17	8	Foolish Games/You Were Meant…	Jewel	Atlantic	15	(32)	G
18	20	Butta Love	Next	Arista	9		F
19	-	A Song For Mama	Boyz II Men	Motown	13	(34)	GL
20	15	Sock It 2 Me	Missy "Misdemeanor" Elliott/Da Brat	east west	10	(33)	

US 1997 OCT-DEC

◆ Sean 'Puffy' Combs produces five of America's ten Number One hits of the year. He even performs on three of them! Not content with that, his single 'I'll Be Missing You' becomes the best-selling rap song of all time, with over seven million sales.

◆ After countless video highlights and mimed TV appearances, the Spice Girls play their first ever live concerts in Istanbul. Shock! Horror! They can actually sing!

◆ R.E.M. suffer their first ever personnel upheaval when drummer Bill Berry calls it a day after almost 20 years. The band decides to carry on as a three-piece.

UK 1998 JAN-MAR

◆ 1998 Brit winners include Finley Quaye, soul newcomer Shola Ama and the reformed Verve who grab a Best Album Award.

◆ Celine Dion becomes the first woman to sell over a million copies of two separate singles in the UK. The latest, 'My Heart Will Go On', is featured on her Number One album *Let's Talk About Love* – the second to sell over 20 million copies globally – and on the soundtrack to the record-breaking movie *Titanic*.

◆ First the good news: Elton John grabs himself a Knighthood. Then the bad: recent deaths include Michael Hutchence of INXS, who is found naked after apparently committing suicide in a hotel room.

◆ After years of speculation about his sexuality, George Michael is 'outed' in spectacular fashion when he is arrested after an incident in a public toilet in Beverly Hills. A few days later, the star tells the world he is gay.

January 1998

This Mnth	Prev Mnth	Title	Artist	Label	Wks 20	(US Pos)	
1	5	Never Ever	All Saints	London	17		G L
2	1	Perfect Day	Various	Chrysalis	11		FGL
3	8	Together Again	Janet Jackson	Virgin	13	(1)	
4	10	Too Much	Spice Girls	Virgin	5	(9)	
5	9	Angels	Robbie Williams	Chrysalis	14		
6	-	High	Lighthouse Family	Polydor	8		L
7	-	Bamboogie	Bamboo	VC	5		FL
8	-	Renegade Master 98	Wildchild	Hi-Life	5		L
9	-	All Around The World	Oasis	Creation	3		L
10	3	Teletubbies Say Eh-Oh!	Teletubbies	BBC Worldwide	6		FGL
11	-	You Make Me Wanna	Usher	Laface	5	(2)	L
12	7	Torn	Natalie Imbruglia	RCA	13		F
13	-	Avenging Angels	Space	Gut	3		
14	-	Mulder And Scully	Catatonia	Blanco Y Negro	4		FL
15	-	No Surprises	Radiohead	Parlophone	1		L
16	-	My Star	Ian Brown	Polydor	2		F L
17	2	Barbie Girl	Aqua	Universal	13	(7)	F G
18	4	Baby Can I Hold You/ Shooting Star	Boyzone	Polydor	8		L
19	12	Candle In The Wind 1997/ Something About The...	Elton John	Rocket	17	(1)	P L
20	-	Amnesia	Chumbawamba	EMI	2		L

February 1998

1	-	Doctor Jones	Aqua	Universal	7		L
2	1	Never Ever	All Saints	London	17		G L
3	-	Gettin' Jiggy Wit It	Will Smith	Columbia	6	(1)	L
4	5	Angels	Robbie Williams	Chrysalis	14		
5	11	You Make Me Wanna	Usher	Laface	5	(2)	F L
6	-	My Heart Will Go On	Celine Dion	Epic	14	(1)	G L
7	-	All I Have To Give	Backstreet Boys	Jive	3		L
8	-	Cleopatra's Theme	Cleopatra	WEA	4		F L
9	6	High	Lighthouse Family	Polydor	8		L
10	-	Brimful Of Asha	Cornershop	Wiiija	8		F L
11	-	Let Me Show You	Camisra	VC	3		F L
12	-	Truly Madly Deeply	Savage Garden	Columbia	*14	(1)	L
13	3	Together Again	Janet Jackson	Virgin	13	(1)	
14	-	When I Need You	Will Mellor	Unity	2		F L
15	14	Mulder And Scully	Catatonia	Blanco Y Negro	4		F L
16	-	Be Alone No More	Another Level	Northwestside	3		F L
17	-	Crazy Little Party Girl	Aaron Carter	Ultra Pop	2		L
18	7	Bamboogie	Bamboo	VC	5		F L
19	-	You're Still The One	Shania Twain	Mercury	4	(2)	F L
20	-	Solomon Bites The Worm	Bluetones	Superior Quality	1		L

March 1998

1	6	My Heart Will Go On	Celine Dion	Epic	14	(1)	G L
2	-	Frozen	Madonna	Maverick	7	(2)	L
3	10	Brimful Of Asha	Cornershop	Wiiija	8		F L
4	-	It's Like That	Run-DMC Vs Jason Nevins	Sm:)e Comms	10		G L
5	12	Truly Madly Deeply	Savage Garden	Columbia	*14	(1)	L
6	-	Stop	Spice Girls	Virgin	6		L
7	-	Big Mistake	Natalie Imbruglia	RCA	3		L
8	-	The Ballad Of Tom Jones	Space With Cerys Of Catatonia	Gut	3		L
9	-	When The Lights Go Out	5ive	RCA	4		L
10	-	How Do I Live	LeAnn Rimes	Curb	*13	(2)	F L
11	-	Say What You Want/Insane	Texas featuring Wu-Tang Clan	Mercury	2		L
12	1	Doctor Jones	Aqua	Universal	7		L
13	-	Let Me Entertain You	Robbie Williams	Chrysalis	5		L
14	-	Everlasting Love	Cast From Casualty	Warner	2		F L
15	-	No, No, No	Destiny's Child	Columbia	3	(3)	F L
16	-	Here's Where The Story Ends	Tin Tin Out featuring Shelley Nelson	VC	5		L
17	-	Show Me Love	Robyn	RCA	2	(7)	F L
18	16	Be Alone No More	Another Level	Northwestside	3		F L
19	-	Angel St	M People	M People	2		L
20	-	Uh La La La	Alexia	Dance Pool	3		F L

January 1998

This Mnth	Prev Mnth	Title	Artist	Label	Wks 20	(UK Pos)	
1	14	Truly Madly Deeply	Savage Garden	Columbia	36	(4)	
2	1	Candle In The Wind/ 1997	Elton John	Rocket	19	(1)	LP
3	13	Together Again	Janet	Virgin	18	(4)	
4	10	It's All About The Benjamins/Been Around The World	Puff Daddy & The Family	Bad Boy	14	(18)	G
5	2	How Do I Live	LeAnn Rimes	Curb	37	(7)	FP
6	4	My Body	LSG	east west	15	(21)	FGL
7	3	You Make Me Wanna…	Usher	Laface	28	(1)	FG
8	8	Show Me Love	Robyn	RCA	14	(8)	L
9	7	Tubthumping	Chumbawamba	Republic	19	(2)	FL
10	19	A Song For Mama	Boyz II Men	Motown	13	(34)	GL
11	5	Feels So Good	Mase	Bad Boy	13		FG
12	-	I Don't Ever Want To See You Again	Uncle Sam	Stonecreek	13	(30)	FGL
13	12	I Don't Want To Wait	Paula Cole	Imago	19	(43)	L
14	6	My Love Is The Shhh!	Somethin' For The People/ Trina & Tamara	Warner Bros	16	(64)	FGL
15	-	Nice & Slow	Usher	Laface	16	(24)	G
16	-	We're Not Making Love Anymore	Dru Hill	Island	7		
17	9	I Will Come To You	Hanson	Mercury	8	(5)	L
18	-	Dangerous	Busta Rhymes	Elektra	6	(32)	
19	-	How's It Going To Be	Third Eye Blind	Elektra	11	(51)	
20	15	The One I Gave My Heart To	Aaliyah	Blackground	15		L

February 1998

This Mnth	Prev Mnth	Title	Artist	Label	Wks 20	(UK Pos)	
1	15	Nice & Slow	Usher	Laface	16	(24)	G
2	3	Together Again	Janet	Virgin	18	(4)	
3	5	How Do I Live	LeAnn Rimes	Curb	37	(7)	FP
4	1	Truly Madly Deeply	Savage Garden	Columbia	36	(4)	
5	4	It's All About The Benjamins/Been Around The World	Puff Daddy & The Family	Bad Boy	14	(18)	G
6	12	I Don't Ever Want To See You Again	Uncle Sam	Stonecreek	13	(30)	FGL
7	10	A Song For Mama	Boyz II Men	Motown	13	(34)	GL
8	-	No, No, No	Destiny's Child	Columbia	18	(5)	FGL
9	19	How's It Going To Be	Third Eye Blind	Elektra	11	(51)	
10	7	You Make Me Wanna…	Usher	Laface	16	(1)	FG
11	18	Dangerous	Busta Rhymes	Elektra	6	(32)	
12	-	My Heart Will Go On	Celine Dion	550 Music	10	(1)	
13	9	Tubthumping	Chumbawamba	Republic	19	(2)	FL
14	13	I Don't Want To Wait	Paula Cole	Imago	19	(43)	L
15	-	What You Want	Mase/Total	Bad Boy	12	(15)	
16	-	Too Much	Spice Girls	Virgin	4	(1)	
17	8	Show Me Love	Robyn	RCA	15	(8)	L
18	-	Gettin' Jiggy With It	Will Smith	Columbia	9	(3)	F
19	-	Gone Till November	Wyclef Jean	Ruffhouse	13	(3)	FGL
20	-	Kiss The Rain	Billie Myers	Universal	5	(4)	FL

March 1998

This Mnth	Prev Mnth	Title	Artist	Label	Wks 20	(UK Pos)	
1	18	Gettin' Jiggy With It	Will Smith	Columbia	9	(3)	F
2	12	My Heart Will Go On	Celine Dion	550 Music	10	(1)	
3	1	Nice & Slow	Usher	Laface	16	(24)	G
4	8	No, No, No	Destiny's Child	Columbia	18	(5)	FGL
5	4	Truly Madly Deeply	Savage Garden	Columbia	36	(4)	
6	15	What You Want	Mase/Total	Bad Boy	12	(15)	
7	2	Together Again	Janet	Virgin	18	(4)	
8	19	Gone Till November	Wyclef Jean	Ruffhouse	13	(3)	FGL
9	-	Swing My Way	K.P & Envyi	east west	6	(14)	FL
10	-	Deja Vu (Uptown Baby)	Lord Tariq & Peter Gunz	Codeine	10		FL
11	3	How Do I Live	LeAnn Rimes	Curb	37	(4)	FP
12	-	Frozen	Madonna	Maverick	13		
13	6	I Don't Ever Want To See You Again	Uncle Sam	Stonecreek	13	(30)	FGL
14	-	Too Close	Next	Arista	36	(24)	GL
15	-	Are You Jimmy Ray?	Jimmy Ray	Epic	7	(13)	FL
16	-	Body Bumpin' Yippie-Yi-Yo	Public Announcement	A&M	16	(38)	FGL
17	16	Too Much	Spice Girls	Virgin	4	(1)	
18	-	Let's Ride	Montell Jordan/Master P/Silkk	Def Jam	14	(25)	G
19	5	It's All About The Benjamins/Been Around The World	Puff Daddy & The Family	Bad Boy	14	18	G
20	9	How's It Going To Be	Third Eye Blind	Elektra	11	(51)	

▲ Fans and accountants are shocked by the news that multi-platinum R&B singer Toni Braxton has filed for bankruptcy. The case seems to have arisen out of Braxton's desire to be released from her Arista/LaFace record contract.

◆ Leonardo DiCaprio doesn't get an Oscar, but no one seems to mind. The film *Titanic* becomes one of the biggest-grossing films in history with its soundtrack doing similarly brisk business.

◆ Superstar Madonna plays her first live show in over four years when she turns up for a 2am gig at the Roxy in New York. Highlights include a preview of tunes from her forthcoming album, *Ray Of Light*.

UK 1998 APR-JUN

◆ The world is shocked by the sad death of Linda McCartney. A noted animal rights activist and devoted wife of former Beatle Sir Paul, she finally loses a long battle against breast cancer in April.

◆ Teenage girls cry into their lemonade as they learn that Ginger Spice has decided to quit the band. Although credited as the driving force behind the sacking of their former manager, Ginger – aka Geri Halliwell – reveals there are still "differences between us" in her press statement.

▲ Remember Run DMC? Well, the veteran rap stars are back, thanks to a beefed-up remix of their classic track 'It's Like That' by DJ-ing newcomer Jason Nevins. The success of the track also heralds a renaissance for that other lost hip-hop art, breakdancing.

April 1998

This Mnth	Prev Mnth	Title	Artist	Label	Wks 20	(US Pos)	
1	4	It's Like That	Run-DMC Vs Jason Nevins	Sm:)e Comms	10		G L
2	1	My Heart Will Go On	Celine Dion	Epic	14	(1)	G L
3	-	La Primavera	Sash!	Multiply	5		L
4	5	Truly Madly Deeply	Savage Garden	Columbia	*14	(1)	L
5	-	Turn It Up/Fire It Up	Busta Rhymes	Elektra	5		L
6	-	Kiss The Rain	Billie Myers	Universal	5	(15)	F L
7	13	Let Me Entertain You	Robbie Williams	Chrysalis	5		L
8	10	How Do I Live	Leann Rimes	Curb	*14	(2)	F L
9	-	All I Want Is You	911	Virgin	3		L
10	-	I Get Lonely	Janet Jackson	Virgin	4		L
11	6	Stop	Spice Girls	Virgin	6		L
12	-	Feel It	Tamperer featuring Maya	Pepper	*6		F L
13	-	Found A Cure	Ultra Nate	AM:PM	3		L
14	-	Give A Little Love	Daniel O'Donnell	Ritz	2		L
15	16	Here's Where The Story Ends	Tin Tin Out featuring Shelley Nelson	VC	5		L
16	-	All My Life	K-Ci & Jojo	MCA	4	(1)	F L
17	15	No, No, No	Destiny's Child	Columbia	3	(3)	F L
18	-	Kung-Fu	187 Lockdown	east west	1		L
19	-	Say You Do	Ultra	east west	2		F L
20	-	All That Matters	Louise	EMI	2		L

May 1998

This Mnth	Prev Mnth	Title	Artist	Label	Wks 20	(US Pos)	
1	12	Feel It	The Tamperer Featuring Maya	Pepper	9		F
2	-	Under The Bridge/ Lady Marmalade	All Saints	London	7		
3	-	Last Thing On My Mind	Steps	Jive	8		
4	-	Dance The Night Away	Mavericks	MCA Nashville	10		FL
5	-	Turn Back Time	Aqua	Universal	5		
6	-	All That I Need	Boyzone	Poly	3		
7	4	Truly Madly Deeply	Savage Garden	Columbia	14		
8	8	How Do I Live	LeAnn Rimes	Hit Label/ London/Curb	14	(2)	FL
9	-	Ray Of Light	Madonna	Maverick	4	(5)	
10	1	It's Like That	Run DMC Vs Jason Nevins	Sm:)e Comms	10		
11	-	Gone Till November	Wyclef Jean	Columbia	4	(7)	
12	-	Life Ain't Easy	Cleopatra	WEA	3	(81)	
13	-	Dreams	The Corrs	Atlantic	4		
14	-	Stranded	Lutricia McNeal	Wildstar	7		
15	-	Road Rage	Catatonia	Blanco Y Negro	3		
16	2	My Heart Will Go On	Celine Dion	Epic	14		G
17	-	Sound Of Drums	Kula Shaker	Columbia	2		
18	-	Say You Love Me	Simply Red	east west	2		
19	5	Turn It Up/Fire It Up	Busta Rhymes	Elektra	5		
20	-	Hot Stuff	Arsenal FC	Grapevine	2		L

June 1998

This Mnth	Prev Mnth	Title	Artist	Label	Wks 20	(US Pos)	
1	-	C'Est La Vie	B*Witched	Glow Worm/Epic	12	(9)	F
2	-	Horny	Mousse T Vs Hot 'n' Juicy	AM:PM	10		FL
3	-	3 Lions '98	Baddiel & Skinner	Epic	5		L
4	-	The Boy Is Mine	Brandy & Monica	Atlantic	14	(1)	FL
5	4	Dance The Night Away	Mavericks	MCA Nashville	10		FL
6	1	Feel It	The Tamperer featuring Maya	Pepper	9		F
7	14	Stranded	Lutricia McNeal	Wildstar	7		
8	-	Vindaloo	Fat Les	Telstar	4		FL
9	-	Got The Feelin'	5ive	RCA	8		
10	-	Kung Fu Fighting	Bus Stop/Carl Douglas	All Around The World	6		
11	8	How Do I Live	LeAnn Rimes	Hit Label	14	(2)	FL
12	2	Under The Bridge/ Lady...	All Saints	London	7		
13	-	My All	Mariah Carey	Columbia	3	(1)	
14	-	Carnaval De Paris	Dario G	Eternal	4		
15	3	Last Thing On My Mind	Steps	Jive	8		
16	-	The Rockafeller Skank	Fatboy Slim	Skint	3	(78)	F
17	-	Life	Des'Ree	Sony S2	5		
18	-	Ghetto Superstar That	Pras Michel/Is What You Are	Interscope ODB/Mya	11	(15)	
19	-	Come Back To What You Know	Embrace	Hut/Virgin	1		
20	-	Lost In Space	Lighthouse Family	Polydor	4		L

364

April 1998

This Mnth	Prev Mnth	Title	Artist	Label	Wks 20	(UK Pos)	
1	-	All My Life	K-Ci & JoJo	MCA	22	(8)	FL
2	14	Too Close	Next	Arista	36	(24)	GL
3	18	Let's Ride	Montell Jordan/Master P/Silkk The Shocker	Def Jam	14	(25)	G
4	12	Frozen	Madonna	Maverick	13	(1)	
5	3	Nice & Slow	Usher	Laface	16	(24)	G
6	5	Truly Madly Deeply	Savage Garden	Columbia	36	(4)	
7	2	My Heart Will Go On	Celine Dion	550 Music	10	(1)	
8	-	Romeo And Juliet Chill	Sylk-E Fyne/Chill	Grand Jury	8		FL
9	8	Gone Till November	Wyclef Jean	Ruffhouse	13	(3)	FGL
10	4	No, No, No	Destiny's Child	Columbia	18	(5)	FGL
11	16	Body Bumpin' Yippie-Yi-Yo	Public Announcement	A&M	16	(38)	FGL
12	10	Deja Vu (Uptown Baby)	Lord Tariq & Peter Gunz	Codeine	10		FL
13	-	You're Still The One	Shania Twain	Mercury (Nashville)	30	(10)	FG
14	-	Sex And Candy	Marcy	Capitol Playground	16	(29)	FL
15	1	Getting' Jiggy Wit It	Will Smith	Columbia	9	(3)	F
16	6	What You Want	Mase/Total	Bad Boy	12	(15)	
17	-	I Want You Back	'N Sync	RCA	14	(5)	F
18	-	Bitter Sweet Symphony	Verve	VC/Hut	4	(2)	FL
19	-	Everybody (Backstreet's Back)	Backstreet Boys	Jive	15	(3)	G
20	7	Together Again	Janet	Virgin	18	(4)	

May 1998

This Mnth	Prev Mnth	Title	Artist	Label	Wks 20	(UK Pos)	
1	2	Too Close	Next	Arista	36	(24)	GL
2	13	You're Still The One	Shania Twain	Mercury (Nashville)	30	(10)	FG
3	-	My All	Mariah Carey	Columbia	13	(4)	G
4	19	Everybody (Backstreet's Back)	Backstreet Boys	Jive	15	(3)	G
5	6	Truly Madly Deeply	Savage Garden	Columbia	36	(4)	
6	11	Body Bumpin' Yippie-Yi-Yo	Public Announcement	A&M	16	(38)	FGL
7	1	All My Life	K-Ci & JoJo	MCA	22	(8)	FL
8	-	It's All About Me	Mya & Sisqo	University	9		F
9	3	Let's Ride	Montell Jordan/Master P./Silkk The Shocker	Def Jam	14	(25)	G
10	4	Frozen	Madonna	Maverick	13	(1)	
11	14	Sex And Candy	Marcy Playground	Capitol	16	(29)	FL
12	-	The Arms Of The One Who Loves You	Xscape	So So Def	9	(46)	
13	17	I Want You Back	'N Sync	RCA	14	(5)	F
14	-	Turn It Up (Remix)/ Fire It Up	Busta Rhymes	Elektra	7	(2)	L
15	-	I Get Lonely	Janet/Blackstreet	Virgin	8	(5)	L
16	8	Romeo And Juliet	Sylk-E Fyne/Chill	Grand Jury	8		FL
17	10	No, No, No	Destiny's Child	Columbia	18	(5)	FGL
18	9	Gone Till November	Wyclef Jean	Ruffhouse	13	(3)	FGL
19	-	Money, Power & Respect	The Lox/DMX/Lil' Kim	Bad Boy	6		FL
20	5	Nice & Slow	Usher	Laface	16	(24)	G

June 1998

This Mnth	Prev Mnth	Title	Artist	Label	Wks 20	(UK Pos)	
1	-	The Boy Is Mine	Brandy & Monica	Atlantic	20	(2)	P
2	1	Too Close	Next	Arista	36	(24)	GL
3	2	You're Still The One	Shania Twain	Mercury (Nashville)	30	(10)	FG
4	3	My All	Mariah Carey	Columbia	13	(4)	G
5	15	I Get Lonely	Janet/Blackstreet	Virgin	8	(5)	L
6	4	Everybody (Backstreet's Back)	Backstreet Boys	Jive	15	(3)	
7	7	All My Life	K-Ci & JoJo	MCA	22	(8)	FL
8	5	Truly Madly Deeply	Savage Garden	Columbia	36	(4)	
9	12	The Arms Of The One Who Loves You	Xscape	So So Def	9	(46)	
10	-	Adia	Sarah McLachlan	Arista	18	(18)	L
11	11	Sex And Candy	Marcy Playground	Capitol	16	(29)	FL
12	-	They Don't Know	Jon B	Yab Yum	7	(32)	GL
13	6	Body Bumpin' Yippie-Yi-Yo	Public Announcement	A&M	16	(38)	FGL
14	8	It's All About Me	Mya & Sisqo	University	9		F
15	9	Let's Ride	Montell Jordan/Master P/Silkk	Def Jam	14	(25)	G
16	-	My Way	Usher	Laface	20		GL
17	13	I Want You Back	'N Sync	RCA	14	(5)	F
18	-	Come With Me	Puff Daddy/Jimmy Page	Epic	11	(2)	GL
19	-	I Got The Hook Up! Of Funk	Master P/Sons	No Limit	8		L
20	10	Frozen	Madonna	Maverick	13	(1)	

US 1998

APR-JUN

◆ Those ol' blue eyes closed for the last time in May as the world bids a fond farewell to the man they called the Chairman Of The Board, Frank Sinatra. Dogged by ill health for several years, Sinatra will nevertheless be remembered for his charismatic charm and classic hits like 'New York New York' and 'Come Fly With Me'.

◆ Gloria Estefan is joined by Aretha, Celine, Mariah and Shania for the all-singing, all-dancing, all-pouting VH1 *Divas Live Special*. The show becomes the station's biggest rating hit ever.

◆ Former Stray Cat Brian Setzer spearheads the US swing revival. His Brian Setzer Orchestra, The Squirrel Nut Zippers and Cherry Poppin' Daddies have audiences jitterbuggin' like crazy.

◆ Beach Boy genius Brian Wilson announces he's the happiest in years and releases the rather splendid *Imagination* album. And he performs his first ever solo show in Chicago.

◆ Spice Girl Mel B becomes Mel G after she marries her dancer boyfriend Jimmy Gulzar in a lavish *Hello*-style wedding in Buckinghamshire. The couple's relationship runs into problems in mid-99, after it's alleged that Jimmy is running up a few too many credit card bills.

◆ It's time for more teeny action as 16-year-old Billie tops the charts with the bubblegum delights of 'Because We Want To'. Young Billie was first seen in an advertising campaign for the pop mag. *Smash Hits*.

◆ John Travolta's quiff is in top form as a re-released 'You're The One That I Want' takes him and Olivia Newton John back into the Top 20.

◆ Pras Michel proves it's not just Wyclef and Lauryn who can do the solo thing. 'Ghetto Superstar', based on the Kenny Rogers/Dolly Parton hit, 'Islands In The Stream', is a big hit on both sides of the Atlantic.

July 1998

This Mnth	Prev Mnth	Title	Artist	Label	Wks 20	(US Pos)	
1	18	Ghetto Superstar That Is What You Are	Pras Michel/ODB/Mya	Interscope	11	(15)	
2	1	C'Est La Vie	B*Witched	Glow Worm/Epic	12	(9)	F
3	-	Because We Want To	Billie	Innocent	6		F
4	-	Save Tonight	Eagle-Eye Cherry	Polydor	9	(5)	F
5	3	3 Lions '98	Baddiel & Skinner	Epic	5		L
6	-	Freak Me	Another Level	Northwestside	7		
7	4	The Boy Is Mine	Brandy & Monica	Atlantic	14	(1)	FL
8	-	Looking For Love	Karen Ramirez	Manifesto	6		FL
9	2	Horny	Mousse T Vs Hot 'n' Juicy	AM:PM	10		FL
10	8	Vindaloo	Fat Les	Telstar	4		FL
11	-	Intergalactic	Beastie Boys	Grand Royal/Parlophone	3	(28)	
12	-	Deeper Underground	Jamiroquai	Sony S2	4		L
13	9	Got The Feelin'	5ive	RCA	8		
14	-	Immortality	Celine Dion	Epic	4		
15	-	Be Careful	Sparkle/R. Kelly	Jive	2		FL
16	17	Life	Des'Ree	Sony S2	5		
17	-	You're The One That I Want	John Travolta & Olivia Newton...	Polydor	2		
18	-	Life Is A Flower	Ace Of Base	London	6		
19	-	Legacy EP	Mansun	Parlophone	1		
20	20	Lost In Space	Lighthouse Family	Polydor	4		L

August 1998

This Mnth	Prev Mnth	Title	Artist	Label	Wks 20	(US Pos)	
1	-	Viva Forever	Spice Girls	Virgin		(6)	
2	-	No Matter What	Boyzone	Polydor		(10)	
3	1	Ghetto Superstar That Is What You Are	Pras Michel/ODB/MYA	Interscope	11	(15)	
4	6	Freak Me	Another Level	Northwestside	7		
5	18	Life Is A Flower	Ace Of Base	London	6		
6	-	Come With Me	Puff Daddy featuring Jimmy Page	Epic	4	(4)	
7	-	Mysterious Times	Sash! featuring Tina Cousins	Multiply	6		
8	-	Lost In Space	Apollo 440	Epic	4		
9	4	Save Tonight	Eagle-Eye Cherry	Polydor	9	(5)	F
10	-	Just The Two Of Us	Will Smith	Columbia	4	(20)	L
11	-	Music Sounds Better With You	Stardust	Virgin	8	(62)	FL
12	-	To The Moon And Back	Savage Garden	Columbia	9	(24)	
13	12	Deeper Underground	Jamiroquai	Sony S2	4		L
14	7	The Boy Is Mine	Brandy & Monica	Atlantic	14	(1)	FL
15	-	Everything's Gonna Be Alright	Sweetbox	RCA	6	(46)	L
16	2	C'Est La Vie	B*Witched	Glow Worm/Epic	12	(9)	F
17	-	I Want You Back	Cleopatra	WEA	3		
18	-	The Air That I Breath	Simply Red	east west	3		L
19	-	My Oh My	Aqua	Universal	2		
20	-	Pure Morning	Placebo	Hut/Virgin	2		

September 1998

This Mnth	Prev Mnth	Title	Artist	Label	Wks 20	(US Pos)	
1	2	No Matter What	Boyzone	Polydor	10		
2	-	One For Sorrow	Steps	Jive	6		
3	-	Finally Found	Honeyz	1st Avenue/Mercury	7		F
4	-	If You Tolerate This Your Children Will Be Next	The Manic Street Preachers	Epic	4		
5	11	Music Sounds Better With You	Stardust	Virgin	8	(62)	FL
6	-	Bootie Call	All Saints	London	3		
7	-	Crush	Jennifer Paige	EAR/Edel	5	(3)	FL
8	-	Millennium	Robbie Williams	Chrysalis	5		
9	12	To The Moon And Back	Savage Garden	Columbia	9	(24)	
10	-	Everybody Get Up	5ive	RCA	3		
11	-	Sex On The Beach	T-Spoon	Control/Edel	7		FL
12	-	I Want You Back	Melanie B feat. Missy Elliott	Virgin		(3)	FL
13	15	Everything's Gonna Be Alright	Sweetbox	RCA	6	(46)	L
14	-	I Don't Want To Miss A Thing	Aerosmith	Columbia	14	(1)	L
15	-	God Is A DJ	Faithless	Cheeky	4		
16	-	What Can I Do (Remix)	The Corrs	Atlantic	4		
17	7	Mysterious Times	Sash! featuring Tina Cousins	Multiply	6		
18	-	The Incidentals	Alisha's Attic	Mercury	3		L
19	-	Someone Loves You Honey	Lutricia McNeal	Wildstar		(2)	
20	-	My Favorite Mistake	Sheryl Crow	A&M/Polydor	2	(20)	

US 1998 JULY-SEPT

This Mnth	Prev Mnth	Title	Artist	Label	Wks 20	(UK Pos)	
1	1	The Boy Is Mine	Brandy & Monica	Atlantic	20	(2)	P
2	3	You're Still The One	Shania Twain	Mercury (Nashville)	30	(10)	FG
3	16	My Way	Usher	Laface	20		GL
4	2	Too Close	Next	Arista	36	(24)	GL
5	18	Come With Me	Puff Daddy/Jimmy Page	Epic	11	(2)	G
6	10	Adia	Sarah McLachlan	Arista	18	(18)	
7	4	My All	Mariah Carey	Columbia	13	(4)	G
8	-	Make It Hot	Nicole/Missy "Misdemeanor" Elliott/Mocha	The Gold Mind, Inc/east west	12	(22)	FL
9	6	Everybody (Backstreet's Back)	Backstreet Boys	Jive	15	(3)	G
10	-	Ray Of Light	Madonna	Maverick	5	(2)	
11	12	They Don't Know	Jon B	Yab Yum	7	(32)	GL
12	-	Say It Theory	Voices Of	H.O.L.A.	12		FL
13	7	All My Life	K-Ci & JoJo	MCA	22	(8)	FL
14	8	Truly Madly Deeply	Savage Garden	Columbia	36	(4)	
15	11	Sex And Candy	Marcy Playground	Capitol	16	(29)	FL
16	-	Ghetto Superstar (That Is What You Are)	Pras Michel/Ol' Dirty Bastard/Mya	Interscope	7	(2)	FL
17	5	I Get Lonely	Janet/Blackstreet	Virgin	8	(5)	L
18	-	When The Lights Go Out	5ive	Arista	18	(4)	FL
19	-	Stop	Spice Girls	Virgin	4	(2)	
20	-	Never Ever	All Saints	London	17	(1)	FL

August 1998

This Mnth	Prev Mnth	Title	Artist	Label	Wks 20	(UK Pos)	
1	1	The Boy Is Mine	Brandy & Monica	Atlantic	20	(2)	P
2	3	My Way	Usher	Laface	20		GL
3	2	You're Still The One	Shania Twain	Mercury (Nashville)	30	(10)	FG
4	6	Adia	Sarah McLachlan	Arista	18	(18)	
5	20	Never Ever	All Saints	London	17	(1)	FL
6	8	Make It Hot	Nicole/Missy "Misdemeanor" Elliott/Mocha	The Gold Mind, Inc/east west	12	(22)	FL
7	4	Too Close	Next	Arista	36	(24)	GL
8	-	Crush	Jennifer Paige	Edel America	18	(4)	FL
9	18	When The Lights Go Out	5ive	Arista	18	(4)	FL
10	5	Come With Me	Puff Daddy/Jimmy Page	Epic	11	(2)	G
11	-	Cruel Summer	Ace Of Base	Arista	9	(8)	L
12	-	The First Night	Monica	Arista	20	(6)	GL
13	-	Friend Of Mine	Kelly Price	T-Neck	9	(25)	FL
14	-	Lookin' At Me	Mase/Puff Daddy	Bad Boy	9		
15	-	Daydreamin'	Tatyana Ali	MJJ	11	(6)	FL
16	12	Say It Theory	Voices Of	H.O.L.A.	12		FL
17	10	Ray Of Light	Madonna	Maverick	5	(2)	
18	16	Ghetto Superstar (That Is What You Are)	Pras Michel/Ol' Dirty Bastard/Mya	Interscope	7	(2)	FL
19	13	All My Life	K-Ci & JoJo	MCA	22	(8)	FL
20	-	Time After Time	Inoj	So So Def	10		FL

September 1998

This Mnth	Prev Mnth	Title	Artist	Label	Wks 20	(UK Pos)	
1	-	I Don't Want To Miss A Thing	Aerosmith	Columbia	14	(4)	L
2	12	The First Night	Monica	Arista	20	(6)	GL
3	8	Crush	Jennifer Paige	Edel America	18	(4)	FL
4	2	My Way	Usher	Laface	20		GL
5	1	The Boy Is Mine	Brandy & Monica	Atlantic	20	(3)	P
6	15	Daydreamin'	Tatyana Ali	MJJ	11	(6)	FL
7	3	You're Still The One	Shania Twain	Mercury	30	(10)	FG
8	20	Time After Time	Inoj	So So Def	10		FL
9	14	Lookin' At Me	Mase/Puff Daddy	Bad Boy	9		
10	9	When The Lights Go Out	5ive	Arista	18	(4)	FL
11	5	Never Ever	All Saints	London	17	(1)	FL
12	4	Adia	Sarah McLachlan	Arista	18	(18)	
13	7	Too Close	Next	Arista	36	(24)	GL
14	-	This Kiss	Faith Hill	Warner Bros	22	(13)	GL
15	-	Thinkin' Bout It	Gerald Levert	east west	7		F
16	11	Cruel Summer	Ace Of Base	Arista	9	(8)	L
17	-	I Still Love You	Next	Arista	12		
18	-	I Can Do That	Montell Jordan	Def Jam	4		L
19	-	I'll Be	Edwin McCain	Lava	10		FL
20	6	Make It Hot	Nicole/Missy "Misdemeanor"...	The Gold Mind,...	12	(22)	FL

▲ The Beastie Boys are back! Once the bad boys of rap, Ad Rock, MCA and Mike D are now more likely to be organising benefit concerts and being nice to people. Their new album, *Hello Nasty*, is applauded as a classic.

◆ The surprise cinema hit of the year, *There's Something About Mary*, also sparks interest in veteran cult star Jonathan Richman after several of his songs are featured on the soundtrack.

◆ As if he hadn't broken enough records already, Garth Brooks releases the biggest selling country album ever in the US. *No Fences* sold a staggering 16 million copies.

UK 1998 OCT-DEC

◆ The most-requested karaoke hit of the year is The Beautiful South's 'Perfect 10', a song about penis size. That says a lot about us Brits, eh!

◆ George Michael releases his first single since that slight mis-understanding in a public loo. The 'Outside' video features lots of steamy dance routines and even the odd gay policeman.

◆ Sixties, Seventies and Eighties star Cher may have made more headlines for her surgery than her singing, but she also scores her biggest hit of the Nineties when she takes 'Believe' to Number One – a feat repeated in the US in 1999.

◆ The coolest Christmas hit has to be 'Chocolate Salty Balls (PS I Love You)', a funky little number released by *South Park*'s overweight gastronomic hero, Chef.

October 1998

This Mnth	Prev Mnth	Title	Artist	Label	Wks 20	(US Pos)	
1	-	Rollercoaster	B*Witched	Epic	6		
2	14	I Don't Want To Miss A Thing	Aerosmith	Columbia	14	(1)	L
3	-	Perfect 10	The Beautiful South	Go! Discs/Mercury	6		
4	-	Girlfriend	Billie	Innocent	4		
5	11	Sex On The Beach	T-Spoon	Control/Edel	7		FL
6	-	Doo Wop (That Thing)	Lauryn Hill	Ruffhouse/Columbia	4	(1)	
7	-	Gym And Tonic	Spacedust	east west	3		F
8	-	Gangster Trippin'	Fatboy Slim	Skint	4		
9	-	Top Of The World	Brandy featuring Mase	Atlantic	3		
10	8	Millennium	Robbie Williams	Chrysalis	5		
11	-	Believe	Cher	WEA	13	(1)	G
12	-	More Than A Woman	911	Virgin	3		
13	3	Finally Found	Honeyz	1st Avenue/Mercury	7		F
14	-	Stand By Me	4 The Cause	RCA	3	(82)	FL
15	12	I Want You Back	Melanie B feat. Missy Elliott	Virgin	3		FL
16	-	Cruel Summer	Ace Of Base	London	2		
17	1	No Matter What	Boyzone	Polydor	10		
18	-	The First Night	Monica	Rowdy/Arista	2	(1)	L
19	-	Outside	George Michael	Epic	4		
20	-	How Deep Is Your Love	Dru Hill	Island/Black Music	2	(3)	

November 1998

This Mnth	Prev Mnth	Title	Artist	Label	Wks 20	(US Pos)	
1	11	Believe	Cher	WEA	13	(1)	G
2	-	Would You...?	Touch And Go	Oval/V2	4		FL
3	-	If You Buy This Record Your Life Will Be Better	The Tamperer featuring Maya	Pepper	5		L
4	2	I Don't Want To Miss A Thing	Aerosmith	Columbia	14	(1)	L
5	-	Each Time	E-17	Telstar	3		
6	19	Outside	George Michael	Epic	4		
7	-	Blue Angels	Pras	Ruffhouse	4		L
8	-	Heartbeat/Tragedy	Steps	Jive	18		
9	-	Sweetest Thing	U2	Island	4		L
10	-	I Just Wanna Be Loved	Culture Club	Virgin	4		L
11	-	Another One Bites The Dust	Queen With Wyclef Jean	Dreamworks	2		L
12	-	Guess I Was A Fool	Another Level	Northwestside	3		
13	-	The Bartender And The Thief	Stereophonics	V2	2		
14	-	Falling In Love Again	Eagle-Eye Cherry	Polydor	2		L
15	-	Daydreamin'	Tatyana Ali	Epic	2		F
16	-	Sit Down (Remix)	James	Fontana	2		L
17	-	Until The Time Is Through	5ive	RCA	3		
18	-	This Kiss	Faith Hill	Warner Bros	3	(7)	FL
19	-	I'm Your Angel	Celine Dion & R Kelly	Epic	4	(1)	L
20	-	Up And Down	Vengaboys	Positiva	8		F

December 1998

This Mnth	Prev Mnth	Title	Artist	Label	Wks 20	(US Pos)	
1	1	Believe	Cher	WEA	13	(1)	G
2	8	Heartbeat/Tragedy	Steps	Ebul/Jive	18		
3	-	I Love The Way You Love Me	Boyzone	Polydor	7		
4	-	Miami	Will Smith	Columbia	7	(17)	
5	-	When You're Gone	Bryan Adams feat. Melanie C	A&M/Mercury	12		
6	-	To You I Belong	B*Witched	Glow Worm/Epic	5		
7	-	Hard Knock Life (Ghetto Anthem)	Jay Z	Northwestside	5	(13)	
8	20	Up And Down	Vengaboys	Positiva	8		F
9	-	Big Big World	Emilia	Universal	7	(92)	FL
10	-	Goodbye	Spice Girls	Virgin	6	(11)	L
11	-	She Wants You	Billie	Innocent	4		
12	-	End Of The Line	Honeyz	1st Avenue/Mercury	7		
13	-	No Regrets	Robbie Williams	Chrysalis	5		
14	-	When You Believe	Mariah Carey & Whitney Houston	Columbia	4	(15)	
15	19	I'm Your Angel	Celine Dion & R Kelly	Epic	4	(1)	
16		War Of Nerves	All Saints	London	4		L
17	-	Take Me There	Blackstreet & Mya/Mase	Interscope	4	(14)	
18	-	Chocolate Salty Balls	Chef	Columbia	8		FL
19	-	The Power Of Good-Bye/ Little Star	Madonna	Maverick	2		
20	17	Until The Time Is Through	5ive	RCA	3		

October 1998

This Mnth	Prev Mnth	Title	Artist	Label	Wks 20	(UK Pos)	
1	2	The First Night	Monica	Arista	20	(6)	GL
2	-	One Week	Barenaked Ladies	Reprise	11	(5)	FL
3	1	I Don't Want To Miss A Thing	Aerosmith	Columbia	14	(4)	L
4	3	Crush	Jennifer Paige	Edel America	18	(4)	FL
5	19	I'll Be	Edwin McCain	Lava	10		FL
6	-	How Deep Is Your Love	Dru Hill/Redman Jam	Island/Def	11	(9)	L
7	14	This Kiss	Faith Hill	Warner Bros (Nashville)	22	(13)	GL
8	-	Because Of You	98 Degrees	Motown	17	(36)	GL
9	4	My Way	Usher	Laface	20		GL
10	-	Lately	Divine	Pendulum	17		FGL
11	8	Time After Time	Inoj	So So Def	10		FL
12	10	When The Lights Go Out	5ive	Arista	18	(4)	FL
13	-	Touch It	Monifah	Uptown	8	(29)	FL
14	13	Too Close	Next	Arista	36	(24)	GL
15	-	I Still Love You	Next	Arista	12		
16	5	The Boy Is Mine	Brandy & Monica	Atlantic	20	(2)	P
17	-	Westside	TQ	Clockwork	7	(4)	FL
18	6	Daydreamin'	Tatyana Ali	MJJ	11	(6)	FL
19	-	My Little Secret	Xscape	So So Def	4		L
20	11	Never Ever	All Saints	London	17	(1)	FL

November 1998

This Mnth	Prev Mnth	Title	Artist	Label	Wks 20	(UK Pos)	
1	10	Lately	Divine	Pendulum	19		FGL
2	1	The First Night	Monica	Arista	20	(6)	GL
3	-	Doo Wop (That Thing)	Lauryn Hill	Ruffhouse	12	(3)	FL
4	8	Because Of You	98 Degrees	Motown	17	(36)	GL
5	2	One Week	Barenaked Ladies	Reprise	11	(5)	FL
6	6	How Deep Is Your Love	Dru Hill/Redman	Island/Def Jam	11	(9)	L
7	-	Nobody's Supposed To Be Here	Deborah Cox	Arista	22		GL
8	4	Crush	Jennifer Paige	Edel America	18	(4)	FL
9	7	This Kiss	Faith Hill	Warner Bros (Nashville)	22	(13)	GL
10	5	I'll Be	Edwin McCain	Lava	10		FL
11	3	I Don't Want To Miss A Thing	Aerosmith	Columbia	14	(4)	L
12	-	The Power Of Good-Bye	Madonna	Maverick	5	(6)	L
13	13	Touch It	Monifah	Uptown	8	(29)	FL
14	17	Westside	TQ	Clockwork	7	(4)	FL
15	-	Come And Get With Me	Keith Sweat/Snoop Dogg	Elektra	6	(58)	
16	-	Love Like This	Faith Evans	Bad Boy	10	(24)	
17	14	Too Close	Next	Arista	36	(24)	GL
18	-	...Baby One More Time	Britney Spears	Jive	25	(1)	FGL
19	-	Love Me	112/Mase	Bad Boy	10		
20	19	My Little Secret	Xscape	So So Def	4		L

December 1998

This Mnth	Prev Mnth	Title	Artist	Label	Wks 20	(UK Pos)	
1	-	I'm Your Angel	R Kelly/Celine Dion	Jive	13	(3)	GL
2	7	Nobody's Supposed To Be Here	Deborah Cox	Arista	22		GL
3	1	Lately	Divine	Pendulum	19	(9)	FGL
4	-	From This Moment On	Shania Twain	Mercury (Nashville)	9		L
5	3	Doo Wop (That Thing)	Lauryn Hill	Ruffhouse	12	(3)	FL
6	4	Because Of You	98 Degrees	Motown	17	(36)	GL
7	16	Love Like This	Faith Evans	Bad Boy	10	(24)	
8	-	Lullaby	Shawn Mullins	SMG	13	(9)	FL
9	18	...Baby One More Time	Britney Spears	Jive	25	(1)	FGL
10	-	Have You Ever?	Brandy	Atlantic	18	(13)	L
11	9	This Kiss	Faith Hill	Warner Bros (Nashville)	22	(13)	GL
12	-	Iris	Goo Goo Dolls	Warner Bros	24	(50)	
13	2	The First Night	Monica	Arista	20	(6)	GL
14	-	Save Tonight	Eagle-Eye Cherry	Work	12	(6)	FL
15	-	Trippin'	Total/Missy Elliott	Bad Boy	10		L
16	6	How Deep Is Your Love	Dru Hill/Redman	Island/Def Jam	11	(9)	L
17	-	Jumper	Third Eye Blind	Elektra	14		L
18	-	Hands	Jewel	Atlantic	12	(41)	L
19	5	One Week	Barenaked Ladies	Reprise	11	(5)	FL
20	-	Goodbye	Spice Girls	Virgin	3	(1)	L

US 1998

OCT-DEC

▲ Hip-hop has a mighty good year as the Fugees' Lauryn Hill tops the charts with her debut solo album, *The Miseducation Of Lauryn Hill*. The album is eventually knocked off the Number One spot by fellow rapper Jay-Z *(pictured above)*.

◆ Ex-multi-platinum rapper Vanilla Ice isn't so lucky, though. Having grown a beard and put on some beach shorts, he decides to get into thrash metal and releases an album called *Hard To Swallow*. Indeed it was.

◆ Everybody might laugh at their geeky looks and silly names, but Canada's Barenaked Ladies silence the critics when they grab the top spot with their infectious single 'One Week'.

369

UK 1999 JAN-MAR

▲ It's official! Big Beat is in. Fatboy Slim – aka Norman Cook of The Housemartins, Beats International and Freakpower fame – takes top spot with 'Praise You'. His album, *You've Come A Long Way, Baby* also makes Number One.

◆ One of the world's greatest pop icons, Debbie Harry, returns with her old band, Blondie. Their comeback single, 'Maria', shoots straight to the top of the UK charts and tickets for London dates sell out in hours.

◆ Talking of comebacks, Lenny Kravitz enjoys his first big hit in years when 'Fly Away' reaches Number One after it's used as the music for a car advert.

January 1999

This Mnth	Prev Mnth	Title	Artist	Label	Wks 20	(US Pos)	
1	2	Heartbeat/Tragedy	Steps	Ebul/Jive	18		
2	18	Chocolate Salty Balls	Chef	Columbia	8		FL
3	5	When You're Gone	Bryan Adams feat. Melanie C	A&M/Mercury	12		
4	10	Goodbye	Spice Girls	Virgin	6	(11)	L
5	-	Praise You	Fatboy Slim	Skint	6		
6	1	Believe	Cher	WEA	13	(1)	G
7	12	End Of The Line	Honeyz	1st Avenue/Mercury	7		
8	-	You Should Be…	Blockster	Sound Of Ministry	4		FL
9	6	To You I Belong	B*Witched	Glow Worm/Epic	5		
10	-	A Little Bit More	911	Virgin	3		
11	-	Especially For You	Denise and Johnny	RCA		(4)	FL
12	4	Miami	Will Smith	Columbia	7	(17)	
13	-	I Want You For Myself	Another Level	Northwestside	3		
14	9	Big Big World	Emilia	Universal	7	(92)	FL
15	-	Pretty Fly (For A White Guy)	The Offspring	Columbia	5	(53)	F
16	-	More Than This	Emmie	Indirect/Manifesto	3		FL
17	3	I Love The Way You Love Me	Boyzone	Polydor		(7)	
18	-	Cassius 1999	Cassius	Virgin		(2)	F
19	8	Up And Down	Vengaboys	Positiva		(8)	F
20	-	Tequila	Terrorvision	Total Vegas	4		L

February 1999

This Mnth	Prev Mnth	Title	Artist	Label	Wks 20	(US Pos)	
1	-	You Don't Know Me	Armand Van Harden	ffrr Helden/Duane		(5)	F
2	-	Maria	Blondie	Beyond/RCA	6	(82)	L
3	15	Pretty Fly (For A White Guy)	The Offspring	Columbia Ebul/Jive	5	(52)	F
4	1	Heartbeat/Tragedy	Steps	Ebul/Jive	18		
5	3	When You're Gone	Bryan Adams feat. Melanie C	A&M/Mercury	12		
6	-	Fly Away	Lenny Kravitz	Virgin	4	(12)	L
7	-	Westside	TQ	Epic	5	(12)	F
8	-	Boy You Knock Me Out	Tatyana Ali/ Will Smith	MJJ/Epic	3		L
9	-	Changes	2 Pac	Jive	6	(32)	L
10	-	Protect Your Mind (For The Love Of A Princess)	DJ Sakin & Friends	Positiva	4		F
11	-	Baby One More Time	Britney Spears	Jive	12	(1)	FGL
12	20	Tequila	Terrorvision	Total Vegas	4		L
13	-	These Are The Times	Dru Hill	Island Black Music	2	(21)	L
14	-	Enjoy Yourself	A+	Universal	3	(63)	FL
15	-	One Week	Barenaked Ladies	Reprise	5	(1)	FL
16	-	National Express	The Divine Comedy	Setanta	2		L
17	-	Runaway (Remix)	The Corrs	Atlantic	5		L
18	-	Can't Get Enough	Soulsearcher	Defected	2		FL
19	-	Ex-Factor	Lauryn Hill	Columbia	2	(21)	L
20	-	I Want You Back	'N-Sync	Transcontinental/ Northwestside	2	(13)	FL

March 1999

This Mnth	Prev Mnth	Title	Artist	Label	Wks 20	(US Pos)	
1	11	Baby One More Time	Britney Spears	Jive	12	(1)	FGL
2	-	When The Going Gets Tough	Boyzone	Polydor	6		L
3	-	It's Not Right But It's OK	Whitney Houston	Arista	8		L
4	-	Tender	Blur	Food/Parlophone	5		L
5	-	Strong Enough	Cher	WEA	5		
6	-	We Like To Party! (The Vengabus)	Vengaboys	Positiva	8	(26)	L
7	-	As	George Michael & Mary J. Blige	Epic	3		L
8	17	Runaway (Remix)	The Corrs	Atlantic	5		L
9	-	Better Best Forgotten	Steps	Ebul/Jive	6		L
10	-	Blame It On The Weatherman	B*Witched	Glow Worm/Epic	4		L
11	-	Just Looking	Stereophonics	V2	2		
12	9	Changes	2 Pac	Jive	6	(32)	L
13	-	You Stole The Sun From My Heart	Manic Street Preachers	Epic	2		L
14	6	Fly Away	Lenny Kravitz	Virgin	4	(12)	L
15	-	Nothing Really Matters	Madonna	Maverick	2	(93)	L
16	2	Maria	Blondie	Beyond/RCA	6	(82)	L
17	-	Erase/Rewind	The Cardigans	Stockholm/Polydor	2		L
18	-	Strong	Robbie Williams	Chrysalis	2		L
19	-	Lullaby	Shawn Mullins	Columbia	2	(7)	FL
20	-	My Love	Kele Le Roc	1st Avenue/ Wild Card/Polydor	2		L

January 1999

This Mnth	Prev Mnth	Title	Artist	Label	Wks 20	(UK Pos)	
1	1	I'm Your Angel	R Kelly/Celine Dion	Jive	13	(3)	LG
2	10	Have You Ever?	Brandy	Atlantic	18	(13)	L
3	9	...Baby One More Time	Britney Spears	Jive	25	(1)	FGL
4	2	Nobody's Supposed To Be Here	Deborah Cox	Arista	22		GL
5	3	Lately	Divine	Pendulum	19		FGL
6	5	Doo Wop (That Thing)	Lauryn Hill	Ruffhouse	12	(3)	FL
7	14	Save Tonight	Eagle-Eye Cherry	Work	12	(6)	FL
8	8	Lullaby	Shawn Mullins	SMG	13	(9)	FL
9	6	Because Of You	98 Degrees	Motown	17	(36)	GL
10	15	Trippin'	Total/Missy Elliott	Bad Boy	10		L
11	18	Hands	Jewel	Atlantic	12	(41)	L
12	4	From This Moment On	Shania Twain	Mercury (Nashville)	9	(9)	L
13	-	Slide	Goo Goo Dolls	Warner Bros.	24		L
14	17	Jumper	Third Eye Blind	Elektra	14		L
15	7	Love Like This	Faith Evans	Bad Boy	10	(24)	
16	-	Angel	Sarah McLachlan	Arista/Warner Sunset	17		L
17	20	Goodbye	Spice Girls	Virgin	3	(1)	L
18	11	This Kiss	Faith Hill	Warner Bros	22	(13)	GL
19	-	Take Me There	Blackstreet & Mya/Mase & Blinky Blink	Interscope	4	(7)	L
20	-	Angel Of Mine	Monica	Arista	16		GL

February 1999

This Mnth	Prev Mnth	Title	Artist	Label	Wks 20	(UK Pos)	
1	20	Angel Of Mine	Monica	Arista	16		GL
2	3	...Baby One More Time	Britney Spears	Jive	25	(1)	FGL
3	4	Nobody's Supposed To Be Here	Deborah Cox	Arista	22		GL
4	-	Believe	Cher	Warner Bros.	18	(1)	GL
5	2	Have You Ever?	Brandy	Atlantic	18	(13)	L
6	-	All I Have To Give	Backstreet Boys	Jive	12	(2)	GL
7	16	Angel	Sarah McLachlan	Arista/Warner Sunset	17		L
8	-	Heartbreak Hotel	Whitney Houston/Faith Evans/Kelly Price	Arista	16		GL
9	13	Slide	Goo Goo Dolls	Warner Bros.	24		L
10	14	Jumper	Third Eye Blind	Elektra	14		L
11	7	Save Tonight	Eagle-Eye Cherry	Work	12	(6)	FL
12	1	I'm Your Angel	R Kelly/Celine Dion	Jive	13	(3)	GL
13	-	Taking Everything	Gerald Levert	east west	5		L
14	-	Faded Pictures	Case & Joe	Def Jam	5		L
15	11	Hands	Jewel	Atlantic	12	(41)	L
16	8	Lullaby	Shawn Mullins	SMG	13	(9)	FL
17	-	You	Jesse Powell	Silas	6		L
18	-	(God Must Have Spent) A Little More Time On You	'N Sync	RCA	5		L
19	-	Every Morning	Sugar Ray	Lava	16	(10)	FL
20	-	I Don't Want To Miss A Thing	Mark Chesnutt	Decca	4		FL

March 1999

This Mnth	Prev Mnth	Title	Artist	Label	Wks 20	(UK Pos)	
1	4	Believe	Cher	Warner Bros.	18	(1)	GL
2	1	Angel Of Mine	Monica	Arista	16		GL
3	8	Heartbreak Hotel	Whitney Houston/Faith Evans	Arista	16		GL
4	7	Angel	Sarah McLachlan	Arista/Warner Sunset	17		L
5	6	All I Have To Give	Backstreet Boys	Jive	12	(2)	GL
6	-	I Still Believe	Mariah Carey	Columbia	8	(16)	GL
7	2	...Baby One More Time	Britney Spears	Jive	25	(1)	FGL
8	19	Every Morning	Sugar Ray	Lava	16	(10)	FL
9	-	No Scrubs	TLC	Laface	13	(3)	L
10	3	Nobody's Supposed To Be Here	Deborah Cox	Arista	22		GL
11	-	Kiss Me	Sixpence None The Richer	Squint	13	(4)	FL
12	9	Slide	Goo Goo Dolls	Warner Bros	24		L
13	18	(God Must Have Spent) A Little...	'N Sync	RCA	5		L
14	17	You	Jesse Powell	Silas	6		L
15	5	Have You Ever?	Brandy	Atlantic	18	(13)	L
16	14	Faded Pictures	Case & Joe	Def Jam	5		L
17	-	What's It Gonna Be?!	Busta Rhymes/Janet	Flipmode/Elektra	10	(6)	L
18	-	All Night Long	Faith Evans/Puff Daddy	Bad Boy	6	(23)	L
19	-	Stay The Same	Joey McIntyre	C2	7		FL
20	11	Save Tonight	Eagle-Eye Cherry	Work	12	6	FL

◆ The normally dull and boring Grammys Ceremony gets a bit of kick up the backside as the ladies sweep the board. Biggest winner is Lauryn Hill who takes home five awards. Other successes include Celine Dion and Sheryl Crow.

◆ Something strange is happening to country and western music. After years in the style doldrums, it suddenly becomes hip. Bands like the Dixie Chicks and Shania Twain are adding a cool, contemporary edge that is even outselling the likes of Madonna.

◆ As well as being Madonna's current beau, Mark McGrath and his band, Sugar Ray, score a huge worldwide hit with the semi-acoustic and soulful 'Every Morning'.

UK 1999 APR-JUNE

◆ The season's biggest star is not Robbie or the Spice Girls, it's Flat Eric, an 18-inch yellow puppet who starred in a Levi TV ad. Ericmania sweeps the country as the ad's background music, 'Flat Beat', by French techno act Mr Oizo, goes to Number One.

◆ Martine 'Tiffany' McCutcheon's dramatic departure from *EastEnders* at Christmas cleared the way for a sparkling pop career. Her debut single, 'Perfect Moment', enters the UK chart at Number One on its first week of release.

◆ The music biz celebrates 25 years since Abba first won the Eurovision Song contest. A repackaged hits album makes Number One and the London West End welcomes *Mamma Mia!*, a musical written by Benny and Bjorn.

April 1999

This Mnth	Prev Mnth	Title	Artist	Label	Wks 20	(US Pos)	
1	-	Flat Beat	Mr Oizo	F Comm/PIAS	6		FL
2	-	Witch Doctor	Cartoons	Flex/EMI	7		F
3	-	Perfect Moment	Martine McCutcheon	Innocent	6		F
4	1	Baby One More Time	Britney Spears	Jive	12	(1)	FG
5	-	My Name Is	Eminem	Interscope/Polydor	5	(36)	F
6	-	Turn Around	Phats & Small	Multiply	10		F
7	-	You Get What You Give	New Radicals	MCA	10	(36)	FL
8	-	No Scrubs	TLC	LaFace	11	(1)	
9	-	Thank Abba For The Music	Various Artists	Epic	5		
10	6	We Like To Party!	Vengaboys	Positiva	8	(26)	
11	-	Honey To The Bee	Billie	Innocent	3		
12	2	When The Going Gets Tough	Boyzone	Polydor	6		
13	-	Dead From The Waist Down	Catatonia	Blanco Y Negro	3		
14	10	Blame It On The Weatherman	B*Witched	Glow Worm/Epic	4		
15	-	Taboo	Glamma Kid/Shola Ama	WEA	3		F
16	9	Better Best Forgotten	Steps	Ebul/Jive	6		
17	-	Electricity	Suede	Nude	1		
18	-	Girlfriend/Boyfriend	Blackstreet/Janet	Interscope/Polydor	2		L
19	3	It's Not Right But It's Okay	Whitney Houston	Arista	7		
20	-	Love Of A Lifetime	Honeyz	1st Avenue/Mercury	3		

May 1999

This Mnth	Prev Mnth	Title	Artist	Label	Wks 20	(US Pos)	
1	-	Swear It Again	Westlife	RCA	5		F
2	8	No Scrubs	TLC	LaFace	11	(1)	
3	6	Turn Around	Phats & Small	Multiply	9		
4	-	I Want It That Way	Backstreet Boys	Jive	8		
5	-	Red Alert	Basement Jaxx	XL Recordings	5		
6	-	Right Here Right Now	Fatboy Slim	Skint	4		
7	-	You Needed Me	Boyzone	Polydor	7		
8	3	Perfect Moment	Martine McCutcheon	Innocent	6		F
9	-	Why Don't You Get A Job?	The Offspring	Columbia	3		
10	-	That Don't Impress Me Much	Shania Twain	Mercury	13	7	F
11	-	Look At Me	Geri Halliwell	EMI	7		F
12	-	Pick A Part That's New	Stereophonics	V2	3		
13	-	Sweet Like Chocolate	Shanks & Bigfoot	Chocolate Boy/Pepper	7		F
14	-	Private Number	911	Virgin	2		
15	-	In Our Lifetime	Texas	Mercury	3		
16	-	Cloud Number 9	Bryan Adams	A&M/Mercury	3		L
17	-	What's It Gonna Be?!	Busta Rhymes/Janet	Elektra	3		L
18	7	You Get What You Give	New Radicals	MCA	11	36	FL
19	-	Bye Bye Baby	TQ	Epic	2		
20	2	Witch Doctor	Cartoons	Flex/EMI	7		FL

June 1999

This Mnth	Prev Mnth	Title	Artist	Label	Wks 20	(US Pos)	
1	13	Sweet Like Chocolate	Shanks & Bigfoot	Chocolate Boy/Pepper	7		F
2	10	That Don't Impress Me Much	Shania Twain	Mercury	13	(12)	
3	-	Everybody's Free (Sunscreen)	Baz Luhrmann	EMI	4		FL
4	-	Ooh La La	Wiseguys	Wall Of Sound	4		FL
5	-	Saltwater	Chicane featuring Maire Brennan of Clannad	Xtravaganza	4		
6	-	Kiss Me	Sixpence None The Richer	Elektra	6		F
7	-	Hey Boy Hey Girl	Chemical Brothers	Virgin	4		
8	4	I Want It That Way	Backstreet Boys	Jive	8		
9	-	Bring It All Back	S Club 7	Polydor	8		
10	-	Canned Heat	Jamiroquai	Sony	3		
11	-	Beautiful Stranger	Madonna	Maverick/Warner	7		
12	-	From The Heart	Another Level	Northwestside	3		
13	-	Doodah!	Cartoons	Flex/EMI	3		
14	11	Look At Me	Geri Halliwell	EMI	5		F
15	8	You Needed Me	Boyzone	Polydor	5		F
16	8	No Scrubs	TLC	LaFace	12	(1)	
17	-	Boom, Boom, Boom Boom!	Vengaboys	Positiva	9		
18	-	Say It Again	Precious	EMI	3		F
19	-	Sometimes	Britney Spears	Jive	10		
20	-	Pumping On Your Stereo	Supergrass	Parlophone	2		

April 1999

This Mnth	Prev Mnth	Title	Artist	Label	Wks 20	(UK Pos)	
1	9	No Scrubs	TLC	Laface	13	(3)	L
2	1	Believe	Cher	Warner Bros	18	(1)	L
3	8	Every Morning	Sugar Ray	Lava	16	(10)	FL
4	17	What's It Gonna Be?!	Busta Rhymes/Janet	Flipmode/Elektra	10	(6)	L
5	3	Heartbreak Hotel	Whitney Houston/Faith Evans/Kelly Price	Arista	16	(25)	L
6	11	Kiss Me	Sixpence None The Richer	Squint	13	(4)	FL
7	6	I Still Believe	Mariah Carey	Columbia	8	(16)	L
8	2	Angel Of Mine	Monica	Arista	16	(55)	L
9	19	Stay The Same	Joey McIntyre	C2	7		FL
10	18	All Night Long	Faith Evans/Puff Daddy	Bad Boy	6	(23)	L
11	-	C'Est La Vie	B*Witched	Epic	5	(1)	FL
12	12	Slide	Goo Goo Dolls	Warner Bros	24	(43)	L
13	5	All I Have To Give	Backstreet Boys	Jive	12	(2)	L
14	-	When I Close My Eyes	Shanice	Laface	4		L
15	-	If You (Lovin' Me)	Silk	Elektra	8		L
16	4	Angel	Sarah McLachlan	Arista/Warner Sunset	25		L
17	7	Hit Me Baby…	Britney Spears	Jive	25	(1)	FL
18	-	Please Remember Me	Tim McGraw	Curb	7		L
19	-	Sweet Lady	Tyrese	RCA	7	(55)	L
20	-	The Animal Song	Savage Garden	Hollywood	2	(16)	L

May 1999

This Mnth	Prev Mnth	Title	Artist	Label	Wks 20	(UK Pos)	
1	-	Livin' La Vida Loca	Ricky Martin	C2	22	(1)	FG
2	1	No Scrubs	TLC	Laface	17	(3)	L
3	6	Kiss Me	Sixpence None The Richer	Squint	14	(4)	FL
4	3	Every Morning	Sugar Ray	Lava	16	(10)	FL
5	2	Believe	Cher	Warner Bros	21	(1)	L
6	5	Heartbreak Hotel	Houston/Evans/Price	Arista	17		L
7	4	What's It Gonna Be?!	Busta Rhymes/Janet	Flipmode/Elektra	11	(6)	L
8	-	Who Dat	JT Money/Sole	Tony Mercedes/Freeworld	9		L
9	12	Slide	Goo Goo Dolls	Warner Bros	25		L
10	-	Fortunate	Maxwell	Rock Land	17		L
11	18	Please Remember Me	Tim McGraw	Curb	11		L
12	-	Give It To You	Jordan Knight	Interscope	17	(5)	FL
13	-	Where My Girls At?	702	Motown	16	(22)	L
14	-	What It's Like	Everlast	Tommy Boy	8	(34)	FL
15	8	Angel Of Mine	Monica	Arista	16	(55)	L
16	-	Fly Away	Lenny Kravitz	Virgin	3	(1)	L
17	19	Sweet Lady	Tyrese	RCA	7		FL
18	-	808	Blaque	Track Masters	11	(31)	L
19	-	Anywhere	112/Lil'Z	Bad Boy	7		L
20	15	If You (Lovin' Me)	Silk	Elektra	4		L

June 1999

This Mnth	Prev Mnth	Title	Artist	Label	Wks 20	(UK Pos)	
1	-	If You Had My Love	Jennifer Lopez	Work/ERG	21	(4)	G
2	8	Who Dat	JT Money/Sole	Tony Mercedes/Freeworld	17		
3	13	Where My Girls At?	702	Motown	16		L
4	10	Fortunate	Maxwell	Rock Land	17		L
5	18	808	Blaque	Track Masters	11		L
6	-	Chante's Got A Man	Chante Moore	Silas/MCA	11		FL
7	1	Livin' La Vida Loca	Ricky Martin	C2	22	(1)	F
8	12	Give It To You	Jordan Knight	Interscope	9	(14)	F
9	-	Happily Ever After	Case	DefJam/Mercury	9		FL
10	-	Holla Holla	Ja Rule	Murder Inc/Def Jam/Mercury	11		FL
11	-	My Favorite Girl	Dave Hollister	Dreamworks	6		FL
12	-	That Don't Impress Me Much	Shania Twain	Mercury	7	(3)	F
13	-	It Ain't My Fault 2	Silkk The Shocker feat. Mystikal	No Limit/Priority	6		
14	-	All I Have To Give	Backstreet Boys	Jive	9	(2)	
15	-	Last Kiss	Pearl Jam	Epic	14	(42)	
16	-	No Pigeons	Sporty Thievz feat. Mr Woods	Ruffhouse/Columbia	12	(22)	FL
17	-	Rollercoaster	B*witched	Epic	12	(1)	
18	20	If You (Lovin' Me)	Silk	Elektra	4		L
19	-	What'd You Come Here For	Trina & Tamara	Columbia	3	(46)	FL
20	-	The Hardest Thing	98 Degrees	Universal	11	(29)	

▲ After the US success of UK teen stars B*Witched and 5ive, 17-year-old Billie enjoys a Clubplay dance chart hit with her debut American release, 'She Wants You'.

◆ America goes Ricky Martin crazy as the Puerto Rican singing sensation enjoys his first Number One hit, the energetic 'Livin' La Vida Loca'. His latest album also features a duet with Madonna.

◆ Taking a break from fatherhood, the King Of Pop Michael Jackson tells the world he's about to record a special millennium single with fellow superstar Lauryn Hill.

UK 1999
JULY-SEPT

▲ Ronan Keating is a busy lad. Not content with handling most of Boyzone's lead vocals, he is also purported to be playing a non-specific managerial role in the increasingly successful career of fellow country-men Westlife. And to prove that everything he touches turns to gold, his solo career takes off with a No. 1 hit.

◆ In the wake of 'Livin La Vida Loca', Britain goes Latin crazy. One of those to benefit is Enrique "son of Julio" Iglesias, getting his first taste of chart action with 'Bailamos'.

◆ Almost 20 years after his death, Bob Marley is back in the charts with a suitably respectful club remix of one of his lesser-known songs, 'Sun Is Shining'.

July 1999

This Mnth	Prev Mnth	Title	Artist	Label	Wks 20	(US Pos)	
1	-	Livin' La Vida Loca	Ricky Martin	Columbia	10	(1)	
2	-	9PM (Till I Come)	ATB	Sound of Ministry	8		F
3	-	My Love Is Your Love	Whitney Houston	Arista	9	(2)	
4	17	Boom, Boom, Boom Boom!	Vengaboys	Positiva	4		
5	19	Sometimes	Britney Spears	Jive	9		
6	-	Wild Wild West	Will Smith	Columbia	10		
7	9	Bring It All Back	S Club 7	Polydor	7		
8	-	If You Had My Love	Jennifer Lopez	Columbia	6	(1)	F
9	2	That Don't Impress Me Much	Shania Twain	Mercury	13	(12)	F
10	11	Beautiful Stranger	Madonna	Maverick/Warner	9		
11	-	Love's Got A Hold On My Heart	Steps	Ebul/Jive	5		
12	-	I Breathe Again	Adam Rickitt	Polydor	4		F
13	-	Bills, Bills, Bills	Destiny's Child	Columbia	3	(3)	
14	-	Synth & Strings	Yomanda	First Avenue	4		F
15	-	Be The First To Believe	A1	Columbia	3		F
16	-	Viva La Radio	Lolly	Polydor	3		F
17	-	Secret Smile	Semisonic	MCA	3		FL
18	-	If Ya Gettin' Down	5ive	RCA	6		
19	-	Better Off Alone	DJ Jurgen presents Alice Deejay	Positiva	10		FL
20	1	Sweet Like Chocolate	Shanks & Bigfoot	Chocolate Boy/Pepper	7		F

August 1999

This Mnth	Prev Mnth	Title	Artist	Label	Wks 20	(US Pos)	
1	-	When You Say Nothing At All	Ronan Keating	Polydor	6		F
2	19	Better Off Alone	DJ Jurgen presents Alice Deejay	Positiva	8		FL
3	1	Livin' La Vida Loca	Ricky Martin	Columbia	13	(1)	FL
4	18	If Ya Gettin' Down	5ive	RCA	5		
5	3	My Love Is Your Love	Whitney Houston	Arista	11	(2)	
6	-	Guilty Conscience	Eminem	Interscope	3		L
7	-	If I Let You Go	Westlife	RCA	5		
8	-	Rendez-Vu	Basement Jaxx	XL	3		L
9	-	Drinking In LA	Bran Van 3000	Capitol	5		FL
10	2	9PM (Till I Come)	ATB	Sound of Ministry	8		F
11	11	Love's Got A Hold On My Heart	Steps	Ebul/Jive	5		
12	-	Mi Chico Latino	Geri Halliwell	EMI	5		
13	6	Wild Wild West	Will Smith	Columbia	8		
14	-	Feel Good	Phats & Small	Multiply	3		L
15	-	Why Does It Always Rain On Me?	Travis	Independiente	3		F
16	4	Boom, Boom, Boom Boom!	Vengaboys	Positiva	9		
17	-	Summer Sun	Texas	Mercury	3		
18	-	Unpretty	TLC	LaFace/Arista	5	(2)	L
19	-	Straight From The Heart	Doolally	XL	2		L
20	-	Let Forever Be	Chemical Brothers	Virgin	2		L

September 1999

This Mnth	Prev Mnth	Title	Artist	Label	Wks 20	(US Pos)	
1	-	Mambo No. 5 (A Little Bit Of...)	Lou Bega	RCA	8		FL
2	-	(Mucho Mambo) Sway	Shaft	Wonderboy	6		F
3	12	Mi Chico Latino	Geri Halliwell	EMI	7		
4	-	The Launch	DJ Jean	AM:PM	6		FL
5	2	Better Off Alone	DJ Jurgen presents Alice Deejay	Positiva	8		FL
6	7	If I let You Go	Westlife	RCA	9		
7	-	Bailamos	Enrique Iglesias	Interscope/Polydor	5		F
8	-	We're Going To Ibiza!	Vengaboys	Positiva	6		
9	-	Sing It Back	Moloko	Echo	3		F
10	-	Mickey	Lolly	Polydor	5		
11	18	Unpretty	TLC	LaFace/Arista	7	(2)	L
12	-	Friends Forever	Thunderbugs	First Avenue	3		FL
13	9	Drinking In LA	Bran Van 3000	Capitol	8		FL
14	-	Blue (Da Ba Dee)	Eiffel 65	Eternal	9		F
15	3	Livin' La Vida Loca	Ricky Martin	Columbia	13	(1)	FL
16	-	Summertime	Another Level	Northwestside	2		
17	-	Sun Is Shining	Bob Marley vs. Funkstar de Luxe	Club Tools	5		F
18	-	Afrika Shox	Leftfield/Bambaataa	Higher Ground	2		L
19	-	Get Get Down	Paul Johnson	Defected	3		FL
20	-	Moving	Supergrass	Parlophone	2		L

US 1999 JULY-SEPT

July 1999

This Mnth	Prev Mnth	Title	Artist	Label	Wks 20	(UK Pos)	
1	15	Last Kiss	Pearl Jam	Epic	14		L
2	1	If You Had My Love	Jennifer Lopez	Work/ERG	21	(8)	
3	-	Bills, Bills, Bills	Destiny's Child	Columbia	11	(6)	
4	16	No Pigeons	Sporty Thievz feat. Mr Woods	Ruffhouse/Columbia	12		FL
5	-	It's Not Right But It's Okay	Whitney Houston	Arista	13	(3)	G
6	-	Genie In A Bottle	Christina Aguilera	RCA	13	(1)	FG
7	20	The Hardest Thing	98 Degrees	Universal	11		
8	-	You'll Be In My Heart	Phil Collins	Walt Disney/Hollywood	9	(17)	L
9	4	Fortunate	Maxwell	Rock Land	11		
10	5	808	Blaque	Track Masters	11		L
11	8	Give It To You	Jordan Knight	Interscope	9	(14)	F
12	-	Summer Girls	LFO	Logic/Arista	18	(16)	FG
13	-	Jamboree	Naughty By Nature feat. Zhane	Arista	13	(51)	L
14	6	Chante's Got A Man	Chante Moore	Silas/MCA	11		FL
15	9	Happily Ever After	Case	DefJam/Mercury	9		FL
16	-	Spend My Life With You	Eric Benet feat. Tamia	Warner Bros	21		L
17	3	Where My Girls At?	702	Motown	16		L
18	17	Rollercoaster	B*witched	Epic	12		
19	10	Holla Holla	JA Rulel	Murder Inc/Def Jam/Mercury	11		FL
20	7	Livin' La Vida Loca	Ricky Martin	C2	22	(1)	F

August 1999

This Mnth	Prev Mnth	Title	Artist	Label	Wks 20	(UK Pos)	
1	6	Genie In A Bottle	Christina Aguilera	RCA	13	(3)	F
2	12	Summer Girls	LFO	Logic/Arista	18		F
3	-	Tell Me It's Real	K-Cl & Jojo	MCA	9	(40)	FL
4	3	Bills, Bills, Bills	Destiny's Child	Columbia	11	(13)	
5	13	Jamoboree	Naughty By Nature feat. Zhane	Arista	13		L
6	-	Wild Wild West	Will Smith	Columbia	7	(2)	
7	-	The Day The World Went Away	Nine Inch Nails	Nothing/Interscope	5		FL
8	16	Spend My Life With You	Eric Benet feat. Tamia	Warner Bros	21		L
9	-	It's All About You (Not About...)	Tracie Spencer	Capitol	9	(65)	F
10	-	Smile	Vitamin C Feat. Lady Saw	Elektra	11		FL
11	4	No Pigeons	Sporty Thievz feat. Mr Woods	Ruffhouse/Columbia	12		FL
12	1	Last Kiss	Pearl Jam	Epic	14		
13	-	I Will Go WIth You	Donna Summer	Epic	4	(44)	L
14	9	Fortunate	Maxwell	Rock Land	11		
15	5	It's Not Right But It's Okay	Whitney Houston	Arista	13		
16	-	I'll Be Your Everything	Youngstown	Hollywood	5		FL
17	-	Smooth	Santana feat. Rob Thomas	Arista	31	(3)	G
18	7	The Hardest Thing	98 Degrees	Universal	11		
19	-	Bailamos	Enrique Iglesias	Overbrook	15	(4)	F
20	2	If You Had My Love	Jennifer Lopez	Work/ERG	21		

September 1999

This Mnth	Prev Mnth	Title	Artist	Label	Wks 20	(UK Pos)	
1	2	Summer Girls	LFO	Logic/Arista	18		F
2	-	Unpretty	TLC	Laface/Arista	9	(16)	
3	19	Bailamos	Enrique Iglesias	Overbrook	15		F
4	17	Smooth	Santana feat. Rob Thomas	Arista	31		
5	-	Lost In You	Garth Brooks as Chris Gaines	Capitol	11	(70)	FL
6	10	Smile	Vitamin C feat. Lady Saw	Elektra	11		FL
7	9	It's All About You (Not Me)	Tracie Spencer	Capitol	9		F
8	-	Never Gonna Let Go	Faith Evans	Bad Boy/Arista	11		
9	5	Jamoboree	Naughty By Nature feat. Zhane	Arista	13		L
10	-	Jigga My N****	Jay-Z	Interscope	8		
11	-	I Love You Came Too Late	Joey McIntyre	C2	9		
12	-	She's All I Ever Had	Ricky Martin	C2	11		
13	8	Spend My Life With You	Eric Benet feat. Tamia	Warner Bros	21		L
14	16	I'll Be Your Everything	Youngstown	Hollywood	5		FL
15	1	Genie In A Bottle	Christina Aguilera	RCA	13	(3)	F
16	-	Get Gone	Ideal	Noontime/Virgin	20		FL
17	-	Candy	Mandy Moore	550 Music/ERG	17	(6)	
18	-	My Love Is Your Love	Whitney Houston	Arista	23	(2)	G
19	-	I Want It All	Warren G feat. Mack 10	G-Funk/Restless	18		L
20	-	Southern Girl	Erykah Badu	Motown	3		

▲ Comeback of this (or any other) year goes to Carlos Santana, whose *Supernatural* album shifts an amazing six million copies and wins an unprecedented nine Grammy awards. In the words of the fifty-something guitar legend, the album "was designed to assault the radio airwaves…for the purpose of rearranging the molecular structure in the listener." Who would argue with that?

◆ Almost as weird is country legend Garth Brooks' notion to invent himself a rocking alter ego. Under the name Chris Gaines, he takes a break from a country career which has shifted close to one hundred million albums, to record, perform and act out his new guise.

375

UK 1999 OCT-DEC

▲ With Britney fever still running high, a new rival emerges in the shape of Christina Aguilera. Spookily, in their early teens, both girls were Mickey Mouse Club singers at the same time.

◆ When Cliff Richard's record company refuses to put out his annual Xmas offering, he takes it to an independent label. The veteran singer has the last laugh, though, when 'The Millennium Prayer' becomes one the year's top sellers.

◆ Tom Jones continues to amaze as, 35 years after his debut single, he records the chart-topping *Reload* album. A series of duets with hip young talent, it yields the old belter four top 20 hits.

October 1999

This Mnth	Prev Mnth	Title	Artist	Label	Wks 20	(US Pos)	
1	15	Blue (Da Ba De)	Eiffel 65	Eternal	10		F
2	-	Man! I Feel Like A Woman	Shania Twain	Mercury	7		
3	-	Genie In A Bottle	Christina Aguilera	RCA	8	(1)	F
4	-	S Club Party	S Club 7	Polydor	4		
5	-	(You Drive Me) Crazy	Britney Spears	Jive	6		
6	-	2 Times	Ann Lee	Systematic/London	6		FL
7	1	Mambo No. 5 (A Little Bit Of…)	Lou Bega	RCA	11		FL
8	-	I Try	Macy Gray	Epic	15		F
9	17	Sun Is Shining	Bob Marley vs. Funkstar de Luxe	Club Tools	4		L
10	-	Jesse Hold On	B*Witched	Epic	4		
11	8	We're Going To Ibiza!	Vengaboys	Positiva	7		
12	-	Don't Stop	ATB	Sound Of Ministry	3		
13	-	Flying Without Wings	Westlife	RCA	6		
14	-	Give It To You	Jordan Knight	Interscope	3	(2)	FL
15	4	The Launch	DJ Jean	AM:PM	7		FL
16	-	Goin' Down	Melanie C	Virgin	2		F
17	19	Get Get Down	Paul Johnson	Defected	9		FL
18	-	After The Love Has Gone	Steps	Jive	3		
19	-	If I Could Turn Back The Hands Of Time	R Kelly	Jive	13		
20	-	Burning Down The House	Tom Jones & The Cardigans	Gut	3		

November 1999

This Mnth	Prev Mnth	Title	Artist	Label	Wks 20	(US Pos)	
1	19	If I Could Turn Back The Hands Of Time	R Kelly	Jive	11		
2	-	Keep On Movin'	5ive	RCA	9		
3	8	I Try	Macy Gray	Epic	13		FL
4	-	Lift Me Up	Geri Halliwell	EMI	4		
5	-	She's The One/It's Only Us	Robbie Williams	Chrysalis	7		
6	-	What I Am	Tin Tin Out feat. Emma Bunton	VC Recordings	3		L
7	3	Genie In A Bottle	Christina Aguilera	RCA	9	(1)	F
8	-	Will 2K	Will Smith	Columbia	4		L
9	13	Flying Without Wings	Westlife	RCA	9		
10	-	Waiting For Tonight	Jennifer Lopez	Columbia	4		
11	-	Everytime/Ready Or Not	A1	Columbia	3		
12	-	King Of My Castle	Wamdue Project	AM:PM	8		FL
13	6	2 Times	Ann Lee	Systematic/London	7		FL
14	-	The Millennium Prayer	Cliff Richard	Papillon	8		L
15	1	Blue (Da Ba De)	Eiffel 65	Eternal	10		F
16	-	Heartbreaker	Mariah Carey	Columbia	2		
17	-	Bomb Diggy	Another Level	Northwestside	3		L
18	-	Turn	Travis	Independiente	2		
19	-	Larger Than Life	Backstreet Boys	Jive	3		
20	-	Not Over You Yet	Diana Ross	EMI	2		L

December 1999

This Mnth	Prev Mnth	Title	Artist	Label	Wks 20	(US Pos)	
1	14	The Millennium Prayer	Cliff Richard	Papillon	11		L
2	-	Back In My Life	Alice Deejay	Positiva	10		F
3	12	King Of My Castle	Wamdue Project	AM:PM	11		FL
4	-	"Re-wind The Crowd Say Bo Selecta"	Artful Dodger feat. Craig David	Public Demand	10		F
5	1	If I could Turn Back…	R Kelly	Jive	11		
6	-	I Have A Dream/Seasons In The Sun	Westlife	RCA	6		
7	3	I Try	Macy Gray	Epic	13		FL
8	-	Northern Star	Melanie C	Virgin	3		
9	-	Everyday I Love You	Boyzone	Polydor	7		L
10	-	Talking In Your Sleep/Love Me	Martine McCutcheon	Innocent	3		
11	-	Kiss (When The Sun Don't Shine)	Vengaboys	Positiva	7		
12	-	Barber's Adagio For Strings	William Orbit	WEA	7		FL
13	-	Big Boys Don't Cry/Rockin' …	Lolly	Polydor	3		L
14	5	She's The One/It's Only Us	Robbie Williams	Chrysalis	9		
15	-	Communication	Mario Piu	Incentive	2		F
16	-	Imagine	John Lennon	Parlophone	5		F
17	-	Cognoscenti Vs Intelligentsia	Cuban Boys	EMI	4		FL
18	-	Two In A Million/You're My No. 1	S Club 7	Polydor	6		
19	-	Steal My Sunshine	Len	Columbia	9		FL
20	-	Everybody	Progress Presents The Boy Wunda	Manifesto	5		FL

US 1999 OCT-DEC

October 1999

This Mnth	Prev Mnth	Title	Artist	Label	Wks 20	(UK Pos)	
1	4	Smooth	Santana feat. Rob Thomas	Arista	31		
2	18	My Love Is Your Love	Whitney Houston	Arista	23	(3)	
3	-	I Need To Know	Marc Anthony	Columbia	17	(28)	F
4	5	Lost In You	Garth Brooks as Chris Gaines	Capitol	11		FL
5	-	We Can't Be Friends	Deborah Cox with RL	Arista	9		FL
6	-	Heartbreaker	Mariah Carey feat. Jay-Z	Columbia	11	(5)	
7	-	Music of My Heart	'N Sync & Gloria Estefan	Miramax	11		
8	-	If I Could Turn Back The Hands Of Time	R Kelly	Jive	19	(34)	
9	19	I Want It All	Warren G feat. Mack 10	G-Funk/Restless	18	(2)	L
10	1	Summer Girls	LFO	Logic/Arista	18		F
11	12	She's All I Ever Had	Ricky Martin	C2	11		
12	2	Unpretty	TLC	Laface/Arista	9	(11)	
13	16	Get Gone	Ideal	Noontime/Virgin	20		FL
14	-	Satisfy You	Puff Daddy feat. R Kelly	Bad Boy/Arista	9	(8)	
15	-	Stay The Night	IMX	MCA	23		FL
16	17	Candy	Mandy Moore	550 Music/ERG	17		
17	3	Bailamos	Enrique Iglesias	Overbrook	15		F
18	-	I Wanna Love You Forever	Jessica Simpson	Columbia	21	(7)	FGL
19	8	Never Gonna Let Go	Faith Evans	Bad Boy/Arista	11		
20	13	Spend My Life With You	Eric Benet feat. Tamia	Warner Bros	21		L

November 1999

This Mnth	Prev Mnth	Title	Artist	Label	Wks 20	(UK Pos)	
1	1	Smooth	Santana feat. Rob Thomas	Arista	31		
2	2	My Love Is Your Love	Whitney Houston	Arista	23		
3	18	I Wanna Love You Forever	Jessica Simpson	Columbia	21		FL
4	14	Satisfy You	Puff Daddy feat. R Kelly	Bad Boy/Arista	9		
5	3	I Need To Know	Marc Anthony	Columbia	17		F
6	8	If I Could Turn Back The Hands Of Time	R Kelly	Jive	19		
7	6	Heartbreaker	Mariah Carey feat. Jay-Z	Columbia	11		
8	13	Get Gone	Ideal	Noontime/Virgin	20		FL
9	9	I Want It All	Warren G feat. Mack 10	G-Funk/Restless	18		L
10	5	We Can't Be Friends	Deborah Cox with RL	Arista	9		FL
11	15	Stay The Night	IMX	MCA	23		FL
12	-	U Know What's Up	Donell Jones	LaFace/Arista	11		L
13	-	If You Love Me	Mint Condition	Elektra	11	(2)	FL
14	-	Don't Say You Love Me	M2M	Atlantic	16	(16)	
15	16	Candy	Mandy Moore	550 Music/ERG	17		
16	-	4, 5, 6	Sole feat. JT Money & Kandi	Dreamworks	8		
17	-	Girl On TV	LFO	Arista	22	(6)	F
18	7	Music of My Heart	'N Sync & Gloria Estefan	Miramax	11		
19	-	15 Minutes	Marc Nelson	Columbia	7		FL
20	-	Hot Boyz	Missy "Misdemeanor" Elliott	East West/EEG	23	(18)	GL

December 1999

This Mnth	Prev Mnth	Title	Artist	Label	Wks 20	(UK Pos)	
1	3	I Wanna Love You Forever	Jessica Simpson	Columbia	21		FL
2	17	Girl On TV	LFO	Arista	22		F
3	20	Hot Boyz	Missy "Misdemeanor" Elliott	East West/EEG	23		L
4	1	Smooth	Santana feat. Rob Thomas	Arista	31		
5	2	My Love Is Your Love	Whitney Houston	Arista	23		
6	14	Don't Say You Love Me	M2M	Atlantic	16		
7	16	4, 5, 6	Sole feat. JT Money & Kandi	Dreamworks	8		
8	12	U Know What's Up	Donell Jones	LaFace/Arista	11		L
9	-	24/7	Kevon Edmonds	RCA	7		FL
10	5	I Need To Know	Marc Anthony	Columbia	17		F
11	11	Stay The Night	IMX	MCA	23		FL
12	-	He Can't Love U	Jagged Edge	So So Def	18		
13	19	15 Minutes	Marc Nelson	Columbia	7		FL
14	8	Get Gone	Ideal	Noontime/Virgin	20		FL
15	13	If You Love Me	Mint Condition	Elektra	11		FL
16	-	Dancin'	Guy	MCA	9		FL
17	15	Candy	Mandy Moore	550 Music/ERG	17		
18	6	If I Could Turn Back The Hands Of Time	R Kelly	Jive	19		
19	-	Caught Out There	Kelis	Virgin	7	(4)	FL
20	9	I Want It All	Warren G feat. Mack 10	G-Funk/Restless	18		L

▲ The Lord moves in mysterious ways. As contemporary Christian music becomes big business in the US, an increasing number of its stars are crossing over to the mainstream charts. The latest success is 20-year-old Jessica Simpson who has already sold hundreds of thousands of albums in America's specialist Christian stores.

◆ With its plaintively screamed chorus of "I HATE YOU SO MUCH RIGHT NOW", 'Caught Out There' by Kelis is one of the most striking hits of the year. The 20-year-old (whose name is pronounced "KelEEEs") is a graduate of the Fame-style La Guardia High School for the Performing Arts in Harlem, New York.

UK 2000
JAN-MAR

▲ REM provide three songs for the soundtrack album of the film *Man On The Moon* – the life story of American comic Andy Kaufman. One of them 'The Great Unknown' provides the band with an unexpected top three single.

◆ Vengaboys continue to bombard the charts with novelty dance anthems. While DJs Danski and Delmondo stay home in Spain creating the music, a group of singers and dancers perform as Vengaboys all over the world.

◆ The latest cult club sound to go mainstream is "UK Garage". Top dogs are Southampton's Artful Dodger who introduce the impressive vocal skills of 19-year-old Craig David.

January 2000

This Mnth	Prev Mnth	Title	Artist	Label	Wks 20	(US Pos)
1	5	I Have A Dream/Seasons…	Westlife	RCA	9	
2	4	Re-wind The Crowd Say…	Artful Dodger feat. Craig David	Public Demand	9	
3	18	Two In A Million/You're My No. 1	S Club 7	Polydor	8	
4	2	Back In My Life	Alice Deejay	Positiva	9	F
5	11	Kiss (When The Sun Don't Shine)	Vengaboys	Positiva	5	
6	-	Say You'll Be Mine/Better The Devil You Know	Steps	Jive	6	
7	12	Barber's Adagio For Strings	William Orbit	WEA	6	FL
8	-	Born To Make You Happy	Britney Spears	Jive	6	(3)
9	19	Steal My Sunshine	Len	Columbia	8	FL
10	-	A Little Bit Of Luck	DJ Luck & MC Neat	Red Rose	10	F
11	16	Imagine	John Lennon	Parlophone	4	L
12	-	U Know What's Up	Donell Jones	LaFace	5	F
13	1	The Millennium Prayer	Cliff Richard	Papillon	11	L
14	-	You Only Tell Me You Love Me When You're Drunk	Petshop Boys	Parlophone	2	L
15	17	Cognoscenti Vs Intelligentsia	Cuban Boys	EMI	6	FL
16	-	More Than I Needed To Know	Scooch	Accolade	2	F
17	7	I Try	Macy Gray	Epic	13	FL
18	3	King Of My Castle	Wamdue Project	AM:PM	11	FL
19	-	Stand Tough	Point Break	Eternal	2	F
20	-	Because Of You	Scanty Sandwich	Southern Fried	3	FL

February 2000

This Mnth	Prev Mnth	Title	Artist	Label	Wks 20	(US Pos)
1	-	Rise	Gabrielle	Go-Beat	8	
2	8	Born To Make You Happy	Britney Spears	Jive	9	(3)
3	-	The Great Beyond	REM	Warner Bros	4	L
4	-	Glorious	Andreas Johnson	WEA	4	FL
5	-	Adelante	Sash!	Multiply	4	
6	10	A Little Bit Of Luck	DJ Luck & MC Neat	Red Rose	9	F
7	-	Go Let It Out	Oasis	Big Brother	3	
8	12	U Know What's Up	Donell Jones	LaFace	7	FL
9	-	Ooh Stick You	Daphne & Celeste	Universal	5	F
10	-	Pure Shores	All Saints	London	8	
11	-	Girl On TV	Lyte Funkie Ones	Logic	4	L
12	-	Move Your Body	Eiffel 65	Eternal	4	L
13	-	Sweet Love 2K	Fierce	Wildstar	3	L
14	-	Hammer To The Heart	The Tamperer feat. Maya	Pepper	2	L
15	-	Dolphins Were Monkeys	Ian Brown	Polydor	2	L
16	-	What A Girl Wants	Christina Aguilera	RCA	3	(1)
17	-	Don't Be Stupid (You Know I Love You)	Shania Twain	Mercury	2	L
18	20	Because Of You	Scanty Sandwich	Southern Fried	3	FL
19	-	In Your Arms (Rescue Me)	Nu-Generation	Concept	4	FL
20	-	Must Be The Music	Joey Negro feat. Taka Boom	Incentive	1	FL

March 2000

This Mnth	Prev Mnth	Title	Artist	Label	Wks 20	(US Pos)
1	10	Pure Shores	All Saints	London	9	
2	-	Movin' Too Fast	Artful Dodger & Romina Johnson	Locked On/XL	5	
3	-	American Pie	Madonna	Maverick	6	
4	-	Sitting Down Here	Lene Marlin	Virgin	6	F
5	-	Sha La La La La	Vengaboys	Positiva	4	
6	-	Show Me The Meaning Of Being Lonely	Backstreet Boys	Jive	4	
7	-	Don't Give Up	Chicane feat. Bryan Adams	Xtravaganza	5	L
8	-	Bye Bye Bye	'N Sync	Jive	4	
9	-	Caught Out There	Kelis	Virgin	3	F
10	-	Satisfy You	Puff Daddy feat. R Kelly	Puff Daddy/Arista	3	L
11	1	Rise	Gabrielle	Go-Beat	11	
12	-	Money	Jamelia feat. Beenie Man	Parlophone	3	F
13	-	Mama Told Me Not To Come	Tom Jones & Stereophonics	Gut	3	
14	-	Bag It Up	Geri Halliwell	EMI	4	L
15	-	Won't Take It Lying Down	Honeyz	1st Avenue	2	L
16	-	All The Small Things	Blink 182	MCA	5	L
17	-	Don't Wanna Let You Go	5ive	RCA	2	
18	-	Killer	ATB	Ministry Of Sound	3	L
19	-	Still D.R.E	Dr Dre feat. Snoop Dogg	Interscope	4	F
20	-	Cartoon Heroes	Aqua	Universal	4	L

US 2000 JAN-MAR

January 2000

This Mnth	Prev Mnth	Title	Artist	Label	Wks 20	(UK Pos)	
1	3	Hot Boyz	Missy "Misdemeanor" Elliott	East West/EEG	23		L
2	1	I Wanna Love You Forever	Jessica Simpson	Columbia	21		FL
3	2	Girl On TV	LFO	Arista	22		F
4	-	What A Girl Wants	Christina Aguilera	RCA	11	(3)	
5	12	He Can't Love U	Jagged Edge	So So Def	18		
6	4	Smooth	Santana feat. Rob Thomas	Arista	31		
7	5	My Love Is Your Love	Whitney Houston	Arista	23		
8	-	Auld Lang Syne	Kenny G	Arista	4		
9	9	24/7	Kevon Edmonds	RCA	7		FL
10	-	You Can Do It	Ice Cube	Best Side/Priority	12		L
11	6	Don't Say You Love Me	M2M	Atlantic	16		
12	-	I Knew I Loved You	Savage Garden	Columbia	11	(10)	
13	19	Caught Out There	Kelis	Virgin	7		FL
14	16	Dancin'	Guy	MCA	9		FL
15	7	4, 5, 6	Sole feat. JT Money & Kandi	Dreamwork	11		L
16	8	U Know What's Up	Donell Jones	LaFace/Arista	14		FL
17	-	One Night Stand	J-Shin feat. Latocha Scott	Atlantic	13		FL
18	11	Stay The Night	IMX	MCA	23		FL
19	-	I Like It	Sammie	Free World/Capitol	24		FL
20	-	It Feels So Good	Sonique	Universal	15	(1)	

February 2000

This Mnth	Prev Mnth	Title	Artist	Label	Wks 20	(UK Pos)	
1	-	Get It On Tonite	Montell Jordan	Def Soul	19	(15)	L
2	1	Hot Boyz	Missy "Misdemeanor" Elliott	East West/EEG	23		L
3	5	He Can't Love U	Jagged Edge	So So Def	18		
4	12	I Knew I Loved You	Savage Garden	Columbia	11		
5	-	All The Small Things	Blink-182	MCA	15	(2)	L
6	-	Thank God I Found You	Mariah Carey feat. Joe & 98 Degrees	Columbia	13	(10)	
7	-	Maria Maria	Santana feat. The Product G&B	Arista	23	(6)	GL
8	-	Shake Your Bon-Bon	Ricky Martin	C2	11	(12)	
9	19	I Like It	Sammie	Free World/Capitol	24		FL
10	20	It Feels So Good	Sonique	Universal	15		
11	4	What A Girl Wants	Christina Aguilera	RCA	11		
12	-	G'd Up	Snoop Dogg presents Tha Eastsidaz	Dogg House/TVT	7		
13	-	Best Friend	Puff Daddy	Bad Boy/Arista	9	(24)	
14	17	One Night Stand	J-Shin feat. Latocha Scott	Atlantic	13		FL
15	6	Smooth	Santana feat. Rob Thomas	Arista	31		
16	3	Girl On TV	LFO	Arista	22		F
17	-	Take A Picture	Filter	Reprise	6	(25)	FL
18	-	From The Bottom Of My Broken Heart	Britney Spears	Jive	19		G
19	-	Amazed	Lonestar	BNA	17	(21)	FL
20	-	Breathe	Faith Hill	Warner Bros	23	(33)	L

March 2000

This Mnth	Prev Mnth	Title	Artist	Label	Wks 20	(UK Pos)	
1	7	Maria Maria	Santana feat. The Product G&B	Arista	23	(6)	L
2	19	Amazed	Lonestar	BNA	17		FL
3	18	From The Bottom Of My Broken Heart	Britney Spears	Jive	19		
4	6	Thank God I Found You	Mariah Carey feat. Joe & 98 Degrees	Columbia	13		
5	-	There You Go	Pink	LaFace/Arista	11	(6)	F
6	20	Breathe	Faith Hill	Warner Bros	23		L
7	1	Get It On Tonite	Montell Jordan	Def Soul	19		L
8	-	Another Dumb Blonde	Hoku	Geffen/Interscope	13		FL
9	5	All The Small Things	Blink-182	MCA	15		L
10	9	I Like It	Sammie	Free World/Capitol	24		FL
11	2	Hot Boyz	Missy "Misdemeanor" Elliott	East West/EEG	23		L
12	-	I Learned From The Best	Whitney Houston	Arista	11	(19)	
13	-	Say My Name	Destiny's Child	Columbia	11	(3)	
14	-	Goodbye Earl	Dixie Chicks	Monument	18		FL
15	14	One Night Stand	J-Shin feat. Latocha Scott	Atlantic	13		FL
16	10	It Feels So Good	Sonique	Universal	15		
17	17	Take A Picture	Filter	Reprise	6		FL
18	3	He Can't Love U	Jagged Edge	So So Def	18		
19	-	U Don't Love Me	Kumbia Kings	EMI Latin/Capitol	3		FL
20	-	Still In My Heart	Tracie Spencer	Capitol	6		L

▲ Some critics have called it a case of arrested development, but Blink-182's mix of adolescent attitude and California thrash clearly appeals to a massive audience. The band claim their new album showcases a growing maturity… even though they called it *Enema Of The People*.

◆ Hard graft can pay off big time, as shown by the chart success of ex-pat Texans Lonestar. They spent most of the 1990s touring the US in a Jeep Cherokee.

◆ While most kids will have spent last summer playing with their pals, 12-year-old Sammie was hard at work in a studio. The latest R&B singing sensation is being touted by some as the new Stevie Wonder.

UK 2000

APR-JUN

▲ With the Spice Girls on hold, the remaining members take time out to get their solo careers into gear. Although they all manage top five hits, Melanie C (formerly "Sporty" Spice) looks set for the most enduring career when her album *Northern Star* charts for well over a year.

◆ The latest musical crossover to hit the mainstream is "Nu-Metal" – a mix of traditional metal riffing with sampling and rap. Bloodhound Gang are the first band to take this sound into the charts.

◆ Ten years after getting together in Glasgow, Travis finally hit pay dirt with their second album, *The Man Who*. It tops the charts, scoops numerous awards and provides three hit singles.

April 2000

This Mnth	Prev Mnth	Title	Artist	Label	Wks 20	(US Pos)	
1	-	Never Be The Same Again	Melanie C feat.Lisa…Lopes	Virgin	7		
2	-	Fill Me In	Craig David	Wildstar	8		F
3	-	Toca's Miracle	Fragma	Positiva1	7		
4	-	The Time Is Now	Moloko	Echo	4		L
5	-	Flowers	Sweet Female Attitude	WEA	6		FL
6	-	Smooth	Santana feat. Rob Thomas	Arista	4	(1)	
7	-	Deeper Shade Of Blue	Steps	Jive	4		
8	-	Fool Again	Westlife	RCA	3		
9	-	Say My Name	Destiny's Child	Columbia	5	(8)	
10	-	The Bad Touch	Bloodhound Gang	Geffen	9		F
11	7	Don't Give Up	Chicane feat. Bryan Adams	Xtravaganza	7		FL
12	3	American Pie	Madonna	Maverick	9		
13	14	Bag It Up	Geri Halliwell	EMI	6		L
14	16	All The Small Things	Blink 182	MCA	7		F
15	-	Thong Song	Sisqo	Def Soul	8		
16	19	Still D.R.E	Dr Dre feat. Snoop Dogg	Interscope	4		
17	-	A Song For Lovers	Richard Ashcroft	Hut/Virgin	3		F
18	1	Pure Shores	All Saints	London	9		
19	-	I Wanna Love You Forever	Jessica Simpson	Columbia	3	(1)	F
20	-	Who Feels Love?	Oasis	Big Brother	2		

May 2000

This Mnth	Prev Mnth	Title	Artist	Label	Wks 20	(US Pos)	
1	-	Oops!...I Did It Again	Britney Spears	Jive	8		
2	-	Bound 4 Da Reload (Casualty)	Oxide & Neutrino	East West	5		F
3	10	The Bad Touch	Bloodhound Gang	Geffen	9		L
4	3	Toca's Miracle	Fragma	Positiva	13		F
5	-	Don't Call Me Baby	Madison Avenue	VC Recordings	6		F
6	15	Thong Song	Sisqo	Def Soul	8		L
7		Heart Of Asia	Watergate	Positiva	5		FL
8	-	Day & Night	Billie Piper	Innocent	3		
9	2	Fill Me In	Craig David	Wildstar	9		
10	-	He Wasn't Man Enough	Toni Braxton	LaFace/Arista	5	(1)	L
11	-	Sex Bomb	Tom Jones & Mousse T	Gut	4		L
12	-	Buggin	True Steppers feat. Dane Bowers	Nulife	3		F
13	5	Flowers	Sweet Female Attitude	WEA	11		FL
14	-	Candy	Mandy Moore	Epic	2	(15)	FL
15	-	Koochy	Armand Van Helden	ffrr	3		L
16	-	Tell Me Why (The Riddle)	Paul Van Dyk feat. Saint Etienne	Deviant	2		
17	-	Crazy Love	MJ Cole	Talkin Loud	3		F
18	-	Achilles Heel	Toploader	S2	3		
19	-	The Wicker Man	Iron Maiden	EMI	2		
20	-	Masterblaster 2000	DJ Luck & MC Neat feat. JJ	Red Rose	3		

June 2000

This Mnth	Prev Mnth	Title	Artist	Label	Wks 20	(US Pos)	
1	-	It Feels So Good	Sonique	Universal	8		F
2	-	Reach	S Club 7	Polydor	7		
3	-	On The Beach	York	Manifesto	5		L
4	-	It's My Life	Bon Jovi	Mercury	5		
5	-	Shackles (Praise You)	Mary Mary	Columbia	6	(8)	FL
6	1	Oops!...I Did It Again	Britney Spears	Jive	11		
7	11	Sex Bomb	Tom Jones & Mousse T	Gut	5		L
8	5	Don't Call Me Baby	Madison Avenue	VC Recordings	9		FL
9	-	Forgot About Dre	Dr Dre feat. Eminem	Interscope	4		L
10	-	Mama – Who Da Man?	Richard Blackwood	east west	3		F
11	8	Day & Night	Billie Piper	Innocent	4		L
12	-	There You Go	Pink	LaFace/Arista	4		F
13	-	Jerusalem	Fat Les 2000	Parlophone	2		L
14	-	When A Woman	Gabrielle	Go Beat	3		L
15	-	Girls Like Us	B15 Project feat. Crissy D &…	Ministry Of Sound	3		FL
16	10	The Bad Touch	Bloodhound Gang	Geffen	9		L
17	20	Masterblaster 2000	DJ Luck & MC Neat	Red Rose	5		L
18	-	Coming Round	Travis	Independiente	1		L
19	-	Sandstorm	Darude	Neo	10		F
20	-	Porcelain	Moby	Mute	2		

April 2000

This Mnth	Prev Mnth	Title	Artist	Label	Wks 20	(UK Pos)	
1	1	Maria Maria	Santana feat. The Product G&B	Arista	23	(6)	L
2	6	Breathe	Faith Hill	Warner Bros	23		L
3	5	There You Go	Pink	LaFace/Arista	11		F
4	10	I Like It	Sammie	Free World/Capitol	24		FL
5	14	Goodbye Earl	Dixie Chicks	Monument	18		FL
6	3	From The Bottom Of My Broken Heart	Britney Spears	Jive	19		
7	8	Another Dumb Blonde	Hoku	Geffen/Interscope	13		FL
8	13	Say My Name	Destiny's Child	Columbia	11		
9	7	Get It On Tonite	Montell Jordan	Def Sou	19		
10	2	Amazed	Lonestar	BNA	17		FL
11	12	I Learned From The Best	Whitney Houston	Arista	11		
12	-	Mirror Mirror	M2M	Atlantic	21		
13	-	Wobble Wobble	504 Boyz	No Limit/Priority	8		FL
14	-	This Time Around	Hanson	Island	13		L
15	-	I Don't Wanna Kiss You Goodnight	LFO	Arista	8		
16	-	Shackles (Praise You)	Mary Mary	C2	12	(5)	L
17	-	He Wasn't Man Enough	Toni Braxton	LaFace/Arista	14	(5)	L
18	9	All The Small Things	Blink-182	MCA	15		L
19	-	Swear It Again	Westlife	Arista	21	(1)	
20	4	Thank God I Found You	Mariah Carey feat. Joe & 98 Degrees	Columbia	13		

May 2000

This Mnth	Prev Mnth	Title	Artist	Label	Wks 20	(UK Pos)	
1	17	He Wasn't Man Enough	Toni Braxton	LaFace/Arista	14		L
2	1	Maria Maria	Santana feat. The Product G&B	Arista	23	(6)	L
3	-	Separated	Avant	Magic Johnson/MCA	8		FL
4	2	Breathe	Faith Hill	Warner Bros	23		L
5	13	Wobble Wobble	504 Boyz	No Limit/Priority	8		FL
6	14	This Time Around	Hanson	Island	13		L
7	12	Mirror Mirror	M2M	Atlantic	21		
8	16	Shackles (Praise You)	Mary Mary	C2	12	(5)	L
9	19	Swear It Again	Westlife	Arista	21		
10	6	From The Bottom Of My...	Britney Spears	Jive	19		
11	5	Goodbye Earl	Dixie Chicks	Monument	18		FL
12	7	Another Dumb Blonde	Hoku	Geffen/Interscope	13		FL
13	-	Feelin' So Good	Jennifer Lopez	Work	7	(15)	
14	-	(Hot S**t) Country Grammar	Nelly	Fo' Reel/Universal	9	(7)	FL
15	-	You Sang To Me	Marc Anthony	Columbia	13		FL
16	4	I Like It	Sammie	Free World/Capitol	24		FL
17	-	Back Here	BBMak	Hollywood	13	(5)	L
18	15	I Don't Wanna Kiss You Goodnight	LFO	Arista	8		
19	9	Get It On Tonite	Montell Jordan	Def Soul	19		L
20	-	Nothing As It Seems	Pearl Jam	Epic	3	(22)	

June 2000

This Mnth	Prev Mnth	Title	Artist	Label	Wks 20	(UK Pos)	
1	15	You Sang To Me	Marc Anthony	Columbia	13		FL
2	9	Swear It Again	Westlife	Arista	21		
3	14	(Hot S**t) Country Grammar	Nelly	Fo' Reel/Universal	9		FL
4	1	He Wasn't Man Enough	Toni Braxton	LaFace/Arista	14		L
5	7	Mirror Mirror	M2M	Atlantic	21		
6	2	Maria Maria	Santana feat. The Product G&B	Arista	23	(6)	L
7	17	Back Here	BBMak	Hollywood	13		L
8	10	From The Bottom Of My...	Britney Spears	Jive	19		
9	8	Shackles (Praise You)	Mary Mary	C2	12	(5)	L
10	13	Feelin' So Good	Jennifer Lopez	Work	7		
11	-	Monica	Before Dark	RCA	13		L
12	-	Otherside	Red Hot Chili Peppers	Warner Bros	9	(33)	L
13	4	Breathe	Faith Hill	Warner Bros	23		L
14	3	Separated	Avant	Magic Johnson/MCA	8		FL
15	6	This Time Around	Hanson	Island	13		L
16	-	Be With You	Enrique Iglesias	Interscope	7		L
17	-	Crybaby	Mariah Carey feat. Snoop Dogg	Columbia	13		
18	11	Goodbye Earl	Dixie Chicks	Monument	18		FL
19	-	Purest Of Pain (A Puro Dolor)	Son By Four	Sony Discos	8		FL
20	-	Someday Out Of The Blue	Elton John	Dreamworks	3		L

▲ Who would have thought that a trio of cute Texan babes singing along to the sound of a fiddle, banjo and dobro had much mainstream appeal? But after racking up six million sales for their debut album, Dixie Chicks are now country's biggest draw. The track 'Goodbye Earl' is the first country song of this kind to make it into the national Top 10 for over two decades. The key to the girls' success can be seen at the their live shows, which draw their audiences from every possible age group.

◆ After gaining attention on the soundtracks to *Dr Doolitle* and *Prince Of Egypt*, gospel/R&B duo Mary Mary score their first big transatlantic hit with the self-penned 'Shackles (Praise You)'.

UK 2000
JUL-SEP

▲ His mother named him Marshall Mathers III, but as Eminem, the white boy from Kansas City becomes one of rap's biggest stars. Widely criticized for his lyrics, he tops the charts twice with 'The Real Slim Shady' and 'Stan'. He's a good lad really, though, as he shows by dueting with Elton John at the Grammy awards.

◆ After a brief dalliance with indie, 80s starlet Kylie Minogue delights her fans with an album of cheesy disco hits, like 'Spinning Around', the ex-*Neighbours* star's first chart-topper in 10 years.

◆ Coldplay enjoy their first hit with 'Yellow'. Their acclaimed debut album *Parachute* quickly sells 1.5 million copies in the UK alone.

July 2000

This Mnth	Prev Mnth	Title	Artist	Label	Wks 20	(US Pos)	
1	19	Sandstorm	Darude	Neo	13		
2	-	The Real Slim Shady	Eminem	Interscope	10		
3	-	Spinning Around	Kylie Minogue	Parlophone	5		
4	-	Gotta Tell You	Samantha Mumba	Wild Card	7		F
5	-	You See The Trouble With Me	Black Legend	Eternal/WEA	4		FL
6	-	Breathless	The Corrs	Atlantic	6		
7	-	Take A Look Around	Limp Bizkit	Interscope	7		F
8	-	When I Said Goodbye/Summer Of Love	Steps	Ebul/Jive	4		
9	1	It Feels So Good	Sonique	Universal	9		
10	5	Shackles (Praise You)	Mary Mary	Columbia	9	(8)	FL
11	-	Life Is A Rollercoaster	Ronan Keating	Polydor	8		
12	-	Yellow	Coldplay	Parlophone	3		F
13	-	Uncle John From Jamaica	Vengaboys	Positiva	3		
14	-	Will I Ever	Alice Deejay	Positiva	4		
15	-	Woman Trouble	Artful Dodger feat. Robbie Craig	Public Demand	4		
16	-	Sunday Morning Call	Oasis	Big Brother	3		L
17	2	Reach	S Club 7	Polydor	9		
18	-	The Power Of Love	Frankie Goes To Hollywood	ZTT	2		
19	-	Ghetto Romance	Damage	Cooltempo	2		
20	-	I Want Your Love	Atomic Kitten	Innocent	2		

August 2000

This Mnth	Prev Mnth	Title	Artist	Label	Wks 20	(US Pos)	
1	-	Rock DJ	Robbie Williams	Chrysalis	8		
2	11	Life Is A Rollercoaster	Ronan Keating	Polydor	9		
3	-	We Will Rock You	5ive & Queen	RCA	6		L
4	2	The Real Slim Shady	Eminem	Interscope	6		
5	-	7 Days	Craig David	Wildstar	7		
6	-	Maria Maria	Santana feat. The Product G&B	Arista	4	(1)	L
7	-	I Turn To You	Melanie C	Virgin	5		
8	-	Freestyler	Bomfunk MCs	Dancepool	8		F
9	-	Jumpin' Jumpin'	Destiny's Child	Columbia	5		
10	-	2 Faced	Louise	1st Avenue	4		
11	-	Time To Burn	Storm	Data	5		FL
12	7	Take A Look Around	Limp Bizkit	Interscope	9		F
13	-	Out Of Your Mind	True Steppers & Dane Bowers feat. Victoria Beckham	NuLife	5		L
14	-	Lucky	Britney Spears	Jive	4		
15	6	Breathless	The Corrs	Atlantic	5		
16	1	Sandstorm	Darude	Neo	13		
17	-	Try Again	Aaliyah	Virgin	4		L
18	-	Affirmation	Savage Garden	Columbia	3		
19	14	Will I Ever	Alice Deejay	Positiva	7		L
20	-	I Can Only Disappoint U	Mansun	Parlophone	1		L

September 2000

This Mnth	Prev Mnth	Title	Artist	Label	Wks 20	(US Pos)	
1	-	Music	Madonna	Maverick	6		
2	-	Groovejet (If This Ain't Love)	Spiller	Positiva	7		FL
3	-	Lady (Hear Me Tonight)	Modjo	Sound Of Barclay	8		FL
4	1	Rock DJ	Robbie Williams	Chrysalis	9		
5	-	'Big Brother' UK TV Theme	Element Four	Channel 4 Music	3		FL
6	13	Out Of Your Mind	True Steppers & Dane Bowers feat. Victoria Beckham	NuLife	7		FL
7	-	Take On Me	A1	Columbia	3		
8	-	Sky	Sonique	Serious	5		
9	14	Lucky	Britney Spears	Jive	7		
10	7	I Turn To You	Melanie C	Virgin	9		
11	-	It Doesn't Matter	Wyclef Jean	Columbia	3		
12	-	On A Night Like This	Kylie Minogue	Parlophone	3		
13	-	Natural	S Club 7	Polydor	3		
14	-	Against All Odds	Mariah Carey & Westlife	Columbia	6		L
15	8	Freestyler	Bomfunk MCs	Dancepool	7		FL
16	5	7 Days	Craig David	Wildstar	9		
17	-	Ordinary World	Aurora feat. Naimee Coleman	Positiva	2		L
18	-	Overload	Sugababes	London	4		F
19	-	Absolutely Everybody	Vanessa Amorosi	Mercury	4		FL
20	-	Kernkraft 400	Zombie Nation	Data	5		FL

US 2000 JUL-SEP

July 2000

This Mnth	Prev Mnth	Title	Artist	Label	Wks 20	(UK Pos)	
1	-	I Turn To You	Christina Aguilera	RCA	13	(19)	
2	2	Swear It Again	Westlife	Arista	21		
3	16	Be With You	Enrique Iglesias	Interscope	7		L
4	17	Crybaby	Mariah Carey feat. Snoop Dogg	Columbia	13		
5	-	No More	Ruff Endz	Epic	11	(11)	L
6	-	Simple Kind Of Life	No Doubt	Trauma/Interscope	7	(69)	L
7	5	Mirror Mirror	M2M	Atlantic	21		
8	7	Back Here	BBMak	Hollywood	13		L
9	-	One Voice	Billy Gilman	Epic	15		F
10	-	Everything You Want	Vertical Horizon	RCA	9	(42)	FL
11	1	You Sang To Me	Marc Anthony	Columbia	13		FL
12	-	Take That	Torry Carter	East West	5		FL
13	19	Purest Of Pain (A Puro Dolor)	Son By Four	Sony Discos	8		FL
14	-	Bent	Matchbox Twenty	Lava/Atlantic	15		FL
15	-	Dancing Queen	A*Teens	MCA	3		L
16	11	Monica	Before Dark	RCA	13		L
17	-	Callin' Me	Lil' Zane feat. 112	Priority	17		L
18	-	Let's Get Married	Jagged Edge	So So Def	11		
19	12	Otherside	Red Hot Chili Peppers	Warner Bros	9		L
20	-	It's Gonna Be Me	'N Sync	Jive	7	(9)	

August 2000

This Mnth	Prev Mnth	Title	Artist	Label	Wks 20	(UK Pos)	
1	-	Incomplete	Sisqo	Soul/IDJMG	22	(13)	GL
2	20	It's Gonna Be Me	'N Sync	Jive	7		
3	14	Bent	Matchbox Twenty	Lava/Atlantic	15		FL
4	-	I Need You	Leann Rimes	Curb	14	(13)	
5	5	No More	Ruff Endz	Epic	11		L
6	17	Callin' Me	Lil' Zane feat. 112	Priority	17		L
7	-	West Side Story	LFO	Arista	5		L
8	9	One Voice	Billy Gilman	Epic	15		F
9	2	Swear It Again	Westlife	Arista	21		
10	-	Faded	Souldecision feat. Thrust	MCA	9		L
11	18	Let's Get Married	Jagged Edge	So So Def	11		
12	1	I Turn To You	Christina Aguilera	RCA	13		
13	10	Everything You Want	Vertical Horizon	RCA	9		FL
14	-	Dance With Me	Debelah Morgan	Atlantic	29	(10)	FL
15	-	Bounce With Me	Lil Bow Wow	So So Def	7		L
16	-	Doesn't Really Matter	Janet	Def Jam	19	(5)	L
17	7	Mirror Mirror	M2M	Atlantic	21		
18	4	Crybaby	Mariah Carey feat. Snoop Dogg	Columbia	13		
19	-	Who Let The Dogs Out	Baha Men	S-Curve	3	(2)	F
20	-	Daily	TQ	Clockwork/Epic	1	(14)	L

September 2000

This Mnth	Prev Mnth	Title	Artist	Label	Wks 20	(UK Pos)	
1	16	Doesn't Really Matter	Janet	Def Jam	19		L
2	1	Incomplete	Sisqo	Soul/IDJMG	22		L
3	-	Aaron's Party (Come Get It)	Aaron Carter	Jive	15	(51)	L
4	-	Music	Madonna	Maverick	23	(1)	G
5	-	Wifey	Next	Arista	9	(19)	L
6	6	Callin' Me	Lil' Zane feat. 112	Priority	17		L
7	4	I Need You	Leann Rimes	Curb	14		
8	15	Bounce With Me	Lil Bow Wow	So So Def	7		L
9	3	Bent	Matchbox Twenty	Lava/Atlantic	15		FL
10	5	No More	Ruff Endz	Epic	11		L
11	-	Can't Fight The Moonlight	Leann Rimes	Curb	25	(1)	L
12	8	One Voice	Billy Gilman	Epic	15		F
13	10	Faded	Souldecision feat. Thrust	MCA	9		L
14	-	Liar	Profyle	Motown/Universal	13		L
15	14	Dance With Me	Debelah Morgan	Atlantic	29		FL
16	11	Let's Get Married	Jagged Edge	So So Def	11		
17	-	The Hardest Part Of Breaking Up	2Gether	TVT	5		L
18	-	Give Me Just One Night (Una Noche)	98 Degrees	Universal	13	(61)	L
19	-	Wonderful	Everclear	Capitol	13	(36)	L
20	-	Desert Rose	Sting feat. Cheb Mami	A&M/Interscope	3	(15)	L

▲ Peroxide "yodelling" rapper Sisqo scores his first solo number one hit away from his pals in the multiplatinum Dru Hill. Although he writes, performs and produces his new material, it's on stage where he scores, his jet-propelled dance routines never failing to set audiences alight.

◆ It seems that America can't resist child stars right now. Kid rapper 'Lil Bow Wow is barely 13 and already has two Top 10 hits behind him. On the other hand, 12-year-old country sensation Billy Gilman is no novelty. He's already won plenty of awards, with critics describing him as the greatest new vocal talent to have emerged in 20 years.

UK 2000 OCT-DEC

◆ Christmas is a time for novelty hits. And this year it's the BBC's animated star Bob The Builder that takes the honours.

◆ Catchiest chorus of all time goes to Baha Men's 'Who Let The Dogs Out' – among the biggest-selling hits of the year, even though it fails to top the charts during any single week.

◆ One of the unlikely stars of the year turns out to be a piece of studio equipment meant for keeping singers in tune. Used successfully on Cher's 'Believe', Antares Autotune creates the "robotic" vocal effect used on numerous chart hits, such as Daft Punk's deliciously sublime 'One More Time'.

October 2000

This Mnth	Prev Mnth	Title	Artist	Label	Wks 20	(US Pos)	
1	14	Against All Odds	Mariah Carey & Westlife	Columbia	6		FL
2	-	Body Groove	Architechs feat. Nana	Go Beat	7		FL
3	20	Kernkraft 400	Zombie Nation	Data	7		FL
4	-	Black Coffee	All Saints	London	4		
5	-	Silence (Remixes)	Delerium feat. Sarah McLachlan	Nettwerk	6		FL
6	-	I'm Outta Love	Anastacia	Epic	9		F
7	-	Could I Have This Kiss Forever	Whitney Houston/Enrique Iglesias	Arista	4		
8	-	Beautiful Day	U2	Island	3		
9	-	Kids	Robbie Williams/Kylie Minogue	Chrysalis	4		
10	3	Lady (Hear Me Tonight)	Modjo	Sound Of Barclay	11		FL
11	-	Tell Me	Melanie B	Virgin	2		
12	-	The Way I Am	Eminem	Interscope	4		
13	-	Stomp	Steps	Ebul/Jive	4		
14	-	Most Girls	Pink	LaFace/Arista	3		
15	-	In Demand	Texas	Mercury	2		
16	-	Ain't No Stoppin Us	DJ Luck & MC Neat feat. JJ	Red Rose	2		
17	18	Overload	Sugababes	London	6		L
18	-	Dooms Night	Azzido Da Bass	Club Tools	2		FL
19	-	Body II Body	Samantha Mumba	Wildcard	3		
20	-	I Believe	Stephen Gately	Polydor	1		L

November 2000

		Title	Artist	Label	Wks 20	(US Pos)	
1	-	Who Let The Dogs Out	Baha Men	Edel	15		F
2	-	Holler/Let Love Lead The Way	Spice Girls	Virgin	3		L
3	-	I'm Over You	Martine McCutcheon	Innocent	4		
4	-	She Bangs	Ricky Martin	Columbia	5		
5	-	My Love	Westlife	RCA	6		
6	-	Number 1	Tweenies	BBC Music	10		F
7	-	Same Old Brand New You	A1	Columbia	3		
8	5	Silence (Remixes)	Delerium feat. Sarah McLachlan	Nettwerk	11		FL
9	13	Stomp	Steps	Ebul/Jive	10		L
10	6	I'm Outa Love	Anastacia	Epic	9		FL
11	-	Don't Think I'm Not	Kandi	Columbia	4		FL
12	-	Shape Of My Heart	Backstreet Boys	Jive	3		
13	-	(Hot S**T) Country Grammar	Nelly	Universal	3		F
14	9	Kids	Robbie Williams	Chrysalis	9		
15	-	Come On Over Baby (All I Want Is You)	Christina Aguilera	RCA	2	(1)	L
16	-	Can't Fight The Moonlight	LeAnn Rimes	Curb/London	10	(11)	
17	-	One More Time	Daft Punk	Virgin	4		L
18	-	Please Don't Turn Me On	Artful Dodger feat. Lifford	ffrr	3		
19	-	Original Prankster	The Offspring	Columbia	2		
20	-	Feel The Beat	Darude	Neo	3		L

December 2000

		Title	Artist	Label	Wks 20	(US Pos)	
1	-	Can We Fix It	Bob The Builder	BBC Music	8		FL
2	-	Stan	Eminem	Interscope	8		L
3	16	Can't Fight The Moonlight	LeAnn Rimes	Curb/London	9	(11)	L
4	-	Independent Women Part 1	Destiny's Child	Columbia	8	(4)	
5	1	Who Let The Dogs Out	Baha Men	Edel	14		F
6	-	Operation Blade (Bass...Place)	Public Domain	Xtravaganza	8		FL
7	-	Never Had A Dream Come True	S Club 7	Polydor	8		L
8	6	Number 1	Tweenies	BBC Music	13		FL
9	-	Don't Tell Me	Madonna	Maverick	6	(3)	L
10	-	Walking Away	Craig David	Wildstar	7		
11	17	One More Time	Daft Punk	Virgin	6		FL
12	-	I Put A Spell On You	Sonique	Universal	3		L
13	-	Wassuup	Da Muttz	Eternal	5		FL
14	-	Stronger	Britney Spears	Jive	5	(1)	L
15	-	Supreme	Robbie Williams	Chrysalis	4		L
16	-	Phatt Bass	Warp Brothers Vs Aquagen	Nulife	2		F
17	-	The Way You Make Me Feel	Ronan Keating	Polydor	3		L
18	20	Feel The Beat	Darude	Neo	7		L
19	18	Please Don't Turn Me On	Artful Dodger feat. Lifford	ffrr	11		L
20	-	911	Wyclef Jean	Columbia	5		L

October 2000

This Mnth	Prev Mnth	Title	Artist	Label	Wks 20	(UK Pos)	
1	4	Music	Madonna	Maverick	23	(1)	
2	-	Bag Lady	Erykah Badu	Motown/Universal	13		L
3	18	Give Me Just One Night (Una Noche)	98 Degrees	Universal	13		L
4	14	Liar	Profyle	Motown/Universal	13		L
5	-	Come On Over Baby (All I Want Is You)	Christina Aguilera	RCA	17	(8)	L
6	3	Aaron's Party (Come Get It)	Aaron Carter	Jive	15		L
7	19	Wonderful	Everclear	Capitol	13		L
8	2	Incomplete	Sisqo	Soul/IDJMG	22		L
9	1	Doesn't Really Matter	Janet	Def Jam	19		L
10	15	Dance With Me	Debelah Morgan	Atlantic	29		FL
11	-	The Way You Love Me	Faith Hill	Warner Bros	23	(15)	L
12	-	Gotta Tell You	Samantha Mumba	Interscope	18	(2)	L
13	8	Bounce With Me	Lil Bow Wow	So So Def	11		L
14	-	With Arms Wide Open	Creed	Wind-up	7	(13)	L
15	5	Wifey	Next	Arista	9		L
16	-	Can't Go For That	Tamia	Elektra/EEG	3		L
17	11	Can't Fight The Moonlight	Leann Rimes	Curb	25	(3)	FL
18	-	Most Girls	Pink	LaFace/Arista	9	(50	L
19	7	I Need You	Leann Rimes	Curb	14		
20	6	Callin' Me	Lil' Zane feat. 112	Priority	17		L

November 2000

This Mnth	Prev Mnth	Title	Artist	Label	Wks 20	(UK Pos)	
1	5	Come On Over Baby (All I Want Is You)	Christina Aguilera	RCA	17	(15)	L
2	12	Gotta Tell You	Samantha Mumba	Interscope	18		L
3	1	Music	Madonna	Maverick	23	(1)	
4	2	Bag Lady	Erykah Badu	Motown/Universal	13		L
5	10	Dance With Me	Debelah Morgan	Atlantic	29		FL
6	-	He Loves U Not	Dream	Bad Boy/Arista	22+	(17)	FL
7	8	Incomplete	Sisqo	Soul/IDJMG	22		L
8	6	Aaron's Party (Come Get It)	Aaron Carter	Jive	15		L
9	3	Give Me Just One Night…	98 Degrees	Universal	13		L
10	4	Liar	Profyle	Motown/Universal	13		L
11	11	The Way You Love Me	Faith Hill	Warner Bros	23		L
12	17	Can't Fight The Moonlight	Leann Rimes	Curb	25	(3)	L
13	9	Doesn't Really Matter	Janet	Def Jam	19		L
14	7	Wonderful	Everclear	Capitol	13		L
15	-	Oklahoma	Billy Gilman	Epic	15		L
16	18	Most Girls	Pink	LaFace/Arista	9		L
17	-	Souljas	Master P	No Limit/Priority	11		L
18	-	Pinch Me	Barenaked Ladies	Reprise	7		L
19	14	With Arms Wide Open	Creed	Wind-up	7		L
20	-	It's OK	Slimm Calhoun	East West/EEG	3		L

December 2000

This Mnth	Prev Mnth	Title	Artist	Label	Wks 20	(UK Pos)	
1	-	Case Of The Ex (Watcha Gonna Do)	Mya	Interscope	9	(3)	L
2	6	He Loves U Not	Dream	Bad Boy/Arista	22+		FL
3	5	Dance With Me	Debelah Morgan	Atlantic	29		FL
4	2	Gotta Tell You	Samantha Mumba	Interscope	18		L
5	1	Come On Over Baby…	Christina Aguilera	RCA	17	(15)	L
6	11	The Way You Love Me	Faith Hill	Warner Bros	23		L
7	-	The Itch	Vitamin C	Elektra/EEG	14		L
8	-	So In Love With Two	Mikaila	Island/IDJMG	14		LI
9	4	Bag Lady	Erykah Badu	Motown/Universa	13		
10	3	Music	Madonna	Maverick	23	(1)	
11	15	Oklahoma	Billy Gilman	Epic	15		L
12	-	Liquid Dreams	O-Town	J	17+		FL
13	-	Independent Women Part 1	Destiny's Child	Columbia	14	(1)	L
14	7	Incomplete	Sisqo	Soul/IDJMG	22		L
15	12	Can't Fight The Moonlight	Leann Rimes	Curb	25	(3)	L
16	9	Give Me Just One Night…	98 Degrees	Universal	13		L
17	-	Mamacita	Public Announcement	RCA	19		L
18	17	Souljas	Master P	No Limit/Priority	11		L
19	18	Pinch Me	Barenaked Ladies	Reprise	7		L
20	-	Could It Be	Jaheim	Warner Bros	17+		F

▲ Talk about taking coals to Newcastle, 18-year-old Dubliner Samantha Mumba becomes the latest R&B sensation to hit the US charts.

◆ At 4 feet 8 inches and barely 12 years old, Aaron Carter has already had a good chart run for his money. Of course, it helps if your big brother is one of the Backstreet Boys, and he lets you make the odd special appearance on stage.

◆ With men-bashing classics such as 'No Scrubs' and 'Bills, Bills, Bills', R&B quartet Destiny's Child have carved a reputation as babes with BIG attitude. Which makes them a perfect choice for taking the lead song on the forthcoming *Charlie's Angels* soundtrack album.

UK 2001 JAN-MAR

▲ Contrivance reaches new heights with *Pop Stars*, a TV series in which a new boy/girl band is "designed" from scratch. Millions of viewers watch thousands of wannabes culled down to a crucial five – named Hear'Say. At the end of March, both debut single and album top the charts.

◆ British singer Dido reaps the benefits of appearing on Eminem's 'Stan', as sales of her first album *No Angel* edge towards a million.

◆ Britain also takes to Eva Cassidy, an obscure US singer who died in 1996 having seen little real success. After a clip of her performing 'Somewhere Over The Rainbow' is shown by the BBC, her album *Songbird* tops the charts.

January 2001

This Mnth	Prev Mnth	Title	Artist	Label	Wks 20	(US Pos)	
1	-	Touch Me	Rui Da Silva feat. Cassandra	Kismet/Arista	6		FL
2	1	Can We Fix It	Bob The Builder	BBC Music	12		FL
3	2	Stan	Eminem	Interscope	13		L
4	-	Every Time You Need Me	Fragma feat. Maria Rubia	Positiva	7		L
5	-	Love Don't Cost A Thing	Jennifer Lopez	Epic	4	(15)	L
6	7	Never Had A Dream Come True	S Club 7	Polydor	11		L
7	-	No Good 4 Me	Oxide & Neutrino	East West	4		FL
8	5	Who Let The Dogs Out	Baha Men	Edel	14		F
9	-	What Makes A Man	Westlife	RCA	6		FL
10	6	Operation Blade (Bass...Place)	Public Domain	Xtravaganza	7		FL
11	4	Independent Women Part 1	Destiny's Child	Columbia	9	(4)	L
12	-	Rollin'	Limp Bizkit	Interscope	7		L
13	-	Buck Rogers	Feeder	Echo	2		L
14	-	Inner Smile	Texas	Mercury	2		L
15	-	Why	Mis-Teeq	Inferno	3		FL
16	3	Can't Fight The Moonlight	LeAnn Rimes	Curb/London	9	(11)	
17	14	Stronger	Britney Spears	Jive	9	(1)	L
18	15	Supreme	Robbie Williams	Chrysalis	7		L
19	8	Number 1	Tweenies	BBC Music	13		FL
20	-	Camels	Santos	Incentive	2		FL

February 2001

1	12	Rollin'	Limp Bizkit	Interscope	9		FL
2	-	Whole Again	Atomic Kitten	Innocent	7+		L
3	-	The Next Episode	Dr Dre feat.Snoop Dogg	Interscope	5		L
4	-	Pop Ya Collar	Usher	LaFace/Arista	4		L
5	4	Every Time You Need Me	Fragma feat. Maria Rubia	Positiva	7		L
6	-	Case Of The Ex	Mya	Interscope	4	(1)	FL
7	-	Teenage Dirtbag	Wheatus	Columbia	8+		FL
8	1	Touch Me	Rui Da Silva	Kismet/Arista	9		FL
9	-	Played Alive (The Bongo Song)	Safri Duo	AM:PM	4		FL
10	-	Last Resort	Papa Roach	Dreamworks	3		FL
11	-	Things I've Seen	Spooks	Artemis	4		FL
12	5	Love Don't Cost A Thing	Jennifer Lopez	Epic	11	(15)	L
13	-	Chase The Sun	Planet Funk	Virgin	2		FL
14	-	Stuck In A Moment You Can't Get Out Of	U2	Island	2		L
15	-	On The Radio	Martine McCutcheon	Innocent	2		L
16	-	Dream To Me	Dario G	Manifesto	2		L
17	-	Stutter	Joe feat. Mystikal	Jive	3	(1)	L
18	-	Loco	Fun Lovin' Criminals	Chrysalis	2		L
19	-	American Dream	Jakatta	Rulin	4+		FL
20	-	Here With Me	Dido	Cheeky/Arista	6+		FL

March 2001

1	2	Whole Again	Atomic Kitten	Innocent	7+		L
2	-	It Wasn't Me	Shaggy feat. Rikrok	MCA	5+	(5)	GL
3	-	Uptown Girl	Westlife	RCA	5+		L
4	7	Teenage Dirtbag	Wheatus	Columbia	8+		FL
5	-	Always Come Back To Your Love	Samantha Mumba	Wild Card	2+		L
6	-	Ms Jackson	Outkast	LaFace/Arista	5+	(4)	FL
7	-	Pure And Simple	Hear'Say	Polydor	3+		GFL
8	-	I'm Like A Bird	Nelly Furtado	Dreamworks	4+		FL
9	-	Clint Eastwood	Gorillaz	Parlophone	3+		FL
10	20	Here With Me	Dido	Cheeky/Arista	8+		FL
11	-	Nobody Wants To Be Lonely	Ricky Martin with Christina Aguilera	Columbia	4+		L
12	-	I Wanna Be U	Chocolate Puma	Cream/Parlophone	4+		FL
13	-	Feels So Good	Melanie B	Virgin	3+		L
14	19	American Dream	Jakatta	Rulin	7+		L
15	-	Shut Up And Forget About It	Dane	Arista	2+		FL
16	-	The Ladyboy Is Mine	Stuntmasterz	East West	2+		FL
17	-	Dancing In The Moonlight	Toploader	S2	9+		L
18	-	Mr Writer	Stereophonics	V2	4+		L
19	-	Shit On You	D12	Interscope	2+		FL
20	-	No More	A1	Columbia	1+		L

January 2001

This Mnth	Prev Mnth	Title	Artist	Label	Wks 20	(UK Pos)	
1	2	He Loves U Not	Dream	Bad Boy/Arista	22+		FL
2	12	Liquid Dreams	O-Town	J	17+		FL
3	17	Mamacita	Public Announcement	RCA	19	(4)	L
4	13	Independent Woman Part 1	Destiny's Child	Columbia	14		L
5	8	So In Love With Two	Mikaila	Island/IDJMG	14		L
6	-	Stronger	Britney Spears	Jive	13+	(7)	L
7	3	Dance With Me	Debelah Morgan	Atlantic	29		FL
8	7	The Itch	Vitamin C	Elektra/EEG	14		L
9	1	Case Of The Ex (Watcha Gonna Do)	Mya	Interscope	9		L
10	-	South Side	Moby feat. Gwen Stefani	V2	10+		FL
11	6	The Way You Love Me	Faith Hill	Warner Bros	23		L
12	-	Stutter	Joe feat. Mystikal	Jive	14+	(7)	FL
13	20	Could It Be	Jaheim	Warner Bros	17+		FL
14	-	Bouncing Off The Ceiling (Upside Down)	A*Teens	MCA	12		L
15	10	Music	Madonna	Maverick	23	(1)	
16	11	Oklahoma	Billy Gilman	Epic	15		L
17	15	Can't Fight The Moonlight	Leann Rimes	Curb	25	(3)	L
18	4	Gotta Tell You	Samantha Mumba	Interscope	18		L
19	-	Soul Sista	Bilal	Moyo/Interscope	13+		L
20	-	I Hope You Dance	Lee Ann Womack	Universal	12+		L

February 2001

This Mnth	Prev Mnth	Title	Artist	Label	Wks 20	(UK Pos)	
1	6	Stronger	Britney Spears	Jive	13+	(14)	L
2	12	Stutter	Joe feat. Mystikal	Jive	14+	(17)	FL
3	-	Don't Tell Me	Madonna	Maverick	9+	(4)	L
4	-	Ms Jackson	Outkast	LaFace/Arista	13+	(2)	FL
5	2	Liquid Dreams	O-Town	J	17+		FL
6	20	I Hope You Dance	Lee Ann Womack	Universal	12+		L
7	13	Could It Be	Jaheim	Warner Bros	17+		FL
8	10	South Side	Moby feat. Gwen Stefani	V2	10+		FL
9	5	So In Love With Two	Mikaila	Island/IDJMG	14		L
10	19	Soul Sista	Bilal	Moyo/Interscope	13+		L
11	3	Mamacita	Public Announcement	RCA	14		L
12	-	You All Dat	Baha Men	S-Curve	5	(14)	L
13	7	Dance With Me	Debelah Morgan	Atlantic	29		FL
14	17	Can't Fight The Moonlight	Leann Rimes	Curb	25	(3)	L
15	8	The Itch	Vitamin C	Elektra/EEG	14		L
16	1	He Loves U Not	Dream	Bad Boy/Arista	22+		FL
17	14	Bouncing Off The Ceiling (Upside Down)	A*Teens	MCA	12		L
18	-	It Wasn't Me	Shaggy	MCA	8+	(1)	L
19	11	The Way You Love Me	Faith Hill	Warner Bros	23		L
20	4	Independent Woman Part 1	Destiny's Child	Columbia	19	(4)	L

March 2001

This Mnth	Prev Mnth	Title	Artist	Label	Wks 20	(UK Pos)	
1	2	Stutter	Joe feat. Mystikal	Jive	14+	(17)	FL
2	7	Could It Be	Jaheim	Warner Bros	17+		FL
3	-	It's Over Now	112	Bad Boy/Arista	5+		L
4	-	Bow Wow (That's My Name)	Lil Bow Wow	So So Def	4+		L
5	18	It Wasn't Me	Shaggy	MCA	8+		L
6	3	Don't Tell Me	Madonna	Maverick	9+		L
7	-	Butterfly	Crazy Town	Columbia	3+		L
8	-	Crazy For The Girl	Evan And Jaron	Columbia	4+		FL
9	4	Ms Jackson	Outkast	LaFace/Arista	13+	(6)	FL
10	-	Promise	Jagged Edge	So So Def	3+		L
11	1	Stronger	Britney Spears	Jive	13+	(14)	L
12	8	South Side	Moby feat. Gwen Stefani	V2	10+		FL
13	10	Soul Sista	Bilal	Moyo/Interscope	13+		L
14	5	Liquid Dreams	O-Town	J	17+		FL
15	-	Love Don't Cost A Thing	Jennifer Lopez	Epic	4+	(1)	L
16	-	What Would You Do?	City High	Interscope	2+		FL
17	6	I Hope You Dance	Lee Ann Womack	Universal	12+		L
18	-	Get Over Yourself	Eden's Crush	London/Sire	4+		L
19	-	That's How I Beat Shaq	Aaron Carter	Jive	2+		L
20	16	He Loves U Not	Dream	Bad Boy/Arista	22+		FL

US 2001
JAN-MAR

▲ Most Hollywood celebs fancy their chances at pop stardom at some point, but nobody in recent years has sustained as credible a pop career as Jennifer Lopez who enjoys her fifth hit single in a year.

◆ A smash hit on both sides of the Atlantic, Joe's 'Stutter' is a supremely catchy slice of R&B featuring New Orleans rapper Mystikal, who – oddly for a hip-hop star – is also a veteran of the Gulf War.

◆ Also scoring well on both sides of the pond is Outkast's inventive 'Ms Jackson'. Although rap is often branded as violent and misogynistic, this one's an apology to a girfriend's mother for upsetting her daughter. Ah, bless!

UK 2001 APR-JUNE

◆ The youngest British male to top the charts with two singles, Craig David, picked up three prestigious Ivor Novello songwriters awards. Meanwhile Shaggy, Ricky Martin, the Backstreet Boys and Christina Aguilera were among winners at the World Music Awards.

◆ Shaggy became the first Jamaican to simultaneously top the UK singles and album charts. In total, 11 singles have reached No. 1 by Jamaican artists and four of these were by Shaggy. Across the Atlantic his album, 'Hot Shot', became the first ever by an artist from that country to head the chart.

◆ One of the few UK acts to sell well across the Atlantic, Radiohead, scored their second UK No. 1 album in a year, 'Amnesiac' – which reached runner-up spot Stateside. Their previous release, 'Kid A', had topped both the US and UK charts.

April 2001

This Mnth	Prev Mnth	Title	Artist	Label	Wks 20	(US Pos)	
1	2	It Wasn't Me	Shaggy featuring Rikrok	MCA	12	(1)	G
2	7	Pure And Simple	Hear'say	Polydor	7		FG
3		What Took You So Long	Emma Bunton	Virgin	6		
4		Butterfly	Crazy Town	Columbia	8	(1)	FL
5	9	Clint Eastwood	Gorillaz	Parlophone	11	(57)	F
6	3	Uptown Girl	Westlife	RCA	7		
7	1	Whole Again	Atomic Kitten	Innocent	15		
8		All For You	Janet Jackson	Virgin	4	(1)	
9		Survivor	Destiny's Child	Columbia	6	(2)	
10		Out Of Reach	Gabrielle	Go. Beat/Polydor	8		
11		Lovin' Each Day	Ronan Keating	Polydor	5		
12	4	Teenage Dirtbag	Wheatus	Columbia	15		F
13		Liquid Dreams	O-Town	J/RCA	4	(10)	F
14		Salsoul Nugget (If U Wanna)	M&S Presents Girl Next Door	ffrr	3		FL
15		Bow Wow (That's My Name)	Lil Bow Wow	So So Def/Columbia	3	(21)	FL
16		Get Ur Freak On	Missy 'Misdemeanor' Elliott	East West/Elektra	6	(8)	
17	8	I'm Like A Bird	Nelly Furtado	Dreamworks	8	(9)	F
18		What It Feels Like For A Girl	Madonna	Maverick	2	(23)	
19	18	Mr Writer	Stereophonics	V2	3		
20		Let Love Be Your Energy	Robbie Williams	Chrysalis	1		

May 2001

This Mnth	Prev Mnth	Title	Artist	Label	Wks 20	(US Pos)	
1		Don't Stop Movin'	S Club 7	Polydor	11		
2		It's Raining Men	Geri Halliwell	EMI	7		
3	9	Survivor	Destiny's Child	Columbia	6	(2)	
4	10	Out Of Reach	Gabrielle	Go. Beat/Polydor	8		
5	11	Lovin' Each Day	Ronan Keating	Polydor	5		
6		Cold As Ice	M.O.P.	Epic	5		F
7		Play	Jennifer Lopez	Epic	5	(18)	
8		8 Get Ur Freak On	Missy 'Misdemeanor' Elliott	East West/Elektra	6	(8)	
9		Ride Wit Me	Nelly featuring City Spud	Universal	5	(3)	
10		You Are Alive	Fragma	Positiva	4		L
11	1	It Wasn't Me	Shaggy featuring Rikrok	MCA	12	(1)	G
12		Who's That Girl	Eve	Interscope	3	(47)	
13	13	Liquid Dreams	O-Town	J/RCA	4	(10)	F
14	5	Clint Eastwood	Gorillaz	Parlophone	11	(57)	F
15		Imitation Of Life	REM	Warner Bros.	2	(83)	L
16		Dream On	Depeche Mode	Mute	1		
17		Up Middle Finger	Oxide & Neutrino	East West	2		
18		Still On Your Side	BBMak	Telstar	1		L
19		Star 69	Fatboy Slim	Skint	2		L
29	3	What Took You So Long	Emma Bunton	Virgin	6		

June 2001

This Mnth	Prev Mnth	Title	Artist	Label	Wks 20	(US Pos)	
1		Do You Really Like It	DJ Pied Piper/Masters Of Ceremonies	Relentless/MoS	7		FL
2		Angel	Shaggy featuring Rayvon	MCA	9	(1)	
3	1	Don't Stop Movin'	S Club 7	Polydor	11		
4		All Rise	Blue	Innocent	8		F
5		Thank You	Dido	Cheeky/Arista	5	(3)	
6		We Come 1	Faithless	Cheeky	4		
7		All I Want	Mis-Teeq	Inferno/Telstar	5		
8		Another Day In Paradise	Brandy & Ray J	WEA	5		
9		Sing	Travis	Independiente	5		
10		Lady Marmalade	Christina Aguilera, Lil' Kim, Mya & Pink	Interscope/Polydor	8	(1)	
11		Until The End Of Time	2Pac	Interscope/Polydor	4	(52)	L
12		Electric Avenue (Remix)	Eddy Grant	Ice/East West	4		L
13		Here And Now/You'll Be Sorry	Steps	Ebul/Jive	3		
14		Romeo	Basement Jaxx	XL Recordings	4		
15		There You'll Be	Faith Hill	Warner Brothers	7	(10)	L
16		Have A Nice Day	Stereophonics	V2	3		
17	2	It's Raining Men	Geri Halliwell	EMI	7		
18		No More (Baby I'm A Do Right)	3LW	Epic	3	(23)	FL
19		My Way	Limp Bizkit	Interscope	3	(75)	
20		Pyramid Song	Radiohead	Parlophone	2		

US 2001 APR-JUNE

April 2001

This Mnth	Prev Mnth	Title	Artist	Label	Wks 20	(UK Pos)	
1		All For You	Janet	Virgin	16	(3)	
2		Survivor	Destiny's Child	Columbia	14	(1)	
3	7	Butterfly	Crazy Town	Columbia	13	(3)	FL
4		Angel	Shaggy featuring Rayvon	MCA	18	(1)	L
5		Thank You	Dido	Arista	18	(3)	FL
6		Again	Lenny Kravitz	Virgin	22		L
7		Missing You	Case	Def Soul/DJMG	8		L
8	1	Stutter	Joe featuring Mystikal	Jive	20	(7)	L
9		Hanging By A Moment	Lifehouse	Dreamworks	32	(25)	FL
10		Jaded	Aerosmith	Columbia	11	(13)	L
11	18	Get Over Yourself	Eden's Crush	London-Sire	5		FL
12		Ride Wit Me	Nelly featuring City Spud	Fo' Reel/Universal	16	(3)	
13		Stranger In My House	Tamia	Elektra	5		L
14		Put It On Me	Ja Rule featuring Lil' Mo Murder Inc	Def Jam	15		
15		Crazy	K-Ci & JoJo	MCA	12	(35)	L
16	10	Promise	Jagged Edge	So So Def	9		
17		Bizounce	Olivia	J	5		FL
18		If You're Gone	Matchbox Twenty	Lava	21	(50)	
19		Follow Me	Uncle Kracker	Top Dog/Lava	13	(3)	F
20	15	Love Don't Cost A Thing	Jennifer Lopez	Epic	15	(1)	

May 2001

This Mnth	Prev Mnth	Title	Artist	Label	Wks 20	(UK Pos)	
1	1	All For You	Janet	Virgin	16	(3)	
2	2	Survivor	Destiny's Child	Columbia	14	(1)	
3	5	Thank You	Dido	Arista	18	(3)	FL
4	9	Hanging By A Moment	Lifehouse	Dreamworks	32	(25)	FL
5		Lady Marmalade	Christina Aguilera, Lil'Kim, Mya & Pink	Interscope	14	(1)	
6	12	Ride Wit Me	Nelly featuring City Spud	Fo' Reel/Universal	16	(3)	
7	19	Follow Me	Uncle Kracker	Top Dog/Lava	13	(3)	F
8	4	Angel	Shaggy featuring Rayvon	MCA	18	(1)	L
9	7	Missing You	Case	Def Soul/DJMG	8		L
10	8	Stutter	Joe featuring Mystikal	Jive	20	(7)	L
11		What Would You Do?	City High	Booga Basement	19	(3)	F
12		I'm Like A Bird	Nelly Furtado	Dreamworks	9	(5)	F
13		Get Ur Freak On	Missy 'Misdemeanor' Elliott	Gold Mind/Eastwest	14	(4)	
14		Never Had A Dream Come True	S Club 7	A&M/Interscope	3	(1)	FL
15	6	Again	Lenny Kravitz	Virgin	22		L
16	3	Butterfly	Crazy Town	Columbia	13	(3)	FL
17		South Side	Moby featuring Gwen Stefani	V2	10		FL
18	13	Stranger In My House	Tamia	Elektra	5		L
19		Peaches & Cream	112	Bad Boy/Arista	20	(32)	L
20	17	Bizounce	Olivia	J	5		FL

June 2001

This Mnth	Prev Mnth	Title	Artist	Label	Wks 20	(UK Pos)	
1	5	Lady Marmalade	Christina Aguilera, Lil'Kim, Mya & Pink	Interscope	14	(1)	
2	4	Hanging By A Moment	Lifehouse	Dreamworks	32	(25)	FL
3	6	Ride Wit Me	Nelly featuring City Spud	Fo' Reel/Universal	16	(3)	
4	1	All For You	Janet	Virgin	16	(3)	
5		My Baby	Lil' Romeo	Soulja/No Limit	7	(67)	FL
6	7	Follow Me	Uncle Kracker	Top Dog/Lava	13	(3)	F
7		Fiesta	R. Kelly featuring Jay-Z	Jive	9	(23)	
8		Drops Of Jupiter (Tell Me)	Train	Columbia	25	(10)	L
9	13	Get Ur Freak On	Missy 'Misdemeanor' Elliot	Gold Mind/Eastwest	14	(4)	
10	19	Peaches & Cream	112	Bad Boy/Arista	20	(32)	L
11	2	Survivor	Destiny's Child	Columbia	14	(1)	
12	3	Thank You	Dido	Arista	18	(3)	FL
13		Let Me Blow Ya Mind	Eve featuring Gwen Stefani	Ruff Ryders	23	(4)	
14		There You'll Be	Faith Hill	Hollywood/Warner	6	(3)	L
15	11	What Would You Do?	City High	Booga Basement	19	(3)	F
16		Superwoman Pt. II	Lil' Mo featuring Fabolous	Eastwest	8		F
17	12	I'm Like A Bird	Nelly Furtado	Dreamworks	9	(5)	F
18		Drive	Incubus	Immortal/Epic	15	(40)	FL
19	9	Missing You	Case	Def Soul/DJMG	8		L
20		Irresistible	Jessica Simpson	Columbia	6	(11)	L

◆ Mariah Carey, who claimed world-wide record sales of 150 million, signed a multi-million dollar four album deal with EMI/Virgin Records, which included a twenty-million dollar signing on fee (then in January 2002 the record company paid her a reported $28 million to end the deal after just one album).

◆ Madonna was in the midst of her very successful 'Drowned World' tour when her gold disc for 'Music' put her level with the Beatles and second only to Elvis Presley in the Gold disc stakes.

▲ A rare 21st Century occurrence happened in May – the US Top 20 contained two British acts when S Club 7 joined Dido.

UK 2001 JULY-SEPT

◆ The song 'Lady Marmalade' (first recorded with little success in 1975 by US group Eleventh Hour) topped the chart for the second time in just three years – earlier it had been a UK No. 1 by All Saints, and this time after being featured in the film 'Moulin Rouge', it was a transatlantic topper by a quartet of top American divas.

◆ Shortly before they called it a day, boy band Five (who had first been seen in a "Neighbours From Hell" TV show) scored their third and last chart topper with 'Let's Dance'.

◆ Bob The Builder, DJ Otzi, Blue and Atomic Kitten, clocked up No.1s with revivals of previous hits; 'Mambo No. 5' (Lou Bega), 'Hey Baby' (Bruce Channel), 'Too Close' (Next) and 'Eternal Flame' (Bangles), respectively. The last was the first song ever to reach No.1 by two different girl groups.

July 2001

This Mnth	Prev Mnth	Title	Artist	Label	Wks 20	(US Pos)	
1	10	Lady Marmalade	Christina Aguilera, Lil' Kim, Mya & Pink	Interscope/Polydor	8	(1)	
2		Another Chance	Roger Sanchez	Defected	6		FL
3		The Way To Your Love	Hear'say	Polydor	4		
4		U Remind Me	Usher	LaFace	6	(1)	
5		Eternity/The Road To Mandalay	Robbie Williams	Chrysalis	8		
6	2	Angel	Shaggy featuring Rayvon	MCA	9	(1)	
7		Purple Hills/Purple Pills	D12	Shady/Interscope	7	(19	
8		A Little Respect	Wheatus	Columbia	5		L
9		Heaven Is A Halfpipe	OPM	Atlantic	9		F
10	15	There You'll Be	Faith Hill	Warner Brothers	7	(10)	L
11		Perfect Gentleman	Wyclef Jean	Columbia	9		
12		Castles In The Sky	Ian Van Dahl	Nulife	9	(91)	F
13		19/2000	Gorillaz	Parlophone	4		
14		Elevation	U2	Island	2		
15	7	All I Want	Mis-Teeq	Inferno/Telstar	5		
16		Dance For Me	Sisqo	Def Soul	3		L
17	8	Another Day In Paradise	Brandy & Ray J	WEA	5		
18		Pop	'N Sync	Jive	2	(19)	
19		Another Lover	Dane	Arista	2		L
20	1	Do You Really Like It	DJ Pied Piper/Masters of Ceremonies	Relentless/MoS	7		FL

August 2001

1		Eternal Flame	Atomic Kitten	Innocent	6		
2	5	Eternity/The Road To Mandalay	Robbie Williams	Chrysalis	8		
3	12	Castles In The Sky	Ian Van Dahl	Nulife	9	(91)	F
4		Bootylicious	Destiny's Child	Columbia	5	(1)	
5	11	Perfect Gentleman	Wyclef Jean	Columbia	9		
6		21 Seconds	So Solid Crew	Relentless	6		F
7	7	Purple Hills/Purple Pills	D12	Shady/Interscope	7	(19)	
8	9	Heaven Is A Halfpipe	OPM	Atlantic	9		F
9		All Or Nothing	O-Town	J	3	(3)	
10		Ain't It Funny	Jennifer Lopez	Epic	4	(1)	
11		Let's Dance	Five	RCA	6		
12		Take Me Home (A Girl Like Me)	Sophie Ellis-Bextor	Polydor	6		F
13		Let Me Blow Ya Mind	Eve featuring Gwen Stefani	Interscope/Polydor	7	(3)	
14		Little L	Jamiroquai	Sony S2	4		
15		Ante Up	M.O.P. featuring Busta Rhymes	Epic	2		L
16		Scream If You Wanna Go Faster	Geri Halliwell	EMI	2		
17		Fire Wire	Cosmic Gate	Data	2		FL
18	1	Lady Marmalade	Christina Aguilera, Lil' Kim, Mya & Pink	Interscope/Polydor	8	(1)	
19		Crystal	New Order	London	1		
20		Drops Of Jupiter (Tell Me)	Train	Columbia	4	(5)	FL

September 2001

1	11	Let's Dance	Five	RCA	6		
2		Too Close	Blue	Innocent	5		
3		Mambo No. 5	Bob The Builder	BBC Music	6		L
4		Follow Me	Uncle Kracker	Atlantic	9	(5)	f
5	6	21 Seconds	So Solid Crew	Relentless	6		F
6		Starlight	Supermen Lovers	Independiente	6		fl
7	12	Take Me Home (A Girl Like Me)	Sophie Ellis-Bextor	Polydor	6		F
8	13	Let Me Blow Ya Mind	Eve featuring Gwen Stefani	Interscope/Polydor	7	(3)	
9		Hey Baby (Uhh, Ahh)	DJ Otzi	EMI	16		F
10		Turn Off The Light	Nelly Furtado	Dreamworks	5	(5)	
11		Stuck In The Middle With You	Louise	1st Avenue/EMI	4		L
12		Can't Get You Out Of My Head	Kylie Minogue	Parlophone	13	(7)	G
13		Set You Free (Remix)	N-Trance	All Around The World	4		
14		Smooth Criminal	Alien Ant Farm	Dreamworks/Polydor	7	(23)	F
15		Baby Come On Over	Samantha Mumba	Wild Card/Polydor	3		
16		Take My Breath Away	Emma Bunton	Virgin	2		
17		Twentyfourseven	Artful Dodger Featuring Melanie Blatt	ffrr/Public Demand	3		
18		Hide U	Kosheen	Arista	2		F
19	14	Little L	Jamiroquai	Sony S2	4		
20		Luv Me Luv Me	Shaggy	MCA	4	(76)	

US 2001 JULY-SEPT

July 2001

This Mnth	Prev Mnth	Title	Artist	Label	Wks 20	(UK Pos)	
1		U Remind Me	Usher	Arista	18	(3)	
2	2	Hanging By A Moment	Lifehouse	Dreamworks	32	(25)	FL
3	13	Let Me Blow Ya Mind	Eve featuring Gwen Stefani	Ruff Ryders	23	(4)	
4	1	Lady Marmalade	Christina Aguilera, Lil'Kim, Mya & Pink	Interscope	14	(1)	
5	10	Peaches & Cream	112	Bad Boy/Arista	20	(32)	L
6		Hit 'em Up Style (Oops!)	Blu Cantrell	Redzone/Arista	18	(12)	FL
7	8	Drops Of Jupiter (Tell Me)	Train	Columbia	25	(10)	L
8		All Or Nothing	O-Town	J	11	(4)	L
9		Bootylicious	Destiny's Child	Columbia	9	(2)	
10	9	Get Ur Freak On	Missy 'Misdemeanor' Elliott	Gold Mind/Eastwest	14	(4)	
11	3	Ride Wit Me	Nelly featuring City Spud	Fo' Reel/Universal	16	(3)	
12	18	Drive	Incubus	Immortal/Epic	15	(40)	FL
13	15	What Would You Do?	City High	Booga Basement	19	(3)	F
14	5	My Baby	Lil' Romeo	Soulja/No Limit	7	(67)	FL
15	7	Fiesta	R. Kelly featuring Jay-Z	Jive	9	(23)	
16	16	Superwoman Pt. II	Lil' Mo featuring Fabolous	Eastwest	8		F
17		Where The Party At	Jagged Edge With Nelly	So So Def	18	(25)	L
18	6	Follow Me	Uncle Kracker	Top Dog/Lava	13	(3)	F
19		It's Been Awhile	Staind	Flip/Elektra	22	(15)	FL
20	14	There You'll Be	Faith Hill	Hollywood/Warner	6	(3)	L

August 2001

This Mnth	Prev Mnth	Title	Artist	Label	Wks 20	(UK Pos)	
1	3	Let Me Blow Ya Mind	Eve Featuring Gwen Stefani	Ruff Ryders	23	(4)	
2		Fallin'	Alicia Keys	J	23	(3)	F
3	9	Bootylicious	Destiny's Child	Columbia	9	(2)	
4	6	Hit 'em Up Style (Oops!)	Blu Cantrell	Redzone/Arista 1	8	(12)	FL
5		I'm Real	Jennifer Lopez featuring Ja Rule	Epic	23	(4)	F
6	1	U Remind Me	Usher	Arista	18	(3)	
7		Loverboy	Mariah Carey featuring Cameo	Virgin	3	(12)	L
8	8	All Or Nothing	O-Town	J	11	(4)	L
9	17	Where The Party At	Jagged Edge with Nelly	So So Def	8	(25)	L
10	7	Drops Of Jupiter (Tell Me)	Train	Columbia	25	(10)	L
11	2	Hanging By A Moment	Lifehouse	Dreamworks	32	(25)	FL
12	19	It's Been Awhile	Staind	Flip/Elektra	22	(15)	FL
13	5	Peaches & Cream	112	Bad Boy/Arista	20	(32)	L
14		Someone To Call My Lover	Janet	Virgin	13	(11)	L
15		When It's Over	Sugar Ray	Lava/Atlantic	10	(32)	L
16	12	Drive	Incubus	Immortal/Epic	15	(40)	FL
17	13	What Would You Do?	City High	Booga Basement	19	(3)	F
18		Fill Me In	Craig David	Wildstar/Atlantic	20	(1)	F
19		Izzo (H.O.V.A.)	Jay-Z	Roc-A-Fella	11	(21)	
20		Purple Hills	D12	Shady/Interscope	4	(2)	FL

September 2001

This Mnth	Prev Mnth	Title	Artist	Label	Wks 20	(UK Pos)	
1	5	I'm Real	Jennifer Lopez featuring Ja Rule	Epic	23	(4)	F
2	2	Fallin'	Alicia Keys	J	23	(3)	F
3	9	Where The Party At	Jagged Edge with Nelly	So So Def	18	(25)	L
4	14	Someone To Call My Lover	Janet	Virgin	13 (	11)	L
5	4	Hit 'em Up Style (Oops!)	Blu Cantrell	Redzone/Arista	18	(12)	FL
6	6	U Remind Me	Usher	Arista	18	(3)	
7	1	Let Me Blow Ya Mind	Eve featuring Gwen Stefani	Ruff Ryders	23 (	4)	
8	12	It's Been Awhile	Staind	Flip/Elektra	22	(15)	FL
9	10	Drops Of Jupiter (Tell Me)	Train	Columbia	25 (	10)	L
10	11	Hanging By A Moment	Lifehouse	Dreamworks	32	(25)	FL
11		Family Affair	Mary J. Blige	MCA	23	(8)	
12	19	Izzo (H.O.V.A.)	Jay-Z	Roc-A-Fella	11	(21)	
13	13	Peaches & Cream	112	Bad Boy/Arista	20	(32)	L
14		You Rock My World	Michael Jackson	Epic	5	(2)	
15	8	All Or Nothing	O-Town	J	11	(4)	L
16	15	When It's Over	Sugar Ray	Lava/Atlantic	10	(32)	L
17		One Minute Man	Missy 'Misdemeanor' Elliott	Gold Mind	7	(10)	
18		Because I Got High	Afroman	Universal	4	(1)	FL
19		Differences	Ginuwine	Epic	20		L
20	18	Fill Me In	Craig David	Wildstar/Atlantic	20	(1)	F

◆ Napster, the internet downloading outfit which had revolutionized the way that people accessed music was closed down. However, it did not halt the amount of records being downloaded free of charge and the decline in singles sales. On the subject of singles, Sony Records head (and ex-Mr. Mariah Carey) Tommy Mottolo said 'We try not to put singles out – we may release 12 a year'.

◆ 22-year-old R&B vocalist-turned-actress Aaliyah died in a plane crash in the Bahamas after filming the video for 'Rock The Boat'. Her current self-titled album jumped from 19 to 1 on the chart – making her the first posthumous No. 1 artist since John Lennon.

◆ Hottest new act on the charts was Alicia Keys who not only topped the singles chart with 'Fallin'' but also headed the albums with her debut release 'Songs In A Minor'.

UK 2001 OCT-DEC

◆ Hottest album of the quarter was Robbie Williams' collection of big band favourites, 'Swing When You're Winning', which sold 1.5 million in the UK alone in six weeks. It included his chart topping update of Frank & Nancy Sinatra's 'Somethin' Stupid'.

◆ The most publicised chart battle of the year was won by Westlife when their 'World Of Our Own' beat Madonna's hits compilation 'GHV2' album to the top.

▲ As their 15th successive Top 10 single, 'Words Are Not Enough', charted Steps announced that they were disbanding. The five-piece had sold over four million singles and 3.5 million albums in the United Kingdom.

October 2001

This Mnth	Prev Mnth	Title	Artist	Label	Wks 20	(US Pos)	
1	12	Can't Get You Out Of My Head	Kylie Minogue	Parlophone	13	(7)	G
2		Hey Baby (Uhh, Ahh)	DJ Otzi	EMI	16		F
3		Chain Reaction/One For Sorrow	Steps	Ebul/Jive	5		
4		What Would You Do?	City High	Interscope/Polydor	9	(8)	F
5	14	Smooth Criminal	Alien Ant Farm	Dreamworks/ Polydor	7	(23)	F
6		You Rock My World	Michael Jackson	Epic	4	(10)	L
7		Thinking It Over	Liberty	V2	4		F
8		Because I Got High	Afroman	Universal	10	(13)	F
9		Family Affair	Mary J. Blige	MCA	8	(1)	
10		U Got It Bad	Usher	LaFace	4	(1)	
11		3 Mambo No. 5	Bob The Builder	BBC Music	6		L
12		I'm A Slave 4 U	Britney Spears	Jive	4	(27)	
13		Sven Sven Sven	Bell & Spurling	Eternal	3		FL
14		One Night Stand	Mis-Teeq	Inferno/Telstar	5		
15		Flawless	Ones	Positiva	3		FL
16		Follow Me	Uncle Kracker	Atlantic	9	(5)	FL
17		Fat Lip	Sum 41	Mercury	3	(66)	F
18		In The End	Linkin Park	Warner Brothers	3	(2)	
19		I Want Love	Elton John	Rocket/Mercury	3		
20		Luv Me Luv Me	Shaggy	MCA	4		

November 2001

This Mnth	Prev Mnth	Title	Artist	Label	Wks 20	(US Pos)	
1	8	Because I Got High	Afroman	Universal	10	(13)	F
2	2	Hey Baby (Uhh, Ahh)	DJ Otzi	EMI	16		F
3	1	Can't Get You Out Of My Head	Kylie Minogue	Parlophone	13	(7)	G
4		Rapture	Iio	Made/Data/MoS	5		FL
5		Fallin'	Alicia Keys	J	6	(1)	F
6		Queen Of My Heart	Westlife	RCA	5		
7		I'm Real	Jennifer Lopez featuring Ja Rule	Epic	5	(1)	
8	4	What Would You Do?	City High	Interscope/Polydor	9	(8)	F
9		Closer To Me	Five	RCA	3		L
10		They Don't Know	So Solid Crew	Relentless	3		
11		If You Come Back	Blue	Innocent	4		
12		Bohemian Like You	Dandy Warhols	Parlophone/Capitol	3		L
13	14	One Night Stand	Mis-Teeq	Inferno/Telstar	5		
14		Emotion	Destiny's Child	Columbia	3	(10)	L
15		What's Going On	Artists Against Aids Worldwide	Columbia	2	(27)	FL
16	12	I'm A Slave 4 U	Britney Spears	Jive	4	(27)	
17		(I Wish I Knew…) Free – One	Lighthouse Family	Wild Card/Polydor	2		L
18		Ugly	Bubba Sparxxx	Interscope/Polydor	2	(15)	FL
19	6	You Rock My World	Michael Jackson	Epic	4	(10)	L
20		The Music's No Good Without You	Cher	WEA	2		L

December 2001

This Mnth	Prev Mnth	Title	Artist	Label	Wks 20	(US Pos)	
1		Have You Ever	S Club 7	Polydor	7		
2		Gotta Get Thru This	Daniel Bedingfield	Relentless	11	(10)	F
3		Murder On The Dancefloor	Sophie Ellis-Bextor	Polydor	10		
4		Resurrection	PPK	Perfecto	7		FL
5		Who Do You Love Now (Stringer)	Riva featuring Dannii Minogue	ffrr	7		FL
6		Somethin' Stupid	Robbie Williams & Nicole Kidman	Chrysalis	5		
7		Handbags And Gladrags	Stereophonics	V2	9		
8	2	Hey Baby (Uhh, Ahh)	DJ Otzi	EMI	16		F
8	11	If You Come Back	Blue	Innocent	4		
9		What If	Kate Winslet	EMI/Liberty	8		FL
10	6	Queen Of My Heart	Westlife	RCA	5		
11		Everybody	Hear'say	Polydor	4		
12		How Wonderful You Are	Gordon Haskell	Flying Sparks	3		FL
13		Will I	Ian Van Dahl	Nulife	6		
14		Words Are Not Enough/ I Know Him	Steps	Ebul/Jive	5		L
15		Country Roads	Hermes House Band	EMI/Liberty	6		FL
16	5	Fallin'	Alicia Keys	J	6	(1)	F
17		Lately	Samantha Mumba	Wild Card/Polydor	6		
18	I	Believe In Christmas	Tweenies	BBC Music	4		
19		Walk On	U2	Island	1		
20		Because I Got High	Afroman	Universal	10	(13)	F

October 2001

This Mnth	Prev Mnth	Title	Artist	Label	Wks 20	(UK Pos)	
1	2	Fallin'	Alicia Keys	J	23	(3)	F
2	1	I'm Real	Jennifer Lopez feat. Ja Rule	Epic	23	(4)	F
3	11	Family Affair	Mary J. Blige	MCA	23	(8)	
4	3	Where The Party At	Jagged Edge with Nelly	So So Def	18	(25)	L
5	5	Hit 'em Up Style (Oops!)	Blu Cantrell	Redzone/Arista	18 (	12)	FL
6	8	It's Been Awhile	Staind	Flip/Elektra	22	(15)	FL
7	19	Differences	Ginuwine	Epic	20		
8	6	U Remind Me	Usher	Arista	18	(3)	
9	12	Izzo (H.O.V.A.)	Jay-Z	Roc-A-Fella	11	(21)	
10	7	Let Me Blow Ya Mind	Eve featuring Gwen Stefani	Ruff Ryders	23	(4)	
11		The Star Spangled Banner	Whitney Houston	Arista	3		L
12		Hero	Enrique Iglesias	Interscope	19	(1)	
13	10	Hanging By A Moment	Lifehouse	Dreamworks	32	(25)	FL
14		Turn Off The Light	Nelly Furtado	Dreamworks	15	(4)	L
15	4	Someone To Call My Lover	Janet	Virgin	13	(11)	L
16		Livin' It Up	Ja Rule featuring Case	Murder Inc/Def Jam	18	(27)	L
17	9	Drops Of Jupiter (Tell Me)	Train	Columbia	25	(10)	L
18	14	You Rock My World	Michael Jackson	Epic	5	(2)	
19		Only Time	Enya	Reprise/Warner	14	(32)	FL
20	20	Fill Me In	Craig David	Wildstar/Atlanic	20	(1)	F

November 2001

This Mnth	Prev Mnth	Title	Artist	Label	Wks 20	(UK Pos)	
1	3	Family Affair	Mary J. Blige	MCA	23	(8)	
2	3	I'm Real	Jennifer Lopez featuring Ja Rule	Epic	23	(4)	F
3	12	Hero	Enrique Iglesias	Interscope	19	(1)	
4		U Got It Bad	Usher	Arista	23	(5)	
5	1	Fallin'	Alicia Keys	J	23	(3)	F
6	7	Differences	Ginuwine	Epic	20		L
7	14	Turn Off The Light	Nelly Furtado	Dreamworks	15	(4)	L
8		How You Remind Me	Nickelback	Roadrunner	29	(4)	FL
9	16	Livin' It Up	Ja Rule featuring Case	Murder Inc/Def Jam	18	(27)	L
10	6	It's Been Awhile	Staind	Flip/Elektra	22	(15)	FL
11	19	Only Time	Enya	Reprise/Warner	14	(32)	FL
12	4	Where The Party At	Jagged Edge with Nelly	So So Def	18	(25)	L
13		Everywhere	Michelle Branch	Maverick	7	(18)	F
14		Emotion	Destiny's Child	Columbia	6	(3)	L
15		Gone	'N Sync	Jive	12	(24)	
16	5	Hit 'em Up Style (Oops!)	Blu Cantrell	Redzone/Arista	18	(12)	FL
17		Rock The Boat	Aaliyah	Blackground	12	(12)	
18		Ugly	Bubba Sparxxx	Beat Club	5	(7)	FL
19	9	Izzo (H.O.V.A.)	Jay-Z	Roc-A-Fella	11	(21)	
20		Fill Me In	Craig David	Wildstar/Atlantic	20	(1)	F

December 2001

This Mnth	Prev Mnth	Title	Artist	Label	Wks 20	(UK Pos)	
1	4	U Got It Bad	Usher	Arista	23	(5)	
2	1	Family Affair	Mary J. Blige	MCA	23	(8)	
3	8	How You Remind Me	Nickelback	Roadrunner	29	(4)	FL
4	3	Hero	Enrique Iglesias	Interscope	19	(1)	
5		Get The Party Started	Pink	Arista	16	(2)	
6	7	Turn Off The Light	Nelly Furtado	Dreamworks	15	(4)	L
7	6	Differences	Ginuwine	Epic	20		
8	9	Livin' It Up	Ja Rule featuring Case	Murder Inc/Def Jam	18	(27)	L
9	2	I'm Real	Jennifer Lopez featuring Ja Rule	Epic	23	(4)	F
10		Whenever, Wherever	Shakira	Epic	14	(2)	F
11		Always On Time	Ja Rule featuring Ashanti	Murder Inc/Def Jam	20	(6)	F
12	15	Gone	'N Sync	Jive	12	(24)	
13		My Sacrifice	Creed	Wind-Up	18	(18)	
14	5	Fallin'	Alicia Keys	J	23	(3)	F
15	14	Emotion	Destiny's Child	Columbia	6	(3)	L
16	11	Only Time	Enya	Reprise/Warner	14	(32)	FL
17		A Woman's Worth	Alicia Keys	J	12	(18)	L
18		Superman (It's Not Easy)	Five For Fighting	Aware/Columbia	9	(48)	FL
19	17	Rock The Boat	Aaliyah	Blackground	12	(12)	
20		Do!!	Toya	Arista	7		FL

◆ Paul McCartney hosted a September 11th benefit show at New York's Madison Square Gardens. Acts appearing included Billy Joel, Bon Jovi, John Mellencamp, Destiny's Child, James Taylor and Janet Jackson, plus fellow Brits David Bowie, Eric Clapton, Elton John, The Who and Mick and Keith from the Stones. They raised over $12 million.

◆ Most heard singles after the 9-11 tragedy were ''Hero'' by Enrique Iglesias, 'Only Time' by Enya and Whitney's Houston's re-issued ''Star Spangled Banner''.

◆ No. 1 albums included 'God Bless America', with patriotic old tracks from such as Bob Dylan, Pete Seeger, Frank Sinatra and Mahalia Jackson.

◆ The telethon 'A Tribute To Heroes', which included Bruce Springsteen, Billy Joel, Celine Dion, Mariah Carey and Alicia Keys, raised $150 million - $1 million of which was donated by the rap legend Dr. Dre.

UK 2002 JAN-MAR

◆ Pop Idol proved to be the most successful TV pop music talent show of all time. At a time when sales were low, the winner, Will Young (who received over four million votes), smashed all records when his debut disc 'Evergreen'/'Anything Is Possible' sold a staggering 385,000 on its first day, and over 1.1 million in the first week.

◆ Irish boy band Westlife had the best chart start of any act. Their 'World Of Our Own' gave them their 10th No.1 from 11 releases. The Beatles were the only other group to have so many chart toppers and it took them a year longer to achieve them.

◆ The year started with posthumous No.1 for Aaliyah (who died in August 2001) and George Harrison (who died in December). The latter becoming the first solo artist to top the singles chart on two different occasions with the same record, 'My Sweet Lord'.

January 2002

This Mnth	Prev Mnth	Title	Artist	Label	Wks 20	(US Pos)	
1	2	Gotta Get Thru This	Daniel Bedingfield	Relentless	11	(10)	F
2	3	Murder On The Dancefloor	Sophie Ellis-Bextor	Polydor	10		
3	6	Somethin' Stupid	Robbie Williams & Nicole Kidman	Chrysalis	5		
4		More Than A Woman	Aaliyah	Blackground/Virgin	5	(25)	
5	7	Handbags And Gladrags	Stereophonics	V2	9		
6		Addicted To Bass	Puretone	Gusto	8		FL
7		My Sweet Lord	George Harrison	Parlophone	4		L
8	12	How Wonderful You Are	Gordon Haskell	Flying Sparks	3		FL
9	13	Will I	Ian Van Dahl	Nulife	6		
10	17	Lately	Samantha Mumba	Wild Card/Polydor	6		
11		Bad Intentions	Dr. Dre featuring Knoc-Turn'al	Interscope	2		L
12		Get The Party Started	Pink	LaFace/Arista	9	(4)	
13		The Whistle Song (Blow My Whistle Bitch)	DJ Aligator Project	All Around The World	5		FL
14		AM To PM	Christina Milian	Def Soul	6	(27)	FL
15		Drowning	Backstreet Boys	Jive	2	(28)	L
16	9	What If	Kate Winslet	EMI/Liberty	8		FL
17		It's Love (Trippin')	Goldtrix Presents Andrea Brown	AM:PM/Serious/ Evolve	5		FL
18	1	Have You Ever	S Club 7	Polydor	7		
19	20	Because I Got High	Afroman	Universal	10	(13)	F
20		Haters	So Solid Crew Presents Mr Shabz	Relentless	2		

February 2002

1		Hero	Enrique	Interscope	11	(3)	
2	12	Get The Party Started	Pink	La Face/Arista	9	(4)	
3		Caught In The Middle	a1	Columbia	4		
4	6	Addicted To Bass	Puretone	Gusto	8		FL
5		Overprotected	Britney Spears	Jive	5	(86)	
6		Always On Time	Ja Rule featuring Ashanti	Def Jam	6	(1)	F
7		Hey Baby	No Doubt	Interscope	3	(5)	
8	7	My Sweet Lord	George Harrison	Parlophone	4		L
9		True Love Never Dies	Flip & Fill featuring Kelly Llorenna	All Around The World	4		F
10		You	S Club 7	Polydor	4		
11		Point Of View	DB Boulevard	Illustrious	5		FL
12		Movies	Alien Ant Farm	Dreamworks/Polydor	3		L
13	14	AM To PM	Christina Milian	Def Soul	6	(27)	F
14		What About Us?	Brandy	Atlantic	3	(7)	
15	1	Think I Love You	Kaci	Curb/London	4		L
16		A Mind Of Its Own	Victoria Beckham	Virgin	2		L
17		So Lonely	Jakatta	Rulin	2		
18	1	Gotta Get Thru This	Daniel Bedingfield	Relentless	11	(10)	F
19		Crazy Rap	Afroman	Universal	3		L
20		Moi...Lolita	Alizee	Polydor	2		FL

March 2002

1		Evergreen/Anything Is Possible	Will Young	S	9		FG
2	1	Hero	Enrique	Interscope	11	(3)	
3		Whenever, Wherever	Shakira	Epic	12	(6)	F
4		World Of Our Own	Westlife	S/RCA	4		
5		How You Remind Me	Nickelback	Roadrunner	13	(1)	F
6		Something	Lasgo	Positiva	9	(35)	F
7		The World's Greatest	R. Kelly	Jive	6	(34)	
8		Me Julie	Ali G & Shaggy	Island	8		FL
9		In Your Eyes	Kylie Minogue	Parlophone	3		
10		Unchained Melody	Gareth Gates	S	8		FG
11		Ain't It Funny (Remix)	Jennifer Lopez featuring Ja Rule	Epic	7	(1)	
12		B With Me	Mis-Teeq	Inferno/Telstar	3		
13		I Will Always Love You	Rik Waller	EMI/Liberty	3		FL
14	11	Point Of View	DB Boulevard	Illustrious	5		FL
15	10	You	S Club 7	Polydor	4		
16		Tainted Love	Marilyn Manson	Maverick/ Warner Bros	4		L
17	2	Get The Party Started	Pink	La Face/Arista	9	(4)	
18		A New Day Has Come	Celine Dion	Epic	4	(22)	
19		Fly By II	Blue	Innocent	5		
20		Caramel	City High featuring Eve	Interscope/Polydor	3	(19)	L

This Mnth	Prev Mnth	Title	Artist	Label	Wks 20	(UK Pos)	
1	3	How You Remind Me	Nickelback	Roadrunner	29	(4)	FL
2	1	U Got It Bad	Usher	Arista	23	(5)	
3	2	Family Affair	Mary J. Blige	MCA	23	(8)	
4	11	Always On Time	Ja Rule featuring Ashanti	Murder Inc/Def Jam	20	(6)	F
5	5	Get The Party Started	Pink	Arista	16	(2)	
6	13	My Sacrifice	Creed	Wind-Up	18	(18)	
7	4	Hero	Enrique Iglesias	Interscope	19	(1)	
8	10	Whenever, Wherever	Shakira	Epic	14	(2)	F
9	17	A Woman's Worth	Alicia Keys	J	12	(18)	L
10	7	Differences	Ginuwine	Epic	20		L
11		Wherever You Will Go	Calling	RCA	21	(3)	FL
12		In The End	Linkin Park	Warner Bros.	21	(8)	FL
13	8	Livin' It Up	Ja Rule featuring Case	Murder Inc/Def Jam	18	(27)	L
14	12	Gone	'N Sync	Jive	12	(24)	
15		Hey Baby	No Doubt featuring Bounty Killer	Interscope	12	(2)	
16		Butterflies	Michael Jackson	Epic	7		L
17	19	Rock The Boat	Aaliyah	Blackground	12	(12)	
18	18	Superman (It's Not Easy)	Five For Fighting	Aware/Columbia	9	(48)	FL
19		We Thuggin'	Fat Joe featuring R. Kelly	Terror Squad	3	(48)	F
20	6	Turn Off The Light	Nelly Furtado	Dreamworks	15	(4)	L

This Mnth	Prev Mnth	Title	Artist	Label	Wks 20	(UK Pos)	
1	2	U Got It Bad	Usher	Arista	23	(5)	
2	4	Always On Time	Ja Rule featuring Ashanti	Murder Inc/Def Jam	20	(6)	F
3	1	How You Remind Me	Nickelback	Roadrunner	29	(4)	FL
4	6	My Sacrifice	Creed	Wind-Up	18	(18)	
5	12	In The End	Linkin Park	Warner Bros.	21	(8)	FL
6	5	Get The Party Started	Pink	Arista	16	(2)	
7		Ain't It Funny (Remix)	Jennifer Lopez featuring Ja Rule	Epic	18	(4)	L
8	15	Hey Baby	No Doubt featuring Bounty Killer	Interscope	12	(2)	F
9	11	Wherever You Will Go	Calling	RCA	21	(3)	FL
10	9	A Woman's Worth	Alicia Keys	J	12	(18)	L
11	8	Whenever, Wherever	Shakira	Epic	14	(2)	F
12		What About Us?	Brandy	Atlantic	10	(4)	
13	3	Family Affair	Mary J. Blige	MCA	23	(8)	
14		7 Days	Craig David	Wildstar/Atlantic	9	(1)	L
15	7	Hero	Enrique Iglesias	Interscope	19	(1)	
16	16	Butterflies	Michael Jackson	Epic	7		L
17		Can't Fight The Moonlight	LeAnn Rimes	Curb	10	(1)	L
18		No More Drama	Mary J. Blige	MCA	4	(9)	
19	10	Differences	Ginuwine	Epic	20		L
20		Can't Get You Out Of My Head	Kylie Minogue	Capitol	11	(1)	L

This Mnth	Prev Mnth	Title	Artist	Label	Wks 20	(UK Pos)	
1	7	Ain't It Funny (Remix)	Jennifer Lopez featuring Ja Rule	Epic	18	(4)	L
2	2	Always On Time	Ja Rule featuring Ashanti	Murder Inc/Def Jam	20	(6)	F
3	3	How You Remind Me	Nickelback	Roadrunner	29	(4)	FL
4	5	In The End	Linkin Park	Warner Bros.	21	(8)	FL
5	9	Wherever You Will Go	Calling	RCA	21	(3)	FL
6	8	Hey Baby	No Doubt featuring Bounty Killer	Interscope	12	(2)	
7		Blurry	Puddle Of Mudd	Flawless/Geffen	20	(8)	F
8	12	What About Us?	Brandy	Atlantic	10	(4)	
9	1	U Got It Bad	Usher	Arista	23	(5)	
10	20	Can't Get You Out Of My Head	Kylie Minogue	Capitol	11	(1)	L
11		What's Luv?	Fat Joe featuring Ashanti	Terror Squad	20	(4)	L
12	4	My Sacrifice	Creed	Wind-Up	18	(18)	
13		Girlfriend	'N Sync Featuring Nelly	Jive	11	(2)	L
14		Oops (Oh My)	Tweet	Gold Mind	13	(5)	FL
15	17	Can't Fight The Moonlight	LeAnn Rimes	Curb	10	(1)	L
16		Foolish	Ashanti	Murder Inc/Def Jam	22	(4)	
17	14	7 Days	Craig David	Wildstar/Atlantic	9	(1)	L
18		U Don't Have To Call	Usher	Arista	16		
19		Lights, Camera, Action!	Mr. Cheeks	Universal	5		F
20	6	Get The Party Started	Pink	Arista	16	(2)	

US 2002
JAN-MAR

◆ American music continued to ride high internationally with almost every US Top 20 entry repeating that feat in the UK. Craig David and Kylie Minogue were the only artists recording in the UK to reach the top end of the US charts – with the latter enjoying her first major American hit since 1988.

▲ Newcomer Ashanti saw her first three singles simultaneously in the Top 10 – a feat not achieved since the Beatles in 1964. And Ja Rule became one of a handful of acts to replace themselves at the No.1 slot.

◆ The acclaimed Grammy winning bluegrass soundtrack album 'O Brother Where Art Thou' was 63 weeks in the chart before reaching No.1.

UK 2002 APR-JUNE

▲ Pop Idol winner Will's follow-up, a revival of 'Light My Fire', sold just under 200,000 in its first week, while runner–up, Gareth Gates, sold over 850,000 copies of 'Unchained Melody' in seven days. It was the fourth time the latter song had headed the UK chart and made 17 year-old Gareth the youngest UK male to reach No. 1.

◆ PopStars winners Hear'say recruited a new member after Kym Marsh left, and runners up Liberty had the first of several big hits under their new name, Liberty X, with 'Just A Little'.

◆ The all-star 'Party at The Palace', which celebrated the Queen's Golden Jubilee, was watched by 12.3 million television viewers.

April 2002

This Mnth	Prev Mnth	Title	Artist	Label	Wks 20	(US Pos)	
1	10	Unchained Melody	Gareth Gates	S	8		FG
2	3	Whenever, Wherever	Shakira	Epic	12	(6)	F
3	8	Me Julie	Ali G & Shaggy	Island	8		FL
4	5	How You Remind Me	Nickelback	Roadrunner	13	(1)	F
5		I'm Not A Girl, Not Yet A Woman	Britney Spears	Jive	5		
6	4	My People	Missy 'Misdemeanor' Elliott	Goldmind/Elektra	7		
7		Lazy	X-Press 2 featuring David Byrne	Skint	6		FL
8		Evergreen/Anything Is Possible	Will Young	S	9		FG
9		The Hindu Times	Oasis	Big Brother	3		
10		Girlfriend	'N Sync featuring Nelly	Jive	5	(5)	L
11		There Goes The Fear	Doves	Heavenly	1		FL
12		Shake Ur Body	Shy FX & T-Power featuring Di	Positiva	4		F
13	19	Fly By II	Blue	Innocent	5		
14	6	Something	Lasgo	Positiva	9	(35)	F
15	16	Tainted Love	Marilyn Manson	Maverick /Warner Bros	4		L
16		One Step Too Far	Faithless featuring Dido	Cheeky/Arista	1		L
17		Insatiable	Darren Hayes	Columbia	8		F
18		It's Goin' Down	X-Ecutioners featuring Mike Shinoda	Epic	1		FL
19		My Culture	1 Giant Leap	Palm Pictures	3		FL
20		Beautiful	Matt Darey featuring Marcella Woods	Incentive	2		L

May 2002

This Mnth	Prev Mnth	Title	Artist	Label	Wks 20	(US Pos)	
1		One Step Closer	S Club Juniors	Polydor	7		F
2		Freak Like Me	Sugababes	Island	5		
3		Kiss Kiss	Holly Valance	London	8		F
4	10	Girlfriend	'N Sync featuring Nelly	Jive	5	(5)	L
5		If Tomorrow Never Comes	Ronan Keating	Polydor	10		
6	4	How You Remind Me	Nickelback	Roadrunner	13	(1)	F
7	2	Whenever, Wherever	Shakira	Epic	12	(6)	F
8		Just A Little	Liberty X	V2	11		
9		DJ	H & Claire	WEA	2		F
10		Oops (Oh My)	Tweet	Elektra	3	(7)	FL
11	9	The Hindu Times	Oasis	Big Brother	3		
12		Follow Da Leader	Nigel & Marvin	Relentless	4		FL
13		Escape	Enrique	Interscope	7		
14	7	Lazy	X-Press 2 featuring David Byrne	Skint	6	(12)	FL
15		What's Luv?	Fat Joe Featuring Ashanti	Atlantic	4	(2)	L
16		At Night	Shakedown	Defected	3		FL
17	1	Unchained Melody	Gareth Gates	S	8		FG
18		Don't Let Me Get Me	Pink	Arista	4	(8)	
19	6	4 My People	Missy 'Misdemeanor' Elliott	Goldmind/Elektra	7		
20		No More Drama	Mary J. Blige	MCA	2	(15)	

June 2002

This Mnth	Prev Mnth	Title	Artist	Label	Wks 20	(US Pos)	
1		Without Me	Eminem	Interscope	11	(2)	
2	8	Just A Little	Liberty X	V2	11		
3		Light My Fire	Will Young	S	5		
4		If Tomorrow Never Comes	Ronan Keating	Polydor	10		
5	5	It's OK!	Atomic Kitten	Innocent	6		
6		We're On The Ball	Ant And Dec	Columbia	4		L
7		A Little Less Conversation	Elvis Vs JXL	RCA	7	(50)	L
8		Love At First Sight	Kylie Minogue	Parlophone	3	(23)	
9	13	Escape	Enrique	Interscope	7	(12)	
10		Get Over You/ Move This Mountain	Sophie Ellis-Bextor	Polydor	4		
11		Hero	Chad Kroeger featuring Josey Scott	Roadrunner	8	(3)	FL
12		Stop Crying Your Heart Out	Oasis	Big Brother	3		
13		The Logical Song	Scooter	Sheffield Tunes	10		
14		When You Look At Me	Christina Milian	Def Soul	6		
15	3	Kiss Kiss	Holly Valance	London	8		F
16		Bop Bop Baby	Westlife	S	2		
17		Hot In Herre	Nelly	Universal	9	(1)	
18	15	What's Luv?	Fat Joe featuring Ashanti	Atlantic	4	(2)	L
19		It Takes More	Ms Dynamite	Polydor	3		F
20		Be Cool	Paffendorf	Data	2		FL

April 2002

This Mnth	Prev Mnth	Title	Artist	Label	Wks 20	(UK Pos)	
1	1	Ain't It Funny (Remix)	Jennifer Lopez featuring Ja Rule	Epic	18	(4)	L
2	16	Foolish	Ashanti	Murder Inc/Def Jam	22	(4)	F
3	11	What's Luv?	Fat Joe featuring Ashanti	Terror Squad	20	(4)	L
4	4	In The End	Linkin Park	Warner Bros.	21	(8)	FL
5	18	U Don't Have To Call	Usher	Arista	16		L
6	13	Girlfriend	'N Sync featuring Nelly	Jive	11	(2)	L
7	7	Blurry	Puddle Of Mudd	Flawless/Geffen	20	(8)	F
8	3	How You Remind Me	Nickelback	Roadrunner	29	(4)	FL
9	14	Oops (Oh My)	Tweet	Gold Mind	13	(5)	FL
10		I Need A Girl (Part 1)	P.Diddy feat.Usher & Loon Bad Boy	Arista	15	(4)	
11		A Thousand Miles	Vanessa Carlton	A&M	26	(6)	FL
12	5	Wherever You Will Go	Calling	RCA	21	(3)	FL
13	2	Always On Time	Ja Rule featuring Ashanti	Murder Inc/Def Jam	20	(6)	F
14		Don't Let Me Get Me	Pink	Arista	11	(6)	
15	10	Can't Get You Out Of My Head	Kylie Minogue	Capitol	11	(1)	L
16		Escape	Enrique Iglesias	Interscope	7	(3)	L
17		I Love You	Faith Evans	Bad Boy/Arista	8		L
18	8	What About Us?	Brandy	Atlantic	10	(4)	
19		All You Wanted	Michelle Branch	Maverick	16	(33)	L
20		Pass The Courvoisier Part II	Busta Rhymes featuring P.Diddy	J	8	(16)	

May 2002

This Mnth	Prev Mnth	Title	Artist	Label	Wks 20	(UK Pos)	
1	2	Foolish	Ashanti	Murder Inc/Def Jam	22	(4)	F
2	3	What's Luv?	Fat Joe featuring Ashanti	Terror Squad	20	(4)	L
3	10	I Need A Girl (Part 1)	P.Diddy feat.Usher & Loon Bad Boy	Arista	15	(4)	
4	5	U Don't Have To Call	Usher	Arista	16		
5	7	Blurry	Puddle Of Mudd	Flawless/Geffen	20	(8)	F
6	11	A Thousand Miles	Vanessa Carlton	A&M	26	(6)	FL
7	19	All You Wanted	Michelle Branch	Maverick	16	(33)	L
8	1	Ain't It Funny (Remix)	Jennifer Lopez featuring Ja Rule	Epic	18	(4)	L
9	14	Don't Let Me Get Me	Pink	Arista	11	(6)	
10	9	Oops (Oh My)	Tweet	Gold Mind	13	(5)	FL
11	6	Girlfriend	'N Sync featuring Nelly	Jive	11	(2)	L
12		Underneath Your Clothes	Shakira	Epic	6	(3)	L
13		The Middle	Jimmy Eat World	Dreamworks	19	(26)	FL
14	4	In The End	Linkin Park	Warner Bros.	21	(8)	FL
15	20	Pass The Courvoisier Part II	Busta Rhymes featuring P. Diddy	J	8	(16)	
16		Without Me	Eminem	Web/Aftermath	14	(1)	
17		Rainy Dayz	Mary J. Blige featuring Ja Rule	MCA	8	(4)	L
18		Hot In Herre	Nelly	Fo' Reel/Universal	20	(4)	
19	8	How You Remind Me	Nickelback	Roadrunner	29	(4)	FL
20	16	Escape	Enrique Iglesias	Interscope	7	(3)	L

June 2002

This Mnth	Prev Mnth	Title	Artist	Label	Wks 20	(UK Pos)	
1	1	Foolish	Ashanti	Murder Inc/Def Jam	22	(4)	F
2	3	I Need A Girl (Part 1)	P.Diddy feat.Usher & Loon Bad Boy	Arista	15	(4)	
3	18	Hot In Herre	Nelly	Fo' Reel/Universal	20	(4)	
4	16	Without Me	Eminem	Web/Aftermath	14	(1)	
5	2	What's Luv?	Fat Joe featuring Ashanti	Terror Squad	20	(4)	L
6	6	A Thousand Miles	Vanessa Carlton	A&M	26	(6)	FL
7	13	The Middle	Jimmy Eat World	Dreamworks	19	(26)	FL
8	4	U Don't Have To Call	Usher	Arista	1	6	L
9		Oh Boy	Cam'ron featuring Juelz Santana	Roc-A-Fella	12	(13)	F
10		Addictive	Truth Hurts featuring Rakim	Aftermath	11	(3)	FL
11	7	All You Wanted	Michelle Branch	Maverick	16	(33)	L
12		Hero	Chad Kroeger featuring Josey Scott	Columbia	16	(4)	FL
13	5	Blurry	Puddle Of Mudd	Flawless/Geffen	20	(8)	F
14		I'm Gonna Be Alright	Jennifer Lopez featuring Nas	Epic	13	(3)	
15		Hella Good	No Doubt	Interscope	7	(12)	
16	27	Rainy Dayz	Mary J. Blige featuring Ja Rule	MCA	8	(17)	L
17		Wasting My Time	Default	Tvt	6	(73)	FL
18	9	Don't Let Me Get Me	Pink	Arista	11	(6)	
19		Still Fly	Big Tymers	Cash Money	9		FL
20		Days Go By	Dirty Vegas	Credence/Capitol	6	(27)	FL

US 2002 APR-JUNE

◆ Ashanti broke the record for first week sales of a female artist's debut album with over 500,000 copies, and became the first female to have singles simultaneously at No. 1 & 2 (which she did for 5 weeks). In addition, her producer Irv Gotti held the top slot for 18 successive weeks!

◆ It was reported that 18 million people downloaded music from the internet every month – far more than at the height of Napster. To combat this the five major record companies had allegedly spent $1.96 billion dollars on developing a digital service system.

▲ Heavy metal hero Ozzy Osbourne was given his own star on the celebrated Hollywood Walk Of Fame.

◆ Elton John's revival of his first ever hit, 'Your Song', did better second time around. Other old songs also faring better on their chart returns were 'The Logical Song' (Scooter-Supertramp) 'Crossroads' (Blazin' Squad – Bone Thugs-N-Harmony), 'Got To Have Your Love' (Liberty X – Mantronix) while Atomic Kitten equalled Blondie by taking 'The Tide Is High' to No.1.

◆ Other old favourites back on the chart included Kelly Llorenna's update of Taylor Dayne's 'Tell It To My Heart' and two past Madonna hits 'Papa Don't Preach' and 'Like A Prayer' by Kelly Osbourne and Mad'House, respectively.

◆ As UK acts Paul McCartney, The Rolling Stones and The Who (despite the death of John Entwistle) pulled huge audiences on their US tours, Fatboy Slim attracted over 250,000 people to a show on Brighton Beach.

July 2002

This Mnth	Prev Mnth	Title	Artist	Label	Wks 20	(US Pos)	
1	7	A Little Less Conversation	Elvis Vs JXL	RCA	7	(50)	L
2	13	The Logical Song	Scooter	Sheffield Tunes	10		
3		Wherever You Will Go	Calling	RCA	7	(5)	F
4		Anyone Of Us (Stupid Mistake)	Gareth Gates	S	8		
5	17	Hot In Herre	Nelly	Universal	9	(1)	
6		I'm Gonna Be Alright	Jennifer Lopez featuring Nas	Epic	5	(10)	
7		By The Way	Red Hot Chili Peppers	Warner Bros.	3	(34)	
8	14	When You Look At Me	Christina Milian	Def Soul	6		
9		Foolish	Ashanti	Murder Inc./Mercury	5	(1)	
10	11	Hero	Chad Kroeger featuring Josey Scott	Roadrunner	8	(3)	FL
11	12	Stop Crying Your Heart Out	Oasis	Big Brother	3		
12		Here I Am	Bryan Adams	A&M	3		L
13	1	Without Me	Eminem	Interscope	11	(2)	
14		Shooting Star	Flip & Fill	All Around The World	3		
15		Your Song	Elton John & Alessandro Safina	Mercury	2		L
16		Baby's Got A Temper	Prodigy	XL Recordings	1		L
17		Tell It To My Heart	Kelly Llorenna	All Around The World	4		
18	2	Just A Little	Liberty X	V2	11		
19		Work It Out	Beyonce	Columbia	3		FL
20		Forever	Dee Dee	Incentive	2		FL

August 2002

This Mnth	Prev Mnth	Title	Artist	Label	Wks 20	(US Pos)	
1	4	Anyone Of Us (Stupid Mistake)	Gareth Gates	S	8		
2		Colourblind	Darius	Mercury	7		F
3		Underneath Your Clothes	Shakira	Epic	8	(9)	
4		Automatic High	S Club Juniors	Polydor	5		
5		Black Suits Comin'(Nod Ya Head)	Will Smith featuring Tra-Knox	Columbia	5	(77)	L
6		Like A Prayer	Mad'house	Serious	6		FL
7		Round Round	Sugababes	Island	7		
8		I Need A Girl (Part One)	P. Diddy featuring Usher & Loon Puff Daddy	Arista	4	(2)	
9	2	The Logical Song	Scooter	Sheffield Tunes	10		
10		A Thousand Miles	Vanessa Carlton	A&M	8	(5)	FL
11		In My Place	Coldplay	Parlophone	2		
12		Romeo Dunn	Romeo	Relentless	4		FL
13		Crossroads	Blazin' Squad	East West	4		F
14		James Dean (I Wanna Know)	Daniel Bedingfield	Polydor	3		
15		Livin' It Up	Ja Rule featuring Case	Def Jam	3	(6)	
16	5	Hot In Herre	Nelly	Universal	9	(1)	
17		Addictive	Truth Hurts featuring Rakim	Interscope	6	(9)	FL
18		What You Got	Abs	S	4		FL
19		Boys	Britney Spears featuring Pharrell Williams	Jive	2		
20		Starry Eyed Surprise	Oakenfold	Perfecto	4	(41)	L

September 2002

This Mnth	Prev Mnth	Title	Artist	Label	Wks 20	(US Pos)	
1		The Tide Is High (Get TheFeeling)	Atomic Kitten	Innocent	10		
2	7	Round Round	Sugababes	Island	7		
3	13	Crossroads	Blazin' Squad	East West	4		F
4	17	Addictive	Truth Hurts featuring Rakim	Interscope	6	(9)	FL
5		Got To Have Your Love	Liberty X	V2	4		
6		Fantasy	Appleton	Polydor	3		F
7		Just Like A Pill	Pink	Arista	7	(8)	
8		Papa Don't Preach	Kelly Osbourne	Epic	3	(74)	F
9		Nessaja	Scooter	Sheffield Tunes	4		
10		Dy-Na-Mi-Tee	Ms Dynamite	Polydor	3		
11	2	Colourblind	Darius	Mercury	7		F
12		What I Go To School For	Busted	Universal	6		F
13		Cleanin' Out My Closet	Eminem	Interscope	4	(4)	
14		When I Lost You	Sarah Whatmore	RCA	4		F
15		I Love It When We Do	Ronan Keating	Polydor	2		
16		Forever	N-Trance	All Around The World	2		L
17	18	What You Got	Abs	S	4		fl
18	6	Like A Prayer	Mad'house	Serious	6		fl
19		Fantasy	Appleton	Polydor	3		F
20		Everyday	Bon Jovi	Mercury	2		L

July 2002

This Mnth	Prev Mnth	Title	Artist	Label	Wks 20	(UK Pos)	
1	3	Hot In Herre	Nelly	Fo' Reel/Universal	20	(4)	
2	4	Without Me	Eminem	Web/Aftermath	14	(1)	
3	12	Hero	Chad Kroeger featuring Josey Scott	Columbia	16	(4)	FL
4	9	Oh Boy	Cam'ron featuring Juelz Santana	Roc-A-Fella	12	(13)	F
5		Complicated	Avril Lavigne	Arista	22	(3)	F
6	1	Foolish	Ashanti	Murder Inc/Def Jam	22	()	F
7	7	The Middle	Jimmy Eat World	Dreamworks	19	(26)	FL
8		I Need A Girl (Part Two)	P. Diddy & Ginuwine	Bad Boy/Arista 1	6	(4)	L
9	6	A Thousand Miles	Vanessa Carlton	A&M	26	(6)	FL
10	14	I'm Gonna Be Alright	Jennifer Lopez featuring Nas	Epic	13	(3)	
11	10	Addictive	Truth Hurts featuring Rakim	Aftermath	11	(3)	FL
12	2	I Need A Girl (Part 1)	P.Diddy feat.Usher & Loon Bad Boy	Arista	15	(4)	
13	19	Still Fly	Big Tymers	Cash Money	9		FL
14		Dilemma	Nelly featuring Kelly Rowland	Fo' Reel/Universal	22	(1)	
15		Down 4 U	Irv Gotti Presents The Inc.	Murder Inc	12		FL
16	5	What's Luv?	Fat Joe featuring Ashanti	Terror Squad	20	(4)	L
17		Just A Friend 2002	Mario	J	12	(18)	FL
18	20	Days Go By	Dirty Vegas	Credence/Capitol	6	(27)	FL
19		Heaven	DJ Sammy & Yanou Feat Do	Robbins	11	(1)	FL
20		Halfcrazy	Musiq	Def Soul/DJMG	7		F

August 2002

This Mnth	Prev Mnth	Title	Artist	Label	Wks 20	(UK Pos)	
1	14	Dilemma	Nelly featuring Kelly Rowland	Fo' Reel/Universal	22	(1)	
2	1	Hot In Herre	Nelly	Fo' Reel/Universal	20	(4)	
3	5	Complicated	Avril Lavigne	Arista	22	(3)	F
4	8	I Need A Girl (Part Two)	P. Diddy & Ginuwine	Bad Boy/Arista	16		L
5	17	Just A Friend 2002	Mario	J	12	(18)	FL
6	15	Down 4 U	Irv Gotti Presents The Inc	Murder Inc	12	(4)	FL
7	3	Hero	Chad Kroeger featuring Josey Scott	Columbia	16	(4)	FL
8	19	Heaven	DJ Sammy & Yanou featuring Do	Robbins	11	(1)	FL
9		Gangsta Lovin'	Eve featuring Alicia Keys	Rough Ryders	15	(6)	L
10		Just Like A Pill	Pink	Arista	10	(1)	
11	2	Without Me	Eminem	Web/Aftermath	14	(1)	
12		Happy	Ashanti	Murder Inc	12	(13)	
13		Nothin'	N.O.R.E.	Def Jam	12	(11)	FL
14		Long Time Gone	Dixie Chicks	Monument	3		
15	10	I'm Gonna Be Alright	Jennifer Lopez featuring Nas	Epic	13	(3)	
16	7	The Middle	Jimmy Eat World	Dreamworks	19	(26)	FL
17	4	Oh Boy	Cam'ron featuring Juelz Santana	Roc-A-Fella	12	(13)	F
18		Cleanin' Out My Closet	Eminem	Web/Aftermath	9	(4)	
19	9	A Thousand Miles	Vanessa Carlton	A&M	26	(6)	FL
20		No Such Thing	John Mayer	Aware/Columbia	10		F

September 2002

This Mnth	Prev Mnth	Title	Artist	Label	Wks 20	(UK Pos)	
1	1	Dilemma	Nelly featuring Kelly Rowland	Fo' Reel/Universal	22	(1)	
2	9	Gangsta Lovin'	Eve featuring Alicia Keys	Rough Ryders	15	(6)	L
3	3	Complicated	Avril Lavigne	Arista	22	(3)	F
4	2	Hot In Herre	Nelly	Fo' Reel/Universal	20	(4)	
5	18	Cleanin' Out My Closet	Eminem	Web/Aftermath	9	(4)	
6	4	I Need A Girl (Part Two)	P. Diddy & Ginuwine	Bad Boy/Arista	16		L
7		One Last Breath	Creed	Wind-Up	18	(47)	L
8	5	Just A Friend 2002	Mario	J	12	(18)	FL
9	12	Happy	Ashanti	Murder Inc	12	(13)	
10	10	Just Like A Pill	Pink	Arista	10	(1)	
11	13	Nothin'	N.O.R.E.	Def Jam	12	(11)	FL
12		Gotta Get Thru This	Daniel Bedingfield	Island/A&M	10	(1)	F
13	6	Down 4 U	Irv Gotti Presents The Inc	Murder Inc	12	(4)	FL
14		Move Bitch	Ludacris featuring Mystikal	Disturbing Tha Peace	11		
15	20	No Such Thing	John Mayer	Aware/Columbia	10		F
16		Hey Ma	Cam'ron featuring Juelz Santana	Roc-A-Fella	15	(8)	L
17	8	Heaven	DJ Sammy & Yanou featuring Do	Robbins	11	(1)	FL
18		If I Could Go!	Angie Martinez featuring Lil' Mo	Elektra	9	(61)	L
19	19	A Thousand Miles	Vanessa Carlton	A&M	26	(6)	FL
20	7	Hero	Chad Kroeger featuring Josey Scott	Columbia	16	(4)	FL

▲ Nelly hogged the No. 1 slot for the complete quarter when 'Dilemma' (which featured Destiny Child's Kelly Rowland) replaced 'Hot In Herre' at the summit. His album 'Nellyville' also topped the chart with first week sales of over 700,000.

◆ Eminem, whose 'The Eminem Show' album topped the charts right around the globe, picked up five MTV awards. Other winners included fellow international hitmakers Jennifer Lopez, Linkin Park, Pink, Coldplay and Canadian teenage sensation Avril Lavigne.

◆ Elvis Presley's 1968 flop, 'A Little Less Conversation', topped the charts in twenty countries, and was the No.1 seller in the US.

UK 2002 OCT-DEC

◆ As Pop Idols Will and Gareth teamed together to score their third No.1 in less than six months with a revival of The Beatles' 'The Long And Winding Road', the latest TV talent search show Popstars – The Rivals gave us Top 3 acts Girls Aloud, One True Voice and Transylvanian twins, The Cheeky Girls.

◆ There was still plenty of room in 2002 for new acts who did not have the benefit of a TV talent show behind them, and the year ended with three of the best breaking through: Avril Lavigne (who became the youngest female to top the UK album chart), Busted and Big Brovaz. Equally successful, if less likely to last, were new European acts Las Ketchup and DJ Sammy.

◆ Chart veterans Lulu and Elton John scored their biggest hits for some time by teaming up with current chart champions Ronan Keating and Blue, respectively.

October 2002

This Mnth	Prev Mnth	Title	Artist	Label	Wks 20	(US Pos)	
1		The Long And Winding Road/ Suspicious Minds	Will Young & Gareth Gates	S	6		
2		Complicated	Avril Lavigne	Arista	7	(2)	F
3	7	Just Like A Pill	Pink	Arista	7	(8)	
4		Little By Little/She Is Love	Oasis	Big Brother	4		
5		The Ketchup Song (Asereje)	Las Ketchup	Columbia	14	(54)	FL
6		Down Boy	Holly Valance	London	4		
7	1	The Tide Is High (Get The Feeling)	Atomic Kitten	Innocent	10		
8		New Direction	S Club Juniors	Polydor	4		
9		Down 4 U	Irv Gotti Presents Ja Rule,	Murder Inc	3	(6)	FL
10		Dilemma	Nelly featuring Kelly Rowland	Universal	13	(1)	
11		My Vision	Jakatta featuring Seal	Rulin	4		L
12		Gangsta Lovin'	Eve featuring Alicia Keys	Ruff Ryders/Interscope	4	(2)	L
13	12	What I Go To School For	Busted	Universal	6		F
14		Nu Flow	Big Brovaz	Epic	8		F
15		All My Life	Foo Fighters	RCA	2	(43)	
16		I'm Right Here	Samantha Mumba	Wild Card/Polydor	3		L
17	13	Cleanin' Out My Closet	Eminem	Interscope	4	(4)	
18		There By The Grace Of God	Manic Street Preachers	Epic	1		L
19		Luv U Better	LL Cool J	Def Jam	2	(4)	
20		Strange And Beautiful	Aqualung	B Unique	2		FL

November 2002

This Mnth	Prev Mnth	Title	Artist	Label	Wks 20	(US Pos)	
1	10	Dilemma	Nelly featuring Kelly Rowland	Universal	13	(1)	
2		Heaven	DJ Sammy & Yanou featuring Do	Data/MOS	8	(8)	F
3	5	The Ketchup Song (Asereje)	Las Ketchup	Columbia	14	(54)	FL
4		Like I Love You	Justin Timberlake	Jive	6	(11)	F
5		Unbreakable	Westlife	S	4		
6		One Love	Blue	Innocent	5		
7		Dirrty	Christina Aguilera featuring Redman	RCA	6	(48)	
8	14	Nu Flow	Big Brovaz	Epic	8		F
9		I'm Gonna Getcha Good!	Shania Twain	Mercury	4	(34)	
10		Die Another Day	Madonna	Warner Bros.	6	(8)	
11		Don't Let Me Down/You And I	Will Young	S	3		L
12		Jenny From The Block	Jennifer Lopez	Epic	6	(3)	
13		Electrical Storm	U2	Island	2	(77)	L
14	2	Complicated	Avril Lavigne	Arista	7	(2)	F
15		Love On The Line	Blazin' Squad	East West	2		
16		Work It	Missy Elliott	Goldmind/Elektra	2	(2)	
17		Stronger/Angels With Dirty Faces	Sugababes	Island	4		
18		Alive	S Club	Polydor	2		
19		Put The Needle On It	Dannii Minogue	London	2		
20	3	Just Like A Pill	Pink	Arista	7	(8)	

December 2002

This Mnth	Prev Mnth	Title	Artist	Label	Wks 20	(US Pos)	
1		If You're Not The One	Daniel Bedingfield	Polydor	15	(17+)	
2		Lose Yourself	Eminem	Interscope	15	(1)	
3		Cheeky Song (Touch My Bum)	Cheeky Girls	Multiply	9		F
4		The Last Goodbye/Be With You	Atomic Kitten	Innocent	6		
5		We've Got Tonight	Ronan Keating featuring Lulu	Polydor	6		
6	7	Dirrty	Christina Aguilera featuring Redman	RCA	6	(48)	
7		Sorry Seems To Be The Hardest Word	Blue featuring Elton John	Innocent	6		
8		Feel	Robbie Williams	Chrysalis	6		
9	3	The Ketchup Song (Asereje)	Las Ketchup	Columbia	14		FL
10	1	Dilemma	Nelly featuring Kelly Rowland	Universal	13	(1)	
11		Sound Of The Underground	Girls Aloud	Polydor	10		F
12		Sacred Trust/After You're Gone	One True Voice	Ebul/Jive	5		FL
13		Holding On For You	Liberty X	V2	5		
14		Rushes	Darius	Mercury	2		
15		What My Heart Wants To Say	Gareth Gates	S	4		
16		Puppy Love/Sleigh Ride	S Club Juniors	Polydor	4		L
17	12	Jenny From The Block	Jennifer Lopez	Epic	6	(3)	
18		You're A Superstar	Love Inc.	Nulife/Arista	7		FL
19	11	Don't Let Me Down/You And I	Will Young	S	3		L
20		United States Of Whatever	Liam Lynch	Global Warming	3		FL

October 2002

This Mnth	Prev Mnth	Title	Artist	Label	Wks 20	(UK Pos)	
1	1	Dilemma	Nelly featuring Kelly Rowland	Fo' Reel/Universal	22	(1)	
2		A Moment Like This	Kelly Clarkson	RCA	8		FL
3	2	Gangsta Lovin'	Eve featuring Alicia Keys	Rough Ryders	15	(6)	L
4	16	Hey Ma	Cam'ron featuring Juelz Santana	Roc-A-Fella	15	(8)	L
5	3	Complicated	Avril Lavigne	Arista	22	(3)	F
6		Work It	Missy 'Misdemeanor' Elliott	Gold Mind	19	(6)	
7	7	One Last Breath	Creed	Wind-Up	18	(47)	L
8	5	Cleanin' Out My Closet	Eminem	Web/Aftermath	9	(4)	
9		Underneath It All	No Doubt Feat Lady Saw	Interscope	17	(18)	L
10		Lose Yourself	Eminem	Shady S/track	18	(1)	
11	6	I Need A Girl (Part Two)	P. Diddy & Ginuwine	Bad Boy/Arista	16		L
12		Luv U Better	Ll Cool J	Def Jam/DJMG	12	(7)	L
13	14	Move Bitch	Ludacris featuring Mystikal	Disturbing Tha Peace	11		L
14	4	Hot In Herre	Nelly	Fo' Reel/Universal	20	(4)	
15		Like I Love You	Justin Timberlake	Jive	10	(2)	F
16		Sk8er Boi	Avril Lavigne	Arista	9	(8)	
17	10	Just Like A Pill	Pink	Arista	10	(1)	
18	12	Gotta Get Thru This	Daniel Bedingfield	Island/A&M	10	(1)	F
19		The Game Of Love	Santana featuring Michelle Branch	Arista	21	(16)	L
20		Gimme The Light	Sean Paul	Black Shadow	12	(5)	F

November 2002

This Mnth	Prev Mnth	Title	Artist	Label	Wks 20	(UK Pos)	
1	10	Lose Yourself	Eminem	Shady S/track	18	(1)	
2	6	Work It	Missy 'Misdemeanor' Elliott	Gold Mind	19	(6)	
3	1	Dilemma	Nelly featuring Kelly Rowland	Fo' Reel/Universal	22	(1)	
4	4	Hey Ma	Cam'ron featuring Juelz Santana	Roc-A-Fella	15	(8)	L
5	9	Underneath It All	No Doubt featuring Lady Saw	Interscope	17	(18)	L
6	12	Luv U Better	LL Cool J	Def Jam/DJMG	12	(7)	L
7	2	The Game Of Love	Santana featuring Michelle Branch	Arista	21	(16)	L
8		A Moment Like This	Kelly Clarkson	RCA	8		FL
9	20	Jenny From The Block	Jennifer Lopez featuring Jadakiss	Epic	15	(3)	
10		Gimme The Light	Sean Paul	Black Shadow	12	(5)	F
11		Die Another Day	Madonna	Maverick	7	(3)	L
12	3	Gangsta Lovin'	Eve featuring Alicia Keys	Rough Ryders	15	(6)	L
3	16	Sk8er Boi	Avril Lavigne	Arista	9	(8)	
14	7	One Last Breath	Creed	Wind-Up	18	(47)	L
15		'03 Bonnie & Clyde	Jay-Z featuring Beyonce Knowles	Roc-A-Fella	16	(2)	
16	5	Complicated	Avril Lavigne	Arista	22	(3)	F
17	15	Like I Love You	Justin Timberlake	Jive	10	(2)	F
18		Air Force One	Nelly featuring St. Lunatics	Reel/Universal	14		L
19		Love Of My Life	Erykah Badu featuring Common	Fox/MCA	10		L
20		Baby	Ashanti	Murder Inc/Def Jam	5		

December 2002

This Mnth	Prev Mnth	Title	Artist	Label	Wks 20	(UK Pos)	
1	1	Lose Yourself	Eminem	Shady S/track	18	(1)	
2	2	Work It	Missy 'Misdemeanor' Elliott	Gold Mind	19	(6)	
3	9	Jenny From The Block	Jennifer Lopez featuring Jadakiss	Epic	15	(3)	
4	5	Underneath It All	No Doubt featuring Lady Saw	Interscope	17	(18)	L
5	15	'03 Bonnie & Clyde	Jay-Z featuring Beyonce Knowles	Roc-A-Fella	16	(2)	
6	18	Air Force One	Nelly featuring St. Lunatics	Reel/Universal	14		L
7	7	The Game Of Love	Santana featuring Michelle Branch	Arista	21	(16)	L
8	10	Gimme The Light	Sean Paul	Black Shadow	12	(5)	F
9		Don't Mess With My Man	Nivea featuring Brian & Brandon Casey	Jive	15	(41)	L
10	6	Luv U Better	LL Cool J	Def Jam/DJMG	12	(7)	L
11		Beautiful	Christina Aguilera	RCA	18	(1)	L
12		Bump, Bump, Bump	B2K & P. Diddy	T.U.G./Epic	15	(11)	FL
13	19	Love Of My Life	Erykah Badu featuring Common	Fox/MCA	10		FL
14	4	Hey Ma	Cam'ron featuring Juelz Santana	Roc-A-Fella	15	(8)	L
15		Landslide	Dixie Chicks	Monument	20	(55)	L
16	3	Dilemma	Nelly featuring Kelly Rowland	Fo' Reel/Universal	22	(1)	
17		She Hates Me	Puddle Of Mudd	Flawless/Geffen	11	(14)	L
18	11	Die Another Day	Madonna	Maverick	7	(3)	L
19		Miss You	Aaliyah	Blackground	22		L
20	14	One Last Breath	Creed	Wind-Up	18	(47)	L

◆ Fifteen million people voted in the final of American Idol.. The winner, Kelly Clarkson's first single, 'A Moment Like This', broke a record set by The Beatles by leaping from No. 52 to No.1. It sold 236,000 in its first week – when 10,000 copies was usually enough to top the sales chart.

◆ A 28 city US tour of 10,000 seat arenas featuring all the 10 American Idol finalists did 'great business' and was over 80% sold out.

◆ The Dixie Chicks were rare country music visitors to the pop Top 20, thanks to their re-working of Fleetwood Mac's 'Landslide'. They also equalled the record for female groups, set by The Supremes, when 'Home' (which sold over 750,000 in its first week) became their second No.1 album. It was one of six country albums to top the pop chart in 2002 – an all time record.

◆ Although Fame Academy had less viewers than earlier 21st century TV talent shows, it's winner David Sneddon hit the top with his own compostion 'Stop Living A Lie', while other finalists, Sinead Quinn and Ainslie Henderson, also had major hits.

◆ British-born Asian artist Rajinder Singh, better known as Panjabi MC, had the first world wide bhangra hit with 'Mundian To Bach Ke' ('Beware of the Boys'). The track, which he originally recorded in 1998, was a huge hit in Germany before spreading around Europe and finally cracking the US charts (when Jay-Z added a rap).

▲ Female duo t.A.T.u. became the first Russian act to top the British chart and reach the Top 20 in the United States.

January 2003

This Mnth	Prev Mnth	Title	Artist	Label	Wks 20	(US Pos)	
1	11	Sound Of The Underground	Girls Aloud	Polydor	10		F
2	3	Cheeky Song (Touch My Bum)	Cheeky Girls	Multiply	9		F
3	2	Lose Yourself	Eminem	Interscope	15	(1)	
4	1	If You're Not The One	Daniel Bedingfield	Polydor	15	(17+)	
5	12	Sacred Trust/After You're Gone	One True Voice	Ebul/Jive	5		FL
6	7	Sorry Seems To Be The Hardest Word	Blue featuring Elton John	Innocent	6		
7		Danger! High Voltage	Electric Six	XL Recordings	4		F
8	18	You're A Superstar	Love Inc.	Nulife/Arista	7		FL
9		Stop Living The Lie	David Sneddon	Mercury	6		F
10		Year 3000	Busted	Universal	9		
11		Sk8er Boi	Avril Lavigne	Arista	6	(10)	
12		The Way (Put Your Hand In My Hand)	Divine Inspiration	Data/MOS	3		FL
13		True	Jaimeson featuring Angel Blu	V2/J-Did	4		FL
14	9	The Ketchup Song (Aserejé)	Las Ketchup	Columbia	14		FL
15		Mundian To Bach Ke	Panjabi MC	Showbiz/Instant Karma	4	(33+)	FL
11	10	Dilemma	Nelly featuring Kelly Rowland	Universal	13	(1)	
17	8	Feel	Robbie Williams	Chrysalis	6		
18		Love Story (Vs Finally)	Layo & Bushwacka!	XL Recordings	2		FL
19		Just The Way I'm Feeling	Feeder	Echo	2		L
20		Solsbury Hill	Erasure	Mute	1		L

February 2003

This Mnth	Prev Mnth	Title	Artist	Label	Wks 20	(US Pos)	
1	9	Stop Living The Lie	David Sneddon	Mercury	6		F
2		All The Things She Said	t.A.T.u.	Interscope	8	(20)	FL
3		'03 Bonnie & Clyde	Jay-Z featuring Beyonce Knowles	Roc-A-Fella	6	(4)	L
4		Stole	Kelly Rowland	Columbia	6	(27)	F
5		The Opera Song (Brave New World)	Jurgen Vries featuring CMC	Direction	4		L
6	10	Year 3000	Busted	Universal	9		
7	3	Lose Yourself	Eminem	Interscope	15	(1)	
8		Cry Me A River	Justin Timberlake	Jive	6	(3)	
9		Songbird	Oasis	Big Brother	3		L
10	4	If You're Not The One	Daniel Bedingfield	Polydor	15	(17+)	
11	1	Sound Of The Underground	Girls Aloud	Polydor	10		F
12		I Can't Break Down	Sinead Quinn	Mercury	4		FL
13		Gimme The Light	Sean Paul	VP/Atlantic	3	(7)	F
14	15	Mundian To Bach Ke	Panjabi MC	Showbiz/Instant Karma	4	(33+)	FL
15		Don't Worry	Appleton	Polydor	3		L
16		OK	Big Brovaz	Epic	3		
17		Hey Ma	Cam'ron featuring Juelz Santana	Roc-A-Fella	4	(3)	L
18	13	True	Jaimeson featuring Angel Blu	V2/J-Did	4		FL
19		Reminisce/Where The Story Ends	Blazin' Squad	East West	1		L
20		Hidden Agenda	Craig David	Wildstar	2		

March 2003

This Mnth	Prev Mnth	Title	Artist	Label	Wks 20	(US Pos)	
1	2	All The Things She Said	t.A.T.u.	Interscope	8	(20)	FL
2		Beautiful	Christina Aguilera	RCA	7	(2)	
3		Move Your Feet	Junior Senior	Mercury	11		FL
4	8	Cry Me A River	Justin Timberlake	Jive	6	(3)	
5		The Boys Of Summer	DJ Sammy	Data/MoS	4		
6		Spirit In The Sky	Gareth Gates featuring The Kumars	S	8		L
7		I Begin To Wonder	Dannii Minogue	London	3		
8		All I Have	Jennifer Lopez featuring LL Cool J	Epic	8	(1)	
9	12	I Can't Break Down	Sinead Quinn	Mercury	4		FL
10	4	Stole	Kelly Rowland	Columbia	6	(27)	F
11		Born To Try	Delta Goodrem	Epic	8		F
12		In Da Club	50 Cent	Interscope	9+	(1)	FL
13		Scandalous	Mis-Teeq	Telstar	6		L
14	7	Lose Yourself	Eminem	Interscope	15	(1)	
15	6	Year 3000	Busted	Universal	9		
16		Being Nobody	Richard X Vs Liberty X	Virgin	4		FL
17		Keep Me A Secret	Ainslie Henderson	Mercury	2		FL
18		U Make Me Wanna	Blue	Innocent	4		L
19		Sing For The Moment	Eminem	Interscope	2	(6)	L
20		Pain Killer	Turin Brakes	Source	2		FL

January 2003

This Mnth	Prev Mnth	Title	Artist	Label	Wks 20	(UK Pos)	
1	1	Lose Yourself	Eminem	Shady S/track	18	(1)	
2	2	Work It	Missy 'Misdemeanor' Elliott	Gold Mind	19	(6)	
3	6	Air Force One	Nelly featuring St.Lunatics	Fo' Reel/Universal	14	()	L
4	12	Bump, Bump, Bump	B2K & P. Diddy	T.U.G./Epic	15	(11)	FL
5	5	'03 Bonnie & Clyde	Jay-Z featuring Beyonce Knowles	Roc-A-Fella	16	(2)	
6	11	Beautiful	Christina Aguilera	RCA	18	(1)	L
7	3	Jenny From The Block	Jennifer Lopez featuring Jadakiss	Epic	15	(3)	
8	9	Don't Mess With My Man	Nivea feat. Brian & Brandon Casey	Jive	15	(41)	L
9		I'm With You	Avril Lavigne	Arista	17	(7)	L
10	7	The Game Of Love	Santana featuring Michelle Branch	Arista	21	(16)	L
11	15	Landslide	Dixie Chicks	Monument	20	(55)	L
12		Cry Me A River	Justin Timberlake	Jive	14	(2)	
13	19	Miss You	Aaliyah	Blackground	22		
14		All I Have	Jennifer Lopez featuring LL Cool J	Epic	17	(2)	L
15	13	Love Of My Life	Erykah Badu featuring Common	Fox/MCA	10	(18)	L
16	4	Underneath It All	No Doubt featuring Lady Saw	Interscope	17		L
17	17	She Hates Me	Puddle Of Mudd	Flawless/Geffen	11	(14)	L
18		Mesmerize	Ja Rule Feat Ashanti	Murder Inc/Def Jam	14	(12)	L
19		Thugz Mansion	2Pac	Amaru/Death Row	5	(24)	F
20	8	Gimme The Light	Sean Paul	Black Shadow	12	(5)	F

February 2003

This Mnth	Prev Mnth	Title	Artist	Label	Wks 20	(UK Pos)	
1	14	All I Have	Jennifer Lopez featuring LL Cool J	Epic	17	(2)	L
2	4	Bump, Bump, Bump	B2K & P. Diddy	T.U.G./Epic	15	(11)	FL
3	6	Beautiful	Christina Aguilera	RCA	18	(1)	L
4	18	Mesmerize	Ja Rule featuring Ashanti	Murder Inc/Def Jam	14	(12)	L
5	12	Cry Me A River	Justin Timberlake	Jive	14	(2)	
6	9	I'm With You	Avril Lavigne	Arista	17	(7)	L
7		In Da Club	50 Cent	Shady/Aftermath	22	(4)	
8	5	'03 Bonnie & Clyde	Jay-Z featuring Beyonce Knowles	Roc-A-Fella	16	(2)	
9	13	Miss You	Aaliyah	Blackground	22		
10	3	Air Force One	Nelly featuring St. Lunatics	Fo' Reel/Universal	14	()	L
11	11	Landslide	Dixie Chicks	Monument	20	(55)	L
12		Gossip Folks	Missy 'Misdemeanor'	Elliott Goldmind	11	(9)	L
13	8	Don't Mess With My Man	Nivea feat.Brian & Brandon Casey	Jive	15	(41)	L
14	1	Lose Yourself	Eminem	Shady S/track	18	(1)	
15		Ignition	R. Kelly	Jive	23	(1)	
16		Picture	Kid Rock featuring Sheryl Crow or Alison Moorer	Lava/Atlantic or Universal South	20		L
17	10	The Game Of Love	Santana featuring Michelle Branch	Arista	21	(16)	L
18	2	Work It	Missy 'Misdemeanor' Elliott	Gold Mind	19	(6)	
19		Wanksta	50 Cent	G Unit/Shady	7		
20	17	She Hates Me	Puddle Of Mudd	Flawless/Geffen	11	(14)	L

March 2003

This Mnth	Prev Mnth	Title	Artist	Label	Wks 20	(UK Pos)	
1	7	In Da Club	50 Cent	Shady/Aftermath	22	(4)	
2	1	All I Have	Jennifer Lopez featuring LL Cool J	Epic	17	(2)	L
3	4	Mesmerize	Ja Rule featuring Ashanti	Murder Inc/Def Jam	14	(12)	L
4	19	Miss You	Aaliyah	Blackground	22		L
5	15	Ignition	R. Kelly	Jive	23	(1)	L
6	5	Cry Me A River	Justin Timberlake	Jive	14	(2)	
7	16	Picture	Kid Rock featuring Sheryl Crow or Alison Moorer	Lava/Atlantic or Universal South	20		L
8	2	Bump, Bump, Bump	B2K & P. Diddy	T.U.G./Epic	15	(11)	FL
9	11	Landslide	Dixie Chicks	Monument	20	(55)	L
10	6	I'm With You	Avril Lavigne	Arista	17	(7)	L
11	12	Gossip Folks	Missy 'Misdemeanor' Elliott	Gold Mind	11	(9)	L
12		How You Gonna Act Like That	Tyrese	J	15		L
13	3	Beautiful	Christina Aguilera	RCA	18	(1)	L
14		When I'm Gone	3 Doors Down	Republic/Universal	22		
15		Excuse Me Miss	Jay-Z	Roc-A-Fella	10	(17)	L
16	19	Wanksta	50 Cent	G Unit/Shady	7		
17		Beautiful	Snoop Dogg featuring Pharrell	Doggy Style	12	(23)	L
18		Get Busy	Sean Paul	VP/Atlantic	21+		L
19		Superman	Eminem	Web/Aftermath	6		L
20		'03 Bonnie & Clyde	Jay-Z featuring Beyonce Knowles	Roc-A-Fella	16	(2)	

◆ At a time when almost half the US hits 'featured' at least two separate artists, Kid Rock topped the best sellers with 'Picture', which featured pop vocalist Sheryl Crow on the much played album version and country singer Alison Moorer on the single.

◆ The hottest new act of early 2003 was Oscar winning Eminem's protégé 50 Cent (Curtis Jackson) who simultaneously had two singles in the pop Top 20 and at times as many as nine different tracks in the R&B Top 100.

◆ Other top news items included: Norah Jones grabbing five Grammy awards for her No. 1 album, 'Come Away With Me', and Eminem being the big winner at the AMA awards… Dixie Chicks records being boycotted by radio after their anti-war comments… American Idol 2 grabbing even bigger viewing figures… Phil Spector being arrested on a murder charge and the death of Bee Gee Maurice Gibb.

UK 2003 APR-JUNE

◆ UK TV shows Popstars and Pop Idol, and their countless international clones, were still responsible for millions of global sales – they were truly the musical phenomenon of the time. The UK charts were still full of winners, losers and rejects from such shows, including the first solo hit from Kym Marsh, ex-member of the very first winners, Hear'say.

▲ S Club (previously S Club 7) called it a day. All their 11 singles had reached the Top 5. The act had sold four million singles and three million albums in the UK since 1999.

◆ Other news: US R&B vocalist Oliver Cheatham had his first Top 20 entry at the age of 54… in the Eurovision Song Contest , the UK entry, 'Cry Baby' by Jemini, scored "nul points".

April 2003

This Mnth	Prev Mnth	Title	Artist	Label	Wks 20	(US Pos)	
1		Make Luv	Room 5 featuring Oliver Cheatham	Positiva	7		FL
2	6	Spirit In The Sky	Gareth Gates featuring The Kumars	S	8		L
3	3	Move Your Feet	Junior Senior	Mercury	11		FL
4		In Da Club	50 Cent	Interscope	14	(1)	FL
5	13	Scandalous	Mis-Teeq	Telstar	6	(1)	L
6		Tonight/Miss You Nights	Westlife	S	4		L
7		Cry	Kym Marsh	Island	5		FL
8	8	All I Have	Jennifer Lopez featuring LL Cool J	Epic	8	(1)	
9		American Life	Madonna	Maverick	3	(37)	L
10		Love Doesn't Have To Hurt	Atomic Kitten	Innocent	2		L
11	16	Being Nobody	Richard X Vs Liberty X	Virgin	4		FL
12	11	Born To Try	Delta Goodrem	Epic	8		F
13		I'm With You	Avril Lavigne	Arista	3	(4)	L
14		Come Undone	Robbie Williams	Chrysalis	3		L
15		I Can't Read You	Daniel Bedingfield	Polydor	3		L
16		Out Of Time	Blur	Parlophone	2		L
17		Sunrise	Simply Red	Simplyred.Com	5		L
18		Clocks	Coldplay	Parlophone	2	(29)	L
19		Speechless	D-Side	WEA	2		FL
20		Weekend!	Scooter	Sheffield Tune	3		L

May 2003

This Mnth	Prev Mnth	Title	Artist	Label	Wks 20	(US Pos)	
1		Loneliness	Tomcraft	Data/Ministry	6		FL
2		Ignition	R. Kelly	Jive	13	(2)	L
3		You Said No	Busted	Universal	5		L
4		Rise & Fall	Craig David featuring Sting	Wildstar	5		L
5		Favourite Things	Big Brovaz	Epic	6		L
6		In Da Club	50 Cent	Interscope	14	(1)	F
7		All Over	Lisa Maffia	Independiente	4		FL
8		Take Your Shoes Off	Cheeky Girls	Multiply	4		L
9		No Good Advice	Girls Aloud	Polydor	4		L
10		X Gon' Give It To Ya	DMX	Def Jam	6	(60)	FL
11	1	Make Luv	Room 5 featuring Oliver Cheatham	Positiva	7		FL
12		Don't Let Go	David Sneddon	Mercury	2		L
13		Get Busy	Sean Paul	VP/Atlantic	6	(1)	L
14		The Long Goodbye	Ronan Keating	Polydor	2		L
15		Rock Your Body	Justin Timberlake	Jive	5	(5)	L
16		Can't Nobody	Kelly Rowland	Columbia	3	(97)	L
17		Girls And Boys	Good Charlotte	Epic	3	(55+)	L
18		Husan	Bhangra Knights Vs Husan	Positiva	3		FL
19		Madame Helga	Stereophonics	V2	1		L
20		Lately	Lisa Scott-Lee	Fontana	2		FL

June 2003

This Mnth	Prev Mnth	Title	Artist	Label	Wks 20	(US Pos)	
1	2	Ignition	R. Kelly	Jive	13	(2)	L
2		Bring Me To Life	Evanescence	Epic	9+	(5)	FL
3		I Know What You Want	Busta Rhymes/Mariah Carey	J	7	(3)	L
4		Say Goodbye/Love Ain't Gonna..	S Club	Polydor	4		L
5		Fighter	Christina Aguilera	RCA	4	(20)	L
6		Get Busy	Sean Paul	VP/Atlantic	6	(1)	L
7		Fly On The Wings Of Love	XTM & DJ Chucky	Serious	10+		FL
8		Fast Food Song	Fast Food Rockers	Better The Devil	7+		FL
9	15	Rock Your Body	Justin Timberlake	Jive	5	(5)	L
10		Free Me	Emma	19/Universal	3		L
11		Forever And For Always	Shania Twain	Mercury	3	(30+)	L
12		There There	Radiohead	Parlophone	2		L
13		Lost Without You	Delta Goodrem	Epic	6		L
14		Gay Bar	Electric Six	XL Recordings	2		L
15		Misfit	Amy Studt	Polydor	4		L
16		Don't Wanna Lose This Feeling	Dannii Minogue	London	2		L
17		No Letting Go	Wayne Wonder	VP/Atlantic	7+	(11)	FL
18	5	Favourite Things	Big Brovaz	Epic	6		L
19		Baby I Don't Care	Jennifer Ellison	East West	3		FL
20		Sunlight	DJ Sammy	Data/MoS	3		L

404

April 2003

This Mnth	Prev Mnth	Title	Artist	Label	Wks 20	(UK Pos)
1	1	In Da Club	50 Cent	G-Unit/Shady	22	(3)
2	5	Ignition	R. Kelly	Jive	23	(1)
3	18	Get Busy	Sean Paul	VP/Atlantic	21+	(4)
4	4	Miss You	Aaliyah	Blackground	22	
5	7	Picture	Kid Rock featuring Sheryl Crow or Alison Moorer	Lava/Atlantic Universal South	20	
6	14	When I'm Gone	3 Doors Down	Republic	22	
7	17	Beautiful	Snoop Dogg featuring Phar	Doggy Style	12	(23)
8	2	All I Have	Jennifer Lopez featuring LL Cool J	Epic	17	(2)
9	12	How You Gonna Act Like That	Tyrese	J	15	(30)
10	21	Questions	50 Cent featuring Nate Dogg	G Unit/Shady	16	(6)
11	15	Excuse Me	Jay-Z	Roc-A-Fella	10	(17)
12		I Know What You Want	Busta Rhymes & Mariah Carey	J	18	(3)
13		Can't Let You Go	Fabolous featuring Mike S	Desert Storm	16	
14	3	Mesmerize	Ja Rule featuring Ashanti	Murder Inc	14	(12)
15	10	I'm With You	Avril Lavigne	Arista	17	(7)
16		Rock Your Body	Justin Timberlake	Jive	12	(2)
17		I Can	Nas	Ill Will	9	(19)
18	11	Gossip Folks	Missy 'Misdemeanor' Elliott	Goldmind	11	(9)
19	6	Cry Me A River	Justin Timberlake	Jive	14	(2)
20		Bring Me To Life	Evanescence/Paul McCoy	Wind-Up	16+	(1)

May 2003

This Mnth	Prev Mnth	Title	Artist	Label	Wks 20	(UK Pos)
1	3	Get Busy	Sean Paul	VP/Atlantic	21+	(4)
2	10	21 Questions	50 Cent featuring Nate Dogg	G Unit/Shady	16	(6)
3	1	In Da Club	50 Cent	G-Unit/Shady	22	(3)
4	2	Ignition	R. Kelly	Jive	23	(1)
5	12	I Know What You Want	Busta Rhymes & Mariah Carey	J	18	(3)
6	13	Can't Let You Go	Fabolous featuring Mike S	Desert Storm	16	
7	16	Rock Your Body	Justin Timberlake	Jive	12	(2)
8	6	When I'm Gone	3 Doors Down	Republic	22	
9	20	Bring Me To Life	Evanescence/Paul McCoy	Wind-Up	16+	(1)
10	5	Picture	Kid Rock featuring Sheryl Crow or Alison Moorer	Lava/Atlantic Universal South	20	
11	7	Beautiful	Snoop Dogg featuring Pharrell	Doggy Style	12	(23)
12		God Bless The USA	American Idol Finalists	RCA	2	
13		No Letting Go	Wayne Wonder	Greensleeves	11	
14		Magic Stick	Lil' Kim featuring 50 Cent	Queen Bee	13+	
15	17	I Can	Nas	Ill Will	9	(19)
16	9	How You Gonna Act Like That	Tyrese	J	15	(30)
17	4	Miss You	Aaliyah	Blackground	22	
18		Unwell	Matchbox Twenty	Atlantic	14+	
19		Sing For The Moment	Eminem	Web/Aftermath	7	(6)
20		If You're Not The One	Daniel Bedingfield	Island/A&M	4	(1)

June 2003

This Mnth	Prev Mnth	Title	Artist	Label	Wks 20	(UK Pos)
1	2	21 Questions	50 Cent featuring Nate Dogg	G Unit/Shady	16	(6)
2	1	Get Busy	Sean Paul	VP/Atlantic	21+	(4)
3	5	I Know What You Want	Busta Rhymes & Mariah Carey	J	18	(3)
4	14	Magic Stick	Lil' Kim featuring 50 Cent	Queen Bee	13+	
5	6	Can't Let Go	Fabolous featuring Mike S	Desert Storm	16	
6	9	Bring Me To Life	Evanescence/Paul McCoy	Wind-Up	16+	(1)
7		Crazy in Love	Beyonce featuring Jay-Z	Columbia	10+	(1)
8	4	Ignition	R. Kelly	Jive	23	(1)
9		This Is Your Night	Clay Aiken	RCA	5	
10	7	Rock Your Body	Justin Timberlake	Jive	12	(46)
11	18	Unwell	Matchbox Twenty	Atlantic	14+	
12		Flying Without Wings	Ruben Studdard	J	4	( )
13		Rock Wit U (Aww Baby)	Ashanti	Murder Inc	10+	(7)
14	8	When I'm Gone	3 Doors Down	Republic	22	
15		So Gone	Monica	J	11+	
16	3	In Da Club	50 Cent	G-Unit/shady	22	(3)
17	13	No Letting Go	Wayne Wonder	Greensleeves	11	
18		Drift Away	Uncle Kracker/Dobie Gray	Lava	11+	
19	10	Picture	Kid Rock featuring Sheryl Crow or Alison Moorer	Lava/Atlantic Universal South	20	
20		Snake	R. Kelly featuring Big Tigger	Jive	3	

◆ For the first time ever, the top two on the US chart were new entries: American Idol 2 runner-up Clay Aiken's 'This Is The Night' and American Idol 2 winner Ruben Studdard's 'Flying Without Wings'. Aiken's first week tally of 398,000 was the biggest weekly sale since Elton's record-shattering 'Candle In The Wind 1997'.

◆ The biggest selling 'Iraq war' single was 'God Bless The USA' by the American Idol Finalists. However, aside from American Idol entrants, the sales of singles were very low, with many erstwhile buyers choosing to download tracks rather than buy them.

◆ Other news: Producer/ songwriter/ vocalist R. Kelly continued his almost unique seamless string of hits, which started in 1992…Motown composers Holland, Dozier & Holland received an award for 100 million radio plays in the USA… Eminem became the first rapper to win an Oscar.

UK 2003 JULY-SEPT

▲ Robbie Williams attracted 375,000 fans to his performance at Knebworth. His album 'Escapology' revisited the No.1 position and he celebrated his 19th Top 20 single since leaving Take That with 'Something Beautiful'. Fellow Take That member Mark Owen returned to the Top 10 after six years with 'Four Minute Warning'.

◆ Destiny's Child vocalist Beyoncé Knowles became the youngest female singer to simultaneously head the UK singles and albums charts with 'Crazy In Love' and 'Dangerously In Love'.

◆ Elton John topped the chart with a re-mix of his minor hit from 1979, 'Are You Ready For Love'. Surprisingly, of his six UK No.1s two were re-mixes and three re-makes.

July 2003

This Mnth	Prev Mnth	Title	Artist	Label	Wks 20	(US Pos)	
1	2	Bring Me To Life	Evanescence featuring Paul McCoy	Epic	11	(6)	F
2		Crazy In Love	Beyoncé	Columbia	9	(1)	
3	8	Fast Food Song	Fast Food Rockers	Better The Devil	7		F
4	17	No Letting Go	Wayne Wonder	VP/Atlantic	7	(11)	F
5	1	Ignition	R. Kelly	Jive	13	(2)	
6		Feel Good Time	P!nk featuring William Orbit	Columbia	4	(60)	
7		Hollywood	Madonna	Maverick	2		
8		We Just Be Dreamin'	Blazin' Squad	East West	3		
9		Real Things	Javine	Innocent	4		F
10	7	Fly On The Wings Of Love	XTM & DJ Chucky presents Annia	Serious	12		F
11		Satisfaction	Benny Benassi presents The Biz	Data/MOS	5		F
12	13	Lost Without You	Delta Goodrem	Epic	6		
13		Fool No More	S Club 8	Polydor	3		
14		21 Questions	50 Cent featuring Nate Dogg	Interscope	4	(1)	
15		Business	Eminem	Interscope	4		
16	3	I Know What You Want	Busta Rhymes and Mariah Carey (feat. Flipmode Squad)	J	7	(3)	
17		Pass It On	The Coral	Deltasonic	2		
18		Can't Get It Back	Mis-Teeq	Telstar	4		
19		Invisible	D-Side	Blacklist/Edel/WEA	2		
20		Rock Wit U (Awww Baby)	Ashanti	Murder Inc./Mercury	3	(2)	

August 2003

This Mnth	Prev Mnth	Title	Artist	Label	Wks 20	(US Pos)	
1		Breathe	Blu Cantrell featuring Sean Paul	Arista	12	(70)	
2		Never Leave You – Uh Ooh, Uh Oooh!	Lumidee	Universal	7	(3)	F
3		Never Gonna Leave Your Side	Daniel Bedingfield	Polydor	5		
4	2	Crazy In Love	Beyoncé	Columbia	9	(1)	
5		Pretty Green Eyes	Ultrabeat	All Around The World	9		F
6	11	Satisfaction	Benny Benassi presents The Biz	Data/MOS	5		F
7		Four Minute Warning	Mark Owen	Universal	5		
8		Something Beautiful	Robbie Williams	Chrysalis	3		
9		Hooray Hooray (It's A Cheeky Holiday)	Cheeky Girls	Multiply	3		
10		Sleeping With The Light On	Busted	Universal	3		
11		Maybe Tomorrow	Stereophonics	V	2	(3)	
12	1	Bring Me To Life	Evanescence featuring Paul McCoy	Epic	11	(6)	F
13		Complete	Jaimeson	V2/J-Did	4		
14		Frontin'	Pharrell Williams featuring Jay-Z	Arista	4	(5)	
15		Dance (With U)	Lemar	Sony Music	4		F
16		Life Got Cold	Girls Aloud	Polydor	3		
17	10	Fly On The Wings Of Love	Xtm & DJ Chucky presents Annia	Serious	12		F
18		Deepest Blue	Deepest Blue	Data/MOS	3		F
19	4	No Letting Go	Wayne Wonder	VP/Atlantic	7	(11)	F
20		All In My Head	Kosheen	Moksha/Arista	2		

September 2003

This Mnth	Prev Mnth	Title	Artist	Label	Wks 20	(US Pos)	
1		Are You Ready For Love	Elton John	Southern Fried	7		
2		Where Is The Love?	The Black Eyed Peas	A&M	12	(8)	F
3	1	Breathe	Blu Cantrell featuring Sean Paul	Arista	12	(70)	
4		White Flag	Dido	Cheeky/Arista	10	(18)	
5	5	Pretty Green Eyes	Ultrabeat	All Around The World	9		F
6		Baby Boy	Big Brovaz	Epic	7		
7		Like Glue	Sean Paul	VP/Atlantic	3	(13)	
8		Sunshine	Gareth Gates	S	2		
9		Sweet Dreams My L.A. Ex	Rachel Stevens	19/Polydor	6		F
10		Miss Perfect	Abs featuring Nodesha	BMG	3		
11		Miss Independent	Kelly Clarkson	S	3	(9)	F
12	15	Dance (With U)	Lemar	Sony Music	4		F
13		Hey Whatever	Westlife	S	3		
14		Can't Hold Us Down	Christina Aguilera featuring Lil' Kim	RCA	3	(12)	
15		Pandora's Kiss/Don't Give Up	Louise	Positive	2		
16		Someday	Nickelback	Roadrunner	3	(7)	
17		Wildest Dreams	Iron Maiden	EMI	1		
18	16	Life Got Cold	Girls Aloud	Polydor	3		
19	2	Never Leave You – Uh Ooh, Uh Oooh!	Lumidee	Universal	7	(3)	F
20		Time Is Running Out	Muse	East West	2		

July 2003

This Mnth	Prev Mnth	Title	Artist	Label	Wks 20	(UK Pos)	F
1	7	Crazy In Love	Beyoncé featuring Jay-Z	Music World/Columbia	20	(1)	
2	4	Magic Stick	Lil' Kim featuring 50 Cent	Queen Bee/Atlantic	16		
3	13	Rock Wit U (Awww Baby)	Ashanti	Murder Inc./Def Jam	14	(7)	
4	9	This Is The Night	Clay Aiken	RCA	5		F
5		Right Thurr	Chingy	Disturbing Tha Peace	20	(17)	F
6	11	Unwell	matchbox twenty	Atlantic	29		
7	2	Get Busy	Sean Paul	Black Shadow/2 Hard	22	(4)	
8	1	21 Questions	50 Cent featuring Nate Dogg	G Unit/Shady/Interscope	16	(6)	
9	6	Bring Me To Life	Evanescence featuring Paul McCoy	Wind-Up	19	(1)	F
10	12	Flying Without Wings	Ruben Studdard	J	4		F
11		Never Leave You – Oh Ooh,	Lumidee	Universal/UMRG	12	(2)	F
12		Miss Independent	Kelly Clarkson	RCA	11	(6)	
13	15	So Gone	Monica	J	12		
14	3	I Know What You Want	Busta Rhymes & Mariah Carey	J	18	(3)	
15	18	Drift Away	Uncle Kracker featuring Dobie Gray	Lava	18		F
16		In Those Jeans	Ginuwine	Epic	10		
17		P.I.M.P.	50 Cent	Shady/Aftermath	18	(5)	
18	5	Can't Let You Go	Fabolous feat. Mike Shorey & Lil' Mo	Desert Storm/Elektra	16	(14)	
19		Where Is The Love?	The Black Eyed Peas	A&M/Interscope	15	(1)	F
20		Into You	Fabolous featuring Tamia or Ashanti	Desert Storm/Elektra	18		

August 2003

This Mnth	Prev Mnth	Title	Artist	Label	Wks 20	(UK Pos)	F
1	1	Crazy In Love	Beyoncé featuring Jay-Z	Music World/Columbia	20	(1)	
2	5	Right Thurr	Chingy	Disturbing Tha Peace	20	(17)	F
3	17	P.I.M.P.	50 Cent	Shady/Aftermath	18	(5)	
4	11	Never Leave You - Uh Ooh, Uh Oooh!	Lumidee	Universal/UMRG	12	(2)	F
5	3	Rock Wit U (Awww Baby)	Ashanti	Murder Inc./Def Jam	14	(7)	
6	6	Unwell	matchbox twenty	Atlantic	29		
7		Shake Ya Tailfeather	Nelly, P. Diddy & Murphy Lee	Bad Boy/UMRG	18	(10)	
8	2	Magic Stick	Lil' Kim featuring 50 Cent	Queen Bee/Atlantic	16		
9	20	Into You	Fabolous featuring Tamia or Ashanti	Desert Storm/Elektra	18		
10		Get Low	Lil Jon & The East Side Boyz feat. Ying Yang Twins	BME	27	(10)	F
11	19	Where Is The Love?	The Black Eyed Peas	A&M/Interscope	15	(1)	F
12	16	In Those Jeans	Ginuwine	Epic	10		
13		Frontin'	Pharrell featuring Jay-Z	Star Trak/Arista	14	(6)	
14	15	Drift Away	Uncle Kracker featuring Dobie Gray	Lava	18		F
15	12	Miss Independent	Kelly Clarkson	RCA	11	(6)	
16	7	Get Busy	Sean Paul	Black Shadow/2 Hard	22	(4)	
17	9	Bring Me To Life	Evanescence featuring Paul McCoy	Wind-Up	19	(1)	F
18		Like Glue	Sean Paul	VP/Atlantic	6	(3)	
19		Baby Boy	Beyoncé featuring Sean Paul	Columbia	22	(2)	
20	13	So Gone	Monica	J	12		

September 2003

This Mnth	Prev Mnth	Title	Artist	Label	Wks 20	(UK Pos)	F
1	7	Shake Ya Tailfeather	Nelly, P. Diddy & Murphy Lee	Bad Boy/UMRG	18	(10)	
2	2	Right Thurr	Chingy	Disturbing Tha Peace	20	(17)	F
3	19	Baby Boy	Beyoncé featuring Sean Paul	Columbia	22	(2)	
4	1	Crazy In Love	Beyoncé featuring Jay-Z	Music World/Columbia	20	(1)	
5	9	Into You	Fabolous featuring Tamia or Ashanti	Desert Storm/Elektra	18		
6	10	Get Low	Lil Jon & The East Side Boyz feat. Ying Yang Twins	BME	27	(10)	F
7	3	P.I.M.P.	50 Cent	Shady/Aftermath	18	(5)	
8	13	Frontin'	Pharrell featuring Jay-Z	Star Trak/Arista	14	(6)	
9	6	Unwell	matchbox twenty	Atlantic	29		
10	11	Where Is The Love?	The Black Eyed Peas	A&M/Interscope	15	(1)	F
11		My Love Is Like... Wo	Mya	A&M/Interscope	8	(33)	
12	4	Never Leave You - Uh Ooh, Uh Oooh!	Lumidee	Universal/UMRG	12	(22)	F
13		Can't Hold Us Down	Christina Aguilera featuring Lil' Kim	RCA	8	(6)	
14		Damn!	YoungBloodZ featuring Lil Jon	So So Def/Arista	19		F
15	12	In Those Jeans	Ginuwine	Epic	10		
16	14	Drift Away	Uncle Kracker featuring Dobie Gray	Lava	18		F
17		Let's Get Down	Bow Wow featuring Baby	Columbia	4		
18		Why Don't You & I	Santana feat. Alex Band or Chad Kroeger	Arista	14		
19		The Remedy (I Won't Worry)	Jason Mraz	Elektra	5		F
20	18	Like Glue	Sean Paul	VP/Atlantic	6	(3)	

◆ Madonna, the most successful female singer of all time, published her first children's book entitled 'English Rose'. However, she missed the Hot 100 for the first time with the single 'Hollywood', although, across the Atlantic, the self-penned and produced track became her eleventh No. 2 hit.

◆ R&B/hip hop and rap continued to rule the US charts with some of the most exciting newcomers on the scene being Chingy (Howard Bailey Jr.), Lumidee (Cadino) and The Black Eyed Peas, who had really taken off since recruiting vocalist Stacy 'Fergie' Ferguson.

◆ East Coast rapper, and Roc-A-Fella Records owner, Jay-Z (Shawn Carter) clocked up his 36th chart entry in just six years. Beyoncé, his vocal partner on 'Crazy In Love', walked off with three MTV awards - a total only equalled by Justin Timberlake.

UK 2003 OCT-DEC

Jamaican dancehall reggae rapper Sean Paul became the first person since Madonna in 1985 to have two singles in the Top 3. He clocked up his fifth Top 5 entry in just eight months with the US No.1 hit 'Baby Boy', which was duet partner Beyoncé's 11th successive Top 10 entry.

Westlife's revival of the Barry Manilow/Scott English hit 'Mandy' was voted Record of the Year by TV viewers. It gave the Irish group their twelfth No.1 from just 16 releases, while 'Turnaround' made them the first act to amass four No.1 albums in the 21st century.

At a time when MPs criticised the harshness of pop TV show juries, previous contestants Gareth Gates, Girls Aloud, Lemar, Liberty X and Alex Parks enjoyed more chart successes, and original Pop Idol Will Young's 'Friday's Child' album sold over a million, as 'Leave Right Now' gave him his fourth No.1 from five singles.

October 2003

This Mnth	Prev Mnth	Title	Artist	Label	Wks 20	(US Pos)	
1	2	Where Is The Love?	The Black Eyed Peas	A&M	12	(8)	F
2	9	Sweet Dreams My L.A. Ex	Rachel Stevens	19/Polydor	6		F
3		I Believe In A Thing Called Love	The Darkness	Must Destroy	7		
4		Superstar	Jamelia	Parlophone	10		
5	4	White Flag	Dido	Cheeky/Arista	10	(18)	
6		Baby Boy	Beyoncé featuring Sean Paul	Columbia	3	(1)	
7		Sundown	S Club 8	Polydor	3		
8		Hole In The Head	Sugababes	Island	5		
9	6	Baby Boy	Big Brovaz	Epic	7		
10		Rubberneckin'	Elvis Presley	RCA	3	(94)	
11		Turn Me On	Kevin Lyttle	Atlantic	10	(4)	F
12		P.I.M.P.	50 Cent	Interscope	3	(3)	
13		Maybe	Emma	19/Universal	4		
14		Re-Offender	Travis	Independiente	2		
15		Going Under	Evanescence	Epic/Wind-up	(2)		
16		Mixed Up World	Sophie Ellis-Bextor	Polydor	1		
17		12:51	The Strokes	Rough Trade	1		
18	3	Breathe	Blu Cantrell featuring Sean Paul	Arista	12	(70)	
19		Innocent Eyes	Delta Goodrem	Epic	2		
20		Bad Day	R.E.M.	Warner Bros.	1		

November 2003

This Mnth	Prev Mnth	Title	Artist	Label	Wks 20	(US Pos)	
1		Be Faithful	Fatman Scoop featuring The Crooklyn Clan	Def Jam	7		F
2	11	Turn Me On	Kevin Lyttle	Atlantic	10	(4)	F
3	1	Where Is The Love?	The Black Eyed Peas	A&M	12	(8)	F
4		Guilty	Blue	Innocent	4		
5		Slow	Kylie Minogue	Parlophone	4		
6		Crashed The Wedding	Busted	Universal	4		
7		Flip Reverse	Blazin' Squad	East West	4		
8		If You Come To Me	Atomic Kitten	Innocent	3		
9		Me Against The Music	Britney Spears featuring Madonna	Jive	4	(35)	
10	8	Hole In The Head	Sugababes	Island	5		
11		Mandy	Westlife	S	6		
12		Jump	Girls Aloud	Polydor	7		
13		Trouble	P!nk	Arista	4	(68)	
14		Jumpin'	Liberty X	V	2	(3)	
15	4	Superstar	Jamelia	Parlophone	10		
16		Maybe That's What It Takes	Alex Parks	Polydor	3		F
17		Hey Ya!	OutKast	Arista	17	(1)	
18		50:50/Lullaby	Lemar	Sony Music	3		
19		State Of Mind	Holly Valance	London	2		
20		Got Some Teeth	Obie Trice	Interscope	3	(54)	F

December 2003

This Mnth	Prev Mnth	Title	Artist	Label	Wks 20	(US Pos)	
1		Leave Right Now	Will Young	S	10		
2		I'm Your Man	Shane Richie	BMG	7		F
3	11	Mandy	Westlife	S	6		
4		Shut Up	The Black Eyed Peas	A&M	9		
5		Changes	Kelly & Ozzy Osbourne	Sanctuary	11		
6	12	Jump	Girls Aloud	Polydor	7		
7		Mad World	Michael Andrews featuring Gary Jules	Adventures In Music	8		F
8		Say It Isn't So	Gareth Gates	S	2		
9		Christmas Time (Don't Let The Bells End)	The Darkness	Must Destroy	3		
10		Santa's List	Cliff Richard	EMI	2		
11		Proper Crimbo	Bo Selecta	BMG	3		F
12	2	Turn Me On	Kevin Lyttle	Atlantic	10	(4)	F
13	16	Maybe That's What It Takes	Alex Parks	Polydor	3		F
14		Happy Xmas (War Is Over)	The Idols	S	3		F
15		One More Chance	Michael Jackson	Epic	1	(83)	
16		You Make Me Feel Brand New	Simply Red	Simplyred.Com	2		
17	6	Crashed The Wedding	Busted	Universal	4		
18		My Immortal	Evanescence	Epic	4	(7)	
19	17	Hey Ya!	OutKast	Arista	17	(1)	
20		Clap Back/Reigns	Ja Rule	Def Jam/Mercury	2	(44)	

October 2003

This Mnth	Prev Mnth	Title	Artist	Label	Wks 20	(UK Pos)	
1	3	Baby Boy	Beyoncé featuring Sean Paul	Columbia	22	(2)	
2	1	Shake Ya Tailfeather	Nelly, P. Diddy & Murphy Lee	Bad Boy/UMRG	18	(10)	
3	6	Get Low	Lil Jon & The East Side Boyz feat. Ying Yang Twins	BME	27	(10)	F
4	2	Right Thurr	Chingy	Disturbing Tha Peace	20	(17)	F
5	14	Damn!	YoungBloodZ featuring Lil Jon	So So Def/Arista	19		F
6		Stand Up	Ludacris featuring Shawnna	Disturbing Tha Peace	19	(14)	
7	8	Frontin'	Pharrell featuring Jay-Z	Star Trak/Arista	14	(6)	
8	5	Into You	Fabolous featuring Tamia or Ashanti	Desert Storm/Elektra	18		
9	7	P.I.M.P.	50 Cent	Shady/Aftermath	18	(5)	
10		Here Without You	3 Doors Down	Republic/Universal	22		
11	18	Why Don't You & I	Santana feat. Alex Band or Chad Kroeger	Arista	14		
12	9	Where Is The Love?	The Black Eyed Peas	A&M/Interscope	15	(1)	F
13	10	Unwell	matchbox twenty	Atlantic	29		
14		Rain On Me	Ashanti	Murder Inc./Def Jam	9	(19)	
15		Holidae In	Chingy feat. Ludacris & Snoop Dogg	Disturbing Tha Peace	14	(35)	
16	4	Crazy In Love	Beyoncé featuring Jay-Z	Music World/Columbia	20	(1)	
17		Thoia Thoing	R. Kelly	Jive	5	(14)	
18		Can't Stop, Won't Stop	Young Gunz	Roc-A-Fella/Def Jam	5		F
19	13	Can't Hold Us Down	Christina Aguilera featuring Lil' Kim	RCA	8	(6)	
20		Suga Suga	Baby Bash featuring Frankie J	Universal	18		F

November 2003

This Mnth	Prev Mnth	Title	Artist	Label	Wks 20	(UK Pos)	
1	1	Baby Boy	Beyoncé featuring Sean Paul	Columbia	22	(2)	
2	6	Stand Up	Ludacris featuring Shawnna	Disturbing Tha Peace	19	(14)	
3	15	Holidae In	Chingy feat. Ludacris & Snoop Dogg	Disturbing Tha Peace	14	(35)	
4	5	Damn!	YoungBloodZ featuring Lil Jon	So So Def/Arista	19		F
5	3	Get Low	Lil Jon & The East Side Boyz feat. Ying Yang Twins	BME	27	(10)	F
6	10	Here Without You	3 Doors Down	Republic/Universal	22		
7		The Way You Move	OutKast featuring Sleepy Brown	Arista	30	(7)	
8		Hey Ya!	OutKast	Arista	21	(3)	
9	14	Rain On Me	Ashanti	Murder Inc./Def Jam	9	(19)	
10	2	Shake Ya Tailfeather	Nelly, P. Diddy & Murphy Lee	Bad Boy/UMRG	18	(10)	
11	20	Suga Suga	Baby Bash featuring Frankie J	Universal	18		F
12	11	Why Don't You & I	Santana feat. Alex Band or Chad Kroeger	Arista	14		
13		Walked Outta Heaven	Jagged Edge	Columbia	15	(21)	
14		Step In The Name Of Love	R. Kelly	Jive	13	(14)	
15	4	Right Thurr	Chingy	Disturbing Tha Peace	20	(17)	F
16	13	Unwell	matchbox twenty	Atlantic	29		
17		Milkshake	Kelis	Star Trak/Arista	12	(2)	F
18		Headstrong	Trapt	Warner Bros.	5		F
19		Stunt 101	G-Unit	G-Unit/Shady	5	(25)	F
20	9	P.I.M.P.	50 Cent	Shady/Aftermath	18	(5)	

December 2003

This Mnth	Prev Mnth	Title	Artist	Label	Wks 20	(UK Pos)	
1	8	Hey Ya!	OutKast	Arista	21	(3)	
2	2	Stand Up	Ludacris featuring Shawnna	Disturbing Tha Peace	19	(14)	
3	7	The Way You Move	OutKast featuring Sleepy Brown	Arista	30	(7)	
4	17	Milkshake	Kelis	Star Trak/Arista	12	(2)	F
5	1	Baby Boy	Beyoncé featuring Sean Paul	Columbia	22	(2)	
6	6	Here Without You	3 Doors Down	Republic/Universal	22		
7	3	Holidae In	Chingy feat. Ludacris & Snoop Dogg	Disturbing Tha Peace	14	(35)	
8	13	Walked Outta Heaven	Jagged Edge	Columbia	15	(21)	
9	11	Suga Suga	Baby Bash featuring Frankie J	Universal	18		F
10		You Don't Know My Name	Alicia Keys	J	14	(19)	
11	14	Step In The Name Of Love	R. Kelly	Jive	13	(14)	
12	4	Damn!	YoungBloodZ featuring Lil Jon	So So Def/Arista	19		F
13		Change Clothes	Jay-Z	Roc-A-Fella/Def Jam	8	(32)	
14	5	Get Low	Lil Jon & The East Side Boyz feat. Ying Yang Twins	BME	27	(10)	F
15	19	Stunt 101	G-Unit	G-Unit/Shady	5	(25)	F
16		It's My Life	No Doubt	Interscope	12	(20)	
17	12	Why Don't You & I	Santana feat. Alex Band or Chad Kroeger	Arista	14		
18		Someday	Nickelback	Roadrunner	14	(6)	
19		Wat Da Hook Gon Be	Murphy Lee featuring Jermaine Dupri	Fo' Reel/Universal	6		
20		Me, Myself And I	Beyoncé	Columbia	14	(11)	

US 2003
OCT-DEC

◆ Twenty-one-year-old Britney Spears became the youngest recording artist ever to have a star on the famous Hollywood Walk of Fame. Together with her "kiss and tell" partner Madonna she scored with 'Me Against The Music', which, despite a video that cost $1.75 million, sold disappointingly.

▲ 'Hey Ya!' by OutKast became the first download to outsell all CD singles in the US in a week with total sales of 8,500. Within a couple of years sales of ten times this amount were average for a top-selling download.

◆ A concert inspired by Nelson Mandela took place in Cape Town for World Aids Day. Among the artists appearing were Beyoncé, Peter Gabriel, Bob Geldof, Eurythmics, Queen and U2.

UK 2004 JAN-MAR

▲ UK acts who picked up BRIT awards included Daniel Bedingfield, The Darkness, Dido, Duran Duran, Lemar and Annie Lennox. Coldplay, The Beatles, George Harrison and Radiohead all won a Grammy each.

◆ The Christmas No.1 battle was won by one-hit wonders Michael Andrews and Gary Jules. They beat The Darkness, The Idols (the last 12 acts in 'Pop Idol') and 'EastEnder' Shane Richie.

◆ 'Pop Idol' winner, Michelle McManus, scored the 13th No.1 for the series with 'All This Time'. Runners-up Sam & Mark joined forces and hit the top with a little help from a Beatles song and 'I'm A Celebrity...' star Peter André repeated that feat with his No.2 hit from 1996, 'Mysterious Girl'.

January 2004

This Mnth	Prev Mnth	Title	Artist	Label	Wks 20	(US Pos)	
1	7	Mad World	Michael Andrews featuring Gary Jules	Adventures In Music	8		F
2	5	Changes	Kelly & Ozzy Osbourne	Sanctuary	11		
3		All This Time	Michelle	S	8		F
4	4	Shut Up	The Black Eyed Peas	A&M	9		
5		Milkshake	Kelis	Virgin	9	(3)	
6	19	Hey Ya!	OutKast	Arista	17	(1)	
7		Somebody To Love	Boogie Pimps	Data	9		F
8	1	Leave Right Now	Will Young	S	10		
9		This Groove/Let Your Head Go	Victoria Beckham	19/Telstar	4		
10	9	Christmas Time (Don't Let The Bells End)	The Darkness	Must Destroy	3		
11		Take Me Out	Franz Ferdinand	Domino	4		
12		I'm Still In Love With You	Sean Paul featuring Sasha	VP/Atlantic	7	(14)	
13	11	Proper Crimbo	Bo Selecta	BMG	3		F
14		Bring It On/My Lover's Prayer	Alistair Griffin	UMTV	3		F
15		So Confused	2Play featuring Raghav & Jucxi	2PSL	7		F
16	2	I'm Your Man	Shane Richie	BMG	7		F
17		Ladies Night	Atomic Kitten featuring Kool & The Gang	Innocent	4		
18	14	Happy Xmas (War Is Over)	The Idols	S	3		F
19		Too Lost In You	Sugababes	Universal	5		
20		Feelin' Fine	Ultrabeat	All Around The World	6		

February 2004

This Mnth	Prev Mnth	Title	Artist	Label	Wks 20	(US Pos)	
1		Take Me To The Clouds Above	LMC vs U2	All Around The World	7		F
2	5	Milkshake	Kelis	Virgin	9	(3)	
3	6	Hey Ya!	OutKast	Arista	17	(1)	
4	3	All This Time	Michelle	S	8		F
5	7	Somebody To Love	Boogie Pimps	Data	9		F
6		With A Little Help From My Friends/Measure Of A Man	Sam & Mark	19	3		F
7		She Believes (In Me)	Ronan Keating	Polydor	3		
8	15	So Confused	2Play featuring Raghav & Jucxi	2PSL	7		F
9		Who's David	Busted	Universal	3		
10		Run	Snow Patrol	Fiction/Polydor	3		F
11		Somewhere Only We Know	Keane	Island	5		F
12		Moviestar	Stereophonics	V	2	(2)	
13	12	I'm Still In Love With You	Sean Paul featuring Sasha	VP/Atlantic	7	(14)	
14		I'll Be There	Emma	19/Universal	3		
15		Here 4 One	Blazin' Squad	East West	2		
16		Last Train Home	Lostprophets	Visible Noise	2		
17		It Takes Scoop	Fatman Scoop featuring The Crooklyn Clan	Def Jam	2		
18	2	Changes	Kelly & Ozzy Osbourne	Sanctuary	11		
19		Give It Away	Deepest Blue	Data/MOS	2		
20		Can't Get Enough	Raghav	A&R	2		

March 2004

This Mnth	Prev Mnth	Title	Artist	Label	Wks 20	(US Pos)	
1		Mysterious Girl	Peter Andre	A&E	6		
2		Cha Cha Slide	DJ Casper	All Around The World	10		F
3		Thank You	Jamelia	Parlophone	7		
4		Toxic	Britney Spears	Jive	8	(9)	
5		Amazing	George Michael	Aegean	4		
6		Obvious	Westlife	S	3		
7		Baby I Love U	Jennifer Lopez	Epic	4	(72)	
8		Red Blooded Woman	Kylie Minogue	Parlophone	4		
9		Yeah!	Usher featuring Lil' Jon & Ludacris	Arista	9	(1)	
10		Not In Love	Enrique featuring Kelis	Interscope	4		
11	1	Take Me To The Clouds Above	LMC vs U2	All Around The World	7		F
12		Your Game	Will Young	S	3		
13	3	Hey Ya!	OutKast	Arista	17	(1)	
14	9	Who's David	Busted	Universal	3		
15		Dude	Beenie Man featuring Ms Thing	Virgin	4	(52)	
16		Hey Mama	The Black Eyed Peas	A&M	3	(23)	
17		She Wants To Move	N*E*R*D	Virgin	7		
18		Love You Like Mad	Vs	Innocent	2		F
19	11	Somewhere Only We Know	Keane	Island	5		F
20		I Miss You	Blink-182	Geffen	3	(42)	

410

January 2004

This Mnth	Prev Mnth	Title	Artist	Label	Wks 20	(UK Pos)	
1	1	Hey Ya!	OutKast	Arista	21	(3)	
2	3	The Way You Move	OutKast featuring Sleepy Brown	Arista	30	(7)	
3	4	Milkshake	Kelis	Star Trak/Arista	12	(2)	F
4	10	You Don't Know My Name	Alicia Keys	J	14		
5		Slow Jamz	Twista feat. Kanye West & Jamie Foxx	Atlantic	14	(3)	F
6	2	Stand Up	Ludacris featuring Shawnna	Disturbing Tha Peace	19	(14)	
7	8	Walked Outta Heaven	Jagged Edge	Columbia	15	(21)	
8	20	Me, Myself And I	Beyoncé	Columbia	14	(11)	
9	9	Suga Suga	Baby Bash featuring Frankie J	Universal	18		F
10	6	Here Without You	3 Doors Down	Republic/Universal	22		
11	18	Someday	Nickelback	Roadrunner	14	(6)	
12	16	It's My Life	No Doubt	Interscope	12	(20)	
13		Yeah!	Usher featuring Lil Jon & Ludacris	Arista	28	(1)	
14	5	Baby Boy	Beyoncé featuring Sean Paul	Columbia	22	(2)	
15	14	Get Low	Lil Jon & The East Side Boyz feat. Ying Yang Twins	BME	27	(10)	F
16		Read Your Mind	Avant	Geffen	7		F
17	7	Holidae In	Chingy feat. Ludacris & Snoop Dogg	Disturbing Tha Peace	14	(35)	
18	12	Damn!	YoungBloodZ featuring Lil Jon	So So Def/Arista	19		F
19		Numb	Linkin Park	Warner Bros.	11	(14)	
20	11	Step In The Name Of Love	R. Kelly	Jive	13	(14)	

February 2004

This Mnth	Prev Mnth	Title	Artist	Label	Wks 20	(UK Pos)	
1	5	Slow Jamz	Twista feat. Kanye West & Jamie Foxx	Atlantic	16	(3)	F
2	2	The Way You Move	OutKast featuring Sleepy Brown	Arista	30	(7)	
3	13	Yeah!	Usher featuring Lil Jon & Ludacris	Arista	28	(1)	
4	1	Hey Ya!	OutKast	Arista	21	(3)	
5	8	Me, Myself And I	Beyoncé	Columbia	14	(11)	
6	4	You Don't Know My Name	Alicia Keys	J	14	(19)	
7	11	Someday	Nickelback	Roadrunner	14	(6)	
8		Hotel	Cassidy featuring R. Kelly	Full Surface	14	(3)	F
9		Salt Shaker	Ying Yang Twins feat. Lil Jon & East Side Boyz	Collipark	9		
10		One Call Away	Chingy featuring J. Weav	Disturbing Tha Peace	13	(26)	
11		Sorry 2004	Ruben Studdard	J	10		
12	3	Milkshake	Kelis	Star Trak/Arista	12	(2)	F
13	10	Here Without You	3 Doors Down	Republic/Universal	22		
14	12	It's My Life	No Doubt	Interscope	12	(20)	
15	19	Numb	Linkin Park	Warner Bros.	11	(14)	
16		Tipsy	J-Kwon	So So Def	20	(4)	F
17	9	Suga Suga	Baby Bash featuring Frankie J	Universal	18		F
18		Through The Wire	Kanye West	Roc-A-Fella/Def Jam	8	(9)	F
19		Splash Waterfalls	Ludacris	Disturbing Tha Peace	11		
20	7	Walked Outta Heaven	Jagged Edge	Columbia	15	(21)	

March 2004

This Mnth	Prev Mnth	Title	Artist	Label	Wks 20	(UK Pos)	
1	3	Yeah!	Usher featuring Lil Jon & Ludacris	Arista	28	(1)	
2	10	One Call Away	Chingy featuring J. Weav	Disturbing Tha Peace	13	(26)	
3	1	Slow Jamz	Twista feat. Kanye West & Jamie Foxx	Atlantic	16		F
4	16	Tipsy	J-Kwon	So So Def	20	(4)	F
5	2	The Way You Move	OutKast featuring Sleepy Brown	Arista	30	(7)	
6	8	Hotel	Cassidy featuring R. Kelly	Full Surface	14	(3)	F
7	19	Splash Waterfalls	Ludacris	Disturbing Tha Peace	11		
8	4	Hey Ya!	OutKast	Arista	21	(3)	
9	5	Me, Myself And I	Beyoncé	Columbia	14	(11)	
10		Dirt Off Your Shoulder	Jay-Z	Roc-A-Fella/Def Jam	17	(12)	
11	11	Sorry 2004	Ruben Studdard	J	10		
12		Toxic	Britney Spears	Jive	12	(1)	
13		My Immortal	Evanescence	Wind-Up	16	(7)	
14	15	Numb	Linkin Park	Warner Bros.	11	(14)	
15	9	Salt Shaker	Ying Yang Twins feat. Lil Jon & East Side Boyz	Collipark	9		
16		With You	Jessica Simpson	Columbia	6	(7)	
17		I Don't Wanna Know	Mario Winans feat. Enya & P. Diddy	Bad Boy	18	(1)	
18		This Love	Maroon5	Octone/J	24	(3)	
19		The First Cut Is The Deepest	Sheryl Crow	A&M/Mercury/Interscope	11	(37)	
20	7	Someday	Nickelback	Roadrunner	14	(6)	

◆ Rap duo OutKast entered the record books when they hogged the top two places on the US singles chart with the same tracks ('Hey Ya!' and 'The Way You Move') for eight consecutive weeks.

◆ A sign of the times – with downloads outselling CD singles by 16-1, the US Singles Sales chart was reduced to a Top 25 and the Digital Sales chart increased to a Top 50. Digital sales were now up to two million tracks a week with 24 million being registered in this three-month period.

◆ On what would have been Elvis Presley's 69th birthday, it was announced that he had earned 25 multi platinum, 55 platinum and 97 gold albums, as well as 7 multi platinum, 27 platinum and 51 gold singles.

◆ The biggest-selling American single in the UK in 2004 was 'F**k It (I Don't Want You Back)' by New Yorker Eamon (Doyle). The track, which sold over 550,000 copies, contained a record-breaking 33 expletives. It was soon followed by an answer record from Frankee (who claimed to be his girlfriend) with 'F.U.R.B. – F U Right Back', which replaced Eamon at No.1 in the UK. Eamon's record was also the first No.1 on the newly launched Ringtones chart.

◆ A survey showed that the most played artist on UK radio in the last 20 years was George Michael. Elton John took the runner-up slot and Robbie Williams completed the Top 3.

◆ Three of the 21st century's most successful recording acts made their UK chart debuts this quarter: boy band McFly, rapper Kanye West and singer/songwriter Natasha Bedingfield, who followed in her brother Daniel's footsteps.

April 2004

This Mnth	Prev Mnth	Title	Artist	Label	Wks 20	(US Pos)	
1	9	Yeah!	Usher featuring Lil' Jon & Ludacris	Arista	9	(1)	
2	2	Cha Cha Slide	DJ Casper	All Around The World	10		F
3		Left Outside Alone	Anastacia	Epic	15		
4		5 Colours In Her Hair	McFly	Universal	6		F
5		Breathe Easy	Blue	Innocent	6		
6		Slow Jamz	Twista	Atlantic	5	(1)	F
7		In The Shadows	The Rasmus	Universal	9		F
8		F**k It (I Don't Want You Back)	Eamon	Jive	11	(16)	F
9	4	Toxic	Britney Spears	Jive	8	(9)	
10		My Band	D12	Shady/Interscope	7	(6)	
11		The Way You Move	OutKast featuring Sleepy Brown	Arista	3	(1)	
12		Love Is Only A Feeling	The Darkness	Must Destroy	2		
13		Come With Me	Special D	All Around The World	5		F
14		Through The Wire	Kanye West	Roc-A-Fella/Def Jam	3	(15)	F
15	17	She Wants To Move	N*E*R*D	Virgin	7		
16		In The Middle	Sugababes	Island	3		
17		For Lovers	Wolfman featuring Peter Doherty	Rough Trade	2		F
18		Someone Like Me/Right Now 2004	Atomic Kitten	Innocent	2		
19		I Like It	Narcotic Thrust	Free 2 Air	4		F
20	3	Thank You	Jamelia	Parlophone	7		

May 2004

This Mnth	Prev Mnth	Title	Artist	Label	Wks 20	(US Pos)	
1	8	F**k It (I Don't Want You Back)	Eamon	Jive	11	(16)	F
2	10	My Band	D12	Shady/Interscope	7	(6)	
3	3	Left Outside Alone	Anastacia	Epic	15		
4		This Love	Maroon5	J	7	(5)	
5	7	In The Shadows	The Rasmus	Universal	9		F
6		Dip It Low	Christina Milian	Def Jam	5	(50)	
7		F.U.R.B. - F U Right Back	Frankee	All Around The World	8	(63)	F
8		Single	Natasha Bedingfield	Phonogenic/BMG	4	(57)	F
9		Air Hostess	Busted	Universal	2		
10	1	Yeah!	Usher featuring Lil' Jon & Ludacris	Arista	9	(1)	
11		Fit But You Know It	The Streets	Locked On/679 Recordings	1		
12		Irish Blood, English Heart	Morrissey	Attack	2		
13		Don't Tell Me	Avril Lavigne	Arista	3	(22)	
14		Hotel	Cassidy featuring R. Kelly	J	7	(4)	F
15		Everybody's Changing	Keane	Island	2		
16		Last Thing On My Mind	Ronan Keating & LeAnn Rimes	Polydor/Curb	2		
17		On My Knees	411 featuring Ghostface Killah	Sony Music	4		F
18		Summer Sunshine	The Corrs	Atlantic	3		
19	4	5 Colours In Her Hair	McFly	Universal	6		F
20		It Can't Be Right	2Play featuring Raghav & Naila Boss	2PSL/Inferno	2		

June 2004

This Mnth	Prev Mnth	Title	Artist	Label	Wks 20	(US Pos)	
1	7	F.U.R.B. – F U Right Back	Frankee	All Around The World	8	(63)	F
2		Trick Me	Kelis	Virgin	9		
3		I Don't Wanna Know	Mario Winans feat. Enya & P. Diddy	Bad Boy	10	(2)	F
4	1	F**k It (I Don't Want You Back)	Eamon	Jive	11	(16)	F
5	14	Hotel	Cassidy featuring R. Kelly	J	7	(4)	F
6		Come On England	4-4-2	Gut	3		F
7		Dragostea Din Tei	O-Zone	Jive	12		F
8		All Together Now 2004	The Farm feat. SFX Boys' Choir, Liverpool	DMG	3		
9		Everytime	Britney Spears	Jive	8	(15)	
10		Insania	Peter Andre	East West	2		
11	17	On My Knees	411 featuring Ghostface Killah	Sony Music	4		F
12	3	Left Outside Alone	Anastacia	Epic	15		
13		Blood Sweat And Tears	V	Universal	2		F
14	6	Dip It Low	Christina Milian	Def Jam	5	(5)	
15		Talk About Our Love	Brandy featuring Kanye West	Atlantic	3	(36)	
16		Mass Destruction	Faithless	Cheeky/Arista	2		
17		With You	Jessica Simpson	Columbia	2	(14)	
18		Ch-Check It Out	Beastie Boys	Capitol	2	(68)	
19		Story Of My Life	Kristian Leontiou	Polydor	2		F
20		All Falls Down	Kanye West feat. Syleena Johnson	Roc-A-Fella	2	(7)	

April 2004

This Mnth	Prev Mnth	Title	Artist	Label	Wks 20	(UK Pos)	
1	1	Yeah!	Usher featuring Lil Jon & Ludacris	Arista	28	(1)	
2	4	Tipsy	J-Kwon	So So Def	20	(4)	F
3	2	One Call Away	Chingy featuring J. Weav	Disturbing Tha Peace	13	(26)	
4	17	I Don't Wanna Know	Mario Winans feat. Enya & P. Diddy	Bad Boy	18	(1)	
5	18	This Love	Maroon5	Octone/J	24	(3)	
6	10	Dirt Off Your Shoulder	Jay-Z	Roc-A-Fella/Def Jam	17	(12)	
7		Burn	Usher	Arista	21	(1)	
8	6	Hotel	Cassidy featuring R. Kelly	Full Surface	14	(3)	F
9	13	My Immortal	Evanescence	Wind-Up	16	(7)	
10	7	Splash Waterfalls	Ludacris	Disturbing Tha Peace	11		
11		Naughty Girl	Beyoncé	Columbia	14	(10)	
12		Solitaire	Clay Aiken	RCA	1		
13	12	Toxic	Britney Spears	Jive	12	(1)	
14		If I Ain't Got You	Alicia Keys	J 30 18			
15		My Band	D12	Shady/Interscope	10	(2)	
16	5	The Way You Move	OutKast featuring Sleepy Brown	Arista	30	(7)	
17		All Falls Down	Kanye West feat. Syleena Johnson	Roc-A-Fella/Def Jam	12	(10)	
18	3	Slow Jamz	Twista feat. Kanye West & Jamie Foxx	Atlantic	16		F
19		Freek-A-Leek	Petey Pablo	Jive	16		F
20		I'm Still In Love With You	Sean Paul featuring Sasha	VP/Atlantic	10	(6)	

May 2004

This Mnth	Prev Mnth	Title	Artist	Label	Wks 20	(UK Pos)	
1	1	Yeah!	Usher featuring Lil Jon & Ludacris	Arista	28	(1)	
2	7	Burn	Usher	Arista	21	(1)	
3	4	I Don't Wanna Know	Mario Winans featuring Enya & P. Diddy	Bad Boy	18	(1)	
4	11	Naughty Girl	Beyoncé	Columbia	14	(10)	
5	5	This Love	Maroon5	Octone/J	24	(3)	
6	2	Tipsy	J-Kwon	So So Def	20	(4)	F
7		Overnight Celebrity	Twista	Atlantic	14	(16)	
8	15	My Band	D12	Shady/Interscope	10	(2)	
9	14	If I Ain't Got You	Alicia Keys	J	30	18	
10		The Reason	Hoobastank	Island	24	(12)	F
11	17	All Falls Down	Kanye West featuring Syleena Johnson	Roc-A-Fella/Def Jam	12	(10)	
12	19	Freek-A-Leek	Petey Pablo	Jive	16		F
13	6	Dirt Off Your Shoulder	Jay-Z	Roc-A-Fella/Def Jam	17	(12)	
14		Confessions Part II	Usher	LaFace/Zomba	18	(5)	
15	9	My Immortal	Evanescence	Wind-Up	16	(7)	
16		The Game Over (Flip)	Lil' Flip	Sucka Free/Columbia	7		F
17	3	One Call Away	Chingy featuring J. Weav	Disturbing Tha Peace	13	(26)	
18	20	I'm Still In Love With You	Sean Paul featuring Sasha	VP/Atlantic	10	(6)	
19		Roses	OutKast	LaFace/Zomba	8	(4)	
20	16	The Way You Move	OutKast featuring Sleepy Brown	Arista	30	(7)	

June 2004

This Mnth	Prev Mnth	Title	Artist	Label	Wks 20	(UK Pos)	
1	2	Burn	Usher	Arista	21	(1)	
2	3	I Don't Wanna Know	Mario Winans featuring Enya & P. Diddy	Bad Boy	18	(1)	
3	10	The Reason	Hoobastank	Island	24	(12)	F
4	4	Naughty Girl	Beyoncé	Columbia	14	(10)	
5	14	Confessions Part II	Usher	LaFace/Zomba	18	(5)	
6	1	Yeah!	Usher featuring Lil Jon & Ludacris	Arista	28	(1)	
7	7	Overnight Celebrity	Twista	Atlantic	14	(16)	
8	9	If I Ain't Got You	Alicia Keys	J	30	(18)	
9	5	This Love	Maroon5	Octone/J	24	(3)	
10	12	Freek-A-Leek	Petey Pablo	Jive	16		F
11	19	Roses	OutKast	LaFace/Zomba	8	(4)	
12	11	All Falls Down	Kanye West featuring Syleena Johnson	Roc-A-Fella/Def Jam	12	(10)	
13		Slow Motion	Juvenile featuring Soulja Slim	Cash Money/UMRG	20		
14	6	Tipsy	J-Kwon	So So Def	20	(4)	F
15		Move Ya Body	Nina Sky featuring Jabba	Next Plateau/Universal	18	(6)	F
16		On Fire	Lloyd Bank$	G-Unit/Interscope	10	(19)	F
17	8	My Band	D12	Shady/Interscope	10	(2)	
18	13	Dirt Off Your Shoulder	Jay-Z	Roc-A-Fella/Def Jam	17		
19	15	My Immortal	Evanescence	Wind-Up	16	(7)	
20		Jesus Walks	Kanye West	Roc-A-Fella/Def Jam	12	(16)	

◆ Usher's album 'Confessions' sold a remarkable 1.1 million copies in its first week, and went on to sell over nine million. He also equalled the Beatles' and Bee Gees' record by having three singles together in the Top 10. In the UK, Usher became the first American male to simultaneously top the singles and album charts for over ten years.

▲ Madonna kicked off her 55-date 'Re-Invention' tour. In total it attracted 880,000 fans who paid out £124.5 million. Other noteworthy live shows included Paul McCartney and Oasis at Glastonbury, The Who at the Isle of Wight and Rock In Rio (in Lisbon), which was seen by 385,000 people.

UK 2004 JULY–SEPT

◆ In August, sales of singles were the lowest since records began in 1969 and at times were only one third of the sales of just four years earlier. However, sales of downloads in the UK had passed two million for the year.

◆ Elvis Presley's first ever single 'That's All Right' was re-issued 50 years after it had initially been released and this time it was a hit – making it the oldest Top 3 entry of all time. It also topped the US physical singles sales chart.

▲ Other news: Katie Melua's debut album 'Call Off The Search' became the year's first million seller… Blue announced they were taking a break and rap superstar Jay-Z retired (he returned in 2006).

July 2004

This Mnth	Prev Mnth	Title	Artist	Label	Wks 20	(US Pos)	
1	9	Everytime	Britney Spears	Jive	8	(15)	
2		Burn	Usher	Arista	7	(1)	
3	3	I Don't Wanna Know	Mario Winans feat. Enya & P. Diddy	Bad Boy	10	(2)	F
4		Obviously	McFly	Universal	7		
5	7	Dragostea Din Tei	O-Zone	Jive	12		F
6		The Show	Girls Aloud	Polydor	4		
7		Lola's Theme	Shapeshifters	Positiva	7		F
8		Some Girls	Rachel Stevens	Polydor	6		
9		Roses	OutKast	Arista	3	(9)	
10		Tipsy	J-Kwon	LaFace	7	(2)	F
11		Dry Your Eyes	The Streets	Locked On/ 679 Recordings	6		
12		Move Ya Body	Nina Sky	Universal	6	(4)	F
13	2	Trick Me	Kelis	Virgin	9		
14		See It In A Boy's Eyes	Jamelia	Parlophone	4		
15		Eyes On You	Jay Sean feat. The Rishi Rich Project	Relentless	4		
16		That's All Right	Elvis Presley	RCA	2		
17		Friday's Child	Will Young	S	2		
18		First Of The Gang To Die	Morrissey	Attack	3		
19		Never Felt Like This Before	Shaznay Lewis	London	5		F
20		Chocolate	Kylie	Parlophone	2		

August 2004

This Mnth	Prev Mnth	Title	Artist	Label	Wks 20	(US Pos)	
1		Thunderbirds/3AM	Busted	Universal	7		
2	11	Dry Your Eyes	The Streets	Locked On/ 679 Recordings	6		
3	7	Lola's Theme	Shapeshifters	Positiva	7		F
4		Baby Cakes	3 Of A Kind	Relentless	9		F
5		How Come	D12	Shady/Interscope	4	(27)	
6		Sick And Tired	Anastacia	Epic	4		
7	8	Some Girls	Rachel Stevens	Polydor	6		
8		Can't Stand Me Now	The Libertines	Rough Trade	2		
9		My Happy Ending	Avril Lavigne	Arista	4	(9)	
10	10	Tipsy	J-Kwon	LaFace	7	(2)	F
11		These Words	Natasha Bedingfield	Phonogenic/BMG	7	(17)	
12		Guns Don't Kill People, Rappers Do	Goldie Lookin Chain	Atlantic	5		F
13		Hip To Hip/Can You Feel It?	V	Universal	2		
14	5	Dragostea Din Tei	O-Zone	Jive	12		F
15	2	Burn	Usher	Arista	7	(1)	
16		Put 'em High	Stonebridge featuring Therese	Hed Kandi	2		F
17		We Are	Ana Johnsson	Epic	3		F
18	1	Everytime	Britney Spears	Jive	8	(15)	
19	14	See It In A Boy's Eyes	Jamelia	Parlophone	4		
20	12	Move Ya Body	Nina Sky	Universal	6	(4)	F

September 2004

This Mnth	Prev Mnth	Title	Artist	Label	Wks 20	(US Pos)	
1	11	These Words	Natasha Bedingfield	Phonogenic/BMG	7	(17)	
2	4	Baby Cakes	3 Of A Kind	Relentless	9		F
3		My Place/Flap Your Wings	Nelly	Universal	7	(4)	
4		Leave (Get Out)	JoJo	Mercury	5	(12)	F
5		Dumb	The 411	Sony/Streetside	5		
6		She Will Be Loved	Maroon5	J	6	(5)	
7		Sunshine	Twista featuring Anthony Hamilton	Atlantic	5		
8		Real To Me	Brian McFadden	Modest!/Sony Music	4		F
9		That Girl	McFly	Universal	3		
10		Call On Me	Eric Prydz	Data	12		
11	12	Guns Don't Kill People, Rappers Do	Goldie Lookin Chain	Atlantic	5		F
12		Love Machine	Girls Aloud	Polydor	4		
13		American Idiot	Green Day	Reprise	4	(61)	
14	1	Thunderbirds/3AM	Busted	Universal	7		
15		You Should Really Know	Pirates feat. Enya, Shola Ama, Naila Boss & Ishani	Relentless	4		F
16		Gravity	Embrace	Independiente	2		
17		Is It Cos I'm Cool?	Mousse T featuring Emma Lanford	Free 2 Air	4		
18	2	Dry Your Eyes	The Streets	Locked On/ 679 Recordings	6		
19		Caught In A Moment	Sugababes	Universal	2		
20		You Had Me	Joss Stone	Relentless/Virgin	3		

July 2004

This Mnth	Prev Mnth	Title	Artist	Label	Wks 20	(UK Pos)	
1	5	Confessions Part II	Usher	LaFace/Zomba	18	(5)	
2	1	Burn	Usher	Arista	21	(1)	
3	13	Slow Motion	Juvenile featuring Soulja Slim	Cash Money/UMRG	20		
4	3	The Reason	Hoobastank	Island	24	(12)	F
5	8	If I Ain't Got You	Alicia Keys	J	30	(18)	
6	15	Move Ya Body	Nina Sky featuring Jabba	Next Plateau/Universal	18	(6)	F
7		I Believe	Fantasia	J	3		F
8	10	Freek-A-Leek	Petey Pablo	Jive	16		F
9		Lean Back	Terror Squad	SRC/Universal	20	(24)	F
10	16	On Fire	Lloyd Bank$	G-Unit/Interscope	10	(19)	F
11	6	Yeah!	Usher featuring Lil Jon & Ludacris	Arista	28	(1)	
12		Turn Me On	Kevin Lyttle featuring Spragga Benz	VP/Atlantic	15	(2)	F
13	2	I Don't Wanna Know	Mario Winans feat. Enya & P. Diddy	Bad Boy	18	(1)	
14	9	This Love	Maroon5	Octone/J	24	(3)	
15	20	Jesus Walks	Kanye West	Roc-A-Fella/Def Jam	12	(16)	
16	7	Overnight Celebrity	Twista	Atlantic	14	(16)	
17		Dip It Low	Christina Milian	Island/IDJMG	14	(2)	
18		Leave (Get Out)	JoJo	Da Family/Background	10	(2)	F
19	4	Naughty Girl	Beyoncé	Columbia	14	(10)	
20		Everytime	Britney Spears	Jive	5	(1)	

August 2004

This Mnth	Prev Mnth	Title	Artist	Label	Wks 20	(UK Pos)	
1	9	Lean Back	Terror Squad	SRC/Universal	20	(24)	F
2	3	Slow Motion	Juvenile featuring Soulja Slim	Cash Money/UMRG	20		
3	1	Confessions Part II	Usher	LaFace/Zomba	18	(5)	
4		Sunshine	Lil' Flip featuring Lea	Sucka Free/Columbia	14	(14)	
5	12	Turn Me On	Kevin Lyttle feat. Spragga Benz	VP/Atlantic	15	(2)	F
6	17	Dip It Low	Christina Milian	Island/IDJMG	14	(2)	
7	6	Move Ya Body	Nina Sky featuring Jabba	Next Plateau/Universal	18	(6)	F
8		Goodies	Ciara featuring Petey Pablo	Sho'Nuff/LaFace	23	(1)	F
9	5	If I Ain't Got You	Alicia Keys	J	30	(18)	
10		My Place	Nelly	Derrty/Fo' Reel	13	(1)	
11	4	The Reason	Hoobastank	Island	24	(12)	F
12		I Like That	Houston feat. Chingy, Nate Dogg & I-20	Capitol /Interscope	2	(4)	F
13		Pieces Of Me	Ashlee Simpson	Geffen/Interscope	12	(4)	F
14	2	Burn	Usher	Arista	21	(1)	
15	15	Jesus Walks	Kanye West	Roc-A-Fella/Def Jam	12	(16)	
16	18	Leave (Get Out)	JoJo	Da Family/Background	10	(2)	F
17	10	On Fire	Lloyd Bank$	G-Unit/Interscope	10	(19)	F
18		Diary	Alicia Keys featuring Tony! Toni! Tone!	J	16		
19		She Will Be Loved	Maroon5	Octone/J	23	(4)	
20	14	This Love	Maroon5	Octone/J	24	(3)	

September 2004

This Mnth	Prev Mnth	Title	Artist	Label	Wks 20	(UK Pos)	
1	8	Goodies	Ciara featuring Petey Pablo	Sho'Nuff/LaFace	23	(1)	F
2	1	Lean Back	Terror Squad	SRC/Universal	20	(24)	F
3	4	Sunshine	Lil' Flip featuring Lea	Sucka Free/Columbia	14	(14)	
4	10	My Place	Nelly	Derrty/Fo' Reel	14	(1)	
5	14	Pieces Of Me	Ashlee Simpson	Geffen/Interscope	12	(4)	F
6	6	Dip It Low	Christina Milian	Island/IDJMG	14	(2)	
7	5	Turn Me On	Kevin Lyttle featuring Spragga Benz	VP/Atlantic	15	(2)	F
8	20	She Will Be Loved	Maroon5	Octone/J	23	(4)	
9	2	Slow Motion	Juvenile featuring Soulja Slim	Cash Money/UMRG	20		
10	19	Diary	Alicia Keys featuring Tony! Toni! Tone!	J	16		
11	9	If I Ain't Got You	Alicia Keys	J	30	(18)	
12		Locked Up	Akon featuring Styles P.	SRC/Universal	13	(5)	F
13	7	Move Ya Body	Nina Sky featuring Jabba	Next Plateau/Universal	18	(6)	F
14	12	I Like That	Houston feat. Chingy, Nate Dogg & I-20	Capitol	10	(11)	F
15		My Boo	Usher & Alicia Keys	LaFace/Zomba	21	(5)	
16		Why?	Jadakiss featuring Anthony Hamilton	Ruff Ryders/Interscope	7		
17	3	Confessions Part II	Usher	LaFace/Zomba	18	(5)	
18		My Happy Ending	Avril Lavigne	RCA	12	(5)	
19	11	The Reason	Hoobastank	Island	24	(12)	F
20		Headsprung	LL Cool J	Def Jam	7	(25)	

◆ A record-breaking 71 million Americans voted in the final of 'American Idol 3'. The winner was Fantasia (Barrino), whose recording of 'I Believe' became the first debut single by an artist to enter the US Top 100 at No.1 (despite having the lowest reported radio play of any No.1).

◆ Usher continued to astound when he replaced himself at the top of the US chart for the second time in 2004, and he became the first act in history to have three consecutive No.1s on the Airplay chart.

◆ Sixty-five thousand 'Phish-Heads' turned out to watch the last live show by Phish. The group, which had reached the US chart with 28 albums, had yet to make their chart debut in the UK.

UK 2004 OCT–DEC

◆ A re-recording of the twenty-year-old, 3.6 million-selling charity single 'Do They Know It's Christmas?' by a current collection of stars topped the chart, as did a DVD of the original 1985 Live Aid concert.

◆ There was no shortage of old hits being successfully revived this quarter. Numbered among them were 'Car Wash' (Christina Aguilera/Rose Royce), 'More More More' (Rachel Stevens/Andrea True Connection), 'My Prerogative' (Britney Spears/Bobby Brown), the Children In Need chart-topper 'I'll Stand By You' (Girls Aloud/The Pretenders) and Ronan Keating's rendition of 'Father And Son', on which he was joined by original hit act Yusuf (Cat Stevens).

◆ On the album front, Robbie Williams sold over 320,000 copies of his Greatest Hits album in the first week, and 17-year-old Devon soul singer Joss Stone became the youngest female to top the chart.

October 2004

This Mnth	Prev Mnth	Title	Artist	Label	Wks 20	(US Pos)	
1	10	Call On Me	Eric Prydz	Data	12		F
2		Flashdance	Deep Dish	Positiva	6		F
3		Radio	Robbie Williams	Chrysalis	4		
4		My Neck, My Back (Lick It)	Khia	Direction	7	(42)	F
5		More More More	Rachel Stevens	Polydor	4		
6	12	Love Machine	Girls Aloud	Polydor	4		
7		I Believe My Heart	Duncan James & Keedie	Innocent	4		F
8		I Hope You Dance	Ronan Keating	Polydor/Curb	3		
9	3	My Place/Flap Your Wings	Nelly	Universal	7	(4)	
10	4	Leave (Get Out)	JoJo	Mercury	5	(12)	F
11		The Love Of Richard Nixon	Manic Street Preachers	Sony Music	1		
12		Pieces Of Me	Ashlee Simpson	Geffen	3	(5)	F
13	13	American Idiot	Green Day	Reprise	4	(61)	
14		Millionaire	Kelis featuring André 3000	Virgin	4		
15		(Reach Up For The) Sunrise	Duran Duran	Epic	2		
16		What You're Made Of...	Lucie Silvas	Mercury	3		F
17		Do You Know (I Go Crazy)	Angel City	Data	3		
18	8	Real To Me	Brian McFadden	Modest!/Sony Music	4		F
19	2	Baby Cakes	3 Of A Kind	Relentless	9		F
20		Leaving New York	R.E.M.	Warner Bros.	1		

November 2004

This Mnth	Prev Mnth	Title	Artist	Label	Wks 20	(US Pos)	
1		Just Lose It	Eminem	Interscope	9	(6)	
2		Lose My Breath	Destiny's Child	Columbia	9	(3)	
3	1	Call On Me	Eric Prydz	Data	12		F
4		Wonderful	Ja Rule featuring R. Kelly & Ashanti	Def Jam	3	(5)	
5		Vertigo	U2	Island	3	(31)	
6		Car Wash	Christina Aguilera feat. Missy Elliott	Dreamworks	9	(63)	F
7		My Prerogative	Britney Spears	Jive	3		
8		Confessions Part II/My Boo	Usher	LaFace/Arista	5	(1)	
9		I'll Stand By You	Girls Aloud	Polydor	7		
10		Nothing Hurts Like Love	Daniel Bedingfield	Polydor	2		
11	4	My Neck, My Back (Lick It)	Khia	Direction	7	(42)	F
12		Curtain Falls	Blue	Innocent	3		
13		Stolen	Jay Sean	Relentless	2		
14		If There's Any Justice	Lemar	Sony Music	8		
15	14	Millionaire	Kelis featuring André 3000	Virgin	4		
16		What You Waiting For?	Gwen Stefani	Interscope	10	(47)	
17		The Weekend	Michael Gray	Eye Industries/UMTV	3		F
18		Room On The 3rd Floor	McFly	Island	2		
19		DJ/Stop	Jamelia	Parlophone	4		
20		You Won't Forget About Me	Dannii Minogue vs Flower Power	All Around The World	2		

December 2004

This Mnth	Prev Mnth	Title	Artist	Label	Wks 20	(US Pos)	
1	9	I'll Stand By You	Girls Aloud	Polydor	7		
2	2	Lose My Breath	Destiny's Child	Columbia	9	(3)	
3		Do They Know It's Christmas?	Band Aid 20	Mercury	6		F
4	14	If There's Any Justice	Lemar	Sony Music	8		
5		You Can Do It	Ice Cube feat. Mack 10 + Ms Toi	All Around The World	7	(35)	F
6		I Believe In You	Kylie	Parlophone	5		
7		Tilt Ya Head Back	Nelly & Christina Aguilera	Universal	7	(58)	
8		Boulevard Of Broken Dreams	Green Day	Reprise	11	(2)	
9		Unwritten	Natasha Bedingfield	Phonogenic	5	(5)	
10		Father And Son	Ronan Keating featuring Yusuf	Polydor	4		
11	16	What You Waiting For?	Gwen Stefani	Interscope	10		
12		Ride It	Geri	Innocent	3		
13	1	Just Lose It	Eminem	Interscope	9	(6)	
14		Irish Son	Brian McFadden	Modest!/Sony Music	3		
15		I Got You Babe/Soda Pop	Merrion, McCall & Kensit	BMG	3		F
16		Baby It's You	JoJo featuring Bow Wow	Mercury	4	(22)	
17		Drop It Like It's Hot	Snoop Dogg featuring Pharrell	Geffen	6	(1)	
18		Misunderstood	Robbie Williams	Chrysalis	2		
19		Killamangiro	Baby Shambles	Rough Trade	1		F
20		Out Of Touch	Uniting Nations	Gusto	13		F

October 2004

This Mnth	Prev Mnth	Title	Artist	Label	Wks 20	(UK Pos)	
1	1	Goodies	Ciara featuring Petey Pablo	Sho'Nuff/LaFace	23	(1)	F
2	15	My Boo	Usher & Alicia Keys	LaFace/Zomba	21	(5)	
3	2	Lean Back	Terror Squad	SRC/Universal	20	(24)	F
4		Lose My Breath	Destiny's Child	Columbia	17	(2)	
5	4	My Place	Nelly	Derrty/Fo' Reel	14	(1)	
6	8	She Will Be Loved	Maroon5	Octone/J	23	(4)	
7	3	Sunshine	Lil' Flip featuring Lea	Sucka Free/Columbia	14	(14)	
8	12	Locked Up	Akon featuring Styles P.	SRC/Universal	13	(5)	F
9	18	My Happy Ending	Avril Lavigne	RCA	12	(5)	
10	10	Diary	Alicia Keys featuring Tony! Toni! Tone!	J		16	
11		Just Lose It	Eminem	Shady/Aftermath/Interscope	10	(1)	
12		Drop It Like It's Hot	Snoop Dogg featuring Pharrell	Doggystyle/Geffen	21	(10)	
13	11	If I Ain't Got You	Alicia Keys	J	30	(18)	
14		Breakaway	Kelly Clarkson	Walt Disney Soundtrack	28	(22)	
15		Over And Over	Nelly featuring Tim McGraw	Curb/Derrty	19	(1)	
16	5	Pieces Of Me	Ashlee Simpson	Geffen/Interscope	12	(4)	F
17	9	Slow Motion	Juvenile featuring Soulja Slim	Cash Money/UMRG	20		
18	16	Why?	Jadakiss featuring Anthony Hamilton	Ruff Ryders/Interscope	7		
19		On The Way Down	Ryan Cabrera	E.V.L.A./Atlantic	7		F
20	6	Dip It Low	Christina Milian	Island/IDJMG	14	(2)	

November 2004

This Mnth	Prev Mnth	Title	Artist	Label	Wks 20	(UK Pos)	
1	2	My Boo	Usher & Alicia Keys	LaFace/Zomba	21	(5)	
2	12	Drop It Like It's Hot	Snoop Dogg featuring Pharrell	Doggystyle/Geffen	21	(10)	
3	1	Goodies	Ciara featuring Petey Pablo	Sho'Nuff/LaFace	23	(1)	F
4	4	Lose My Breath	Destiny's Child	Columbia	17	(2)	
5	15	Over And Over	Nelly featuring Tim McGraw	Curb/Derrty	19	(1)	
6	6	She Will Be Loved	Maroon5	Octone/J	23	(4)	
7	14	Breakaway	Kelly Clarkson	Walt Disney Soundtrack	28	(22)	
8	11	Just Lose It	Eminem	Shady/Aftermath/Interscope	10	(1)	
9		Let's Go	Trick Daddy featuring Lil Jon & Twista	Slip-N-Slide	13	(26)	
10		Wonderful	Ja Rule featuring R. Kelly & Ashanti	The Inc./Def Jam	12	(1)	
11	3	Lean Back	Terror Squad	SRC/Universal	20	(24)	F
12		Breathe	Fabolous	Desert Storm/Atlantic	8	(28)	
13		Oye Mi Canto	N.O.R.E. featuring Daddy Yankee, Nina Sky, Gem Star & Big Mato	Roc-A-Fella/Def Jam	10		
14		Let Me Love You	Mario	3rd Street/J	24	(2)	
15	8	Locked Up	Akon featuring Styles P.	SRC/Universal	13	(5)	F
16	9	My Happy Ending	Avril Lavigne	RCA	12	(5)	
17		Go D.J.	Lil Wayne	Cash Money/UMRG	7		F
18		1, 2 Step	Ciara featuring Missy Elliott	Sho'Nuff/LaFace	23	(3)	
19	10	Diary	Alicia Keys featuring Tony! Toni! Tone!	J		16	
20	5	My Place	Nelly	Derrty/Fo' Reel	14	(1)	

December 2004

This Mnth	Prev Mnth	Title	Artist	Label	Wks 20	(UK Pos)	
1	2	Drop It Like It's Hot	Snoop Dogg featuring Pharrell	Doggystyle/Geffen	21	(10)	
2	1	My Boo	Usher & Alicia Keys	LaFace/Zomba	21	(5)	
3	14	Let Me Love You	Mario	3rd Street/J	24	(2)	
4	5	Over And Over	Nelly featuring Tim McGraw	Curb/Derrty	19	(1)	
5	18	1, 2 Step	Ciara featuring Missy Elliott	Sho'Nuff/LaFace	23	(3)	
6	4	Lose My Breath	Destiny's Child	Columbia	17	(2)	
7	10	Wonderful	Ja Rule featuring R. Kelly & Ashanti	The Inc./Def Jam	12	(1)	
8	9	Let's Go	Trick Daddy featuring Lil Jon & Twista	Slip-N-Slide	13		
9		Lovers And Friends	Lil Jon & The East Side Boyz feat. Usher & Ludacris	BME/TVT	18		
10	7	Breakaway	Kelly Clarkson	Walt Disney Soundtrack	28	(22)	
11	3	Goodies	Ciara featuring Petey Pablo	Sho'Nuff/LaFace	23	(1)	F
12		Soldier	Destiny's Child feat. T.I. & Lil Wayne	Columbia	17	(4)	
13	12	Breathe	Fabolous	Desert Storm/Atlantic	8	(28)	
14		I Don't Want To Be	Gavin DeGraw	J	12	(38)	F
15	6	She Will Be Loved	Maroon5	Octone/J	23	(4)	
16	13	Oye Mi Canto	N.O.R.E. featuring Daddy Yankee, Nina Sky, Gem Star & Big Mato	Roc-A-Fella/Def Jam	10		
17		Disco Inferno	50 Cent	Shady/Aftermath	22		
18	8	Just Lose It	Eminem	Shady/Aftermath/Interscope	10	(1)	
19	17	Go D.J.	Lil Wayne	Cash Money/UMRG	7		F
20		Only U	Ashanti	The Inc./Def Jam	7	(2)	

US 2004 OCT-DEC

◆ Texas-born rapper Nelly became the first artist in history to have two albums – 'Suit' and 'Sweat' – enter the US chart simultaneously in positions 1 and 2.

▲ The big winners at the American Music Awards were Usher (above) with four trophies and OutKast with three. At the Billboard Music Awards Usher grabbed 11 and OutKast, again runners-up, five.

◆ Other news: US acts inducted into the newly launched British Hall of Fame were Michael Jackson, Madonna and Elvis Presley. Rod Stewart became the first British solo act to top the US album chart for ten years with his 'Stardust – The Great American Songbook Volume III'.

UK 2005
JAN-MAR

▲ Steve Brookstein, the first winner of TV series 'X Factor', opened the year with the No.1 single – an update of Phil Collins' No.2 hit 'Against All Odds'. Oddly, the runners-up, vocal group G4, sold far more albums than Brookstein, who gave his royalties to the Tsunami appeal.

◆ Elvis Presley's previous 17 No. 1 singles were issued weekly in chronological order and all reached the Top 5 and the month's Top 20s (excluding the first, 'All Shook Up', which was excluded due to its packaging). His 'One Night'/'I Got Stung' was the 1000th UK No.1.

◆ The Best Song of the Last 25 Years BRIT went to 'Angels' – giving Robbie Williams his record 15th award.

January 2005

This Mnth	Prev Mnth	Title	Artist	Label	Wks 20	(US Pos)	
1		Against All Odds	Steve Brookstein	Syco Music	5		F
2	3	Do They Know It's Christmas?	Band Aid 20	Mercury	6		F
3	8	Boulevard Of Broken Dreams	Green Day	Reprise	11	(2)	
4	6	I Believe In You	Kylie	Parlophone	5		
5	10	Father And Son	Ronan Keating featuring Yusuf	Polydor	4		
6	20	Out Of Touch	Uniting Nations	Gusto	13		F
7		Jailhouse Rock	Elvis Presley	RCA	2		
8		Somebody Told Me	The Killers	Lizard King	3	(51)	
9		The Number Of The Beast	Iron Maiden	EMI	2		
10	5	You Can Do It	Ice Cube featuring Mack 10 + Ms Toi	All Around The World	7		F
11		One Night/I Got Stung	Elvis Presley	RCA	2		
12		Goodies	Ciara featuring Petey Pablo	LaFace	5	(1)	F
13	4	If There's Any Justice	Lemar	Sony Music	8		
14		A Fool Such As I/I Need Your Love Tonight	Elvis Presley	RCA	2		
15		Empty Souls	Manic Street Preachers	Columbia	1		
16		Breathe	Erasure	Mute	2		
17		Filthy/Gorgeous	Scissor Sisters	Polydor	3		
18		Staring At The Sun	Rooster	Brightside	3		
19		Galvanize	The Chemical Brothers	Virgin	5		
20		Wires	Athlete	Parlophone	4		F

February 2005

This Mnth	Prev Mnth	Title	Artist	Label	Wks 20	(US Pos)	
1		Like Toy Soldiers	Eminem	Interscope	5		
2		Only U	Ashanti	The Inc./Mercury	4	(13)	
3	12	Goodies	Ciara featuring Petey Pablo	LaFace	5	(1)	F
4		Almost Here	Brian McFadden & Delta Goodrem	Modest!/Sony Music	5		
5		Sometimes You Can't Make It On Your Own	U2	Island	3	(97)	
6	19	Galvanize	The Chemical Brothers	Virgin	5		
7		It's Now Or Never	Elvis Presley	RCA	2		
8		Get Right	Jennifer Lopez	Epic	7	(12)	
9		Soldier	Destiny's Child feat. T.I. & Lil Wayne	Columbia	3	(3)	
10		Grief Never Grows Old	One World Project	One World	2		F
11		Are You Lonesome To-night?	Elvis Presley	RCA	2		
12		Surrender	Elvis Presley	RCA	2		
13		Wooden Heart	Elvis Presley	RCA	1		
14		Hush	LL Cool J featuring 7 Aurelius	Def Jam	4	(26)	
15	20	Wires	Athlete	Parlophone	4		F
16		So Here We Are/Positive Tension	Bloc Party	Wichita Recordings	2		F
17		How We Do	The Game featuring 50 Cent	Interscope	4	(4)	F
18		Shine	The Lovefreekz	Positiva	2		F
19		Black And White Town	Doves	Heavenly	2		
20		Angel Eyes	Raghav	A&R/V2	2		

March 2005

This Mnth	Prev Mnth	Title	Artist	Label	Wks 20	(US Pos)	
1		Over And Over	Nelly featuring Tim McGraw	Curb/Derrty/Island	6	(3)	
2	8	Get Right	Jennifer Lopez	Epic	7	(12)	
3		Dakota	Stereophonics	V2	3		
4		All About You/You've Got A Friend	McFly	Island	7		
5		Locked Up	Akon featuring Styles P.	Universal	5	(8)	F
6		Star To Fall	Cabin Crew	Data	4		F
7		Falling Stars	Sunset Strippers	Direction	6		F
8		Wake Me Up	Girls Aloud	Polydor	3		
9		(Is This The Way To) Amarillo	Tony Christie featuring Peter Kay	Universal TV	14		
10		Good Luck Charm	Elvis Presley	RCA	1		
11	14	Hush	LL Cool J featuring 7 Aurelius	Def Jam	4	(26)	
12		Rock-A-Hula Baby	Elvis Presley	RCA	1	(S)	
13		His Latest Flame	Elvis Presley	RCA	1		
14		She's Not You	Elvis Presley	RCA	1		
15		Oh My God	Kaiser Chiefs	B-Unique	3		F
16		Do Somethin'	Britney Spears	Jive	3		
17		Rich Girl	Gwen Stefani featuring Eve	Interscope	6	(8)	
18		An Honest Mistake	The Bravery	Loog	2		F
19		They	Jem	Ato	7		F
20		Caught Up	Usher	LaFace	3	(8)	

January 2005

This Mnth	Prev Mnth	Title	Artist	Label	Wks 20	(UK Pos)	
1	3	**Let Me Love You**	Mario	3rd Street/J	24	(2)	
2	5	**1, 2 Step**	Ciara featuring Missy Elliott	Sho'Nuff/LaFace	23	(3)	
3	1	**Drop It Like It's Hot**	Snoop Dogg featuring Pharrell	Doggystyle/Geffen	21	(10)	
4	9	**Lovers And Friends**	Lil Jon & The East Side Boyz feat. Usher & Ludacris	BME/TVT	18		
5	12	**Soldier**	Destiny's Child feat. T.I. & Lil Wayne	Columbia	17	(4)	
6	2	**My Boo**	Usher & Alicia Keys	LaFace/Zomba	21	(5)	
7	4	**Over And Over**	Nelly featuring Tim McGraw	Curb/Derrty	19	(1)	
8	17	**Disco Inferno**	50 Cent	Shady/Aftermath	22		
9		**How We Do**	The Game featuring 50 Cent	Aftermath/G-Unit	16	(5)	F
10	7	**Wonderful**	Ja Rule featuring R. Kelly & Ashanti	The Inc./Def Jam	12	(1)	
11	14	**I Don't Want To Be**	Gavin DeGraw	J	12	(38)	F
12	10	**Breakaway**	Kelly Clarkson	Walt Disney Soundtrack	28	(22)	
13		**Boulevard Of Broken Dreams**	Green Day	Reprise	23	(5)	F
14	6	**Lose My Breath**	Destiny's Child	Columbia	17	(2)	
15		**Get Back**	Ludacris	Disturbing Tha Peace	11		
16	20	**Only U**	Ashanti	The Inc./Def Jam	7	(2)	
17		**Bring Em Out**	T.I.	Grand Hustle/Atlantic	11	(59)	F
18	8	**Let's Go**	Trick Daddy featuring Lil Jon & Twista	Slip-N-Slide	13		
19	15	**She Will Be Loved**	Maroon5	Octone/J	23	(4)	
20		**Karma**	Lloyd Bank$ featuring Avant	G-Unit/Interscope	4		

February 2005

This Mnth	Prev Mnth	Title	Artist	Label	Wks 20	(UK Pos)	
1	1	**Let Me Love You**	Mario	3rd Street/J	24	(2)	
2	2	**1, 2 Step**	Ciara featuring Missy Elliott	Sho'Nuff/LaFace	23	(3)	
3	13	**Boulevard Of Broken Dreams**	Green Day	Reprise	23	(5)	F
4	4	**Lovers And Friends**	Lil Jon & The East Side Boyz feat. Usher & Ludacris	BME/TVT	18		
5	5	**Soldier**	Destiny's Child feat. T.I. & Lil Wayne	Columbia	17	(4)	
6	9	**How We Do**	The Game featuring 50 Cent	Aftermath/G-Unit	16	(5)	F
7	8	**Disco Inferno**	50 Cent	Shady/Aftermath	22		
8	3	**Drop It Like It's Hot**	Snoop Dogg featuring Pharrell	Doggystyle/Geffen	21	(10)	
9		**Candy Shop**	50 Cent featuring Olivia	Shady/Aftermath	17	(4)	
10		**Since U Been Gone**	Kelly Clarkson	RCA	25	(5)	G
11	17	**Bring Em Out**	T.I.	Grand Hustle/Atlantic	11	(59)	F
12		**Caught Up**	Usher	LaFace/Zomba	13	(9)	
13	12	**Breakaway**	Kelly Clarkson	Walt Disney Soundtrack	28	(22)	
14	7	**Over And Over**	Nelly featuring Tim McGraw	Curb/Derrty	19	(1)	
15		**Get Right**	Jennifer Lopez	Epic	6	(1)	
16		**Rich Girl**	Gwen Stefani featuring Eve	Interscope	12	(4)	
17		**Mockingbird**	Eminem	Shady/Aftermath	10	(4)	
18	6	**My Boo**	Usher & Alicia Keys	LaFace/Zomba	21	(5)	
19	11	**I Don't Want To Be**	Gavin DeGraw	J	12	(38)	F
20	15	**Get Back**	Ludacris	Disturbing Tha Peace	11		

March 2005

This Mnth	Prev Mnth	Title	Artist	Label	Wks 20	(UK Pos)	
1	9	**Candy Shop**	50 Cent featuring Olivia	Shady/Aftermath	17	(4)	
2	3	**Boulevard Of Broken Dreams**	Green Day	Reprise	23	(5)	F
3	1	**Let Me Love You**	Mario	3rd Street/J	24	(2)	
4	7	**Disco Inferno**	50 Cent	Shady/Aftermath	22		
5	6	**How We Do**	The Game featuring 50 Cent	Aftermath/G-Unit	16	(5)	F
6	10	**Since U Been Gone**	Kelly Clarkson	RCA	25	(5)	G
7	2	**1, 2 Step**	Ciara featuring Missy Elliott	Sho'Nuff/LaFace	23	(3)	
8		**Obsession (No Es Amor)**	Frankie J. featuring Baby Bash	Columbia	14		
9	16	**Rich Girl**	Gwen Stefani featuring Eve	Interscope	12	(4)	
10	12	**Caught Up**	Usher	LaFace/Zomba	13	(9)	
11	4	**Lovers And Friends**	Lil Jon & The East Side Boyz feat. Usher & Ludacris	BME/TVT	18		
12	17	**Mockingbird**	Eminem	Shady/Aftermath	10	(4)	
13	5	**Soldier**	Destiny's Child feat. T.I. & Lil Wayne	Columbia	17	(4)	
14		**Hate It Or Love It**	The Game featuring 50 Cent	Aftermath/G-Unit	15	(4)	
15	13	**Breakaway**	Kelly Clarkson	Walt Disney Soundtrack	28	(22)	
16	11	**Bring Em Out**	T.I.	Grand Hustle/Atlantic	11	(59)	F
17		**Some Cut**	Trillville featuring Cutty	BME/Reprise	9		F
18	20	**Get Back**	Ludacris	Disturbing Tha Peace	11		
19	15	**Get Right**	Jennifer Lopez	Epic	6	(1)	
20		**It's Like That**	Mariah Carey	Island/IDJMG	7	(4)	

US 2005 JAN-MAR

◆ The late Ray Charles was the big winner at the Grammy Awards with eight trophies to add to the 12 he amassed in his lifetime. Ray also returned to the top of the album chart after a 40-year absence with 'Genius Loves Company', and it was announced that he had sold 3.7 million albums in the US in the nine months since his death.

◆ Paul McCartney provided the half-time entertainment on America's most watched TV show, The Super Bowl. Meanwhile, Usher equalled a record set over 40 years earlier by Paul's old band, The Beatles, when he achieved three singles simultaneously in the Top 5.

◆ Lifetime Achievement Grammy award recipients included Led Zeppelin, Janis Joplin and Jerry Lee Lewis, and the Rock & Roll Hall of Fame welcomed U2, The Pretenders, The O'Jays, Percy Sledge and Buddy Guy.

UK 2005 APR-JUNE

◆ On April 23rd, for the first time, digital sales were included in the UK chart – which almost doubled the number of total sales. The first combined No.1 was Tony Christie's re-issued 1971 hit '(Is This The Way To) Amarillo'. In its first week it sold over 175,000 copies - more records than there are people living in Amarillo itself!

◆ All 112,000 tickets for the Glastonbury Festival were sold in just three hours, and tickets for the four Royal Albert Hall shows by the re-united Cream sold in only two. In addition, Oasis sold all 250,000 tickets for their world tour in a day.

◆ The hottest UK act internationally were Coldplay, whose 'X&Y' sold a staggering 464,471 copies in the first week in the UK. Over five million albums were shipped worldwide and it entered charts at No.1 in 22 countries including the US.

April 2005

This Mnth	Prev Mnth	Title	Artist	Label	Wks 20	(US Pos)	
1	9	(Is This The Way To) Amarillo	Tony Christie featuring Peter Kay	Universal TV	14		
2		Let Me Love You	Mario	J	8	(1)	
3		Switch	Will Smith	Interscope	11	(7)	
4		Candy Shop	50 Cent	Interscope	7	(4)	
5	4	All About You/You've Got A Friend	McFly	Island	7		
6		It's Like That	Mariah Carey	Def Jam	5	(16)	
7		Somewhere Else	Razorlight	Vertigo	5		
8	17	Rich Girl	Gwen Stefani featuring Eve	Interscope	6	(8)	
9		1, 2 Step	Ciara featuring Missy Elliott	LaFace	5	(2)	
10		(You're The) Devil In Disguise	Elvis Presley	RCA	1		
11		Crying In The Chapel	Elvis Presley	RCA	1		
12		Way Down	Elvis Presley	RCA	1		
13		I Like The Way	Bodyrockers	Mercury	13		F
14		Shiver	Natalie Imbruglia	Brightside	5		
15		Time To Grow	Lemar	Sony Music	5		
16		The Wonder Of You	Elvis Presley	RCA	1		
17		Return To Sender	Elvis Presley	RCA	1		
18		Giving You Up	Kylie	Parlophone	2		
19		Why Do You Love Me	Garbage	Mushroom	2		
20	7	Falling Stars	Sunset Strippers	Direction	6		F

May 2005

This Mnth	Prev Mnth	Title	Artist	Label	Wks 20	(US Pos)	
1	1	(Is This The Way To) Amarillo	Tony Christie featuring Peter Kay	Universal TV	14		
2		Signs	Snoop Dogg featuring Charlie Wilson and Justin Timberlake	Geffen	7	(46)	
3		Lonely	Akon	Universal	10	(4)	
4	13	I Like The Way	Bodyrockers	Mercury	13		F
5		Feel Good Inc	Gorillaz	Parlophone	14	(14)	
6	3	Switch	Will Smith	Interscope	11	(7)	
7		Mockingbird	Eminem	Interscope	3	(11)	
8		Lyla	Oasis	Big Brother	3		
9		Hate It Or Love It	The Game featuring 50 Cent	Interscope	5	(2)	
10		Girl	Destiny's Child	Columbia	3	(23)	
11	9	1, 2 Step	Ciara featuring Missy Elliott	LaFace	5	(2)	
12		Don't Phunk With My Heart	The Black Eyed Peas	Interscope	7	(3)	
13		A Little Less Conversation	Elvis vs JXL	RCA	1	(50)	
14		In The Morning	The Coral	Deltasonic	3		
15	7	Somewhere Else	Razorlight	Vertigo	5		
16		Hold You Down	Jennifer Lopez featuring Fat Joe	Epic	2	(64)	
17		One Word	Kelly Osbourne	Sanctuary	2		
18	2	Let Me Love You	Mario	J	8	(1)	
19		Beverly Hills	Weezer	Geffen	2	(13)	
20		Owner Of A Lonely Heart	Max Graham vs Yes	Data	2		F

June 2005

This Mnth	Prev Mnth	Title	Artist	Label	Wks 20	(US Pos)	
1		Axel F	Crazy Frog	Gusto	12	(50)	F
2	3	Lonely	Akon	Universal	10	(4)	
3	5	Feel Good Inc	Gorillaz	Parlophone	14	(14)	
4		1 Thing	Amerie	Columbia	6	(8)	
5		Shot You Down	Audio Bullys featuring Nancy Sinatra	Source	11		
6		You're Beautiful	James Blunt	Atlantic	15	(1)	F
7		Speed Of Sound	Coldplay	Parlophone	3	(8)	
8	12	Don't Phunk With My Heart	The Black Eyed Peas	Interscope	7	(3)	
9		Best Of You	Foo Fighters	RCA	3	(18)	
10		City Of Blinding Lights	U2	Island	2		
11		Hollaback Girl	Gwen Stefani	Interscope	6	(1)	
12	8	Lyla	Oasis	Big Brother	3		
13		N Dey Say	Nelly	Universal	3	(64)	
14	1	(Is This The Way To) Amarillo	Tony Christie featuring Peter Kay	Universal TV	14		
15		Why	DJ Sammy	Data	2		
16		Feels Just Like It Should	Jamiroquai	Sony S	2	(2)	
17		Wake Me Up When September Ends	Green Day	Reprise	8	(6)	
18		Blue Orchid	The White Stripes	XL Recordings	2	(43)	
19	9	Hate It Or Love It	The Game featuring 50 Cent	Interscope	5	(2)	
20		Paint Your Target	Fightstar	Island	1		F

US 2005 APR-JUNE

April 2005

This Mnth	Prev Mnth	Title	Artist	Label	Wks 20	(UK Pos)	
1	1	Candy Shop	50 Cent featuring Olivia	Shady/Aftermath	17	(4)	
2	14	Hate It Or Love It	The Game featuring 50 Cent	Aftermath/G-Unit	15	(4)	
3	6	Since U Been Gone	Kelly Clarkson	RCA	25	(5)	G
4	2	Boulevard Of Broken Dreams	Green Day	Reprise	23	(5)	F
5	8	Obsession (No Es Amor)	Frankie J. featuring Baby Bash	Columbia	14		
6	4	Disco Inferno	50 Cent	Shady/Aftermath	22		
7		Lonely	Akon	SRC/Universal	11	(1)	
8	3	Let Me Love You	Mario	3rd Street/J	24	(2)	
9		Hollaback Girl	Gwen Stefani	Interscope	20	(8)	G
10	9	Rich Girl	Gwen Stefani featuring Eve	Interscope	12	(4)	
11	10	Caught Up	Usher	LaFace/Zomba	13	(9)	
12	5	How We Do	The Game featuring 50 Cent	Aftermath/G-Unit	16	(5)	F
13		1 Thing	Amerie	Columbia	7	(4)	F
14		Lonely No More	Rob Thomas	Melisma/Atlantic	16	(11)	
15	7	1, 2 Step	Ciara featuring Missy Elliott	Sho'Nuff/LaFace	23	(3)	
16		Mr. Brightside	The Killers	Island/IDJMG	17	(10)	F
17		Oh	Ciara featuring Ludacris	Sho'Nuff Musicline/ LaFace	16	(4)	
18		Switch	Will Smith	Overbrook/Interscope	18	(4)	
19	17	Some Cut	Trillville featuring Cutty	BME/Reprise	9		F
20		Goin' Crazy	Natalie	Latium/Universal	7		F

May 2005

This Mnth	Prev Mnth	Title	Artist	Label	Wks 20	(UK Pos)	
1	9	Hollaback Girl	Gwen Stefani	Interscope	20	(8)	G
2	2	Hate It Or Love It	The Game featuring 50 Cent	Aftermath/G-Unit	15	(4)	
3	17	Oh	Ciara featuring Ludacris	Sho'Nuff Musicline/ LaFace	16	(4)	
4		We Belong Together	Mariah Carey	Island/IDJMG	27	(2)	
5	7	Lonely	Akon	SRC/Universal	11	(1)	
6	1	Candy Shop	50 Cent featuring Olivia	Shady/Aftermath	17	(4)	
7		Just A Lil Bit	50 Cent	Shady/Aftermath	15	(10)	
8	14	Lonely No More	Rob Thomas	Melisma/Atlantic	16	(11)	
9	3	Since U Been Gone	Kelly Clarkson	RCA	25	(5)	G
10		Slow Down	Bobby Valentino	DTP/Def Jam	10	(4)	F
11		Don't Phunk With My Heart	The Black Eyed Peas	A&M/Interscope	16	(3)	
12	5	Obsession (no Es Amor)	Frankie J. featuring Baby Bash	Columbia	14		
13		Speed Of Sound	Coldplay	Capitol	5	(2)	
14	16	Mr. Brightside	The Killers	Island/IDJMG	17	(10)	F
15	13	1 Thing	Amerie	Columbia	7	(4)	F
16	4	Boulevard Of Broken Dreams	Green Day	Reprise	23	(5)	F
17	18	Switch	Will Smith	Overbrook/Interscope	18	(4)	
18		Incomplete	Backstreet Boys	Jive	7	(8)	
19	6	Disco Inferno	50 Cent	Shady/Aftermath	22		
20		Let Me Go	3 Doors Down	Republic/Universal	6		

June 2005

This Mnth	Prev Mnth	Title	Artist	Label	Wks 20	(UK Pos)	
1	4	We Belong Together	Mariah Carey	Island/IDJMG	27	(2)	
2	1	Hollaback Girl	Gwen Stefani	Interscope	20	(8)	G
3	3	Oh	Ciara featuring Ludacris	Sho'Nuff Musicline/ LaFace	16	(4)	
4	7	Just A Lil Bit	50 Cent	Shady/Aftermath	15	(10)	
5	11	Don't Phunk With My Heart	The Black Eyed Peas	A&M/Interscope	16	(3)	
6		Behind These Hazel Eyes	Kelly Clarkson	RCA	21	(9)	
7	17	Switch	Will Smith	Overbrook/Interscope	18	(4)	
8	2	Hate It Or Love It	The Game featuring 50 Cent	Aftermath/G-Unit	15	(4)	
9	9	Since U Been Gone	Kelly Clarkson	RCA	25	(5)	G
10		Grind With Me	Pretty Ricky	Atlantic	12	(26)	F
11	8	Lonely No More	Rob Thomas	Melisma/Atlantic	16	(11)	
12	12	Mr. Brightside	The Killers	Island/IDJMG	17	(10)	F
13	10	Slow Down	Bobby Valentino	DTP/Def Jam	10	(4)	F
14	18	Incomplete	Backstreet Boys	Jive	7	8	
15	13	Speed Of Sound	Coldplay	Capitol	5	(2)	
16	20	Let Me Go	3 Doors Down	Republic/Universal	6		
17		Don't Cha	Pussycat Dolls featuring Busta Rhymes	A&M/Interscope	21	(1)	F
18	5	Lonely	Akon	SRC/Universal	11	(1)	
19		Wait (The Whisper Song)	Ying Yang Twins	Collipark	4	(47)	
20	6	Candy Shop	50 Cent featuring Olivia	Shady/Aftermath	17	(4)	

▲ There were almost as many 50 Cent singles on the US Top 20 this quarter as there were Elvis singles in the UK chart. Also racking up simultaneous hits were Ciara, Kelly Clarkson and Gwen Stefani.

◆ R&B producer Scott Storch completed a record-breaking run of 18 successive weeks at the top of the pop chart, the records coming from Mario and 50 Cent.

◆ Other news: Destiny's Child announced that they were splitting up... Cher's record-breaking farewell tour finally ended with the 323 shows grossing $200 million... The Beatles became the first act to be awarded six Diamond albums – these are given for sales of over 10 million.

UK 2005 JULY-SEPT

◆ Ten all-star shows were staged around the World as part of Live 8. Over one million people saw these shows and an estimated two billion watched on TV or listened to them. It was the biggest global music event since Live Aid twenty years earlier.

▲ The UK Live 8 show was held at Hyde Park and was seen by over 200,000 fans. Artists performing included Coldplay, Elton John, Madonna, George Michael, Pink Floyd (their first show together for 24 years), Robbie Williams and The Who.

◆ The first ringtone-turned-hit, 'Axel F' by Crazy Frog, which supposedly drove many people to the brink of insanity, was a world-wide best-seller.

July 2005

This Mnth	Prev Mnth	Title	Artist	Label	Wks 20	(US Pos)	
1		Ghetto Gospel	2Pac (featuring Elton John)	Interscope	9		
2	6	You're Beautiful	James Blunt	Atlantic	15	(1)	F
3	1	Axel F	Crazy Frog	Gusto	12	(50)	F
4		Crazy Chick	Charlotte Church	Sony BMG	7		
5		Roc Ya Body 'Mic Check 1,2'	M.V.P.	Positiva	9		F
6		We Belong Together	Mariah Carey	Def Jam/Island	7	(1)	
7	5	Shot You Down	Audio Bullys featuring Nancy Sinatra	Source	11		
8		Slow Down	Bobby Valentino	Def Jam	5	(8)	F
9		Lose Control	Missy Elliott feat. Ciara & Fat Man Scoop	Atlantic	7	(3)	
10		Since U Been Gone	Kelly Clarkson	RCA	9	(2)	
11	3	Feel Good Inc	Gorillaz	Parlophone	14	(14)	
12		Army Of Lovers	Lee Ryan	Brightside	4		F
13		Electricity	Elton John	Rocket/Mercury	1		
14		Diamonds From Sierra Leone	Kanye West	Roc-A-Fella	3	(83)	
15		Gasolina	Daddy Yankee	Machete	5	(32)	F
16		From The Floorboards Up	Paul Weller	V2	1		
17		Incomplete	Backstreet Boys	Jive	2	(13)	
18	17	Wake Me Up When September Ends	Green Day	Reprise	8	(6)	
19		Nasty Girl	Inaya Day	All Around The World	2		F
20		Just A Lil Bit	50 Cent	Interscope	3	(3)	

August 2005

This Mnth	Prev Mnth	Title	Artist	Label	Wks 20	(US Pos)	
1	2	You're Beautiful	James Blunt	Atlantic	15	(1)	F
2		Bad Day	Daniel Powter	Warner Bros.	18	(1)	F
3	1	Ghetto Gospel	2Pac (featuring Elton John)	Interscope	9		
4	10	Since U Been Gone	Kelly Clarkson	RCA	9	(2)	
5	6	We Belong Together	Mariah Carey	Def Jam/Island	7	(1)	
6		Ass Like That	Eminem	Interscope	4	(60)	
7		Oh	Ciara featuring Ludacris	LaFace	4	(2)	
8		All The Way	Craig David	Warner Bros.	2		
9		I'll Be OK	McFly	Island	3		
10		Ooh La La	Goldfrapp	Mute	4		
11		Belly Dancer (Bananza)	Akon	Universal	3	(30)	
12	15	Gasolina	Daddy Yankee	Machete	5	(37)	F
13	5	Roc Ya Body 'Mic Check 1,2'	M.V.P.	Positiva	9		F
14		Fuck Forever	Baby Shambles	Rough Trade	2		
15		The Trooper	Iron Maiden	EMI	1		
16		Getaway	Texas	Mercury	2		
17		Dreams	The Game	Interscope	3	(32)	
18		This Town Ain't Big Enough For Both Of Us	British Whale	Atlantic	1		F
19	12	Army Of Lovers	Lee Ryan	Brightside	4		F
20	3	Axel F	Crazy Frog	Gusto	12	(50)	F

September 2005

This Mnth	Prev Mnth	Title	Artist	Label	Wks 20	(US Pos)	
1		Pon De Replay	Rihanna	Def Jam	6	(2)	F
2	2	Bad Day	Daniel Powter	Warner Bros.	18	(1)	F
3		Dare	Gorillaz	Parlophone	9	(87)	
4		The Importance Of Being Idle	Oasis	Big Brother	5		
5		Don't Cha	Pussycat Dolls featuring Busta Rhymes	A&M	13	(2)	F
6		Lay Your Hands	Simon Webbe	Innocent	4		F
7		Doctor Pressure	Mylo vs Miami Sound Machine	Breastfed	7		
8		These Boots Are Made For Walkin'	Jessica Simpson	Columbia	4	(14)	
9		Don't Lie	The Black Eyed Peas	Interscope	4	(14)	
10		Fix You	Coldplay	Parlophone	4	(59)	
11		We Be Burnin'	Sean Paul	Atlantic/VP	9	(6)	
12	1	You're Beautiful	James Blunt	Atlantic	15	(1)	F
13		The One I Love	David Gray	Atlantic	4		
14		Long Hot Summer	Girls Aloud	Polydor	2		
15		Outta Control	50 Cent featuring Mobb Deep	Interscope	3	(6)	
16		Have A Nice Day	Bon Jovi	Mercury	2	(53)	
17		I Predict A Riot/Sink That Ship	Kaiser Chiefs	B-Unique	4		
18	9	I'll Be Ok	McFly	Island	3		
19		Jacques Your Body (Make Me Sweat)	Les Rythmes Digitales	Data	2		F
20		My Doorbell	The White Stripes	XL Recordings	2		

This Mnth	Prev Mnth	Title	Artist	Label	Wks 20	(UK Pos)	
1	1	We Belong Together	Mariah Carey	Island/IDJMG	27	(2)	
2	2	Hollaback Girl	Gwen Stefani	Interscope	20	(8)	G
3	5	Don't Phunk With My Heart	The Black Eyed Peas	A&M/Interscope	16	(3)	
4		Inside Your Heaven	Carrie Underwood	Arista/RMG	5		F
5		Pon De Replay	Rihanna	SRP/Def Jam	15	(2)	F
6	17	Don't Cha	Pussycat Dolls featuring Busta Rhymes	A&M/Interscope	21	(1)	F
7	4	Just A Lil Bit	50 Cent	Shady/Aftermath	15	(10)	
8	6	Behind These Hazel Eyes	Kelly Clarkson	RCA	21	(9)	
9		Inside Your Heaven	Bo Bice	RCA/RMG	3		F
10		Lose Control	Missy Elliott featuring Ciara & Fat Man Scoop	The Gold Mind/Atlant	16	(7)	
11	10	Grind With Me	Pretty Ricky	Atlantic	12	(26)	F
12	3	Oh	Ciara featuring Ludacris	Sho'Nuff Musicline/ LaFace	16	(4)	
13		Get It Poppin'	Fat Joe featuring Nelly	Terror Squad/Atlantic	11	(34)	
14	7	Switch	Will Smith	Overbrook/Interscope	18	(4)	
15		Let Me Hold You	Bow Wow featuring Omarion	Columbia	13	(27)	
16		Pimpin' All Over The World	Ludacris featuring Bobby Valentino	DTP/Def Jam South	11		
17		You And Me	Lifehouse	Geffen	21		
18	9	Since U Been Gone	Kelly Clarkson	RCA	25	(5)	G
19		Listen To Your Heart	D.H.T.	Robbins	12	(7)	F
20		These Boots Are Made For Walkin'	Jessica Simpson	Columbia	2	(4)	

This Mnth	Prev Mnth	Title	Artist	Label	Wks 20	(UK Pos)	
1	1	We Belong Together	Mariah Carey	Island/IDJMG	27	(2)	
2	6	Don't Cha	Pussycat Dolls featuring Busta Rhymes	A&M/Interscope	21	(1)	F
3	5	Pon De Replay	Rihanna	SPR/Def Jam	15	(2)	F
4	15	Let Me Hold You	Bow Wow featuring Omarion	Columbia	13	(27)	
5	10	Lose Control	Missy Elliott feat. Ciara & Fat Man Scoop	The Gold Mind/Atlantic	16	(7)	
6	17	You And Me	Lifehouse	Geffen	21		
7	2	Hollaback Girl	Gwen Stefani	Interscope	20	(8)	G
8	8	Behind These Hazel Eyes	Kelly Clarkson	RCA	21	(9)	
9	19	Listen To Your Heart	D.H.T.	Robbins	13	7	F
10	16	Pimpin' All Over The World	Ludacris featuring Bobby Valentino	DTP/Def Jam South	11		
11	3	Don't Phunk With My Heart	The Black Eyed Peas	A&M/Interscope	16	(3)	
12		Shake It Off	Mariah Carey	Island/IDJMG	18		
13	13	Get It Poppin'	Fat Joe featuring Nelly	Terror Squad/Atlantic	11	(34)	
14	11	Grind With Me	Pretty Ricky	Atlantic	12	(26)	F
15		Feel Good Inc	Gorillaz	Parlophone/Virgin	13	(20)	
16		Like You	Bow Wow featuring Ciara	Columbia	14	(17)	
17		Beverly Hills	Weezer	Geffen	16	(9)	F
18		Cater 2 U	Destiny's Child	Columbia	6		
19	7	Just A Lil Bit	50 Cent	Shady/Aftermath	15	(10)	
20		Scars	Papa Roach	El Tonal/Geffen	5		F

This Mnth	Prev Mnth	Title	Artist	Label	Wks 20	(UK Pos)	
1	1	We Belong Together	Mariah Carey	Island/IDJMG	27	(2)	
2	12	Shake It Off	Mariah Carey	Island/IDJMG	18		
3	2	Don't Cha	Pussycat Dolls featuring Busta Rhymes	A&M/Interscope	21	(1)	F
4	5	Lose Control	Missy Elliott feat. Ciara & Fat Man Scoop	The Gold Mind/Atlantic	16	(7)	
5	3	Pon De Replay	Rihanna	SPR/Def Jam	15	(2)	F
6	16	Like You	Bow Wow featuring Ciara	Columbia	14	(17)	
7		Gold Digger	Kanye West featuring Jamie Foxx	Roc-A-Fella/Def Jam	23	(2)	G
8	4	Let Me Hold You	Bow Wow featuring Omarion	Columbia	13	(27)	
9	6	You And Me	Lifehouse	Geffen	21		
10	8	Behind These Hazel Eyes	Kelly Clarkson	RCA	21	(9)	
	11	Sugar, We're Goin Down	Fall Out Boy	Fueled By Ramen	20	(8)	F
12	9	Listen To Your Heart	D.H.T.	Robbins	13	(7)	F
13		My Humps	The Black Eyed Peas	A&M/Interscope	21	(3)	
14		Wake Me Up When September Ends	Green Day	Reprise	13	(8)	
15	17	Beverly Hills	Weezer	Geffen	16	(9)	F
16		Just The Girl	The Click Five	Lava	3		F
17		Outta Control	50 Cent featuring Mobb Deep	Shady/Aftermath	4	(6)	
18	10	Pimpin' All Over The World	Ludacris featuring Bobby Valentino	DTP/Def Jam South	11		
19		Don't Lie	The Black Eyed Peas	A&M/Interscope	5	(6)	
20		Play	David Banner	S.R.C./Universal/UMRG	10		F

US 2005 JULY-SEPT

◆ The US leg of Live 8 attracted an estimated one million fans to Philadelphia to see such varied acts as The Black Eyed Peas, Bon Jovi, Def Leppard, Destiny's Child, Toby Keith, Alicia Keys, Linkin Park, Maroon5, Dave Matthews, Will Smith, Kanye West and Stevie Wonder.

◆ Many top recording artists performed in aid of the Hurricane Katrina victims. New Orleans had been a major source of popular music since the early days of jazz and among those rescued from the floods was the legendary R&B artist Fats Domino. Tragically, Barry Cowsill from 70s hit-makers The Cowsills drowned. On a fundraising Katrina TV special rap superstar Kanye West accused President Bush of 'not caring about black people'.

◆ Female singers ruled the roost this quarter, with newcomers The Pussycat Dolls, Rihanna and American Idol winner Carrie Underwood scoring the first of their many hits.

UK 2005 OCT-DEC

◆ Sheffield band the Arctic Monkeys became the first "internet made" band to top the download chart. The buzz for their single, 'I Bet You Look Good On The Dancefloor', was built up in cyberspace rather than through the normal promotional routes.

◆ Westlife scored their 13th UK No. 1 single with 'You Raise Me Up' – a record only bettered by Elvis, The Beatles and Cliff Richard. The group also broke a record by scoring their 18th successive Top 5 entry. In the UK alone, they had amassed sales of over 5 million singles and 7 million albums.

◆ The UK Music Hall of Fame inductees this year were Bob Dylan, Aretha Franklin, Jimi Hendrix, Joy Division/ New Order, The Kinks, Pink Floyd and The Who.

October 2005

This Mnth	Prev Mnth	Title	Artist	Label	Wks 20	(US Pos)	
1	5	Don't Cha	Pussycat Dolls featuring Busta Rhymes	A&M	13	(2)	F
2		Push The Button	Sugababes	Island	9		
3		Gold Digger	Kanye West featuring Jamie Foxx	Roc-A-Fella	8	(1)	
4	11	We Be Burnin'	Sean Paul	Atlantic/VP	9	(6)	
5		Tripping	Robbie Williams	Chrysalis	9		
6	2	Bad Day	Daniel Powter	Warner Bros.	18	(1)	F
7		Song 4 Lovers	Liberty X featuring Rev Run from Run DMC	EMI Virgin/Unique	5		
8		Nine Million Bicycles	Katie Melua	Dramatico	5		
9		I Bet You Look Good On The Dancefloor	Arctic Monkeys	Domino Recordings	9		F
10	7	Doctor Pressure	Mylo vs Miami Sound Machine	Breastfed	7		
11		Baby Goodbye	Friday Hill	Longside	4		F
12		Do You Want To	Franz Ferdinand	Domino Recordings	2	(83)	
13		I Wanna Hold You	McFly	Island	2		
14		Precious	Depeche Mode	Mute	2		
15	3	Dare	Gorillaz	Parlophone	9	(87)	
16		All Because Of You	U2	Island	2		
17		Get Your Number/Shake It Off	Mariah Carey	Def Jam/Island	4	(2)	
18		Behind These Hazel Eyes	Kelly Clarkson	RCA	4	(6)	
19		Two More Years	Bloc Party	Wichita Recordings	2		
20		All About Us	t.A.T.u.	Interscope	2		

November 2005

This Mnth	Prev Mnth	Title	Artist	Label	Wks 20	(US Pos)	
1		You Raise Me Up	Westlife	S	9		
2	9	I Bet You Look Good On The Dancefloor	Arctic Monkeys	Domino Recordings	9		F
3	2	Push The Button	Sugababes	Island	9		
4		Hung Up	Madonna	Warner Bros.	16	(7)	
5	5	Tripping	Robbie Williams	Chrysalis	9		
6	1	Don't Cha	Pussycat Dolls featuring Busta Rhymes	A&M	13	(2)	F
7		Can I Have It Like That	Pharrell featuring Gwen Stefani	Virgin	4	(49)	
8		Don't Love You No More	Craig David	Warner Bros.	6		
9		No Worries	Simon Webbe	Innocent	10		
10		Ticket Outta Loserville	Son Of Dork	Mercury	3		F
11		King Of The Mountain	Kate Bush	EMI	2		
12		My Humps	The Black Eyed Peas	A&M	11	(3)	
13		Wake Up	Hilary Duff	Angel	3		
14		Biology	Girls Aloud	Polydor	4		
15		Switch It On	Will Young	Sony BMG	2		
16		A Night To Remember	Liberty X	EMI Virgin/Unique	3		
17		One Way Ticket	The Darkness	Atlantic	2		
18		Just Want You To Know	Backstreet Boys	Jive	1	(70)	
19	3	Gold Digger	Kanye West featuring Jamie Foxx	Roc-A-Fella	8	(1)	
20		Love Generaton	Bob Sinclar featuring Gary Pine	Defected	6		

December 2005

This Mnth	Prev Mnth	Title	Artist	Label	Wks 20	(US Pos)	
1	4	Hung Up	Madonna	Warner Bros.	16	(7)	
2		Stickwitu	The Pussycat Dolls	A&M	8	(5)	
3	1	You Raise Me Up	Westlife	S	9		
4	12	My Humps	The Black Eyed Peas	A&M	11	(3)	
5	9	No Worries	Simon Webbe	Innocent	10		
6		JCB Song	Nizlopi	FDM	11		F
7		Ugly	Sugababes	Island	8		
8		When You Tell Me That You Love Me	Westlife with Diana Ross	S	4		
9		Let There Be Love	Oasis	Big Brother	3		
10	14	Biology	Girls Aloud	Polydor	4		
11		That's My Goal	Shayne Ward	Syco Music	9		FG
12		Dirty Harry	Gorillaz	Parlophone	5		
13		Jingle Bells/U Can't Touch This	Crazy Frog	Gusto	3		
14		Because Of You	Kelly Clarkson	RCA	7	(7)	
15		Fairytale Of New York	The Pogues feat. Kirsty MacColl	Warner Bros.	3		
16	2	I Bet You Look Good On The Dancefloor	Arctic Monkeys	Domino Recordings	9		F
17		Juicebox	The Strokes	Rough Trade	2	(98)	
18		When I'm Gone	Eminem	Interscope	5	(8)	
19		Listen To Your Heart	DHT featuring Edmée	Data	3	(8)	F
20	16	A Night To Remember	Liberty X	EMI Virgin/Unique	3		

October 2005

This Mnth	Prev Mnth	Title	Artist	Label	Wks 20	(UK Pos)	
1	7	Gold Digger	Kanye West featuring Jamie Foxx	Roc-A-Fella/Def Jam	23	(2)	G
2	2	Shake It Off	Mariah Carey	Island/IDJMG	18		
3	6	Like You	Bow Wow featuring Ciara	Columbia	14	(17)	
4	13	My Humps	The Black Eyed Peas	A&M/Interscope	21	(3)	
5		Photograph	Nickelback	Roadrunner	18	(29)	
6	14	Wake Me Up When September Ends	Green Day	Reprise	13	(8)	
7	1	We Belong Together	Mariah Carey	Island/IDJMG	27	(2)	
8		Run It!	Chris Brown	Jive/Zomba	22	(2)	F
9	20	Play	David Banner	S.R.C./UMRG	10		F
10		Soul Survivor	Young Jeezy featuring Akon	Corporate Thugs/Def Jam	17	(16)	F
11	11	Sugar, We're Goin Down	Fall Out Boy	Fueled By Ramen	20	(8)	F
12	3	Don't Cha	Pussycat Dolls featuring Busta Rhymes	A&M/Interscope	21	(1)	F
13	15	Beverly Hills	Weezer	Geffen	16	(9)	F
14	17	Outta Control	50 Cent featuring Mobb Deep	Shady/Aftermath	4	(6)	
15		Because Of You	Kelly Clarkson	RCA	22	(7)	
16	4	Lose Control	Missy Elliott feat. Ciara & Fat Man Scoop	The Gold Mind/Atlantic	16	(7)	
17	9	You And Me	Lifehouse	Geffen	21		
18		Your Body	Pretty Ricky	Atlantic	7	(37)	
19	5	Pon De Replay	Rihanna	SPR/Def Jam	15	(2)	F
20		We Be Burnin'	Sean Paul	VP/Atlantic	13	(2)	

November 2005

This Mnth	Prev Mnth	Title	Artist	Label	Wks 20	(UK Pos)	
1	1	Gold Digger	Kanye West featuring Jamie Foxx	Roc-A-Fella/Def Jam	23	(2)	G
2	8	Run It!	Chris Brown	Jive/Zomba	22	(2)	F
3	4	My Humps	The Black Eyed Peas	A&M/Interscope	21	(3)	
4	10	Soul Survivor	Young Jeezy featuring Akon	Corporate Thugs/Def Jam	17	(16)	F
5	5	Photograph	Nickelback	Roadrunner	18	(29)	
6	20	We Be Burnin'	Sean Paul	VP/Atlantic	13	(2)	
7	15	Because Of You	Kelly Clarkson	RCA	22	(7)	
8	2	Shake It Off	Mariah Carey	Island/IDJMG	18		
9	3	Like You	Bow Wow featuring Ciara	Columbia	14	(17)	
10		I'm Sprung	T-Pain	Konvict Muzik/Jive	11		F
11	11	Sugar, We're Goin' Down	Fall Out Boy	Fueled By Ramen	20	(8)	F
12	6	Wake Me Up When September Ends	Green Day	Reprise	13	(8)	
13		Laffy Taffy	D4L	Deemoney/Asylum/Atlantic	14	(29)	F
14		Stickwitu	The Pussycat Dolls	A&M/Interscope	16	(1)	
15	18	Your Body	Pretty Ricky	Atlantic	7	(37)	
16	17	You And Me	Lifehouse	Geffen	21		
17		Stay Fly	Three 6 Mafia feat. Young Buck & Eightball & MJG	Hypnotize Minds	12		F
18	13	Beverly Hills	Weezer	Geffen	16	(9)	F
19		Girl Tonite	Twista featuring Trey Songz	Atlantic	4	(47)	
20	9	Play	David Banner	S.R.C./UMRG	10		F

December 2005

This Mnth	Prev Mnth	Title	Artist	Label	Wks 20	(UK Pos)	
1	2	Run It!	Chris Brown	Jive/Zomba	22	(2)	F
2	13	Laffy Taffy	D4L	Deemoney/Asylum/Atlantic	14	(29)	F
3	1	Gold Digger	Kanye West featuring Jamie Foxx	Roc-A-Fella/Def Jam	23	(2)	G
4		Don't Forget About Us	Mariah Carey	Island/IDJMG	14	(11)	
5	5	Photograph	Nickelback	Roadrunner	18	(29)	
6	3	My Humps	The Black Eyed Peas	A&M/Interscope	21	(3)	
7	4	Soul Survivor	Young Jeezy featuring Akon	Corporate Thugs/Def Jam	17	(16)	F
8	14	Stickwitu	The Pussycat Dolls	A&M/Interscope	16	(1)	
9		Grillz	Nelly featuring Paul Wall, Ali & Gipp	Fo' Reel/Derrty	19	(24)	
10	7	Because Of You	Kelly Clarkson	RCA	22	(7)	
11	6	We Be Burnin'	Sean Paul	VP/Atlantic	13	(2)	
12		Hung Up	Madonna	Warner Bros.	6	(1)	
13		When I'm Gone	Eminem	Shady/Aftermath/Interscope	6	(4)	
14		There It Go! (The Whistle Song)	Juelz Santana	Diplomats/Def Jam	12		
15	10	I'm Sprung	T-Pain	Konvict Muzik/Jive	11		F
16		Check On It	Beyoncé featuring Slim Thug	Columbia	18	(3)	
17	17	Stay Fly	Three 6 Mafia feat. Young Buck & Eightball & MJG	Hypnotize Minds	12		F
18		One Wish	Ray J	Knockout/Sanctuary	7	(26)	F
19		I Think They Like Me	Dem Franchize Boyz feat. Jermaine Dupri, Da Brat & Bow Wow	So So Def/Virgin	9		F
20	11	Sugar, We're Goin Down	Fall Out Boy	Fueled By Ramen	20	(8)	F

▲ For the fourth year running an 'American Idol' artist had the biggest-selling single ('Inside Your Heaven' by Carrie Underwood). Billboard's end-of-year survey listed 50 Cent as Top Male, Green Day as Top Group and Kelly Clarkson as the year's Top Female.

◆ For the first time, sales of downloads in a single week passed the 20 million mark and 'Laffy Taffy' by D4L broke the weekly sales record when it sold over 175,000 downloads.

◆ Luck of the Irish?: U2's Vertigo tour was the most successful of the year grossing over $260 million … Van Morrison's 'Brown Eyed Girl' joined the handful of singles to amass over seven million radio plays in America.

425

UK 2006 JAN-MAR

◆ 'X Factor' winner Shayne Ward sold 283,446 copies of 'That's My Goal' on its first day of release (Dec 28) and 742,180 before the year's end. Amazingly, these four days' sales made him the No.2 selling singles artist of 2005 behind Tony Christie (Elvis was third).

▲ James Blunt's debut album 'Back To Bedlam' sold 2,367,758 copies in the UK in 2005 – a figure never matched in a calendar year. It went on to sell over 10 million worldwide.

◆ BRIT award-winners included Blunt, Coldplay, Green Day, Kaiser Chiefs, Madonna, Paul Weller and the Arctic Monkeys, whose album 'Whatever People Say I Am, That's What I'm Not' sold 363,735 in its first week – a record for a debut album.

January 2006

This Mnth	Prev Mnth	Title	Artist	Label	Wks 20	(US Pos)	
1	11	That's My Goal	Shayne Ward	Syco Music	9		FG
2	6	JCB Song	Nizlopi	FDM	11		F
3	1	Hung Up	Madonna	Warner Bros.	16	(7)	
4		George Best - A Tribute	Brian Kennedy and Peter Corry	Curb	5		F
5	18	When I'm Gone	Eminem	Interscope	5	(8)	
6	4	My Humps	The Black Eyed Peas	A&M	11	(3)	
7		Break The Night With Colour	Richard Ashcroft	Parlophone	4		
8		When The Sun Goes Down	Arctic Monkeys	Domino Recordings	5		
9		I'll Be Ready	Sunblock	Manifesto	6		F
10	2	Stickwitu	The Pussycat Dolls	A&M	8	(5)	
11		Nasty Girl	The Notorious B.I.G. featuring Diddy, Nelly, Jagged Edge & Avery Storm	Bad Boy	10	(44)	
12	7	Ugly	Sugababes	Island	8		
13		All Time Love	Will Young	Sony BMG	6		
14	15	Fairytale Of New York	The Pogues featuring Kirsty MacColl	Warner Bros.	3		
15		Check On It	Beyoncé featuring Slim Thug	Columbia	6	(1)	
16		Goodbye My Lover	James Blunt	Atlantic	6	(100)	
17		Sleep	Texas	Mercury	3		
18		Say Say Say (Waiting 4 U)	Hi_Tack	Gusto	7		F
19		Heartbeats	Jose Gonzalez	Peace Frog	4		F
20	14	Because Of You	Kelly Clarkson	RCA	7	(7)	

February 2006

This Mnth	Prev Mnth	Title	Artist	Label	Wks 20	(US Pos)	
1	11	Nasty Girl	The Notorious B.I.G. featuring Diddy, Nelly, Jagged Edge & Avery Storm	Bad Boy	10	(44)	
2		Boys Will Be Boys	The Ordinary Boys	B-Unique	6		
3	15	Check On It	Beyoncé featuring Slim Thug	Columbia	6	(1)	
4		Run It!	Chris Brown featuring Juelz Santana	Jive	6	(1)	F
5	18	Say Say Say (Waiting 4 U)	Hi_Tack	Gusto	7		F
6		Thunder In My Heart Again	Meck featuring Leo Sayer	Apollo/Free 2 Air	7		F
7	8	When The Sun Goes Down	Arctic Monkeys	Domino Recordings	5		
8	13	All Time Love	Will Young	Sony BMG	6		
9		You Spin Me Round	Dead Or Alive	Epic	4		
10	1	That's My Goal	Shayne Ward	Syco Music	9		FG
11	2	JCB Song	Nizlopi	FDM	11		F
12	9	I'll Be Ready	Sunblock	Manifesto	6		F
13		You Got The Love	The Source featuring Candi Staton	Positiva	6		
14		Woman In Love/ I Get The Sweetest Feeling	Liz McClarnon	All Around The World	2		F
15		Sugar, We're Goin Down	Fall Out Boy	Mercury	4	(8)	F
16	7	Break The Night With Colour	Richard Ashcroft	Parlophone	4		
17		Analogue (All I Want)	A-Ha	Polydor	2		
18	3	Hung Up	Madonna	Warner Bros.	16	(7)	
19		Boyfriend	Ashlee Simpson	Geffen	2	(19)	
20	4	George Best - A Tribute	Brian Kennedy and Peter Corry	Curb	5		F

March 2006

This Mnth	Prev Mnth	Title	Artist	Label	Wks 20	(US Pos)	
1		It's Chico Time	Chico	Sony BMG	6		F
2		No Tomorrow	Orson	Mercury	10		F
3		Beep	The Pussycat Dolls featuring Will.I.Am	A&M	9	(13)	
4		Put Your Records On	Corinne Bailey Rae	EMI	10	(64)	F
5		Sorry	Madonna	Warner Bros.	7	(58)	
6		Red Dress	Sugababes	Island	4		
7	6	Thunder In My Heart Again	Meck featuring Leo Sayer	Apollo/Free 2 Air	7		F
8		Pump It	The Black Eyed Peas	A&M	9	(18)	
9		Sewn	The Feeling	Island	5		F
10		Touch The Sky	Kanye West featuring Lupe Fiasco	Roc-A-Fella	5	(42)	F
11	1	Nasty Girl	The Notorious B.I.G. featuring Diddy, Nelly, Jagged Edge & Avery Storm	Bad Boy	10	(44)	
12		Whole Lotta History	Girls Aloud	Polydor	2		
13		Don't Bother	Shakira	Epic	2	(74)	
14	4	Run It!	Chris Brown featuring Juelz Santana	Jive	6	(1)	F
15	13	You Got The Love	The Source featuring Candi Staton	Positiva	6		
16		Amazing	Westlife	S	2		
17		Billie Jean	Michael Jackson	Epic	1		
18		Incredible	The Shapeshifters	Positiva	1		
19	2	Boys Will Be Boys	The Ordinary Boys	B-Unique	6		
20		One Wish	Ray J	Sanctuary Urban	2	(11)	

US 2006 JAN-MAR

January 2006

This Mnth	Prev Mnth	Title	Artist	Label	Wks 20	(UK Pos)	
1	9	Grillz	Nelly featuring Paul Wall, Ali & Gipp	Fo' Reel/Derrty	19	(24)	
2	1	Run It!	Chris Brown	Jive/Zomba	22	(2)	F
3	4	Don't Forget About Us	Mariah Carey	Island/DJMJ	14	(11)	
4	2	Laffy Taffy	D4L	Deemoney/Asylum/Atlantic	14	(29)	F
5	16	Check On It	Beyoncé featuring Slim Thug	Columbia	18	(3)	
6	5	Photograph	Nickelback	Roadrunner	18	(29)	
7	3	Gold Digger	Kanye West featuring Jamie Foxx	Roc-A-Fella/Def Jam	23	(2)	G
8	8	Stickwitu	The Pussycat Dolls	A&M/Interscope	16	(1)	
9	14	There It Go! (The Whistle Song)	Juelz Santana	Diplomats/Def Jam	12		
10	6	My Humps	The Black Eyed Peas	A&M/Interscope	21	(3)	
11		Dance, Dance	Fall Out Boy	Fueled By Ramen/Island	14	(8)	
12		Dirty Little Secret	The All-American Rejects	Doghouse/Interscope	10	(18)	F
13		Be Without You	Mary J. Blige	Geffen/Interscope	21	(32)	
14	10	Because Of You	Kelly Clarkson	RCA	22	(7)	
15	18	One Wish	Ray J	Knockout/Sanctuary	7	(26)	F
16	20	Sugar, We're Goin Down	Fall Out Boy	Fueled By Ramen	20		F
17	7	Soul Survivor	Young Jeezy featuring Akon	Corporate Thugs/Def Jam	17	(16)	F
18		You're Beautiful	James Blunt	Custard/Atlantic	20	(1)	FG
19		Beverly Hills	Weezer	Geffen	16	9	F
20		So Sick	Ne-Yo	Def Jam/IDJMG	15	(1)	F

February 2006

This Mnth	Prev Mnth	Title	Artist	Label	Wks 20	(UK Pos)	
1	5	Check On It	Beyoncé featuring Slim Thug	Columbia	18	(3)	
2	1	Grillz	Nelly featuring Paul Wall, Ali & Gipp	Fo' Reel/Derrty	19	(24)	
3	18	You're Beautiful	James Blunt	Custard/Atlantic	20	(1)	FG
4	13	Be Without You	Mary J. Blige	Geffen/Interscope	21	(32)	
5	2	Run It!	Chris Brown	Jive/Zomba	22	(2)	F
6	20	So Sick	Ne-Yo	Def Jam/IDJMG	15	(1)	F
7	8	Stickwitu	The Pussycat Dolls	A&M/Interscope	16	(1)	
8		I'm N Luv (Wit A Stripper)	T-Pain featuring Mike Jones	Konvict Muzik/Jive	11		
9		Yo (Excuse Me Miss)	Chris Brown	Jive/Zomba	13	(13)	
10		Unpredictable	Jamie Foxx featuring Ludacris	J/RMG	10	(16)	
11		Shake That	Eminem featuring Nate Dogg	Shady/Aftermath/Interscope		(9)	
12		Breaking Free	Zac Efron, Andrew Seeley & Vanessa Anne Hudgens	Walt Disney	2	(9)	F
13	9	There It Go! (The Whistle Song)	Juelz Santana	Diplomats/Def Jam	12		
14	12	Dirty Little Secret	The All-American Rejects	Doghouse/Interscope	10	(18)	FG
15		Unwritten	Natasha Bedingfield	Epic	21	(6)	G
16	3	Don't Forget About Us	Mariah Carey	Island/DJMJ	14	(11)	
17		Temperature	Sean Paul	VP/Atlantic	20	(11)	
18	11	Dance, Dance	Fall Out Boy	Fueled By Ramen/Island	14	(8)	
19	4	Laffy Taffy	D4L	Deemoney/Asylum/Atlantic	14	(29)	F
20		Lean Wit It, Rock Wit It	Dem Franchize Boyz feat. Lil Peanut & Charlay	So So Def/Virgin	14		

March 2006

This Mnth	Prev Mnth	Title	Artist	Label	Wks 20	(UK Pos)	
1	3	You're Beautiful	James Blunt	Custard/Atlantic	20	(1)	FG
2	17	Temperature	Sean Paul	VP/Atlantic	20	(11)	
3	1	Check On It	Beyoncé featuring Slim Thug	Columbia	18	(3)	
4	6	So Sick	Ne-Yo	Def Jam/IDJMG	15	(1)	F
5	4	Be Without You	Mary J. Blige	Geffen/Interscope	21	(32)	
6	2	Grillz	Nelly featuring Paul Wall, Ali & Gipp	Fo' Reel/Derrty	19	(24)	
7	8	I'm N Luv (Wit A Stripper)	T-Pain featuring Mike Jones	Konvict Muzik/Jive	11		
8	9	Yo (Excuse Me Miss)	Chris Brown	Jive/Zomba	13	(13)	
9	15	Unwritten	Natasha Bedingfield	Epic	21	(6)	G
10	20	Lean Wit It, Rock Wit It	Dem Franchize Boyz feat. Lil Peanut & Charlay	So So Def/Virgin	14		
11		Bad Day	Daniel Powter	Warner Bros.	20	(2)	FG
12	11	Shake That	Eminem featuring Nate Dogg	Shady/Aftermath/Interscope	9		
13		Everytime We Touch	Cascada	Robbins	12	(2)	F
14	10	Unpredictable	Jamie Foxx featuring Ludacris	J/RMG	10	(16)	
15		Stupid Girls	P!nk	LaFace/Zomba	3	(4)	
16	14	Dirty Little Secret	The All-American Rejects	Doghouse/Interscope	10	(18)	FG
17	18	Dance, Dance	Fall Out Boy	Fueled By Ramen/Island	14	(8)	
18		New Booty	Bubba Sparxxx feat. Ying Yang Twins & Mr. Collipark	New South/Purple Ribbon	14		
19		Touch It	Busta Rhymes	Aftermath/Interscope	8	(6)	
20		Beep	The Pussycat Dolls featuring Will.I.Am	A&M/Interscope	7	(2)	

◆ Perhaps surprisingly, the Grammy Awards attracted 11 million viewers less than a heat of American Idol. In other words, people preferred to watch unknowns rather than superstars like Christina Aguilera, Mary J. Blige, Mariah Carey, Coldplay, Paul McCartney, Bruce Springsteen, U2, Kanye West and original American Idol Kelly Clarkson.

◆ Nine tracks from the chart-topping Walt Disney soundtrack album 'High School Musical' were simultaneously in the US Top 100, with six of them being in the Top 20 on the digital sales chart. Top seller was 'Breaking Free', which broke a chart record by jumping from position 86 to 4.

◆ Billy Joel broke the record for successive shows at New York's famed Madison Square Garden. His 12 performances at the prestigious venue were seen by over 200,000 fans and grossed a record-breaking $20 million.

◆ 2006's biggest-selling single was 'Crazy' by US duo Gnarls Barkley, which was also the first recording to top the UK chart on download sales alone. It was deleted as a physical record while still No.1, but was still among the Top 40 downloads at the end of 2006.

◆ Following in the footsteps of his ex-wife Lisa Marie's dad, one previous Michael Jackson hit was released every week for four months. Unlike Elvis though, not many fared well enough to reach these Top 20s. However, in Spain they clogged the chart with eight of them simultaneously in the Top 10 at one time.

◆ Other news: Recently knighted Tom Jones returned to the chart as vocalist with dance act Chicane… The first three acts on X Factor, Shayne Ward, Journey South and Andy Abraham, all sold over 175,000 in the first week with their debut albums.

April 2006

This Mnth	Prev Mnth	Title	Artist	Label	Wks 20	(US Pos)	
1		So Sick	Ne-Yo	Def Jam	8	(1)	F
2		Crazy	Gnarls Barkley	Warner Bros.	11	(2)	F
3	2	No Tomorrow	Orson	Mercury	10		F
4		Natures Law	Embrace	Independiente	4		
5		One	Mary J. Blige and U2	Geffen	8	(86)	
6	8	Pump It	The Black Eyed Peas	A&M	9	(18)	
7		Stupid Girls	P!nk	LaFace	5	(15)	
8		Naive	The Kooks	Virgin	9		
9	3	Beep	The Pussycat Dolls featuring Will.I.Am	A&M	9	(13)	
10	4	Put Your Records On	Corinne Bailey Rae	EMI	10	(64)	F
11		No Promises	Shayne Ward	Syco Music	7		
12		SOS	Rihanna	Def Jam	9	(1)	
13		You Have Killed Me	Morrissey	Attack	2		
14		From Paris To Berlin	Infernal	Apollo/Europa	13		F
15		When You Wasn't Famous	The Streets	679 Recordings	3		
16	1	It's Chico Time	Chico	Sony BMG	6		F
17	10	Touch The Sky	Kanye West featuring Lupe Fiasco	Roc-A-Fella	5	(42)	F
18		Temperature	Sean Paul	Atlantic/VP	4	(2)	
19		Dance, Dance	Fall Out Boy	Mercury	4	(9)	
20		Why Won't You Give Me Your Love?	The Zutons	Deltasonic	2		

May 2006

This Mnth	Prev Mnth	Title	Artist	Label	Wks 20	(US Pos)	
1	2	Crazy	Gnarls Barkley	Warner Bros.	11	(2)	F
2	14	From Paris To Berlin	Infernal	Apollo/Europa	13		F
3	12	SOS	Rihanna	Def Jam	9		
4		Dani California	Red Hot Chili Peppers	Warner Bros.	6	(6)	
5		Somebody's Watching Me	Beatfreakz	Data	5		F
6		Control Myself	LL Cool J featuring Jennifer Lopez and Jermaine Dupri	Def Jam	5	(4)	
7		Steady As She Goes	The Raconteurs	XL Recordings	4	(54)	F
8	11	No Promises	Shayne Ward	Syco Music	7		
9		Stoned In Love	Chicane featuring Tom Jones	Manifesto	4		F
10		Bang Bang You're Dead	Dirty Pretty Things	Vertigo	3		F
11		You're All I Have	Snow Patrol	Fiction	4		
12		Say I	Christina Milian featuring Young Jeezy	Def Jam	4	(21)	
13	8	Naive	The Kooks	Virgin	9		
14	5	One	Mary J. Blige and U2	Geffen	8	(86)	
15		Touch It	Busta Rhymes	Interscope	4	(16)	
16		I'm With Stupid	Pet Shop Boys	Parlophone	1		
17		Who Am I	Will Young	Sony BMG	4		
18		First Time	Sunblock featuring Robin Beck	Manifesto	2		
19		Teenage Life	Daz Sampson	Ebul/Jive	3		F
20		Bright Idea	Orson	Mercury	1		F

June 2006

This Mnth	Prev Mnth	Title	Artist	Label	Wks 20	(US Pos)	
1		I Wish I Was A Punk Rocker (With Flowers In My Hair)	Sandi Thom	RCA	13		F
2	2	From Paris To Berlin	Infernal	Apollo/Europa	13		F
3	1	Crazy	Gnarls Barkley	Warner Bros.	11	(2)	F
4		Maneater	Nelly Furtado	Geffen	9	(16)	
5		Is It Any Wonder?	Keane	Island	5	(78)	
6		Who Knew	P!nk	LaFace	8		
7		World At Your Feet	Embrace	Independiente	3		F
8		Monster	The Automatic	B-Unique/Polydor	7		F
9	6	Control Myself	LL Cool J featuring Jennifer Lopez and Jermaine Dupri	Def Jam	5	(4)	
10		Country Girl	Primal Scream	Columbia	3		
11		Hips Don't Lie	Shakira featuring Wyclef Jean	Epic	19	(1)	
12		Faster Kill Pussycat	Oakenfold featuring Brittany Murphy	Perfecto	5		
13		(Is This The Way To) The World Cup	Tony Christie	Tug	3		
14		Nine2Five	The Ordinary Boys vs Lady Sovereign	B-Unique	2		F
15		Who Says You Can't Go Home	Bon Jovi	Mercury	1	(23)	
16		All Over Again	Ronan Keating and Kate Rusby	Polydor	1		
17		3 Lions	Baddiel, Skinner & The Lightning Seeds	Epic	4		
18		Up All Night	Matt Willis	Mercury	1		F
19		Fill My Little World	The Feeling	Island	6		F
20	3	SOS	Rihanna	Def Jam	9	(1)	

US 2006 APR–JUNE

April 2006

This Mnth	Prev Mnth	Title	Artist	Label	Wks 20	(UK Pos)	
1	11	Bad Day	Daniel Powter	Warner Bros.	20	(2)	FG
2	2	Temperature	Sean Paul	VP/Atlantic	20	(11)	
3	1	You're Beautiful	James Blunt	Custard/Atlantic	20	(1)	FG
4	4	So Sick	Ne-Yo	Def Jam/IDJMG	15	(1)	F
5	5	Be Without You	Mary J. Blige	Geffen/Interscope	21	(32)	
6	9	Unwritten	Natasha Bedingfield	Epic	21	(6)	G
7		What You Know	T.I.	Grand Hustle/Atlantic	(10)		
8	10	Lean Wit It, Rock Wit It	Dem Franchize Boyz feat. Lil Peanut & Charlay	So So Def/Virgin	14		
9	18	Ms. New Booty	Bubba Sparxxx feat, Ying Yang Twins & Mr. Collipark	New South/Purple Ribbon	14		
10	7	I'm N Luv (Wit A Stripper)	T-Pain featuring Mike Jones	Konvict Muzik/Jive	11		
11	8	Yo (Excuse Me Miss)	Chris Brown	Jive/Zomba	13	(13)	
12		What Hurts The Most	Rascal Flatts	Lyric Street	4		F
13		Control Myself	LL Cool J featuring Jennifer Lopez	Def Jam	2	(2)	
14	13	Everytime We Touch	Cascada	Robbins	12	(2)	F
15	3	Check On It	Beyoncé featuring Slim Thug	Columbia	18	(3)	
16		Walk Away	Kelly Clarkson	RCA	9	(21)	
17	20	Beep	The Pussycat Dolls feat. Will.I.Am	A&M/Interscope	7	(2)	
18		Dani California	Red Hot Chili Peppers	Warner Bros.	15	(2)	
19		Ridin'	Chamillionaire featuring Krayzie Bone	Universal Motown	17	(2)	F
20	6	Grillz	Nelly featuring Paul Wall, Ali & Gipp	Fo' Reel/Derrty	19	(24)	

May 2006

This Mnth	Prev Mnth	Title	Artist	Label	Wks 20	(UK Pos)	
1	1	Bad Day	Daniel Powter	Warner Bros.	20	(2)	FG
2	2	Temperature	Sean Paul	VP/Atlantic	20	(11)	
3	19	Ridin'	Chamillionaire featuring Krayzie Bone	Universal Motown	17	(2)	F
4		SOS	Rihanna	SRP/Def Jam	9	(2)	
5	7	What You KnoW	T.I.	Grand Hustle/Atlantic	10		
6	6	Unwritten	Natasha Bedingfield	Epic	21	(6)	G
7	18	Dani California	Red Hot Chili Peppers	Warner Bros.	15	(2)	
8		Where'd You Go	Fort Minor featuring Holly Brook	Shop/Warner Bros.	11		F
9	9	Ms. New Booty	Bubba Sparxxx feat. Ying Yang Twins & Mr. Collipark	New South/Purple Ribbon	14		
10		What's Left Of Me	Nick Lachey	Jive/Zomba	7		F
11	3	You're Beautiful	James Blunt	Custard/Atlantic	20	(1)	FG
12	8	Lean Wit It, Rock Wit It	Dem Franchize Boyz feat. Lil Peanut & Charlay	So So Def/Virgin	14		
13		Over My Head (Cable Car)	The Fray	Epic/Sony Music	17		FG
14		Snap Yo Fingers	Lil Jon feat. E-40 & Sean Paul of YoungBloodZ	BME/TVT	15		
15	13	Control Myself	LL Cool J featuring Jennifer Lopez	Def Jam	2	(2)	
16	5	Be Without You	Mary J. Blige	Geffen/Interscope	21	(32)	
17		Hips Don't Lie	Shakira featuring Wyclef Jean	Epic/Sony	17	(1)	G
18		Let U Go	Ashley Parker Angel	Blackground/Universal	(2)		F
19	12	What Hurts The Most	Rascal Flatts	Lyric Street	4		F
20	16	Walk Away	Kelly Clarkson	RCA	9	(21)	

June 2006

This Mnth	Prev Mnth	Title	Artist	Label	Wks 20	(UK Pos)	
1	3	Ridin'	Chamillionaire featuring Krayzie Bone	Universal Motown	17	(2)	F
2	1	Bad Day	Daniel Powter	Warner Bros.	20	(2)	FG
3		Promiscuous	Nelly Furtado featuring Timbaland	Mosley/Geffen	19	(3)	G
4	17	Hips Don't Lie	Shakira featuring Wyclef Jean	Epic/Sony	17	(1)	G
5	8	Where'd You Go	Fort Minor featuring Holly Brook	Machine Shop/warner	11		F
6	4	SOS	Rihanna	SPR/Def Jam	9	(2)	
7	2	Temperature	Sean Paul	VP/Atlantic	20	(11)	
8		Me & U	Cassie	Next Selection/Bad Boy	17	(6)	F
9		It's Goin' Down	Yung Joc	Block/Bad Boy/South/Atlantic	12		FG
10	7	Dani California	Red Hot Chili Peppers	Warner Bros.	15	(2)	
11	14	Snap Yo Fingers	Lil Jon feat. E-40 & Sean Paul of YoungBloodZ	BME/TVT	15		
12		Unfaithful	Rihanna	SRP/Def Jam	14	(2)	
13	13	Over My Head (Cable Car)	The Fray	Epic/Sony Music	18		FG
14	5	What You Know	T.I.	Grand Hustle/Atlantic	10		
15	10	What's Left Of Me	Nick Lachey	Jive/Zomba	7		F
16		So What	Field Mob featuring Ciara	DTP/Geffen/Interscope	9	(56)	
17	9	Ms. New Booty	Bubba Sparxxx feat. Ying Yang Twins & Mr.Collipark	New South/Purple Ribbon	14		
18		Gimme That	Chris Brown featuring Lil' Wayne	Jive/Zomba	7		
19	6	Unwritten	Natasha Bedingfield	Epic	21	(6)	G
20		Crazy	Gnarls Barkley	Downtown/Atlantic	17	(1)	FG

▲ Shakira and Wyclef Jean's 'Hips Don't Lie' sold an unprecedented 266,500 downloads in one week. The record topped charts in 16 countries and was No.1 on the last ever 'Top Of The Pops', which had run in the UK for 42 years.

◆ Following its huge 2005 success in Europe, Canadian singer/songwriter Daniel Powter's 'Bad Day' finally clicked in the US. He became the fourth male soloist to head the chart in 2006 and it joined the digital million-sellers club.

◆ Record-breakers: 64 million votes were cast in the American Idol final with Taylor Hicks the winner... 'Rolling Stone' mag published its 1000th edition, and Pink Floyd's 'The Dark Side Of The Moon' celebrated 1500 weeks on the US album charts.

429

UK 2006 JULY-SEPT

▲ Madonna's 'Get Together' was her record 33rd No.1 on the UK Dance Chart. Her eight shows at Wembley Arena grossed over $22 million, while The Rolling Stones' two Twickenham Stadium shows were seen by over 100,000 fans and took over $13.5 million.

◆ Robbie Williams' album 'Rudebox' passed the two million sales mark in Europe, as did the Kaiser Chiefs' debut album 'Employment', while new UK act Corinne Bailey Rae saw her eponymous album exceed a million sales.

◆ Other news: Ronan Keating's amazing run of 30 successive Top 10 singles (with Boyzone and as a soloist) ended when his revival of The Goo Goo Dolls' 'Iris' stalled at No.15.

July 2006

This Mnth	Prev Mnth	Title	Artist	Label	Wks 20	(US Pos)	F
1	11	Hips Don't Lie	Shakira featuring Wyclef Jean	Epic	19	(1)	
2	4	Maneater	Nelly Furtado	Geffen	9	(16)	
3	1	Wish I Was A Punk Rocker (With Flowers In My Hair)	Sandi Thom	RCA	13		F
4		Smile	Lily Allen	Regal Recordings	9		F
5		Buttons	The Pussycat Dolls feat. Snoop Dogg	A&M	5	(3)	
6		In The Morning	Razorlight	Vertigo	7		
7	8	Monster	The Automatic	B-Unique/Polydor	7		F
8		Sexy Love	Ne-Yo	Def Jam	6	(7)	
9		Voodoo Child	Rogue Traders	Ariola	10		F
10		Last Request	Paolo Nutini	Atlantic	7		F
11		She Moves In Her Own Way	The Kooks	Virgin	9		
12		Don't Stop Me Now/ Please, Please	McFly	Universal	3		
13		Unfaithful	Rihanna	Def Jam	8	(6)	
14		Supermassive Black Hole	Muse	A&E	3		
15		Mas Que Nada	Sergio Mendes feat. The Black Eyed Peas	Concord/UCJ	3		F
16	2	From Paris To Berlin	Infernal	Apollo/Europa	13		F
17		Valerie	The Zutons	Deltasonic	5		
18		You Give Me Something	James Morrison	Polydor	9		F
19		I Love My Chick	Busta Rhymes featuring Will.I.Am & Kelis	Interscope	3		
20		Rooftops (A Liberation Broadcast)	Lostprophets	Visible Noise	3		

August 2006

This Mnth	Prev Mnth	Title	Artist	Label	Wks 20	(US Pos)	F
1	1	Hips Don't Lie	Shakira featuring Wyclef Jean	Epic	19	(1)	
2		Ain't No Other Man	Christina Aguilera	RCA	8	(6)	
3	13	Unfaithful	Rihanna	Def Jam	8	(6)	
4		Everytime We Touch	Cascada	All Around The World	15	(10)	F
5	18	You Give Me Something	James Morrison	Polydor	9		F
6	4	Smile	Lily Allen	Regal Recordings	9		F
7	9	Voodoo Child	Rogue Traders	Ariola	10		F
8		Stars Are Blind	Paris	Warner Bros.	4	(18)	F
9		Ridin'	Chamillionaire featuring Krayzie Bone	Universal	7	(1)	F
10		Love Don't Let Me Go (Walking Away)	David Guetta vs The Egg	Gusto	6		
11		Leave Before The Lights Come On	Arctic Monkeys	Domino Recordings	4		
12	10	Last Request	Paolo Nutini	Atlantic	7		F
13	12	Don't Stop Me Now/Please, Please	McFly	Universal	3		
14		Empire	Kasabian	Columbia	6		
15		Chasing Cars	Snow Patrol	Fiction	13	(5)	
16		Me & U	Cassie	Bad Boy	6	(3)	F
17		Get Together	Madonna	Warner Bros.	2		
18	3	I Wish I Was A Punk Rocker (With Flowers In My Hair)	Sandi Thom	RCA	13		F
19	11	She Moves In Her Own Way	The Kooks	Virgin	9		
20	2	Maneater	Nelly Furtado	Geffen	9	(16)	

September 2006

This Mnth	Prev Mnth	Title	Artist	Label	Wks 20	(US Pos)	F
1		Sexyback	Justin Timberlake	Jive	10	(1)	
2	1	Hips Don't Lie	Shakira featuring Wyclef Jean	Epic	19	(1)	
3		I Don't Feel Like Dancin'	Scissor Sisters	Polydor	14		
4		Deja Vu	Beyoncé featuring Jay-Z	Columbia	5	(4)	
5		Promiscuous	Nelly Furtado featuring Timbaland	Geffen	8	(1)	
6	9	Ridin'	Chamillionaire featuring Krayzie Bone	Universal	7	(1)	F
7	15	Chasing Cars	Snow Patrol	Fiction	13	(5)	
8	4	Everytime We Touch	Cascada	All Around The World	15	(10)	F
9		When You Were Young	The Killers	Vertigo	6	(14)	
10	10	Love Don't Let Me Go (Walking Away)	David Guetta Vs The Egg	Gusto	6		
11		Rudebox	Robbie Williams	Chrysalis	3		
12		London Bridge	Fergie	A&M	3	(1)	F
13		Chelsea Dagger	The Fratellis	Fallout	7		
14	16	Me & U	Cassie	Bad Boy	6	(3)	F
15		Never Be Lonely	The Feeling	Island	5		
16		It's Not That Easy	Lemar	Sony Music	4		
17		U & Ur Hand	P!nk	LaFace	6		
18	11	Leave Before The Lights Come On	Arctic Monkeys	Domino Recordings	4		
19		Something About You	Jamelia	Parlophone	4		
20	5	You Give Me Something	James Morrison	Polydor	9		F

July 2006

This Mnth	Prev Mnth	Title	Artist	Label	Wks 20	(UK Pos)	
1	3	Promiscuous	Nelly Furtado featuring Timbaland	Mosley/Geffen	19	(3)	G
2	4	Hips Don't Lie	Shakira featuring Wyclef Jean	Epic/Sony	17	(1)	G
3	20	Crazy	Gnarls Barkley	Downtown/Atlantic	17	(1)	FG
4	8	Me & U	Cassie	Next Selection/Bad Boy	17	(6)	F
5	9	It's Goin' Down	Yung Joc	Block/Bad Boy South/Atlantic	12		FG
6	1	Ridin'	Chamillionaire featuring Krayzie Bone	Universal Motown	17	(2)	F
7	12	Unfaithful	Rihanna	SPR/Def Jam	14	(2)	
8		Do I Make You Proud	Taylor Hicks	Arista/RMG	3		F
9		Ain't No Other Man	Christina Aguilera	RCA	15	(2)	
10	11	Snap Yo Fingers	Lil Jon feat. E-40 & Sean Paul of YoungBloodZ	BME/TVT	15		
11		Life Is A Highway	Rascal Flatts	Walt Disney/Lyric Street	5		
12	13	Over My Head (Cable Car)	The Fray	Epic/Sony Music	18		FG
13	16	So What	Field Mob featuring Ciara	DTP/Geffen/Interscope	9	(56)	
14		Buttons	The Pussycat Dolls feat. Snoop Dogg	A&M/Interscope	18	(3)	
15	10	Dani California	Red Hot Chili Peppers	Warner Bros.	15	(2)	
16	2	Bad Day	Daniel Powter	Warner Bros.	20	(2)	FG
17	5	Where'd You Go	Fort Minor featuring Holly Brook	Machine Shop/Warner Bros.	11		F
18		I Write Sins Not Tragedies	Panic! At The Disco	Decaydance/Fueled By Ramen	14	(25)	FG
19		Somewhere Over The Rainbow	Katharine McPhee	RCA	1		F
20		Do It To It	Cherish feat. Sean Paul of YoungBloodZ	Sho'Nuff/Capitol	9	(30)	F

August 2006

This Mnth	Prev Mnth	Title	Artist	Label	Wks 20	(UK Pos)	
1	1	Promiscuous	Nelly Furtado featuring Timbaland	Mosley/Geffen	19	(3)	G
2	3	Crazy	Gnarls Barkley	Downtown/Atlantic	17	(1)	FG
3	4	Me & U	Cassie	Next Selection/Bad Boy	17	(6)	F
4		London Bridge	Fergie	A&M/Interscope	14	(3)	F
5	14	Buttons	The Pussycat Dolls feat. Snoop Dogg	A&M/Interscope	18	(3)	
6	5	It's Goin' Down	Yung Joc	Block/Bad Boy South/Atlantic	12		FG
7		Deja Vu	Beyoncé featuring Jay-Z	Columbia	4	(1)	
8	9	Ain't No Other Man	Christina Aguilera	RCA	15	(2)	
9		(When You Gonna) Give It Up To Me	Sean Paul featuring Keyshia Cole	VP/Atlantic	11	(31)	
10	18	I Write Sins Not Tragedies	Panic! At The Disco	Decaydance/Fueled By Ramen	14	(25)	FG
11	2	Hips Don't Lie	Shakira featuring Wyclef Jean	Epic/Sony	17	(1)	G
12	7	Unfaithful	Rihanna	SPR/Def Jam	14	(2)	
13	12	Over My Head (cable Car)	The Fray	Epic/sony Music	18		FG
14		Shoulder Lean	Young Dro featuring T.I.	Grand Hustle/Atlantic	10		F
15		Sexy Love	Ne-Yo	Def Jam/IDJMG	11	(5)	
16	10	Snap Yo Fingers	Lil Jon feat. E-40 & Sean Paul of YoungBloodZ	BME/TVT	15		
17	20	Do It To It	Cherish feat. Sean Paul of Youngbloodz	Sho'Nuff/Capitol	9	(30)	F
18		U And Dat	E-40 featuring T-Pain & Kandi Girl	Sick Wid' It	9		
19	13	So What	Field Mob featuring Ciara	DTP/Geffen/Interscope	9	(56)	
20		A Public Affair	Jessica Simpson	Epic	2		

September 2006

This Mnth	Prev Mnth	Title	Artist	Label	Wks 20	(UK Pos)	
1	4	London Bridge	Fergie	A&M/Interscope	14	(3)	F
2		Sexyback	Justin Timberlake	Jive	17	(1)	
3	2	Crazy	Gnarls Barkley	Downtown/Atlantic	17	(1)	FG
4	5	Buttons	The Pussycat Dolls feat. Snoop Dogg	A&M/Interscope	18	(3)	
5	9	(When You Gonna) Give It Up To Me	Sean Paul featuring Keyshia Cole	VP/Atlantic	11	(31)	
6	1	Promiscuous	Nelly Furtado featuring Timbaland	Mosley/Geffen	19	(3)	G
7	15	Sexy Love	Ne-Yo	Def Jam/IDJMG	11	(5)	
8		Chasing Cars	Snow Patrol	Polydor/A&M	17	(6)	F
9		Far Away	Nickelback	Roadrunner	18	(40)	
10		Money Maker	Ludacris featuring Pharrell	DTP/Def Jam	15		
11	3	Me & U	Cassie	Next Selection/Bad Boy	17	(6)	F
12		Lips Of An Angel	Hinder	Universal Republic	16		F
13		Too Little Too Late	JoJo	Da Family/Blackground	10		
14		Chain Hang Low	Jibbs	Geffen/Interscope	9		F
15	8	Ain't No Other Man	Christina Aguilera	RCA	15	(2)	
16		Get Up	Ciara featuring Chamillionaire	LaFace/Jive/Zomba	4		
17		How To Save A Life	The Fray	Epic/Sony Music	15		G
18	10	I Write Sins Not Tragedies	Panic! At The Disco	Decaydance/Fueled By Ramen	14	(25)	FG
19		Show Stopper	Danity Kane	Bad Boy/Atlantic	11		F
20		Call Me When You're Sober	Evanescence	Wind-Up	11	(4)	

US 2006 JULY-SEPT

◆ Taylor Hicks' debut single 'Do I Make You Proud' was the 15th single by an American Idol singer to top the US chart. Unusually, its 190,000 first-week sales were mainly on CD rather than downloads. Also, this year's runner up, Katharine McPhee, had the highest placed version ever of the old favourite 'Over The Rainbow'.

◆ Both Bob Dylan and fellow veteran Johnny Cash entered the US album chart at No.1 for the first time. Dylan's 'Modern Times' was his first chart-topper for thirty years, and the late country singer's 'American V: A Hundred Highways' was his first since 1969.

◆ British rock legends Iron Maiden topped charts in 28 countries with their album 'A Matter Of Life And Death', which gave them their first US Top 10 entry in their long and successful career.

431

UK 2006 OCT-DEC

◆ Few reunions or comebacks have proved as successful as Take That's. They packed out the UK's biggest venues and ended the year with a No.1 single, album and music DVD.

▲ Elton John co-wrote and played piano on the Scissor Sisters' No.1 'I Don't Feel Like Dancin''. The US group, who sold relatively few records at home, also had their second UK million-selling album with 'Ta-Dah'.

◆ The battle for Xmas No.1 was easily won by 'X Factor' winner Leona (Lewis) with her version of 'American Idol' Kelly Clarkson's debut hit 'A Moment Like This'. Meanwhile, Girls Aloud, winners of 'PopStars – The Rivals', scored their 13th Top 10 hit in a row – a record for a female group.

October 2006

This Mnth	Prev Mnth	Title	Artist	Label	Wks 20	(US Pos)	
1	3	I Don't Feel Like Dancin'	Scissor Sisters	Polydor	14		
2		America	Razorlight	Vertigo	11		
3		Checkin' It Out	Lil' Chris	RCA	6		F
4	9	When You Were Young	The Killers	Vertigo	6	(14)	
5		Rock This Party	Bob Sinclar & Cutee B feat. Dollarman & Big Ali	Defected	7		
6		Welcome To The Black Parade	My Chemical Romance	Reprise	8	(13)	
7		Come To Me	P. Diddy featuring Nicole Scherzinger	Bad Boy	5	(9)	
8	1	Sexyback	Justin Timberlake	Jive	10	(1)	
9		LDN	Lily Allen	Regal Recordings	4		
10		Jump In My Car	David Hasselhoff	Skintight	2		F
11		Call Me When You're Sober	Evanescence	Wind-Up	3	(10)	
12	5	Promiscuous	Nelly Furtado featuring Timbaland	Geffen	8	(1)	
13		I Don't Need A Man	The Pussycat Dolls	A&M	3		
14		Something Kinda Ooooh	Girls Aloud	Fascination	8		
15		Superfreak	Beatfreakz	Data	2		
16		It's All Coming Back To Me Now	Meat Loaf featuring Marion Raven	Mercury	3		
17	2	Hips Don't Lie	Shakira featuring Wyclef Jean	Epic	19	(1)	
18		Breaking Free	Cast of High School Musical	Walt Disney	3	(4)	F
19		Wonderful World	James Morrison	Polydor	3		
20	8	Everytime We Touch	Cascada	All Around The World	15	(10)	F

November 2006

This Mnth	Prev Mnth	Title	Artist	Label	Wks 20	(US Pos)	
1		Put Your Hands Up For Detroit	Fedde Le Grand	Data	9		F
2		Irreplaceable	Beyoncé	Columbia	9	(1)	
3		Yeah Yeah	Bodyrox featuring Luciana	Eye Industries/UMTV	7		F
4	14	Something Kinda Ooooh	Girls Aloud	Fascination	8		
5		The Saints Are Coming	U2 and Green Day	Mercury	3	(51)	
6	6	Welcome To The Black Parade	My Chemical Romance	Reprise	8	(13)	
7		The Rose	Westlife	S	4		
8		Star Girl	McFly	Island	3		
9		Rock Steady	All Saints	Parlophone	5		
10		Smack That	Akon featuring Eminem	Universal	7	(2)	
11	2	America	Razorlight	Vertigo	11		
12		My Love	Justin Timberlake featuring T.I.	Jive	7	(1)	
13		Rehab	Amy Winehouse	Island	7		F
14		Patience	Take That	Polydor	6		
15	5	Rock This Party	Bob Sinclar & Cutee B feat. Dollarman & Big Ali	Defected	7		
16		Easy	Sugababes	Island	2		
17		Lovelight	Robbie Williams	Chrysalis	2		
18	16	It's All Coming Back To Me Now	Meat Loaf featuring Marion Raven	Mercury	3		
19	1	I Don't Feel Like Dancin'	Scissor Sisters	Polydor	14		
20		Jump	Madonna	Warner Bros.	2		

December 2006

This Mnth	Prev Mnth	Title	Artist	Label	Wks 20	(US Pos)	
1	14	Patience	Take That	Polydor	6		
2	10	Smack That	Akon featuring Eminem	Universal	7	(2)	
3		Boogie 2nite	Booty Luv	Hed Kandi	5		F
4	12	My Love	Justin Timberlake featuring T.I.	Jive	7	(1)	
5		All Good Things (Come To An End)	Nelly Furtado	Geffen	5		
6		Downtown	Emma Bunton	19 Recordings	3		
7		Wind It Up	Gwen Stefani	Interscope	3	(6)	
8	2	Irreplaceable	Beyoncé	Columbia	9	(1)	
9		21st Century Christmas/Move It	Cliff Richard with Brian May and Brian Bennett	EMI	2		
10		Bing Bang (Time To Dance)	Lazy Town	GTV	3		F
11		Truly Madly Deeply	Cascada	All Around The World	3		
12	1	Put Your Hands Up For Detroit	Fedde Le Grand	Data	9		F
13		A Moment Like This	Leona	Syco Music	1		
14		Sorry's Not Good Enough	McFly	Island	1		
15	7	The Rose	Westlife	S	4		
16		You Know My Name	Chris Cornell	Interscope	3	(79)	F
17		Fairytale Of New York	The Pogues feat. Kirsty MacColl	Warner Bros.	3		
18		I Think We're Alone Now	Girls Aloud	Fascination	1		
19		Tell Me	P. Diddy featuring Christina Aguilera	Bad Boy	3	(47)	
20	11	America	Razorlight	Vertigo	11		

This Mnth	Prev Mnth	Title	Artist	Label	Wks 20	(UK Pos)	
1	2	Sexyback	Justin Timberlake	Jive	17	(1)	
2	10	Money Maker	Ludacris featuring Pharrell	DTP/Def Jam	15		
3	12	Lips Of An Angel	Hinder	Universal Republic	16		F
4	17	How To Save A Life	The Fray	Epic/Sony Music	15		G
5	8	Chasing Cars	Snow Patrol	Polydor/A&M	17	(6)	F
6	1	London Bridge	Fergie	A&M/Interscope	14	(3)	F
7		Smack That	Akon featuring Eminem	SRC/Konvict/ Universal Motown	11	(1)	
8	4	Chain Hang Low	Jibbs	Geffen/Interscope	9		F
9	13	Too Little Too Late	JoJo	Da Family/Blackground	10		
10	9	Far Away	Nickelback	Roadrunner	40		
11		Pullin' Me Back	Chingy featuring Tyrese	Slot-A-Lot/Capitol	10	(44)	
12		My Love	Justin Timberlake featuring T.I.	Jive/Zomba	12	(2)	
13		White & Nerdy	"Weird" Al Yankovic	Way Moby/Volcano	4		
14	4	Buttons	The Pussycat Dolls feat. Snoop Dogg	A&M/Interscope	18	(3)	
15	20	Call Me When You're Sober	Evanescence	Wind-Up	11	(4)	
16	19	Show Stopper	Danity Kane	Bad Boy/Atlantic	11		F
17	7	Sexy Love	Ne-Yo	Def Jam/IDJMG	11	(5)	
18		Say Goodbye	Chris Brown	Jive/Zomba	10		
19	5	(When You Gonna) Give It Up To Me	Sean Paul featuring Keyshia Cole	VP/Atlantic	11	(31)	
20		Ring The Alarm	Beyoncé	Columbia	5		

This Mnth	Prev Mnth	Title	Artist	Label	Wks 20	(UK Pos)	
1	12	My Love	Justin Timberlake featuring T.I.	Jive/Zomba	12	(2)	
2	7	Smack That	Akon featuring Eminem	SRC/Konvict/ Universal Motown	11	(1)	
3	2	Money Maker	Ludacris featuring Pharrell	DTP/Def Jam	15		
4	3	Lips Of An Angel	Hinder	Universal Republic	16		F
5	1	Sexyback	Justin Timberlake	Jive	17	(1)	
6		Fergalicious	Fergie	Will.I.Am/A&M/Interscope	9		
7	4	How To Save A Life	The Fray	Epic/Sony Music	15		G
8	5	Chasing Cars	Snow Patrol	Polydor/A&M	17	(6)	F
9	9	Too Little Too Late	JoJo	Da Family/Blackground	10		
10		Irreplaceable	Beyoncé	Columbia	7	(4)	
11	18	Say Goodbye	Chris Brown	Jive/Zomba	10		
12	10	Far Away	Nickelback	Roadrunner	18	(40)	
13		Come To Me	Diddy featuring Nicole Scherzinger	Bad Boy/Atlantic	5	(4)	
14		Show Me What You Got	Jay-Z	Roc-A-Fella/Def Jam	3	(38)	
15	16	Show Stopper	Danity Kane	Bad Boy/Atlantic	11		F
16	8	Chain Hang Low	Jibbs	Geffen/Interscope	9		F
17		It Ends Tonight	The All-American Rejects	Doghouse/Interscope	7		
18		Welcome To The Black Parade	My Chemical Romance	Reprise	2	(1)	F
19	15	Call Me When You're Sober	Evanescence	Wind-Up	11	(4)	
20		Shortie Like Mine	Bow Wow feat. Chris Brown & Johnta Austin	Columbia	8		

This Mnth	Prev Mnth	Title	Artist	Label	Wks 20	(UK Pos)	
1	10	Irreplaceable	Beyoncé	Columbia	7	(4)	
2		I Wanna Love You	Akon featuring Snoop Dogg	SRC/Universal Motown	7		
3	2	Smack That	Akon featuring Eminem	SRC/Konvict/ Universal Motown	11	(1)	
4	6	Fergalicious	Fergie	Will.I.Am/A&M/Interscope	9		
5	1	My Love	Justin Timberlake featuring T.I.	Jive/Zomba	12	(2)	
6	7	How To Save A Life	The Fray	Epic/Sony Music	15		G
7	4	Lips Of An Angel	Hinder	Universal Republic	16		F
8		Wind It Up	Gwen Stefani	Interscope	4	(3)	
9		We Fly High	Jim Jones	Diplomats/Koch	6		F
10	3	Money Maker	Ludacris featuring Pharrell	DTP/Def Jam	15		
11	20	Shortie Like Mine	Bow Wow feat. Chris Brown & Johnta Austin	Columbia	8		
12		Say It Right	Nelly Furtado	Mosley/Geffen	3		
13	8	Chasing Cars	Snow Patrol	Polydor/A&M	17	(6)	F
14	5	Sexyback	Justin Timberlake	Jive	17	(1)	
15	17	It Ends Tonight	The All-American Rejects	Doghouse/Interscope	7		
16		Walk It Out	Unk	Big Oomp/Koch	7		F
17		Promise	Ciara	LaFace/Zomba	2		
18	14	Show Me What You Got	Jay-Z	Roc-A-Fella/Def Jam	3	(38)	
19		You Don't Know	Eminem, 50 Cent, Lloyd Bank$, Cashis	Shady/Interscope	1		
20	11	Say Goodbye	Chris Brown	Jive/Zomba	10		

US 2006 OCT-DEC

◆ Justin Timberlake replaced himself at the top in the November chart. Soon after, the two tracks concerned also simultaneously occupied places in the UK Top 5. 'Sexyback' also joined the expanding group of million-selling ringtones.

◆ At times, Senegal-born Aliaune Thiam, better known as Akon, held the top two rungs on the singles chart. His 'Smack That' (on which he was joined by Eminem) broke the US chart jump record by leaping from 95 to 7.

◆ Chart chat: The 700th album to top the chart in America, 'The Open Door' by Evanescence, also entered the European chart at No.1… Snow Patrol became the first UK guitar band to reach the US Top 10 since 1993… A record six tracks from the TV movie 'Hannah Montana' simultaneously debuted in the US Top 100… 80-year-old Tony Bennett became the oldest person to record a Top 20 album.

UK 2007 JAN-MAR

◆ The singles chart fully embraced the digital age to allow all downloadable songs - past and present - to chart without a CD release. The new rules' most immediate and noteworthy beneficiary, Snow Patrol's six-month-old 'Chasing Cars', returned to the Top 10 on its way to an incredible 96 weeks and counting in the Top 75.

◆ Lebanon-born, London-based singer-songwriter Mika topped the BBC's 'Sound of 2007' poll and quickly repaid the critics' faith with the long-running No.1 'Grace Kelly'.

◆ The BRIT Awards were broadcast live for the first time since 1989's infamous Samantha Fox/Mick Fleetwood spectacle. Host Russell Brand attracted 435 complaints for cracking jokes about the Queen, Robbie Williams and the Iraq war while the Arctic Monkeys and The Killers bagged two awards apiece and Oasis were lauded for their outstanding contribution to British music.

January 2007

This Mnth	Prev Mnth	Title	Artist	Label	Wks 20	(US Pos)	
1	13	A Moment Like This	Leona	Syco Music	7		F
2	1	Patience	Take That	Polydor	18		
3		Proper Education	Eric Prydz Vs Floyd	Data/Positiva	6		
4	2	Smack That	Akon Featuring Eminem	Universal	13	(2)	
5		Grace Kelly	Mika	Casablanca/Island	14	(57)	F
6	3	Boogie 2nite	Booty Luv	Hed Kandi	13		F
7	11	Truly Madly Deeply	Cascada	All Around The World	9		
8		Starz In Their Eyes	Just Jack	Mercury	9		F
9		Same Jeans	The View	1965	7		
10		Too Little Too Late	Jojo	Mercury	8	(3)	
11		P.A.T.T. - Party All The Time	Sharam	Data	5		F
12		Window In The Skies	U2	Mercury	2		
13		Different World	Iron Maiden	EMI	1		
14	18	I Think We're Alone Now	Girls Aloud	Fascination	3		
15	16	You Know My Name	Chris Cornell	Interscope	6	(79)	F
16		I Luv U	Ordinary Boys	B-Unique/Polydor	5		
17	5	All Good Things (Come To An End)	Nelly Furtado	Geffen	8	(86)	
18	19	Tell Me	P. Diddy Featuring Christina Aguilera	Bad Boy	8	47)	
19		Chasing Cars	Snow Patrol	Fiction	15	(5)	
20		Calm Down Dearest	Jamie.T	Virgin	1		

February 2007

This Mnth	Prev Mnth	Title	Artist	Label	Wks 20	(US Pos)	
1	5	Grace Kelly	Mika	Casablanca/Island	14	(57)	F
2	8	Starz In Their Eyes	Just Jack	Mercury	9		F
3		It Ain't A Scene, It's An Arms Race	Fall Out Boy	Mercury	7	(2)	
4		Exceeder	Mason	Data	7		F
5	10	Too Little Too Late	Jojo	Mercury	8	(3)	
6		I Wanna Love You	Akon Featuring Snoop Dogg	Universal	9	(1)	
7	9	Same Jeans	The View	1965	7		
8		Ruby	Kaiser Chiefs	B-Unique	11		
9		How To Save A Life	The Fray	Epic	15	(3)	F
10		The Prayer	Bloc Party	Wichita Recordings	3		
11		Golden Skans	Klaxons	Polydor	5		F
12	16	I Luv U	The Ordinary Boys	B-Unique/Polydor	5		
13		The Sweet Escape	Gwen Stefani Featuring Akon	Interscope	14	(2)	
14		Famous Last Words	My Chemical Romance	Reprise	2	(88)	
15	3	Proper Education	Eric Prydz Vs Floyd	Data/Positiva	6		
16	2	Patience	Take That	Polydor	18		
17	6	Boogie 2nite	Booty Luv	Hed Kandi	13		F
18		Shine	Take That	Polydor	9		
19	1	A Moment Like This	Leona	Syco Music	7		F
20		Lil Star	Kelis Featuring Cee-Lo	Virgin	8		

March 2007

This Mnth	Prev Mnth	Title	Artist	Label	Wks 20	(US Pos)	
1	8	Ruby	Kaiser Chiefs	B-Unique	11		
2	13	The Sweet Escape	Gwen Stefani Featuring Akon	Interscope	14	(2)	
3	18	Shine	Take That	Polydor	9		
4	1	Grace Kelly	Mika	Casablanca/Island	14	(57)	F
5	9	How To Save A Life	The Fray	Epic	15	(3)	F
6	20	Lil Star	Kelis Featuring Cee-Lo	Virgin	8		
7		What Goes Around Comes Around	Justin Timberlake	Jive	10	(1)	
8		Walk This Way	Sugababes Vs Girls Aloud	Fascination/Island	3		
9		(I'm Gonna Be) 500 Miles	The Proclaimers Featuring Brian Potter & Andy Pipkin	EMI	7		
10	6	I Wanna Love You	Akon Featuring Snoop Dogg	Universal	9	(1)	
11		Standing In The Way Of Control	Gossip	Back Yard Recordings	7		F
12		The Creeps	Camille Jones Vs Fedde Le Grand	Data	6		F
13		Girlfriend	Avril Lavigne	Arista	11	(1)	
14		Say It Right	Nelly Furtado	Polydor	9	(1)	
15	2	Starz In Their Eyes	Just Jack	Mercury	9		F
16		Destination Calabria	Alex Gaudino Featuring Crystal Waters	Data	8		F
17		Miracle	Cascada	Incentive/Product	3		
18	3	It Ain't A Scene, It's An Arms Race	Fall Out Boy	Mercury	7	(2)	
19		Catch You	Sophie Ellis-Bextor	Fascination	3		
20		Acceptable In The 80s	Calvin Harris	Columbia	5		F

This Mnth	Prev Mnth	Title	Artist	Label	Wks 20	(UK Pos)	
1	1	Irreplaceable	Beyoncé	Columbia	20	(4)	P
2	2	I Wanna Love You	Akon Featuring Snoop Dogg	SRC/Universal Motown	17	(3)	P
3	4	Fergalicious	Fergie	Will.I.Am/A&M/Interscope	17		P
4	3	Smack That	Akon Featuring Eminem	SRC/Universal Motown	19	(1)	P
5	12	Say It Right	Nelly Furtado	Mosley/Geffen	20	(10)	G
6	5	My Love	Justin Timberlake Featuring T.I.	Jive	20	(2)	G
7	6	How To Save A Life	The Fray	Epic/Sony Music	22	(4)	P
8	9	We Fly High	Jim Jones	Diplomats/Koch	16		GF
9	15	It Ends Tonight	All-American Rejects	Doghouse/Interscope	12	(66)	
10	11	Shortie Like Mine	Bow Wow Featuring Chris Brown & Johnta Austin	Columbia	13		G
11	7	Lips Of An Angel	Hinder	Universal Republic	20		PF
12		Welcome To The Black Parade	My Chemical Romance	Reprise	7	(1)	G
13	14	Sexyback	Justin Timberlake	Jive	21	(1)	P
14	16	Walk It Out	Unk	Big Oomp/Koch	18		GF
15		What Goes Around... Comes Around	Justin Timberlake	Jive/Zomba	14	(4)	G
16		Runaway Love	Ludacris Featuring Mary J. Blige	DTP/Def Jam	11	(52)	
17	10	Money Maker	Ludacris Featuring Pharrell	DTP/Def Jam	18		G
18	17	Promise	Ciara	LaFace/Zomba	4		G
19	13	Chasing Cars	Snow Patrol	Polydor/A&M	20	(6)	F
20	8	Wind It Up	Gwen Stefani	Interscope	5	(3)	

This Mnth	Prev Mnth	Title	Artist	Label	Wks 20	(UK Pos)	
1	1	Irreplaceable	Beyoncé	Columbia	20	(4)	P
2	5	Say It Right	Nelly Furtado	Mosley/Geffen	20	(10)	G
3		It's Not A Scene, It's An Arms Race	Fall Out Boy	Fueled By Ramen	11	(2)	G
4		It's Not Over	Daughtry	RCA	14		GF
5	2	I Wanna Love You	Akon Featuring Snoop Dogg	SRC/Universal Motown	17	(3)	P
6		The Sweet Escape	Gwen Stefani Featuring Akon	Interscope	21	(2)	
7	16	Runaway Love	Ludacris Featuring Mary J. Blige	DTP/Def Jam	11	(52)	
8	8	We Fly High	Jim Jones	Diplomats/Koch	16		GF
9	15	What Goes Around... Comes Around	Justin Timberlake	Jive/Zomba	14	(4)	G
10	3	Fergalicious	Fergie	Will.I.Am/A&M/Interscope	17		P
11		You	Lloyd Featuring Lil Wayne	The Inc/Universal Motown	11	(45)	F
12		Cupid's Chokehold/ Breakfast In America	Gym Class Heroes Featuring Patrick Stump	Decaydance/Fueled By Ramen	14	(3)	GF
13	4	Smack That	Akon Featuring Eminem	SRC/Universal Motown	19	(1)	P
14	14	Walk It Out	Unk	Big Oomp/Koch	18		GF
15	7	How To Save A Life	The Fray	Epic/Sony Music	22	(4)	P
16		Glamorous	Fergie Featuring Ludacris	Will.I.Am/A&M/Interscope	15	(6)	P
17	12	Welcome To The Black Parade	My Chemical Romance	Reprise	7	(1)	G
18		On The Hotline	Pretty Ricky	Bluestar/Atlantic	6		G
19		Make It Rain	Fat Joe Featuring Lil Wayne	Terror Squad	10		G
20	6	My Love	Justin Timberlake Featuring T.I.	Jive	20	(2)	G

This Mnth	Prev Mnth	Title	Artist	Label	Wks 20	(UK Pos)	
1		Don't Matter	Akon	Konvict/Upfront/SRC	15	(3)	P
2	9	What Goes Around... Comes Around	Justin Timberlake	Jive/Zomba	14	(4)	G
3		This Is Why I'm Hot	Mims	Capitol	11	(18)	GF
4	6	The Sweet Escape	Gwen Stefani Featuring Akon	Interscope	21	(2)	
5	12	Cupid's Chokehold/ Breakfast In America	Gym Class Heroes Featuring Patrick Stump	Decaydance/Fueled By Ramen	14	(3)	GF
6	2	Say It Right	Nelly Furtado	Mosley/Geffen	20	(10)	G
7	16	Glamorous	Fergie Featuring Ludacris	Will.I.Am/A&M/Interscope	15	(6)	P
8	7	Runaway Love	Ludacris Featuring Mary J. Blige	DTP/Def Jam	11	(52)	
9	3	It's Not A Scene, It's An Arms Race	Fall Out Boy	Fueled By Ramen	11	(2)	G
10	4	It's Not Over	Daughtry	RCA	14		GF
11		Girlfriend	Avril Lavigne	RCA	20	(2)	P
12	1	Irreplaceable	Beyoncé	Columbia	20	(4)	P
13		Not Ready To Make Nice	Dixie Chicks	Columbia	2	(70)	G
14		Break It Off	Rihanna & Sean Paul	SRP/Def Jam	3		
15		Ice Box	Omarion	T.U.G./Columbia	10	(14)	
16		Throw Some D's	Rich Boy Featuring Polow Da Don	Zone 4/Interscope	3		GF
17	11	You	Lloyd Featuring Lil Wayne	The Inc/Universal Motown	11	(45)	F
18	5	I Wanna Love You	Akon Featuring Snoop Dogg	SRC/Universal Motown	17	(3)	P
19		Lost Without U	Robin Thicke	Overbrook/Star Trak	9	(11)	GF
20	21	Make It Rain	Fat Joe Featuring Lil Wayne	Terror Squad	10		G

US 2007 JAN-MAR

◆ For 10 consecutive weeks, Beyoncé was 'Irreplaceable' at No.1. It was the longest-running No.1 of her solo career, eclipsing nine-week chart champ 'Baby Boy'. In Billboard magazine's end-of-year charts, 'Irreplaceable' will be crowned top Hot 100 song of 2007.

◆ Multiple winners at the 49th Grammy Awards in Los Angeles included the Bush-bashing Dixie Chicks (five statues), the Red Hot Chili Peppers (four) and eight-time nominee Mary J Blige (three). The Doors picked up a Lifetime Achievement award and fans copped a look at the reformed Police.

◆ British invasion ... UK females Corinne Bailey Rae, Amy Winehouse (highest debut by a British female solo newcomer - No.7 - with 'Back To Black') and Joss Stone (highest new entry ever by a British female solo act - No.2 - with 'Introducing Joss Stone') crashed into the Top 10 of the album chart.

UK 2007 APR-JUNE

◆ The Proclaimers celebrated their first chart-topper with the re-recorded 'I'm Gonna Be (500 Miles)'. With a little help from their comedy friends, Brian Potter (Peter Kay) and Andy Pipkin (Matt Lucas), they outsold the official Comic Relief single, 'Walk This Way', a feisty collaboration between the UK's biggest girl groups, Sugababes and Girls Aloud.

◆ McFly's double-A side, 'Baby's Coming Back'/'Transylvania', plummeted from No.1 to No.20 to match the unenviable record set by Elvis' 2005 re-issue 'One Night'/'I Got Stung' for the biggest drop from the top.

◆ Rihanna and Jay-Z's unstoppable 'Umbrella' began its 10-week stay at No.1 - the longest sojourn at the summit since Wet Wet Wet's 15-weeker, 'Love Is All Around', in 1994. Ironically, the track heralded the onset of one of the wettest UK summers on record.

April 2007

This Mnth	Prev Mnth	Title	Artist	Label	Wks 20	(US Pos)	
1	9	(I'm Gonna Be) 500 Miles	The Proclaimers Featuring Brian Potter & Andy Pipkin	EMI	7		
2	13	Girlfriend	Avril Lavigne	Arista	11	(1)	
3	2	The Sweet Escape	Gwen Stefani Featuring Akon	Interscope	14	(2)	
4		Give It To Me	Timbaland Featuring Nelly Furtado	Interscope	12	(1)	
5		Beautiful Liar	Beyoncé & Shakira	Columbia	16	(3)	
6		Stop Me	Mark Ronson Featuring Daniel Merriweather	Columbia	6		
7	5	How To Save A Life	The Fray	Epic	15	(3)	F
8	16	Destination Calabria	Alex Gaudino Featuring Crystal Waters	Data	8		F
9		Brianstorm	Arctic Monkeys	Domino Recordings	5		
10		Glamorous	Fergie Featuring Ludacris	A&M	8	(1)	
11	1	Ruby	Kaiser Chiefs	B-Unique	11		
12		Because Of You	Ne-Yo	Def Jam	9	(2)	
13		I Wanna Have Your Babies	Natasha Bedingfield	Phonogenic	4		
14	7	What Goes Around Comes Around	Justin Timberlake	Jive	10	(1)	
15	3	Shine	Take That	Polydor	9		
16		Away From Here	The Enemy	Warner Bros.	2		F
17	4	Grace Kelly	Mika	Casablanca/Island	14	(57)	F
18	12	The Creeps	Camille Jones Vs Fedde Le Grand	Data	6		F
19		Thnks Fr Th Mmrs	Fall Out Boy	Mercury	3	(11)	
20	20	Acceptable In The 80s	Calvin Harris	Columbia	5		F

May 2007

This Mnth	Prev Mnth	Title	Artist	Label	Wks 20	(US Pos)	
1	5	Beautiful Liar	Beyoncé & Shakira	Columbia	16	(3)	
2	4	Give It To Me	Timbaland Featuring Nelly Furtado	Interscope	12	(1)	
3		Cupid's Chokehold/Breakfast In America	Gym Class Heroes	Atlantic	10	(4)	F
4	2	Girlfriend	Avril Lavigne	Arista	11	(1)	
5		Don't Matter	Akon	Universal	10	(1)	
6	12	Because Of You	Ne-Yo	Def Jam	9	(2)	
7		Your Love Alone Is Not Enough	Manic Street Preachers	Columbia	4		
8		Baby's Coming Back/ Transylvania	McFly	Island	2		
9		Here (In Your Arms)	Hellogoodbye	Drive Thru	8	(14)	F
10		Umbrella	Rihanna Featuring Jay-Z	Def Jam	18	(1)	
11	6	Stop Me	Mark Ronson Featuring Daniel Merriweather	Columbia	6		
12		Love Today	Mika	Casablanca/Island	7	(92)	
13		Makes Me Wonder	Maroon5	A&M	7	(1)	
14		Flying The Flag (For You)	Scooch	Warner Bros.	2		
15		What I've Done	Linkin Park	Warner Bros.	8	(7)	
16		Signal Fire	Snow Patrol	Fiction	5	(65)	
17	9	Brianstorm	Arctic Monkeys	Domino Recordings	5		
18	13	I Wanna Have Your Babies	Natasha Bedingfield	Phonogenic	4		
19		Take Control	Amerie	Columbia	4		
20		Get Down	Groove Armada Featuring Stush	Columbia	2		

June 2007

This Mnth	Prev Mnth	Title	Artist	Label	Wks 20	(US Pos)	
1	10	Umbrella	Rihanna Featuring Jay-Z	Def Jam	18	(1)	
2		Real Girl	Mutya Buena	4th & Broadway	6		F
3	1	Beautiful Liar	Beyoncé & Shakira	Columbia	16	(3)	
4	13	Makes Me Wonder	Maroon5	A&M	7	(1)	
5	3	Cupid's Chokehold/Breakfast In America	Gym Class Heroes	Atlantic	10	(4)	F
6		The Girls	Calvin Harris	Columbia	6		
7	9	Here (In Your Arms)	Hellogoodbye	Drive Thru	8	(14)	F
8		Do You Know (The Ping Pong Song)	Enrique Iglesias	Polydor	11		
9		Icky Thump	The White Stripes	XL Recordings	3		
10		Like This	Kelly Rowland Featuring Eve	Columbia	7	(30)	
11	2	Give It To Me	Timbaland Featuring Nelly Furtado	Interscope	12	(1)	
12	5	Don't Matter	Akon	Universal	10	(1)	
13		Any Dream Will Do	Lee Mead	Fascination/Rug	4		F
14		Heavyweight Champion Of The World	Reverend And The Makers	Wall Of Sound	6		
15	16	Signal Fire	Snow Patrol	Fiction	5	(65)	
16		Never Again	Kelly Clarkson	RCA	3	(8)	
17		Smokers Outside The Hospital Doors	Editors	Kitchenware	2		
18		Either Way	The Twang	B-Unique	3		
19		Shine	Booty Luv	Hed Kandi	4		
20	4	Girlfriend	Avril Lavigne	Arista	11	(1)	

April 2007

This Mnth	Prev Mnth	Title	Artist	Label	Wks 20	(UK Pos)	
1	1	Don't Matter	Akon	Konvict/Upfront/SRC	15	(3)	P
2	7	Glamorous	Fergie Featuring Ludacris	Will.I.Am/A&M/Interscope	15	(6)	P
3	4	The Sweet Escape	Gwen Stefani Featuring Akon	Interscope	21	(2)	
4	3	This Is Why I'm Hot	Mims	Capitol	11	(18)	GF
5	11	Girlfriend	Avril Lavigne	RCA	20	(2)	P
6		Beautiful Liar	Beyoncé & Shakira	Columbia	6	(1)	G
7		Give It To Me	Timbaland Feat. Nelly Furtado & Justin Timberlake	Mosley/Blackground/Interscope	10		
8	5	Cupid's Chokehold/ Breakfast In America	Gym Class Heroes Featuring Patrick Stump	Decaydance/Fueled By Ramen	14	(3)	GF
9	2	What Goes Around... Comes Around	Justin Timberlake	Jive/Zomba	14	(4)	G
10		Buy You A Drank (Shawty Snappin')	T-Pain Featuring Yung Joc	Konvict/Nappy Boy/Jive	22		P
11	10	It's Not Over	Daughtry	RCA	14		GF
12		Last Night	Diddy Featuring Keyshia Cole	Bad Boy/Atlantic	11	(14)	
13		What I've Done	Linkin Park	Machine Shop/Warner Bros	5	(6)	P
14	16	Throw Some D's	Rich Boy Featuring Polow Da Don	Zone 4/Interscope	3		GF
15	6	Say It Right	Nelly Furtado	Mosley/Geffen	20	(10)	G
16		U & Ur Hand	P!nk	LaFace/Zomba	14	(10)	G
17		I'm A Flirt	R. Kelly Or Bow Wow Featuring T.I. & T-Pain	Columbia/Jive/Zomba	12	(18)	
18	15	Ice Box	Omarion	T.U.G./Columbia	10	(14)	
19		Last Dollar (Fly Away)	Tim McGraw	Curb	2		
20	19	Lost Without U	Robin Thicke	Overbrook/Star Trak	9	(11)	GF

May 2007

This Mnth	Prev Mnth	Title	Artist	Label	Wks 20	(UK Pos)	
1	5	Girlfriend	Avril Lavigne	RCA	20	(2)	P
2	10	Buy You A Drank (Shawty Snappin')	T-Pain Featuring Yung Joc	Konvict/Nappy Boy/Jive	22		P
3	7	Give It To Me	Timbaland Feat. Nelly Furtado & Justin Timberlake	Mosley/Blackground/Interscope	10		
4		Makes Me Wonder	Maroon5	A&M/Octone/Interscope	12	(2)	
5		Because Of You	Ne-Yo	Def Jam/IDJMG	4	(4)	
6	1	Don't Matter	Akon	Konvict/Upfront/SRC	15	(3)	P
7	2	Glamorous	Fergie Featuring Ludacris	Will.I.Am/A&M/Interscope	15	(6)	P
8		I Tried	Bone Thugs-N-Harmony Featuring Akon	Full Surface/Interscope	9	(69)	G
9	3	The Sweet Escape	Gwen Stefani Featuring Akon	Interscope	21	(2)	
10		Pop Lock And Drop It	Huey	Hitz Committee/Jive	12		PF
11		I'll Stand By You	Carrie Underwood	Freemantle/19	3		
12	16	U & Ur Hand	P!nk	LaFace/Zomba	14	(10)	G
13		Never Again	Kelly Clarkson	RCA	9	(9)	
14		Before He Cheats	Carrie Underwood	Arista/BMG	5		P
15	4	This Is Why I'm Hot	Mims	Capitol	11	(18)	GF
16	8	Cupid's Chokehold/ Breakfast In America	Gym Class Heroes Featuring Patrick Stump	Decaydance/Fueled By Ramen	14	(3)	GF
17	12	Last Night	Diddy Featuring Keyshia Cole	Bad Boy/Atlantic	11		
18	17	I'm A Flirt	R. Kelly Or Bow Wow Featuring T.I. & T-Pain	Columbia/Jive/Zomba	12	(18)	
19	6	Beautiful Liar	Beyoncé & Shakira	Columbia	6	(1)	G
20		Home	Daughtry	RCA	11		G

June 2007

This Mnth	Prev Mnth	Title	Artist	Label	Wks 20	(UK Pos)	
1	4	Makes Me Wonder	Maroon5	A&M/Octone/Interscope	12	(2)	
2	2	Buy You A Drank (Shawty Snappin')	T-Pain Featuring Yung Joc	Konvict/Nappy Boy/Jive	22		P
3		Umbrella	Rihanna Featuring Jay-Z	SRP/Def Jam	16	(1)	P
4		Party Like A Rockstar	Shop Boyz	Ondeck/Universal Republic	12		PF
5	1	Girlfriend	Avril Lavigne	RCA	20	(2)	P
6		Big Girls Don't Cry	Fergie	Will.I.Am/A&M/Interscope	28	(2)	P
7	20	Home	Daughtry	RCA	11		G
8		Summer Love	Justin Timberlake	Jive/Zomba	12		G
9	10	Pop Lock And Drop It	Huey	Hitz Committee/Jive	12		PF
10	3	Give It To Me	Timbaland Feat. Nelly Furtado & Justin Timberlake	Mosley/Blackground/Interscope	10		
11		Hey There Delilah	Plain White T's	Hollywood	20	(2)	GF
12	14	Before He Cheats	Carrie Underwood	Arista/BMG	5		P
13	8	I Tried	Bone Thugs-N-Harmony Featuring Akon	Full Surface/Interscope	9	(69)	G
14	13	Never Again	Kelly Clarkson	RCA	9	(9)	
15	12	U & Ur Hand	P!nk	LaFace/Zomba	14	(10)	G
16		Rehab	Amy Winehouse	Universal Republic	7	(7)	F
17		Thnks Fr Th Mmrs	Fall Out Boy	Fueled By Ramen	10	(12)	
18	7	Glamorous	Fergie Featuring Ludacris	Will.I.Am/A&M/Interscope	15	(6)	P
19		Lip Gloss	Lil Mama	Jive/Zomba	3		F
20		What I've Done	Linkin Park	Machine Shop/Warner Bros	7	(6)	P

▲ In July 2008, Avril Lavigne's 'Girlfriend' will become the most watched music video of all-time on YouTube with more than 100 million views, surpassing the mark set by Judson Laipply with his 'Evolution Of Dance'.

◆ Due to the song's temporary removal from iTunes and its subsequent return, Fergie's 'Glamorous' recorded two visits to the Top 10 before becoming the second No.1 for the solo Black Eyed Pea.

◆ More than five years since the last Hot 100 rock No.1 (Nickelback's 'How You Remind Me'), Maroon 5 rung the top bell with 'Makes Me Wonder', setting a new record – for the biggest jump to No.1 (from No.64).

437

UK 2007 JULY-SEPT

▲ In one of the closest chart battles for years, Timbaland and Keri Hilson's 'The Way I Are' denied Kate Nash a debut No.1 with 'Foundations' by just 16 copies, forcing a sales recount before the run-down was released to the media.

◆ A galaxy of stars descended on Wembley Stadium for the Diana Memorial Concert, watched by an average TV audience of 11.4 million, and, in the same month, Al Gore's Live Earth - The Concert for a Climate in Crisis, headlined by Madonna.

◆ Prince completed a 21-date residency in London with 351,527 tickets sold and £10,971,157 in the bank. It was the UK's top-grossing tour of 2007.

July 2007

This Mnth	Prev Mnth	Title	Artist	Label	Wks 20	(US Pos)	
1	1	Umbrella	Rihanna Featuring Jay-Z	Def Jam	18	(1)	
2		Foundations	Kate Nash	Fiction	13		F
3	8	Do You Know (The Ping Pong Song)	Enrique Iglesias	Polydor	11		
4		The Way I Are	Timbaland Featuring Keri Hilson & D.O.E.	Interscope	18	(3)	
5		When You're Gone	Avril Lavigne	RCA	8	(24)	
6		Worried About Ray	The Hoosiers	RCA	10		F
7	13	Any Dream Will Do	Lee Mead	Fascination/Rug	4		F
8		Fluorescent Adolescent	Arctic Monkeys	Domino Recordings	4		
9		Soulmate	Natasha Bedingfield	Phonogenic	5		
10		Had Enough	The Enemy	Warner Bros	3		
11		Big Girls Don't Cry	Fergie	Polydor	15	(1)	
12	10	Like This	Kelly Rowland Featuring Eve	Columbia	7	(30)	
13		Torn On The Platform	Jack Penate	XL Recordings	3		F
14		Teenagers	My Chemical Romance	Reprise	5	(67)	
15		Oh My God	Mark Ronson Featuring Lily Allen	Columbia	6		
16		Lovestoned	Justin Timberlake	Jive	5	(17)	
17	6	The Girls	Calvin Harris	Columbia	6		
18	14	Heavyweight Champion Of The World	Reverend And The Makers	Wall Of Sound	6		F
19		Do It Again	The Chemical Brothers	Virgin	4		
20	3	Beautiful Liar	Beyoncé & Shakira	Columbia	16	(3)	

August 2007

This Mnth	Prev Mnth	Title	Artist	Label	Wks 20	(US Pos)	
1	4	The Way I Are	Timbaland Featuring Keri Hilson & D.O.E.	Interscope	18	(3)	
2	2	Foundations	Kate Nash	Fiction	13		F
3	11	Big Girls Don't Cry	Fergie	Polydor	15	(1)	
4		With Every Heartbeat	Robyn With Kleerup	Konichiwa	9		
5	1	Umbrella	Rihanna Featuring Jay-Z	Def Jam	18	(1)	
6		Stronger	Kanye West	Roc-A-Fella	10	(1)	
7	3	Do You Know (The Ping Pong Song)	Enrique Iglesias	Polydor	11		
8		Hey There Delilah	Plain White T's	Angel	13	(1)	F
9	6	Worried About Ray	The Hoosiers	RCA	10		F
10		Dream Catch Me	Newton Faulkner	Ugly Truth	6		F
11	5	When You're Gone	Avril Lavigne	RCA	8	(24)	
12		Song 4 Mutya (Out Of Control)	Groove Armada	Columbia	5		
13		Big Girl (You Are Beautiful)	Mika	Casablanca/Island	5		
14		I Found U	Axwell Featuring Max C	Positiva	3		
15		Shut Up And Drive	Rihanna	Mercury	12	(15)	
16		Clothes Off!!	Gym Class Heroes	Decaydance/Fueled By Ramen	5	(46)	
17		Love Is Gone	David Guetta Featuring Chris Willis	Charisma	5		
18	15	Oh My God	Mark Ronson Featuring Lily Allen	Columbia	6		
19		Autumnsong	Manic Street Preachers	Columbia	1		
20		Suspicious Minds	Elvis Presley	RCA Victor	1		

September 2007

This Mnth	Prev Mnth	Title	Artist	Label	Wks 20	(US Pos)	
1		Beautiful Girls	Sean Kingston	Beluga Heights/Epic	10	(1)	F
2	6	Stronger	Kanye West	Roc-A-Fella	10	(1)	
3	8	Hey There Delilah	Plain White T's	Angel	13	(1)	F
4		Ayo Technology	50 Cent Featuring Justin Timberlake & Timbaland	Interscope	13	(5)	
5	4	With Every Heartbeat	Robyn With Kleerup	Konichiwa	9		
6	1	The Way I Are	Timbaland Featuring Keri Hilson & D.O.E.	Interscope	18	(3)	
7		1973	James Blunt	Atlantic	7	(73)	
8	15	Shut Up And Drive	Rihanna	Mercury	12	(15)	
9	16	Clothes Off!!	Gym Class Heroes	Decaydance/Fueled By Ramen	5	(46)	
10		Sexy! No No No...	Girls Aloud	Fascination	3		
11	3	Big Girls Don't Cry	Fergie	Polydor	15	(1)	
12		She's So Lovely	Scouting For Girls	Epic	9		F
13	2	Foundations	Kate Nash	Fiction	13		F
14		Suburban Knights	Hard-Fi	Atlantic/Necessary	4		
15		Delivery	Babyshambles	Parlophone	1		
16		The Creeps (Get On The Dancefloor)	Freaks	Azuli	3		F
17		The Pretender	Foo Fighters	RCA	3	(37)	
18	10	Dream Catch Me	Newton Faulkner	Ugly Truth	6		F
19		Don't Mess With My Man	Booty Luv	Hed Kandi	2		
20	17	Love Is Gone	David Guetta Featuring Chris Willis	Charisma	5		

This Mnth	Prev Mnth	Title	Artist	Label	Wks 20	(UK Pos)	
1	3	**Umbrella**	Rihanna Featuring Jay-Z	SRP/Def Jam	16	(1)	P
2	11	**Hey There Delilah**	Plain White T's	Hollywood	20	(2)	GF
3	4	**Party Like A Rockstar**	Shop Boyz	Ondeck/Universal Republic	12		PF
4	6	**Big Girls Don't Cry**	Fergie	Will.I.Am/A&M/ Interscope	28	(2)	P
5	2	**Buy You A Drank (Shawty Snappin')**	T-Pain Featuring Yung Joc	Konvict/Nappy Boy/Jive	22		P
6	1	**Makes Me Wonder**	Maroon5	A&M/Octone/Interscope	12	(2)	
7		**The Way I Are**	Timbaland Featuring Keri Hilson	Mosley/Blackground	26	(1)	
8	5	**Girlfriend**	Avril Lavigne	RCA	20	(2)	P
9	8	**Summer Love**	Justin Timberlake	Jive/Zomba	12		G
10		**A Bay Bay**	Hurricane Chris	Polo Grounds/J/RMG	11		PF
11		**Bartender**	T-Pain Featuring Akon	Konvict/Nappy Boy/Jive	15		G
12		**Make Me Better**	Fabolous Featuring Ne-Yo	Desert Storm/Def Jam	12		G
13	16	**Rehab**	Amy Winehouse	Universal Republic	7	(7)	F
14		**Big Things Poppin' (Do It)**	T.I.	Grand Hustle/Atlantic	7		
15	17	**Thnks Fr Th Mmrs**	Fall Out Boy	Fueled By Ramen	10	(12)	
16	12	**Before He Cheats**	Carrie Underwood	Arista/BMG	5		P
17	9	**Pop Lock And Drop It**	Huey	Hitz Committee/Jive	12		PF
18	20	**What I've Done**	Linkin Park	Machine Shop/Warner Bros	5	(6)	P
19	19	**Lip Gloss**	Lil Mama	Jive/Zomba	3		F
20		**Get It Shawty**	Lloyd	The Inc/Universal Motown	6	(72)	

1	2	**Hey There Delilah**	Plain White T's	Hollywood	20	(2)	GF
2	4	**Big Girls Don't Cry**	Fergie	Will.I.Am/A&M/Interscope	28	(2)	P
3		**Beautiful Girls**	Sean Kingston	Beluga Heights/Epic	8	(1)	PF
4	7	**The Way I Are**	Timbaland Featuring Keri Hilson	Mosley/Blackground	26	(1)	
5	1	**Umbrella**	Rihanna Featuring Jay-Z	SRP/Def Jam	16	(1)	P
6	11	**Bartender**	T-Pain Featuring Akon	Konvict/Nappy Boy/Jive	15		G
7	3	**Party Like A Rockstar**	Shop Boyz	Ondeck/Universal Republic	12		PF
8	10	**A Bay Bay**	Hurricane Chris	Polo Grounds/J/RMG	11		PF
9	12	**Make Me Better**	Fabolous Featuring Ne-Yo	Desert Storm/Def Jam	12		G
10	5	**Buy You A Drank (Shawty Snappin')**	T-Pain Featuring Yung Joc	Konvict/Nappy Boy/Jive	22		P
11		**Stronger**	Kanye West	Roc-A-Fella/Def Jam	22	(1)	P
12		**Sorry, Blame It On Me**	Akon	Konvict/Upfront/SRC	6		
13		**Shawty**	Plies Featuring T-Pain	Slip-N-Slide/Atlantic	14		GF
14		**What Time Is It**	Cast Of High School Musical 2	Walt Disney	1		F
15		**Crank Dat (Soulja Boy)**	Soulja Boy Tellem	Collipark/Interscope	24	(2)	PF
16		**Wait For You**	Elliott Yamin	Hickory	10		GF
17	6	**Makes Me Wonder**	Maroon5	A&M/Octone/Interscope	16	(2)	
18	14	**Big Things Poppin' (Do It)**	T.I.	Grand Hustle/Atlantic	7		
19		**Shut Up And Drive**	Rihanna	SRP/Def Jam	5	(5)	
20		**Me Love**	Sean Kingston	Beluga Heights/Epic	5	(32)	

1	15	**Crank Dat (Soulja Boy)**	Soulja Boy Tellem	Collipark/Interscope	24	(2)	PF
2	2	**Big Girls Don't Cry**	Fergie	Will.I.Am/A&M/Interscope	28	(2)	P
3	11	**Stronger**	Kanye West	Roc-a-Fella/Def Jam	22	(1)	P
4	4	**The Way I Are**	Timbaland Featuring Keri Hilson	Mosley/Blackground	26	(1)	
5	3	**Beautiful Girls**	Sean Kingston	Beluga Heights/Epic	8	(1)	PF
6	1	**Hey There Delilah**	Plain White T's	Hollywood	20	(2)	GF
7	6	**Bartender**	T-Pain Featuring Akon	Konvict/Nappy Boy/Jive	15		G
8		**Rockstar**	Nickelback	Roadrunner	12	(2)	
9		**Let It Go**	Keyshia Cole Featuring Missy Elliott & Lil' Kim	Imani/Geffen	12		G
10	13	**Shawty**	Plies Featuring T-Pain	Slip-N-Slide/Atlantic	14		GF
11	9	**Make Me Better**	Fabolous Featuring Ne-Yo	Desert Storm/Def Jam	12		G
12		**Bed**	J. Holiday	Music Line/Capitol	15	(75)	F
13	5	**Umbrella**	Rihanna Featuring Jay-Z	SRP/Def Jam	16	(1)	P
14		**Ayo Technology**	50 Cent Feat. Justin Timberlake & Timbaland	Shady/Aftermath/ Interscope	12	(2)	
15		**Who Knew**	P!nk	LaFace/Zomba	14	(5)	G
16	8	**A Bay Bay**	Hurricane Chris	Polo Grounds/J/RMG	11		PF
17	16	**Wait For You**	Elliott Yamin	Hickory	10		GF
18		**How Far We've Come**	Matchbox Twenty	Melisma/Atlantic	13		G
19	20	**Me Love**	Sean Kingston	Beluga Heights/Epic	5	(32)	
20		**Good Life**	Kanye West Featuring T-Pain	Roc-a-Fella/Def Jam	17	(23)	G

US 2007 JULY-SEPT

◆ Worldwide smash 'Hey There Delilah' was inspired by Plain White T's Tom Higgenson's meeting with athlete Delilah DiCrescenzo.

◆ The Grammy-nominated internet sensation 'Crank That (Soulja Boy)', an ubiquitous mobile ringtone in 2007, will become one of only five songs to top the four million mark in paid downloads (as of November 2009).

◆ In other news: Fans marked the 30th anniversary of Elvis' death with a candlelight vigil at Graceland and a tribute concert featuring footage of 'The King'… Britney Spears kicked off the MTV Video Music Awards with a version of 'Gimme More'… Kanye West's 'Graduation' and 50 Cent's 'Curtis' debuted at No.1 and No.2 with 957,000 and 691,000 copies respectively, the first time since 1991 that two albums sold more than 650,000 copies in the same week.

◆ Leon Jackson completed a hat-trick of X Factor Xmas No.1s. Whitney Houston/ Mariah Carey cover 'When You Believe' headed a festive chart featuring "golden oldies" from The Pogues and Mariah Carey.

◆ Leona Lewis' 'Bleeding Love' registered the longest-running No.1 by a British female solo artist in UK chart history (seven weeks) and was named the biggest-selling single of 2007 (788,000 copies sold in 10 weeks). Due to the flourishing digital market, 2007 was the fourth highest year on record for singles sales (86.6 million).

◆ In other news: Radiohead's 'In Rainbows' was initially offered as a 'pay-what-you like' download on the band's website. 62% of fans paid nothing for it; Led Zeppelin's long awaited reunion in London paid tribute to Atlantic Records founder Ahmet Ertegun, who died in December 2006.

October 2007

This Mnth	Prev Mnth	Title	Artist	Label	Wks 20	(US Pos)	
1		About You Now	Sugababes	Island	15		
2		Let Me Think About It	Ida Corr Vs Fedde Le Grand	Data	7		F
3		No U Hang Up/If That's OK With You	Shayne Ward	Syco Music	6		
4		Valerie	Mark Ronson Featuring Amy Winehouse	Columbia	21		
5	4	Ayo Technology	50 Cent Featuring Justin Timberlake & Timbaland	Interscope	13	(5)	
6	1	Beautiful Girls	Sean Kingston	Beluga Heights/Epic	10	(1)	F
7	3	Hey There Delilah	Plain White T's	Angel	13	(1)	F
8		Goodbye Mr A	The Hoosiers	RCA	11		
9	12	She's So Lovely	Scouting For Girls	Epic	9		F
10	2	Stronger	Kanye West	Roc-A-Fella	10	(1)	
11		Gimme More	Britney Spears	Jive	7	(3)	
12		1,2,3,4	Feist	Polydor	4	(8)	F
13		Apologize	Timbaland Presents OneRepublic	Polydor	18	(2)	
14		Happy Ending	Mika	Casablanca/Island	5		
15	7	1973	James Blunt	Atlantic	7	(73)	
16	8	Shut Up And Drive	Rihanna	Mercury	12	(15)	
17		Uninvited	Freemasons Featuring Bailey Tzuke	Loaded	8		
18		Do It Well	Jennifer Lopez	Epic	3	(31)	
19	6	The Way I Are	Timbaland Feat. Keri Hilson & D.O.E.	Interscope	18	(3)	
20	17	The Pretender	Foo Fighters	RCA	3	(37)	

November 2007

This Mnth	Prev Mnth	Title	Artist	Label	Wks 20	(US Pos)	
1		Bleeding Love	Leona Lewis	Syco Music	14	(1)	
2		Rule The World	Take That	Polydor	16		
3	13	Apologize	Timbaland Presents OneRepublic	Polydor	18	(2)	
4	4	Valerie	Mark Ronson Featuring Amy Winehouse	Columbia	21		
5	1	About You Now	Sugababes	Island	15		
6		Home	Westlife	S	8		
7	11	Gimme More	Britney Spears	Jive	7	(3)	
8		The Heart Never Lies	McFly	Island	2		
9	17	Uninvited	Freemasons Featuring Bailey Tzuke	Loaded	8		
10		2 Hearts	Kylie Minogue	Parlophone	6		
11		No One	Alicia Keys	J	11	(1)	
12	8	Goodbye Mr A	The Hoosiers	RCA	11		
13		Hot Stuff (Let's Dance)	Craig David	Warner Bros	5		
14	2	Let Me Think About It	Ida Corr Vs Fedde Le Grand	Data	7		F
15		Flux	Bloc Party	Wichita Recordings	4		
16		Loch Lomond - Hampden Remix	Runrig With The Tartan Army	Ridge	2		
17		Lord Don't Slow Me Down	Oasis	Big Brother	1		
18	14	Happy Ending	Mika	Casablanca/Island	5		
19	5	Ayo Technology	50 Cent Featuring Justin Timberlake & Timbaland	Interscope	13	(5)	
20	3	No U Hang Up/If That's Ok With You	Shayne Ward	Syco Music	6		

December 2007

This Mnth	Prev Mnth	Title	Artist	Label	Wks 20	(US Pos)	
1	1	Bleeding Love	Leona Lewis	Syco Music	14	(1)	
2		Heartbroken	T2 Featuring Jodie Aysha	2NV/AATW/BNB	11		F
3	2	Rule The World	Take That	Polydor	16		
4		Call The Shots	Girls Aloud	Fascination	10		
5	3	Apologize	Timbaland Presents OneRepublic	Polydor	18	(2)	
6	4	Valerie	Mark Ronson Featuring Amy Winehouse	Columbia	21		
7		Crank That (Soulja Boy)	Soulja Boy Tellem	Polydor	13	(1)	F
8		What A Wonderful World	Eva Cassidy & Katie Melua	Dramatico	3		F
9	11	No One	Alicia Keys	J	11	(1)	
10		Breathless	Shayne Ward	Syco Music	6		
11		All I Want For Christmas Is You	Mariah Carey	Columbia	4		
12		Fairytale Of New York	The Pogues Featuring Kirsty MacColl	Warner Bros	4		
13		When You Believe	Leon Jackson	Syco Music	5		F
14	10	2 Hearts	Kylie Minogue	Parlophone	6		
15	5	About You Now	Sugababes	Island	15		
16	6	Home	Westlife	S	8		
17		What Hurts The Most	Cascada	All Around The World	6	(52)	
18	15	Flux	Bloc Party	Wichita Recordings	4		
19		Headlines (Friendship Never Ends)	Spice Girls	Virgin	2	(90)	
20		An American Trilogy	Elvis Presley	RCA Victor	1		

October 2007

This Mnth	Prev Mnth	Title	Artist	Label	Wks 20	(UK Pos)	
1	1	Crank Dat (Soulja Boy)	Soulja Boy Tellem	Collipark/Interscope	24	(2)	PF
2	3	Stronger	Kanye West	Roc-a-Fella/Def Jam	22	(1)	P
3	4	The Way I Are	Timbaland Featuring Keri Hilson	Mosley/Blackground	26	(1)	
4	2	Big Girls Don't Cry	Fergie	Will.I.Am/A&M/Interscope	28	(2)	P
5		Gimme More	Britney Spears	Jive	6	(3)	G
6		Apologize	Timbaland Featuring Onerepublic	Mosley/Blackground	31	(3)	P
7	12	Bed	J. Holiday	Music Line/Capitol	15	(75)	F
8		Bubbly	Colbie Caillat	Universal Republic	23	(72)	GF
9		No One	Alicia Keys	J/RMG	32	(6)	P
10	14	Ayo Technology	50 Cent Featuring Justin Timberlake & Timbaland	Shady/Aftermath/Interscope	12	(2)	
11	9	Let It Go	Keyshia Cole Featuring Missy Elliott & Lil' Kim	Imani/Geffen	12		G
12	8	Rockstar	Nickelback	Roadrunner	12	(2)	
13	15	Who Knew	P!nk	LaFace/Zomba	14	(5)	G
14	20	Good Life	Kanye West Featuring T-Pain	Roc-a-Fella/Def Jam	17	(23)	G
15	18	How Far We've Come	Matchbox Twenty	Melisma/Atlantic	13		G
16		1,2,3,4	Feist	Cherrytree/Polydor	1	(8)	F
17		Cyclone	Baby Bash Featuring T-Pain	Arista/RMG	16		G
18	10	Shawty	Plies Featuring T-Pain	Slip-N-Slide/Atlantic	14		GF
19	6	Hey There Delilah	Plain White T's	Hollywood	20	(2)	GF
20		Hate That I Love You	Rihanna Featuring Ne-Yo	SRP/Def Jam	16	(15)	G

November 2007

This Mnth	Prev Mnth	Title	Artist	Label	Wks 20	(UK Pos)	
1		Kiss Kiss	Chris Brown Featuring T-Pain	Jive/Zomba	16	(38)	P
2	1	Crank Dat (Soulja Boy)	Soulja Boy Tellem	Collipark/Interscope	24	(2)	PF
3	6	Apologize	Timbaland Featuring Onerepublic	Mosley/Blackground	31	(3)	P
4	9	No One	Alicia Keys	J/RMG	32	(6)	P
5	8	Bubbly	Colbie Caillat	Universal Republic	23	(72)	GF
6	2	Stronger	Kanye West	Roc-a-Fella/Def Jam	22	(1)	P
7	14	Good Life	Kanye West Featuring T-Pain	Roc-a-Fella/Def Jam	17	(23)	G
8	17	Cyclone	Baby Bash Featuring T-Pain	Arista/RMG	16		G
9	20	Hate That I Love You	Rihanna Featuring Ne-Yo	SRP/Def Jam	16	(15)	G
10	3	The Way I Are	Timbaland Featuring Keri Hilson	Mosley/Blackground	26	(1)	
11	7	Bed	J. Holiday	Music Line/Capitol	15	(75)	F
12		Low	Flo Rida Featuring T-Pain	Poe Boy/Atlantic	28	(2)	PF
13	4	Big Girls Don't Cry	Fergie	Will.I.Am/A&M/Interscope	28	(2)	P
14		Paralyzer	Finger Eleven	Wind-Up	15		P
15	10	Ayo Technology	50 Cent Featuring Justin Timberlake & Timbaland	Shady/Aftermath/Interscope	12	(2)	
16	5	Gimme More	Britney Spears	Jive	6	(3)	G
17	15	How Far We've Come	Matchbox Twenty	Melisma/Atlantic	13		G
18		Clumsy	Fergie	Will.I.Am/A&M/Interscope	17	(62)	G
19	13	Who Knew	P!nk	LaFace/Zomba	14	(5)	G
20	12	Rockstar	Nickelback	Roadrunner	12	(2)	

December 2007

This Mnth	Prev Mnth	Title	Artist	Label	Wks 20	(UK Pos)	
1	4	No One	Alicia Keys	J/RMG	32	(6)	P
2	3	Apologize	Timbaland Featuring Onerepublic	Mosley/Blackground	31	(3)	P
3	1	Kiss Kiss	Chris Brown Featuring T-Pain	Jive/Zomba	16	(38)	P
4	12	Low	Flo Rida Featuring T-Pain	Poe Boy/Atlantic	28	(2)	PF
5	5	Bubbly	Colbie Caillat	Universal Republic	23	(72)	GF
6	18	Clumsy	Fergie	Will.I.Am/A&M/Interscope	17	(62)	G
7	2	Crank Dat (Soulja Boy)	Soulja Boy Tellem	Collipark/Interscope	24	(2)	PF
8	7	Good Life	Kanye West Featuring T-Pain	Roc-a-Fella/Def Jam	17	(23)	G
9	9	Hate That I Love You	Rihanna Featuring Ne-Yo	SRP/Def Jam	16	(15)	G
10	14	Paralyzer	Finger Eleven	Wind-Up	15		P
11		Tattoo	Jordin Sparks	Jive/zomba	16	(24)	G
12	8	Cyclone	Baby Bash Featuring T-Pain	Arista/RMG	16		G
13	6	Stronger	Kanye West	Roc-a-Fella/Def Jam	22	(1)	P
14	10	The Way I Are	Timbaland Featuring Keri Hilson	Mosley/Blackground	26	(1)	
15	11	Bed	J. Holiday	Music Line/Capitol	15	(75)	F
16		Can't Help But Wait	Trey Songz	Song Book/Atlantic	3		
17		Like You'll Never See Me Again	Alicia Keys	MBK/J/RMG	13	(53)	G
18	17	How Far We've Come	Matchbox Twenty	Melisma/Atlantic	13		G
19		Hypnotized	Plies Featuring Akon	Big Gates/Slip-N-Slide	3	(66)	
20		Duffle Bag Boy	Playaz Circle Featuring Lil Wayne	DTP/Def Jam	3		GF

◆ T-Pain (Faheem Rasheed Najm) was the name to drop in 2007. 'Buy You A Drank (Shawty Snappin')', 'Bartender', 'Shawty', 'Good Life', 'Cyclone', 'Kiss Kiss' and 'Low' all carried his name – either as lead or featured vocalist – on this year's Top 20s.

◆ Music industry website MediaBase reported that Timbaland and OneRepublic's 'Apologize' had shattered the Top 40 radio weekly airplay record in North America with 10,331 spins. Leona Lewis' 'Bleeding Love' – co-written by OneRepublic vocalist Ryan Tedder – will set the bar even higher in 2008.

◆ 'No One' was ever likely to deny Alicia Keys a chart-topping comeback. The track, which won Best R&B Song and Best Female R&B Vocal Performance at the 2008 Grammys, was, according to *Rolling Stone* magazine, the most listened to song on US radio in 2008 with 3.08 billion listeners.

UK 2008 JAN-MAR

◆ EMI faced a musicians' mutiny with Robbie Williams refusing to make another album in protest at the label axing 2,000 staff in the wake of Terra Firma's £2.4 billion takeover. Robbie was still reeling from news that one million unsold copies of the critically-panned 'Rudebox' would be crushed and recycled for road surfaces and street lighting … in China.

◆ Six million viewers tuned in to see the Sharon and (a frequently AWOL) Ozzy show at the BRITs. Award-winners included Mark Ronson (British Male), Kate Nash (British Female) and the Arctic Monkeys (British Group and British Album).

◆ Soul singer Aimée Duffy drew favourable comparisons with Aretha Franklin, Dusty Springfield and Amy Winehouse when she became the first Welsh singer to top the singles chart since Bonnie Tyler in 1983. 'Mercy' was from 2008's top-selling album 'Rockferry'.

January 2008

This Mnth	Prev Mnth	Title	Artist	Label	Wks 20	(US Pos)	
1	7	Crank That (Soulja Boy)	Soulja Boy Tellem	Polydor	13	(1)	F
2	13	When You Believe	Leon Jackson	Syco Music	5		F
3		Now You're Gone	Basshunter Featuring DJ Mental Theo's Bazzheadz	Hard2beat	14		F
4	1	Bleeding Love	Leona Lewis	Syco Music	14	(1)	
5		Rockstar	Nickelback	Roadrunner	19	(6)	
6		Piece Of Me	Britney Spears	Jive	9		
7	3	Rule The World	Take That	Polydor	16		
8	5	Apologize	Timbaland Presents OneRepublic	Polydor	18	(2)	
9	6	Valerie	Mark Ronson Featuring Amy Winehouse	Columbia	21		
10		Don't Stop The Music	Rihanna	Def Jam	14	(3)	
11		Superstar	Lupe Fiasco Featuring Matthew Santos	Atlantic	7		
12	4	Call The Shots	Girls Aloud	Fascination	10		
13		Chasing Pavements	Adele	XL Recordings	9	(21)	F
14	2	Heartbroken	T2 Featuring Jodie Aysha	2NV/AATW/BNB	11		F
15		Elvis Ain't Dead	Scouting For Girls	Epic	6		
16	9	No One	Alicia Keys	J	11	(1)	
17		Homecoming	Kanye West Featuring Chris Martin	Def Jam	4	(69)	
18		Goodbye Mr A	The Hoosiers	RCA	11		
19	12	Fairytale Of New York	The Pogues Featuring Kirsty MacColl	Warner Bros	4		
20		Be Mine	Robyn	Konichiwa	3		

February 2008

This Mnth	Prev Mnth	Title	Artist	Label	Wks 20	(US Pos)	
1	3	Now You're Gone	Basshunter Featuring DJ Mental Theo's Bazzheadz	Hard2beat	14		F
2	5	Rockstar	Nickelback	Roadrunner	19	(6)	
3	13	Chasing Pavements	Adele	XL Recordings	9	(21)	F
4	10	Don't Stop The Music	Rihanna	Def Jam	14	(3)	
5		Work	Kelly Rowland	RCA	7		
6		Sun Goes Down	David Jordan	Mercury	6		F
7	11	Superstar	Lupe Fiasco Featuring Matthew Santos	Atlantic	7		
8	6	Piece Of Me	Britney Spears	Jive	9		
9		Mercy	Duffy	A&M	14	(27)	F
10		Ready For The Floor	Hot Chip	EMI	4		F
11	15	Elvis Ain't Dead	Scouting For Girls	Epic	6		
12	1	Crank That (Soulja Boy)	Soulja Boy Tellem	Polydor	13	(1)	F
13		Just For Tonight	One Night Only	Vertigo	5		F
14		What's It Gonna Be	H Two O Featuring Platnum	Hard2beat	8		F
15		I Thought It Was Over	The Feeling	Fiction	4		
16	20	Be Mine	Robyn	Konichiwa	3		
17		Ride It	Jay Sean	2point9	3		
18		A&E	Goldfrapp	Mute	4		
19		Weightless	Wet Wet Wet	Dry	1		
20		The Journey Continues	Mark Brown Featuring Sarah Cracknell	Positiva	2		F

March 2008

This Mnth	Prev Mnth	Title	Artist	Label	Wks 20	(US Pos)	
1	9	Mercy	Duffy	A&M	14	(27)	F
2	14	What's It Gonna Be	H Two O Featuring Platnum	Hard2beat	8		F
3	2	Rockstar	Nickelback	Roadrunner	19	(6)	
4		Stop And Stare	OneRepublic	Interscope	10	(12)	
5	1	Now You're Gone	Basshunter Featuring DJ Mental Theo's Bazzheadz	Hard2beat	14		F
6		Better In Time/Footprints In The Sand	Leona Lewis	Syco Music	8	(11)	
7		Come On Girl	Taio Cruz Featuring Luciana	4th & Broadway	6		F
8		Wow	Kylie Minogue	Parlophone	6		
9		Low	Flo Rida Featuring T-Pain	Atlantic	17	(1)	F
10	4	Don't Stop The Music	Rihanna	Def Jam	14	(3)	
11		American Boy	Estelle Featuring Kanye West	Atlantic	14	(10)	
12	3	Chasing Pavements	Adele	XL Recordings	9	(21)	F
13		Fascination	Alphabeat	Charisma	10		F
14	6	Sun Goes Down	David Jordan	Mercury	6		F
15		Something Good '08	Utah Saints	Data	8		
16		4 Minutes	Madonna Featuring Justin Timberlake	Warner Bros	17	(3)	
17	5	Work	Kelly Rowland	RCA	7		
18		Us Against The World	Westlife	S	2		
19		Can't Speak French	Girls Aloud	Fascination	6		
20		Scream	Timbaland Featuring Keri Hilson & Nicole Scherzinger	Interscope	5		

January 2008

This Mnth	Prev Mnth	Title	Artist	Label	Wks 20	(UK Pos)	
1	4	Low	Flo Rida Featuring T-Pain	Poe Boy/Atlantic	28	(2)	PF
2	1	No One	Alicia Keys	J/RMG	32	(6)	P
3	2	Apologize	Timbaland Featuring Onerepublic	Mosley/Blackground	31	(3)	P
4	3	Kiss Kiss	Chris Brown Featuring T-Pain	Jive/Zomba	16	(38)	P
5	6	Clumsy	Fergie	Will.I.Am/A&M/Interscope	17	(62)	G
6	5	Bubbly	Colbie Caillat	Universal Republic	23	(72)	GF
7	10	Paralyzer	Finger Eleven	Wind-Up	15		P
8	7	Crank Dat (Soulja Boy)	Soulja Boy Tellem	Collipark/Interscope	24	(2)	PF
9	11	Tattoo	Jordin Sparks	Jive/Zomba	16	(24)	G
10		Love Song	Sara Bareilles	Epic/Sony	27	(4)	PF
11		With You	Chris Brown	Jive/Zomba	22	(8)	P
12	9	Hate That I Love You	Rihanna Featuring Ne-Yo	SRP/Def Jam	16	(15)	G
13		Take You There	Sean Kingston	Beluga Heights/Epic	14	(47)	G
14	12	Cyclone	Baby Bash Featuring T-Pain	Arista/RMG	16		G
15		Sweetest Girl (Dollar Bill)	Wyclef Jean Featuring Akon, Lil Wayne & Niia	In Ya Face/Columbia	7	(66)	
16		Sensual Seduction	Snoop Dogg	Doggystyle/Geffen	10	(24)	
17	9	Good Life	Kanye West Featuring T-Pain	Roc-a-Fella/Def Jam	17	(23)	G
18		Don't Stop The Music	Rihanna	SRP/Def Jam	17	(4)	G
19	13	Stronger	Kanye West	Roc-a-Fella/Def Jam	22	(1)	P
20		Our Song	Taylor Swift	Big Machine	4		P

February 2008

This Mnth	Prev Mnth	Title	Artist	Label	Wks 20	(UK Pos)	
1	1	Low	Flo Rida Featuring T-Pain	Poe Boy/Atlantic	28	(2)	PF
2	11	With You	Chris Brown	Jive/Zomba	22	(8)	P
3	2	No One	Alicia Keys	J/RMG	32	(6)	P
4	3	Apologize	Timbaland Featuring Onerepublic	Mosley/Blackground	31	(3)	P
5	18	Don't Stop The Music	Rihanna	SRP/Def Jam	17	(4)	G
6	5	Clumsy	Fergie	Will.I.Am/A&M/Interscope	17	(62)	G
7	10	Love Song	Sara Bareilles	Epic/Sony	27	(4)	PF
8	13	Take You There	Sean Kingston	Beluga Heights/Epic	14	(47)	G
9	16	Sensual Seduction	Snoop Dogg	Doggystyle/Geffen	10	(24)	
10	4	Kiss Kiss	Chris Brown Featuring T-Pain	Jive/Zomba	16	(38)	P
11		New Soul	Yael Naim	Tot Au Tard	4	(30)	F
12	7	Paralyzer	Finger Eleven	Wind-Up	16		P
13		Like You'll Never See Me Again	Alicia Keys	MBK/J/RMG	13	(53)	G
14		Sorry	Buckcherry	Eleven Seven/Atlantic	12		GF
15	9	Tattoo	Jordin Sparks	Jive/Zomba	16	(24)	G
16	9	Bubbly	Colbie Caillat	Universal Republic	23	(72)	GF
17		Love Like This	Natasha Bedingfield Featuring Sean Kingston	Phonogenic/Epic	9	(20)	G
18		Teardrops On My Guitar	Taylor Swift	Big Machine/Universal	10	(51)	PF
19		Independent	Webbie, Lil' Phat & Lil' Boosie	Trill/Asylum	13		F
20		See You Again	Miley Cyrus	Hollywood	15	(11)	F

March 2008

This Mnth	Prev Mnth	Title	Artist	Label	Wks 20	(UK Pos)	
1	1	Low	Flo Rida Featuring T-Pain	Poe Boy/Atlantic	28	(2)	PF
2	2	With You	Chris Brown	Jive/Zomba	22	(8)	P
3	5	Don't Stop The Music	Rihanna	SRP/Def Jam	17	(4)	G
4	7	Love Song	Sara Bareilles	Epic/Sony	27	(4)	PF
5		Love In This Club	Usher Featuring Young Jeezy	LaFace/Zomba	18	(4)	G
6	3	No One	Alicia Keys	J/RMG	32	(6)	P
7	4	Apologize	Timbaland Featuring Onerepublic	Mosley/Blackground	31	(3)	P
	8	No Air	Jordin Sparks Duet With Chris Brown	19/Jive/Zomba	20	(3)	G
9	9	Sensual Seduction	Snoop Dogg	Doggystyle/Geffen	10	(24)	
10	19	Independent	Webbie, Lil' Phat & Lil' Boosie	Trill/Asylum	13		F
11		Sexy Can I	Ray J & Yung Berg	Deja 34/Knockout/Koch	18		G
12		Superstar	Lupe Fiasco Featuring Matthew Santos	1st & 15th/Atlantic	9	(4)	F
13	14	Sorry	Buckcherry	Eleven Seven/Atlantic	12		GF
14	8	Take You There	Sean Kingston	Beluga Heights/Epic	14	(47)	G
15	20	See You Again	Miley Cyrus	Hollywood	15	(11)	F
16		Bleeding Love	Leona Lewis	Syco/J/RMG	24	(1)	PF
17	18	Teardrops On My Guitar	Taylor Swift	Big Machine/Universal	10	(51)	PF
18	13	Like You'll Never See Me Again	Alicia Keys	MBK/J/RMG	13	(53)	G
19		Shadow Of The Day	Linkin Park	Warner Bros	8	(46)	G
20		Touch My Body	Mariah Carey	Island/IDJMG	13	(5)	G

US 2008 JAN-MAR

◆ 'Low', by Flo Rida and T-Pain, dominated 2008's first quarter. The track smashed the record for one-week digital sales (467,000; previous record-holder 'Fergalicious' clocked up 295,000 units in the first week of 2007) and topped the digital chart for a record 13 consecutive weeks. 'Low' will become the top-selling download in the US with 5.1 million units sold (as of November '09).

◆ Amy Winehouse filled her mantlepiece with five Grammys: Song of the Year, Record of the Year, Best Female Pop Vocal Performance (all for 'Rehab'), Best Pop Vocal (for 'Back To Black') and Best New Act.

◆ Sara Bareilles, the woman from Eureka, California with an impressive vocal range, took her 'Love Song' up the chart after it was featured as the free 'Song of the Week' on iTunes. 'Love Song' topped both the Hot Adult Top 40 Tracks and Hot Adult Contemporary Tracks charts in 2008.

UK 2008

APR-JUNE

◆ 'Violet Hill' was downloaded an incredible two million times in a week after being made available, free of charge, on Coldplay's website. The first single from 'Viva La Vida ...' would have outsold the entire Top 40 four times over had it been eligible for the chart.

◆ Rapper Jay-Z covered Oasis' 'Wonderwall' in his well-received Glastonbury set, which included the broadcast of a tape of Noel's "I'm not having hip-hop at Glastonbury" quote. Kings Of Leon and The Verve joined Jay-Z as festival headliners.

◆ MOBO award-winner Estelle enlisted the help of 'American Boy' Kanye West on their Grammy-winning No.1, complete with eight song-writing credits and a sample from producer/co-writer Will.I.Am's track 'Impatient'. 'American Boy' was the fastest-selling digital song to date with 51,857 units in week 1.

April 2008

This Mnth	Prev Mnth	Title	Artist	Label	Wks 20	(US Pos)	
1	11	American Boy	Estelle Featuring Kanye West	Atlantic	14	(10)	
2	9	Low	Flo Rida Featruing T-Pain	Atlantic	17	(1)	
3		Black & Gold	Sam Sparro	Island	19		F
4	16	4 Minutes	Madonna Featuring Justin Timberlake	Warner Bros	17	(3)	
5	1	Mercy	Duffy	A&M	14	(27)	F
6		Always Where I Need To Be	The Kooks	Virgin	4		
7	6	Better In Time/Footprints In The Sand	Leona Lewis	Syco Music	8	(11)	
8		Touch My Body	Mariah Carey	Def Jam	5	(1)	
9		With You	Chris Brown	RCA	12	(2)	
10		Cry For You	September	Hard2beat	13	(74)	F
11		Love In This Club	Usher Featuring Young Jeezy	RCA	13	(1)	
12	3	Rockstar	Nickelback	Roadrunner	19	(6)	
13	13	Fascination	Alphabeat	Charisma	10		F
14	4	Stop And Stare	OneRepublic	Interscope	10	(12)	
15	15	Something Good '08	Utah Saints	Data	8		
16		The Age Of The Understatement	The Last Shadow Puppets	Domino	1		F
17	19	Can't Speak French	Girls Aloud	Fascination	6		
18		I'm Not Gonna Teach Your Boyfriend How To Dance With You	Black Kids	Almost Gold	2		F
19	7	Come On Girl	Taio Cruz Featuring Luciana	4th & Broadway	6		F
20	2	What's It Gonna Be	H Two O Featuring Platnum	Hard2beat	8		F

May 2008

This Mnth	Prev Mnth	Title	Artist	Label	Wks 20	(US Pos)	
1	4	4 Minutes	Madonna Featuring Justin Timberlake	Warner Bros	17	(3)	
2	3	Black & Gold	Sam Sparro	Island	19		F
3		Wearing My Rolex	Wiley	Asylum	11		F
4		Heartbreaker	Will.I.Am Featuring Cheryl Cole	Interscope	13		
5	1	American Boy	Estelle Featuring Kanye West	Atlantic	14	(10)	
6	11	Love In This Club	Usher Featuring Young Jeezy	RCA	13	(1)	
7	10	Cry For You	September	Hard2beat	13	(74)	F
8		Take A Bow	Rihanna	Def Jam	13	(1)	
9		That's Not My Name	The Ting Tings	Columbia	13	(39)	F
10	2	Low	Flo Rida Featruing T-Pain	Atlantic	17	(1)	F
11		Propane Nightmares	Pendulum	Warner Bros	7		F
12		Violet Hill	Coldplay	Parlophone	7	(40)	
13		Warwick Avenue	Duffy	A&M	13		
14	5	Mercy	Duffy	A&M	14	(27)	F
15		Heartbeat	Scouting For Girls	Epic	7		
16		In My Arms	Kylie Minogue	Parlophone	2		
17	13	Fascination	Alphabeat	Charisma	10		F
18	8	Touch My Body	Mariah Carey	Def Jam	5	(1)	
19	9	With You	Chris Brown	RCA	12	(2)	
20		Closer	Ne-Yo	Def Jam	15	(7)	

June 2008

This Mnth	Prev Mnth	Title	Artist	Label	Wks 20	(US Pos)	
1	8	Take A Bow	Rihanna	Def Jam	13	(1)	
2	9	That's Not My Name	The Ting Tings	Columbia	13	(39)	F
3	20	Closer	Ne-Yo	Def Jam	15	(7)	
4		Singin' In The Rain	Mint Royale	Syco Music	4		
5	13	Warwick Avenue	Duffy	A&M	13		
6		Love Song	Sara Bareilles	Columbia	10	(4)	F
7	1	4 Minutes	Madonna Featuring Justin Timberlake	Warner Bros	17	(3)	
8	4	Heartbreaker	Will.I.Am Featuring Cheryl Cole	Interscope	13		
9		Sweet About Me	Gabriella Cilmi	Island	18		F
10		Forever	Chris Brown	Jive	11	(2)	
11	2	Black & Gold	Sam Sparro	Island	19		F
12		Viva La Vida	Coldplay	Parlophone	13	(1)	
13	6	Love In This Club	Usher Featuring Young Jeezy	RCA	13	(1)	
14	12	Violet Hill	Coldplay	Parlophone	7	(40)	
15	7	Cry For You	September	Hard2beat	13	(74)	F
16	3	Wearing My Rolex	Wiley	Asylum	11		F
17		No Air	Jordin Sparks Featuring Chris Brown	Jive	14	(3)	F
18	10	Low	Flo Rida Featuring T-Pain	Atlantic	17	(1)	F
19	5	American Boy	Estelle Featuring Kanye West	Atlantic	14	(10)	
20		We Made It	Busta Rhymes Featuring Linkin Park	Interscope	6	(65)	

April 2008

This Mnth	Prev Mnth	Title	Artist	Label	Wks 20	(UK Pos)	
1	16	Bleeding Love	Leona Lewis	Syco/J/RMG	24	(1)	PF
2	5	Love In This Club	Usher Featuring Young Jeezy	Laface/Zomba	18	(4)	G
3	20	Touch My Body	Mariah Carey	Island/IDJMG	13	(5)	G
4		Lollipop	Lil Wayne Featuring Static Major	Cash Money/Universal	21		P
5	8	No Air	Jordin Sparks Duet With Chris Brown	19/Jive/Zomba	20	(3)	G
6	11	Sexy Can I	Ray J & Yung Berg	Deja 34/Knockout/Koch	18		G
7	2	With You	Chris Brown	Jive/Zomba	22	(8)	P
8		4 Minutes	Madonna Featuring Justin Timberlake	Warner Bros	12	(1)	P
9	4	Love Song	Sara Bareilles	Epic/Sony	27	(4)	PF
10	1	Low	Flo Rida Featuring T-Pain	Poe Boy/Atlantic	28	(2)	PF
11	3	Don't Stop The Music	Rihanna	SRP/Def Jam	17	(4)	G
12	15	See You Again	Miley Cyrus	Hollywood	15	(11)	F
13	7	Apologize	Timbaland Featuring Onerepublic	Mosley/Blackground	31	(3)	P
14		Stop And Stare	Onerepublic	Mosley/Interscope	10	(4)	
15		Shawty Get Loose	Lil Mama Featuring Chris Brown & T-Pain	Familiar Faces/Jive	2	(57)	
16	12	Superstar	Lupe Fiasco Featuring Matthew Santos	1st & 15th/Atlantic	9	(4)	F
17		You're Gonna Miss This	Trace Adkins	Capitol Nashville	2		F
18	6	No One	Alicia Keys	J/RMG	32	(6)	P
19	10	Independent	Webbie, Lil' Phat & Lil' Boosie	Trill/Asylum	13		F
20	13	Sorry	Buckcherry	Eleven Seven/Atlantic	12		GF

May 2008

This Mnth	Prev Mnth	Title	Artist	Label	Wks 20	(UK Pos)	
1	1	Bleeding Love	Leona Lewis	Syco/J/RMG	24	(1)	PF
2	4	Lollipop	Lil Wayne Featuring Static Major	Cash Money/Universal	21		P
3	5	No Air	Jordin Sparks Duet With Chris Brown	19/Jive/Zomba	20	(3)	G
4	2	Love In This Club	Usher Featuring Young Jeezy	Laface/Zomba	18	(4)	G
5	8	4 Minutes	Madonna Featuring Justin Timberlake	Warner Bros	12	(1)	P
6	6	Sexy Can I	Ray J & Yung Berg	Deja 34/Knockout/Koch	18		G
7	3	Touch My Body	Mariah Carey	Island/IDJMG	13	(5)	G
8		Take A Bow	Rihanna	SRP/Def Jam	18	(1)	G
9	9	Love Song	Sara Bareilles	Epic/Sony	27	(4)	PF
10		Pocketful Of Sunshine	Natasha Bedingfield	Phonogenic/Epic	17		P
11		Damaged	Danity Kane	Bad Boy/Atlantic	13		G
12	7	With You	Chris Brown	Jive/Zomba	22	(8)	P
13	10	Low	Flo Rida Featuring T-Pain	Poe Boy/Atlantic	28	(2)	PF
14		Leavin'	Jesse McCartney	Hollywood	20	(66)	G
15		Say	John Mayer	Aware/Columbia	5		G
16	12	See You Again	Miley Cyrus	Hollywood	15	(11)	F
17		Forever	Chris Brown	Jive/Zomba	18	(4)	
18	11	Don't Stop The Music	Rihanna	SRP/Def Jam	17	(4)	G
19		Bust It Baby (Part 2)	Plies Featuring Ne-Yo	Big Gates/Slip-N-Slide	13		
20		What You Got	Colby O'Donis Featuring Akon	Konlive/Geffen/Interscope	9		F

June 2008

This Mnth	Prev Mnth	Title	Artist	Label	Wks 20	(UK Pos)	
1	2	Lollipop	Lil Wayne Featuring Static Major	Cash Money/Universal	21		P
2	1	Bleeding Love	Leona Lewis	Syco/J/RMG	24	(1)	PF
3		Viva La Vida	Coldplay	Capitol	21	(1)	P
4	8	Take A Bow	Rihanna	SRP/Def Jam	18	(1)	G
5		I Kissed A Girl	Katy Perry	Capitol	16	(1)	PF
6	3	No Air	Jordin Sparks Duet With Chris Brown	19/Jive/Zomba	20	(3)	G
7	4	Love In This Club	Usher Featuring Young Jeezy	Laface/Zomba	18	(4)	G
8	10	Pocketful Of Sunshine	Natasha Bedingfield	Phonogenic/Epic	17		P
9	6	Sexy Can I	Ray J & Yung Berg	Deja 34/Knockout/Koch	18		G
10		The Time Of My Life	David Cook	Fremantle/19/RCA/RMG	3	(61)	GF
11	5	4 Minutes	Madonna Featuring Justin Timberlake	Warner Bros	12	(1)	P
12	17	Forever	Chris Brown	Jive/Zomba	18	(4)	
13	11	Damaged	Danity Kane	Bad Boy/Atlantic	13		G
14	19	Bust It Baby (Part 2)	Plies Featuring Ne-Yo	Big Gates/Slip-N-Slide	13		
15	14	Leavin'	Jesse Mccartney	Hollywood	20	(66)	G
16		Shake It	Metro Station	Red Ink/Red/Columbia	9	(6)	PF
17	20	What You Got	Colby O'donis Featuring Akon	Konlive/Geffen/Interscope	9		F
18	17	Touch My Body	Mariah Carey	Island/IDJMG	13	(5)	G
19		Got Money	Lil Wayne Featuring T-Pain	Cash Money/Universal	9		G
20		Dream Big	David Cook	Fremantle/19/RCA/RMG	1		

▲ Mariah Carey was crowned the most successful solo artist in the history of the Hot 100 with her 18th No.1 single, 'Touch My Body', surpassing Elvis' 17 chart-toppers. In a bad week for 'The King', Madonna eclipsed his record of 36 Top 10 singles in the rock era with '4 Minutes'.

◆ Neil Diamond became America's oldest ever chart champ at 67 years and three months with, remarkably, his first No.1 album, 'Home Before Dark'. Bob Dylan will reclaim the 'oldie' crown in 2009 with 'Together Through Life'.

◆ With 'Viva La Vida', Coldplay were the first British band since the Spice Girls in 1997 to reach the top rung of the Billboard Hot 100.

July 2008

This Mnth	Prev Mnth	Title	Artist	Label	Wks 20	(US Pos)	
1	3	Closer	Ne-Yo	Def Jam	15	(7)	
2	17	No Air	Jordin Sparks Featuring Chris Brown	Jive	14	(3)	F
3		Dance Wiv Me	Dizzee Rascal Featuring Calvin Harris & Chrome	Dirtee Stank	12		
4		All I Ever Wanted	Basshunter	Hard2beat	8		
5	12	Viva La Vida	Coldplay	Parlophone	13	(1)	
6	10	Forever	Chris Brown	Jive	11	(2)	
7		Stay With Me	Ironik	Asylum	9		F
8	1	Take A Bow	Rihanna	Def Jam	13	(1)	
9		All Summer Long	Kid Rock	Atlantic	12		F
10	9	Sweet About Me	Gabriella Cilmi	Island	18		F
11	6	Love Song	Sara Bareilles	Columbia	10	(4)	F
12		One For The Radio	McFly	Super	1		
13	2	That's Not My Name	The Ting Tings	Columbia	13	(39)	F
14	20	We Made It	Busta Rhymes Featuring Linkin Park	Interscope	6	(65)	
15	5	Warwick Avenue	Duffy	A&M	13		
16		Give It 2 Me	Madonna	Warner Bros	8	(57)	
17		Shut Up And Let Me Go	The Ting Tings	Columbia	8	(55)	
18	11	Black & Gold	Sam Sparro	Island	19		F
19		SOS	Jonas Brothers	Hollywood	2		F
20	7	4 Minutes	Madonna Featuring Justin Timberlake	Warner Bros	17	(3)	

August 2008

This Mnth	Prev Mnth	Title	Artist	Label	Wks 20	(US Pos)	
1	9	All Summer Long	Kid Rock	Atlantic	12		F
2	3	Dance Wiv Me	Dizzee Rascal Featuring Calvin Harris & Chrome	Dirtee Stank	12		
3		I Kissed A Girl	Katy Perry	Virgin	15	(1)	F
4		The Man Who Can't Be Moved	The Script	RCA	11		
5	2	No Air	Jordin Sparks Featuring Chris Brown	Jive	14	(3)	F
6	1	Closer	Ne-Yo	Def Jam	15	(7)	
7	4	All I Ever Wanted	Basshunter	Hard2beat	8		
8		Love Is Noise	The Verve	Parlophone	6		
9		5 Years Time	Noah And The Whale	Vertigo	8		F
10		Disturbia	Rihanna	Def Jam	13	(1)	
11	17	Shut Up And Let Me Go	The Ting Tings	Columbia	8	(55)	
12	7	Stay With Me	Ironik	Asylum	9		F
13		Beggin'	Madcon	RCA	9	(79)	F
14	10	Sweet About Me	Gabriella Cilmi	Island	18		F
15	5	Viva La Vida	Coldplay	Parlophone	13	(1)	
16		If This Is Love	The Saturdays	Fascination	3		F
17	8	Take A Bow	Rihanna	Def Jam	13	(1)	
18	16	Give It 2 Me	Madonna	Warner Bros	8	(57)	
19		I Like You So Much Better When You're Naked	Ida Maria	Waterfall	5		F
20	18	Black & Gold	Sam Sparro	Island	19		F

September 2008

This Mnth	Prev Mnth	Title	Artist	Label	Wks 20	(US Pos)	
1	3	I Kissed A Girl	Katy Perry	Virgin	15	(1)	F
2		Pjanoo	Eric Prydz	Data	5		
3	10	Disturbia	Rihanna	Def Jam	13	(1)	
4	4	The Man Who Can't Be Moved	The Script	RCA	11		
5		When I Grow Up	Pussycat Dolls	A&M	9	(9)	
6		Sex On Fire	Kings Of Leon	Hand Me Down	23	(56)	
7	13	Beggin'	Madcon	RCA	9	(79)	F
8	1	All Summer Long	Kid Rock	Atlantic	12		F
9		Mountains	Biffy Clyro	14th Floor	5		
10		Thank You For A Lifetime	Cliff Richard	EMI	2		
11		Cookie Jar	Gym Class Heroes	Decaydance/Fueled By Ramen	7	(59)	
12	2	Dance Wiv Me	Dizzee Rascal Featuring Calvin Harris & Chrome	Dirtee Stank	12		
13		Lies	McFly	Super	2		
14	8	Love Is Noise	The Verve	Parlophone	6		
15		Miss Independent	Ne-Yo	Def Jam	9	(7)	
16	9	5 Years Time	Noah And The Whale	Vertigo	8		F
17	5	No Air	Jordin Sparks Featuring Chris Brown	Jive	14	(3)	F
18		See You Again	Miley Cyrus	Walt Disney	3	(10)	F
19		Changes	Will Young	19/RCA	3		
20	15	Viva La Vida	Coldplay	Parlophone	13	(1)	

▲ Eighteen years after forming and seven years since their first nomination, Elbow claimed the Nationwide Music Prize and £20,000 for 'The Seldom Seen Kid'. The band gave the award to the mother of the musician Bryan Glancy, inspiration for the title.

◆ Abba's indefatigable 'Gold – Greatest Hits' was the oldest album to reach No.1, returning to the top spot for the fourth time since 1992 following the success of the Abba-inspired musical *Mamma Mia*.

◆ A chance encounter in Preston resulted in the Dizzee Rascal/Calvin Harris collaboration 'Dance Wiv Me', although the pair never actually met while working on the song – they communicated over the telephone.

July 2008

This Mnth	Prev Mnth	Title	Artist	Label	Wks 20	(UK Pos)	
1	5	I Kissed A Girl	Katy Perry	Capitol	16	(1)	PF
2	1	Lollipop	Lil Wayne Featuring Static Major	Cash Money/Universal	21		P
3	4	Take A Bow	Rihanna	SRP/Def Jam	18	(1)	G
4	2	Bleeding Love	Leona Lewis	Syco/J/RMG	24	(1)	PF
5	12	Forever	Chris Brown	Jive/Zomba	18	(4)	
6	3	Viva La Vida	Coldplay	Capitol	21	(1)	P
7	8	Pocketful Of Sunshine	Natasha Bedingfield	Phonogenic/Epic	17		P
8	14	Bust It Baby (Part 2)	Plies Featuring Ne-Yo	Big Gates/Slip-N-Slide	13		
9		Burnin' Up	Jonas Brothers	Hollywood	8		
10		7 Things	Miley Cyrus	Hollywood	6	(26)	
11		When I Grow Up	The Pussycat Dolls	Interscope	13	(3)	
12		A Milli	Lil Wayne	Cash Money/Universal	10		G
13		This Is Me	Demi Lovato & Joe Jonas	Walt Disney	2	(33)	F
14	15	Leavin'	Jesse Mccartney	Hollywood	20	(66)	G
15		Disturbia	Rihanna	SRP/Def Jam	26	(3)	P
16	16	Shake It	Metro Station	Red Ink/Red/Columbia	9	(6)	PF
17	6	No Air	Jordin Sparks Duet With Chris Brown	19/Jive/Zomba	20	(3)	G
18		Dangerous	Kardinal Offishall Featuring Akon	Konlive/Geffen/Interscope	13	(16)	F
19	13	Damaged	Danity Kane	Bad Boy/Atlantic	13		G
20	7	Love In This Club	Usher Featuring Young Jeezy	Laface/Zomba	18	(4)	G

August 2008

This Mnth	Prev Mnth	Title	Artist	Label	Wks 20	(UK Pos)	
1	1	I Kissed A Girl	Katy Perry	Capitol	16	(1)	PF
2	5	Forever	Chris Brown	Jive/Zomba	18	(4)	
3	15	Disturbia	Rihanna	SRP/Def Jam	26	(3)	P
4	3	Take A Bow	Rihanna	SRP/Def Jam	18	(1)	G
5	6	Viva La Vida	Coldplay	Capitol	21	(1)	P
6	12	A Milli	Lil Wayne	Cash Money/Universal	10		G
7	18	Dangerous	Kardinal Offishall Featuring Akon	Konlive/Geffen/Interscope	13	(16)	F
8	2	Lollipop	Lil Wayne Featuring Static Major	Cash Money/Universal	21		P
9	4	Bleeding Love	Leona Lewis	Syco/J/RMG	24	(1)	PF
10		Paper Planes	M.I.A.	XL/Interscope	13	(19)	PF
11		Crush	David Archuleta	19/Jive/Zomba	6		F
12	11	When I Grow Up	The Pussycat Dolls	Interscope	13	(3)	
13		Closer	Ne-Yo	Big Gates/Slip-N-Slide	16	(1)	G
14	9	Burnin' Up	Jonas Brothers	Hollywood	8		
15	14	Leavin'	Jesse Mccartney	Hollywood	20	(66)	G
16	7	Pocketful Of Sunshine	Natasha Bedingfield	Phonogenic/Epic	17		P
17		American Boy	Estelle Featuring Kanye West	Home School/Atlantic	7	(1)	GF
18		Tonight	Jonas Brothers	Hollywood	1		
19		Change	Taylor Swift	Big Machine	1		
20		A Little Bit Longer	Jonas Brothers	Hollywood	1		

September 2008

This Mnth	Prev Mnth	Title	Artist	Label	Wks 20	(UK Pos)	
1		Whatever You Like	T.I.	Grand Hustle/Atlantic	23	(47)	P
2	3	Disturbia	Rihanna	SRP/Def Jam	26	(3)	P
3		So What	P!nk	LaFace/Zomba	22	(1)	
4	2	Forever	Chris Brown	Jive/Zomba	18	(4)	
5	10	Paper Planes	M.I.A.	XL/Interscope	13	(19)	PF
6	7	Dangerous	Kardinal Offishall Featuring Akon	Konlive/Geffen/Interscope	13	(16)	F
7	13	Closer	Ne-Yo	Big Gates/Slip-N-Slide	16	(1)	G
8	5	Viva La Vida	Coldplay	Capitol	21	(1)	P
9	1	I Kissed A Girl	Katy Perry	Capitol	16	(1)	PF
10		I'm Yours	Jason Mraz	Atlantic	27	(11)	P
11		Can't Believe It	T-Pain Featuring Lil Wayne	Nappy Boy/Konvict/Jive	15		G
12		Swagga Like Us	Jay-Z & T.I. Featuring Kanye West & Lil Wayne	Grand Hustle/Atlantic	1	(33)	
13		Got Money	Lil Wayne Featuring T-Pain	Cash Money/Universal	9		G
14	12	When I Grow Up	The Pussycat Dolls	Interscope	13	(3)	
15		In The Ayer	Flo Rida Featuring Will.I.Am	Poe Boy/Atlantic	3	(29)	G
16	4	Take A Bow	Rihanna	SRP/Def Jam	18	(1)	G
17	17	American Boy	Estelle Featuring Kanye West	Home School/Atlantic	7	(1)	GF
18		Put On	Young Jeezy Featuring Kanye West	CTE/Def Jam	5		
19		Hot N Cold	Katy Perry	Capitol	24	(4)	P
20		Just Stand Up!	Artists Stand Up To Cancer	Suc2/IDJMG	1	(26)	F

◆ On the 1,000th No.1 of the 'rock era' and one of the most parodied songs of all-time, Katy Perry admitted: "I kissed a girl and I liked it!". The song, about "appreciating the beauty of women", was, surprisingly, the first ever No.1 for co-writer Cathy Dennis as a singer or songwriter.

◆ T.I.'s 'Whatever You Like' recorded the biggest jump to No.1 in Hot 100 history (from No.71) and was the first song on the Hot 100 to return to No.1 after an act's follow-up single ('Live Your Life', which replaced 'Whatever You Like' at the top) had reached No.1.

◆ The impossibly catchy 'I'm Yours', which will rack up digital sales of more than 4.4 million, will send Jason Mraz into the record books in 2009 for the longest stay on the Hot 100 - an incredible 76 weeks.

447

UK 2008
OCT-DEC

◆ In March 2009, 'Sex On Fire' becomes the UK's top-selling digital single (550,000) and will rack up 60+ weeks on the singles chart by the end of the year. The track was replaced at No.1 by P!nk's 'So What', which recorded the biggest ever jump to No.1 inside the Top 40 (from No.38).

◆ Alexandra Burke's 'Hallelujah' (576,046 units sold in week one) set a new benchmark for the fastest-selling single in the UK. In January 2009, she will become the first British female solo singer to sell more than one million copies of a single'. And with Jeff Buckley's 'Hallelujah' at No.2, different versions of the same song were at Nos.1 and 2 for the first time since Tommy Steele and Guy Mitchell dominated with 'Singing The Blues' in 1957.

◆ 115 million singles (95.8% of them digital) were sold in the UK in 2008, more than any other year on record. The previous best was 1979's 89.1 million.

October 2008

This Mnth	Prev Mnth	Title	Artist	Label	Wks 20	(US Pos)	
1	6	Sex On Fire	Kings Of Leon	Hand Me Down	23	(56)	
2		So What	P!nk	LaFace	11	(1)	
3	3	Disturbia	Rihanna	Def Jam	13	(1)	
4		Girls	Sugababes	Island	6		
5	1	I Kissed A Girl	Katy Perry	Virgin	15	(1)	F
6	5	When I Grow Up	Pussycat Dolls	A&M	9	(9)	
7	15	Miss Independent	Ne-Yo	Def Jam	9	(7)	
8		In This City	Iglu & Hartly	Mercury	5		F
9	11	Cookie Jar	Gym Class Heroes	Decaydance/Fueled By Ramen	7	(59)	
10		The Winners Song	Geraldine	Polydor	3		
11		The Shock Of The Lightning	Oasis	Big Brother	2	(93)	
12		I Love You Anyway	Boyzone	Polydor	3		
13		Don't Call This Love	Leon Jackson	Syco Music	3		
14		Never Miss A Beat	Kaiser Chiefs	B-Unique	3		
15		Take Back The City	Snow Patrol	Fiction	4		
16		Up	The Saturdays	Fascination	5		
17		You Make It Real	James Morrison	Polydor	3		
18		Spotlight	Jennifer Hudson	RCA	8	(24)	F
19		Love Lockdown	Kanye West	Def Jam	10	(3)	
20		Raindrops (Encore Une Fois)	Sash! Featuring Stunt	Hard2beat	4		

November 2008

This Mnth	Prev Mnth	Title	Artist	Label	Wks 20	(US Pos)	
1		The Promise	Girls Aloud	Fascination	11		
2		Hero	The X Factor Finalists	Syco Music	9		F
3		Infinity 2008	Guru Josh Project	Maelstrom	11		
4	2	So What	P!nk	LaFace	11	(1)	
5		If I Were A Boy	Beyoncé	Columbia	13	(3)	
6		Hot N Cold	Katy Perry	Virgin	15	(3)	
7	1	Sex On Fire	Kings Of Leon	Hand Me Down	23	(56)	
8		Live Your Life	T.I. Featuring Rihanna	Atlantic	9	(1)	
9		Womanizer	Britney Spears	Jive	10	(1)	
10		The Boy Does Nothing	Alesha Dixon	Asylum	10		F
11		Human	The Killers	Vertigo	14	(32)	
12	19	Love Lockdown	Kanye West	Def Jam	10	(3)	
13		Forgive Me	Leona Lewis	Syco Music	4		
14	16	Up	The Saturdays	Fascination	5		
15		Wire To Wire	Razorlight	Vertigo	3		
16		Another Way To Die	Jack White & Alicia Keys	RCA	4	(81)	F
17	20	Raindrops (Encore Une Fois)	Sash! Featuring Stunt	Hard2beat	4		
18	10	The Winners Song	Geraldine	Polydor	3		
19	18	Spotlight	Jennifer Hudson	RCA	8	(24)	F
20	7	Miss Independent	Ne-Yo	Def Jam	9	(7)	

December 2008

This Mnth	Prev Mnth	Title	Artist	Label	Wks 20	(US Pos)	
1		Greatest Day	Take That	Polydor	7		
2	5	If I Were A Boy	Beyoncé	Columbia	13	(3)	
3		Run	Leona Lewis	Syco Music	9		
4	9	Womanizer	Britney Spears	Jive	10	(1)	
5		Use Somebody	Kings Of Leon	Hand Me Down	20	(4)	
6	11	Human	The Killers	Vertigo	14	(32)	
7	6	Hot N Cold	Katy Perry	Virgin	15	(3)	
8	8	Live Your Life	T.I. Featuring Rihanna	Atlantic	9	(1)	
9		Right Now	Akon	Island	11	(17)	
10	10	The Boy Does Nothing	Alesha Dixon	Asylum	10		F
11		Hallelujah	Alexandra Burke	Syco Music	6		F
12		Little Drummer Boy/ Peace On Earth	Bandaged (Sir Terry Wogan & Aled Jones)	Warner Bros.	2		F
13		Hallelujah	Jeff Buckley	Columbia	2		F
14	2	Hero	The X Factor Finalists	Syco Music	9		F
15		Once Upon A Christmas Song	Geraldine	Polydor	2		
16		Broken Strings	James Morrison Featuring Nelly Furtado	Polydor	16		
17		Listen	Beyoncé	Columbia	1	(61)	
18	1	The Promise	Girls Aloud	Fascination	11		
19	3	Infinity 2008	Guru Josh Project	Maelstrom	11		
20		Fairytale Of New York	The Pogues Featuring Kirsty MacColl	Warner Bros	4		

This Mnth	Prev Mnth	Title	Artist	Label	Wks 20	(UK Pos)	
1	1	Whatever You Like	T.I.	Grand Hustle/Atlantic	23	(47)	P
2	3	So What	P!nk	LaFace/Zomba	22	(1)	
3	2	Disturbia	Rihanna	SRP/Def Jam	26	(3)	P
4		Love Lockdown	Kanye West	Rock-A-Fella/Def Jam	17	(8)	P
5	19	Hot N Cold	Katy Perry	Capitol	24	(4)	P
6		Live Your Life	T.I. Featuring Rihanna	Def Jam/Grand Hustle	20	(2)	P
7	5	Paper Planes	M.I.A.	XL/Interscope	13	(19)	PF
8	11	Can't Believe It	T-Pain Featuring Lil Wayne	Nappy Boy/Konvict/Jive	15		G
9		Love Story	Taylor Swift	Big Machine	33	(2)	P
10		Womanizer	Britney Spears	Jive	17	(3)	
11		Let It Rock	Kevin Rudolf Featuring Lil Wayne	Cash Money/Univeral Republic	20	(5)	PF
12	7	Closer	Ne-Yo	Big Gates/Slip-N-Slide	16	(1)	G
13		Miss Independent	Ne-Yo	Def Jam/IDJMG	18	(6)	G
14		Keeps Gettin' Better	Christina Aguilera	RCA/RMG	2	(14)	
15	17	American Boy	Estelle Featuring Kanye West	Home School/Atlantic	7	(1)	GF
16	10	I'm Yours	Jason Mraz	Atlantic	27	(11)	P
17		Better In Time	Leona Lewis	Syco/J/RMG	11	(2)	
18	4	Forever	Chris Brown	Jive/Zomba	18	(4)	
19		Gotta Be Somebody	Nickelback	Roadrunner/RRP	17	(20)	
20	13	Got Money	Lil Wayne Featuring T-Pain	Cash Money/Universal	9		G

This Mnth	Prev Mnth	Title	Artist	Label	Wks 20	(UK Pos)	
1	6	Live Your Life	T.I. Featuring Rihanna	Def Jam/Grand Hustle	20	(2)	P
2	1	Whatever You Like	T.I.	Grand Hustle/Atlantic	23	(47)	P
3	2	So What	P!nk	LaFace/Zomba	22	(1)	
4	5	Hot N Cold	Katy Perry	Capitol	24	(4)	P
5	10	Womanizer	Britney Spears	Jive	17	(3)	
6		If I Were A Boy	Beyoncé	Music World/Columbia	11	(1)	P
7	11	Let It Rock	Kevin Rudolf Featuring Lil Wayne	Cash Money/Univeral Republic	20	(5)	PF
8	13	Miss Independent	Ne-Yo	Def Jam/IDJMG	18	(6)	G
9	3	Disturbia	Rihanna	SRP/Def Jam	26	(3)	P
10	16	I'm Yours	Jason Mraz	Atlantic	27	(11)	P
11		Right Now (Na Na Na)	Akon	SRC/Universal Motown	1	(6)	G
12		Heartless	Kanye West	Rock-A-Fella/Def Jam	22	(11)	P
13	4	Love Lockdown	Kanye West	Rock-A-Fella/Def Jam	17	(8)	P
14	8	Can't Believe It	T-Pain Featuring Lil Wayne	Nappy Boy/Konvict/Jive	15		G
15	17	Better In Time	Leona Lewis	Syco/J/RMG	11	(2)	
16		Fearless	Taylor Swift	Big Machine	1		
17	9	Love Story	Taylor Swift	Big Machine	33	(2)	P
18		You're Not Sorry	Taylor Swift	Big Machine	1		
19		You Belong With Me	Taylor Swift	Big Machine		(30)	P
20		White Horse	Taylor Swift	Big Machine	1	(60)	G

This Mnth	Prev Mnth	Title	Artist	Label	Wks 20	(UK Pos)	
1	1	Live Your Life	T.I. Featuring Rihanna	Def Jam/Grand Hustle	20	(2)	P
2		Single Ladies (Put A Ring On It)	Beyoncé	Music World/Columbia	16	(7)	P
3		Just Dance	Lady Gaga Featuring Colby O'donis	Streamline/Konlive/Interscope	26	(1)	PF
4	2	Whatever You Like	T.I.	Grand Hustle/Atlantic	23	(47)	P
5	6	If I Were A Boy	Beyoncé	Music World/Columbia	11	(1)	P
6	4	Hot N Cold	Katy Perry	Capitol	24	(4)	P
7		Circus	Britney Spears	Jive	17	(13)	
8	5	Womanizer	Britney Spears	Jive	17	(3)	
9	13	Love Lockdown	Kanye West	Rock-A-Fella/Def Jam	17	(8)	P
10	8	Miss Independent	Ne-Yo	Def Jam/IDJMG	18	(6)	G
11	3	So What	P!nk	LaFace/Zomba	22	(1)	
12	10	I'm Yours	Jason Mraz	Atlantic	27	(11)	P
13	11	Right Now (Na Na Na)	Akon	SRC/Universal Motown	1	(6)	G
14	12	Heartless	Kanye West	Rock-A-Fella/Def Jam	22	(11)	P
15	17	Love Story	Taylor Swift	Big Machine	33	(2)	P
16	7	Let It Rock	Kevin Rudolf Featuring Lil Wayne	Cash Money/Univeral Republic	20	(5)	PF
17		Gotta Be Somebody	Nickelback	Roadrunner/RRP	17	(20)	
18	14	Can't Believe It	T-Pain Featuring Lil Wayne	Nappy Boy/Konvict/Jive	15		G
19		Mrs. Officer	Lil Wayne Featuring Bobby Valentino & Kidd Kidd	Cash Money	11		
20		You Found Me	The Fray	Epic/Sony Music	23	(35)	P

US 2008 OCT-DEC

◆ Taylor Swift parked five songs from 'Fearless' in November's Top 20, including 'Love Story', country music's most popular paid download. Among her other chart records: most Top 20 debuts on the Hot 100 (six in 2008); most Top 40 hits from one album (13 from 'Fearless'); first country artist to sell two million downloads with four different songs; most songs simultaneously on the Hot 100 by a female (9); most Top 40 hits this decade by a female (19).

◆ T.I. and Rihanna's 'Live Your Life' (No.80–No.1) and Britney Spears' 'Womanizer' (No.96-No.1) made record-breaking jumps to No.1. The latter sold a female record 286,000 downloads in week 1.

◆ Lady Gaga crowned the Hot 100 with 'Just Dance', which will shift 4.5 million units by November 2009. The song took 22 weeks to reach the summit, five weeks short of Creed's record-breaking climb with the 2000 anthem 'With Arms Wide Open'.

UK
2009
JAN-MAR

◆ Internet savvy Londoner Lily Allen was one of a number of female singers dominating the singles chart. 'The Fear', which rose from No.168 to No.1, was released as a single nine months after Allen posted a demo of the song – then called 'I Don't Know' – on her MySpace page.

◆ BRIT award-winners included Duffy (British Female, Breakthrough Act, British Album for 'Rockferry'), Elbow (British Group), Paul Weller (British Male) and Kings Of Leon (International Group, International Album for 'Only By The Night'). The Pet Shop Boys, meanwhile, bagged the Outstanding Contribution to British Music accolade.

◆ Michael Jackson caused fan hysteria when he visited London's O2 Arena to announce his ill-fated 10-date residency (later extended to 50 shows), billed as his last live performances on British soil. 750,000 tickets were immediately snapped up at a rate of 11 per second.

January 2009

This Mnth	Prev Mnth	Title	Artist	Label	Wks 20	(US Pos)	
1	11	Hallelujah	Alexandra Burke	Syco Music	6		F
2	16	Broken Strings	James Morrison Featuring Nelly Furtado	Polydor	16		
3		Just Dance	Lady Gaga feat. Colby O'Donis	Interscope	17	(1)	F
4	3	Run	Leona Lewis	Syco Music	9		
5	5	Use Somebody	Kings Of Leon	Hand Me Down	20	(4)	
6	2	If I Were A Boy	Beyoncé	Columbia	13	(3)	
7		Issues	The Saturdays	Fascination	6		
8		Day 'n' Nite	Kid Cudi Vs Crookers	Data	8	(3)	F
9		Single Ladies (Put A Ring On It)	Beyoncé	RCA	12	(1)	
10		Let It Rock	Kevin Rudolf Featuring Lil Wayne	Island	7	(5)	F
11	7	Hot N Cold	Katy Perry	Virgin	15	(3)	
12	6	Human	The Killers	Vertigo	14	(32)	
13		Take Me Back	Tinchy Stryder Featuring Taio Cruz	4th & Broadway	7		F
14	1	Greatest Day	Take That	Polydor	7		
15		Sex On Fire	Kings Of Leon	Hand Me Down	23	(56)	
16	4	Womanizer	Britney Spears	Jive	10	(1)	
17		Heartless	Kanye West	Roc-A-Fella	3	(2)	
18	13	Hallelujah	Jeff Buckley	Columbia	2		F
19	15	Once Upon A Christmas Song	Geraldine	Polydor	2		
20		The Loving Kind	Girls Aloud	Fascination	2		

February 2009

This Mnth	Prev Mnth	Title	Artist	Label	Wks 20	(US Pos)	
1		The Fear	Lily Allen	EMI	12	(80)	
2	3	Just Dance	Lady Gaga feat. Colby O'Donis	Interscope	17	(1)	F
3		Breathe Slow	Alesha Dixon	Asylum	9		
4	13	Take Me Back	Tinchy Stryder Featuring Taio Cruz	4th & Broadway	7		F
5	8	Day 'n' Nite	Kid Cudi Vs Crookers	Data	8	(3)	F
6	2	Broken Strings	James Morrison Featuring Nelly Furtado	Polydor	16		
7	5	Use Somebody	Kings Of Leon	Hand Me Down	20	(4)	
8		Crack A Bottle	Eminem/Dr. Dre/50 Cent	Interscope	5	(1)	
9	9	Single Ladies (Put A Ring On It)	Beyoncé	RCA	12	(1)	
10		Omen	The Prodigy	Take Me To The Hospital	7		
11		T-Shirt	Shontelle	Universal	6	(36)	F
12	10	Let It Rock	Kevin Rudolf Featuring Lil Wayne	Island	7	(5)	
13	7	Issues	The Saturdays	Fascination	6		
14		Change	Daniel Merriweather	Allido	2		
15		Whatcha Think About That	The Pussycat Dolls Featuring Missy Elliott	Interscope	6		
16		I'm Yours	Jason Mraz	Elektra	3	(6)	F
17		Circus	Britney Spears	Jive	6	(3)	
18		Sober	P!nk	LaFace	4	(16)	
19		Get On Your Boots	U2	Vertigo	2	(37)	
20	15	Sex On Fire	Kings Of Leon	Hand Me Down	23	(56)	

March 2009

This Mnth	Prev Mnth	Title	Artist	Label	Wks 20	(US Pos)	
1		Poker Face	Lady Gaga feat. Colby O'Donis	Interscope	18	(1)	
2		My Life Would Suck Without You	Kelly Clarkson	RCA	8	(1)	
3		Love Story	Taylor Swift	Mercury	8	(4)	F
4		Right Round	Flo Rida Featuring Ke$ha	Atlantic	9	1)	
5		Just Can't Get Enough	The Saturdays	Fascination	5		
6		Dead And Gone	T.I. Featuring Justin Timberlake	Atlantic	9	(2)	
7		Barry Islands In The Stream	Vanessa Jenkins & Bryn West Feat. Tom Jones & Robin Gibb	Mercury	2		F
8	1	The Fear	Lily Allen	EMI	12	(80)	
9	2	Just Dance	Lady Gaga	Interscope	17	(1)	F
10	7	Use Somebody	Kings Of Leon	Hand Me Down	20	(4)	
11	11	T-Shirt	Shontelle	Universal	6	(36)	F
12		Beautiful	Akon Featuring Colby O'Donis & Kardinal Offishall	Universal	7		
13	15	Whatcha Think About That	The Pussycat Dolls Featuring Missy Elliott	Interscope	6		
14	3	Breathe Slow	Alesha Dixon	Asylum	9		
15	10	Omen	The Prodigy	Take Me To The Hospital	7		
16		Halo	Beyoncé	Columbia	12	(5)	
17		Falling Down	Oasis	Big Brother	1		
18	6	Broken Strings	James Morrison Featuring Nelly Furtado	Polydor	16		
19		In For The Kill	La Roux	Polydor	19		F
20	8	Crack A Bottle	Eminem/Dr. Dre/50 Cent	Interscope	5	(1)	

![US 2009 JAN-MAR logo]

US 2009 JAN-MAR

January 2009

This Mnth	Prev Mnth	Title	Artist	Label	Wks 20	(UK Pos)	
1	3	Just Dance	Lady Gaga Featuring Colby O'donis	Streamline/Konlive/Interscope	26	(1)	PF
2	2	Single Ladies (Put A Ring On It)	Beyoncé	Music World/Columbia	16	(7)	P
3	1	Live Your Life	T.I. Featuring Rihanna	Def Jam/Grand Hustle	20	(2)	P
4	14	Heartless	Kanye West	Rock-A-Fella/Def Jam	22	(11)	P
5	15	Love Story	Taylor Swift	Big Machine	33	(2)	P
6	6	Hot N Cold	Katy Perry	Capitol	24	(4)	P
7	8	Womanizer	Britney Spears	Jive	17	(3)	
8	12	I'm Yours	Jason Mraz	Atlantic	27	(11)	P
9	9	Love Lockdown	Kanye West	Rock-A-Fella/Def Jam	17	(8)	P
10	16	Let It Rock	Kevin Rudolf Featuring Lil Wayne	Cash Money/Univeral Republic	20	(5)	PF
11	4	Whatever You Like	T.I.	Grand Hustle/Atlantic	23	(47)	P
12		Gives You Hell	All-American Rejects	Doghouse/DGC/Interscope	22	(18)	
13	7	Circus	Britney Spears	Jive	17	(13)	
14	5	If I Were A Boy	Beyoncé	Music World/Columbia	11	(1))	P
15	13	Right Now (Na Na Na)	Akon	SRC/Universal Motown	1	(6)	G
16		I Hate This Part	The Pussycat Dolls	Interscope	6	(12)	
17	11	So What	P!nk	LaFace/Zomba	22	(1)	
18	10	Miss Independent	Ne-Yo	Def Jam/IDJMG	18	(6)	G
19	17	Gotta Be Somebody	Nickelback	Roadrunner/RRP	17	(20)	
20	20	You Found Me	Fray	Epic/Sony Music	23	(35)	P

February 2009

This Mnth	Prev Mnth	Title	Artist	Label	Wks 20	(UK Pos)	
1		My Life Would Suck Without You	Kelly Clarkson	RCA	16	(1)	
4	2	Heartless	Kanye West	Rock-A-Fella/def Jam	22	(11)	P
3	1	Just Dance	Lady Gaga Featuring Colby O'donis	Streamline/Konlive/Interscope	26	(1)	PF
4	2	Single Ladies (Put A Ring On It)	Beyoncé	Music World/Columbia	16	(7)	P
5		Dead And Gone	T.I. Featuring Justin Timberland	Grand Hustle/Atlantic	18	(4)	P
6	5	Love Story	Taylor Swift	Big Machine	33	(2)	P
7	12	Gives You Hell	All-American Rejects	Doghouse/DGC/Interscope	22	(18)	
8		Crack A Bottle	Eminem/Dr. Dre/50 Cent	Shady/Aftermath/Interscope	6	(4)	
9	20	You Found Me	Fray	Epic/Sony Music	23	(35)	P
10		Right Round	Flo Rida	Poe Boy/Atlantic	18	(1)	P
11	3	Live Your Life	T.I. Featuring Rihanna	Def Jam/Grand Hustle	20	(2)	P
12	13	Circus	Britney Spears	Jive	17	(13)	
13	8	I'm Yours	Jason Mraz	Atlantic	27	(11)	P
14		Poker Face	Lady Gaga	Streamline/Konlive/Interscope	24	(1)	
15	16	I Hate This Part	The Pussycat Dolls	Interscope	6	(12)	
16	10	Let It Rock	Kevin Rudolf Featuring Lil Wayne	Cash Money/Univeral Republic	20	(5)	PF
17	6	Hot N Cold	Katy Perry	Capitol	24	(4)	P
18		Mad	Ne-Yo	Def Jam/IDJMG	12	(19)	G
19		Viva La Vida	Coldplay	Capitol	21	(1)	P
20		Sober	P!nk	LaFace/JLG	11	(9)	

March 2009

This Mnth	Prev Mnth	Title	Artist	Label	Wks 20	(UK Pos)	
1	10	Right Round	Flo Rida	Poe Boy/Atlantic	18	(1)	P
2	5	Dead And Gone	T.I. Featuring Justin Timberland	Grand Hustle/Atlantic	18	(4)	P
3	14	Poker Face	Lady Gaga	Streamline/Konlive/Interscope	24	(1)	
4	2	Heartless	Kanye West	Rock-A-Fella/def Jam	22	(11)	P
5	7	Gives You Hell	All-American Rejects	Doghouse/DGC/Interscope	22	(18)	
6		Kiss Me Thru The Phone	Soulja Boy Tell'em Featuring Sammie	Collipark/Interscope	15	(6)	
7	1	My Life Would Suck Without You	Kelly Clarkson	RCA	16	(1)	
8	3	Just Dance	Lady Gaga Featuring Colby O'donis	Streamline/Konlive/Interscope	26	(1)	PF
9	8	Crack A Bottle	Eminem, Dr. Dre & 50 Cent	Shady/Aftermath/Interscope	6	(4)	
10	6	Love Story	Taylor Swift	Big Machine	33	(2)	P
11		Blame It	Jamie Foxx Featuring T-Pain	J/RMG	18		G
12		The Climb	Miley Cyrus	Walt Disney/Hollywood	20	(11)	P
13	18	Mad	Ne-Yo	Def Jam/IDJMG	12	(19)	G
14	9	You Found Me	Fray	Epic/Sony Music	23	(35)	P
15	12	Circus	Britney Spears	Jive	17	(13)	
16	4	Single Ladies (Put A Ring On It)	Beyoncé	Music World/Columbia	16	(7)	P
17		Here Comes Goodbye	Rascal Flatts	Lyric Street	1		
18		Turnin' Me On	Keri Hilson Featuring Lil Wayne	Mosley/Zone 4/Interscope	8		
19	20	Sober	P!nk	LaFace/JLG	11	(9)	
20		Jai Ho! (You Are My Destiny)	A R Rahman & The Pussycat Dolls Featuring Nicole Scherzinger	Interscope	1	(3)	F

▲ Robert Plant and Alison Krauss scooped five Grammy awards, including Album of the Year for 'Raising Sand'.

◆ Kelly Clarkson won the first season of *American Idol*. Her "blast of rock-tinged pop" rose from No.97 to No.1, making Clarkson the first person to set two records for the biggest climb to No.1 on the Hot 100 ('A Moment Like This' jumped from No.52 to No.1 in 2002).

◆ Based on a sample of Dead Or Alive's 'You Spin Me Round (Like A Record)', Flo Rida's broke his own one-week digital sales record with an incredible 636,000 units for 'Right Round', which will become the fastest one-, two- and three-million selling download in chart history.

UK 2009
APR–JUNE

◆ Tinchy Stryder's prophetic 'Number 1', the first song title containing the words 'number one' to reach the top spot, brought back memories of The Verve's 'Bitter Sweet Symphony' by sampling the strings from 'The Last Time' by the Andrew Oldham Orchestra.

◆ Bob Dylan's seventh No.1 album, 'Together Through Life', gave him the longest span of UK No.1s in chart history, 44 years and one month since 'The Freewheelin' Bob Dylan' hit No.1 in April 1965.

◆ Michael Jackson's 'Number Ones' (2003) collection topped the album chart following his sudden death on 25th June. The following week, it will be replaced at No.1 by 'The Essential Michael Jackson' (2005), the UK's best-selling album for seven consecutive weeks. On the singles side, 'Man In The Mirror', a No.21 hit from 1988, will be the most successful of his numerous re-entries, stalling at No.2.

April 2009

This Mnth	Prev Mnth	Title	Artist	Label	Wks 20	(US Pos)	
1	1	Poker Face	Lady Gaga	Interscope	18	(1)	
2		Don't Upset The Rhythm (Go Baby Go)	Noisettes	Vertigo	7		F
3		Jai Ho! (You Are My Destiny)	A.R. Rahman & The Pussycat Dolls Feat. Nicole Scherzinger	Polydor	12	(15)	F
4	19	In For The Kill	La Roux	Polydor	19		F
5	16	Halo	Beyoncé	Columbia	12	(5)	
6	4	Right Round	Flo Rida Featuring Ke$ha	Atlantic	9	(1)	
7		I'm Not Alone	Calvin Harris	Columbia	9		
8		Shake It	Metro Station	Columbia	8	(10)	F
9	3	Love Story	Taylor Swift	Mercury	8	(4)	F
10		Love Sex Magic	Ciara Featuring Justin Timberlake	Geffen	8	(10)	
11	6	Dead And Gone	T.I. Featuring Justin Timberlake	Atlantic	9	(2)	
12	12	Beautiful	Akon Featuring Colby O' Donis & Kardinal Offishall	Universal	7		
13		Not Fair	Lily Allen	Regal	12		
14	2	My Life Would Suck Without You	Kelly Clarkson	RCA	8	(1)	
15		We Made You	Eminem	Polydor	9	(9)	
16		Show Me Love	Steve Angello & Laidback Luke Featuring Robin S	Data	3		F
17		Takin' Back My Love	Enrique Iglesias Featuring Ciara	Interscope	8		
18	9	Just Dance	Lady Gaga	Interscope	17	(1)	F
19		Fields Of Anfield Road	Liverpool Collective/The Kop Choir	Robot	3		F
20	5	Just Can't Get Enough	The Saturdays	Fascination	5		

May 2009

This Mnth	Prev Mnth	Title	Artist	Label	Wks 20	(US Pos)	
1		Number 1	Tinchy Stryder Featuring N-Dubz	4th & Broadway	10		
2	4	In For The Kill	La Roux	Polydor	19		F
3	7	I'm Not Alone	Calvin Harris	Columbia	9		
4	15	We Made You	Eminem	Polydor	9	(9)	
5	1	Poker Face	Lady Gaga	Interscope	18	(1)	
6		Tiny Dancer (Hold Me Closer)	Ironik Featuring Chipmunk & Elton John	Asylum	5		
7	13	Not Fair	Lily Allen	Regal	12		
8	10	Love Sex Magic	Ciara Featuring Justin Timberlake	Geffen	8	(10)	
9		Boom Boom Pow	The Black Eyed Peas	Interscope	14	(1)	
10	3	Jai Ho! (You Are My Destiny)	A.R. Rahman & The Pussycat Dolls Feat. Nicole Scherzinger	Polydor	12	(15)	F
11		Bonkers	Dizzee Rascal Featuring Armand Van Helden	Dirtee Stank	10		
12	5	Halo	Beyoncé	Columbia	12	(5)	
13		Warrior's Dance	The Prodigy	Take Me To The Hospital	7		
14		Red	Daniel Merriweather	J	11		
15		The Climb	Miley Cyrus	Polydor	5	(6)	
16		Kiss Me Thru The Phone	Soulja Boy Tell'em Featuring Sammie	Interscope	7	(3)	
17	2	Don't Upset The Rhythm (Go Baby Go)	Noisettes	Vertigo	7		F
18		Please Don't Leave Me	P!nk	RCA	4	(17)	
19	8	Shake It	Metro Station	Columbia	8	(10)	F
20		Rubber Lover	Marmaduke Duke	14th Floor	4		F

June 2009

This Mnth	Prev Mnth	Title	Artist	Label	Wks 20	(US Pos)	
1	9	Boom Boom Pow	The Black Eyed Peas	Interscope	14	(1)	
2	11	Bonkers	Dizzee Rascal Featuring Armand Van Helden	Dirtee Stank	10		
3		Release Me	Agnes	3 Beat	10		F
4	14	Red	Daniel Merriweather	J	11		
5		Mama Do (Uh Oh, Uh Oh)	Pixie Lott	Mercury	5		F
6		Knock You Down	Keri Hilson Featuring Kanye West & Ne-Yo	Polydor	11	(3)	
7	1	Number 1	Tinchy Stryder Featuring N-Dubz	4th & Broadway	10		
8		When Love Takes Over	David Guetta Featuring Kelly Rowland	Positiva	11	(76)	
9		Fire	Kasabian	Columbia	4		
10	16	Kiss Me Thru The Phone	Soulja Boy Tell'em Featuring Sammie	Interscope	7	(3)	
11		Untouched	The Veronicas	Sire	8	(17)	F
12	2	In For The Kill	La Roux	Polydor	19		F
13		Paparazzi	Lady Gaga	Interscope	12	(6)	
14	7	Not Fair	Lily Allen	Regal	12		
15	4	We Made You	Eminem	Polydor	9	(9)	
16	5	Poker Face	Lady Gaga	Interscope	18	(1)	
17		Said It All	Take That	Polydor	1		
18		New In Town	Little Boots	Sixsevenine	3		F
19		Battlefield	Jordin Sparks	Jive	8	(10)	
20		We Are The People	Empire Of The Sun	EMI	3		F

April 2009

This Mnth	Prev Mnth	Title	Artist	Label	Wks 20	(UK Pos)	
1	3	Poker Face	Lady Gaga	Streamline/Konlive/Interscope	24	(1)	
2	1	Right Round	Flo Rida	Poe Boy/Atlantic	18	(1)	P
3	6	Kiss Me Thru The Phone	Soulja Boy Tell'em Featuring Sammie	Collipark/Interscope	15	(6)	
4	2	Dead And Gone	T.I. Featuring Justin Timberlake	Grand Hustle/Atlantic	18	(4)	P
5	11	Blame It	Jamie Foxx Featuring T-Pain	J/RMG	18		G
6		Boom Boom Pow	The Black Eyed Peas	Will.I.Am/Interscope	24	(1)	P
7	5	Gives You Hell	All-American Rejects	Doghouse/DGC/Interscope	22	(18)	
8	7	My Life Would Suck Without You	Kelly Clarkson	RCA	16	(1)	
9	12	The Climb	Miley Cyrus	Walt Disney/Hollywood	20	(11)	P
10		Day 'n' Nite	Kid Cudi	Fool's Gold/Universal	14	(2)	F
11	8	Just Dance	Lady Gaga Feat. Colby O'Donis	Streamline/Konlive/Interscope	26	(1)	PF
12	14	You Found Me	Fray	Epic/Sony Music	23	(35)	P
13	4	Heartless	Kanye West	Rock-A-Fella/Def Jam	22	(11)	P
14		Love Sex Magic	Ciara Featuring Justin Timberlake	LaFace/JLG	3	(5)	
15		I Love College	Asher Roth	Schoolboy/Loud/SCR	6	(26)	GF
16		I Told You So	Carrie Underwood Featuring Randy Travis	19/Arista Nashville	1		
17	10	Love Story	Taylor Swift	Big Machine	33	(2)	P
18	13	Mad	Ne-Yo	Def Jam/IDJMG	12	(19)	G
19	18	Turnin' Me On	Keri Hilson Featuring Lil Wayne	Mosley/Zone 4/Interscope	8		
20		Halo	Beyoncé	Music World/Columbia	17	(4)	G

May 2009

This Mnth	Prev Mnth	Title	Artist	Label	Wks 20	(UK Pos)	
1	6	Boom Boom Pow	Black Eyed Peas	Will.I.Am/Interscope	24	(1)	P
2	1	Poker Face	Lady Gaga	Streamline/Konlive/Interscope	24	(1)	
3	5	Blame It	Jamie Foxx Featuring T-Pain	J/RMG	18		G
4	10	Day 'n' Nite	Kid Cudi	Fool's Gold/Universal	14	(2)	F
5	2	Right Round	Flo Rida	Poe Boy/Atlantic	18	(1)	P
6	3	Kiss Me Thru The Phone	Soulja Boy Tell'em Featuring Sammie	Collipark/Interscope	15	(6)	
7	9	The Climb	Miley Cyrus	Walt Disney/Hollywood	20	(11)	P
8	20	Halo	Beyoncé	Music World/Columbia	17	(4)	G
9		Sugar	Flo Rida Featuring Wynter	Poe Boy/Atlantic	10	(18)	G
10		I Know You Want Me (Calle Ocho)	Pitbull	Ultra	18	(4)	F
11		Don't Trust Me	3oh!3	Photo Finish/Atlantic	16	(21)	PF
12	4	Dead And Gone	T.I. Featuring Justin Timberlake	Grand Hustle/Atlantic	18	(4)	P
13		We Made You	Eminem	Web/Shady/Aftermath/Interscope	3	(4)	
14	7	Gives You Hell	All-American Rejects	Doghouse/DGC/Interscope	22	(18)	
15		Birthday Sex	Jeremih	Mick Shultz/Def Jam	14	(15)	F
16	12	You Found Me	Fray	Epic/Sony Music	23	(35)	P
17	8	My Life Would Suck Without You	Kelly Clarkson	RCA	16	(1)	
18		Second Chance	Shinedown	Atlantic	13	(74)	GF
19	11	Just Dance	Lady Gaga Feat. Colby O'Donis	Streamline/Konlive/Interscope	26	(1)	PF
20		Waking Up In Vegas	Katy Perry	Capitol	17	(19)	

June 2009

This Mnth	Prev Mnth	Title	Artist	Label	Wks 20	(UK Pos)	
1	1	Boom Boom Pow	Black Eyed Peas	Will.I.Am/Interscope	24	(1)	P
2	10	I Know You Want Me (Calle Ocho)	Pitbull	Ultra	18	(4)	F
3	2	Poker Face	Lady Gaga	Streamline/Konlive/Interscope	24	(1)	
4		Knock You Down	Keri Hilson Featuring Kanye West & Ne-Yo	Mosley/Zone 4/Interscope	21	(5)	
5	15	Birthday Sex	Jeremih	Mick Shultz/Def Jam	14	(15)	F
6	3	Blame It	Jamie Foxx Featuring T-Pain	J/RMG	18		G
7	8	Halo	Beyoncé	Music World/Columbia	17	(4)	G
8		Lovegame	Lady Gaga	Streamline/Konlive/Interscope	13		
9	4	Day 'n' Nite	Kid Cudi	Fool's Gold/Universal	14	(2)	F
10		Fire Burning	Sean Kingston	Beluga Heights/Epic	16	(12)	G
11		I Gotta Feeling	Black Eyed Peas	Interscope		(1)	P
12	18	Second Chance	Shinedown	Atlantic	13	(74)	GF
13		Don't Stop Believin'	Glee Cast	Fox/Columbia	1		F
14	20	Waking Up In Vegas	Katy Perry	Capitol	17	(19)	
15		New Divide	Linkin Park	Machine Shop/Warner Bros	7	(19)	G
16	7	The Climb	Miley Cyrus	Walt Disney/Hollywood	20	(11)	P
17	11	Don't Trust Me	3oh!3	Photo Finish/Atlantic	16	(21)	PF
18		No Boundaries	Kris Allen	19/Jive/JLG	1		F
19	9	Sugar	Flo Rida Featuring Wynter	Poe Boy/Atlantic	10		G
20		Goodbye	Kristinia Debarge	Sodapop/Island/IDJMG	4.		F

US
2009
APR-JUNE

▲ The death of Michael Jackson, 50, stunned the world. Posthumous records set – he died less than three weeks before the scheduled start of his residency at the O2 Arena – included the most entries on the Hot Digital Songs chart (26) and the first act to sell more than one million downloads in a week (2.6 million).

◆ 'Wall of Sound' producer Phil Spector was found guilty of murdering actress Lana Clarkson and was jailed for 19 years.

◆ Jamie Foxx and T-Pain racked up 14 consecutive weeks at No.1 on the Hot R&B/Hip-Hop Songs chart with the heavily Auto-Tuned 'Blame It' - a male record equalled later in 2009 by Maxwell's 'Pretty Wings'.

UK 2009 JULY-SEPT

▲ JLS (Jack the Lad Swing) scored the second fastest-selling single of 2009 to date with 'Beat Again', which debuted at No.1 with sales of 106,299. Only Dizzee Rascal's 'Bonkers' had a healthier opening week.

◆ 'Evacuate The Dancefloor', the song that denied Michael Jackson a posthumous No.1, was the first UK chart-topper for Cascada, fronted by German-born Natalie Horler.

◆ At 92 years and five months, 'Forces Sweetheart' Vera Lynn became the oldest living artist in the world to have a chart-topping album. 'The Very Best Of Vera Lynn – We'll Meet Again' outsold the the Arctic Monkeys, Jamie.T, the Kings Of Leon and a host of Beatles re-issues.

July 2009

This Mnth	Prev Mnth	Title	Artist	Label	Wks 20	(US Pos)	
1		Bulletproof	La Roux	Polydor	10		
2	8	When Love Takes Over	David Guetta Featuring Kelly Rowland	Positiva	11	(76)	
3		Evacuate The Dancefloor	Cascada	All Around The World	9		
4		Man In The Mirror	Michael Jackson	Epic	5		
5	13	Paparazzi	Lady Gaga	Interscope	12	(6)	
6	1	Boom Boom Pow	The Black Eyed Peas	Interscope	14	(1)	
7	6	Knock You Down	Keri Hilson Featuring Kanye West & Ne-Yo	Polydor	11	(3)	
8	3	Release Me	Agnes	3 Beat	10		F
9		I Gotta Feeling	The Black Eyed Peas	Polydor		(1)	
10		Beat Again	JLS	Epic	8		F
11	5	Mama Do (Uh Oh, Uh Oh)	Pixie Lott	Mercury	5		F
12		Diamond Rings	Chipmunk Featuring Emeli Sande	Jive	5		
13	4	Red	Daniel Merriweather	J	11		
14	2	Bonkers	Dizzee Rascal Featuring Armand Van Helden	Dirtee Stank	10		
15	11	Untouched	The Veronicas	Sire	8		F
16		Poppiholla	Chicane	Modena	5		
17		I Know You Want Me (Calle Ocho)	Pitbull	Positiva/Virgin	8	(4)	F
18	19	Battlefield	Jordin Sparks	Jive	8	(10)	
19		Billie Jean	Michael Jackson	Epic	1		
20		Rabbit Heart (Raise It Up)	Florence + The Machine	Island	7		F

August 2009

This Mnth	Prev Mnth	Title	Artist	Label	Wks 20	(US Pos)	
1	9	I Gotta Feeling	The Black Eyed Peas	Polydor		(1)	
2	10	Beat Again	JLS	Epic	8		F
3		Supernova	Mr Hudson Featuring Kanye West	Mercury	8		F
4		Sweet Dreams	Beyoncé	RCA	10		
5		Never Leave You	Tinchy Stryder Feat. Amelle	4th & Broadway	7		
6	17	I Know You Want Me (Calle Ocho)	Pitbull	Positiva/Virgin	8	(4)	F
7	3	Evacuate The Dancefloor	Cascada	All Around The World	9		
8	1	Bulletproof	La Roux	Polydor	10		
9		Ready For The Weekend	Calvin Harris	Columbia	5		
10	2	When Love Takes Over	David Guetta Featuring Kelly Rowland	Positiva	11	(76)	
11	5	Paparazzi	Lady Gaga	Interscope	12	(6)	
12		Sexy Chick	David Guetta Featuring Akon	Positiva/Virgin			
13		Behind Closed Doors	Peter Andre	Conehead	2		
14		Remedy	Little Boots	Atlantic	8		
15		Get Shaky	Ian Carey Project	All Around The World	6		F
16	16	Poppiholla	Chicane	Modena	5		
17		Outta Here	Esmée Denters	Interscope	4		F
18	12	Diamond Rings	Chipmunk Featuring Emeli Sande	Jive	5		
19	18	Battlefield	Jordin Sparks	Jive	8	(10)	
20	6	Boom Boom Pow	The Black Eyed Peas	Interscope	14	(1)	

September 2009

This Mnth	Prev Mnth	Title	Artist	Label	Wks 20	(US Pos)	
1	12	Sexy Chick	David Guetta Featuring Akon	Positiva/Virgin			
2		Holiday	Dizzee Rascal	Dirtee Stank	6		
3	1	I Gotta Feeling	The Black Eyed Peas	Polydor		(1)	
4		Run This Town	Jay-Z Featuring Rihanna & Kanye West	Roc Nation	7	(2)	
5		Get Sexy	Sugababes	Island	5		
6		Boys And Girls	Pixie Lott	Mercury	6		
7	14	Remedy	Little Boots	Atlantic	8		
8	5	Never Leave You	Tinchy Stryder Feat. Amelle	4th & Broadway	7		
9		Break Your Heart	Taio Cruz	Island			
10	9	Ready For The Weekend	Calvin Harris	Columbia	5		
11		We Are Golden	Mika	Island	3		
12	4	Sweet Dreams	Beyoncé	RCA	10		
13		Celebration	Madonna	Warner Bros	3		
14		Sex On Fire	Kings Of Leon	Hand Me Down	23	(56)	
15	17	Outta Here	Esmée Denters	Interscope	4		F
16		Left My Heart In Tokyo	Mini Viva	Xenomania/Geffen	4		F
17		She Wolf	Shakira	Epic		(11)	
18	3	Supernova	Mr Hudson Featuring Kanye West	Mercury	8		F
19		Uprising	Muse	Helium 3/Warner Bros	3	(37)	
20		Fire Burning	Sean Kingston	Epic	7	(5)	

This Mnth	Prev Mnth	Title	Artist	Label	Wks 20	(UK Pos)	
1	11	I Gotta Feeling	The Black Eyed Peas	Interscope		(1)	P
2	1	Boom Boom Pow	The Black Eyed Peas	Will.I.Am/Interscope	24	(1)	P
3		Best I Ever Had	Drake	Young Money/Cash Money	16		F
4	4	Knock You Down	Keri Hilson Featuring Kanye West & Ne-Yo	Mosley/Zone 4/Interscope	21	(5)	
5	8	Lovegame	Lady Gaga	Streamline/Konlive/Interscope	13		
6	10	Fire Burning	Sean Kingston	Beluga Heights/Epic	16	(12)	G
7	2	I Know You Want Me (Calle Ocho)	Pitbull	Ultra	18	(4)	F
8	5	Birthday Sex	Jeremih	Mick Shultz/Def Jam	14	(15)	F
9		You Belong With Me	Taylor Swift	Big Machine		(30)	P
10	14	Waking Up In Vegas	Katy Perry	Capitol	17	(19)	
11	15	New Divide	Linkin Park	Machine Shop/Warner Bros	7	(19)	G
12	12	Second Chance	Shinedown	Atlantic	13	(74)	GF
13	17	Don't Trust Me	3oh!3	Photo Finish/Atlantic	16	(21)	PF
14		Every Girl	Young Money	Young Money/Cash Money	8		F
15	3	Poker Face	Lady Gaga	Streamline/Konlive/Interscope	24	(1)	
16	7	Halo	Beyoncé	Music World/Columbia	17	(4)	G
17		He Could Be The One	Hannah Montana	Walt Disney	1		F
18		Obsessed	Mariah Carey	Island/IDJMG	16	(56)	
19		Fallin' For You	Colbie Caillat	Universal Republic	3		
20	16	The Climb	Miley Cyrus	Walt Disney/Hollywood	20	(11)	P

This Mnth	Prev Mnth	Title	Artist	Label	Wks 20	(UK Pos)	
1	1	I Gotta Feeling	The Black Eyed Peas	Interscope	1		P
2	3	Best I Ever Had	Drake	Young Money/Cash Money	16		F
3	9	You Belong With Me	Taylor Swift	Big Machine	30		P
4	4	Knock You Down	Keri Hilson Featuring Kanye West & Ne-Yo	Mosley/Zone 4/Interscope	21	(5)	
5		Use Somebody	Kings Of Leon	RCA	2		GF
6	6	Fire Burning	Sean Kingston	Beluga Heights/Epic	16	(12)	G
7	2	Boom Boom Pow	Black Eyed Peas	Will.I.Am/Interscope	24	(1)	P
8		Good Girls Go Bad	Cobra Starship Featuring Leighton Meester	Decaydance/Fueled By Ramen	11	(17)	GF
9	5	Lovegame	Lady Gaga	Streamline/Konlive/Interscope	13		
10		Down	Jay Sean Featuring Lil Wayne	Cash Money/Universal	3		GF
11	10	Waking Up In Vegas	Katy Perry	Capitol	17	(19)	
12		Party In The U.S.A.	Miley Cyrus	Hollywood		(11)	
13	7	I Know You Want Me (Calle Ocho)	Pitbull	Ultra	18	(4)	F
14		Run This Town	Jay-Z, Rihanna & Kanye West	Roc Nation	1		
15		Hotel Room Service	Pitbull	Mr./Polo Grounds/J/RMG	10	(9)	
16	8	Birthday Sex	Jeremih	Mick Shultz/Def Jam	14	(15)	F
17		Battlefield	Jordin Sparks	19/Jive/Zomba	8	(11)	
18	18	Obsessed	Mariah Carey	Island/IDJMG	16	(56)	
19	14	Every Girl	Young Money	Young Money/Cash Money	8		F
20		She Wolf	Shakira	Sony Music Latin/Epic	9	(4)	

This Mnth	Prev Mnth	Title	Artist	Label	Wks 20	(UK Pos)	
1	1	I Gotta Feeling	The Black Eyed Peas	Interscope	1		P
2	10	Down	Jay Sean Featuring Lil Wayne	Cash Money/Universal	3		GF
3	12	Party In The U.S.A.	Miley Cyrus	Hollywood	11		
4	14	Run This Town	Jay-Z, Rihanna & Kanye West	Roc Nation	1		
5	5	Use Somebody	Kings Of Leon	RCA	2		GF
6	3	You Belong With Me	Taylor Swift	Big Machine	30		P
7	2	Best I Ever Had	Drake	Young Money/Cash Money	16		F
8	18	Obsessed	Mariah Carey	Island/IDJMG	16	(56)	
9	15	Hotel Room Service	Pitbull	Mr./Polo Grounds/J/RMG	10	(9)	
10	4	Knock You Down	Keri Hilson Featuring Kanye West & Ne-Yo	Mosley/Zone 4/Interscope	21	(5)	
11		Whatcha Say	Jason Derulo	Beluga Heights/Warner Bros			F
12	8	Good Girls Go Bad	Cobra Starship Featuring Leighton Meester	Decaydance/Fueled By Ramen	11	(17)	GF
13	20	She Wolf	Shakira	Sony Music Latin/Epic	9	(4)	
14	17	Battlefield	Jordin Sparks	19/Jive/Zomba	8	(11)	
15		Break Up	Mario Feat. Gucci Mane & Sean Garrett	3rd Street/J/RMG	10		
16	11	Waking Up In Vegas	Katy Perry	Capitol	17	(19)	
17		Throw It In The Bag	Fabolous Featuring The-Dream	Desert Storm/Def Jam	6		
18	7	Boom Boom Pow	Black Eyed Peas	Will.I.Am/Interscope	24	(1)	P
19		Fallin' For You	Colbie Caillat	Universal Republic	3		
20	6	Fire Burning	Sean Kingston	Beluga Heights/Epic	16	(12)	G

US
2009
JULY-SEPT

◆ Mariah Carey, Usher and Stevie Wonder were among the performers at Michael Jackson's star-studded memorial concert at the Staples Center in Los Angeles, where his family and friends paid emotional tributes to the 'King of Pop'.

◆ The Black Eyed Peas smashed the record (previously held by Usher) for consecutive weeks at No.1 on the Billboard Hot 100, locking down the top spot for 26 weeks with 'Boom Boom Pow' (12 weeks) and 'I Gotta Feeling' (14 weeks). Chart headlines in the Peas' record-breaking 20th week on top were shared with Jason Mraz's 'I'm Yours', which spent its 70th week on the countdown to oust LeAnn Rimes' 'How Do I Live' from the record books.

◆ The Black Eyed Peas' No.1 reign was extinguished by Jay Sean, the first British urban artist to crown the Hot 100. 'Down' went up to No.1 in its 14th chart week.

455

◆ Boyzone singer Stephen Gately, 33, died suddenly at his apartment in Majorca. A post mortem revealed that he died due to pulmonary oedema.

◆ Surprisingly, Rage Against The Machine's 1993 hit 'Killing In The Name', the first download-only Christmas No.1, shifted more than 500,000 units in the wake of a Facebook campaign supported by 'friends' determined to end the X Factor's Xmas No.1 monopoly. The X Factor final attracted 19 million viewers and more than 10 million votes, but Joe McElderry's 'The Climb' had to settle for No.2 (although it climbed to No.1 the following week).

◆ Lady Gaga's 'Poker Face' (800,000) and Susan Boyle's I Dreamed A Dream (1.5 million) were the top-selling single and album of 2009. A record 4.22 million singles (98% of them digital) were sold in the last week of 2009.

October 2009

This Mnth	Prev Mnth	Title	Artist	Label	Wks 20	(US Pos)	
1	9	Break Your Heart	Taio Cruz	Island	7		
2		Empire State Of Mind	Jay-Z + Alicia Keys	Roc Nation	12	(1)	
3	1	Sexy Chick	David Guetta Featuring Akon	Positiva/Virgin	11	(6)	
4	17	She Wolf	Shakira	Epic	7	(11)	
5	3	I Gotta Feeling	The Black Eyed Peas	Polydor	20	(1)	
6		Oopsy Daisy	Chipmunk	Jive	5		
7		Bad Boys	Alexandra Burke Featuring Flo Rida	Syco Music	7		
8		Forever Is Over	The Saturdays	Fascination	3		
9		Sweet Disposition	The Temper Trap	Infectious	7		F
10		Bodies	Robbie Williams	Virgin	3		
11	4	Run This Town	Jay-Z Featuring Rihanna & Kanye West	Roc Nation	7	(2)	
12		Fight For This Love	Cheryl Cole	Fascination	9		
13		Million Dollar Bill	Whitney Houston	Arista	6	(100)	
14	6	Boys And Girls	Pixie Lott	Mercury	6		
15		Hotel Room Service	Pitbull	J	5	(8)	
16	13	Celebration	Madonna	Warner Bros	3	(71)	
17		Haven't Met You Yet	Michael Bublé	Reprise	6	(65)	
18	2	Holiday	Dizzee Rascal	Dirtee Stank	6		
19		Dirtee Cash	Dizzee Rascal	Dirtee Stank	3		
20	16	Left My Heart In Tokyo	Mini Viva	Xenomania/Geffen	4		F

November 2009

This Mnth	Prev Mnth	Title	Artist	Label	Wks 20	(US Pos)	
1		Meet Me Halfway	The Black Eyed Peas	Interscope	9	(7)	
2	12	Fight For This Love	Cheryl Cole	Fascination	9		
3		Everybody In Love	JLS	Epic	5		
4		Down	Jay Sean Featuring Lil Wayne	Island	6	(1)	
5	7	Bad Boys	Alexandra Burke Featuring Flo Rida	Syco Music	7		
6		What About Now	Westlife	S	5		
7		Happy	Leona Lewis	Syco Music	4	(50)	
8		Tik Tok	Ke$ha	RCA	6	(2)	
9		You Are Not Alone	The X Factor Finalists	Syco Music	5		
10	17	Haven't Met You Yet	Michael Bublé	Reprise	6	(65)	
11		Bad Romance	Lady Gaga	Interscope	8	(2)	
12		I Need You	N-Dubz	AATW/UMTV	3		
13		Whatcha Say	Jason Derulo	Warner Bros	5	(1)	F
14		3	Britney Spears	Jive	3	(1)	
15	6	Oopsy Daisy	Chipmunk	Jive	5		
16	13	Million Dollar Bill	Whitney Houston	Arista	6	(100)	
17	5	I Gotta Feeling	The Black Eyed Peas	Polydor	20	(1)	
18		About A Girl	Sugababes	Island	2		
19	2	Empire State Of Mind	Jay-Z + Alicia Keys	Roc Nation	12	(1)	
20		End Credits	Chase & Status Featuring Plan B	Vertigo	2		F

December 2009

This Mnth	Prev Mnth	Title	Artist	Label	Wks 20	(US Pos)	
1		The Official Children In Need Medley	Peter Kay's All Star Band	Epic	5		
2	11	Bad Romance	Lady Gaga	Interscope	8	(2)	
3		Russian Roulette	Rihanna	Def Jam	4	(9)	
4	9	You Are Not Alone	The X Factor Finalists	Syco Music	5		
5	1	Meet Me Halfway	The Black Eyed Peas	Interscope	9	(7)	
6	13	Whatcha Say	Jason Derulo	Warner Bros	5	(1)	F
7	8	Tik Tok	Ke$ha	RCA	6	(2)	
8		Killing In The Name	Rage Against The Machine	Epic	1		
9		The Climb	Joe McElderry	Syco Music	1		F
10		Morning After Dark	Timbaland Featuring Nelly Furtado	Interscope	3	(61)	
11	2	Fight For This Love	Cheryl Cole	Fascination	9		
12		Doesn't Mean Anything	Alicia Keys	J	3	(60)	
13		You Know Me	Robbie Williams	Virgin	5		
14		Starstrukk	3OH!3 Featuring Katy Perry	Photo Finish/Atlantic	1	(66)	F
15		3 Words	Cheryl Cole Feat. Will.I.Am	Fascination	2		
16		Wild Horses	Susan Boyle	Syco Music	2	(98)	F
17		Let The Bass Kick In Miami Girl	Chuckie & LMFAO	CR2	2		F
18	7	Happy	Leona Lewis	Syco Music	4	(50)	
19		Don't Stop Believin'	Journey	Columbia	2		F
20		Cry Me Out	Pixie Lott	Mercury	4		

October 2009

This Mnth	Prev Mnth	Title	Artist	Label	Wks 20	(UK Pos)	
1	2	Down	Jay Sean Featuring Lil Wayne	Cash Money/Universal	20	(3)	GF
2	1	I Gotta Feeling	The Black Eyed Peas	Interscope	27	(1)	P
3	3	Party In The U.S.A.	Miley Cyrus	Hollywood	18	(11)	
4	4	Run This Town	Jay-Z, Rihanna & Kanye West	Roc Nation	15	(1)	
5	11	Whatcha Say	Jason Derulo	Beluga Heights/Warner Bros	16	(3)	F
6	6	You Belong With Me	Taylor Swift	Big Machine	26	(30)	P
7		Paparazzi	Lady Gaga	Streamline/Konlive	14	(4)	
8		Empire State Of Mind	Jay-Z + Alicia Keys	Roc Nation	13	(2)	
9		3	Britney Spears	Jive	10	(7)	
10	5	Use Somebody	Kings Of Leon	RCA	23	(2)	GF
11	8	Obsessed	Mariah Carey	Island/IDJMG	16	(56)	
12		Forever	Drake Featuring Kanye West, Lil Wayne & Eminem	Harvey Mason/Zone 4	13	(43)	
13		Fireflies	Owl City	Universal Republic	11		GF
14		Sweet Dreams	Beyoncé	Music World/Columbia	13	(5)	
15		Meet Me Halfway	The Black Eyed Peas	Interscope	10	(1)	
16		Cowboy Casanova	Carrie Underwood	19/Arista Nashville	4		
17	9	Hotel Room Service	Pitbull	Mr./Polo Grounds	10	(9)	
18	13	She Wolf	Shakira	Sony Music Latin/Epic	9	(4)	
19		Replay	Iyaz	Beluga Heights/Reprise	10		F
20	18	Boom Boom Pow	The Black Eyed Peas	Will.I.Am/Interscope	24	(1)	P

November 2009

This Mnth	Prev Mnth	Title	Artist	Label	Wks 20	(UK Pos)	
1	13	Fireflies	Owl City	Universal Republic	11		GF
2	5	Whatcha Say	Jason Derulo	Beluga Heights/Warner Bros	16	(3)	F
3	8	Empire State Of Mind	Jay-Z + Alicia Keys	Roc Nation	13	(2)	
4	1	Down	Jay Sean Featuring Lil Wayne	Cash Money/Universal	20	(3)	GF
5	3	Party In The U.S.A.	Miley Cyrus	Hollywood	18	(11)	
6	19	Replay	Iyaz	Beluga Heights/Reprise	10		F
7	7	Paparazzi	Lady Gaga	Streamline/Konlive	14	(4)	
8	9	3	Britney Spears	Jive	10	(7)	
9	4	Run This Town	Jay-Z, Rihanna & Kanye West	Roc Nation	15	(1)	
10	15	Meet Me Halfway	The Black Eyed Peas	Interscope	10	(1)	
11		Need You Now	Lady Antebellum	Capitol Nashville	5		
12	14	Sweet Dreams	Beyoncé	Music World/Columbia	13	(5)	
13	2	I Gotta Feeling	The Black Eyed Peas	Interscope	27	(1)	P
14		Bad Romance	Lady Gaga	Streamline/Konlive/c	7	(1)	
15	6	You Belong With Me	Taylor Swift	Big Machine	26	(30)	P
16		Tik Tok	Ke$ha	Kasz Money/RCA/RMG	7	(5)	F
17		Russian Roulette	Rihanna	SRP/Def Jam/IDJMG	3	(2)	
18		Sexy Chick	David Guetta Featuring Akon	Gum/Astralwerks	8	(1)	F
19		Jump Then Fall	Taylor Swift	Big Machine	1		
20	12	Forever	Drake Featuring Kanye West, Lil Wayne & Eminem	Harvey Mason/Zone 4	13	(43)	

December 2009

This Mnth	Prev Mnth	Title	Artist	Label	Wks 20	(UK Pos)	
1	3	Empire State Of Mind	Jay-Z + Alicia Keys	Roc Nation	13	(2)	
2	14	Bad Romance	Lady Gaga	Streamline/Konlive	7	(1)	
3	16	Tik Tok	Ke$ha	Kasz Money/RCA/RMG	7	(5)	F
4	1	Fireflies	Owl City	Universal Republic	11		GF
5	6	Replay	Iyaz	Beluga Heights/Reprise	10		F
6	2	Whatcha Say	Jason Derulo	Beluga Heights/Warner Bros	16	(3)	F
7	18	Sexy Chick	David Guetta Featuring Akon	Gum/Astralwerks	8	(1)	F
8	10	Meet Me Halfway	The Black Eyed Peas	Interscope	10	(1)	
9	7	Paparazzi	Lady Gaga	Streamline/Konlive	14	(4)	
10	8	3	Britney Spears	Jive	10	(7)	
11	4	Down	Jay Sean Featuring Lil Wayne	Cash Money/Universal	20	(3)	GF
12	5	Party In The U.S.A.	Miley Cyrus	Hollywood	18	(11)	
13	12	Sweet Dreams	Beyoncé	Music World/Columbia	13	(5)	
14		Already Gone	Kelly Clarkson	19/RCA/RMG	3	(75)	
15	20	Forever	Drake Featuring Kanye West, Lil Wayne & Eminem	Harvey Mason/Zone 4	13	(43)	
16	11	Need You Now	Lady Antebellum	Capitol Nashville	5		
17		How Low	Ludacris	DTP/Def Jam/IDJMG	1		
18	13	I Gotta Feeling	The Black Eyed Peas	Interscope	27	(1)	P
19	15	You Belong With Me	Taylor Swift	Big Machine	26	(30)	P
20		Do You Remember	Jay Sean Featuring Sean Paul & Lil Jon	Cash Money/Universal	2		

◆ Owl City (Adam Young), who channelled his insomnia into music-making in his parents' Minnesota basement, soared to the top with 'Fireflies', the most-downloaded song from the US iTunes store.

◆ Scottish singer Susan Boyle, who dreamed a dream on reality TV show Britain's Got Talent, became the fastest-selling female debutant in US chart history with first-week sales of 701,000 for 'I Dreamed A Dream'. Snoop Doggy Dogg's 'Doggystyle' (1993), the fastest-selling debut album in the US, sold 803,000 copies in the first week.

◆ '1' by The Beatles was the top-selling US album of the noughties (11,499,000 units), according to Nielsen Soundscan. 'No Strings Attached' (*NSync), 'Come Away With Me' (Norah Jones) and 'The Marshall Mathers LP' (Eminem) also sold more than 10 million copies during the decade.

Code to Nationalities

A	Austria	JAP	Japan
AUS	Australia	KEN	Kenya
B	Belgium	L	Lebanon
BA	Barbados	M	Moldova
BRA	Brazil	N	Norway
C	Canada	NZ	New Zealand
CO	Colombia	P	Puerto Rica
CZ	Czech Rep.	R	Romania
D	Denmark	S	Sweden
F	France	SA	South Africa
FIN	Finland	SE	Senegal
G	Germany	SPA	Spain
GRE	Greece	SWI	Switzerland
GUY	Guyana	TUR	Turkey
H	Holland	UK	United Kingdom
HUN	Hungary	US	United States
I	Ireland	WI	West Indies
ICE	Iceland	Y	Yugoslavia
ISR	Israel	ZIM	Zimbabwe
ITA	Italy	❖	Shared hit
J	Jamaica	★	Re-entry

	US Top 20 Ent	UK Top 20 Ent
A+ (US)		
Enjoy Yourself		2/99
A*Teens (S)		
Bouncing Off The Ceiling	1/01	
Dancing Queen	7/00	
A1 (UK/N)		
Be The First To Believe		7/99
Caught In The Middle		2/02
Everytime/Ready Or Not		11/99
No More		3/01
Same Old Brand New You		11/00
Take On Me		09/00
AALIYAH (US)		
At Your Best (You Are Love)	9/94	
Back & Forth	5/94	
If Your Girl Only Knew	9/96	
Miss You	12/02	
More Than A Woman		1/02
Rock The Boat	11/01	
The One I Gave My Heart To	10/97	
Try Again		08/00
ABBA (S/N)		
Angel Eyes/Voulez Vous		8/79
Chiquitita		2/79
Dancing Queen	2/77	9/76
Does Your Mother Know		5/79
Fernando	11/76	4/76
Gimme Gimme Gimme (A Man After Midnight)		10/79
I Do, I Do, I Do, I Do, I Do	4/76	
I Have A Dream		12/79
Knowing Me Knowing You	7/77	3/77
Lay All Your Love On Me		7/81
Mamma Mia		1/76
Money Money Money		12/76
The Name Of The Game	3/78	11/77
One Of Us		12/81
S.O.S.		10/75
Summer Night City		9/78
Super Trouper		11/80
Take A Chance On Me	5/78	2/78
Waterloo	7/74	4/74
The Winner Takes It All	2/81	8/80
Russ ABBOT (UK)		
Atmosphere		1/85
Gregory ABBOTT (US)		
Shake You Down	12/86	12/86
ABC (UK)		
All of My Heart		9/82
Be Near Me	11/85	
The Look Of Love (Part 1)		5/82
Poison Arrow		3/82
When Smokey Sings	9/87	6/87
Paula ABDUL (US)		
Blowing Kisses In The Wind	11/91	
Cold Hearted	8/89	
Forever Your Girl	5/89	
(It's Just) The Way You Love Me	11/89	
The Promise Of A New Day	8/91	
Rush Rush	6/91	7/91
Straight Up	1/89	3/89
Vibeology	2/92	
Paula ABDUL (duet with The Wild Pair) (US)		
Opposites Attract	1/90	4/90
Colonel ABRAMS (US)		
Trapped		10/85
ABS (UK)		
What You Got		8/02
ABS (UK) featuring NODESHA		
Miss Perfect		9/3
ABSOLUTELY FABULOUS (UK)		
Absolutely Fabulous		6/94
AC/DC (AUS/UK)		
Heatseeker		1/88
Let's Get It Up		2/82
Rock 'n' Roll Ain't Noise Pollution		12/80
ACE OF BASE (S)		
All That She Wants	10/93	5/93
Cruel Summer	8/98	10/98
Don't Turn Around	5/94	6/94
Life Is A Flower		7/98
The Sign	2/94	2/94
ACE (UK)		
How Long	5/75	
Johnny ACE (US)		
Pledging My Love	3/55	

	US Top 20 Ent	UK Top 20 Ent
AD LIBS (US)		
The Boy From New York City	2/65	
ADAM & THE ANTS (UK)		
Ant Rap		12/81
Antmusic		12/80
Deutscher Girls		3/82
Dog Eat Dog		11/80
Kings Of The Wild Frontier		3/81
Prince Charming		9/81
Stand And Deliver		5/81
Young Parisians		2/81
ADAM ANT (UK)		
Friend Or Foe		10/82
Goody Two Shoes	1/83	5/82
Puss 'n' Boots		11/83
Room At The Top	5/90	
Bryan ADAMS (C)		
Can't Stop This Thing We Started	10/91	
Cloud Number 9		5/99
Do I Have To Say The Words?	9/92	
(Everything I Do) I Do It For You	7/91	7/91
Have You Ever Really Loved A Woman?	5/95	4/95
Heat Of The Night	5/87	
Heaven	5/85	
Here I Am		7/02
One Night Love Affair	11/85	
Please Forgive Me	11/93	10/93
Run To You	12/84	2/85
Somebody	4/85	
Straight From The Heart	5/83	
Summer Of '69	8/85	
Thought I'd Died And Gone To Heaven	5/92	2/92
Bryan ADAMS & Mel C (C/UK)		
When You're Gone		12/98
Bryan ADAMS & Tina Turner (C/US)		
It's Only Love	1/86	
Bryan ADAMS/Rod Stewart/Sting (C/UK)		
All For Love	12/93	1/94
Oleta ADAMS (US)		
Get Here	3/91	2/91
ADAMSKI (UK)		
Killer		4/90
The Space Jungle		9/90
Cannonball ADDERLEY (US)		
Mercy, Mercy, Mercy	2/67	
ADELE (UK)		
Chasing Pavements		1/08
Trace ADKINS (US)		
You're Gonna Miss This	4/08	
ADVENTURES OF STEVIE V (UK)		
Dirty Cash		5/90
AEROSMITH (US)		
Angel	4/88	
Cryin'	9/93	
Dream On	3/76	
Dude (Looks Like A Lady)	12/87	
Jaded	4/01	
Janie's Got A Gun	1/90	
I Don't Want To Miss A Thing	9/98	9/98
Love In An Elevator	10/89	
Walk This Way	1/77	
What It Takes	4/90	
AFTER 7 (US)		
Can't Stop	10/90	
Ready Or Not	6/90	
AFTER THE FIRE (UK)		
Der Kommissar	4/83	
AFTERSHOCK (US)		
Slave To The Vibe		9/93
AFROMAN (US)		
Because I Got High	9/01	10/01
Crazy Rap		2/02
AGNES (US)		
Release Me		6/09
Christina AGUILERA (US)		
Ain't No Other Man	7/06	9/03
Beautiful	12/02	3/03
Come On Over Baby	10/00	11/00
Fighter		6/03
Genie In A Bottle	7/99	10/99
I Turn To You	7/00	
Keeps Gettin' Better	10/08	
What A Girl Wants	1/00	2/00
featuring Lil' Kim		
Can't Hold Us Down	9/03	9/03
❖ *featuring Redman*		
Dirrty		11/02
featuring Missy Elliott		

	US Top 20 Ent	UK Top 20 Ent
Car Wash		11/04
❖ Christina AGUILERA, LIL' KIM, MYA & PINK (US)		
Lady Marmalade	5/01	6/01
A-HA (N)		
AN		
Analogue (All I Want)	7/06	2/06
Cry Wolf		12/86
Hunting High And Low		6/86
I've Been Losing You		10/86
The Living Daylights		7/87
Stay On These Roads		4/88
The Sun Always Shines On TV		1/86
Take On Me	9/85	10/85
Touchy!		9/88
Train Of Thought		4/86
You Are The One		1/89
Clay AIKEN (US)		
Solitaire	4/04	
This Is The Night	6/03	
AIR SUPPLY (AUS/UK)		
All Out Of Love	8/80	11/80
Even The Nights Are Better	7/82	
Every Woman In The World	12/80	
Here I Am (Just When You Thought I Was Over You)	10/81	
Lost In Love	4/80	
Making Love Out Of Nothing At All	9/83	
The One That You Love	6/81	
Sweet Dreams	2/82	
Jewel AKENS (US)		
The Birds And The Bees	3/65	
AKON (SE)		
Belly Dancer (Bananza)	/	8/5
Lonely	4/5	5/5
featuring Eminem		
Smack That	10/6	11/6
featuring Snoop Dogg		
I Wanna Love You	12/6	2/07
featuring Styles P. (SE)		
Locked Up	9/04	3/05
AKON (US)		
Don't Matter	3/07	5/07
Right Now (Na Na Na)	11/08	12/08
Sorry, Blame It On Me	8/07	
AKON feat. Colby O'DONIS & Kardinal OFFISHALL (US)		
Beautiful	3/09	
Morris ALBERT (BRA)		
Feelings	10/75	10/75
ALESSI (US)		
Oh Lori		7/77
Tatyana ALI (US)		
Daydreamin'	8/98	11/98
Tatyana ALI & Will Smith (US)		
Boy You Knock Me Out	2/99	
ALIAS (US)		
More Than Words Can Say	11/90	
Waiting For Love	3/91	
ALICE DEEJAY (H)		
Back In My Life		12/99
Will I Ever		7/00
ALIEN ANT FARM (US)		
Movies		2/02
Smooth Criminal		9/1
ALISHA'S ATTIC (UK)		
The Incidentals		9/98
ALIVE & KICKING (US)		
Tighter, Tighter	7/70	
ALIZEE (F)		
Moi...Lolita	2/02	
ALL ABOUT EVE (UK)		
Martha's Harbour		8/88
ALL-AMERICAN REJECTS (US)		
Gives You Hell	1/09	
All-4-One (US)		
I Can Love You Like That	7/95	
I Swear	5/94	6/94
So Much In Love	2/94	
Donna ALLEN (US)		
Serious		6/87
Allisons (UK)		
Are You Sure		3/61
ALLMAN BROTHERS BAND (US)		
Ramblin' Man	9/73	
ALL SAINTS (UK/C)		
Black Coffee		10/00
Bootie Call		9/98
Never Ever		7/98
Pure Shores		2/00
Rock Steady		11/06
Under The Bridge/Lady Marmalade		**5/98**
War Of Nerves		12/98
ALL-AMERICAN REJECTS (US)		
Dirty Little Secret	1/06	
It Ends Tonight	11/06	
ALLURE with 112 (US)		
All Cried Out	9/97	
Kris ALLEN (US)		
No Boundaries	6/09	
Lily ALLEN (UK)		
Ldn		10/06
Not Fair		4/09
The Fear		2/09
Smile		7/06
Marc ALMOND (UK)		
The Days Of Pearly Spencer		5/92
❖ with Bronski Beat		
I Feel Love		4/85
Marc ALMOND featuring Gene Pitney (UK/US)		
Something's Gotten Hold Of My Heart		1/89
Herb ALPERT (US)		
Diamonds	6/87	
The Lonely Bull	11/62	
Rise	9/79	
Spanish Flea		1/66
A Taste Of Honey	11/65	
This Guy's In Love With You	6/68	7/68
Zorba The Greek	2/66	
ALPHABEAT (D)		
Fascination		3/08
ALPHAVILLE (G)		
Big In Japan		9/84
ALTERED IMAGES (UK)		
Don't Talk To Me About Love		4/83
Happy Birthday		10/81
I Could Be Happy		1/82
See Those Eyes		4/82
ALTERN 8 (UK)		
Activ 8 (Come With Me)		11/91
Evapor 8		4/92
ALTHIA AND DONNA (J)		
Uptown Top Ranking		1/78
Shola AMA (UK)		
You Might Need Somebody		4/97
You're The One I Love		8/97
AMAZING RHYTHM ACES (US)		
Third Rate Romance	9/75	
AMAZULU (UK)		
Excitable		8/85
Montego Bay		10/86
Too Good To Be Forgotten		6/86
AMBASSADORS OF FUNK featuring MC Mario (US)		
Supermarioland		11/92
AMBOY DUKES (US)		
Journey To The Center Of The Mind	8/68	
AMBROSIA (US)		
Biggest Part Of Me	5/80	
How Much I Feel	10/78	
You're The Only Woman (You & I)	9/80	
AMEN CORNER (UK)		
Bend Me, Shape Me		2/68
Gin House Blues		8/67
Hello Susie		7/69
High In The Sky		8/68
(If Paradise Is) Half As Nice		2/69
AMERICA (US)		
A Horse With No Name	3/72	1/72
I Need You	7/72	
Lonely People	2/75	
Sister Golden Hair	5/75	
Tin Man	11/74	
Ventura Highway	11/72	
You Can Do Magic	9/82	
AMERICAN BREED (US)		
Bend Me, Shape Me	12/67	
AMERICAN IDOL FINALISTS (US)		
God Bless The USA	5/03	
AMERIE (US)		
1 Thing	4/05	6/05
Take Control	5/07	
AMES BROTHERS (US)		
It Only Hurts For A Little While	7/56	
The Man With The Banjo	4/54	
Melodie D'Amour	11/57	
My Bonnie Lassie	10/55	
The Naughty Lady Of Shady Lane	12/54	2/55
You You You	1/54	
Ed AMES (US)		
My Cup Runneth Over	3/67	
Vanessa AMOROSI (AUS)		
Absolutely Everybody		09/00
Tori AMOS (US)		
Cornflake Girl		1/94
Pretty Good Year		3/94
ANASTACIA (US)		
I'm Outta Love		10/00
Left Outside Alone		4/04
Sick And Tired		8/04
Angry ANDERSON (AUS)		
Suddenly		12/88
Bill ANDERSON (US)		
Still	6/63	
Carl ANDERSON with Gloria Loring (US)		
❖ Friends And Lovers	8/86	
Laurie ANDERSON (US)		
O Superman		10/81
Lynn ANDERSON (US)		
Rose Garden	1/71	3/71
Peter ANDRE (UK)		
All About Us		8/97
Behind Closed Doors		8/09
Flava		9/96
I Feel You		12/96
Insania		6/04
Lonely		11/97
Mysterious Girl		3/04
Natural		3/97
featuring Bubbler Ranx		
Mysterious Girl		6/96
Chris ANDREWS (UK)		
To Whom It Concerns		1/66
Yesterday Man		10/65
Michael ANDREWS featuring Gary Jules (US)		
Mad World		12/03
ANEKA (UK)		
Japanese Boy		8/81
Steve ANGELLO & Laidback Luke FEAT. Robin S (GRE/H/US)		
Show Me Love		4/09
ANGELS (US)		
My Boyfriend's Back	8/63	
ANGEL CITY (US)		
Do You Know (I Go Crazy)		10/04
Ashley Parker ANGEL (US)		
Let U Go	5/06	
ANIMALS (UK)		
Bring It On Home To Me		5/65
Don't Bring Me Down	7/66	6/66
Don't Let Me Be Misunderstood		2/65
House Of The Rising Sun	8/64	7/64
House Of The Rising Sun		10/82
I'm Crying		10/64
Inside-Looking Out		3/66
It's My Life		11/65
We Gotta Get Out Of This Place		7/65
Eric Burdon & The ANIMALS (UK)		
Help Me Girl		11/66
Monterey	1/68	
San Franciscan Nights	9/67	11/67
See See Rider	10/66	
When I Was Young	5/67	
ANIMOTION (US)		
Obsession	4/85	6/85
Room To Move	4/89	
Paul ANKA (C)		
(All Of A Sudden) My Heart Sings	2/59	2/59
Dance On Little Girl	7/61	
Diana	8/57	8/57
I Love You Baby		11/57
It's Time To Cry	12/59	
Lonely Boy	6/59	8/59
Love Me Warm And Tender	4/62	
My Home Town	6/60	
Puppy Love	3/60	
Put Your Head On My Shoulder	9/59	11/59
Times Of Your Life	12/75	
You Are My Destiny	2/58	2/58
Paul ANKA with Odia COATES (C/US)		
I Believe There's Nothing Stronger Than Our Love	9/75	
I Don't Like To Sleep Alone	5/75	
One Man Woman/One Woman Man	1/75	
(You're) Having My Baby	8/74	10/74

	US Top 20 Ent	UK Top 20 Ent
STEVIE B (US)		
Because I Love You (The Postman Song)	11/90	3/91
B-15 Project featuring Crissy D & Lady G. (UK)		
Girls Like Us		6/00
B.V.S.M.P. (US)		
I Need You		8/88
BABY D (UK)		
(Everybody's Got To Learn Sometime) I Need		
Your Loving		6/95
Let Me Be Your Fantasy		11/94
So Pure		1/96
BABY BASH (US)		
❖ *featuring FRANKIE J*		
Suga Suga	10/03	
BABY BASH (US) featuring T-PAIN		
Cyclone	10/07	
BABY SHAMBLES (UK)		
Delivery		9/07
Fuck Forever		8/05
Killamangiro		12/04
BABYFACE (US)		
Everytime I Close My Eyes	2/97	
It's No Crime	10/89	
❖ *with Jon B.*		
Someone To Love	6/95	
When Can I See You	8/94	
BABYFACE with LL Cool J (US)		
This Is For The Lover In You	10/96	
Whip Appeal	4/90	
BABYLON ZOO (UK)		
Spaceman		1/96
BABYS (UK)		
Every Time I Think Of You	3/79	
Isn't It Time	12/77	
BACCARA (SPA)		
Sorry I'm A Lady		2/78
Yes Sir I Can Boogie		10/77
Burt BACHARACH (US)		
Trains And Boats And Planes		6/65
BACHELORS (I)		
Charmaine		3/63
Diane	6/64	2/64
I Believe		4/64
I Wouldn't Trade You For The World		9/64
Marie		6/65
No Arms Could Ever Hold You		12/64
Ramona		6/64
The Sound Of Silence		4/66
BACHMAN-TURNER OVERDRIVE (C)		
Takin' Care Of Business	8/74	
You Ain't Seen Nothin' Yet	10/74	12/74
BACKSTREET BOYS (US)		
All I Have To Give	2/99	
Drowning		1/02
Everybody (Backstreet's Back)	4/98	
I Want It That Way		5/99
Incomplete	5/05	7/05
Just Want You To Know		11/05
Larger Than Life		11/99
Quit Playing Games With My Heart	7/97	
Shape Of My Heart		11/00
Show Me The Meaning Of Being Lonely		3/00
BAD BOYS INC (UK)		
More To This World		5/94
BAD COMPANY (UK)		
Can't Get Enough	10/74	
Feel Like Makin' Love	9/75	
Rock 'n' Roll Fantasy	6/79	
BADDIEL, SKINNER & THE LIGHTNING SEEDS (UK)		
3 Lions		6/06
3 Lions 98		6/98
Three Lions		6/96
BAD ENGLISH (UK/US)		
Price Of Love	2/90	
When I See You Smile	10/89	
BAD MANNERS (UK)		
Can Can		7/81
Just A Feeling		4/81
Lip Up Fatty		8/80
My Girl Lollipop (My Boy Lollipop)		8/82
Special Brew		11/80
Walkin' In The Sunshine		10/81
BADFINGER (UK)		
Baby Blue	4/72	
Come And Get It	4/70	1/70
Day After Day	1/72	2/72
No Matter What	12/70	12/71
Erykah BADU (US)		
Bag Lady	10/00	
On & On	2/97	
Southern Girl	09/99	
❖ *featuring Common*		
Love Of My Life (An Ode To Hip Hop)	11/02	
Joan BAEZ (US)		
The Night They Drove Old Dixie Down	9/71	11/71
There But For Fortune		7/65
BAHA MEN (Bar)		
Who Let The Dogs Out	8/00	11/00
You All Dat	2/01	
Corinne BAILEY RAE (UK)		
Put Your Records On		3/06
Philip BAILEY with Phil Collins (US/UK)		
Easy Lover	1/85	3/85
Merril BAINBRIDGE (AUS)		
Mouth	10/96	
Adrian BAKER (UK)		
Sherry		8/75
Anita BAKER (US)		
Giving You The Best That I Got	11/88	
Sweet Love	10/86	
George BAKER SELECTION (H)		
Paloma Blanca		10/75
Lavern BAKER (US)		
I Cried A Tear	2/59	
Long John BALDRY (UK)		
Let The Heartaches Begin		11/67
Mexico		11/68
Marty BALIN (US)		
Hearts	7/81	
Kenny BALL (UK)		
The Green Leaves Of Summer		6/62
March Of The Siamese Children		2/62
Midnight In Moscow	3/62	11/61
Samantha		3/61
So Do I		8/62
Sukiyaki		2/63
Michael BALL (UK)		
Love Changes Everything		2/89
HANK BALLARD & THE MIDNIGHTERS (UK)		
Finger Poppin' Time	8/60	
Let's Go, Let's Go, Let's Go	11/60	
BALTIMORA (I)		
Tarzan Boy		8/85
BAMBOO (I)		
Bamboogie		1/98
BANANARAMA (UK)		
Cruel Summer	9/84	7/83
I Heard A Rumour	9/87	
I Want You Back		4/88
Love In The First Degree		10/87
Na Na Hey Hey Kiss Him Goodbye		3/83
Robert De Niro's Waiting		3/84
Shy Boy		7/82
Venus	8/86	7/86
❖ *with Fun Boy Three (UK)*		
It Ain't What You Do It's The Way That You Do It		3/82
Really Saying Something		5/82
BANANARAMA/LA NA NEE NEE NOO NOO (UK)		
Help		3/89
BAND AID (UK/I)		
Do They Know It's Christmas?	1/85	12/84
★ Do They Know It's Christmas?		12/85
BAND AID II (UK/AUS)		
Do They Know It's Christmas?		12/89
BAND AID 20 (UK)		
Do They Know It's Christmas?		12/04
BANDAGED (SIR TERRY WOGAN & ALED JONES) (UK)		
Little Drummer Boy/Peace On Earth		12/08
BANGLES (US)		
Eternal Flame	3/89	4/89
Hazy Shade Of Winter	1/88	3/88
In Your Room	12/88	
Manic Monday	3/86	3/86
Walk Like An Egyptian	11/86	10/86
Walking Down Your Street	4/87	
Lloyd BANK$ (US)		
On Fire	6/04	
Lloyd BANK$ featuring Avant		
Karma	1/05	
David BANNER (US)		
Play	9/05	
Pato BANTON (UK)		
Baby Come Back		10/94
Chris BARBER JAZZ BAND (UK)		
Petite Fleur (Little Flower)	2/59	2/59
BARDO (UK)		
One Step Further		4/82
BOBBY Bare (US)		
All American Boy	1/59	
500 Miles Away From Home	11/63	
Sara BAREILLES (US)		
Love Song	1/08	6/08
BARENAKED LADIES (C)		
One Week	10/98	2/99
Pinch Me	11/00	
Gary BARLOW (UK)		
Forever Love		7/96
Love Won't Wait		5/97
Open Road		11/97
JJ BARRIE (C)		
No Charge		5/76
BARRON KNIGHTS (UK)		
Call Up The Groups		7/64
Live In Trouble		11/77
Merrie Gentle Pops		1/66
Pop Go The Workers		4/65
A Taste Of Aggro		12/78
John BARRY SEVEN (UK)		
Walk Don't Run		9/60
Len BARRY (US)		
Like A Baby		2/66
1-2-3	11/65	11/65
BASEMENT JAXX (UK)		
Red Alert		5/99
Rendez-Vu		8/99
Romeo		6/01
TONI BASIL (US)		
Mickey	11/82	3/82
Fontella BASS (US)		
Rescue Me	11/65	12/65
BASS-O-MATIC (UK)		
Fascinating Rhythm		10/90
Shirley BASSEY (UK)		
As I Love You		1/59
As Long As He Needs Me		8/60
Banana Boat Song		3/57
Climb Ev'ry Mountain		8/61
For All We Know		9/71
Goldfinger	3/65	
I (Who Have Nothing)		10/63
I'll Get By		12/61
Kiss Me Honey Honey Kiss Me		1/59
Never Never Never		3/73
Reach For The Stars		8/61
Something		7/70
What Now My Love		10/62
You'll Never Know		5/61
BASSHEADS (UK)		
Is There Anybody Out There?		11/91
BASSHUNTER (S)		
All I Ever Wanted		7/08
BASSHUNTER Feat. DJ MENTAL THEO'S BAZZHEADZ (S/H)		
Now You're Gone		1/08
Mike BATT (UK)		
Summertime City		9/75
Les BAXTER (US)		
The High And The Mighty	8/54	
The Poor People Of Paris	2/56	
Unchained Melody	4/55	5/55
Wake The Town And Tell The People	8/55	
BAY CITY ROLLERS (US)		
All Of Me Loves All Of You		10/74
Bye Bye Baby		3/75
Give A Little Love		7/75
I Only Want To Be With You	10/76	9/76
Keep On Dancing		10/71
Love Me Like I Love You		4/76
Money Honey	3/76	11/75
Remember (Sha-La-La)		3/74
Saturday Night	12/75	
Shang-A-Lang		5/74
Summerlove Sensation		8/74
You Made Me Believe In Magic	7/77	
BAZUKA (US)		
Dynomite	7/75	
BBMAK (UK)		
Back Here	5/00	
Still On Your Side		5/01
BEACH BOYS (US)		
Barbara Ann	1/66	3/66
Be True To Your School	12/63	

	US Top 20 Ent	UK Top 20 Ent
Think Twice	3/61	
with Dinah Washington		
Baby (You Got What It Takes)	2/60	
A Rockin' Good Way	6/60	
BERLIN (US)		
Take My Breath Away	8/86	11/86
Take My Breath Away		11/90
Elmer BERNSTEIN (US)		
Main Title From 'The Man With The Golden Arm'	4/56	
Staccato's Theme		12/59
BERRI (UK)		
The Sunshine After The Rain		9/95
Chuck BERRY (US)		
Johnny B. Goode	5/58	
Maybellene	8/55	
Memphis Tennessee		10/63
My Ding-A-Ling	10/72	11/72
No Particular Place To Go	7/64	6/64
Rock & Roll Music	11/57	
School Day	4/57	
Sweet Little Sixteen	3/58	
Dave BERRY (UK)		
The Crying Game		9/64
Little Things		4/65
Mama		8/66
Mike BERRY (UK)		
Don't You Think It's Time		1/63
Sunshine Of Your Smile		8/80
Nick BERRY (UK)		
Every Loser Wins		10/86
Heartbeat		6/92
BEVERLEY SISTERS (UK)		
I Saw Mommy Kissing Santa Claus		1/54
Little Donkey		12/59
The Little Drummer Boy		2/59
BEYONCE (US)		
Crazy In Love		7/03
Halo	4/09	3/09
If I Were A Boy	11/08	11/08
Irreplaceable	11/06	11/06
Listen		12/08
Me Myself And I	12/03	
Naughty Girl	4/04	
Ring The Alarm	10/06	
Single Ladies (Put A Ring On It)	12/08	1/09
Sweet Dreams	10/09	8/09
Work It Out		7/02
❖ *featuring Jay-Z (US)*		
Crazy In Love	6/03	
Deja Vu	8/06	9/06
❖ *featuring Sean Paul*		
Baby Boy	8/03	10/03
❖ *featuring Slim Thug*		
Check It On	12/05	1/06
❖ *& SHAKIRA (US/CO)*		
Beautiful Liar	4/07	4/07
B-52'S (US)		
Love Shack	11/89	3/90
Roam	2/90	
BC-52'S (US)		
(Meet) The Flintstones		7/94
BHANGRA KNIGHTS vs HUSAN (UK/H)		
❖ *Husan*		5/03
Bo BICE (US)		
Inside Your Heaven		
BIFFY CLYRO (UK)		
Mountains		9/08
BIG AUDIO DYNAMITE (UK)		
E=MC^2		4/86
BIG BEN BANJO BAND (UK)		
Let's Get Together No. 1		12/54
BIG BOPPER (US)		
Chantilly Lace	10/58	1/59
BIG BROTHER & The Holding Company (US)		
Piece Of My Heart	10/68	
BIG BROVAZ (UK)		
Baby Boy		9/03
Favourite Things		5/03
Nu Flow		10/02
OK		2/3
BIG COUNTRY (UK)		
Chance		9/83
Fields Of Fire (400 Miles)		4/83
Look Away		4/86
Wonderland		1/84
BIG FUN (UK)		
Blame It On The Boogie		8/89
Can't Shake The Feeling		12/89
BIG MOUNTAIN (US)		
Baby I Love Your Way	4/94	6/94
BIG TYMERS (US)		
Still Fly	6/02	
Barry BIGGS (J)		
Side Show		1/77
BILAL (US)		
Soul Sista	01/01	
Acker BILK (UK)		
Aria		9/76
Buona Sera		1/61
Lonely		10/62
Stranger On The Shore	4/62	8/62
Summer Set		2/60
That's My Home		8/61
BILLIE (PIPER) (UK)		
Because We Want To		7/98
Day & Night		5/00
Girlfriend		10/98
Honey To The Bee		4/99
She Wants You		12/98
BILLY & LILLIE (US)		
La Dee Dah		1/58
BILLY JOE & The Checkmates (US)		
Percolator (Twist)	3/62	
BIMBO JET (F)		
El Bimbo		8/75
Jane BIRKIN & Serge GAINSBOURG (UK/F)		
Je T'Aime…Moi Non Plus		9/69
Elvin BISHOP (US)		
Fooled Around And Fell In Love	4/76	
Stephen BISHOP (US)		
On And On	9/77	
BIZ MARKIE (US)		
Just A Friend	3/90	
BIZARRE INC (UK)		
Playing With Knives		11/91
Such A Feeling		10/91
BIZARRE INC featuring Angie Brown (UK)		
I'm Gonna Get You		10/92
BIZZ NIZZ (US/B)		
Don't Miss The Partyline		4/90
BJÖRK (ICE)		
Hyperballad		2/96
It's Oh So Quiet		11/95
BJÖRK & David ARNOLD (Ice/UK)		
Play Dead		10/93
BLACK (UK)		
Sweetest Smile		7/87
Wonderful Life		9/87
Bill BLACK('S) COMBO (US)		
Don't Be Cruel	10/60	
Smokie-Part 2	1/60	
White Silver Sands	4/60	
Cilla BLACK (UK)		
Alfie		4/66
Anyone Who Had A Heart		2/64
Conversations		8/69
Don't Answer Me		6/66
A Fool Am I		11/66
It's For You		8/64
Love's Just A Broken Heart		2/66
Something Tells Me (Something Is Gonna Happen Tonight)		12/71
Step Inside Love		4/68
Surround Yourself With Sorrow		3/69
You're My World		5/64
You've Lost That Lovin' Feelin'		1/65
Jeanne BLACK (US)		
He'll Have To Stay	5/60	
BLACK BOX (Ita)		
Everybody Everybody	10/90	
Fantasy		11/90
I Don't Know Anybody Else		2/90
Ride On Time		8/89
Strike It Up	6/91	
The Total Mix		1/91
BLACKBYRDS (US)		
Walking In Rhythm	4/75	
BLACK EYED PEAS (US)		
Boom Boom Pow	4/09	5/09
Don't Lie	9/05	9/05
Don't Phunk With My Heart	5/05	5/05
Hey Mama		3/04
I Gotta Feeling	6/09	7/09
Meet Me Halfway	10/09	12/09
My Humps	9/05	
Pump It		3/06
Shut Up		12/03
Where Is The Love?	7/03	9/03
My Humps		11/05
BLACK KIDS (US)		
I'm Not Gonna Teach Your Boyfriend How To Dance With You		4/08
BLACKFOOT SUE (UK)		
Standing In The Road		9/72
BLACK GRAPE (UK)		
In The Name Of The Father		8/95
Reverend Black Grape		6/95
BLACK LACE (UK)		
Agadoo		8/84
Do The Conga		12/84
Superman (Gioca Jouer)		10/83
BLACK LEGEND (Ita/UK)		
You See The Trouble With Me		7/00
BLACK SABBATH (UK)		
Paranoid		10/70
BLACK SLATE (UK/J)		
Amigo		10/80
BLACKSTREET (US)		
Before I Let You Go	12/94	
BLACKSTREET AND DR DRE (US)		
No Diggity	10/96	
BLACKSTREET AND MYA		
featuring Ma$e and Blinky Blink (US)		
Take Me There	1/99	12/98
BLACKSTREET AND JANET JACKSON (US)		
Girlfriend/Boyfriend		4/99
Richard BLACKWOOD (UK)		
Mama – Who Da Man?		6/00
Band Of The BLACK WATCH (UK)		
Scotch On The Rocks		10/75
BLANCMANGE (UK)		
Blind Vision		5/83
Don't Tell Me		4/84
Living On The Ceiling		11/82
Billy BLAND (US)		
Let The Little Girl Dance	5/60	5/60
Marcie BLANE (US)		
Bobby's Girl	11/62	
BLAQUE (US)		
808	5/99	
BLAZIN' SQUAD (UK)		
Crossroads		8/02
Flip Reverse		11/03
Here 4 One		2/04
Love On The Line		11/02
Reminisce/Where The Story Ends		2/03
We Just Be Dreamin'		7/03
BLESSID UNION OF SOULS (US)		
I Believe	4/95	
Archie BLEYER (US)		
Hernando's Hideaway	6/54	
Mary J BLIGE (US)		
Be Without You	1/06	
Family Affair	9/01	10/01
No More Drama	2/02	5/02
Not Gon' Cry	2/96	
Real Love	10/92	
❖ *with Method Man*		
I'll Be There For You/You're All I Need To Get By	5/95	
❖ *featuring Ja Rule*		
Rainy Dayz	5/02	
Mary J BLIGE and U2 (US/I)		
One		4/06
BLINK-182 (US)		
All The Small Things	2/00	3/00
I Miss You		3/04
BLOC PARTY (UK)		
Flux		11/07
So Here We Are/Positive Tension		2/05
The Prayer		2/07
Two More Years		10/05
BLOCKSTER (UK/Ita)		
You Should Be…		1/99
BLONDIE (US/UK)		
Atomic		2/80
Call Me	3/80	4/80
Denis		3/78
Dreaming		10/79
Hanging On The Telephone		11/78
Heart Of Glass	4/79	1/79

	US Top 20 Ent	UK Top 20 Ent
(I'm Always Touched By Your) Presence Dear		5/78
Island Of Lost Souls		6/82
Maria		2/99
Picture This		9/78
Rapture	3/81	2/81
Sunday Girl		5/79
The Tide Is High	12/80	11/80
Union City Blue		12/79
BLOOD SWEAT & TEARS (US)		
And When I Die	11/69	
Hi-De-Ho	9/70	
Spinning Wheel	6/69	
You've Made Me So Very Happy	4/69	
BLOODHOUND GANG (US)		
The Bad Touch		4/00
BLOODSTONE (US)		
Natural High	7/73	
Bobby BLOOM (US)		
Montego Bay	11/70	9/70
BLOW MONKEYS (UK)		
Digging Your Scene		3/86
It Doesn't Have To Be This Way	2/87	
BLUE (UK)		
All Rise		6/01
Breath Easy		4/04
Curtain Falls		11/04
Fly By II		3/02
Guilty		11/03
If You Come Back		11/01
One Love	11/02	
Too Close		9/01
U Make Me Wanna		3/03
❖ featuring Elton John		
Sorry Seems To Be The Hardest Word		12/02
Barry BLUE (UK)		
(Dancing) On A Saturday Night		8/73
Do You Wanna Dance		11/73
School Love		3/74
BLUE BOY (UK)		
Remember Me		2/97
BLUE CHEER (US)		
Summertime Blues	4/68	
BLUE MAGIC (US)		
Sideshow	7/74	
BLUE MINK (UK/US)		
Banner Man		6/71
Good Morning Freedom		4/70
Melting Pot		12/69
Randy		7/73
Stay With Me		12/72
BLUE OYSTER CULT (US)		
(Don't Fear) The Reaper	10/76	
BLUE PEARL (UK/US)		
(Can You) Feel The Passion		1/92
Naked In The Rain		7/90
BLUE SWEDE (S)		
Hooked On A Feeling	3/74	
Never My Love	10/74	
BLUEBELLS (UK)		
I'm Falling		5/84
Young At Heart		7/84
★ Young At Heart		3/93
BLUES BROTHERS (US)		
Everybody Needs Somebody To Love		4/90
Soul Man	2/79	
BLUES IMAGE (US)		
Ride Captain Ride	6/70	
BLUES MAGOOS (US)		
(We Ain't Got) Nothin' Yet	1/67	
BLUES TRAVELER (US)		
Run-Around	6/95	
BLUETONES (UK)		
Slight Return		2/96
Colin BLUNSTONE (UK)		
Say You Don't Mind		3/72
James BLUNT (UK)		
Goodbye My Lover		1/06
1973		9/07
You're Beautiful	1/06	6/05
BLUR (UK)		
Country House		8/95
Girls And Boys		3/94
Out Of Time		4/03
Parklife		9/94
Stereotypes		2/96
There's No Other Way		5/91

	US Top 20 Ent	UK Top 20 Ent
Tender		3/99
The Universal		11/95
BO SELECTA (UK)		
Proper Crimbo		12/03
BOB & EARL (US)		
Harlem Shuffle		4/69
BOB & MARCIA (J)		
Pied Piper		7/71
Young Gifted And Black		3/70
BOB THE BUILDER (UK)		
Can We Fix It?		12/00
Mambo No. 5		9/01
BOBBETTES (US)		
Mr Lee	9/57	
BODYROCKERS (UK/A)		
I Like The Way		4/05
BODYROX featuring Luciana (UK)		
Yeah Yeah		11/06
Hamilton BOHANNON (US)		
Disco Stomp		6/75
Marc BOLAN (UK) see T-Rex		
Michael BOLTON (US)		
Can I Touch You...There?		9/95
How Am I Supposed To Live Without You	12/89	2/90
How Can We Be Lovers	4/90	5/90
Love Is A Wonderful Thing	5/91	
Missing You Now	3/92	
Said I Love You...But I Lied	11/93	11/93
(Sittin' On) The Dock Of The Bay	3/88	
Time, Love And Tenderness	8/91	
To Love Somebody	12/92	
When A Man Loves A Woman	11/91	11/91
When I'm Back On My Feet Again	7/90	
BOMB THE BASS (UK)		
Beat Dis		2/88
Megablast/Don't Make Me Wait		9/88
Say A Little Prayer		12/88
Winter In July		8/91
BOMBALURINA (UK)		
Itsy Bitsy Teeny Weeny Yellow Polka Dot Bikini		8/90
BOMFUNK MCs (FIN)		
Freestyler		8/00
BONE THUGS-N-HARMONY (US)		
1st Of Tha Month	9/95	
Look Into My Eyes	6/97	
Tha Crossroads	5/96	
BON JOVI (US)		
Always	10/94	9/94
Bad Medicine	11/88	
Bed Of Roses	3/93	
Born To Be My Baby	1/89	
Dry County		4/94
Everyday		9/02
Have A Nice Day		9/05
I'll Be There For You	4/89	
In These Arms		5/93
It's My Life		6/00
Keep The Faith		10/92
Lay Your Hands On Me	7/89	
Lie To Me		12/95
Livin' On A Prayer	1/87	11/86
Living In Sin	12/89	
Please Come Home For Christmas		12/94
Someday I'll Be Saturday Night		2/95
Something For The Pain		10/95
These Days		3/96
This Ain't A Love Song	8/95	6/95
Wanted Dead Or Alive	5/87	4/87
Who Says You Can't Go Home		6/06
You Give Love A Bad Name	11/86	9/86
Jon BON JOVI (US)		
Blaze Of Glory	8/90	8/90
Miracle	12/90	
Gary US BONDS (US)		
Dear Lady Twist	2/62	
New Orleans	11/60	
Quarter To Three	6/61	8/61
School Is Out	8/61	
This Little Girl	6/81	
Twist, Twist Senora	4/62	
BONE THUGS-N-HARMONY		
❖ featuring AKON (US)		
I Tried	5/07	
BONEY M (WI)		
Belfast		12/77
Boney M Megamix		12/92
Daddy Cool		2/77

	US Top 20 Ent	UK Top 20 Ent
Gotta Go Home/El Lute		9/79
Hooray Hooray It's A Holi-Holiday		5/79
Ma Baker		7/77
Mary's Boy Child-Oh My Lord		12/78
Painter Man		3/79
Rasputin		10/78
Rivers Of Babylon/Brown Girl In The Ring		5/78
Sunny		4/77
Graham BONNETT (UK)		
Night Games		4/81
BONZO DOG DOO-DAH BAND (UK)		
I'm The Urban Spaceman		12/68
Betty BOO (UK)		
Doin' The Doo		6/90
❖ with Beatmasters		
Hey DJ I Can't Dance To That Music You're Playing		8/89
Where Are You Baby?		8/90
BOO RADLEYS (UK)		
Wake Up Boo!		3/95
BOOGIE BOX HIGH (UK)		
Jive Talkin'		7/87
BOOGIE PIMPS (G)		
Somebody To Love		1/04
BOOKER T & The MG's (US)		
Green Onions	9/62	1/80
Hang 'Em High	2/69	
Time Is Tight	4/69	6/69
BOOMTOWN RATS (I)		
Banana Republic		12/80
I Don't Like Mondays		7/79
Like Clockwork		7/78
Looking After Number One		9/77
Mary Of The Fourth Form		12/77
Rat Trap		10/78
She's So Modern		5/78
Someone's Looking At You		2/80
Debby BOONE (US)		
You Light Up My Life	10/77	
Pat BOONE (US)		
Ain't That A Shame	7/55	11/55
April Love/When The Swallows Come Back To Capistrano	11/57	12/57
At My Front Door (Crazy Little Mama)	11/55	
Don't Forbid Me	1/57	2/57
Friendly Persuasion/Chains Of Love	10/56	1/57
I Almost Lost My Mind	6/56	8/56
I'll Be Home	2/56	5/56
If Dreams Came True	8/58	
It's Too Soon To Know	2/58	4/58
Johnny Will		12/61
Love Letters In The Sand	5/57	7/57
The Main Attraction		12/62
Moody River	6/61	7/61
Remember You're Mine/There's A Gold Mine In The Sky	8/57	10/57
Speedy Gonzales	7/62	7/62
Sugar Moon/Cherie I Love You	5/58	7/58
Two Hearts	5/55	
Why Baby Why	3/57	
A Wonderful Time Up There/It's Too Soon To Know	2/58	4/58
Ken BOOTHE (J)		
Crying Over You		1/75
Everything I Own		10/74
BOOTY LUV (UK)		
Boogie 2nite		12/06
Don't Mess With My Man		9/07
Shine		6/07
Boston (US)		
Amanda	10/86	
Don't Look Back	9/78 •	
More Than A Feeling	11/76	
We're Ready	2/87	
Eve BOSWELL (HUN)		
Pickin' A Chicken		1/56
Judy BOUCHER (UK)		
Can't Be With You Tonight		4/87
BOW WOW featuring Chris Brown & Johnta Austin		
Shortie Like Mine	11/06	
BOW WOW featuring Ciara		
Like You	8/05	
BOW WOW featuring Omarion		
Let Me Hold You	7/05	
BOW WOW WOW (UK)		
Go Wild In The Country		3/82
I Want Candy		6/82
Jimmy BOWEN (US)		

	US Top 20 Ent	UK Top 20 Ent
Chris BROWN featuring Lil' Wayne		
Gimme That	6/06	
Chris BROWN featuring T-PAIN (US)		
Kiss Kiss	11/ 07	
Foxy BROWN AND JAY Z (US)		
I'll Be	3/97	
Ian BROWN (UK)		
Dolphins Were Monkeys		2/00
James BROWN (US)		
Cold Sweat (Part 1)	8/67	
Hot Pants (She Got To Use What She Got To Get What She Wants)	8/71	
I Got The Feelin'	4/68	
I Got You (I Feel Good)	11/65	
It's A Man's Man's Man's World	6/66	
Living In America	2/86	2/86
Mother Popcorn (You Got To Have A Mother For Me)	7/69	
Papa's Got A Brand New Bag	8/65	
Say It Loud-I'm Black And I'm Proud	10/68	
Super Bad (Pts 1 & 2)	11/70	
Jocelyn BROWN (US)		
Somebody Else's Guy	5/84	
❖ with Incognito		
Always There	7/91	
❖ with Kym Mazelle		
No More Tears (Enough Is Enough)	6/94	
❖ with Right Said Fred		
Don't Talk Just Kiss		12/91
Joe BROWN & The Bruvvers (UK)		
It Only Took A Minute		12/62
A Picture Of You		6/62
That's What Love Will Do		2/63
Mark BROWN featuring Sarah Cracknell (UK)		
The Journey Continues		2/08
Peter BROWN (US)		
Dance With Me	6/78	
Roy Chubby BROWN (US) see Smokie		
Sam BROWN (UK)		
Stop		2/89
Jackson BROWNE (US)		
Doctor My Eyes	4/72	
Lawyers In Love	8/83	
Runnin' On Empty	4/78	
Somebody's Baby	9/82	
Stay		8/78
Tom BROWNE (US)		
Funkin' For Jamaica (N.Y.)		8/80
BROWNS (US)		
The Old Lamplighter	4/60	
Scarlet Ribbons	12/59	
The Three Bells	8/59	9/59
BROWNSTONE (US)		
If You Love Me	2/95	4/95
BROWNSVILLE STATION (US)		
Smokin' In The Boys Room	12/73	
Dave BRUBECK Quartet (US)		
Take Five		11/61
Tommy BRUCE & The Bruisers (UK)		
Ain't Misbehavin'		6/60
Dora BRYAN (UK)		
All I Want For Christmas Is A Beatle		12/63
Anita BRYANT (US)		
In My Little Corner Of The World	8/60	
Paper Roses	5/60	
Peabo BRYSON (US)		
If Ever You're In My Arms Again	8/84	
❖ with Celine Dion		
Beauty And The Beast	3/92	5/92
Peabo BRYSON & Regina Belle (US)		
A Whole New World (Aladdin's Theme)	1/93	1/94
Peabo BRYSON & Roberta Flack (US)		
Tonight I Celebrate My Love	11/83	9/83
BT EXPRESS (US)		
Do It ('Til You're Satisfied)	11/74	
Express	3/75	
BUBBLE PUPPY (US)		
Hot Smoke & Sasafrass	4/69	
Michael BUBLE (C)		
Haven't Met You Yet		10/09
BUCHANAN & GOODMAN (US)		
The Flying Saucer (Parts 1 & 2)	8/56	
BUCKCHERRY (US)		
Sorry	2/08	
BUCKETHEADS (US)		
The Bomb! (These Sounds Fall Into		

	US Top 20 Ent	UK Top 20 Ent
My Mind)		3/95
Lindsey BUCKINGHAM (US)		
Trouble		12/81
BUCKINGHAMS (US)		
Don't You Care	4/67	
Hey Baby (They're Playing Our Song)	10/67	
Kind Of A Drag	1/67	
Mercy, Mercy, Mercy	7/67	
Susan	1/68	
Jeff BUCKLEY (US)		
Hallelujah		12/08
BUCKNER & GARCIA (US)		
Pac-Man Fever	3/82	
BUCKS FIZZ (UK)		
If You Can't Stand The Heat		1/83
Land Of Make Believe		12/81
Making Your Mind Up		4/81
My Camera Never Lies		4/82
New Beginning (Mamba Seyra)		6/86
Now Those Days Are Gone		7/82
Piece Of The Action		7/81
When We Were Young		7/83
Mutya BUENA (UK)		
Real Girl		6/07
BUFFALO SPRINGFIELD (US)		
For What It's Worth (Stop, Hey What's That Sound)	3/67	
Jimmy BUFFETT (US)		
Margaritaville	6/77	
BUGGLES (UK)		
Video Killed The Radio Star		10/79
B BUMBLE & The Stingers (US)		
Nut Rocker		4/62
Emma BUNTON (UK)		
Downtown		12/06
Take My Breath Away		9/01
What Took You So Long		4/01
Eric BURDON & War (UK/US)		
Spill The Wine	8/70	
Alexandra BURKE (UK)		
Hallelujah		12/08
Alexandra BURKE featuring FLO RIDA (UK/US)		
Bad Boys		10/09
Johnny BURNETTE (US)		
Dreamin'	8/60	10/60
Little Boy Sad	3/61	
You're Sixteen	12/60	1/61
Rocky BURNETTE (US)		
Tired Of Toein' The Line	7/80	
Ray BURNS (UK)		
Mobile		2/55
That's How A Love Song Was Born		9/55
Malandra BURROWS (UK)		
Just This Side Of Love		12/90
Lou BUSCH (US)		
Zambesi		2/56
Kate BUSH (UK)		
Babooshka		7/80
Kate Bush On Stage E.P.		10/79
King Of The Mountain		11/05
Man With The Child In His Eyes		7/78
Rocket Man (I Think It's Going To Be A Long Long Time)		12/91
Rubberband Girl		9/93
Running Up That Hill		8/85
Sat In Your Lap		7/81
Wow		4/79
Wuthering Heights		3/78
❖ with Peter Gabriel		
Don't Give Up		11/86
BUS STOP/CARL DOUGLAS (US/UK)		
Kung Fu Fighting		6/98
BUSTED (UK)		
Air Hostess		5/04
Crashed The Wedding		11/03
Sleeping With The Light On		8/03
Thunderbirds/3AM		8/04
What I Go To School For		9/02
Who's David		2/04
Year 3000		1/03
You Said No		5/03
Jerry BUTLER (US)		
He Will Break Your Heart	11/60	
Moon River	12/61	
Only The Strong Survive	4/69	
Jerry BUTLER & Betty Everett (US)		
Let It Be Me	10/64	
Jerry BUTLER & The Impressions (US)		

	US Top 20 Ent	UK Top 20 Ent
For Your Precious Love	7/58	
Max BYGRAVES (UK)		
Deck Of Cards		11/73
Fings Ain't What They Used T'Be		3/60
Gilly Gilly Ossenfeffer Katzenellenbogen By The Sea		9/54
Heart		4/57
Heart Of My Heart		5/54
Jingle Bell Rock		12/59
Meet Me On The Corner		11/55
You Need Hands/Tulips From Amsterdam		5/58
Max BYGRAVES & The Tanner Sisters (UK)		
Friends And Neighbours		6/54
Charlie BYRD (US) see Stan Getz & Charlie Byrd		
Gary BYRD & The GB Experience (US)		
The Crown		8/83
BYRDS (US)		
All I Really Want To Do	8/65	
Eight Miles High	5/66	
Mr. Tambourine Man	6/65	7/65
Turn! Turn! Turn!	11/65	
Edward BYRNES & Connie Stevens (US)		
Kookie, Kookie (Lend Me Your Comb)	5/59	
Fantastic Johnny C (US)		
Boogaloo Down Broadway	12/67	
Melanie C (UK)		
Goin' Down		10/99
I Turn To You		08/00
Northern Star		12/99
featuring Lisa "Lefteye" Lopes		
Never Be The Same Again		4/00
C&C MUSIC FACTORY feat. Freedom Williams (US)		
Gonna Make You Sweat	1/91	1/91
Things That Make You Go Hmmmm…	8/91	7/91
C&C MUSIC FACTORY feat. Freedom Williams & Zelma Davis (US)		
Here We Go	4/91	
C.C.S. (UK)		
Tap Turns On The Water		9/71
Walkin'		4/71
CABIN CREW (A)		
Star To Fall		3/05
Ryan CABRERA (US)		
On The Way Down	10/04	
CADETS (US)		
Stranded In The Jungle	7/56	
Susan CADOGAN (UK)		
Hurt So Good		5/75
John CAFFERTY & The Beaver Brown Band (US)		
On The Dark Side	10/84	
Bobby CALDWELL (US)		
What You Won't Do For Love	3/79	
Slimm CALHOUN (US)		
It's OK	11/00	
Colbie CAILLAT (US)		
Bubbly	10/07	
Fallin' For You	9/09	
CALLING (US)		
Wherever You Will Go	1/02	7/02
CALLOWAY (US)		
I Wanna Be Rich	4/90	
Eddie CALVERT (UK)		
Cherry Pink And Apple Blossom White		4/55
John And Julie		8/55
Mandy		2/58
Midnight		8/54
Oh, Mein Papa	1/54	1/54
Stranger In Paradise		5/55
Zambesi		3/56
CAMEO (US)		
Back And Forth	5/87	
Single Life		10/85
Word Up	11/86	9/86
Andy CAMERON (UK)		
Ally's Tartan Army		3/78
Ali CAMPBELL (UK)		
That Look In Your Eye		5/95
Glen CAMPBELL (UK)		
Country Boy (You Got Your Feet In LA)	1/76	
Galveston	3/69	6/69
Honey Come Back		5/70
It's Only Make Believe	10/70	12/70
Rhinestone Cowboy	8/75	11/75
Southern Nights	4/77	
Wichita Lineman	11/68	3/69
❖ with Bobbie Gentry		
All I Have To Do Is Dream		12/69
Junior CAMPBELL (UK)		

	US Top 20 Ent	UK Top 20 Ent
Everlasting Love		03/98
CAST OF HIGH SCHOOL MUSICAL (US)		
Breaking Free		10/6
CASUALS (UK)		
Jesamine		9/68
CATATONIA (UK)		
Dead From The Waist Down		4/99
Mulder and Scully		1/98
Road Rage		5/98
George CATES (US)		
Moonglow And Theme From 'Picnic'	5/56	
CATHY JEAN & The Roommates (US)		
Please Love Me Forever	4/61	
CERRONE (F)		
Supernatura		8/78
Peter CETERA (US) with Cher		
After All	5/89	
Glory Of Love	7/86	9/86
One Good Woman	9/88	
Peter CETERA & Amy Grant (US)		
The Next Time I Fall	11/86	
Frank CHACKSFIELD (UK)		
Ebb Tide	1/54	2/54
In Old Lisbon		3/56
CHAD & JEREMY (UK)		
A Summer Song	10/64	
Willow Weep For Me	1/65	
CHAIRMEN OF THE BOARD (US)		
Everything's Tuesday		3/71
Give Me Just A Little More Time	3/70	9/70
Pay To The Piper	1/71	
You've Got Me Dangling On A String		12/70
CHAKACHAS (B)		
Jungle Fever	3/72	
Richard CHAMBERLAIN (US)		
Theme From 'Doctor Kildare' (Three Stars Will Shine Tonight)	7/62	6/62
CHAMBERS BROTHERS (US)		
Time Has Come Today	9/68	
CHAMILLIONAIRE featuring Krayzie Bone (US)		
Ridin'	4/06	8/06
CHAMPAIGN (US)		
How 'Bout Us	5/81	6/81
CHAMPS (US)		
Tequila	3/58	4/58
Gene CHANDLER (US)		
Duke Of Earl	2/62	
Get Down		3/79
Groovy Situation	9/70	
CHANGE (US)		
Searching		10/80
CHANGING FACES (US)		
G.H.E.T.T.O.U.T	5/97	
Stroke You Up	8/94	
Bruce CHANNEL (US)		
Hey! Baby	2/62	3/62
Keep On		8/68
CHANTAYS (US)		
Pipeline	4/63	
CHANTELS (US)		
Look In My Eyes	10/61	
Maybe	2/58	
Harry CHAPIN (US)		
Cat's In The Cradle	11/74	
Tracy CHAPMAN (US)		
Fast Car	8/88	7/88
Give Me One Reason	5/96	
CHARLATANS (UK)		
The Only One I Know		6/90
CHARLENE (US)		
I've Never Been To Me	5/82	6/82
CHARLES & EDDIE (US)		
Would I Lie To You?	11/92	11/92
Jimmy CHARLES (US)		
A Million To One	9/60	
Ray CHARLES (US)		
Busted	10/63	
Crying Time	2/66	
Georgia On My Mind	10/60	
Here We Go Again	7/67	
Hit The Road Jack	10/61	10/61
I Can't Stop Loving You	5/62	6/62
One Mint Julep	4/61	
Take These Chains From My Heart	5/63	5/63
Unchain My Heart	1/62	

	US Top 20 Ent	UK Top 20 Ent
What'd I Say (Pt. 1)	8/59	
You Are My Sunshine	12/62	
You Don't Know Me	8/62	9/62
Your Cheatin' Heart		12/62
Ray CHARLES SINGERS (US)		
Love Me With All Your Heart	5/64	
Sonny CHARLES & The Checkmates, Ltd. (US)		
Black Pearl	6/69	
Tina CHARLES (UK)		
Dance Little Lady Dance		9/76
Dr. Love		12/76
I Love To Love (But My Baby Loves To Dance)		2/76
CHARMS (US)		
Hearts Of Stone	12/54	
Ivory Tower	5/56	
CHAS & DAVE (UK)		
Ain't No Pleasing You		4/82
Rabbit		1/81
❖ **with The Matchroom Mob**		
Snooker Loopy		5/86
CHASE & STATUS featuring PLAN B (UK)		
End Credits		11/09
CHEAP TRICK (US)		
Can't Stop Falling Into Love	9/90	
Don't Be Cruel	9/88	
The Flame	6/88	
I Want You To Want Me	7/79	
Chubby CHECKER (US)		
Birdland	6/63	
Dancin' Party	7/62	
The Fly	10/61	
The Hucklebuck	11/60	
Let's Twist Again	7/61	1/62
★ Let's Twist Again		12/75
Limbo Rock	11/62	
Loddy Lo	12/63	
Pony Time	2/61	
Popeye (The Hitchhiker)	10/62	
Slow Twistin'	3/62	
The Twist	8/60	
★ The Twist	12/61	1/62
❖ **with The Fat Boys**		
The Twist (Yo, Twist)	8/88	6/88
CHEECH & CHONG (US)		
Basketball Jones Featuring Tyrone Shoelaces	10/73	
Earache My Eye Featuring Alice Bowie	9/74	
CHEEKY GIRLS (R)		
Cheeky Song (Touch My Bum)		12/02
Hooray Hooray (It's A Cheeky Holiday)		8/03
Take Your Shoes Off		5/03
CHEERS (US)		
(Bazoom) I Need Your Lovin'	11/54	
Black Denim Trousers	10/55	
CHEF (US)		
Chocolate Salty Balls (PS I Love You)		12/98
CHELSEA F.C. (UK)		
Blue Is The Colour		3/72
CHEMICAL BROTHERS (UK)		
Block Rockin' Beats		4/97
Do It Again		7/07
Galvanize		1/05
Hey Boy Hey Girl		6/99
Let Forever Be		8/99
Setting Sun		10/96
CHER (US)		
All I Really Want To Do	8/65	9/65
Bang Bang (My Baby Shot Me Down)	4/66	4/66
Believe	2/99	10/98
Dark Lady	3/74	
Gypsys Tramps & Thieves	10/71	11/71
Half-Breed	9/73	
I Found Someone	2/88	1/88
If I Could Turn Back Time	9/89	10/89
Just Like Jesse James	12/89	2/90
Love And Understanding		7/91
The Music's No Good Without You		11/01
One By One		1/96
The Shoop Shoop Song (It's In His Kiss)		4/91
Strong Enough		3/99
Take Me Home	4/79	
Walking In Memphis		10/95
The Way Of Love	3/72	
We All Sleep Alone	6/88	
You Better Sit Down Kids	12/67	
CHER & Peter Cetera (US)		
After All	5/89	

	US Top 20 Ent	UK Top 20 Ent
CHER, Chrissie Hynde & Neneh Cherry with Eric Clapton (US/UK)		
Love Can Build A Bridge		3/95
CHERELLE & Alexander O'Neal (US)		
Saturday Love		1/86
CHERISH featuring Sean Paul of The YoungBloodZ (US)		
Do It To It	7/06	
Don CHERRY (US)		
Band Of Gold	12/55	2/56
Eagle-Eye CHERRY (S)		
Save Tonight	12/98	7/98
Falling In Love Again		11/98
Neneh CHERRY (US)		
Buffalo Stance	6/89	12/88
Kisses On The Wind	9/89	
Manchild		5/89
❖ **with Cher, Chrissie Hynde & Eric Clapton**		
Love Can Build A Bridge		3/95
❖ **with Youssou N'dour**		
7 Seconds		8/94
Mark CHESNUTT (US)		
I Don't Want To Miss A Thing	2/99	
CHIC (US)		
Dance, Dance, Dance (Yowsah, Yowsah, Yowsah)	2/78	1/78
Everybody Dance		5/78
Good Times	7/79	7/79
I Want Your Love	4/79	3/79
Le Freak	11/78	12/78
CHICAGO (US)		
Alive Again	12/78	
Along Comes A Woman	4/85	
Baby What A Big Surprise	11/77	
Beginnings/Colour My World	8/71	
Call On Me	8/74	
Does Anybody Really Know What Time It Is	12/70	
Feelin' Stronger Every Day	8/73	
Hard Habit To Break	9/84	11/84
Hard To Say I'm Sorry	7/82	10/82
Harry Truman	4/75	
I Don't Wanna Live Without Your Love	8/88	
I'm A Man		2/70
(I've Been) Searchin' So Long	5/74	
If You Leave Me Now	9/76	10/76
Just You 'n' Me	11/73	
Look Away	11/88	
Make Me Smile	6/70	
No Tell Lover	2/79	
Old Days	5/75	
Saturday In The Park	9/72	
Stay The Night	6/84	
25 Or 6 To 4	8/70	8/70
What Kind Of Man Would I Be?	2/90	
Will You Still Love Me	2/87	
Wishing You Were Here	12/74	
You're Not Alone	3/89	
You're The Inspiration	12/84	
CHICANE (UK)		
Poppiholla		7/09
CHICANE featuring Bryan ADAMS (UK/C)		
Don't Give Up		3/00
CHICANE featuring Maire BRENNAN (UK/I)		
Saltwater		6/99
CHICANE featuring Tom JONES		
Stoned In Love		5/6
CHICKEN SHACK (UK)		
I'd Rather Go Blind		6/69
CHICO (UK)		
It's Chico Time		3/06
CHICORY TIP (UK)		
Son Of My Father		2/72
CHIFFONS (US)		
He's So Fine	3/63	5/63
One Fine Day	6/63	
Sweet Talkin' Guy	6/66	4/72
CHILD (UK)		
It's Only Make Believe		9/78
Jane CHILD (US)		
Don't Wanna Fall In Love	3/90	
CHILDLINERS (UK/Aus)		
The Gift Of Christmas		12/95
CHI-LITES (US)		
Have You Seen Her	11/71	2/72
★ Have You Seen Her/Oh Girl		7/75
Homely Girl		4/74
It's Time For Love		10/75

	US Top 20 Ent	UK Top 20 Ent
Oh Girl	5/72	
Too Good To Be Forgotten		12/74
You Don't Have To Go		8/76
CHIMES (UK)		
I Still Haven't Found What I'm Looking For		5/90
CHIMES (US)		
Once In A While	1/61	
CHINA BLACK (UK)		
Searching		7/94
CHINA CRISIS (UK)		
Christian		2/83
Wishful Thinking		1/84
CHINGY (US)		
Right Thurr	7/03	
featuring J. Weav		
One Call Away	2/04	
featuring Ludacris & Snoop Dogg		
Holidae In	10/3	
featuring Tyrese		
Pullin' Me Back	10/6	
CHIPMUNK (UK)		
Oopsy Daisy		10/09
CHIPMUNK featuring Emeli Sande (UK)		
Diamond Rings		7/09
CHIPMUNKS (US)		
Alvin's Harmonica	3/59	
The Chipmunk Song	12/58	
Ragtime Cowboy Joe		8/59
CHOCOLATE PUMA (H)		
I Wanna Be U		3/01
CHORDETTES (US)		
Born To Be With You	7/56	9/56
Lollipop	3/58	4/58
Mr Sandman	11/54	1/55
Never On Sunday	8/61	
CHORDS (US)		
Sh-Boom	7/54	
CHRISTIANS (UK)		
Harvest For The World		10/88
CHRISTIANS, Holly Johnson, Paul McCartney, Gerry Marsden & Stock Aitken Waterman (UK)		
Ferry 'Cross The Mersey		5/89
CHRISTIE (UK)		
San Bernadino		11/70
Yellow River		5/70
David CHRISTIE (F)		
Saddle Up		9/82
Lou CHRISTIE (US)		
I'm Gonna Make You Mine	10/69	10/69
Lightnin' Strikes	2/66	3/66
Two Faces Have I	5/63	
Tony CHRISTIE (UK)		
I Did What I Did For Maria		6/71
(Is This The Way To) The World Cup		6/06
Tony CHRISTIE featuring Peter KAY		
(Is This The Way To) Amarillo		3/05
CHUCKIE & LMFAO (H/US/UK)		
Let The Bass Kick In Miami Girl		12/09
CHUMBAWAMBA (UK)		
Amnesia		1/98
Tubthumping		10/97
Charlotte CHURCH (UK)		
Crazy Chick		7/05
CIARA (US)		
Promise	12/06	
featuring Chamillionaire		
Get Up	9/06	
featuring Ludacris		
Oh	4/05	8/05
featuring Missy Elliott		
1, 2 Step	11/04	4/05
featuring Petey Pablo (US)		
Goodies	8/04	1/05
CIARA featuring Justin TIMBERLAKE (US)		
Love Sex Magic	4/09	4/09
Gabriella CILMI (AUS)		
Sweet About Me		6/08
CINDERELLA (US)		
Don't Know What You Got (Till It's Gone)	11/88	
Nobody's Fool	2/87	
Gigliola CINQUETTI (ITA)		
Go (Before You Break My Heart)		6/74
Non Ho L'Eta Per Amarti		6/64
CITY BOY (UK)		
5-7-0-5		8/78
CITY HIGH (US)		

	US Top 20 Ent	UK Top 20 Ent
What Would You Do?	5/01	10/01
❖ *featuring Eve* (US)		
Caramel		3/02
Gary CLAIL ON-U SOUND SYSTEM (UK)		
Human Nature		4/91
CLAIRE & FRIENDS (UK)		
It's 'orrible Being In Love (When You're 8 1/2)		7/86
CLANNAD (I)		
Theme From 'Harry's Game'		11/82
Jimmy CLANTON (US)		
Go Jimmy Go	1/60	
Just A Dream	8/58	
Venus In Blue Jeans	10/62	
Eric CLAPTON (UK)		
Change The World	7/96	
I Can't Stand It	4/81	
I Shot The Sheriff	8/74	8/74
Lay Down Sally	2/78	
Layla	11/92	
Promises	12/78	
Tears In Heaven	2/92	3/92
❖ *with Cher, Chrissie Hynde & Neneh Cherry*		
Love Can Build A Bridge		3/95
Claudine CLARK (US)		
Party Lights	8/62	
Dave CLARK FIVE (UK)		
Any Way You Want It	1/65	
Because	8/64	
Bits And Pieces	4/64	2/64
Can't You See That She's Mine	7/64	6/64
Catch Us If You Can	9/65	8/65
Come Home	3/65	
Do You Love Me	6/64	
Everybody Get Together		3/70
Everybody Knows		11/67
Glad All Over	3/64	12/63
Good Old Rock 'n' Roll		1/70
I Like It Like That	7/65	
Over And Over	12/65	
Red Balloon		10/68
You Got What It Takes	5/67	
Dee CLARK (US)		
Raindrops	6/61	
Petula CLARK (UK)		
Alone		11/57
Baby Lover		3/58
Don't Sleep In The Subway	7/67	7/67
Downtown	1/65	12/64
★ Downtown '88		12/88
I Couldn't Live Without Your Love	8/66	7/66
I Know A Place	4/65	
The Little Shoemaker		6/54
Majorca		2/55
My Friend The Sea		12/61
My Love	2/66	2/66
Romeo		7/61
Sailor		1/61
A Sign Of The Times	4/66	
Suddenly There's A Valley		12/55
This Is My Song	4/67	2/67
With All My Heart		8/57
Ya Ya Twist		7/62
Sanford CLARK (US)		
The Fool	8/56	
Kelly CLARKSON (US)		
Already Gone	12/09	
A Moment Like This	10/02	
Because Of You	10/5	12/05
Behind These Hazel Eyes	6/05	10/05
Breakaway	10/04	
Miss Independent	7/03	9/03
My Life Would Suck Without You	2/09	3/09
Never Again	5/07	6/07
Since U Been Gone	2/05	7/05
Walk Away	4/06	
CLASH (UK)		
Bank Robber		9/80
London Calling		1/80
Rock The Casbah	12/82	
Should I Stay Or Should I Go		3/91
CLASSICS IV (US)		
Spooky	1/68	
Stormy	11/68	
Traces	3/69	
CLASSIX NOUVEAUX (UK)		
Is It A Dream		4/82
Judy CLAY & William BELL (US)		

	US Top 20 Ent	UK Top 20 Ent
Private Number		12/68
Tom CLAY (US)		
What The World Needs Now Is Love/Abraham, Martin & John	8/71	
ADAM CLAYTON & LARRY MULLEN (I)		
Theme From 'Mission Impossible'		6/96
CLEOPATRA (UK)		
Cleopatra's Theme		2/98
I Want You Back		8/98
Life Ain't Easy		5/98
CLICK FIVE (US)		
Just The Girl	9/05	
Jimmy CLIFF (J)		
Wild World		9/70
Wonderful World Beautiful People		11/69
Buzz CLIFFORD (US)		
Baby Sittin' Boogie	2/61	4/61
Mike CLIFFORD (US)		
Close To Cathy	11/62	
CLIMAX (US)		
Precious And Few	2/72	
CLIMAX BLUES BAND (UK)		
Couldn't Get It Right	4/77	11/76
I Love You	6/81	
CLIMIE FISHER (UK)		
Love Changes (Everything)		4/88
Rise To The Occasion		1/88
Patsy CLINE (US)		
Crazy	11/61	
I Fall To Pieces	8/61	
CLOCK (UK)		
Axel F/Keep Pushin'		3/95
Everybody		8/95
Whoomph! (There It Is)		7/95
Rosemary CLOONEY (US)		
Hey There	7/54	10/55
Mambo Italiano	11/54	1/55
Man		2/54
This Ole House	8/54	12/54
Where Will The Baby's Dimple Be		5/55
CLOUT (SA)		
Substitute		7/78
CLUBHOUSE featuring Carl (ITA)		
Light My Fire		4/94
CLUB NOUVEAU (US)		
Lean On Me	3/87	4/87
COAST TO COAST (UK)		
(Do) The Hucklebuck		2/81
COASTERS (US)		
Along Came Jones	6/59	
Charlie Brown	2/59	4/59
Poison Ivy	9/59	
Searchin'/Young Blood	6/57	
Yakety Yak	6/58	9/58
Odia COATES (US) see Paul Anka with Odia Coates		
COBRA STARSHIP featuring Leighton Meester (US)		
Good Girls Go Bad	8/09	
Eddie COCHRAN (US)		
C'mon Everybody		3/59
Summertime Blues	9/58	
Three Steps To Heaven		5/60
Weekend		7/61
Tom COCHRANE (C)		
Life Is A Highway	7/92	
Joe COCKER (UK)		
Cry Me A River		11/70
Delta Lady		11/69
The Letter	5/70	
When The Night Comes	1/90	
With A Little Help From My Friends		11/68
You Are So Beautiful	3/75	
Joe COCKER & Jennifer WARNES (UK/US)		
Up Where We Belong	10/82	2/83
COCKNEY REBEL (UK) see Steve Harley		
CO-CO (UK)		
Bad Old Days		5/78
Commander CODY & His Lost Planet Airmen (US)		
Hot Rod Lincoln	5/72	
COFFEE (US)		
Casanova		10/80
Dennis COFFEY & The Detroit Guitar Band (US)		
Scorpio	12/71	
Alma COGAN (UK)		
Bell Bottom Blues		3/54
Dreamboat		6/55
Go On By		10/55
I Can't Tell A Waltz From A Tango		12/54

	US Top 20 Ent	UK Top 20 Ent
Billy COTTON & His Band (UK)		
Friends And Neighbours		4/54
John COUGAR (US) see John (Cougar) Mellencamp		
COUNT FIVE (US)		
Psychotic Reaction	10/66	
COURSE (H)		
Ain't Nobody		7/97
Ready Or Not		4/97
COVER GIRLS (US)		
We Can't Go Wrong	2/90	
Wishing On A Star	6/92	
Julie COVINGTON (UK)		
Don't Cry For Me Argentina		1/77
Only Women Bleed		1/78
COWBOY CHURCH SUNDAY SCHOOL (US)		
Open Up Your Heart (And Let The Sunshine In)	2/55	
COWSILLS (US)		
Hair	4/69	
Indian Lake	7/68	
The Rain, The Park & Other Things	11/67	
Deborah COX (US)		
Nobody's Supposed To Be Here	11/98	
We Can't Be Friends	10/99	
Michael COX (UK)		
Angela Jones		7/60
Floyd CRAMER (US)		
Last Date	11/60	
On The Rebound	3/61	5/61
San Antonio Rose	7/61	
CRANBERRIES (I)		
Linger	12/93	
Les CRANE (US)		
Desiderata	11/71	3/72
CRASH TEST DUMMIES (C)		
Mmm Mmm Mmm Mmm	3/94	4/94
Beverley CRAVEN (UK)		
Promise Me		5/91
Johnny CRAWFORD (US)		
Cindy's Birthday	6/62	
Rumors	12/62	
Michael CRAWFORD (UK)		
The Music Of The Night		2/87
Randy CRAWFORD (US)		
Almaz		2/87
One Day I'll Fly Away		9/80
You Might Need Somebody		7/81
CRAZY ELEPHANT (US)		
Gimme Gimme Good Lovin'	4/69	7/69
CRAZY FROG (G/S)		
Axel F		6/05
Jingle Bells/U Can't Touch This		12/05
CRAZY TOWN (US)		
Butterfly	4/01	4/01
CRAZY WORLD OF ARTHUR BROWN (UK) see Arthur Brown		
CREAM (UK)		
I Feel Free		1/67
Sunshine Of Your Love	8/68	
White Room	11/68	
CREED (US)		
My Sacrifice	12/01	
One Last Breath	9/02	
With Arms Wide Open	10/00	
CREEDENCE CLEARWATER REVIVAL (US)		
Bad Moon Rising	6/69	9/69
Down On The Corner/Fortunate Son	11/69	
Green River	8/69	
Have You Ever Seen The Rain	2/71	
Lookin' Out My Back Door/Long As I Can See The Light	9/70	
Proud Mary	2/69	7/69
Suzie Q. (Pt. 1)	10/68	
Sweet Hitch-Hiker	8/71	
Travelin' Band/Who'll Stop The Rain	2/70	5/70
Up Around The Bend/Run Through The Jungle	5/70	7/70
KID CREOLE & The Coconuts (US)		
Annie I'm Not Your Daddy		10/82
I'm A Wonderful Thing (Baby)		6/82
Stool Pigeon		8/82
CRESCENDOS (US)		
Oh Julie	2/58	
CRESTS (US)		
16 Candles	1/59	
Step By Step	4/60	
CREW-CUTS (C)		
Angels In The Sky	1/56	
Crazy 'Bout You, Baby	6/54	
Don't Be Angry	5/55	
Earth Angel	2/55	4/55
Gum Drop	9/55	
Ko Ko Mo (I Love You So)	2/55	
Oop-Shoop	10/54	
Sh-Boom	7/54	10/54
A Story Untold	7/55	
Bernard CRIBBINS (UK)		
Hole In The Ground		3/62
Right Said Fred		7/62
CRICKETS (US)		
Don't Ever Change		7/62
Maybe Baby		3/58
Oh, Boy!	1/58	1/58
That'll Be The Day	8/57	10/57
Think It Over		8/58
Jim CROCE (US)		
Bad, Bad Leroy Brown	6/73	
I Got A Name	11/73	
I'll Have To Say I Love You In A Song	4/74	
Time In A Bottle	12/73	
You Don't Mess Around With Jim	8/72	
Bing CROSBY (US)		
Around The World		6/57
Changing Partners		3/54
Count Your Blessings		1/55
White Christmas		12/77
❖ with David Bowie		
Peace On Earth-Little Drummer Boy		12/82
❖ with Grace Kelly		
True Love	10/56	12/56
CROSBY, STILLS & NASH (US/UK)		
Just A Song Before I Go	8/77	
Wasted On The Way	7/82	
CROSBY, STILLS, NASH & YOUNG (US/UK/C)		
Ohio	8/70	
Woodstock	5/70	
Christopher CROSS (US)		
All Right	2/83	
Arthur's Theme (Best That You Can Do)	9/81	2/82
Never Be The Same	12/80	
Ride Like The Wind	3/80	
Sailing	8/80	
Think Of Laura	1/84	
Sheryl CROW (US)		
All I Wanna Do	9/94	11/94
Every Day Is A Winding Road	4/97	
The First Cut Is The Deepest	3/04	
If It Makes You Happy	10/96	
My Favorite Mistake		8/98
Strong Enough	2/95	
CROWD (UK)		
You'll Never Walk Alone		6/85
CROWDED HOUSE (AUS/NZ)		
Don't Dream It's Over	3/87	
Something So Strong	7/87	
Weather With You		3/92
CROWN HEIGHTS AFFAIR (US)		
You Gave Me Love		6/80
Julee CRUISE (US)		
Falling		12/90
CRUSADERS (US)		
Street Life		9/79
Taio CRUZ (UK)		
Break Your Heart		9/09
Taio CRUZ featuring Luciana (UK)		
Come On Girl		3/08
CRYSTALS (US)		
Da Doo Ron Ron	6/63	6/63
He's A Rebel	10/62	
He's Sure The Boy I Love	2/63	
Then He Kissed Me	9/63	9/63
Uptown	5/62	
Kid CUDI (US)		
Day 'n' Nite	4/09	1/09
CUFF LINKS (US)		
Tracy	10/69	12/69
When Julie Comes Around		4/70
CUBAN BOYS (UK)		
Cognoscenti Vs Intelligentsia		12/99
CULT (UK)		
Lil' Devil		5/87
CULTURE BEAT (G/UK/US)		
Anything		1/94
Got To Get It		11/93
Mr Vain		8/93
CULTURE CLUB (UK)		
Church Of The Poison Mind	11/83	4/83
Do You Really Want To Hurt Me	2/83	10/82
I Just Wanna Be Loved		11/98
I'll Tumble 4 Ya	8/83	
It's A Miracle	6/84	3/84
Karma Chameleon	1/84	9/83
Miss Me Blind	3/84	
Move Away	5/86	3/86
Time (Clock Of The Heart)	5/83	12/82
Victims		12/83
The War Song		10/84
Smiley CULTURE (UK)		
Police Officer		1/85
Burton CUMMINGS (C)		
Stand Tall	12/76	
CUPID'S INSPIRATION (UK)		
Yesterday Has Gone		7/68
CURE (UK)		
Close To Me		11/90
Friday, I'm In Love		6/92
The Love Cats		11/83
Love Song	9/89	
Lullaby		4/89
CURIOSITY KILLED THE CAT (aka Curiosity) (UK)		
Down To Earth		1/87
Hang On In There Baby		5/92
Misfit		7/87
Name And Number		10/89
Ordinary Day		4/87
CURVED AIR (UK)		
Back Street Luv		9/71
CUTTING CREW (UK)		
(I Just) Died In Your Arms	4/87	9/86
I've Been In Love Before	11/87	
CYRKLE (US)		
Red Rubber Ball	6/66	
Billy Ray CYRUS (US)		
Achy Breaky Heart	6/92	8/92
Miley CYRUS (US)		
7 Things		7/08
Party In The U.S.A.	8/09	
See You Again	2/08	9/08
The Climb	3/09	5/09
Heavy D (US)		
Big Daddy	4/97	
D-SIDE (I)		
Speechless		4/03
Invisible		7/03
D12 (US)		
How Come		8/04
My Band	4/04	4/04
Shit On You		3/01
Purple Hills/Purple Pills	8/1	7/01
D4L (US)		
Laffy Taffy	11/05	
D'ANGELO (US)		
Lady	3/96	
D MOB featuring Cathy Dennis (UK)		
C'mon And Get My Love	3/90	11/89
D MOB featuring Gary Haisman (UK)		
We Call It Acieed		10/88
D MOB featuring LRS (UK)		
It Is Time To Get Funky		6/89
D MOB featuring Nuff Juice (UK)		
Put Your Hands Together		1/90
D:REAM (UK)		
Shoot Me With Your Love		7/95
Things Can Only Get Better		1/94
U R The Best Thing		3/94
DA BRAT (US)		
Funkdafied	7/94	
DA MUTTZ (UK)		
Wassuup		12/00
Terry DACTYL & The Dinosaurs (UK)		
Seaside Shuffle		7/72
DADDY DEWDROP (US)		
Chick-A-Boom	5/71	
DADDY YANKEE (P)		
Gasolina		7/05
Ricardo DA FORCE (UK) see N-Trance featuring Ricardo Da Force		
DAFT PUNK (F)		
Around The World		4/97
Da Funk/Musique		2/97
One More Time	11/00	

	US Top 20 Ent	UK Top 20 Ent
DALE & GRACE (US)		
I'm Leaving It Up To You	11/63	
Stop And Think It Over	2/64	
Alan DALE (US)		
Sweet And Gentle	7/55	
Jim DALE (UK)		
Be My Girl		11/57
Roger DALTREY (UK)		
Giving It All Away		5/73
DAMAGE (UK)		
Forever		12/96
Ghetto Romance		7/00
Love Guaranteed		3/97
Wonderful Tonight		5/97
DAMIAN (UK)		
The Time Warp		9/89
Michael DAMIAN (US)		
Rock On	5/89	
DAMITA JO (US)		
I'll Be There	8/61	
DAMN YANKEES (US)		
High Enough	12/90	
DAMNED (UK)		
Eloise		2/86
Vic DAMONE (US)		
On The Street Where You Live	6/56	5/58
DANA (UK)		
All Kinds Of Everything		4/70
Fairytale		1/77
It's Gonna Be A Cold Cold Christmas		12/75
Please Tell Him I Said Hello		3/75
Who Put The Lights Out		3/71
Vic DANA (US)		
Red Roses For A Blue Lady	4/65	
DANDY WARHOLS (US)		
Bohemian Like You		11/01
DANE (UK)		
Shut Up And Forget About It		3/01
Another Lover		7/01
D'ANGELO (US)		
Lady	4/96	
Charlie DANIELS BAND (US)		
The Devil Went Down To Georgia	8/79	
In America	7/80	
Uneasy Rider	8/73	
DANITY KANE (US)		
Damaged	5/08	
Show Stopper	9/06	
Johnny DANKWORTH (UK)		
African Waltz		4/61
Experiments With Mice		7/56
DANNY & The Juniors (US)		
At The Hop	12/57	1/58
DANNY WILSON (UK)		
Mary's Prayer		4/88
DANTE & The Evergreens (US)		
Alley-Oop	7/60	
Steven DANTE (UK) see Jellybean feat. Steven Dante		
DAPHNE & CELESTE (US)		
Ooh Stick You!		2/00
Terence Trent D'ARBY (US)		
If You Let Me Stay		4/87
Sign Your Name	7/88	1/88
Wishing Well	4/88	7/87
Matt DAREY featuring Marcella Woods (UK)		
❖Beautiful		4/02
Bobby DARIN (US)		
Beyond The Sea	2/60	2/60
Clementine		4/60
Dream Lover	5/59	6/59
18 Yellow Roses	6/63	
If I Were A Carpenter	10/66	11/66
Irresistible You	2/62	
Lazy River		3/61
Mack The Knife	9/59	10/59
Multiplication		1/62
Queen Of The Hop	11/58	
Splish Splash	7/58	
Things	8/62	8/62
You Must Have Been A Beautiful Baby	10/61	10/61
You're The Reason I'm Living	2/63	
DARIUS (UK)		
Colourblind		8/02
Rushes		12/02
DARKNESS (UK)		
Christmas Time (Don't Let The Bells End)		12/03
I Believe In A Thing Called Love		10/03
Love Is Only A Feeling		4/04
One Way Ticket		11/05
James DARREN (US)		
Conscience	5/62	
Goodbye Cruel World	11/61	
Her Royal Majesty	3/62	
DARTELLS (US)		
Hot Pastrami	5/63	
DARTS (UK)		
Boy From New York City		5/78
Come Back My Love		2/78
Daddy Cool/The Girl Can't Help It		11/77
Duke Of Earl		8/79
Get It		3/79
It's Raining		8/78
Let's Hang On		7/80
DARUDE (FIN)		
Feel The Beat		11/00
Sandstorm		6/00
DAUGHTRY (US)		
Home	5/07	
It's Not Over	2/07	
DAVID & JONATHAN (UK)		
Lovers Of The World Unite		8/66
Michelle		2/66
Ann-Marie DAVID (F)		
Wonderful Dream		5/73
Craig DAVID (UK)		
All The Way		8/05
Hot Stuff (Let's Dance)		11/07
Don't Love You No More		11/05
7 Days	2/02	08/00
Fill Me In	8/01	4/00
Hidden Agenda		2/03
Walking Away		12/00
❖ featuring STING		
Rise & Fall		5/03
FR DAVID (F)		
Words		4/83
Paul DAVIDSON (J)		
Midnight Rider		2/76
Dave DAVIES (UK)		
Death Of A Clown		8/67
Windsor DAVIES & Don ESTELLE (UK)		
Whispering Grass		5/75
Billie DAVIS (UK)		
Tell Him		3/63
❖ with Mike Sarne Will I What		9/62
Mac DAVIS (US)		
Baby Don't Get Hooked On Me	8/72	
One Hell Of A Woman	7/74	
Stop And Smell The Roses	10/74	
Paul DAVIS (US)		
Cool Night	1/82	
I Go Crazy	2/78	
'65 Love Affair	4/82	
Sammy DAVIS JR (US)		
The Candy Man	5/72	
Hey There	9/54	
I've Gotta Be Me	3/69	
Love Me Or Leave Me	6/55	9/55
Something's Gotta Give	6/55	9/55
Skeeter DAVIS (US)		
The End Of The World	3/63	
I Can't Stay Mad At You	10/63	
Spencer DAVIS GROUP (UK)		
Gimme Some Lovin'	2/67	11/66
I'm A Man	4/67	2/67
Keep On Runnin'		1/66
Somebody Help Me		4/66
When I Come Home		9/66
Tyrone DAVIS (US)		
Can I Change My Mind	2/69	
Turn Back The Hands Of Time	4/70	
DAWN (US)		
Candida	9/70	2/71
Knock Three Times	12/70	5/71
Tie A Yellow Ribbon Round The Ole Oak Tree	4/73	4/73
What Are You Doing Sunday		8/71
DAWN featuring Tony Orlando (US)		
Say, Has Anybody Seen My Sweet Gypsy Rose	8/73	9/73
Tony Orlando & DAWN (US)		
He Don't Love You (Like I Love You)	4/75	
Look In My Eyes Pretty Woman	2/75	
Mornin' Beautiful	8/75	
Steppin' Out (Gonna Boogie Tonight)	10/74	
Dana DAWSON (US)		
3 Is Family		7/95
Bobby DAY (US)		
Rock-In' Robin/Over And Over	9/58	
Doris DAY (US)		
Black Hills Of Dakota		8/54
Deadwood Stage		5/54
Everybody Loves A Lover	8/58	
I'll Never Stop Loving You		8/55
If I Give My Heart To You	9/54	10/54
Move Over Darling		4/64
Ready Willing And Able		4/55
Secret Love	1/54	4/55
Whatever Will Be, Will Be (Que Sera, Sera)	7/56	7/56
Inaya DAY (US)		
Nasty Girl		7/05
Taylor DAYNE (US)		
Can't Get Enough Of Your Love		7/93
Don't Rush Me	12/88	
Heart Of Stone	9/90	
I'll Always Love You	9/88	
I'll Be Your Shelter	6/90	
Love Will Lead You Back	3/90	
Prove Your Love	4/88	4/88
Tell It To My Heart	12/87	2/88
With Every Beat Of My Heart	12/89	
DAZZ BAND (US)		
Let It Whip	6/82	
DB BOULEVARD (ITA)		
Point Of View		2/02
DeBARGE (US)		
Rhythm Of The Night	4/85	5/85
Who's Holding Donna Now	7/85	
El DeBARGE (US)		
Who's Johnny	6/86	
Kristinia DEBARGE (US)		
Goodbye	6/09	
Chris De Burgh (I)		
Lady In Red	5/87	7/86
Missing You		11/88
DE CASTRO SISTERS (US)		
Teach Me Tonight	10/54	
DE JOHN SISTERS (US)		
(My Baby Don't Love Me) No More	1/55	
DE LA SOUL (US)		
The Magic Number/Buddy		1/90
❖ with Queen Latifah		
Mamma Gave Birth To The Soul Children		4/90
Ring Ring Ring (Ha Ha Hey)		5/91
DE'LACY (US)		
Hideaway		9/95
DEACON BLUE (UK)		
Four Bacharach & David Songs (EP)		9/90
Real Gone Kid		11/88
Twist & Shout		8/91
DEAD END KIDS (UK)		
Have I The Right?		4/77
DEAD OR ALIVE (UK)		
Brand New Lover	3/87	
Lover Come Back To Me		5/85
You Spin Me Round		2/06
You Spin Me Round (Like A Record)	8/85	2/85
Hazell DEAN (UK)		
Searchin' (I Gotta Find A Man)		6/84
Whatever I Do (Wherever I Go)		8/84
Who's Leaving Who		4/88
Jimmy DEAN (US)		
Big Bad John	10/61	11/61
P.T. 109	5/62	
Diana DECKER (UK)		
Poppa Piccolino		1/54
Dave DEE, DOZY, BEAKY, MICK & TICH (UK)		
Bend It		10/66
Hideaway		7/66
Hold Tight		4/66
Last Night In Soho		8/68
Legend Of Xanadu		3/68
Okay!		6/67
Save Me		12/66
Touch Me Touch Me		4/67
Zabadak		10/67
Joey DEE & The Starliters (US)		
Peppermint Twist (Pt. 1)	12/61	2/62
Shout (Pt. 1)	4/62	
Kiki DEE (UK)		
I've Got The Music In Me		11/74
Loving And Free/Amoureuse		12/73

	US Top 20 Ent	UK Top 20 Ent
Loving And Free/Amoureuse		10/76
Star		3/81
❖ with Elton John		
Don't Go Breaking My Heart	7/76	7/76
True Love		11/93
Tommy DEE (US)		
Three Stars	5/59	
DEE DEE (B)		
Forever		7/02
DEEE-LITE (US)		
Groove Is In The Heart	11/90	9/90
Alice DEEJAY (UK)		
Back In My Life		12/99
Will I Ever		7/00
DEELE (US)		
Two Occasions	5/88	
DEEP BLUE SOMETHING (US)		
Breakfast At Tiffany's		12/95
DEEP DISH (US)		
Flashdance		10/04
DEEP FOREST (Fra)		
Sweet Lullaby		2/94
DEEP PURPLE (UK)		
Black Night		9/70
Fireball		12/71
Hush	9/68	
Smoke On The Water	7/73	
Strange Kind Of Woman		3/71
DEEPEST BLUE(ISR)		
Deepest Blue		8/03
Give It Away		2/04
Rick DEES & HIS CAST OF IDIOTS (US)		
Disco Duck	9/76	10/76
DEF LEPPARD (UK)		
Animal		8/87
Armageddon It	12/88	
Have You Ever Needed Someone So Bad	10/92	
Hysteria	3/88	
Let's Get Rocked	5/92	3/92
Love Bites	9/88	7/88
Photograph	5/83	
Pour Some Sugar On Me	6/88	
Rocket	4/89	
Two Steps Behind	10/93	
When Love & Hate Collide		10/95
DEFAULT (US)		
Wasting My Time	6/02	
DEFRANCO FAMILY (C)		
Heartbeat – It's A Lovebeat	10/73	
Gavin DeGRAW (US)		
I Don't Want To Be	12/04	
DEGREES OF MOTION (US)		
Shine On		3/94
Desmond DEKKER & The Aces (J)		
The Israelites	6/69	4/69
★ The Israelites		6/75
It Mek		7/69
You Can Get It If You Really Want		9/70
DEL AMITRI (UK)		
Nothing Ever Happens		2/90
Roll To Me	11/95	
DELANEY & BONNIE & Friends (US)		
Never Ending Song Of Love	7/71	
DELEGATES (US)		
Convention '72	11/72	
DELERIUM feat. SARAH MCLACHLAN (C)		
Silence (Remixes)		10/00
DELFONICS (US)		
Didn't I (Blow Your Mind This Time)	3/70	
La-La Means I Love You	3/68	
DELL-VIKINGS (US)		
Come Go With Me	3/57	
Whispering Bells	8/57	
DELLS (US)		
Oh What A Nite	9/69	
Stay In My Corner	8/68	
DEM FRANCHIZE BOYZ featuring Jermaine DUPRI, DA BRAT & BOW WOW (US)		
I Think They Like Me	12/05	
DEM FRANCHIZE BOYZ featuring LIL PEANUT & CHARLAY		
Lean Wit It, Rock Wit It	2/06	
Chaka DEMUS & PLIERS (J)		
She Don't Let Nobody		9/93
Tease Me		6/93
Chaka DEMUS & PLIERS with Jack Radics & Taxi Gang (J)		

	US Top 20 Ent	UK Top 20 Ent
Twist And Shout		12/93
DENISE AND JOHNNY (UK)		
Especially For You		1/99
Cathy DENNIS (UK)		
Just Another Dream	1/91	
Too Many Walls	8/91	
Touch Me (All Night Long)	4/91	5/91
❖ with D.Mob C'mon And Get My Love	3/90	11/89
Jackie DENNIS (UK)		
La Dee Dah		3/58
Esmee DENTERS (H)		
Outta Here		8/09
Martin DENNY (US)		
Quiet Village	5/59	John
DENVER (US)		
Annie's Song	7/74	9/74
Back Home Again	11/74	
Fly Away	1/76	
I'm Sorry/Calypso	9/75	
Rocky Mountain High	2/73	
Sunshine On My Shoulders	3/74	
Sweet Surrender	2/75	
Take Me Home, Country Roads	7/71	
Thank God I'm A Country Boy	5/75	
Karl DENVER (UK)		
A Little Love, A Little Kiss		6/62
Marcheta		8/61
Mexicali Rose		10/61
Never Goodbye		4/62
Still		9/63
Wimoweh		2/62
DEODATA (US)		
Also Sprach Zarathustra (2001)	3/73	5/73
Lynsey DE PAUL (UK)		
No Honestly		11/74
Sugar Me		9/72
Won't Somebody Dance With Me		11/73
DEPECHE MODE (UK)		
Dream On		5/01
Enjoy The Silence	7/90	2/90
Everything Counts		8/83
I Feel You		2/93
In Your Room		1/94
Just Can't Get Enough		10/81
Master And Servant		9/84
New Life		8/81
People Are People	8/85	4/84
Personal Jesus		9/89
Precious		10/5
See You		3/82
DEREK (US)		
Cinnamon	12/68	
DEREK & The Dominoes (UK/US)		
Layla	7/72	8/72
★ Layla		3/82
Jason DERULO (US)		
Whatcha Say	9/09	11/09
DES'REE (UK)		
Feel So High		1/92
You Gotta Be	12/94	3/95
Life		6/98
Teri DESARIO with KC (US)		
Yes, I'm Ready	2/80	
Jackie DESHANNON (US)		
Put A Little Love In Your Heart	8/69	
What The World Needs Now Is Love	7/65	
DESIRELESS (F)		
Voyage Voyage		6/88
Johnny DESMOND (US)		
Play Me Hearts And Flowers (I Wanna Cry)	4/55	
The Yellow Rose Of Texas	8/55	
DESTINY'S CHILD (US)		
Bills, Bills, Bills	7/99	7/99
Bootylicious	7/01	8/01
Cater 2 U	8/05	
Emotion	11/01	11/01
Girl		5/05
Independent Women Part 1	12/00	12/00
Jumpin' Jumpin'		08/00
Lose My Breath	10/04	11/04
No, No, No	2/98	
Say My Name	3/00	4/00
Survivor	4/01	4/01
featuring T.I. & Lil Wayne		
Soldier	12/04	2/05
Stephanie DE SYKES (UK)		
Born With A Smile On My Face		7/74
DETROIT EMERALDS (US)		

	US Top 20 Ent	UK Top 20 Ent
Feel The Need In Me		3/73
★ Feel The Need In Me		7/77
DETROIT SPINNERS (US) see Spinners		
DEUCE (UK)		
Call It Love		2/95
William DEVAUGHN (US)		
Be Thankful For What You Got	6/74	
DEVO (US)		
Whip It	11/80	
Barry DEVORZON & Perry Botkin (US)		
Nadia's Theme (The Young & The Restless)	11/76	
DEXY'S MIDNIGHT RUNNERS (UK)		
Come On Eileen	3/83	7/82
Geno		4/80
Jackie Wilson Said		10/82
There There My Dear		8/80
Dennis DEYOUNG (US)		
Desert Moon	11/84	
DHT featuring EDMEE (B)		
Listen To Your Heart	7/05	12/05
Tony DI BART (UK)		
The Real Thing		4/94
Jim DIAMOND (UK)		
Hi Ho Silver		3/86
I Should Have Known Better		11/84
Neil DIAMOND (US)		
America	5/81	
Beautiful Noise		11/76
Cherry Cherry	10/66	
Cracklin' Rosie	9/70	11/70
Desiree	2/78	
Girl, You'll Be A Woman Soon	5/67	
Heartlight	10/82	
Hello Again	2/81	
Holly Holy	12/69	
I Am…I Said	4/71	6/71
If You Know What I Mean	7/76	
Longfellow Serenade	11/74	
Love On The Rocks	11/80	
Play Me	9/72	
Song Sung Blue	6/72	
Stones	12/71	
Sweet Caroline	7/69	2/71
Yesterday's Songs	12/81	
❖ with Barbra Streisand		
You Don't Bring Me Flowers	11/78	12/78
DIAMONDS (C)		
The Church Bells May Ring	6/56	
Little Darlin'	3/57	6/57
The Stroll	1/58	
DICK & DEEDEE (US)		
The Mountain's High	9/61	
Thou Shalt Not Steal	1/65	
DICKIES (US)		
Banana Splits (Tra La La Song)		5/79
Barbara DICKSON (UK)		
January February		4/80
❖ with Elaine Paige		
I Know Him So Well		1/85
DIDDY featuring Keyshia COLE (US)		
Last Night	4/07	
DIGITAL UNDERGROUND (US)		
The Humpty Dance	5/90	
Mark DINNING (US)		
Teen Angel	1/60	
DIDO (UK)		
Here With Me		2/01
Thank You	4/01	6/01
White Flag		9/03
DINO (US)		
I Like It	7/89	
Romeo	10/90	
DION & THE BELMONTS (US)		
A Teenager In Love	5/59	
Where Or When	1/60	
DION (US)		
Abraham, Martin And John	11/68	
Donna The Prima Donna	10/63	
Drip Drop	12/63	
Little Diane	8/62	
Lonely Teenager	12/60	
Love Came To Me	12/62	
Lovers Who Wander	5/62	
Ruby Baby	2/63	
Runaround Sue	10/61	11/61
The Wanderer	1/62	3/62
Celine DION (C)		
All By Myself	3/97	

	US Top 20 Ent	UK Top 20 Ent
EDEN'S CRUSH (US)		
Get Over Yourself	03/01	
EDISON LIGHTHOUSE (UK)		
Love Grows (Where My Rosemary Goes)	3/70	1/70
EDITORS (UK)		
Smokers Outside The Hospital Doors		6/07
Kevon EDMONDS (US)		
24/7	12/99	
Dave EDMUNDS (UK)		
Baby I Love You		2/73
Born To Be With You		7/73
Girls Talk		7/79
I Hear You Knocking	1/71	11/70
Queen Of Hearts		10/79
EDWARD BEAR (C)		
Last Song	2/73	
Bobby EDWARDS (US)		
You're The Reason	11/61	
Jonathan EDWARDS (US)		
Sunshine	1/72	
Rupie EDWARDS (J)		
Ire Feelings (Skanga)		12/74
Tommy EDWARDS (US)		
It's All In The Game	9/58	10/58
Love Is All We Need	12/58	
Please Mr. Sun	3/59	
Zac EFRON, Andrew SEELEY & Vanessa Anne HUDGENS (US)		
Breaking Free	2/06	
Walter EGAN (US)		
Magnet And Steel	8/78	
808 STATE (UK)		
Cubik/Olympic		11/90
In Yer Face		2/91
Pacific		12/89
❖ with MC Tunes The Only Rhyme		
That Bites		6/90
8TH DAY (US)		
She's Not Just Another Woman	7/71	
EIFFEL 65 (ITA)		
Blue (Da Ba Dee)		9/99
Move Your Body		2/00
EIGHTH WONDER (UK)		
I'm Not Scared		4/88
Donnie ELBERT (US)		
I Can't Help Myself		3/72
Where Did Our Love Go	12/71	1/72
ELECTRIC LIGHT ORCHESTRA (UK)		
All Over The World	9/80	
Can't Get It Out Of My Head	3/75	
Confusion/Last Train To London		12/79
The Diary Of Horace Wimp		8/79
Don't Bring Me Down	8/79	9/79
Evil Woman	1/76	2/76
Hold On Tight	9/81	8/81
I'm Alive	7/80	
Livin' Thing	1/77	12/76
Mr. Blue Sky		2/78
10538 Overture		8/72
Rock 'n' Roll Is King		7/83
Rockaria		3/77
Roll Over Beethoven		2/73
Shine A Little Love	7/79	6/79
Showdown		10/73
Strange Magic	5/76	
Sweet Talkin' Woman		10/78
Telephone Line	8/77	6/77
Turn To Stone	1/78	
Wild West Hero		7/78
❖ with Olivia Newton-John		
Xanadu	9/80	7/80
ELECTRIC PRUNES (US)		
I Had Too Much To Dream (Last Night)	2/67	
ELECTRIC SIX (US)		
Danger! High Voltage		1/03
Gay Bar		6/03
ELECTRONIC (UK)		
Disappointed		7/92
Get The Message		5/91
ELEGANTS (US)		
Little Star	8/58	
ELEMENT FOUR (UK)		
'Big Brother' UK TV Theme		09/00
ELGINS (US)		
Heaven Must Have Sent You		5/71
ELIAS & His Zigzag Jive Flutes (SA)		
Tom Hark		5/58
Yvonne ELLIMAN (US)		
Hello Stranger	5/77	
If I Can't Have You	3/78	5/78
Love Me	12/76	12/76
Duke ELLINGTON (US)		
Skin Deep		3/54
Missy 'Misdemeanor' ELLIOTT (US)		
4 My People		4/02
Get Ur Freak On	5/01	4/01
Hot Boyz	11/99	
One Minute Man	9/01	
❖ with Da Brat & Mariah Carey		
Sock It 2 Me	11/97	
❖ featuring Ludacris		
Gossip Folks	2/03	
Missy ELLIOTT (US)		
Work It	10/02	11/02
❖ featuring Ciara & Fat Man Scoop		
Lose Control	7/05	7/05
Shirley ELLIS (US)		
The Clapping Song	4/65	5/65
The Name Game	1/65	
The Nitty Gritty	1/64	
Jennifer ELLISON (UK)		
Baby I Don't Care		6/03
Sophie ELLIS-BEXTOR (UK)		
Catch You		3/07
Get Over You/Move This Mountain		6/02
Mixed Up World		10/03
Murder On The Dancefloor		12/01
Take Me Home (A Girl Like Me)		8/01
EMBRACE (UK)		
Come Back To What You Know		6/98
Gravity		9/04
Natures Law		4/06
World At Your Feet		6/06
EMERSON, LAKE & PALMER (UK)		
Fanfare For The Common Man		6/77
EMF (UK)		
I Believe		2/91
Unbelievable	6/91	11/90
EMF/REEVES AND MORTIMER (UK)		
I'm A Believer		7/95
EMILIA (S)		
Big Big World		12/98
EMINEM (US)		
Ass Like That		8/05
Business		7/03
Cleanin' Out My Closet	8/02	9/02
Guilty Conscience		8/99
Just Lose It	10/04	11/04
Like Toy Soldiers		2/05
Lose Yourself	10/02	12/02
Mockingbird	2/05	5/05
My Name Is		4/99
Sing For The Moment	5/03	3/03
Stan		1/01
Superman	3/03	
The Real Slim Shady		7/00
The Way I Am		10/00
We Made You	5/09	4/09
When I'm Gone	12/05	12/05
Without Me	5/02	6/02
EMINEM, DR. DRE & 50 CENT (US)		
Crack A Bottle	2/09	2/09
EMINEM featuring Nate DOGG		
Shake That	2/06	
EMINEM, 50 CENT, Lloyd BANK$, CASHIS		
You Don't Know	12/06	
EMMA (UK)		
Free Me		6/03
I'll Be There		2/04
Maybe		10/03
EMMIE (UK)		
More Than This		1/99
EMOTIONS (US)		
Best Of My Love	7/77	9/77
❖ with Earth, Wind & Fire		
Boogie Wonderland	6/79	6/79
EMPIRE OF THE SUN (AUS)		
We Are The People		6/09
EN VOGUE (US)		
Don't Let Go (Love)	11/96	
Free Your Mind	10/92	11/92
Giving Him Something He Can Feel	8/92	11/92
Hold On	6/90	5/90
My Lovin' (You're Never Gonna Get It)	4/92	5/92
Whatever		7/97
❖ with Salt-N-Pepa		
Whatta Man	2/94	3/94
ENEMY (UK)		
Away From Here		4/07
Had Enough		7/07
Harry ENFIELD (UK)		
Loadsamoney (Doin' Up The House)		5/88
ENGLAND DAN & John Ford Coley (US)		
I'd Really Love To See You Tonight	8/76	
Love Is The Answer	5/79	
Nights Are Forever Without You	11/76	
We'll Never Have To Say Goodbye Again	4/78	
ENGLAND WORLD CUP SQUAD (UK)		
Back Home		5/70
This Time (We'll Get It Right)/ England We'll Fly The Flag		5/82
ENGLANDNEWORDER (UK)		
World In Motion...		6/90
Scott ENGLISH (US)		
Brandy		11/71
ENIGMA (UK)		
Ain't No Stoppin'		6/81
ENIGMA (R/G)		
Return To Innocence	4/94	1/94
Sadness Part 1	3/91	12/90
ENYA (I)		
Anywhere Is		11/95
Book Of Days		8/92
Only Time	10/01	
Orinoco Flow		10/88
EQUALS (UK/GUY)		
Baby Come Back		6/68
Black Skin Blue Eyed Boys		1/71
Viva Bobbie Joe		8/69
ERASURE (UK)		
Abba-Esque (E.P.)		6/92
Always		5/94
Blue Savannah		3/90
Breath Of Life		4/92
Breathe		1/05
Chains Of Love		6/88
Chorus		6/91
The Circus		10/87
Crackers International (E.P.)		12/88
Drama!		10/89
It Doesn't Have To Be		3/87
A Little Respect		10/88
Love To Hate You		9/91
Run To The Sun		7/94
Ship Of Fools		3/88
Solsbury Hill		1/03
Sometimes		12/86
Star		6/90
Victim Of Love		6/87
Who Needs Love (Like That)		11/92
ERNIE (US)		
Rubber Duckie	9/70	
ERUPTION (US)		
I Can't Stand The Rain		3/78
One Way Ticket		5/79
ESCAPE CLUB (UK)		
I'll Be There	8/91	
Wild Wild West	10/88	
ESQUIRES (US)		
Get On Up	10/67	
ESSEX (US)		
Easier Said Than Done	6/63	
A Walkin' Miracle	9/63	
David ESSEX (UK)		
Gonna Make You A Star		10/74
Hold Me Close		9/75
If I Could		1/76
Lamplight		12/73
Oh What A Circus		9/78
Rock On	2/74	9/73
Rollin' Stone		7/75
Silver Dream Machine (Pt. 1)		4/80
Stardust		1/75
Tahiti (From 'Mutiny On The Bounty')		10/83
A Winter's Tale		12/82
Gloria ESTEFAN (US)		
Coming Out Of The Dark	3/91	
Don't Wanna Lose You	8/89	7/89
Get On Your Feet	11/89	
Go Away		4/93
Hold Me, Thrill Me, Kiss Me		12/94
Here We Are	2/90	

	US Top 20 Ent	UK Top 20 Ent
Miami Hit Mix/Christmas Through Your Eyes		12/92
Turn The Beat Around	11/94	
Gloria ESTEFAN & The Miami Sound Machine (US)		
Anything For You	4/88	9/88
Bad Boy	4/86	
Can't Stay Away From You	2/88	3/89
Conga	1/86	
Dr. Beat		9/84
1-2-3	7/88	11/88
Rhythm Is Gonna Get You	7/87	
Words Get In The Way	9/86	
ESTELLE featuring Kanye WEST (UK/US)		
American Boy	8/08	3/08
Deon ESTUS (US)		
Heaven Help Me	4/89	
ETERNAL (UK)		
I Am Blessed		12/95
Just A Step From Heaven		5/94
Oh Baby I...		11/94
Power Of A Woman		10/95
Save Our Love		1/94
So Good		8/94
Stay		10/93
Melissa ETHERIDGE (US)		
I'm The Only One	11/94	
If I Wanted To/Like The Way I Do	3/95	
EUROPE (S)		
Carrie	9/87	
The Final Countdown	3/87	11/86
EURYTHMICS (UK)		
Here Comes The Rain Again	3/84	2/84
It's Alright (Baby's Coming Back)		1/86
Love Is A Stranger		4/83
Missionary Man	10/86	
Right By Your Side		12/83
Sexcrime (Nineteen Eighty Four)		11/84
Sweet Dreams (Are Made Of This)	7/83	3/83
There Must Be An Angel		7/85
Thorn In My Side		9/86
Who's That Girl		7/83
Would I Lie To You?	6/85	
EURYTHMICS & Aretha Franklin (UK/US)		
Sisters Are Doin' It For Themselves		11/85
EVAN AND JARON (US)		
Crazy For The Girl	03/01	
EVANESCENCE (US)		
Call Me When You're Sober	9/6	10/6
Going Under		10/03
My Immortal	3/04	12/03
❖ featuring Paul McCoy		
Bring Me To Life	4/03	6/03
Faith EVANS (US)		
I Love You	4/02	
Love Like This	11/98	
Never Gonna Let Go	09/99	
Faith EVANS with Puff Daddy (US)		
All Night Long	3/99	
Maureen EVANS (UK)		
Like I Do		1/63
Paul EVANS (US)		
Happy-Go-Lucky-Me	6/60	
Hello This Is Joannie (The Telephone Answering Machine Song)		1/79
Midnite Special	3/60	
Paul EVANS & The Curls (US)		
Seven Little Girls Sitting In The Back Seat	11/59	
EVE (US)		
Who's That Girl		5/01
❖ featuring Alicia KEYS (C)		
Gangsta Lovin'	8/02	10/2
❖ featuring Gwen STEFANI (C)		
Let Me Blow Ya Mind	6/01	8/01
Betty EVERETT (US)		
Shoop Shoop Song (It's In His Kiss)	4/64	
❖ with Jerry Butler Let It Be Me	10/64	
Kenny EVERETT (UK)		
Snot Rap		4/83
EVERCLEAR (US)		
Wonderful	09/00	
EVERLAST (US)		
What It's Like	5/99	
EVERLY BROTHERS (US)		
All I Have To Do Is Dream	5/58	6/58
Bird Dog	8/58	9/58
Bye Bye Love	6/57	7/57
Cathy's Clown	5/60	4/60
Cryin' In The Rain	2/62	1/62
Devoted To You	9/58	
Ebony Eyes	2/61	
Let It Be Me	2/60	
Love Is Strange		11/65
No One Can Make My Sunshine Smile		11/62
Poor Jenny	7/59	
The Price Of Love		6/65
Problems	12/58	1/59
So Sad (To Watch Good Love Go Bad)	9/60	10/60
Take A Message To Mary	5/59	
Temptation		6/61
That's Old Fashioned (That's The Way Love Should Be)	6/62	
('Til) I Kissed You	9/59	9/59
Wake Up Little Susie	10/57	11/57
Walk Right Back	3/61	2/61
When Will I Be Loved	7/60	7/60
Phil EVERLY & Cliff Richard (US/UK)		
She Means Nothing To Me		3/83
EVERY MOTHERS' SON (US)		
Come On Down To My Boat	6/67	
EVERYTHING BUT THE GIRL (UK)		
I Don't Want To Talk About It		7/88
Missing	12/95	10/95
EXCITERS (US)		
Tell Him	1/63	
EXILE (US)		
Kiss You All Over	8/78	9/78
EXPOSE (US)		
Come Go With Me	3/87	
I'll Never Get Over You (Getting Over Me)	6/93	
Let Me Be The One	10/87	
Point Of No Return	6/87	
Seasons Change	1/88	
Tell Me Why	2/90	
What You Don't Know	7/89	
When I Looked At Him	10/89	
EXTREME (US)		
Hole Hearted	10/91	
More Than Words	5/91	7/91
Rest In Peace		9/92
Song For Love		5/92
FAB featuring MC PARKER (UK)		
Thunderbirds Are Go		7/90
Shelley FABARES (US)		
Johnny Angel	3/62	
FABIAN (US)		
Hound Dog Man	12/59	
Tiger	7/59	
Turn Me Loose	4/59	
FABOLOUS featuring NE-YO (US)		
Make Me Better	7/07	
FABOLOUS featuring The-Dream (US)		
Throw It In The Bag	9/09	
Bent FABRIC (N)		
Alley Cat	9/62	
FABOLOUS (US)		
Breathe		11/04
FABOLOUS Featuring Mike SHOREY & LIL' MO (US)		
Can't Let You Go	4/03	
FABOLOUS featuring TAMIA or ASHANTI		
Into You	7/03	
FABULOUS THUNDERBIRDS (US)		
Tuff Enuff	7/86	
FACES (UK)		
Cindy Incidentally		2/73
Pool Hall Richard/I Wish It Would Rain		1/74
Stay With Me	2/72	1/72
Rod STEWART & The Faces (UK)		
You Can Make Me Dance Sing Or Anything...		12/74
Joe FAGIN (UK)		
That's Living (Alright)		1/84
Yvonne FAIR (US)		
It Should Have Been Me		2/76
FAIRGROUND ATTRACTION (UK)		
Find My Love		8/88
Perfect		5/88
FAIR WEATHER (UK)		
Natural Sinner		8/70
Andy FAIRWEATHER-LOW (UK)		
Reggae Tune		10/74
Wide Eyed And Legless		12/75
FAITH NO MORE (US)		
Epic	8/90	
I'm Easy/Be Aggressive		1/93
Midlife Crisis		6/92
Adam FAITH (UK)		
As You Like It		5/62
Don't That Beat All		9/62
Don't You Know It		7/61
Easy Going Me		5/61
The First Time		10/63
How About That		9/60
Lonely Pup (In A Christmas Shop)		12/60
Lonesome		2/62
Made You		7/60
Message To Martha (Kentucky Bluebird)		12/64
Poor Me		2/60
Someone Else's Baby		4/60
The Time Has Come		11/61
We Are In Love		1/64
What Do You Want		11/59
When Johnny Comes Marching Home		7/60
Who Am I/This Is It		2/61
Horace FAITH (J)		
Black Pearl		10/70
Percy FAITH (US)		
Theme From 'A Summer Place'	2/60	3/60
Marianne FAITHFULL (UK)		
As Tears Go By		9/64
Come And Stay With Me		3/65
Summer Nights		8/65
This Little Bird		5/65
FAITHLESS (UK)		
God Is A DJ		9/98
Insomnia		10/96
Mass Destruction		6/04
We Come 1		6/01
❖ featuring DIDO (UK)		
One Step Too Far		4/02
FALCO (A)		
Rock Me Amadeus	3/86	4/86
Vienna Calling		6/86
FALL OUT BOY (US)		
Dance, Dance	1/06	4/06
It's Not A Scene, It's An Arms Race	2/07	2/07
Sugar, We're Goin Down	9/05	2/06
Thnks Fr Th Mmrs	6/07	4/07
Harold FALTERMEYER (G)		
Axel F	5/85	6/85
FAME AND PRICE TOGETHER (UK)		
Rosetta		5/71
Georgie FAME (UK)		
The Ballad Of Bonnie And Clyde	3/68	1/68
Get Away		7/66
Sittin' In The Park		1/67
Sunny		10/66
Yeh Yeh		1/65
FAMILY STAND (US)		
Ghetto Heaven		4/90
FAMILY (UK)		
Burlesque		11/72
In My Own Time		8/71
Strange Band		10/70
FAMILY DOGG (UK)		
Way Of Life		7/69
FANTASIA (US)		
I Believe	7/04	
FANTASTICS (US)		
Something Old, Something New		4/71
FAR CORPORATION (UK/US/G/Swi)		
Stairway To Heaven		11/85
Don FARDON (UK)		
Indian Reservation		11/70
Donna FARGO (US)		
Funny Face	12/72	
The Happiest Girl In The Whole U.S.A.	8/72	
Chris FARLOWE (UK)		
Out Of Time		7/66
FARM (UK)		
All Together Now		12/90
Groovy Train		9/90
FARM featuring SFX BOYS' CHOIR, LIVERPOOL		
All Together Now 2004		6/04
John FARNHAM (AUS)		
You're The Voice		6/87
Dionne FARRIS (US)		
I Know	3/95	
FAST FOOD ROCKERS (UK)		
Fast Food Song		6/03
FAT BOYS & The Beach Boys (US)		
Wipeout	9/87	9/87
FAT BOYS & CHUBBY CHECKER (US)		

	US Top 20 Ent	UK Top 20 Ent
In The Ayer	9/08	
FLO RIDA featuring Wynter (US)		
Sugar	5/09	
FLOATERS (US)		
Float On	8/77	8/77
A FLOCK OF SEAGULLS (UK)		
I Ran (So Far Away)	10/82	
Wishing (If I Had A Photograph Of You)		12/82
FLORENCE + THE MACHINE (UK)		
Rabbit Heart (Raise It Up)	7/09	
FLOWERPOT MEN (UK)		
Let's Go To San Francisco		9/67
Mike FLOWERS POPS (UK)		
Wonderwall		12/95
Eddie FLOYD (US)		
Bring It On Home To Me	12/68	
FLYING LIZARDS (UK)		
Money		9/79
FLYING MACHINE (UK)		
Smile A Little Smile For Me	11/69	
FLYING PICKETS (UK)		
Only You		12/83
When You're Young And In Love		5/84
FOCUS (H)		
Hocus Pocus	5/73	
Sylvia		2/73
Dan FOGELBERG (US)		
Hard To Say	10/81	
The Language Of Love	3/84	
Leader Of The Band	2/82	
Longer	2/80	
Same Old Lang Syne	2/81	
John FOGERTY (US)		
The Old Man Down The Road	2/85	
Wayne FONTANA (UK)		
Pamela Pamela		1/67
Wayne FONTANA & THE MINDBENDERS (UK)		
Game Of Love	4/65	2/65
Um Um Um Um Um Um		11/64
FONTANE SISTERS (US)		
Daddy-O	12/55	
Eddie My Love	4/56	
Hearts Of Stone	12/54	
Seventeen	9/55	
FOO FIGHTERS (US)		
All My Life		10/02
Best Of You		6/05
The Pretender		9/07
This Is A Call		7/95
Steve FORBERT (US)		
Romeo's Tune	2/80	
FORCE MD'S (US)		
Tender Love	4/86	
Emile FORD & THE CHECKMATES (UK)		
Counting Teardrops		12/60
On A Slow Boat To China		2/60
What Do You Want To Make Those Eyes At Me For		11/59
Frankie FORD (US)		
Sea Cruise	4/59	
Lita FORD (US)		
Kiss Me Deadly	6/88	
Lita FORD (& Ozzy Osbourne) (US/UK)		
Close My Eyes Forever	5/89	
Tennessee Ernie FORD (US)		
Ballad Of Davy Crockett	3/55	1/56
Give Me Your Word		1/55
Sixteen Tons	11/55	1/56
FOREIGNER (UK/US)		
Cold As Ice	9/77	
Dirty White Boy	10/79	
Double Vision	10/78	
Feels Like The First Time	5/77	
Head Games	12/79	
Hot Blooded	7/78	
I Don't Want To Live Without You	5/88	
I Want To Know What Love Is	1/85	1/85
Say You Will	2/88	
That Was Yesterday	5/85	
Urgent	8/81	
Waiting For A Girl Like You	11/81	1/82
FORREST (US)		
Rock The Boat		3/83
FORT MINOR featuring Holly BROOK (US)		
Where'd You Go	5/06	
Lance FORTUNE (UK)		

	US Top 20 Ent	UK Top 20 Ent
Be Mine		3/60
FORTUNES (UK)		
Freedom Come Freedom Go		10/71
Here Comes That Rainy Day Feeling Again	7/71	
Here It Comes Again		10/65
Storm In A Teacup		2/72
This Golden Ring		3/66
You've Got Your Troubles	9/65	7/65
49ERS (ITA)		
Touch Me		1/90
FOUNDATIONS (UK)		
Baby Now That I've Found You	2/68	10/67
Build Me Up Buttercup	2/69	12/68
In The Bad Bad Old Days		4/69
4-4-2 (UK)		
Come On England		6/04
411 featuring GHOSTFACE KILLAH (US)		
On My Knees		54/04
The 411		
Dumb		9/04
FOUR ACES (US)		
The Gang That Sang 'Heart Of My Heart'	1/54	
Love Is A Many-Splendored Thing	9/55	11/55
Melody Of Love	2/55	
Mr Sandman	11/54	1/55
Stranger In Paradise	1/54	5/55
Three Coins In The Fountain	5/54	7/54
FOUR KNIGHTS (US)		
I Get So Lonely	2/54	6/54
FOUR LADS (US)		
Moments To Remember	9/55	
No, Not Much!	2/56	
Skokiaan	9/54	
Standing On The Corner	5/56	
4 NON BLONDES (US)		
What's Up	7/93	7/93
FOUR PENNIES (UK)		
I Found Out The Hard Way		8/64
Juliet		5/64
4 P.M. (US)		
Sukiyaki	12/94	
FOUR PREPS (US)		
Big Man	5/58	6/58
Down By The Station	2/60	
26 Miles	3/58	
FOUR SEASONS (US)		
Big Girls Don't Cry	11/62	2/63
Bye, Bye, Baby (Baby Goodbye)	2/65	
C'mon Marianne	7/67	
Candy Girl	8/63	
Dawn (Go Away)	2/64	
December '63 (Oh What A Night)	2/76	2/76
★ December '63 (Oh What A Night)		10/94
Don't Think Twice (as Wonder Who)	12/65	
I've Got You Under My Skin	10/66	11/66
Let's Hang On!	11/65	12/65
Opus 17 (Don't You Worry 'Bout Me)	6/66	
Rag Doll	7/64	9/64
Ronnie	5/64	
Save It For Me	9/64	
Sherry	9/62	10/62
Silver Star		5/76
Tell It To The Rain	1/67	
Walk Like A Man	2/63	4/63
Who Loves You	10/75	10/75
Working My Way Back To You	2/66	
Frankie Valli & FOUR SEASONS (US)		
The Night		5/75
4 THE CAUSE (US)		
Stand By Me		10/98
FOUR TOPS (US)		
Ain't No Woman (Like The One I've Got)	3/73	
Baby I Need Your Loving	10/64	
Bernadette	4/67	4/67
Do What You Gotta Do		10/69
I Can't Help Myself	6/65	4/70
If I Were A Carpenter		3/68
It's All In The Game		6/70
It's The Same Old Song	8/65	
Keeper Of The Castle	12/72	
Loco In Acapulco		12/88
Reach Out I'll Be There	10/66	10/66
★ Reach Out I'll Be There		8/88
Seven Rooms Of Gloom	6/67	7/67
Simple Game		10/71
Standing In The Shadows Of Love	1/67	1/67
Still Water (Love)	10/70	10/70
Walk Away Renee		12/67

	US Top 20 Ent	UK Top 20 Ent
When She Was My Girl	10/81	11/81
❖ with The Supremes		
River Deep-Mountain High	1/71	7/71
FOUR TUNES (US)		
I Understand Just How You Feel	6/54	
FOURMOST (UK)		
Hello Little Girl		10/63
A Little Loving		5/64
FOX (UK)		
Only You Can		3/75
S-S-S-Single Bed		4/76
Samantha FOX (UK)		
Do Ya Do Ya (Wanna Please Me)		7/86
I Wanna Have Some Fun	2/89	
Naughty Girls (Need Love Too)	5/88	
Nothing's Gonna Stop Me Now		6/87
Touch Me (I Want Your Body)	1/87	3/86
Inez FOXX (US)		
Mockingbird	8/63	
Jamie FOXX featuring LUDACRIS (US)		
Unpredictable	2/06	
Jamie FOXX featuring T-PAIN (US)		
Blame It	3/09	
FOXY (US)		
Get Off	10/78	
FPI PROJECT (ITA)		
Going Back To My Roots/Rich In Paradise		1/90
FRAGMA (G/Spa)		
Toca's Miracle		4/00
Every Time You Need Me		1/01
You Are Alive		5/01
Peter FRAMPTON (UK)		
Baby, I Love Your Way	8/76	
Do You Feel Like We Do	11/76	
I Can't Stand It No More	7/79	
I'm In You	7/77	
Show Me The Way	4/76	6/76
Connie FRANCIS (US)		
Among My Souvenirs	12/59	12/59
Breakin' In A Brand New Broken Heart	5/61	7/61
Carolina Moon/Stupid Cupid		8/58
Don't Break The Heart That Loves You	3/62	
Everybody's Somebody's Fool	6/60	8/60
Frankie	6/59	
I'm Sorry I Made You Cry		7/58
Lipstick On Your Collar	6/59	7/59
Mama	3/60	5/60
Many Tears Ago	12/60	2/61
My Happiness	12/58	2/59
My Heart Has A Mind Of Its Own	9/60	11/60
Robot Man		6/60
Second Hand Love	6/62	
Together	7/61	9/61
Vacation	8/62	8/62
When The Boy In Your Arms (Is The Boy In Your Heart)	1/62	
Where The Boys Are	2/61	4/61
Who's Sorry Now	3/58	4/58
You Always Hurt The One You Love		1/59
FRANK AND WALTERS (I)		
After All		1/93
FRANKE & The Knockouts (US)		
Sweetheart	5/81	
FRANKEE (US)		
F.U.R.B – F U Right Back		5/04
FRANKIE GOES TO HOLLYWOOD (UK)		
The Power Of Love		12/84
★The Power Of Love		12/93
★The Power Of Love		7/00
Rage Hard		9/86
Relax	3/85	1/84
★Relax		10/93
Two Tribes		6/84
Welcome To The Pleasure Dome		4/85
Aretha FRANKLIN (US)		
Baby I Love You	8/67	
Bridge Over Troubled Water/Brand New Me	5/71	
Call Me	4/70	
Chain Of Fools	1/68	
Day Dreaming	4/72	
A Deeper Love		2/94
Don't Play That Song	9/70	9/70
Freeway Of Love	8/85	
The House That Jack Built	9/68	
I Never Loved A Man (The Way I Love You)	4/67	
I Say A Little Prayer	9/68	8/68
A Natural Woman (You Make Me Feel Like)	10/67	
Respect	5/67	7/67

	US Top 20 Ent	UK Top 20 Ent
Rock Steady	11/71	
See Saw	12/68	
Share Your Love With Me	9/69	
Spanish Harlem	8/71	
(Sweet Sweet Baby) Since You've Been Gone	3/68	
Think	6/68	
Until You Come Back To Me (That's What I'm Gonna Do)	1/74	
Who's Zoomin' Who	11/85	1/86
❖ *with Eurythmics*		
Sisters Are Doin' It For Themselves		11/85
Aretha FRANKLIN & George Michael (US/UK)		
I Knew You Were Waiting (For Me)	3/87	1/87
Rodney FRANKLIN (US)		
The Groove		5/80
FRANTIQUE (US)		
Strut Your Funky Stuff		9/79
FRANZ FERDINAND (UK)		
Do You Want To		10/05
Take Me Out		1/04
FRATELLIS (UK)		
Chelsea Dagger		9/06
FRAY (US)		
How To Save A Life	9/06	2/07
Over My Head (Cable Car)	5/06	
You Found Me	12/08	
FREAK NASTY (US)		
Da' Dip	5/97	
FREAK POWER (UK/Can)		
Turn On, Tune In, Cop Out		3/95
FREAKS (UK)		
The Creeps (Get On The Dancefloor)		9/07
Stan FREBERG (US)		
Sh-Boom		11/54
John FRED & His Playboy Band (US)		
Judy In Disguise (With Glasses)	12/67	1/68
FREDDIE & THE DREAMERS (UK)		
I Understand		12/64
I'm Telling You Now	4/65	8/63
If You Gotta Make A Fool Of Somebody		6/63
Over You		3/64
You Were Made For Me		11/63
FREE (UK)		
All Right Now	10/70	6/70
★ All Right Now		8/73
★ All Right Now		2/91
Free (E.P.)		3/78
Little Bit Of Love		7/72
My Brother Jake		5/71
Wishing Well		1/73
FREEEZ (UK)		
I.O.U.		7/83
Southern Freeez		3/81
Bobby FREEMAN (US)		
C'mon And Swim	8/64	
Do You Want To Dance	6/58	
Ernie FREEMAN (US)		
Raunchy	11/57	
FREEMASONS featuring Bailey Tzuke (UK)		
Uninvited		10/07
FREE MOVEMENT (US)		
I've Found Someone Of My Own	10/71	
Ace FREHLEY (US)		
New York Groove	1/79	
FREIHEIT (G)		
Keeping The Dream Alive		1/89
Nicki FRENCH (UK)		
Total Eclipse Of The Heart	5/95	1/95
FRESH 4 featuring Lizz E (UK)		
Wishing On A Star		10/89
Doug E FRESH & The Get Fresh Crew (US)		
The Show		11/85
Glenn FREY (US)		
The Heat Is On	2/85	4/85
The One You Love	11/82	
Smuggler's Blues	6/85	
True Love	10/88	
You Belong To The City	10/85	
FRIDA (N)		
I Know There's Something Going On	3/83	
FRIDAY HILL (UK)		
Baby Goodbye		10/05
Dean FRIEDMAN (US)		
Lucky Stars		10/78
FRIEND AND LOVER (US)		

	US Top 20 Ent	UK Top 20 Ent
Reach Out Of The Darkness	6/68	
FRIENDS OF DISTINCTION (US)		
Going In Circles	11/69	
Grazin' In The Grass	5/69	
Love Or Let Me Be Lonely	4/70	
FRIJID PINK (US)		
House Of The Rising Sun	3/70	5/70
FUGEES (UK)		
Killing Me Softly		6/96
No Woman No Cry		11/96
Ready Or Not		9/96
Rumble In The Jungle		3/97
FULL FORCE (US)		
Alice I Want You Just For Me		1/86
Bobby FULLER FOUR (US)		
I Fought The Law	3/66	
FUN BOY THREE (UK)		
Our Lips Are Sealed		5/83
The Tunnel Of Love		2/83
❖ *with Bananarama*		
Really Saying Something		5/82
FUN BOY THREE & BANANARAMA (UK)		
It Ain't What You Do It's The Way…		3/82
FUN LOVIN' CRIMINALS (US)		
Loco		2/01
FARLEY 'JACKMASTER' FUNK (US)		
Love Can't Turn Around		9/86
FUNKADELIC (US)		
One Nation Under A Groove (Pt. 1)		1/79
FUNK MASTERS (UK)		
It's Over		7/83
FUNKY WORM (UK)		
Hustle! (To The Music…)		8/88
FUREYS & Davey Arthur (UK)		
When You Were Sweet Sixteen		11/81
Nelly FURTADO (US)		
All Good Things (Come To An End)		12/06
I'm Like A Bird	5/01	3/01
Maneater		6/06
Say It Right	12/06	3/07
Turn Off The Light	10/01	9/01
featuring Timbaland		
Promiscuous	6/06	9/06
Billy FURY (UK)		
Halfway To Paradise		6/61
I Will		5/64
I'd Never Find Another You		12/61
In Summer		8/63
In Thoughts Of You		8/65
It's Only Make Believe		8/64
Jealousy		9/61
Last Night Was Made For Love		5/62
Like I've Never Been Gone		3/63
Once Upon A Dream		8/62
When Will You Say I Love You		5/63
FUZZBOX (UK)		
International Rescue		4/89
Sylk-E FYNE AND CHILL (US)		
Romeo And Juliet	4/98	
Ali G & SHAGGY (UK)		
❖ Me Julie		3/02
Dario G (UK)		
Carnaval De Paris		6/98
Dream To Me		2/01
Sunchyme		9/97
Kenny G (US)		
Auld Lang Syne	01/00	
Songbird	6/87	
Gina G (AUS)		
Fresh		3/97
I Belong To You		11/96
Ooh Aah…Just A Little Bit	2/97	
Warren G (US)		
This D.J.	8/94	11/94
❖ *feat. Mack 10*		
I Want It All	09/99	
Warren G & Nate Dogg (US)		
Regulate	5/94	7/94
G-UNIT (US)		
Stunt 101	11/03	
Peter GABRIEL (UK)		
Big Time	2/87	4/87
Games Without Frontiers		3/80
Sledgehammer	6/86	5/86
Solsbury Hill		5/77
Steam		1/93
Peter GABRIEL & Kate Bush (UK)		
Don't Give Up		11/86

	US Top 20 Ent	UK Top 20 Ent
GABRIELLE (UK)		
Dreams		6/93
Give Me A Little More Time		3/96
Going Nowhere		10/93
Out Of Reach		4/01
Rise		2/00
Walk On By		2/97
When A Woman		6/00
Rosie GAINES (US)		
Closer Than Close		5/97
GALA (ITA)		
Freed From Desire		7/97
Let A Boy Cry		12/97
GALAXY (UK) see Phil Fearon & Galaxy		
GALLAGHER & LYLE (UK)		
Heart On My Sleeve		6/76
I Wanna Stay With You		3/76
Patsy GALLANT (C)		
From New York To L.A.		10/77
GALLERY (US)		
Nice To Be With You	6/72	
James GALWAY (UK)		
Annie's Song		6/78
GAME featuring 50 CENT (US)		
Hate It Or Love It	3/05	5/05
How We Do	1/05	2/05
The GAME (US)		
Dreams		8/05
GAP BAND (US)		
Big Fun		12/86
Oops Upside Your Head		8/80
GARBAGE (US/UK)		
Stupid Girl		3/96
Why Do You Love Me		4/05
Boris GARDINER (J)		
I Want To Wake Up With You		8/86
Art GARFUNKEL (US)		
All I Know	10/73	
Bright Eyes		4/79
I Only Have Eyes For You		9/75
Art GARFUNKEL, James TAYLOR & Paul SIMON (US)		
Wonderful World		3/78
Gale GARNETT (US)		
We'll Sing In The Sunshine	10/64	
Leif GARRETT (US)		
I Was Made For Dancin'	2/79	2/79
Runaround Sue	1/78	
GARY'S GANG (US)		
Keep On Dancin'		3/79
GAT DECOR (UK)		
Passion		3/96
Stephen GATELY (I)		
I Believe		10/00
David GATES (US)		
Goodbye Girl	4/78	
Gareth GATES (UK)		
Anyone Of Us (Stupid Mistake)		7/02
Say It Isn't So		12/03
Sunshine		9/03
Suspicious Minds		10/02
Unchained Melody		3/02
What My Heart Wants To Say		12/02
❖ *featuring The KUMARS (UK)*		
Spirit In The Sky		3/03
Alex GAUDINO featuring Crystal WATERS (ITA/US)		
Destination Calabria		3/07
Marvin GAYE (US)		
Abraham Martin & John		6/70
Ain't That Peculiar	11/65	
Got To Give It Up (Pt.1)	5/77	5/77
How Sweet It Is To Be Loved By You	1/65	
I Heard It Through The Grapevine	12/68	3/69
★ I Heard It Through The Grapevine		5/86
I Want You	6/76	
I'll Be Doggone	5/65	
Inner City Blues (Makes Me Wanna Holler)	11/71	
Let's Get It On	8/73	
Mercy Mercy Me (The Ecology)	8/71	
Pride And Joy	7/63	
Sexual Healing	12/82	11/82
That's The Way Love Is	10/69	
Too Busy Thinking About My Baby	6/69	8/69
Trouble Man	1/73	
Try It Baby	7/64	
What's Going On	3/71	
❖ *with Diana Ross* You Are Everything		4/74
You're A Wonderful One	4/64	
Marvin GAYE & Diana ROSS (US)		

	US Top 20 Ent	UK Top 20 Ent
Dickie GOODMAN (US)		
Mr Jaws	10/75	
Delta GOODREM (AUS)		
Born To Try		3/03
Innocent Eyes		10/03
Lost Without You		6/03
GOOMBAY DANCE BAND (G/UK)		
Seven Tears		3/82
GOONS (UK)		
Bloodnok's Rock 'n' Roll Call/		
Ying Tong Song		9/56
I'm Walking Backwards For Christmas/		
Bluebottle Blues		7/56
★ Ying Tong Song		8/73
Barry GORDON (US)		
Nuttin' For Christmas	12/55	
Lonnie GORDON (US)		
Happenin' All Over Again		2/90
Lesley GORE (US)		
It's My Party	6/63	6/63
Judy's Turn To Cry	8/63	
She's A Fool	11/63	
That's The Way Boys Are	4/64	
You Don't Own Me	2/64	
GORILLAZ (UK)		
Clint Eastwood		3/01
Dare		9/05
Dirty Harry		12/05
Feel Good Inc	8/05	5/05
19/2000		7/01
Eydie GORME (US)		
Blame It On The Bossa Nova	2/63	
Yes My Darling Daughter		7/62
❖ *with Steve Lawrence*		
I Want To Stay Here		9/63
GOSSIP (US)		
Standing In The Way Of Control		3/07
Irv GOTTI Presents JA RULE, ASHANTI, Charli BALTIMORE & VITA (US)		
❖ Down 4 U	7/02	10/02
G.Q. (US)		
Disco Nights (Rock Freak)	5/79	
GRACE (UK)		
Not Over Yet		4/95
Charlie GRACIE (US)		
Butterfly	3/57	5/57
Fabulous		6/57
Wanderin' Eyes/I Love You So Much		
It Hurts		9/57
Jaki GRAHAM (UK)		
❖ *with David Grant*		
Could It Be I'm Falling In Love		4/85
Round And Round		7/85
Set Me Free		6/86
Larry GRAHAM (US)		
One In A Million You	9/80	
Max GRAHAM vs YES (C)		
Owner Of A Lonely Heart		5/05
Lou GRAMM (US)		
Just Between You And Me	1/90	
Midnight Blue	4/87	
Billy GRAMMER (US)		
Gotta Travel On	12/58	
Fedde LE GRAND (H)		
Put Your Hands Up For Detroit		11/06
GRAND FUNK (US)		
Bad Time	5/75	
The Loco-Motion	4/74	
Shinin' On	8/74	
Some Kind Of Wonderful	1/75	
We're An American Band	9/73	
GRANDPUBA (US) see Shaggy featuring Grand Puba		
GRANDMASTER FLASH, Melle Mel & The Furious Five US)		
The Message		9/82
White Lines (Don't Don't Do It)		7/84
GRANDMASTER MELLE MEL & The Furious Five (US)		
Step Off (Pt 1)		1/85
GRANGE HILL CAST (UK)		
Just Say No		4/86
Amy GRANT (US)		
Baby Baby	4/91	5/91
Every Heartbeat	7/91	
Good For Me	2/92	
That's What Love Is For	11/91	
❖ *with Peter Cetera*		
The Next Time I Fall	11/86	
David GRANT (UK)		
Watching You Watching Me		8/83
David GRANT & Jaki Graham (UK)		
Could It Be I'm Falling In Love		4/85
Earl GRANT (US)		
The End	10/58	
Eddy GRANT (GUY)		
Do You Feel My Love		12/80
Electric Avenue	6/83	1/83
Electric Avenue (Remix)		6/01
Gimme Hope Jo'anna		2/88
I Don't Wanna Dance		11/82
Living On The Front Line		7/79
Gogi GRANT (US)		
Suddenly There's A Valley	10/55	
The Wayward Wind	5/56	7/56
GRASS ROOTS (US)		
I'd Wait A Million Years	9/69	
Let's Live For Today	6/67	
Midnight Confessions	10/68	
Sooner Or Later	7/71	
Temptation Eyes	3/71	
GRATEFUL DEAD (US)		
Touch Of Grey	9/87	
David GRAY (UK)		
The One I Love		9/5
Dobie GRAY (US)		
Drift Away	4/73	
The "In" Crowd	2/65	
Macy GRAY (US)		
I Try		10/99
Michael GRAY (UK)		
The Weekend		11/04
Charles RANDOLPH GREAN SOUNDE (US)		
Quentin's Theme (from TV Series 'Dark Shadows')	8/69	
GREAT WHITE (US)		
Once Bitten Twice Shy	7/89	
R B GREAVES (US)		
Take A Letter Maria	11/69	
GREEN DAY (US)		
American Idiot		9/04
Basket Case		1/95
Boulevard Of Broken Dreams	1/05	12/04
Wake Me Up When September Ends	9/05	6/05
GREEN JELLY (US)		
Three Little Pigs		6/93
Al GREEN (US)		
Call Me (Come Back Home)	3/73	
Here I Am (Come And Take Me)	8/73	
I'm Still In Love With You	8/72	
L-O-V-E (Love)	4/75	
Let's Stay Together	1/72	1/72
Look What You Done For Me	4/72	
Sha-La-La (Make Me Happy)	12/74	
Tired Of Being Alone	10/71	11/71
You Ought To Be With Me	11/72	
❖ *with Annie Lennox* Put A Little Love In Your Heart	1/89	
Robson GREEN & Jerome Flynn (UK)		
I Believe/Up On The Roof		11/95
Unchained Melody/White Cliffs Of Dover		5/95
Norman GREENBAUM (US)		
Spirit In The Sky	3/70	4/70
Lorne GREENE (US)		
Ringo	11/64	
GREYHOUND (UK)		
Black And White		7/71
Moon River		2/72
GRID (UK)		
Swamp Thing		6/94
Alistair GRIFFIN (UK)		
Bring It On/My Lover's Prayer		1/04
Andy GRIFFITH (US)		
What Is Was, Was Football	1/54	
Larry GROCE (US)		
Junk Food Junkie	3/76	
GROOVE ARMADA featuring Stush (UK)		
Get Down		5/07
GROOVE THEORY (US)		
Tell Me	11/95	
Henry GROSS (US)		
Shannon	5/76	
GTR (UK)		
When The Heart Rules The Mind	7/86	
GUESS WHO (C)		
American Woman/No Sugar Tonight	4/70	
Clap For The Wolfman	9/74	
Laughing		8/69
No Time		2/70
Share The Land		12/70
These Eyes		5/69
David GUETTA featuring AKON (F/US)		
Sexy Chick	11/09	8/09
David GUETTA featuring Chris WILLIS (F/US)		
Love Is Gone		8/07
David GUETTA featuring Kelly ROWLAND (F/US)		
When Love Takes Over		6/09
David GUETTA vs The EGG (F)		
Love Don't Let Me Go (WaAlking Away)		8/06
Greg GUIDRY (US)		
Goin' Down	5/82	
Bonnie GUITAR (US)		
Dark Moon	5/57	
GUN (UK)		
Race With The Devil		12/68
GUN (UK)		
Word Up		7/94
GUNS N' ROSES (US)		
Ain't It Fun		11/93
Don't Cry	11/91	9/91
Knockin' On Heaven's Door		5/92
Live And Let Die		12/91
November Rain	7/92	3/92
Paradise City	3/89	3/89
Patience	5/89	7/89
Since I Don't Have You		6/94
Sweet Child O' Mine	8/88	6/89
Sympathy For The Devil		1/95
Welcome To The Jungle	12/88	
Yesterdays/November Rain		11/92
You Could Be Mine		7/91
GURU JOSH (UK)		
Infinity		3/90
GURU JOSH PROJECT (UK)		
Infinity 2008		11/08
Adrian GURVITZ (UK)		
Classic		3/82
Gwen GUTHRIE (US)		
Ain't Nothing Goin' On But The Rent		8/86
A GUY CALLED GERALD (UK)		
Voodoo Ray EP		7/89
GUY (US)		
Dancin'	12/99	
GUYS & DOLLS (UK)		
There's A Whole Lot Of Loving		3/75
You Don't Have To Say You Love Me		3/76
GYM CLASS HEROES (US)		
Clothes Off!!		8/07
Cookie Jar		9/08
GYM CLASS HEROES featuring Patrick Stump (US)		
Breakfast In America	2/07	5/07
Cupid's Chokehold	2/07	5/07
H & CLAIRE (UK)		
DJ		5/02
H TWO O featuring Platnum (UK)		
What's It Gonna Be		2/08
H-TOWN (US)		
Knockin' Da Boots	5/93	
HADDAWAY (WI)		
I Miss You		1/94
Life		10/93
Rock My Heart		4/94
What Is Love	10/93	6/93
Sammy HAGAR (US)		
Your Love Is Driving Me Crazy	2/83	
HAIRCUT 100 (UK)		
Fantastic Day		5/82
Favourite Shirts (Boy Meets Girl)		11/81
Love Plus One		2/82
Nobody's Fool		9/82
Curtis HAIRSTON (US)		
I Want Your Lovin' (Just A Little Bit)		5/85
HALE & PACE & The Stonkers (UK)		
The Stonk		3/91
Bill HALEY & HIS COMETS (US)		
Dim, Dim The Lights (I Want Some Atmosphere)		12/54
Don't Knock The Rock		2/57
Razzle Dazzle		10/56
Rip It Up		11/56
★ Rock Around The Clock	5/55	10/55
★ Rock Around The Clock		9/56
★ Rock Around The Clock		4/74
Rock-A-Beatin' Boogie		1/56
Rockin' Through The Rye		8/56

	US Top 20 Ent	UK Top 20 Ent
The Saints Rock 'n Roll		6/56
See You Later, Alligator	1/56	3/56
★ See You Later, Alligator		10/56
Shake, Rattle And Roll	9/54	12/54
Aaron HALL(US)		
I Miss You	7/94	
Daryl HALL & John OATES (US)		
Adult Education	3/84	
Did It In A Minute	5/82	
Everything Your Heart Desires	5/88	
Family Man	6/83	
I Can't Go For That (No Can Do)	12/81	2/82
Kiss On My List	3/81	
Maneater	11/82	11/82
Method Of Modern Love	2/85	
One On One	3/83	
Out Of Touch	11/84	
Private Eyes	10/81	
Rich Girl	3/77	
Sara Smile	5/76	
Say It Isn't So	11/83	
She's Gone	10/76	
So Close	11/90	
You Make My Dreams	6/81	
You've Lost That Lovin' Feeling	11/80	
Daryl HALL (US)		
Dreamtime	9/86	
Larry HALL (US)		
Sandy	1/60	
Tom T HALL (US)		
I Love	2/74	
Geri HALLIWELL (UK)		
Look At Me		5/99
Bag It Up		3/00
It's Raining Men		5/01
Lift Me Up		11/99
Mi Chico Latino		8/99
Scream If You Wanna Go Faster		8/01
HALO JAMES (UK)		
Could Have Told You So		1/90
George HAMILTON IV (US)		
A Rose And A Baby Ruth	11/56	
HAMILTON, Joe Frank & Reynolds (US)		
Don't Pull Your Love	6/71	
Fallin' In Love	8/75	
Lynne HAMILTON (AUS)		
On The Inside (Theme From Prisoner: Cell Block H')		6/89
Roy HAMILTON (US)		
Don't Let Go	2/58	
Unchained Melody	5/55	
You Can Have Her	3/61	
Russ HAMILTON (UK)		
Rainbow	8/57	
We Will Make Love		6/57
Marvin HAMLISCH (US)		
The Entertainer	5/74	
HAMMER (US) see also MC Hammer		
Addams Groove	1/92	12/91
2 Legit 2 Quit	12/91	
MC HAMMER (US)		
Have You Seen Her	8/90	10/90
Pray	10/90	12/90
U Can't Touch This	5/90	7/90
Jan HAMMER (CZ)		
Crockett's Theme		10/87
Miami Vice Theme	10/85	10/85
Albert HAMMOND (UK)		
It Never Rains In Southern California	12/72	
Herbie HANCOCK (US)		
Rockit		8/83
HANSON (US)		
I Will Come To You	12/97	11/97
Mmmbop	5/97	6/97
This Time Around	04/00	
Where's The Love		9/97
HAPPENINGS (US)		
I Got Rhythm	5/67	
My Mammy	8/67	
See You In September	8/66	
HAPPY CLAPPERS (UK)		
I Believe		11/95
HAPPY MONDAYS (UK)		
Kinky Afro		10/90
Step On		4/90
HARD-FI (UK)		
Suburban Knights		9/07
Paul HARDCASTLE (UK)		
Don't Waste My Time		3/86
19	7/85	5/85
Steve HARLEY (UK)		
Here Comes The Sun		8/76
❖ with Sarah Brightman		
The Phantom Of The Opera		2/86
Steve HARLEY & COCKNEY REBEL (UK)		
Judy Teen		6/74
Make Me Smile (Come Up And See Me)		2/75
Mr Soft		8/74
Jimmy HARNEN With Sync (US)		
Where Are You Now	6/89	
HARPERS BIZARRE (US)		
The 59th Street Bridge Song (Feelin' Groovy)	4/67	
Anita HARRIS (US)		
Just Loving You		8/67
Calvin HARRIS (UK)		
Acceptable In The 80s		3/07
I'm Not Alone		4/09
Ready For The Weekend		8/09
The Girls		6/07
Jet HARRIS (UK)		
Main Title Theme From 'Man With The Golden Arm'		9/62
Jet HARRIS & Tony Meehan (UK)		
Applejack		9/63
Diamonds		1/63
Scarlett O'Hara		5/63
Keith HARRIS & Orville (UK)		
Orville's Song		1/83
Major HARRIS (US)		
Love Won't Let Me Wait	5/75	
Max HARRIS (UK)		
Gurney Slade		12/60
Richard HARRIS (UK)		
MacArthur Park	6/68	7/68
Rolf HARRIS (AUS)		
Stairway To Heaven		2/93
Sun Arise		11/62
Tie Me Kangaroo Down, Sport	7/63	8/60
Two Little Boys		12/69
Ronnie HARRIS (UK)		
Story Of Tina		9/54
Thurston HARRIS (US)		
Little Bitty Pretty One	11/57	
George HARRISON (UK)		
All Those Years Ago	6/81	
Bangla Desh		8/71
Give Me Love (Give Me Peace On Earth)	6/73	6/73
Got My Mind Set On You	12/87	11/87
My Sweet Lord/Isn't It A Pity	12/70	1/71
★ My Sweet Lord		1/02
What Is Life	3/71	
Noel HARRISON (UK)		
Windmills Of Your Mind		4/69
Wilbert HARRISON (US)		
Kansas City	5/59	
HARRY J. ALL STARS (J)		
Liquidator		11/69
Deborah HARRY (US)		
French Kissin' In The USA		11/86
I Want That Man		11/89
Corey HART (C)		
Never Surrender	7/85	
Sunglasses At Night	8/84	
Freddie HART (US)		
Easy Loving	11/71	
Richard HARTLEY/Michael Reed Orchestra (UK)		
The Music Of Torvill & Dean EP		3/84
Dan HARTMAN (US)		
I Can Dream About You	7/84	9/85
Instant Replay		11/78
Sensational Alex HARVEY BAND (UK)		
Delilah		8/75
Gordon HASKELL (UK)		
How Wonderful You Are		12/01
David HASSELHOFF (US)		
Jump In My Car		10/6
Richie HAVENS (US)		
Here Comes The Sun	5/71	
Chesney HAWKES (UK)		
The One And Only	11/91	3/91
Edwin HAWKINS SINGERS (US)		
Oh Happy Day	5/69	6/69
Sophie B HAWKINS (US)		
As I Lay Me Down	9/95	
Damn I Wish I Was Your Lover	5/92	
Right Beside You		9/94
HAWKWIND (UK)		
Silver Machine		8/72
Bill HAYES (US)		
The Ballad Of Davy Crockett	3/55	1/56
Darren HAYES (AUS)		
Insatiable		4/02
Isaac HAYES (US)		
Disco Connection		5/76
Theme From 'Shaft'	10/71	12/71
Richard HAYMAN & Jan August (US)		
A Theme From 'The Three Penny Opera' (Moritat)	3/56	
HAYSI FANTAYZEE (UK)		
John Wayne Is Big Leggy		8/82
Justin HAYWARD (UK)		
Forever Autumn		8/78
Justin HAYWARD & John Lodge (UK)		
Blue Guitar		11/75
Leon HAYWOOD (US)		
Don't Push It, Don't Force It		4/80
I Want'a Do Something Freaky To You	12/75	
Murray HEAD (UK)		
One Night In Bangkok	4/85	12/84
Superstar	5/71	
Roy HEAD (US)		
Treat Her Right	10/65	
Jeff HEALEY BAND (C)		
Angel Eyes	8/89	
HEAR'SAY (UK)		
Everybody		12/01
Pure And Simple		3/01
The Way To Your Love		7/01
HEART (US)		
All I Wanna Do Is Make Love To You	4/90	4/90
Alone	6/87	7/87
Barracuda	8/77	
Magic Man	10/76	
Never	11/85	3/88
Nothin' At All	6/86	
Straight On	12/78	
Stranded	12/90	
Tell It Like It Is	12/80	
There's The Girl	1/88	
These Dreams	3/86	3/88
What About Love?	8/85	
Who Will You Run To	9/87	
Ted HEATH (UK)		
Skin Deep		2/54
Swingin' Shepherd Blues		4/58
HEATWAVE (US)		
Always And Forever/ Mind Blowing Decisions		12/78
Boogie Nights	10/77	2/77
The Groove Line	6/78	2/78
Mind Blowing Decisions		7/78
Too Hot To Handle/Slip Your Disc To This		6/77
HEAVEN 17 (UK)		
Come Live With Me		7/83
Temptation		5/83
★ Temptation		11/92
HEAVY D & The Boyz (US)		
Now That We Found Love	9/91	7/91
Bobby HEBB (US)		
Sunny	8/66	10/66
HEDGEHOPPERS ANONYMOUS (UK)		
It's Good News Week		10/65
HEIGHTS (US)		
How Do You Talk To An Angel	10/92	
HEINZ (UK)		
Just Like Eddie		9/63
Armand Van HELDEN (H)		
Koochy		5/00
HELLO (UK)		
New York Groove		11/75
Tell Him		12/74
HELLOGOODBYE (US)		
Here (In Your Arms)		5/07
Bobby HELMS (US)		
Jingle Bell Rock	1/58	
My Special Angel	11/57	
Jimmy HELMS (US)		
Gonna Make You An Offer You Can't Refuse		3/73

	US Top 20 Ent	UK Top 20 Ent
Holy Smoke		9/90
Infinite Dreams		11/89
The Number Of The Beast		1/05
Run To The Hills		3/82
The Trooper		7/83
★ The Trooper		8/05
The Wicker Man		5/00
Wildest Dreams		9/3
IRONIK (UK)		
Stay With Me		7/08
IRONIK featuring CHIPMUNK & Elton JOHN (UK)		
Tiny Dancer (Hold Me Closer)		5/09
Big Dee IRWIN (US)		
Swinging On A Star		12/63
Chris ISAAK (US)		
Wicked Game	2/91	12/90
ISLANDERS (US)		
The Enchanted Sea	11/59	
ISLEY BROTHERS (US)		
Behind A Painted Smile		5/69
Fight The Power Pt. 1	8/75	
Harvest For The World		8/76
I Guess I'll Always Love You		2/69
It's Your Thing	4/69	
That Lady	9/73	10/73
This Old Heart Of Mine	4/66	11/68
ISOTONIK (UK)		
Different Strokes		1/92
IT BITES (UK)		
Calling All The Heroes		8/86
Burl IVES (US)		
Funny Way Of Laughin'	5/62	
A Little Bitty Tear	1/62	2/62
IVY LEAGUE (UK)		
Funny How Love Can Be		2/65
Tossing And Turning		7/65
IVY THREE (US)		
Yogi	9/60	
IYAZ (US)		
Replay	10/09	
FRANKIE J. featuring BABY BASH (US)		
Obsession (No Es Amor)	3/05	
Ray J (US)		
One Wish	12/05	
Ray J & Yung BERG (US)		
Sexy Can I	3/08	
J-KWON (US)		
Tipsy	2/04	
J-SHIN feat. LATOCHA SCOTT (US)		
One Night Stand	01/00	
JA RULE (US)		
Holla Holla	06/99	
Clap Back/Reigns		12/03
featuring ASHANTI (US)		
❖Always On Time	12/01	2/02
❖Mesmerize	1/03	
featuring CASE (US)		
❖ Livin' It Up	10/01	8/02
featuring LIL' MO & VITA (US)		
❖ Put It On Me	4/01	
featuring R. KELLY & ASHANTI (US)		
Wonderful	11/04	11/04
JACK 'N' CHILL (UK)		
The Jack That House Built		2/88
Terry JACKS (US)		
If You Go Away		7/74
Seasons In The Sun	2/74	3/74
Chad JACKSON (UK)		
Hear The Drummer (Get Wicked)		6/90
Dee D JACKSON (UK)		
Automatic Lover		5/78
Deon JACKSON (US)		
Love Makes The World Go Round	3/66	
Freddie JACKSON (US)		
You Are My Lady	11/85	
Janet JACKSON (US)		
Again	10/93	11/93
All For You	4/01	4/01
Alright	5/90	
Because Of Love	2/94	3/94
Any Time, Any Place/And On And On	6/94	6/94
Together Again	12/97	
Black Cat	10/90	
Come Back To Me	8/90	
Control	12/86	
Escapade	2/90	
If	8/93	
Let's Wait Awhile	3/87	4/87
Love Will Never Do (Without You)	12/90	
Miss You Much	9/89	
Nasty	6/86	
Rhythm Nation	12/89	
Runaway	9/95	9/95
Someone To Call My Lover	8/01	
That's The Way Love Goes	5/93	5/93
What Have You Done For Me Lately	4/86	4/86
When I Think Of You	9/86	9/86
Whoops Now/What'll I Do		3/95
You Want This/70's Love Groove	11/94	
❖ with Blackstreet I Get Lonely	5/98	
❖ with Michael Jackson Scream	6/96	6/95
❖ with Luther Vandross		
The Best Things In Life Are Free	6/92	8/92
★ ❖ with Luther Vandross		
The Best Things In Life Are Free		12/95
Jermaine JACKSON (US)		
Daddy's Home	2/73	
Do What You Do	1/85	3/85
Dynamite	9/84	
I Think It's Love	4/86	
Let's Get Serious	6/80	6/80
Joe JACKSON (UK)		
It's Different For Girls		2/80
Steppin' Out	11/82	1/83
You Can't Get What You Want (Till You Know What You Want)	6/84	
Leon JACKSON (UK)		
Don't Call This Love		10/08
When You Believe		12/07
Michael JACKSON (US)		
Ain't No Sunshine		9/72
Another Part Of Me	9/88	
Bad	10/87	9/87
Beat It	4/83	4/83
Ben	9/72	12/72
Billie Jean	2/83	2/83
★ Billie Jean		3/06
Billie Jean		7/09
Black Or White	11/91	11/91
Butterflies	1/02	
Dirty Diana	6/88	7/88
Don't Stop Till You Get Enough	9/79	10/79
Earth Song		12/95
Farewell My Summer Love		6/84
Give In To Me		2/93
Got To Be There	11/71	2/72
Heal The World		12/92
Human Nature	8/83	
I Just Can't Stop Loving You	8/87	8/87
In The Closet	5/92	5/92
Jam		9/92
Leave Me Alone		2/89
Man In The Mirror	3/88	
Man In The Mirror		7/09
Off The Wall	4/80	12/79
One Day In Your Life		6/81
One More Chance		12/03
P.Y.T. (Pretty Young Thing)	11/83	4/84
Remember The Time	2/92	2/92
Rock With You	12/79	2/80
Rockin' Robin	4/72	6/72
She's Out Of My Life	6/80	5/80
Smooth Criminal	1/89	12/88
Thriller	2/84	12/83
Wanna Be Startin' Something	6/83	6/83
The Way You Make Me Feel	12/87	12/87
Who Is It	5/93	8/92
Will You Be There	8/93	7/93
You Are Not Alone	9/95	9/95
You Rock My World	9/01	10/01
❖ with Paul McCartney		
Say Say Say	11/83	11/83
Michael JACKSON & Janet JACKSON (US)		
Scream/Childhood	6/95	6/95
Michael JACKSON & Paul MCCARTNEY (US/UK)		
The Girl Is Mine	11/82	11/82
Michael JACKSON with THE JACKSON FIVE (US)		
I Want You Back '88		4/88
Stonewall JACKSON (US)		
Waterloo	7/59	
JACKSON FIVE (US) see also Jacksons		
ABC	3/70	6/70
Dancing Machine	4/74	
Doctor My Eyes		3/73
I Want You Back	12/69	2/70
I'll Be There	10/70	12/70
Little Bitty Pretty One	5/72	
Lookin' Through The Windows		12/72
The Love You Save	6/70	8/70
Mama's Pearl	2/71	
Never Can Say Goodbye	4/71	
Sugar Daddy	1/72	
JACKSONS (US)		
Blame It On The Boogie		10/78
Can You Feel It		4/81
Enjoy Yourself	1/77	
Lovely One	11/80	
Shake Your Body (Down To The Ground)	4/79	4/79
Show You The Way To Go		6/77
State Of Shock	7/84	
Walk Right Now		8/81
JACKY (UK)		
White Horses		5/68
JADAKISS featuring Anthony HAMILTON (US)		
Why?	9/04	
JADE (US)		
Don't Walk Away	2/93	4/93
I Wanna Love You		7/93
JAGGED EDGE (US)		
He Can't Love U	1/00	
Let's Get Married	7/00	
Promise	3/01	
Walked Outta Heaven	11/03	
JAGGED EDGE with NELLY (US)		
❖ Where The Party At	7/01	
Mick JAGGER (UK)		
❖ with David Bowie		
Dancing In The Street	9/85	9/85
Just Another Night	3/85	
JAGGERZ (US)		
The Rapper	2/70	
JAHEIM (US)		
Could It Be	1/01	
JAIMESON (UK)		
Complete		8/03
JAIMESON featuring Angel BLU (UK)		
❖ True		1/03
JAKATTA (UK)		
American Dream		2/01
So Lonely		2/02
❖ featuring SEAL (UK)		
My Vision		10/02
JAM (UK)		
Absolute Beginners		10/81
Beat Surrender		12/82
The Bitterest Pill (I Ever Had To Swallow)		9/82
The Eton Rifles		11/79
Funeral Pyre		6/81
Going Underground/Dreams Of Children		3/80
Just Who Is The Five O'Clock Hero		7/82
Start		8/80
Town Called Malice/Precious		2/82
JAM & SPOON featuring Plavka (G)		
Right In The Night (Fall In Love With Music)		6/95
JAMELIA (UK)		
DJ/Stop		11/04
Money		3/00
See It In A Boy's Eyes		7/04
Something About You		9/06
Superstar		10/03
Thank You		3/04
JAMES (UK)		
Sit Down		4/91
Sound		12/91
Sit Down (Remix)		11/98
Dick JAMES (UK)		
Robin Hood		2/56
Duncan JAMES & KEEDIE (UK)		
I Believe My Heart		10/4
Etta JAMES (US)		
I Just Want To Make Love To You		2/96
Jimmy JAMES & THE VAGABONDS (UK)		
Now Is The Time		8/76
Joni JAMES (US)		
How Important Can It Be?	3/55	
Rick JAMES (US)		
Super Freak (Pt. 1)	10/81	
You And I	9/78	
Sonny JAMES (US)		
Young Love	1/57	3/57
Tommy JAMES (US)		
Draggin' The Line	7/71	

	US Top 20 Ent	UK Top 20 Ent
Tommy JAMES & The Shondells (US)		
Crimson & Clover	1/69	
Crystal Blue Persuasion	7/69	
Hanky Panky	7/66	
I Think We're Alone Now	3/67	
Mirage	6/67	
Mony Mony	5/68	7/68
Sweet Cherry Wine	4/69	
JAMIE.T (UK)		
Calm Down Dearest		1/07
JAMIROQUAI (UK)		
Blow Your Mind		6/93
Canned Heat		6/99
Deeper Underground		7/98
Feels Just Like It Should		6/05
Little L		8/01
Stillness In Time		7/95
Too Young To Die		3/93
JAN & ARNIE (US)		
Jennie Lee	6/58	
JAN & DEAN (US)		
Baby Talk	9/59	
Dead Man's Curve	4/64	
Drag City	1/64	
Honolulu Lulu	10/63	
The Little Old Lady (From Pasadena)	7/64	
Surf City	7/63	
JANET (US)		
Doesn't Really Matter	08/00	
Horst JANKOWSKI (G)		
A Walk In The Black Forest	6/65	8/65
JAPAN (UK)		
Ghosts		4/82
I Second That Emotion		8/82
JARMELS (US)		
A Little Bit Of Soap	9/61	
Jean-Michel JARRE (F)		
Oxygene Part IV		9/77
Al JARREAU (US)		
Moonlighting ('Theme')		3/87
We're In This Love Together	11/81	
JAVINE (UK)		
Real Things		7/03
JAY & The Americans (US)		
Cara Mia	7/65	
Come A Little Bit Closer	11/64	
Let's Lock The Door…	2/65	
She Cried	5/62	
Some Enchanted Evening	10/65	
This Magic Moment	2/69	
JAY & THE TECHNIQUES (US)		
Apples Peaches Pumpkin Pie	9/67	
Keep The Ball Rollin'	12/67	
JAY-Z (US)		
Change Clothes	12/03	
Dirt Off Your Shoulder	3/04	
Hard Knock Life (Ghetto Anthem)		12/98
Excuse Me Miss	3/03	
Izzo (H.O.V.A.)	8/01	
Jigga My N****	9/99	
Show Me What You Got	11/06	
❖ featuring Beyoncé KNOWLES (US)		
'03 Bonnie & Clyde	11/02	2/03
JAY-Z & T.I. featuring Kanye WEST & LIL WAYNE (US)		
Swagga Like Us	9/08	
JAY-Z + Alicia KEYS (US)		
Empire State Of Mind	10/09	10/09
JAY-Z, RIHANNA & Kanye WEST (US/BA)		
Run This Town	8/09	9/09
JAYNETTS (US)		
Sally, Go 'Round The Roses	9/63	
Wyclef JEAN		
Gone Till November	2/98	5/98
911		12/00
It Doesn't Matter		09/00
Perfect Gentleman		7/01
Wyclef JEAN featuring AKON, LIL WAYNE & Niia (US)		
Sweetest Girl (Dollar Bill)	1/08	
JEFFERSON AIRPLANE (US)		
Somebody To Love	6/67	
White Rabbit	7/67	
JEFFERSON STARSHIP (US)		
Count On Me	4/78	
Jane	1/80	
Miracles	10/75	
Runaway	7/78	
With Your Love	9/76	
JELLY BEANS (US)		
I Wanna Love Him So Bad	8/64	
JELLYBEAN featuring Elisa Fiorillo (US)		
Who Found Who		12/87
JELLYBEAN featuring Steven Dante (US/UK)		
The Real Thing		10/87
JEM (UK)		
They	3/05	
Vanessa JENKINS & Bryn WEST feat. Tom JONES & Robin GIBB (UK)		
Barry Islands In The Stream		3/09
JEREMIH (US)		
Birthday Sex	5/09	
JESUS AND MARY CHAIN (UK)		
April Skies		5/87
JESUS JONES (UK)		
International Bright Young Thing		1/91
Real Real Real	10/91	
Right Here, Right Now	6/91	
JETHRO TULL (UK)		
Bungle In The Jungle	1/75	
Life Is A Long Song/Up The Pool		10/71
Living In The Past	1/73	6/69
Sweet Dream		11/69
The Witch's Promise/Teacher		2/70
JETS (US)		
Cross My Broken Heart	7/87	
Crush On You	6/86	3/87
Make It Real	5/88	
Rocket 2 U	3/88	
You Got It All	2/87	
Joan JETT & The Blackhearts (US)		
Crimson And Clover	6/82	
I Hate Myself For Loving You	9/88	
I Love Rock 'n' Roll	2/82	5/82
JEWEL (US)		
Foolish Games/You Were Meant For Me	9/97	
Hands	12/98	
Who Will Save Your Soul	7/96	
You Were Meant For Me	2/97	
JIBBS (US)		
Chain Hang Low	9/06	
JIGSAW (UK)		
Sky High	11/75	11/75
JILTED JOHN (UK)		
Jilted John		9/78
JIMMY EAT WORLD (US)		
The Middle	5/02	
JIMMY RAY (US)		
Are You Jimmy Ray?	3/98	
JIVE BUNNY & The Mastermixers (UK)		
Can Can You Party		9/90
Let's Party		12/89
Swing The Mood	1/90	8/89
That Sounds Good To Me		3/90
That's What I Like		10/89
JIVE FIVE (US)		
My True Story	9/61	
JLS (UK)		
Beat Again		7/09
Everybody In Love		11/09
JOBOXERS (UK)		
Boxer Beat		4/83
Just Got Lucky		6/83
Yung JOC (US)		
It's Goin' Down	6/06	
JODECI (US)		
Come & Talk To Me	6/92	
Freek'n You	7/95	6/95
Lately	7/93	
JOE (US)		
All The Things (Your Man Won't Do)	3/96	
❖ featuring MYSTIKAL (US)		
Stutter	01/01	2/01
JOE PUBLIC (US)		
Live And Learn	4/92	
Billy JOEL (US)		
Allentown	2/83	
Big Shot	3/79	
I Go To Extremes	3/90	
An Innocent Man	2/84	3/84
It's Still Rock And Roll To Me	6/80	9/80
Just The Way You Are	1/78	
The Longest Time	5/84	
A Matter Of Trust	10/86	
Modern Woman	7/86	
My Life	12/78	2/79
The River Of Dreams	9/93	8/93
Tell Her About It	9/83	12/83
Uptown Girl	10/83	11/83
We Didn't Start The Fire	11/89	10/89
You May Be Right	4/80	
You're Only Human (Second Wind)	8/85	
Elton JOHN (UK)		
Are Yor Ready For Love?		9/03
Believe	4/95	3/95
Bennie And The Jets	3/74	
The Bitch Is Back	10/74	
Blue Eyes	9/82	4/82
Can You Feel The Love Tonight	6/94	7/94
Candle In The Wind		3/74
Candle In The Wind (Live)	12/87	2/88
Something About the Way You LookTonight/ Candle In The Wind 1997		10/97
Circle Of Life		10/94
Crocodile Rock	1/73	11/72
Daniel	5/73	2/73
Don't Let The Sun Go Down On Me	7/74	
Electricity		7/05
Empty Garden (Hey Hey Johnny)	5/82	
Goodbye Yellow Brick Road	11/73	10/73
Grow Some Funk Of Your Own	2/76	
Healing Hands	10/89	6/90
Honky Cat	9/72	
I Don't Wanna Go On With You Like That	8/88	
I Guess That's Why They Call It The Blues	12/83	6/83
I'm Still Standing	7/83	8/83
Island Girl	10/75	
I Want Love		10/01
Little Jeannie	6/80	
Lucy In The Sky With Diamonds	12/74	12/74
Mama Can't Buy You Love	8/79	
Nikita	3/86	10/85
The One	8/92	6/92
Passengers		9/84
Philadelphia Freedom	3/75	4/75
Pinball Wizard		4/76
Rocket Man	7/72	5/72
Sacrifice/Healing Hands		6/90
Sad Songs (Say So Much)	7/84	6/84
Saturday Night's Alright For Fighting	9/73	7/73
Someday Out Of The Blue	06/00	
Someone Saved My Life Tonight	7/75	
Song For Guy		12/78
Sorry Seems To Be The Hardest Word	12/76	12/76
Your Song	1/71	2/71
❖ *with George Michael* Don't Let The Sun Go Down On Me	1/92	12/91
Elton JOHN & Kiki Dee (UK)		
Don't Go Breaking My Heart	7/76	7/76
True Love		11/93
Elton JOHN & RuPaul (UK/US)		
Don't Go Breaking My Heart		3/94
Elton JOHN & Alessandro SAFINA (UK)		
❖Your Song		7/02
Little Willie JOHN (US)		
Sleep	11/60	
Robert JOHN (US)		
The Lion Sleeps Tonight	2/72	
Sad Eyes	8/79	
JOHNNIE & JOE (US)		
Over The Mountain; Across The Sea	7/57	
Johnny & THE HURRICANES (US)		
Beatnik Fly	3/60	3/60
Down Yonder		6/60
Ja-Da		3/61
Red River Rock	9/59	10/59
Reveille Rock		1/60
Rocking Goose		10/60
JOHNNY HATES JAZZ (UK)		
I Don't Want To Be A Hero		9/87
Shattered Dreams	5/88	5/87
Sammy JOHNS (US)		
Chevy Van	4/75	
Andreas JOHNSON (S)		
Glorious		2/00
Don JOHNSON (US)		
Heartbeat	10/86	
Holly JOHNSON (UK)		
Americanos		4/89
❖ with The Christians, Paul McCartney, Gerry Marsden & Stock Aitken Waterman		
Ferry 'Cross The Mersey		5/89
Love Train		2/89
Johnny JOHNSON & THE BANDWAGON (US)		

	US Top 20 Ent	UK Top 20 Ent
Blame It On The Pony Express		12/70
Breakin' Down The Walls Of Heartache		11/68
Sweet Inspiration		8/70
Laurie JOHNSON (UK)		
Sucu-Sucu		10/61
Marv JOHNSON (US)		
I Love The Way You Love	4/60	
I'll Pick A Rose For My Rose		2/69
You Got What It Takes	1/60	2/60
Michael JOHNSON (US)		
Bluer Than Blue	7/78	
Paul JOHNSON (US)		
Get Get Down		10/99
Sabrina JOHNSON (US)		
Peace		9/91
Ana JOHNSSON (S)		
We Are		8/04
JOHNSTON BROTHERS (UK)		
Hernando's Hideaway		10/55
JOJO (US)		
Leave (Get Out)	7/4	9/04
Too Little Too Late	9/06	1/07
JOJO featuring BOW WOW		
Baby It's You		12/04
JO JO GUNNE (US)		
Run Run Run		4/72
France JOLI (C)		
Come To Me	11/79	
JON & VANGELIS (UK/Gre)		
I Hear You Now		2/80
I'll Find My Way Home		1/82
JONAS BROTHERS (US)		
A Little Bit Longer	8/08	
Burnin' Up	7/08	
SOS		7/08
Tonight	8/08	
Aled JONES (UK)		
Walking In The Air		12/85
Camille JONES vs Fedde Le GRAND (D/H)		
The Creeps		3/07
Donell JONES (US)		
U Know What's Up		1/00
Grace JONES (US)		
Pull Up To The Bumper/La Vie En Rose		2/86
Slave To The Rhythm		10/85
Howard JONES (UK)		
Everlasting Love	5/89	
Hide And Seek		3/84
Like To Get To Know You Well		8/84
New Song		10/83
No One Is To Blame	6/86	
Pearl In The Shell		6/84
Things Can Only Get Better	5/85	2/85
What Is Love		12/83
Jack JONES (UK)		
The Race Is On	4/65	
Wives And Lovers	1/64	
Jim JONES (US)		
We Fly High	12/06	
Jimmy JONES (US)		
Good Timin'	5/60	6/60
Handy Man	2/60	4/60
Joe JONES (US)		
You Talk Too Much	10/60	
Oran 'JUICE' Jones (US)		
The Rain	11/86	12/86
Paul JONES (UK)		
High Time		11/66
I've Been A Bad Bad Boy		2/67
Quincy JONES (US)		
Razzamatazz		7/81
Quincy JONES featuring James INGRAM (US)		
One Hundred Ways	4/82	
Rickie Lee JONES (US)		
Chuck E.'s In Love	6/79	
Tammy JONES (UK)		
Let Me Try Again		5/75
Tom JONES (UK)		
A Boy From Nowhere		5/87
Daughter Of Darkness	6/70	5/70
Delilah		3/68
Detroit City		3/67
Funny Familiar Forgotten Feelings		5/67
Green Green Grass Of Home	2/67	11/66
Help Yourself		8/68
I (Who Have Nothing)	9/70	
If I Only Knew		11/94
I'll Never Fall In Love Again	9/69	8/67
I'm Comin' Home		12/67
It's Not Unusual	5/65	3/65
Love Me Tonight	6/69	5/69
A Minute Of Your Time		12/68
She's A Lady	3/71	2/71
Till		11/71
What's New Pussycat?	7/65	9/65
With These Hands		8/65
Without Love (There Is Nothing)	1/70	12/69
The Young New Mexican Puppeteer		4/72
❖ with The Art Of Noise		
Kiss		11/88
❖ with The Cardigans		
Burning Down The House		10/99
❖ with Mousse T		
Sex Bomb		5/00
❖ with Stereophonics		
Mama Told Me Not To Come		3/00
Janis JOPLIN (US)		
Me And Bobby McGee	3/71	
David JORDAN (UK)		
Sun Goes Down		2/08
Jeremy JORDAN (US)		
The Right Kind Of Love	3/93	
Montell JORDAN (US)		
I Can Do That	9/98	
Falling	12/96	
Get It On Tonite	02/00	
This Is How We Do It	3/95	5/95
Montell JORDAN featuring Master P and Silkk The Shocker (US)		
Let's Ride	3/98	
JOURNEY (US)		
Be Good To Yourself	5/86	
Don't Stop Believin'	12/81	12/09
Faithfully	6/83	
Only The Young	3/85	
Open Arms	2/82	
Separate Ways (Worlds Apart)	3/83	
When You Love A Woman	11/96	
Who's Crying Now	8/81	
JOY DIVISION (UK)		
Love Will Tear Us Apart		7/80
JT & THE BIG FAMILY (ITA)		
Moments In Soul		3/90
JT MONEY/SOLE (US)		
Who Dat	06/99	
JUDAS PRIEST (UK)		
Breaking The Law		6/80
Living After Midnight		4/80
JUDGE DREAD (UK)		
Big Eight		5/73
Big Seven		1/73
Big Six		10/72
Big Ten		10/75
Je T'Aime (Moi Non Plus)		7/75
JUMP 'N THE SADDLE (US)		
The Curly Shuffle	1/84	
Rosemary JUNE (US)		
Apple Blossom Time		2/59
JUNIOR (UK)		
Mama Used To Say		6/82
❖ with Kim Wilde		
Another Step (Closer To You)		5/87
JUNIOR M.A.F.I.A. (US)		
Player's Anthem	8/95	
JUNIOR SENIOR (D)		
Move Your Feet		3/03
JUST JACK (UK)		
Starz In Their Eyes		1/07
Jimmy JUSTICE (UK)		
Ain't That Funny		6/62
When My Little Girl Is Smiling		4/62
Bill JUSTIS (US)		
Raunchy	11/57	2/58
JUVENILE featuring SOULJA SLIM (US)		
Slow Motion	6/04	
JX (UK)		
Son Of A Gun		8/95
K-KLASS (UK)		
Rhythm Is A Mystery		11/91
K7 (US)		
Come Baby Come	12/93	1/94
KACI (US)		
I Think I Love You		2/02
Bert KAEMPFERT (G)		
Red Roses For A Blue Lady	3/65	
Wonderland By Night	12/60	
KAISER CHIEFS (UK)		
Fire		6/09
I Predict A Riot/Sink That Ship		9/05
Never Miss A Beat		10/08
Oh My God		3/05
Ruby		2/07
KAJAGOOGOO (UK)		
Big Apple		10/83
Hang On Now		6/83
Ooh To Be Ah		4/83
Too Shy	6/83	2/83
KALIN TWINS (US)		
Forget Me Not	11/58	
When	7/58	8/58
Kitty KALLEN (US)		
In The Chapel In The Moonlight	7/54	
Little Things Mean A Lot	4/54	7/54
Nick KAMEN (UK)		
Each Time You Break My Heart		11/86
Ini KAMOZE (J)		
Here Comes The Hotstepper	10/94	1/95
Kiri Te KANAWA (NZ)		
World In Union		10/91
KANDI (US)		
Don't Think I'm Not		11/00
KANDIDATE (UK)		
I Don't Wanna Lose You		4/79
Eden KANE (UK)		
Boys Cry		3/64
Forget Me Not		1/62
Get Lost		9/61
I Don't Know Why		5/62
Well I Ask You		6/61
KANE GANG (UK)		
Closest Thing To Heaven		8/84
KANSAS (US)		
Carry On Wayward Son	3/77	
Dust In The Wind	4/78	
KAOMA (F)		
Lambada		12/89
KASABIAN (UK)		
Empire		8/06
KATRINA & THE WAVES (US/UK)		
Walking On Sunshine	6/85	6/85
KAVANA (UK)		
I Can Make You Feel Good		1/97
Janet KAY (UK)		
Silly Games		7/79
Peter KAY'S ALL STAR BAND (UK)		
The Official Children In Need Medley		12/09
KAYE SISTERS (UK)		
Paper Roses		8/60
with Frankie Vaughan		
❖ Come Softly To Me		5/59
❖ Gotta Have Something In The Bank Frank		11/57
KC & THE SUNSHINE BAND (US)		
Get Down Tonight	8/75	
Give It Up		8/83
I'm Your Boogie Man	5/77	
Keep It Comin' Love	9/77	
Please Don't Go	10/79	1/80
Queen Of Clubs		9/74
(Shake, Shake, Shake) Shake Your Booty	8/76	
That's The Way (I Like It)	11/75	8/75
❖ with Teri DeSario		
Yes, I'm Ready	2/80	
K-CI AND JOJO (US)		
All My Life	4/98	
Crazy	4/01	
Tell Me It's Real	8/99	
Ernie K-DOE (US)		
Mother-In-Law	4/61	
KE$HA (US)		
Tik Tok	11/09	11/09
KEANE (UK)		
Everybody's Changing		5/04
Is It Any Wonder?		6/06
Somewhere Only We Know		2/04
Ronan KEATING (I)		
I Hope You Dance		10/04
I Love It When We Do		9/02
If Tomorrow Never Comes		5/02
Life Is A Rollercoaster		7/00
The Long Goodbye		5/03
Lovin' Each Day		4/01

	US Top 20 Ent	UK Top 20 Ent
Hula Love	10/57	
Party Doll	3/57	
KOKOMO (US)		
Asia Minor	4/61	
KON KAN (C)		
I Beg Your Pardon	3/89	4/89
John KONGOS (SA)		
He's Gonna Step On You Again		6/71
Tokoloshe Man		12/71
KOOKS (UK)		
Always Where I Need To Be		4/08
Naive		4/06
She Moves In Her Own Way		7/06
KOOL & THE GANG (US)		
Celebration	1/81	11/80
Cherish	8/85	6/85
Fresh	5/85	12/84
Get Down On It	5/82	1/82
Hollywood Swinging	6/74	
Joanna	1/84	3/84
Jungle Boogie	2/74	
Ladies Night	12/79	11/79
Misled	2/85	
Ooh La La La (Let's Go Dancing)		11/82
Stone Love	4/87	
Tonight	4/84	3/84
Too Hot	3/80	
Victory	12/86	
(When You Say You Love Somebody) In The Heart	4/84	
KORGIS (UK)		
Everybody's Got To Learn Sometime		6/80
KOSHEEN (UK)		
All In My Head		8/03
Hide U		9/01
K P AND ENVYI (US)		
Swing My Way	3/98	
KRAFTWERK (G)		
Autobahn		6/75
The Model/Computer Love		1/82
Billy J KRAMER & The Dakotas (UK)		
Bad To Me	6/64	8/63
Do You Want To Know A Secret		5/63
From A Window		8/64
I'll Keep You Satisfied		11/63
Little Children	5/64	3/64
Trains And Boats And Planes		6/65
Lenny KRAVITZ (US)		
Again	4/01	
Are You Gonna Go My Way		2/93
Fly Away	5/99	2/99
It Ain't Over 'Til It's Over	7/91	7/91
KRIS KROSS (US)		
Jump	4/92	6/92
Tonite's Tha Night	2/96	
Warm It Up	7/92	
Kris KRISTOFFERSON (US)		
Why Me	11/73	
Chad KROEGER featuring Josey SCOTT (US)		
Hero	6/02	6/02
KRUSH (UK)		
House Arrest		1/88
Bob KUBAN & The In-Men (US)		
The Cheater	3/66	
KULA SHAKER (UK)		
Govinda		11/96
Hey Dude		9/96
Sound Of Drums		5/98
Tattva		7/96
KUMBIA KINGS (US)		
U Don't Love Me	3/00	
KURSAAL FLYERS (UK)		
Little Does She Know		12/76
KWS (UK)		
Please Don't Go	9/92	5/92
Rock Your Baby		8/92
LA MIX (UK)		
Check This Out		6/88
LA ROUX (UK)		
Bulletproof		7/09
In For The Kill		3/09
LL COOL J (US)		
Around The Way Girl	2/91	
Doin It	4/96	
Headsprung	9/04	
Hey Lover	11/95	1/96
I Need Love	9/87	10/87
I'm That Type Of Guy	8/89	
Loungin'	7/96	
Luv U Better	10/02	10/02
featuring 7 Aurelius		
Hush		2/05
featuring Jennifer Lopez		
Control Myself	4/06	5/06
LSG (US)		
My Body	11/97	
L.T.D. (US)		
Back In Love Again	11/77	
LA BELLE EPOQUE (F)		
Black Is Black		10/77
LA BOUCHE (US)		
Be My Lover	1/96	
Sweet Dreams	6/96	
Julius LA ROSA (US)		
Domani (Tomorrow)	8/55	
Eh Cumpari	1/54	
Denise LA SALLE (US)		
My Toot Toot		7/85
Trapped By A Thing Called Love	10/71	
LABELLE (US)		
Lady Marmalade		3/75
Patti LABELLE & Michael McDonald (US)		
On My Own	5/86	5/86
Nick LACHEY (US)		
What's Left Of Me	5/06	
LADY ANTEBELLUM (US)		
Need You Now	11/09	
LADY GAGA (US)		
Bad Romance	11/09	11/09
Lovegame	6/09	
Paparazzi	10/09	6/09
Poker Face	2/09	3/09
LADY GAGA featuring Colby O'DONIS (US)		
Just Dance	12/08	1/09
Cleo LAINE (UK)		
You'll Answer To Me		9/61
Frankie LAINE (US)		
Answer Me		1/54
Blowing Wild		1/54
Cool Water		6/55
Granada		3/54
Hawkeye		12/55
The Kid's Last Fight		4/54
Moonlight Gambler	1/57	12/56
My Friend		8/54
Rain Rain Rain		10/54
Rawhide		12/59
Sixteen Tons		1/56
Some Day		9/54
Strange Lady In Town		7/55
There Must Be A Reason		10/54
A Woman In Love		9/56
Greg LAKE (UK)		
I Believe In Father Christmas		12/75
LAMBRETTAS (UK)		
D-a-a-ance		6/80
Poison Ivy		4/80
Major LANCE (US)		
Hey Little Girl	11/63	
The Monkey Time	9/63	
Um, Um, Um, Um, Um, Um	1/64	
LANDSCAPE (UK)		
Einstein A Go-Go		4/81
Ronnie LANE (UK)		
How Come		2/74
Don LANG (UK)		
Witch Doctor		6/58
Mario LANZA (US)		
Drinking Song		2/55
LARKS (US)		
The Jerk	12/64	
Nicolette LARSON (US)		
Lotta Love	1/79	
LAS KETCHUP (SPA)		
The Ketchup Song (Aserejé)		10/02
LASGO (B)		
Something		3/02
LAST SHADOW PUPPETS (UK)		
The Age Of The Understatement		4/08
LATINO RAVE (Various)		
Deep Heat '89		1/90
Stacy LATTISAW (US)		
Jump To The Beat		7/80
Cyndi LAUPER (US)		
All Through The Night	11/84	
Change Of Heart	1/87	
Girls Just Want To Have Fun	2/84	2/84
The Goonies 'R' Good Enough		7/85
Hey Now (Girls Just Want To Have Fun)		9/94
I Drove All Night	6/89	6/89
She Bop	8/84	
Time After Time	5/84	7/84
True Colors	10/86	10/86
What's Going On	5/87	
LAUREL & HARDY with The Avalon Boys (US)		
The Trail Of The Lonesome Pine		12/75
Avril LAVIGNE (C)		
Complicated	7/02	10/02
Don't Tell Me	5/04	
Girlfriend	3/07	3/07
I'm With You	1/03	4/03
My Happy Ending	9/4	8/04
Sk8er Boi	10/02	1/03
When You're Gone		7/07
Joey LAWRENCE (US)		
Nothin' My Love Can't Fix		7/93
Lee LAWRENCE (UK)		
Crying In The Chapel		1/54
Suddenly There's A Valley		12/55
Steve LAWRENCE (US)		
Footsteps	4/60	4/60
Go Away Little Girl	12/62	
Party Doll	4/57	
Portrait Of My Love	5/61	
Pretty Blue Eyes	12/59	
Steve LAWRENCE & Eydie GORME (US)		
I Want To Stay Here		9/63
Vicki LAWRENCE (US)		
The Night The Lights Went Out In Georgia	3/73	
LAYO & BUSHWACKA! (UK)		
Love Story (Vs Finally)		1/03
Lindy LAYTON (UK) see Beats International featuring Lindy Layton		
LAZY TOWN (ICE)		
Bing Bang (Time To Dance)		12/06
Vicky LEANDROS (GRE)		
Come What May		4/72
LEBLANC & CARR (US)		
Falling	3/78	
LED ZEPPELIN (UK)		
Black Dog	2/72	
Whole Lotta Love	12/69	
Ann LEE (UK)		
2 Times		10/99
Brenda LEE (US)		
All Alone Am I	10/62	2/63
As Usual	1/64	1/64
Break It To Me Gently	2/62	
Coming On Strong	11/66	
Dum Dum	7/61	
Emotions	1/61	
Everybody Loves Me But You	5/62	
Fool #1	11/61	
Here Comes That Feeling		6/62
I Want To Be Wanted	10/60	
I'm Sorry	6/60	8/60
It Started All Over Again		10/62
Let's Jump The Broomstick		3/61
Losing You	5/63	5/63
Rockin' Around The Christmas Tree		12/62
Speak To Me Pretty		4/62
Sweet Nothin's	3/60	4/60
That's All You Gotta Do	7/60	
Too Many Rivers		7/65
You Can Depend On Me	4/61	
Curtis LEE (US)		
Pretty Little Angel Eyes	8/61	
Dee C LEE (UK)		
See The Day		11/85
Dickey LEE (US)		
I Saw Linda Yesterday	1/63	
Laurie (Strange Things Happen)	7/65	
Patches	9/62	
Jackie LEE (US)		
The Duck	1/66	
Rupert		2/71
Johnny LEE (US)		
Lookin' For Love	9/80	
Leapy LEE (UK)		
Little Arrows		9/68
Murphy LEE featuring Jermaine DUPRI (US)		
Wat Da Hook Gon Be	12/03	

	US Top 20 Ent	UK Top 20 Ent
Peggy LEE (US)		
Fever	8/58	8/58
Is That All There Is	11/69	
Mr Wonderful		5/57
LEEDS UNITED FC (UK)		
Leeds United		5/72
LEFT BANKE (US)		
Walk Away Renee	10/66	
LEFTFIELD/BAMBAATAA (UK/Ken)		
Afrika Shox		9/99
LEMAR (UK)		
50:50/Lullaby		11/03
Dance (With U)		8/03
If There's Any Justice		11/04
It's Not That Easy		9/06
Time To Grow		4/05
LEMON PIPERS (US)		
Green Tambourine	1/68	3/68
LEN (C)		
Steal My Sunshine		12/99
John LENNON/Yoko Ono/Plastic Ono Band (UK/Jap)		
Cold Turkey		11/69
Give Peace A Chance		7/69
Happy Xmas (War Is Over)		12/72
★ Happy Xmas (War Is Over)		12/80
Imagine	11/71	11/75
★ Imagine		1/81
★ Imagine		12/99
Instant Karma (We All Shine On)	3/70	2/70
(Just Like) Starting Over	11/80	11/80
No 9 Dream	2/75	
Nobody Told Me	2/84	1/84
Power To The People	5/71	3/71
Watching The Wheels	5/81	
Whatever Gets You Thru The Night	11/74	
Woman	2/81	1/81
Julian LENNON (UK)		
Saltwater		10/91
Too Late For Goodbyes	3/85	11/84
Valotte	12/84	
Annie LENNOX (UK)		
Little Bird/Love Song For A Vampire		2/93
No More 'I Love You's'		2/95
Walking On Broken Glass	11/92	9/92
Why		4/92
Annie LENNOX & Al Green (UK/US)		
Put A Little Love In Your Heart	1/89	
LEONA (UK)		
A Moment Like This		12/06
Kele LE ROC (UK)		
My Love		3/99
Kristian LEONTIOU (UK)		
Story of My Life		6/04
LES RYTHMES DIGITALES (UK)		
Jacques Your Body (Make Me Sweat)		9/05
Ketty LESTER (US)		
Love Letters	4/62	4/62
LET LOOSE (UK)		
Best In Me		4/95
Crazy For You		7/94
One Night Stand		2/95
Seventeen		10/94
LETTERMEN (US)		
Goin' Out Of My Head/Can't Take My Eyes Off You	2/68	
Hurt So Bad	9/69	
The Way You Look Tonight	10/61	
When I Fall In Love	12/61	
LEVEL 42 (UK)		
It's Over		9/87
Lessons In Love	6/87	5/86
Running In The Family		2/87
Something About You	5/86	11/85
The Sun Goes Down (Living It Up)		9/83
To Be With You Again		5/87
LEVERT (US)		
Casanova	10/87	9/87
Gerald LEVERT (US)		
Taking Pictures	2/99	
Thinkin' 'Bout It	9/98	
General LEVY (UK) see M-Beat feat. General Levy		
Jona LEWIE (UK)		
Stop The Cavalry		12/80
Barbara LEWIS (US)		
Baby, I'm Yours	8/65	
Hello Stranger	6/63	
Make Me Your Baby	11/65	
Bobby LEWIS (US)		
One Track Mind	9/61	
Tossin' And Turnin'	6/61	
CJ LEWIS (UK)		
Everything Is Alright (Uptight)		7/94
Sweets For My Sweet		4/94
DONNA LEWIS (UK)		
I Love You Always Forever	8/96	9/96
Gary LEWIS & The Playboys (US)		
Count Me In	5/65	
Everybody Loves A Clown	10/65	
Green Grass	6/66	
My Heart's Symphony	8/66	
Save Your Heart For Me	7/65	
She's Just My Style	1/66	
Sure Gonna Miss Her	4/66	
This Diamond Ring	2/65	
Huey LEWIS & The News (US)		
Couple Days Off	6/91	
Do You Believe In Love	4/82	3/86
Doing It All For My Baby	9/87	
Heart And Soul	11/83	
The Heart Of Rock 'n' Roll	5/84	
Hip To Be Square	11/86	
I Know What I Like	5/87	
I Want A New Drug	3/84	
If This Is It	8/84	
Jacob's Ladder	2/87	
Perfect World	8/88	
The Power Of Love	8/85	9/85
★ The Power Of Love/Do You Believe In Love		3/86
Stuck With You	8/86	10/86
Jerry LEWIS (US)		
Rock-A-Bye Your Baby With A Dixie Melody	12/56	2/57
Jerry Lee LEWIS (US)		
Breathless	3/58	4/58
Great Balls Of Fire	12/57	12/57
High School Confidential		2/59
What'd I Say		5/61
Whole Lot Of Shakin' Going On	8/57	10/57
Leona LEWIS (UK)		
Better In Time	10/08	3/08
Bleeding Love	3/08	11/07
Footprints In The Sand		3/08
Forgive Me		11/08
Happy		11/09
Run		12/08
Linda LEWIS (UK)		
It's In His Kiss		8/75
Ramsey LEWIS TRIO (US)		
Hang On Sloopy	12/65	
The "In" Crowd	9/65	
Shaznay LEWIS (UK)		
Never Felt Like This Before		7/04
John LEYTON (UK)		
Johnny Remember Me		8/61
Wild Wind		10/61
LFO (UK)		
LFO		8/90
LFO (US)		
Girl On TV	01/00	2/00
I Don't Wanna Kiss You	04/00	
Summer Girls	07/99	
The LIBERTINES (UK)		
Can't Stand Me Now		8/04
LIBERTY (UK)		
Thinking It Over		10/01
LIBERTY X (UK)		
A Night To Remember		11/05
Got To Have Your Love		9/02
Holding On For You		12/02
Jumpin'		11/03
Just A Little		5/02
LIBERTY X featuring REV RUN from RUN DMC		
Song 4 Lovers		10/05
LIEUTENANT PIGEON (UK)		
Mouldy Old Dough		10/72
LIFEHOUSE (C)		
Hanging By A Moment	4/01	
You And Me	7/05	
Gordon LIGHTFOOT (C)		
Carefree Highway	11/74	
If You Could Read My Mind	2/71	
Sundown	6/74	
The Wreck Of The Edmund Fitzgerald	10/76	
LIGHTHOUSE FAMILY (UK)		
(I Wish I Knew How It Would Feel To Be) Free – One		11/01
Lifted		2/96
Lost In Space		6/98
LIL BOW WOW (US)		
Bounce WIth Me	08/00	
Bow Wow (That's My Name)	03/01	4/01
LIL' CHRIS (UK)		
Checkin' It Out		10/06
LIL' FLIP (US)		
Game Over (Flip)	5/04	
LIL' FLIP featuring LEA		
Sunshine	8/04	
LIL JON & The EAST SIDE BOYZ featuring USHER & LUDICRIS (US)		
Lovers And Friends	12/04	
LIL JON & The EAST SIDE BOYZ featuring YING YANG TWINS (US)		
Get Low	8/03	
LIL JON featuring E-40 & Sean PAUL of The YOUNGBLOODZ		
Snap Yo Fingers	5/06	
LIL' KIM featuring 50 CENT (US)		
❖ Magic Stick	5/03	
LIL' KIM and PUFF DADDY (US)		
No Time	1/97	
LIL' KIM with DA BRAT, LEFT EYE, MISSY ELLIOTT and ANGIE MARTINEZ (US)		
Not Tonight	8/97	
LIL LOUIS (US)		
French Kiss		8/89
LIL MAMA (US)		
Lip Gloss	6/07	
LIL MAMA featuring Chris BROWN & T-PAIN (US)		
Shawty Get Loose	4/08	
LIL' MO featuring FABOLOUS (US)		
❖ Superwoman Pt. II	6/01	
LIL' ROMEO (US)		
My Baby	6/01	
LIL WAYNE (US)		
A Milli	7/08	
Go D.J.	11/04	
LIL WAYNE featuring Static Major (US)		
Lollipop	4/08	
LIL WAYNE featuring T-PAIN (US)		
Got Money	9/08	
LIL WAYNE feat. Bobby VALENTINO & Kidd Kidd (US)		
Mrs. Officer	12/08	
LIL' ZANE feat. 112 (US)		
Callin' Me	07/00	
LIMAHL (UK)		
Never Ending Story		11/84
LIMMIE & THE FAMILY COOKIN' (US)		
A Walkin' Miracle		4/74
You Can Do Magic		8/73
LIMP BIZKIT (US)		
My Way		6/01
Rollin'		1/01
Take A Look Around		08/00
Bob LIND (US)		
Elusive Butterfly	3/66	3/66
Kathy LINDEN (US)		
Goodbye Jimmy, Goodbye	6/59	
LINDISFARNE (UK)		
Lady Eleanor		6/72
Meet Me On The Corner		3/72
Run For Home		7/78
❖ with Gazza Fog On The Tyne (Revisited)		11/90
Mark LINDSAY (US)		
Arizona	2/70	
LINEAR (US)		
Sending All My Love	4/90	
Laurie LINGO & THE DIPSTICKS (UK)		
Convoy GB		5/76
LINKIN PARK (US)		
In The End	1/02	10/01
New Divide	6/09	
Numb	1/04	
Shadow Of The Day	3/08	
What I've Done	6/07	5/07
LINX (UK)		
Intuition		4/81
LIPPS INC. (US)		
Funkytown	5/80	6/80
LIQUID GOLD (UK)		
Dance Yourself Dizzy		3/80
Substitute		6/80
LISA LISA & Cult Jam (US)		
Head To Toe	5/87	
Lost In Emotion	9/87	

	US Top 20 Ent	UK Top 20 Ent
LISA LISA & CULT JAM with Full Force (US)		
All Cried Out	10/86	
LITTLE ANTHONY & The Imperials (US)		
Goin' Out Of My Head	12/64	
Hurt So Bad	3/65	
Tears On My Pillow	9/58	
LITTLE BOOTS (UK)		
New In Town		6/09
Remedy		8/09
LITTLE CAESAR & The Romans (US)		
Those Oldies But Goodies (Remind Me Of You)	6/61	
LITTLE DIPPERS (US)		
Forever	3/60	
LITTLE EVA (US)		
Keep Your Hands Off My Baby	12/62	
Let's Turkey Trot		4/63
The Loco-Motion	8/62	9/62
★ The Loco-Motion		8/72
LITTLE RICHARD (US)		
Baby Face	1/59	
By The Light Of The Silvery Moon		4/59
The Girl Can't Help It		3/57
Good Golly, Miss Molly	3/58	3/58
Jenny, Jenny/Miss Ann	7/57	9/57
Keep A Knockin'	10/57	
Long Tall Sally	4/56	3/57
Lucille		7/57
LITTLE RIVER BAND (AUS)		
Cool Change	12/79	
Happy Anniversary	3/78	
Help Is On Its Way	11/77	
Lady	3/79	
Lonesome Loser	9/79	
Man On Your Mind	5/82	
The Night Owls	10/81	
The Other Guy	1/83	
Reminiscing	9/78	
Take It Easy On Me	2/82	
LIVERPOOL COLLECTIVE / THE KOP CHOIR (UK)		
Fields Of Anfield Road		4/09
LIVERPOOL EXPRESS (UK)		
You Are My Love		7/76
LIVERPOOL FC (UK)		
Anfield Rap (Red Machine In Full Effect)		5/88
LIVIN' JOY (US/Ita)		
Dreamer		5/95
LIVING COLOUR (US)		
Cult Of Personality	5/89	
Love Rears It's Ugly Head		3/91
LIVING IN A BOX (UK)		
Blow The House Down		3/89
Living In A Box		4/87
Room In Your Heart		10/89
Dandy LIVINGSTONE (O)		
Suzanne Beware Of The Devil		10/72
Kelly LLORENNA (UK)		
Tell It To My Heart		7/02
LLOYD (US)		
Get It Shawty	7/07	
LLOYD featuring LIL WAYNE (US)		
You	2/07	
LMC vs U2 (UK)		
Take Me To The Clouds Above		2/04
LOBO (H)		
Caribbean Disco Show		8/81
LOBO (US)		
Don't Expect Me To Be Your Friend	2/73	
I'd Love To Want Me	11/72	6/74
Me And You And A Dog Named Boo	5/71	7/71
Los LOBOS (US)		
La Bamba	8/87	7/87
Hank LOCKLIN (US)		
Please Help Me, I'm Falling	7/60	10/60
Lisa LOEB & Nine Stories (US)		
Stay	6/94	9/94
Johnny LOGAN (I)		
Hold Me Now		5/87
What's Another Year		5/80
LOGGINS & MESSINA (US)		
Your Mama Don't Dance	12/72	
Dave LOGGINS (US)		
Please Come To Boston	7/74	
Kenny LOGGINS (US)		
Danger Zone	7/86	
Footloose	3/84	5/84

	US Top 20 Ent	UK Top 20 Ent
Heart To Heart	1/83	
I'm Alright	9/80	
Meet Me Half Way	6/87	
Nobody's Fool	9/88	
This Is It	1/80	
Whenever I Call You 'Friend'	9/78	
LOLLY (UK)		
Big Boys Don't Cry/Rockin' Robin		12/99
Mickey		9/99
Viva La Radio		7/99
LOLITA (A)		
Sailor (Your Home Is The Sea)	12/60	
LONDON BOYS (UK)		
London Nights		7/89
Requiem		5/89
Laurie LONDON (UK)		
He's Got The Whole World (In His Hands)	4/58	12/57
LONDONBEAT (UK/US)		
I've Been Thinking About You	3/91	9/90
LONESTAR (US)		
Amazed	02/00	
Shorty LONG (US)		
Here Comes The Judge	6/68	
LOOK (UK)		
I Am The Beat		1/81
LOOKING GLASS (US)		
Brandy (You're A Fine Girl)	7/72	
Jennifer LOPEZ (US)		
Ain't It Funny	8/01	
Baby I Love U	3/04	
Do It Well	10/07	
Feelin' So Good	5/00	
Get Right	2/05	2/05
If You Had My Love	6/99	7/99
Love Don't Cost A Thing	3/01	1/01
Play	5/01	
Waiting For Tonight	11/99	
❖ featuring FAT JOE		
Hold You Down		5/05
❖ featuring JA RULE		
I'm Real	8/01	11/01
❖ featuring JA RULE & CADDILLAC TAH		
Ain't It Funny (Remix)	2/02	3/02
❖ featuring JADAKISS & STYLES		
Jenny From The Block	11/2	11/02
❖ featuring LL COOL J		
All I Have	1/03	3/03
❖ featuring NAS		
I'm Gonna Be Alright	6/02	7/02
Trini LOPEZ (US)		
If I Had A Hammer	8/63	9/63
Denise LOR (US)		
If I Give My Heart To You	10/54	
A'me LORAIN (US)		
Whole Wide World	4/90	
Jerry LORDAN (US)		
Who Could Be Bluer		3/60
LORD TARIQ & PETER GUNZ (US)		
Déjà Vu (Uptown Baby)	3/98	
Gloria LORING & Carl Anderson (US)		
Friends And Lovers	8/86	
LOS DEL RIO (SPA)		
Macarena (Bayside Boys Remix)	6/96	7/96
LOSTPROPHETS (UK)		
Last Train Home		2/04
Rooftops (A Liberation Broadcast)		7/06
Pixie LOTT (UK)		
Boys And Girls		9/09
Cry Me Out		12/09
Mama Do (Uh Oh, Uh Oh)		6/09
Bonnie LOU (US)		
Tennessee Wig Walk		2/54
LOUCHIE LOU & Michie One (UK)		
Shout		6/93
John D LOUDERMILK (US)		
Language Of Love	1/62	
LOUISE (UK)		
All That Matters		4/98
Arms Around The World		10/97
Light Of My Life		10/95
Naked		6/96
Pandora's Kiss/Don't Give Up		9/03
Stuck In The Middle With You		9/01
2 Faced		08/00
Undivided Love		8/96
LOVE AFFAIR (UK)		
Bringing On Back The Good Times		8/69
A Day Without Love		10/68

	US Top 20 Ent	UK Top 20 Ent
Everlasting Love		1/68
Rainbow Valley		5/68
LOVE AND ROCKETS (UK)		
So Alive	7/89	
LOVE CITY GROOVE (UK)		
Love City Groove		5/95
LOVE INC. (J/C)		
You're A Superstar		12/02
LOVE SCULPTURE (UK)		
Sabre Dance		12/68
LOVE UNLIMITED (US)		
It May Be Winter Outside (But In My Heart It's Spring)		3/75
Walkin' In The Rain With The One I Love	6/72	7/72
LOVE UNLIMITED ORCHESTRA (US)		
Love's Theme	1/74	3/74
Monie LOVE featuring True Image (UK)		
It's A Shame (My Sister)		10/90
LOVEBUG STARSKI (US)		
Amityville (The House On The Hill)		6/86
The LOVEFREEKZ (UK)		
Shine		2/05
Bill LOVELADY (UK)		
Reggae For It Now		9/79
LOVERBOY (US)		
Heaven In Your Eyes	10/86	
Hot Girls In Love	8/83	
Lovin' Every Minute Of It	10/85	
This Could Be The Night	3/86	
Lene LOVICH (US)		
Lucky Number		3/79
LOVIN' SPOONFUL (US)		
Daydream	3/66	5/66
Did You Ever Have To Make Up Your Mind	5/66	
Do You Believe In Magic	10/65	
Nashville Cats	1/67	
Rain On The Roof	11/66	
Summer In The City	8/66	8/66
You Didn't Have To Be So Nice	1/66	
Demi LOVATO & Joe Jonas (US)		
This Is Me	7/08	
Jim LOWE (US)		
The Green Door	10/56	11/56
Nick LOWE (UK)		
Cruel To Be Kind	9/79	10/79
I Love The Sound Of Breaking Glass		3/78
THE LOX/DMX/LIL' KIM (US)		
Money, Power & Respect	5/98	
LUDACRIS (US)		
Get Back	1/05	
How Low	12/09	
Splash Waterfalls	2/04	
LUDACRIS featuring Bobby VALENTINO		
Pimpin' All Over The World	7/05	
LUDACRIS featuring Mary J. BLIGE (US)		
Runaway Love	1/07	
LUDACRIS featuring MYSTIKAL & INFAMOUS 2.0 (US)		
❖ Move Bitch	9/02	
LUDACRIS featuring PHARRELL		
Money Maker	9/06	
LUDACRIS featuring SHAWNNA		
Stand Up	10/03	
Baz LUHRMANN (AUS)		
Everybody's Free (To Wear Sunscreen)		6/99
Robin LUKE (US)		
Susie Darlin'	9/58	
LULU (UK)		
The Boat That I Row		5/67
Boom Bang-A-Bang		4/69
I'm A Tiger		12/68
Independence		2/93
Leave A Little Love		7/65
Let's Pretend		8/67
The Man Who Sold The World		2/74
Me The Peaceful Heart		3/68
Shout		6/64
★ Shout		8/86
To Sir With Love	10/67	
❖ with Take That		
Relight My Fire		10/93
Bob LUMAN (US)		
Let's Think About Living	10/60	10/60
LUMIDEE (US)		
Never Leave You – Uh Ooh, Uh Oooh!	7/03	8/03
Victor LUNDBERG (US)		
An Open Letter To My Teenage Son	12/67	
LUNIZ (US)		

	US Top 20 Ent	UK Top 20 Ent
I Got 5 On It	8/95	2/96
LV (US) see Coolio featuring LV		
Arthur LYMAN (US)		
Yellow Bird	6/61	
Frankie LYMON & The Teenagers (US)		
Baby Baby		4/57
I Want You To Be My Girl	5/56	
I'm Not A Juvenile Delinquent		4/57
Why Do Fools Fall In Love	2/56	7/56
Kenny LYNCH (UK)		
Up On The Roof		12/62
You Can Never Stop Me Loving You		7/63
Liam LYNCH (UK)		
United States Of Whatever		12/02
Barbara LYNN (US)		
You'll Lose A Good Thing	8/62	
Cheryl LYNN (US)		
Got To Be Real	2/79	
Tami LYNN (US)		
I'm Gonna Run Away From You		6/71
LYTE FUNKIE ONES (US) see LFO (US)		
M (UK)		
Pop Muzik	9/79	4/79
Kevin LYTTLE (WI)		
Turn Me On	7/04	10/03
M&S presents GIRL NEXT DOOR (UK)		
❖ Salsoul Nugget (If U Wanna)		4/01
M.I.A. (UK)		
Paper Planes	8/08	
M2M (US)		
Don't Say You Love Me	01/00	
Mirror Mirror	04/00	
M.O.P. (US)		
Cold As Ice		5/01
❖ **featuring Busta RHYMES**		
Ante Up		8/01
M PEOPLE (UK)		
Don't Look Any Further		12/93
How Can I Love You More?		2/93
Moving On Up		9/93
One Night In Heaven		6/93
Open Your Heart		2/95
Renaissance		3/94
Search For The Hero		6/95
Sight For Sore Eyes		11/94
M.V.P. (US)		
Roc Ya Body 'Mic Check 1,2'		7/05
M-BEAT featuring General Levy (UK)		
Incredible		9/94
M/A/R/R/S (UK)		
Pump Up The Volume	2/88	9/87
MAC BAND featuring The McCampbell Brothers (US)		
Roses Are Red		7/88
Kirsty MacCOLL (UK)		
Days		8/89
New England		2/85
❖ **with The Pogues**		
Fairytale Of New York		12/87
Byron MacGREGOR (US)		
Americans	1/74	
Mary MacGREGOR (US)		
Torn Between Two Lovers	1/77	3/77
Lonnie MACK (US)		
Memphis	7/63	
Giselle MacKENZIE (C)		
Hard To Get	7/55	
Ken MacKINTOSH (UK)		
The Creep		1/54
Patrick MacNEE & HONOR BLACKMAN (UK)		
Kinky Boots		12/90
MAD COBRA (J)		
Flex	1/93	
MADCON (N)		
Beggin'		8/08
MAD'HOUSE (F/H)		
Like A Prayer		8/02
Johnny MADDOX (US)		
The Crazy Otto (Medley)	2/55	
MADISON AVENUE (UK)		
Don't Call Me Baby		5/00
MADNESS (UK)		
Baggy Trousers		9/80
Cardiac Arrest		3/82
Driving In My Car		7/82
Embarrassment		12/80
Grey Day		5/81
House Of Fun		5/82
It Must Be Love		12/81
★ It Must Be Love		2/92
Michael Caine		2/84
My Girl		1/80
One Step Beyond		12/79
Our House	7/83	12/82
Return Of The Los Palmas 7		2/81
Shut Up		10/81
The Sun And The Rain		11/83
Tomorrow's (Just Another Day)/Madness (Is All In The Mind)		3/83
Wings Of A Dove		8/83
Work Rest & Play (E.P.)		4/80
MADONNA (US)		
American Life		4/03
American Pie		3/00
Angel	6/85	9/85
Bad Girl		3/93
Beautiful Stranger		6/99
Bedtime Story		2/95
Borderline	6/84	2/86
Causing A Commotion	10/87	9/87
Cherish	9/89	9/89
Celebration		9/09
Crazy For You	4/85	6/85
★ Crazy For You		3/91
Dear Jessie		12/89
Deeper And Deeper	12/92	12/92
Die Another Day	11/02	11/02
Don't Cry For Me Argentina	3/97	
Don't Tell Me	2/01	12/00
Dress You Up	9/85	12/85
Erotica	10/92	10/92
Express Yourself	7/89	6/89
Fever		4/93
Frozen	3/98	
Gambler		10/85
Get Together		8/06
Give It 2 Me		7/08
Hanky Panky	7/90	7/90
Holiday		2/84
★ Holiday		8/85
★ Holiday		6/91
Hollywood		7/03
Human Nature	8/95	
Hung Up	12/05	11/05
Jump	11/06	
I'll Remember	4/94	4/94
Into The Groove		7/85
Justify My Love	12/90	12/90
Keep It Together	3/90	
La Isla Bonita	4/87	4/87
Like A Prayer	4/89	3/89
Like A Virgin	12/84	12/84
Live To Tell	5/86	5/86
The Look Of Love		12/87
Lucky Star	10/84	
Material Girl	3/85	3/85
Music	01/01	09/00
Nothing Really Matters		3/99
Open Your Heart	1/87	12/86
Papa Don't Preach	7/86	7/86
The Power Of Goodbye/Little Star	11/98	12/98
Rain	9/93	8/93
Ray Of Light	7/98	5/95
Rescue Me	3/91	4/91
Secret	10/94	10/94
Sorry		3/06
Take A Bow	12/94	
This Used To Be My Playground	7/92	7/92
True Blue	11/86	10/86
Vogue	5/90	4/90
What It Feels Like For A Girl		4/01
Who's That Girl	8/87	7/87
You'll See 12/95		11/95
MADONNA featuring Justin TIMBERLAKE (US)		
4 Minutes	4/08	3/08
MAD STUNTMAN see Reel 2 Real featuring the Mad Stuntman		
Lisa MAFFIA (UK)		
All Over		5/03
MAGOO & TIMBALAND (US)		
Up Jumps Da Boogie	9/97	
MAI TAI (H)		
Body And Soul		9/85
History		6/85
MAIN INGREDIENT (US)		
Everybody Plays The Fool	9/72	
Just Don't Want To Be Lonely	4/74	
MAISONETTES (UK)		
Heartache Avenue		1/83
Miriam MAKEBA (SA)		
Pata Pata	11/67	
Carl MALCOLM (J)		
Fattie Bum-Bum		9/75
Richard MALTBY (US)		
Themes From 'The Man With The Golden Arm'	4/56	
MAMA CASS (US)		
Dream A Little Dream Of Me	8/68	9/68
MAMAS & THE PAPAS (US)		
California Dreamin'		2/66
Creeque Alley	5/67	8/67
Dedicated To The One I Love	3/67	5/67
I Saw Her Again	7/66	8/66
Monday Monday	4/66	5/66
Words Of Love	1/67	
MAN 2 MAN MEET MAN PARRISH (US)		
Male Stripper		2/87
Melissa MANCHESTER (US)		
Don't Cry Out Loud	3/79	
Midnight Blue	7/75	
You Should Hear How She Talks About You	8/82	
MANCHESTER UNITED FOOTBALL SQUAD (UK)		
Come On You Reds		5/94
We're Gonna Do It Again		5/95
Henry MANCINI & His Orchestra (US)		
How Soon		10/64
Love Theme From Romeo & Juliet	6/69	
Moon River	12/61	
Theme From Love Story	2/71	
MANFRED MANN (UK/SA)		
Come Tomorrow		1/65
Do Wah Diddy Diddy	9/64	7/64
5-4-3-2-1		2/64
Fox On The Run		1/69
Ha Ha Said The Clown		4/67
Hubble Bubble Toil And Trouble		5/64
If You Gotta Go Go Now		10/65
Just Like A Woman		9/66
Mighty Quinn	3/68	2/68
My Name Is Jack		7/68
Oh No Not My Baby		5/65
Pretty Flamingo		4/66
Ragamuffin Man		5/69
Semi-Detached Surburban Mr. James		11/66
Sha La La	12/64	11/64
MANFRED MANN'S EARTH BAND (UK/SA)		
Blinded By The Light	1/77	9/76
Davy's On The Road Again		6/78
Joybringer		10/73
Chuck MANGIONE (US)		
Feels So Good	5/78	
MANHATTAN TRANSFER (US)		
The Boy From New York City	7/81	
Chanson D'Amour		2/77
Walk In Love		4/78
MANHATTANS (US)		
Hurt		10/76
Kiss And Say Goodbye	6/76	7/76
Shining Star	6/80	
MANIC STREET PREACHERS (UK)		
Empty Souls		1/05
If You Tolerate This Your Children Will Be Next		9/98
The Love Of Richard Nixon		10/04
Theme From M*A*S*H (Suicide Is Painless)		9/92
There By The Grace Of God		10/02
You Stole The Sun From My Heart		3/99
Your Love Alone Is Not Enough		5/07
Barry MANILOW (US)		
Can't Smile Without You	3/78	
Copacabana (At The Copa)	7/78	
Could It Be Magic	8/75	
I Made It Through The Rain	1/81	
I Wanna Do It With You		11/82
I Write The Songs	12/75	
It's A Miracle	5/75	
Looks Like We Made It	6/77	
Mandy	12/74	3/75
The Old Songs	11/81	
Ready To Take A Chance Again	11/78	
Ships	11/79	
Somewhere In The Night	2/79	
Tryin' To Get The Feeling Again	5/76	
Weekend In New England	2/77	

	US Top 20 Ent	UK Top 20 Ent
Barry MANN (US)		
Who Put The Bomp…	9/61	
Johnny MANN SINGERS (US)		
Up Up And Away		8/67
MANSUN (UK)		
Legacy EP		7/98
I Can Only Disappoint U		8/00
MANTOVANI (UK)		
Shadow Waltz		5/54
Swedish Rhapsody		1/54
MANTRONIX featuring WONDRESS (US/J)		
Got To Have Your Love		1/90
Take Your Time		5/90
MANUEL & HIS MUSIC OF THE MOUNTAINS (UK)		
Rodrigo's Guitar Concierto De Aranjuez		2/76
MARBLES (UK)		
Only One Woman		10/68
MARCELS (US)		
Blue Moon	3/61	4/61
Heartaches	11/61	
Little Peggy MARCH (US)		
I Will Follow Him	4/63	
MARCY PLAYGROUND (US)		
Sex And Candy	4/98	
Benny MARDONES (US)		
Into The Night	8/80	
Ernie MARESCA (US)		
Shout! Shout! (Knock Yourself Out)	5/62	
Ida MARIA (N)		
I Like You So Much Better When You're Naked		8/08
Kelly MARIE (UK)		
Feels Like I'm In Love		8/80
Teena MARIE (US)		
Behind The Groove		6/80
Lovergirl	3/85	
MARILLION (UK)		
Incommunicado		5/87
Kayleigh		5/85
Lavender		9/85
MARILYN (UK)		
Calling Your Name		11/83
MARILYN MANSON (US)		
Tainted Love		3/02
MARINO Marini (ITA)		
Come Prima		10/58
Volare		10/58
MARIO (US)		
Just A Friend 2002	7/02	
Let Me Love You	11/04	4/05
MARIO featuring Gucci Mane & Sean Garrett (US)		
Break Up	9/09	
MARKY MARK & THE FUNKY BUNCH featuring Loleatta HOLLOWAY (US)		
Good Vibrations	9/91	9/91
Wildside	12/91	
MARKETTS (US)		
Out Of Limits	1/64	
MAR-KEYS (US)		
Last Night	7/61	
Yannis MARKOPOULOS (GRE)		
Who Pays The Ferryman		1/78
BOB MARLEY & THE WAILERS (J)		
Buffalo Soldier		6/83
Could You Be Loved		7/80
Iron Lion Zion		9/92
Is This Love		3/78
Jamming/Funky Reggae Party		1/78
No Woman No Cry		7/81
One Love/People Get Ready		5/84
Sun Is Shining		9/99
MARMADUKE DUKE (UK)		
Rubber Lover		5/09
Lene MARLIN (N)		
Sitting Down Here		3/00
MARMALADE (UK)		
Baby Make It Soon		7/69
Cousin Norman		9/71
Falling Apart At The Seams		3/76
Lovin' Things		6/68
Ob-La-Di Ob-La-Da		12/68
Radancer		5/72
Rainbow		8/70
Reflections Of My Life	5/70	1/70
MAROON5 (US)		
Makes Me Wonder	5/07	5/07

	US Top 20 Ent	UK Top 20 Ent
She Will Be Loved	8/04	9/04
This Love	3/04	5/04
Kym MARSH (UK)		
Cry		4/03
MARSHALL HAIN (UK)		
Dancing In The City		7/78
MARSHALL TUCKER BAND (US)		
Heard It In A Love Song	6/77	
Keith MARSHALL (UK)		
Only Crying		5/81
Lena MARTELL (UK)		
One Day At A Time		10/79
Ralph MARTERIE (US)		
Skokiaan	9/54	
MARTHA & THE MUFFINS (C)		
Echo Beach		4/80
MARTHA (REEVES) & THE VANDELLAS (US)		
Dancing In The Street	9/64	2/69
Forget Me Not		3/71
Heat Wave	9/63	
Honey Chile	1/68	
I'm Ready For Love	12/66	
Jimmy Mack	4/67	
Nowhere To Run	4/65	
Quicksand	12/63	
MARTIKA (US)		
I Feel The Earth Move		11/89
Love…Thy Will Be Done	10/91	9/91
Toy Soldiers	7/89	8/89
Billie Ray MARTIN (G)		
Your Loving Arms		5/95
Bobbi MARTIN (US)		
For The Love Of Him	5/70	
Dean MARTIN (US)		
The Door Is Still Open To My Heart	10/64	
Everybody Loves Somebody	7/64	9/64
Gentle On My Mind		3/69
I Will	12/65	
Let Me Go, Lover		3/55
Mambo Italiano		2/55
Memories Are Made Of This	12/55	2/56
Naughty Lady Of Shady Lane		2/55
Return To Me	5/58	8/58
Sway	8/54	10/54
That's Amore	1/54	1/54
Under The Bridges Of Paris		4/55
Volare		9/58
Juan MARTIN (SPA)		
Love Theme From 'The Thorn Birds'		2/84
Ray MARTIN (UK)		
Swedish Rhapsody		1/54
Ricky MARTIN (Puerto Rico)		
Livin' La Vida Loca	5/99	7/99
Shake Your Bon-Bon	2/00	
She Bangs		11/00
She's All I Ever Had	9/99	
(Un Dos Tres) Maria		9/97
❖ with Christina Aguilera		
Nobody Wants To Be Lonely		3/01
Tony MARTIN (US)		
Here	4/54	
Stranger In Paradise	1/54	4/55
Walk Hand In Hand		7/56
Vince MARTIN with THE TARRIERS (US)		
Cindy, Oh Cindy	10/56	
Wink MARTINDALE (US)		
Deck Of Cards	10/59	5/63
ANGIE MARTINEZ featuring LIL' MO & SACARIO (US)		
❖ If I Could Go!	9/02	
Al MARTINO (US)		
I Love You Because	5/63	
I Love You More And More Every Day	3/64	
Spanish Eyes		8/73
The Story Of Tina		10/54
Wanted		6/54
MARVELETTES (US)		
Don't Mess With Bill	2/66	
The Hunter Gets Captured By The Game	3/67	
Playboy	6/62	
Please Mr. Postman	11/61	
Lee MARVIN (US)		
Wand'rin' Star		2/70
Richard MARX (US)		
Angelia	11/89	
Children Of The Night	6/90	
Don't Mean Nothing	8/87	
Endless Summer Nights	3/88	
Hazard	4/92	6/92

	US Top 20 Ent	UK Top 20 Ent
Hold On To The Nights	7/88	
Keep Coming Back	12/91	
Now And Forever	2/94	1/94
Right Here Waiting	8/89	9/89
Satisfied	6/89	
Should've Known Better	11/87	
Take This Heart		9/92
Too Late To Say Goodbye	3/90	
MARY JANE GIRLS (US)		
In My House	5/85	
MARY MARY (US)		
Shackles (Praise You)	4/00	6/00
MA$E (US)		
Feels So Good	11/97	12/97
MA$E & TOTAL (US)		
What You Want	2/98	
MA$E & PUFF DADDY (US)		
Lookin' At Me	8/98	
Hugh MASEKELA (SA)		
Grazing In The Grass	7/68	
MASH (US)		
Theme From M*A*S*H (Suicide Is Painless)		5/80
MASON (H)		
Exceeder	2/07	
Barbara MASON (US)		
Yes, I'm Ready	7/65	
Dave MASON (UK)		
We Just Disagree	11/77	
MASTER P (US)		
Souljas	11/00	
MATCHBOX (UK)		
Midnite Dynamos		6/80
When You Ask About Love		10/80
MATCHBOX TWENTY (US)		
Bent	07/00	
How Far We've Come	9/07	
If You're Gone	4/01	
Unwell	5/03	
MATCHROOM MOB with Chas & Dave (UK)		
Snooker Loopy		5/86
Johnny MATHIS (US)		
A Certain Smile		10/58
Chances Are/The Twelfth Of Never	9/57	
Gina	10/62	
I'm Stone In Love With You		3/75
It's Not For Me To Say	6/57	
Misty	11/59	2/60
My Love For You		10/60
Someone		8/59
What Will My Mary Say	3/63	
When A Child Is Born (Soleado)		12/76
Johnny MATHIS & Deniece WILLIAMS (US)		
Too Much, Too Little, Too Late	5/78	4/78
MATT BIANCO (UK)		
Don't Blame It On That Girl/Wap Bam Boogie		7/88
Ian MATTHEWS (UK)		
Shake It	2/79	
MATTHEWS' SOUTHERN COMFORT (UK)		
Woodstock		10/70
Susan MAUGHAN (UK)		
Bobby's Girl		11/62
MAUREEN (UK)		
Thinking Of You		7/90
Paul MAURIAT (F)		
Love Is Blue	2/68	4/68
MAVERICKS (US)		
Dance The Night Away		5/98
MAXWELL (US)		
Fortunate	5/99	
Robert MAXWELL, HIS HARP & HIS ORCHESTRA (US)		
Shangri-La	5/64	
MAXX (UK/S/G)		
Get-A-Way		5/94
No More (I Can't Stand It)		8/94
Billy MAY (US)		
Main Title Theme From 'The Man With The Golden Arm'		5/56
Brian MAY (UK)		
Driven By You		12/91
Too Much Love Will Kill You		9/92
Simon MAY (UK)		
Summer Of My Life		10/76
John MAYER (US)		
No Such Thing	8/02	
Say	5/08	
Curtis MAYFIELD (US)		

	US Top 20 Ent	UK Top 20 Ent
R.O.C.K In The U.S.A. (A Salute To 60's Rock)	3/86	
Small Town	12/85	
John MELLENCAMP & Me'shell Ndegeocello (US)		
Wild Night	7/94	
Will MELLOR (UK)		
When I Need You		2/98
MELLOW MAN ACE (US)		
Mentirosa	7/90	
Katie MELUA (UK)		
Nine Million Bicycles		10/05
Harold MELVIN & THE BLUE NOTES (US)		
Bad Luck (Pt. 1)	6/75	
Don't Leave Me This Way		2/77
If You Don't Know Me By Now	11/72	2/73
The Love I Lost (Part 1)	11/73	
Wake Up Everybody (Pt. 1)	2/76	
MEMBERS (UK)		
Sound Of The Suburbs		3/79
MEN AT WORK (AUS)		
Down Under	12/82	1/83
It's A Mistake	8/83	
Overkill	4/83	
Who Can It Be Now?	9/82	
MEN WITHOUT HATS (C)		
The Safety Dance	8/83	10/83
Sergio MENDES (BRA)		
Never Gonna Let You Go	6/83	
Sergio MENDES & BRASIL '66 (BRA)		
The Fool On The Hill	9/68	
The Look Of Love	6/68	
Scarborough Fair	12/68	
Sergio MENDES featuring The BLACK EYED PEAS		
Mas Que Nada	7/06	
MENTAL AS ANYTHING (AUS)		
Live It Up		3/87
Natalie MERCHANT (US)		
Carnival	11/95	
Freddie MERCURY (UK)		
The Great Pretender		3/87
I Was Born To Love You		5/85
In My Defence		12/92
Living On My Own		7/93
Love Kills		10/84
Freddie MERCURY & Montserrat CABALLE (UK/Spa)		
Barcelona		11/87
★ Barcelona		8/92
MERCY (US)		
Love (Can Make You Happy)	5/69	
MERRION, McCALL & KENSIT (UK)		
I Got You Babe/Soda Pop		12/04
Daniel MERRIWEATHER (AUS)		
Change		2/09
Red		5/09
MERSEYBEATS (UK)		
Don't Turn Around		5/64
I Think Of You		2/64
Wishin' And Hopin'		8/64
MERSEYS (UK)		
Sorrow		5/66
METALLICA (US/D)		
Enter Sandman	10/91	8/91
Nothing Else Matters		5/92
Until It Sleeps	6/96	
METHOD MAN (US)		
❖ with Redman		
How High	9/95	
METHOD MAN/Mary J. Blige (US)		
I'll Be There For You/You're All I Need To Get By	5/95	
METRO STATION (US)		
Shake It	6/08	4/09
MFSB featuring The Three Degrees (US)		
TSOP (The Sound Of Philadelphia)	4/74	
George MICHAEL (UK)		
Amazing		3/04
Careless Whisper	1/85	8/84
A Different Corner	6/86	4/86
Faith	11/87	10/87
Fastlove	6/96	
Father Figure	2/88	
Freedom	12/90	
I Want Your Sex	7/87	6/87
Jesus To A Child	2/96	1/96
Kissing A Fool	11/88	
Monkey	8/88	
One More Try	5/88	
Outside		10/98
Praying For Time	9/90	9/90
Toofunky	7/92	6/92
❖ with Mary J. Blige		
As		3/99
❖ with Aretha Franklin		
I Knew You Were Waiting (For Me)	3/87	1/87
George MICHAEL & QUEEN (UK)		
Five Live (EP)		5/93
George MICHAEL & ELTON JOHN (UK)		
Don't Let The Sun Go Down On Me	1/92	12/91
Lee MICHAELS (US)		
Do You Know What I Mean	9/71	
MICHELLE (US)		
All This Time		1/04
MICHEL'LE (US)		
No More Lies	2/90	
Keith MICHEL (AUS)		
Captain Beaky/Wilfred The Weasel		2/80
Pras MICHEL/ODB/MYA (US)		
Blue Angels		11/98
Ghetto Supastar That Is What You Are	7/98	6/98
MICK & PAT (UK) see Pat & Mick		
MICKEY & SYLVIA (US)		
Love Is Strange	2/57	
MIDDLE OF THE ROAD (UK)		
Chirpy Chirpy Cheep Cheep		6/71
Soley Soley		12/71
Tweedle Dee Tweedle Dum		9/71
Bette MIDLER (US)		
Boogie Woogie Bugle Boy	7/73	
From A Distance	11/90	
The Rose	6/80	
Wind Beneath My Wings	5/89	7/89
MIDNIGHT OIL (AUS)		
Beds Are Burning		5/89
MIDNIGHT STAR (US)		
Midas Touch		11/86
MIGHTY MORPH'N POWER RANGERS (US)		
Power Rangers		12/94
MIGIL FIVE (UK)		
Mockingbird Hill		4/64
MIKA (L)		
Grace Kelly		1/07
Happy Ending		10/07
Love Today		5/07
We Are Golden		9/09
MIKAILA (US)		
So In Love With Two	12/00	
MIKE + THE MECHANICS (UK)		
All I Need Is A Miracle	5/86	
The Living Years	2/89	1/89
Over My Shoulder		3/95
Silent Running (On Dangerous Ground)	2/86	
John MILES (UK)		
Music		4/76
Slow Down		7/77
Robert MILES (ITA)		
Children		2/96
Christina MILIAN (US)		
AM To PM		1/02
Dip It Low	7/4	5/04
When You Look At Me		6/02
Christina MILIAN featuring YOUNG JEEZY		
Say I	5/06	
MILK & HONEY (ISR)		
Hallelujah		4/79
Chuck MILLER (US)		
The House Of Blue Lights	7/55	
Frankie MILLER (UK)		
Darlin'		11/78
Gary MILLER (UK)		
Garden Of Eden		1/57
Robin Hood		2/56
Story Of My Life		1/58
Yellow Rose Of Texas		11/55
Glenn MILLER (US)		
Moonlight Serenade		3/54
Moonlight Serenade/Little Brown Jug/In The Mood		2/76
Mitch MILLER (US)		
The Children's Marching Song	2/59	
Theme Song From 'Song For A Summer Night'	8/56	
The Yellow Rose Of Texas	8/55	10/55
Ned MILLER (US)		
From A Jack To A King	2/63	3/63
Roger MILLER (US)		
Chug-A-Lug	10/64	
Dang Me	7/64	
Engine Engine #9	6/65	
England Swings	12/65	
King Of The Road	2/65	5/65
Steve MILLER Band (US)		
Abracadabra	7/82	7/82
Fly Like An Eagle	2/77	
Jet Airliner	6/77	
The Joker	12/73	9/90
Rock'n Me	10/76	12/76
Take The Money And Run	7/76	
MILLI VANILLI (F/G)		
All Or Nothing		2/90
Baby Don't Forget My Number	6/89	
Blame It On The Rain	11/89	
Girl I'm Gonna Miss You	9/89	10/89
Girl You Know It's True	3/89	11/88
MILLIE (J) see Millie Small		
Frank MILLS (US)		
Music Box Dancer	4/79	
Garry MILLS (UK)		
Look For A Star		7/60
Hayley MILLS (UK)		
Let's Get Together	10/61	11/61
Stephanie MILLS (US)		
Never Knew Love Like This Before	10/80	11/80
Ronnie MILSAP (US)		
Any Day Now	7/82	
(There's) No Gettin' Over Me	8/81	
Garnet MIMMS & THE ENCHANTERS (US)		
Cry Baby	9/63	
MIMS (US)		
This Is Why I'm Hot	3/07	
MINDBENDERS (UK)		
A Groovy Kind Of Love	5/66	2/66
Sal MINEO (US)		
Start Movin' (In My Direction)	6/57	8/57
Marcello MINERBI (ITA)		
Zorba's Dance		8/65
MINI VIVA (UK)		
Left My Heart In Tokyo		9/09
Liza MINNELLI (US)		
Losing My Mind		8/89
Dannii MINOGUE (AUS)		
Baby Love		10/91
Don't Wanna Lose This Feeling		6/03
I Begin To Wonder		3/03
Jump To The Beat		8/91
Love & Kisses		4/91
Put The Needle On It		11/02
Success		6/91
This Is It		7/93
Dannii MINOGUE vs FLOWER POWER		
You Won't Forget About Me		11/04
Kylie MINOGUE (AUS)		
2 Hearts		11/07
Better The Devil You Know		5/90
Can't Get You Out Of My Head	2/02	9/01
Chocolate		7/04
Confide In Me		9/94
Give Me Just A Little More Time		1/92
Giving You Up		4/05
Got To Be Certain		5/88
Hand On Your Heart		5/89
I Believe In You		12/04
I Should Be So Lucky		2/88
In My Arms		5/08
In Your Eyes		3/02
Je Ne Sais Pas Pourquoi		10/88
Love At First Sight		6/02
The Loco-Motion	10/88	8/88
Never Too Late		11/89
On A Night Like This		09/00
Red Blooded Woman		3/04
Shocked		6/91
Slow		11/03
Spinning Around		7/00
Step Back In Time		11/90
Tears On My Pillow		1/90
What Do I Have To Do		2/91
Wouldn't Change A Thing		8/89
Wow		3/08
Kylie MINOGUE & Jason DONOVAN (AUS)		
Especially For You		12/88
Kylie MINOGUE & Keith WASHINGTON (AUS/US)		
If You Were Here With Me Now		11/91

	US Top 20 Ent	UK Top 20 Ent
Sugar MINOTT (UK)		
Good Thing Going		4/81
MINT CONDITION (US)		
Breakin' My Heart (Pretty Brown Eyes)	3/92	
If You Love Me	11/99	
What Kind Of Man Would I Be	12/96	
MINT ROYALE (UK)		
Singin' In The Rain		6/08
MIRACLES (US)		
Do It Baby	10/74	
Going To A Go-Go	2/66	
Love Machine	1/76	1/76
Mickey's Monkey	9/63	
Shop Around	1/61	
You've Really Got A Hold On Me	2/63	
Smokey Robinson & THE MIRACLES (US)		
Baby, Baby Don't You Cry	2/69	
(Come 'Round Here) I'm The One You Need		2/71
I Don't Blame You At All		7/71
I Second That Emotion	12/67	
If You Can Want	4/68	
The Tears Of A Clown	11/70	8/70
The Tracks Of My Tears		6/69
MIRAGE (UK)		
Jack Mix II		6/87
Jack Mix IV		11/87
Danny MIRROR (H)		
I Remember Elvis Presley (The King Is Dead)		10/77
MISSION (UK)		
Tower Of Strength		2/88
MIS-TEEQ (UK)		
All I Want		6/01
B With Me		3/02
Can't Get It Back		7/03
One Night Stand		10/01
Scandalous		3/03
Why		1/01
MR. BEAN & SMEAR CAMPAIGN (UK)		
(I Want To Be) Elected		4/92
MR. BIG (US)		
Just Take My Heart	6/92	
To Be With You	2/92	3/92
MR. BIG (UK)		
Romeo		2/77
MR. BLOBBY (UK)		
Mr. Blobby		12/93
MR. BLOE (UK)		
Groovin' With Mr. Bloe		6/70
MR. CHEEKS (US)		
Lights, Camera, Action!	3/02	
MR. MISTER (US)		
Broken Wings	11/85	1/86
Is It Love	5/86	
Kyrie	2/86	3/86
MR OIZO (F)		
Flat Beat		4/99
Guy MITCHELL (US)		
Call Rosie On The Phone		10/57
Chika Boom		1/54
Cloud Lucky Seven		1/54
Cuff Of My Shirt		2/54
Dime And A Dollar		4/54
Heartaches By The Number	11/59	1/60
Knee Deep In The Blues		3/57
Rock-A-Billy	5/57	5/57
Singing The Blues	11/56	12/56
Sippin' Soda		2/54
Joni MITCHELL (C)		
Big Yellow Taxi		8/70
Help Me	5/74	
MIXMASTER (ITA)		
Grand Piano		11/89
MIXTURES (AUS)		
The Pushbike Song		1/71
Hank MIZELL (US)		
Jungle Rock		4/76
MN8 (UK/WI)		
Happy		7/95
I've Got A Little Something For You		2/95
If You Only Let Me In		4/95
MOBILES (UK)		
Drowning In Berlin		2/82
MOBY (US)		
Go		11/91
James Bond Theme		11/97
Porcelain		6/00
❖ *featuring Gwen Stefani*		
South Side		01/01
MOCEDADES (SPA)		
Eres Tu (Touch The Wind)	3/74	
MODERN ROMANCE (UK)		
Ay Ay Ay Ay Moosey		12/81
Best Years Of Our Lives		12/82
Everybody Salsa		9/81
High Life		3/83
Walking In The Rain		9/83
MODERN TALKING (G)		
Brother Louie		8/86
MODJO (F)		
Lady (Hear Me Tonight)		09/00
Domenico MODUGNO (ITA)		
Nel Blu Dipinto Di Blu (Volare)	8/58	9/58
MOJOS (UK)		
Everything's Alright		4/64
MOKENSTEF (US)		
He's Mine	8/95	
MOLELLA featuring The Outhere Brothers (Ita/US)		
If You Wanna Party		1/96
MOLOKO (UK/I)		
Sing It Back		9/99
The Time Is Now		4/00
MOMENTS (US)		
Dolly My Love		8/75
Jack In The Box		2/77
Love On A Two-Way Street	5/70	
MOMENTS AND WHATNAUTS (US)		
Girls		3/75
Eddie MONEY (US)		
Baby Hold On	5/78	
I Wanna Go Back	3/87	
Peace In Our Time	2/90	
Take Me Home Tonight	11/86	
Think I'm In Love	9/82	
Walk On Water	12/88	
JT MONEY with SOLE (US)		
Who Dat	5/99	
MONICA (US)		
Angel Of Mine	1/99	
Before You Walk Out Of My Life/Like This And Like That	12/95	
Don't Take It Personal (Just One Of Dem Days)	5/95	
The First Night	8/98	10/98
For You I Will	3/97	
So Gone	6/03	
Why I Love You So Much/Ain't Nobody	6/96	
MONIFAH (US)		
Touch It	10/98	
MONKEES (US/UK)		
Alternate Title		7/67
Daydream Believer	11/67	12/67
I'm A Believer	12/66	1/67
Last Train To Clarksville	10/66	
A Little Bit Me, A Little Bit You	4/67	4/67
Pleasant Valley Sunday	8/67	8/67
Valleri	3/68	4/68
Words	9/67	
MONOTONES (US)		
Book Of Love	4/58	
Matt MONRO (UK)		
My Kind Of Girl		3/61
Portrait Of My Love		1/61
Softly As I Leave You		3/62
Walk Away		10/64
Yesterday		11/65
Gerry MONROE (UK)		
It's A Sin To Tell A Lie		5/71
My Prayer		12/70
Sally		6/70
Vaughn MONROE (US)		
They Were Doin' The Mambo	8/54	
Hannah MONTANA (US)		
He Could Be The One	7/09	
Lou MONTE (US)		
At The Darktown Strutters' Ball	2/54	
Pepino The Italian Mouse	1/63	
Hugo MONTENEGRO & HIS ORCHESTRA (US)		
The Good, The Bad & The Ugly	5/68	10/68
Chris MONTEZ (US)		
Let's Dance	9/62	10/62
★ Let's Dance		11/72
The More I See You	6/66	7/66
MOODY BLUES (UK)		
Gemini Dream	7/81	
Go Now!	4/65	1/65
I'm Just A Singer (In A Rock 'n' Roll Band)	3/73	
Isn't Life Strange		6/72
★ Nights In White Satin	10/72	12/72
Question		5/70
Your Wildest Dreams	7/86	
Art MOONEY (US)		
Honey-Babe	5/55	
Bob MOORE & HIS ORCHESTRA (US)		
Mexico	10/61	
Chante MOORE (US)		
Chante's Got A Man	06/99	
Dorothy MOORE (US)		
Misty Blue	5/76	7/76
GARY MOORE (UK)		
Parisienne Walkways		5/79
Gary MOORE & Phil LYNOTT (UK/I)		
Out In The Fields		6/85
Mandy MOORE		
Candy	9/99	5/00
Melba MOORE (US)		
This Is It		6/76
Tina Moore (US)		
Never Gonna Let You Go		8/97
Debelah MORGAN (US)		
Dance With Me	08/00	
Jane MORGAN (US)		
The Day The Rains Came		12/58
Fascination	10/57	
Jaye P. MORGAN (US)		
The Longest Walk	9/55	
That's All I Want From You	12/54	
Alanis MORISSETTE (C)		
Ironic	3/96	
You Learn/You Oughta Know	7/96	
MORMON TABERNACLE CHOIR (US)		
Battle Hymn Of The Republic	10/59	
Giorgio MORODER & Phil OAKEY (Ita/UK)		
Together In Electric Dreams		10/84
Ennio MORRICONE (ITA)		
Chi Mai Theme		4/81
MORRIS MINOR & THE MAJORS (UK)		
Stutter Rap (No Sleep 'Til Bedtime)		1/88
James MORRISON (UK)		
Wonderful World		10/06
You Give Me Something		7/06
You Make It Real		10/08
James MORRISON featuring Nelly FURTADO (UK/US)		
Broken Strings		12/08
Mark MORRISON (UK)		
Return Of The Mack	4/97	3/96
Van MORRISON (UK)		
Brown Eyed Girl	9/67	
Domino	12/70	
MORRISSEY (UK)		
Everyday Is Like Sunday		6/88
First Of The Gang To Die		7/04
Irish Blood, English Heart		5/04
Last Of The Famous International Playboys		2/89
The More You Ignore Me, The Closer I Get		3/94
November Spawned A Monster		5/90
Suedehead		2/88
You Have Killed Me		4/06
MOTELS (US)		
Only The Lonely	7/82	
Suddenly Last Summer	10/83	
Wendy MOTEN (US)		
Come In Out Of The Rain		2/94
MOTLEY CRUE (US)		
Dr. Feelgood	10/89	
Girls Girls Girls	7/87	
Smokin' In The Boys Room	9/85	
Without You	4/90	
MOTORHEAD (UK)		
The Golden Years (E.P.)		5/80
Motörhead Live		7/81
MOTORHEAD & GIRLSCHOOL (UK)		
St. Valentine's Day Massacre E.P.		2/81
MOTORS (UK)		
Airport		7/78
Forget About You		9/78
MOTT THE HOOPLE (UK)		
All The Way From Memphis		10/73
All The Young Dudes		8/72
Honaloochie Boogie		7/73
Roll Away The Stone		12/73

	US Top 20 Ent	UK Top 20 Ent
Hello Mary Lou	5/61	6/61
I Got A Feeling	11/58	
It's Late	3/59	5/59
Just A Little Too Much	7/59	9/59
Lonesome Town	11/58	
Never Be Anyone Else But You	3/59	
Poor Little Fool	7/58	8/58
Someday		11/58
Stood Up/Waitin' In School	1/58	
Sweeter Than You	8/59	
A Teenagers Romance/I'm Walkin'	5/57	
Teenage Idol	9/62	
Travelin' Man	5/61	6/61
A Wonder Like You	11/61	
Young Emotions	6/60	
Sandy NELSON (US)		
Let There Be Drums	12/61	12/61
Teen Beat	9/59	11/59
Willie NELSON (US)		
Always On My Mind	5/82	
❖ with Julio Iglesias		
To All The Girls I've Loved Before	4/84	
NENA (G)		
99 Luftballons (99 Red Balloons)	2/84	2/84
NERVOUS NORVUS (US)		
Transfusion	6/56	
Robbie NEVIL (US)		
C'est La Vie	12/86	1/87
Wot's It To Ya	8/87	
Aaron NEVILLE (US)		
Everybody Plays The Fool	10/91	
Tell It Like It Is	12/66	
with Linda Ronstadt		
❖ All My Life	4/90	
❖ Don't Know Much	11/89	11/89
NEW ATLANTIC (UK)		
I Know		3/92
NEW EDITION (US)		
Candy Girl		5/83
Cool It Now	11/84	
Hit Me Off	8/96	
If It Isn't Love	9/88	
I'm Still In Love With You	11/96	
Mr. Telephone Man	2/85	
NEW KIDS ON THE BLOCK (US)		
Cover Girl	10/89	5/90
Didn't I (Blow Your Mind)	11/89	
Hangin' Tough	8/89	1/90
If You Go Away	3/92	12/91
I'll Be Loving You (Forever)	5/89	3/90
Let's Try Again/Didn't I Blow Your Mind		10/90
Please Don't Go Girl	10/88	
Step By Step	6/90	6/90
This One's For The Children	12/89	12/90
Tonight	9/90	8/90
You Got It (The Right Stuff)	2/89	11/89
NEW MUZIK (UK)		
Living By Numbers		2/80
NEW ORDER (UK)		
Blue Monday		4/83
★ Blue Monday		10/83
★ Blue Monday 1988		5/88
Confusion		9/83
Crystal		8/01
Fine Time		12/88
Regret		4/93
True Faith		8/87
★ True Faith – 94		11/94
❖ Englandneworder		
World In Motion…		6/90
NEW SEEKERS (UK)		
Beg Steal Or Borrow		3/72
Circles		7/72
I Get A Little Sentimental Over You		3/74
I'd Like To Teach The World To Sing	1/72	12/71
Never Ending Song Of Love		7/71
You Won't Find Another Fool Like Me		12/73
NEW SEEKERS featuring Eve Graham (UK)		
Look What They've Done To My Song Ma	10/70	
NEW VAUDEVILLE BAND (UK)		
Finchley Central		6/67
Peek-A-Boo		2/67
Winchester Cathedral	11/66	10/66
NEW WORLD (AUS)		
Rose Garden		3/71
Sister Jane		6/72

	US Top 20 Ent	UK Top 20 Ent
Tom-Tom Turnaround		7/71
NEWBEATS (US)		
Bread And Butter	9/64	
Run, Baby Run (Back Into My Arms)	11/65	11/71
Booker NEWBERRY III (US)		
Love Town		6/83
Anthony NEWLEY (UK)		
And The Heavens Cried		3/61
Do You Mind		4/60
I've Waited So Long		5/59
Idle On Parade (EP)		5/59
If She Should Come To You		7/60
Personality		7/59
Pop Goes The Weasel		6/61
Strawberry Fair		12/60
Why		1/60
Randy NEWMAN (US)		
Short People	1/78	
NEW RADICALS (US)		
You Get What You Give		4/99
Juice NEWTON (US)		
Angel Of The Morning	4/81	
Break It To Me Gently	10/82	
Love's Been A Little Bit Hard On Me	6/82	
Queen Of Hearts	7/81	
The Sweetest Thing (I've Ever Known)	12/81	
Wayne NEWTON (US)		
Daddy Don't You Walk So Fast	7/72	
Danke Schoen	8/63	
Olivia NEWTON-JOHN (UK)		
Banks Of The Ohio		11/71
Deeper Than The Night	6/79	
Have You Never Been Mellow	2/75	
Heart Attack	10/82	
Hopelessly Devoted To You	8/78	11/78
I Honestly Love You	9/74	
If Not For You		4/71
If You Love Me (Let Me Know)	6/74	
Let Me Be There	1/74	
A Little More Love	1/79	1/79
Long Live Love		4/74
Magic	7/80	
Make A Move On Me	3/82	
Physical	11/81	11/81
Please Mr. Please	7/75	
Sam		7/77
Something Better To Do	10/75	
Twist Of Fate	12/83	
❖ with Andy Gibb		
I Can't Help It	5/80	
with John Travolta		
❖ The Grease Megamix		12/90
❖ Summer Nights	9/78	9/78
❖ You're The One That I Want	4/78	6/78
Olivia NEWTON-JOHN & ELECTRIC LIGHT ORCHESTRA (UK)		
Xanadu	9/80	7/80
NEXT (US)		
Butta Love	11/97	
I Still Love You	9/98	
Too Close	3/98	
Wifey	09/00	
NE-YO (US)		
Because Of You	5/07	4/07
Closer	8/08	5/08
Mad	2/09	
Miss Independent	10/08	9/08
Paul NICHOLAS (UK)		
Dancing With The Captain		11/76
Grandma's Party		1/77
Heaven On The 7th Floor	10/77	
NICKELBACK (C)		
Far Away	9/06	
Gotta Be Somebody	12/08	
How You Remind Me	11/01	3/02
Photograph	10/05	
Rockstar	9/07	1/08
Someday	12/03	9/03
Stevie NICKS (US)		
Edge Of Seventeen (Just Like The White Winged Dove)	4/82	
I Can't Wait	4/86	
If Anyone Falls	10/83	
Leather And Lace	12/81	
Stand Back	7/83	
Talk To Me	12/85	
Stevie NICKS with Tom PETTY & THE HEARTBREAKERS (US)		

	US Top 20 Ent	UK Top 20 Ent
Stop Draggin' My Heart Around	8/81	
NICOLE (G)		
A Little Peace		5/82
NICOLE with Missy Misdemeanor Elliott and Mocha (US)		
Make It Hot	7/98	
NIGEL & MARVIN (WI)		
Follow Da Leader		5/02
NIGHTCRAWLERS (UK)		
Push The Feeling On		3/95
NIGHTCRAWLERS featuring John Reid (UK)		
Surrender Your Love		5/95
Maxine NIGHTINGALE (UK)		
Lead Me On	8/79	
Love Hit Me		4/77
Right Back Where We Started From	3/76	11/75
NIGHT RANGER (US)		
Sentimental Street	7/85	
Sister Christian	5/84	
NILSSON (US)		
Coconut	8/72	
Everybody's Talkin'	10/69	
Without You	2/72	2/72
NINA & FREDERIK (D)		
Little Donkey		12/60
NINA SKY featuring JABBA (US)		
Move Ya Body	6/04	7/04
NINE INCH NAILS (US)		
The Day The World Went Away	08/99	
911 (UK)		
A Little Bit More		1/99
All I Want Is You		4/98
Bodyshakin'		5/97
The Day We Find Love		2/97
The Journey		7/97
More Than A Woman		10/98
Party People/Friday Night		11/97
Private Number		5/99
1910 FRUITGUM CO. (US)		
Indian Giver	3/69	
1 2 3 Red Light	9/68	
Simon Says	2/68	4/68
95 SOUTH (US)		
Whoot, There It Is	7/93	
98 DEGREES (US)		
Because Of You	10/98	
Invisible Man	8/97	
The Hardest Thing	6/99	
Give Me Just One Night	11/00	
NIRVANA (US)		
Come As You Are		3/92
Heart-Shaped Box		9/93
Smells Like Teen Spirit	12/91	12/91
NITTY GRITTY DIRT BAND (US)		
An American Dream	2/80	
Mr. Bojangles	2/71	
NKOTB (US) see New Kids On The Block		
Cliff NOBLES & CO. (US)		
The Horse	6/68	
NIVEA featuring BRIAN & BRANDON CASEY (US)		
❖ Don't Mess With My Man		12/02
NIZLOPI (UK)		
JCB Song		12/05
NO DOUBT (US)		
Don't Speak		2/97
Hella Good	6/02	
❖ Hey Baby	1/02	2/02
It's My Life		12/03
Just A Girl		7/97
Simple Kind Of Life	07/00	
❖ featuring LADY SAW		
Underneath It All		10/02
NOAH AND THE WHALE (UK)		
5 Years Time		8/08
NOISETTES (UK)		
Don't Upset The Rhythm (Go Baby Go)		4/09
Kenny NOLAN (US)		
I Like Dreamin'	2/77	
NOLANS (UK)		
Attention To Me		4/81
Don't Make Waves		5/80
Gotta Pull Myself Together		10/80
I'm In The Mood For Dancing		1/80
NOMAD featuring MC Mikee Freedom (UK)		
(I Wanna Give You) Devotion		2/91
NO MERCY (US)		
Please Don't Go		6/97
Where Do You Go	9/96	1/97
Peter NOONE (UK)		

	US Top 20 Ent	UK Top 20 Ent
PLIES featuring T-PAIN (US)		
Shawty	8/07	
POGUES & THE DUBLINERS (I/UK)		
The Irish Rover		4/87
POGUES featuring KIRSTY MacCOLL (I/UK)		
Fairytale Of New York		12/87
★ Fairytale Of New York		12/05
★ Fairytale Of New York		12/06
Fairytale Of New York		12/07
Fairytale Of New York		12/08
POINT BREAK (UK)		
Stand Tough		1/00
POINTER SISTERS (US)		
American Music	8/82	
Automatic	3/84	5/84
Dare Me	9/85	
Fairytale	12/74	
Fire	1/79	
He's So Shy	10/80	
I'm So Excited	10/84	11/84
Jump (For My Love)	6/84	7/84
Neutron Dance	2/85	
Should I Do It	3/82	
Slow Hand	7/81	9/81
Yes We Can Can	10/73	
Bonnie POINTER (US)		
Heaven Must Have Sent You	9/79	
POISON (US)		
Every Rose Has Its Thorn	12/88	3/89
I Won't Forget You	11/87	
Nothin' But A Good Time	6/88	
Something To Believe In	11/90	
Talk Dirty To Me	5/87	
Unskinny Bop	8/90	
Your Mama Don't Dance	4/89	5/89
POLICE (UK/US)		
Can't Stand Losing You		8/79
De Do Do Do, De Da Da Da	12/80	12/80
Don't Stand So Close To Me	3/81	9/80
Every Breath You Take	6/83	5/83
Every Little Thing She Does Is Magic	11/81	11/81
Invisible Sun		10/81
King Of Pain	9/83	
Message In A Bottle		9/79
Roxanne		5/79
So Lonely		3/80
Spirits In The Material World	3/82	12/81
Synchronicity II	12/83	
Walking On The Moon		12/79
Wrapped Around Your Finger	2/84	7/83
Su POLLARD (UK)		
Starting Together		2/86
PONI-TAILS (US)		
Born Too Late	8/58	9/58
Brian POOLE & THE TREMELOES (UK)		
Candy Man		2/64
Do You Love Me		9/63
Someone Someone		6/64
Twist And Shout		7/63
POPPY FAMILY (C)		
Which Way You Goin' Billy	5/70	9/70
PORTISHEAD (UK)		
Glory Box		1/95
PORTRAIT (US)		
Here We Go Again!	2/93	
Sandy POSEY (US)		
Born A Woman	9/66	
Single Girl	1/67	
POSITIVE K (US)		
I Got A Man	3/93	
MIKE POST (US)		
The Rockford Files	8/75	
Mike POST featuring Larry CARLTON (US)		
The Theme From Hill Street Blues	11/81	
Frank POURCEL'S FRENCH FIDDLES (F)		
Only You	5/59	
Cozy POWELL (UK)		
Dance With The Devil		1/74
Na Na Na		9/74
Jane POWELL (US)		
True Love	10/56	
Jesse POWELL (US)		
You	2/99	
POWER STATION (UK/US)		
Get It On (Bang A Gong)	7/85	
Some Like It Hot	4/85	

	US Top 20 Ent	UK Top 20 Ent
Joey POWERS (US)		
Midnight Mary	1/64	
Daniel POWTER (C)		
Bad Day	3/06	8/05
PPK (RU)		
Resurection		12/01
Perez PRADO (US)		
Cherry Pink And Apple Blossom White	3/55	4/55
Guaglione		5/95
Patricia	6/58	8/58
PRAISE (UK)		
Only You		2/91
PRATT & McCLAIN (US)		
Happy Days	5/76	
PRECIOUS (UK)		
Say It Again		6/99
PREFAB SPROUT (UK)		
The King Of Rock 'n' Roll		5/88
PRESIDENTS (US)		
5-10-15-20 (25-30 Years Of Love)	12/70	
Elvis PRESLEY (US)		
All Shook Up	4/57	6/57
Always On My Mind		1/73
An American Trilogy		7/72
An American Trilogy		12/07
Are You Lonesome Tonight?	11/60	1/61
★ Are You Lonesome Tonight?		2/05
Ask Me	11/64	
Big Hunk O' Love	7/59	7/59
Blue Christmas		12/64
Blue Moon		11/56
Blue Suede Shoes		6/56
Bossa Nova Baby	11/63	
Burning Love	10/72	10/72
Can't Help Falling In Love	12/61	2/62
Crying In The Chapel	5/65	6/65
★ Crying In The Chapel		4/05
Don't Cry Daddy/Rubberneckin'	1/70	3/70
Don't/I Beg Of You	2/58	3/58
Follow That Dream E.P.		6/62
A Fool Such As I	4/59	4/59
★ A Fool Such As I/★ I Need Your Love Tonight		1/05
Girl Of My Best Friend		8/60
★ Girl Of My Best Friend		10/76
Good Luck Charm	3/62	5/62
★ Good Luck Charm		3/05
Hard Headed Woman	7/58	7/58
Heartbreak Hotel	3/56	5/56
★ Heartbreak Hotel		8/71
★ His Latest Flame		3/05
Hound Dog/Don't Be Cruel	8/56	9/56
I Feel So Bad	5/61	
I Got Stung	11/58	1/59
I Just Can't Help Believing		1/72
I Need Your Love Tonight	4/59	4/59
I Want You, I Need You, I Love You	6/56	9/56
I'm Yours	10/65	
I've Lost You		11/70
If Every Day Was Like Christmas		12/66
If I Can Dream	2/69	3/69
In The Ghetto	5/69	6/69
It's Now Or Never	8/60	11/60
★ It's Now Or Never		2/05
It's Only Love/Beyond The Reef		9/80
Jailhouse Rock	10/57	1/58
★ Jailhouse Rock		1/05
Kid Galahad E.P.		11/62
King Creole		10/58
Kiss Me Quick		1/64
Kissin' Cousins	3/64	7/64
Little Sister	9/61	
Love Letters		7/66
Love Me	12/56	
Love Me Tender	10/56	12/56
(Marie's The Name) His Latest Flame	9/61	11/61
A Mess Of Blues		8/60
Moody Blue		3/77
My Boy		12/74
My Way		12/77
My Wish Came True	8/59	
One Broken Heart For Sale	3/63	3/63
One Night	11/58	1/59
★ One Night/★ I Got Stung		1/05
Paralysed		9/57
Party	10/57	
Promised Land		2/75
Rags To Riches		6/71
Return To Sender	11/62	11/62

	US Top 20 Ent	UK Top 20 Ent
★ Return To Sender		4/05
Rock-A-Hula-Baby		2/62
★ Rock-A-Hula Baby		3/05
Rubberneckin'		10/03
Santa Bring My Baby Back To Me		11/57
She's Not You	8/62	9/62
★ She's Not You		3/05
Stuck On You	4/60	4/60
(Such An) Easy Question	7/65	
Such A Night		9/64
Surrender	2/61	5/61
★ Surrender		2/05
Suspicion		2/77
Suspicious Minds	10/69	12/69
Suspicious Minds		8/07
Teddy Bear	7/57	7/57
Tell Me Why		12/65
That's All Right		7/04
There Goes My Everything		4/71
Too Much	2/57	5/57
Until It's Time For You To Go		4/72
Viva Las Vegas		4/64
Way Down		8/77
★ Way Down		4/05
Wear My Ring Around Your Neck	4/58	5/58
Wild In The Country		9/61
★ The Wonder Of You		4/05
The Wonder Of You/Mama Liked The Roses	6/70	7/70
Wooden Heart		3/61
★ Wooden Heart		2/05
You Don't Have To Say You Love Me/Patch It Up	11/70	1/71
(You're The) Devil In Disguise	7/63	7/63
★ (You're The) Devil In Disguise		4/05
❖ vs JXL (US)		
A Little Less Conversation		6/02
★ A Little Less Conversation		5/05
Billy PRESTON (US)		
❖ with The Beatles Get Back	5/69	4/69
Nothing From Nothing	9/74	
Outa-Space	6/72	
Space Race	11/73	
That's The Way God Planned It		7/69
Will It Go Round In Circles	6/73	
Billy PRESTON & SYREETA (US)		
With You I'm Born Again	4/80	1/80
Johnny PRESTON (US)		
Cradle Of Love	4/60	5/60
Feel So Fine	8/60	
Running Bear	1/60	2/60
Mike PRESTON (UK)		
Mr. Blue		11/59
PRETENDERS (C)		
Back On The Chain Gang	3/83	
Brass In Pocket	6/80	12/79
Don't Get Me Wrong	12/86	11/86
Hymn To Her		1/87
I Go To Sleep		11/81
I'll Stand By You		4/94
Message Of Love		2/81
Talk Of The Town		4/80
PRETTY POISON (US)		
Catch Me I'm Falling	12/87	
PRETTY RICKY (US)		
Grind With Me	6/05	
On The Hotline	2/07	
Your Body	10/5	
PRETTY THINGS (UK)		
Don't Bring Me Down		11/64
Honey I Need		3/65
Alan PRICE (UK)		
Jarrow Song		6/74
❖ with Georgie Fame		
Rosetta		5/71
Alan PRICE SET (UK)		
Don't Stop The Carnival		2/68
Hi-Lili-Hi-Lo		8/66
The House That Jack Built		8/67
I Put A Spell On You		4/66
Simon Smith & His Amazing Dancing Bear		3/67
Kelly PRICE (US)		
Friend Of Mine	8/98	
Lloyd PRICE (US)		
I'm Gonna Get Married	8/59	
Lady Luck	3/60	
Personality	6/59	7/59
Stagger Lee	1/59	3/59

	US Top 20 Ent	UK Top 20 Ent
Ray PRICE (US)		
For The Good Times	1/71	
Maxi PRIEST (UK)		
Close To You	9/90	7/90
Some Guys Have All The Luck		12/87
Wild World		6/88
❖ with Roberta Flack		
Set The Night To Music	11/91	
❖ with Shabba Ranks		
Housecall		5/93
Louis PRIMA (US)		
Wonderland By Night	1/61	
PRIMAL SCREAM (UK)		
Country Cirl		6/06
Dixie-Narco (EP)		2/92
Rocks/Funky Jam		3/94
PRIMITIVES (UK)		
Crash		3/88
PRINCE (US)		
Alphabet Street	6/88	5/88
Batdance	7/89	6/89
Controversy		12/93
Cream	10/91	
Delirious	10/83	
Diamonds And Pearls	1/92	
Gett Off		9/91
Gold		12/95
I Could Never Take The Place Of Your Man	1/88	
I Hate U	9/95	9/95
I Wanna Be Your Lover	1/80	
I Would Die 4 U	1/85	
Kiss	3/86	3/86
Let's Go Crazy	9/84	3/85
Little Red Corvette	4/83	1/85
The Most Beautiful Girl In The World	3/94	4/94
My Name Is Prince		10/92
1999	7/83	1/85
Pop Life	9/85	
Purple Rain	10/84	10/84
Raspberry Beret	6/85	
7	1/93	
Sexy MF/Strollin'		7/92
Sign 'O' The Times	4/87	3/87
Thieves In The Temple	9/90	8/90
U Got The Look	9/87	9/87
When Doves Cry	6/84	7/84
PRINCESS (UK)		
Say I'm Your No. 1		8/85
P.J. PROBY (US)		
Hold Me		7/64
I Apologise		3/65
Maria		12/65
Somewhere		12/64
Together		10/64
PROCLAIMERS (UK)		
I'm Gonna Be (500 Miles)	7/93	9/88
King Of The Road (E.P.)		12/90
Letter From America		12/87
PROCLAIMERS feat. Brian POTTER & Andy PIPKIN (UK)		
(I'm Gonna Be) 500 Miles		3/07
PROCOL HARUM (UK)		
Homburg		10/67
A Whiter Shade Of Pale	7/67	6/67
★ A Whiter Shade Of Pale		6/72
PRODIGY (UK)		
Baby's Got A Temper		7/02
Charly		8/91
Everybody In The Place (EP)		1/92
Fire/Jericho		9/92
Firestarter		3/96
No Good (Start The Dance)		5/94
Omen		2/09
One Love		10/93
Out Of Space/Ruff In The Jungle Bizness		11/92
Warrior's Dance		5/09
Wind It Up (Rewound)		4/93
PROFYLE (US)		
Liar	09/00	
PROGRESS PRESENTS THE BOY WUNDA (UK)		
Everybody		12/99
Dorothy PROVINE (US)		
Don't Bring Lulu		12/61
Eric PRYDZ (S)		
Call On Me		9/04
Pjanoo		9/08
Eric PRYDZ vs Floyd (S/UK)		
Proper Education		1/07
PSEUDO ECHO (AUS)		
Funky Town	7/87	8/87
PUBLIC ANNOUNCEMENT (US)		
Body Bumpin' Yippie-Yi-Yo	3/98	
Mamacita	12/00	
PUBLIC DOMAIN (UK)		
Operation Blade (Bass In The Place)		12/00
PUBLIC IMAGE LTD. (UK)		
Public Image		11/78
Rise		2/86
This Is Not A Love Song		10/83
Gary PUCKETT & THE UNION GAP (US)		
Don't Give In To Him	4/69	
Lady Willpower	7/68	9/68
Over You	10/68	
This Girl Is A Woman Now	9/69	
Woman, Woman	12/67	
Young Girl	3/68	5/68
★ Young Girl		7/74
PUDDLE OF MUDD (US)		
Blurry	3/02	
She Hates Me	12/02	
PUFF DADDY (US)		
Best Friend	02/00	
featuring FAITH EVANS		
I'll Be Missing You	6/97	
featuring MA$E		
Can't Nobody Hold Me Down	2/97	
featuring JIMMY PAGE		
Come With Me	6/98	8/98
featuring R KELLY		
Satisfy You	10/99	3/00
PUFF DADDY AND THE FAMILY (US)		
It's All About The Benjamins	12/97	
PULP (UK)		
Common People		6/95
Disco 2000		12/95
Mis-Shapes/Sorted For E's & Wizz		10/95
PURE PRAIRIE LEAGUE (US)		
Let Me Love You Tonight	6/80	
PURETONE (AUS)		
Addicted To Bass		1/02
James & Bobby PURIFY (US)		
I'm Your Puppet	11/66	
PURSELL (US)		
Our Winter Love	3/63	
PUSSYCAT (H)		
Mississippi		9/76
PUSSYCAT DOLLS (US)		
I Don't Need A Man		10/06
I Hate This Part	1/09	
Stickwitu	11/05	12/05
When I Grow Up	7/08	9/08
featuring Busta RHYMES		
Don't Cha	6/05	9/05
featuring SNOOP DOGG		
Buttons	7/06	7/06
featuring WILL.I.AM		
Beep	3/06	3/06
PUSSYCAT DOLLS featuring Missy ELLIOTT (US)		
Whatcha Think About That	2/09	
PYTHON LEE JACKSON (AUS)		
In A Broken Dream		10/72
Monty PYTHON (UK)		
Always Look On The Bright Side Of Life		10/91
Stacey Q (US)		
Two Of Hearts	9/86	
QUAD CITY DJS (US)		
C'Mon N' Ride It (The Train)	7/96	
QUADROPHONIA (B)		
Quadrophonia		5/91
QUANTUM JUMP (UK)		
The Lone Ranger		6/79
QUARTERFLASH (US)		
Find Another Fool	4/82	
Harden My Heart	12/81	
Take Me To Heart	8/83	
QUARTZ INTRODUCING DINA CARROLL (UK)		
It's Too Late		3/91
Suzi QUATRO (US)		
Can The Can		5/73
Devil Gate Drive		2/74
48 Crash		8/73
If You Can't Give Me Love		4/78
She's In Love With You		11/79
The Wild One		11/74
Suzi QUATRO & Chris NORMAN (US/UK)		
Stumblin' In		4/79
QUEEN LATIFAH & DE LA SOUL (US)		
Mamma Gave Birth To The Soul Children		4/90
QUEEN (UK)		
Another One Bites The Dust	9/80	9/80
Bicycle Race/Fat Bottomed Girls		11/78
Body Language	6/82	
Bohemian Rhapsody	4/76	11/75
★ Bohemian Rhapsody/These Are The Days Of Our Lives	4/92	12/91
Breakthru'		7/89
Crazy Little Thing Called Love	1/80	11/79
Don't Stop Me Now		3/79
Flash		12/80
Heaven For Everyone		11/95
I Want It All		5/89
I Want To Break Free		4/84
Innuendo		1/91
It's A Hard Life		8/84
Killer Queen	5/75	11/74
A Kind Of Magic		4/86
Now I'm Here		2/75
One Vision		11/85
Radio Ga Ga		2/84
Seven Seas Of Rhye		4/74
Somebody To Love	1/77	11/76
We Are The Champions	1/78	11/77
A Winter's Tale		12/95
You're My Best Friend		7/76
❖ with 5ive		
We Will Rock You		8/00
❖ with George Michael		
Five Live (EP)		5/93
QUEEN & DAVID BOWIE (UK)		
Under Pressure		11/81
QUEEN with Wyclef Jean featuring Pras Michel (UK/US)		
Another One Bites The Dust		11/98
QUEENSRYCHE (US)		
Silent Lucidity	5/91	
? (QUESTION MARK) & THE MYSTERIANS (US)		
96 Tears	9/66	
QUIET RIOT (US)		
Cum On Feel The Noize	11/83	
Sinead QUINN (UK)		
I Can't Break Down		2/03
Eddie RABBITT (US)		
Drivin' My Life Away	9/80	
I Love A Rainy Night	1/81	
Someone Could Lose A Heart Tonight	1/82	
Step By Step	9/81	
You And I	12/82	
RACEY (UK)		
Lay Your Love On Me		12/78
Some Girls		4/79
RACONTEURS (US)		
Steady As She Goes		5/06
RADHA KRISHNA TEMPLE (UK)		
Hare Krishna		10/69
RADIOHEAD (UK)		
Creep		9/93
Pyramid Song		6/01
Street Spirit (Fade Out)		2/96
There There		6/03
Gerry RAFFERTY (UK)		
Baker Street	6/78	3/78
Night Owl		6/79
Right Down The Line	10/78	
RAGE (UK)		
Run To You		11/92
RAGE AGAINST THE MACHINE (US)		
Killing In The Name		12/09
RAGHAV (C)		
Angel Eyes		2/05
Can't Get Enough		2/04
RAH BAND (UK)		
Clouds Across The Moon		4/85
The Crunch		8/77
A R RAHMAN & THE PUSSYCAT DOLLS feat. Nicole Scherzinger (IND/US)		
Jai Ho! (You Are My Destiny)	3/09	4/09
RAINBOW (UK)		
All Night Long		3/80
I Surrender		2/81
Since You've Been Gone		10/79
Marvin RAINWATER (US)		
Whole Lotta Woman		3/58
Bonnie RAITT (US)		
Something To Talk About	9/91	

	US Top 20 Ent	UK Top 20 Ent
RAM JAM (US)		
Black Betty		10/77
★ Black Betty		3/90
RAMBLERS (UK)		
The Sparrow		11/79
Karen RAMIREZ (UK)		
Looking For Love		7/98
RAMRODS (US)		
Riders In The Sky		2/61
RANDY & THE RAINBOWS (US)		
Denise	8/63	
Shabba RANKS (J)		
Mr. Loverman		3/93
Shabba RANKS featuring Maxi Priest (J/UK)		
Housecall		5/93
RARE EARTH (US)		
Get Ready	5/70	
I Just Want To Celebrate	9/71	
(I Know) I'm Losing You	9/70	
RASCAL FLATTS (US)		
Here Comes Goodbye	3/09	
Life Is A Highway	7/06	
What Hurts The Most	4/06	
RASCALS (US)		
A Beautiful Morning	5/68	
A Girl Like You	8/67	
Good Lovin'	4/66	
Groovin'	5/67	6/67
How Can I Be Sure	10/67	
People Got To Be Free	8/68	
RASMUS (FIN)		
In The Shadows		4/04
RASPBERRIES (US)		
Go All The Way	9/72	
RATT (US)		
Round And Round	8/84	
RATTLES (G)		
The Witch		11/70
Lou RAWLS (US)		
Love Is A Hurtin' Thing	11/66	
You'll Never Find Another Love Like Mine	8/76	8/76
RAY, GOODMAN & BROWN (US)		
Special Lady	3/80	
Johnnie RAY (US)		
Build Your Love		9/57
Destiny		8/54
Hernando's Hideaway		10/55
Hey There		10/55
If You Believe		5/55
Just Walking In The Rain	9/56	10/56
Look Homeward Angel		4/57
Song Of The Dreamer		11/55
Such A Night		4/54
Yes Tonight Josephine		5/57
You Don't Owe Me A Thing	2/57	2/57
RAYDIO (US) see Ray Parker Jr. & Raydio		
RAYS (US)		
Silhouettes	10/57	
RAYVON (US) see Shaggy featuring Rayvon		
RAZORLIGHT (UK)		
America		10/06
In The Morning		7/06
Somewhere Else		4/05
Wire To Wire		11/08
Chris REA (UK)		
Fool (If You Think It's Over)	9/78	
Let's Dance		7/87
The Road To Hell (Pt. 2)		10/89
READY FOR THE WORLD (US)		
Love You Down	2/87	
Oh Sheila	9/85	
REAL McCOY (G/US)		
Another Night	10/94	
Run Away	3/95	2/95
REAL ROXANNE with Hitman Howie Tee (US)		
(Bang Zoom) Let's Go Go		7/86
REAL THING (UK)		
Can You Feel The Force		3/79
Can't Get By Without You		9/76
★ Can't Get By Without You		6/86
You To Me Are Everything		6/76
★ You To Me Are Everything		4/86
REBEL MC (UK)		
❖ with Double Trouble		
Just Keep Rockin'		6/89
REBEL MC & DOUBLE TROUBLE (UK)		
Street Tuff		10/89
REBELS (US)		
Wild Weekend	2/63	
RED BOX (UK)		
For America		11/86
Lean On Me (Ah-Li-Ayo)		9/85
RED DRAGON with Brian & Tony Gold (J)		
Compliments On Your Kiss		8/94
RED HOT CHILI PEPPERS (US)		
By The Way		7/02
Dani California	4/06	5/06
Give It Away		2/94
Under The Bridge	5/92	5/94
Otherside		06/00
REDBONE (US)		
Come And Get Your Love	3/74	
Witch Queen Of New Orleans		10/71
Otis REDDING (US)		
Hard To Handle		9/68
My Girl		1/66
(Sittin' On) The Dock Of The Bay	2/68	3/68
Helen REDDY (AUS)		
Ain't No Way To Treat A Lady	9/75	
Angie Baby	12/74	2/75
Delta Dawn	8/73	
I Am Woman	11/72	
I Don't Know How To Love Him	6/71	
Leave Me Alone (Ruby Red Dress)	12/73	
Peaceful	4/73	
You And Me Against The World	8/74	
REDHEAD KINGPIN & THE FBI (US)		
Do The Right Thing		8/89
REDMAN/METHOD MAN (US)		
How High	9/95	
REDNEX (S)		
Cotton Eye Joe		12/94
Jerry REED (US)		
Amos Moses	2/71	
When You're Hot, You're Hot	6/71	
Lou REED (US)		
Walk On The Wild Side		6/73
Michael REED ORCHESTRA (UK) see Richard Hartley/Michael Reed Orchestra		
REEL 2 REAL featuring The Mad Stuntman (US)		
Go On Move		7/94
I Like To Move It		2/94
Della REESE (US)		
Don't You Know	10/59	
Not One Minute More	1/60	
Jim REEVES (US)		
Distant Drums		9/66
Four Walls	6/57	
He'll Have To Go	2/60	6/60
I Love You Because		3/64
I Won't Come In While He's There		2/67
I Won't Forget You		7/64
It Hurts So Much		2/65
There's A Heartache Following Me		11/64
Welcome To My World		7/63
Martha REEVES (US) see Martha & The Vandellas		
REEVES & MORTIMER		
❖ with EMF		
I'm A Believer		7/95
Vic REEVES & THE ROMAN NUMERALS (UK)		
Born Free		5/91
Vic REEVES & THE WONDER STUFF (UK)		
Dizzy		10/91
REFLECTIONS (US)		
(Just Like) Romeo & Juliet	5/64	
Joan REGAN (UK)		
If I Give My Heart To You		10/54
May You Always		6/59
Prize Of Gold		4/55
Ricochet		1/54
Someone Else's Roses		5/54
REGENTS (US)		
Barbara Ann	6/61	
7 Teen		2/80
REGINA (US)		
Baby Love	8/86	
John REID (UK) see Nightcrawlers featuring John Reid		
Mike REID (UK)		
The Ugly Duckling		4/75
Neil REID (UK)		
Mother Of Mine		1/72
R.E.M. (US)		
Bad Day		10/03
Everybody Hurts		5/93
Imitation Of Life		5/01
Leaving New York		10/04
Losing My Religion	5/91	
The One I Love	11/87	
Shiny Happy People	9/91	6/91
Stand	4/89	
The Great Beyond		5/00
What's The Frequency, Kenneth?		9/94
REMBRANDTS (US)		
I'll Be There For You/This House Is Not A Home	10/95	9/95
★ I'll Be There For You		5/97
RENAISSANCE (UK)		
Northern Lights		8/78
Diane RENAY (US)		
Navy Blue	2/64	
RENE & RENE (US)		
Lo Mucho Que Te Quiero (The More I Love You)	1/69	
Henri RENE (US)		
The Happy Wanderer		5/54
RENEE AND RENATO (UK/Ita)		
Save Your Love		12/82
Mike RENO & Ann WILSON (US)		
Almost Paradise...Love Theme From Footloose	6/84	
REO SPEEDWAGON (US)		
Can't Fight This Feeling	2/85	
Keep On Loving You	2/81	5/81
Keep The Fire Burnin'	7/82	
Take It On The Run	5/81	
REPARATA & THE DELRONS (US)		
Captain Of Your Ship		4/68
RESTLESS HEART (US)		
When She Cries	1/93	
REUNION (US)		
Life Is A Rock (But The Radio Rolled Me)	11/74	
Paul REVERE & THE RAIDERS (US)		
Good Thing	1/67	
Him Or Me - What's It Gonna Be	5/67	
Hungry	7/66	
Indian Reservation (The Lament Of The Cherokee Reservation Indian)	6/71	
Just Like Me	1/66	
Kicks	4/66	
REVEREND AND THE MAKERS (UK)		
Heavyweight Champion Of The World		6/07
REYNOLDS GIRLS (UK)		
I'd Rather Jack		3/89
Debbie REYNOLDS (US)		
Tammy	8/57	9/57
Jody REYNOLDS (US)		
Endless Sleep	6/58	
Busta RHYMES (UK)		
Dangerous	1/98	
❖ I Know What You Want	4/03	6/03
Touch It	3/06	5/06
Turn It Up/Fire It Up	5/98	5/98
Woo-Hah!! Got You All In Check/Everything Remains Raw	4/96	
❖ featuring P. DIDDY & PHARRELL (UK/US)		
I Need A Girl (Part 1)	4/02	8/02
featuring will.i.am & KELIS		
I Love My Chick		7/06
Busta RHYMES & Mariah CAREY featuring FLIPMODE SQUAD		
I Know What You Want	4/03	6/03
Busta RHYMES & Janet JACKSON (US)		
Who's It Gonna Be?!	3/99	5/99
Busta RHYMES featuring LINKIN PARK (US)		
We Made It		6/08
RHYTHM HERITAGE (US)		
Theme From S.W.A.T.	2/76	
RICH BOY featuring Polow Da Don (US)		
Throw Some D's	3/07	
Charlie RICH (US)		
Behind Closed Doors	7/73	
The Most Beautiful Girl	11/73	3/74
A Very Special Love Song	4/74	
Tony RICH PROJECT (US)		
Nobody Knows	1/96	5/96
RICHARD X vs LIBERTY X (UK)		
❖ Being Nobody		3/03
Cliff RICHARD (UK)		
All My Love		12/67
Bachelor Boy		12/62
The Best Of Me		6/89

	US Top 20 Ent	UK Top 20 Ent
Big Ship		6/69
Carrie		2/80
Congratulations		4/68
Constantly		5/64
Daddy's Home		12/81
The Day I Met Marie		9/67
Devil Woman	9/76	6/76
Do You Wanna Dance		6/62
Don't Talk To Him		11/63
Dreaming	11/80	9/80
Fall In Love With You		4/60
From A Distance		10/90
Gee Whiz It's You		4/61
A Girl Like You		6/61
Good Times (Better Times)		3/69
Goodbye Sam Hello Samantha		6/70
High Class Baby		12/58
I Could Easily Fall		12/64
I Just Don't Have The Heart		9/89
I Love You		12/60
I Still Believe In You		12/92
I'm Looking Out The Window		5/62
I'm The Lonely One		2/64
In The Country		1/67
It'll Be Me		9/62
It's All In The Game		8/63
It's All Over		4/67
A Little In Love	3/81	
Living Doll		7/59
Living In Harmony		9/72
Lucky Lips		5/63
Mean Streak		5/59
The Millennium Prayer		11/99
The Minute You're Gone		3/65
Miss You Nights		3/76
Mistletoe And Wine		12/88
Move It		10/58
My Pretty One		7/87
The Next Time		12/62
Nine Times Out Of Ten		9/60
On My Word		7/65
On The Beach		7/64
The Only Way Out		8/82
Peace In Our Time		3/93
Please Don't Fall In Love		12/83
Please Don't Tease		7/60
Power To All Our Friends		3/73
Santa's List		12/03
Saviour's Day		12/90
Silhouettes		9/90
Sing A Song Of Freedom		12/71
Some People		9/87
Summer Holiday		2/63
Thank You For A Lifetime		9/08
Theme For A Dream		3/61
Throw Down A Line		9/69
Time Drags By		11/66
Travellin' Light		10/59
True Love Ways		5/83
The Twelfth Of Never		10/64
21st Century Christmas/Move It		12/06
Visions		8/66
Voice In The Wilderness		1/60
We Don't Talk Anymore	12/79	8/79
We Should Be Together		12/91
When The Girl In Your…		10/61
Wind Me Up (Let Me Go)		11/65
Wired For Sound		9/81
The Young Ones		1/62

❖ **with Phil Everly**

	US Top 20 Ent	UK Top 20 Ent
She Means Nothing To Me		3/83

Cliff RICHARD & Sarah BRIGHTMAN (UK)

All I Ask Of You		10/86

Cliff RICHARD & THE YOUNG ONES (UK)

Living Doll		3/86

Lionel RICHIE (US)

All Night Long (All Night)	10/93	10/83
Ballerina Girl	2/87	
Dancing On The Ceiling	8/86	8/86
Hello	4/84	3/84
Love Will Conquer All	11/86	
My Destiny		9/92
My Love	5/83	
Penny Lover	11/84	
Running With The Night	1/84	1/84
Say You, Say Me	12/85	12/85
Stuck On You	8/84	7/84
Truly	11/82	12/82
You Are	3/83	

❖ **with Diana Ross**

Endless Love	8/81	9/81

SHANE RICHIE (UK)

I'm Your Man		12/03

Jonathan RICHMAN & THE MODERN LOVERS (US)

Egyptian Reggae		12/77
Roadrunner		8/77

Adam RICKITT (UK)

I Breathe Again		7/99

Nelson RIDDLE (US)

Lisbon Antigua	1/56	

Stan RIDGWAY (US)

Camouflage		7/86

RIGHT SAID FRED (UK)

Deeply Dippy		3/92
I'm Too Sexy	1/92	8/91

RIGHT SAID FRED & FRIENDS (UK)

Stick It Out		3/93

RIGHT SAID FRED featuring Jocelyn Brown (UK/US)

Don't Talk Just Kiss		12/91

RIGHTEOUS BROTHERS (US)

Ebb Tide	12/65	
Just Once In My Life	5/65	
Rock And Roll Heaven	7/74	
Unchained Melody	8/65	9/65
★ Unchained Melody	10/90	10/90
(You're My) Soul And Inspiration	3/66	
You've Lost That Lovin' Feelin'	1/65	1/65
★ You've Lost That Lovin' Feelin'		3/69
★ You've Lost That Lovin' Feelin'/Ebb Tide		12/90

RIHANNA (BA)

Disturbia	7/08	8/08
Don't Stop The Music	1/08	1/08
Pon De Replay	7/05	9/05
Russian Roulette	11/09	12/09
Shut Up And Drive	8/07	8/4
SOS	5/06	4/06
Take A Bow	5/08	5/08
Unfaithful	6/06	7/06

RIHANNA & Sean PAUL (BA/J)

Break It Off	3/07	

RIHANNA featuring JAY-Z (BA/US)

Umbrella	6/07	5/07

RIHANNA featuring NE-YO (BA/US)

Hate That I Love You	10/07	

Jeannie C. RILEY (US)

Harper Valley P.T.A.	9/68	12/68

LeAnn RIMES (US)

How Do I Live	8/97	5/98
Can't Fight The Moonlight	10/00	12/00
★ Can't Fight The Moonlight	2/02	
I Need You	8/00	

Miguel RIOS (SPA)

A Song Of Joy	7/70	

Waldo De Los RIOS (BRA)

Mozart Symphony No. 40 In G Minor		4/71

RIP CHORDS (US)

Hey Little Cobra	1/64	

Minnie RIPERTON (US)

Lovin' You	3/75	4/75

RITCHIE FAMILY (US)

The Best Disco In Town		10/76
Brazil	10/75	

Tex RITTER (US)

Wayward Wind		7/56

RIVER CITY PEOPLE (UK)

California Dreamin'/Carry The Blame		8/90

RIVA featuring Dannii MINOGUE (H)

❖ Who Do You Love Now (Stringer)		12/01

Johnny RIVERS (US)

Baby I Need Your Lovin'	2/67	
Maybelline	9/64	
Memphis	6/64	
Mountain Of Love	11/64	
Poor Side Of Town	10/66	
Rockin' Pneumonia & The Boogie Woogie Flu	12/72	
Secret Agent Man	4/66	
Seventh Son	6/65	
Summer Rain	1/68	
Swayin' To The Music (Slow Dancin')	9/77	
The Tracks Of My Tears	7/67	

RIVIERAS (US)

California Sun	2/64	

ROACHFORD (UK)

Cuddly Toy		1/89

ROB 'N' RAZ Featuring Leila K (S)

Got To Get		12/89

Kate ROBBINS & BEYOND (UK)

More Than In Love		6/81

Marty ROBBINS (US)

Devil Woman		11/62
Don't Worry	2/61	
El Paso	12/59	
A White Sport Coat (And A Pink Carnation)	5/57	

Austin ROBERTS (US)

Rocky	10/75	
Something's Wrong With Me	12/72	

Malcolm ROBERTS (UK)

Love Is All		12/69
May I Have The Next Dream With You		12/68

B.A. ROBERTSON (UK)

Bang Bang		8/79
Knocked It Off		11/79
To Be Or Not To Be		7/80

B.A. ROBERTSON & Maggie BELL (UK)

Hold Me		11/81

Don ROBERTSON (US)

The Happy Whistler	5/56	5/56

Ivo ROBIC (Y)

Morgen	9/59	

Floyd ROBINSON (US)

Makin' Love		10/59

Smokey ROBINSON (US) see also The Miracles

Being With You	4/81	6/81
Cruisin'	1/80	
Just To See Her	6/87	
One Heartbeat	10/87	

Tom ROBINSON BAND (UK)

2-4-6-8 Motorway		11/77
War Baby		7/83

Vicki Sue ROBINSON (US)

Turn The Beat Around	8/76	

ROBYN (S)

Be Mine		1/08
Do You Know (What It Takes)		6/97
Show Me Love	11/97	3/98

ROBYN with Kleerup (US)

With Every Heartbeat		8/07

ROCK FOLLIES (UK)

O.K.		6/77

ROCKER'S REVENGE (US)

Walking On Sunshine		9/82

ROCKIN' BERRIES (UK)

He's In Town		11/64
Poor Man's Son		5/65

Lord ROCKINGHAM'S XI (UK)

Hoots Mon		10/58

ROCKSTEADY CREW (US)

(Hey You) The Rocksteady Crew		10/83

ROCKWELL (US)

Somebody's Watching Me	2/84	2/84

Clodagh RODGERS (I)

Come Back And Shake Me		4/69
Goodnight Midnight		8/69
Jack In The Box		3/71

Jimmie RODGERS (US)

Are You Really Mine	9/58	
Bimbombey	12/58	
English Country Garden		7/62
Honeycomb	9/57	
Kisses Sweeter Than Wine	12/57	1/58
Secretly	5/58	

RODS (UK)

Do Anything You Wanna Do		9/77

Tommy ROE (US)

Dizzy	3/69	5/69
Everybody	11/63	10/63
The Folk Singer		4/63
Hooray For Hazel	10/66	
Jam Up Jelly Tight	1/70	
Sheila	8/62	9/62
Sweet Pea	7/66	

ROGER (US)

I Want To Be Your Man	1/88	

Julie ROGERS (UK)

The Wedding	12/64	9/64

Kenny ROGERS/FIRST EDITION (US)

Coward Of The County	1/80	2/80
I Don't Need You	7/81	
Just Dropped In (To See What Condition My Condition Was In)	3/68	
Lady	10/80	12/80

	US Top 20 Ent	UK Top 20 Ent
Paul & Barry RYAN (UK)		
Don't Bring Me Your Heartaches		12/65
Bobby RYDELL (US)		
The Cha Cha Cha	11/62	
Forget Him	12/63	6/63
Good Time Baby	3/61	
I'll Never Dance Again	7/62	
Kissin' Time	9/59	
Sway	12/60	1/61
Swingin' School	6/60	
Volare	8/60	
We Got Love	11/59	
Wild One	2/60	4/60
Mitch RYDER & THE DETROIT WHEELS (US)		
Devil With A Blue Dress On &		
Good Golly Miss Molly	11/66	
Jenny Take A Ride!	2/66	
Sock It To Me-Baby!	3/67	
RYTHM SYNDICATE (US)		
P.A.S.S.I.O.N.	7/91	
S CLUB (UK)		
Alive		11/02
Say Goodbye/Love Ain't Gonna Wait For You		6/03
S CLUB JUNIORS (UK)		
Automatic High		8/02
New Direction		10/02
One Step Closer		5/02
Puppy Love/Sleigh Ride		12/02
S CLUB 7 (UK)		
Bring It All Back		6/99
Don't Stop Movin'		5/01
Have You Ever		12/01
Natural		09/00
Never Had A Dream Come True	5/01	1/01
Reach		6/00
S Club Party		10/99
Two In A Million/You're My No. 1		12/99
You		2/02
S CLUB 8		
Fool No More		7/03
Sundown		10/03
Robin S (US)		
Luv 4 Luv		8/93
Show Me Love	6/93	4/93
S'EXPRESS (UK)		
Hey Music Lover		3/89
Superfly Guy		8/88
Theme From S'Express		4/88
SABRINA (ITA)		
Boys (Summertime Love)		6/88
SAD CAFE (UK)		
Every Day Hurts		10/79
SADE (UK)		
Smooth Operator	4/85	
The Sweetest Taboo	2/86	
Your Love Is King		3/84
SSGT. BARRY SADLER (US)		
The Ballad Of The Green Berets	2/66	
SAFARIS (US)		
Image Of A Girl	7/60	
SA-FIRE (US)		
Thinking Of You	5/89	
SAFRI DUO (D)		
Played-A-Live (The Bongo Song)		2/01
Carole Bayer SAGER (US)		
You're Moving Out Today		6/77
SAIGON KICK (US)		
Love Is On The Way	11/92	
SAILCAT (US)		
Motorcycle Mama	8/72	
SAILOR (UK)		
Girls Girls Girls		4/76
Glass Of Champagne		1/76
ST. CECILIA (UK)		
Leap Up And Down (Wave Your Knickers In The Air)		8/71
SAINT ETIENNE (UK)		
He's On The Phone		11/95
You're In A Bad Way		2/93
ST. LOUIS UNION (UK)		
Girl		2/66
Crispian ST. PETERS (UK)		
The Pied Piper	7/66	4/66
You Were On My Mind		2/66
ST. WINIFRED'S SCHOOL CHOIR (UK)		
There's No One Quite Like Grandma		12/80

	US Top 20 Ent	UK Top 20 Ent
Buffy SAINTE-MARIE (C)		
Soldier Blue		8/71
Kyu SAKAMOTO (JAP)		
Sukiyaki	6/63	7/63
SAKKARIN (UK)		
Sugar Sugar		5/71
SALT-N-PEPA (US)		
Do You Want Me		6/91
Let's Talk About Sex	11/91	9/91
Push It/Tramp		7/88
Shoop	11/93	
Twist And Shout		11/88
SALT-N-PEPA featuring En Vogue (US)		
Whatta Man	2/94	3/94
SAM & DAVE (US)		
I Thank You	3/68	
Soul Man	10/67	
SAM & MARK (UK)		
With A Little Help From My Friends/		
Measure Of A Man		2/04
SAM THE SHAM & THE PHARAOHS (US)		
Lil' Red Riding Hood	7/66	
Wooly Bully	5/65	7/65
SAMMIE (US)		
I Like It	01/00	
Daz SAMPSON (UK)		
Teenage Life		5/06
SAN JOSE (UK)		
Argentine Melody (Cancion De Argentina)		7/78
Roger SANCHEZ (US)		
Another Chance		7/01
SANDPIPERS (US)		
Guantanamera	9/66	10/66
Jodie SANDS (US)		
Someday		11/58
Tommy SANDS (US)		
Teen-Age Crush	3/57	
SANFORD/TOWNSEND BAND (US)		
Smoke From A Distant Fire	8/77	
Samantha SANG (AUS)		
Emotion	2/78	3/78
SANTA ESMERALDA (US/F)		
Don't Let Me Be Misunderstood	2/78	
Mongo SANTAMARIA (US)		
Watermelon Man	4/63	
SANTANA (US)		
Black Magic Woman	12/70	
Everybody's Everything	11/71	
Evil Ways	3/70	
Hold On	10/82	
Oye Como Va	4/71	
She's Not There		11/77
Winning	7/81	
❖ featuring Alex BAND or Chad KROEGER		
Why Don't You & I	9/03	
❖ featuring Michelle BRANCH		
The Game Of Love	10/02	
❖ featuring The Product G&B		
Maria Maria	02/00	08/00
❖ featuring Rob THOMAS		
Smooth	08/99	4/00
Juelz SANTANA (US)		
There It Go! (The Whistle Song)	12/05	
SANTO & JOHNNY (US)		
Sleep Walk	8/59	
SANTOS (ITA)		
Camels		1/01
Mike SARNE with BILLIE DAVIS (UK)		
Will I What		9/62
Mike SARNE with WENDY RICHARD (UK)		
Come Outside		5/62
Peter SARSTEDT (UK)		
Frozen Orange Juice		7/69
Where Do You Go To My Lovely		2/69
Robin SARSTEDT (UK)		
My Resistance Is Low		5/76
SASH! (G)		
Adelante		2/00
feat. Rodriguez Ecuador		3/97
Encore Une Fois		3/97
La Primavera		4/98
Mysterious Times		8/98
feat. La Trec Stay		10/97
SASH! featuring Stunt (G)		
Raindrops (Encore Une Fois)		10/08
SATURDAYS (UK/I)		
Forever Is Over		10/09
If This Is Love		8/08

	US Top 20 Ent	UK Top 20 Ent
Issues		1/09
Just Can't Get Enough		3/09
Up		10/08
SAVAGE GARDEN (AUS)		
The Animal Song	4/99	
Affirmation		08/00
I Knew I Loved You	01/00	
I Want You	3/97	
To The Moon And Back		8/98
Truly Madly Deeply	12/97	5/98
Telly SAVALAS (US)		
If		3/75
SAXON (UK)		
And The Bands Played On		4/81
747 (Strangers In The Night)		7/80
Leo SAYER (UK)		
Have You Ever Been In Love		4/82
How Much Love		5/77
I Can't Stop Lovin' You (Though I Try)		10/78
Long Tall Glasses (I Can Dance)	4/75	9/74
Moonlighting		9/75
More Than I Can Say	11/80	7/80
One Man Band		6/74
The Show Must Go On		12/73
When I Need You	4/77	2/77
You Make Me Feel Like Dancing	12/76	11/76
SCAFFOLD (UK)		
Lily The Pink		11/68
Liverpool Lou		6/74
Thank U Very Much		12/67
Boz SCAGGS (US)		
Breakdown Dead Ahead	5/80	
Lido Shuffle	4/77	6/77
Look What You've Done To Me	10/80	
Lowdown	9/76	
Miss Sun	2/81	
What Can I Say		3/77
SCANDAL featuring PATTY SMYTH (US)		
The Warrior	8/84	
SCANTY SANDWICH (UK)		
Because Of You		1/00
Joey SCARBURY (US)		
Theme From 'Greatest American Hero' (Believe It Or Not)	6/81	
SCARFACE featuring 2PAC AND JOHNNY P (US)		
Smile	7/97	
SCARLET (UK)		
Independent Love Song		2/95
SCATMAN JOHN (US)		
Scatman (Ski-Ba-Bop-Ba-Dop-Bop)		5/95
Scatman's World		9/95
Lalo SCHIFRIN (US)		
Jaws		11/76
Peter SCHILLING (G)		
Major Tom (Coming Home)	12/83	
John SCHNEIDER (US)		
It's Now Or Never	8/81	
SCISSOR SISTERS (US)		
Filthy/Gorgeous		1/05
I Don't Feel Like Dancin'		9/06
SCOOCH (UK)		
Flying The Flag (For You)		5/07
More Than I Needed To Know		1/00
SCOOTER (G)		
Nessaja		9/02
The Logical Song		6/02
Weekend!		4/03
SCORPIONS (G)		
Wind Of Change	8/91	10/91
SCOTLAND WORLD CUP SQUAD (UK)		
We Have A Dream		5/82
Freddie SCOTT (US)		
Hey, Girl	9/63	
Jack SCOTT (US)		
Burning Bridges	5/60	
Goodbye Baby	1/59	
My True Love/Leroy	7/58	11/58
What In The World's Come Over You	2/60	3/60
Linda SCOTT (US)		
Don't Bet Money Honey	8/61	
I've Told Every Little Star	4/61	6/61
Lisa SCOTT-LEE (UK)		
Lately		5/03
SCOUTING FOR GIRLS (UK)		
Elvis Ain't Dead		1/08
Heartbeat		5/08
She's So Lovely		9/07
SCRIPT (I)		

	US Top 20 Ent	UK Top 20 Ent
The Man Who Can't Be Moved		8/08
SCRITTI POLITTI (UK)		
Perfect Way	12/85	
Wood Beez (Pray Like Aretha Franklin)		4/84
SCRITTI POLITTI featuring Ranking Ann (UK)		
The Word Girl		6/85
SEAL (UK)		
Crazy	8/91	1/91
Fly Like An Eagle	12/96	
Future Love (EP)		5/91
Killer (EP)		11/91
Kiss From A Rose	7/95	7/95
SEALS & CROFTS (US)		
Diamond Girl	7/73	
Get Closer	7/76	
Summer Breeze	11/72	
Jay SEAN (UK)		
Ride It	2/08	
Stolen	11/04	
Jay SEAN featuring LIL WAYNE (UK/US)		
Down	8/09	11/09
Jay SEAN featuring The Rishi RICH PROJECT		
Eyes On You		7/04
Jay SEAN featuring Sean PAUL & LIL JON (UK/J/US)		
Do You Remember	12/09	
SEARCHERS (UK)		
Ain't Gonna Kiss Ya (E.P.)		10/63
Don't Throw Your Love Away		4/64
Goodbye My Love		3/65
He's Got No Love		8/65
Love Potion Number Nine	12/64	
Needles And Pins	4/64	1/64
Someday We're Gonna Love Again		8/64
Sugar And Spice		11/63
Sweets For My Sweet		7/63
What Have They Done To The Rain		1/65
When You Walk In The Room		10/64
John SEBASTIAN (US)		
Welcome Back	4/76	
Jon SECADA (US)		
Do You Believe In Us	12/92	
If You Go	6/94	
Just Another Day	6/92	8/92
Harry SECOMBE (UK)		
On With The Motley		12/55
This Is My Song		3/67
Neil SEDAKA (US)		
Bad Blood	10/75	
Breaking Up Is Hard To Do	2/76	
Breaking Up Is Hard To Do	7/62	8/62
Calendar Girl	1/61	2/61
Happy Birthday, Sweet Sixteen	12/61	12/61
I Go Ape		5/59
Laughter In The Rain	12/74	
Little Devil	5/61	6/61
Next Door To An Angel	11/62	
Oh! Carol	11/59	11/59
Stairway To Heaven	5/60	5/60
SEDUCTION (US)		
Could This Be Love	8/90	
Heartbeat	4/90	
Two To Make It Right	1/90	
SEEKERS (AUS)		
The Carnival Is Over		11/65
Georgy Girl	1/67	3/67
I'll Never Find Another You	4/65	2/65
Morningtown Ride		12/66
Someday One Day		4/66
Walk With Me		10/66
When Will The Good Apples Fall		10/67
A World Of Our Own		5/65
Bob SEGER & THE SILVER BULLET BAND (US)		
Against The Wind	5/80	
American Storm	4/86	
Even Now	4/83	
Fire Lake	4/80	
Hollywood Nights	9/78	
Like A Rock	7/86	
Night Moves	2/77	
Shakedown	6/87	
Shame On The Moon	1/83	
Still The Same	6/78	
Tryin' To Live My Life Without You	10/81	
We've Got Tonite	1/79	
You'll Accomp'ny Me	9/80	

	US Top 20 Ent	UK Top 20 Ent
SELECTER (UK)		
On My Radio		11/79
Peter SELLERS (UK)		
A Hard Day's Night		1/66
Peter SELLERS & Sophia LOREN (UK/Ita)		
Goodness Gracious Me		11/60
Michael SEMBELLO (US)		
Maniac	7/83	
SEMISONIC (US)		
Secret Smile		7/99
SENSATIONS (US)		
Let Me In	3/62	
SEPTEMBER (US)		
Cry For You		4/08
SERENDIPITY SINGERS (US)		
Don't Let The Rain Come Down (Crooked Little Man)	4/64	
Taja SEVELLE (US)		
Love Is Contagious		3/88
702 (US)		
Get It Together	3/97	
Where My Girls At	5/99	
❖ **with Subway**		
This Lil' Game We Play 4/95		
SEVERINE (F)		
Un Banc, Un Arbre, Une Rue		5/71
David SEVILLE (US)		
Witch Doctor	4/58	6/58
SEX PISTOLS (UK)		
C'mon Everybody		7/79
God Save The Queen		6/77
Holidays In The Sun		10/77
No One Is Innocent/My Way		7/78
Pretty Vacant		7/77
Silly Thing/Who Killed Bambi		4/79
Something Else/Friggin' In The Riggin'		3/79
SHADES OF BLUE (US)		
Oh How Happy	6/66	
SHADOWS OF KNIGHT (US)		
Gloria	5/66	
SHADOWS (UK)		
Apache		8/60
Atlantis		6/63
Dance On		12/62
Don't Cry For Me Argentina		2/79
Don't Make My Baby Blue		8/65
F.B.I.		2/61
Foot Tapper		3/63
Frightened City		5/61
Geronimo		12/63
Guitar Tango		8/62
Kon-Tiki		9/61
Let Me Be The One		4/75
Man Of Mystery		11/60
Riders In The Sky		3/80
The Rise & Fall Of Flingel Bunt		5/64
The Savage		11/61
Shindig		9/63
The Stranger		11/60
Theme For Young Lovers		3/64
Theme From The Deer Hunter (Cavatina)		6/79
Wonderful Land		3/62
SHAFT (US)		
(Mucho Mambo) Sway		9/99
SHAG (UK)		
Loop Di Love		11/72
SHAGGY (J)		
Boombastic	7/95	9/95
Oh Carolina		3/93
It Wasn't Me	2/01	3/01
Luv Me Luv Me		9/01
featuring Grand Puba (J/US)		
Why You Treat Me So Bad		1/96
featuring Rayvon (J/UK)		
❖ Angel	4/01	6/01
In The Summertime	7/95	7/95
SHAI (US)		
Baby I'm Yours	9/93	
Comforter	3/93	
If I Ever Fall In Love	11/92	
SHAKATAK (UK)		
Dark Is The Night		6/83
Down On The Street		8/84
Easier Said Than Done		2/82
Night Birds		4/82
SHAKEDOWN (US)		
At Night	5/02	
SHAKESPEAR'S SISTER (UK/US)		

	US Top 20 Ent	UK Top 20 Ent
Hello (Turn Your Radio On)		11/92
I Don't Care		5/92
Stay	8/92	2/92
You're History		8/89
SHAKIRA (CO)		
Don't Bother		3/06
She Wolf	8/09	9/09
Underneath Your Clothes	5/02	8/02
Whenever, Wherever	12/01	3/02
SHAKIRA featuring Wyclef JEAN		
Hips Don't Lie	5/06	6/06
SHALAMAR (US)		
Dead Giveaway		7/83
Friends		12/82
I Can Make You Feel Good		5/82
A Night To Remember		7/82
The Second Time Around	3/80	
There It Is		9/82
SHAM 69 (UK)		
Hersham Boys		8/79
Hurry Up Harry		11/78
If The Kids Are United		8/78
SHAMEN (UK)		
Boss Drum		11/92
Ebeneezer Goode		9/92
L.S.I.		7/92
Move Any Mountain		7/91
Phorever People		12/92
SHAMPOO (UK)		
Trouble		8/94
SHANGRI-LAS (US)		
I Can Never Go Home Anymore	12/65	
Leader Of The Pack	11/64	2/65
★ Leader Of The Pack		11/72
★ Leader Of The Pack		7/76
Remember (Walkin' In The Sand)	9/64	11/64
SHANICE (US)		
I Love Your Smile	1/92	2/92
Saving Forever For You	12/92	
When I Close My Eyes	4/99	
SHANKS & BIGFOOT (UK)		
Sweet Like Chocolate		5/99
SHANNON (US)		
Let The Music Play	2/84	
Del SHANNON (US)		
Hats Off To Larry	7/61	9/61
Hey Little Girl		3/62
Keep Searchin' (We'll Follow The Sun)	1/65	2/65
Little Town Flirt	2/63	1/63
Runaway	4/61	5/61
So Long Baby		12/61
Swiss Maid		10/62
Two Kinds Of Teardrops		5/63
SHAPESHIFTERS (UK/S)		
Lola's Theme		7/04
The SHAPESHIFTERS		
Incredible		3/06
Helen SHAPIRO (UK)		
Don't Treat Me Like A Child		4/61
Let's Talk About Love		5/62
Little Miss Lonely		8/62
Tell Me What He Said		3/62
Walkin' Back To Happiness		10/61
You Don't Know		7/61
SHARAM (US)		
P.A.T.T. - Party All The Time		1/07
Feargal SHARKEY (UK)		
A Good Heart		11/85
I've Got News For You		4/91
You Little Thief		1/86
Dee Dee SHARP (US)		
Do The Bird	4/63	
Gravy (For My Mashed Potatoes)	7/62	
Mashed Potato Time	4/62	
Ride	11/62	
Georgie SHAW (US)		
Till We Two Are One	1/54	
Sandie SHAW (UK)		
Girl Don't Come		1/65
I'll Stop At Nothing		3/65
Long Live Love		5/65
Message Understood		10/65
Monsieur Dupont		3/69
Nothing Comes Easy		6/66
Puppet On A String		4/67
(There's) Always Something There To Remind Me		10/64
Tomorrow		2/66

	US Top 20 Ent	UK Top 20 Ent
Gary SHEARSTON (UK)		
I Get A Kick Out Of You		10/74
SHEER ELEGANCE (UK)		
Life Is Too Short Girl		5/76
Duncan SHEIK (UK)		
Barely Breathing	4/97	
SHEILA B. DEVOTION (F)		
Singin' In The Rain (Pt. 1)		4/78
Peter SHELLEY (UK)		
Gee Baby		10/74
Love Me Love My Dog		4/75
Anne SHELTON (UK)		
Lay Down Your Arms		9/56
Sailor		2/61
SHEP & THE LIMELITES (US)		
Daddy's Home	5/61	
SHERBET (AUS)		
Howzat		10/76
SHERIFF (US)		
When I'm With You	1/89	
Allan SHERMAN (US)		
Hello Mudduh, Hello Fadduh	8/63	
Bobby SHERMAN (US)		
Cried Like A Baby	3/71	
Easy Come, Easy Go	3/70	
Julie, Do Ya Love Me	9/70	
La La La (If I Had You)	12/69	
Little Woman	9/69	
Pluto SHERVINGTON (J)		
Dat		2/76
SHIELDS (US)		
You Cheated	10/58	
SHINEDOWN (US)		
Second Chance	5/09	
SHIRELLES (US)		
Baby It's You	1/62	
Dedicated To The One I Love	2/61	
Foolish Little Girl	5/63	
Mama Said	5/61	
Soldier Boy	4/62	
Will You Love Me Tomorrow	1/61	2/61
SHIRLEY & COMPANY (US)		
Shame Shame Shame	3/75	2/75
SHOCKING BLUE (H)		
Venus	1/70	2/70
Troy SHONDELL (US)		
This Time	10/61	
SHONTELLE (BA)		
T-Shirt		2/09
SHOP BOYZ (US)		
Party Like A Rockstar	6/07	
SHOWADDYWADDY (UK)		
Dancin' Party		11/77
Heartbeat		9/75
Hey Rock And Roll		6/74
I Wonder Why		4/78
A Little Bit Of Soap		7/78
Pretty Little Angel Eyes		11/78
Rock 'n' Roll Lady		9/74
Three Steps To Heaven		5/75
Under The Moon Of Love		11/76
When		3/77
You Got What It Takes		8/77
SHOWSTOPPERS (US)		
Ain't Nothin' But A Houseparty		4/68
SHY FX & T-POWER featuring DI (UK)		
❖ Shake Ur Body		4/02
Labi SIFFRE (UK)		
Crying Laughing Loving Lying		4/72
It Must Be Love		12/71
(Something Inside) So Strong		5/87
SIGUE SIGUE SPUTNIK (UK)		
Love Missile F1-11		3/86
SILHOUETTES (US)		
Get A Job	1/58	
SILK (US)		
Freak Me	3/93	
If You (Lovin Me)	4/99	
SILKIE (UK)		
You've Got To Hide Your Love Away	11/65	
SILKK THE SHOCKER feat. MYSTIKAL (US)		
It Ain't My Fault 2	06/99	
Rui Da SILVA feat. Cassandra (Port/UK)		
Touch Me		1/01
Lucie SILVAS (UK)		
What You're Made Of...		10/04

	US Top 20 Ent	UK Top 20 Ent
SILVER CONVENTION (G/US)		
Fly Robin Fly	11/75	
Get Up And Boogie	5/76	5/76
Harry SIMEONE CHORALE (US)		
Little Drummer Boy		2/59
Gene SIMMONS (US)		
Haunted House	9/64	
SIMON & GARFUNKEL (US)		
At The Zoo	4/67	
The Boxer	5/69	5/69
Bridge Over Troubled Water	2/70	3/70
Cecilia	5/70	
A Hazy Shade Of Winter	12/66	
Homeward Bound	3/66	5/66
I Am A Rock	5/66	
Mrs. Robinson	5/68	7/68
Mrs. Robinson (E.P.)		2/69
My Little Town	11/75	
Scarborough Fair/Canticle	4/68	
The Sounds Of Silence	12/65	
Carly SIMON (US)		
Anticipation	2/72	
Coming Around Again		2/87
Jesse	10/80	
Nobody Does It Better	9/77	8/77
That's The Way I've Always Heard It Should Be	7/71	
Why		9/82
You Belong To Me	6/78	
You're So Vain	12/72	1/73
Carly SIMON & James TAYLOR (US)		
Mockingbird	3/74	
Joe SIMON (US)		
The Chokin' Kind	5/69	
Drowning In The Sea Of Love	1/72	
Get Down, Get Down (Get On The Floor)	6/75	
Power Of Love	9/72	
Step By Step		7/73
Paul SIMON (US)		
50 Ways To Leave Your Lover	1/76	
Kodachrome	6/73	
Late In The Evening	8/80	
Loves Me Like A Rock	9/73	
Mother And Child Reunion	3/72	3/72
Slip Slidin' Away	12/77	
Take Me To The Mardi Gras		7/73
You Can Call Me Al		10/86
❖ with James Taylor & Art Garfunkel		
Wonderful World		3/78
Nina SIMONE (US)		
Ain't Got No – I Got Life		11/68
My Baby Just Cares For Me		11/87
To Love Somebody		2/69
SIMPLE MINDS (UK)		
Alive & Kicking	12/85	10/85
All The Things She Said		4/86
Belfast Child		2/89
Don't You (Forget About Me)	4/85	4/85
Let There Be Love		3/91
★ Love Song/Alive And Kicking		10/92
Sanctify Yourself	3/86	2/86
She's A River		1/95
SIMPLY RED (UK)		
Ev'ry Time We Say Goodbye		12/87
Fairground		9/95
For Your Babies		2/92
Holding Back The Years	6/86	6/86
If You Don't Know Me By Now	6/89	4/89
It's Only Love		2/89
Money's Too Tight (To Mention)		7/85
Montreux EP		11/92
The Right Thing		3/87
Something Got Me Started		9/91
Stars		12/91
Say You Love Me		5/98
Sunrise		4/03
The Air That I Breathe		8/98
You Make Me Feel Brand New		12/03
Ashlee SIMPSON		
Boyfriend		2/06
Pieces Of Me	8/04	10/04
Jessica SIMPSON (US)		
A Public Affair	8/06	
I Wanna Love You Forever	10/99	4/00
Irresistible	6/01	
These Boots Are Made For Walkin'	7/05	9/05
With You	3/04	6/04
SIMPSONS (US)		

	US Top 20 Ent	UK Top 20 Ent
Do The Bartman		2/91
SIMPSONS featuring Bart & Homer (US)		
Deep, Deep Trouble		4/91
Joyce SIMS (US)		
Come Into My Life		1/88
Kym SIMS (US)		
Take My Advice		4/92
Too Blind To See It		12/91
Frank SINATRA (US)		
All The Way/Chicago	12/57	12/57
Ev'rybody's Twistin'		4/62
From Here To Eternity	3/54	
Granada		10/61
Hey! Jealous Lover	11/56	
High Hopes	9/59	
Learnin' The Blues	6/55	8/55
Love And Marriage	11/55	1/56
Love's Been Good To Me		11/69
My Way		5/69
Ol' Macdonald	12/60	
Songs For Swinging Lovers (L.P.)		6/56
Strangers In The Night	6/66	5/66
The Tender Trap		1/56
That's Life	12/66	
Theme From 'New York, New York'		3/86
Three Coins In The Fountain	6/54	7/54
Witchcraft		2/58
You My Love	6/55	
Young-At-Heart	2/54	7/54
Nancy & Frank SINATRA (US)		
Somethin' Stupid	4/67	4/67
Nancy SINATRA (US)		
How Does That Grab You Darlin'	5/66	
Sugar Town	12/66	2/67
These Boots Are Made For Walkin'	2/66	2/66
You Only Live Twice/Jackson		7/67
Nancy SINATRA & Lee HAZLEWOOD (US)		
Did You Ever		9/71
Jackson	8/67	
Bob SINCLAR & CUTEE B featuring DOLLARMAN & BIG ALI (F)		
Rock This Party		10/06
Bob SINCLAR featuring Gary PINE		
Love Generation		11/05
SINGING DOGS (D/US)		
The Singing Dogs (Medley)		12/55
SINGING NUN (soeur Sourire) (B)		
Dominique	11/63	12/63
SINITTA (US)		
Cross My Broken Heart		4/88
Right Back Where We Started From		6/89
So Macho/Cruising		8/86
Toy Boy		8/87
SIOUXSIE & THE BANSHEES (UK)		
Dear Prudence		10/83
Hong Kong Garden		9/78
SIR DOUGLAS QUINTET (US)		
She's About A Mover	6/65	
SIR MIX-A-LOT (US)		
Baby Got Back	5/92	
SISQO (US)		
Dance For Me	7/01	
Incomplete	08/00	
Thong Song	4/00	
SISTER HAZEL (US)		
All For You	8/97	
SISTER SLEDGE (US)		
Frankie		6/85
He's The Greatest Dancer	4/79	4/79
★ Lost In Music		9/84
Thinking Of You		6/84
We Are Family	5/79	6/79
★ We Are Family		1/93
SISTERS OF MERCY (UK)		
Temple Of Love (1992)		5/92
This Corrosion		10/87
SIXPENCE NONE THE RICHER (US)		
Kiss Me	3/99	
69 BOYZ (US)		
Tootsie Roll	9/94	
SKEE-LO (US)		
I Wish	8/95	12/95
Peter SKELLERN (UK)		
You're A Lady		10/72
SKID ROW (US)		
18 And Life	9/89	2/90
I Remember You	1/90	
SKIDS (UK)		

	US Top 20 Ent	UK Top 20 Ent
Into The Valley		3/79
Masquerade		6/79
SKIP & FLIP (US)		
Cherry Pie	5/60	
It Was I	8/59	
SKY (UK)		
Toccata		5/80
SKYLARK (US)		
Wildflower	5/73	
SKYLINERS (US)		
Since I Don't Have You	4/59	
SL2 (UK)		
DJs Take Control/Way In My Brain		11/91
On A Ragga Tip		4/92
SLADE (UK)		
Bangin' Man		7/74
Coz I Luv You		11/71
Cum On Feel The Noize		3/73
Everyday		4/74
Far Far Away		10/74
Get Down And Get With It		8/71
Gudbuy T'Jane		12/72
In For A Penny		12/75
Look Wot You Dun		2/72
Mama Weer All Crazee Now		9/72
Merry Xmas Everybody		12/73
My Friend Stan		10/73
My Oh My		12/83
Run Runaway		3/84
Skweeze Me Pleeze Me		6/73
Take Me Bak 'Ome		6/72
Thanks For The Memory (Wham Bam Thank You Mam)		5/75
We'll Bring The House Down		2/81
Percy SLEDGE (US)		
Take Time To Know Her	5/68	
When A Man Loves A Woman	5/66	6/66
★ When A Man Loves A Woman		2/87
SLIK (UK)		
Forever & Ever		1/76
SLY & THE FAMILY STONE (US)		
Dance To The Music	3/68	8/68
Everyday People	1/69	
Family Affair	11/71	
Hot Fun In The Summertime	9/69	
If You Want Me To Stay	8/73	
Thank You (Falettinme Be Mice Elf Agin)/Everybody Is A Star	1/70	
SLY AND ROBBIE (J)		
Boops (Here To Go)		5/87
SLY FOX (US)		
Let's Go All The Way	3/86	7/86
SMALL FACES (UK)		
All Or Nothing		8/66
Here Come The Nice		7/67
Hey Girl		5/66
Itchycoo Park	2/68	9/67
★ Itchycoo Park		1/76
Lazy Sunday		5/68
My Mind's Eye		12/66
Sha La La La Lee		2/66
Tin Soldier		1/68
What Cha Gonna Do About It		10/65
Millie SMALL (J)		
My Boy Lollipop	6/64	4/64
SMART E'S (UK)		
Sesame's Treet		7/92
SMASHING PUMPKINS (US)		
1979	3/96	2/96
1979	4/96	
SMITH (US)		
Baby It's You	10/69	
Huey (Piano) SMITH & THE CLOWNS (US)		
Don't You Just Know It	4/58	
Hurricane SMITH (UK)		
Don't Let It Die		6/71
Oh Babe What Would You Say	1/73	5/72
Keely SMITH (US)		
You're Breakin' My Heart		4/65
Mel SMITH (UK) See Kim Wilde		
Michael W. SMITH (US)		
Place In This World	7/91	
O.C. SMITH (US)		
Little Green Apples	10/68	
The Son Of Hickory Holler's Tramp		6/68
Patti SMITH GROUP (US)		

	US Top 20 Ent	UK Top 20 Ent
Because The Night	6/78	5/78
Rex SMITH (US)		
You Take My Breath Away	6/79	
Sammi SMITH (US)		
Help Me Make It Through The Night	3/71	
Somethin' SMITH & THE REDHEADS (US)		
It's A Sin To Tell A Lie	6/55	
Whistling Jack SMITH (UK)		
I Was Kaiser Bill's Batman		3/67
Will SMITH (US)		
Getting Jiggy Wit It	2/98	
Just The Two Of Us	8/98	
Men In Black		8/97
Miami	12/98	
Switch	4/05	4/05
Wild Wild West	8/99	7/99
Will 2K		11/99
❖ *featuring TRA-KNOX (US)*		
Black Suits Comin' (Nod Ya Head)		8/02
SMITHS (UK)		
Heaven Knows I'm Miserable Now		6/84
Panic		8/86
Shoplifters Of The World Unite		2/87
This Charming Man		8/92
What Difference Does It Make		2/84
SMOKIE/SMOKEY (UK)		
Don't Play Your Rock 'n' Roll To Me		10/75
I'll Meet You At Midnight		10/76
If You Think You Know How To Love Me		8/75
It's Your Life		8/77
Lay Back In The Arms Of Someone		4/77
Living Next Door To Alice		12/76
Needles And Pins		11/77
Oh Carol		6/78
SMOKIE featuring Roy Chubby Brown (UK)		
Who The F**k Is Alice?		9/95
Father Abraham & The SMURFS (H)		
Dippety Day		11/78
The Smurf Song		6/78
Patty SMYTH with Don Henley (US) see also Scandal featuring Patty Smyth		
Sometimes Love Just Ain't Enough	9/92	
SNAP! (G/US)		
Cult Of Snap!		10/90
Mary Had A Little Boy		12/90
Oops Up		6/90
The Power	7/90	3/90
Rhythm Is A Dancer	10/92	7/92
Snap! Mega Mix		4/91
SNAP! featuring Niki Haris (G/US)		
Do You See The Light (Looking For)		6/93
Exterminate!		1/93
SNAP! featuring Summer (G/US)		
Welcome To Tomorrow		10/94
David SNEDDON (UK)		
Don't Let Go		5/03
Stop Living The Lie		1/03
SNOOP DOGG (US)		
Sensual Seduction	1/08	
SNOOP DOGG PRESENTS THA EASTSIDAZ (US)		
G'd Up	02/00	
SNOOP DOGG featuring PHARRELL		
Drop It Like It's Hot	10/04	12/04
SNOOP DOGG featuring PHARRELL & UNCLE CHARLIE WILSON (US)		
Beautiful	3/03	
SNOOP DOGG feat. Charlie WILSON & JUSTIN TIMBERLAKE		
Signs		5/05
SNOOP DOGGY DOGG (US)		
What's My Name?	12/93	
SNOW (C)		
Informer	2/93	3/93
SNOW PATROL (UK)		
Chasing Cars	9/06	8/06
Run		2/04
Signal Fire		5/07
Take Back The City		10/08
You're All I Have		5/06
Mark SNOW (US)		
The X Files		3/96
Phoebe SNOW (US)		
Poetry Man	3/75	
SO SOLID CREW (UK)		
21 Seconds		8/01
They Don't Know		11/01
SO SOLID CREW presents MR SHABZ featuring MBD & The REELISTS (UK)		
❖ Haters		102

	US Top 20 Ent	UK Top 20 Ent
SOFT CELL (UK)		
Bed Sitter		11/81
Say Hello Wave Goodbye		2/82
Tainted Love	6/82	8/81
★ Tainted Love		5/91
Torch		6/82
What		8/82
SOHO (UK)		
Hippychick	11/90	2/91
SOLE FEAT. JT MONEY & KANDI (US)		
4, 5, 6	01/00	
Jimmy SOMERVILLE (UK)		
To Love Somebody		11/90
You Make Me Feel (Mighty Real)		1/90
SOMETHIN' FOR THE PEOPLE with Trina & Tamara (US)		
My Love Is The Shhh!	10/97	
Joanie SOMMERS (US)		
Johnny Get Angry	7/62	
SON BY FOUR (US)		
Purest Of Pain (A Puro Dolor)	06/00	
SON OF DORK (UK)		
Ticket Outta Loserville		11/05
Trey SONGZ (US)		
Can't Help But Wait	12/07	
SONIA (UK)		
Listen To Your Heart		1/90
Only Fools (Never Fall In Love)		6/91
You'll Never Stop Me Loving You		7/89
SONIQUE (UK)		
I Put A Spell On You		12/00
It Feels So Good		6/00
Sky		09/00
SONNY & CHER (US) see also Cher		
All I Ever Need Is You	12/71	2/72
Baby Don't Go	10/65	10/65
The Beat Goes On	2/67	
But You're Mine	11/65	
A Cowboys Work Is Never Done	4/72	
I Got You Babe	8/65	8/65
Little Man		9/66
What Now My Love	3/66	
SONNY (US)		
Laugh At Me	9/65	9/65
S.O.S. BAND (US)		
Take Your Time (Do It Right) (Pt. 1)	7/80	
SOUL ASYLUM (US)		
Runaway Train	8/93	11/93
SOULDECISION feat. THRUST (US)		
Faded	08/00	
SOUL FOR REAL (US)		
Candy Rain 2/95		
SOUL II SOUL (UK)		
A Dream's A Dream		5/90
Get A Life		12/89
Joy		4/92
SOUL II SOUL featuring Caron Wheeler (UK)		
Back To Life (However Do You Want Me)	11/89	6/89
Keep On Movin'	8/89	3/89
SOULJA BOY TELL'EM (US)		
Crank Dat (Soulja Boy)	8/07	12/07
SOULJA BOY TELL'EM featuring SAMMIE (US)		
Kiss Me Thru The Phone	3/09	5/09
SOULSEARCHER (US)		
Can't Get Enough		2/99
SOUL SURVIVORS (US)		
Expressway To Your Heart	10/67	
David SOUL (US)		
Don't Give Up On Us	3/77	1/77
Going In With My Eyes Open		3/77
It Sure Brings Out The Love In Your Eyes		6/78
Let's Have A Quiet Night In		1/78
Silver Lady		9/77
Jimmy SOUL (US)		
If You Wanna Be Happy	5/63	
SOUNDGARDEN (US)		
Black Hole Sun	8/94	
SOUNDS ORCHESTRAL (UK)		
Cast Your Fate To The Wind	5/65	1/65
SOUP DRAGONS (UK)		
I'm Free		7/90
SOURCE featuring Candi Staton (UK/US)		
You Got The Love		2/91
★ You Got The Love		2/06
Joe SOUTH (US)		
Games People Play	2/69	3/69
Walk A Mile In My Shoes	2/70	
J. D. SOUTHER (US)		
You're Only Lonely	11/79	

	US Top 20 Ent	UK Top 20 Ent
❖ **with James Taylor**		
Her Town Too	4/81	
RED SOVINE (US)		
Teddy Bear		6/81
BOB B. SOXX & THE BLUE JEANS (US)		
Zip-A-Dee Doo-Dah	12/62	
SPACE (F)		
Magic Fly		9/77
SPACE (UK)		
Avenging Angels		1/98
with Cerys of Catatonia		
The Ballad of Tom Jones		3/98
Me And You Versus The World		9/96
SPACEDUST (UK)		
Gym And Tonic		10/98
SPAGNA (ITA)		
Call Me		8/87
SPANDAU BALLET (UK)		
Chant No.1 (I Don't Need This Pressure On)		7/81
Communication		3/83
Gold		8/83
I'll Fly For You		9/84
Instinction		5/82
Lifeline		10/82
Musclebound/Glow		5/81
Only When You Leave		6/84
Through The Barricades		11/86
To Cut A Long Story Short		12/80
True	9/83	4/83
SPANKY & OUR GANG (US)		
Sunday Will Never Be The Same	6/67	
SPARKLE/R. KELLY (US)		
Be Careful		7/98
SPARKS (US)		
Amateur Hour		8/74
Beat The Clock		8/79
Never Turn Your Back On Mother Earth		11/74
This Town Ain't Big Enough For Both Of Us		5/74
Jordin SPARKS (US)		
Battlefield	8/09	6/09
Tattoo	12/07	
Jordin SPARKS duet with Chris BROWN (US)		
No Air	3/08	6/08
Sam SPARRO (AUS)		
Black & Gold		4/08
Bubba SPARXXX (US)		
Ugly	11/01	
11/01 **Bubba SPARXXX feat. YING YANG TWINS & MR. COLLIPARK** Ms. New Booty	3/06	
Billie Jo SPEARS (US)		
Blanket On The Ground		8/75
What I've Got In Mind		8/76
Britney SPEARS (US)		
3	10/09	11/09
Born To Make You Happy		1/00
Circus	12/08	2/09
(You Drive Me) Crazy		10/99
Do Somethin'		3/05
Everytime	7/04	6/04
From The Bottom Of My Broken Heart	2/00	6/00
...Baby One More Time	11/98	2/99
Gimme More	10/07	10/07
I'm A Slave 4 U		10/01
I'm Not A Girl, Not Yet A Woman		4/02
Lucky		8/00
My Prerogative		11/04
Oops!… I Did It Again		5/00
Overprotected		2/02
Piece Of Me		1/08
Stronger	1/01	12/00
Sometimes		6/99
Toxic	3/04	3/04
Womanizer	10/08	11/08
❖ **featuring MADONNA (US)**		
Me Against The Music		11/03
❖ **featuring Pharrell WILLIAMS (US)**		
Boys		8/02
SPECIAL AKA (UK)		
Nelson Mandela		4/84
SPECIAL D (G)		
Come With Me		4/04
SPECIALS (UK)		
Do Nothing/Maggie's Farm		1/81
Gangsters		8/79
Ghost Town		6/81
A Message To You Rudy/Nite Klub		11/79
Rat Race/Rude Boys Outa Jail		6/80
Stereotype/International Jet Set		10/80
Too Much Too Young E.P.		2/80
Chris SPEDDING (UK)		
Motor Biking		9/75
Johnny SPENCE (UK)		
Dr. Kildare Theme		4/62
Tracie SPENCER (US)		
This House	3/91	
It's All About You (Not Me)	08/99	
Still In My Heart	03/00	
SPICE GIRLS (UK)		
Goodbye	12/98	12/98
Headlines (Friendship Never Ends)		12/07
Holler/Let Love Lead The Way		11/00
Mama/Who Do You Think You Are?		3/97
Say You'll Be There	5/97	10/96
Stop	7/98	3/98
Too Much		2/98
2 Become 1	8/97	12/96
Viva Forever		8/98
Wannabe	1/97	7/96
SPILLER (ITA)		
Groovejet (If This Ain't Love)		09/00
SPIN DOCTORS (US)		
Little Miss Can't Be Wrong	12/92	
Two Princes	3/93	6/93
(Detroit) SPINNERS (US)		
Could It Be I'm Falling In Love	2/73	
Cupid-I've Loved You For A Long Time (Medley)	6/80	7/80
Ghetto Child		10/73
I'll Be Around	11/72	
It's A Shame	10/70	
One Of A Kind (Love Affair)	6/73	
The Rubberband Man	11/76	
They Just Can't Stop It The (Games People Play)	10/75	
Working My Way Back To You- Forgive Me, Girl	2/80	3/80
SPIRAL STAIRCASE (US)		
More Today Than Yesterday	6/69	
SPITTING IMAGE (UK)		
The Chicken Song		5/86
SPLODGENESSABOUNDS (UK)		
Simon Templar/Two Pints Of Lager And A Packet Of Crisps Please		6/80
SPOOKS (US)		
Things I've Seen		2/01
SPORTY THIEVZ feat. MR WOODS (US)		
No Pigeons	06/99	
Dusty SPRINGFIELD (UK)		
All I See Is You		10/66
Goin' Back		7/66
I Close My Eyes And Count To Ten		7/68
I Just Don't Know What To Do With Myself		7/64
I Only Want To Be With You	3/64	11/63
In Private		12/89
In The Middle Of Nowhere		7/65
Losing You		12/64
Some Of Your Lovin'		10/65
Son-Of-A Preacher Man	1/69	1/69
Stay Awhile		3/64
Wishin' And Hopin'	7/64	
You Don't Have To Say You Love Me	6/66	4/66
❖ **with Pet Shop Boys**		
What Have I Done To Deserve This	2/88	8/87
Rick SPRINGFIELD (AUS)		
Affair Of The Night	5/83	
Don't Talk To Strangers	4/82	
I've Done Everything For You	10/81	
Jessie's Girl	6/81	
Love Somebody	4/84	
Speak To The Sky	10/72	
SPRINGFIELDS (UK)		
Island Of Dreams		2/63
Say I Won't Be There		4/63
Bruce SPRINGSTEEN (US)		
Born In The U.S.A.	12/84	7/85
Brilliant Disguise	10/87	
Cover Me	9/84	
Dancing In The Dark	6/84	2/85
Glory Days	7/85	
Human Touch/Better Days	4/92	3/92
Hungry Heart	12/80	
I'm Goin' Down	10/85	
I'm On Fire	4/85	7/85
My Hometown	1/86	12/85
One Step Up	4/88	
Santa Claus Is Comin' To Town/My Hometown		12/85
Streets Of Philadelphia	3/94	3/94
Tougher Than The Rest		7/88
Tunnel Of Love	2/88	
War	12/86	
SPRINGWATER (UK)		
I Will Return		11/71
SQUEEZE (UK)		
Cool For Cats		4/79
Labelled With Love		11/81
Up The Junction		6/79
Billy SQUIER (US)		
Rock Me Tonite	9/84	
Jim STAFFORD (US)		
My Girl Bill	6/74	
Spiders & Snakes	2/74	5/74
Wildwood Weed	8/74	
Jo STAFFORD (US)		
Make Love To Me!	2/54	5/54
Suddenly There's A Valley		12/55
Terry STAFFORD (US)		
Suspicion	3/64	
STAIND (US)		
It's Been Awhile	7/01	
STAKKA BO (S)		
Here We Go		10/93
Frank STALLONE (US)		
Far From Over	9/83	
STAMPEDERS (C)		
Sweet City Woman	10/71	
STANDELLS (US)		
Dirty Water	7/66	
Lisa STANSFIELD (UK)		
All Around The World	3/90	11/89
Change		10/91
In All The Right Places		6/93
Live Together		2/90
Someday (I'm Coming Back)		1/93
Time To Make You Mine		4/92
You Can't Deny It	7/90	
❖ **with Coldcut**		
People Hold On		4/89
STAPLE SINGERS (US)		
I'll Take You There	5/72	
If You're Ready Come Go With Me	12/73	
Let's Do It Again	11/75	
Respect Yourself	12/71	
Cyril STAPLETON (UK)		
Blue Star		9/55
The Children's Marching Song		2/59
STARBUCK (US)		
Moonlight Feels Right	7/76	
STARDUST (F)		
Music Sounds Better With You		8/98
Alvin STARDUST (UK)		
I Feel Like Buddy Holly		6/84
I Won't Run Away		12/84
Jealous Mind		2/74
My Coo-Ca-Choo		12/73
Pretend		9/81
Red Dress		5/74
You You You		9/74
STARGAZERS (UK)		
Close The Door		9/55
Crazy Otto Rag		6/55
Happy Wanderer		4/54
I See The Moon		2/54
Twenty Tiny Fingers		11/55
STARLAND VOCAL BAND (US)		
Afternoon Delight	6/76	
STARLIGHT (ITA)		
Numero Uno		9/89
Brenda K. STARR (US)		
I Still Believe	6/88	
Edwin STARR (US)		
Contact		2/79
H.A.P.P.Y. Radio		6/79
Stop Her On Sight (SOS)/Headline News		1/69
Twenty Five Miles	4/69	
War	8/70	11/70
Freddie STARR (UK)		
It's You		3/74
Kay STARR (US)		
Changing Partners	1/54	3/54
If You Love Me (Really Love Me)	5/54	
Man Upstairs	4/54	

	US Top 20 Ent	UK Top 20 Ent
Rock And Roll Waltz	1/56	2/56

Ringo STARR (UK)

	US Top 20 Ent	UK Top 20 Ent
Back Off Boogaloo	5/72	4/72
It Don't Come Easy	5/71	5/71
No No Song/Snookeroo	3/75	
Oh My My	4/74	
Only You	12/74	
Photograph	11/73	11/73
You're Sixteen	1/74	3/74

STARS ON 45 (H) see Starsound

STARSHIP (US)

	US Top 20 Ent	UK Top 20 Ent
It's Not Enough	10/89	
It's Not Over ('Til It's Over)	8/87	
Nothing's Gonna Stop Us Now	3/87	5/87
Sara	2/86	
We Built This City	10/85	12/85

STARSOUND (H)

	US Top 20 Ent	UK Top 20 Ent
STARS ON 45 (Medley)	**5/81**	**5/81**
Stars On 45 (Vol 2)		7/81

STAR TURN ON 45 PINTS (UK)

	US Top 20 Ent	UK Top 20 Ent
Pump Up The Bitter		5/88

STATLER BROTHERS (US)

	US Top 20 Ent	UK Top 20 Ent
Flowers On The Wall	1/66	

Candi STATON (US)

	US Top 20 Ent	UK Top 20 Ent
Nights On Broadway		8/77
Young Hearts Run Free		6/76

❖ **with The Source**

	US Top 20 Ent	UK Top 20 Ent
You Got The Love		2/91

STATUS QUO (UK)

	US Top 20 Ent	UK Top 20 Ent
Again And Again		9/78
The Anniversary Waltz - Part 1		10/90
Break The Rules		5/74
Burning Bridges (On And Off And On Again)		12/88
Caroline		10/73
Caroline (Live At The N.E.C.)		11/82
Dear John		4/82
Down Down		12/74
Down The Dustpipe		6/70
Ice In The Sun		10/68
In The Army Now		10/86
Lies/Don't Drive My Car		12/80
Marguerita Time		12/83
Mystery Song		8/76
Ol' Rag Blues		9/83
Paper Plane		2/73
Pictures Of Matchstick Men	8/68	2/68
Rain		2/76
Rock 'n' Roll		12/81
Rockin' All Over The World		10/77
Roll Over Lay Down		6/75
Rolling Home		5/86
Something 'Bout You Baby I Like		3/81
The Wanderer		11/84
What You're Proposing		10/80
Whatever You Want		10/79
Wild Side Of Life		1/77

STEALER'S WHEEL (UK)

	US Top 20 Ent	UK Top 20 Ent
Stuck In The Middle With You	4/73	6/73

STEAM (US)

	US Top 20 Ent	UK Top 20 Ent
Na Na Hey Hey Kiss Him Goodbye	11/69	3/70

STEEL BREEZE (US)

	US Top 20 Ent	UK Top 20 Ent
You Don't Want Me Anymore	11/82	

Anthony STEEL & THE RADIO REVELLERS (UK)

	US Top 20 Ent	UK Top 20 Ent
West Of Zanzibar		9/54

Tommy STEELE (UK)

	US Top 20 Ent	UK Top 20 Ent
Butterfingers		5/57
Come On Let's Go		11/58
Little White Bull		12/59
Nairobi		3/58
Shiralee		9/57
Singing The Blues		1/57
Tallahassee Lassie		8/59
Water Water/Handful Of Songs		9/57
What A Mouth		7/60

STEELEYE SPAN (UK)

	US Top 20 Ent	UK Top 20 Ent
All Around My Hat		12/75

STEELY DAN (US)

	US Top 20 Ent	UK Top 20 Ent
Do It Again	1/73	
Hey Nineteen	1/81	
Peg	2/78	
Reeling In The Years	5/73	
Rikki Don't Lose That Number	7/74	

Gwen STEFANI (US)

	US Top 20 Ent	UK Top 20 Ent
Hollaback Girl	4/05	6/05
What You Waiting For?		11/04
Wind It Up	12/06	12/06

Gwen STEFANI featuring AKON (US)

	US Top 20 Ent	UK Top 20 Ent
The Sweet Escape	2/07	2/07

Gwen STEFANI featuring EVE

	US Top 20 Ent	UK Top 20 Ent
Rich Girl	2/05	3/05

STEPPENWOLF (US)

	US Top 20 Ent	UK Top 20 Ent
Born To Be Wild	8/68	
Magic Carpet Ride	11/68	
Rock Me	4/69	

STEPS (UK)

	US Top 20 Ent	UK Top 20 Ent
After The Love Has Gone		10/99
Better Best Forgotten		3/99
Chain Reaction/One For Sorrow (Remix)		10/01
Deeper Shade Of Blue		4/00
Heartbeat/Tragedy		11/98
Here And Now/You'll Be Sorry		6/01
Last Thing On My Mind		5/98
Love's Got A Hold On My Heart		7/99
One For Sorrow		9/98
Say You'll Be Mine/Better The Devil You Know		1/00
Stomp		10/00
When I Said Goodbye/Summer Of Love		7/00
Words Are Not Enough/I Know Him So Well		12/01

STEREO MCS (UK)

	US Top 20 Ent	UK Top 20 Ent
Step It Up		12/92

STEREOPHONICS (UK)

	US Top 20 Ent	UK Top 20 Ent
The Bartender And The Thief		11/98
Dakota		3/05
Handbags And Gladrags		12/01
Have A Nice Day		6/01
Just Looking		3/99
Madame Helga		5/03
Maybe Tomorrow		8/03
Mr Writer		3/01
Movie Star		2/04
Pick A Part That's New		5/99

Cat STEVENS (UK)

	US Top 20 Ent	UK Top 20 Ent
Another Saturday Night	9/74	
Can't Keep It In		1/73
I'm Gonna Get Me A Gun		4/67
Lady D'Arbanville		7/70
Matthew And Son		1/67
Morning Has Broken	5/72	1/72
Oh Very Young	5/74	
Peace Train	10/71	
Wild World	4/71	

Connie STEVENS (US)

	US Top 20 Ent	UK Top 20 Ent
Sixteen Reasons	4/60	6/60

❖ **with Edward Byrnes**

	US Top 20 Ent	UK Top 20 Ent
Kookie, Kookie (Lend Me Your Comb)	5/59	

Dodie STEVENS (US)

	US Top 20 Ent	UK Top 20 Ent
Pink Shoe Laces	3/59	

Rachel STEVENS (UK)

	US Top 20 Ent	UK Top 20 Ent
More More More		10/04
Some Girls		7/04
Sweet Dreams My L.A. Ex		9/03

Ray STEVENS (US)

	US Top 20 Ent	UK Top 20 Ent
Ahab, The Arab	7/62	
Bridget The Midget (The Queen Of The Blues)	3/71	
Everything Is Beautiful	5/70	6/70
Gitarzan	5/69	
Misty	7/75	7/75
The Streak	5/74	6/74

Ricky STEVENS (UK)

	US Top 20 Ent	UK Top 20 Ent
I Cried For You		12/61

Shakin' STEVENS (UK)

	US Top 20 Ent	UK Top 20 Ent
Cry Just A Little Bit		11/83
Give Me Your Heart Tonight		9/82
Green Door		8/81
I'll Be Satisfied		11/82
It's Late		8/83
It's Raining		10/81
A Letter To You		9/84
A Love Worth Waiting For		4/84
Merry Christmas Everyone		12/85
Oh Julie		1/82
The Shakin' Stevens E.P.		12/82
Shirley		5/82
Teardrops		12/84
This Ole House		3/81
What Do You Want To Make Those Eyes…		12/87
You Drive Me Crazy		5/81

Shaky & Bonny (Shakin' STEVENS & Bonnie TYLER) (UK)

	US Top 20 Ent	UK Top 20 Ent
A Rockin' Good Way		1/84

B.W. STEVENSON (US)

	US Top 20 Ent	UK Top 20 Ent
My Maria	9/73	

Al STEWART (UK)

	US Top 20 Ent	UK Top 20 Ent
Time Passages	11/78	
Year Of The Cat	2/77	

Amii STEWART (US)

	US Top 20 Ent	UK Top 20 Ent
Friends		1/85
Knock On Wood	3/79	5/79
★ Knock On Wood/Light My Fire		9/85
Light My Fire/137 Disco Heaven (Medley)		7/79

Andy STEWART with the Michael Sammes Singers (UK)

	US Top 20 Ent	UK Top 20 Ent
Donald Where's Your Troosers		12/89

Billy STEWART (US)

	US Top 20 Ent	UK Top 20 Ent
Summertime	8/66	

Dave STEWART & Barbara GASKIN (UK)

	US Top 20 Ent	UK Top 20 Ent
It's My Party		10/81

David A. STEWART introducing Candy Dulfer (UK/H)

	US Top 20 Ent	UK Top 20 Ent
Lily Was Here	7/91	3/90

Jermaine STEWART (US)

	US Top 20 Ent	UK Top 20 Ent
Say It Again		2/88
We Don't Have To Take Your Out Clothes Off…	8/86	8/86

John STEWART (US)

	US Top 20 Ent	UK Top 20 Ent
Gold	7/79	

Rod STEWART (UK)

	US Top 20 Ent	UK Top 20 Ent
Angel/What Made Milwaukee Famous		12/72
Baby Jane	7/83	6/83
Crazy About Her	7/89	
Da Ya Think I'm Sexy?	1/79	11/78
Downtown Train	1/90	3/90
Every Beat Of My Heart		7/86
Farewell/Bring It On Home To Me		10/74
Forever Young	10/88	
Get Back		12/76
Have I Told You Lately	5/93	6/93
Hotlegs/I Was Only Joking		2/78
I Don't Want To Talk About It/First Cut Is The Deepest		5/77
Infatuation	7/84	
The Killing Of Georgie		9/76
Lost In You	7/88	
Love Touch	7/86	
Maggie May/Reason To Believe	9/71	9/71
The Motown Song	9/91	6/91
My Heart Can't Tell You No	3/89	
Oh No Not My Baby		9/73
Ole Ola (Mulher Brasileira)		6/78
Passion	12/80	
Rhythm Of My Heart	4/91	3/91
Ruby Tuesday		2/93
Sailing		8/75
★ Sailing		10/76
Some Guys Have All The Luck	10/84	
This Old Heart Of Mine		11/75
Tom Traubert's Blues (Waltzing Matilda)		12/92
Tonight I'm Yours (Don't Hurt Me)		11/81
Tonight's The Night (Gonna Be Alright)	11/76	6/76
What Am I Gonna Do		9/83
You Wear It Well	10/72	8/72
You're In My Heart	12/77	10/77
Young Turks	11/81	1/82

Rod STEWART & Tina TURNER (UK/US)

	US Top 20 Ent	UK Top 20 Ent
It Takes Two		12/90

ROD STEWART with Ronald ISLEY (UK/US)

	US Top 20 Ent	UK Top 20 Ent
This Old Heart Of Mine		5/90

Curtis STIGERS (US)

	US Top 20 Ent	UK Top 20 Ent
I Wonder Why	11/91	2/92
You're All That Matters To Me		4/92

STILTSKIN (UK)

	US Top 20 Ent	UK Top 20 Ent
Inside		5/94

STING (UK)

	US Top 20 Ent	UK Top 20 Ent
All This Time	3/91	
Be Still My Beating Heart	3/88	
Fortress Around Your Heart	10/85	
If You Love Somebody Set Them Free	7/85	
Russians		1/86
We'll Be Together	11/87	
When We Dance		10/94

❖ **with Bryan Adams & Rod Stewart**

	US Top 20 Ent	UK Top 20 Ent
All For Love		12/93

❖ **featuring Cheb Mami**

	US Top 20 Ent	UK Top 20 Ent
Desert Rose		09/00

STOCK AITKEN WATERMAN (UK)

	US Top 20 Ent	UK Top 20 Ent
Mr Sleaze		10/87

❖ **with Christians, Holly Johnson, Paul McCartney, Gerry Marsden**

	US Top 20 Ent	UK Top 20 Ent
Ferry 'Cross The Mersey		5/89

Morris STOLOFF (US)

	US Top 20 Ent	UK Top 20 Ent
Moonglow And Theme From 'Picnic'	4/56	6/56

Joss STONE

	US Top 20 Ent	UK Top 20 Ent
You Had Me		9/04

	US Top 20 Ent	UK Top 20 Ent
R & J STONE (UK)		
We Do It		1/76
STONE PONEYS (US)		
Different Drum	1/68	
STONE ROSES (UK)		
Elephant Stone		3/90
Fool's Gold/What The World Is Waiting For		12/89
Love Spreads		12/94
One Love		7/90
STONEBRIDGE featuring THERESE (S)		
Put 'Em High		8/04
STORIES (US)		
Brother Louie	8/73	
STORM (G)		
Time To Burn		08/00
Gale STORM (US)		
Dark Moon	5/57	
I Hear You Knocking	11/55	
Teenage Prayer	1/56	
Why Do Fools Fall In Love	3/56	
STRANGELOVES (US)		
I Want Candy	8/65	
STRANGLERS (UK)		
All Day And All Of The Night		1/88
European Female		1/83
Golden Brown		1/82
No More Heroes		10/77
Peaches/Go Buddy Go		7/77
Something Better Change/Straighten Out		8/77
Strange Little Girl		8/82
STRAWBERRY ALARM CLOCK (US)		
Incense And Peppermints	10/67	
STRAWBERRY SWITCHBLADE (UK)		
Since Yesterday		1/85
STRAWBS (UK)		
Lay Down		12/72
Part Of The Union		2/73
STRAY CATS (US)		
Rock This Town	11/82	2/81
Runaway Boys		12/80
(She's) Sexy + 17	9/83	
Stray Cat Strut	2/83	5/81
The STREETS (UK)		
Dry Your Eyes		7/04
Fit But You Know It		5/04
When You Wasn't Famous		4/06
Barbra STREISAND (US)		
Comin' In And Out Of Your Life	12/81	
Evergreen (From 'A Star Is Born')	2/77	5/77
The Main Event/Fight	7/79	
My Heart Belongs To Me	6/77	
People	6/64	
Stoney End	1/71	
The Way We Were	1/74	
Woman In Love	9/80	10/80
❖ **with Bryan Adams**		
I Finally Found Someone	11/96	
❖ **with Donna Summer**		
No More Tears (Enough Is Enough)	11/79	11/79
BARBRA STREISAND & NEIL DIAMOND (US)		
You Don't Bring Me Flowers	11/78	12/78
Barbra STREISAND & Barry GIBB (US/UK)		
Guilty	12/80	
What Kind Of Fool	3/81	
STRING-A-LONGS (US)		
Wheels	2/61	3/61
The STROKES (US)		
12:51		10/03
Juicebox		12/05
Jud STRUNK (US)		
Daisy A Day	5/73	
Tinchy STRYDER featuring Amelle (UK)		
Never Leave You		8/09
Tinchy STRYDER featuring N-DUBZ (UK)		
Number 1		5/09
Tinchy STRYDER featuring Taio CRUZ (UK)		
Take Me Back		1/09
Ruben STUDDARD (US)		
Flying Without Wings	6/03	
Sorry 2004	2/04	
Amy STUDT (UK)		
Misfit		6/03
STUNTMASTERZ (UK)		
The Ladyboy Is Mine		3/01
STYLE COUNCIL (UK)		
Groovin' (You're The Best Thing)/Big Boss		
Groove		6/84
It Didn't Matter		1/87
The Lodgers		10/85
Long Hot Summer		8/83
Money Go Round (Pt.1)		6/83
My Ever Changing Moods		2/84
Shout To The Top		10/84
Solid Bond In Your Heart		11/83
Speak Like A Child		3/83
Walls Come Tumbling Down!		5/85
STYLISTICS (US)		
Betcha By Golly, Wow	4/72	
Break Up To Make Up	3/73	
Can't Give You Anything		
(But My Love)		8/75
Can't Help Falling In Love		5/76
Funky Weekend		3/76
I'm Stone In Love With You	12/72	11/72
Let's Put It All Together		11/74
Na Na Is The Saddest Word		12/75
Rockin' Roll Baby	12/73	2/74
Sing Baby Sing		5/75
16 Bars		9/76
Star On A TV Show		2/75
You Are Everything	12/71	
You Make Me Feel Brand New	5/74	8/74
STYX (US)		
Babe	11/79	1/80
The Best Of Times	2/81	
Come Sail Away	12/77	
Don't Let It End	6/83	
Lady	3/75	
Mr. Roboto	3/83	
Show Me The Way	3/91	
Too Much Time On My Hands	5/81	
SUB SUB featuring Melanie Williams (UK)		
Ain't No Love (Ain't No Use)		4/93
SUBWAY See 702 featuring Subway		
SUEDE (UK)		
Animal Nitrate		3/93
Electricity		4/99
Stay Together		2/94
SUGABABES (UK)		
About A Girl		11/09
About You Now		10/07
Caught In A Moment		9/04
Easy		11/06
Freak Like Me		5/02
Get Sexy		9/09
Girls		10/08
Hole In The Head		10/03
In The Middle		4/04
Overload		09/00
Push The Button		10/05
Red Dress		3/06
Round Round		8/02
Stronger/Angels With Dirty Faces		11/02
Too Lost In You		1/04
Ugly		12/05
SUGABABES vs GIRLS ALOUD (UK)		
Walk This Way		3/07
SUGAR RAY (US)		
Every Morning	2/99	
When It's Over	8/01	
SUGARHILL GANG (US)		
Rapper's Delight		12/79
SUGARLOAF (US)		
Green Eyed Lady	10/70	
SUGARLOAF/JERRY CORBETTA (US)		
Don't Call Us We'll Call You	3/75	
SUGGS (UK)		
I'm Only Sleeping/Off On Holiday		8/95
SUM 41 (US)		
Fat Lip	10/01	
SUMMER (US) see Snap! featuring Summer		
Donna SUMMER (US)		
Bad Girls	6/79	
Deep Down Inside		9/77
Dim All The Lights	10/79	
Heaven Knows	2/79	
Hot Stuff	5/79	6/79
I Don't Wanna Get Hurt		6/89
I Feel Love	10/77	7/77
★ I Feel Love	9/95	
I Love You		1/78
I Remember Yesterday		10/77
I Will Go WIth You	08/99	
Last Dance	7/78	
Love Is In Control (Finger On The Trigger)	8/82	
Love To Love You Baby	1/76	2/76
Love's Unkind		12/77
MacArthur Park	10/78	10/78
On The Radio	2/80	
She Works Hard For The Money	7/83	
This Time I Know It's For Real	6/89	3/89
Unconditional Love		11/83
The Wanderer	10/80	
Donna SUMMER & BARBRA STREISAND (US)		
No More Tears (Enough Is Enough)	11/79	11/79
SUNBLOCK (UK)		
I'll Be Ready		1/06
SUNBLOCK featuring Robin BECK		
First Time		5/06
SUNNY (UK)		
Doctor's Orders		4/74
SUNNY & THE SUNGLOWS (US)		
Talk To Me	10/63	
SUNSET STRIPPERS (UK)		
Falling Stars		3/05
SUPERGRASS (UK)		
Alright/Time		7/95
Going Out		3/96
Moving		9/99
Pumping On Your Stereo		6/99
SUPERMEN LOVERS (F)		
Starlight		9/01
SUPERTRAMP (UK)		
Breakfast In America		7/79
Dreamer	11/80	3/75
Goodbye Stranger	9/79	
It's Raining Again	12/82	
The Logical Song	5/79	4/79
Take The Long Way Home	11/79	
DIANA ROSS & The SUPREMES (US)		
★ Baby Love		9/74
I'm Livin' In Shame	2/69	5/69
In And Out Of Love	12/67	1/68
Love Child	11/68	1/69
Reflections	8/67	9/67
Someday We'll Be Together	12/69	1/70
DIANA ROSS, The SUPREMES & the TEMPTATIONS (US)		
I'm Gonna Make You Love Me	12/68	2/69
SUPREMES (US)		
Automatically Sunshine		8/72
Baby Love	10/64	11/64
Back In My Arms Again	5/65	
Come See About Me	12/64	
Floy Joy		3/72
The Happening	4/67	6/67
I Hear A Symphony	11/65	
Love Is Here And Now You're Gone	2/67	
Love Is Like An Itching In My Heart	5/66	
My World Is Empty Without You	2/66	
Nathan Jones	6/71	9/71
Nothing But Heartaches	9/65	
Stoned Love	12/70	2/71
Stop! In The Name Of Love	3/65	4/65
Up The Ladder To The Roof	4/70	5/70
Where Did Our Love Go	8/64	9/64
You Can't Hurry Love	9/66	9/66
You Keep Me Hangin' On	11/66	12/66
SUPREMES & FOUR TOPS (US)		
River Deep-Mountain High	1/71	7/71
AL B. SURE! (US)		
Nite And Day	7/88	
SURFACE (US)		
The First Time	1/91	
Shower Me With Your Love	8/89	
SURFARIS (US)		
Wipe Out	7/63	8/63
SURVIVOR (US)		
Burning Heart	12/85	2/86
Eye Of The Tiger	7/82	8/82
High On You	3/85	
I Can't Hold Back	12/84	
Is This Love	12/86	
The Search Is Over	6/85	
SUTHERLAND BROTHERS AND QUIVER (UK)		
Arms Of Mary		5/76
Billy SWAN (US)		
I Can Help	11/74	1/75
Patrick SWAYZE (with Wendy Fraser) (US)		
She's Like The Wind	2/88	
Keith SWEAT (US)		
I Want Her	3/88	
I'll Give All My Love To You		1/91

	US Top 20 Ent	UK Top 20 Ent
Make You Sweat	8/90	
Twisted	7/96	
Keith SWEAT and Athena CAGE (US)		
Nobody	10/96	
Keith SWEAT and SNOOP DOGG (US)		
Come And Get With Me	11/98	
SWEET DREAMS (UK)		
Honey Honey		8/74
SWEETBOX (G/US)		
Everything's Gonna Be Alright		8/98
SWEET PEOPLE (F)		
Et Les Oiseaux Chantaient (And The Birds Were Singing)		10/80
SWEET SENSATION (US)		
If Wishes Came True	7/90	
Love Child	5/90	
SWEET SENSATION (UK)		
Purely By Coincidence		2/75
Sad Sweet Dreamer	3/75	10/74
SWEET (UK)		
Ballroom Blitz	9/75	9/73
Blockbuster!		1/73
Co-Co		6/71
Fox On The Run	12/75	4/75
Funny Funny		4/71
Hell Raiser		5/73
Little Willy	4/73	7/72
Love Is Like Oxygen	5/78	2/78
Poppa Joe		3/72
The Six Teens		**7/74**
Teenage Rampage		1/74
Wig Wam Bam		9/72
SWEET FEMALE ATTITUDE (UK)		
Flowers		4/00
Taylor SWIFT (US)		
Change	8/08	
Fearless	11/08	
Jump Then Fall	11/09	
Love Story	10/08	3/09
Our Song	1/08	
Teardrops On My Guitar	2/08	
White Horse	11/08	
You Belong With Me	7/09	
You're Not Sorry	11/08	
SWING OUT SISTER (UK)		
Breakout	10/87	11/86
Surrender		1/87
SWINGING BLUE JEANS (UK)		
Good Golly Miss Molly		4/64
Hippy Hippy Shake		1/64
You're No Good		6/64
SWV (US)		
I'm So Into You	4/93	
Right Here (Human Nature)	8/93	8/93
Weak	5/93	
You're The One	4/96	
SYBIL (US)		
Walk On By		2/90
When I'm Good And Ready		4/93
❖ with West End		
The Love I Lost		1/93
SYLVERS (US)		
Boogie Fever	4/76	
Hot Line	12/76	
SYLVESTER (US)		
You Make Me Feel (Mighty Real)		10/78
SYLVIA (US)		
Pillow Talk	5/73	
SYLVIA (Swe)		
Y Viva Espana		9/74
SYLVIA (US)		
Nobody	11/82	
SYNDICATE OF SOUND (US)		
Little Girl	7/66	
SYREETA (US) See Billy Preston & Syreeta		
SYSTEM (US)		
Don't Disturb The Groove	6/87	
T-BONES (US)		
No Matter What Shape (Your Stomach's In)	1/66	
T-CONNECTION (US)		
Do What You Wanna Do		7/77
T-PAIN (US)		
I'm Sprung	11/05	
T-PAIN featuring AKON (US)		
Bartender	7/07	
T-PAIN featuring LIL WAYNE (US)		
Can't Believe It	9/08	
T-PAIN featuring Mike JONES		
I'm N Luv (Wit A Stripper)		
T-PAIN featuring Yung Joc (US)		
Buy You A Drank (Shawty Snappin')	4/07	
T-REX (UK)		
Bang A Gong (Get It On)	3/72	7/71
Children Of The Revolution		9/72
Debora/One Inch Rock		4/72
The Groover		6/73
Hot Love		3/71
I Love To Boogie		7/76
Jeepster		11/71
Metal Guru		5/72
Ride A White Swan		2/71
Solid Gold Easy Action		12/72
Teenage Dream		2/74
Telegram Sam		1/72
Truck On (Tyke)		12/73
20th Century Boy		3/73
★ 20th Century Boy		9/91
T-SPOON (H)		
Sex On The Beach		9/98
T99 (B)		
Anasthasia		5/91
t.A.T.u. (RU)		
All About Us		10/05
All The Things She Said		2/03
T.I. (US)		
Big Things Poppin' (Do It)	7/07	
Bring Em Out	1/05	
What You Know	4/06	
Whatever You Like	9/08	
T.I. featuring Justin TIMBERLAKE (US)		
Dead And Gone	2/09	3/09
T.I. featuring RIHANNA (US/BA)		
Live Your Life	10/08	11/08
T2 featuring Jodie Aysha (UK)		
Heartbroken		12/07
TACO (H)		
Puttin' On The Ritz	8/83	
TAFFY (US)		
I Love My Radio		2/87
TAG TEAM (US)		
Whoomp! (There It Is)	6/93	
TAKE THAT (UK)		
Babe		12/93
Back For Good	11/95	4/95
Could It Be Magic		12/92
Everything Changes		4/94
Greatest Day		12/08
How Deep Is Your Love		3/96
It Only Takes A Minute		6/92
Love Ain't Here Anymore		7/94
A Million Love Songs (EP)		10/92
Never Forget		8/95
Patience		11/06
Pray		7/93
Rule The World		11/07
Said It All		6/09
Shine		2/07
Sure		10/94
Why Can't I Wake Up With You?		2/93
TAKE THAT featuring Lulu (UK)		
Relight My Fire		10/93
TALK TALK (UK)		
Today		9/82
TALKING HEADS (US)		
Burning Down The House	10/83	
Once In A Lifetime		3/81
Road To Nowhere		11/85
TAMIA (US)		
Can't Go For That	10/00	
Stranger In My House	4/01	
The TAMPERER featuring Maya (Ita/US)		
Feel It		5/98
Hammer To The Heart		2/00
If You Buy This Record…		11/98
TAMS (US)		
Hey Girl Don't Bother Me		8/71
What Kind Of Fool (Do You Think I Am)	2/64	
TARRIERS (US)		
The Banana Boat Song	12/56	
❖ with Vince Martin Cindy, Oh Cindy	10/56	
TASTE OF HONEY (US)		
Boogie Oogie Oogie	8/78	7/78
Sukiyaki		5/81
TAVARES (US)		
Don't Take Away The Music		10/76
Heaven Must Be Missing An Angel	9/76	7/76
It Only Takes A Minute		10/75
More Than A Woman		5/78
Whodunit		5/77
Felice TAYLOR (US)		
I Feel Love Comin' On		11/67
James TAYLOR (US)		
Don't Let Me Be Lonely Tonight	1/73	
Fire And Rain	10/70	
Handy Man	8/77	
How Sweet It Is (To Be Loved By You)	8/75	
You've Got A Friend	7/71	9/71
❖ with Art Garfunkel & Paul Simon		
Wonderful World	3/78	
❖ with Carly Simon		
Mockingbird	3/74	
James TAYLOR & J. D. SOUTHER (US)		
Her Town Too	4/81	
Johnnie TAYLOR (US)		
Disco Lady	3/76	
I Believe In You (You Believe In Me)	8/73	
Who's Making Love	11/68	
R. Dean TAYLOR (C)		
Indiana Wants Me	10/70	5/71
There's A Ghost In My House		6/74
TEARDROP EXPLODES (UK)		
Reward		3/81
TEARS FOR FEARS (UK)		
Change		2/83
Everybody Wants To Rule The World	5/85	4/85
Everybody Wants To Run The World		6/86
Head Over Heels	10/85	7/85
Mad World		10/82
Pale Shelter		5/83
Shout	7/85	1/85
Sowing The Seeds Of Love	10/89	9/89
TECHNOHEAD (UK)		
I Wanna Be A Hippy		2/96
TECHNOTRONIC (B)		
Get Up! (Before The Night Is Over)	3/90	2/90
Megamix		10/90
Move That Body		6/91
Move This	8/92	
Pump Up The Jam	12/89	9/89
Rockin' Over The Beat		7/90
This Beat Is Technotronic		4/90
TEDDY BEARS (US)		
To Know Him, Is To Love Him	10/58	1/59
TEE SET (H)		
Ma Belle Amie	2/70	
TEEN QUEENS (US)		
Eddie My Love	3/56	
TEMPER TRAP (A)		
Sweet Disposition		10/09
TEMPERANCE SEVEN (UK)		
Pasadena		6/61
You're Driving Me Crazy		4/61
Nino TEMPO & April STEVENS (US)		
Deep Purple	10/63	
Whispering	1/64	
TEMPTATIONS (US)		
Ain't Too Proud To Beg	7/66	
All I Need	6/67	
Ball Of Confusion (That's What The World Is Today)	6/70	10/70
Beauty Is Only Skin Deep	9/66	
Cloud Nine	12/68	9/69
Get Ready		4/69
I Can't Get Next To You	9/69	2/70
I Could Never Love Another (After Loving You)	6/68	
(I Know) I'm Losing You	12/66	
I Wish It Would Rain	1/68	
Just My Imagination (Running Away With Me)	3/71	7/71
(Loneliness Made Me Realize) It's You That I Need	11/67	
Masterpiece	4/73	
My Girl	2/65	2/92
Papa Was A Rollin' Stone	11/72	
Psychedelic Shack	2/70	
Run Away Child, Running Wild	3/69	
Take A Look Around		5/72
The Way You Do The Things You Do	4/64	

	US Top 20 Ent	UK Top 20 Ent
Mountain Greenery		5/56
TORNADOS (UK)		
Globetrotter		1/63
The Ice Cream Man		6/63
Robot		4/63
Telstar	12/62	9/62
Mitchell TOROK (US)		
When Mexico Gave Up The Rumba		10/56
TOTAL (US)		
Kissin' You	7/97	
What About Us	11/97	
TOTAL featuring Missy Elliott (US)		
Trippin'	12/98	
TOTAL featuring The Notorious B.I.G. (US)		
Can't You See	6/95	
TOTO (US)		
Africa	12/82	2/83
Hold The Line	12/78	
I Won't Hold You Back	5/83	
I'll Be Over You	11/86	
Rosanna	6/82	
TOTO COELO (UK)		
I Eat Cannibals Pt. 1		8/82
TOTTENHAM HOTSPUR F.A. CUP FINAL SQUAD (UK)		
Ossie's Dream (Spurs Are On Their Way		
To Wembley)		5/81
TOUCH & GO (UK)		
Would You…		11/98
TOURISTS (UK)		
I Only Want To Be With You		12/79
So Good To Be Back Home Again		3/80
Ed TOWNSEND (US)		
For Your Love	5/58	
Pete TOWNSHEND (UK)		
Let My Love Open The Door	8/80	
TOXIC TWO (US)		
Rave Generator		3/92
TOY DOLLS (UK)		
Nellie The Elephant		12/84
TOYA (US)		
I Do!!	12/01	
TOYAH (UK)		
Four From Toyah E.P.		3/81
Four More From Toyah E.P.		12/81
I Want To Be Free		5/81
Thunder In Mountains		10/81
TOYS (US)		
A Lovers Concerto	10/65	11/65
T'PAU (UK)		
China In Your Hand		11/87
Heart And Soul	7/87	9/87
Valentine		2/88
TQ (US)		
Bye Bye Baby		5/99
Daily	08/00	
Westside	10/98	2/99
TRACIE (UK)		
The House That Jack Built		4/83
TRAFFIC (UK)		
Here We Go Round The Mulberry Bush		12/67
Hole In My Shoe		9/67
Paper Sun		6/67
TRAIN (US)		
Drops Of Jupiter (Tell Me)	6/01	8/01
TRAMMPS (US)		
Disco Inferno	5/78	
Hold Back The Night		11/75
TRANSVISION VAMP (UK)		
Baby I Don't Care		4/89
I Want Your Love		7/88
TRANS-X (C)		
Living On Video		7/85
TRAPT (US)		
Headstrong	11/03	
TRASHMEN (US)		
Surfin' Bird	1/64	
TRAVIS (UK)		
Coming Round		6/00
Re-Offender		10/03
Sing		6/01
Turn		11/99
Why Does It Always Rain On Me?		8/99
TRAVIS & BOB (US)		
Tell Him No	4/59	
John TRAVOLTA (US)		
Greased Lightning		12/78

	US Top 20 Ent	UK Top 20 Ent
Let Her In	7/76	
Sandy		10/78
John TRAVOLTA &		
Olivia NEWTON-JOHN (US/UK)		
The Grease Megamix		12/90
Summer Nights	9/78	9/78
You're The One That I Want	4/78	6/78
You're The One That I Want		7/98
TREMELOES (UK) see also Brian Poole		
(Call Me) Number One		11/69
Even The Bad Times Are Good		8/67
Helule Helule		6/68
Here Comes My Baby	6/67	2/67
Me And My Life		10/70
My Little Lady		10/68
Silence Is Golden	8/67	5/67
Suddenly You Love Me		2/68
Jackie TRENT (UK)		
Where Are You Now (My Love)		5/65
Ralph TRESVANT (US)		
Sensitivity	12/90	
Obie TRICE (US)		
Got Some Teeth	11/03	
TRICK DADDY featuring LIL JON & TWISTA (US)		
Let's Go	11/04	
TRICKY DISCO (UK)		
Tricky Disco		8/90
TRILLVILLE featuring CUTTY (US)		
Some Cut	3/05	
TRINA & TAMARA (US)		
What'd You Come Here For	06/99	
TRIO (G)		
Da Da Da		7/82
TRIPLETS (US)		
You Don't Have To Go Home Tonight	5/91	
Kathy TROCCOLI (US)		
Everything Changes	4/92	
TROGGS (UK)		
Any Way That You Want Me		1/67
Give It To Me		3/67
I Can't Control Myself		10/66
Love Is All Around	5/68	11/67
Wild Thing	7/66	5/66
With A Girl Like You		7/66
Doris TROY (US)		
Just One Look	7/63	
TRUE STEPPERS feat. Dane Bowers (UK)		
Buggin		5/00
Out Of Your Mind		8/00
Andrea TRUE CONNECTION (US)		
More, More, More (Pt. 1)	6/76	5/76
TRUTH HURTS featuring RAKIM (US)		
❖ Addictive	6/02	8/02
TUBES (US)		
She's A Beauty	6/83	
TUBEWAY ARMY (UK) See Gary Numan		
Tommy TUCKER (US)		
Hi-Heel Sneakers	3/64	
TUNE WEAVERS (US)		
Happy, Happy Birthday Baby	9/57	
TURIN BRAKES (UK)		
Pain Killer		3/03
Ike & Tina TURNER (US)		
Nutbush City Limits		10/73
Proud Mary	3/71	
River Deep Mountain High		6/66
Sammy TURNER (US)		
Lavender-Blue	7/59	
Spyder TURNER (US)		
Stand By Me	2/67	
Tina TURNER (US) see also Ike & Tina Turner		
The Best	9/89	
Better Be Good To Me	11/84	
Disco Inferno		9/93
Goldeneye		11/95
I Don't Wanna Fight	7/93	5/93
I Don't Wanna Lose You		12/89
Let's Stay Together		12/83
Private Dancer	3/85	
Typical Male	10/86	
We Don't Need Another Hero		
(Thunderdome)	8/85	8/85
What You Get Is What You See	4/87	
What's Love Got To Do With It	7/84	7/84
❖ with Bryan Adams		
It's Only Love	1/86	
❖ with Rod Stewart		
It Takes Two		12/90

	US Top 20 Ent	UK Top 20 Ent
TURTLES (US)		
Elenore	10/68	11/68
Happy Together	3/67	4/67
It Ain't Me Babe	9/65	
She'd Rather Be With Me	6/67	7/67
You Know What I Mean	9/67	
You Showed Me	2/69	
TV CAST (UK)		
Army Game		6/58
Shania TWAIN (C)		
Don't Be Stupid (You Know I Love You)		2/00
Forever And For Always		6/03
From This Moment On	12/98	
I'm Gonna Getcha Good!		11/02
Man! I Feel Like A Woman		10/99
That Don't Impress Me Much		5/99
You're Still The One	4/98	2/98
TWANG (UK)		
Either Way		6/07
TWEENIES (UK)		
I Believe In Christmas		12/01
Number 1		11/00
TWEET (US)		
Oops (Oh My)	3/02	5/02
TWEETS (US)		
The Birdie Song (Birdie Dance)		10/81
TWENTY 4 SEVEN featuring Captain Hollywood (US/G/H)		
I Can't Stand It		10/90
Dwight TWILLEY (US)		
Girls	4/84	
TWINKLE (UK)		
Terry		12/64
TWISTA (US)		
Overnight Celebrity	5/04	
featuring Anthony HAMILTON		
Sunshine		9/04
featuring Kanye WEST & Jamie FOXX		
Slow Jamz	1/04	4/04
featuring Trey SONGZ		
Girl Tonite	11/05	
Conway TWITTY (US)		
Danny Boy	11/59	
It's Only Make Believe	10/58	11/58
Lonely Blue Boy	2/60	
Mona Lisa		8/59
TWO COWBOYS (ITA)		
Everybody Gonfi Gon		7/94
2GETHER (US)		
The Hardest Part Of Breaking Up	9/00	
2 IN A ROOM (US)		
Wiggle It	12/90	2/91
2PAC (US)		
Changes		2/99
Thugz Mansion	1/03	
Until The End Of Time		6/01
(featuring Elton JOHN)		
Ghetto Gospel		7/05
2PAC & KC AND JOJO (US)		
How Do You Want It/California Love	6/96	
2PLAY featuring RAGHAV & JUCXI (UK)		
So Confused		1/04
2PLAY featuring RAGHAV & Naila BOSS (UK)		
It Can't Be Right		5/04
2 UNLIMITED (H)		
Faces		9/93
Get Ready For This		10/91
Let The Beat Control Your Body		2/94
Magic Friend		8/92
No Limit		1/93
The Real Thing		5/94
Tribal Dance		5/93
Twilight Zone		1/92
Workaholic		5/92
2PAC (US)		
Dear Mama/Old School	4/95	
I Get Around	9/93	
Keep Ya Head Up	11/93	
Bonnie TYLER (UK)		
Holding Out For A Hero		9/85
It's A Heartache	6/78	12/77
Lost In France		11/76
Total Eclipse Of The Heart	9/83	3/83
❖ with Shakin' Stevens		
A Rockin' Good Way		1/84
TYMES (US)		
Ms Grace		1/75
So Much In Love	7/63	

	US Top 20 Ent	UK Top 20 Ent
Wonderful! Wonderful!	9/63	
You Little Trustmaker	10/74	
TYPICALLY TROPICAL (UK)		
Barbados		7/75
TYRANNOSAURUS REX (UK) see T-Rex		
TYREE featuring Kool Rock Steady (US)		
Turn Up The Bass		3/89
TYRESE (US)		
How You Gonna Act Like That	3/03	
Sweet Lady	4/99	
UB40 (UK)		
I Can't Help Falling In Love With You	6/93	5/93
Cherry Oh Baby		4/84
Don't Break My Heart		11/85
The Earth Dies Screaming/Dream A Lie		11/80
Here I Am (Come And Take Me)		6/91
Higher Ground		8/93
Homely Girl		12/89
If It Happens Again		10/84
King/Food For Thought		4/80
Kingston Town		4/90
My Way Of Thinking/I Think It's Going To Rain		7/80
One In Ten		9/81
Please Don't Make Me Cry		11/83
Red Red Wine	10/88	9/83
Sing Our Own Song		7/86
The Way You Do The Things You Do	12/90	
❖ with Robert Palmer		
I'll Be Your Baby Tonight		11/90
UB40 & Chrissie HYNDE (UK/US)		
Breakfast In Bed		7/88
I Got You Babe		8/85
UGLY KID JOE (US)		
Cat's In The Cradle	3/93	3/93
Everything About You	5/92	5/92
UK MIXMASTERS (UK)		
The Bare Necessities Megamix		12/91
Tracey ULLMAN (UK)		
Breakaway		4/83
Move Over Darling		12/83
They Don't Know	4/84	10/83
ULTIMATE KAOS (UK)		
Some Girls		11/94
ULTRABEAT (UK)		
Feelin' Fine		1/04
Pretty Green Eyes		8/03
ULTRAVOX (UK)		
All Stood Still		6/81
Dancing With Tears In My Eyes		6/84
Hymn		12/82
Love's Great Adventure		11/84
The Thin Wall		9/81
Vienna		2/81
Piero UMILIANI (ITA)		
Mah Na Mah Na		5/77
UNCLE KRACKER (US)		
Follow Me	4/01	9/01
❖ featuring Dobie GRAY		
Drift Away	6/03	
UNCLE SAM (US)		
I Don't Ever Want To See You Again	1/98	
UNDERCOVER (UK)		
Baker Street		8/92
Never Let Her Slip Away		11/92
UNDERTONES (UK)		
My Perfect Cousin		5/80
Carrie UNDERWOOD (US)		
Before He Cheats	5/07	
Cowboy Casanova	10/09	
I'll Stand By You	5/07	
Inside Your Heaven	5/07	
Carrie UNDERWOOD featuring Randy Travis (US)		
I Told You So	4/09	
UNDISPUTED TRUTH (US)		
Smiling Faces Sometime	8/71	
UNION GAP (US) see Gary Puckett		
UNIT 4 PLUS 2 (UK)		
Concrete And Clay		3/65
You've Never Been In Love Like This Before		6/65
UNITING NATIONS (UK)		
Out Of Touch		12/04
UNK (US)		
Walk It Out	12/06	
UPSETTERS (J)		

	US Top 20 Ent	UK Top 20 Ent
The Return Of Django		11/69
UPSIDE DOWN (UK)		
Change Your Mind		2/96
URBAN HYPE (UK)		
A Trip To Trumpton		7/92
URBAN COOKIE COLLECTIVE (UK)		
Feels Like Heaven		11/93
The Key The Secret		8/93
Midge URE (UK)		
If I Was		9/85
No Regrets		7/82
USA FOR AFRICA (US)		
We Are The World	4/85	4/85
USHER (US)		
Burn	4/04	7/04
Caught Up	2/05	3/05
Confessions Part II	5/04	11/04
My Way	6/98	
Nice & Slow	1/98	
Pop Ya Collar		2/01
U Don't Have To Call	3/02	
U Got It Bad	11/01	10/01
U Remind Me	7/01	7/01
You Make Me Wanna…	9/97	1/98
USHER & ALICIA KEYS		
My Boo	9/04	11/04
USHER featuring LIL' JON & LUDACRIS		
Yeah!	1/04	3/04
USHER featuring YOUNG JEEZY (US)		
Love In This Club	3/08	4/08
US3 (UK)		
Cantaloop (Flip Fantasia)	2/94	
USURA (ITA)		
Open Your Mind		1/93
UTAH SAINTS (UK)		
Believe In Me		5/93
Something Good	3/08	6/92
What Can You Do For Me		9/91
U2 (I)		
All Because Of You		10/05
All I Want Is You		7/89
Angel Of Harlem	2/89	12/88
Beautiful Day		10/00
City Of Blinding Lights		6/05
Desire	11/88	10/88
Discotheque		2/97
Electrical Storm		11/02
Elevation		7/01
Even Better Than The Real Thing		6/92
Get On Your Boots		2/09
The Fly		11/91
Hold Me, Thrill Me, Kiss Me, Kill Me		6/95
I Still Haven't Found What I'm Looking For	7/87	6/87
Mysterious Ways		1/92
New Year's Day		2/83
One	5/92	
Pride (In The Name Of Love)		9/84
Sometimes You Can't Make It On Your Own		2/05
Stay (Faraway, So Close!)		12/93
Stuck In A Moment You		2/01
The Unforgettable Fire		5/85
Vertigo		11/04
Walk On		12/01
Where The Streets Have No Name	11/87	9/87
With Or Without You	4/87	3/87
Window In The Skies		1/07
U2 and GREEN DAY		
The Saints Are Coming		11/06
U2 with B.B. KING (I/US)		
When Love Comes To Town		4/89
The Sweetest Thing		11/98
V (UK)		
Blood Sweat And Tears		6/04
Hip To Hip/Can You Feel It?		8/04
Holly VALANCE (AUS)		
Down Boy		10/02
Kiss Kiss		5/02
State Of Mind		11/03
Ricky VALANCE (UK)		
Tell Laura I Love Her		9/60
Jerry VALE (US)		
You Don't Know Me	9/56	
Ritchie VALENS (US)		
Donna	1/59	
Caterina VALENTE (F)		
The Breeze And I	4/55	8/55
Dickie VALENTINE (UK)		
A Blossom Fell		2/55

	US Top 20 Ent	UK Top 20 Ent
Christmas Alphabet		12/55
Christmas Island		12/56
Finger Of Suspicion		12/54
I Wonder		6/55
Mr. Sandman		1/55
One More Sunrise (Morgen)		11/59
Bobby VALENTINO (US)		
Slow Down	5/05	7/05
Joe VALINO (US)		
Garden Of Eden	11/56	
Frankie VALLI (US) see also Four Seasons		
Can't Take My Eyes Off You	6/67	
Grease	7/78	9/78
My Eyes Adored You	2/75	3/75
Our Day Will Come	12/75	
Swearin' To God	7/75	
You're Ready Now		1/71
June VALLI (US)		
I Understand	7/54	
Ian VAN DAHL (B)		
Castles In The Sky		7/01
Will I		12/01
Leroy VAN DYKE (US)		
Walk On By	12/61	1/62
VAN HALEN (US/H)		
Dance The Night Away		7/79
Finish What Ya Started		12/88
I'll Wait		6/84
Jump	2/84	3/84
(Oh) Pretty Woman		4/82
Panama		8/84
When It's Love		8/88
Why Can't This Be Love	4/86	5/86
Armand VAN HELDEN/Duane Harden (US)		
You Don't Know Me		2/99
Luther VANDROSS (US)		
Don't Want To Be A Fool	10/91	
Here And Now	4/90	
Never Too Much		11/89
Power Of Love-Love Power	6/91	
Stop To Love	2/87	
Luther VANDROSS & Mariah CAREY (US)		
Endless Love	9/94	9/94
Luther VANDROSS & Janet JACKSON (US)		
The Best Things In Life Are Free	6/92	8/92
★ The Best Things In Life Are Free		12/95
VANGELIS (GRE) see also Jon & Vangelis		
Chariots Of Fire	3/82	6/81
VANILLA FUDGE (US)		
(You Keep Me) Hangin' On		8/68
VANILLA ICE (US)		
Ice Ice Baby	10/90	11/90
Play That Funky Music	1/91	2/91
VANITY FARE (UK)		
Early In The Morning	1/70	8/69
Hitchin' A Ride	6/70	
Gino VANNELLI (US)		
I Just Wanna Stop	11/78	
Living Inside Myself	4/81	
Randy VANWARMER (US)		
Just When I Needed You Most	5/79	9/79
VAPORS (UK)		
Turning Japanese		3/80
VARIOUS ARTISTS (UK)		
All Star Hit Parade		7/56
VARIOUS ARTISTS (UK)		
The BRITs 1990		3/90
VARIOUS ARTISTS (UK)		
Thank Abba For The Music		4/99
Frankie VAUGHAN (UK)		
Can't Get Along Without You/We're Not Alone		3/58
Garden Of Eden		1/57
Green Door		11/56
Happy Days And Lonely Nights		2/55
The Heart Of A Man		8/59
Heartless		5/54
Kewpie Doll		5/58
Kisses Sweeter Than Wine		1/58
Loop De Loop		2/63
Man On Fire/Wanderin' Eyes		10/57
There Must Be A Way		9/67
Tower Of Strength		11/61
Frankie VAUGHAN & THE KAYE SISTERS (UK)		
Come Softly To Me		5/59
Gotta Have Something In The Bank Frank		11/57
Malcolm VAUGHAN (UK)		
Chapel Of The Roses		5/57

	US Top 20 Ent	UK Top 20 Ent
Hopeless	8/63	
I Like Your Kind Of Love	6/57	7/57
It's So Easy		9/70
Lonely Street	10/59	
Solitaire		1/74
The Village Of St. Bernadette	1/60	
(Where Do I Begin) Love Story	3/71	4/71
Billy WILLIAMS (US)		
I'm Gonna Sit Right Down And Write Myself A Letter	7/57	
Danny WILLIAMS (UK)		
Moon River		11/61
White On White	5/64	
Wonderful World Of The Young		4/62
Deniece WILLIAMS (US)		
Free		4/77
It's Gonna Take A Miracle	6/82	
Let's Hear It For The Boy	4/84	5/84
That's What Friends Are For		8/77
❖ with Johnny Mathis		
Too Much, Too Little, Too Late	5/78	4/78
John WILLIAMS (US)		
Theme From 'Close Encounters Of The Third Kind'	2/78	
John WILLIAMS & THE LSO (US/UK)		
Star Wars (Main Title)	9/77	
Larry WILLIAMS (US)		
Bony Moronie/You Bug Me, Baby	12/57	2/58
Short Fat Fannie	7/57	
Mason WILLIAMS (US)		
Classical Gas	7/68	9/68
Maurice WILLIAMS & THE ZODIACS (US)		
Stay	11/60	1/61
Robbie WILLIAMS (UK)		
Bodies		10/09
Come Undone		4/03
Eternity/The Road To Mandalay		7/01
Feel		12/02
Kids		10/00
Let Love Be Your Energy		4/01
Lovelight		11/06
Millennium		9/98
Misunderstood		12/04
No Regrets		12/98
Radio		10/04
Rock DJ		8/00
Rudebox		9/06
It's Only Us/She's The One		11/99
Something Beautiful		8/03
Strong		3/99
Supreme		12/00
Tripping		10/05
You Know Me		12/09
Robbie WILLIAMS & Nicole KIDMAN (UK)		
❖ Somethin' Stupid		12/01
Roger WILLIAMS (US)		
Autumn Leaves	9/55	
Born Free	11/66	
Near You	9/58	
Vanessa WILLIAMS (US)		
Colours Of The Wind	7/95	
Dreamin'	3/89	
Save The Best For Last	2/92	4/92
Vanessa WILLIAMS & Brian McKNIGHT (US)		
Love Is	4/93	
Vesta WILLIAMS (US)		
Once Bitten Twice Shy		2/87
Bruce WILLIS (US)		
Respect Yourself	2/87	3/87
Under The Boardwalk		6/87
Chuck WILLIS (US)		
C.C. Rider	7/57	
What Am I Living For	6/58	
Matt WILLIS (UK)		
Up All Night		
Viola WILLS (US)		
Gonna Get Along Without You Now		11/79
WILSON PHILLIPS (US)		
The Dream Is Still Alive	7/91	
Hold On	5/90	6/90
Impulsive	12/90	
Release Me	8/90	
You're In Love	3/91	
AL WILSON (US)		
Show And Tell	12/73	
Ann WILSON (US)		
❖ with Mike Reno		
Almost Paradise	6/84	
Ann WILSON & Robin ZANDER (US)		
Surrender To Me	2/89	
J. Frank WILSON & THE CAVALIERS (US)		
Last Kiss	10/64	
Jackie WILSON (US)		
Alone At Last	11/60	
Baby Workout	3/63	
Higher And Higher	9/67	6/69
★ Higher And Higher		7/87
I Get The Sweetest Feeling		9/72
★ I Get The Sweetest Feeling		3/87
Lonely Teardrops	1/59	
My Empty Arms	2/61	
Night	4/60	
Reet Petite		12/57
★ Reet Petite		12/86
Whispers (Gettin' Louder)	12/66	
(You Were Made For) All My Love	8/60	
Mari WILSON (UK)		
Just What I Always Wanted		10/82
Meri WILSON (US)		
Telephone Man	9/77	
Nancy WILSON (US)		
(You Don't Know) How Glad I Am	8/64	
Mario WINANS featuring ENYA & P. DIDDY (US)		
I Don't Wanna Know	3/04	6/04
Kai WINDING (US)		
More	8/63	
Amy WINEHOUSE (UK)		
Rehab	6/07	11/06
WINGER (US)		
Miles Away	1/91	
Pete WINGFIELD (UK)		
Eighteen With A Bullet		7/75
WINGS (UK) see Paul McCartney		
Josh WINK (US)		
Higher State Of Consciousness		10/95
Kate WINSLET (UK)		
What If		12/01
WINSTONS (US)		
Color Him Father	7/69	
Edgar WINTER GROUP (US)		
Frankenstein	5/73	
Free Ride	10/73	
Hugo WINTERHALTER (US)		
The Little Shoemaker	7/54	
Hugo WINTERHALTER & Eddie HEYWOOD (US)		
Canadian Sunset	8/56	
Ruby WINTERS (US)		
Come To Me		6/78
I Will		12/77
Steve WINWOOD (UK)		
Back In The High Life Again	8/87	
Don't You Know What The Night Can Do	10/88	
The Finer Things	4/87	
Higher Love	8/86	7/86
Holding On	1/89	
Roll With It	7/88	
Valerie	12/87	
While You See A Chance	3/81	
Norman WISDOM (UK)		
Don't Laugh At Me		2/54
Wisdom Of A Fool		3/57
WISEGUYS (UK)		
Ooh La La		6/99
Bill WITHERS (US)		
Ain't No Sunshine	9/71	
Lean On Me	6/72	
Lovely Day		1/78
★ Lovely Day		9/88
Use Me	9/72	
WIZZARD (UK)		
Angel Fingers		9/73
Are You Ready To Rock		1/75
Ball Park Incident		1/73
I Wish It Could Be Christmas Everyday		12/73
Rock 'n' Roll Winter		5/74
See My Baby Jive		5/73
Peter WOLF (US)		
Lights Out	9/84	
WOLFMAN featuring Peter DOHERTY (UK)		
For Lovers		4/04
WOMACK & WOMACK (US)		
Teardrops		9/88
Bobby WOMACK (US)		
Lookin' For A Love	4/74	
Lee Ann WOMACK (US)		
I Hope You Dance	01/01	
WOMBLES (UK)		
Banana Rock		7/74
Remember You're A Womble		4/74
The Wombling Song		2/74
Wombling Merry Christmas		12/74
WONDER STUFF (UK)		
The Size Of A Cow		4/91
Welcome To The Cheap Seats (EP)		2/92
❖ with Vic Reeves		
Dizzy		10/91
Stevie WONDER (US)		
Blowin' In The Wind	8/66	
Boogie On Reggae Woman	12/74	2/75
Do I Do	7/82	6/82
Fingertips (Pt. 2)	7/63	
For Once In My Life	11/68	1/69
Go Home	1/86	
Happy Birthday		8/81
He's Misstra Know It All		5/74
Heaven Help Us All	11/70	
Higher Ground	9/73	
I Ain't Gonna Stand For It	2/81	1/81
I Just Called To Say I Love You	9/84	8/84
I Was Made To Love Her	7/67	8/67
I Wish	12/76	1/77
I'm Wondering	11/67	
If You Really Love Me	10/71	
Lately		3/81
Living For The City	12/73	
Master Blaster (Jammin')	11/80	9/80
My Cherie Amour	7/69	8/69
Never Had A Dream Come True	4/70	
Part Time Lover	10/85	9/85
A Place In The Sun	12/66	
Send One Your Love	11/79	
Shoo-Be-Doo-Be-Doo-Da-Day	5/68	
Signed Sealed Delivered I'm Yours	7/70	8/70
Sir Duke	4/77	4/77
Superstition	1/73	2/73
That Girl	2/82	
Uptight (Everything's Alright)	2/66	
Yester-Me, Yester-You, Yesterday	11/69	11/69
You Are The Sunshine Of My Life	4/73	6/73
You Haven't Done Nothin	9/74	
❖ with Julio Iglesias		
My Love		8/88
❖ with Paul McCartney		
Ebony And Ivory	4/82	4/82
Wayne WONDER (J)		
No Letting Go	5/03	6/03
WONDER WHO? (aka Four Seasons) (US)		
Don't Think Twice	12/65	
Brenton WOOD (US)		
Gimme Little Sign	10/67	2/68
Roy WOOD (UK)		
Forever		12/73
Going Down The Road		7/74
Oh What A Shame		6/75
Sheb WOOLEY (US)		
The Purple People Eater	6/58	7/58
WRECKX-N-EFFECT (US)		
Rump Shaker	11/92	
Betty WRIGHT (US)		
Clean Up Woman	1/72	
Charles WRIGHT & THE WATTS 103RD STREET RHYTHM BAND (US)		
Do Your Thing	4/69	
Express Yourself	10/70	
Gary WRIGHT (UK)		
Dream Weaver	2/76	
Love Is Alive	6/76	
Really Wanna Know You	9/81	
Ruby WRIGHT (US)		
Bimbo		4/54
WURZELS (UK)		
Combine Harvester (Brand New Key)		5/76
I Am A Cider Drinker (Paloma Blanca)		9/76
WWF SUPERSTARS (US)		
Slam Jam		12/92
Wrestlemania		4/93
Tammy WYNETTE (US/UK)		
D.I.V.O.R.C.E.		7/75
❖ with KLF		
Justified And Ancient	3/92	12/91
Stand By Your Man		5/75

	US Top 20 Ent	UK Top 20 Ent

Mark WYNTER (UK)
Go Away Little Girl — 1/63
It's Almost Tomorrow — 11/63
Venus In Blue Jeans — 10/62
X-ECUTIONERS FEATURING MIKE SHINODA & MR. HAHN OF LINKIN PARK (US)
❖ It's Goin' Down — 4/02
X FACTOR FINALISTS (UK)
Hero — 11/08
You Are Not Alone — 11/09
X-PRESS 2 FEATURING DAVID BYRNE (UK)
❖ Lazy — 4/02
XPANSIONS (UK)
Move Your Body (Elevation) — 3/91
XSCAPE (US)
The Arms Of The One Who Loves You — 5/98
Just Kickin' It — 10/93
My Little Secret — 10/98
Understanding — 1/94
Who Can I Run To — 11/95
XTC (UK)
Senses Working Overtime — 2/82
XTM & DJ Chucky Presents Annia (Spa/Jap)
❖ Fly On The Wings Of Love — 6/03

"Weird Al" YANKOVIC (US)
Eat It — 4/84
White & Nerdy — 10/06
Elliott YAMIN (US)
Wait For You — 8/07
YARBROUGH & PEOPLES (US)
Don't Stop The Music — 1/81
Glenn YARBROUGH (US)
Baby The Rain Must Fall — 5/65
YARDBIRDS (UK)
Evil Hearted You/Still I'm Sad — 10/65
For Your Love — 6/65 — 4/65
Heart Full Of Soul — 9/65 — 7/65
Over Under Sideways Down — 8/66 — 6/66
Shapes Of Things — 5/66 — 3/66
YAZOO (UK)
Don't Go — 7/82
Nobody's Diary — 5/83
Only You — 5/82
The Other Side Of Love — 12/82
YAZZ (UK)
Fine Time — 2/89
Stand Up For Your Love Rights — 11/88
Where Has All The Love Gone — 5/89
YAZZ & THE PLASTIC POPULATION (UK)
The Only Way Is Up — 8/88
❖ with Coldcut
Doctorin' The House — 3/88
YELL! (UK)
Instant Replay — 2/90
YELLO (SWI)
The Race — 9/88
YELLOW DOG (UK)
Just One More Night — 2/78
YES (UK/SA)
Owner Of A Lonely Heart — 12/83
Roundabout — 4/72
Wondrous Stories — 9/77
YING YANG TWINS (US)
Wait (The Whisper Song) — 6/05
YING YANG TWINS featuring LIL JON & EAST SIDE BOYZ
Salt Shaker — 2/04
YOMANDA (UK)
Synth & Strings — 7/99
YORK (G)
On The Beach — 6/00
YOUNG DRO featuring T.I. (US)
Shoulder Lean — 8/06
YOUNG GUNZ (US)
Can't Stop, Won't Stop — 10/03
YOUNG JEEZY featuring AKON (US)
Soul Suvivor — 10/05
YOUNG JEEZY featuring Kanye WEST (US)
Put On — 9/08
YOUNG M.C. (US)
Bust A Move — 10/89
YOUNG MONEY (US)
Every Girl — 7/09
YOUNG ONES (UK) see Cliff Richard & The Young Ones
Faron YOUNG (US)
Hello Walls — 6/61

It's Four In The Morning — 8/72
Jimmy YOUNG (UK)
Chain Gang — 3/56
Little Things Mean A Lot — 9/54
The Man From Laramie — 9/55
More — 10/56
Someone On Your Mind — 1/56
Unchained Melody — 5/55
John Paul YOUNG (AUS)
Love Is In The Air — 9/78 — 5/78
Karen YOUNG (US)
Nobody's Child — 10/69
Kathy YOUNG with The Innocents (US)
A Thousand Stars — 11/60
Neil YOUNG (C)
Heart Of Gold — 3/72 — 4/72
Paul YOUNG (UK)
Come Back And Stay — 9/83
Everything Must Change — 12/84
Everytime You Go Away — 7/85 — 3/85
I'm Gonna Tear Your Playhouse Down — 10/85 — 10/84
Love Of The Common People — 11/83
Oh Girl — 9/90
Wherever I Lay My Hat (That's My Home) — 7/83
❖ with Zucchero
Senza Una Donna (Without A Woman) — 5/91
Victor YOUNG (US)
The High And The Mighty — 8/54
Will YOUNG (UK)
All Time Love — 1/06
Changes — 9/08
Don't Let Me Down/You And I — 11/02
Evergreen/Anything Is Possible — 3/02
Friday's Child — 7/04
Leave Right Now — 12/03
Light My Fire — 6/02
Switch It On — 11/05
Who Am I — 5/06
Your Game — 3/04
Will YOUNG & Gareth GATES (UK)
❖ The Long And Winding Road — 10/02
YOUNG-HOLT UNLIMITED (US)
Soulful Strut — 1/69
Sydney YOUNGBLOOD (US)
If Only I Could — 9/89
YOUNGBLOODS (US)
Get Together — 8/69
YOUNGBLOODZ featuring LIL JON (US)
Damn! — 9/03
YOUNG RASCALS (US) see Rascals
YOUNGSTOWN (US)
I'll Be Your Everything — 08/99
Timi YURO (US)
Hurt — 8/61
Helmut ZACHARIAS ORCHESTRA (G)
Tokyo Melody — 11/64
John ZACHERLE (US)
Dinner With Drac (Part 1) — 3/58
ZAGER & EVANS (US)
In The Year 2525 (Exordium and Terminus) — 7/69 — 8/69
Michael ZAGER Band (US)
Let's All Chant — 5/78
Gheorghe ZAMFIR (R)
(Light Of Experience) Doina De Jale — 9/76
Lena ZAVARONI (UK)
Ma He's Making Eyes At Me — 3/74
ZHANE (US)
Hey Mr. D.J. — 10/93
ZOE (UK)
Sunshine On A Rainy Day
ZOMBIE NATION (G)
Kernkraft 400 — 09/00
ZOMBIES (UK)
She's Not There — 11/64 — 9/64
Tell Her No — 2/65
Time Of The Season — 3/69
ZUCCHERO/Paul YOUNG (Ita/UK)
Senza Una Donna (Without A Woman) — 5/91
ZUTONS (UK)
Valerie — 7/06
Why Won't You Give Me Your Love? — 4/06
ZZ TOP (US)
Gimme All Your Lovin' — 11/84
Legs — 7/84
Sleeping Bag — 11/85
Viva Las Vegas — 4/92

Title	Artist
A&E	Goldfrapp
Aaron's Party (Come Get It)	Aaron Carter
Abacab	Genesis
Abba-Esque (EP)	Erasure
ABC	Jackson Five
About A Girl	Sugababes
About You Now	Sugababes
Abracadabra	Steve Miller Band
Abraham, Martin And John	Dion
Abraham Martin & John	Marvin Gaye
Absolute Beginners	David Bowie
Absolute Beginners	Jam
Absolutely Fabulous	Absolutely Fabulous
Acceptable In The 80s	Calvin Harris
Achilles Heel	Toploader
Achy Breaky Heart	Billy Ray Cyrus
Action	Freddy Cannon
Activ 8 (Come With Me)	Altern 8
Adalante	Sash!
Addams Groove	Hammer
Addicted To Bass	Puretone
Addicted To Love	Robert Palmer
Addictive	Truth Hurts featuring Rakim
Adia	Sarah McLachlan
Admiral Halsey	Paul & Linda McCartney
Adoration Waltz	David Whitfield
Adult Education	Daryl Hall & John Oates
Affair Of The Night	Rick Springfield
Affirmation	Savage
Africa	Toto
African Waltz	Johnny Dankworth
Afrika Shox	Leftfield/Bambaataa
After All	Cher & Peter Cetera
After All	Frank And Walters
After The Love Has Gone	Earth, Wind & Fire
After The Love Has Gone	Steps
After The Lovin'	Engelbert Humperdinck
After The Rain	Nelson
After You're Gone (I'll Still Be Loving You)	One True Voice
Afternoon Delight	Starland Vocal Band
Agadoo	Black Lace
Again	Janet Jackson
Again	Lenny Kravitz
Again And Again	Status Quo
Against All Odds (Take A Look At Me Now)	Phil Collins
Against All Odds	Mariah Carey & Westlife
Against All Odds	Steve Brookstein
Against The Wind	Bob Seger & The Silver Bullet Band
The Age Of The Understatement	The Last Shadow Puppets
Ahab, The Arab	Ray Stevens
Ain't Gonna Bump No More (With No Big Fat Woman)	Joe Tex
Ain't Gonna Kiss Ya (E.P.)	Searchers
Ain't Got No - I Got Life	Nina Simone
Ain't It Fun	Guns N' Roses
Ain't It Funny	Jennifer Lopez
Ain't It Funny (Remix)	Jennifer Lopez featuring Ja Rule & Caddillac Tah
Ain't Misbehavin'	Tommy Bruce & The Bruisers
Ain't No Doubt	Jimmy Nail
Ain't No Love (Ain't No Use)	Sub Sub featuring Melanie Williams
Ain't No Mountain High Enough	Diana Ross
Ain't No Other Man	Christina Aguilera
Ain't No Pleasing You	Chas & Dave
Ain't No Stoppin'	Enigma
Ain't No Stoppin' Us Now	McFadden & Whitehead
Ain't No Stoppin Us	DJ Luck & MC Neat Feat. JJ
Ain't No Sunshine	Michael Jackson
Ain't No Sunshine	Bill Withers
Ain't No Way To Treat A Lady	Helen Reddy
Ain't No Woman (Like The One I've Got)	Four Tops
Ain't Nobody	Rufus & Chaka Khan
Ain't Nothin' But A Houseparty	Showstoppers
Ain't Nothing Goin' On But The Rent	Gwen Guthrie
Ain't Nothing Like The Real Thing	Marvin Gaye & Tammi Terrell
Ain't That A Shame	Pat Boone
Ain't That Funny	Jimmy Justice
Ain't That Peculiar	Marvin Gaye
Ain't Too Proud 2 Beg	TLC
Ain't Too Proud To Beg	Temptations
The Air That I Breathe	Hollies
The Air That I Breathe	Simply Red
Air Force One	Nelly Feat St. Lunatics
Air Hostess	Busted
Airport	Motors
Al Di La	Emilio Pericoli
Albatross	Fleetwood Mac
Alfie	Cilla Black
Alice I Want You Just For Me	Full Force
Alive	S Club
Alive Again	Chicago
Alive & Kicking	Simple Minds
All About Us	t.A.T.u.
All About You	McFly
All Alone Am I	Brenda Lee
All Along The Watchtower	Jimi Hendrix Experience
All American Boy	Bill Parsons
All Around My Hat	Steeleye Span
All Around The World	Lisa Stansfield
All Because Of You	Geordie
All Because Of You	U2
All By Myself	Eric Carmen

Title	Artist
All By Myself	Celine Dion
All Cried Out	Allure/112
All Cried Out	Lisa Lisa & Cult Jam With Full Force
All Cried Out	Alison Moyet
All Day And All Of The Night	Kinks
All Day And All Of The Night	Stranglers
All 4 Love	Color Me Badd
All Falls Down	Kanye West featuring Syleena Johnson
All For Love	Bryan Adams/Rod Stewart/Sting
All For You	Janet
All For You	Sister Hazel
All Good Things (Come To An End)	Nelly Furtado
All I Ask Of You	Cliff Richard
All I Ever Need Is You	Sonny & Cher
All I Ever Wanted	Basshunter
All I Have	Jennifer Lopez featuring LL Cool J
All I Have To Do Is Dream	Everly Brothers
All I Have To Do Is Dream	Bobbie Gentry & Glen Campbell
All I Have To Give	Backstreet Boys
All I Know	Art Garfunkel
All I Need	Temptations
All I Need	Jack Wagner
All I Need Is A Miracle	Mike + The Mechanics
All I Really Want To Do	Byrds
All I Really Want To Do	Cher
All I See Is You	Dusty Springfield
All I Wanna Do	Sheryl Crow
All I Wanna Do Is Make Love To You	Heart
All I Want	Mis-Teeq
All I Want	Toad The Wet Sprocket
All I Want For Christmas Is A Beatle	Dora Bryan
All I Want For Christmas Is You	Mariah Carey
All I Want Is You	Roxy Music
All I Want Is You	U2
All In My Head	Kosheen
All Kinds Of Everything	Dana
All My Life	Foo Fighters
All My Life	K-Ci & JoJo
All My Life	Linda Ronstadt (featuring Aaron Neville)
All My Love	Cliff Richard
All Night Long	Faith Evans/Puff Daddy
All Night Long	Rainbow
All Night Long (All Night)	Lionel Richie
(All Of A Sudden) My Heart Sings	Paul Anka
All Of Me Loves All Of You	Bay City Rollers
All Of My Heart	ABC
All Of My Life	Diana Ross
All Or Nothing	Milli Vanilli
All Or Nothing	O-Town
All Or Nothing	Small Faces
All Out Of Love	Air Supply
All Over	Lisa Maffia
All Over Again	Ronan Keating and Kate Rusby
All Over The World	Electric Light Orchestra
All Right	Christopher Cross
All Right Now	Free
All Rise	Blue
All She Wants Is	Duran Duran
All She Wants To Do Is Dance	Don Henley
All Shook Up	Elvis Presley
All Star Hit Parade	Various Artists
All Stood Still	Ultravox
All Summer Long	Kid Rock
All That I Need	Boyzone
All That She Wants	Ace Of Base
All The Love In The World	Dionne Warwick
All The Man That I Need	Whitney Houston
All The Small Things	Blink-182
All The Things She Said	Simple Minds
All The Things She Said	t.A.T.U.
All The Things (Your Man Won't Do)	Joe
All The Way	Craig David
All The Way	Frank Sinatra
All The Way From Memphis	Mott The Hoople
All The Young Dudes	Mott The Hoople
All This Time	Michelle
All This Time	Sting
All This Time	Tiffany
All Those Years Ago	George Harrison
All Through The Night	Cyndi Lauper
All Time Love	Will Young
All Together Now	Farm
All Together Now 2004	Farm featuring SFX Boys' Choir, Liverpool
All You Need Is Love	Beatles
All You Wanted	Michelle Branch
Allegheny Moon	Patti Page
Allentown	Billy Joel
Alley Cat	Bent Fabric
Alley-Oop	Dante & The Evergreens
Alley-Oop	Hollywood Argyles
Ally's Tartan Army	Andy Cameron
Almaz	Randy Crawford
Almost Here	Brian McFadden & Delta Goodrem
Almost Paradise...Love Theme From Footloose	Mike Reno & Ann Wilson
Almost There	Andy Williams
Almost Unreal	Roxette
Alone	Petula Clark
Alone	Heart
Alone Again (Naturally)	Gilbert O'Sullivan
Alone At Last	Jackie Wilson
Alone Without You	King

Title	Artist
Back And Forth	Cameo
Back For Good	Take That
Back Here	BBMak
Back Home	England World Cup Squad
Back Home Again	John Denver
Back In Love Again	L.T.D.
Back In My Arms Again	Supremes
Back In My Life	Alice Deejay
Back In The High Life Again	Steve Winwood
Back In The U.S.A.	Linda Ronstadt
Back Off Boogaloo	Ringo Starr
Back On The Chain Gang	Pretenders
Back Stabbers	O'Jays
Back Street Luv	Curved Air
Back To Life	Soul II Soul (featuring Caron Wheeler)
Back To The Sixties	Tight Fit
Back Together Again	Roberta Flack & Donny Hathaway
Backfield In Motion	Mel & Tim
Backstage	Gene Pitney
Bad	Michael Jackson
Bad	Nazareth
Bad, Bad Leroy Brown	Jim Croce
Bad Blood	Neil Sedaka
Bad Boy	Miami Sound Machine
Bad Boy	Marty Wilde
Bad Boys	Alexandra Burke Featuring Flo Rida
Bad Boys	Inner Circle
Bad Boys	Wham!
Bad Case Of Loving You (Doctor, Doctor)	Robert Palmer
Bad Day	Daniel Powter
Bad Day	Rem
Bad Girl	Madonna
Bad Girls	Donna Summer
Bad Intentions	Dr. Dre featuring Knoc-Turn'al
Bad Luck (Pt. 1)	Harold Melvin & The Blue Notes
Bad Medicine	Bon Jovi
Bad Moon Rising	Creedence Clearwater Revival
Bad Old Days	Coco
Bad Romance	Lady Gaga
Bad Time	Grand Funk
Bad To Me	Billy J. Kramer & The Dakotas
The Bad Touch	Bloodhound Gang
Baggy Trousers	Madness
Bag It Up	Geri Haliwell
Bailamos	Enrique Iglesias
Baggy Trousers	Madness
Baker Street	Gerry Rafferty
Baker Street	Undercover
Ball Of Confusion (That's What The World Is Today)	Temptations
Ball Park Incident	Wizzard
The Ballad Of Bonnie And Clyde	Georgie Fame
Ballad Of Davy Crockett	Tennessee Ernie Ford
Ballad Of Davy Crockett	Fess Parker
The Ballad Of Davy Crockett	Bill Hayes
Ballad Of John And Yoko	Beatles
Ballad Of Paladin	Duane Eddy
The Ballad Of The Green Berets	SSgt. Barry Sadler
Ballerina Girl	Lionel Richie
Ballroom Blitz	Sweet
Banana Boat Song	Shirley Bassey
Banana Boat (Day-O)	Harry Belafonte
The Banana Boat Song	Tarriers
Banana Republic	Boomtown Rats
Banana Rock	Wombles
Banana Splits (Tra La La Song)	Dickies
Band Of Gold	Don Cherry
Band Of Gold	Freda Payne
Band On The Run	Paul McCartney
Bang A Gong (Get It On)	T. Rex
Bang Bang	B.A. Robertson
Bang Bang (My Baby Shot Me Down)	Cher
Bang Bang You're Dead	Dirty Pretty Things
(Bang Zoom) Let's Go Go	Real Roxanne With Hitman Howie
Bangin' Man	Slade
Bangla Desh	George Harrison
Bank Robber	Clash
Banks Of The Ohio	Olivia Newton-John
Banner Man	Blue Mink
Barbados	Typically Tropical
Barbara Ann	Beach Boys
Barbara Ann	Regents
Barber's Adagio For Strings	William Orbit
Barbie Girl	Aqua
Barcelona	Monserrat Caballé
Barcelona	Freddie Mercury & Monserrat Caballé
Barely Breathing	Duncan Sheik
The Bare Necessities Megamix	UK Mixmasters
Barefootin'	Robert Parker
Barracuda	Heart
Barry Islands In The Stream	Vanessa Jenkins & Bryn West Feat.Tom Jones & Robin Gibb
Bartender	T-Pain Featuring Akon
The Bartender And The Thief	Stereophonics
Basket Case	Green Day
Basketball Jones Feat Tyrone Shoelaces	Cheech & Chong
Batdance	Prince
Battle Hymn Of The Republic	Mormon Tabernacle Choir
The Battle Of Kookamonga	Homer & Jethro
Battle Of New Orleans	Lonnie Donegan
Battle Of New Orleans	Johnny Horton
Battlefield	Jordin Sparks
A Bay Bay	Hurricane Chris

Title	Artist
(Bazoom) I Need Your Lovin'	Cheers
Be Aggressive	Faith No More
Be Cool	Paffendorf
Be Faithful	Fatman Scoop featuring The Crooklyn Clan
Be Good To Yourself	Journey
Be Mine	Lance Fortune
Be Mine	Robyn
Be My Baby	Vanessa Paradis
Be My Baby	Ronettes
Be My Girl	Jim Dale
Be My Guest	Fats Domino
Be My Lover	La Bouche
Be Near Me	ABC
Be Quick Or Be Dead	Iron Maiden
Be Still My Beating Heart	Sting
Be Thankful For What You Got	William DeVaughn
Be True To Your School	Beach Boys
Be The First To Believe	A1
Be With You	Atomic Kitten
Be With You	Enrique Iglesias
Be Without You	Mary J. Blige
Beat Again	JLS
Be-Bop Baby	Ricky Nelson
Be-Bop-A-Lula	Gene Vincent & His Blue Caps
Beach Baby	First Class
Beach Boy Gold	Gidea Park
The Beach Boys Medley	Beach Boys
Beast Of Burden	Rolling Stones
Beat Dis	Bomb The Bass
The Beat Goes On	Sonny & Cher
Beat It	Michael Jackson
Beat Surrender	Jam
Beat The Clock	Sparks
Beatles Hits E.P.	Beatles
The Beatles Movie Medley	Beatles
Beatnik Fly	Johnny & The Hurricanes
Beautiful	Akon Feat. Colby O'Donis & Kardinal Offishall
Beautiful	Christina Aguilera
Beautiful	Matt Darey featuring Marcella Woods
Beautiful	Snoop Dogg featuring Pharrell & Uncle Charlie Wilson
A Beautiful Morning	Rascals
Beautiful Day	U2
Beautiful Girls	Sean Kingston
Beautiful Liar	Beyonce & Shakira
Beautiful Noise	Neil Diamond
Beautiful Stranger	Madonna
Beauty And The Beast	Celine Dion & Peabo Bryson
Beauty Is Only Skin Deep	Temptations
Be Careful	Sparkle/R.Kelly
Because	Dave Clark Five
Because I Got High	Afroman
Because I Love You (The Postman Song)	Stevie B
Because Of Love	Janet Jackson
Because Of You	Kelly Clarkson
Because Of You	98 Degrees
Because Of You	Ne-Yo
Because Of You	Scanty Sandwich
Because The Night	Patti Smith Group
Because The Night	10,000 Maniacs
Because They're Young	Duane Eddy
Because We Want To	Billie
Because You Loved Me	Celine Dion
Bed	J. Holiday
Bed Of Roses	Bon Jovi
Bed Sitter	Soft Cell
Beds Are Burning	Midnight Oil
Bedtime Story	Madonna
Beep	Pussycat Dolls featuring will.i.am
Beep Beep	Playmates
Before He Cheats	Carrie Underwood
Before I Let You Go	Blackstreet
Before The Next Teardrop Falls	Freddy Fender
Before You Walk Out Of My Life/Like This And Like That	Monica
Beg Steal Or Borrow	New Seekers
Beggin'	Madcon
Begin The Beguine (Volver A Empezar)	Julio Iglesias
Beginnings	Chicago
Behind A Painted Smile	Isley Brothers
Behind Closed Doors	Charlie Rich
Behind Closed Doors	Peter Andre
Behind The Groove	Teena Marie
Behind These Hazel Eyes	Kelly Clarkson
Bein' Boiled	Human League
Being Nobody	Richard X Vs Liberty X
Being With You	Smokey Robinson
Belfast	Boney M
Belfast Child	Simple Minds
Believe	Cher
Believe	Elton John
Believe	Utah Saints
Believe In Me	Ricky Nelson
Believe What You Say	Alma Cogan
Bell Bottom Blues	Originals
The Bells	Originals
Belly Dancer (Bananza)	Akon
Ben	Michael Jackson
Ben	Marti Webb
Bend It	Dave Dee, Dozy, Beaky, Mick & Tich
Bend Me, Shape Me	American Breed
Bend Me, Shape Me	Amen Corner
Bennie And The Jets	Elton John
Bent	Matchbox Twenty

Title	Artist
Bernadette	Four Tops
The Best	Tina Turner
The Best Disco In Town	Ritchie Family
Best Friend	Puff Daddy
Best I Ever Had	Drake
Best In Me	Let Loose
The Best Of Me	Cliff Richard
Best Of My Love	Eagles
Best Of My Love	Emotions
The Best Of Times	Styx
Best Of You	Foo Fighters
Best Of You	Kenny Thomas
Best Thing That Ever Happened To Me	Gladys Knight & The Pips
The Best Things In Life Are Free	Luther Vandross & Janet Jackson
Best Years Of Our Lives	Modern Romance
Betcha By Golly, Wow	Stylistics
Beth	Kiss
Bette Davis Eyes	Kim Carnes
Better Be Good To Me	Tina Turner
Better Best Forgotten	Steps
Better Days	Bruce Springsteen
Better Do It Salsa	Gibson Brothers
Better In Time	Leona Lewis
Better Love Next Time	Dr. Hook
Better Off Alone	DJ Jurgen
Better The Devil You Know	Kylie Minogue
Betty, Betty, Betty	Lonnie Donegan
Beverly Hills	Weezer
Beyond The Reef	Elvis Presley
Beyond The Sea	Bobby Darin
Beyond The Stars	David Whitfield
The Bible Tells Me So	Don Cornell
Bicycle Race	Queen
Big Apple	Kajagoogoo
Big Area	Then Jericho
Big Bad John	Jimmy Dean
Big Big World	Emilia
Big Daddy	Heavy D
Big Boys Don't Cry	Lolly
Big Brother UK TV Theme	Element Four
Big Eight	Judge Dread
Big Fun	Gap Band
Big Fun	Inner City
Big Girls Don't Cry	Fergie
Big Girls Don't Cry	Four Seasons
Big Hunk O' Love	Elvis Presley
The Big Hurt	Miss Toni Fisher
Big In Japan	Alphaville
Big Log	Robert Plant
Big Love	Fleetwood Mac
Big Man	Four Preps
Big Poppa/Warning	Notorious B.I.G.
Big Seven	Judge Dread
Big Ship	Cliff Richard
Big Shot	Billy Joel
Big Six	Judge Dread
Big Ten	Judge Dread
Big Things Poppin' (Do It)	T.I.
Big Time	Peter Gabriel
Big Yellow Taxi	Joni Mitchell
Biggest Part Of Me	Ambrosia
Billie Jean	Michael Jackson
Billie Jean	Michael Jackson
Billy, Don't Be A Hero	Bo Donaldson & The Heywoods
Bills, Bills, Bills	Destiny's Child
Bimbo	Ruby Wright
Bimbombey	Jimmie Rodgers
Bing Bang (Time To Dance)	Lazy Town
Biology	Girls Aloud
Bionic Santa	Chris Hill
Bird Dog	Everly Brothers
Bird Of Paradise	Snowy White
Birdhouse In Your Soul	They Might Be Giants
The Birdie Song (Birdie Dance)	Tweets
Birdland	Chubby Checker
The Birds And The Bees	Jewel Akens
Birthday Sex	Jeremih
Bitch	Meredith Brooks
The Bitch Is Back	Elton John
Bitter Sweet Symphony	Verve
Bits And Pieces	Dave Clark Five
The Bitterest Pill (I Ever Had To Swallow)	Jam
Bizounce	Olivia
Black & Gold	Sam Sparro
Black & White	Three Dog Night
Black And White	Greyhound
Black And White Town	Doves
Black Betty	Ram Jam
Black Cat	Janet Jackson
Black Coffee	All Saints
Black Denim Trousers	Cheers
Black Dog	Led Zeppelin
The Black Eyed Boys	Paper Lace
Black Hills Of Dakota	Doris Day
Black Hole Sun	Soundgarden
Black Is Black	Los Bravos
Black Is Black	La Belle Epoque
Black Magic Woman	Santana
Black Night	Deep Purple
Black Or White	Michael Jackson
Black Pearl	Sonny Charles & The Checkmates, Ltd.
Black Pearl	Horace Faith

Title	Artist
Damaged	Danity Kane
Damn!	YoungBloodZ featuring Lil Jon
Damn I Wish I Was Your Lover	Sophie B. Hawkins
Damned Don't Cry	Visage
Damned On 45	Captain Sensible
Dance Away	Roxy Music
Dance, Dance	Fall Out Boy
Dance, Dance, Dance	Beach Boys
Dance, Dance, Dance (Yowsah, Yowsah, Yowsah)	Chic
Dance For Me	Sisqo
Dance Little Lady Dance	Tina Charles
Dance On	Kathy Kirby
Dance On	Shadows
Dance On Little Girl	Paul Anka
Dance The Night Away	Mavericks
Dance The Night Away	Van Halen
Dance To The Music	Sly & The Family Stone
(Dance With The) Guitar Man	Duane Eddy
Dance With Me	Peter Brown
Dance With Me	Debelah Morgan
Dance With Me	Orleans
Dance With Me Henry (Wallflower)	Georgia Gibbs
Dance With The Devil	Cozy Powell
Dance (With U)	Lemar
Dance Wiv Me	Dizzee Rascal Feat. Calvin Harris & Chrome
Dance Yourself Dizzy	Liquid Gold
Dancin	Guy
Dancin' In The Moonlight	Thin Lizzy
Dancin' In The Moonlight	Toploader
Dancin' Party	Chubby Checker
Dancin' Party	Showaddywaddy
Dancing Girls	Nik Kershaw
Dancing In The City	Marshall Hain
Dancing In The Dark	Bruce Springsteen
Dancing In The Moonlight	King Harvest
Dancing In The Street	David Bowie
Dancing In The Street	Mick Jagger & David Bowie
Dancing In The Street	Martha & The Vandellas
Dancing Machine	Jackson Five
(Dancing) On A Saturday Night	Barry Blue
Dancing On The Ceiling	Lionel Richie
Dancing On The Floor (Hooked On Love)	Third World
Dancing Queen	Abba
Dancing Queen	A*Teens
Dancing Tight	Galaxy featuring Phil Fearon
Dancing With Tears In My Eyes	Ultravox
Dancing With The Captain	Paul Nicholas
Dandelion	Rolling Stones
Dandy	Herman's Hermits
Dang Me	Roger Miller
Danger Games	Pinkees
Danger! High Voltage	Electric Six
Danger Zone	Kenny Loggins
Dangerous	Kardinal Offishall Featuring Akon
Dangerous	Busta Rhymes
Dangerous	Roxette
Dani California	Red Hot Chili Peppers
Daniel	Elton John
Danke Schoen	Wayne Newton
Danny Boy	Conway Twitty
Danny's Song	Anne Murray
Da Pip	Freak Nasty
Dare	Gorillaz
Dare Me	Pointer Sisters
Dark Is The Night	Shakatak
Dark Lady	Cher
Dark Moon	Bonnie Guitar
Dark Moon	Gale Storm
Darlin'	Beach Boys
Darlin'	Frankie Miller
Darling Je Vous Aime Beaucoup	Nat 'King' Cole
Dat	Pluto Shervington
Daughter Of Darkness	Tom Jones
Davy's On The Road Again	Manfred Mann's Earth Band
Dawn (Go Away)	Four Seasons
Day After Day	Badfinger
Day & Night	Billie Piper
Day Dreaming	Aretha Franklin
The Day I Met Marie	Cliff Richard
Day 'n' Nite	Kid Cudi
The Day The Rains Came	Jane Morgan
The Day The World Went Away	Nine Inch Nails
Day Trip To Bangor (Didn't We Have A Lovely Time)	Fiddler's Dram
Day Tripper	Beatles
A Day Without Love	Love Affair
Daydream	Lovin' Spoonful
Daydream Believer	Monkees
Daydream Believer	Anne Murray
Daydreamer	David Cassidy
Daydreamin'	Tatyana Ali
Days	Kinks
Days	Kirsty MacColl
Days Go By	Dirty Vegas
The Days Of Pearly Spencer	Marc Almond
Dazz	Brick
Dazzey Duks	Duice
De Do Do Do, De Da Da Da	Police
Dead And Gone	T.I. Featuring Justin Timberlake
Dead End Street	Kinks
Dead From The Waist Down	Catatonia
Dead Giveaway	Shalamar
Dead Man's Curve	Jan & Dean
Dead Or Alive	Lonnie Donegan
Dead Ringer For Love	Meat Loaf
Deadwood Stage	Doris Day
The Dean And I	10cc
Dear Jessie	Madonna
Dear John	Status Quo
Dear Lady Twist	Gary U.S. Bonds
Dear Lonely Hearts	Nat 'King' Cole
Dear Mama/Old School	2Pac
Dear One	Larry Finnegan
Dear Prudence	Siouxsie & The Banshees
Death Of A Clown	Dave Davies
Debora	Tyrannosaurus Rex
December '63 (Oh What A Night)	Four Seasons
Deck Of Cards	Max Bygraves
Deck Of Cards	Wink Martindale
Dede Dinah	Frankie Avalon
Dedicated Follower Of Fashion	Kinks
Dedicated To The One I Love	Mamas & The Papas
Dedicated To The One I Love	Bitty McLean
Dedicated To The One I Love	Shirelles
Deep	East 17
Deep, Deep Trouble	Simpsons
Deep Down Inside	Donna Summer
Deep Heat '89	Latino Rave
Deep Purple	Donny & Marie Osmond
Deep Purple	Nino Tempo & April Stevens
Deeper And Deeper	Madonna
A Deeper Love	Aretha Franklin
Deeper Shade Of Blue	Steps
Deeper Than The Night	Olivia Newton-John
Deeper Underground	Jamiroquai
Deepest Blue	Deepest Blue
Deeply Dippy	Right Said Fred
Deja Vu	Beyoncé featuring Jay-Z
Deja Vu	Dionne Warwick
Déjà vu (Uptown Baby)	Lord Tariq & Peter Gunz
Delaware	Perry Como
Delilah	Sensational Alex Harvey Band
Delilah	Tom Jones
Delirious	Prince & The Revolution
Delivery	Babyshambles
Delta Dawn	Helen Reddy
Delta Lady	Joe Cocker
Denis	Blondie
Denise	Randy & The Rainbows
Der Kommissar	After The Fire
Desafinado	Stan Getz & Charlie Byrd
Desert Moon	Dennis DeYoung
Desert Rose	Sting Feat. Cheb Mami
Desiderata	Les Crane
Desire	Andy Gibb
Desire	U2
Desiree	Neil Diamond
Destination Calabria	Alex Gaudino Featuring Crystal Waters
Destiny	Johnnie Ray
Detroit City	Tom Jones
Deutscher Girls	Adam & The Ants
Devil Gate Drive	Suzi Quatro
Devil Inside	Inxs
Devil Or Angel	Bobby Vee
The Devil Went Down To Georgia	Charlie Daniels Band
Devil With A Blue Dress On & Good Golly Miss Molly	Mitch Ryder & The Detroit Wheels
Devil Woman	Cliff Richard
Devil Woman	Marty Robbins
Devil's Answer	Atomic Rooster
Devoted To You	Everly Brothers
Dial My Heart	Boys
Diamond Girl	Seals & Crofts
Diamond Rings	Chipmunk Featuring Emeli Sande
Diamonds	Herb Alpert
Diamonds	Jet Harris & Tony Meehan
Diamonds And Pearls	Prince
Diamonds From Sierra Leone	Kanye West
Diana	Paul Anka
Diane	Bachelors
Diary	Bread
Diary	Alicia Keys featuring Tony! Toni! Tone!
The Diary Of Horace Wimp	Electric Light Orchestra
Did It In A Minute	Daryl Hall & John Oates
Did You Ever	Nancy Sinatra & Lee Hazlewood
Did You Ever Have To Make Up Your Mind	Lovin' Spoonful
Didn't I (Blow Your Mind This Time)	Delfonics
Didn't I (Blow Your Mind)	New Kids On The Block
Didn't We Almost Have It All	Whitney Houston
Die Another Day	Madonna
Differences	Ginuwine
A Different Corner	George Michael
Different Drum	Stone Poneys
Different Strokes	Isotonik
Different World	Iron Maiden
Diggin' On You	TLC
Digging Your Scene	Blow Monkeys
Dilemma	Nelly featuring Kelly Rowland
Dim All The Lights	Donna Summer
Dim, Dim The Lights (I Want Some Atmosphere)	Bill Haley & His Comets
Dime And A Dollar	Guy Mitchell
Dinner With Drac (Part 1)	John Zacherle
Dip It Low	Christina Milian
Dippety Day	Father Abraham & The Smurfs
Dirt Off Your Shoulder	Jay-Z
Dirrty	Christina Aguilera featuring Redman
Dirtee Cash	Dizzee Rascal
Dirty Cash	Adventures Of Stevie V
Dirty Diana	Michael Jackson
Dirty Harry	Gorillaz
Dirty Laundry	Don Henley
Dirty Little Secret	All-American Rejects
Dirty Water	Standells
Dirty White Boy	Foreigner
Disappear	Inxs
Disappointed	Electronic
D.I.S.C.O.	Ottawan
Disco 2000	Pulp
Disco Connection	Isaac Hayes
Disco Duck	Rick Dees & His Cast Of Idiots
Disco Inferno	50 Cent
Disco Inferno	Trammps
Disco Inferno	Tina Turner
Disco Lady	Johnnie Taylor
Disco Nights (Rock Freak)	G.Q.
Disco Queen	Hot Chocolate
Disco Stomp	Hamilton Bohannon
Discotheque	U2
Distant Drums	Jim Reeves
Disturbia	Rihanna
Ditty	Paperboy
Divine Emotions	Narada
D.I.V.O.R.C.E.	Billy Connolly
D.I.V.O.R.C.E.	Tammy Wynette
Dixie-Narco (EP)	Primal Scream
Dixieland	Winifred Atwell
Dizzy	Vic Reeves & The Wonder Stuff
Dizzy	Tommy Roe
DJ	H & Claire
DJ	Jamelia
DJs Take Control	SL2
Do Anything	Natural Selection
Do Anything You Wanna Do	Rods
Do Anything You Want To	Thin Lizzy
Do I Do	Stevie Wonder
Do I Have To Say The Words?	Bryan Adams
Do I Like It	Nat 'King' Cole
Do I Make You Proud	Taylor Hicks
Do It ('Til You're Satisfied)	B.T. Express
Do It Again	Beach Boys
Do It Again	The Chemical Brothers
Do It Again	Raffaella Carra
Do It Again	Steely Dan
Do It Any Way You Wanna	Peoples Choice
Do It Baby	Miracles
Do It To It	Cherish featuring Sean Paul of The YoungBloodZ
Do It Well	Jennifer Lopez
Do Me	Bell Biv Devoe
Do Nothing	Specials
Do Somethin'	Britney Spears
Do That To Me One More Time	Captain & Tennille
Do The Bartman	Simpsons
Do The Bird	Dee Dee Sharp
Do The Conga	Black Lace
(Do) The Hucklebuck	Coast To Coast
Do The Right Thing	Redhead Kingpin & The FBI
(Do The) Spanish Hustle	Fatback Band
Do They Know It's Christmas?	Band Aid
Do They Know It's Christmas?	Band Aid II
Do They Know It's Christmas?	Band Aid 20
Do U Still?	East 17
Do Wah Diddy Diddy	Manfred Mann
Do What You Do	Jermaine Jackson
Do What You Gotta Do	Four Tops
Do What You Gotta Do	Nina Simone
Do What You Wanna Do	T-Connection
Do Ya Do Ya (Wanna Please Me)	Samantha Fox
Do You Believe In Love	Huey Lewis & The News
Do You Believe In Magic	Lovin' Spoonful
Do You Believe In Us	Jon Secada
Do You Feel Like We Do	Peter Frampton
Do You Feel My Love	Eddy Grant
Do You Know (I Go Crazy)	Angel City
Do You Know (The Ping Pong Song)	Enrique Iglesias
Do You Know The Way To San Jose	Dionne Warwick
Do You Know What I Mean	Lee Michaels
Do You Know What It Takes	Robyn
Do You Love Me	Dave Clark Five
Do You Love Me	Contours
Do You Love Me	Brian Poole & The Tremeloes
Do You Mind	Anthony Newley
Do You Really Like It	DJ Pied Piper & The Masters Of Ceremonies
Do You Really Want To Hurt Me	Culture Club
Do You Remember?	Phil Collins
Do You Remember	Jay Sean Featuring Sean Paul & Lil Jon
Do You See The Light (Looking For)	Snap!
Do You Wanna Dance	Barry Blue
Do You Wanna Dance	Cliff Richard
Do You Wanna Dance?	Beach Boys
Do You Wanna Make Love	Peter McCann
Do You Wanna Touch Me? (Oh Yeah)	Gary Glitter

Title	Artist
Do You Want Me	Salt-N-Pepa
Do You Want To	Franz Ferdinand
Do You Want To Dance	Bobby Freeman
Do You Want To Know A Secret	Beatles
Do You Want To Know A Secret	Billy J. Kramer & The Dakotas
Do Your Thing	Watts 103rd Street Band
The Doctor	Doobie Brothers
Dr. Beat	Miami Sound Machine
Doctor! Doctor!	Thompson Twins
Dr. Feelgood	Motley Crue
Dr. Kildare Theme	Johnny Spence
Dr. Love	Tina Charles
Doctor My Eyes	Jackson Browne
Doctor My Eyes	Jackson Five
Doctor Pressure	Mylo vs Miami Sound Machine
Doctor's Orders	Carol Douglas
Doctor's Orders	Sunny
Doctorin' The House	Coldcut featuring Yazz & The Plastic Poulation
Doctorin' The Tardis	Timelords
Does Anybody Really Know What Time It Is	Chicago
Does Your Chewing Gum Lose Its Flavour (On The Bedpost Overnight)	Lonnie Donegan
Does Your Mother Know	Abba
Doesn't Mean Anything	Alicia Keys
Doesn't Really Matter	Janet
Doesn't Somebody Want To Be Wanted	Partridge Family
Dog Eat Dog	Adam & The Ants
Dion In	LL Cool J
Doin' The Doo	Betty Boo
Doing Alright With The Boys	Gary Glitter
Doing It All For My Baby	Huey Lewis & The News
Dolce Vita	Ryan Paris
Dolly My Love	Moments
Dolphins Were Monkeys	Ian Brown
Domani (Tomorrow)	Julius La Rosa
Dominique	Singing Nun (Soeur Sourire)
Domino	Van Morrison
Domino Dancing	Pet Shop Boys
Don Quixote	Nik Kershaw
Don't	Elvis Presley
Don't Answer Me	Cilla Black
Don't Be Angry	Crew-Cuts
Don't Be Cruel	Bill Black's Combo
Don't Be Cruel	Bobby Brown
Don't Be Cruel	Cheap Trick
Don't Be Cruel	Elvis Presley
Don't Be Stupid (You Know I Love You)	Shania Twain
Don't Believe A Word	Thin Lizzy
Don't Bet Money Honey	Linda Scott
Don't Blame It On That Girl	Matt Bianco
Don't Blame Me	Frank Ifield
Don't Bother	Shakira
Don't Break My Heart	UB40
Don't Break The Heart That Loves You	Connie Francis
Don't Bring Lulu	Dorothy Provine
Don't Bring Me Down	Animals
Don't Bring Me Down	Electric Light Orchestra
Don't Bring Me Down	Pretty Things
Don't Bring Me Your Heartaches	Paul & Barry Ryan
Don't Call Me Baby	Madison Avenue
Don't Call This Love	Leon Jackson
Don't Call Us We'll Call You	Sugarloaf/Jerry Corbetta
Don't Cha	Pussycat Dolls featuring Busta Rhymes
Don't Close You Eyes	Kix
Don't Come Around Here No More	Tom Petty & The Heartbreakers
Don't Cry	Asia
Don't Cry	Guns N' Roses
Don't Cry Daddy	Elvis Presley
Don't Cry For Me Argentina	Julie Covington
Don't Cry For Me Argentina	Madonna
Don't Cry For Me Argentina	Shadows
Don't Cry Out Loud	Elkie Brooks
Don't Cry Out Loud	Melissa Manchester
Don't Disturb The Groove	System
Don't Do It Baby	Mac & Katie Kissoon
Don't Do Me Like That	Tom Petty & The Heartbreakers
Don't Dream It's Over	Crowded House
Don't Drive My Car	Status Quo
Don't Ever Change	Crickets
Don't Expect Me To Be Your Friend	Lobo
Don't Fall In Love With A Dreamer	Kenny Rogers & Kim Carnes
(Don't Fear) The Reaper	Blue Oyster Cult
Don't Forbid Me	Pat Boone
Don't Forget About Us	Mariah Carey
Don't Forget To Remember	Bee Gees
Don't Forget Me (When I'm Gone)	Glass Tiger
Don't Get Me Wrong	Pretenders
Don't Give In To Him	Gary Puckett & The Union Gap
Don't Give Me Your Life	Alex Party
Don't Give Up	Chicane featuring Bryan Adams
Don't Give Up	Peter Gabriel & Kate Bush
Don't Give Up	Louise
Don't Give Up On Us	David Soul
Don't Go	Yazoo
Don't Go Breaking My Heart	Elton John & Kiki Dee
Don't Go Breaking My Heart	Elton John & Rupaul
Don't Hang Up	Orlons
Don't It Make My Brown Eyes Blue	Crystal Gayle
Don't Just Stand There	Patty Duke
Don't Knock The Rock	Bill Haley & His Comets

Title	Artist
Don't Knock My Love (Pt. 1)	Wilson Pickett
Don't Know Much	Linda Ronstadt (featuring Aaron Neville)
Don't Know What You Got (Till It's Gone)	Cinderella
Don't Laugh At Me	Norman Wisdom
Don't Leave Me This Way	Communards
Don't Leave Me This Way	Thelma Houston
Don't Leave Me This Way	Harold Melvin & The Blue Notes
Don't Let Go	Roy Hamilton
Don't Let Go	David Sneddon
Don't Let Go (Love)	En Vogue
Don't Let It Die	Hurricane Smith
Don't Let It End	Styx
Don't Let Me Be Lonely Tonight	James Taylor
Don't Let Me Be Misunderstood	Animals
Don't Let Me Be Misunderstood	Santa Esmeralda
Don't Let Me Down	Will Young
Don't Let Me Get Me	P!nk
Don't Let The Sun Catch You Crying	Gerry & The Pacemakers
Don't Let The Sun Go Down On Me	Elton John
Don't Let The Sun Go Down On Me	George Michael & Elton John
Don't Lie	Serendipity Singers
Don't Lie	The Black Eyed Peas
Don't Look Any Further	M People
Don't Look Back	Boston
Don't Look Back In Anger	Fine Young Cannibals
Don't Look Back In Anger	Oasis
Don't Look Down-The Sequel	Go West
Don't Love You No More	Craig David
Don't Lose My Number	Phil Collins
Don't Make Me Wait	Bomb The Bass
Don't Make My Baby Blue	Shadows
Don't Make Waves	Nolans
Don't Matter	Akon
Don't Mean Nothing	Richard Marx
Don't Mess With Bill	Marvelettes
Don't Mess With My Man	Booty Luv
Don't Mess With My Man	Nivea Feat Brian & Brandon Casey
Don't Miss The Partyline	Bizz Nizz
Don't Phunk With My Heart	Black Eyed Peas
Don't Play That Song	Aretha Franklin
Don't Play That Song (You Lied)	Ben E. King
Don't Play Your Rock 'n' Roll To Me	Smokey
Don't Pull Your Love	Hamilton, Joe Frank & Reynolds
Don't Push It, Don't Force It	Leon Haywood
Don't Rush Me	Taylor Dayne
Don't Say Nothin' (Bad About My Baby)	Cookies
Don't Say You Don't Remember	Beverly Bremmers
Don't Say You Love Me	M2M
Don't Shed A Tear	Paul Carrack
Don't Sleep In The Subway	Petula Clark
Don't Stand So Close To Me	Police
Don't Stay Away Too Long	Peters & Lee
Don't Stop	ATP
Don't Stop	Fleetwood Mac
Don't Stop Believin'	Glee Cast
Don't Stop Believin'	Journey
Don't Stop It Now	Hot Chocolate
Don't Stop Me Now	McFly
Don't Stop Me Now	Queen
Don't Stop Movin'	S Club 7
Don't Stop The Carnival	Alan Price Set
Don't Stop The Music	Rihanna
Don't Stop The Music	Yarbrough & Peoples
Don't Stop Till You Get Enough	Michael Jackson
Don't Stop (Wiggle Wiggle)	Outhere Brothers
Don't Take Away The Music	Tavares
Don't Take It Personal (Just One Of Dem Days)	Monica
Don't Take The Girl	Tim McGraw
Don't Talk Just Kiss	Right Said Fred/Jocelyn Brown
Don't Talk To Him	Cliff Richard
Don't Talk To Me About Love	Altered Images
Don't Talk To Strangers	Rick Springfield
Don't Tell Me	Blancmange
Don't Tell Me	Avril Lavigne
Don't Tell Me	Madonna
Don't Tell Me Lies	Breathe
Don't That Beat All	Adam Faith
Don't Think I'm Not	Kandi
Don't Think Twice	Wonder Who?
Don't Think Twice It's All Right	Peter, Paul & Mary
Don't Throw Your Love Away	Searchers
Don't Treat Me Like A Child	Helen Shapiro
Don't Trust Me	3OH!3
Don't Turn Around	Ace Of Base
Don't Turn Around	Aswad
Don't Turn Around	Merseybeats
Don't Upset The Rhythm (Go Baby Go)	Noisettes
Don't Walk Away	Jade
Don't Wanna Fall In Love	Jane Child
Don't Wanna Lose This Feeling	Dannii Minogue
Don't Wanna Lose You	Gloria Estefan
Don't Want To Be A Fool	Luther Vandross
Don't Want To Forgive Me Now	Wet Wet Wet
Don't Want To Let You Go	5ive
Don't Waste My Time	Paul Hardcastle
Don't Worry	Kim Appleby
Don't Worry	Appleton
Don't Worry	Marty Robbins
Don't Worry Be Happy	Bobby McFerrin
Don't You Care	Buckinghams
Don't You (Forget About Me)	Simple Minds
Don't You Just Know It	Huey (Piano) Smith & The Clowns

Title	Artist
Don't You Know	Della Reese
Don't You Know It	Adam Faith
Don't You Know What The Night Can Do	Steve Winwood
Don't You Rock Me Daddy-O	Lonnie Donegan
Don't You Rock Me Daddy-O	Vipers Skiffle Group
Don't You Think It's Time	Mike Berry
Don't You Want Me	Felix
Don't You Want Me	Human League
Don't You Want Me	Jody Watley
Donald Where's Your Troosers	Andy Stewart with The Michael Sammes Singers
Donna	10cc
Donna	Ritchie Valens
Donna	Marty Wilde
Donna The Prima Donna	Dion
Doo Doo Doo Doo Doo (Heartbreaker)	Rolling Stones
Doo Wop (That Thing)	Lauryn Hill
Doodah!	Cartoons
Dooms Night	Azzido Da Bass
Doop	Doop
The Door Is Still Open To My Heart	Dean Martin
Double Barrel	Dave & Ansil Collins
Double Dutch	Malcolm McLaren
Double Lovin'	Osmonds
Double Vision	Foreigner
Down	Jay Sean Featuring Lil Wayne
(Down At) Papa Joe's	Dixiebelles
Down Boy	Holly Valance
Down By The Lazy River	Osmonds
Down By The Station	Four Preps
Down Down	Status Quo
Down 4 U	Irv Gotti Presents The Inc. Feat. Ja Rule, Ashanti, Charli Baltimore & Vita
Down In The Boondocks	Billy Joe Royal
Down Low (Nobody Has To Know)	R. Kelly featuring Ronald Isley
Down On The Beach Tonight	Drifters
Down On The Corner	Creedence Clearwater Revival
Down On The Street	Shakatak
Down The Dustpipe	Status Quo
Down To Earth	Curiosity Killed The Cat
Down Under	Men At Work
Down Yonder	Johnny & The Hurricanes
Downtown	Emma Bunton
Downtown	Petula Clark
Downtown Train	Rod Stewart
Dr Kiss Kiss	5000 Volts
Drag City	Jan & Dean
Draggin' The Line	Tommy James
Dragging Me Down	Inspiral Carpets
Dragnet	Ray Anthony
Dragnet	Ted Heath
Dragostea Din Tei	O-Zone
Drama!	Erasure
Dre Day	Dr. Dre
Dreadlock Holiday	10cc
Dream A Lie	UB40
Dream A Little Dream Of Me	Mama Cass
Dream Baby	Roy Orbison
Dream Big	David Cook
Dream Catch Me	Newton Faulkner
The Dream Is Still Alive	Wilson Phillips
Dream Lover	Bobby Darin
Dream On	Aerosmith
Dream On	Depeche Mode
Dream To Me	Dario G
Dream Weaver	Gary Wright
A Dream's A Dream	Soul II Soul
Dreamboat	Alma Cogan
Dreamer	Supertramp
Dreamin'	Johnny Burnette
Dreamin'	Vanessa Williams
Dreaming	Blondie
Dreaming	Orchestral Manoeuvres In The Dark
Dreaming	Cliff Richard
Dreamlover	Mariah Carey
Dreams	The Corrs
Dreams	Fleetwood Mac
Dreams	Gabrielle
Dreams	The Game
Dreams Can Tell A Lie	Nat 'King' Cole
Dreamtime	Daryl Hall
Dress You Up	Madonna
Drift Away	Dobie Gray
Drift Away	Uncle Kracker featuring Dobie Gray
Drinking In LA	Bran Van 3000
Drinking Song	Mario Lanza
Drip Drop	Dion
Drive	Cars
Drive	Incubus
Drive-In Saturday	David Bowie
Driven By You	Brian May
Drivin' My Life Away	Eddie Rabbitt
Driving My Car	Madness
Drop It Like It's Hot	Snoop Dogg featuring Pharrell
Drop The Boy	Bros
Drops Of Jupiter (Tell Me)	Train
Drowning	Backstreet Boys
Drowning In Berlin	Mobiles
Drowning In The Sea Of Love	Joe Simon
Drummer Man	Tonight
Dry County	Bon Jovi

Title	Artist
Falling Stars	Sunset Strippers
Fame	David Bowie
Fame	Irene Cara
Family Affair	Mary J. Blige
Family Affair	Sly & The Family Stone
Family Man	Daryl Hall & John Oates
The Family Of Man	Three Dog Night
Famous Last Words	My Chemical Romance
Fancy Pants	Kenny
Fanfare For The Common Man	Emerson, Lake & Palmer
Fanny (Be Tender With My Love)	Bee Gees
Fantastic Day	Haircut 100
Fantastic Voyage	Coolio
Fantasy	Appleton
Fantasy	Black Box
Fantasy	Mariah Carey
Fantasy	Earth, Wind & Fire
Fantasy Island	Tight Fit
Far Away	Nickelback
Far Far Away	Slade
Far From Over	Frank Stallone
Farewell	Rod Stewart
Farewell Is A Lonely Sound	Jimmy Ruffin
Farewell My Summer Love	Michael Jackson
Fascinating Rhythm	Bass-O-Matic
Fascination	Alphabeat
Fascination	Jane Morgan
Fashion	David Bowie
Fast Car	Tracy Chapman
Fast Food Song	Fast Food Rockers
Faster Kill Pussycat	Oakenfold featuring Brittany Murphy
Fastlove	George Michael
Fat Bottomed Girls	Queen
Fat Lip	Sum 41
Father And Son	Boyzone
Father And Son	Ronan Keating featuring Yusuf
Father Christmas Do Not Touch Me	Goodies
Father Figure	George Michael
Fattie Bum-Bum	Carl Malcolm
Favourite Shirts (Boy Meets Girl)	Haircut 100
Favourite Things	Big Brovaz
F.B.I.	Shadows
The Fear	Lily Allen
Fear Of The Dark (Live)	Iron Maiden
Fearless	Taylor Swift
Feel	Robbie Williams
Feel Good	Phats & Small
Feel Good Inc	Gorillaz
Feel Good Time	P!nk featuring William Orbit
Feel It	The Tamperer featuring Maya
Feel Like Makin' Love	Bad Company
Feel Like Makin' Love	Roberta Flack
Feel Like Making Love	Pauline Henry
Feel So Fine	Johnny Preston
Feel So High	Des'ree
Feel So Real	Steve Arrington
Feel The Beat	Darude
Feel The Need In Me	Detroit Emeralds
Feelin' Fine	Ultrabeat
Feelin' So Good	Jennifer Lopez
Feelin' Stronger Every Day	Chicago
Feelings	Morris Albert
Feel Good	Phats & Small
Feels	Tony! Toni! Tone!
Feels Just Like It Should	Jamiroquai
(Feels Like) Heaven	Fiction Factory
Feels Like Heaven	Urban Cookie Collective
Feels Like I'm In Love	Kelly Marie
Feels Like The First Time	Foreigner
Feels So Good	Chuck Mangione
Feels So Good	Mase
Feels So Good	Melanie B
Fernando	Abba
Fergalicious	Fergie
Ferry 'cross The Mersey	Marsden/McCartney/Johnson/Christians
Ferry 'cross The Mersey	Gerry & The Pacemakers
Fever	Peggy Lee
Fever	Madonna
Fever	McCoys
Fields Of Anfield Road	Liverpool Collective / The Kop Choir
Fields Of Fire (400 Miles)	Big Country
Fiesta	R. Kelly featuring Jay-Z
A Fifth Of Beethoven	Walter Murphy & The Big Apple Band
50:50	Lemar
The 59th Street Bridge Song (Feelin' Groovy)	Harpers Bizarre
15 Minutes	Marc Nelson
50 Ways To Leave Your Lover	Paul Simon
Figaro	Brotherhood Of Man
Fight	Barbra Streisand
Fight For This Love	Cheryl Cole
Fight The Power Pt. 1	Isley Brothers
Fighter	Christina Aguilera
Fill Me In	Craig David
Fill My Little World	The Feeling
The Final Countdown	Europe
Finally	Ce Ce Peniston
Finally Found	Honeyz
Finchley Central	New Vaudeville Band
Find Another Fool	Quarterflash
Find My Love	Fairground Attraction
Find The Time	Five Star
Fine Time	New Order
Fine Time	Yazz
The Finer Things	Steve Winwood
Finger Of Suspicion	Dickie Valentine
Finger Poppin' Time	Hank Ballard & The Midnighters
Fingertips (Pt. 2)	Stevie Wonder
Fings Ain't What They Used T'be	Max Bygraves
Finish What Ya Started	Van Halen
Fire	Crazy World Of Arthur Brown
Fire	Kasabian
Fire	Ohio Players
Fire	Pointer Sisters
Fire	Prodigy
Fire And Rain	James Taylor
Fire Brigade	Move
Fire Burning	Sean Kingston
Fire Lake	Bob Seger & The Silver Bullet Band
Fire Wire	Cosmic Gate
Fireball	Deep Purple
Fireflies	Owl City
Firestarter	Prodigy
The First Cut Is The Deepest	Sheryl Crow
First Cut Is The Deepest	Rod Stewart
First Of May	Bee Gees
1st Of Tha Month	Bone Thugs-N-Harmony
First Of The Gang To Die	Morrissey
The First Night	Monica
The First Time Ever I Saw Your Face	Roberta Flack
The First Time	Robin Beck
The First Time	Adam Faith
First Time	Sunblock featuring Robin Beck
The First Time	Surface
Fit But You Know It	The Streets
5 Colours In Her Hair	McFly
5-4-3-2-1	Manfred Mann
500 Miles Away From Home	Bobby Bare
Five Live (EP)	George Michael & Queen
Five O'clock World	Vogues
5-7-0-5	City Boy
5-10-15-20 (25-30 Years Of Love)	Presidents
5 Years Time	Noah And The Whale
Fix You	Coldplay
The Flame	Cheap Trick
Flap Your Wings	Nelly
Flash	Queen
Flashdance	Deep Dish
Flashdance....What A Feeling	Irene Cara
Flat Beat	Mr Oizo
Flawless	Ones
Flex	Mad Cobra
Flip Reverse	Blazin' Squad
F.L.M.	Mel & Kim
Float On	Floaters
The Floral Dance	Brighouse And Rastrick Brass Band
Flowers	Sweet Female Attitude
Flowers In The Rain	Move
Flowers On The Wall	Statler Brothers
Floy Joy	Supremes
Fluorescent Adolescent	Arctic Monkeys
Flux	Bloc Party
The Fly	Chubby Checker
The Fly	U2
Fly Away	John Denver
Fly Away	Lenny Kravitz
Fly By II	Blue
Fly Like An Eagle	Steve Miller Band
Fly Like An Eagle	Seal
Fly On The Wings Of Love	XTM & DJ Chucky presents Annia
Fly Robin Fly	Silver Convention
Flying The Flag (For You)	Scooch
Flying Without Wings	Ruben Studdard
Flying Without Wings	Westlife
The Flying Saucer (Parts 1 & 2)	Buchanan & Goodman
Fog On The Tyne (Revisited)	Gazza And Lindisfarne
The Folk Singer	Tommy Roe
Follow Da Leader	Nigel & Marvin
Follow Me	Uncle Kracker
Follow That Dream (E.P.)	Elvis Presley
Follow You Down	Gin Blossoms
Follow You Follow Me	Genesis
Food For Thought	UB40
The Fool	Sanford Clark
A Fool Am I	Cilla Black
Fool (If You Think It's Over)	Chris Rea
A Fool Never Learns	Andy Williams
Fool No More	S Club 8
Fool # 1	Brenda Lee
Fool Again	Westlife
The Fool On The Hill	Sergio Mendes & Brasil '66
A Fool Such As I	Elvis Presley
Fool To Cry	Rolling Stones
Fool's Gold	Stone Roses
Fooled Around And Fell In Love	Elvin Bishop
Foolish	Ashanti
Foolish Beat	Debbie Gibson
Foolish Games/You Were Meant For Me	Jewel
Foolish Little Girl	Shirelles
Fools Rush In	Rick Nelson
Foot Tapper	Shadows
Footloose	Kenny Loggins
Footprints In The Sand	Leona Lewis
Footsee	Wigan's Chosen Few
Footsteps	Steve Lawrence
For All We Know	Shirley Bassey
For All We Know	Carpenters
For America	Red Box
4 My People	Missy 'Misdemeanor' Elliott
For Lovers	Wolfman featuring Peter Doherty
For Once In My Life	Stevie Wonder
For The Good Times	Perry Como
For The Good Times	Ray Price
For The Love Of Him	Bobbi Martin
For The Love Of Money	O'Jays
For What It's Worth (Stop, Hey What's That Sound)	Buffalo Springfield
For Whom The Bell Tolls	Bee Gees
For You	Rick Nelson
For You Blue	Beatles
For You I Will	Monica
For Your Babies	Simply Red
For Your Eyes Only	Sheena Easton
For Your Love	Ed Townsend
For Your Love	Yardbirds
For Your Precious Love	Jerry Butler & The Impressions
Forever	Chris Brown
Forever	Dee Dee
Forever	Drake Featuring Kanye West, Lil Wayne & Eminem
Forever	Kiss
Forever	Little Dippers
Forever	N-Trance
Forever	Roy Wood
Forever & Ever	Slik
Forever And For Always	Shania Twain
Forever Autumn	Justin Hayward
Forever Is Over	The Saturdays
A Forever Kind Of Love	Bobby Vee
(Forever) Live And Die	Orchestral Manoeuvres In The Dark
Forever Lov	Color Me Badd
Forever Young	Rod Stewart
Forever Your Girl	Paula Abdul
Forget About You	Motors
Forget About Dre	Dr Dre
Forget Him	Bobby Rydell
Forget Me Not	Kalin Twins
Forget Me Not	Eden Kane
Forget Me Not	Martha & The Vandellas
Forget Me Nots	Patrice Rushen
Forgive Me	Leona Lewis
Forgive Me, Girl	Spinners
Forgive My Heart	Nat 'King' Cole
Fort Worth Jail	Lonnie Donegan
Fortress Around Your Heart	Sting
Fortunate	Maxwell
Fortunate Son	Creedence Clearwater Revival
48 Crash	Suzi Quatro
Forty Miles Of Bad Road	Duane Eddy
Foundations	Kate Nash
Four Bacharach & David Songs (EP)	Deacon Blue
4, 5, 6	Sole Feat. JT Money & Kandi
Four From Toyah E.P.	Toyah
Four Letter Word	Kim Wilde
Four Minute Warning	Mark Owen
4 Minutes	Madonna Featuring Justin Timberlake
Four More From Toyah E.P.	Toyah
Four Walls	Jim Reeves
4 Seasons Of Loneliness	Boyz II Men
Fox On The Run	Manfred Mann
Fox On The Run	Sweet
Frankenstein	Edgar Winter Group
Frankie	Connie Francis
Frankie	Sister Sledge
Frankie And Johnny	Sam Cooke
Freak Like Me	Adina Howard
Freak Like Me	Sugababes
Freak Me	Another Level
Freak Me	Silk
Freddie's Dead	Curtis Mayfield
Free	Deniece Williams
Free As A Bird	Beatles
Free E.P.	Free
Free Fallin'	Tom Petty
Free Me	Emma
Free Ride	Edgar Winter Group
Free Your Mind	En Vogue
Freebird	Will To Power
Freedom	George Michael
Freedom	Wham!
Freedom Come Freedom Go	Fortunes
Freek-A-Leek	Petey Pablo
Freek'n You	Jodeci
Freestyler	Bomfunk MCs
Freeway Of Love	Aretha Franklin
Freeze-Frame	J. Geils Band
Freight Train	Chas McDevitt Skiffle Group
French Kiss	Lil Louis
French Kissin' In The USA	Debbie Harry
Fresh	Kool & The Gang
The Freshmen	The Verve Pipe
Friday, I'm In Love	Cure
Friday Night (Live Version)	Kids From 'Fame'
Friday On My Mind	Easybeats
Friday's Child	Will Young
Friend Of Mine	Kelly Price
Friend Or Foe	Adam Ant

Friendly Persuasion	Pat Boone
Friends	Arrival
Friends	Shalamar
Friends	Amii Stewart
Friends	Jody Watley With Erik B & Rakim
Friends And Lovers	Gloria Loring & Carl Anderson
Friends And Neighbours	Max Bygraves & The Tanner Sisters
Friends And Neighbours	Billy Cotton & His Band
Friends Forever	Thunderbugs
Friggin' In The Riggin'	Sex Pistols
Frightened City	Shadows
From A Distance	Bette Midler
From A Distance	Cliff Richard
From A Jack To A King	Ned Miller
From A Window	Billy J. Kramer & The Dakotas
From Here To Eternity	Frank Sinatra
From Me To You	Beatles
From New York To L.A.	Patsy Gallant
From Paris To Berlin	Infernal
From The Bottom Of My Broken Heart	Britney Spears
From The Floorboards Up	Paul Weller
From The Heart	Another Level
From The Underworld	Herd
From The Vine Came The Grape	Gaylords
From The Vine Came The Grape	Hilltoppers
From This Moment On	Shania Twain
Frontin'	Pharrell featuring Jay-Z
Frozen	Madonna
Frozen Orange Juice	Peter Sarstedt
Fuck Forever	Baby Shambles
Full Metal Jacket (I Wanna Be Your Drill Instructor)	Abigail Mead & Nigel Goulding
Fun, Fun, Fun	Beach Boys
Funeral Pyre	Jam
Funkdafied	Da Brat
Funkin' For Jamaica (N.Y.)	Tom Browne
Funky Broadway	Wilson Pickett
Funky Cold Medina	Tone Loc
Funky Gibbon	Goodies
Funky Jam	Primal Scream
Funky Moped	Jasper Carrott
Funky Street	Arthur Conley
Funky Town	Pseudo Echo
Funky Weekend	Stylistics
Funky Worm	Ohio Players
Funkytown	Lipps Inc.
Funny	Joe Hinton
Funny Face	Donna Fargo
Funny Familiar Forgotten Feeling	Tom Jones
Funny Funny	Sweet
Funny How Love Can Be	Ivy League
Funny Way Of Laughin'	Burl Ives
Future Love (EP)	Seal
Gal With The Yaller Shoes	Michael Holliday
Galvanize	Chemical Brothers
Galveston	Glen Campbell
Gambler	Madonna
Gamblin' Man	Lonnie Donegan
Game Of Love	Wayne Fontana & The Mindbenders
The Game Of Love	Santana featuring Michelle Branch
Game Over (Flip)	Lil' Flip
Games People Play	Alan Parsons Project
Games People Play	Joe South
Games Without Frontiers	Peter Gabriel
The Gang That Sang 'Heart Of My Heart'	Four Aces
Gangsta Lean	DRS
Gangsta Lovin'	Eve featuring Alicia Keys
Gangsta's Paradise	Coolio featuring L.V.
Gangsters	Specials
Gangster Trippin'	Fatboy Slim
Garden Of Eden	Gary Miller
Garden Of Eden	Joe Valino
Garden Of Eden	Frankie Vaughan
Garden Party	Rick Nelson
Gasoline	Daddy Yankee
Gasoline Alley Bred	Hollies
Gay Bar	Electric Six
Gaye	Clifford T. Ward
G'd Up	Snoop Dogg Presents Tha Eastsidaz
Gee Baby	Peter Shelley
Gee Whiz (Look At His Eyes)	Carla Thomas
Gee Whiz It's You	Cliff Richard
Gemini Dream	Moody Blues
Geno	Dexy's Midnight Runners
Genie In A Bottle	Christina Aguilera
Gentle On My Mind	Dean Martin
George Best – A Tribute	Brian Kennedy and Peter Corry
Georgia On My Mind	Ray Charles
Georgy Girl	Seekers
Geronimo	Shadows
Get A Job	Silhouettes
Get A Life	Soul II Soul
Get Away	Bobby Brown
Get Away	Georgie Fame
Get Back	Beatles
Get Back	Ludacris
Get Back	Rod Stewart
Get Busy	Sean Paul
Get Closer	Seals & Crofts
Get Dancin'	Disco Tex & The Sex-O-Lettes
Get Down	Gene Chandler
Get Down	Gilbert O'Sullivan

Get Down	Groove Armada Featuring Stush
Get Down And Get With It	Slade
Get Down, Get Down (Get On The Floor)	Joe Simon
Get Down On It	Kool & The Gang
Get Down Tonight	KC & The Sunshine Band
Get Down	Paul Johnson
Get Gone	Ideal
Get Here	Oleta Adams
Get It	Darts
Get It On Tonite	Montell Jordan
Get It On (Bang A Gong)	Power Station
Get It Poppin'	Fat Joe featuring Nelly
Get It Shawty	Lloyd
Get It Together	702
Get Lost	Eden Kane
Get Low	Lil Jon & The East Side Boys featuring Ying Yang Twins
Get Off	Foxy
Get Off Of My Cloud	Rolling Stones
Get On Up	Esquires
Get On Your Feet	Gloria Estefan
Get Outta My Dreams Get Into My Car	Billy Ocean
Get Over You	Sophie Ellis-Bextor
Get Over Yourself	Eden's Crush
Get Ready	Rare Earth
Get Ready	Temptations
Get Ready For This	2 Unlimited
Get Right	Jennifer Lopez
Get The Message	Electronic
Get The Party Started	P!nk
Get Together	Madonna
Get Together	Youngbloods
Get Up	Ciara featuring Chamillionaire
Get Up And Boogie	Silver Convention
Get Up I Feel Like Being A Sex Machine (Part 1)	James Brown
Get Up! (Before The Night Is Over)	Technotronic
Get Ur Freak On	Missy 'Misdemeanor' Elliot
Get Your Number	Mariah Carey
Get-A-Way	Maxx
Getaway	Earth, Wind & Fire
Getaway	Texas
Get Off	Prince
Get On Your Boots	U2
Get Sexy	Sugababes
Get Shaky	Ian Carey Project
Getting Jiggy Wit It	Will Smith
Getto Jam	Domino
Ghetto Child	Detroit Spinners
Ghetto Gospel	2Pac featuring Elton John
Ghetto Heaven	Family Stand
Ghetto Romance	Damage
Ghetto Supastar (That Is What You Are)	Pras Michel With ODB and Mya
G.H.E.T.T.O.U.T	Changing Faces
Ghost Town	Specials
Ghostbusters	Ray Parker Jr.
Ghosts	Japan
Giddy-Up-A-Ding-Dong	Freddie Bell & The Bellboys
The Gift Of Christmas	Childliners
Gigi	Billy Eckstine
Gilly Gilly Ossenfeffer Katzenellen Bogen By The Sea	Max Bygraves
Gimme All Your Lovin'	ZZ Top
Gimme Dat Ding	Pipkins
Gimme Gimme Good Lovin'	Crazy Elephant
Gimme Gimme Gimme (A Man After Midnight)	Abba
Gimme Hope Jo'anna	Eddy Grant
Gimme Little Sign	Brenton Wood
Gimme More	Britney Spears
Gimme Some	Brendon
Gimme Some Lovin'	Spencer Davis Group
Gimme That	Chris Brown featuring Lil' Wayne
Gimme The Light	Sean Paul
Gin And Juice	Snoop Doggy Dogg
Gin House Blues	Amen Corner
Gina	Johnny Mathis
Ginger Bread	Frankie Avalon
Ginny Come Lately	Brian Hyland
Girl	Destiny's Child
Girl	St. Louis Union
A Girl, A Girl	Eddie Fisher
The Girl Can't Help It	Darts
The Girl Can't Help It	Little Richard
Girl Crazy	Hot Chocolate
Girl Don't Come	Sandie Shaw
The Girl From Ipanema	Stan Getz/Astrud Gilberto
Girl I'm Gonna Miss You	Milli Vanilli
The Girl Is Mine	Michael Jackson
The Girl Is Mine	Paul McCartney & Michael Jackson
A Girl Like You	Edwyn Collins
A Girl Like You	Young Rascals
A Girl Like You	Cliff Richard
Girl Of My Best Friend	Elvis Presley
Girl Of My Dreams	Tony Brent
Girl On TV	LFO
Girl Tonite	Twista featuring Trey Songz
Girl Watcher	O'Kaysions
Girl You Know It's True	Milli Vanilli
Girl, You'll Be A Woman Soon	Neil Diamond
Girlfriend	Avril Lavigne
Girlfriend	Billie
Girlfriend	'N Sync featuring Nelly
Girlfriend	Pebbles

Girlfriend/Boyfriend	Blackstreet/Janet
Girlie Girlie	Sophia George
Girls	Moments And Whatnauts
Girls	Dwight Twilley
Girls	Sugababes
The Girls	Calvin Harris
Girls And Boys	Blur
Girls And Boys	Good Charlotte
Girls Girls Girls	Motley Crue
Girls Girls Girls	Sailor
Girls Just Want To Have Fun	Cyndi Lauper
Girls Like Us	B15 Feat. Chrissy D & Lady G
Girls Nite Out	Tyler Collins
Girls On Film	Duran Duran
Girls' School	Wings
Girls Talk	Dave Edmunds
Gitarzan	Ray Stevens
Give A Little Love	Aswad
Give A Little Love	Bay City Rollers
Give In To Me	Michael Jackson
Give It Away	Deepest Blue
Give It Away	Red Hot Chili Peppers
Give It To Me	Troggs
Give It To Me	Timbaland Feat. Nelly Furtado & Justin Timberlake
Give It 2 Me	Madonna
Give It To You	Jordan Knight
Give It Up	Goodmen
Give It Up	KC & The Sunshine Band
Give Me A Little More Time	Gabrielle
Give Me Back My Heart	Dollar
Give Me Just A Little More Time	Chairmen Of The Board
Give Me Just A Little More Time	Kylie Minogue
Give Me Love (Give Me Peace On Earth)	George Harrison
Give Me Just One Night	98 Degrees
Give Me One Reason	Tracy Chapman
Give Me The Night	George Benson
Give Me Your Heart Tonight	Shakin' Stevens
Give Me Your Word	Tennessee Ernie Ford
Give Peace A Chance	Plastic Ono Band
Gives You Hell	All-American Rejects
Givin' Up Givin' In	Three Degrees
Giving Him Something He Can Feel	En Vogue
Giving It All Away	Roger Daltrey
Giving It Up For Your Love	Delbert McClinton
Giving You The Benefit	Pebbles
Giving You The Best That I Got	Anita Baker
Giving You Up	Kylie
G.L.A.D.	Kim Appleby
Glad All Over	Dave Clark Five
Glad It's All Over	Captain Sensible
Glamorous	Fergie Featuring Ludacris
The Glamorous Life	Sheila E
Glass Of Champagne	Sailor
Globetrotter	Tornados
Gloria	Laura Branigan
Gloria	Shadows Of Knight
Glorious	Andreas Johnson
Glory Box	Portishead
Glory Days	Bruce Springsteen
Glory Of Love	Peter Cetera
Glow	Spandau Ballet
Go	Moby
Go All The Way	Raspberries
Go Away	Gloria Estefan
Go Away Little Girl	Steve Lawrence
Go Away Little Girl	Donny Osmond
Go Away Little Girl	Mark Wynter
Go (Before You Break My Heart)	Gigliola Cinquetti
Go Buddy Go	Stranglers
Go D.J.	Lil Wayne
Go Home	Stevie Wonder
Go Jimmy Go	Jimmy Clanton
Gone Till November	Wyclef Jean
Go Let It Out	Oasis
Go Now!	Moody Blues
Go On By	Alma Cogan
Go On Move	Reel 2 Real
Go On With The Wedding	Patti Page
Go West	Pet Shop Boys
Go Wild In The Country	Bow Wow Wow
Go Your Own Way	Fleetwood Mac
God Bless The USA	American Idol Finalists
God Is A DJ	Faithless
God Gave Rock & Roll To You II	Kiss
(God Must Have Spent) A Little More Time On You	'N-Sync
God Only Knows	Beach Boys
God Save The Queen	Sex Pistols
Goin' Back	Dusty Springfield
Goin' Crazy	Natalie
Goin' Down	Greg Guidry
Goin' Down	Melanie C
Goin' Out Of My Head	Lettermen
Goin' Out Of My Head	Little Anthony & The Imperials
Going Back To My Roots	FPI Project
Going Back To My Roots	Odyssey
Going Down The Road	Roy Wood
Going Home	Osmonds
Going In Circles	Friends Of Distinction
Going In With My Eyes Open	David Soul
Going Nowhere	Gabrielle
Going Out	Supergrass
Going To A Go-Go	Miracles

Hazard	Richard Marx
Hazy Shade Of Winter	Bangles
A Hazy Shade Of Winter	Simon & Garfunkel
He	Al Hibbler
He	McGuire Sisters
He Ain't Heavy, He's My Brother	Hollies
He Ain't No Competition	Brother Beyond
He Can't Love U	Jagged Edge
He Could Be The One	Hannah Montana
He Don't Love You (Like I Love You)	Tony Orlando & Dawn
He Will Break Your Heart	Jerry Butler
He'll Have To Go	Jim Reeves
He'll Have To Stay	Jeanne Black
He's A Rebel	Crystals
He's Gonna Step On You Again	John Kongos
He's Got No Love	Searchers
He's Got The Whole World (In His Hands)	Laurie London
He's In Town	Rockin' Berries
He Loves U Not	Dream
He's Mine	Mokenstef
He's Mine	Platters
He's Misstra Know It All	Stevie Wonder
He's On The Phone	Saint Etienne
He's So Fine	Chiffons
He's So Shy	Pointer Sisters
He's Sure The Boy I Love	Crystals
He's The Greatest Dancer	Sister Sledge
He Wasn't Man Enough	Toni Braxton
Head Games	Foreigner
Head Over Heels	Go-Go's
Head Over Heels	Tears For Fears
Head To Toe	Lisa Lisa & Cult Jam
Headline News	Edwin Starr
Headlines (Friendship Never Ends)	Spice Girls
Headsprung	LL Cool J
Headstrong	Trapt
Heal The World	Michael Jackson
Healing Hands	Elton John
Hear The Drummer (Get Wicked)	Chad Jackson
Heard It In A Love Song	Marshall Tucker Band
Heart	Max Bygraves
Heart	Eddie Fisher
Heart	Pet Shop Boys
Heart And Soul	Huey Lewis & The News
Heart And Soul	T'Pau
Heart Attack	Olivia Newton-John
Heart Full Of Soul	Yardbirds
The Heart Never Lies	McFly
The Heart Of A Man	Frankie Vaughan
Heart Of A Teenage Girl	Craig Douglas
Heart Of Asia	Watergate
Heart Of Glass	Blondie
Heart Of Gold	Neil Young
Heart Of My Heart	Max Bygraves
The Heart Of Rock 'n' Roll	Huey Lewis & The News
Heart Of Stone	Taylor Dayne
Heart Of Stone	Kenny
Heart On My Sleeve	Gallagher & Lyle
Heart To Heart	Kenny Loggins
Heart-Shaped Box	Nirvana
Heartache	Pepsi & Shirlie
Heartache Avenue	Maisonettes
Heartache Tonight	Eagles
Heartaches	Marcels
Heartaches By The Number	Guy Mitchell
Heartbeat	Nick Berry
Heartbeat	Don Johnson
Heartbeat	Ruby Murray
Heartbeat	Scouting For Girls
Heartbeat	Seduction
Heartbeat	Showaddywaddy
Heartbeat - It's A Lovebeat	DeFranco Family
Heartbeat/Tragedy	Steps
Heartbeats	Jose Gonzalez
Heartbreak Hotel	Whitney Houston/Faith Evans/Kelly Price
Heartbreak Hotel	Elvis Presley
Heartbreaker	Mariah Carey Feat. Jay-Z
Heartbreaker	Dionne Warwick
Heartbreaker	Will.I.Am Featuring Cheryl Cole
Heartbroken	T2 Featuring Jodie Aysha
Heartless	Frankie Vaughan
Heartless	Kanye West
Heartlight	Neil Diamond
Hearts	Marty Balin
Hearts Of Stone	Charms
Hearts Of Stone	Fontane Sisters
The Heat Is On	Glenn Frey
Heat Of The Moment	Asia
Heat Of The Night	Bryan Adams
Heat Wave	Martha & The Vandellas
Heat Wave	Linda Ronstadt
Heatseeker	AC/DC
Heaven	Bryan Adams
Heaven	DJ Sammy & Yanou Featuring Do
Heaven	Warrant
Heaven For Everyone	Queen
Heaven Help Me	Deon Estus
Heaven Help Us All	Stevie Wonder
Heaven In Your Eyes	Loverboy
Heaven Is A Halfpipe	OPM
Heaven Is A Place On Earth	Belinda Carlisle
Heaven Knows	Donna Summer
Heaven Knows I'm Miserable Now	Smiths
Heaven Must Be Missing An Angel	Tavares
Heaven Must Have Sent You	Elgins
Heaven Must Have Sent You	Bonnie Pointer
Heaven On The 7th Floor	Paul Nicholas
Heavyweight Champion Of The World	Reverend And The Makers
Helen Wheels	Paul McCartney
Hell Raiser	Sweet
Hella Good	No Doubt Featuring Bounty Killer
Hello	Lionel Richie
Hello Again	Neil Diamond
Hello, Dolly!	Louis Armstrong
Hello Goodbye	Beatles
Hello Happiness	Drifters
Hello! Hello! I'm Back Again	Gary Glitter
Hello, I Love You	Doors
Hello It's Me	Todd Rundgren
Hello Little Girl	Fourmost
Hello Mary Lou	Ricky Nelson
Hello Mudduh, Hello Fadduh	Allan Sherman
Hello Stranger	Yvonne Elliman
Hello Stranger	Barbara Lewis
Hello Susie	Amen Corner
Hello This Is Joannie (The Telephone Answering Machine)	Paul Evans
Hello (Turn Your Radio On)	Shakespear's Sister
Hello Walls	Faron Young
Help	Bananarama
Help!	Beatles
Help Is On Its Way	Little River Band
Help Me	Joni Mitchell
Help Me Girl	Eric Burdon & The Animals
Help Me Make It Through The Night	John Holt
Help Me Make It Through The Night	Gladys Knight & The Pips
Help Me Make It Through The Night	Sammi Smith
Help Me, Rhonda	Beach Boys
Help Yourself	Tom Jones
Helule Helule	Tremeloes
Her Royal Majesty	James Darren
Her Town Too	James Taylor & J. D. Souther
Here	Tony Martin
Here And Now	Steps
Here And Now	Luther Vandross
Here Come The Nice	Small Faces
Here Comes Goodbye	Rascal Flatts
Here Comes My Baby	Tremeloes
Here Comes Summer	Jerry Keller
Here Comes That Feeling	Brenda Lee
Here Comes That Rainy Day Feeling Again	Fortunes
Here Comes The Hotstepper	Ini Kamoze
Here Comes The Judge	Shorty Long
Here Comes The Night	Them
Here Comes The Rain Again	Eurythmics
Here Comes The Sun	Steve Harley
Here Comes The Sun	Richie Havens
Here 4 One	Blazin' Squad
Here I Am	Bryan Adams
Here I Am (Come And Take Me)	Al Green
Here I Am (Come And Take Me)	UB40
Here I Am (Just When You Thought I Was Over You)	Air Supply
Here I Go Again	Archie Bell & The Drells
Here I Go Again	Hollies
Here I Go Again	Whitesnake
Here I Stand	Bitty McLean
Here (In Your Arms)	Hellogoodbye
Here It Comes Again	Fortunes
Here We Are	Gloria Estefan
Here We Go	C&C Music Factory feat. Freedom Williams & Zelma Davis
Here We Go	Stakka Bo
Here We Go Again	Ray Charles
Here We Go Again!	Portrait
Here We Go Round The Mulberry Bush	Traffic
Here With Me	Dido
Here Without You	3 Doors Down
Here You Come Again	Dolly Parton
Hernando's Hideaway	Johnston Brothers
Hernando's Hideaway	Johnnie Ray
Hernando's Hideaway	Archie Bleyer
Hero	Mariah Carey
Hero	Enrique Iglesias
Hero	Chad Kroeger featuring Josey Scott
Hero	The X Factor Finalists
Heroes And Villains	Beach Boys
Hersham Boys	Sham 69
Hey! Baby	Bruce Channel
Hey Baby	No Doubt featuring Bounty Killer
Hey Baby (They're Playing Our Song)	Buckinghams
Hey Baby (Uhh, Ahh)	DJ Otzi
Hey Boy Hey Girl	Chemical Brothers
Hey Deanie	Shaun Cassidy
Hey D.J. I Can't Dance To...	Beatmasters featuring Betty Boo
Hey Girl	Donny Osmond
Hey Girl	Small Faces
Hey, Girl	Freddie Scott
Hey Girl Don't Bother Me	Tams
Hey! Jealous Lover	Frank Sinatra
Hey Joe	Jimi Hendrix Experience
Hey Jude	Beatles
Hey Little Cobra	Rip Chords
Hey Little Girl	Major Lance
Hey Little Girl	Del Shannon
Hey Lover	LL Cool J
Hey Ma	Cam'ron featuring Juelz Santana, Freekey Zeke
Hey Mama	Black Eyed Peas
Hey Mr. D.J.	Zhane
Hey Music Lover	S'Express
Hey Nineteen	Steely Dan
Hey Now (Girls Just Want To Have Fun)	Cyndi Lauper
Hey Paula	Paul & Paula
Hey Rock And Roll	Showaddywaddy
Hey There	Rosemary Clooney
Hey There	Sammy Davis Jr.
Hey There	Johnnie Ray
Hey There Delilah	Plain White T's
Hey There Lonely Girl	Eddie Holman
Hey Whatever	Westlife
(Hey Won't You Play) Another Somebody Done Somebody Wrong Song	B.J. Thomas
Hey Ya!	OutKast
(Hey You) The Rocksteady Crew	Rocksteady Crew
Hi-De-Ho	Blood Sweat & Tears
Hi-Fidelity	Kids From 'Fame'
Hi-Heel Sneakers	Tommy Tucker
Hi, Hi, Hi	Paul McCartney
Hi Ho Silver	Jim Diamond
Hi-Ho Silver Lining	Jeff Beck
Hi-Lili-Hi-Lo	Alan Price Set
Hi Tension	Hi Tension
Hidden Agenda	Craig David
Hide And Seek	Howard Jones
Hide U	Kosheen
Hideaway	De'lacy
Hideaway	Dave Dee, Dozy, Beaky, Mick & Tich
The High And The Mighty	Les Baxter
The High And The Mighty	Leroy Holmes
The High And The Mighty	Victor Young
High Class Baby	Cliff Richard
High Energy	Evelyn Thomas
High Enough	Damn Yankees
High Hopes	Frank Sinatra
High In The Sky	Amen Corner
High Life	Modern Romance
High On You	Survivor
High School Confidential	Jerry Lee Lewis
High Time	Paul Jones
Higher Ground	UB40
Higher Ground	Stevie Wonder
Higher Love	Steve Winwood
Higher State Of Consciousness	Josh Wink
Him	Rupert Holmes
Him Or Me – What's It Gonna Be	Paul Revere & The Raiders
The Hindu Times	Oasis
Hip Hop Hurray	Naughty By Nature
Hip To Be Square	Huey Lewis & The News
Hip To Hip	V
Hippy Hippy Shake	Swinging Blue Jeans
Hippychick	Soho
Hips Don't Lie	Shakira featuring Wyclef Jean
History	Mai Tai
Hit 'em Up Style (Oops!)	Blu Cantrell
Hit Me Off	New Edition
Hit Me With Your Best Shot	Pat Benatar
Hit Me With Your Rhythm Stick	Ian & The Blockheads
Hit That Perfect Beat	Bronski Beat
Hit The Road Jack	Ray Charles
Hitchin' A Ride	Vanity Fare
Hocus Pocus	Focus
Hold Back The Night	Trammps
Hold Her Tight	Osmonds
Hold Me	Fleetwood Mac
Hold Me	P.J. Proby
Hold Me	B.A. Robertson
Hold Me Close	David Essex
Hold Me In Your Arms	Rick Astley
Hold Me Now	Johnny Logan
Hold Me Now	Thompson Twins
Hold Me Thrill Me Kiss Me	Mel Carter
Hold Me Tight	Johnny Nash
Hold Me, Thrill Me, Kiss Me	Gloria Estefan
Hold Me, Thrill Me, Kiss Me, Kill Me	U2
Hold My Hand	Don Cornell
Hold My Hand	Hootie & The Blowfish
Hold On	En Vogue
Hold On	Santana
Hold On	Wilson Phillips
Hold On My Heart	Genesis
Hold On Tight	Electric Light Orchestra
Hold On To My Love	Jimmy Ruffin
Hold On To The Nights	Richard Marx
Hold The Line	Toto
Hold Tight	Dave Dee, Dozy, Beaky, Mick & Tich
Hold What You've Got	Joe Tex
Hold You Down	Jennifer Lopez featuring Fat Joe
Hold You Tight	Tara Kemp
Hold Your Head Up	Argent
Holding Back The Years	Simply Red
Holding On	Steve Winwood
Holding On For You	Liberty X
Holding Out For A Hero	Bonnie Tyler
Hole Hearted	Extreme
Hole In My Shoe	neil

Hole In My Shoe	Traffic
Hole In The Ground	Bernard Cribbins
Hole In The Head	Sugababes
Holidae In	Chingy featuring Ludacris and Snoop Dog
Holiday	Dizzee Rascal
Holiday	Madonna
Holiday Rap	M.C. Miker 'G' & Deejay Sven
Holidays In The Sun	Sex Pistols
Holla Holla	JA Rule
Hollaback Girl	Gwen Stefani
Holler	Spice Girls
Holly Holy	Neil Diamond
Hollywood	Madonna
Hollywood Nights	Bob Seger & The Silver Bullet Band
Hollywood Swinging	Kool & The Gang
Holy Cow	Lee Dorsey
Holy Smoke	Iron Maiden
Homburg	Procol Harum
Home	Daughtry
Home	Westlife
Home Lovin' Man	Andy Williams
Homecoming	Kanye West Featuring Chris Martin
Homely Girl	Chi-Lites
Homely Girl	UB40
Homeward Bound	Simon & Garfunkel
Honaloochie Boogie	Mott The Hoople
An Honest Mistake	The Bravery
Honey	Bobby Goldsboro
Honey	Mariah Carey
Honey Chile	Martha & The Vandellas
Honey Come Back	Glen Campbell
Honey Honey	Sweet Dreams
Honey I Need	Pretty Things
Honey-Babe	Art Mooney
Honey To The Bee	Billie
Honeycomb	Jimmie Rodgers
Hong Kong Garden	Siouxsie & The Banshees
Honky Cat	Elton John
Honky Tonk (Parts 1 & 2)	Bill Doggett
Honky Tonk Women	Rolling Stones
Honolulu Lulu	Jan & Dean
Hooked On A Feeling	Blue Swede
Hooked On A Feeling	B.J. Thomas
Hooked On Classics	Royal Philharmonic Orchestra
Hooray For Hazel	Tommy Roe
Hooray Hooray (It's A Cheeky Holiday)	Cheeky Girls
Hooray Hooray It's A Holi-Holiday	Boney M
Hoots Mon	Lord Rockingham's XI
Hopeless	Andy Williams
Hopelessly Devoted To You	Olivia Newton-John
The Horse	Cliff Nobles & Co.
Horny	Mousse T Vs Hot 'n' Juicy
A Horse With No Name	America
Hot Blooded	Foreigner
Hot Boyz	Missy "Misdemeanor" Elliott
Hot Child In The City	Nick Gilder
Hot Diggity	Michael Holliday
Hot Diggity (Dog Ziggity Boom)	Perry Como
Hot Fun In The Summertime	Sly & The Family Stone
Hot Girls In Love	Loverboy
Hot In The City	Billy Idol
Hot In Herre	Nelly
Hot Line	Sylvers
Hot Love	T. Rex
Hot N Cold	Katy Perry
Hot Pants (She Got To Use What She Got To Get What She Wants)	James Brown
Hot Pastrami	Dartells
Hot Rod Hearts	Robbie Dupree
Hot Rod Lincoln	Commander Cody & His Lost Planet Airmen
(Hot S**T) Country Grammar	Nelly
Hot Smoke & Sasafrass	Bubble Puppy
Hot Stuff	Arsenal FC
Hot Stuff	Donna Summer
Hot Stuff (Let's Dance)	Craig David
Hot Tracks E.P. (Love Hurts Etc.)	Nazareth
Hotel	Cassidy featuring R. Kelly
Hotel California	Eagles
Hotel Happiness	Brook Benton
Hotel Room Service	Pitbull
Hotlegs	Rod Stewart
Hound Dog	Elvis Presley
Hound Dog Man	Fabian
House Arrest	Krush
House Nation	House Master Boyz & The Rude Boy Of House
The House Of Blue Lights	Chuck Miller
House Of Fun	Madness
House Of Love	East 17
House Of The Rising Sun	Animals
House Of The Rising Sun	Frijid Pink
The House That Jack Built	Aretha Franklin
The House That Jack Built	Alan Price Set
The House That Jack Built	Tracie
A House With Love In It	Vera Lynn
Housecall	Shabba Ranks featuring Maxi Priest
How 'Bout Us	Champaign
How About That	Adam Faith
How Am I Supposed To Live Without You	Michael Bolton
How Am I Supposed To Live Without You	Laura Branigan
How Can I Be Sure	David Cassidy
How Can I Be Sure	Young Rascals
How Can I Ease The Pain	Lisa Fischer

How Can I Fall	Breathe
How Can I Love You More?	M People
How Can We Be Lovers	Michael Bolton
How Can You Mend A Broken Heart	Bee Gees
How Come	D12
How Come	Ronnie Lane
How Deep Is Your Love	Bee Gees
How Deep Is Your Love	Dru Hill
How Deep Is Your Love	Take That
How Do I Live	LeAnn Rimes
How Do I Make You	Linda Ronstadt
How Do You Do It?	Gerry & The Pacemakers
How Do You Do!	Roxette
How Do You Do?	Mouth & McNeal
How Do You Talk To An Angel	Heights
How Do You Want It/California Love	2Pac/KC And JoJo
How Does That Grab You Darlin'	Nancy Sinatra
How Far We've Come	Matchbox Twenty
How High	Redman/Method Man
How Important Can It Be?	Joni James
How Long	Ace
How Low	Ludacris
How Many Tears	Bobby Vee
How Much I Feel	Ambrosia
How Much Love	Leo Sayer
How Soon	Henry Mancini & His Orchestra
How Sweet It Is To Be Loved By You	Marvin Gaye
How Sweet It Is (To Be Loved By You)	James Taylor
How Time Flies	Jerry Wallace
How To Save A Life	Fray
How We Do	Game featuring 50 Cent
How Will I Know	Whitney Houston
How Wonderful You Are	Gordon Haskell
How You Gonna Act Like That	Tyrese
How You Gonna See Me Now	Alice Cooper
How You Remind Me	Nickelback
How's It Going To Be	Third Eye Blind
Howzat	Sherbet
Hubble Bubble Toil And Trouble	Manfred Mann
The Hucklebuck	Chubby Checker
Hula Love	Buddy Knox
Human	Human League
Human	The Killers
Human Nature	Gary Clail On-U Sound System
Human Nature	Michael Jackson
Human Nature	Madonna
Human Touch	Bruce Springsteen
Hummingbird	Les Paul & Mary Ford
Humpin' Around	Bobby Brown
The Humpty Dance	Digital Underground
A Hundred Pounds Of Clay	Craig Douglas
A Hundred Pounds Of Clay	Gene McDaniels
Hung Up	Madonna
Hung Up	Paul Weller
Hungry	Paul Revere & The Raiders
Hungry Eyes	Eric Carmen
Hungry Heart	Bruce Springsteen
Hungry Like The Wolf	Duran Duran
The Hunter Gets Captured By The Game	Marvelettes
Hunting High And Low	A-Ha
Hurdy Gurdy Man	Donovan
Hurry Up Harry	Sham 69
Hurt	Manhattans
Hurt	Timi Yuro
Hurt So Bad	Lettermen
Hurt So Bad	Little Anthony & The Imperials
Hurt So Bad	Linda Ronstadt
Hurt So Good	Susan Cadogan
Hurting Each Other	Carpenters
Hurts So Good	John Cougar
Husan	Bhangra Knights Vs Husan
Hush	Deep Purple
Hush	LL Cool J featuring 7 Aurelius
Hush, Hush Sweet Charlotte	Patti Page
Hush Not A Word To Mary	John Rowles
The Hustle	Van McCoy
Hustle! (To The Music...)	Funky Worm
Hymn	Ultravox
Hymn To Her	Pretenders
Hyperballad	Björk
Hypnotize	Notorious B.I.G.
Hypnotized	Plies Featuring Akon
Hysteria	Def Leppard
I Adore Mi Amor	Color Me Badd
I Ain't Gonna Stand For It	Stevie Wonder
I Almost Lost My Mind	Pat Boone
I Am	Tony Bennett
I Am A Cider Drinker (Paloma Blanca)	Wurzels
I Am A Rock	Simon & Garfunkel
I Am Blessed	Eternal
I Am ...I Said	Neil Diamond
I Am The Beat	Look
I Am Woman	Helen Reddy
I Apologise	P.J. Proby
I Beg Of You	Elvis Presley
I Beg Your Pardon	Kon Kan
I Begin To Wonder	Dannii Minogue
I Believe	Bachelors
I Believe	Blessid Union Of Souls
I Believe	EMF
I Believe	Fantasia
I Believe	Stephen Gately

I Believe	Happy Clappers
I Believe I Can Fly	R.Kelly
I Believe In Christmas	Tweenies
I Believe In Father Christmas	Greg Lake
I Believe (In Love)	Hot Chocolate
I Believe In A Thing Called Love	The Darkness
I Believe In You	Kylie
I Believe In You (You Believe In Me)	Johnnie Taylor
I Believe My Heart	Duncan James & Keedie
I Believe There's Nothing Stronger Than Our Love	Paul Anka with Odia Coates
I Believe/Up On The Roof	Robson Green & Jerome Flynn
I Belong To You	Rome
I Bet You Look Good On The Dancefloor	Arctic Monkeys
I Breathe Again	Adam Rickitt
I Can	Nas
I Can Do It	Rubettes
I Can Do That	Montell Jordan
I Can Dream About You	Dan Hartman
I Can Hear Music	Beach Boys
I Can Hear The Grass Grow	Move
I Can Help	Billy Swan
I Can Love You Like That	All-4-One
I Can Make You Feel Good	Shalamar
I Can Never Go Home Anymore	Shangri-Las
I Can Only Disappoint U	Mansun
I Can Prove It	Phil Fearon
I Can See Clearly Now	Johnny Nash
I Can See For Miles	Who
I Can Take Or Leave Your Lovin'	Herman's Hermits
I Can't Break Down	Sinead Quinn
I Can't Control Myself	Troggs
I Can't Dance	Genesis
I Can't Explain	Who
(I Can't Get No) Satisfaction	Rolling Stones
I Can't Get Next To You	Temptations
I Can't Go For That (No Can Do)	Daryl Hall & John Oates
I Can't Help Falling In Love With You	UB40
I Can't Help It	Andy Gibb & Olivia Newton-John
I Can't Help Myself	Donnie Elbert
I Can't Help Myself	Four Tops
I Can't Hold Back	Survivor
I Can't Leave You Alone	George McCrae
I Can't Let Go	Hollies
I Can't Let Maggie Go	Honeybus
I Can't Read You	Daniel Bedingfield
I Can't Sleep Baby (If I)	R.Kelly
I Can't Stand It	Eric Clapton
I Can't Stand It	Twenty 4 Seven
I Can't Stand It No More	Peter Frampton
I Can't Stand The Rain	Eruption
I Can't Stand Up For Falling Down	Elvis Costello
I Can't Stay Mad At You	Skeeter Davis
I Can't Stop	Osmonds
I Can't Stop Dancing	Archie Bell & The Drells
I Can't Stop Lovin' You	Don Gibson
I Can't Stop Loving You	Ray Charles
I Can't Stop Lovin' You (Though I Try)	Leo Sayer
I Can't Take The Power	Off-Shore
I Can't Tell A Waltz From A Tango	Alma Cogan
I Can't Tell The Bottom From The Top	Hollies
I Can't Tell You Why	Eagles
I Can't Wait	Stevie Nicks
I Can't Wait	Nu Shooz
I Can't Wait Another Minute	Hi-Five
I Close My Eyes And Count To Ten	Dusty Springfield
I Could Be Happy	Altered Images
I Could Be So Good For You	Dennis Waterman
I Could Easily Fall	Cliff Richard
I Could Never Take The Place Of Your Man	Prince
I Could Never Love Another (After Loving You)	Temptations
I Couldn't Live Without Your Love	Petula Clark
I Cried A Tear	Lavern Baker
I Cried For You	Ricky Stevens
I Did What I Did For Maria	Tony Christie
I Didn't Know I Loved You (Till I Saw You Rock 'n' Roll)	Gary Glitter
I Didn't Mean To Turn You On	Robert Palmer
I Die:You Die	Gary Numan
I Dig Rock And Roll Music	Peter, Paul & Mary
I Do!!	Toya
I Do, I Do, I Do, I Do, I Do	Abba
I Don't Believe In If Anymore	Roger Whittaker
I Don't Blame You At All	Smokey Robinson & The Miracles
I Don't Care	Shakespear's Sister
I Don't Ever Want To See You Again	Uncle Sam
I Don't Feel Like Dancin'	Scissor Sisters
I Don't Have The Heart	James Ingram
I Don't Know Anybody Else	Black Box
I Don't Know How To Love Him	Helen Reddy
I Don't Know Why	Eden Kane
I Don't Know Why	Linda Scott
I Don't Like Mondays	Boomtown Rats
I Don't Like To Sleep Alone	Paul Anka with Odia Coates
I Don't Need A Man	Pussycat Dolls
I Don't Need You	Kenny Rogers
I Don't Think That Man Should Sleep Alone	Ray Parker Jr.
I Don't Wanna Cry	Mariah Carey
I Don't Wanna Dance	Eddy Grant
I Don't Wanna Fight	Tina Turner
I Don't Wanna Get Hurt	Donna Summer

Title	Artist
I Don't Wanna Go On Like That	Elton John
I Don't Wanna Kiss You	LFO
I Don't Wanna Know	Mario Winans featuring Enya & P. Diddy
I Don't Wanna Live Without Your Love	Chicago
I Don't Wanna Lose You	Kandidate
I Don't Wanna Lose You	Tina Turner
I Don't Want A Lover	Texas
I Don't Want Our Loving To Die	Herd
I Don't Want To Be	Gavin DeGraw
I Don't Want To Be A Hero	Johnny Hates Jazz
I Don't Want To Do Wrong	Gladys Knight & The Pips
I Don't Want To Live Without You	Foreigner
I Don't Want To Miss A Thing	Aerosmith
I Don't Want To Miss A Thing	Mark Chesnutt
I Don't Want To Put A Hold On You	Berni Flint
I Don't Want To Talk About It	Everything But The Girl
I Don't Want To Talk About It	Rod Stewart
I Don't Want to Wait	Paula Cole
I Don't Want Your Love	Duran Duran
I Drove All Night	Cyndi Lauper
I Drove All Night	Roy Orbison
I Eat Cannibals Pt. 1	Toto Coelo
I Fall To Pieces	Patsy Cline
I Feel Fine	Beatles
I Feel For You	Chaka Khan
I Feel Free	Cream
I Feel Like A Bullet	Elton John
I Feel Like Buddy Holly	Alvin Stardust
I Feel Love	Bronski Beat & Marc Almond
I Feel Love	Donna Summer
I Feel Love Comin' On	Felice Taylor
I Feel So Bad	Elvis Presley
I Feel The Earth Move	Carole King
I Feel The Earth Move	Martika
I Feel You	Depeche Mode
I Finally Found Someone	Barbra Streisand and Bryan Adams
I Fought The Law	Bobby Fuller Four
I Found Lovin'	Fatback Band
I Found Out The Hard Way	Four Pennies
I Found Someone	Cher
I Found U	Axwell Featuring Max C
I Get A Kick Out Of You	Gary Shearston
I Get A Little Sentimental Over You	New Seekers
I Get Around	Beach Boys
I Get Around	2Pac
I Get Lonely	Janet/Blackstreet
I Get So Lonely	Four Knights
I Get The Sweetest Feeling	Liz McClarnon
I Get The Sweetest Feeling	Jackie Wilson
I Get Weak	Belinda Carlisle
I Go Ape	Neil Sedaka
I Go Crazy	Paul Davis
I Go To Extremes	Billy Joel
I Go To Pieces	Peter & Gordon
I Go To Sleep	Pretenders
I Got 5 On It	Luniz
I Got A Feeling	Ricky Nelson
I Got A Man	Positive K
I Got A Name	Jim Croce
I Got ID/Long Road	Pearl Jam
I Got Rhythm	Happenings
I Got Stung	Elvis Presley
I Got The Feelin'	James Brown
I Got The Hook Up!	Master P/Sons of Funk
I Got You Babe	Merrion, McCall & Kensit
I Got You Babe	Sonny & Cher
I Got You Babe	UB40
I Got You (I Feel Good)	James Brown
I Gotcha	Joe Tex
I Gotta Feeling	The Black Eyed Peas
I Guess I'll Always Love You	Isley Brothers
I Guess That's Why They Call It The Blues	Elton John
I Had Too Much To Dream (Last Night)	Electric Prunes
I Hate Myself For Loving You	Joan Jett & The Blackhearts
I Hate This Part	The Pussycat Dolls
I Hate U	TAFKAP
I Have A Dream	Abba
I Have A Dream	Westlife
I Have Nothing	Whitney Houston
I Haven't Stopped Dancing Yet	Pat & Mick
I Hear A Symphony	Supremes
I Hear You Knocking	Dave Edmunds
I Hear You Knocking	Gale Storm
I Hear You Now	Jon & Vangelis
I Heard A Rumour	Bananarama
I Heard It Through The Grapevine	Marvin Gaye
I Heard It Through The Grapevine	Gladys Knight & The Pips
I Honestly Love You	Olivia Newton-John
I Hope You Dance	Ronan Keating
I Hope You Dance	Lee Ann Womack
I Just Called To Say I Love You	Stevie Wonder
I Just Can't Help Believing	Elvis Presley
I Just Can't Help Believing	B.J. Thomas
I Just Can't Stop Loving You	Michael Jackson
	(duet with Seidah Garrett)
(I Just) Died In Your Arms	Cutting Crew
I Just Don't Have The Heart	Cliff Richard
I Just Don't Know What To Do	
With Myself	Dusty Springfield
I Just Fall In Love Again	Anne Murray
I Just Wanna Be Loved	Culture Club
I Just Wanna Stop	Gino Vannelli
I Just Want To Be Your Everything	Andy Gibb
I Just Want To Celebrate	Rare Earth
I Just Want To Make Love To You	Etta James
I Keep Forgettin' (Everytime You're Near)	Michael McDonald
I Kissed A Girl	Katy Perry
I Knew I Loved You	Savage Garden
I Knew You Were Waiting (For Me)	Aretha Franklin & George Michael
I Knew You When	Donny Osmond
I Knew You When	Billy Joe Royal
I Know	Perry Como
I Know	Dionne Farris
I Know	New Atlantic
I Know A Place	Petula Clark
I Know Him So Well	Elaine Paige & Barbara Dickson
I Know Him So Well	Steps
(I Know) I'm Losing You	Rare Earth
(I Know) I'm Losing You	Temptations
I Know There's Something Going On	Frida
I Know What I Like	Huey Lewis & The News
I Know What You Want	Busta Rhymes & Mariah
Carey	
featuring Flipmode Squad	
I Know (You Don't Love Me No More)	Barbara George
I Know You Want Me (Calle Ocho)	Pitbull
I Learned From The Best	Whitney Houston
I Like Dreamin'	Kenny Nolan
I Like It	Dino
I Like It	Gerry & The Pacemakers
I Like It	Narcotic Thrust
I Like It	Sammie
I Like It Like That	Dave Clark Five
I Like It Like That (Pt.1)	Chris Kenner
I Like That	Houston featuring Chingy, Nate Dog & I-20
I Like The Way	Bodyrockers
I Like The Way (The Kissing Game)	Hi-Five
I Like To Move It	Reel 2 Real featuring The Mad Stuntman
I Like You So Much Better When You're Naked	Ida Maria
I Like Your Kind Of Love	Andy Williams
I Live For Your Love	Natalie Cole
I Lost My Heart To A Starship Trooper	Sarah Brightman
I Love	Tom T. Hall
I Love A Rainy Night	Eddie Rabbitt
I Love College	Asher Roth
I Love How You Love Me	Paris Sisters
I Love How You Love Me	Bobby Vinton
I Love It When We Do	Ronan Keating
I Love Music (Pt. 1)	O'Jays
I Love My Chick	Busta Rhymes featuring will-i-am & Kelis
I Love My Radio	Taffy
I Love Rock 'n' Roll	Joan Jett & The Blackhearts
I Love The Night Life (Disco 'Round)	Alicia Bridges
I Love The Sound Of Breaking Glass	Nick Lowe &
	His Cowboy Outfit
I Love The Way You Love	Marv Johnson
I Love The Way You Love Me	Boyzone
I Love To Boogie	T. Rex
I Love To Love (But My Baby Loves To Dance)	Tina Charles
I Love You	The Ordinary Boys
I Love You	Climax Blues Band
I Love You	Faith Evans
I Love You	People
I Love You	Cliff Richard
I Love You	Donna Summer
I Love You Always Forever	Donna Lewis
I Love You Anyway	Boyzone
I Love You Baby	Paul Anka
I Love You Because	Al Martino
I Love You Because	Jim Reeves
I Love You Came Too Late	Joey McIntyre
I Love You Love Me Love	Gary Glitter
I Love You More And More Every Day	Al Martino
I Love You So Much It Hurts	Charlie Gracie
I Love Your Smile	Shanice
I Luv U Baby	Original
I Made It Through The Rain	Barry Manilow
I May Never Pass This Way Again	Perry Como
I May Never Pass This Way Again	Robert Earl
I Miss You	Haddaway
I Miss You	Blink-182
I Miss You	Aaron Hall
I Miss You	Klymaxx
I Missed Again	Phil Collins
I Must Be Seeing Things	Gene Pitney
I Need Love	LL Cool J
I Need A Girl (Part 1)	P.Diddy featuring Usher & Loon
I Need A Girl (Part Two)	P. Diddy & Ginuwine feat. Loon, Mario Winans
I Need To Know	Marc Anthony
I Need You	America
I Need You	B.V.S.M.P.
I Need You	Leann Rimes
I Need You	N-Dubz
I Need You Now	Eddie Fisher
I Need Your Love Tonight	Elvis Presley
I Need Your Lovin'	Alyson Williams
I Never Cry	Alice Cooper
I Never Loved A Man (The Way I Love You)	Aretha Franklin
I Only Have Eyes For You	Flamingos
I Only Have Eyes For You	Art Garfunkel
I Only Want To Be With You	Bay City Rollers
I Only Want To Be With You	Dusty Springfield
I Only Want To Be With You	Tourists
I Owe You Nothing	Bros
I Predict A Riot	Kaiser Chiefs
I Pretend	Des O'Connor
I Put A Spell On You	Alan Price Set
I Put A Spell On You	Sonique
I Quit	Bros
I Ran (So Far Away)	Flock Of Seagulls
I Remember Elvis Presley (The King Is Dead)	Danny Mirror
I Remember Holding You	Boys Club
I Remember Yesterday	Donna Summer
I Remember You	Frank Ifield
I Remember You	Skid Row
I Saw Her Again	Mamas & The Papas
I Saw Him Standing There	Tiffany
I Saw Linda Yesterday	Dickey Lee
I Saw Mommy Kissing Santa Claus	Beverley Sisters
I Saw Mommy Kissing Santa Claus	Jimmy Boyd
I Saw Red	Warrant
I Saw The Light	Todd Rundgren
I Say A Little Prayer	Aretha Franklin
I Say A Little Prayer	Dionne Warwick
I Second That Emotion	Japan
I Second That Emotion	Smokey Robinson & The Miracles
I See A Star	Mouth & McNeal
I See The Moon	Stargazers
I Shot The Sheriff	Eric Clapton
I Should Be So Lucky	Kylie Minogue
I Should Have Known Better	Jim Diamond
I Shoulda Loved Ya	Narada Michael Walden
I Started A Joke	Bee Gees
I Still Believe	Mariah Carey
I Still Believe	Ronnie Hilton
I Still Believe	Brenda K. Starr
I Still Believe In You	Cliff Richard
I Still Can't Get Over You	Ray Parker Jr.
I Still Haven't Found What I'm Looking For	Chimes
I Still Haven't Found What I'm Looking For	U2
I Still Love You	Next
I Surrender	Rainbow
I Swear	All-4-One
I Thank You	Sam & Dave
I Think I Love You	Kaci
I Think I Love You	Partridge Family
I Think It's Going To Rain	UB40
I Think It's Love	Jermaine Jackson
I Think Of You	Perry Como
I Think Of You	Merseybeats
I Think They Like Me	Dem Franchize Boyz featuring Jermaine Dupri
I Think We're Alone Now	Girls Aloud
I Think We're Alone Now	Tommy James & The Shondells
I Think We're Alone Now	Tiffany
I Thought It Was Over	The Feeling
I Told You So	Carrie Underwood Featuring Randy Travis
I Tried	Bone Thugs-N-Harmony Featuring Akon
I Try	Macy Gray
I Turn To You	Christina Aguilera
I Turn To You	Melanie C
I Touch Myself	Divinyls
I Understand	Freddie & The Dreamers
I Understand	June Valli
I Understand Just How You Feel	Four Tunes
I Understand (Just How You Feel)	G-Clefs
I Walk The Line	Johnny Cash
I Wanna Be A Cowboy	Boys Don't Cry
I Wanna Be A Hippy	Technohead
I Wanna Be Down	Brandy
I Wanna Be Rich	Calloway
I Wanna Be U	Chocolate Puma
I Wanna Be Your Lover	Prince
I Wanna Be Your Man	Rolling Stones
I Wanna Dance Wit Choo'	Disco Tex & The Sex-O-Lettes
I Wanna Dance With Somebody	
(Who Loves Me)	Whitney Houston
I Wanna Do It With You	Barry Manilow
I Wanna Get Next To You	Rose Royce
(I Wanna Give You) Devotion	Nomad featuring MC Mikee Freedom
I Wanna Go Back	Eddie Money
I Wanna Go Home	Lonnie Donegan
I Wanna Have Some Fun	Samantha Fox
I Wanna Have Your Babies	Natasha Bedingfield
I Wanna Hold You	McFly
I Wanna Love Him So Bad	Jelly Beans
I Wanna Love You	Akon featuring Snoop Dogg
I Wanna Love You	Jade
I Wanna Love You Forever	Jessica Simpson
I Wanna Sex You Up	Color Me Badd
I Wanna Stay With You	Gallagher & Lyle
I Want A New Drug	Huey Lewis & The News
I Want Candy	Bow Wow Wow
I Want Candy	Strangeloves
I Want Her	Keith Sweat
I Want It All	Warren G Feat. Mack 10
I Want It All	Queen
I Want It That Way	Backstreet Boys
I Want Love	Elton John
I Want That Man	Deborah Harry
(I Want To Be) Elected	Mr. Bean & Smear Campaign
I Want To Be Free	Toyah
I Want To Be Wanted	Brenda Lee
I Want To Be Your Man	Roger
I Want To Break Free	Queen
I Want To Hold Your Hand	Beatles
I Want To Know What Love Is	Foreigner

Just Stand Up!	Artists Stand Up To Cancer
Just Take My Heart	Mr. Big
Just The Girl	Click Five
Just The Two Of Us	Will Smith
Just The Two Of Us	Grover Washington Jr.
Just The Way I'm Feeling	Feeder
Just The Way You Are	Billy Joel
Just The Way You Are	Barry White
Just This Side Of Love	Malandra Burrows
Just To Be Close To You	Commodores
Just To See Her	Smokey Robinson
Just Walking In The Rain	Johnnie Ray
Just Want You To Know	Backstreet Boys
Just What I Always Wanted	Mari Wilson
Just When I Needed You Most	Randy Vanwarmer
Just Who Is The Five O'Clock Hero	Jam
Just You 'n' Me	Chicago
Justified And Ancient	KLF
Justify My Love	Madonna
Kansas City	Wilbert Harrison
Karma	Lloyd Bank$ featuring Avant
Karma Chameleon	Culture Club
Kate Bush On Stage E.P.	Kate Bush
Kayleigh	Marillion
Keep A Knockin'	Little Richard
Keep Coming Back	Richard Marx
(Keep Feeling) Fascination	Human League
Keep It Comin' Love	KC & The Sunshine Band
Keep It Together	Madonna
Keep Me A Secret	Ainslie Henderson
Keep On	Bruce Channel
Keep On Dancin'	Gary's Gang
Keep On Dancing	Bay City Rollers
Keep On Dancing	Gentrys
Keep On Keepin' On	MC Lyte & Xscape
Keep On Loving You	REO Speedwagon
Keep On Movin'	5ive
Keep On Movin'	Soul II Soul
Keep On Pushing	Impressions
Keep On Runnin'	Spencer Davis Group
Keep On Smilin'	Wet Willie
Keep On Truckin' (Pt 1)	Eddie Kendricks
Keep On Walkin'	Ce Ce Peniston
Keep Pushin'	Clock
Keep Searchin' (We'll Follow The Sun)	Del Shannon
Keep The Ball Rollin'	Jay & The Techniques
Keep The Faith	Bon Jovi
Keep The Fire Burnin'	REO Speedwagon
Keep Their Heads Ringin'	Dr. Dre
Keep Ya Head Up	2Pac
Keep Your Hands Off My Baby	Little Eva
Keep Your Hands To Yourself	Georgia Satellites
Keeper Of The Castle	Four Tops
Keeping The Dream Alive	Freiheit
Keeps Gettin' Better	Christina Aguilera
Kernkraft 400	Zombie Nation
The Ketchup Song (Asereje)	Las Ketchup
Kewpie Doll	Perry Como
Kewpie Doll	Frankie Vaughan
Key Largo	Bertie Higgins
The Key The Secret	Urban Cookie Collective
Key To My Life	Boyzone
Key West Intermezzo (I Saw You First)	John Mellencamp
Kicks	Paul Revere & The Raiders
Kid Galahad E.P.	Elvis Presley
Kids	Robbie Williams
The Kid's Last Fight	Frankie Laine
Kiddio	Brook Benton
Kids In America	Kim Wilde
Killer	ATP
Killamangiro	Baby Shambles
Killer	Adamski
Killer (EP)	Seal
Killer On The Loose	Thin Lizzy
Killer Queen	Queen
Killing In The Name	Rage Against The Machine
Killing Me Softly With His Song	Roberta Flack
The Killing Moon	Echo & The Bunnymen
The Killing Of Georgie	Rod Stewart
Kind Of A Drag	Buckinghams
A Kind Of Magic	Queen
King	UB40
King Creole	Elvis Presley
King For A Day	Thompson Twins
The King Is Gone	Ronnie McDowell
King Of My Castle	Wamdue Project
King Of Pain	Police
The King Of Rock 'n' Roll	Prefab Sprout
King Of The Cops	Billy Howard
King Of The Mountain	Kate Bush
King Of The Road	Roger Miller
King Of The Road	Proclaimers
King Of Wishful Thinking	Go West
King Rocker	Generation X
Kings Of The Wild Frontier	Adam & The Ants
Kingston Town	UB40
Kinky Afro	Happy Mondays
Kinky Boots	Patrick McNee & Honor Blackman
Kiss	Art Of Noise & Tom Jones
Kiss	Prince & The Revolution
Kiss And Say Goodbye	Manhattans

Kiss Him Goodbye	Nylons
Kiss Kiss	Chris Brown Featuring T-Pain
Kiss Kiss	Holly Valance
Kiss Me	Stephen 'Tin Tin' Duffy
Kiss Me	Sixpence None The Richer
Kiss Me Deadly	Lita Ford
Kiss Me Honey Honey Kiss Me	Shirley Bassey
Kiss Me Quick	Elvis Presley
Kiss Me Thru The Phone	Soulja Boy Tell'em Featuring Sammie
Kiss On My List	Daryl Hall & John Oates
Kiss The Rain	Billie Myers
Kiss (When The Sun Don't Shine)	Vengaboys
Kiss You All Over	Exile
Kisses On The Wind	Neneh Cherry
Kisses Sweeter Than Wine	Jimmie Rodgers
Kisses Sweeter Than Wine	Frankie Vaughan
Kissin' Cousins	Elvis Presley
Kissin' In The Back Row Of The Movies	Drifters
Kissin' Time	Bobby Rydell
Kissin You	Total
Kissing A Fool	George Michael
Kites	Simon Dupree & The Big Sound
Knee Deep In The Blues	Guy Mitchell
Knock Knock Who's There	Mary Hopkin
Knock On Wood	David Bowie
Knock On Wood	Amii Stewart
Knock Three Times	Dawn
Knock You Down	Keri Hilson Featuring Kanye West & Ne-Yo
Knocked It Off	B.A. Robertson
Knockin' Boots	Candyman
Knockin' Da Boots	H-Town
Knockin' On Heaven's Door	Bob Dylan
Knockin' On Heaven's Door	Guns N' Roses
Knowing Me Knowing You	Abba
Ko Ko Mo (I Love You So)	Perry Como
Ko Ko Mo (I Love You So)	Crew-Cuts
Kodachrome	Paul Simon
Kokomo	Beach Boys
Kommotion	Duane Eddy
Kon-Tiki	Shadows
Koochy	Armand Van Helden
Kookie, Kookie (Lend Me Your Comb)	Edward Byrnes & Connie Stevens
Kung Fu Fighting	Bus Stop featuring Carl Douglas
Kung Fu Fighting	Carl Douglas
Kyrie	Mr. Mister
La Bamba	Los Lobos
La Dee Dah	Billy & Lillie
La Dee Dah	Jackie Dennis
La Isla Bonita	Madonna
La La La Hey Hey	Outhere Brothers
La La La (If I Had You)	Bobby Sherman
La-La Means I Love You	Delfonics
La Vie En Rose	Grace Jones
Labelled With Love	Squeeze
Labour Of Love	Hue & Cry
Ladies Night	Atomic Kitten featuring Kool & The Gang
Ladies Night	Kool & The Gang
Lady	D'Angelo
Lady	Little River Band
Lady	Kenny Rogers
Lady	Styx
Lady Barbara	Herman's Hermits
Lady D'Arbanville	Cat Stevens
Lady Eleanor	Lindisfarne
Lady Godiva	Peter & Gordon
Lady In Red	Chris De Burgh
Lady (Hear Me Tonight)	Modjo
Lady Love Me (One More Time)	George Benson
Lady Luck	Lloyd Price
Lady Lynda	Beach Boys
Lady Madonna	Beatles
Lady Marmalade	Christina Aguilera, Lil' Kim, Mya & P!nk
Lady Marmalade (Voulez-Vous Coucher Avec Moi)	Labelle
Lady Rose	Mungo Jerry
Lady Willpower	Gary Puckett & The Union Gap
Lady You Bring Me Up	Commodores
The Ladyboy Is Mine	Stuntmasterz
Laffy Taffy	D4L
Lambada	Kaoma
Lamplight	David Essex
Lana	Roy Orbison
Land Of Confusion	Genesis
Land Of Make Believe	Bucks Fizz
Land Of 1,000 Dances	Wilson Pickett
Landslide	Dixie Chicks
Language Of Love	John D. Loudermilk
The Language Of Love	Dan Fogelberg
Larger Than Life	Backstreet Boys
Last Chance To Turn Around	Gene Pitney
Last Christmas	Wham!
Last Dance	Donna Summer
Last Date	Floyd Cramer
Last Dollar (Fly Away)	Tim McGraw
The Last Farewell	Roger Whittaker
The Last Goodbye	Atomic Kitten
Last Kiss	J. Frank Wilson & The Cavaliers
Last Kiss	Pearl Jam
The Last Kiss	David Cassidy
Last Night	Az Yet
Last Night	Diddy Featuring Keyshia Cole
Last Night	Mar-Keys

Last Night A D.J. Saved My Life	Indeep
Last Night In Soho	Dave Dee, Dozy, Beaky, Mick & Tich
(Last Night) I Didn't Get To Sleep At All	Fifth Dimension
Last Night Was Made For Love	Billy Fury
Last Of The Famous International Playboys	Morrissey
Last Resort	Papa Roach
Last Request	Paolo Nutini
Last Song	Edward Bear
Last Thing On My Mind	Ronan Keating & LeAnn Rimes
The Last Thing On My Mind	Steps
The Last Time	Rolling Stones
Last Train Home	Lostprophets
Last Train To Clarksville	Monkees
Last Train To London	Electric Light Orchestra
Last Train To San Fernando	Johnny Duncan & The Blue Grass Boys
Last Train To Trancentral	KLF
The Last Waltz	Engelbert Humperdinck
Late In The Evening	Paul Simon
Lately	Divine
Lately	Jodeci
Lately	Samantha Mumba
Lately	Lisa Scott-Lee
Lately	Stevie Wonder
Laugh At Me	Sonny
Laugh, Laugh	Beau Brummels
Laughing	Guess Who
The Laughing Gnome	David Bowie
Laughter In The Rain	Neil Sedaka
The Launch	DJ Jean
Laurie (Strange Things Happen)	Dickey Lee
Lavender	Marillion
Lavender-Blue	Sammy Turner
Lawyers In Love	Jackson Browne
Lay A Little Lovin' On Me	Robin McNamara
Lay All Your Love On Me	Abba
Lay Back In The Arms Of Someone	Smokie
Lay Down	Strawbs
Lay Down (Candles In The Rain)	Melanie
Lay Down Sally	Eric Clapton
Lay Down Your Arms	Anne Shelton
Lay Lady Lay	Bob Dylan
Lay Your Hands	Simon Webbe
Lay Your Hands On Me	Bon Jovi
Lay Your Hands On Me	Thompson Twins
Lay Your Love On Me	Racey
Layla	Eric Clapton
Layla	Derek & The Dominoes
Lazy	X-Press 2 Featuring David Byrne
Lazy River	Bobby Darin
Lazy Sunday	Small Faces
Ldn	Lily Allen
Le Freak	Chic
Lead Me On	Maxine Nightingale
Leader Of The Band	Dan Fogelberg
Leader Of The Pack	Shangri-Las
Lean Back	Terror Squad
Lean On Me	Club Nouveau
Lean On Me	Mud
Lean On Me	Bill Withers
Lean On Me (Ah-Li-Ayo)	Red Box
Lean Wit It, Rock Wit It	Dem Franchize Boyz featuring Lil Peanut & Charlay
Leaning On The Lamp Post	Herman's Hermits
Leap Up And Down (Wave Your Knickers In The Air)	St. Cecilia
Learnin' The Blues	Frank Sinatra
Leather And Lace	Stevie Nicks
Leave A Light On	Belinda Carlisle
Leave A Little Love	Lulu
Leave Before The Lights Come On	Arctic Monkeys
Leave (Get Out)	JoJo
Leave Me Alone	Michael Jackson
Leave Me Alone (Ruby Red Dress)	Helen Reddy
Leave Right Now	Will Young
Leavin'	Jesse McCartney
Leaving New York	R.E.M.
Leaving On A Jet Plane	Peter, Paul & Mary
The Lebanon	Human League
Leeds United	Leeds United F.C.
Left Bank	Winifred Atwell
Left My Heart In Tokyo	Mini Viva
Left Outside Alone	Anastacia
Left Right Out Of Your Heart	Patti Page
Left To My Own Devices	Pet Shop Boys
Legacy EP	Mansun
Legend Of Xanadu	Dave Dee, Dozy, Beaky, Mick & Tich
Legs	ZZ Top
Leroy	Jack Scott
Les Bicyclettes De Belsize	Engelbert Humperdinck
Lessons In Love	Level 42
Let 'Em In	Paul McCartney
Let Forever Be	Chemical Brothers
Let Her Cry	Hootie & The Blowfish
Let Her In	John Travolta
Let It Be	Beatles
Let It Be	Ferry Aid
Let It Be Me	Jerry Butler & Betty Everett
Let It Be Me	Everly Brothers
Let It Go	Keyshia Cole Feat. Missy Elliott & Lil' Kim
Let It Out (Let It All Hang Out)	Hombres
Let It Rain	East 17

Title	Artist
Let It Rock	Kevin Rudolf Featuring Lil Wayne
Let It Whip	Dazz Band
Let Love Be Your Energy	Robbie Williams
Let Me Be The One	Exposé
Let Me Be The One	Shadows
Let Me Be There	Olivia Newton-John
Let Me Be Your Fantasy	Baby D
Let Me Blow Ya Mind	Eve Featuring Gwen Stefani
Let Me Cry On Your Shoulder	Ken Dodd
Let Me Go	3 Doors Down
Let Me Go, Lover	Kathy Kirby
Let Me Go, Lover	Dean Martin
Let Me Go, Lover	Ruby Murray
Let Me Go, Lover	Joan Weber
Let Me Go, Lover!	Teresa Brewer
Let Me Hold You	Bow Wow featuring Omarion
Let Me In	Osmonds
Let Me In	Sensations
Let Me Love You	Mario
Let Me Love You Tonight	Pure Prairie League
Let Me Think About It	Ida Corr Vs Fedde Le Grand
Let Me Try Again	Tammy Jones
Let My Love Open The Door	Pete Townshend
Let The Bass Kick In Miami Girl	Chuckie & LMFAO
Let The Beat Control Your Body	2 Unlimited
Let The Four Winds Blow	Fats Domino
Let The Heartaches Begin	Long John Baldry
Let The Little Girl Dance	Billy Bland
Let The Music Play	Shannon
Let The Music Play	Barry White
Let The Sunshine In	Fifth Dimension
Let There Be Drums	Sandy Nelson
Let There Be Love	Nat 'King' Cole
Let There Be Love	Oasis
Let There Be Love	Simple Minds
Let U Go	Ashley Parker Angel
Let Your Head Go	Victoria Beckham
Let Your Love Flow	Bellamy Brothers
Let Your Yeah Be Yeah	Pioneers
Let's All Chant	Mick And Pat
Let's All Chant	Michael Zager Band
Let's Dance	David Bowie
Let's Dance	Five
Let's Dance	Chris Montez
Let's Dance	Chris Rea
Let's Do It Again	Staple Singers
Let's Get Down	Bow Wow featuring Baby
Let's Get It On	Marvin Gaye
Let's Get It Up	AC/DC
Let's Get Married	Jagged Edge
Let's Get Ready To Rumble	PJ And Duncan
Let's Get Rocked	Def Leppard
Let's Get Serious	Jermaine Jackson
Let's Get Together	Hayley Mills
Let's Get Together Again	Glitter Band
Let's Get Together No. 1	Big Ben Banjo Band
Let's Go	Cars
Let's Go	Trick Daddy featuring Lil Jon & Twista
Let's Go	Wang Chung
Let's Go All The Way	Sly Fox
Let's Go Crazy	Prince & The Revolution
Let's Go, Let's Go, Let's Go	Hank Ballard & The Midnighters
Let's Go Round Again Pt. 1	Average White Band
Let's Go To San Francisco	Flowerpot Men
Let's Groove	Earth, Wind & Fire
Let's Hang On	Darts
Let's Hang On!	Four Seasons
Let's Have A Ball	Winifred Atwell
Let's Have A Ding Dong	Winifred Atwell
Let's Have A Party	Winifred Atwell
Let's Have A Quiet Night In	David Soul
Let's Have Another Party	Winifred Atwell
Let's Hear It For The Boy	Deniece Williams
Let's Jump The Broomstick	Brenda Lee
Let's Live For Today	Grass Roots
Let's Lock The Door (And Throw Away The Key)	Jay & The Americans
Let's Party	Jive Bunny & The Mastermixers
Let's Pretend	Lulu
Let's Put It All Together	Stylistics
Let's Ride	Monetell Jordan/Master P/Silkk The Shocker
Let's Spend The Night Together	Rolling Stones
Let's Stay Together	Al Green
Let's Stay Together	Tina Turner
Let's Stick Together	Bryan Ferry
Let's Talk About Love	Helen Shapiro
Let's Talk About Sex	Salt-N-Pepa
Let's Think About Living	Bob Luman
Let's Try Again	New Kids On The Block
Let's Turkey Trot	Little Eva
Let's Twist Again	Chubby Checker
Let's Wait Awhile	Janet Jackson
Let's Work Together	Canned Heat
The Letter	Box Tops
The Letter	Joe Cocker
Letter From America	Proclaimers
A Letter To You	Shakin' Stevens
LFO	LFO
Liar	Three Dog Night
Liar	Profyle
Liar, Liar	Castaways
Licence To Kill	Gladys Knight
Lido Shuffle	Boz Scaggs
Lie To Me	Bon Jovi
Liechtensteiner Polka	Will Glahe
Lies	McFly
Lies	Status Quo
Life	Des'ree
Life	Haddaway
Life Ain't Easy	Cleopatra
Life Got Cold	Girls Aloud
Life In A Northern Town	Dream Academy
Life In The Fast Lane	Eagles
Life Is A Flower	Ace Of Base
Life Is A Highway	Tom Cochrane
Life Is A Highway	Rascal Flatts
Life Is A Long Song	Jethro Tull
Life Is A Minestrone	10cc
Life Is A Rock (But The Radio Rolled Me)	Reunion
Life Is A Rollercoaster	Ronan Keating
Life Is Too Short Girl	Sheer Elegance
Life On Mars	David Bowie
Life's Been Good	Joe Walsh
Lifeline	Spandau Ballet
Lifted	Lighthouse Family
Lift Me Up	Geri Haliwell
Light My Fire	Clubhouse featuring Carl
Light My Fire	Doors
Light My Fire	José Feliciano
Light My Fire	Will Young
Light My Fire/137 Disco Heaven (Medley)	Amii Stewart
(Light Of Experience) Doina De Jale	Gheorghe Zamfir
Light Of My Life	Louise
Lightnin' Strikes	Lou Christie
Lights, Camera, Action!	Mr. Cheeks
Lights Of Cincinati	Scott Walker
Lights Out	Peter Wolf
(The Lights Went Out In) Massachusetts	Bee Gees
Like A Baby	Len Barry
Like A Prayer	Mad'house
Like A Prayer	Madonna
Like A Rock	Bob Seger & The Silver Bullet Band
Like A Rolling Stone	Bob Dylan
Like A Virgin	Madonna
Like Clockwork	Boomtown Rats
Like Glue	Sean Paul
Like I Do	Maureen Evans
Like I Love You	Justin Timberlake
Like I've Never Been Gone	Billy Fury
Like Sister And Brother	Drifters
Like The Way I Do	Melissa Etheridge
Like This	Kelly Rowland Featuring Eve
Like This And Like That	Monica
Like To Get To Know You Well	Howard Jones
Like Toy Soldiers	Eminem
Like You	Bow Wow featuring Ciara
Like You'll Never See Me Again	Alicia Keys
Lil' Devil	Cult
Lil' Red Riding Hood	Sam The Sham & The Pharaohs
Lil Star	Kelis Featuring Cee-Lo
Lily The Pink	Scaffold
Lily Was Here	David A. Stewart Introducing Candy Dulfer
Limbo Rock	Chubby Checker
Linger	Cranberries
The Lion Sleeps Tonight	Robert John
The Lion Sleeps Tonight	Tight Fit
The Lion Sleeps Tonight	Tokens
Lip Gloss	Lil Mama
Lip Up Fatty	Bad Manners
Lips Of An Angel	Hinder
Lipstick On Your Collar	Connie Francis
Liquid Dreams	O-Town
Liquidator	Harry J. & The All Stars
Liquid Dreams	O-Town
Lisbon Antigua	Nelson Riddle
Listen	Beyonce
Listen People	Herman's Hermits
Listen To Me	Hollies
Listen To The Music	Doobie Brothers
Listen To What The Man Said	Paul McCartney
Listen To Your Heart	DHT featuring Edmée
Listen To Your Heart	Roxette
Listen To Your Heart	Sonia
Little Arrows	Leapy Lee
Little Bird	Annie Lennox
A Little Bit Longer	Jonas Brothers
A Little Bit Me, A Little Bit You	Monkees
A Little Bit More	Dr. Hook
A Little Bit More	911
A Little Bit Of Luck	DJ Luck & MC Neat
A Little Bit Of Love	Free
Little Bit O' Soul	Music Explosion
A Little Bit Of Soap	Jarmels
A Little Bit Of Soap	Showaddywaddy
Little Bitty Pretty One	Thurston Harris
Little Bitty Pretty One	Jackson Five
A Little Bitty Tear	Burl Ives
A Little Boogie Woogie (In The Back Of My Mind)	Shakin' Stevens
Little Boy Sad	Johnny Burnette
Little Brown Jug	Glenn Miller
Little By Little	Oasis
Little Children	Billy J. Kramer & The Dakotas
Little Darlin'	Diamonds
Little Devil	Neil Sedaka
Little Diane	Dion
Little Does She Know	Kursaal Flyers
Little Donkey	Beverley Sisters
Little Donkey	Nina & Frederik
Little Drummer Boy	David Bowie
Little Drummer Boy	Royal Scots Dragoon Guards
Little Drummer Boy	Harry Simeone Chorale
The Little Drummer Boy	Beverley Sisters
Little Drummer Boy/Peace On Earth	Bandaged (Sir Terry Wogan & Aled Jones)
Little Fluffy Clouds	Orb
Little Girl	Syndicate Of Sound
Little Green Apples	O.C. Smith
Little Honda	Hondells
A Little In Love	Cliff Richard
Little Jeannie	Elton John
Little L	Jamiroquai
A Little Less Conversation	Elvis vs JXL
Little Lies	Fleetwood Mac
A Little Love, A Little Kiss	Karl Denver
A Little Love And Understanding	Gilbert Becaud
A Little Loving	Fourmost
Little Man	Sonny & Cher
Little Miss Can't Be Wrong	Spin Doctors
Little Miss Lonely	Helen Shapiro
A Little More Love	Olivia Newton-John
The Little Old Lady (From Pasadena)	Jan & Dean
Little Ole Man (Uptight-Everything's Alright)	Bill Cosby
A Little Peace	Nicole
Little Red Corvette	Prince & The Revolution
Little Red Rooster	Sam Cooke
Little Red Rooster	Rolling Stones
A Little Respect	Erasure
A Little Respect	Wheatus
The Little Shoemaker	Petula Clark
The Little Shoemaker	Gaylords
The Little Shoemaker	Frank Weir
The Little Shoemaker	Hugo Winterhalter
Little Sister	Elvis Presley
Little Star	Elegants
Little Things	Dave Berry
Little Things	Bobby Goldsboro
Little Things Mean A Lot	Alma Cogan
Little Things Mean A Lot	Kitty Kallen
Little Things Mean A Lot	Jimmy Young
A Little Time	Beautiful South
Little Town Flirt	Del Shannon
Little White Bull	Tommy Steele
Little Willy	Sweet
Little Woman	Bobby Sherman
Live And Learn	Joe Public
Live And Let Die	Guns N' Roses
Live And Let Die	Paul McCartney
Live Forever	Oasis
Live In Trouble	Barron Knights
Live Is Life	Opus
Live It Up	Mental As Anything
Live To Tell	Madonna
Live Together	Lisa Stansfield
Live Your Life	T.I. Featuring Rihanna
Live Your Life Be Free	Belinda Carlisle
Lively	Lonnie Donegan
Liverpool Lou	Scaffold
Livin' It Up	Ja Rule featuring Case
Livin' It Up (Friday Night)	Bell & James
Livin' La Vida Loca	Ricky Martin
Livin' On A Prayer	Bon Jovi
Livin' Thing	Electric Light Orchestra
Living After Midnight	Judas Priest
Living By Numbers	New Muzik
The Living Daylights	A-Ha
Living Doll	Cliff Richard
Living Doll	Cliff Richard & The Young Ones
Living For The City	Stevie Wonder
Living In A Box	Living In A Box
Living In America	James Brown
Living In Harmony	Cliff Richard
Living In Sin	Bon Jovi
Living In The Past	Jethro Tull
Living Inside Myself	Gino Vannelli
Livin' La Vida Loca	Ricky Martin
Living Next Door To Alice	Smokie
Living On My Own	Freddie Mercury
Living On The Ceiling	Blancmange
Living On The Front Line	Eddy Grant
Living On Video	Trans-X
The Living Years	Mike + The Mechanics
L-L-Lucy	Mud
Lo Mucho Que Te Quiero (The More I Love You)	Rene & Rene
Loadsamoney (Doin' Up The House)	Harry Enfield
Loch Lomond – Hampden Remix	Runrig With The Tartan Army
Locked Up	Akon featuring Styles P.
Loco	Fun Lovin' Criminals
Loco In Acapulco	Four Tops
The Loco-Motion	Grand Funk
The Loco-Motion	Little Eva
The Loco-Motion	Kylie Minogue
Locomotion	Orchestral Manoeuvres In The Dark
Loddy Lo	Chubby Checker
The Lodgers	Style Council
The Logical Song	Scooter

Title	Artist
The Logical Song	Supertramp
Lola	Kinks
Lola's Theme	Shapeshifters
Lollipop	Chordettes
Lollipop	Lil Wayne Featuring Static Major
Lollipop	Mudlarks
London Bridge	Fergie
London Calling	Clash
London Nights	London Boys
The Lone Ranger	Quantum Jump
Loneliness	Tomcraft
(Loneliness Made Me Realize) It's You That I Need	Temptations
Lonely	Akon
Lonely	Acker Bilk
Lonely Blue Boy	Conway Twitty
Lonely Boy	Paul Anka
Lonely Boy	Andrew Gold
Lonely Boy	Donny Osmond
The Lonely Bull	Herb Alpert
Lonely Days	Bee Gees
Lonely Night (Angel Face)	Captain & Tennille
Lonely No More	Rob Thomas
Lonely Ol' Night	John Cougar Mellencamp
Lonely People	America
Lonely Pup (In A Christmas Shop)	Adam Faith
Lonely Street	Andy Williams
Lonely Teardrops	Jackie Wilson
Lonely Teenager	Dion
Lonely This Christmas	Mud
Lonesome	Adam Faith
Lonesome Loser	Little River Band
Lonesome Town	Ricky Nelson
The Long And Winding Road	Beatles
The Long And Winding Road	Will Young & Gareth Gates
Long As I Can See The Light	Creedence Clearwater Revival
Long Cool Woman (In A Black Dress)	Hollies
The Long Goodbye	Ronan Keating
Long Haired Lover From Liverpool	Little Jimmy Osmond
Long Hot Summer	Girls Aloud
Long Hot Summer	Style Council
Long Legged Woman Dressed In Black	Mungo Jerry
Long Live Love	Olivia Newton-John
Long Live Love	Sandie Shaw
Long Road	Pearl Jam
The Long Run	Eagles
Long Tall Glasses (I Can Dance)	Leo Sayer
Long Tall Sally	Little Richard
Long Time Gone	Dixie Chicks
Long Train Running	Doobie Brothers
Longer	Dan Fogelberg
The Longest Time	Billy Joel
The Longest Walk	Jaye P. Morgan
Longfellow Serenade	Neil Diamond
The Look	Roxette
Look Around	Vince Hill
Look At Me	Geri Halliwell
Look Away	Big Country
Look Away	Chicago
Look For A Star	Garry Mills
Look Homeward Angel	Johnnie Ray
Look In My Eyes	Chantels
Look In My Eyes Pretty Woman	Tony Orlando & Dawn
Look Into My Eyes	Bone Thugs-N-Harmony
The Look Of Love (Part 1)	ABC
The Look Of Love	Madonna
The Look Of Love	Sergio Mendes & Brasil '66
Look Through Any Window	Hollies
Look What They've Done To My Song Ma	New Seekers featuring Eve Graham
Look What You Done For Me	Al Green
Look What You've Done To Me	Boz Scaggs
Look Wot You Dun	Slade
Lookin' At Me	Mase/Puff Daddy
Lookin' For A Love	Bobby Womack
Lookin' For Love	Johnny Lee
Lookin' Out My Back Door	Creedence Clearwater Revival
Lookin' Through The Eyes Of Love	Partridge Family
Lookin' Through The Windows	Jackson Five
Looking After Number One	Boomtown Rats
Looking Back	Nat 'King' Cole
Looking For A New Love	Jody Watley
Looking for Love	Karen Ramirez
Looking Through Patient Eyes	P.M. Dawn
Looking Through The Eyes Of Love	Gene Pitney
Looking Up	Michelle Gayle
Looks Like We Made It	Barry Manilow
Loop De Loop	Johnny Thunder
Loop De Loop	Frankie Vaughan
Loop Di Love	Shag
Lord Don't Slow Me Down	Oasis
The Lord's Prayer	Sister Janet Mead
Lose Control	Missy Elliott featuring Ciara & Fat Man Scoop
Lose My Breath	Destiny's Child
Lose Yourself	Eminem
Loser	Beck
Losing My Mind	Liza Minnelli
Losing My Religion	R.E.M.
Losing You	Brenda Lee
Losing You	Dusty Springfield
Lost In Emotion	Lisa Lisa & Cult Jam
Lost In France	Bonnie Tyler
Lost In Space	Apollo 440
Lost In Space	The Lighthouse Family
Lost In Love	Air Supply
Lost In You	Rod Stewart
Lost In You	Garth Brooks as Chris Gaines
Lost In Your Eyes	Debbie Gibson
Lost John	Lonnie Donegan
Lost Without U	Robin Thicke
Lost Without You	Delta Goodrem
Lost Without Your Love	Bread
Lotta Love	Nicolette Larson
Lotta Lovin'	Gene Vincent & His Blue Caps
Louie Louie	Kingsmen
Louise	Human League
Loungin'	LL Cool J
Love Action (I Believe In Love)	Human League
Love Ain't Gonna Wait For You	S Club
Love Ain't Here Anymore	Take That
Love And Affection	Joan Armatrading
Love & Kisses	Dannii Minogue
Love And Marriage	Frank Sinatra
Love & Pride	King
Love And Understanding	Cher
Love At First Sight	Kylie Minogue
Love Bites	Def Leppard
A Love Bizarre	Sheila E
Love Came To Me	Dion
Love Can Build A Bridge	Cher, Chrissie Hynde & Neneh Cherry With Eric Clapton
Love (Can Make You Happy)	Mercy
Love Can't Turn Around	Farley 'Jackmaster' Funk
The Love Cats	Cure
Love Changes Everything	Michael Ball
Love Changes (Everything)	Climie Fisher
Love Child	Diana Ross & The Supremes
Love Child	Sweet Sensation
Love City Groove	Love City Groove
Love Come Down	Evelyn 'Champagne' King
Love Doesn't Have To Hurt	Atomic Kitten
Love Don't Cost A Thing	Jennifer Lopez
Love Don't Let Me Go (Walking Away)	David Guetta vs The Egg
Love Don't Live Here Anymore	Jimmy Nail
Love Don't Live Here Anymore	Rose Royce
Love Games	Belle & The Devotions
Love Generation	Bob Sinclar featuring Gary Pine
Love Grows (Where My Rosemary Goes)	Edison Lighthouse
Love Hangover	Diana Ross
Love Her Madly	Doors
Love Hit Me	Maxine Nightingale
Love Hurts	Jim Capaldi
Love Hurts	Nazareth
The Love I Lost (Part 1)	Harold Melvin &The Blue Notes
The Love I Lost	West End featuring Sybil
Love In An Elevator	Aerosmith
Love In The First Degree	Bananarama
Love In The Sun	Glitter Band
Love In This Club	Usher Featuring Young Jeezy
Love Is	Vanessa Williams & Brian McKnight
Love Is A Battlefield	Pat Benatar
Love Is A Hurtin' Thing	Lou Rawls
Love Is A Many-Splendored Thing	Four Aces
Love Is A Rose	Linda Ronstadt
Love Is A Stranger	Eurythmics
Love Is A Wonderful Thing	Michael Bolton
Love Is Alive	Gary Wright
Love Is All	Malcolm Roberts
Love Is All Around	Troggs
Love Is All Around	Wet Wet Wet
Love Is All We Need	Tommy Edwards
Love Is Blue	Paul Mauriat
Love Is Contagious	Taja Sevelle
Love Is Gone	David Guetta Featuring Chris Willis
Love Is Here And Now You're Gone	Supremes
Love Is In Control (Finger On The Trigger)	Donna Summer
Love Is In The Air	John Paul Young
Love Is Life	Hot Chocolate
Love Is Like A Violin	Ken Dodd
Love Is Like An Itching In My Heart	Supremes
Love Is Like Oxygen	Sweet
Love Is Noise	The Verve
Love Is On The Way	Saigon Kick
Love Is Only A Feeling	The Darkness
Love Is Strange	Everly Brothers
Love Is Strange	Mickey & Sylvia
Love Is Strange	Peaches & Herb
(Love Is) Thicker Than Water	Andy Gibb
Love Is The Answer	England Dan & John Ford Coley
Love Is The Drug	Roxy Music
Love Kills	Freddie Mercury
Love Letters	Ketty Lester
Love Letters	Alison Moyet
Love Letters	Elvis Presley
Love Letters In The Sand	Pat Boone
Love Like A Man	Ten Years After
Love Like This	Faith Evans
Love Like This	Natasha Bedingfield Featuring Sean Kingston
L-O-V-E (Love)	Al Green
Love Lockdown	Kanye West
Love Machine	Girls Aloud
Love Machine	Miracles
Love Makes The World Go Round	Perry Como
Love Makes The World Go Round	Deon Jackson
Love Makes Things Happen	Pebbles
Love Me	Yvonne Elliman
Love Me	112/Mase
Love Me	Elvis Presley
Love Me As If There Were No Tomorrow	Nat 'King' Cole
Love Me Do	Beatles
Love Me For A Reason	Boyzone
Love Me For A Reason	Osmonds
Love Me Forever	Marion Ryan
Love Me Like I Love You	Bay City Rollers
Love Me Love My Dog	Peter Shelley
Love Me Or Leave Me	Sammy Davis Jr.
Love Me Tender	Elvis Presley
Love Me To Pieces	Jill Corey
Love Me Tonight	Tom Jones
Love Me Warm And Tender	Paul Anka
Love Me With All Your Heart	Ray Charles Singers
Love Missile F1-11	Sigue Sigue Sputnik
Love Of A Lifetime	Firehouse
Love Of A Lifetime	Honeyz
Love Of My Life	Dooleys
Love Of My Life (An Ode To Hip Hop)	Erykah Badu featuring Common
The Love Of Richard Nixon	Manic Street Preachers
Love Of The Common People	Nicky Thomas
Love Of The Common People	Paul Young
Love On A Mountain Top	Robert Knight
Love On A Two-Way Street	Moments
Love On The Line	Blazin' Squad
Love On The Rocks	Neil Diamond
Love On Your Side	Thompson Twins
Love Or Let Me Be Lonely	Friends Of Distinction
Love Overboard	Gladys Knight & The Pips
Love Plus One	Haircut 100
Love Potion Number Nine	Searchers
Love Power	Luther Vandross
Love Power	Dionne Warwick & Jeffrey Osborne
Love Really Hurts Without You	Billy Ocean
Love Rears Its Ugly Head	Living Colour
Love Resurrection	Alison Moyet
Love Rollercoaster	Ohio Players
Love Sex Magic	Ciara Featuring Justin Timberlake
Love Shack	B-52's
Love So Right	Bee Gees
Love Somebody	Rick Springfield
Love Song	Cure
Love Song	Tesla
A Love Song	Anne Murray
Love Song	Sara Bareilles
Love Song For A Vampire	Annie Lennox
Love Spreads	Stone Roses
Love Story	Taylor Swift
Love Story (Vs Finally)	Layo & Bushwacka!
Love Takes Time	Mariah Carey
Love Takes Time	Orleans
Love Theme From Romeo & Juliet	Henry Mancini & His Orchestra
Love Theme From 'The Thorn Birds'	Juan Martin
Love...Thy Will Be Done	Martika
Love To Hate You	Erasure
Love To Love You Baby	Donna Summer
Love Today	Mika
Love Touch	Rod Stewart
Love Town	Booker Newberry III
Love Train	Holly Johnson
Love Train	O'Jays
Love Will Conquer All	Lionel Richie
Love Will Find A Way	Pablo Cruise
Love Will Keep Us Together	Captain & Tennille
Love Will Lead You Back	Taylor Dayne
Love Will Never Do (Without You)	Janet Jackson
Love Will Save The Day	Whitney Houston
Love Will Tear Us Apart	Joy Division
Love Will Turn You Around	Kenny Rogers
Love Won't Let Me Wait	Major Harris
A Love Worth Waiting For	Shakin' Stevens
Love You Down	Ready For The World
Love You Inside Out	Bee Gees
Love You Like Mad	Vs
The Love You Save	Jackson Five
Love You So	Ron Holden
Love Zone	Billy Ocean
Love's Been A Little Bit Hard On Me	Juice Newton
Love's Been Good To Me	Frank Sinatra
Love's Gotta Hold On Me	Dollar
Love's Gotta Hold On My Heart	Steps
Love's Great Adventure	Ultravox
Love's Just A Broken Heart	Cilla Black
Love's Theme	Love Unlimited Orchestra
Love's Unkind	Donna Summer
Lovegame	Lady Gaga
Lovelight	Robbie Williams
Lovely Day	Bill Withers
Lovely One	Jacksons
Lover Come Back To Me	Dead Or Alive
The Lover In Me	Sheena Easton
Lover Please	Clyde McPhatter
A Lover's Concerto	Toys
A Lover's Question	Clyde McPhatter
Loverboy	Billy Ocean
Lovergirl	Teena Marie
Lovers And Friends	Lil Jon & The East Side Boyz featuring Usher & Ludacris
Lovers Of The World Unite	David & Jonathan

Mind Of A Toy	Visage
A Mind Of Its Own	Victoria Beckham
Minute By Minute	Doobie Brothers
A Minute Of Your Time	Tom Jones
The Minute You're Gone	Cliff Richard
Miracle	Cascada
Miracle	Jon Bon Jovi
Miracle	Whitney Houston
Miracle	Jefferson Starship
Miracles	Tommy James & The Shondells
Mirage	Beat
Mirror In The Bathroom	Human League
Mirror Man	Pinkerton's Assorted Colours
Mirror Mirror	Diana Ross
Mirror Mirror	M2M
Mirror Mirror	Dollar
Mirror Mirror (Mon Amour)	Pulp
Mis-Shapes/Sorted For E's & Wizz	Curiosity Killed The Cat
Misfit	Amy Studt
Misfit	Kool & The Gang
Misled	Little Richard
Miss Ann	Kelly Clarkson
Miss Independent	Ne-Yo
Miss Independent	Culture Club
Miss Me Blind	Abs featuring Nodesha
Miss Perfect	Passengers
Miss Sarajevo	Boz Scaggs
Miss Sun	Aaliyah
Miss You	Rolling Stones
Miss You	Natalie Cole
Miss You Like Crazy	Janet Jackson
Miss You Much	Cliff Richard
Miss You Nights	Westlife
Miss You Nights	Herman's Hermits
Mrs. Brown You've Got A Lovely Daughter	Simon & Garfunkel
Mrs. Robinson (E.P.)	Simon & Garfunkel
Mrs. Robinson	Everything But The Girl
Missing	Case
Missing You	Chris De Burgh
Missing You	Diana Ross
Missing You	John Waite
Missing You	Michael Bolton
Missing You Now	Donnie Brooks
Mission Bell	Eurythmics
Missionary Man	Pussycat
Mississippi	Cliff Richard
Mistletoe And Wine	Johnny Mathis
Misty	Ray Stevens
Misty	Dorothy Moore
Misty Blue	Genesis
Misunderstanding	Robbie Williams
Misunderstood	Rolling Stones
Mixed Emotions	Sophie Ellis-Bextor
Mixed Up World	Hanson
Mmmbop	Crash Test Dummies
Mmm Mmm Mmm Mmm	Notorious B.I.G/Puff Dadddy/Mase
Mo Money Mo Problems	Ray Burns
Mobile	Eminem
Mockingbird	Inez Foxx
Mockingbird	Carly Simon & James Taylor
Mockingbird	Migil Five
Mockingbird Hill	Kraftwerk
The Model	Sheena Easton
Modern Girl	David Bowie
Modern Love	Billy Joel
Modern Woman	Alizée
Moi...Lolita	Kelly Clarkson
A Moment Like This	Leona
A Moment Like This	JT And The Big Family
Moments In Soul	Four Lads
Moments To Remember	Craig McLachlan & Check 1-2
Mona	Conway Twitty
Mona Lisa	Mamas & The Papas
Monday Monday	Flying Lizards
Money	Pink Floyd
Money	Jamelia
Money	Dire Straits
Money For Nothing	Style Council
Money Go Round (Pt.1)	Bay City Rollers
Money Honey	Ludacris featuring Pharrell
Money Maker	Abba
Money Money Money	The Lox/DMX/lLil' Kim
Money, Power & Respect	Simply Red
Money's Too Tight (To Mention)	George Michael
Monkey	Before Dark
Monica	Dave & Ansil Collins
Monkey Spanner	Major Lance
The Monkey Time	Sandie Shaw
Monsieur Dupont	Automatic
Monster	Bobby 'Boris' Pickett & The Crypt Kickers
Monster Mash	Amazulu
Montego Bay	Bobby Bloom
Montego Bay	Eric Burdon & The Animals
Monterey	Simply Red
Montreux (EP)	Billy Idol
Mony Mony	Tommy James & The Shondells
Mony Mony	Elvis Presley
Moody Blue	Pat Boone
Moody River	Jerry Butler
Moon River	Greyhound
Moon River	Henry Mancini
Moon River	Danny Williams

Moonglow And Theme From 'Picnic'	George Cates
Moonglow And Theme From 'Picnic'	Morris Stoloff
Moonlight Feels Right	Starbuck
Moonlight Gambler	Frankie Laine
Moonlight Serenade	Glenn Miller
Moonlight Shadow	Mike Oldfield
Moonlighting	Leo Sayer
Moonlighting ('Theme')	Al Jarreau
Moonshine Sally	Mud
More	Perry Como
More	Kai Winding
More	Jimmy Young
More And More	Captain Hollywood Project
More And More Party Pops	Russ Conway
The More I See You	Chris Montez
More Like The Movies	Dr. Hook
More Love	Kim Carnes
More More More	Rachel Stevens
More, More, More (Pt. 1)	Andrea True Connection
More Party Pops	Russ Conway
More Than A Feeling	Boston
More Than A Woman	Aaliyah
More Than A Woman	911
More Than A Woman	Tavares
More Than Ever	Nelson
More Than Ever (Come Prima)	Malcolm Vaughan
More Than I Can Say	Leo Sayer
More Than I Can Say	Bobby Vee
More Than I Needed To Know	Scooch
More Than In Love	Kate Robbins
More Than This	Emmie
More Than This	Roxy Music
More Than Words	Extreme
More Than Words Can Say	Alias
More To This World	Bad Boys Inc
More Today Than Yesterday	Spiral Staircase
The More You Ignore Me, The Closer I Get	Morrissey
Morgen	Ivo Robic
Moritat (A Theme From 'The Three Penny Opera')	Dick Hyman
Mornin' Beautiful	Tony Orlando & Dawn
Morning	Val Doonican
Morning After Dark	Timbaland Featuring Nelly Furtado
The Morning After (Song From The Poseidon Adventure)	Maureen McGovern
Morning Has Broken	Cat Stevens
Morning Side Of The Mountain	Donny & Marie Osmond
Morning Train (A.K.A. 9 To 5)	Sheena Easton
Morningtown Ride	Seekers
The Most Beautiful Girl In The World	Prince
The Most Beautiful Girl	Charlie Rich
Most Girls	P!nk
Mother And Child Reunion	Paul Simon
Mother-In-Law	Ernie K-Doe
Mother Of Mine	Neil Reid
Mother Popcorn (You Got To Have A Mother Or Me)	James Brown
Mothers Little Helper	Rolling Stones
Motor Biking	Chris Spedding
Motorcycle Mama	Sailcat
Motörhead Live	Motörhead
The Motown Song	Rod Stewart
Motownphilly	Boyz II Men
Mouldy Old Dough	Lieutenant Pigeon
Mountain Greenery	Mel Tormé
Mountain Of Love	Johnny Rivers
Mountain Of Love	Dick & Deedee
The Mountain's High	Biffy Clyro
Mountains	Merril Bainbridge
Mouth	Shamen
Move Any Mountain	Culture Club
Move Away	Phyllis Nelson
Move Closer	Ludacris Feat Mystikal
Move Bitch	Cliff Richard
Move It	Cappella
Move On Baby	Doris Day
Move Over Darling	Tracey Ullman
Move Over Darling	Technotronic featuring Reggie
Move That Body	Technotronic featuring Ya Kid K
Move This	Sophie Ellis-Bextor
Move This Mountain	Nina Sky featuring Jabba
Move Ya Body	Eiffel 65
Move Your Body	Xpansions
Move Your Body (Elevation)	Junior Senior
Move Your Feet	Alien Ant Farm
Movies	Stereophonics
Moviestar	Brass Construction
Movin'	Artful Dodger & Romina Johnson
Movin' Too Fast	Supergrass
Moving	M People
Moving On Up	Waldo De Los Rios
Mozart Symphony No. 40 In G Minor	Jean Knight
Mr. Big Stuff	Mr. Blobby
Mr. Blobby	Fleetwoods
Mr. Blue	Mike Preston
Mr. Blue	Electric Light Orchestra
Mr. Blue Sky	Nitty Gritty Dirt Band
Mr. Bojangles	Killers
Mr. Brightside	Charlie Drake
Mr. Custer	Larry Verne
Mr. Custer	Dickie Goodman
Mr. Jaws	Bobbettes
Mr. Lee	Bobby Vinton
Mr. Lonely	Shabba Ranks
Mr. Loverman	

Mr. Roboto	Styx
Mr. Sandman	Chordettes
Mr. Sandman	Four Aces
Mr. Sandman	Dickie Valentine
Mr. Sleaze	Bananarama
Mr. Soft	Cockney Rebel
Mr. Tambourine Man	Byrds
Mr. Telephone Man	New Edition
Mr. Vain	Culture Beat
Mr. Wendal	Arrested Development
Mr. Wonderful	Peggy Lee
Mr. Writer	Stereophonics
Mrs. Officer	Lil Wayne Feat. Bobby Valentino & Kidd Kidd
Ms Grace	Tymes
Ms Jackson	Outkast
Ms. New Booty	Bubba Sparxxx
	featuring Ying Yang Twins & Mr. Collipark
M.T.A.	Kingston Trio
(Mucho Mambo) Sway	Shaft
Mule Skinner Blues	Fendermen
Mull Of Kintyre/Girls' School	Paul McCartney
Multiplication	Bobby Darin
Mundian To Bach Ke	Panjabi MC
Murder On The Dancefloor	Sophie Ellis-Bextor
Musclebound	Spandau Ballet
Muscles	Diana Ross
Music	John Miles
Music	Madonna
Music And Lights	Imagination
Music Box Dancer	Frank Mills
The Music Of My Heart	'N Sync & Gloria Estefan
The Music Of The Night	Michael Crawford & Sarah Brightman
The Music Of Torvill & Dean EP	Richard Hartley & Michael Reed Orchestra
Music Sounds Better With You	Stardust
The Music's No Good Without You	Cher
Muskrat Love	Captain & Tennille
Muskrat Ramble	McGuire Sisters
Must Be The Music	Joey Negro Feat. Taka Boom
Must Of Got Lost	J. Geils Band
A Must To Avoid	Herman's Hermits
My All	Mariah Carey
My Angel Baby	Toby Beau
My Arms Keep Missing You	Rick Astley
My Baby	Lil' Romeo
My Baby Daddy	B-Rock & The Bizz
(My Baby Don't Love Me) No More	DeJohn Sisters
My Baby Just Cares For Me	Nina Simone
My Baby Loves Lovin'	White Plains
My Band	D12
My Best Friend's Girl	Cars
My Body	LSG
My Bonnie Lassie	Ames Brothers
My Boo	Usher & Alicia Keys
My Boomerang Won't Come Back	Charlie Drake
My Boy	Elvis Presley
My Boy Lollipop	Millie Small
My Boyfriend's Back	Angels
My Brother Jake	Free
My Bucket's Got A Hole In It	Ricky Nelson
My Camera Never Lies	Bucks Fizz
My Cherie Amour	Stevie Wonder
My Coo-Ca-Choo	Alvin Stardust
My Culture	1 Giant Leap
My Cup Runneth Over	Ed Ames
My Dad	Paul Petersen
My Destiny	Lionel Richie
My Ding-A-Ling	Chuck Berry
My Dixie Darling	Lonnie Donegan
My Doorbell	White Stripes
My Empty Arms	Jackie Wilson
My Ever Changing Mood	Style Council
My Eyes Adored You	Frankie Valli
My Favorite Girl	Dave Hollister
My Favorite Mistake	Sheryl Crow
My Favourite Waste Of Time	Owen Paul
My Friend	Frankie Laine
My Friend Stan	Slade
My Friend The Sea	Petula Clark
My Generation	Who
My Girl	Madness
My Girl	Otis Redding
My Girl	Temptations
My Girl Bill	Jim Stafford
My Girl Josephine	Fats Domino
My Girl Lollipop (My Boy Lollipop)	Bad Manners
My Guy	Mary Wells
My Happiness	Connie Francis
My Happy Ending	Avril Lavigne
My Heart Belongs To Me	Barbra Streisand
My Heart Belongs To Only You	Bobby Vinton
My Heart Can't Tell You No	Rod Stewart
My Heart Has A Mind Of Its Own	Connie Francis
My Heart Is An Open Book	Carl Dobkins Jr.
My Heart's Symphony	Gary Lewis & The Playboys
My Heart Will Go On	Celine Dion
My Home Town	Paul Anka
My Hometown	Bruce Springsteen
My Humps	Black Eyed Peas
My Immortal	Evanescence
My Kind Of Girl	Matt Monro
My Life	Billy Joel

Respect	Aretha Franklin
Respect Yourself	Staple Singers
Respect Yourself	Bruce Willis
Respectable	Mel & Kim
Rest In Peace	Extreme
Resurection	PPK
Resurrection Shuffle	Ashton Gardner & Dyke
The Return Of Django	Upsetters
Return Of The Los Palmas 7	Madness
Return Of The Mack	Mark Morrison
Return To Innocence	Enigma
Return To Me	Dean Martin
Return To Sender	Elvis Presley
Reunited	Peaches & Herb
Reveille Rock	Johnny & The Hurricanes
Reverend Black Grape	Black Grape
Reverend Mr. Black	Kingston Trio
Revolution	Arrested Development
Revolution	Beatles
Reward	Teardrop Explodes
Re-wind The Crowd Say	
Bo Selecta	Artful Dodger feat. Craig David
Rhiannon (Will You Ever Win)	Fleetwood Mac
Rhinestone Cowboy	Glen Campbell
Rhythm Is A Dancer	Snap!
Rhythm Is A Mystery	K-Klass
Rhythm Is Gonna Get You	Gloria Estefan & The Miami Sound Machine
Rhythm Nation	Janet Jackson
Rhythm Of My Heart	Rod Stewart
Rhythm Of The Night	DeBarge
Rhythm Of The Rain	Cascades
Rhythm Of The Rain	Jason Donovan
The Rhythm Of The Night	Corona
Rich Girl	Daryl Hall & John Oates
Rich Girl	Gwen Stefani featuring Eve
Rico Suave	Gerardo
Ricochet	Teresa Brewer
Ricochet	Joan Regan
The Riddle	Nik Kershaw
Ride	Dee Dee Sharp
Ride A White Swan	T. Rex
Ride Captain Ride	Blues Image
Ride It	Geri
Ride It	Jay Sean
Ride Like The Wind	Christopher Cross
Ride Like The Wind	East Side Beat
Ride On Time	Black Box
Ride Wit Me	Nelly Featuring City Spud
Riders In The Sky	Ramrods
Riders In The Sky	Shadows
Riders On The Storm	Doors
Ridin'	Chamillionaire featuring Krayzie Bone
Riding On A Train	Pasadenas
Right Back Where We Started From	Maxine Nightingale
Right Back Where We Started From	Sinitta
Right Beside You	Sophie B. Hawkins
Right By Your Side	Eurythmics
Right Down The Line	Gerry Rafferty
Right Here Right Now	Fatboy Slim
Right Here, Right Now	Jesus Jones
Right Here (Human Nature)	SWV
Right Here Waiting	Richard Marx
Right In The Night (Fall In Love With Music)	Jam & Spoon Feat Plavka
The Right Kind Of Love	Jeremy Jordan
Right Now (Na Na Na)	Akon
Right Now 2004	Atomic Kitten
Right On Track	Breakfast Club
Right Place Wrong Time	Dr. John
Right Round	Flo Rida
Right Said Fred	Bernard Cribbins
The Right Thing	Simply Red
Right Thurr	Chingy
Right Time Of The Night	Jennifer Warnes
Rikki Don't Lose That Number	Steely Dan
Ring My Bell	Anita Ward
Ring Ring Ring (Ha Ha Hey)	De La Soul
Ring The Alarm	Beyoncé
Ringo	Lorne Greene
Rinky Dink	Dave 'Baby' Cortez
Rio	Duran Duran
Rip It Up	Bill Haley & His Comets
Rip It Up	Orange Juice
Rise	Gabrielle
Rise	Herb Alpert
Rise	Public Image Ltd.
Rise & Fall	Craig David featuring Sting
The Rise & Fall Of Flingel Bunt	Shadows
Rise To The Occasion	Climie Fisher
Rising Sun	Medicine Head
The River	Ken Dodd
River Deep Mountain High	Ike & Tina Turner
River Deep-Mountain High	Supremes & Four Tops
The River Of Dreams	Billy Joel
Riverdance	Bill Whelan
Rivers Of Babylon	Boney M
The Road To Hell (Pt. 2)	Chris Rea
Road To Nowhere	Talking Heads
Road Rage	Catatonia
The Road To Mandalay	Robbie Williams
Roadrunner	Jonathan Richman & The Modern Lovers
Roam	B-52's

Robert De Niro's Waiting	Bananarama
Robin Hood	Dick James
Robin Hood	Gary Miller
Robot	Tornados
Robot Man	Connie Francis
Rock 'n' Roll Winter	Wizzard
Rock 'n' Roll	Status Quo
Rock 'n' Roll Ain't Noise Pollution	AC/DC
Rock 'n' Roll Fantasy	Bad Company
Rock 'n' Roll Is King	Electric Light Orchestra
Rock 'n' Roll Lady	Showaddywaddy
Rock & Roll Music	Chuck Berry
Rock And Roll Dreams Come Through	Meat Loaf
Rock And Roll Heaven	Righteous Brothers
Rock And Roll Music	Beach Boys
Rock And Roll Part 2	Gary Glitter
Rock And Roll Waltz	Kay Starr
Rock And Roll All Nite (Live Version)	Kiss
Rock DJ	Robbie Williams
R.O.C.K In The U.S.A. (A Salute To 60's Rock)	John Cougar Mellencamp
Rock Island Line	Lonnie Donegan
Rock Me	Steppenwolf
Rock Me Amadeus	Falco
Rock Me Baby	David Cassidy
Rock Me Gently	Andy Kim
Rock Me Tonite	Billy Squier
Rock My Heart	Haddaway
Rock On	Michael Damian
Rock On	David Essex
Rock Steady	All Saints
Rock Steady	Aretha Franklin
Rock Steady	Whispers
Rock The Boat	Aaliyah
Rock The Boat	Forrest
Rock The Boat	Hues Corporation
Rock The Casbah	Clash
Rock This Party	Bob Sinclar & Cutee B featuring Dollarman & Big Ali
Rock This Town	Stray Cats
Rock Wit U (Awww Baby)	Ashanti
Rock Wit'cha	Bobby Brown
Rock With You	Michael Jackson
Rock Ya Body 'Mic Check 1, 2,'	M.V.P.
Rock Your Baby	KWS
Rock Your Baby	George McCrae
Rock Your Body	Justin Timberlake
Rock'n Me	Steve Miller Band
Rock-A-Beatin' Boogie	Bill Haley & His Comets
Rock-A-Billy	Guy Mitchell
Rock-A-Bye Your Baby With A Dixie Melody	Jerry Lewis
Rock-A-Hula-Baby	Elvis Presley
Rock-In' Robin	Bobby Day
The Rockafeller Skank	Fatboy Slim
Rockaria	Electric Light Orchestra
Rocket	Def Leppard
Rocket	Mud
Rocket Man	Elton John
Rocket Man (I Think It's Going To Be A Long Long Time)	Kate Bush
Rocket 2 U	Jets
The Rockford Files	Mike Post
Rockin' All Over The World	Status Quo
Rockin' Around The Christmas Tree	Brenda Lee
Rockin' Around The Christmas Tree	Kim Wilde & Mel Smith
Rockin' Chair	Gwen McCrae
A Rockin' Good Way	Shaky & Bonnie
A Rockin' Good Way	Dinah Washington & Brook Benton
Rockin' Over The Beat	Technotronic featuring Ya Kid K
Rockin' Pneumonia & The Boogie Woogie Flu	Johnny Rivers
Rockin' Robin	Michael Jackson
Rockin' Roll Baby	Stylistics
Rockin' Through The Rye	Bill Haley & His Comets
Rocking Goose	Johnny & The Hurricanes
Rockit	Herbie Hancock
Rocks/Funky Jam	Primal Scream
Rockstar	Nickelback
Rocky	Austin Roberts
Rocky Mountain High	John Denver
Rodrigo's Guitar Concerto De Aranjuez	Manuel & His Music Of The Mountains
Rok Da House	Beatmasters featuring The Cookie Crew
Roll Away The Stone	Mott The Hoople
Rollercoaster	B*Witched
Roll Over Beethoven	Electric Light Orchestra
Roll Over Lay Down	Status Quo
Roll To Me	Del Amitri
Roll With It	Oasis
Roll With It	Steve Winwood
Rollin'	Limp Bizkit
Rollin' Stone	David Essex
Rolling Home	Status Quo
Romantic	Karyn White
Romeo	Basement Jaxx
Romeo	Petula Clark
Romeo	Dino
Romeo	Mr. Big
Romeo And Juliet	Dire Straits
Romeo And Juliet	Silk-E Fyne/Chill
Romeo Dunn	Romeo
Romeo's Tune	Steve Forbert
Roni	Bobby Brown
Ronnie	Four Seasons

Rooftops (A Liberation Broadcast)	Lostprophets
Room At The Top	Adam Ant
Room In Your Heart	Living In A Box
Room On The 3rd Floor	McFly
Room To Move	Animotion
Rosanna	Toto
The Rose	Bette Midler
The Rose	Westlife
A Rose And A Baby Ruth	George Hamilton IV
Rose Garden	Lynn Anderson
Rose Garden	New World
A Rose Has To Die	Dooleys
Rose Marie	Slim Whitman
Roses Are Red	Ronnie Carroll
Roses	OutKast
Roses Are Red	Mac Band featuring The McCampbell Brothers
Roses Are Red (My Love)	Bobby Vinton
Roses Of Picardy	Vince Hill
Rosetta	Fame And Price Together
Rosie	Don Partridge
Roulette	Russ Conway
Round And Round	Tevin Campbell
Round And Round	Perry Como
Round And Round	Jaki Graham
Round And Round	Ratt
Round Round	Sugababes
Roundabout	Yes
The Roussos Phenomenon E.P.	Demis Roussos
Roxanne	Police
Royal Event	Russ Conway
Rub You The Right Way	Johnny Gill
Rubber Ball	Bobby Vee
Rubber Ball	Marty Wilde
Rubber Bullets	10cc
Rubber Duckie	Ernie
Rubber Lover	Marmaduke Duke
Rubberband Girl	Kate Bush
The Rubberband Man	Spinners
Rubberneckin'	Elvis Presley
Ruby	Kaiser Chiefs
Ruby Baby	Dion
Ruby, Don't Take Your Love To Town	Kenny Rogers & The First Edition
Ruby Tuesday	Melanie
Ruby Tuesday	Rolling Stones
Ruby Tuesday	Rolling Stones
Ruby Tuesday	Rod Stewart
Rude Boys Outa Jail	Specials
Rudebox	Robbie Williams
Ruff In The Jungle	Prodigy
Rule The World	Take That
Rumors	Johnny Crawford
Rumors	Timex Social Club
Rump Shaker	Wreckx-N-Effect
Run	Leona Lewis
Run	Snow Patrol
Run Away	Real McCoy
Run Away Child, Running Wild	Temptations
Run, Baby Run (Back Into My Arms)	Newbeats
Run For Home	Lindisfarne
Run It!	Chris Brown
Run Joey Run	David Geddes
Run Run Run	Jo Jo Gunne
Run Runaway	Slade
Run This Town	Jay-Z, Rihanna & Kanye West
Run Through The Jungle	Creedence Clearwater Revival
Run To Him	Bobby Vee
Run To Me	Bee Gees
Run To The Hills	Iron Maiden
Run To The Sun	Erasure
Run To You	Bryan Adams
Run To You	Rage
Run-Around	Blues Traveler
Runaround Sue	Dion
Runaround Sue	Leif Garrett
Runaway (Remix)	Corrs
Runaway	Janet Jackson
Runaway	Jefferson Starship
Runaway	Del Shannon
Runaway Boys	Stray Cats
Runaway Love	Ludacris Featuring Mary J. Blige
Runaway Train	Soul Asylum
The Runner	Three Degrees
Runnin' On Empty	Jackson Browne
Running Bear	Johnny Preston
Running In The Family	Level 42
Running Scared	Roy Orbison
Running Up That Hill	Kate Bush
Running With The Night	Lionel Richie
Rupert	Jackie Lee
Rush Hour	Jane Wiedlin
Rush Rush	Paula Abdul
Rushes	Darius
Russian Roulette	Rihanna
Russians	Sting
S Club Party	S Club 7
S-S-S-Single Bed	Fox
Sabre Dance	Love Sculpture
Sacred Emotion	Donny Osmond
Sacred Trust	One True Voice
Sacrifice	Elton John
Sad Eyes	Robert John

She'd Rather Be With Me	Turtles
She's A Beauty	Tubes
She's A Fool	Lesley Gore
She's A Lady	Tom Jones
She's A River	Simple Minds
She's A Woman	Beatles
She's About A Mover	Sir Douglas Quintet
She's All I Ever Had	Ricky Martin
She's Gone	Daryl Hall & John Oates
She's Got Claws	Gary Numan
She's Got That Vibe	R. Kelly
She's In Love With You	Suzi Quatro
She's Just My Style	Gary Lewis & The Playboys
She's Leaving Home	Wet Wet Wet & Billy Bragg
She's Like The Wind	Patrick Swayze (with Wendy Fraser)
She's Not Just Another Woman	8th Day
She's Not There	Santana
She's Not There	Zombies
She's Not You	Elvis Presley
She's On It	Beastie Boys
She's Out Of My Life	Michael Jackson
She's Playing Hard To Get	Hi-Five
(She's) Sexy + 17	Stray Cats
She's So Lovely	Scouting For Girls
She's So Modern	Boomtown Rats
Sheffield Grinder	Tony Capstick
Sheila	Tommy Roe
Sherry	Adrian Baker
Sherry	Four Seasons
The Shifting, Whispering Sands	Rusty Draper
The Shifting Whispering Sands (Pts 1 & 2)	Billy Vaughn
Shindig	Shadows
Shine	Aswad
Shine	Booty Luv
Shine	Collective Soul
Shine	Take That
Shine	The Lovefreekz
Shine A Little Love	Electric Light Orchestra
Shine On	Degrees Of Motion
Shinin' On	Grand Funk
Shining Star	Earth, Wind & Fire
Shining Star	Manhattans
Shiny Happy People	R.E.M.
Ship Of Fools	Erasure
Ships	Barry Manilow
Shiralee	Tommy Steele
Shirley	Shakin' Stevens
Shit On You	D12
Shiver	Natalie Imbruglia
The Shock Of The Lightning	Oasis
Shocked	Kylie Minogue
Shoo-Be-Doo-Be-Doo-Da-Day	Stevie Wonder
Shoop	Salt-N-Pepa
Shoop Shoop Song (It's In His Kiss)	Betty Everett
The Shoop Shoop Song (It's In His Kiss)	Cher
Shoot Me With Your Love	D:ream
Shooting Star	Flip & Fill
Shop Around	Captain & Tennille
Shop Around	Miracles
Shoplifters Of The World Unite	Smiths
Short Dick Man	20 Fingers
Short Fat Fannie	Larry Williams
Short People	Randy Newman
Short Shorts	Royal Teens
Shortie Like Mine	Bow Wow featuring Chris Brown & Johnta Austin
Shortsharpshock (EP)	Therapy?
Shot You Down	Audio Bullys featuring Nancy Sinatra
Shotgun	Jr. Walker & The All Stars
Shotgun Wedding	Roy 'C'
Should I Do It	Pointer Sisters
Shoulder Lean	Young Dro featuring T.I.
Should've Known Better	Richard Marx
Shout	Louchie Lou & Michie One
Shout	Lulu
Shout	Tears For Fears
Shout (Pt. 1)	Joey Dee & The Starliters
Shout! Shout!	
(Knock Yourself Out)	Ernie Maresca
Shout To The Top	Style Council
The Show	Doug E. Fresh & The Get Fresh Crew
The Show	Girls Aloud
Show And Tell	Al Wilson
Show Me Heaven	Maria McKee
Show Me Love	Robin S.
Show Me Love	Robyn
Show Me Love	Steve Angello & Laidback Luke Feat. Robin S
Show Me The Meaning Of Loneliness	Backstreet Boys
Show Me The Way	Peter Frampton
Show Me The Way	Styx
Show Me What You Got	Jay-Z
Show Me You're A Woman	Mud
The Show Must Go On	Leo Sayer
The Show Must Go On	Three Dog Night
Show Stopper	Danity Kane
Show You The Way To Go	Jacksons
Showdown	Electric Light Orchestra
Shower Me With Your Love	Surface
Showing Out (Get Fresh At The Weekend)	Mel & Kim
The Shuffle	Van McCoy
Shut Up	Black Eyed Peas
Shut Up	Madness
Shut Up And Drive	Rihanna

Shut Up And Forget About It	Dane
Shut Up And Let Me Go	The Ting Tings
Shy Boy	Bananarama
Shy Guy	Diana King
Sick And Tired	Anastacia
Sick Man Blues	Goodies
Side Saddle	Russ Conway
Side Show	Barry Biggs
Sideshow	Blue Magic
Sight For Sore Eyes	M People
The Sign	Ace Of Base
Sign 'O' The Times	Prince
Sign Of The Times	Belle Stars
A Sign Of The Times	Petula Clark
Sign Your Name	Terence Trent D'Arby
Signal Fire	Snow Patrol
Signed Sealed Delivered I'm Yours	Stevie Wonder
Signs	Five Man Electrical Band
Signs	Snoop Dogg featuring Charlie Wilson and Justin Timberlake
Signs	Tesla
Silence (Remixes)	Delerium Feat. Sarah McLachlan
Silence Is Golden	Tremeloes
Silent Lucidity	Queensrÿche
Silent Night	Bros
Silent Running (On Dangerous Ground)	Mike + The Mechanics
Silhouettes	Herman's Hermits
Silhouettes	Rays
Silhouettes	Cliff Richard
Silly Games	Janet Kay
Silly Love Songs	Paul McCartney
Silly Thing	Sex Pistols
Silver Dream Machine (Pt. 1)	David Essex
Silver Lady	David Soul
Silver Machine	Hawkwind
Silver Star	Four Seasons
Simon Says	1910 Fruitgum Co.
Simon Smith & His Amazing Dancing Bear	Alan Price Set
Simon Templar	Splodgenessabounds
Simple Game	Four Tops
Simple Kind Of Life	No Doubt
Simply Irresistible	Robert Palmer
Since I Don't Have You	Guns N' Roses
Since I Don't Have You	Skyliners
Since I Fell For You	Lenny Welch
Since I Met You Baby	Ivory Joe Hunter
Since Yesterday	Strawberry Switchblade
Since U Been Gone	Kelly Clarkson
Since You've Been Gone	Rainbow
Sincerely	McGuire Sisters
Sing	Carpenters
Sing	Travis
Sing A Song	Earth, Wind & Fire
Sing A Song Of Freedom	Cliff Richard
Sing Baby Sing	Stylistics
Sing For The Moment	Eminem
Sing It Back	Moloko
Sing It With Joe	Joe 'Mr. Piano' Henderson
Sing Little Birdie	Pearl Carr & Teddy Johnson
Sing Me	Brothers
Sing Our Own Song	UB40
Singin' In The Rain	Mint Royale
Singin' In The Rain (Pt. 1)	Sheila B. Devotion
The Singing Dogs (Medley)	Singing Dogs
Singing The Blues	Guy Mitchell
Singing The Blues	Tommy Steele
Single	Natasha Bedingfield
Single Girl	Sandy Posey
Single Ladies (Put A Ring On It)	Beyonce
Single Life	Cameo
Sink That Ship	Kaiser Chiefs
Sink The Bismarck	Johnny Horton
Sippin' Soda	Guy Mitchell
Sir Duke	Stevie Wonder
Sister	Bros
Sister Christian	Night Ranger
Sister Golden Hair	America
Sister Jane	New World
Sister Of Mercy	Thompson Twins
Sisters Are Doin' It For Themselves	Eurythmics & Aretha Franklin
Sit Down	James
Sit Down (Remix)	James
Sittin' In The Park	Georgie Fame
(Sittin' On) The Dock Of The Bay	Michael Bolton
(Sittin' On) The Dock Of The Bay	Otis Redding
Sittin' Up In My Room	Brandy
Sitting Down Here	Lene Marlin
The Six Teens	Sweet
634-5789	Wilson Pickett
16 Bars	Stylistics
16 Candles	Crests
Sixteen Reasons	Connie Stevens
Sixteen Tons	Tennessee Ernie Ford
Sixteen Tons	Frankie Laine
'65 Love Affair	Paul Davis
The Size Of A Cow	Wonder Stuff
Ska Train	Beatmasters
Sk8er Boi	Avril Lavigne
Skiing In The Snow	Wigan's Ovation
Skin Deep	Duke Ellington
Skin Deep	Ted Heath
Skin Tight	Ohio Players
Skinny Legs And All	Joe Tex

Skokiaan	Four Lads
Skokiaan	Ralph Marterie
Skweeze Me Pleeze Me	Slade
Sky	Sonique
Sky High	Jigsaw
The Skye Boat Song	Roger Whittaker & Des O'Connor
Slam	Onyx
Slam Jam	WWF Superstars
Slave To Love	Bryan Ferry
Slave To The Rhythm	Grace Jones
Slave To The Vibe	Aftershock
Sledgehammer	Peter Gabriel
Sleep	Little Willie John
Sleep	Texas
Sleep Walk	Santo & Johnny
Sleeping Bag	ZZ Top
Sleeping Satellite	Tasmin Archer
Sleeping With The Light On	Busted
Sleepy Joe	Herman's Hermits
Sleepy Shores	Johnny Pearson Orchestra
Sleigh Ride	S Club Juniors
Slide	Goo Goo Dolls
Slight Return	Bluetones
The Slightest Touch	Five Star
Slip Away	Clarence Carter
Slip Slidin' Away	Paul Simon
Slip Your Disc To This	Heatwave
Slippin' Into Darkness	War
Sloop John B	Beach Boys
Slow	Kylie Minogue
Slow Down	John Miles
Slow Down	Bobby Valentino
Slow Hand	Pointer Sisters
Slow Jamz	Twista featuring Kanye West & Jamie Foxx
Slow It Down	East 17
Slow Motion	Juvenile featuring Soulja Slim
Slow Twistin'	Chubby Checker
Smack That	Akon featuring Eminem
Smackwater Jack	Carole King
Small Town	John Cougar Mellencamp
Smalltown Boy	Bronski Beat
Smarty Pants	First Choice
Smells Like Teen Spirit	Nirvana
Smile	Lily Allen
Smile	Nat 'King' Cole
Smile	Scarface/2Pac/Johnny P
Smile	Vitamin C Feat. Lady Saw
Smile A Little Smile For Me	Flying Machine
Smiling Faces Sometime	Undisputed Truth
Smoke From A Distant Fire	Sanford/Townsend Band
Smoke Gets In Your Eyes	Platters
Smoke On The Water	Deep Purple
Smokers Outside The Hospital Doors	Editors
Smokie- Part 2	Bill Black's Combo
Smokin' In The Boys Room	Brownsville Station
Smokin' In The Boys Room	Mötley Crüe
Smooth	Santana Feat. Rob Thomas
Smooth Criminal	Alien Ant Farm
Smooth Criminal	Michael Jackson
Smooth Operator	Sade
Smuggler's Blues	Glenn Frey
The Smurf Song	Father Abraham & The Smurfs
Snake	R. Kelly Featuring Big Tigger
Snap! Mega Mix	Snap!
Snap Yo Fingers	Lil Jon featuring E-40 & Sean Paul of the YoungBloodZ
Snap Your Fingers	Joe Henderson
Snooker Loopy	Matchroom Mob With Chas & Dave
Snookeroo	Ringo Starr
Snoopy vs. The Red Baron	Hotshots
Snoopy vs. The Red Baron	Royal Guardsmen
Snot Rap	Kenny Everett
Snow Coach	Russ Conway
Snowbird	Anne Murray
So Alive	Love And Rockets
So Close	Daryl Hall John Oates
So Cold The Night	Communards
So Confused	2play featuring Raghav & Jucxi
So Do I	Kenny Ball
So Emotional	Whitney Houston
So Far Away	Carole King
So Fine	Fiestas
So Gone	Monica
So Good	Boyzone
So Good	Eternal
So Good To Be Back Home Again	Tourists
So Hard	Pet Shop Boys
So Here We Are	Bloc Party
So In Love With Two	Mikaila
So In To You	Atlanta Rhythm Section
So Lonely	Jakatta
So Lonely	Police
So Long Baby	Del Shannon
So Macho	Sinitta
So Many Ways	Brook Benton
So Much In Love	All-4-One
So Much In Love	Tymes
So Pure	Baby D
So Rare	Jimmy Dorsey
So Sad (To Watch Good Love Go Bad)	Everly Brothers
So Sick	Ne-Yo
So What	Field Mob featuring Ciara

Song	Artist
So What	P!nk
So You Win Again	Hot Chocolate
Sober	P!nk
Society's Child (Baby I've Been Thinking)	Janis Ian
Sock It 2 Me	Missy Misdemeanor Elliott/Da Brat
Sock It To Me-Baby!	Mitch Ryder & The Detroit Wheels
Soda Pop	Merrion, McCall & Kensit
Soft Summer Breeze	Eddie Heywood
Softly As I Leave You	Matt Monro
Softly Softly	Ruby Murray
Softly Whispering I Love You	Congregation
Soldier	Destiny' Child featuring T.I. & Lil Wayne
Soldier Blue	Buffy Sainte Marie
Soldier Boy	Shirelles
Soldier Of Love	Donny Osmond
Soley Soley	Middle Of The Road
Solid	Ashford & Simpson
Solid Bond In Your Heart	Style Council
Solid Gold Easy Action	T. Rex
Solitaire	Clay Aiken
Solitaire	Laura Branigan
Solitaire	Andy Williams
Solsbury Hill	Erasure
Solsbury Hill	Peter Gabriel
Some Cut	Trillville featuring Cutty
Some Day	Frankie Laine
Some Enchanted Evening	Jay & The Americans
Some Girls	Racey
Some Girls	Rachel Stevens
Some Girls	Ultimate Kaos
Some Guys Have All The Luck	Maxi Priest
Some Guys Have All The Luck	Rod Stewart
Some Kind Of A Summer	David Cassidy
Some Kind Of Lover	Jody Watley
Some Kind Of Wonderful	Grand Funk
Some Kind-A Earthquake	Duane Eddy
Some Like It Hot	Power Station
Some Might Say	Oasis
Some Of Your Lovin'	Dusty Springfield
Some People	Cliff Richard
Somebody	Bryan Adams
Somebody Bad Stole De Wedding Bell	Eartha Kitt
Somebody Else's Guy	Jocelyn Brown
(Somebody) Help Me Out	Beggar & Co
Somebody Help Me	Spencer Davis Group
Somebody To Love	Boogie Pimps
Somebody To Love	Jefferson Airplane
Somebody To Love	Queen
Somebody Told Me	The Killers
Somebody's Baby	Jackson Browne
Somebody's Been Sleeping	100 Proof Aged In Soul
Somebody's Knockin'	Terri Gibbs
Somebody's Watching Me	Beatfreakz
Somebody's Watching Me	Rockwell
Someday	Mariah Carey
Someday	Glass Tiger
Someday	Ricky Nelson
Someday	Nickelback
Someday	Jodie Sands
Someday I'll Be Saturday Night	Bon Jovi
Someday (I'm Coming Back)	Lisa Stansfield
Someday One Day	Seekers
Someday Out Of The Blue	Elton John
Someday We'll Be Together	Diana Ross & The Supremes
Someday We're Gonna Love Again	Searchers
Someone	Johnny Mathis
Someone Could Lose A Heart Tonight	Eddie Rabbitt
Someone Else's Baby	Adam Faith
Someone Else's Roses	Joan Regan
Someone Like Me	Atomic Kitten
Someone Loves You Honey	Lutricia McNeal
Someone On Your Mind	Jimmy Young
Someone Saved My Life Tonight	Elton John
Someone Someone	Brian Poole & The Tremeloes
Someone To Call My Lover	Janet
Someone To Love	Jon B. featuring Babyface
Someone's Looking At You	Boomtown Rats
Somethin' Stupid	Nancy & Frank Sinatra
Somethin' Stupid	Robbie Williams & Nicole Kidman
Something	Shirley Bassey
Something	Beatles
Something	Lasgo
Something 'Bout You Baby	Status Quo
Something About You	Jamelia
Something About You	Level 42
Something Beautiful	Robbie Williams
Something Better Change	Stranglers
Something Better To Do	Olivia Newton-John
Something Else	Sex Pistols
Something For The Pain	Bon Jovi
Something Good	Utah Saints
Something Good '08	Utah Saints
Something Got Me Started	Simply Red
Something Happened On The Way To Heaven	Phil Collins
Something Here In My Heart (Keeps A-Tellin' Me No)	Paper Dolls
(Something Inside) So Strong	Labi Siffre
Something In The Air	Thunderclap Newman
Something Kinda Ooooh	Girls Aloud
Something Old, Something New	Fantastics
Something So Strong	Crowded House
Something Tells Me (Something Is Gonna Happen Tonight)	Cilla Black
Something To Believe In	Poison
Something To Believe In	Bonnie Raitt
Something To Talk About	Kenny Rogers & The First Edition
Something's Burning	Sammy Davis Jr.
Something's Gotta Give	Marc Almond feat. Gene Pitney
Something's Gotten Hold Of My Heart	Gene Pitney
Something's Happening	Herman's Hermits
Something's Wrong With Me	Austin Roberts
Something's Gotta Give	McGuire Sisters
Sometimes	Erasure
Sometimes	Britney Spears
Sometimes Love Just Ain't Enough	Patty Smyth
Sometimes When We Touch	Dan Hill
Sometimes You Can't Make It On Your Own	U2
Somewhere	P.J. Proby
Somewhere Else	Razorlight
Somewhere In My Heart	Aztec Camera
Somewhere In The Night	Barry Manilow
Somewhere, My Love	Ray Conniff & The Singers
Somewhere Only We Know	Keane
Somewhere Out There	Linda Ronstadt
Somewhere Over The Rainbow	Katharine McPhee
Somewhere Somehow	Wet Wet Wet
The Son Of Hickory Holler's Tramp	O.C. Smith
Son Of My Father	Chicory Tip
Son-Of-A Preacher Man	Dusty Springfield
Song For Guy	Elton John
Song For Love	Extreme
A Song For Lovers	Richard Ashcroft
Song 4 Lovers	Liberty X featuring Rev Run from Run DMC
A Song For Mama	Boyz II Men
Song For Whoever	Beautiful South
A Song Of Joy	Miguel Rios
Song Of The Dreamer	Eddie Fisher
Song Of The Dreamer	Johnnie Ray
Song Sung Blue	Neil Diamond
Songbird	Kenny G
Songbird	Oasis
Songs For Swinging Lovers (L.P.)	Frank Sinatra
Sooner Or Later	Grass Roots
Sorrow	David Bowie
Sorrow	Merseys
Sorry	Buckcherry
Sorry	Madonna
Sorry	Akon
Sorry, Blame It On Me	Impalas
Sorry (I Ran All The Way Home)	Baccara
Sorry I'm A Lady	Blue featuring Elton John
Sorry Seems To Be The Hardest Word	Elton John
Sorry Seems To Be The Hardest Word	Hollies
Sorry Suzanne	Ruben Studdard
Sorry 2004	McFly
Sorry's Not Good Enough	Pulp
Sorted For E's & Wizz	Abba
S.O.S.	Jonas Brothers
SOS	Rihanna
SOS	Blues Brothers
Soul Man	Sam & Dave
Soul Man	Bilal
Soul Sista	Young Jeezy featuring Akon
Soul Survivor	Young-Holt Unlimited
Soulful Strut	Master P
Souljas	Natasha Bedingfield
Soulmate	James
Sound	David Bowie
Sound And Vision	Kula Shaker
Sound of Drums	Bachelors
The Sound Of Silence	Members
Sound Of The Suburbs	Simon & Garfunkel
The Sounds Of Silence	Girls Aloud
Sound Of The Underground	Moby feauring Gwen Stefani
South Side	Orlons
South Street	Freeez
Southern Freeez	Erykah Badu
Southern Girl	Glen Campbell
Southern Nights	Orchestral Manoeuvres In The Dark
Souvenir	Tears For Fears
Sowing The Seeds Of Love	Adamski
The Space Jungle	David Bowie
Space Oddity	Billy Preston
Space Race	Babylon Zoo
Spaceman	Al Martino
Spanish Eyes	Herb Alpert
Spanish Flea	Aretha Franklin
Spanish Harlem	Ben E. King
Spanish Harlem	Ramblers
The Sparrow	Style Council
Speak Like A Child	Brenda Lee
Speak To Me Pretty	Rick Springfield
Speak To The Sky	Bad Manners
Special Brew	Ray, Goodman & Brown
Special Lady	Val Doonican
The Special Years	D-Side
Speechless	Coldplay
Speed Of Sound	Pat Boone
Speedy Gonzales	Eric Benet Feat. Tamia
Spend My Life With You	Coolnotes
Spend The Night	Jim Stafford
Spiders & Snakes	Paul McCartney
Spies Like Us	Eric Burdon & War
Spill The Wine	Pearl Jam
Spin The Black Circle	
Spinning Around	Kylie Minogue
Spinning Wheel	Blood Sweat & Tears
Spirit In The Sky	Doctor & The Medics
Spirit In The Sky	Gareth Gates featuring The Kumars
Spirit In The Sky	Norman Greenbaum
Spirits In The Material World	Police
Splash Waterfalls	Ludacris
Splish Splash	Bobby Darin
Splish Splash	Charlie Drake
Spooky	Classics IV
Spot The Pigeon E.P.	Genesis
Spotlight	Jennifer Hudson
Squeeze Box	Who
Staccato's Theme	Elmer Bernstein
Stagger Lee	Lloyd Price
Stairway Of Love	Michael Holliday
Stairway To Heaven	Far Corporation
Stairway To Heaven	Rolf Harris
Stairway To Heaven	Neil Sedaka
Stan	Eminem
Stand	R.E.M.
Stand And Deliver	Adam & The Ants
Stand Back	Stevie Nicks
Stand By Me	4 The Cause
Stand By Me	Ben E. King
Stand By Me	Spyder Turner
Stand By Your Man	Tammy Wynette
Stand Tall	Burton Cummings
Stand Tough	Point Break
Stand Up	Ludacris featuring Shawnna
Stand Up For Your Love Rights	Yazz
Standing In The Road	Blackfoot Sue
Standing In The Shadows Of Love	Four Tops
Standing In The Way Of Control	Gossip
Standing On The Corner	Four Lads
Standing On The Corner	King Brothers
Star	Kiki Dee
Star	Erasure
Star	McFly
Star Girl	Stylistics
Star On A TV Show	Fatboy Slim
Star 69	Whitney Houston
The Star Spangled Banner	Cabin Crew
Star To Fall	Firm
Star Trekkin'	London Symphony Orchestra
Star Wars (Main Title)	Meco
Star Wars Theme/Cantina Band	David Essex
Stardust	Billy Ward & His Dominoes
Stardust	Rooster
Staring At The Sun	Supermen Lovers
Starlight	Kids From 'Fame'
Starmaker	David Bowie
Starman	Michael Holliday
Starry Eyed	Oakenfold
Starry Eyed Surprise	Simply Red
Stars	Paris
Stars Are Blind	Stars On 45
Stars On 45 (Medley)	Starsound
Stars On 45 (Vol 2)	Ronnie Hilton
Stars Shine In Your Eyes	3OH!3 Featuring Katy Perry
Starstrukk	Just Jack
Starz In Their Eyes	Jam
Start	Rolling Stones
Start Me Up	Sal Mineo
Start Movin' (In My Direction)	Su Pollard
Starting Together	Holly Valance
State Of Mind	Jacksons
State Of Shock	Jackson Browne
Stay	Eternal
Stay	Hollies
Stay	Lisa Loeb & Nine Stories
Stay	Shakespear's Sister
Stay	Maurice Williams & The Zodiacs
Stay Another Day	East 17
Stay Awhile	Bells
Stay Awhile	Dusty Springfield
Stay (Faraway, So Close)	U2
Stay Fly	Three 6 Mafia featuring Young Buck & Eightball
Stay In My Corner	Dells
Stay On These Roads	A-Ha
Stay Out Of My Life	Five Star
Stay The Night	Chicago
Stay The Night	IMX
Stay The Same	Joey McIntyre
Stay Together	Suede
Stay With Me	Blue Mink
Stay With Me	Faces
Stay With Me	Ironik
Stay With Me	Notorious B.I.G.
Stayin' Alive	Bee Gees
Stayin' Alive	N-Trance featuring Ricardo Da Force
Steady As She Goes	Raconteurs
Steal Away	Robbie Dupree
Steal My Sunshine	Len
Steam	East 17
Steam	Peter Gabriel
Steam Heat	Patti Page
Step Back In Time	Kylie Minogue
Step By Step	Crests
Step By Step	New Kids On The Block
Step By Step	Eddie Rabbitt
Step By Step	Joe Simon

Step In The Name Of Love	R. Kelly
Step Inside Love	Cilla Black
Step It Up	Stereo MCs
Step Off (Pt. 1)	Grandmaster Melle Mel & The Furious Five
Step On	Happy Mondays
Steppin' Out	Joe Jackson
Steppin' Out (Gonna Boogie Tonight)	Tony Orlando & Dawn
Stereotype	Specials
Stereotypes	Blur
Stewball	Lonnie Donegan
Stick It Out	Right Said Fred
Stick-Up	Honey Cone
Stickwitu	Pussycat Dolls
Still	Bill Anderson
Still	Commodores
Still	Karl Denver
Still D.R.E	Dr Dre Feat. Snoop Dogg
Still Fly	Big Tymers
Still I'm Sad	Yardbirds
Still In My Heart	Tracie Spencer
Still On Your Side	BBMak
Still The One	Orleans
Still The Same	Bob Seger & The Silver Bullet Band
Still Water (Love)	Four Tops
Stillness In Time	Jamiroquai
Stir It Up	Johnny Nash
Stole	Kelly Rowland
Stolen	Jay Sean
Stomp	Steps
Stomp!	Brothers Johnson
Stone Love	Kool & The Gang
Stoned In Love	Chicane featuring Tom Jones
Stoned Love	Supremes
Stoned Soul Picnic	Fifth Dimension
Stones	Neil Diamond
Stoney End	Barbra Streisand
The Stonk	Hale & Pace
Stood Up	Ricky Nelson
Stool Pigeon	Kid Creole & The Coconuts
Stop	Sam Brown
Stop	Spice Girls
Stop	Jamelia
Stop And Smell The Roses	Mac Davis
Stop And Stare	OneRepublic
Stop And Think It Over	Dale & Grace
Stop Crying Your Heart Out	Oasis
Stop Draggin' My Heart Around	Stevie Nicks With Tom Petty & The Heartbreakers
Stop Her On Sight (SOS)	Edwin Starr
Stop Living The Lie	David Sneddon
Stop Me	Mark Ronson Featuring Daniel Merriweather
Stop Me (If You've Heard It All Before)	Billy Ocean
Stop Stop Stop	Hollies
Stop The Cavalry	Jona Lewie
Stop To Love	Luther Vandross
Stop! In The Name Of Love	Supremes
Storm In A Teacup	Fortunes
Stormy	Classics IV
Story Of My Life	Kristian Leontiou
Story Of My Life	Gary Miller
The Story Of My Life	Michael Holliday
The Story Of The Blues	Wah!
The Story Of Three Loves	Winifred Atwell
Story Of Tina	Ronnie Harris
The Story Of Tina	Al Martino
A Story Untold	Crew-Cuts
Stowaway	Barbara Lyon
Straight From The Heart	Bryan Adams
Straight From The Heart	Doolally
Straight On	Heart
Straight Up	Paula Abdul
Straighten Out	Stranglers
Stranded	Heart
Stranded	Lutricia McNeal
Stranded In The Jungle	Cadets
Strange And Beautiful (I'll Put A Spell On You)	Aqualung
Strange Band	Family
Strange Kind Of Woman	Deep Purple
Strange Lady In Town	Frankie Laine
Strange Little Girl	Stranglers
Strange Magic	Electric Light Orchestra
Strange Way	Firefall
The Stranger	Shadows
Stranger In My House	Tamia
Stranger In Paradise	Tony Bennett
Stranger In Paradise	Eddie Calvert
Stranger In Paradise	Four Aces
Stranger In Paradise	Tony Martin
Stranger On The Shore	Acker Bilk
Strangers In The Night	Frank Sinatra
Strawberry Fair	Anthony Newley
Strawberry Fields Forever	Beatles
Strawberry Fields Forever	Candy Flip
Strawberry Letter 23	Brothers Johnson
Stray Cat Strut	Stray Cats
The Streak	Ray Stevens
Street Dance	Break Machine
Street Life	Crusaders
Street Life	Roxy Music
Street Spirit (Fade Out)	Radiohead
Street Tuff	Rebel MC/Double Trouble
Streets Of London	Ralph McTell

Streets Of Philadelphia	Bruce Springsteen
Strike It Up	Black Box
The Stripper	David Rose & His Orchestra
Stroke You Up	Changing Faces
The Stroll	Diamonds
Strollin'	Prince
Strong	Robbie Williams
Strong Enough	Cher
Strong Enough	Sheryl Crow
Stronger	Britney Spears
Stronger	Kanye West
Stronger	Sugababes
Strut	Sheena Easton
Strut Your Funky Stuff	Frantique
Stuck In A Moment You Can't Get Out Of	U2
Stuck In The Middle With You	Louise
Stuck In The Middle With You	Stealer's Wheel
Stuck On You	Elvis Presley
Stuck On You	Lionel Richie
Stuck On You	Trevor Walters
Stuck With You	Huey Lewis & The News
Stumblin' In	Suzi Quatro & Chris Norman
Stunt 101	G-Unit
Stupid Cupid	Connie Francis
Stupid Girl	Garbage
Stupid Girls	P!nk
Stutter	Joe featuring Mystikal
Stutter Rap (No Sleep 'til Bedtime)	Morris Minor & The Majors
Substitute	Clout
Substitute	Liquid Gold
Substitute	Who
Subterranean Homesick Blues	Bob Dylan
Suburban Knights	Hard-Fi
Suburbia	Pet Shop Boys
Success	Dannii Minogue
Such A Feeling	Bizarre Inc
Such A Night	Elvis Presley
Such A Night	Johnnie Ray
(Such An) Easy Question	Elvis Presley
Sucu-Sucu	Laurie Johnson
Suddenly	Angry Anderson
Suddenly	Billy Ocean
Suddenly Last Summer	Motels
Suddenly There's A Valley	Petula Clark
Suddenly There's A Valley	Gogi Grant
Suddenly There's A Valley	Lee Lawrence
Suddenly There's A Valley	Jo Stafford
Suddenly You Love Me	Tremeloes
Suedehead	Morrissey
Suga Suga	Baby Bash featuring Frankie J
Sugar	Flo Rida Featuring Wynter
Sugar And Spice	Searchers
Sugar Baby Love	Rubettes
Sugar Candy Kisses	Mac & Katie Kissoon
Sugar Daddy	Jackson Five
Sugar Me	Lynsey De Paul
Sugar Moon	Pat Boone
Sugar Shack	Jimmy Gilmer & The Fireballs
Sugar, Sugar	Archies
Sugar, Sugar	Sakkarin
Sugar Town	Nancy Sinatra
Sugar Walls	Sheena Easton
Sugar, We're Goin Down	Fall Out Boy
Sugartime	McGuire Sisters
Suicide Blonde	Inxs
Sukiyaki	4 P.M.
Sukiyaki	Kenny Ball
Sukiyaki	Kyu Sakamoto
Sukiyaki	Taste Of Honey
Sultana	Titanic
Sultans Of Swing	Dire Straits
Summer	War
Summer Breeze	Seals & Crofts
Summer Girls	LFO
Summer Holiday	Cliff Richard
Summer In The City	Lovin' Spoonful
Summer Love	Justin Timberlake
Summer Night City	Abba
Summer Nights	Marianne Faithfull
Summer Nights	John Travolta & Olivia Newton-John
Summer Of '69	Bryan Adams
Summer Of My Life	Simon May
Summer Rain	Johnny Rivers
Summer Set	Acker Bilk
A Summer Song	Chad & Jeremy
Summer Sun	Texas
Summer Sunshine	Corrs
Summer (The First Time)	Bobby Goldsboro
Summerlove Sensation	Bay City Rollers
Summertime	D.J. Jazzy Jeff & The Fresh Prince
Summertime	Billy Stewart
Summertime	Another Level
Summertime Blues	Blue Cheer
Summertime Blues	Eddie Cochran
Summertime City	Mike Batt
The Sun Ain't Gonna Shine Anymore	Walker Brothers
The Sun Always Shines On T.V.	A-Ha
The Sun And The Rain	Madness
Sun Arise	Rolf Harris
Sun Goes Down	David Jordan
The Sun Goes Down (Living It Up)	Level 42
Sun Is Shining	Bob Marley

Sunday Girl	Blondie
Sunday Morning Call	Oasis
Sunday Will Never Be The Same	Spanky & Our Gang
Sundown	Gordon Lightfoot
Sundown	S Club 8
Sunglasses At Night	Corey Hart
Sunlight	DJ Sammy
Sunny	Boney M
Sunny	Georgie Fame
Sunny	Bobby Hebb
Sunny Afternoon	Kinks
Sunny Came Home	Shawn Colvin
Sunrise	Simply Red
Sunshine	Jonathan Edwards
Sunshine	Gareth Gates
Sunshine	Lil' Flip featuring Lea
Sunshine	Twista featuring Anthony Hamilton
Sunshine After The Rain	Elkie Brooks
The Sunshine After The Rain	Berri
Sunshine Girl	Herman's Hermits
Sunshine Of Your Love	Cream
Sunshine Of Your Smile	Mike Berry
Sunshine On A Rainy Day	Zoe
Sunshine On My Shoulders	John Denver
Sunshine Superman	Donovan
Super Bad (Pts 1 & 2)	James Brown
Super Freak (Pt. 1)	Rick James
Super Trouper	Abba
Superfly	Curtis Mayfield
Superfly Guy	S'Express
Superfreak	Beatfreakz
Superman	Eminem
Superman (Gioca Jouer)	Black Lace
Superman (It's Not Easy)	Five For Fighting
Supermarioland	Ambassadors Of Funk/MC Mario
Supermassive Black Hole	Muse
Supernatural Thing Part 1	Ben E. King
Supernature	Cerrone
Supernova	Mr Hudson Featuring Kanye West
Superstar	Carpenters
Superstar	Lupe Fiasco Featuring Matthew Santos
Superstar	Murray Head
Superstar	Jamelia
Superstition	Stevie Wonder
Superwoman	Karyn White
Superwoman Pt. II	Lil' Mo Featuring Fabolous
Supreme	Robbie Williams
Sure	Take That
Sure Gonna Miss Her	Gary Lewis & The Playboys
Surf City	Jan & Dean
Surfer Girl	Beach Boys
Surfin' Bird	Trashmen
Surfin' Safari	Beach Boys
Surfin' U.S.A.	Beach Boys
Surrender	Elvis Presley
Surrender	Diana Ross
Surrender	Swing Out Sister
Surrender To Me	Ann Wilson & Robin Zander
Surrender Your Love	Nightcrawlers featuring John Reid
Surround Yourself With Sorrow	Cilla Black
Survivor	Destiny's Child
Susan	Buckinghams
Susie Darlin'	Robin Luke
Suspicion	Elvis Presley
Suspicion	Terry Stafford
Suspicious Minds	Fine Young Cannibals
Suspicious Minds	Gareth Gates
Suspicious Minds	Elvis Presley
Sussudio	Phil Collins
Suzanne Beware Of The Devil	Dandy Livingstone
Suzie Q. (Pt. 1)	Creedence Clearwater Revival
Sven Sven Sven	Bell & Spurling
Swagga Like Us	Jay-Z & T.I. Featuring Kanye West & Lil Wayne
Swamp Thing	Grid
Sway	Dean Martin
Sway	Bobby Rydell
Swayin' To The Music (Slow Dancin')	Johnny Rivers
Swear It Again	Westside
Swearin' To God	Frankie Valli
Sweat (A La La La La Long)	Inner Circle
Swedish Rhapsody	Mantovani
Swedish Rhapsody	Ray Martin
Sweet About Me	Gabriella Cilmi
Sweet And Gentle	Alan Dale
Sweet And Innocent	Donny Osmond
Sweet Blindness	Fifth Dimension
Sweet Caroline	Neil Diamond
Sweet Cherry Wine	Tommy James & The Shondells
Sweet Child O' Mine	Guns N' Roses
Sweet City Woman	Stampeders
Sweet Disposition	Temper Trap
Sweet Dream	Jethro Tull
Sweet Dreams	Air Supply
Sweet Dreams	Beyonce
Sweet Dreams	La Bouche
Sweet Dreams	Tommy McLain
Sweet Dreams (Are Made Of This)	Eurythmics
Sweet Dreams My L.A. Ex	Rachel Stevens
The Sweet Escape	Gwen Stefani Featuring Akon
Sweet Freedom	Michael McDonald
Sweet Harmony	Beloved
Sweet Hitch-Hiker	Creedence Clearwater Revival

Sweet Home Alabama	Lynyrd Skynyrd
Sweet Inspiration	Johnny Johnson & The Bandwagon
Sweet Lady	Tyrese
Sweet Like Chocolate	Shanks & Bigfoot
Sweet Little Mystery	Wet Wet Wet
Sweet Little Sixteen	Chuck Berry
Sweet Love	Anita Baker
Sweet Love	Commodores
Sweet Love 2K	Fierce
Sweet Lullaby	Deep Forest
Sweet Mary	Wadsworth Mansion
Sweet Nothin's	Brenda Lee
A Sweet Old Fashioned Girl	Teresa Brewer
Sweet Pea	Tommy Roe
Sweet Seasons	Carole King
Sweet Soul Music	Arthur Conley
Sweet Surrender	John Denver
Sweet Surrender	Wet Wet Wet
(Sweet Sweet Baby) Since You've Been Gone	Aretha Franklin
Sweet Talkin' Guy	Chiffons
Sweet Talkin' Woman	Electric Light Orchestra
Sweet Thing	Rufus featuring Chaka Khan
Sweeter Than You	Ricky Nelson
Sweetest Girl (Dollar Bill)	Wyclef Jean Featuring Akon, Lil Wayne & Niia
Sweetest Smile	Black
The Sweetest Taboo	Sade
Sweetest Thing	U2
The Sweetest Thing (I've Ever Known)	Juice Newton
Sweetheart	Franke & The Knockouts
Sweetness	Michelle Gayle
Sweets For My Sweet	CJ Lewis
Sweets For My Sweet	Searchers
Swing My Way	K.P. And Envyi
Swing The Mood	Jive Bunny & The Mastermixers
Swing Your Daddy	Jim Gilstrap
Swingin' School	Bobby Rydell
Swingin' Shepherd Blues	Ted Heath
Swinging On A Star	Big Dee Irwin
Swiss Maid	Del Shannon
Switch	Will Smith
Switch It On	Will Young
Swords Of A Thousand Men	Ten Pole Tudor
Sylvia	Focus
Sylvia's Mother	Dr. Hook
Sympathy For The Devil	Guns N' Roses
Synchronicity II	Police
Synth & Strings	Yomanda
System Addict	Five Star
T-Shirt	Shontelle
Taboo	Glamma Kid And Shola Ama
Tahiti (From Mutiny On The Bounty)	David Essex
Tainted Love	Marilyn Manson
Tainted Love	Soft Cell
Take A Bow	Madonna
Take A Bow	Rihanna
Take A Chance On Me	Abba
Take A Letter Maria	R.B. Greaves
(Take A Little) Piece Of My Heart	Erma Franklin
Take A Little Rhythm	Ali Thomson
Take A Look Around	Temptations
Take A Look Around	Limp Bizkit
Take A Message To Mary	Everly Brothers
Take A Picture	Filter
Take Back The City	Snow Patrol
Take Control	Amerie
Take Five	Dave Brubeck Quartet
Take Good Care Of Her	Adam Wade
Take Good Care Of My Baby	Bobby Vee
Take Good Care Of Yourself	Three Degrees
Take It Away	Paul McCartney
Take It Easy	Eagles
Take It Easy On Me	Little River Band
Take It On The Run	REO Speedwagon
Take It To The Limit	Eagles
Take Me Back	Tinchy Stryder Featuring Taio Cruz
Take Me Bak 'Ome	Slade
Take Me Home	Cher
Take Me Home	Phil Collins
Take Me Home (A Girl Like Me)	Sophie Ellis-Bextor
Take Me Home Tonight	Eddie Money
Take Me Home, Country Roads	John Denver
Take Me In Your Arms (Rock Me)	Doobie Brothers
Take Me Out	Franz Ferdinand
Take Me There	Blackstreet & Mya featuring Mase & Blinky Blink
Take Me To Heart	Quarterflash
Take Me To The Clouds	LMC vs U2
Take Me To The Mardi Gras	Paul Simon
Take Me To Your Heart	Rick Astley
Take Me With You	Prince & The Revolution
Take My Advice	Kym Sims
Take My Breath Away	Berlin
Take My Breath Away	Emma Bunton
Take On Me	A-Ha
Take On Me	A1
Take That	Torry Carter
Take That Look Off Your Face	Marti Webb
Take That Situation	Nick Heyward
Take The Long Way Home	Supertramp
Take The Money And Run	Steve Miller Band
Take These Chains From My Heart	Ray Charles

Take This Heart	Richard Marx
Take Time To Know Her	Percy Sledge
Take You There	Sean Kingston
Take Your Shoes Off	Cheeky Girls
Take Your Time	Mantronix featuring Wondress
Take Your Time (Do It Right) (Pt. 1)	S.O.S. Band
Takin' Back My Love	Enrique Iglesias Featuring Ciara
Takin' Care Of Business	Bachman-Turner Overdrive
Takin' It To The Streets	Doobie Brothers
Taking Everything	Gerald Levert
Talk About Our Love	Brandy featuring Kanye West
Talk Back Trembling Lips	Johnny Tillotson
Talk Dirty To Me	Poison
Talk Of The Town	Pretenders
Talk Talk	Music Machine
Talk To Me	Stevie Nicks
Talk To Me	Sunny & The Sunglows
Talking About My Baby	Impressions
Talking In Your Sleep	Crystal Gayle
Talking In Your Sleep	Romantics
Talking In Your Sleep/Love Me	Martine McCutcheon
Talking Loud And Clear	Orchestral Manoeuvres In The Dark
Tall Paul	Annette
Tallahassee Lassie	Freddy Cannon
Tallahassee Lassie	Tommy Steele
Tammy	Debbie Reynolds
Tap Turns On The Water	C.C.S.
Tarzan Boy	Baltimora
A Taste Of Aggro	Barron Knights
A Taste Of Honey	Herb Alpert
The Taste Of Your Tears	King
Tattoo	Jordin Sparks
Tea For Two Cha Cha	Tommy Dorsey Orchestra
Teach Me Tonight	De Castro Sisters
Teacher	Jethro Tull
A Tear Fell	Teresa Brewer
Teardrops	Shakin' Stevens
Teardrops	Womack & Womack
Teardrops On My Guitar	Taylor Swift
Tears	Ken Dodd
The Tears I Cried	Glitter Band
Tears In Heaven	Eric Clapton
Tears Of A Clown	Beat
The Tears Of A Clown	Smokey Robinson & The Miracles
Tears On My Pillow	Little Anthony & The Imperials
Tears On My Pillow	Kylie Minogue
Tears On My Pillow	Johnny Nash
Tease Me	Chaka Demus & Pliers
Teddy Bear	Elvis Presley
Teddy Bear	Red Sovine
Teen Angel	Mark Dinning
Teen Beat	Sandy Nelson
Teen-Age Crush	Tommy Sands
Teenage Dirtbag	Wheatus
Teenage Dream	Marc Bolan & T. Rex
Teenage Idol	Ricky Nelson
Teenage Lament '74	Alice Cooper
Teenage Life	Daz Sampson
Teenage Prayer	Gale Storm
Teenage Rampage	Sweet
A Teenager In Love	Dion & The Belmonts
A Teenager In Love	Craig Douglas
A Teenager In Love	Marty Wilde
Teenagers	My Chemical Romance
A Teenagers Romance	Ricky Nelson
Telefone (Long Distance Love Affair)	Sheena Easton
Telegram Sam	T. Rex
Telephone Line	Electric Light Orchestra
Telephone Man	Meri Wilson
Tell Her About It	Billy Joel
Tell Her No	Zombies
Tell Him	Billie Davis
Tell Him	Exciters
Tell Him	Hello
Tell Him No	Travis & Bob
Tell It Like It Is	Heart
Tell It Like It Is	Aaron Neville
Tell It To My Heart	Taylor Dayne
Tell It To My Heart	Kelly Llorenna
Tell It To The Rain	Four Seasons
Tell Laura I Love Her	Ray Peterson
Tell Laura I Love Her	Ricky Valance
Tell Me	Groove Theory
Tell Me	Melanie B
Tell Me	P. Diddy featuring Christina Aguilera
Tell Me It's Real	K-Ci & Jojo
Tell Me Something Good	Rufus
Tell Me What He Said	Helen Shapiro
Tell Me What You Want Me To Do	Tevin Campbell
Tell Me When	Applejacks
Tell Me When	Human League
Tell Me Why	Exposé
Tell Me Why	Elvis Presley
Tell Me Why	Bobby Vinton
Tell Me Why (The Riddle)	Paul Van Dyke Feat. Saint Etienne
Telstar	Tornados
Temma Harbour	Mary Hopkin
Temperature	Sean Paul
Temple Of Love (1992)	Sisters Of Mercy
Temptation	Corina
Temptation	Everly Brothers
Temptation	Heaven 17

Temptation Eyes	Grass Roots
Tender	Blur
Tender Love	Force M.D's
The Tender Trap	Frank Sinatra
Tenderly	Nat 'King' Cole
Tennessee	Arrested Development
Tennessee Wig Walk	Bonnie Lou
Tequila	Champs
Tequila	Terrorvision
Terry	Twinkle
Tetris	Doctor Spin
Thank Abba For The Music	Various Artists
Thank God I Found You	Mariah Carey Feat. Joe & 98 Degrees
Thank God I'm A Country Boy	John Denver
Thank U Very Much	Scaffold
Thank You	Dido
Thank You	Jamelia
Thank You (Falettinme Be Mice Elf Agin)	Sly & The Family Stone
Thank You For A Lifetime	Cliff Richard
Thanks For The Memory (Wham Bam Thank You Mam)	Slade
That Don't Impress Me Much	Shania Twain
That Girl	McFly
That Girl	Stevie Wonder
That Girl Belongs To Yesterday	Gene Pitney
That Lady	Isley Brothers
That Look In Your Eye	Ali Campbell
That Ole Devil Called Love	Alison Moyet
That Same Old Feeling	Pickettywitch
That Sounds Good To Me	Jive Bunny & The Mastermixers
That Sunday, That Summer	Nat 'King' Cole
That Was Yesterday	Foreigner
That'll Be The Day	Crickets
That'll Be The Day	Linda Ronstadt
That's All I Want From You	Jaye P. Morgan
That's All You Gotta Do	Brenda Lee
That's All!	Genesis
That's Amore	Dean Martin
That's How A Love Song Was Born	Ray Burns
That's How I Beat Shaq	Aaron Carter
That's Life	Frank Sinatra
That's Living (Alright)	Joe Fagin
That's My Goal	Shayne Ward
That's My Home	Acker Bilk
That's Not My Name	The Ting Tings
That's Old Fashioned (That's The Way Love Should Be)	Everly Brothers
That's Rock 'n' Roll	Shaun Cassidy
That's The Way	Honeycombs
That's The Way Boys Are	Lesley Gore
That's The Way God Planned It	Billy Preston
That's The Way I've Always Heard It Should Be	Carly Simon
That's The Way It Is	Mel & Kim
That's The Way Love Goes	Janet Jackson
That's The Way Love Is	Marvin Gaye
That's The Way Love Is	Ten City
That's The Way Of The World	Earth, Wind & Fire
That's The Way (I Like It)	KC & The Sunshine Band
That's What Friends Are For	Dionne Warwick & Friends
That's What Friends Are For	Deniece Williams
That's What I Like	Jive Bunny & The Mastermixers
That's What Love Is For	Amy Grant
That's What Love Will Do	Joe Brown & The Bruvvers
Them Girls Them Girls	Zig and Zag
Theme For A Dream	Cliff Richard
Theme For Young Lovers	Shadows
Theme From 'A Summer Place'	Percy Faith
Theme From 'Close Encounters Of The Third Kind'	John Williams
Theme From Dixie	Duane Eddy
Theme From Doctor Kildare (Three Stars Will Shine Tonight)	Richard Chamberlain
Theme From 'Greatest American Hero' (Believe It Or Not)	Joey Scarbury
Theme From Harry's Game	Clannad
The Theme From Hill Street Blues	Mike Post feat. Larry Carlton
Theme From Love Story	Henry Mancini & His Orchestra
Theme From M*A*S*H* (Suicide Is Painless)	Mash
Theme From Mahogany (Do You Know Where You're Going To)	Diana Ross
Theme From Mission: Impossible	Adam Clayton And Larry Mullen
Theme From 'New York, New York'	Frank Sinatra
Theme From S'Express	S'Express
Theme From S.W.A.T.	Rhythm Heritage
Theme From 'Shaft'	Isaac Hayes
Theme From The Appartment	Ferrante & Teicher
Theme From The Threepenny Opera	Louis Armstrong
Theme From 'The Legion's Last Patrol'	Ken Thorne & His Orchestra
A Theme From 'The Three Penny Opera' (Moritat)	Richard Hayman & Jan August
Theme From 'The Threepenny Opera'	Billy Vaughn
Theme From The Deer Hunter (Cavatina)	Shadows
(Theme From) Valley Of The Dolls	Dionne Warwick
Theme Song From 'Song For A Summer Night'	Mitch Miller
Themes From 'The Man With The Golden Arm'	Richard Maltby
Then Came You	Dionne Warwick
Then He Kissed Me	Crystals
Then I Kissed Her	Beach Boys
Then You Can Tell Me Goodbye	Casinos
There Are More Questions Than Answers	Johnny Nash
There But For Fortune	Joan Baez
There By The Grace Of God	Manic Street Preachers

There Goes My Baby	Drifters
There Goes My Everything	Engelbert Humperdinck
There Goes My Everything	Elvis Presley
There Goes My First Love	Drifters
There Goes The Fear	Doves
There I've Said It Again	Bobby Vinton
There Is A Mountain	Donovan
There It Go! (The Whistle Song)	Juelz Santana
There It Is	Shalamar
There Must Be A Reason	Frankie Laine
There Must Be A Way	Frankie Vaughan
There Must Be An Angel (Playing With My Heart)	Eurythmics
There There	Radiohead
There There My Dear	Dexy's Midnight Runners
There Won't Be Many Coming Home	Roy Orbison
There You Go	P!nk
There You'll Be	Faith Hill
There'll Be No Teardrops Tonight	Tony Bennett
There's A Gold Mine In The Sky	R. Dean Taylor
There's A Gold Mine In The Sky	Pat Boone
There's A Heartache Following Me	Jim Reeves
There's A Kind Of Hush	Herman's Hermits
There's A Kind Of Hush (All Over The World)	Carpenters
There's A Moon Out Tonight	Capris
There's A Whole Lot Of Loving	Guys & Dolls
(There's) Always Something There To Remind Me	Sandie Shaw
There's Always Something There To Remind Me	Naked Eyes
(There's) No Gettin' Over Me	Ronnie Milsap
There's No One Quite Like Grandma	St. Winifred's School Choir
There's No Other Way	Blur
There's The Girl	Heart
These Are the Times	Dru Hill
These Boots Are Made For Walkin'	Jessica Simpson
These Boots Are Made For Walkin'	Nancy Sinatra
These Days	Bon Jovi
These Dreams	Heart
These Eyes	Guess Who
These Words	Natasha Bedingfield
They	Jem
They Don't Know	Jon B
They Don't Know	So Solid Crew
They Don't Know	Tracey Ullman
They Just Can't Stop It (The Games People Play)	Spinners
(They Long To Be) Close To You	Carpenters
They Were Doin' The Mambo	Vaughn Monroe
They'll Be Sad Songs (To Make You Cry)	Billy Ocean
They're Coming To Take Me Away Ha-Haaa!	Napoleon XIV
Thieves In The Temple	Prince
The Thin Wall	Ultravox
A Thing Called Love	Johnny Cash
Things	Bobby Darin
Things Can Only Get Better	D:ream
Things Can Only Get Better	Howard Jones
Things I've Seen	Spooks
Things That Make You Go Hmmmm	C&C Music Factory featuring Freedom Williams
Things We Do For Love	10cc
Think	Aretha Franklin
Think I'm In Love	Eddie Money
Think It Over	Crickets
Think Of Laura	Christopher Cross
Think Of You	Whigfield
Think Twice	Brook Benton
Think Twice	Celine Dion
Thinkin' Bout It	Gerald Levert
Thinking About Your Love	Kenny Thomas
Thinking It Over	Liberty
Thinking Of You	Colour Field
Thinking Of You	Maureen
Thinking Of You	Sa-Fire
Thinking Of You	Sister Sledge
Third Rate Romance	Amazing Rhythm Aces
This Ain't A Love Song	Bon Jovi
This Beat Is Technotronic	Technotronic featuring MC Eric
This Corrosion	Sisters Of Mercy
This Could Be The Night	Loverboy
This D.J.	Warren G
This Diamond Ring	Gary Lewis & The Playboys
This Door Swings Both Ways	Herman's Hermits
This Flight Tonight	Nazareth
This Girl Is A Woman Now	Gary Puckett & The Union Gap
This Girl's In Love With You	Dionne Warwick
This Golden Ring	Fortunes
This Groove	Victoria Beckham
This Guy's In Love With You	Herb Alpert
This House	Tracie Spencer
This House Is Not A Home	Rembrandts
This Is A Call	Foo Fighters
This Is For The Lover In You	Babyface With LL Cool J, H. Hewett, J. Watley and J. Daniels
This Is How We Do It	Montell Jordan
This Is It	Adam Faith
This Is It	Kenny Loggins
This Is It	Dannii Minogue
This Is It	Melba Moore
This Is Me	Demi Lovato & Joe Jonas
This Is My Song	Petula Clark
This Is My Song	Harry Secombe
This Is Not A Love Song	Pil
This Is The Night	Clay Aiken
This Is Tomorrow	Bryan Ferry
This Is Why I'm Hot	Mims

This Kiss	Faith Hill
This Lil' Game We Play	Subway (featuring 702)
This Little Bird	Marianne Faithfull
This Little Girl	Gary U.S. Bonds
This Love	Maroon5
This Magic Moment	Jay & The Americans
This Masquerade	George Benson
This Old Heart Of Mine	Isley Brothers
This Old Heart Of Mine	Rod Stewart with Ronald Isley
This Old Heart Of Mine	Rod Stewart
This Old House	Billie Anthony
This Ole House	Rosemary Clooney
This Ole House	Shakin' Stevens
This One's For The Children	New Kids On The Block
This Time	Troy Shondell
This Time Around	Hanson
This Time I Know It's For Real	Donna Summer
This Time I'm In It For Love	Player
This Time (We'll Get It Right)	England World Cup Squad
This Town Ain't Big Enough For Both Of Us	British Whale
This Town Ain't Big Enough For Both Of Us	Sparks
This Used To Be My Playground	Madonna
This Wheel's On Fire	Julie Driscoll, Brian Auger & The Trinity
This Will Be	Natalie Cole
Thnks Fr Th Mmrs	Fall Out Boy
Thoia Thoing	R. Kelly
Thong Song	Sisqo
Thorn In My Side	Eurythmics
Those Lazy-Hazy-Crazy Days Of Summer	Nat 'King' Cole
Those Oldies But Goodies (Remind Me Of You)	Little Caesar & The Romans
Those Were The Days	Mary Hopkin
Thou Shalt Not Steal	Dick & Deedee
Thought I'd Died And Gone To Heaven	Bryan Adams
A Thousand Miles	Vanessa Carlton
A Thousand Stars	Kathy Young With The Innocents
3	Britney Spears
3 AM	Busted
3 A.M. Eternal	KLF
The Three Bells	Browns
3 X 3 E.P.	Genesis
Three Coins In The Fountain	Tony Brent
Three Coins In The Fountain	Four Aces
Three Coins In The Fountain	Frank Sinatra
3 Is Family	Dana Dawson
3 Lions	Baddiel, Skinner & The Lightning Seeds
Three Little Pigs	Green Jelly
Three Nights A Week	Fats Domino
Three Stars	Tommy Dee
Three Steps To Heaven	Eddie Cochran
Three Steps To Heaven	Showaddywaddy
Three Times A Lady	Commodores
3 Words	Cheryl Cole Feat Will.I.Am
The Thrill Is Gone	B.B. King
Thriller	Michael Jackson
Through The Barricades	Spandau Ballet
Through The Wire	Kanye West
Through The Years	Kenny Rogers
Throw Down A Line	Cliff Richard
Throw It In The Bag	Fabolous Featuring The-Dream
Throw Some D's	Rich Boy Featuring Polow Da Don
Throwing It All Away	Genesis
Thugz Mansion	2Pac
Thunder	East 17
Thunder In Mountains	Toyah
Thunder In My Heart	Meck featuring Leo Sayer
Thunder Island	Jay Ferguson
Thunderbirds	Busted
Thunderbirds Are Go	Fab featuring MC Parker
Ticket Outta Loserville	Son Of Dork
Ticket To Ride	Beatles
The Tide Is High	Blondie
The Tide Is High (Get The Feeling)	Atomic Kitten
Tie A Yellow Ribbon Round The Ole Oak Tree	Dawn
Tie Me Kangaroo Down, Sport	Rolf Harris
Tiger	Fabian
Tiger Feet	Mud
Tight Rope	Leon Russell
Tighten Up	Archie Bell & The Drells
Tighter, Tighter	Alive & Kicking
Tijuana Jail	Kingston Trio
Tik Tok	Ke$ha
('Til) I Kissed You	Everly Brothers
Till	Tom Jones
Till I Hear It From You/Follow You Down	Gin Blossoms
Till The End Of The Day	Kinks
Till Then	Hilltoppers
Till We Two Are One	Georgie Shaw
Tilt Ya Head Back	Nelly & Christina Aguilera
Time	Craig Douglas
Time	Hootie & The Blowfish
Time	Alan Parsons Project
Time	Supergrass
Time After Time	Inoj
Time After Time	Cyndi Lauper
Time (Clock Of The Heart)	Culture Club
Time Drags By	Cliff Richard
The Time Has Come	Adam Faith
Time Has Come Today	Chambers Brothers
Time In A Bottle	Jim Croce
The Time Is Now	Moloko

Time Is On My Side	Rolling Stones
Time Is Running Out	Muse
Time Is Tight	Booker T. & The M.G.'s
Time Is Time	Andy Gibb
Time, Love And Tenderness	Michael Bolton
The Time Of My Life	David Cook
Time Of The Season	Zombies
Time Passages	Al Stewart
Time To Burn	Storm
Time To Grow	Lemar
Time To Make You Mine	Lisa Stansfield
The Time Warp (SAW Remix)	Damian
Time Won't Let Me	Outsiders
Times Of Your Life	Paul Anka
Times They Are A-Changin'	Bob Dylan
Tin Man	America
Tin Soldier	Small Faces
Tina Marie	Perry Como
Tiny Dancer (Hold Me Closer)	Ironik feat. Chipmunk & Elton John
Tipsy	J-Kwon
Tired Of Being Alone	Al Green
Tired Of Toein' The Line	Rocky Burnette
Tired Of Waiting For You	Kinks
To All The Girls I've Loved Before	Julio Iglesias & Willie Nelson
To Be A Lover	Billy Idol
To Be Loved	Malcolm Vaughan
To Be Or Not To Be	B.A. Robertson
To Be With You	Mr. Big
To Be With You Again	Level 42
To Cut A Long Story Short	Spandau Ballet
To Know Him, Is To Love Him	Teddy Bears
To Know You Is To Love You	Peter & Gordon
To Love Somebody	Michael Bolton
To Love Somebody	Nina Simone
To Love Somebody	Jimmy Somerville
To Sir With Love	Lulu
To Whom It Concerns	Chris Andrews
To You I Belong	B*Witched
Tobacco Road	Nashville Teens
Toca's Miracle	Fragma
Toccata	Sky
Today	Talk Talk
Together	Connie Francis
Together	P.J. Proby
Together	Tierra
Together Again	Janet
Together Forever	Rick Astley
Together In Electric Dreams	Giorgio Moroder & Phil Oakey
Together We Are Beautiful	Fern Kinney
Tokoloshe Man	John Kongos
Tokyo Melody	Helmut Zacharias Orchestra
Tom Dooley	Lonnie Donegan
Tom Dooley	Kingston Trio
Tom Hark	Elias & His Zigzag Jive Flutes
Tom Hark	Piranhas
Tom-Tom Turnaround	New World
Tom Traubert's Blues (Waltzing Matilda)	Rod Stewart
Tom's Diner	DNA featuring Suzanne Vega
Tomboy	Perry Como
Tomorrow	Johnny Brandon
Tomorrow	Sandie Shaw
Tomorrow Night	Atomic Rooster
Tomorrow's (Just Another Day)	Madness
Tonight	Ferrante & Teicher
Tonight	Jonas Brothers
Tonight	Kool & The Gang
Tonight	Move
Tonight	New Kids On The Block
Tonight	Rubettes
Tonight	Westlife
Tonight I Celebrate My Love	Peabo Bryson & Roberta Flack
Tonight I Celebrate My Love	Roberta Flack
Tonight I'm Yours (Don't Hurt Me)	Rod Stewart
Tonight She Comes	Cars
Tonight Tonight Tonight	Genesis
Tonight You Belong To Me	Patience & Prudence
Tonight's The Night (Gonna Be Alright)	Rod Stewart
Tonite's Tha Night	Kris Kross
Too Blind To See It	Kym Sims
Too Busy Thinking About My Baby	Marvin Gaye
Too Close	Blue
Too Funky	George Michael
Too Good To Be Forgotten	Amazulu
Too Good To Be Forgotten	Chi-Lites
Too Hot	Coolio
Too Hot	Kool & The Gang
Too Hot To Handle	Heatwave
Too Late For Goodbyes	Julian Lennon
Too Late To Say Goodbye	Richard Marx
Too Late To Turn Back Now	Cornelius Brothers & Sister Rose
2 Legit 2 Quit	Hammer
Too Little Too Late	JoJo
Too Lost In You	Sugababes
Too Many Broken Hearts	Jason Donovan
Too Many Rivers	Brenda Lee
Too Many Walls	Cathy Dennis
Too Much	Bros
Too Much	Elvis Presley
Too Much	Spice Girls
Too Much Heaven	Bee Gees
Too Much Love Will Kill Me	Brian May
Too Much Time On My Hands	Styx

Title	Artist
Too Much, Too Little, Too Late	Johnny Mathis & Deniece Williams
Too Much Too Young (E.P.) (Special Aka Live!)	Specials
Too Nice To Talk To	Beat
Too Shy	Kajagoogoo
Too Soon To Know	Roy Orbison
Too Young	Donny Osmond
Too Young To Die	Jamiroquai
Too Young To Go Steady	Nat 'King' Cole
Tootsie Roll	69 Boyz
Top Of The World	Brandy
Top Of The World	Carpenters
Topsy II	Cozy Cole
Torch	Soft Cell
Torn Between Two Lovers	Mary MacGregor
Torn On The Platform	Jack Penate
Tossin' And Turnin'	Bobby Lewis
Tossing And Turning	Ivy League
Total Eclipse Of The Heart	Nicki French
Total Eclipse Of The Heart	Bonnie Tyler
To The Moon And Back	Savage Garden
The Total Mix	Black Box
Touch It	Busta Rhymes
Touch It	Monifah
Touch Me	Doors
Touch Me	49ers
Touch Me	Rui Da Silva
Touch Me (All Night Long)	Cathy Dennis
Touch Me (I Want Your Body)	Samantha Fox
Touch Me In The Morning	Diana Ross
Touch Me Tease Me	La Bouche
Touch Me Touch Me	Dave Dee, Dozy, Beaky, Mick & Tich
Touch Me When We're Dancing	Carpenters
Touch My Body	Mariah Carey
Touch Of Grey	Grateful Dead
A Touch Too Much	Arrows
Touch The Sky	Kanye West featuring Lupe Fiasco
Touchy!	A-Ha
Tougher Than The Rest	Bruce Springsteen
Tower Of Strength	Mission
Tower Of Strength	Frankie Vaughan
Tower Of Strength	Gene McDaniels
Town Called Malice	Jam
Town Without Pity	Gene Pitney
Toy Balloons	Russ Conway
Toxic	Britney Spears
Toy Boy	Sinitta
Toy Soldiers	Martika
Traces	Classics IV
The Tracks Of My Tears	Smokey Robinson & The Miracles
The Tracks Of My Tears	Johnny Rivers
Tracy	Cuff Links
Tragedy	Bee Gees
Tragedy	Fleetwoods
Tragedy	Thomas Wayne
The Trail Of The Lonesome Pine	Laurel & Hardy
Train Of Thought	A-Ha
Trains And Boats And Planes	Burt Bacharach
Trains And Boats And Planes	Billy J. Kramer & The Dakotas
Tramp	Salt 'n' Pepa
Transfusion	Nervous Norvus
Transylvania	McFly
Trapped	Colonel Abrams
Trapped By A Thing Called Love	Denise La Salle
Travelin' Band	Creedence Clearwater Revival
Travelin' Man	Ricky Nelson
Travellin' Light	Cliff Richard
Treat Her Like A Lady	Cornelius Brothers & Sister Rose
Treat Her Right	Roy Head
Tribal Dance	2 Unlimited
Tribute (Right On)	Pasadenas
Trick Me	Kelis
Tricky Disco	Tricky Disco
A Trip To Trumpton	Urban Base
Trippin'	Total/Missy Elliott
Tripping	Robbie Williams
Troglodyte (Cave Man)	Jimmy Castor Bunch
The Trooper	Iron Maiden
Trouble	Lindsey Buckingham
Trouble	P!nk
Trouble	Shampoo
Trouble Man	Marvin Gaye
Truck On (Tyke)	T. Rex
Trudie	Joe 'Mr. Piano' Henderson
True	Jaimeson featuring Angel Blu
True	Spandau Ballet
True Blue	Madonna
True Colors	Cyndi Lauper
True Faith	New Order
True Love	Bing Crosby
True Love	Glenn Frey
True Love	Elton John & Kiki Dee
True Love	Jane Powell
True Love Never Dies	Flip & Fill featuring Kelly Llorenna
True Love Ways	Peter & Gordon
True Love Ways	Cliff Richard
Truly	Lionel Richie
Truly Madly Deeply	Cascada
Truly Madly Deeply	Savage Garden
Try Again	Aaliyah
Try It Baby	Marvin Gaye
Try Me Out	Corona
Try To Remember	Gladys Knight & The Pips

Title	Artist
Tryin' To Get The Feeling Again	Barry Manilow
Tryin' To Live My Life Without You	Bob Seger & The Silver Bullet Band
Tryin' To Love Two	William Bell
Trying To Hold On To My Woman	Lamont Dozier
TSOP (The Sound Of Philadelphia)	MFSB featuring The Three Degrees
Tu M'Aimes Encore (To Love Me Again)	Celine Dion
Tubthumping	Chumbawamba
Tubular Bells	Mike Oldfield
Tuff Enuff	Fabulous Thunderbirds
Tulane	Steve Gibbons Band
Tulips From Amsterdam	Max Bygraves
Tumbling Dice	Rolling Stones
Tunnel Of Love	Bruce Springsteen
The Tunnel Of Love	Fun Boy Three
Turn	Travis
Turn Around	Phats & Small
Turn Around Look At Me	Vogues
Turn Back The Hands Of Time	Tyrone Davis
Turn Back Time	Aqua
Turn It On Again	Genesis
Turn It Up/Fire it Up	Busta Rhymes
Turn It Up	Conway Brothers
Turn Me Loose	Fabian
Turn Me On	Kevin Lyttle
Turn Off The Light	Nelly Furtado
Turn On, Tune In, Cop Out	Freak Power
Turn The Beat Around	Gloria Estefan
Turn The Beat Around	Vicki Sue Robinson
Turn The Music Up	Players Association
Turn To Stone	Electric Light Orchestra
Turn Up The Bass	Tyree featuring Kool Rock Steady
Turn Your Love Around	George Benson
Turn! Turn! Turn!	Byrds
Turnin' Me On	Keri Hilson Featuring Lil Wayne
Turning Japanese	Vapors
Turtle Power	Partners In Kryme
Tusk	Fleetwood Mac
Tweedle Dee	Georgia Gibbs
Tweedle Dee	Little Jimmy Osmond
Tweedle Dee Tweedle Dum	Middle Of The Road
The Twelfth Of Never	Johnny Mathis
The Twelfth Of Never	Donny Osmond
The Twelfth Of Never	Cliff Richard
12:51	The Strokes
20th Century Boy	T. Rex
25 Or 6 To 4	Chicago
Twenty Five Miles	Edwin Starr
21st Century Christmas	Cliff Richard
24/7	Kevon Edmonds
Twenty Four Hours From Tulsa	Gene Pitney
21 Questions	50 Cent Featuring Nate Dogg
21 Seconds	So Solid Crew
26 Miles	Four Preps
Twenty Tiny Fingers	Stargazers
Twentyfourseven	Artful Dodger featuring Melanie Blatt
Twilight Time	Platters
Twilight Zone	Golden Earring
Twilight Zone	2 Unlimited
Twine Time	Alvin Cash & The Crawlers
The Twist	Chubby Checker
Twist & Shout	Deacon Blue
Twist And Shout	Pliers/Jack Radics/Taxi Gang
Twist And Shout	Brian Poole & The Tremeloes
Twist And Shout	Salt 'n' Pepa
Twist Of Fate	Olivia Newton-John
Twist, Twist Senora	Gary U.S. Bonds
The Twist (Yo, Twist)	Fat Boys
Twisted	Keith Sweat
Twistin' The Night Away	Sam Cooke
2 Become 1	Spice Girls
Two Can Play The Game	Bobby Brown
Two Different Worlds	Ronnie Hilton
2 Faced	Louise
Two Faces Have I	Lou Christie
2-4-6-8 Motorway	Tom Robinson Band
2 Hearts	Kylie Minogue
Two Hearts	Pat Boone
Two Hearts	Phil Collins
Two In A Million/You're My No. 1	S Club 7
Two Kinds Of Teardrops	Del Shannon
Two Little Boys	Rolf Harris
Two Lovers	Mary Wells
Two More Years	Bloc Party
Two Occasions	Deele
Two Of Hearts	Stacey Q
Two Out Of Three Ain't Bad	Meat Loaf
Two Pints Of Lager And A Packet Of Crisps Please	Splodgenessabounds
Two Princes	Spin Doctors
Two Steps Behind	Def Leppard
2 Times	Ann Lee
Two To Make It Right	Seduction
Two Tribes	Frankie Goes To Hollywood
Typical Male	Tina Turner
U & Me	Cappella
U & Ur Hand	P!nk
U And Dat	E-40 featuring T-Pain & Kandi Girl
U And Hand	P!nk
U Can't Touch This	Crazy Frog
U Can't Touch This	M.C. Hammer
U Don't Have To Call	Usher

Title	Artist
U Don't Love Me	Kumbia Kings
U Got It Bad	Usher
U Got The Look	Prince
U Got 2 Know	Cappella
U Got 2 Let The Music	Cappella
U Know What's Up	Donell Jones
U Make Me Wanna	Blue
U R The Best Thing	Dream
U Remind Me	Usher
U Sure Do	Strike
Ugly	Bubba Sparxxx
Ugly	Sugababes
The Ugly Duckling	Mike Reid
Uh! Oh! Part 2	Nutty Squirrels
Uhh Ahh	Boyz II Men
Um, Um, Um, Um, Um, Um	Major Lance
Um Um Um Um Um Um	Wayne Fontana & The Mindbenders
Umbrella	Rihanna Featuring Jay-Z
Un Banc, Un Arbre, Une Rue	Severine
Una Paloma Blanca	Jonathan King
Unbelievable	EMF
Un-Break My Heart	Toni Braxton
Unbreakable	Westlife
Unchain My Heart	Ray Charles
Unchained Melody	Les Baxter
Unchained Melody	Gareth Gates
Unchained Melody	Roy Hamilton
Unchained Melody	Al Hibbler
Unchained Melody	Righteous Brothers
Unchained Melody	Jimmy Young
Unchained Melody/ White Cliffs Of Dover	Robson Green & Jerome Flynn
Uncle Albert/Admiral Halsey	Paul & Linda McCartney
Uncle John From Jamaica	Vengaboys
Unconditional Love	Donna Summer
Under Pressure	Queen & David Bowie
Under The Boardwalk	Drifters
Under The Boardwalk	Bruce Willis
Under The Bridge/Lady Marmalde	All Saints
Under The Bridge	Red Hot Chilli Peppers
Under The Bridges Of Paris	Eartha Kitt
Under The Bridges Of Paris	Dean Martin
Under The Moon Of Love	Showaddywaddy
Under Your Thumb	Godley & Creme
Undercover Angel	Alan O'Day
Undercover Of The Night	Rolling Stones
Underneath It All	No Doubt Featuring Lady Saw
Underneath Your Clothes	Shakira
Understanding	Xscape
Uneasy Rider	Charlie Daniels Band
Unfaithful	Rihanna
Unforgettable	Natalie Cole
The Unforgettable Fire	U2
The Unicorn	Irish Rovers
Uninvited	Freemasons Featuring Bailey Tzuke
Union City Blue	Blondie
Union Of The Snake	Duran Duran
United States Of Whatever	Liam Lynch
United We Stand	Brotherhood Of Man
The Universal	Blur
Unpredictable	Jamie Foxx featuring Ludacris
Unpretty	TLC
Unskinny Bop	Poison
Until It Sleeps	Metallica
Until It's Time For You To Go	Elvis Presley
Until The End Of Time	2Pac
Until The Time Is Through	Five
Until You Come Back To Me (That's What I'm Gonna Do)	Aretha Franklin
Untouched	The Veronicas
Unwell	Matchbox 20
Unwritten	Natasha Bedingfield
Up	The Saturdays
Up All Night	Matt Willis
Up And Down	Vengaboys
Up Around The Bend	Creedence Clearwater Revival
Up Jumps Da Boogie	Magoo And Timbaland
Up Middle Finger	Oxide & Neutrino
Up On The Roof	Drifters
Up On The Roof	Robson Green & Jerome Flynn
Up On The Roof	Kenny Lynch
Up The Junction	Squeeze
Up The Ladder To The Roof	Supremes
Up The Pool	Jethro Tull
Up Up & Away	Fifth Dimension
Up Up And Away	Johnny Mann Singers
Up Where We Belong	Joe Cocker & Jennifer Warnes
Uprising	Muse
Upside Down	Diana Ross
Uptight (Everything's Alright)	Stevie Wonder
Uptown	Crystals
Uptown Girl	Billy Joel
Uptown Girl	Westlife
Uptown Top Ranking	Althia And Donna
Urgent	Foreigner
Us Against The World	Westlife
Use It Up And Wear It Out	Odyssey
Use Me	Bill Withers
Use Somebody	Kings Of Leon
Use Ta Be My Girl	O'Jays
Vacation	Connie Francis
Vacation	Go-Go's

Title	Artist
Valentine	T'Pau
Valerie	Mark Ronson Featuring Amy Winehouse
Valerie	Steve Winwood
Valerie	The Zutons
Valleri	Monkees
Valley Of Tears	Fats Domino
The Valley Road	Bruce Hornsby & The Range
Valotte	Julian Lennon
Vaya Con Dios	Les Paul & Mary Ford
Vehicle	Ides Of March
Veni Vidi Vici	Ronnie Hilton
Ventura Highway	America
Venus	Frankie Avalon
Venus	Bananarama
Venus	Don Pablo's Animals
Venus	Shocking Blue
Venus And Mars Rock Show	Paul McCartney
Venus In Blue Jeans	Jimmy Clanton
Venus In Blue Jeans	Mark Wynter
Vertigo	U2
A Very Special Love Song	Charlie Rich
Vibeology	Paula Abdul
Victim Of Love	Erasure
Victims	Culture Club
Victory	Kool & The Gang
Video Killed The Radio Star	Buggles
Vienna	Ultravox
Vienna Calling	Falco
A View To A Kill	Duran Duran
The Village Of St. Bernadette	Andy Williams
Vincent	Don McLean
Vindaloo	Fat Les
Violet Hill	Coldplay
Virginia Plain	Roxy Music
Vision Of Love	Mariah Carey
Visions	Cliff Richard
Viva Bobbie Joe	Equals
Viva Forever	Spice Girls
Viva La Radio	Lolly
Viva La Vida	Coldplay
Viva Las Vegas	Elvis Presley
Viva Las Vegas	ZZ Top
Vogue	Madonna
Voice In The Wilderness	Cliff Richard
Voices Carry	Til Tuesday
Voices That Care	Voices That Care
Volare	Marino Marini
Volare	Dean Martin
Volare	Bobby Rydell
Voodoo Child	Rogue Traders
Voodoo Chile	Jimi Hendrix Experience
Voodoo Ray (E.P.)	A Guy Called Gerald
Voulez Vous	Abba
Voyage Voyage	Desireless
The Wah-Watusi	Orlons
Wait	Robert Howard & Kym Mazelle
Wait	White Lion
Wait (The Whisper Song)	Ying Yang Twins
Wait For Me	Malcolm Vaughan
Wait For You	Elliott Yamin
Waitin' In School	Ricky Nelson
Waiting For A Girl Like You	Foreigner
Waiting For A Star To Fall	Boy Meets Girl
Waiting For A Train	Flash And The Pan
Waiting For An Alibi	Thin Lizzy
Waiting For Love	Alias
Waiting On A Friend	Rolling Stones
Waiting For Tonight	Jennifer Lopez
Wake Me Up	Girls Aloud
Wake Me Up Before You Go-Go	Wham!
Wake Me Up When September Ends	Green Day
Wake The Town And Tell The People	Les Baxter
Wake Up	Hilary Duff
Wake Up Boo!	Boo Radleys
Wake Up Everybody (Pt. 1)	Harold Melvin & The Blue Notes
Wake Up Little Susie	Everly Brothers
Waking Up In Vegas	Katy Perry
The Walk	Jimmy McCracklin
Walk A Mile In My Shoes	Joe South
Walk Away	Kelly Clarkson
Walk Away	Matt Monro
Walk Away From Love	David Ruffin
Walk Away Renee	Four Tops
Walk Away Renee	Left Banke
Walk Don't Run	John Barry Seven
Walk Hand In Hand	Ronnie Carroll
Walk Hand In Hand	Tony Martin
Walk In Love	Manhattan Transfer
A Walk In The Black Forest	Horst Jankowski
Walk It Out	Unk
Walk Like A Man	Four Seasons
Walk Like An Egyptian	Bangles
Walk Of Life	Dire Straits
Walk On	U2
Walk On By	Sybil
Walk On By	Leroy Van Dyke
Walk On By	Dionne Warwick
Walk On The Wild Side	Lou Reed
Walk On Water	Eddie Money
Walk Right Back	Everly Brothers
Walk Right In	Rooftop Singers
Walk Right Now	Jacksons
Walk Tall	Val Doonican
Walk The Dinosaur	Was (Not Was)
Walk This Way	Aerosmith
Walk This Way	Run D.M.C.
Walk This Way	Sugababes Vs Girls Aloud
Walk With Me	Seekers
Walk-Don't Run	Ventures
Walk-Don't Run '64	Ventures
Walked Outta Heaven	Jagged Edge
Walkin'	C.C.S.
Walkin' Back To Happiness	Helen Shapiro
Walkin' In The Rain With The One I Love	Love Unlimited
Walkin' In The Sunshine	Bad Manners
A Walkin' Miracle	Essex
A Walkin' Miracle	Limmie & The Family Cookin'
Walkin' To New Orleans	Fats Domino
Walking Away	Information Society
Walking Away	Craig David
Walking Down Your Street	Bangles
Walking In Memphis	Cher
Walking In Memphis	Marc Cohn
Walking In Rhythm	Blackbyrds
Walking In The Air	Aled Jones
Walking In The Rain	Modern Romance
Walking In The Rain	Partridge Family
Walking On Broken Glass	Annie Lennox
Walking On Sunshine	Katrina & The Waves
Walking On Sunshine	Rocker's Revenge
Walking On The Moon	Police
Walking The Dog	Rufus Thomas
Wall Street Shuffle	10cc
Walls Come Tumbling Down!	Style Council
Wand'rin' Star	Lee Marvin
The Wanderer	Dion
The Wanderer	Status Quo
The Wanderer	Donna Summer
Wanderin' Eyes	Charlie Gracie
Wanderin' Eyes	Frankie Vaughan
Wanksta	50 Cent
Wanna Be Startin' Something	Michael Jackson
Wannabe	Spice Girls
Want Ads	Honey Cone
Wanted	Perry Como
Wanted	Dooleys
Wanted	Al Martino
Wanted Dead Or Alive	Bon Jovi
Wap Bam Boogie	Matt Bianco
War	Bruce Springsteen
War	Edwin Starr
War Baby	Tom Robinson
War Of Nerves	All Saints
The War Song	Culture Club
Warm It Up	Kris Kross
Warning	Notorious B.I.G.
Warpaint	Brook Brothers
The Warrior	Scandal featuring Patty Smyth
Warrior's Dance	The Prodigy
Warwick Avenue	Duffy
Washington Square	Village Stompers
Wassuup	Da Mutz
Wasted Days And Wasted Nights	Freddy Fender
Wasted On The Way	Crosby, Stills & Nash
Wasting My Time	Default
Wat Da Hook Gon Be	Murphy Lee featuring Jermaine Dupri
Watchin' The Detectives	Elvis Costello
Watching Scotty Grow	Bobby Goldsboro
Watching The Wheels	John Lennon
Watching You Watching Me	David Grant
Water On Glass	Kim Wilde
Water Runs Dry	Boyz II Men
Water Water	Tommy Steele
Waterfalls	Paul McCartney
Waterfalls	TLC
Waterloo	Abba
Waterloo	Stonewall Jackson
Waterloo Sunset	Kinks
Watermelon Man	Mongo Santamaria
The Way (Put Your Hand In My Hand)	Divine Inspiration
Way Down	Elvis Presley
Way Down Yonder In New Orleans	Freddy Cannon
The Way I Am	Eminem
The Way I Feel About You	Karyn White
The Way I Want To Touch You	Captain & Tennille
The Way I Are	Timbaland Featuring Keri Hilson
Way In My Brain	SL2
The Way It Is	Bruce Hornsby & The Range
The Way It Used To Be	Engelbert Humperdinck
Way Of Life	Family Dogg
The Way Of Love	Cher
The Way To Your Love	Hear'say
The Way We Were	Barbra Streisand
The Way We Were/Try To Remember (Medley)	Gladys Knight & The Pips
The Way You Do The Things You Do	Temptations
The Way You Do The Things You Do	UB40
The Way You Look Tonight	Lettermen
The Way You Love Me	Karyn White
The Way You Love Me	Faith Hill
The Way You Make Me Feel	Michael Jackson
The Way You Make Me Feel	Ronan Keating
The Way You Move	OutKast featuring Sleepy Brown
Wayward Wind	Frank Ifield
Wayward Wind	Tex Ritter
The Wayward Wind	Gogi Grant
(We Ain't Got) Nothin' Yet	Blues Magoos
We All Sleep Alone	Cher
We All Stand Together	Paul McCartney
We Are	Ana Johnsson
We Are Detective	Thompson Twins
We Are Family	Sister Sledge
We Are Glass	Gary Numan
We Are Golden	Mika
We Are In Love	Adam Faith
We Are The Champions	Queen
We Are The People	Empire Of The Sun
We Are The World	USA For Africa
We Be Burnin'	Sean Paul
We Belong	Pat Benatar
We Belong Together	Mariah Carey
We Built This City	Starship
We Call It Acieed	D. Mob featuring Gary Haisman
We Can Work It Out	Beatles
We Can't Be Friends	Deborah Cox With RL
We Can't Go Wrong	Cover Girls
We Close Our Eyes	Go West
We Come 1	Faithless
We Didn't Start The Fire	Billy Joel
We Do It	R & J Stone
We Don't Have To Take Our Clothes Off...	Jermaine Stewart
We Don't Need Another Hero (Thunderdome)	Tina Turner
We Don't Talk Anymore	Cliff Richard
We Fly High	Jim Jones
We Got A Love Thang	Ce Ce Peniston
We Got Love	Bobby Rydell
We Got The Beat	Go-Go's
We Gotta Get Out Of This Place	Animals
We Have A Dream	Scotland World Cup Squad
We Have All The Time In The World	Louis Armstrong
We Just Be Dreamin'	Blazin' Squad
We Just Disagree	Dave Mason
We Like To Party! (The Vengabus)	The Vengaboys
We Love You	Rolling Stones
We Made It	Busta Rhymes Featuring Linkin Park
We Made You	Eminem
We Should Be Together	Cliff Richard
We Take Mystery (To Bed)	Gary Numan
We Thuggin'	Fat Joe Featuring R. Kelly
(We Want) The Same Thing	Belinda Carlisle
We Will Make Love	Russ Hamilton
We Will Rock You	5ive & Queen
We'll Be Together	Sting
We'll Bring The House Down	England Dan & John Ford Coley
We'll Sing In The Sunshine	Gale Garnett
We're A Winner	Impressions
We're All Alone	Rita Coolidge
We're An American Band	Grand Funk
We're Going To Ibiza!	Vengaboys
We're Gonna Do It Again	Manchester United 1995 Football Squad Feat Stryker
We're In This Love Together	Al Jarreau
We're Not Alone	Frankie Vaughan
We're Not Making Love Anymore	Dru Hill
We're Ready	Boston
We're Through	Hollies
We've Got Tonight	Kenny Rogers & Sheena Easton
We've Got Tonite	Bob Seger & The Silver Bullet Band
We're On The Ball	Ant And Dec
We've Got Tonight	Ronan Keating featuring Lulu
We've Only Just Begun	Carpenters
Weak	SWV
Weak In The Presence Of Beauty	Alison Moyet
Wear My Ring	Gene Vincent & His Blue Caps
Wear My Ring Around Your Neck	Elvis Presley
Wearing My Rolex	Wiley
Weather With You	Crowded House
The Wedding	Julie Rogers
Wedding Bell Blues	Fifth Dimension
Wedding Bells	Eddie Fisher
Wedding Bells	Godley & Creme
Wee Rule	Wee Papa Girl Rappers
Weekend	Eddie Cochran
The Weekend	Michael Gray
Weekend!	Scooter
Weekend In New England	Barry Manilow
Weightless	Wet Wet Wet
Welcome Back	John Sebastian
	Peters & Lee
Welcome To My World	Jim Reeves
Welcome To The Black Parade	My Chemical Romance
Welcome To The Jungle	Guns N' Roses
Welcome To The Pleasure Dome	Frankie Goes To Hollywood
Welcome To Tomorrow	Snap! featuring Summer
Welcome To The Cheap Seats (EP)	Wonder Stuff
Well I Ask You	Eden Kane
A Well Respected Man	Kinks
West End Girls	Pet Shop Boys
West Of Zanzibar	Anthony Steel & The Radio Revellers
West Side Story	LFO
Western Movies	Olympics
Western Union	Five Americans
Westside	TQ
Wet Dream	Max Romeo
Wham Rap	Wham!
What	Soft Cell
What A Diff'rence A Day Makes	Esther Phillips

Title	Artist
Who's Zoomin' Who	Aretha Franklin
Whodunit	Tavares
Whole Again	Atomic Kitten
Whole Lot Of Shakin' Going On	Jerry Lee Lewis
Whole Lotta History	Girls Aloud
Whole Lotta Love	Goldbug
Whole Lotta Love	Led Zeppelin
Whole Lotta Loving	Fats Domino
Whole Lotta Woman	Marvin Rainwater
A Whole New World	
(Aladdin's Theme)	Peabo Bryson & Regina Belle
The Whole Of The Moon	Waterboys
Whole Wide World	A'me Lorain
Whoomp! (There It Is)	Tag Team
Whoomph! (There It Is)	Clock
Whoops Now/What'll I Do	Janet Jackson
Whoot, There It Is	95 South
Why	Frankie Avalon
Why?	Bronski Beat
Why	DJ Sammy
Why?	Jadakiss featuring Anthony Hamilton
Why	Annie Lennox
Why	Mis-Teeq
Why	Anthony Newley
Why	Donny Osmond
Why	Carly Simon
Why Baby Why	Pat Boone
Why Can't I Wake Up With You?	Take That
Why Can't This Be Love	Van Halen
Why Can't We Be Friends?	War
Why Can't We Live Together	Timmy Thomas
Why Do Fools Fall In Love	Frankie Lymon & The Teenagers
Why Do Fools Fall In Love	Diana Ross
Why Do Fools Fall In Love	Gale Storm
Why Do You Love Me	Garbage
Why Does It Always Rain On Me?	Travis
Why Don't You And I	Santana featuring Alex Band
	or Chad Kroeger
Why Don't You Get A Job	Offspring
Why I Love You So Much/Ain't Nobody	Monica
Why Me	Kris Kristofferson
Why Me?	Irene Cara
Why Oh Why Oh Why	Gilbert O'Sullivan
Why Won't You Give Me Your Love?	The Zutons
Why You Treat Me So Bad	Shaggy featuring Grand Puba
Wichita Lineman	Glen Campbell
Wicked Game	Chris Isaak
The Wicker Man	Iron Maiden
Wide Boy	Nik Kershaw
Wide Eyed And Legless	Andy Fairweather-Low
Wifey	Next
Wig Wam Bam	Sweet
Wiggle It	2 In A Room
The Wild Boys	Duran Duran
Wild Horses	Susan Boyle
Wild In The Country	Elvis Presley
Wild Night	John Mellencamp & Me'shell Ndegeocello
Wild One	Bobby Rydell
The Wild One	Suzi Quatro
Wild Side Of Life	Status Quo
Wild Thing	Tone Loc
Wild Thing	Troggs
Wild Weekend	Rebels
Wild West Hero	Electric Light Orchestra
Wild Wild West	Escape Club
Wild Wild West	Will Smith
Wild Wind	John Leyton
Wild World	Jimmy Cliff
Wild World	Maxi Priest
Wild World	Cat Stevens
Wildest Dreams	Iron Maiden
Wildfire	Michael Murphey
Wildflower	Skylark
Wildside	Marky Mark & The Funky Bunch
Wildwood Weed	Jim Stafford
Wilfred The Weasel	Keith Michel
Will 2K	Will Smith
Will I	Ian Van Dahl
Will I Ever	Alice Deejay
Will I What	Mike Sarne
Will It Go Round In Circles	Billy Preston
Will You	Hazel O'Connor
Will You Be There	Michael Jackson
Will You Love Me Tomorrow	Shirelles
Will You Still Love Me	Chicago
Willie And The Hand Jive	Johnny Otis Show
Willie Can	Alma Cogan
Willow Weep For Me	Chad & Jeremy
Wimoweh	Karl Denver
Winchester Cathedral	New Vaudeville Band
Wind Beneath My Wings	Bette Midler
The Wind Cries Mary	Jimi Hendrix Experience
Wind It Up	Gwen Stefani
Wind It Up (Rewound)	Prodigy
Wind Me Up (Let Me Go)	Cliff Richard
Wind Of Change	Scorpions
Windmills Of Your Mind	Noel Harrison
Window In The Skies	U2
Windy	Association
Wings Of A Dove	Ferlin Husky
Wings Of A Dove	Madness
The Winners Song	Geraldine

Title	Artist
The Winner Takes It All	Abba
Winning	Santana
Winter In July	Bomb The Bass
Winter World Of Love	Engelbert Humperdinck
A Winter's Tale	David Essex
A Winter's Tale	Queen
Wipe Out	Surfaris
Wipeout	Fat Boys & Beach Boys
Wire To Wire	Razorlight
Wired For Sound	Cliff Richard
Wires	Athlete
Wisdom Of A Fool	Norman Wisdom
Wishful Thinking	China Crisis
Wishin' And Hopin'	Merseybeats
Wishin' And Hopin'	Dusty Springfield
Wishing	Buddy Holly
Wishing I Was Lucky	Wet Wet Wet
Wishing (If I Had A Photograph Of You)	Flock Of Seagulls
Wishing On A Star	Cover Girls
Wishing On A Star	Fresh 4
Wishing On A Star	Rose Royce
Wishing Well	Terence Trent D'Arby
Wishing Well	Free
Wishing You Were Here	Chicago
Wishing You Were Somehow	
Here Again	Michael Crawford/Sarah Brightman
The Witch	Rattles
Witch Doctor	Cartoons
Witch Doctor	Don Lang
Witch Doctor	David Seville
Witch Queen Of New Orleans	Redbone
The Witch's Promise	Jethro Tull
Witchcraft	Frank Sinatra
Witchy Woman	Eagles
With A Girl Like You	Troggs
With A Little Help From My Friends	Joe Cocker
With A Little Help From My Friends	Sam & Mark
With A Little Help From My Friends	Wet Wet Wet
With A Little Luck	Paul McCartney
With All My Heart	Petula Clark
With Arms Wide Open	Creed
With Every Beat Of My Heart	Taylor Dayne
With Every Heartbeat	Robyn With Kleerup
With Or Without You	U2
With The Beatles L.P.	Beatles
With These Hands	Tom Jones
With You	Chris Brown
With You	Jessica Simpson
With You I'm Born Again	Billy Preston & Syreeta
With Your Love	Jefferson Starship
Without Love (There Is Nothing)	Tom Jones
Without Me	Eminem
Without You	Mötley Crüe
Without You	Nilsson
Without You	Johnny Tillotson
Without You/Never Forget You	Mariah Carey
Wives And Lovers	Jack Jones
Wobble Wobble	504 Boyz
Wolverton Mountain	Claude King
Woman	John Lennon
Woman In Love	Liz McClarnon
Woman In Love	Barbra Streisand
A Woman In Love	Frankie Laine
A Woman Needs Love (Just Like You Do)	Ray Parker Jr. & Raydio
Woman Trouble	Artful Dodger Feat. Craig David
Woman (Uh-Huh)	Jose Ferrer
Woman, Woman	Union Gap featuring Gary Puckett
A Woman's Worth	Alicia Keys
Womanizer	Britney Spears
Wombling Merry Christmas	Wombles
The Wombling Song	Wombles
Women In Love	Three Degrees
Won't Get Fooled Again	Who
Won't Somebody Dance With Me	Lynsey De Paul
Won't Take It Lying Down	Honeyz
Won't Talk About It	Beats International
A Wonder Like You	Ricky Nelson
The Wonder Of You	Elvis Presley
Wonderful	Everclear
Wonderful	Ja Rule featuring R. Kelly & Ashanti
Wonderful Christmastime	Paul McCartney
Wonderful Dream	Ann-Marie David
Wonderful Land	Shadows
Wonderful Life	Black
Wonderful Secret Of Love	Robert Earl
Wonderful Summer	Robin Ward
A Wonderful Time Up There	Pat Boone
Wonderful World	Sam Cooke
Wonderful World	Art Garfunkel, James Taylor & Paul Simon
Wonderful World	Herman's Hermits
Wonderful World	James Morrison
Wonderful World Beautiful People	Jimmy Cliff
Wonderful World Of The Young	Danny Williams
Wonderful! Wonderful!	Tymes
Wonderland	Big Country
Wonderland By Night	Bert Kaempfert
Wonderland By Night	Louis Prima
Wonderwall	Mike Flowers Pops
Wonderwall	Oasis
Wondrous Stories	Yes
Wood Beez (Pray Like Aretha Franklin)	Scritti Politti
Wooden Heart	Joe Dowell

Title	Artist
Wooden Heart	Elvis Presley
Woodstock	Crosby, Stills, Nash & Young
Woodstock	Matthews' Southern Comfort
Woo-Hah!! Got You All In Check	Busta Rhymes
Wooly Bully	Sam The Sham & The Pharaohs
The Word Girl	Scritti Politti (Feat. Ranking Ann)
Word Up	Cameo
Word Up	Gun
Words	Bee Gees
Words	F.R. David
Words	Monkees
Words Are Not Enough	Steps
Words Get In The Way	Miami Sound Machine
Words Of Love	Mamas & The Papas
Wordy Rappinghood	Tom Tom Club
Work	Kelly Rowland
Work It	Missy 'Misdemeanor' Elliott
Work It Out	Beyoncé
Work Rest & Play E.P.	Madness
Work That Body	Diana Ross
Workaholic	2 Unlimited
Working In The Coal Mine	Lee Dorsey
Working Man	Rita MacNeil
Working My Way Back To You	Four Seasons
Working My Way Back To You/Forgive Me, Girl	Spinners
World	Bee Gees
World At Your Feet	Embrace
World In Motion	Englandneworder
World In Union	Kiri Te Kanawa
The World Is A Ghetto	War
A World Of Our Own	Seekers
World Of Our Own	Westlife
A World Without Love	Peter & Gordon
The World's Greatest	R. Kelly
Worried About Ray	The Hoosiers
Worst That Could Happen	Brooklyn Bridge
Wot's It To Ya	Robbie Nevil
Would I Lie To You?	Charles & Eddie
Would I Lie To You?	Eurythmics
Wouldn't Change A Thing	Kylie Minogue
Wouldn't It Be Good	Nik Kershaw
Wouldn't It Be Nice	Beach Boys
Would You...	Touch And Go
Wow	Kate Bush
Wow	Kylie Minogue
Wrapped Around Your Finger	Police
The Wreck Of The Edmund Fitzgerald	Gordon Lightfoot
Wrestlemania	WWF Superstars
Wringle Wrangle	Fess Parker
The Writing On The Wall	Adam Wade
Wuthering Heights	Kate Bush
The X Files	Mark Snow
X Gon' Give It To Ya	DMX
Xanadu	Olivia Newton-John/Electric Light Orchestra
Y Viva Espana	Sylvia
Ya Ya	Lee Dorsey
Ya Ya Twist	Petula Clark
Yah Mo B There	James Ingram & Michael McDonald
Yakety Yak	Coasters
Yeah!	Usher featuring Ludacris & Lil Jon
Yeah Yeah	Bodyrox featuring Luciana
Year 3000	Busted
Year Of The Cat	Al Stewart
Years May Come, Years May Go	Herman's Hermits
Yeh Yeh	Georgie Fame
Yellow	Coldplay
Yellow Bird	Arthur Lyman
Yellow River	Christie
Yellow Rose Of Texas	Ronnie Hilton
Yellow Rose Of Texas	Gary Miller
The Yellow Rose Of Texas	Johnny Desmond
The Yellow Rose Of Texas	Mitch Miller
Yellow Submarine	Beatles
Yes	McAlmont & Butler
Yes I Will	Hollies
Yes, I'm Ready	Teri DeSario With KC
Yes, I'm Ready	Barbara Mason
Yes My Darling Daughter	Eydie Gorme
Yes Sir I Can Boogie	Baccara
Yes Tonight Josephine	Johnnie Ray
Yes We Can Can	Pointer Sisters
Yester-Me, Yester-You, Yesterday	Stevie Wonder
Yesterday	Beatles
Yesterday	Matt Monro
Yesterday Has Gone	Cupid's Inspiration
Yesterday Man	Chris Andrews
Yesterday Once More	Carpenters
Yesterday's Songs	Neil Diamond
Yesterdays	Guns N' Roses
Ying Tong Song	Goons
Y.M.C.A.	Village People
Yo (Excuse Me Miss)	Chris Brown
Yo-Yo	Osmonds
Yogi	Ivy Three
You	Jesse Powell
You	Lloyd Featuring Lil Wayne
You	S Club 7
You	Ten Sharp
You Ain't Seen Nothin' Yet	Bachman-Turner Overdrive
You All Dat	Baha Men
You Alone	Perry Como
You Always Hurt The One You Love	Connie Francis

Title	Artist
You Always Hurt The One You Love	Clarence 'Frogman' Henry
You And I	Rick James
You And I	Eddie Rabbitt
You And I	Will Young
You And Me	Alice Cooper
You And Me	Lifehouse
You And Me Against The World	Helen Reddy
You And Me Tonight	Aurra
You Are	Lionel Richie
You Are Alive	Fragma
You Are Everything	Diana Ross
You Are Everything	Stylistics
You Are My Destiny	Paul Anka
You Are My Lady	Freddie Jackson
You Are My Love	Liverpool Express
You Are My Sunshine	Ray Charles
You Are Not Alone	Michael Jackson
You Are Not Alone	X Factor Finalists
You Are So Beautiful	Joe Cocker
You Are The One	A-Ha
You Are The Sunshine Of My Life	Stevie Wonder
You Are The Woman	Firefall
You Beat Me To The Punch	Mary Wells
You Belong To Me	Duprees
You Belong To Me	Carly Simon
You Belong To The City	Glenn Frey
You Belong With Me	Taylor Swift
You Better Sit Down Kids	Cher
You Better You Bet	Who
You Bug Me, Baby	Larry Williams
You Came	Kim Wilde
You Can Call Me Al	Paul Simon
You Can Depend On Me	Brenda Lee
You Can Do It	Ice Cube featuring Mack 10 + Ms Toi
You Can Do Magic	America
You Can Do Magic	Limmie & The Family Cookin'
You Can Get It If You Really Want	Desmond Dekker
You Can Have Her	Roy Hamilton
You Can Make Me Dance Sing Or Anything...	Rod Stewart & The Faces
You Can Never Stop Me Loving You	Kenny Lynch
You Can't Be True To Two	Dave King
You Can't Change That	Raydio
You Can't Deny It	Lisa Stansfield
You Can't Get What You Want (Till You Know What You Want)	Joe Jackson
You Can't Hurry Love	Phil Collins
You Can't Hurry Love	Supremes
You Can't Sit Down	Dovells
You Can't Turn Me Off (In The Middle Of Turning Me On)	High Inergy
You Cheated	Shields
You Could Be Mine	Guns N' Roses
You Could Have Been With Me	Sheena Easton
You Decorated My Life	Kenny Rogers
You Didn't Have To Be So Nice	Lovin' Spoonful
You Don't Bring Me Flowers	Barbra & Neil
You Don't Have To Be A Baby To Cry	Caravelles
You Don't Have To Be In The Army To Fight In The War	Mungo Jerry
You Don't Have To Go	Chi-Lites
You Don't Have To Go Home Tonight	Triplets
You Don't Have To Say You Love Me	Guys & Dolls
You Don't Have To Say You Love Me	Elvis Presley
You Don't Have To Say You Love Me	Dusty Springfield
You Don't Have To Be A Star (To Be In My Show)	Marilyn McCoo & Billy Davis Jr
You Don't Know	Eminem, 50 Cent, Lloyd Bank$, Cashis
You Don't Know	Helen Shapiro
(You Don't Know) How Glad I Am	Nancy Wilson
You Don't Know How It Feels	Tom Petty
You Don't Know Me	Ray Charles
You Don't Know Me	Jerry Vale
You Don't Know Me	Armand Van Helden/Duane Harden
You Don't Know My Name	Alicia Keys
You Don't Know What You Got (Until You Lose It)	Ral Donner
You Don't Love Me (No, No, No)	Dawn Penn
You Don't Mess Around With Jim	Jim Croce
You Don't Owe Me A Thing	Johnnie Ray
You Don't Own Me	Lesley Gore
You Don't Want Me Anymore	Steel Breeze
You Drive Me Crazy	Shakin' Stevens
(You Drive Me) Crazy	Britney Spears
You Found Me	Fray
You Gave Me Love	Crown Heights Affair
You Get What You Give	New Radicals
You Give Good Love	Whitney Houston
You Give Love A Bad Name	Bon Jovi
You Give Me Something	James Morrison
You Got It	Roy Orbison
You Got It All	Jets
You Got It (The Right Stuff)	New Kids On The Block
You Got Soul	Johnny Nash
You Got The Love	Rufus featuring Chaka Khan
You Got The Love	Source featuring Candi Staton
You Got What It Takes	Dave Clark Five
You Got What It Takes	Marv Johnson
You Got What It Takes	Showaddywaddy
(You Gotta) Fight For Your Right (To Party)	Beastie Boys
You Had Me	Joss Stone
You Have Killed Me	Morrissey
You Haven't Done Nothin	Stevie Wonder
You Just Might See Me Cry	Our Kid
You Keep It All In	Beautiful South
(You Keep Me) Hangin' On	Vanilla Fudge
You Keep Me Hangin' On	Supremes
You Keep Me Hangin' On	Kim Wilde
You Know Me	Robbie Williams
You Know My Name	Chris Cornell
You Know What I Mean	Turtles
You Learn/You Oughta Know	Alanis Morissette
You Light Up My Life	Debby Boone
You Little Thief	Feargal Sharkey
You Little Trustmaker	Tymes
You Made Me Believe In Magic	Bay City Rollers
You Make It Real	James Morrison
You Make Lovin' Fun	Fleetwood Mac
You Make Me Feel Brand New	Simply Red
You Make Me Feel Brand New	Stylistics
You Make Me Feel Like Dancing	Leo Sayer
You Make Me Feel (Mighty Real)	Jimmy Somerville
You Make Me Feel (Mighty Real)	Sylvester
You Make Me Wanna...	Usher
You Make My Dreams	Daryl Hall & John Oates
You May Be Right	Billy Joel
You Mean The World To Me	Toni Braxton
You Might Need Somebody	Randy Crawford
You Might Think	Cars
You Must Have Been A Beautiful Baby	Bobby Darin
You My Love	Frank Sinatra
You Need Hands	Max Bygraves
You Needed Me	Boyzone
You Needed Me	Anne Murray
You Never Done It Like That	Captain & Tennille
You Only Live Twice	Nancy Sinatra
You Only Tell Me You Love Me When You're Drunk	Pet Shop Boys
You Ought To Be With Me	Al Green
You Raise Me Up	Westlife
You Really Got Me	Kinks
You Remind Me Of Something	R. Kelly
You Rock My World	Michael Jackson
You Said No	Busted
You Sang To Me	Marc Anthony
You See The Trouble With Me	Barry White
You See The Trouble With Me	Black Legend
You Send Me	Sam Cooke
You Sexy Thing	Hot Chocolate
You Should Be...	Blockster
You Should Be Dancing	Bee Gees
You Should Be Mine (The Woo Woo Song)	Jeffrey Osborne
You Should Be Mine (Don't Waste Your Time)	Brian McKnight/Ma$e
You Should Hear How She Talks About You	Melissa Manchester
You Should Really Know	Pirates featuring Enya, Shola Ama, Naila Boss
You Showed Me	Turtles & Ishani
You Spin Me Round (Like A Record)	Dead Or Alive
You Stole The Sun From My Heart	Manic Street Preachers
You Take Me Up	Thompson Twins
You Take My Breath Away	Rex Smith
You Talk Too Much	Joe Jones
You To Me Are Everything	Real Thing
You Turn Me On	Ian Whitcomb
You Want This/70's Love Groove	Janet Jackson
You Wear It Well	Rod Stewart
(You Were Made For) All My Love	Jackie Wilson
You Were Made For Me	Freddie & The Dreamers
You Were Made For Me	Jewel
You Were On My Mind	Crispian St. Peters
You Were On My Mind	We Five
You Win Again	Bee Gees
You Won't Find Another Fool Like Me	New Seekers
You Won't Forget About Me	Dannii Minogue vs Flower Power
You Won't See Me	Anne Murray
You You	Ames Brothers
You You You	Alvin Stardust
You'll Accomp'ny Me	Bob Seger & The Silver Bullet Band
You'll Answer To Me	Cleo Laine
You'll Be In My Heart	Phil Collins
You'll Be Sorry	Steps
You'll Lose A Good Thing	Barbara Lynn
You'll Never Ever Know	Platters
You'll Never Find Another Love Like Mine	Lou Rawls
You'll Never Know	Shirley Bassey
You'll Never Stop Me Loving You	Sonia
You'll Never Walk Alone	Crowd
You'll Never Walk Alone	Gerry & The Pacemakers
You'll See	Madonna
You're A Lady	Peter Skellern
You're A Special Part Of Me	Marvin Gaye & Diana Ross
You're A Superstar	Love Inc.
You're A Wonderful One	Marvin Gaye
You're All I Have	Snow Patrol
You're All I Need To Get By	Marvin Gaye & Tammi Terrell
You're All I Need To Get By	Method Man/Mary J. Blige
You're All That Matters To Me	Curtis Stigers
You're Beautiful	James Blunt
You're Breakin' My Heart	Keely Smith
You're Driving Me Crazy	Temperance Seven
You're Gonna Get Next To Me	Bo Kirkland & Ruth Davis
You're Gonna Miss This	Trace Adkins
(You're) Having My Baby	Paul Anka with Odia Coates
You're History	Shakespear's Sister
You're In A Bad Way	Saint Etienne
You're In Love	Wilson Phillips
You're In My Heart	Rod Stewart
You're Makin' Me High/Let It Flow	Toni Braxton
You're More Than A Number In My Little Red Book	Drifters
You're Moving Out Today	Carole Bayer Sager
You're My Best Friend	Queen
You're My Everything	Temptations
(You're My) Soul And Inspiration	Righteous Brothers
You're My World	Cilla Black
You're No Good	Linda Ronstadt
You're No Good	Swinging Blue Jeans
You're Not Alone	Chicago
You're Not Alone	Olive
You're Not Sorry	Taylor Swift
You're Only Lonely	J.D. Souther
You're Only Human (Second Wind)	Billy Joel
You're Ready Now	Frankie Valli
You're Sixteen	Johnny Burnette
You're Sixteen	Ringo Starr
You're So Vain	Carly Simon
You're Still The One	Shania Twain
You're Such A Good Looking Woman	Joe Dolan
(You're The) Devil In Disguise	Elvis Presley
You're The First, The Last, My Everything	Barry White
You're The Inspiration	Chicago
You're The One	SWV
You're The One	Vogues
You're The One That I Want	John Travolta & Olivia Newton-John
You're The Only Woman (You & I)	Ambrosia
You're The Reason	Bobby Edwards
You're The Reason I'm Living	Bobby Darin
You're The Voice	John Farnham
You've Got A Friend	McFly
You've Got A Friend	James Taylor
You've Got Me Dangling On A String	Chairmen Of The Board
You've Got To Hide Your Love Away	Silkie
(You've Got) The Magic Touch	Platters
You've Got Your Troubles	Fortunes
You've Lost That Lovin' Feelin'	Cilla Black
You've Lost That Lovin' Feelin'	Righteous Brothers
You've Lost That Lovin' Feeling	Daryl Hall & John Oates
You've Made Me So Very Happy	Blood Sweat & Tears
You've Never Been In Love Like This Before	Unit 4 Plus 2
You've Really Got A Hold On Me	Miracles
Young And Foolish	Edmund Hockridge
Young At Heart	Bluebells
Young Blood	Coasters
Young Emotions	Ricky Nelson
Young Gifted And Black	Bob & Marcia
Young Girl	Union Gap featuring Gary Puckett
Young Guns (Go For It)	Wham!
Young Hearts Run Free	Candi Staton
Young Love	Tab Hunter
Young Love	Sonny James
Young Love	Donny Osmond
Young Lovers	Paul & Paula
The Young New Mexican Puppeteer	Tom Jones
The Young Ones	Cliff Richard
Young Parisians	Adam & The Ants
Young Turks	Rod Stewart
Young World	Rick Nelson
Young-At-Heart	Frank Sinatra
Your Body	Pretty Ricky
Your Body's Callin'	R. Kelly
Your Cheatin' Heart	Ray Charles
Your Game	Will Young
Your Love	Outfield
Your Love Alone Is Not Enough	Manic Street Preachers
(Your Love Has Lifted Me) Higher And Higher	Rita Coolidge
Your Love Is Driving Me Crazy	Sammy Hagar
Your Love Is King	Sade
(Your Love Keeps Lifting Me) Higher And Higher	Jackie Wilson
Your Loving Arms	Billie Ray Martin
Your Mama Don't Dance	Loggins & Messina
Your Mama Don't Dance	Poison
Your Precious Love	Marvin Gaye & Tammi Terrell
Your Song	Elton John
Your Song	Elton John & Alessandro Safina
Your Wildest Dreams	Moody Blues
Yummy Yummy Yummy	Ohio Express
Zabadak	Dave Dee, Dozy, Beaky, Mick & Tich
Zambesi	Lou Busch
Zambesi	Eddie Calvert
Zip-A-Dee Doo-Dah	Bob B. Soxx & The Blue Jeans
Zoom	Fat Larry's Band
Zorba The Greek	Herb Alpert
Zorba's Dance	Marcello Minerbi

PICTURE CREDITS

The publishers would like to thank the following sources for their kind permission to reproduce the pictures in this book:

All Action 348, 352, 359, 363, 364. 370. 373
Getty Images /Dave M. Benett: 430; /Jon Furniss: 406; /Scott Gries: 429; /Jo Hale: 413, 414, 418, 426; /Dave Hogan: 432; /John D. McHugh: 422; /Frank Micelotta: 409, 410, 417, 421; /Andrew H. Walker: 425
London Features International 367
Pictorial Press 369
Retna 356, 360
Redferns 389, 392, 394, 396, 397, 398, 399, 402, 404
All other photographs supplied by **London Features International**

Every effort has been made to acknowledge correctly and contact the source and/or copyright holder of each picture and Carlton Books Limited apologises for any unintentional errors or omissions which will be corrected in future editions of this book.